EDITORS

Annette DiMeo Carlozzi and Kelly Baum

BLANTON MUSEUM OF ART
AMERICAN ART SINCE 1900

BLANTON MUSEUM OF ART
THE UNIVERSITY OF TEXAS AT AUSTIN

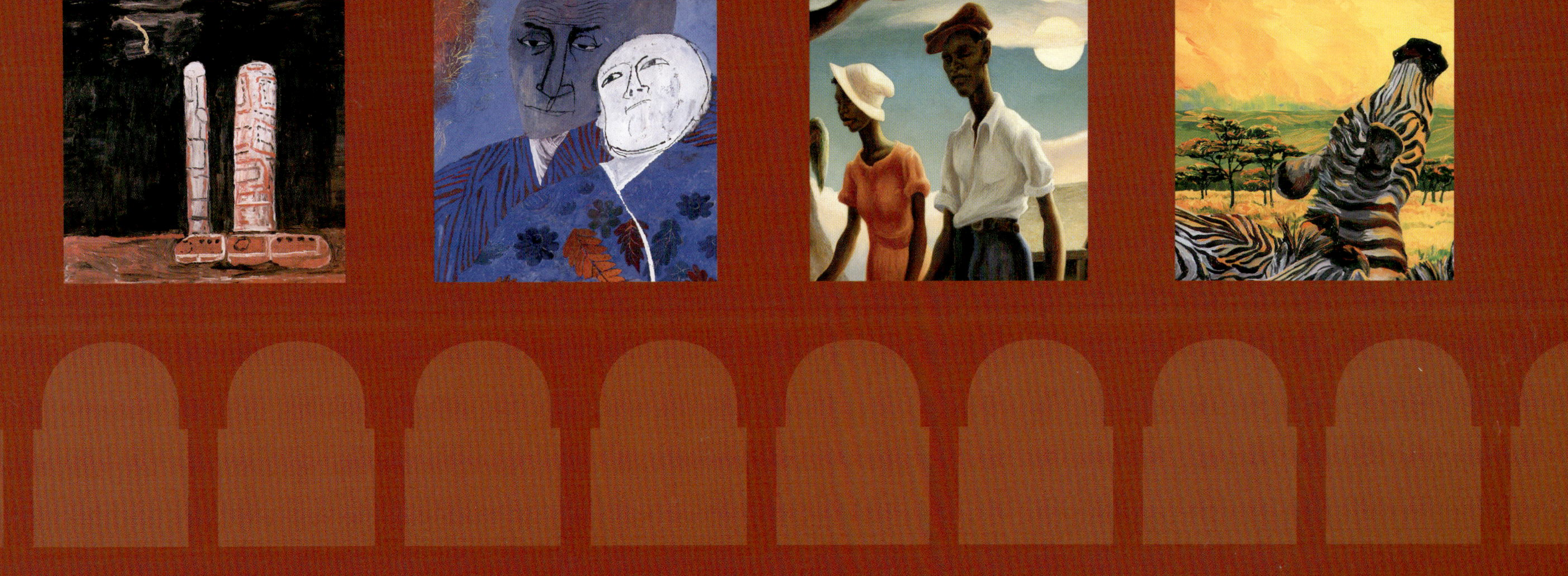

Published by the Blanton Museum of Art (formerly the Archer M. Huntington Art Gallery), The University of Texas at Austin

Distributed by the University of Texas Press

Library of Congress Cataloging-in-Publication Data
Blanton Museum of Art : American art since 1900 / editors, Annette DiMeo Carlozzi and Kelly Baum.
p. cm.
Includes bibliographical references and index.
ISBN 0-9771453-1-X (softcover : alk. paper) 1. Art, American—20th century—Catalogs. 2. Art—Texas—Austin—Catalogs. 3. Blanton Museum of Art—Catalogs. I. Title: American art since 1900. II. Carlozzi, Annette DiMeo. III. Baum, Kelly. IV. Blanton Museum of Art.
N6512.B525 2006
709.73'07476431—dc22 2005036425

Front cover: Louise Nevelson, *Dawn's Presence—Two Columns,* 1969–1975 (detail, plate 133)
Spine: Roy Colmer, *#56,* 1974 (detail, page 399, figure 10)
Page 3 (left to right): Philip Guston, *Two Legs,* 1976 (detail, plate 56); Ben Shahn, *From That Day On,* 1960 (detail, plate 160); Thomas Hart Benton, *Romance,* 1931–1932 (detail, plate 19); Melissa Miller, *Zebras and Hyenas,* 1985 (detail, plate 125)

Co-editors: Annette DiMeo Carlozzi and Kelly Baum
Principle photography: Rick Hall and George Holmes
Researchers: Lynn Boland, Ann Clifton, Erina Duganne, Rina Faletti, Karen Gonzalez, Keith Kristynik, Lara Kuykendall, Laura Lindenberger, Melissa Warak, and Kayaneh T. Wood

Copyeditors: Valerie Ann Leeds, Pam Sachant, Jonathan Smit, and Gina McDaniel Tarver
Proofreader: Louise Chu
Indexer: Candace Hyatt
Designer: Zach Hooker
Separations by iocolor, Seattle
Produced by Marquand Books, Inc., Seattle
www.marquand.com
Printed and bound by CS Graphics Pte., Ltd., Singapore

CONTENTS

CONTRIBUTORS

Erin Aldana
Ken Allan
Gwen Allen
Charity Anderson
Claire Barliant
Jennifer Barrett
Regine Basha
Kelly Baum
Alan C. Braddock
Annette DiMeo Carlozzi
Ann Clifton
Lea Cline
Rebecca S. Cohen
Feay Shellman Coleman
Frances Colpitt
Leo Costello
Charlotte Cousins
Jennifer Davy
Nancy Deffebach
John Devine
Amy Dove
Erina Duganne
Alexander Dumbadze
Teresa Eckmann
Katie Robinson Edwards
Rina Faletti
Jennifer Farrell
Ann Eden Gibson
Mette Gieskes
Karen C. Gonzalez
Sue Graze
Anjali Gupta
Stephanie Hanor
Valerie Hellstein
Dave Hickey
Linda Dalrymple Henderson
Sarah Holian
James Housefield
Madeline Irvine
Kathleen V. Jameson
Jennifer Jankauskas
Robert Kushner
Lara Kuykendall
Rebecca E. Lawton
Mary Leclère
Valerie Ann Leeds
Mariani Lefas-Tetenes
Ann Marie Leimer
Laura A. Lindenberger
Karal Ann Marling
Heather E. Mathews
Dorothy Moss
Sara-Jayne Parsons
Lisa Pasquariello
Justine Price
Karen M. Rapp
Tiffany Rasco
David Reed
Katherine Roeder
R. Sarah Richardson
Raphael Rubinstein
Sue Scott
Cherise Smith
Patrick Tomlin
Melissa Warak
Kayaneh T. Wood

PREFACE AND ACKNOWLEDGMENTS

In 1977, three-quarters of the way through the twentieth century, the Blanton Museum of Art, then known as the University Art Museum, published a catalogue of its Michener Collection of Twentieth Century American Painting. The catalogue, featuring selections from the collection given to the museum by the esteemed writer James A. Michener and his wife, Mari, is an historic document for us. Compiled by Earl A. Powell III—then a young curator here, now the distinguished director of the National Gallery of Art—and created in consultation with the Micheners themselves, that volume, a bit smaller than this one, indicated the institution's pride in its first serious and comprehensive acquisition of major modern paintings. The Michener gift, in turn, helped prompt the generosity of Barbara Duncan, the donor of the Blanton's core collection of modern Latin American art, and together both bodies of work have grounded a collecting and research program in modern and contemporary art of the Americas that is unique in this country.

The Blanton today has entered a new century and, as this publication is readied for press, is poised to enter a significant new era with the opening of its new museum building—appropriately named the Mari and James A. Michener Gallery Building. The building is the first of a two-building complex, the largest of any university art museum in the country, that will greatly expand our acquisitions, exhibitions, programming, teaching, research, and outreach capabilities.

The last edition of the Michener Collection catalogue is long out of print, and the Blanton's collection of modern and contemporary American art has expanded dramatically. We are proud to be able to offer this new, more complete and up-to-date twentieth-century American collection catalogue as a tangible manifestation of the growth of our museum and of this significant collecting area.

Since the late 1970s the Blanton's American collection has grown considerably through gifts, purchases, and commissions. The acquisition of the C. R. Smith Collection of late-nineteenth and early twentieth-century images of the American West, and the publication of its superb catalogue, *Collecting the West* by Richard Saunders in 1988, further strengthened our holdings and reputation. Then, in 1996, staff expansion allowed the hire of our first curator of American and contemporary art, Annette DiMeo Carlozzi. An exhibitions program, research into and re-presentation of the collection, and a careful program of new acquisitions to add contemporary works and fill in historical gaps followed.

Significant new patronage emerged in the form of Jeanne and Michael Klein, both alumni of The University of Texas at Austin, who have joined the Blanton as collecting partners. Their passion for contemporary art and artists reflects the collecting spirit of the Micheners. Their experimental vision perfectly meshed with our goal to build an exciting, provocative collection of international contemporary art so that students and visitors could discover the new territories that artists explore. With their support as well as that of others in Austin's lively, growing contemporary arts scene, the Blanton is on its way to building one of the most distinctive and adventurous collections of contemporary works in the country.

Scholarship also has thrived, thanks in large measure to the Henry S. Luce Foundation, which began its support with a multiyear grant from their American Collections Enhancement initiative. That ACE award, along with a generous grant from our friends and longtime benefactors at the Susan Vaughan Foundation, assisted the research phase for this volume. The Luce Foundation also has funded the publication of this catalogue and the accompanying reinstallation of the collection. We are so grateful for their endorsement and financial support.

A true legion of people has made this book possible. Curator Annette DiMeo Carlozzi conceived the project six years ago, and it is her creative vision and direction that have kept it—and all the department's activities—on track. Ably assisted at first by Stephanie Hanor, then Blanton assistant curator, and a group of graduate research assistants that included Erina Duganne, Rina Faletti, Keith Kristynik, and Kayaneh T. Wood, Carlozzi expanded the original scope of the publication over time, commissioning more than 200 object essays from graduate students, professors, curators, and arts professionals, many of them representing an emerging generation of scholars. Assistant curator Kelly Baum joined the staff in 2002 and gradually took on day-to-day management of the project; her meticulous research standards, acute writing and editing skills, and masterful supervision of the huge team of writers, editors, and researchers were fundamental to the publication's success. During this second phase, graduate research assistants included Lynn Boland, Ann Clifton, Karen Gonzalez, Lara Kuykendall, and especially Laura Lindenberger and Melissa Warak.

We are grateful to the dedicated group of visiting scholars who worked tirelessly with Carlozzi to review and write about the collection, including Ann Eden Gibson, Dave Hickey, Robert Kushner, Karal Ann Marling, David Reed, Raphael Rubinstein, and UT's own Linda Dalrymple Henderson. Fran and Steve Magee, staunch Blanton supporters, provided true Texas-style hospitality to our visiting scholars and we thank them for it.

The inimitable Ed Marquand and his staff at Marquand Books were a pleasure to work with throughout the design and production process. Expert editors for the publication were Valerie Ann Leeds, Pam Sachant, Jonathan Smit, and Gina McDaniel Tarver. Former associate director Paige Bartels assisted Carlozzi in securing initial funding for the publication. Other Blanton staff members whose help was crucial along the way include photographer Rick Hall, registrars Sue Ellen Jeffers and Meredith Sutton, business officer Tanya Walker, Sheree Scarborough and Brady Dyer of the public relations department, and associate director Ann Wilson.

James and Mari Michener would be proud to see the many accomplishments sparked by their gift. When I first met them in 1985, they had recently come here in order for Jim to work on his novel *Texas* for the State's sesquicentennial. We at the museum were blessed to know them as friends and to learn what drove them to build their extraordinary collection. It has expanded in line with their vision for it, and I believe they would be pleased to see that it remains a living, constantly changing record of the moment in which we live. I am delighted to dedicate this book to their memory.

Jessie Otto Hite
Director
Blanton Museum of Art

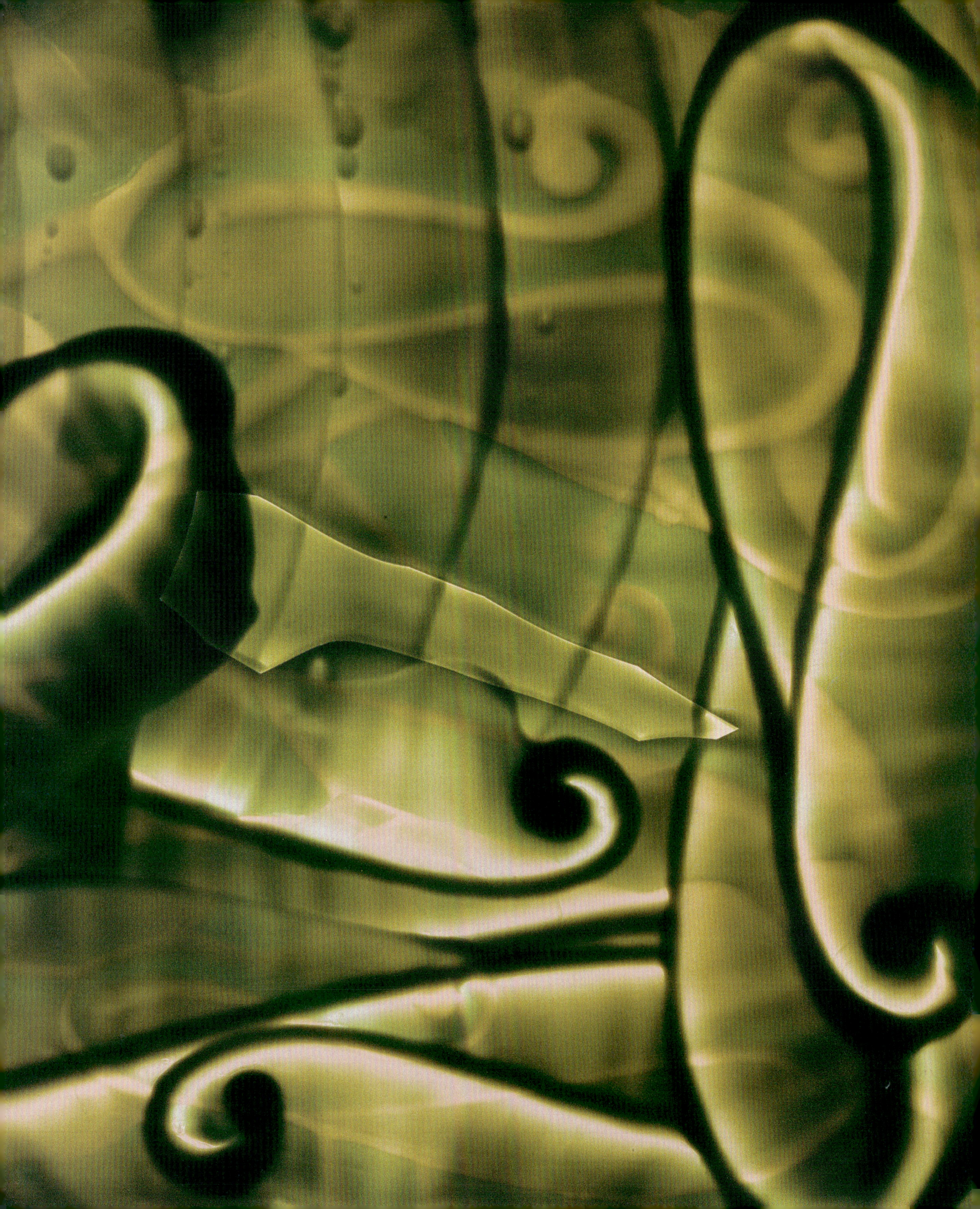

INTRODUCTION TO THE COLLECTION

Annette DiMeo Carlozzi, Curator of American and Contemporary Art

The Blanton's collection of American art since 1900 is chockfull of surprises. Featuring a corpus of more than 400 works that traces the history of achievement in American art, especially painting, from 1900 to the present day, it is a strong teaching collection, and contains significant examples of works from the Ashcan School, early American modernism, Regionalism and Social Realism, Abstract Expressionism, Color Field, Pop, Minimalism, Post-Minimalism, and most contemporary trends. That makes it user-friendly for our primary audience of university students and faculty and an admirable cultural resource for the greater community. But in addition to its excellent survey of works by well-known artists that together illustrate the modernist narrative of twentieth-century American art history, the collection is also filled with unexpected riches—bold and idiosyncratic expressions—that confound expectations and pique the curiosity of scholars and visitors alike. It is rare to find this kind of texture in a university collection, to peruse collection catalogues or museum galleries and encounter a trove of Yayoi Kusamas or Lee Lozanos alongside majestic works by Adolph Gottlieb, Alfred Jensen, and John Wesley commissioned especially for the collection, not far from signature examples by artists like Jacob Lawrence, Alice Neel, Donald Roller Wilson, and Dario Robleto, mavericks all. With a core of historic material acquired and gifted by Mari and James A. Michener, now supplemented by new gifts, purchases, and additional commissions of contemporary art, the collection is rich in masterworks that show artists' production at its most ambitious; experimental works that provide clues to artistic transitions and new directions; strong representative works that capture the essence of an artist's style; and uncommon works that enrich the context of an accepted movement or direction, making clear that history is never simple and that our view of truth is inexorably affected by perspective and circumstance.

Over the past ten years, we have assiduously cultivated this collection, applying curiosity, imagination, and sustained attention, along with a healthy measure of skepticism, open-minded reconsideration of the art historical canon, and the introduction of fresh outside perspectives. We have dedicated time for research and museological experimentation, made strategic new acquisitions, and now, with the advent of our new facility, provided better exhibition space and technologies to the task of its re-presentation. The installations in the galleries and this new publication together presume several assumptions that have guided us: each is grounded in profound respect for the works of art and an earnest desire to champion the stories of the artists who made them. We believe that a work of art, experienced on its own without embellishment of any kind, has something unique and powerful to communicate. And yet understanding the social, historical, and art historical

David Reed, *#476*, 2001 (detail, plate 147)

context in which it was made—even if it was made last year—is extremely relevant, as is knowing the artist's ambitions and intentions, the work that preceded and followed it in the artist's oeuvre, its critical reception, and, most elusive still, its potential meaning to the unending variety of its audiences today. Works of art are artifacts of history; they offer us a parallel language with which to craft a narrative of time, place, and character. In addition to being extraordinary objects capable of inspiring visual, intellectual, and spiritual awareness, they engage the history of ideas and embody the cultural attitudes of a given moment. Put two works of art together in a gallery and the possibilities for meaning expand exponentially. Add two viewers, who focus independently on different aspects of those works, and discussion commences. Support those works, that viewing situation, with new research, as was commissioned for this catalogue, and hopefully we have offered access to the multiple layers of information and the singularly rich experience that a university museum should provide.

The title of this book—*American Art Since 1900*—was determined on the basis of context as well. Generic to most tastes, it describes the particular circumstances that gave shape to the Blanton's collection. "Since 1900" indicates the span of more than a century, allowing us to establish and explore essential reverberations between modern and contemporary art. "American," perhaps a charged term, here suggests complementarity with the Blanton's collection of "Latin American" art—itself a misnomer—whose important new collection catalogue has also just been published.[1] For our purposes, "American" implies the US context in which the work was made, rather than the nationality of the artist. Just as early and mid-twentieth-century "American" artists were as often immigrants as they were first- or second-generation citizens of the United States, so too is a new generation of artists working in New York and Texas as likely to have come from Pakistan or Argentina as they are to have been raised in Michigan or Oregon. Geography is still relevant, but only to the degree that its fluidity and contingency are understood, now that space and time have been effectively collapsed through the ease of worldwide travel and the development of new technologies and economic models.

What the title does not stress is that these works are but a selection of the almost 4,000 American artworks in the Blanton's collection. Evenly distributed over the past century and then some, they constitute many of the most distinctive works acquired before January 2005, showing a range of media and stylistic approaches and a mix of both historic/established and emerging artists. Supplementing these featured works are several hundred additional paintings and sculptures, many of them quite fine; a superb collection of several thousand twentieth-century American prints; as well as a distinctive collection of nineteenth-century and early twentieth-century paintings and sculptures depicting images of the American West, most notably the renowned C. R. Smith Collection, which has its own first-rate catalogue.[2] We invite students, scholars, colleagues, and interested audiences to get to know our collections through these publications, our recently redesigned website, and hopefully, for there is no substitute, visits to our galleries.

HISTORY OF THE COLLECTION: FOUNDATIONS AND THEIR GENEROSITY, COLLECTORS AND THEIR PASSION

The collection began in the usual hodgepodge way: a group of works gifted here, an exhibited work retained there. In 1960, three years prior to the establishment of this institution,[3] the Longview Foundation of New York gave a parcel of paintings to The University of Texas.[4] This donation included recent works by Peter Agostini, Robert Mallary, and other New York–based contemporary artists who were deemed under-recognized at the time, but the most important object was a signature abstraction by Norman Lewis, painted in 1958. Discovered in deep storage in the late 1990s after not having been exhibited in almost forty years, it is a vivacious work by a respected Abstract Expressionist whose career has only recently received the attention it deserves. In some ways, the Lewis painting's experience is emblematic of that which awaits the entire collection now that a handsome new catalogue and state-of-the-art facility in which to showcase it exists.

The core of the collection arrived not long thereafter and still constitutes fully three-quarters of the twentieth-century American painting collection: the Mari and James A. Michener Collection. Tracing critical developments in American painting from 1900 to the mid-1970s, the Michener Collection was actively built by the noted author and his wife during a sixteen-year period, 1959–1975, after which modest acquisitions funds were made available to museum staff.[5] Comprising almost 300 paintings, it ranges from works of singular historical and artistic importance (one of Jacob Lawrence's earliest gouaches, a rare Alfred Jensen commission, one of Hans Hofmann's last and greatest paintings, for example) to groups of works which together illustrate the broad diversity of painting at a particular moment in a particular place (New York in 1960 and 1968, for instance).[6] The Micheners' motivations in building the collection were exceptionally altruistic: while they relished the process of researching, scouting, debating the merits of, and finally purchasing works of art, their vision of the collection was educational and instructive. With no children of their own, they wanted to pass their passion, discipline, and zeal for expanding the boundaries of their visual imaginations (which not incidentally fueled Mr. Michener's extremely successful career as a writer of historical fiction about vivid places) to a younger generation—preferably those who, like Mr. Michener, were raised with few advantages.[7] Their search for a public university with a diverse student body and an art museum that could exhibit and publish their works ended with The University of Texas at Austin. The gift was given in two parcels, one in 1968 and one in 1991. Most of the works the Micheners purchased never hung in their own home but were instead temporarily stored and shipped directly to Austin. The gift immediately put UT's University Art Museum on the map as one of the foremost university collections of American painting, and today the works form the nucleus of a vital cross-disciplinary teaching resource.

The collection has continued to expand as the Blanton has received numerous gifts of modern and contemporary American art from other benefactors and has purchased selectively in the field over the past thirty years. Critical to the success of these efforts has been the support of longtime donors such as Jack S. Blanton and the Blanton family and Mary and Jack Bartholow. The contributions of our constantly evolving affinity group, the Contemporary Circle, have been essential as well. The Judith Rothschild Foundation's support for increasing knowledge of the art of recently deceased, under-recognized artists has been of enormous benefit to the museum, allowing the acquisition of key works by Ana Mendieta, Lee Lozano, and George Sugarman. Visiting scholar and artist David Reed has opened doors to several gracious donors, including Miles Bellamy, the son of legendary gallerist and Michener advisor Richard Bellamy. Scholar and UT professor Linda Henderson also has encouraged the museum to acquire representative examples by artists whose works have enriched the teaching curriculum.

No one has been more devoted to helping the Blanton's contemporary collection grow than Jeanne and Michael Klein, whose passionate risk-taking merges perfectly with the museum's goal to build an exceptional collection of works by emerging artists. Inspired by their own experiences as UT students whose eyes and horizons were widened by exposure to contemporary art at university, the Kleins represent the next generation of enlightened philanthropy. In their own inimitable manner, they have followed the Micheners' sterling example and taken it a step further. Among the first prominent American collectors[8] to propose private/institutional partnerships for collection building, the Kleins have worked in tandem with the museum over the past six years to identify works that are of mutual interest and then to purchase them as partial and pledged gifts to the museum. The advantages of the partnership are manifold. The Kleins expand their knowledge of emerging artists, add to their already extraordinary collection works that otherwise would have been reserved for prestigious private institutions, and enjoy the ongoing pleasures of getting to know the artists personally and living with the works of art for part of the time. Meanwhile, the museum benefits incalculably by their shared enthusiasm for the process of discovery, ongoing commitment to new endeavors, and infusion of financial capital. The Kleins have helped the museum acquire works right out of the studio by such promising young artists as Trenton Doyle Hancock as well as rising art stars like Amy Sillman, Oliver Herring, and Anne Chu. They have allowed the museum to expand its own network of relationships with key galleries by purchasing major pieces from shows of new work by Jeremy Blake, Rachel Harrison, and Arturo Herrera, among many others. And in several instances they have extended their support beyond the museum to include the residency program at Artpace in San Antonio, from whose international exhibitions program significant new commissions by Shahzia Sikander and Robyn O'Neil were purchased. The Kleins' support is fundamental to our success.

HIGHLIGHTS OF THE COLLECTION

The early twentieth-century collection is notable for its excellent examples of work by leading artists and unusual works by lesser-known artists. Certainly, the museum's small grouping of early modernist paintings—with its first-rate Marsden Hartley, Arthur Doves, John Marin, Max Weber, and Stanton Macdonald-Wright, its early Stuart Davis, and its intriguing Marguerite and William Zorach double picture—is distinctive. The Depression era is well represented, for it was both the time of Mr. Michener's young adult years and a political moment that reflected his lifelong commitment to democratic principles. Masterworks by Philip Evergood, Raphael Soyer, and Thomas Hart Benton describe how life was then in unforgettable images; an early painting by Jacob Lawrence indelibly captures the moment as well as the seventeen-year-old artist's incipient style.

Although the collection is missing paintings by some of the major figures of Abstract Expressionism, it features a small yet intriguing Mark Rothko that traces his first attempts at a universal abstract language, both early and late Arshile Gorkys that shed light on that seminal artist's development, and an interesting Bradley Walker Tomlin that stands in for the AbEx group's groundbreaking experimentations with gestural imagery in the mid-1940s. Representing the late 1950s and early 1960s, as the Abstract Expressionist style was fully mature and at the height of its popular acceptance, the collection is dense with major paintings. It includes superb works by Hans Hofmann, Adolph Gottlieb, and William Baziotes as well as signature examples by many artists who espoused the style—Franz Kline, Joan Mitchell, Philip Guston, Alfred Leslie, Norman Lewis, Michael Goldberg, and Jack Tworkov among them. Reactions to the hegemony of the New York School ranged from new developments in geometric abstraction and figuration to the formalist abstractions of the Color Field painters. The collection includes excellent work by Alfred Jensen, Al Held, Elmer Bischoff, Richard Anuszkiewicz, Ellsworth Kelly, Harold Stevenson, Leon Golub, Helen Frankenthaler, Morris Louis, and Kenneth Noland. Proto-Pop and Pop works—the next generation's response—include significant paintings by Robert Indiana, Peter Saul, Larry Rivers, and John Wesley as well as unusual early works by Jim Dine and Lee Lozano and a striking Tom Wesselmann still-life.

The collection possesses an extraordinary resource of late 1960s abstraction. A now-classic Jo Baer diptych, major early works by Brice Marden and Richard Tuttle, and paintings spanning almost a decade of experimentation by David Novros are joined by strong examples of less canonical artists such as Alan Cote, Lawrence Stafford, and Mary Corse. A fine Carl Andre floor piece is one of the few sculptures in the collection that predated recent efforts to expand its focus beyond painting.

The Michener Collection, with its impressive breadth of works from 1900–1975, was built by serious scholars who did their homework, but its assumptions were that painting was primary and that most artists were white men who lived in New York. As a result, acquisitions over the past decade have addressed the need to fill historical gaps and to diversify the collection in terms of media and approach. In order to establish continuity between the existing collection and the new works, a dialogue with the ideas of painting prevailed in the first rounds of selections. Later, moving off the wall became key: noteworthy sculptures by George Sugarman, Louise Nevelson, Stephen Antonakos, George Segal, Alan Saret, Joel Shapiro, James Surls, Jesús Moroles, Anne Chu, and Rachel Harrison now engage the three-dimensional space of the galleries. A strong representation of leading Texas-based artists' work made since the 1980s was acquired to complement works by Melissa Miller, David Bates, Derek Boshier, Jack Mims, and Frank X. Tolbert, among others, which had been purchased earlier. And so a rich assembly of works by Vernon Fisher, Gael Stack, Celia Alvarez Muñoz, Luis Jiménez, Robert Levers, Jesse Amado, John Pomara, Claudia Reese, Benito Huerta, Joseph Guy, Stephen Daly, and the above-mentioned Surls and Moroles have been engaged in conversation with those by a younger generation of artists working here. The new "post-Texas" generation, including Annette Lawrence, Trenton Doyle Hancock, Robyn O'Neil, Dario Robleto, and Brent Steen, shines when placed within the national and international context of our most recent works in the collection.

Indeed, building upon the strong critical response to the Blanton-organized conceptual painting exhibition, *Negotiating Small Truths* (1999), we have now amassed an exciting survey of works made during the past ten years by an international roster of culturally diverse artists working in the United States. This survey brings the collection into the present day with verve and integrity. In addition to those extraordinary contemporary works mentioned in various contexts above, we have acquired brand-new works by Wangechi Mutu, Emily Jacir, Leo Villareal, Terry Adkins, Bill Viola, David Reed, Janine Antoni, Radcliffe Bailey, John Valadez, Amy Globus, and Glenn Ligon and have commissioned works from Byron Kim, Fabian Marcaccio, and Peter Rostovsky. Our newest art is a dynamic and well-balanced representation of contemporary works in all media, including painting, sculpture, animation, video, and mixed media installation.

EXCAVATING THE COLLECTION: THE CURATOR'S PERSPECTIVE AND SCHOLARS' RESPONSES

Of course, it is the curator's job to reassess continually the merits of a collection—to add, to cull, to advocate on its behalf both internally, within an institution's acquisitions and exhibitions priorities, and externally, to colleagues in the field, whose knowledge may lead to greater exposure and a new understanding of the museum's holdings. On staff for more than a year in 1997, but preoccupied with a full slate of temporary exhibitions and the committee work associated with a new museum-wide strategic plan, I headed into the storage rooms with mixed expectations to view works of art that, in many cases, had not been exhibited in years. Some of the findings were extraordinary. They included Joan Semmel's feminist masterwork, *Mythologies and Me,* and Alice Neel's double portrait of David Bourdon and Gregory Battcock, both of which I had seen reproduced and had never forgotten after they debuted in New York in the 1970s. Also, the astonishing compilation of thirteen Yayoi Kusama works was a revelation: almost a dozen exquisitely potent small paintings on paper, an important transitional assemblage that has now traveled from Los Angeles to New York to Tokyo,[9] and the large-scale diptych that was reproduced on the cover of the catalogue for her 1991 New York retrospective.[10] Others were merely unexpected—a small grouping of austere Minimal works that were extremely different from the high-keyed objects that more often appealed to the Micheners' taste. It was clear that the museum possessed an idiosyncratic collection with enough breadth to sustain a series of thematic exhibitions drawn from it on a variety of topics. And so, over the next year or two, we dismantled the conventional chronological installation that had been hanging, with small adjustments, for years and regrouped the works into topical galleries—landscape as metaphor, approaches to the figure, comparisons of artists' early and mature works—in order to read them from, literally, new perspectives. With the remaining Michener funds, we began to acquire some brand-new paintings, which, once installed in the galleries, formed analogous relationships with the historical core of the Michener Collection. Compelling juxtapositions of Luis Cruz Azaceta's biting social commentary, *Sleepless* (1996), with Raphael Soyer's powerful Depression-era group portrait, *Transients* (1936), for instance, or Byron Kim's series of sly monochromatic panels, *Synecdoche* (1991/1998), with Brice Marden's early abstract diptych, *Fave* (1968–1969), allowed fresh, multiple readings of the older, more familiar works, which seemed to come to life again. At the same time, the recent acquisitions achieved greater resonance and depth.

Exhilarated by the interpretive possibilities suggested by these exhibitions and determined to generate a new assessment of the collection's strengths, we sought support for the first extended period of collection research in two decades. In 1999 the Henry Luce Foundation awarded a three-year grant to the Blanton to develop "New Perspectives on American Art," a multifaceted program designed to expand awareness and encourage use of the museum's holdings of twentieth-century American art, especially the Michener Collection. The program allowed us to invite a wide-ranging group of art historians, critics, and artists to visit the Blanton multiple times in order to research, lecture, teach, and write about works for this proposed catalogue. The visiting scholars—art historians Dr. Ann Eden Gibson and Dr. Karal Ann Marling, critics Dave Hickey and Raphael Rubinstein, and artists Robert Kushner and David Reed—were chosen because of the scope and independence of their research interests as well as their specific expertise in modern and contemporary painting. In addition, art historians Richard Shiff and Frances Colpitt, artist Mark Schlesinger, and gallerist Mitchell Algus all provided salient information during short consultations with the visiting scholars. "New Perspectives" provided students and the public the rare opportunity to observe artists, critics, and art historians—all researchers in their respective enterprises—solving related problems within equally valid but different vocabularies and frames of reference. Most importantly, the project allowed the museum to provide alternate forums for ongoing consideration of and debate about the collection over the past several years, while we operated without the proper access to collections that our new facility now affords.

The "New Perspectives" scholars were invited to choose their own research topics, and most delved into storage and the museum's archives looking for connections to subjects they had been thinking about for a while. Ultimately, each chose to focus on lesser-known works in the collection, and each took special care to illuminate the biases, as well as serendipities, that inevitably affect an artist's reputation and place in history. Here the similarities ended, however, for among them the scholars interrogated the works in the collection from every possible perspective. Art historian and American culture expert Karal Ann Marling examined Kenneth Hayes Miller's career-long struggle to master a particularly challenging composition. Her contribution offers both a classic art historical investigation of the painting's previously accepted date, subject matter, and source material as well as a discursive consideration of the social context of downtown painting in 1930s/1940s New York. Cultural critic Dave Hickey wrote about artist Bradley Walker Tomlin, the outsider status that plagued him throughout his career despite his dense network of artistic connections, and the inspired qualities that convince the author that Tomlin's mid-century paintings were ahead of their time. Painter Robert Kushner took on Michener himself and conducted a subjective, spirited, and ultimately sympathetic examination of the inherent patterns, achievements, and weaknesses of his collection. Poet and art critic Raphael Rubinstein traced the overlapping professional and personal connections among three painters—Norman Bluhm, Sam Francis, and Joan Mitchell—who spent substantial portions of their careers abroad and evolved important variants of Abstract Expressionism. Art historian Linda Henderson and painter David Reed both looked at abstract painting in mid-1960s New York: Henderson from a rich art historical perspective and through a lens attuned to the intersections of art, music, and science; and Reed from a critical and painterly perspective that gives the reader an incomparable sense of how painters see and how complicated and sometimes compromised official histories may be. Each reclaimed almost-forgotten works and reestablished their vitality in the context of the museum's collection. Finally, art historian Ann Gibson constructed a comparative theoretical study of two vastly different but contemporaneous artists, Richard Anuszkiewicz and Sam Gilliam. Tracing their motivations, innovations, and critical reception, she uncovered propositions about color that link them, perhaps unexpectedly.[11]

Following the scholars' visits in 1999–2001, the extended process of planning the new facility began, and the museum ceased its regular program of temporary exhibitions—a healthy mix of shows organized by Blanton curatorial staff and loan shows from institutional partners—in favor of small exhibitions drawn exclusively from the collection. What might have been a disappointing task for curators—looking inward only to the museum's own holdings and not outward to the ever-expanding world of temporary loans and presumably new topics of investigation—became an optimal experience of working intensively with the collection, slicing into it from diverse perspectives, and ultimately revealing more of the works in a wider variety of combinations than had ever been seen before. These curatorial experiments included the Blanton's first-ever interweaving of its modern and contemporary American and Latin American collections: a year-long, two-part exhibition on the subject of time titled *Past Present Future: Notions of Time in Twentieth Century Art* (2001) and *time/frame* (2002). With the bulk of its collection in storage, the museum then returned to chronology as an organizing principle that best suited faculty needs. Large exhibitions highlighting popular favorites as well as many rarely exhibited works included *Routes to Modernism: American Painting 1870–1950* (2002); *Painting Explosion 1958–1963* (2003); and *Twister: Moving through Color, 1965–1977* (2004), the latter of which once again juxtaposed American and Latin American works in an exploration of perceptual painting. Finally, the museum organized three exhibitions that grouped works from the collection according to provocative topics: *Cartoon Noir* (2002), a series of recently acquired contemporary works by Jeremy Blake, Ellen Gallagher, Arturo Herrera, and Trenton Doyle Hancock whose comic overtones bely an anxious world view; *Transgressive Women* (2003), which looked at clusters of work by audacious experimenters Yayoi Kusama, Lee Lozano, Ana

Mendieta, and Joan Semmel; and *Visualizing Identity* (2003), a small exhibition of works by Jesse Amado, Radcliffe Bailey, Byron Kim, and Glenn Ligon that offered visitors a platform for exploring notions of personal and cultural identity with the aid of an experimental interactive handheld device.

With the opening of the Blanton's new facility in spring 2006, the museum seized the perfect opportunity to showcase its new collections in every area, from antiquities to the present. The presentation of the modern and contemporary American and Latin American collections was conceived as a special project, titled *America/Americas,* which was several years in the making. Highlights from each collection were interwoven in one dynamic installation featuring more than 200 paintings, sculptures, prints, and other works of art dating from 1875–1985. The integration of these rarely juxtaposed works allowed for exploration of the shared hemispheric histories and cultural dialogues that unite the diverse political and geographic areas of North and South America. Notions of the frontier and the impact of early twentieth-century industrialization, developments in European modernism, scientific discoveries, psychological theories, and the rise of the civil rights movements that spread north and south throughout the century—all had more similarities of effect on artistic practices in North and South America than differences. Without mitigating the distinctions and particularities that do exist in any wide spectrum of creative circumstances, *America/Americas* suggested that geographic readings of content have become increasingly limiting when applied to works made in the mid- and late twentieth century. Indeed, an exhibition called *New Now Next: The Contemporary Blanton,* which presented more than thirty-five recent acquisitions made in the past decade in the United States and South America, put forth a cogent argument that the artistic concerns of the contemporary moment are indistinguishable across continents, and that it would be not only difficult but also pointless to try to distinguish works in one collection from those in another given the global nature of contemporary life.

REPOSITIONING THE COLLECTION: NEW DIRECTIONS

In the past decade, the modern and contemporary American collection has gained new visibility. Masterworks from the collection have traveled to exhibitions at the National Gallery of Art, Washington, D.C.; The Museum of Modern Art, New York; Dia Center for the Arts, New York; the Whitney Museum of American Art, New York; the Los Angeles County Museum of Art; the Peggy Guggenheim Collection in Venice, Italy; the Castello di Rivoli Museo d'Arte Contemporanea in Rivoli, Italy; and the Centro Galego de Arte Contemporánea in Santiago de Compostela, Spain, among other important venues.[12] During the museum's recent construction process, several exhibitions drawn from the Michener Collection have traveled to institutions across the state, including the Grace Museum in Abilene, the Victoria Regional Museum Association, and the Amarillo Art Museum. And, thanks to the efforts of the museum's education department, university faculty from departments within the Colleges of Fine Arts, Education, Communication, Liberal Arts, and Natural Sciences and the Business, Architecture, and Social Work Schools have discovered the interdisciplinary riches of the collection and mined the exhibitions in the galleries as forums for class debate.

The museum's dynamic new collection of contemporary works by emerging and established artists now is considered one of the three most important publicly held collections of contemporary art in Texas. Seen for the first time during the grand opening of the new facility, selections from this collection, along with a lively range of educational and interpretive programs, reflect the museum's renewed engagement with the art and ideas of our time. International by definition and multifaceted in form, the contemporary collection constantly extends into the future, proposing new experiences, experimental concepts, and an open-minded perspective on the world in which we all live.

Notes

1. Gabriel Pérez-Barreiro, ed., *Blanton Museum of Art: Latin American Collection* (Austin: Blanton Museum of Art, 2006).
2. Richard H. Saunders, *Collecting the West: The C. R. Smith Collection of Western American Art* (Austin: Published for the Archer M. Huntington Art Gallery, College of Fine Arts, The University of Texas at Austin by the University of Texas Press, 1988).
3. Founded in 1963, the institution was christened the University Art Museum; in 1980 the name was changed to the Archer M. Huntington Art Gallery. Then, with the advent of a new facility in 1997, we received our final institutional name, the Jack S. Blanton Museum of Art.
4. See the Longview Foundation files in the Blanton Museum of Art Archives, The University of Texas at Austin.
5. For information on Michener's collecting practices, see Robert Kushner's essay, "The Good, The Bad, and The Ugly," in this catalogue.
6. For information on the museum's collection of paintings made in New York in 1968, see David Reed's essay, "New York Painting circa 1968: Notes Toward the Missing History of Experimental Abstraction," in this catalogue.
7. For Michener's own account of the motivations behind and the genesis of his collection, see his essay, "The Collector: An Informal Memoir," in *The James A. Michener Collection: Twentieth Century American Painting,* preface by Earl A. Powell III (Austin: University Art Museum, University of Texas at Austin, 1977), ix–xviii.
8. Jeanne and Michael Klein have been named two of the world's top 200 art collectors for three years in a row. See Milton Esterow, "The ARTnews 200 Top Collectors," *Artnews* 104 (summer 2005): 164.
9. This exhibition, *Love Forever: Yayoi Kusama, 1958–1968,* was organized by the Los Angeles County Museum of Art and the Japan Foundation in collaboration with The Museum of Modern Art, New York. It was co-curated by Lynn Zelevansky and Laura Hoptman.
10. Bhupendra Karia, ed., *Yayoi Kusama: A Retrospective* (New York: CICA, Center for International Contemporary Arts, 1989).
11. Final essays by the scholars can be found at the back of this catalogue. In addition, UT-based art historian, Dr. Linda Dalrymple Henderson, contributed an essay to this section of the catalogue.
12. For example, the museum's William Baziotes painting traveled to Venice in 2004 for *William Baziotes: Paintings and Drawings, 1934–1962* at the Peggy Guggenheim Collection; its Marsden Hartley painting traveled to the National Gallery of Art for the 2001 exhibition, *Modern Art and America: Alfred Stieglitz and His New York Galleries;* one of its works by Arturo Herrera, *Night Before Last,* traveled to Spain for the exhibition, *Arturo Herrera: Keep in Touch,* at the Centro Galego de Arte Contemporánea in 2005; its Alfred Jensen painting traveled to New York for the Dia Art Foundation's 2001–2002 exhibition, *Alfred Jensen: Concordance;* its Franz Kline painting traveled to Rivoli for *Franz Kline 1910–1962,* an exhibition held at the Castello di Rivoli in 2004; and its Oscar Bluemner painting traveled to the Whitney Museum of American Art for the 2005 Bluemner retrospective.

SELECTED WORKS FROM THE COLLECTION

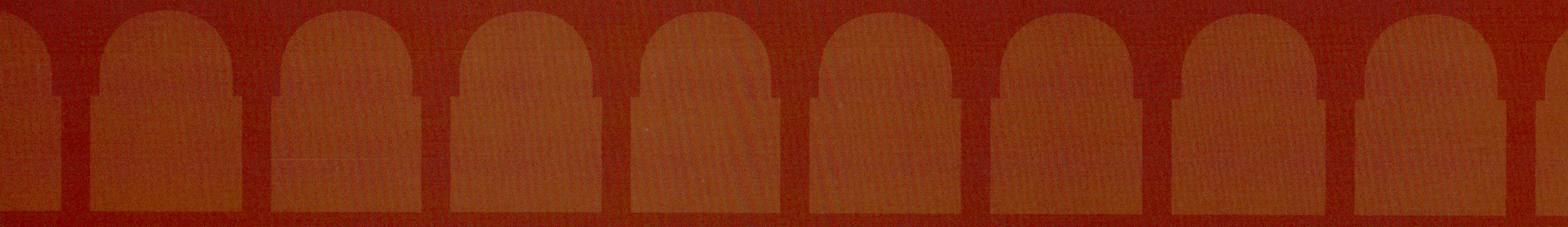

Vito Acconci

b. New York, 1940

w. Des Moines, 1962–1964; New York, 1964–1971; Valencia, California, 1971–1978; Brooklyn, New York, 1978–present

One of the key artists driving the development of performance art in the 1960s, Vito Acconci can be seen as an heir to the legacy of Marcel Duchamp, whose work fundamentally challenged every Western assumption about the status and definition of art. In particular, Acconci has consistently employed his own body, often treated with violence or deprivation mixed with eroticism, as both the subject and source for his art. Acconci's use of his body needs to be understood as a complex response to the modernist paradigm of transcendent male artistic subjectivity.[1] However, more than breaking boundaries—between subject and self in art, between viewer and artist/artwork, between pain and pleasure, between public and private—the artist has fundamentally questioned the validity of such boundaries in the first place.

Acconci was born in New York and attended the graduate program in art at the University of Iowa in the early 1960s. In 1969 he began a series of performance pieces centered upon the body, specifically his own, which established his position as one of the most important Conceptual artists of the time. In addition to performances that have both enacted and questioned the idea of the male self as the source and subject of all transcendent creativity, much of Acconci's work has counteracted the traditional functioning of the male nude as object in art, long considered the most hallowed site of artistic achievement. In *Container* (1970) the artist transformed his body into a sort of vessel by attempting to contain a cat within a space. Acconci's body also concealed the cat from view, a function he further explored in *Steal* of the same year, a performance in which he used his body to block the audience's view of a nude woman. In these two works, the male nude no longer revealed enlightened truths to the viewer, as was the case, for instance, with neoclassical paintings like David's 1775 *Oath of the Horatii,* but was instead a source of frustration and concealment.

Trademarks (plate 1), also of 1970, seems the product of a similar bodily ambivalence. The implicit aggression of performances such as *Proximity Piece* (1969), in which Acconci placed himself physically near viewers of an exhibition at The Jewish Museum in New York, became explicit and self-directed in *Trademarks.* Here Acconci attempted to bite as many parts of his nude body as he could reach. The artist then applied printer's ink to the bite marks, allowing him to capture an impression on paper and make this once private act public: "Therefore, I was turning in on myself, making a closed system and then presenting the possibility of opening that system with the print. Theoretically, this is a secret activity, but the print is a possibility of revealing the secret and sharing it."[2] In one sense, then, *Trademarks* is profoundly solipsistic and self-absorbed, based as it is on a constant and exclusively inward turn and a belief in the fundamental primacy of the self as both the subject and object of knowledge. At the same time, however, it would seem to be full of ambivalence and self-loathing.

From a museological perspective, a work like *Trademarks* poses a significant challenge to curators and art historians as well. Acconci's performance-based art is essentially ephemeral and fleeting. Limited to the present tense, the performances themselves cannot be owned—only their video and photographic documentation (often accompanied by Acconci's deadpan text) remains to be purchased, disseminated, collected, preserved, and researched. Much as Duchamp challenged the traditional definition of a work of art with his ready-mades, therefore, Acconci forces us to grapple with the vexing and important question of what constitutes the actual work of art in the case of *Trademarks.* In 1970 he would most certainly have argued on behalf of the performance, but as his comments about the bite prints suggest, he was also fascinated by the process by which the performance became public. Thus, today the same photographs that Acconci intended primarily to document performances, upon which they are entirely dependent, have acquired an autonomous status as works of art/commodities, and our knowledge of the performances in turn becomes dependent upon the photographs.

Indeed, the effect of looking at the photographs from *Trademarks,* in which we see Acconci's distorted body at precise, sharp intervals, differs considerably from that of witnessing the performance. Aside from formal differences—the photographs take on a clipped, nervous rhythm that is very unlike the fluidity of a moving body—the camera reimposes a layer of distance between viewer and (violent) artistic act that the performance necessarily challenged. While the photographs insulate the viewer from some of the disturbing visceral effects of the performance, they also render the self-inflicted violence permanent, creating a kind of wound that will not heal. In each mode of viewing, therefore, different responses and degrees of discomfort are elicited from the viewer. Although Acconci's performances, *Trademarks* included, exist in a determinedly present tense, they also have the capacity to accrue layers of meaning with the passage of time and with the imposition of filming or photography. These documents, rather than simply re-presenting a performance, continue to perform themselves.

Leo Costello

Notes

1. Amelia Jones, "Dis/playing the phallus: male artists perform their masculinities," *Art History* 17 (December 1994): 564–66.
2. Vito Acconci, "An Interview with Vito Acconci," interview by Cindy Nemser, *Arts Magazine* 45 (March 1971): 20.

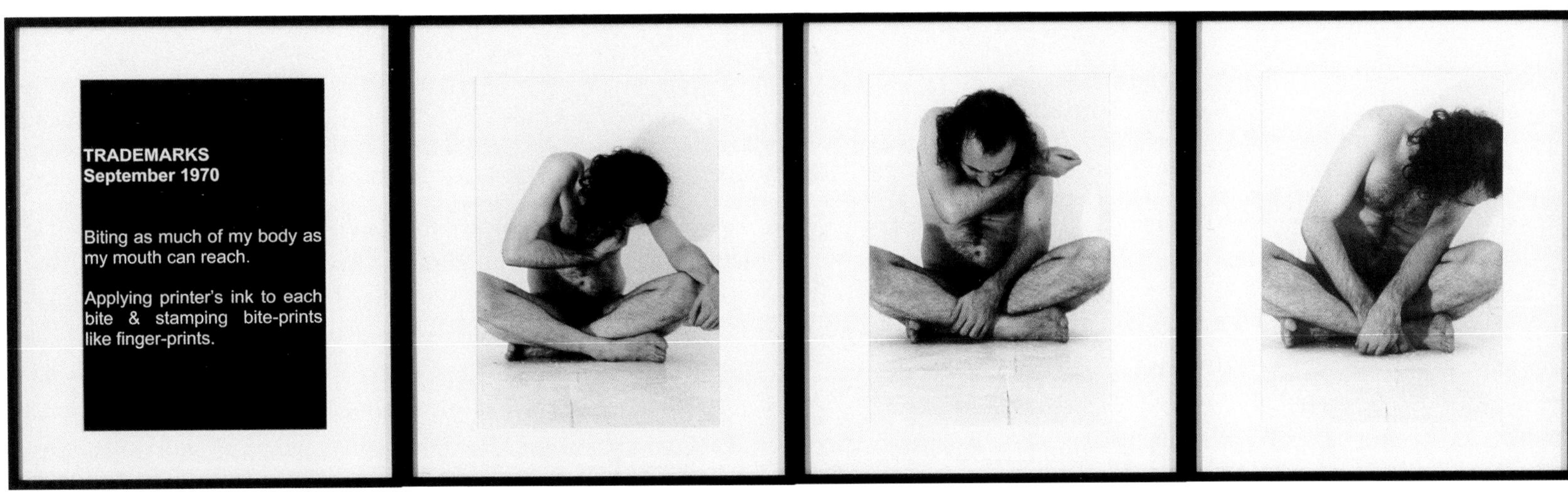

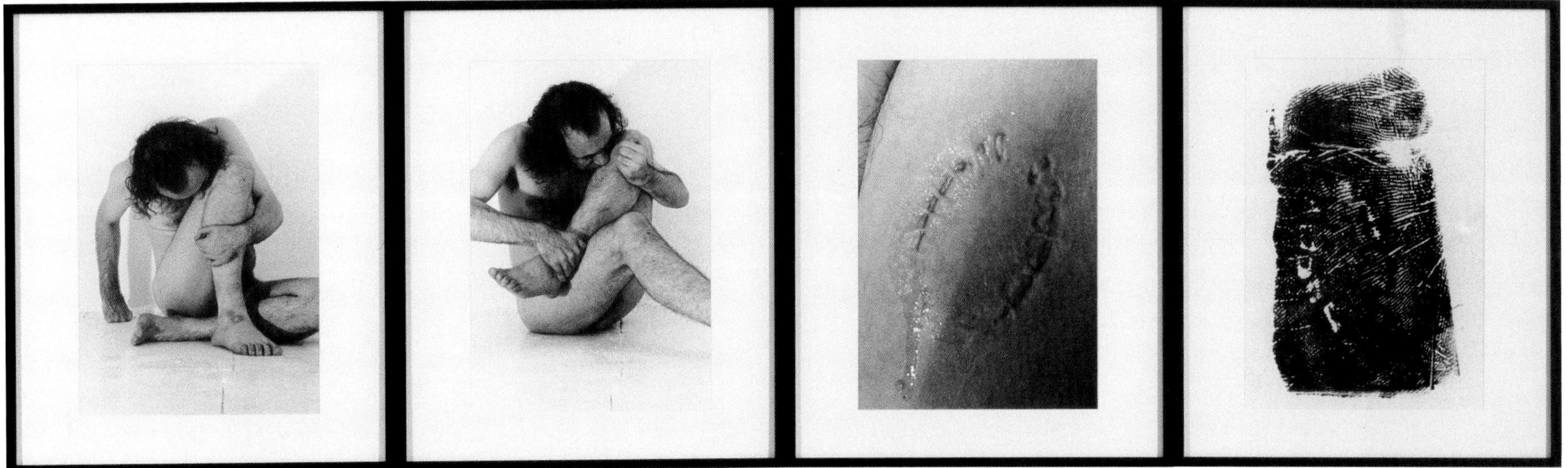

1.

Trademarks, 1970/2001

Suite of seven black and white C-prints and one text panel
Edition 8/10
Overall: 14 × 76 in. (35.6 × 193 cm)
Archer M. Huntington Museum Fund
2001.50.1/8–8/8

Provenance: Purchased from Galerie Lelong, New York, 2001
Each panel signed verso, upper left "VA"
Each panel inscribed verso, upper right with number and description

Terry Adkins

b. Washington, D.C., 1953

w. Nashville, 1971–1975; Normal, Illinois, 1975–1977; Lexington, Kentucky, 1977–1979; Washington, D.C., 1980–1997; New York, 1982/1984–1985; Zurich, 1986–1988; New York, 1988–1997; Brooklyn, New York–Philadelphia, 1997–present

Terry Adkins's large-scale sculptures, which frequently incorporate found objects and everyday materials, succeed as both form and metaphor. The artist's rigorous investigations of space and scale, as well as his fondness for reductive forms and repetition, beg comparisons to an earlier generation of Minimalist artists, whom Adkins acknowledges as an important influence. Yet, in contrast to Minimalism's stubborn self-referentiality, Adkins's work celebrates the allegorical potential of objects and materials. His art frequently references African American southern history and culture, especially blues music—a tradition in which Adkins also participates as an accomplished saxophonist.

To describe his sculptural appropriations of everyday objects, which have included musical instruments, bricks, discarded commercial signs, and architectural fragments, Adkins prefers to use the term "potential disclosure." He maintains, "my creative imagination has always been sparked by the potentialities that exist in other things, and all I try to do is unveil what's already there, sort of polish it, embellish it, to use a musical term."[1] Indeed the artist's use of found objects is less a matter of re-contextualizing them than transforming them, drawing out their latent spiritual or symbolic dimension.

In *Single Bound* (2000, plate 2) Adkins combined industrial detritus from an old factory with dyed black rooster feathers to produce a powerful sculptural experience that simultaneously functions to commemorate an actual historical event. *Single Bound* is a large flat semicircular form that projects perpendicularly out from the wall, concurrently occupying and floating in space. Its surface, a coarse metal screen, is half covered in a dense layer of lustrous black rooster feathers, creating an unexpected collision between the industrial and the organic. Like many of Adkins's sculptures, *Single Bound* is site-specific in process and materials. It belongs to a series of works called Wild Ashes Mute that Adkins created while in residence at the Finesilver Gallery in San Antonio in the summer of 2000. Working on site and using items salvaged from the former factory building from which the gallery was converted, Adkins contemplated the history of the workers who once labored in this space. Wild Ashes Mute also symbolically references the tradition of early Texas blues music and its role as a vernacular form of expression developed by the black working class. The black rooster feathers in *Single Bound*, for example, signify a black male presence, while its shape resembles the capital letter D—the note in which the blues is most frequently played. According to curator Annette DiMeo Carlozzi, "*Single Bound* claims the hero's position for those who never got their due."[2] Indeed the title of Adkins's sculpture is meant to refer to the feats of early blues musicians whose experience and resourcefulness were certainly every bit as courageous as that of our contemporary superheroes. However the title works on another level, as well, for like Superman's legendary ability to leap over buildings in a "single bound," Adkins's sculpture itself performs a redemptive function. In this case, what is being saved and elevated is history itself—the history of those early blues musicians whose accomplishments the artist renders newly available and relevant in our present moment.

Adkins literally reenacted the history of Texas blues music in a concert titled *Blue Recall (Echoes): A Recital in Five Dominions*. Performed in Austin in 2002, this concert or "aural collage" was conceived as a kind of extension of the sculptural investigations begun in the Wild Ashes Mute series. *Blue Recall* combined recordings of early blues musicians Blind Willie Johnson, Leadbelly, Blind Lemon Jefferson, and Mississippi Robert Johnson with live improvisations of local guitarists, accompanied by Adkins's own saxophone solos.

One feature that has distinguished Adkins's artistic career is his simultaneous engagement with music and visual art. Born in Washington, D.C., into a family of musicians and educators, Adkins took up guitar as a child and started to play the saxophone at age nineteen. He studied art formally in college, receiving a BA from Fisk University in Nashville, where he met Harlem Renaissance artist and Professor Emeritus Aaron Douglas. Adkins went on to earn graduate degrees in both music and art, receiving an MS from Illinois State University and an MFA from the University of Kentucky.

Given this background, it is no surprise that Adkins's sculptures and installations have always had a salient musical component. According to the artist, "Music completes the circuit that's left open by the objects. . . . I try to make sculpture that is as immediate and ethereal as music and make music that is as muscular and physical as sculpture."[3] If music appears thematically in Adkins's sculptures, it also pervades his working process in important ways. The artist's emphasis on spontaneity and his method of embellishing found objects and materials draw on a specific form of creativity that is likewise crucial to blues music and other folk traditions, with their emphasis on improvisation and their history as artistic forms that evolved out of limited material resources. As Adkins stated in an interview, "My black Southern heritage is rooted in the tradition of ennobling the worthless. I see myself as a latter-day practitioner of this way of working."[4]

While Adkins's understanding of history is motivated by a desire for social justice, he refrains from imposing a single version of the past on his viewers. Rather he invites them to form their own relationship to the past and find their own significance in history. This acceptance of the indeterminacy of works of art manifests itself as a kind of generosity that pervades Adkins's sculpture. His sculptures inspire dialogue rather than monologue and encourage all those present to join in the conversation.

Gwen Allen

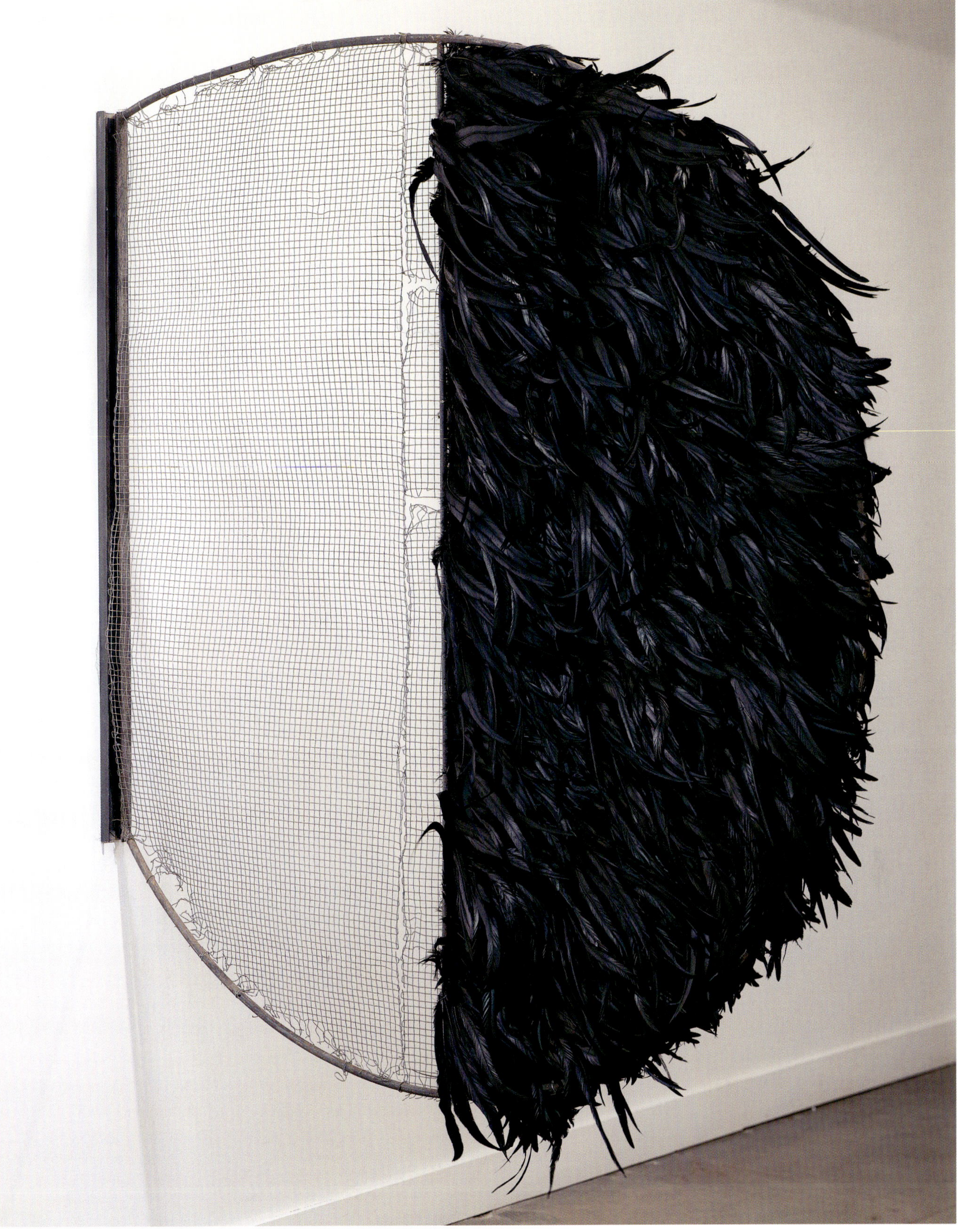

Notes

1. Terry Adkins, interview by Judith Page, *Sculpture* 19 (April 2000): 20.
2. Annette DiMeo Carlozzi, "Might Could Be," in *Terry Adkins: Towering Steep* (Dartmouth, N.H.: Jaffe-Friede & Strauss Galleries, Dartmouth College, 2003), 16.
3. Terry Adkins, quoted in J. C. Van Ryzin, "4 Boomboxes, 4 Guitars, 1 Artist," *Austin American-Statesman*, February 14, 2002, 34.
4. Adkins, 24.

2.

Single Bound, 2000

Metal and feathers
84 × 3 × 69 in. (213.4 × 7.6 × 175.3 cm)
Purchase through the Archer M. Huntington Museum Fund and with support from the Blanton Contemporary Circle
2001.6

Provenance: Purchased from Finesilver Gallery, San Antonio, 2001

John Alexander

b. Beaumont, Texas, 1945

w. Beaumont, Texas, 1964–1968; Dallas, 1968–1970; Houston, 1970–1979; New York–Amagansett, New York, 1979–present (with extended stays in Texas during the 1980s)

John Alexander was one of the most innovative painters to emerge in New York during the 1980s. *Dancing with an Old Pair of Legs* (1984, plate 3), one of Alexander's classic works created during the height of his career, demonstrates his unique style of abstract figuration and reveals a great deal about contemporaneous trends in painting.

The seminal exhibition *New Image Painting*, organized by the Whitney Museum of American Art in 1978, launched the careers of artists such as Susan Rothenburg and Robert Moskowitz. These artists and others departed from the Minimalist aesthetic, which had dominated the art scene for close to a decade, and reintroduced the figure, gesture, and experimentation with materials. Alexander was part of the generation of artists—Neo-Expressionists like Donald Sultan, Julian Schnabel, and David Salle—whose work heralded a return to the expressive possibilities of painting. In his own paintings, Alexander created a type of abstraction that melded imagery with virulent brushwork while referencing personal history and varied art historical precedents.

A native Texan, Alexander grew up exploring the swamps that surrounded his hometown of Beaumont, Texas. He stayed close to home for college, attending Lamar University in Beaumont, where he earned an undergraduate degree in fine arts in 1968. He completed an MFA at Southern Methodist University in Dallas in 1970. In graduate school, Alexander acquired a firm foundation in traditional painting techniques, and at the university's art museum, he discovered the work of the Old Masters, notably that of Francisco Goya and Diego Velázquez. At the same time, the Dallas Museum of Fine Arts exposed him to Abstract Expressionists such as Jackson Pollock and Franz Kline. After graduating from SMU, Alexander moved to Houston and joined the faculty of the University of Houston, where he taught painting for nearly ten years.

As he matured as a painter, Alexander found himself reaching back into art history, taking inspiration from the fantastic realism of Hieronymous Bosch. Indeed, suggestions of Bosch's floating fish and hybrid animals are evident in many of Alexander's paintings throughout the 1980s and early 1990s. But by far it was Willem de Kooning who exerted the greatest influence on Alexander's development. De Kooning's Cubist-derived abstraction *Excavation* (1950), with its gestural markings that extend edge-to-edge across the surface of the painting, became a compositional departure point for most of Alexander's large-scale paintings beginning in the 1970s and continuing for nearly three decades.

During the mid-1970s, when he began to attract increasing national attention, Alexander saw himself as a landscape painter:

> *I went out and observed nature . . . just as a Barbizon painter would have gone out in mid-nineteenth century France and painted what he saw, except I happened to choose very strange looking nature—the bayou country of southeast Texas and southwest Louisiana.*[1]

Upon moving to New York permanently in 1979, Alexander exchanged the untamed, known landscape of the Texas bayou for the unfamiliar wilds of SoHo. Yet the exotic imagery of his youth—birds, snakes, alligators, and mysterious revelers set against lush foliage and tangled vegetation reminiscent of the bayou—remained a primary source of inspiration. Moreover, while his work continued to reference the landscape, Alexander started to remove the horizon line and collapse the image into the center of the work, thereby incorporating not only abstraction, but also certain elements of urban graffiti art as exemplified by the paintings of Jean-Michel Basquiat.

The social consciousness that defined the 1970s was also an important concern for Alexander, who obliquely confronted issues of race, class, and the environment. At the same time, he sought to infuse his paintings with a palpable sense of mystery. As Alexander himself noted: "Me at my best is when I do something completely unexpected and mysterious and weird that allows the viewer to go in and try to find his own meanings."[2] In *Dancing with an Old Pair of Legs*, for example, Alexander interlaces gestural marks over what appears to be a central, luminous figure. Black and white birds surround this human shape, which seems to explode from inside the painting. Black herons do not exist in nature, but Alexander's hybrid black birds juxtaposed against white birds could be interpreted as a metaphor for racial tension, or conversely, as tar-covered birds—a commentary on pollution. Alexander often uses animal imagery in his work, though his intent is to take the meaning beyond simply what the eye sees; as he observed: "I'm capable of rendering a bird to look exactly as it should, that's the easy part. The hard part is to take that bird as a point of departure and then hybridize it in such a way that you can make a creature that has a certain universal appeal."[3] The title of the Blanton's painting is a humorous musing sparked by the artist's memories of the many galas he attended at the Museum of Fine Arts, Houston, a further example of the broad range of sources on which Alexander draws even in a single work.

In the mid-1990s, perhaps ignited by the milestone of his fiftieth birthday, Alexander reevaluated his artistic direction and found himself drawn to the challenge of representing nature in its most perfect state. Today the artist spends most of his time on Long Island, New York, away from the city, making highly realistic and beautiful renditions

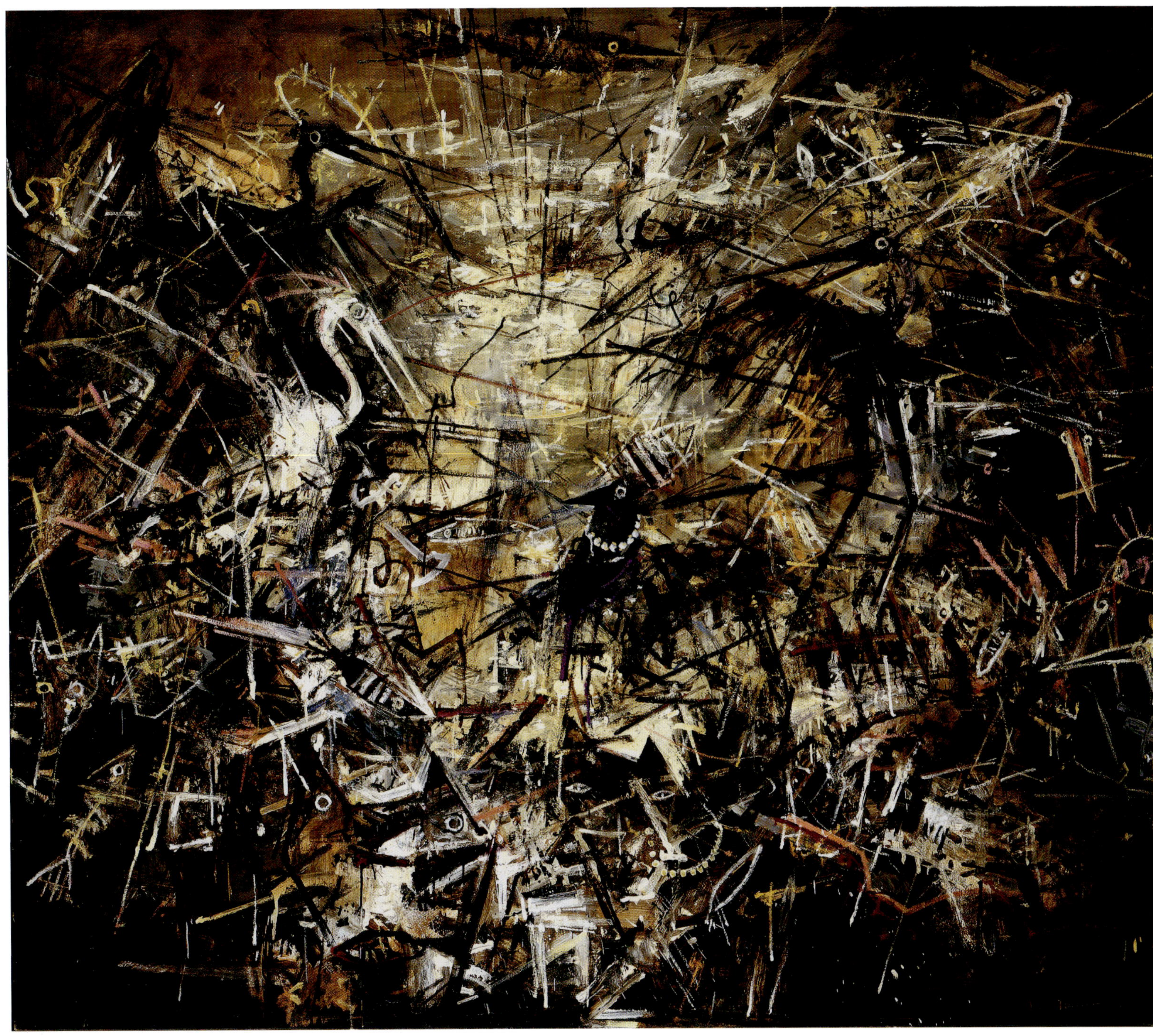

of the sea, landscape, animals, birds, and fish. Alexander continues to blend nature and art history as he has throughout his career. Moving between the influences of de Kooning, Gustave Courbet, Bosch, and Albrecht Dürer, he has nevertheless allowed his painting style to evolve while remaining committed to his original goal of rendering the world around him.

Sue Scott

Notes

1. John Alexander, "Interview with John Alexander," interview by George Plimpton, in *John Alexander: Recent Paintings* (New York: Marlborough Gallery, 1994), 6.
2. Alexander, 4.
3. Alexander, 18.

3.

Dancing with an Old Pair of Legs, 1984

Oil on canvas
90 x 100¼ in. (228.6 x 254.6 cm)
Michener Acquisitions Fund, 1985
1985.24

Provenance: Purchased from Marlborough Gallery, Inc., New York, 1985
Signed lower right "John Alexander"
Inscribed verso "90 x 100/John Alexander/0462-9-84/Dancing w/ an old pair of legs"

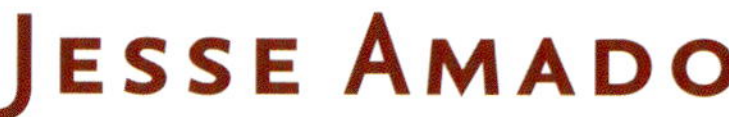

Jesse Amado

b. San Antonio, 1951
w. San Antonio, 1977–present

San Antonio–based artist Jesse Amado defines his work as post-Minimalist. Although he adopts a Minimalist aesthetic, creating forms that are structurally spare and composed of industrial materials, he simultaneously subverts Minimalism by inserting elements that evoke the human body. Of his intent, he asserts: "I attempt to provide opportunities to examine the emotional impact of Minimalism. This allows me a position in which to absorb the world around me: architecture, industry, advertising, politics, and nature."[1] This merging of personal subject matter and formal rigor is beautifully achieved in *I Pray, Then I Play in the Collective Landscape I* (1995, plate 4).

Initially conceived as part of a larger installation that was completed during his residency at ArtPace in San Antonio, *I Pray* consists of three primary components: a large cabinet with a transparent Plexiglas door, a mirror, and a flesh-colored latex suit made to the artist's exact measurements that hangs inside the cabinet. The bottom of the cabinet is lined with boxes of soap purchased from a local botanica, a store that sells natural or indigenous remedies. In an interview conducted while he was in residence at ArtPace, Amado described the symbolic import of the soap, which functioned for him as a metaphor for personal and professional transformation:

> *My neighbor is a botanica. So, I went in there and there was a wonderful display of about one hundred different soaps that one can get in order to wash oneself with the hope of, perhaps, having a better love life. There are so many soaps that are available through this botanica to use to cleanse yourself, and to wash away the things that are impure and that are keeping you from being happier, I suppose . . . I was wanting to change my work, to reevaluate it, to see what was wrong with it and what was strong about it. I thought the perfect metaphor for that would be to just wash away everything that had ever been accumulated in my work.*[2]

Although he assimilates and expands upon the legacy of such Minimalists as Carl Andre and Donald Judd, creating spare, geometric, streamlined works that respond to the architecture of the gallery, Amado also looks to Joseph Beuys, Jannis Kounellis, and David Hammons for inspiration.[3] In the spirit of these artists, he exploits the poignancy of humble materials and infuses them with symbolic meaning. This is the case in *I Pray,* where both latex soaps and a product commonly associated with prophylactics are employed to signify cleanliness, regeneration, and rebirth. Amado reinforced the theme of rebirth when he exhibited *I Pray* in an exhibition titled *Renascence* at the Contemporary Arts Museum, Houston, in 1996. Here the artist took advantage of the museum's pending renovation or "reincarnation" and replaced the soaps at the bottom of *I Pray* with chunks of plaster removed from the museum walls. As is the case with *I Pray,* however, Amado's work rarely specifies exactly whose renewal or transformation is at stake, which accounts for much of its psychological and emotional impact—viewers are free to insert their own narratives or histories into the framework provided by the artist.

The emotional content of Amado's work often draws on his own upbringing as a Catholic Mexican-American. He grew up in San Antonio, and in 1968, at the apogee of a period of great social upheaval in the United States, Amado graduated from high school and joined the Navy. While stationed in Newport, Rhode Island, he nurtured an interest in art by frequenting New York galleries and museums on the weekends. After completing his military service, he studied literature at The University of Texas at Austin, completing his BA in 1977. Amado returned to San Antonio and studied art at the The University of Texas at San Antonio while working as a firefighter. In 1990 he received a graduate degree in fine arts.

Amado has long been interested in the layering of materials, as evidenced in a series of sculptures from 1991 that he fabricated from several layers of black felt. As one critic observed, "The multi-layered nature of Amado's work is derived in part from Beuys's use of felt and in part from Amado's occupation as a firefighter, which requires wearing many layers of protective clothing."[4] The idea of layers surfaces again in *I Pray,* where the latex suit appears to have been cast off from a human body as though it were a husk or chrysalis. The suit hangs lifeless, limp, and utterly exposed—despite the protection of the cabinet, it is always available to the viewer's gaze through the transparent Plexiglas. Amado's garment pays homage to Beuys's felt suit, which likewise evokes the idea of transformation.

The role of the viewer is crucial to *I Pray.* Indeed, Amado insists that the work is not complete until the viewer spies his or her reflection in the mirror. The mirror and the title's emphasis on the first-person pronoun, "I," raise questions about the construction of identity—more specifically, how identity is formulated in relation to others. The distinction between "self" and "other" is apparent in the title, where the "I" first *prays* alone, and then *plays* in a collective landscape. Amado's work thus would seem to suggest that we must first recognize ourselves as autonomous beings before being able to interact and establish connections with others. With a poetic and personal touch, *I Pray* provides the means to facilitate this transition. The mirror embedded in Amado's work captures not just the reflection of the viewer standing before it, but the fleeting reflections of those viewers who traverse the gallery space, thereby positioning the solitary viewer always in relationship to a larger public.

Claire Barliant

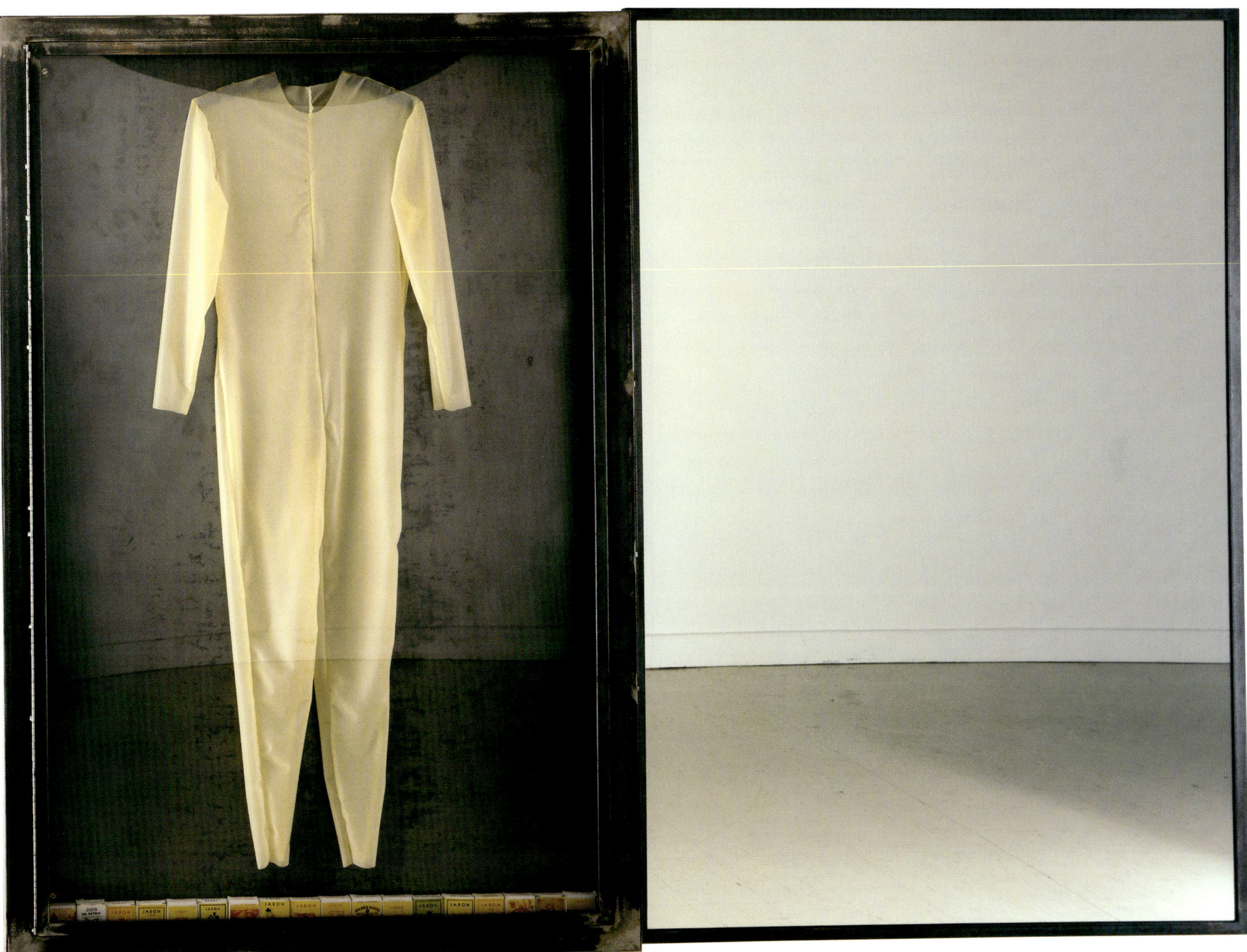

Notes

1. Quoted by MaLin Wilson-Powell, *Beauty Spot* (San Antonio: The Marian Koogler McNay Museum, 2002), 2.
2. Jesse Amado, interview by Frances Colpitt, November 1994, available at http://www.artpace.org/artists/essay.jhtml?ID=4&Previous=/artists/artist.jhtml*ID~4 [September 16, 2004].
3. Dana Friis-Hansen, *Jesse Amado: Renascence* (Houston: Contemporary Arts Museum, 1996), 3.
4. Peter Doroshenko, *Texas Between Two Worlds* (Houston: Contemporary Arts Museum, 1993), 16.

4.

I Pray, Then I Play in the Collective Landscape I, 1995

Mirror, steel, Plexiglas, latex, and soap boxes
72 × 96 × 2 in. (182.88 × 243.84 × 5.08 cm)
Gift of the Artist
1999.57

Provenance: Commissioned by ArtPace, San Antonio

Carl Andre

b. Quincy, Massachusetts, 1935
w. New York, 1957–present

Carl Andre often has been called the quintessential Minimalist. In the mid-1960s, along with Donald Judd, Robert Morris, and Dan Flavin, Andre began to use industrial or commercial materials as the building blocks of sculpture, arranging a work's constituent parts in basic, geometric configurations. Judd memorably described Minimalism as "one thing after another," and Andre offered an equally succinct definition: "the greatest efficiency with the least means."[1]

Usually composed of similar or identical readymade units and produced in small editions, Minimalist sculpture lays bare its own physical properties and encourages a primary focus on the materiality of the object and the viewer's spatial and bodily relationship to it. This relationship—indebted to philosopher Maurice Merleau-Ponty's emphasis on the primacy of sensory perception—is quite direct in *Fourth Copper Corner* (1975, plate 5). Viewers are free to traverse its ten thin copper plates, approximately eighteen inches square each, which occupy the floor of the gallery space, radiating out from one corner. The plates abut one another yet are not affixed to the ground, and they weather and rust over time: "I accept what happens to my material," Andre noted.[2]

Although linking an artist's work to his biography can be risky business, several aspects of Andre's early life suggestively foretell the art he would go on to produce. Born in 1935, he grew up in Quincy, Massachusetts, an industrial suburb south of Boston. Andre remembers the granite quarries, construction sites, and shipyards nearby as well as influences even closer to home: his grandfather's work as a contractor and his own chore of splitting wood in his father's tool shop. He studied art in high school and worked in the early 1960s as a conductor and freight brakeman on the Pennsylvania Railroad, where the task of breaking down and reassembling strings of train cars prefigured the shifting around of similar units that would later characterize his work. In addition to these experiences, Andre cites several formative aesthetic encounters: a trip to Stonehenge that he took as an adolescent; Constantin Brancusi's wood, metal, and stone sculptural combinations; the exposed production and serial forms of Constructivist sculptures by Alexsandr Rodchenko and Vladimir Tatlin; and the industrial paint and deductive symmetrical structure in works by his high school friend and studio mate, Frank Stella.

Andre settled in New York in 1964 and began making the floor-bound work for which he would become best known. These included wooden beams stacked in columns or pyramids, strips of bricks or concrete blocks running across the ground of the exhibition space, and modules of construction metals—aluminum, steel, lead, magnesium, tin, zinc, and copper—shaped in various isometric groupings. Critical recognition followed quickly. His first solo exhibition, at New York's Tibor de Nagy Gallery, took place on the cusp of Minimalism's emergence in 1965. Soon after, Andre exhibited in several important shows: *Primary Structures* (Jewish Museum, New York, 1966), *When Attitudes Become Form* (Kunsthalle, Berne, 1969), and *Art of the Real* (The Museum of Modern Art, New York, 1969).

Some of Andre's early sculptures were asymmetrical and unsystematic, but most were made by arranging interchangeable, repeated geometric units, a method that continues to structure his practice. The artist calls these units of matter "particles"—comparing them at times to the individual linguistic components that comprise the Concrete poetry he also writes—and he orders and reorders them, like words or musical notes, in seemingly infinite variations on a theme. (His *Fifth Copper Corner* [1976] and *Twelfth Copper Corner* [1975], for example, are closely related works.) Crucial to Andre's notion of the particle is that "the rules for joining the particles together is the characteristic of the single particle."[3] Thus, the nested squares of *Fourth Copper Corner* are adjacent to and form other squares, and the exterior angles of its four outermost plates echo the ninety-degree angle of the corner.

Minimalism often is considered spare, even austere in its matter and facture, and indeed, Andre's sculptures are composed of utilitarian, uninflected construction materials. But a work such as *Fourth Copper Corner* is less remarkable for what it lacks—the artist's hand or touch, anthropomorphism, finish—than for what it adds to conventional and historical understandings of sculpture. Andre's emphatically horizontal works upend traditional conceptions of sculptural verticality and introduce architecture and environment into the experience of reception by training our eyes on oft-overlooked parts of gallery space: floors and corners. Spatial specificity becomes as important as material particularity, and one's bodily experience of the work, its placement, and context, are as consequential as form. Although Andre is known for his political activism, beholding and navigating his works sponsors sensations of calm and equilibrium. With *Fourth Copper Corner* he achieved one of his stated goals for art, the creation of "a place of stillness and serenity where we can regather ourselves, not where we're going to be overloaded."[4]

Lisa Pasquariello

Notes

1. Donald Judd, "Specific Objects," *Arts Yearbook* 8 (1965): 82; Carl Andre, quoted in Paul Cummings, *Artists in Their Own Words* (New York: St. Martin's Press, 1979), 191.
2. Carl Andre in "Time: A Panel Discussion," moderated by Lucy Lippard, *Art International* 13 (November 1969): 21.
3. Andre, 23.
4. Andre, 21.

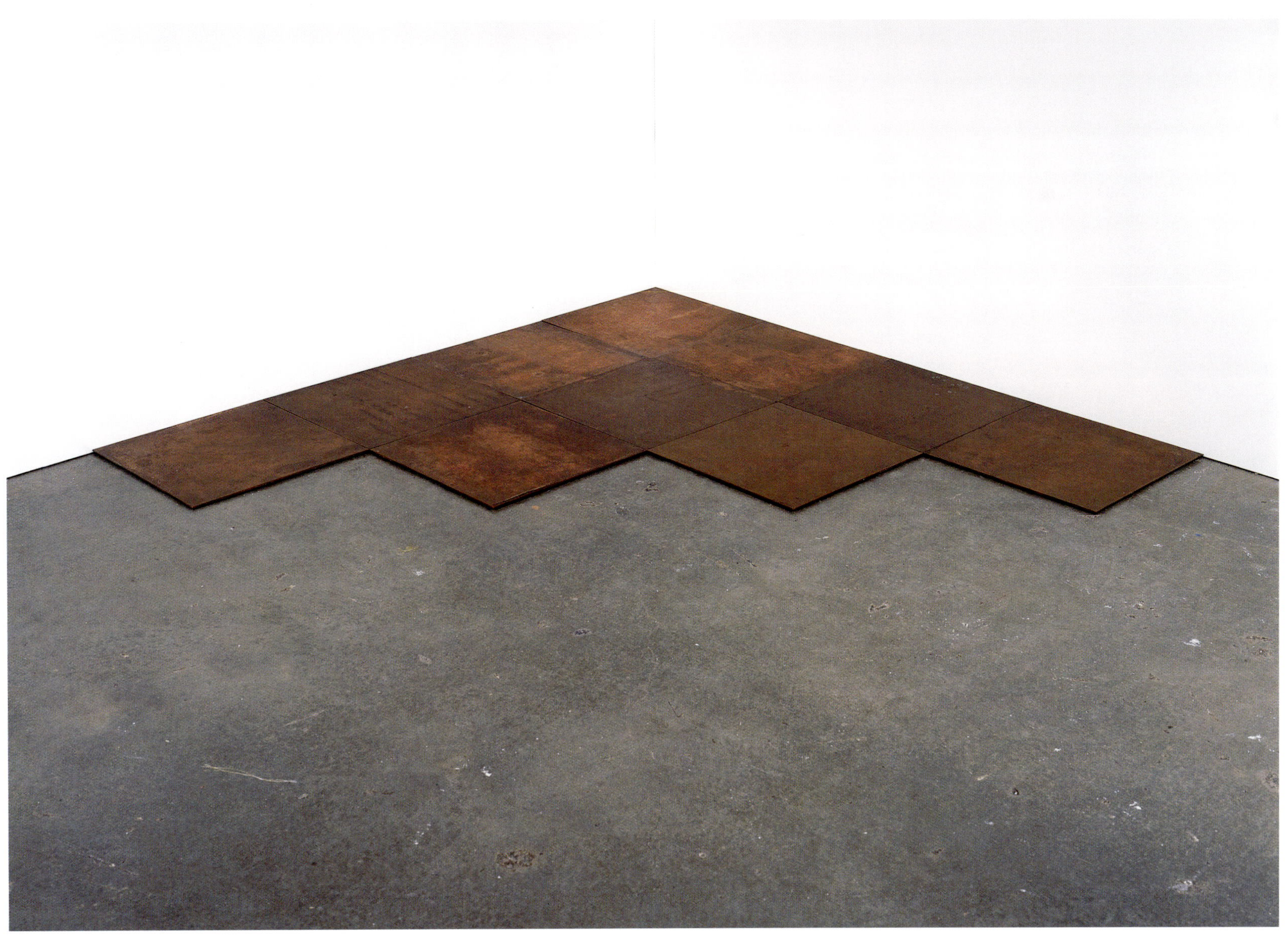

5.

Fourth Copper Corner, 1975

Copper
Overall: 3⁄16 × 79 × 79 in. (.5 × 200 × 200 cm)
Archer M. Huntington Museum Fund
1983.11

Provenance: Galerie Yvon Lambert, 1975; Armand P. Arman; Annina Nosei; Martha White, 1979; Alexander Milliken, New York; purchased from Alexander Milliken, 1983

Stephen Antonakos

b. Agios Nikolaos, Greece, 1926
w. New York (frequent trips to Greece), 1947–present

Stephen Antonakos's *Untitled (Blue Neon Circle)*, c. 1974 (plate 6), traces an unfinished circle in cobalt blue neon tubing: it is missing a fragment of its lower arc just right of center. Antonakos's circle incorporates elements of drawing, painting, sculpture, and environmental art. While its neon lines initially appear rigidly geometric, planes of blue light extend into and transform the physical space around the piece. As Antonakos said of a related sculpture, "You sense that the space of [the sculpture] flows out into the space around it, which you occupy as a viewer. It is distinct, yet it is continuous. . . . The release of the visual into the spatial is one thing this work is about."[1] The artist has attributed his frequent use of cobalt blue neon tubing to the Mediterranean landscape of his Greek heritage.[2]

A self-taught artist, Antonakos learned about art and art making by observing art at public galleries and museums in New York. In the 1940s and 1950s he worked as a commercial artist while simultaneously creating fine art—first drawings, then paintings, and finally, influenced by the work of Alberto Burri and Lucio Fontana and the combines of Robert Rauschenberg, assemblages of found objects.[3] In his Sewlages and Pillow pieces, Antonakos used boxes, umbrellas, and fabric scraps from garment district trash heaps. The artist recalled that at this period, "it was very difficult for me to get shows. I didn't know how to go about it, but I kept working. I was learning about myself and what I was doing."[4]

In 1962, during a late-night walk, Antonakos discovered what was to be become his preferred medium, neon: "I had been looking at the old neon signs on Broadway and Times Square for years and years, but I did not really see them until that moment."[5] He incorporated a piece of neon tubing into his next assemblage, *White Light* (1962), and was instantly taken with the possibilities of the medium. Antonakos's use of neon coincided with the increasingly high profile of Pop art, a movement fascinated by mass culture. However, unlike other artists of the era, such as Andy Warhol, Antonakos was intrigued by the sculptural potential of this medium rather than by its associations with consumer culture.[6]

Accordingly, in his early neons Antonakos explored complex planar and three-dimensional forms as well as straight-edged lines and shapes. Initially, many of these works employed timers that turned the neon tubes on and off at specific intervals, but the artist almost immediately dispensed with them. He preferred to rely on the viewer's own mechanisms of visual perception: "We have a timing device within ourselves, our eyelids opening and closing. The tubes themselves reflect the play of our eyes blinking, resulting in certain colors left and right or up and down, depending on the wall color and the tubes' colors . . . [Y]ou will see the tubes jump around, due to the pulse in your eyes."[7] Antonakos was also interested in how the viewer's experience of pieces such as *Untitled (Blue Neon Circle)* changed from moment to moment as he or she moved through the exhibition space.

Antonakos created *Untitled (Blue Neon Circle)* at a crossroads in his career, as his focus shifted from a concern with creating discrete sculptural objects to a fascination with the ability of light to transform architectural and environmental space. In 1974, the period to which *Untitled (Blue Neon Circle)* belongs, the Fort Worth Art Museum offered Antonakos his first large-scale commission. The viewer-oriented, public character of monumental sculpture appealed to Antonakos's desire to create environments, an interest that he has continued to explore in a variety of public commissions from the 1970s to the present, including *Neon for 42nd Street* (1981) in New York, *Neons for Tachikawa* (1994) in Japan, and *Neons for the Reading Power Station* (1999) in Tel Aviv.

In addition to working with neon, Antonakos has consistently employed other media throughout his career. His "package art" consists of wrapped packages labeled with instructions about when and how they should be opened. Although Antonakos's package art has no formal resemblance to his neon sculpture, it engages the viewer's imagination in similar ways. In both instances, the viewer adds to the piece by attempting to complete the circle or imagine the contents of the package. Antonakos has also recently created meditation rooms and chapels such as his *Chapel of the Saints* neon installation (1993) at the Fortress of Saint George in Rhodes, Greece and *Chapel of the Heavenly Ladder* (1997), originally created for the 1997 Venice Biennale and now in the collection of the State Museum of Contemporary Art in Thessaloniki. These spiritual projects distill the overarching intent of his oeuvre, including *Untitled (Blue Neon Circle):*

> *The thing I hope for and the thing I need are rather a new, perhaps more hopeful, sense of myself, my awareness in the world. I do not want to tell people how to experience art, mine or anyone else's. I simply want to try to find for myself ways of putting things together visually so that the possibility for a kind of higher consciousness may occur in the experience of the art.*[8]

Whether executed in public spaces or private churches, in neon light or in packing paper, Antonakos's work engenders an active, imaginative relationship with viewers. This optimistic approach to the communicative potential of art gestures to its transcendent possibilities.

Karen C. Gonzalez

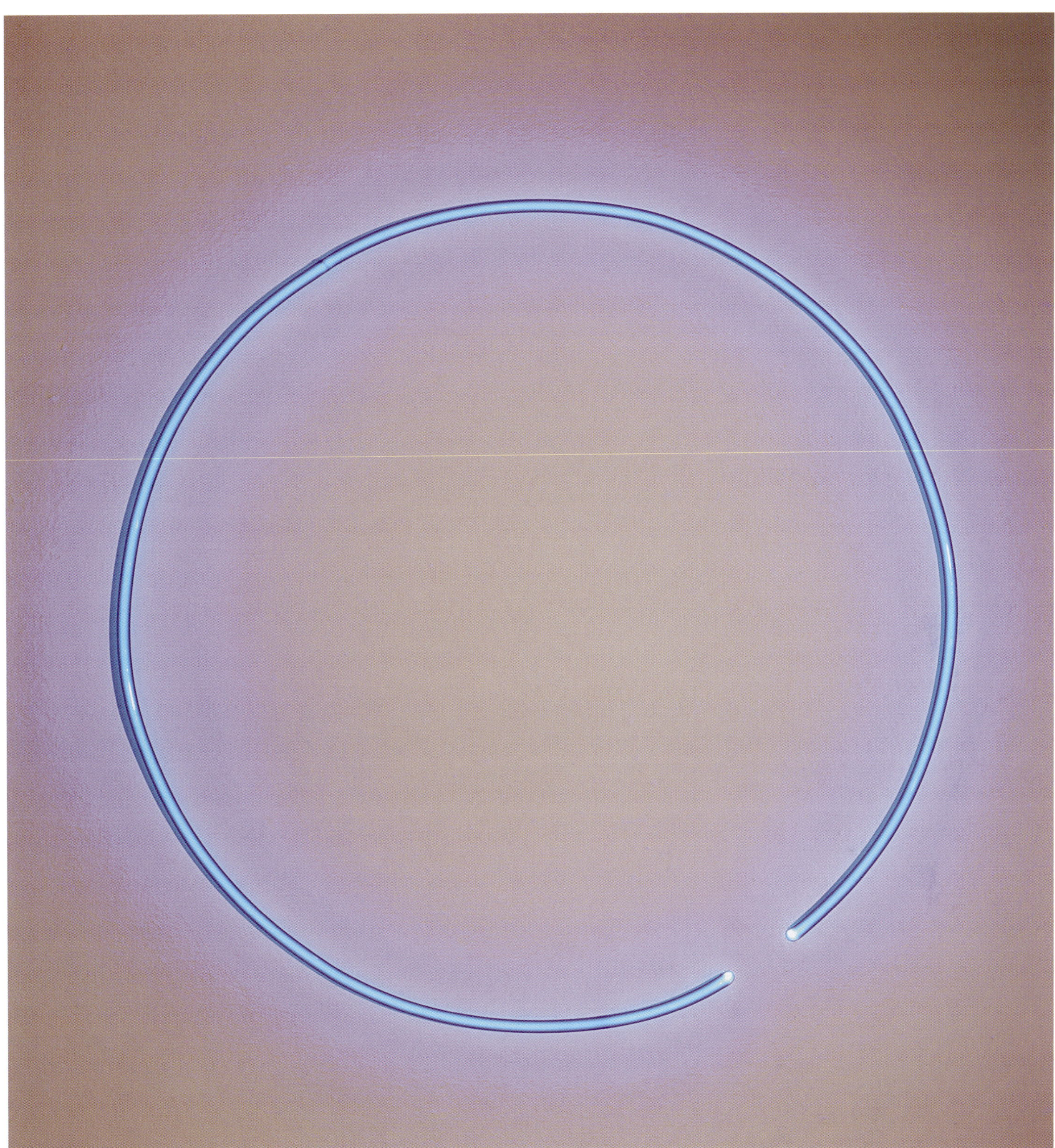

Notes

1. Stephen Antonakos, "The Architecture of Light and Space: An Interview with Stephen Antonakos," interview by Zoe Kosmidou, *Sculpture* 17 (January 1998): 28.
2. Irving Sandler, *Stephen Antonakos* (New York: Hudson Hills Press, 1999), 52.
3. Sandler, 13.
4. Quoted in Isabelle Wasserman, "Neon lights up the life of artist," *New York Times*, August 19, 1984, E1.
5. Quoted in Sandler, 24.
6. Sandler, 39.
7. Quoted in Dan Talley, "Stephen Antonakos," *Art Papers* 11 (January/February 1987): 38.
8. Antonakos, 31.

6.

Untitled (Blue Neon Circle), c. 1974

Neon tube
35 in. diameter (88.9 cm)
Gift of Vera Simon
2000.77

Janine Antoni

b. Freeport, Bahamas, 1964

w. Bronxville, New York, 1982–1986; Providence, Rhode Island, 1987–1989; Brooklyn, New York, 1989–present

Janine Antoni is one of a number of artists who began to explore the poetic, erotic, linguistic, and social currency of the body in the early 1990s, expanding the parameters of "body art" as it had been practiced in the 1960s and 1970s. Antoni employs her own body, often in conjunction with surrogates for her body or the bodies of her friends and family members, to scrutinize issues surrounding gender, cultural identity, and intersubjective relations. Although they tend to be evocative rather than declarative, Antoni's projects are no less incisive for their heightened lyricism.

Since her first solo exhibition at Sandra Gering Gallery in New York in 1992, Antoni has consistently destabilized the boundaries between sculpture and performance and, to a lesser extent, painting and performance, always to poetic effect.[1] Antoni's work constitutes in large part a sustained, productive dialogue with Minimalist sculpture of the 1960s as well as feminist art of the 1970s and 1980s, in particular Hannah Wilke and Ana Mendieta's visceral performances and Sherrie Levine and Barbara Kruger's appropriation strategies.[2]

From chocolate and soap to hair dye and lard, the materials that Antoni used to create some of her earliest works were prosaic in origin but rich in metaphor. Most conjured up associations with the female body and cultural stereotypes of femininity. From these materials, Antoni fashioned paintings and sculptural objects, but she did so in a manner foreign to more conventional artists, substituting her teeth for a chisel, her tongue for her hands, and her hair for a paintbrush. Such methods constituted a subversive twist on the rituals of feminine domesticity, like weaving, mopping, and washing, although some involved more universal bodily functions such as chewing and spitting. Antoni restaged these activities either in private or public, adding a performative dimension to her work.

Historically and conceptually, *Caryatid* (2003, plate 7) is related to a series of projects that explore the psychological connotations of "balance" through the physical act of balancing. In the first such project, a video titled *Touch* (2002), Antoni appears to perform the miraculous task of walking on the ocean outside her childhood home in the Bahamas, an illusion created with the aid of a tightrope. The artist's precarious journey from one end of the rope to the other symbolized the universal desire to transcend the limitations of the body and bring physical reality into synchronicity with the imagination.[3] Antoni had begun to take tightrope-walking lessons two years earlier, as she was completing a project titled *Moor* (2001), in which she wove a 290-foot-long rope out of clothing and other odd materials donated by friends and family members. This rope literalized the artist's interpersonal universe, creating what Antoni described as both "an umbilical cord" as well as a collective diary. The tightrope-walking lessons ultimately enabled her to actually walk this "lifeline" and revisit the memories and relationships comprising her personal history.[4] According to the artist, they taught her to become "more comfortable with being out of balance"—that is, to accept the sensation of occasionally losing control, whether physical or emotional, as not only inevitable but natural.[5]

This, the impossibility of maintaining balance indefinitely, was the subject of Antoni's next major project, *To Draw a Line* (2003). The first part of *To Draw a Line* consisted of a long rope tightly wound around two nine-foot steel reels. Antoni and her assistants fabricated part of the rope themselves, spinning silky brown hemp into fiber and then plaiting the fiber with an antique rope-making device. This handmade rope was then spliced to a piece of industrially manufactured rope. While the end of the former unraveled to form a soft cushion on the floor, the end of the latter acted as a ladder. At that point, the performative dimension of the work commenced: in front of an audience, Antoni climbed the ladder, crossed the rope, and after about ten minutes fell gracefully onto the hemp pillow below, where an imprint of her body remained for the duration of the exhibition.[6]

The circularity of Antoni's project, resulting in the poetic symbiosis of body, performance, and sculpture, also characterizes *Caryatid*. Exhibited alongside *To Draw a Line* at Luhring Augustine Gallery in New York in 2003, *Caryatid* is comprised of two elements, a photograph and a clay vessel, that, while physically distinct from one another, belong to the same temporal and narrative trajectory. The photograph depicts Antoni holding the clay vessel on top of her head, but because it has been inverted and its background digitally erased, the exact opposite appears to be true. This inversion also constitutes an intervention: simply by changing the orientation of the photograph, Antoni has relieved the female body of the tasks it performs as either a domestic laborer or a support structure, literally a column, in the context of classical and neoclassical architecture, most famously in the Porch of the Caryatids at the Erechtheum in Athens.[7]

The same vessel that "supports" Antoni's body, now liberated from gravity as well as labor, rests on the floor in front of the photograph. Vessels are commonly invoked as symbols of the female body. Antoni simultaneously subverts and subscribes to this stereotype by shattering the vessel but preserving its function as a container. "Maturity is epitomized in the vessel holding its broken self," the artist commented, referring to the pieces of clay nestled inside the damaged vessel.[8] Exactly how the vessel came to be broken remains a mystery, however, for Antoni is deliberately reticent on the subject. "For me this is a generous decision. It is the part of the story that I give to the viewer. It is up to them to fill in the blank between the image and the broken vessel," she said.[9] Antoni thus withholds information in an effort to enhance the expressive potential of her work.[10]

Antoni's willingness to relinquish control over interpretation allows a productive dialogue to develop between artist, viewer, and art object. This inherently reciprocal model of communication

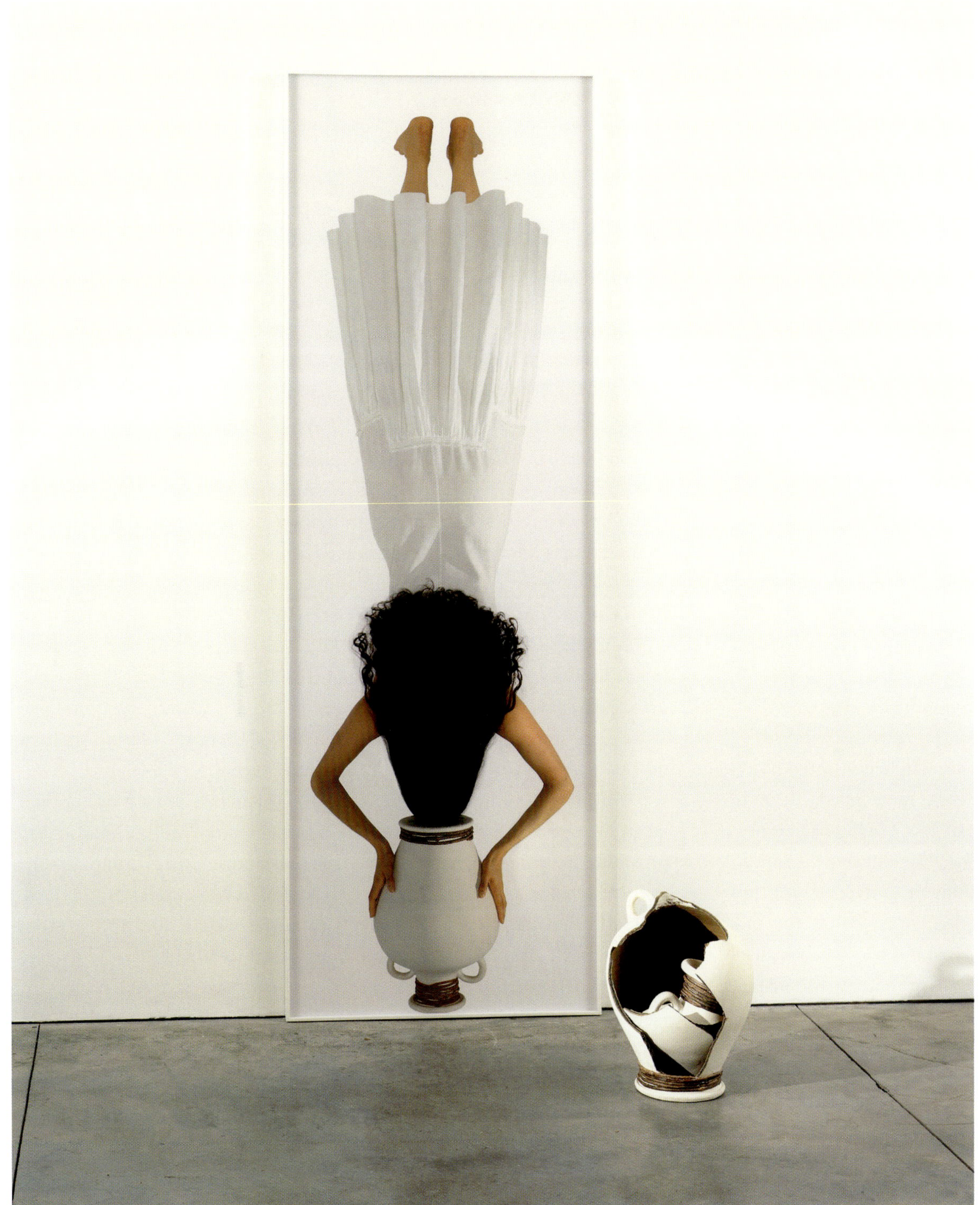

7.

Caryatid (clay amphora with matte creme engobe with neck and base wrapped with twigs), 2003

C-print and broken vessel
Photograph: 91 × 29½ in. (231.14 × 74.93 cm)
Vessel: 19 × 16 × 14 in. (48.26 × 40.64 × 35.56 cm)
Partial and pledged gift of Jeanne and Michael Klein
T2004.1.1/2–2/2

Provenance: Purchased at the request of the museum by Jeanne and Michael Klein from Luhring Augustine Gallery, New York, 2003

exemplifies her work from the early 1990s to the present day, as does its successful, yet nonetheless tenuous, reconciliation between the utopian and the critical, the aspirational and the polemical.

Kelly Baum

Notes

1. Antoni received a BA in painting from Sarah Lawrence College in 1986 and a MFA in sculpture from the Rhode Island School of Design in 1989. Just four years later, she exhibited at both the Whitney Biennial and the Venice Biennale. Antoni was awarded the John D. and Catherine T. MacArthur Fellowship and the Larry Aldrich Foundation Award in 1998 and 1999, respectively.
2. As Antoni said, "I feel attached to my artistic heritage and I want to destroy it: it defines me as an artist and it excludes me as a woman." See Laura Cottingham, "Janine Antoni: Biting sums up my relationship to art history," *Flash Art*, no. 171 (summer 1993): 104. On this issue, see also Ewa Lajer-Burcharth, "Antoni's difference," *differences* 10 (summer 1998).
3. See the interview with Antoni available at http://www.pbs.org/art21/artists/antoni/clip1.html [May 15, 2005].
4. Susan Sollins, *Art 21: Art in the Twenty-First Century 2* (New York: Harry N. Abrams, 2003), 82.
5. Linda Weintraub, "On the Tightrope," *Tema Celeste*, no. 99 (October 2003): 64.
6. For additional information on *To Draw a Line*, see Ginger Danto, "Life as a Tightrope: Weave, Walk and Fall," *New York Times*, August 24, 2003; Jerry Saltz, "The Artist Who Fell to Earth," *Village Voice*, September 29, 2003; and Gregory Volk, "Janine Antoni at Luhring Augustine," *Art in America* 91 (November 2003): 158.
7. Janine Antoni, email conversation with the author, May 17, 2005.
8. Janine Antoni, email conversation with the author.
9. Janine Antoni, email conversation with the author, May 18, 2005.
10. For more information on the manner in which viewers interact and communicate with Antoni's work, see Stuart Horodner, "Janine Antoni," *Bomb*, no. 66 (winter 1999): 50.

Richard Anuszkiewicz

b. Erie, Pennsylvania, 1930

w. Cleveland, 1948–1953; New Haven, Connecticut, 1953–1955; Kent, Ohio, 1955–1956; New York, 1957–1967; Englewood, New Jersey, 1967–present

By 1960 there was a growing interest in moving away from the gestural canvases of Abstract Expressionism toward abstract paintings with vivid color juxtapositions and linear, geometric forms. Art critics and curators at first labeled these paintings hard-edged, purist, or abstract precisionist, but by 1965 the term Optical art, or Op art, became the accepted name for work specifically concerned with the retinal effects of systematically created color and pattern conjunctions.

Richard Anuszkiewicz was America's leading Op artist in the mid-1960s, producing smooth-surfaced, brightly colored abstract canvases. A native of Erie, Pennsylvania, Anuszkiewicz studied at the Cleveland Institute of Art from 1948 to 1953, Yale University's Art School under Josef Albers from 1953 to 1955, and Kent State University from 1955 to 1956. He was deeply influenced by Albers's experiments with color and color theory, and his own work can be seen as an outgrowth of his study with Albers.

Plus Reversed (1960, plate 8) was the first painting Anuskiewicz ever sold, catching James Michener's eye as it hung in the window of the New York gallery The Contemporaries. Michener immediately perceived the overwhelming impact of the work; he recalled, "It quite knocked me over and I bought it on the spot."[1] As Michener's comment suggests, one's perceptual experience of *Plus Reversed* is indeed its defining characteristic. Playing with notions of nineteenth-century color theory, Anuszkiewicz paired the complementary colors red and green. Not only does this juxtaposition serve to intensify the vividness of each color, it produces a flickering of dominant and recessive hues as well. The plus forms literally change from green to red as they expand out from the center of the canvas, causing a constant shifting of ground that in turn generates both a movement of forms across the painting and a vibration in the viewer's eye. The active participation of the viewer thus is required to decipher the ambiguous space created through the interaction of colors and forms.

Albers's color theory classes at Yale exerted a significant impact on Op art in America. Albers, who had taught at the Bauhaus in Germany, spoke of the necessity to "recognize that color deceives continually."[2] At Yale Albers and his students examined the emotive and associative properties of color as well as the changing effects produced by the interaction of two or more colors. However, whereas Albers's paintings of nested squares demonstrate a gentle, luminous use of color, Anuszkiewicz's works from the early and mid-1960s exploit color's potential energy.

Other influences on Op art included works by Piet Mondrian and the artists and designers of the Bauhaus as well as experiments in visual perception being carried out by psychologists and scientists from the 1920s onward. A recognized pioneer of Op art was Victor Vasarely, whose work in Paris from the 1940s and 1950s set an example for other artists. Op art was a movement dominated by Europeans and South Americans living in Europe, although a few artists in the United States, such as Anuszkiewicz, developed related styles. Anuszkiewicz shared the European artists' interest in art as an objective practice akin to science, referring to his paintings as experiments, investigations, and studies of color.[3]

William Seitz included examples of Anuszkiewicz's paintings in his defining exhibition *The Responsive Eye*, held at The Museum of Modern Art in 1965, which displayed the work of an array of international artists concerned with the physiological impact of color, line, and composition. This important show drew from the manifestoes of contemporary European Op art groups such as Zero and GRAV and, in the accompanying catalogue, traced a history of "optical" painting back to Georges Seurat and the Neo-Impressionists, thus giving historical legitimacy to artists such as Anuszkiewicz. The show occurred at a point when Op art was being embraced on the popular front as well. In the months prior to the opening of *The Responsive Eye*, *Time* and *Life* magazines featured major articles on Op art. Commercial interests swiftly co-opted optical patterns and adapted them for everything from fabrics and window displays to utilitarian objects.

Ultimately, geometric approaches to abstraction were more popular in Europe and South America than in the United States, and Op art proved to be a short-lived movement in the States. Critics complained that the work was too easily understood—merely an effect or gimmick. Critical responses to Anuszkiewicz's paintings were mixed. While some critics described them as dazzling, others characterized them as too impersonal or universal in appeal.[4] During the early 1970s, Anuszkiewicz began using pastel tones, concentrating more on relationships between colors rather than on physiological responses to colors. Throughout this period the artist's popularity waned as public taste veered from a style deemed passé by gallery dealers, curators, and collectors. Despite these negative comments, Anuszkiewicz continued to explore the effects of color and patterning in painting. He also became a prolific printmaker, the flat, colored surfaces and precisely drawn lines of his paintings lending themselves well to the printed medium.

While Anuszkiewicz's work still retains some of the basic retinal principles associated with the Op movement, it has continued to suffer from the assumption that it produces an optical, perceptual response alone. Anuszkiewicz insists that pure color was always his chief interest, and he disclaims the term "Op" as being too limiting and superficial. Indeed, today he is recognized as an exceptional colorist.[5] In the early 1990s Anuszkiewicz's work enjoyed a renewed validity, as younger generations of American artists, including Peter Halley, began to create hard-edged geometrical abstractions that recall the constructivist style of Albers. *Plus Reversed* is one of the most frequently reproduced works in the Blanton's collection, and the artist considers it one of his most accomplished early paintings.

Stephanie Hanor

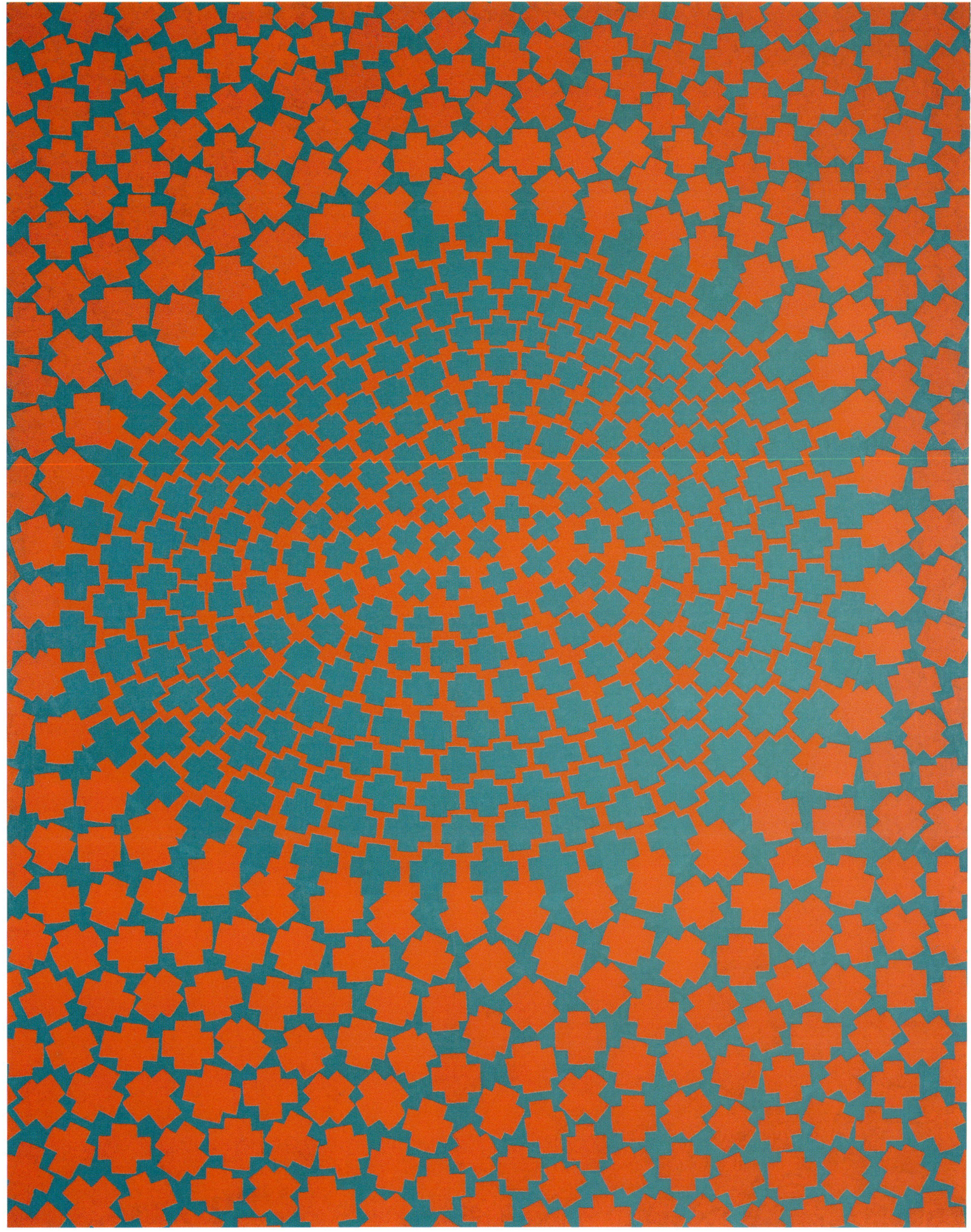

Notes

1. James A. Michener, untitled and undated memorandum, Blanton Museum of Art Archives, The University of Texas at Austin. According to text typed at the bottom of the memo, these comments were transcribed from a taped interview with Michener recorded in the mid- to late 1960s, also located in the Blanton Museum of Art archives.
2. Josef Albers, *Interaction of Color* (New Haven: Yale University Press, 1963); reprinted in Eugen Gomringer, *Josef Albers* (New York: George Wittenborn, 1968), 105.
3. *Americans 1963* (New York: The Museum of Modern Art, 1963), 6.
4. See, for example, "Reviews," *Art in America* 55 (September 1967): 111.
5. See Hayden Herrera, "Richard Anuszkiewicz at Crispo," *Art in America* 65 (May 1977): 118, and Donald Karshan, "Richard Anuszkiewicz," *Art in America* 58 (March 1970): 56.

8.

Plus Reversed, 1960

Oil on canvas
75 × 58 in. (189.6 × 148 cm)
Gift of Mari and James A. Michener
1991.177

Provenance: Purchased by James Michener from The Contemporaries, New York, 1962; long-term loan to The University of Texas at Austin, 1968–1991

Milton Avery

Sand Bank (Altmar), New York, 1893–New York, 1965

w. Hartford, Connecticut (summers in Gloucester, Massachusetts, 1920–1925), 1911–1925; New York (summers in Provincetown, Massachusetts, 1954–1960), 1925–1965

Milton Avery was a largely self-taught artist who doggedly pursued a vision that often ran contrary to the current artistic fashion of the day. Highly idiosyncratic and distinctive, Avery's art reflects his thorough understanding of a wide range of aesthetic approaches.

Avery was born in Sand Bank (now Altmar), New York, in 1885.[1] His family moved to a town near Hartford, Connecticut, in 1898. Beginning in 1905, Avery studied at the Connecticut League of Art Students with Charles Noel Flagg and Albertus E. Jones. He transferred to the School of the Art Society of Hartford in 1918. In 1920 he began visiting Gloucester, Massachusetts, a town where many artists congregated and to which Avery continually returned. It was there that he met his future wife, artist Sally Michel, who became an important force behind Avery's career and whom he followed to New York in 1925.

Like Stuart Davis, Avery explored the course established by the previous generation of American modernists, such as Arthur Dove and John Marin. He had already established the essential elements of his style by the time he moved to New York. There his exposure to European artists further shaped his art. Especially influential were the Fauves, the German Expressionists, and particularly Henri Matisse and Pablo Picasso, whose later work was frequently shown at the Valentine Gallery, which also represented Avery from 1935 until 1943.

Avery remained relatively unknown outside of a small group of artists, critics, and collectors until his first one-person show at the Valentine Gallery in 1935. It was not until 1944, however, when he had his first museum exhibition at the Phillips Memorial Gallery in Washington, D.C., that he began to receive widespread public recognition.

Avery's individual style revolved around the deft assimilation of modernist techniques and recognizable subject matter. He created monumental images from quotidian subjects and invested them with lyricism, formal structure, and timelessness. He remained committed to natural observation and never embraced total abstraction, yet he often simplified his forms and rendered them in emotive color. Like Matisse, Avery placed great importance on an overall sense of design and economy of line, utilizing shapes locked together in complex patterns that resist succumbing to decoration, a flaw for which he criticized the French master.

Avery also exploited the expressive potential of color more extensively than most of his contemporaries, allowing it to occupy a central role in his art. Indeed, he often divorced color from pure description, choosing colors intuitively and arbitrarily. Through the application of layers of thinned pigments in highly saturated and closely valued hues, he constructed complex tonal compositions. About his work Avery once asserted, "I work on two levels. I try to construct a picture in which shapes, spaces, colors form a set of unique relationships, independent of any subject matter. At the same time I try to capture and translate the excitement and emotion aroused in me by the impact with the original idea."[2]

Avery rendered *Clowns* (1935, plate 9), which is characteristic of his early production, in gestural, seemingly spontaneous, brushstrokes (most evident in the central figure that seems to float on the surface of the canvas). Along with brash shades of blue, pink, and green, these brushstrokes imbue the work with energy as well as a sense of underlying anxiety. As he did in his self-portraits and his portraits of friends and colleagues, moreover, Avery invests the clowns with personality and humor, recording the details of their oversized costumes and exaggerated grins.

While his early work typically displays the surface texture and color contrasts found in *Clowns*, in late works such as *The Card Players* (1945, plate 10), Avery employed large blocks of more harmoniously

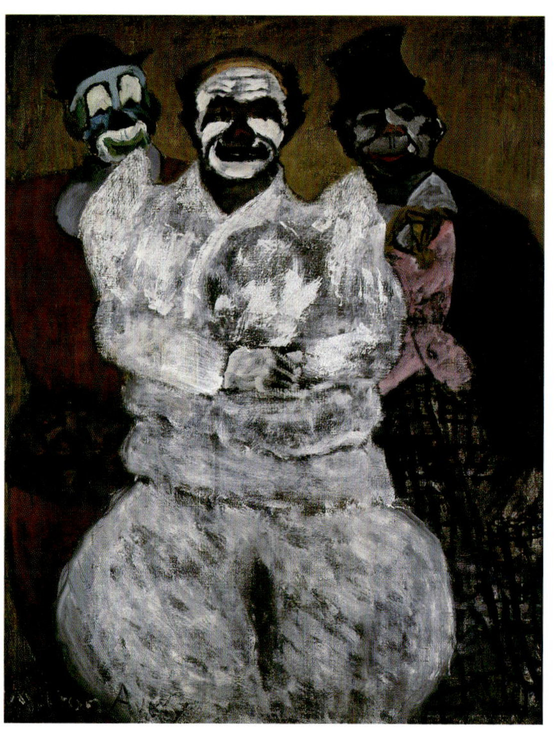

9.
Clowns, 1935
Oil on canvas
50 x 38 in. (127 x 96.5 cm)
Gift of Mari and James A. Michener
1991.179

Provenance: Valentine Gallery, New York; Walter P. Chrysler, Jr.; Parke-Bernet Galleries, Inc., New York, 1950; purchased by James Michener from Parke-Bernet Galleries, 1966; long-term loan to The University of Texas at Austin, 1968–1991

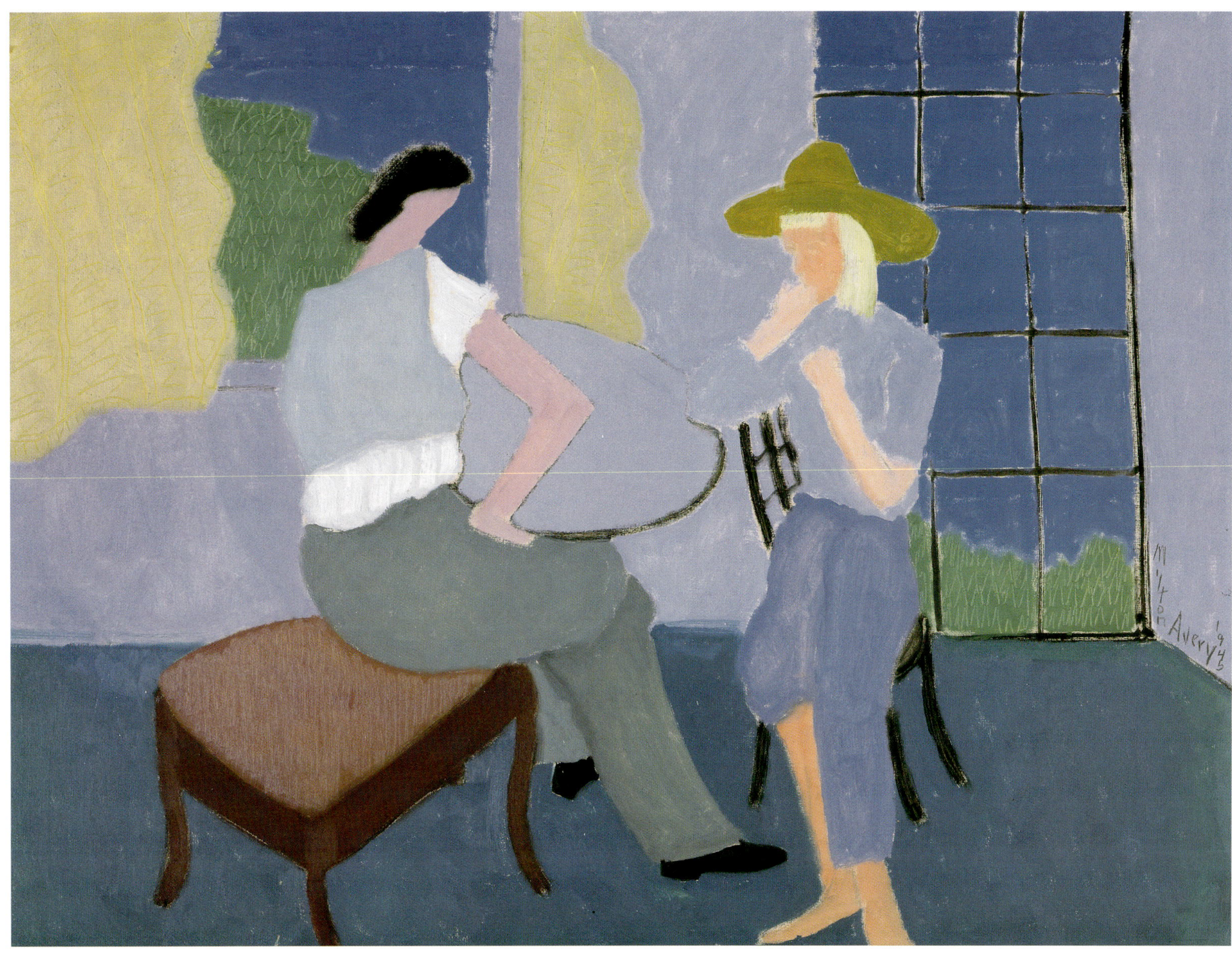

keyed, saturated colors in an arrangement of flat shapes. Delicate variations in blue create a congruous appearance, while accents of pink, mauve, and yellow generate a staccato visual rhythm. Through the repetition of forms and shapes—such as the left figure's bent arm, the table and yellow hat, the legs of the stool and chair, and the back of chair and window grid—Avery constructs a complicated visual puzzle linking the two figures to one another and to their environment. As *The Card Players* suggests, Avery's late works became increasingly distilled and simplified, more and more abstracted, while his color achieved greater harmony and expression.

The rise in popularity of Abstract Expressionism during the early 1950s relegated Avery to a position of critical disfavor. By 1957, however, the influential critic Clement Greenberg had begun to champion his adroit use of color, while others had started to acknowledge his profound impact on a younger generation of artists that included Adolph Gottlieb, Barnett Newman, and Mark Rothko. The major retrospectives and critical acclaim that soon followed placed Avery among the most important and influential artists of the twentieth century.[3]

Kathleen V. Jameson

10.

The Card Players, 1945

Oil on canvas
26 × 34 in. (66 × 86.4 cm)
Gift of Mari and James A. Michener
1991.178

Provenance: Durand-Ruel, New York; Associated American Artists, New York; Mrs. Reeves Lowenthal; purchased by James Michener from Parke-Bernet Galleries, New York, 1966; long-term loan to The University of Texas at Austin, 1968–1991

Notes

1. For further information on Avery's life and work, see Adelyn D. Breeskin, *Milton Avery* (New York: The American Federation of Arts, 1960); Hilton Kramer, *Milton Avery: Paintings, 1930–1960* (New York: Thomas Yoseloff, 1962); *Milton Avery, Drawings and Paintings* (Austin: The University of Texas at Austin, 1976); and Barbara Haskell, *Milton Avery* (New York: Whitney Museum of American Art, 1982).
2. Quoted in *Contemporary American Painting and Sculpture* (Urbana, Ill.: University of Illinois, 1951), 159.
3. Major exhibitions of Avery's art were held at The Baltimore Museum of Art (1953) and the Whitney Museum of American Art (1960 and 1982).

Luis Cruz Azaceta

b. Havana, Cuba, 1942

w. Hoboken, New Jersey, 1960–1963; New York, 1963–1992; New Orleans, 1992–present

Luis Cruz Azaceta's oeuvre is an extended meditation on the human condition. Over the past four decades, this prolific artist has produced a body of work that is at once stylistically rich and consistent in its thematic focus. A scavenger of his own imagery, he revisits and quotes past discoveries within his personal iconography to create anew without falling into formulaic repetition. Like other of Azaceta's works from the 1990s that incorporate found objects, the Blanton's *Sleepless* (1996, plate 11) constitutes both a departure from his Neo-Expressionist painting of the 1980s and a continuation of a principal theme in his art: the psychological state of exile.

"The space of the exile is 'limbatic' [in limbo]; it is not hell and it is not really heaven. . . . We are not here and we are not there psychologically. We don't belong here and we don't belong there anymore," explained Azaceta.[1] Having lived in the United States as an exile since 1960, the artist identifies with the many in society who share this state of displacement and marginality, including the homeless, drug addicts, AIDS victims, political refugees, and the poor. For Azaceta every outcast is a *balsero*, struggling toward a better shore.[2] Because the artist has internalized this collective despair, painting is for him not only an act of exorcism but also one of prayer and hope. "We come here to spend X amount of time doing something positive that would benefit the whole human race. We have to contribute to our humanity," he stated.[3]

Although Azaceta's formation as an artist has taken place entirely in the United States, his Cuban American bi-cultural identity informs his art. Born in Havana, Cuba, in 1942, Azaceta fled conscription into Fidel Castro's militia to live with relatives in Hoboken, New Jersey, upon turning eighteen. Urban life seemed cold, indifferent, and chaotic to the new immigrant, who spoke little English. Fired for union activity in a trophy factory where he had worked for three years, he taught himself to draw and paint to relieve his boredom. He later worked in a button factory and attended night classes at an adult education center in Queens, where a teacher encouraged him to pursue an art career.[4] In 1966 Azaceta enrolled full-time at the School of Visual Arts in New York. His student work there echoed the hard-edged geometric abstraction of Frank Stella and Victor Vasarely. After graduating in 1969 with a BFA, he traveled throughout Europe. At the Prado museum in Spain, Azaceta encountered works by Hieronymus Bosch, Francisco Goya, and Diego Velázquez, which awakened his desire to change his artistic direction and develop a personal iconography.

Once back in the United States, memory, imagination, and everyday occurrences witnessed on the subways and streets of Manhattan fueled Azaceta's art. For example, he based the forty paintings that comprise his 1969 series Car Crash on his recollections of a near-death experience that had occurred three years earlier when, driving his family (newly arrived from Cuba) to a picnic, his 1959 Chevy Impala was rear-ended by a drunken driver. Dismemberment emerged as a constant theme in his work—one that represented psychological fragmentation. Bloody body parts, cigarette butts, and various weapons painted in high-key, lush colors with heavy black outlines crowd Azaceta's urban scenarios of the 1970s. The artist explains that their tragic, sarcastic humor reflects a distinctly Cuban sensibility.[5] These graffiti-like and at times grotesque paintings have been commonly referred to by art critics as "apocalyptic pop," a term coined by the artist.[6]

In the 1980s Azaceta began to incorporate self-portraits into powerful, large-scale, expressionistic oil paintings variously influenced by artists such as Frida Kahlo and Francis Bacon, the work of the German Expressionists, and sources as diverse as African sculpture and Panamanian *molas* (narrative textile panels). Without making preliminary sketches, Azaceta would rely on intuition when approaching the blank canvas that he would staple to the floor. The rawness or crudeness achieved in his work can be attributed to his technique: "I use my whole body to paint. I just don't use my wrist to paint, and my fingers, it's my entire body, so I can dance. I'm really dancing when I paint."[7] While *Homo-Fragile* of 1983 (part of the Blanton's Latin American Collection) typifies the artist's complex and dynamic paintings from this period, *Sleepless* exemplifies his shift in the mid-1990s to a more conceptual approach.[8]

Sleepless challenges the viewer to confront the experience of homelessness. With minimal materials, this poetic visual statement conveys impermanence and discomfort. Azaceta lightly coated a panel, suggesting a hard bed or the raft of a *balsero*, with gesso to accentuate the grain of the wood, which echoes the movement of the ocean's surface. The artist's self-portrait is drawn in charcoal and sealed with visible drips of shellac, creating stains that recall bodily fluids, specifically urine and blood.

Five bent and twisted metal studs extend the length of the eight-foot panel. These sculptural forms suggest limbs that entrap, rather than support, the disembodied head. This notion of entrapment is reinforced by the fact that the metal studs, normally used in construction, serve as containers for repeated photographic images: a shotgun house in silhouette, a street person's makeshift home in Chelsea, and several views of the New York subway. Azaceta points out that the red, white, and blue of the images immediately above the face locate the homeless person (or the exile) in the US by evoking the colors of the American flag.[9] The artist placed coins in the metal stud spanning the lower edge of the panel, as if it were a receptacle for handouts given to a beggar.

Sleepless conveys Azaceta's ongoing dialogue with the extremes of violence, passivity, and helplessness encountered in himself and in society. At its heart lies Azaceta's conviction that, by encouraging greater social awareness and responsibility, art can transform humanity.

Teresa Eckmann

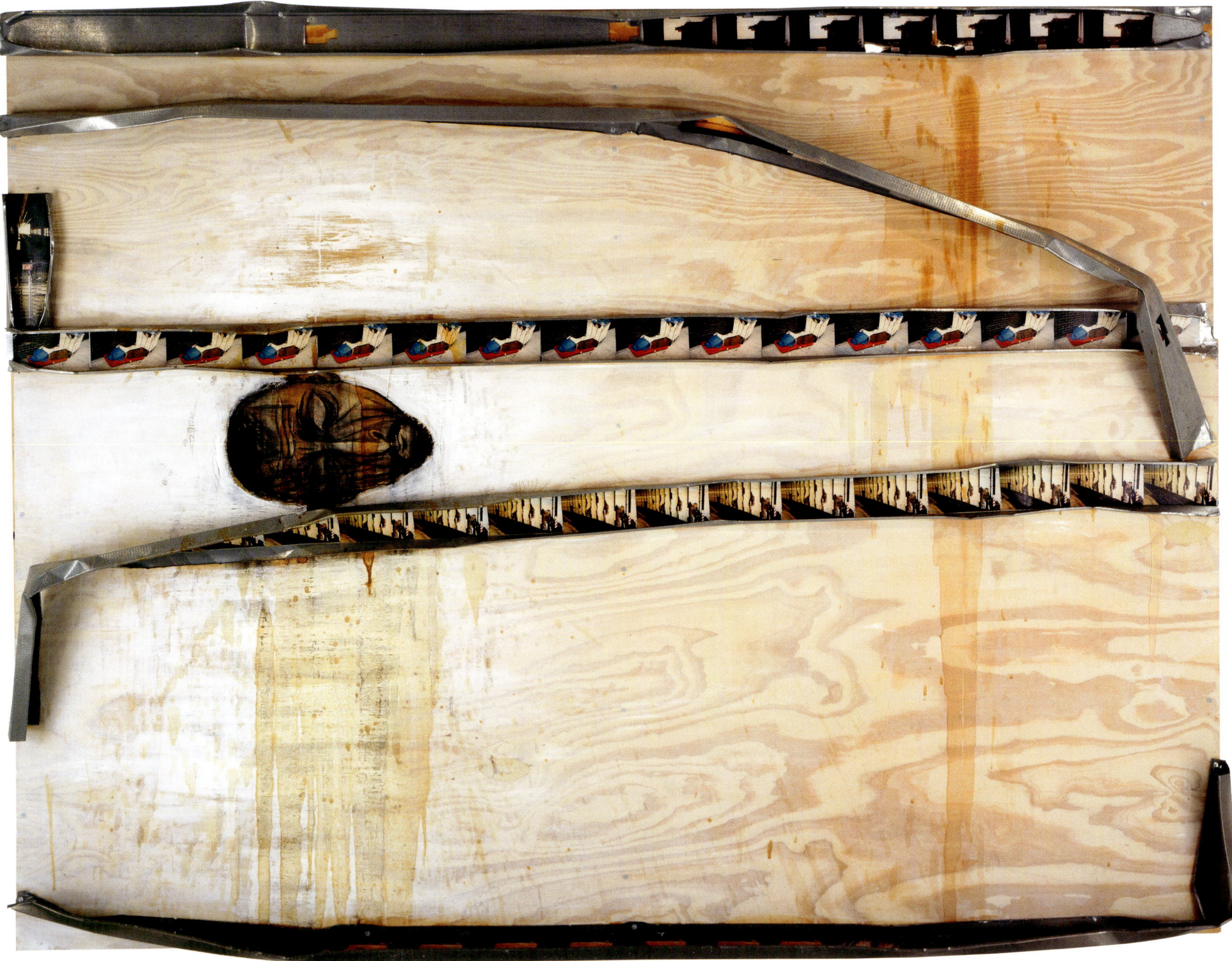

Notes

1. Luis Cruz Azaceta, interview with the author, New Orleans, December 11, 2004.
2. *Balsero* refers to a Cuban refugee who leaves the island on a makeshift raft.
3. Azaceta, interview with the author.
4. Button-shapes later appear as a recurring motif in his work.
5. Azaceta, interview with the author.
6. Azaceta refers to his 1970s paintings as "apocalyptic pop" in Luiz Cruz Azaceta, "Luis Cruz Azaceta: Interviewed by Robert Loescher," in Jeanne Dunning, ed., *Affirmative Actions: Recognizing a Cross-Cultural Practice in Contemporary Art* (Chicago: School of the Art Institute of Chicago, 1990), 21. Art historians and critics including Gerardo Mosquera, Katherine B. Crum, and Victor Zamudio-Taylor employed the term in the 1990s when writing about Azaceta's work.
7. Azaceta, "Luis Cruz Azaceta: Interviewed by Robert Loescher," 24.
8. For more information on *Homo-Fragile,* see Sarah Holian's object essay in Gabriel Pérez-Barreiro, ed., *Blanton Museum of Art: Latin American Collection* (Austin: Blanton Museum of Art, 2006).
9. Azaceta, interview with the author.

11.

Sleepless, 1996

Charcoal, acrylic, gesso, metal studs, photographs, coins, and shellac on plywood
75 × 96¼ × 11¼ in. (190.6 × 244.5 × 28.6 cm)
Michener Acquisitions Fund
1997.46

Provenance: Purchased from the artist, 1997

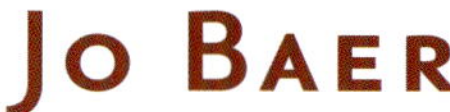

Jo Baer

b. Seattle, 1929

w. New York, 1950–1953; Los Angeles, 1953–1960; New York, 1960–1975; Ardee County, Louth, Ireland, 1975–1982; London, 1982–1984; Amsterdam, 1984–present

A few phrases convey the pictorial structure of Jo Baer's austere *Horizontals Tiered [Vertical Diptych]* (1966, plate 12): two canvases, each approximately 52 × 72 inches, hang stacked with six inches between them.[1] The paintings are essentially identical: each features a large rectangular expanse of white rimmed by a thin strip of ochre, which in turn is framed by a two-inch band of black whose outer edge lies a fraction of an inch away from the edge of the canvas. This schematic description, however, fails to capture the work's hypnotic effects. Nor does it reveal the relation of the work, which collector James Michener bought while visiting the studio Baer shared with her then-husband, Pop painter John Wesley,[2] to the charged contexts of 1960s American artistic production and reception.

Baer's scientific bent offers a first ingress to *Horizontals Tiered*. Born Josephine Kleinberg in Seattle in 1929, Baer studied biology as an undergraduate at the University of Washington. Shortly after moving to New York in 1950, she began working with the Graduate Faculty in Physiological Psychology at the New School of Social Research. Colleagues there introduced Baer to Gestalt theory, the idea that the brain organizes patterns of light and sensory data into simple, symmetrical patterns; configurations such as squareness or roundness thus constitute the bases of perception.

But the Gestalt structure of *Horizontals Tiered* only partly accounts for the retinal reverberations that accompany its beholding. Contrasts of brightness result in heightened chromatic intensities and lingering afterimages, and the milky mustard bands—mediating lambent white and inky black—appear to shimmer and fluoresce. Baer explained this effect, a neural phenomenon known as a Mach band (named for the Austrian philosopher and physicist Ernst Mach):

> *The white, when it's lit, develops a glare, and it expands beyond its boundaries, like a bit of a halo, lending light to the next color. At the same time, the color band is also next to black, and something different happens there. . . . the black side—this is retinal, not strictly physical—will be much blacker, and the lighter side will be much lighter.*[3]

Her technical choices, honed with small, intuitive adjustments, work to magnify optical resonance. Baer limned the color strips by hand and brushed white beading over the black bands. She applied multiple coats of white paint (a blend of acrylic and oil developed with a conservator from the Guggenheim Museum) in flat, even, vertical strokes and covered the canvas with a layer of varnish before adding several more coats. As the viewer's eyes move back and forth between the two panels, the white fields appear to hover and recede simultaneously, while the ochre and black bands seem at once luminescent and matte. Despite these oscillations, however, *Horizontals Tiered* reads as resolutely holistic; those formal tensions that dominated the theory and practice of postwar painting—figure and ground, flatness and depth, physicality and immateriality—dissolve in the act of looking.

Baer's output in the mid-1960s consisted of similar deceptively simple arrangements: flanking and tiered diptychs and triptychs whose component panels contained a central white or gray square or rectangle faced by concentric bands of color and black. A self-taught painter, she arrived at her signature style after a period of imitative Abstract Expressionism and a short Pop interlude of representational paintings dominated by geometric icons. The body of work to which *Horizontals Tiered* belongs—marked by limited pictorial variables, uninflected surfaces, and serial or systemic groupings—aligned Baer with a nascent New York–based Minimalism. Indeed, *Horizontals Tiered* partakes of several concerns that animated the work of Minimalists such as Donald Judd and Robert Morris: a near-ascetic distillation of forms, a non-hierarchical, integrated structural arrangement, and a stringent opposition to illusionism. Baer exhibited (along with Ellsworth Kelly, Agnes Martin, and Robert Ryman) in Lawrence Alloway's 1966 *Systemic Painting* at the Guggenheim Museum, the Dwan Gallery's *10* show that same year (with Morris, Sol LeWitt, and Ad Reinhardt), and the Finch College Museum's *Art in Series* exhibition in 1967.

But two important distinctions measure Baer's distance from Minimalism. Although she also relies on the parameters of the physical support to determine the work's internal structure, and the parallel bands painted on her surfaces recapitulate the shape of the canvas, they are not usually contiguous with its boundaries. This difference separates paintings such as *Horizontals Tiered* from work by those artists, especially Reinhardt and Frank Stella, who strove to articulate the literalness of the canvas support by painting their geometric forms as coterminous with the edge of the canvas, making structure flush with surface. Equally important, Baer's commitment (shared by Brice Marden and Robert Mangold) to the viability of painting has remained unwavering over a half-century-long career. While Morris critiqued painting as an "antique mode," and Judd conceived of the three-dimensional "specific object" that was neither painting nor sculpture, Baer continued to explore the physical constraints of the medium.[4]

Baer's Wraparound and Double Bar series of the late 1960s and early 1970s feature more dominant color forms, diagonal and swerve shapes, and painted curves that radiate around the sides of the canvas. After a mid-career retrospective at the Whitney Museum of American Art in 1975, Baer renounced abstract painting—to which she, like many of her contemporaries, had once attributed a radical, even political, dimension—and moved to Ireland.[5] Working there and later in London and Amsterdam, she has produced what she calls "image work," mining sources as diverse as Paleolithic sculpture and Latin botanical terms.

12.

Horizontals Tiered [Vertical Diptych], 1966

Oil and synthetic resin on canvas
Each panel: 52 × 72 in. (131 × 183 cm)
Gift of Mari and James A. Michener
G1968.31

Provenance: Purchased by James Michener from the artist, 1967
Signed verso, lower right "J. Baer 66–67"

In a 1967 letter to Morris about paintings such as *Horizontals Tiered*, Baer wrote: "There is no hierarchy. There is no ambiguity. There is no illusion. There is no space or interval (time)."[6] Yet if implications of narrative and duration are absent here, "time" is crucial to our experience of this work. Light reflects and refracts, subtleties of hue and facture emerge, optical and physical presence assert themselves in tandem: *Horizontals Tiered* rewards long looking.

Lisa Pasquariello

Notes

1. The work was previously titled *Vertical Diptych*, but in a 1997 letter to the museum, Baer suggested *Horizontals Tiered* (or *Stacked*) instead. Jo Baer to Stephanie Hanor, November 15, 1997, Blanton Museum of Art Archives, The University of Texas at Austin. In keeping with the artist's request, the museum changed the title to *Horizontals Tiered*, but appended *[Vertical Diptych]* since for decades the painting was known and published under this title.
2. The young art dealer Richard Bellamy, who had titled an earlier series of Baer's paintings, accompanied Michener. Michener purchased Wesley's *Annunciations*, also in the Blanton collection, during this visit as well.
3. Jo Baer, "The Adventures of Jo Baer," interview by Judith E. Stein, *Art in America* 91 (May 2003): 107.
4. See Robert Morris, "Notes on Sculpture, Part I," *Artforum* 4 (February 1966), and Donald Judd, "Specific Objects," *Arts Yearbook*, no. 8 (1965).
5. In a 1995 interview, Baer said that her Minimalist paintings were "about identity and the rights of individuals to maintain themselves as individuals." Jo Baer, interview by Linda Boersma, *Bomb*, no. 53 (fall 1995): 63.
6. Jo Baer to Robert Morris, July 29, 1967, quoted in Lynne Cooke, *Jo Baer: The Minimalist Years 1960–1975* (New York: Dia Center for the Arts, 2003), 1.

Radcliffe Bailey

b. Bridgeton, New Jersey, 1968
w. Atlanta, Georgia, 1987–present

In *The Blue Devils of Nada*, critic Albert Murray gives readers this essential criteria for artistic creation: "The condition of man is always a matter of the specific texture of existence in a given place, time, and circumstance. But the point is that the regional particulars—the idiomatic details, the down-home conventions, the provincial customs and folkways—must be *processed* into artistic statement, *stylized* into significance."[1] Only when local conditions attain "universal implications," he argues, can a work of art transcend the dull and repetitive act of reportage. For Murray, strikingly, it is the blues, a contemporary and vernacular form of music, that has consistently affirmed the gamut of human action and sentiment throughout the twentieth century. Through its complex oscillation between tradition and improvisation, simplicity and sophistication, despair and triumph, the blues idiom navigates the vast and often contradictory terrain occupied by both the heroic epic and *la vie quotidienne*—frequently within the course of a single song.

Radcliffe Bailey's *By the River* (1997, plate 13) suggests an association with the blues. Like the blues, the work expresses universal implications through regional particulars. Since the early 1990s, Bailey has incorporated a wide array of materials into his dense and physical artworks. In addition to paint, *By the River* is composed of Georgia clay, beeswax, tar, and a prominently placed bright red gourd. Bailey brings together these heterogeneous ingredients to form a prismatic, haphazard pattern of colors and symbols that evoke the measured energy and stark sobriety of a fully orchestrated blues composition. As the artist himself pointed out, "What I do may not even be called art. It may be called music."[2] That the title supposedly refers to a song by Robert Johnson, an enigmatic blues musician, only reinforces such comparisons.

Like many of Bailey's works, *By the River* is concerned with the intertwined paths of time and memory. The title alludes to a geographical space beyond the confines of the gallery, while the work's imagery evokes a time other than now, or at least a temporality unconcerned with traditional boundaries separating past from present. Bailey aims to preserve the stories and recollections of the African diaspora and restate them within the context of his life experiences. Through the recovery of small and mesmerizing details such as the curvilinear forms found in the wrought iron-work made by early nineteenth-century Adinkran craftsmen, *By the River* excavates and foregrounds fragments of unrecorded and forgotten history. An arc of painted beads roughly paralleling the iron-work suggests West African adornment rituals. Numbers and names inscribed on the right and left sides of *By the River* reference the slave trade and the Middle Passage across the Atlantic. Their elusive forms rise above and sink beneath coats of paint and wax like the lives traded, migrated, assimilated, and lost to record. Against webbed tendrils and rectilinear patches, past and present illuminate each other as they pass back and forth in condensed time.

These overlapping surfaces ultimately play a supporting role to *By the River*'s central element, an arresting reproduction of a carte-de-visite photograph of a young African American woman. Originally given to Bailey by his grandmother, the sepia-toned image of a deceased family member evokes the passing of time even as it serves to preserve its subject against the vagaries of that process. In the 1990s Bailey often used such photographs, including reproductions of bodies of water meant to evoke his father and grandfather, both fishermen, and to pay homage to his own ancestral and cultural history. The enframed, altar-like settings in which the artist placed these images serve as memorial spaces for members of his own family and for other, unknown African Americans. Similar to the writing and objects covering the surface of *By the River*, the photograph refers to the long history of diasporic culture, but on an infinitely more human and poignant scale. It provokes the contemplation of both personal and public memory and the ways in which the two are frequently bound together.

Bailey has referred to himself as a sculptor who paints, and it is easy to see why. *By the River* is bulky and exerts a strong physical presence, incorporating objects that were not designed to adhere to a flat surface or that contradict the pull of gravity by hanging perpendicular to the floor. The diverse processes that Bailey uses to create his mixed media works and installations has led him to collaborate with musicians, poets, and filmmakers. He has also studied the art and spiritual practices of the Congo, Nigeria, the Caribbean, and African American diasporic cultures.

Citing the many forces and identities at play in Bailey's culturally and artistically complex body of work, critics have linked him to Jean-Michel Basquiat, Robert Rauschenberg, and Anselm Kiefer. Like these artists, Bailey utilizes the formal tactic of juxtaposing images in order to create new meanings from otherwise indeterminate, fragmented, or incongruent references. The metaphoric evocations that spring from *By the River*'s particular combinations serve to reaffirm the existence of events and people within a specific history, one connected in immediate ways to the artist. Yet if the initial impact of the work stems from the evocation of that rich and troubled past, its lasting hold over the imagination stems from its ability to occasion more general meditations on the nature of loss, remembrance, and time. As Bailey stated, although his works are "like a self-portrait, where I'm visually writing a story in space," they also accommodate "another level of history that allows viewers to find themselves in the work."[3]

Patrick Tomlin

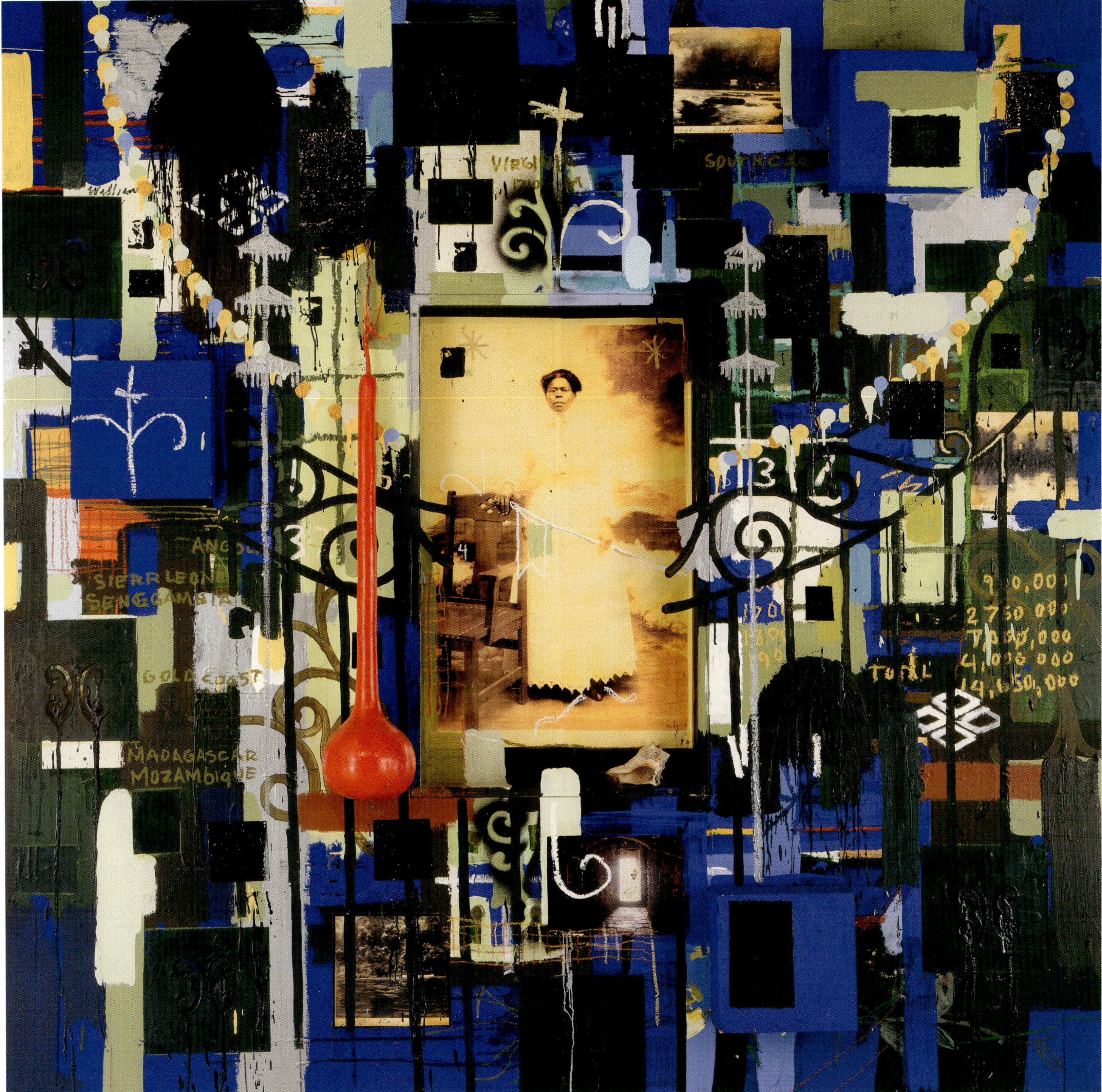

Notes

1. Albert Murray, *The Blue Devils of Nada* (New York: Vintage Books, 1996), 11.
2. Quoted in Mason Klein, "Radcliffe Bailey," *Artforum* 38 (February 2000): 121.
3. Quoted in Jerry Cullum, "Spiritual Migrations: Radcliffe Bailey's Hybrid Identities," *Art Papers* 24 (November/December 2000): 27.

13.

By the River, 1997

Acrylic, oil stick, Plexiglas, photographs, beeswax, gourd, and tar on wood
82 × 82 × 10 in. (208.4 × 208.4 × 25.5 cm)
Michener Acquisitions Fund
1997.36

Provenance: Purchased from David Beitzel Gallery, New York, 1997

David Bates

b. Dallas, 1952
w. Dallas, 1971–present

The energetic portraits, landscapes, and still-lifes of contemporary Texas-based artist David Bates have been linked to various historic influences, such as twentieth-century modernism, German Expressionism, and American folk art. The artist fuels this debate by expressing his admiration for a diverse cadre of "dead guys,"[1] including Giotto de Bondone and Henri Matisse.[2] Bates's folksy Texan manner of speaking echoes the unpretentious yet eloquent and self-aware nature of his paintings. While paying tribute to the intense color of Marsden Hartley, the Cubism of Pablo Picasso, and the patterning of Matisse, among others, Bates remains a rugged individualist. When considering his work, one is inevitably reminded of the honesty and directness of so-called outsider art, especially the black folk art for which he has great admiration. His subjects are most often prosaic and rendered in oil paint on canvas in a stylized yet representational manner.

Born in Dallas in 1952, Bates spent his early years in Garland, a Dallas suburb. His mother, who had attended the Art Institute of Chicago, encouraged him to pursue formal art training at Southern Methodist University, where he received undergraduate and graduate degrees in fine arts. Bates moved to New York in 1977 to attend the Independent Study Program at the Whitney Museum of American Art. While in residence, he experimented with performance and video art. By the end of 1977, he was back in Texas, teaching at Easterfield College in Mesquite and making small-scale painted sculptures and paintings influenced by folk art. In the summer of 1982, while on a fishing expedition, Bates discovered the Grassy Lake area of western Arkansas. It was there that his "art and life came together."[3] Bates himself observed of this epiphany: "It was like a dream, a place of strange beauty and complex compositions that changes completely from sunrise to noon."[4] His work gained new strength from that magical landscape and its denizens. He began to imbue all his subjects from Grassy Lake to the Gulf Coast of Texas as well as those he selected from his immediate environs with a directness that was apt to be playful as well as respectful.

A young whittler's quiet dedication to his craft caught the artist's attention in the Texas Hill Country in 1982. As is his habit, Bates noted details of the scene and later sketched them. Most of his paintings are based on selective memory, which Bates has claimed is often more adept than photography at preserving the essence of a subject.[5] In his studio, he transformed his modest sketch into a monumental oil painting, *The Whittler* (1983, plate 14). If at first glance Bates's ordinary, awkwardly drawn central figure, with his massive shoes and pants, mismatched shoulders, and tiny head, seems to be the product of an unsophisticated eye and untrained hand, that notion is quickly dispelled. The proportions of the young man seated on the porch direct the viewer's gaze upward as if he or she was approaching him from the path below, while the window on the right and the edge of the tree on the left frame this imaginary encounter. One can almost imagine a "Howdy, stranger!" emanating from the whittler's crooked upturned mouth. The raucous pattern of the stone wall contrasts with the boy's simple billowy white shirt, and the pile of crossed sticks in the lower right corner and the small dog in the lower left further anchor the composition. Bates's canvas is slathered with paint and textured with brush strokes that provide a liveliness that might otherwise have been absent from this essentially formal composition.

The Sculptor (1983, plate 15), completed the same year as *The Whittler*, is Bates's paean to outsider artist William Edmondson, the first black man to be given a one-man exhibition at The Museum of Modern Art.[6] Edmondson, described by Bates as the Brancusi of folk artists,[7] died the year before Bates was born, and so *The Sculptor* derives its inspiration from photographs of the artist and his chiseled

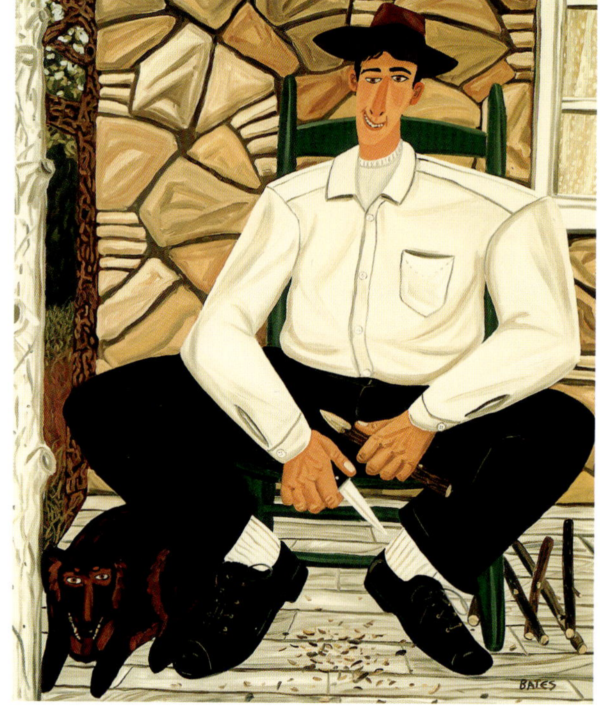

14.
The Whittler, 1983

Oil on canvas
96 × 78 in. (243.9 × 198.1 cm)
Michener Acquisitions Fund
1983.123

Provenance: Purchased from Charles Cowles Gallery, New York, 1983
Signed lower right "BATES" in paint
Inscribed verso, upper stretcher (on canvas) "David Bates—The Whittler—96 × 78" in black paint

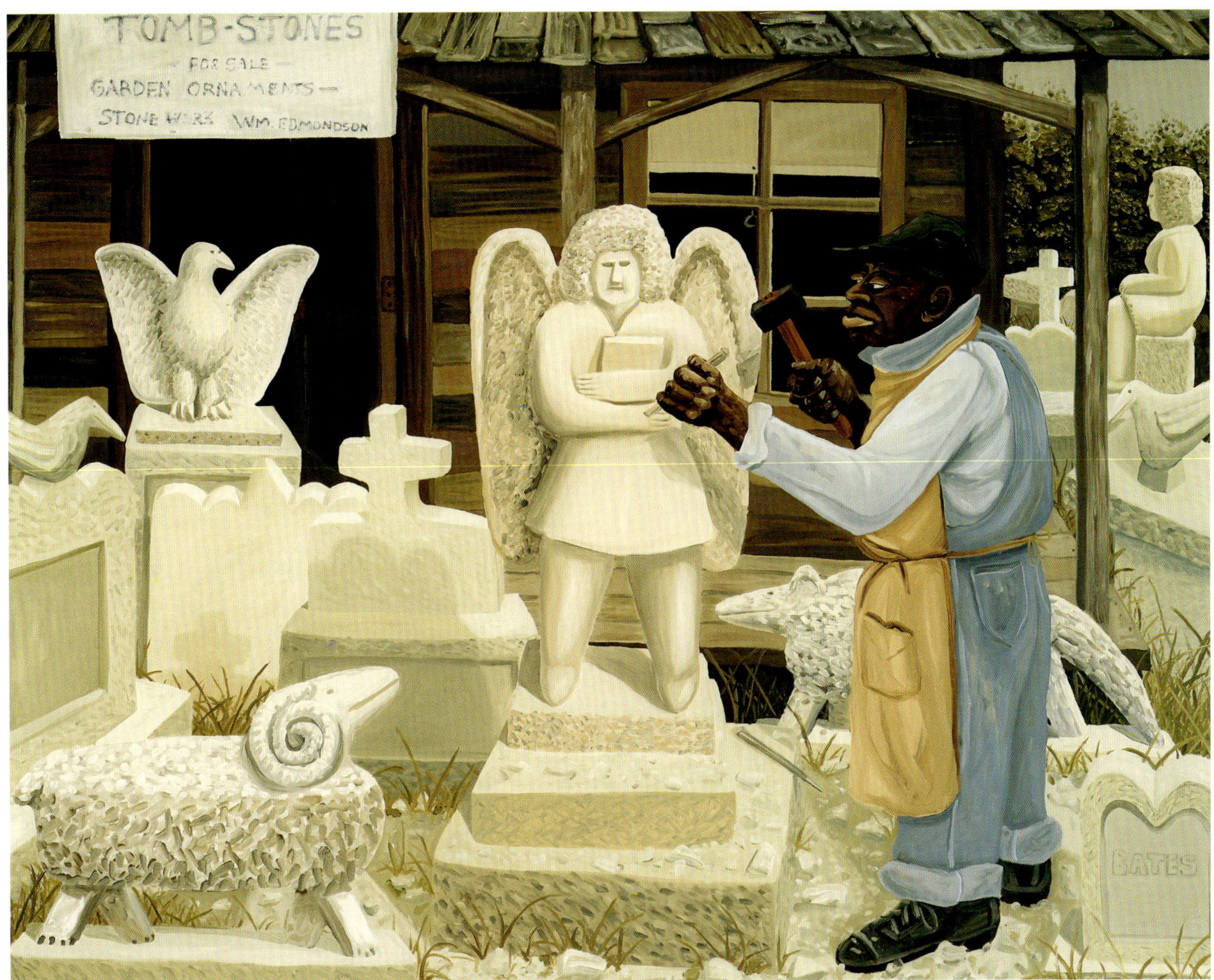

15.
The Sculptor, 1983
Oil on canvas
78 × 96 in. (198.1 × 243.9 cm)
Gift of the American Academy and Institute of Arts and Letters
1984.41
Signed lower right "BATES" in paint (signed as part of image, on tombstone)

limestone animals, winged figures, and workers.[8] Here Bates took liberty with his source material to suit the compositional needs of the painting. He combined, compressed, distilled, and distorted a selection of photographic images, ultimately arriving at a truth that the artist believes supercedes the version recorded by the camera. The central figure in the painting is a sculpture in progress rather than the sculptor himself, who stands to the right with a mallet and chisel in his hands. Edmondson, clad in blue work clothes, regards the winged angel clutching a book intently, as do the surrounding carved creatures and, inevitably, the viewer. The painting is full of ordinary details: the supports of the porch roof, the grass making its way through the ground littered with stones, the carved stone plinths and crosses positioned in stark contrast to the worn boards of the clapboard house in the background. These come together in an arrangement that might have appeared static but for the richness of the painting's surface and Bates's skill in manipulating the viewer's eye through the organization of shapes and color.

Recognition for Bates quickly followed the completion of his first Grassy Lake paintings. In 1983 his work appeared in the 38th Corcoran Biennial of American Paintings, the New Orleans Triennial at the New Orleans Museum of Art, and the exhibition *Southern Fictions,* organized by the Contemporary Arts Museum, Houston. The Blanton Museum purchased *The Whittler* at Bates's first one-person exhibition at Charles Cowles Gallery in New York in 1983. Just four years later, his work was included in the 1987 Whitney Biennial, and the following year the Modern Art Museum of Fort Worth honored Bates with a one-person show.

Bates has continued to explore his very personal universe through his art, asserting that "trying to fit into some world that's not yours is not being successful, or honest."[9]

Rebecca S. Cohen

Notes

1. David Bates, phone conversation with the author, December 23, 2004.
2. *David Bates: Poems* (Dallas: Dunn and Brown Contemporary, 2003), 27.
3. Marla Price, *David Bates: Forty Paintings* (Fort Worth, Tex.: Modern Art Museum of Fort Worth, 1988), 11.
4. Quoted in Price, 10.
5. Bates, phone conversation with the author.
6. The Museum of Modern Art's director, Alfred Barr, selected Edmonson's work for exhibition in 1937.
7. Bates, phone conversation with the author.
8. Paul Arnett and William Arnett, eds., *Souls Grown Deep: African American Vernacular Art of the South*, vol. I (Atlanta: Tinwood Books, 2000), 106–11.
9. *David Bates: Poems*, 22.

William A. Baziotes

Pittsburgh, 1912–New York, 1963
w. New York, 1933–1963

William Baziotes was a central member of the Abstract Expressionists, the group credited with largely determining the course of later twentieth-century art and moving the center of the avant-garde from Paris to New York in the years after World War II. His name is now less familiar than those of his contemporaries, perhaps because Baziotes's paintings remained closer to the organic, deeply personal forms of abstract Surrealism and thus kept a formal distance from the bold abstract statements that make the work of artists like Jackson Pollock and Mark Rothko so immediately recognizable. *Mariner* (1960–1961, plate 16) is typical of Baziotes's late work, in which the dense, thick forms of his 1940s paintings give way to a sense of still mystery created by precisely delineated biomorphic shapes that overlay soft fields of gently glowing colors.

Baziotes was born in Pittsburgh and raised in Reading, Pennsylvania, by Greek immigrant parents. After moving to New York in 1933, he attended classes for three years at the National Academy of Design. Like so many artists of his generation, he worked for the WPA Federal Art Project from 1933 to 1940. In the early 1940s Baziotes came under the influence of Surrealist artists then living in New York, like Max Ernst and Matta. While his contemporaries Rothko and Adolph Gottlieb were primarily concerned with expressing man's sense of terror in the face of war, violence, and genocide in the twentieth century, Baziotes was fascinated by his own complex, multifaceted personality. "I am a strange creature and most of all to myself," he once wrote of his artistic approach. "Evil tempts me as much as the good. I would like to be the purest of men, yet the lewd fascinates me."[1]

As a means of accessing his inner states, Baziotes employed automatic writing, which he learned from Matta and André Masson. Through this technique, and stemming from a variety of personal memories and associations, he created bizarre organic shapes and deformed monster figures. The menacing form of *Cyclops* (1947), for instance, evokes Baziotes's memory of a rhinoceros at the Bronx Zoo as much as it does the mythical myopic creature.[2] According to Irving Sandler, however, Baziotes always balanced this interest in automatism with a careful attention to painterly surface, compositional stability, and the plasticity of forms, qualities he admired in the work of Pablo Picasso and Joan Miró.[3]

Baziotes tended to employ dark, rich hues to invest his canvases with a poetic, mysterious, and sometimes sinister mood. As with the radiant green and blue of *Mariner,* Baziotes's fields of color often seem to glow from within, establishing the pictorial space as one of psychic energy.[4] In *Mariner* that energy appears to radiate outwards from the horizon line, marked by a slight lightening of tone and conspicuously placed in the middle of the canvas. As the triangular form at the left seems to stretch back into the distance, the viewer is asked to enter into the space of the painting, to embark on a journey of introspection.[5]

In this regard, an important aspect of *Mariner* lies in the title's unavoidable reference to Samuel Taylor Coleridge's "Rime of the Ancient Mariner" (1797–1798). While Baziotes claimed in a statement of 1954 that "Music and literature do not inspire any of my works," he went on to say that "I do find brothers in those arts."[6] Along with Robert Motherwell, Baziotes was among the most literary members of the New York School and an avid student of Charles Baudelaire and the French Symbolists.[7] *Mariner* should be seen not as an illustration of a literary source, however, but rather as a kind of parallel but distinct visual project.

As one commentator described Coleridge's poem, "It is about man's attempt to understand the mystery surrounding the human soul in a universe moved by forces and powers at once imminent and transcendent."[8] To the extent that the "Ancient Mariner" can also be seen to describe the journey of the poet and artist, it expresses very much the kind of searching, restless wandering into both internal and external worlds of intense experience that the Abstract Expressionists sought. Furthermore, this poem is famously difficult to analyze with any finality.[9] Coleridge himself remarked that poetry "gives most pleasure when only generally and not perfectly understood."[10] Baziotes, who once quoted Baudelaire's statement, "I have a horror of being easily understood," would certainly have agreed.[11]

In this way, Coleridge's poem is a precedent for Baziotes's desire to create powerful associations and emotions for the viewer without making reference to specific ideas or forms in nature. The horizontal division of *Mariner,* with its preponderance of blue at the bottom and green on the top, undoubtedly evokes a vast space of sea and sky. But if we follow the metaphysics of Coleridge's poem, this landscape is seen best as an equivalent for an internal or spiritual realm. Here the spiritual traveler, whether the artist or viewer, encounters elemental forms, which are themselves representations of essential aspects of the human experience: sin, love, guilt, and redemption. Water, and marine themes in general, had long attracted Baziotes, who perhaps recognized in them an alternative to the crisp, clear rationalism of the land and air. As one writer suggested, "Baziotes saw in the symbol of water the idea of the mirror which reveals the images of otherworldliness through its calm translucent surfaces."[12]

It is the viewer's act of engaging with these ideas and emotions that constitutes the significance of Baziotes's painting, not any specific set of symbolic meanings. Baziotes likely had this kind of journey in mind when he wrote that "the poet must look at the world; must enter into other men's lives; must look at the earth and the sky; must examine the dust in the street; must walk through the world and his mirror."[13]

Leo Costello

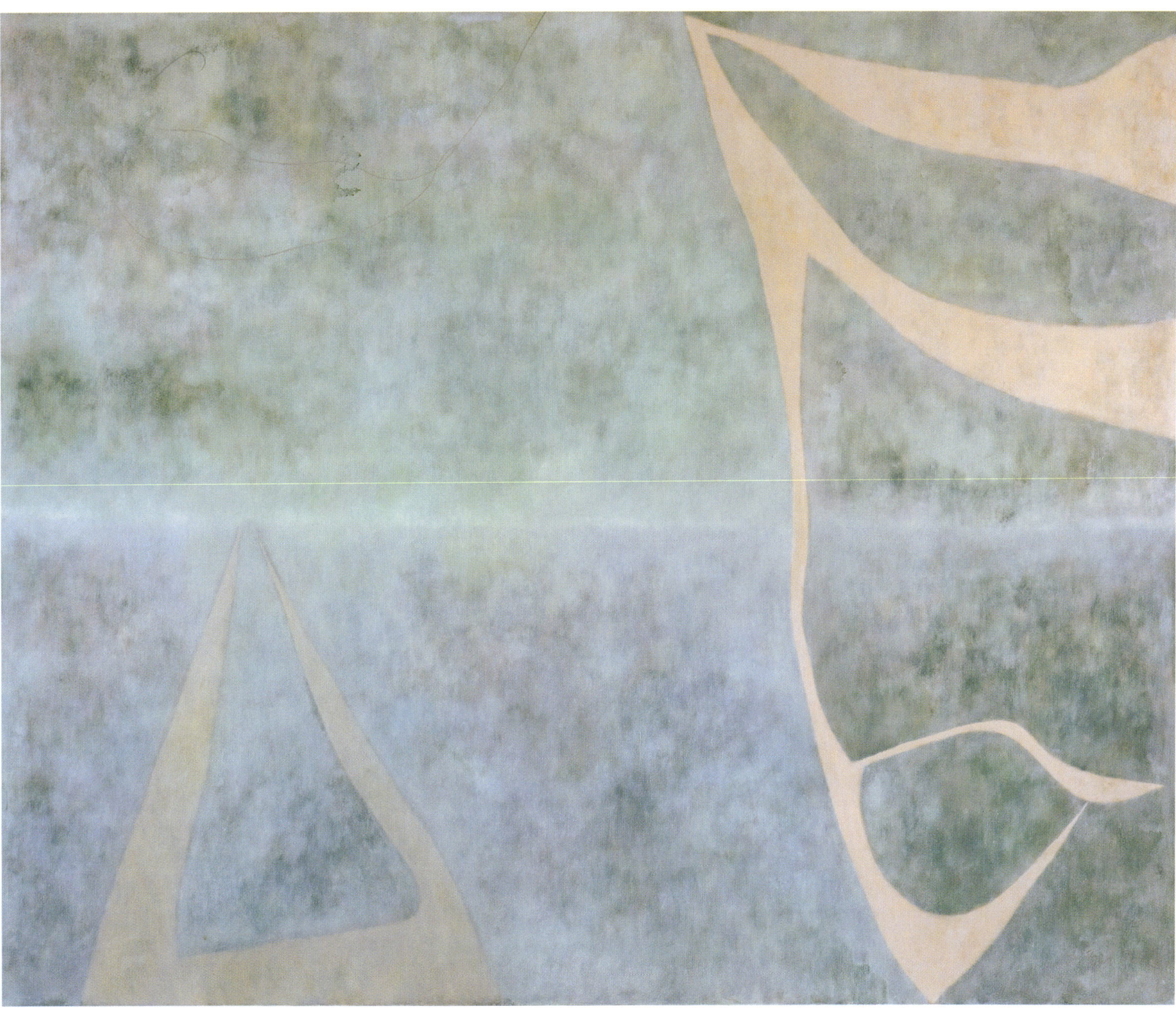

Notes

1. William Baziotes, "The Artist and His Mirror," *Right Angle* 3 (June 1949): 3.
2. Irving Sandler, *The Triumph of American Painting: A History of Abstract Expressionism* (New York: Praeger, 1970), 73–75.
3. Sandler, 72.
4. This quality may also owe something to Baziotes's work creating stained glass windows for churches in the early 1930s. See Barbara Cavaliere, "William Baziotes: The Subtlety of Life for the Artist," in Michael Preble, Barbara Cavaliere, and Mona Hadler, *William Baziotes: A Retrospective Exhibition* (Newport Beach, Calif.: Newport Harbor Art Museum, 1978), 33.
5. In conversation with Blanton curator Kelly Baum, Michael Preble, curator of the 2004 Baziotes retrospective at the Peggy Guggenheim Collection in Venice, mentioned that a similar triangular form is found in Baziotes's 1955 painting *Pompeii*. The Blanton's *Mariner* was included in the Guggenheim exhibition.
6. William Baziotes, in "Symposium: The Creative Process," *Arts Digest* 28 (January 15, 1954): 16.
7. Mona Hatoum, "William Baziotes: Four Sources of Inspiration," in Preble, Cavaliere, and Hadler, 79–82.
8. John Spencer Hill, *A Coleridge Companion* (London: MacMillan, 1983), 156.
9. Hill, 152–55ff.
10. Quoted in Hill, 163.
11. Baziotes, 3.
12. Cavaliere, 54.
13. Baziotes, 3.

16.

Mariner, 1960–1961

Oil on canvas
66 1/16 × 78 in. (167.8 × 198.2 cm)
Gift of Mari and James A. Michener
1991.185

Provenance: Purchased by James Michener from Sidney Janis Gallery, New York, 1962; long-term loan to The University of Texas at Austin, 1968–1991
Signed lower right corner "Baziotes"

Romare Bearden

Charlotte, North Carolina, 1911–New York, 1988
w. Oxford, Pennsylvania, 1929–1930; Boston, 1930–1932; New York (frequent trips to Europe), 1949–1988

Throughout his career, Romare Bearden struggled with the question of how to address social identity in his art while at the same time remaining committed to the formal qualities of his paintings. To confront this issue, he searched for ways of using his artistic vision to reveal universal aspects of his individual experience. Bearden's 1946 painting *Some Drink! Some Drink!* (plate 17) belongs to a period in which he stepped back from the immediacy of his identity as an African American and looked to myth and ritual as vehicles for exploring the universality of human nature.

Born in Charlotte, North Carolina, in 1911, Bearden began to explore art formally in the early 1930s when he entered New York University. After graduating in 1935, he enrolled in classes at the Art Students League, where he studied under the German Expressionist George Grosz. Bearden's approach to art-making was strongly influenced by Grosz's expressive style, as it was by his involvement with the "306 Group," an informal organization of African American artists based in Harlem. From his interactions with this group, Bearden gained a strong understanding of the importance of belonging to an artistic community.

Over the next several years, Bearden primarily painted African American genre scenes, often evoking his southern upbringing in a manner reminiscent of the Social Realist style of such Mexican muralists as Diego Rivera and José Clemente Orozco. In the early 1940s fellow artist William H. Johnson introduced Bearden to Caresse Crosby, who in the 1920s had co-published the avant-garde Parisian journal *Black Sun Press*. Caresse became a pivotal figure in Bearden's career; she exhibited his works in several shows and, in 1944, introduced him to Samuel M. Kootz, a New York art dealer who represented many of the leading American abstractionists of the time, including Adolph Gottlieb, William Baziotes, and Robert Motherwell. Kootz agreed to represent Bearden at his gallery on 57th Street, which was fortunate since government patronage had largely disappeared after the war, leaving a number of artists without a means of support. With Kootz's help, Bearden became one of the few African American artists to join the newly emerging New York art scene.

Early in their association, Kootz asked to see some of Bearden's oil paintings. Since he had been working mainly in gouache, Bearden quickly produced a number of oil paintings, adapting to oil what he had previously done in the opaque watercolor medium. He did so by making an enlarged photographic copy of his initial sketch, the outline of which he traced onto a gessoed panel. To achieve the effect of a watercolor Bearden completed the work using oil paint thinned with turpentine.

The works greatly impressed Kootz, and he arranged to exhibit them. *The Passion of Christ*, held in October 1945, was the first of three exhibitions of Bearden's work at the Kootz Gallery. Within two weeks of the opening, twenty of the twenty-four paintings had sold, in addition to one purchased by The Museum of Modern Art. In 1947 the Whitney Museum of American Art selected *Some Drink! Some Drink!*, which had been exhibited the preceding year in *New Paintings by Bearden*, for inclusion in their *Annual Exhibition of Contemporary American Painting*.

For the subjects of these works, Bearden turned to biblical scenes and to the writing of such authors as Federico García Lorca, François Rabelais, and Homer. *Some Drink! Some Drink!*, for example, took its inspiration from the Frenchman Rabelais's satirical novel *Gargantua and Pantagruel*, written between 1532 and 1542. The novel—which details the exploits and travels of two giants and their companions—questions, reappraises, and redefines man's journey in the world in a manner that praises the human spirit. Through his use of line and color, Bearden translated into paint the intoxicating mood of an episode of drunkenness described by Rabelais. He loosely sketched the outlines of the four figures, who pull and push at each other as if caught in a moment of inebriation. On top of them, he placed blocks of pure color that call attention to the figurative elements and function as a means of exploring the tensions created between the composition's curvilinear and rectilinear forms. The contrast between abstract and representational space allowed Bearden to explore the ritual of drink on a figurative as well as a formal level.

In 1950 Bearden left New York to spend eighteen months in Paris where, among other things, he studied philosophy at the Sorbonne on the GI Bill. After he returned to the US, Bearden experienced a major creative dilemma and abandoned painting for nearly two years. When he decided to paint again in 1954, he experimented with a variety of Abstract Expressionist techniques. Bearden shared formal concerns as well as an interest in the universal significance of myths and rituals with the Abstract Expressionists, yet he never adopted their gestural styles or their preoccupation with existentialism. Instead, he forged an individual approach to Abstract Expressionism, which involved creating a "poetic, serene abstract art."[1]

As the Civil Rights Movement gained increasing visibility in the 1960s, Bearden began to reassess his social responsibilities as an artist and to think about how he could contribute to the movement without necessarily making "protest art." His response was to produce a series of photomontages and photographic copies of his works, a practice that quickly led to his working almost exclusively in the collage medium. Although these works mark Bearden's return to incorporating the specificity of his African American experience into his art, he believed neither in isolating African American culture from the United States as a whole nor in the notion that a mainstream United States culture untouched by an African American style or idiom existed. Bearden's art, as Ralph Ellison has written, "is an

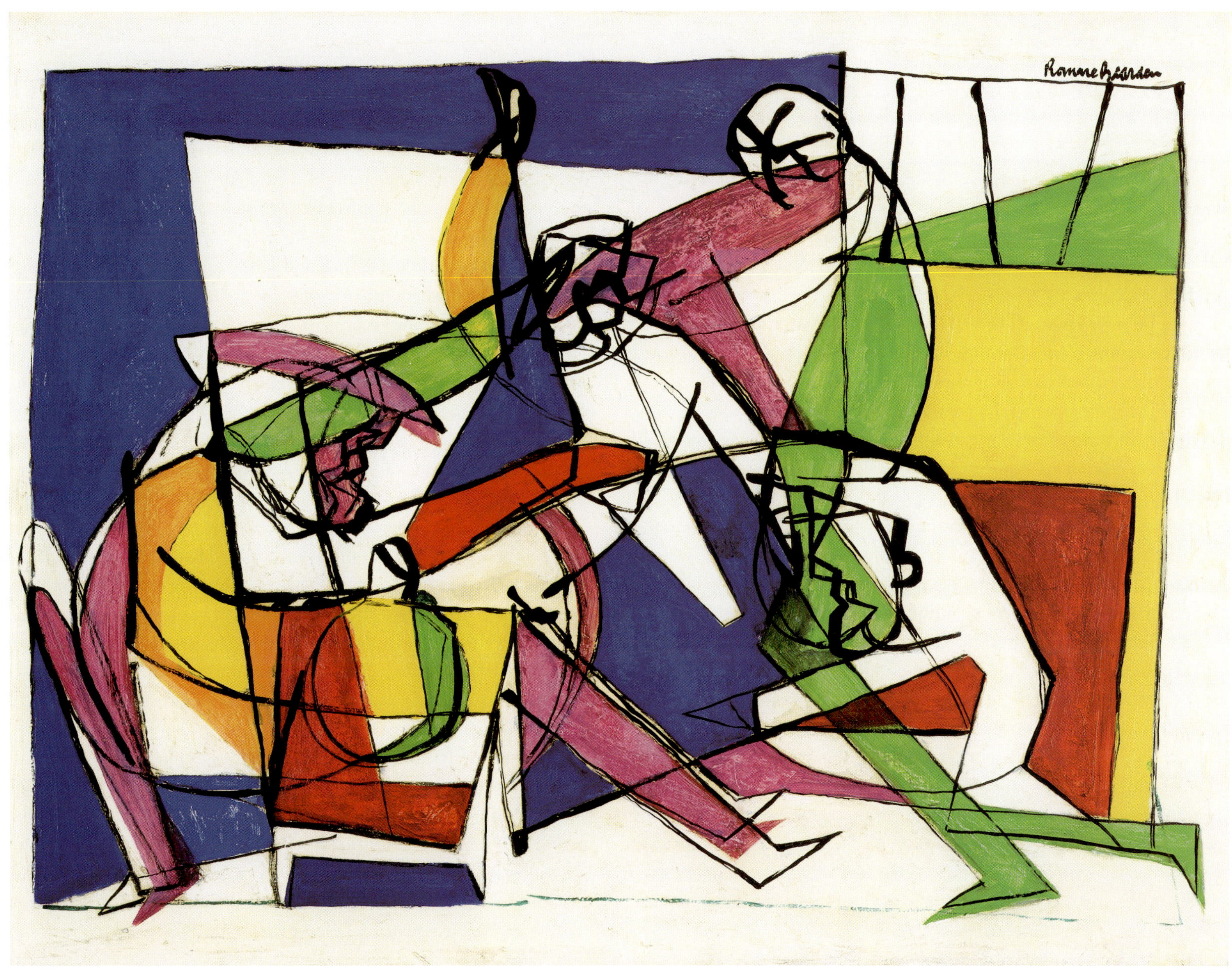

affirmation of the irrelevance of the notion of race as a limiting force in the arts."[2]

Erina Duganne

Notes

1. Sharon F. Patton, *Memory and Metaphor: The Art of Romare Bearden, 1940–1987* (New York and Oxford: Oxford University Press in conjunction with The Studio Museum in Harlem, 1991), 35. For additional information on Bearden's relationship to Abstract Expressionism, see Matthew S. Witkovsky, "Experience vs. Theory: Romare Bearden and Abstract Expressionism," *Black American Literature Forum* 23 (summer 1989): 257–82; and Lowery Sims, "Romare Bearden: An Artist's Odyssey," in *Romare Bearden: Origins and Progressions* (Detroit, Mich.: The Detroit Institute of Arts, 1986), 11–20.
2. Ralph Ellison, "Introduction," in *Romare Bearden: Paintings and Projections* (Albany, N.Y.: The Art Gallery, 1968), n.p.

17.

Some Drink! Some Drink!, 1946

Oil on Masonite
25 × 32 in. (63 × 81 cm)
Michener Acquisitions Fund
P1969.7(1)P

Provenance: Samuel Kootz Gallery, New York; Grand Central Galleries, New York, 1947; private dealer; Hirschl & Adler, New York; purchased from Hirschl & Adler, 1969
Signed upper right corner "Romare Bearden"
Inscribed verso, upper left corner "'Some Drink, Some Drink'
25/32–October 1946 Romare Bearden"

George Wesley Bellows

Columbus, Ohio, 1882–New York, 1925

w. New York (summers in Monhegan Island, Maine, 1911–1916 and Woodstock, New York, 1920–1925), 1904–1925

Although *Rolling Breakers* (1913, plate 18) may not closely resemble works by Robert Henri and the artists associated with him in the Ashcan School, its foundations lie there. George Bellows was born and raised in Columbus, Ohio, where he developed a talent for drawing and athletics in high school. He entered Ohio State University in 1901 and pursued his interest in both sports and art. In 1904 he moved to New York to embark on an art career. Bellows enrolled in William Merritt Chase's New York School of Art, where he studied under Henri.

Bellows's early paintings closely followed Henri's style and themes, focusing on the characters in and life of the city with the immediacy for which members of "The Eight" were known. Bellows soon attained his own voice, however, and achieved almost instant success. He was awarded the prestigious Hallgarten Prize at the National Academy of Design when his work was exhibited there in 1908. The following year, he was elected an associate member, the youngest in the academy's history.[1]

Bellows's first important paintings were unsentimental portraits of young children; these early subjects led to scenes of city life, such as groups of children standing on street corners or swimming in the East River. He created his most famous paintings in his studio in the Lincoln Arcade, across from the Sharkey Athletic Club. Bringing to life the underground world of New York's prizefighting matches, the artist revealed his ability to capture the aggressive action and force of boxing by creating compositions based on the juxtaposition of diagonals within a rectangle, thereby emphasizing the dynamic immediacy of the scene. After his participation in the Armory Show of 1913, however, Bellows came face to face with the avant-garde and its alternative strategies to painting. One historian wrote, "As a kind of compromise with modernism, he focused on new techniques for presenting realist subject matter so that the underlying color organization and compositional design would conform to abstract principles."[2]

For Bellows, children and prizefighters represented the culture of New York and of the United States, but the sea represented something more—something intangible yet monumental. He began painting seascapes in 1911, during summers spent on Monhegan Island off the coast of Maine. Although the artist often traveled there in the succeeding years with colleagues such as Henri, John Sloan, and Randall Davey, the work of Winslow Homer, who spent extended periods of time at Prout's Neck between 1882 and his death in 1910, exerted the greatest influence on Bellows's seascapes. Indeed, it appears Bellows embraced "Homer's dictum on how to paint the sea, 'do it with one wave, not more than two.'"[3]

The sense of power and simplicity found in Homer's seascapes is evidenced in *Rolling Breakers,* one of the more than one hundred canvases Bellows painted in Maine during the summer of 1913. In this small and intimate seascape, two waves move toward the large boulders that fill the foreground. The immediate shoreline forefronts an expansive ocean vista—as if one were standing on a large boulder just behind those seen in the painting. The ocean extends high into the upper portion of the picture plane where it blends in with a slim band of sky. A diffused light illuminates the scene from above, evoking the typically spotty sunlight that pours over the Maine coast through an atmosphere of moving clouds and mist. This light can be seen on the white-flecked boulders in the middle distance and in the myriad patches of blue and green tones into which the ocean is divided.

The deep blues and greens of the ocean are balanced by the white of the waves and the long, horizontal band of blue-gray clouds that meets the sea on the horizon. Adding a heavier undertone are the blue-gray boulders in the foreground and the ochre-green and brown-black of the boulders that extend further out into the sea. Bellows expanded his limited palette by varying the value and density of each hue.

In *Rolling Breakers* the artist relied heavily on short, thick strokes of white paint to render the impact of the waves crashing over boulders and a lighter, more fluid application for the blue, green, and white swirl of the sea. To the right of the breakers, spanning the canvas in a strong diagonal, the artist used wide, upwardly curved strokes of deep green to communicate the force of the imminently cresting wave. For the one behind, Bellows employed dark blue to suggest the growing swells that appear to temporarily pull back, as if to gather force before making their move toward shore.

The subtleties in movement and color—as in the slight touches of high-keyed orange that allude to moss and barnacles on the boulder's surface and the harmonic relationships between the many tones of blue and green—are the key to Bellows's realism. In his later seascapes and portraits, Bellows developed an interest in color systems, in particular that of Hardesty Maratta, a painter from Chicago. Maratta's system of a prearranged array of 144 hues freed the artist from the task of mixing colors while working, thereby permitting greater spontaneity of paint application.[4] Bellows also became interested in compositional theories, specifically Jay Hambridge's concept of dynamic symmetry.[5] Dynamic symmetry posits basic geometric law as the basis of all pictorial composition, which provided the formal structure Bellows intuitively sought in his paintings.[6]

A quintessential American artist, Bellows covered many genres yet maintained a sense of vitality in all his work through his commitment to experimentation and his determined discipline. He was one of the few artists of his time to be honored with a large retrospective at the Metropolitan Museum of Art immediately following his death in 1925; he was also the first artist to be awarded a solo exhibition at the National Gallery of Art in 1957.

Jennifer Davy

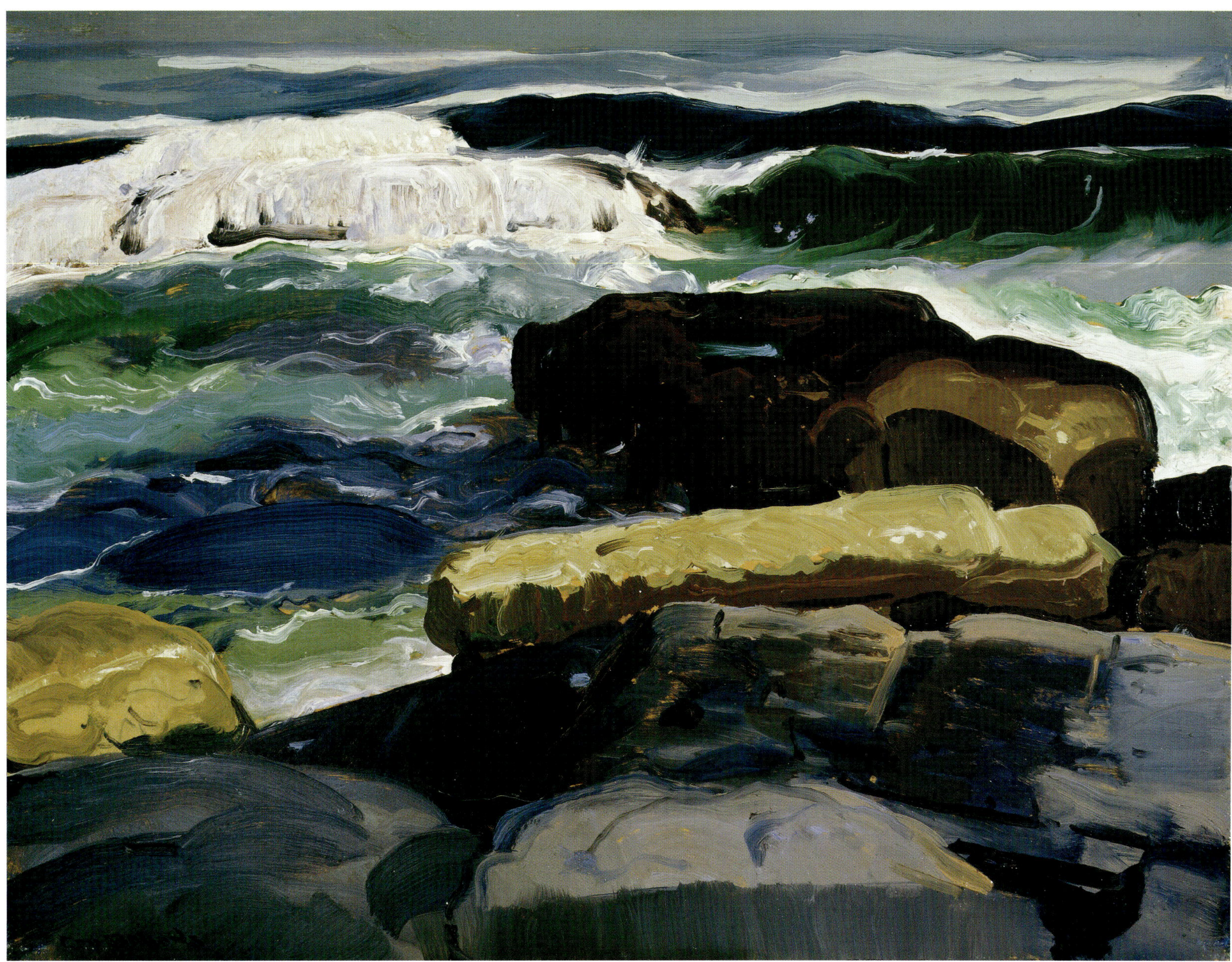

Notes

1. Henry Adams, "The Paintings of George Bellows," *American Artist* 56 (July 1992): 54–55.
2. Adams, 56–57.
3. Charles H. Morgan, *George Bellows: Painter of America* (New York: Reynal and Company, 1965), 171.
4. Frederick A. Sweet, "George Wesley Bellows," in *George Bellows: Paintings, Drawings and Prints* (Chicago: The Art Institute of Chicago, 1946), 21.
5. Hambridge, a painter and illustrator, claimed his theory was based on techniques used by the ancient Greeks. He offered numerous compositional strategies through a complex system that divided the rectangle into parts bearing a relationship both to each other and to the whole. See Adams, 57–58.
6. Sweet, 23.

18.

Rolling Breakers, 1913

Oil on panel
15 x 19 in. (38 x 50 cm)
Michener Acquisitions Fund
P1969.8.1

Provenance: George Wesley Bellows Estate; Emma Bellows; Allison Gallery; Alfredo Valente, New York; purchased from Bernard Danenberg Galleries, New York, 1969
Signed lower left "Geo Bellows"

Thomas Hart Benton

Neosho, Missouri, 1889–Kansas City, Missouri, 1975

w. Chicago, 1907–1908; Paris, 1908–1911; New York (frequent trips to the western, midwestern, and southern United States after 1924), 1912–1935; Kansas City, Missouri, 1935–1975

Along with Grant Wood and John Stuart Curry, Thomas Hart Benton formed the "triumvirate" of American Regionalist painting, a movement that gained considerable momentum throughout the 1920s and almost completely dominated the cultural scene in the 1930s.[1] Each artist was indelibly associated with a particular region: Benton with Missouri, Wood with Iowa, and Curry with Kansas. Above all, the Regionalists sought to identify a uniquely American style of painting that addressed subjects specific to the United States. Benton, Wood, and Curry represented ordinary Americans engaged in ordinary tasks, most of them from rural communities as opposed to urban centers (although Benton never ceased to paint scenes of life in American cities as well). The Regionalists also sought to give visual form to such "American" values as resilience, hard work, stoicism, self-reliance, physical strength, and individualism. As Erika Doss commented, Benton and his colleagues "projected these regional stereotypes as the essence of American national identity. Regionalism's lure of the local was used as the currency of cultural nationalism."[2] Invariably optimistic and aspirational, Regionalist painting was invested with nothing less than the task of revitalizing what Benton and others perceived as America's moribund, bankrupt culture. Benton in particular "aimed to create a modern art which could generate social and political reform in post–world war I America."[3]

The depictions of vernacular culture that critics and collectors greeted with so much enthusiasm did not come easily to Benton. His great-uncle had been a Senator and his father a Representative in the United States Congress; Benton's family expected that, as the oldest son, he too would become a lawyer and a statesman. The artist-to-be and his father struggled in a heated contest of wills for over a decade. Eventually, Benton enrolled at the Art Institute in Chicago; a year later, in 1908, he moved to Paris. It was in Paris that Benton learned the value of copying Old Master paintings, and he often went to the Louvre with his sketching materials. He was particularly enthralled with the sculptural solidity of Michelangelo's figures and the dynamic energy of Baroque composition—qualities he would emulate in his own work. He also discovered European modernism, carefully studying the work of the Impressionists, Cubists, and Paul Cézanne. While living in Paris, Benton met Mexican artist Diego Rivera and befriended American painters John Marin and Stanton Macdonald-Wright, who would exert a profound influence on his subsequent artistic career.

Benton returned from Paris in 1911 and settled in New York one year later. He continued to experiment with the styles he had assimilated while living in Europe, associating with other exemplars of American modernism. Most of Benton's paintings from this period represent recognizable subjects using a pictorial vocabulary borrowed from Macdonald-Wright, but others verge on complete abstraction. In 1916 Benton participated in *The Forum Exhibition of Modern Painters* at the Anderson Galleries in New York. Alongside works by Arthur Dove, Marsden Hartley, and Man Ray, he exhibited a series of paintings that adapt Macdonald-Wright's Synchromism to the depiction of figures inspired by Michelangelo's paintings and sculptures.[4]

While living in New York in the mid- to late 1910s, Benton amassed a variety of experiences that would have a formative impact on his later work. He participated in the People's Art Guild, which helped convince him of the social function of art and of the social responsibility of the artist, mandates he would begin to fulfill in the 1920s and realize fully in the 1930s.[5] He also built and designed sets for the film industry, work he secured through connections with his friend, director Rex Ingram. As Doss argued, Benton's exposure to mainstream cinema deepened his commitment to developing a public art with broad popular appeal at the same time that it offered a viable model for realizing this art visually.[6]

The period between 1918 and 1924 represents a transitional time in Benton's career, as he began to solidify his mature, Regionalist style. Several events precipitated this change. In 1918 Benton worked as a draftsman for the Navy. He was stationed in Norfolk, Virginia, where he devoted a considerable amount of time to sketching his local environs. Benton recalled this as the propitious moment when he "left for good the art-for-art-sake world in which I had hitherto lived."[7] The death of his father in 1924 marked the beginning of Benton's gradual reconciliation with his political heritage—more specifically, with the democratic liberalism (Republicanism) of his great-uncle and father.[8] That year also coincided with the onset of Benton's annual summertime sketching trips through the West, Midwest, and South.[9] There he sketched everything from timber camps, boomtowns, and mining operations—sites of economic and social transition—to bucolic scenes such as the one in *Romance* (1931–1932, plate 19), where time and history seem suspended in a state of arrested development. These sketches would form the basis for much of Benton's Regionalist paintings in the 1920s and 1930s.

A poignant depiction of an African American couple as they stroll hand in hand across a dirt road, *Romance* was likely inspired by one of Benton's rural travels, possibly his trip to the Daufuskee Islands, located just off the coast of South Carolina.[10] However, what probably began as a relatively straightforward observation of the inhabitants of these islands appears in the painting as a scene invested with considerable lyricism and emotional resonance. This is due in no small part to Benton's style, which adapts European and American modernism to narrative, representational painting. As is typical of his work from the 1920s, Benton imbued *Romance* with a sense of gentle rhythm and spatial dynamism, creating a ripple effect across the canvas by repeating certain shapes and by endowing the two figures with a lanky, elastic quality. Thanks to Benton's use of undulating lines and forms,

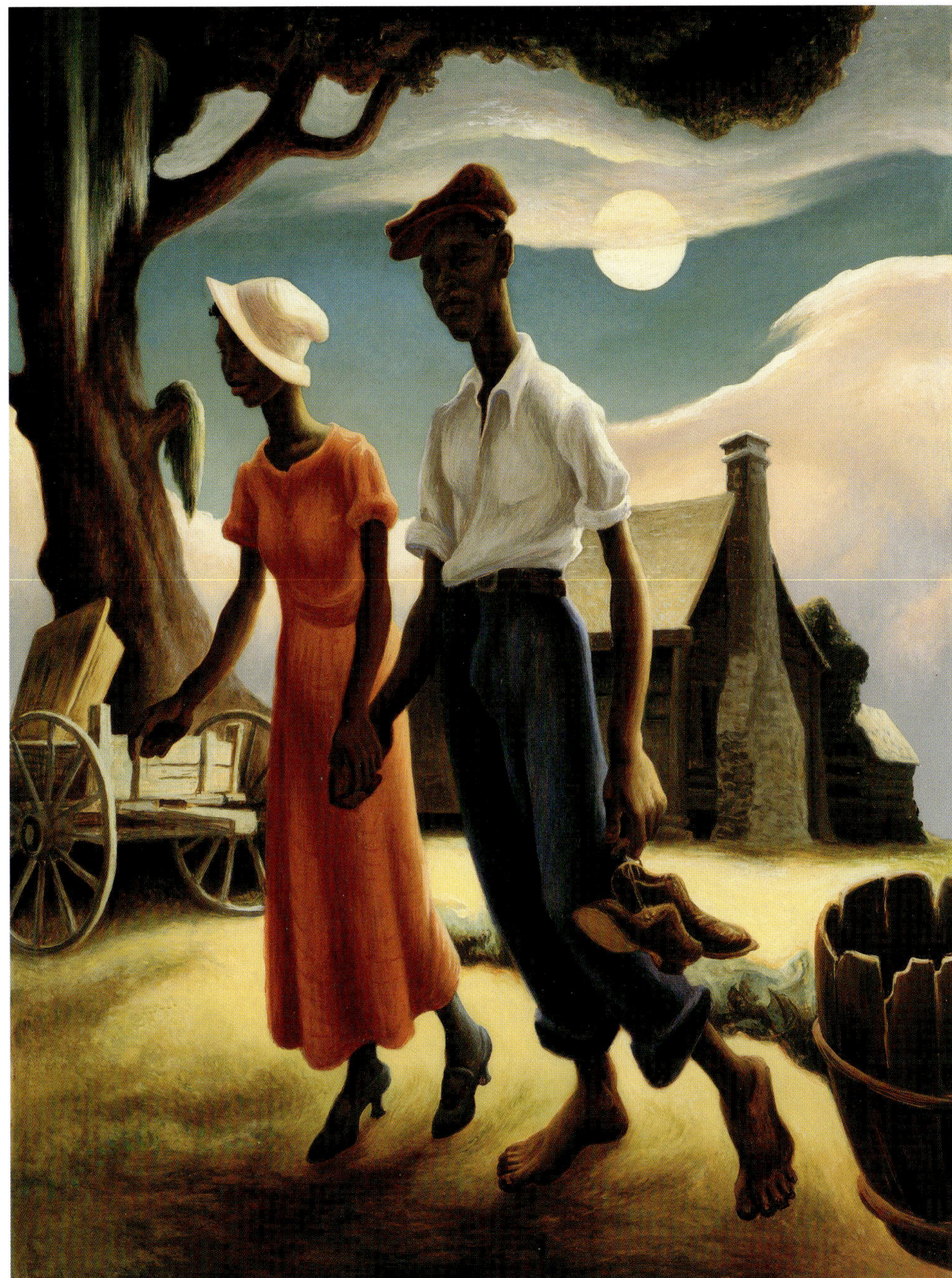

19.

Romance, 1931–1932

Tempera and oil varnish glazes on gesso panel
$45\frac{1}{2} \times 33\frac{1}{4}$ in. (115 × 84 cm)
Gift of Mari and James A. Michener
1991.187

Provenance: Purchased by James Michener from the artist, 1962; long-term loan to The University of Texas at Austin, 1968–1991
Signed recto, lower left "Benton"

everything in the painting appears to be in motion or, at the very least, capable of movement, even when absolutely still.

In addition to his contributions as a painter, Benton was also an influential teacher. In the 1920s and 1930s he taught at the Art Students League in New York, where his students included Alexander Calder and Jackson Pollock, with whom Benton would maintain a close relationship throughout the 1950s, even after Abstract Expressionism had eclipsed Regionalism in the popular imagination and in cultural and critical circles.

Kelly Baum

Notes

1. Benton was the first artist to appear on the cover of *Time* magazine in 1934. Regionalism had parallels in poetry and literature as well. For more information, see Matthew Baigell, "Recovering America for American Art: Benton in the Early Twenties," in *Thomas Hart Benton: Chronicler of America's Folk Heritage* (Annandale-on-Hudson, N.Y.: Edith C. Blum Art Institute, 1984), 12–31.
2. Erika Doss, *Twentieth-Century American Art* (Oxford: Oxford University Press, 2002), 111.
3. Erika Doss, *Benton, Pollock, and the Politics of Modernism: From Regionalism to Abstract Expressionism* (Chicago: The University of Chicago Press, 1991), 56.
4. Matthew Baigell, "Thomas Hart Benton in the 1920's," *Art Journal* 29 (summer 1970): 422.
5. Doss, *Benton, Pollock, and the Politics of Modernism*, 48–49.
6. Doss, *Benton, Pollock, and the Politics of Modernism*, 42–44.
7. Quoted in Baigell, 424.
8. Doss, *Benton, Pollock, and the Politics of Modernism*, 2, 50, 53.
9. Karal Ann Marling claims that Benton "was the first outlander of any stature to suggest that the South and its traditions might warrant respectful attention." See her essay in *Tom Benton and His Drawings: A Biographical Essay and A Collection of His Sketches, Studies, and Mural Cartoons* (Columbia: University of Missouri Press, 1985), 49.
10. Thomas Hart Benton, *An Artist in America* (New York: Robert M. McBride & Company, 1937), 171. I would like to thank Phaedra Siebert for her research on this matter. *Romance* was produced in the interim between the unveiling of Benton's *America Today* murals at the New School for Social Research in 1930 (his first project to attract national attention) and *The Arts of Life* murals at the Whitney Museum of American Art in 1932.

Elmer Bischoff

Berkeley, California, 1916–1991

w. Berkeley, California, 1934–1938; San Francisco, 1946–1952; Marysville, California, 1953–1956; San Francisco, 1957–1959; Berkeley, 1959–1991

Like many artists who came of age in the 1940s, Elmer Bischoff first immersed himself in Abstract Expressionism, the dominant style of the period. On the West Coast, where Bischoff lived and worked, Abstract Expressionism was identified with the work of Clyfford Still, one of its major practitioners. By the early 1950s, however, Bischoff, along with David Park and Richard Diebenkorn, abandoned abstraction in favor of figuration. They went on to form what came to be known as the Bay Area Figurative Movement, which nonetheless incorporated stylistic aspects of Abstract Expressionism.

Born and raised in Berkeley, California, Bischoff spent nearly his entire life in the San Francisco Bay Area. He grew up in the home built by his father, an architect, and attended high school in Berkeley and Oakland. Interested in both athletics and art, Bischoff majored in art at the University of California at Berkeley and was a member of the ROTC as well as the university's wrestling team. Studying under the artists that made up the "Berkeley School"—Earle Loran, Margaret Peterson, and Worth Ryder—Bischoff produced still-lifes, portraits, and abstract paintings that were influenced by a range of artists, from El Greco to Pablo Picasso and Joan Miró. Continuing his studies in the graduate program at Berkeley, the artist received his MFA and exhibited in the San Francisco Art Association Annual in 1939, an event he continued to participate in until 1963.

After serving in World War II, Bischoff began teaching at the California School of Fine Arts (now the San Francisco Art Institute) in the fall of 1945. He joined Park, who had started working there the preceding year; Still and Diebenkorn both followed within the next year. In the midst of this fertile creative environment, Bischoff produced primitivistic and dreamlike abstractions that became the focus of his first solo exhibition in 1947 at the California Palace of the Legion of Honor. He continued to paint abstractly until the end of 1952. Then, disillusioned with the idealism of Abstract Expressionism, whose diverse stylistic qualities he believed had become restrictive and formulaic, Bischoff began exploring recognizable subject matter. As Susan Landauer observed, for Bischoff and his fellow artists, figurative art was the means not of rejecting Abstraction Expressionism outright but rather "a way of preserving what was meaningful in it."[1] Bischoff was also greatly influenced by Susanne Langer's 1953 text, *Feeling and Form: A Theory of Art,* which encouraged artists to develop an intrinsic relationship between form and content.[2]

In the second half of the decade, both Bischoff and Diebenkorn turned to the nude figure as their primary subject matter. They rendered the nude with a variety of Abstract Expressionist painting strategies, such as animated brushwork and gestural movement. Bischoff's new work received critical acclaim; his success in a 1956 solo exhibition at the California School of Fine Arts was reinforced a year later when he was awarded an Oakland Art Museum Purchase Prize for a work in the exhibition *Contemporary Bay Area Figurative Painting*, the group's first show. This event not only showcased the figurative tendency in California as an alternative to abstraction, it gained national recognition for its members, including Park and Diebenkorn, and secured for Bischoff his first solo show in New York, at the Staempfli Gallery in 1960.

The 1960s was a tumultuous decade for Bischoff. Park died of cancer in 1960, and a few years later Diebenkorn left for Santa Monica. In addition to these losses, Bischoff accepted a new position at UC Berkeley, where he was the only figurative painter on the faculty. He increasingly withdrew from his peers and from campus life as student protests escalated throughout the 1960s.[3]

The changes in Bischoff's life are often cited as the impetus behind the unsettling melancholy that infuses his seascapes from the 1960s. *Breakers* (1963, plate 20), the first in this series, is a large oil on canvas that depicts the back of a lone swimmer, who stands with an air of hesitancy amidst the large boulders that separate him or her from the expanse of the sea beyond. The calm water in which the nude figure stands is a brilliant blue with highlights of reflected light, while thick lines of white paint atop a blue of velvety darkness announce the ominous approach of a cresting wave that can be seen in the distance.

Bischoff's mastery of color reveals itself in *Breakers,* which blends a dominant palette of cool harmonies of blues and greens with sparingly applied warm-toned hues—dark brown, gray, red, and orange, each used with absolute economy. *Breakers* also illustrates a hallmark of the Bay Area figurative tradition: gestural abstraction as a representational strategy. Here Bischoff moved swaths of paint across the canvas with an overwhelming sense of spontaneity; traces of his brush, varying in size, articulate the painting's forms and enact a sense of fluidity.

After twenty years of embracing figurative painting, Bischoff returned to a painterly abstraction that combined the qualities of early modernists Wassily Kandinsky and Joan Miró. Although he remained successful throughout his professional life, Bischoff's figurative enterprise and his contribution to the Bay Area School endure as the touchstones of his career.

Jennifer Davy

Notes

1. Susan Landauer, *Elmer Bischoff: The Ethics of Paint* (Berkeley, Calif.: University of California Press; Oakland, Calif.: Oakland Museum, 2001), 62–63.
2. Susanne Langer, *Feeling and Form: A Theory of Art* (New York: Scribner, 1953).
3. Landauer, 126, 128.

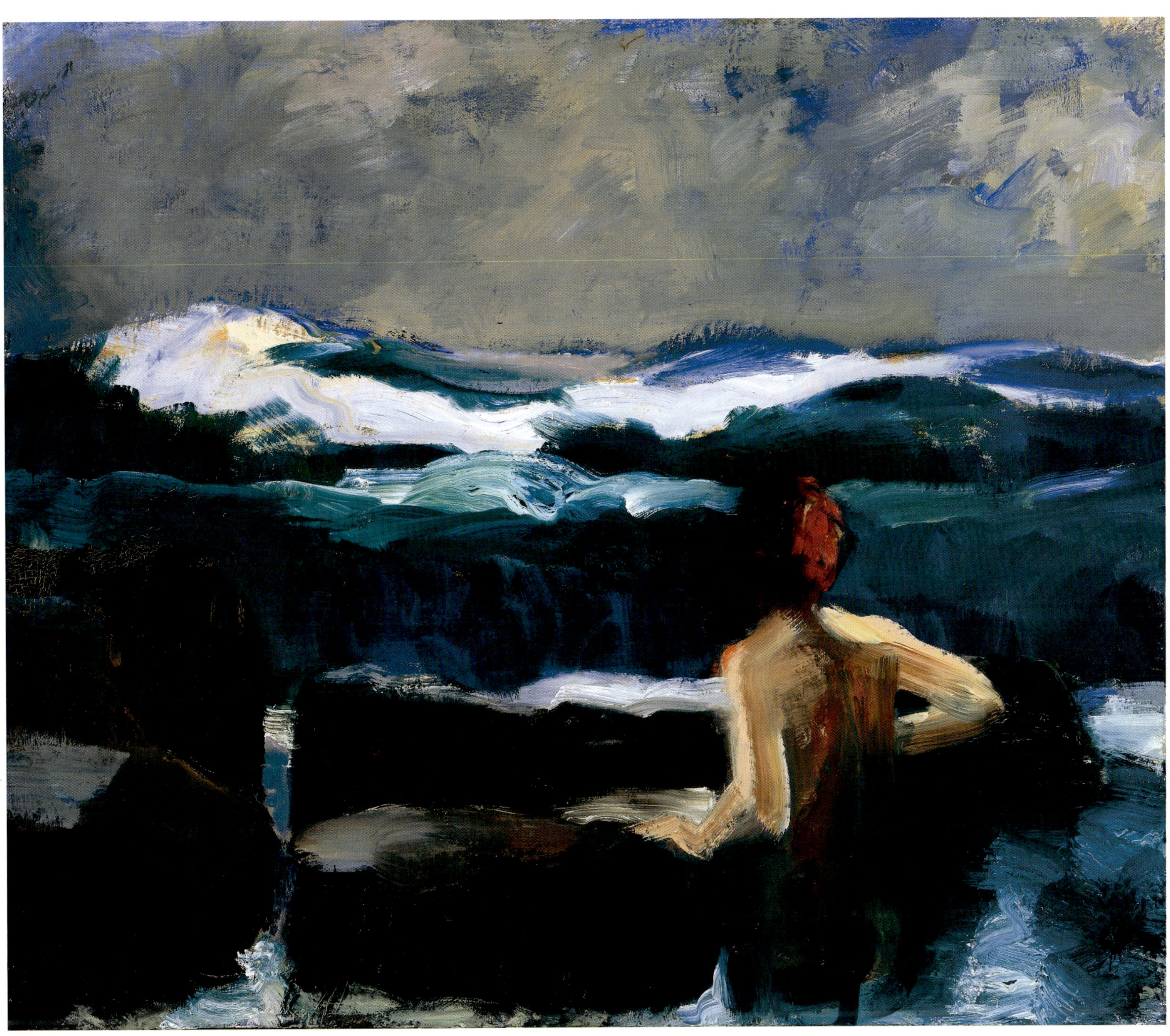

20.

Breakers, 1963

Oil on canvas
61 × 70 in. (155 × 178 cm)
Gift of Mari and James A. Michener
G1968.33

Provenance: Purchased by James Michener from Staempfli Gallery, New York, 1964

Tom Blackwell

b. Chicago, 1938

w. Keene, New Hampshire, 1978; Hanover, New Hampshire, 1980; Tucson, Arizona, 1981; New York, 1985–present

THE ARTIST TOM BLACKWELL has long been interested in reflective surfaces, from the steel and chrome bodies of motorcycles to the gleaming plate glass of shop windows. Blackwell is closely identified with the Photorealist movement, which included such printmakers, sculptors, and painters as Duane Hanson, Richard Estes, and Chuck Close. In an effort to enhance illusionism and verisimilitude, the Photorealists based their work on photographs that they either made themselves or appropriated from preexisting sources. Blackwell's *A Life in Motion II* (1980, plate 21), with its precise attention to detail, highly finished surface, and reference to modern life and consumer culture, is a prime example of Photorealism.

Blackwell, who was born in Chicago and eventually moved to New York, is a self-taught artist.[1] He taught at the School of Visual Arts in the late 1980s and for many years also had a home in southern New Hampshire. Several of his paintings are based on photographs taken in towns near his home.[2]

Strongly influenced by the work of James Rosenquist, Blackwell's initial foray into realism began in 1970, when he combined random magazine images in a manner that approximated collage. He explained, "I was juxtaposing photographic images in an irrational and, I hoped, poetic way. . . . It was a hit or miss situation. Sometimes it worked surprisingly well and other times a painting would end up as the visual equivalent of a bad pun."[3] After painting an image of a motorcycle tail section in the mid- to late 1960s, he decided to concentrate on a single image rather than creating a montage effect in his paintings.[4] Displeased with the quality of magazine reproductions, Blackwell began to take his own photographs around the same time. This filtering of the world through a camera lens led him to a deeper consideration of subject matter:

> *The reflective surface—plate glass windows, chrome, stainless steel, baked enamel, and, of course, the ubiquitous automobile and all it has wrought—has changed our world forever. The subject matter of my painting is the interaction of light on all of these man-made surfaces, the reflections, refractions, distortions, interactions of objects and people with these things—in short, the modern world and the way we see it.*[5]

Having largely focused on motorcycles and car engines at the beginning of his professional career, in the 1980s Blackwell found alternate and equally compelling subject matter in the world of commerce, becoming particularly enchanted with the ubiquitous female mannequin. Art historian Linda Chase described these two approaches in related terms: "If the bikes and engines represented a kind of idealized masculinity basic to our culture, the mannequins . . . represent an idealized femininity whose unreality is played off against the reflections of real people walking by."[6]

A Life in Motion II permitted Blackwell to investigate the aggressive allure of an artificial ideal promoted by the fashion business and its removal from anything resembling real life. The painting depicts an upscale, sophisticated department store in Manhattan. Text etched into the store's glass window—"HUBERT DE GIVENCHY: A LIFE IN MOTION"—inspired the title of the painting. Three mannequins wearing red dresses and elegant black hats stand in a group on the other side of the store window. The two mannequins at the front appear to stare haughtily at pedestrians below, while the third gazes disdainfully into the distance. The stony faces of weary New Yorkers are reflected in the glass and seem equally lifeless. The painting raises the multifaceted question: how do we distinguish between the real and the unreal? The mannequins appear solid and substantial, while the passing pedestrians dissolve into immateriality, their presence momentarily registering on the surface of the window. As they walk by the shop, the window "records" their fleeting images in much the same way a photograph "records" the image of its referent. As Linda Nochlin observed, "The photographed shop window is a readymade hyperrealist subject, flat like the picture surface and yet full of consumer objects at the same time."[7]

The composition of *A Life in Motion II* is replete with angles, corners, and diagonals that provide a geometric framework for the painting, one that alternates between the stable and the dynamic. The composition is characterized by a strong diagonal thrust that propels the eye from the upper left-hand corner, where we see the mannequins' white faces, to the area just right of center, where we see the reflection of a woman wearing glasses and striding purposefully toward her destination, completely unaware of either the camera or the mannequins. The structure of the building's limestone bricks, with their strong verticals and horizontals, anchors the composition. These intersecting lines contribute to the sense of an enclosed grid, a crucial element not only of the design of the painting but of the urban landscape as well.

Although his choice of subject matter might suggest otherwise, Blackwell's intent was not to generate commentary on the alienating effects of the urban landscape. When asked how to define Photorealism, Blackwell responded by saying that it was

> *a posture regarding painting and sculpture that is totally without subjective ramifications, totally cold, objective, unemotional—simply a slice of American Life or an aspect of it, unsentimentalized in any way, not made dramatic. The thing itself, meticulously represented with great technical skill and accuracy, but with none of the artist's subjective feelings.*[8]

In other words, Blackwell's goal was to render the modern world in as detached and straightforward a manner as possible. The viewer, however, is free to draw her own conclusions about the hidden subtexts

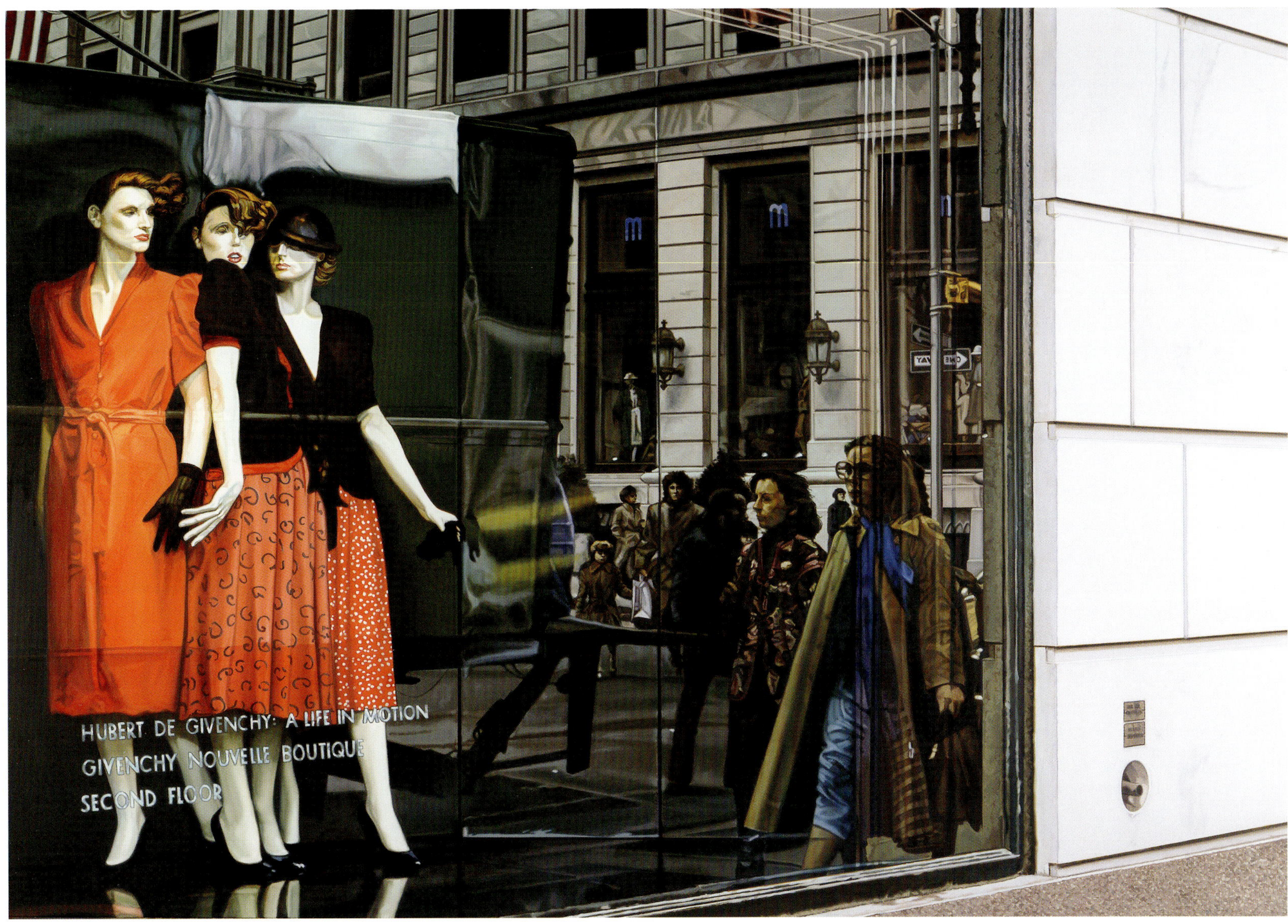

regarding urbanism, consumer culture, and femininity buried in *A Life in Motion II*.

Claire Barliant

Notes

1. Louis Meisel, conversation with the author, New York, December 10, 2004.
2. Linda Chase, "Tom Blackwell: Ten Years," in *Tom Blackwell: Selected Works 1970–1980* (Hanover, N.H.: Dartmouth College, 1980), n.p.
3. Quoted in Chase, n.p.
4. L. Chase and T. McBurnett, "Photo-Realists: 12 Interviews," *Art in America* 60 (November 1972): 74.
5. Tom Blackwell, artist's statement, in *Real, Really Real, Superreal* (San Antonio: The San Antonio Museum Association, 1981), 118.
6. Linda Chase, "Tom Blackwell: 1970–1980," *Arts Magazine* 55 (December 1980): 155.
7. Linda Nochlin, "The Flowering of American Realism," in *Real, Really Real, Superreal*, 29.
8. Chase and McBurnett, 75–76.

21.

A Life in Motion II, 1980

Oil on canvas
60 × 84 in. (152.4 × 213.4 cm)
Archer M. Huntington Museum Fund
1983.2

Provenance: Louis K. Meisel Gallery, New York; Mr. Howard Weingrow; Louis K. Meisel Gallery; purchased from Louis K. Meisel Gallery, 1983

Jeremy Blake

b. Fort Sill, Oklahoma, 1971

w. Chicago, 1989–1993; Valencia, California, 1993–1995; New York, 1995–2001; New York–Venice, California, 2001–present

Morris Louis and Kenneth Noland are not necessarily cool. Not that they are uncool either. It's just that Color Field painting is usually not the first thing on the minds of today's younger artists. But combine the aesthetics of Louis and Noland with the sentiments of a pack of Mods riding their Vespas through the streets of London with The Who's "Tommy" blasting in the background. Now, throw in a splash of L.A. Noir with a deft knowledge of digital technology. That's cool. And that, in essence, is what Jeremy Blake is trying to capture in his digital animations.

It would short-change Blake, though, to assume that he's only after a superficial aesthetic. Indeed, he has grand ambitions for what he calls his "time-based paintings": "I want to reclaim abstraction from its being just a visual style. After all, before abstraction was a visual style, an abstraction was a philosophical concept that called up multiple images. That's what abstraction means to me: the visual demonstration of philosophical nuance."[1] Or, we might say, it is for Blake a conduit for deep thinking and a way to sensually convey his ideas.

Since the late 1990s, Blake has been devising complex, looping animations that bring together architectural elements—from corporate lobbies to hotel rooms to lounges to subways to haunted houses—with emotive abstractions that take their cues from the paintings of Louis and Noland.[2] What holds these seemingly disparate elements together are Blake's intricate, nonlinear narratives. At times, only he knows the details, which forces the viewer to piece together a story line, even if it's not immediately clear.[3] As Blake once said, "I want people to ask questions and walk away focused yet confused."[4] He continued, "It's important to me that the threat of a narrative intrusion transforms the work."[5] And it does.

Transformation or, in more cinematic terms, dissolving has been an important feature of Blake's work since he attended graduate school at CalArts, where he studied with visiting painter David Reed. Blake had always thought of himself as a painter, but he eventually realized that painting could not capture everything he wanted, movement in particular.[6] This realization occurred while he was watching François Truffaut's 1966 film, *Fahrenheit 451*. During the scene where Julie Christie's character sits transfixed before a flat screen broadcasting abstract images that moved and morphed, Blake thought, "What a weird, uncanny, dystopic potential for abstraction. I wanted to make paintings like that. But I couldn't . . . because paintings only move so much."[7] Fortunately for Blake, his desires coincided with advances in computer technology.[8]

Over the last several years, Blake has integrated his training as a painter with his knowledge of video, film, and other time-based media. And he has met with success. Digital animations like *All Mods Cons* (2001) and *Mod Lang* (2001) have captured the attention of critics, most of whom picked up on Blake's references to Modernist painting and design. Some see Blake's digital animations as "psychedelic scenarios with an astute sense of MTV showmanship and art history," while others have characterized him as "more [of] a choreographer of video pleasure than an analgesic practitioner of it."[9]

Blake's digital animation, *Winchester* (2002, plate 22), manifests all these qualities and then some. Originally conceived for the 2002 Whitney Biennial, *Winchester* represents Blake's first foray into the intricacies and wonders of the Winchester Mystery House in San Jose, California. Built by the widow of the Winchester Rifle heir, the Mystery House, with its stairways to nowhere, seemingly endless hallways, and doors that open into thin air, was designed to excise the spirits (killed by her family's guns) that Sarah Winchester believed were haunting her.[10] For Blake, the *Winchester* saga raises issues "fundamental to American national identity," such as the myth of the American West, the Protestant work ethic, violence, and the pursuit of happiness.[11]

Winchester begins with a grainy black and white image of the famed house. At first glance, it seems to be taken from an old film reel. The pictorial field is in constant motion, as the individual frames appear to melt and deteriorate, while the sound of a whirring projector fills the gallery.[12] Yet these effects are all contrived. In fact, they were created through "intricate frame by frame digital retouching," which allowed Blake to occasionally insert a ghostlike "old west" gunman.[13] After a short while, *Winchester* dissolves into abstractions that seemingly evoke the spirit of Louis's paintings from the late 1950s. On the one hand, these colorful, almost organic nonrepresentational forms mitigate (perhaps even aestheticize) the violence underlying the video's subject matter. On the other hand, they give visual form to Sarah Winchester's personal demons and enhance the video's psychological complexities. As Blake said, "I'm taking a space that, in theory, is haunted, and using time-based abstraction to demonstrate that haunting. . . . These abstract passages allow you to process the violence done by the gun, the fear that made the gun seem necessary in the first place—the violent act of going West."[14]

Like Blake's other digital animations, *Winchester* calls into question the process of painting. Is it possible, Blake asks, to integrate painterly qualities and techniques with something so seemingly far removed as digital animation? The answer seems to be yes:

> *I create layers and layers of translucent colors. Images are conceived in my head first. I create a digital print and build a still environment. Then I tell myself a story about the environment. This evolves into an animation, which evolves into a series of animations. Then I have to edit. It's like scraping paint off a canvas or painting over what's already been done. . . . So in fact my work is created with the same process that a painter uses.*[15]

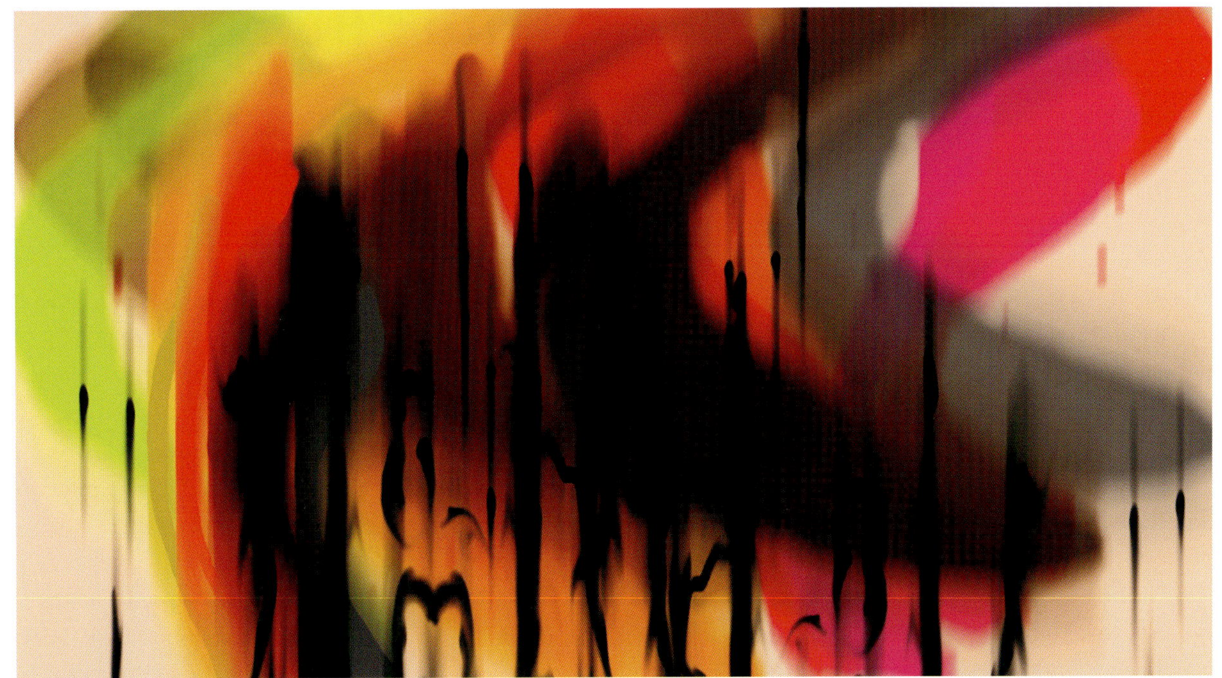

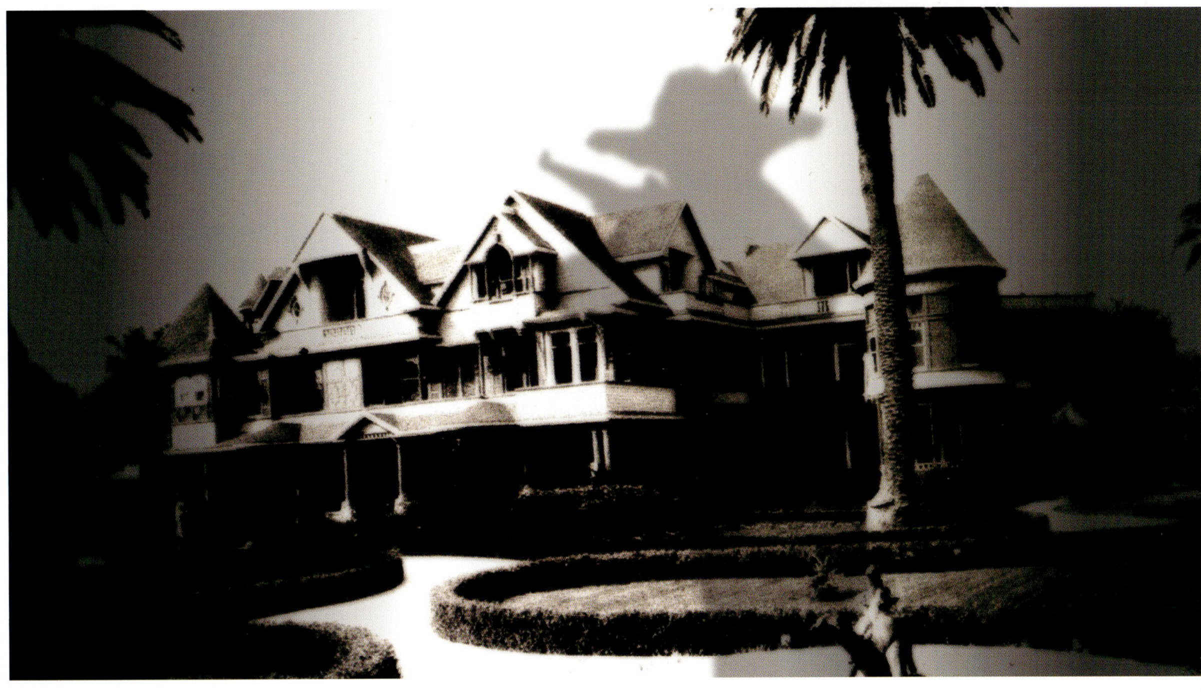

22.

Winchester, 2002

Digital animation with sound on DVD
18-minute continuous loop
Edition 2/8
Partial and pledged gift of Jeanne and Michael Klein
T2003.1

Provenance: Purchased at the request of the museum by Jeanne and Michael Klein from Feigen Contemporary, New York, 2002

Courtesy Feigen Contemporary, New York

So then, if we take Blake for his word, if *Winchester* does indeed successfully adapt painterly process to digital media, what is *Winchester*? A painting? A video?[16] In fact, it is a bit of both, like many things in contemporary art today. As a result, Blake's technique makes us reconceptualize the nature of paintings and videos. It also makes us think about the past, especially high Modernism, in a different light.

Who knew that Morris Louis or Kenneth Noland could be so cool?

Alexander Dumbadze

Notes

1. John Baldessari and Jeremy Blake, "In Conversation," *Artforum* 43 (March 2004): 165.
2. Blake calls these architectural spaces "floating interior territories." Quoted in Doris Saatchi, "State of the Art: USA," *Independent on Sunday*, June 3, 2001.
3. Sarah Valdez, "Attack of the Abstract," *Art in America* 90 (March 2002): 104.
4. Reena Jana, "Jeremy Blake: Politics and Fashion in Buccinan," *Flash Art*, no. 34 (May/June 2001): 118.
5. Tim Griffin, "H-h-h-his Generation," *Time Out New York*, October 18–25, 2001, 76.
6. Jana, 118.
7. Baldessari and Blake, 162.
8. Jana, 118.
9. Adrian Dannatt, "Psychedelic audio-visual art at Feigen," *Art Newspaper*, no. 102 (November 2001): 77; David Hunt, "Jeremy Blake," *Tema Celeste*, no. 89 (January/February 2002): 82.
10. Jeremy Blake, artist's statement for an exhibition at Feigen Contemporary, New York, January 2002, Blanton Museum of Art Archives, The University of Texas at Austin. *Winchester* is the first installment in Blake's *Winchester* trilogy (2002–2004). The second is *1906* (2003) and the third is *Century 21* (2004). The entire trilogy was recently exhibited at the San Francisco Museum of Modern Art. See Benjamin Weil, et al., *Jeremy Blake: Winchester* (San Francisco, Calif.: San Francisco Museum of Modern Art, 2005).
11. Blake, artist's statement.
12. Blake said that "sound in my work functions as mood control." See Griffin, 76.
13. Blake, artist's statement.
14. Baldessari and Blake, 162.
15. Jana, 118.
16. See Lane Relyea, "Jeremy Blake Now Playing," in *Jeremy Blake: All Mods Cons* (Houston: Blaffer Gallery, 2001): 4.

Oscar Florianus Bluemner

Prenzlau, Germany (Breslau, Poland), 1867–South Braintree, Massachusetts, 1938

w. Berlin, 1887–1892; Chicago, 1892–1893; New York, 1893–1895, Chicago, 1895–1899; New York, 1900–1916; Europe, 1912; Bloomfield, New Jersey, 1916–1923; Elizabeth, New Jersey, 1924–1926; South Braintree, Massachusetts, 1926–1938

Oscar Bluemner produced a significant body of work comprised of oil paintings and watercolors as well as a corpus of critical writings on modern art in the United States. As a painter-critic working in New York in the early decades of the twentieth century, Bluemner was part of a seminal moment in American modernist painting and an active participant, along with Georgia O'Keeffe, Arthur Dove, and Charles Sheeler, in an avant-garde milieu fostered by the critic and photographer Alfred Stieglitz. In his lifetime, Bluemner received critical notice for painting abstracted views of his everyday surroundings. The modern industrial buildings of New York and northern New Jersey and small-town landscapes of South Braintree, Massachusetts, are the subjects with which he is most often identified.

It was Bluemner's use of highly charged colors that earned him critical note and the nickname "The Vermillionaire." This moniker—a conscious word play on the wealthy American millionaires of the Roaring Twenties and the roaring reds of his paintings—was tartly ironic. Bluemner experienced intermittent financial troubles for much of his adult life; he was rich in his palette, if little else. Later in life, he adopted the middle name Florianus, an abbreviation of which (Florian) he used to sign the Blanton's painting. It is another play on words: in this case, a Latinate derivation of his German surname, meaning "blossom."

Bluemner was born in Preuzlau, Germany (now Breslau, Poland), in 1867 and received formal training in Berlin in the family profession of architecture before immigrating to New York in 1893.[1] He lived in Chicago for a time but returned to the New York area in 1900, where he remained until 1926. Bluemner did not devote himself to painting full time until about 1910, when he gave up his architectural practice and forged a friendship with Stieglitz, who had been exhibiting avant-garde art from Europe and America at his gallery at 291 Fifth Avenue since 1908. Bluemner exhibited work at 291 and also served as a contributor to Stieglitz's noted art journal, *Camera Work*. It was at 291 in 1911 that Bluemner first saw Paul Cézanne's watercolors, which were of great significance to his artistic development. He met with some initial success in 1913 when he exhibited five paintings at the Armory Show. Bluemner published an essay in defense of this controversial exhibition, "*Audiator et Altera Pars*: Some Plain Sense on the Modern Art Movement."[2] In what was effectively a position paper, Bluemner predicated the success of modern art on having a cooperative (informed) viewer who would not be confounded by the radical aesthetics of modern art. During the 1910s and 1920s, Bluemner continued to exhibit work in other New York galleries, though he achieved little commercial success. The financial hardships he had borne throughout his life worsened in the late 1920s and 1930s with the onset of the Great Depression. He found modest relief through the New Deal programs and participated in the Public Works of Art Project (PWAP).

Landscape without Words (1927, plate 23) is a painterly recollection of the town of Bloomfield, New Jersey, where Bluemner had lived earlier with his wife, Lina.[3] (Following her death in 1926, Bluemner moved to South Braintree, Massachusetts.) The painting depicts a modest house, rendered in severe planes of contrasting reds and blue-blacks and framed by organic forms suggestive of trees and foliage. The sky appears as a light blue square in the center of the composition. *Landscape without Words* was one of the last oil paintings Bluemner executed in the 1920s, after which time he preferred working in watercolor. He first exhibited the painting in 1928 at An Intimate Gallery, another establishment founded by Stieglitz.[4] Critics expressed mixed opinions of the show and some observers, including Stieglitz, thought that perhaps Bluemner's colors were too unwieldy and his works, with their lyrical titles (some with musical allusions), too inscrutable. Bluemner, however, was satisfied with the reviews; as he had noted in his 1913 essay, even Cézanne's work had been previously characterized as "rough" or of "unsound technique." Through his work, Bluemner sought to stir in the beholder feelings akin to those aroused while listening to music. Both kinds of sensory experience, seeing and listening, are outside the realm of language—hence Bluemner's paintings without words.

Elsewhere in his writing, Bluemner argued that he sought emotional equivalents *within* his painting—that is, through the forms and colors of the work itself. He embraced the nineteenth-century color theories of Johann Wolfgang von Goethe, the Romantic poet and essayist, and was especially fond of red, the privileged color in Goethe's theory.[5] For Bluemner, red was the "*chief color and maximum of everything artistic; the strongest attraction, signal, warning, symbol of power, vitality, energy, life. Fire, blood, sunball, passion, struggle.*"[6] Seen in this light, *Landscape without Words,* with its preponderance of reds, can be understood as a possible elegy to the artist's late wife and the home where they once lived. While critics found the references to Goethe obscure, Bluemner maintained that the emotive qualities of his colors were uncomplicated. In an essay published posthumously, Bluemner implored his ideal viewer to look at his work as one would "listen to music—look at the space filled with colors and try to feel: do not insist on 'understanding' what seems strange. When you '*FEEL*' colors, you will understand the '*WHY*' of their forms," he argued. "It is," he concluded, "so simple."[7]

Justine Price

Notes

1. For a chronology of Bluemner's life, see Judith K. Zilczer, *Oscar Bluemner: The Hirshhorn Museum and Sculpture Garden Collection* (Washington, D.C.: Smithsonian Institution Press, 1979), 7–17. For more information on Bluemner, see Barbara Haskell, *Oscar Bleumner: A Passion for Color* (New York: Whitney Museum of American Art, 2005). The Blanton's painting was included in this exhibition.

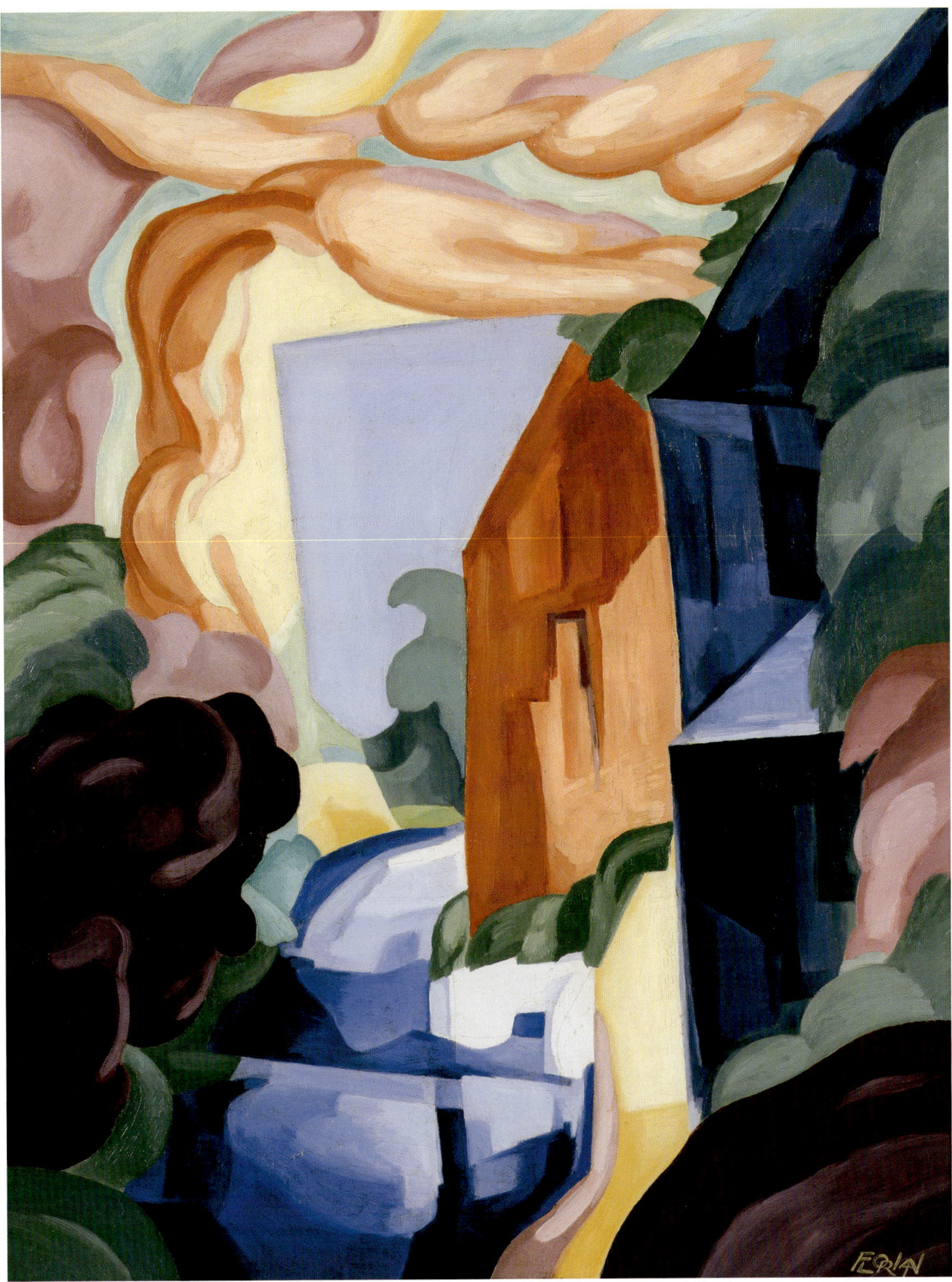

2. Oscar Bluemner, "*Audiator et Altera Pars*: Some Plain Sense on the Modern Art Movement," *Camera Work*, special number (June 1913): 25–38.
3. Jeffrey R. Hayes, *Oscar Bluemner* (Cambridge, Mass.: Cambridge University Press, 1991), 126.
4. The exhibition at An Intimate Gallery was entitled *A Series of "Water Colors" (Synthetic Medium) and 6 Oils of Suns, Moons, Etc.—Facts and Fancy—Strains or Moods.* Bluemner sold four oils from the show and one watercolor. In addition to the provenance assembled by the museum, Jeffrey Hayes argues that *Landscape without Words* was also owned at one point by prominent music critic Paul Rosenfeld. Hayes, *Oscar Bluemner*, 126, 134ff.
5. See Johann Wolfgang von Goethe, *Zur Farbenlehre* (Tübingen, Germany: J. G. Cotta'schen Buchhandlung, 1810).
6. Oscar Florianus Bluemner, introduction to *Oscar Florianus Bluemner* (Minneapolis: University of Minnesota, 1939): n.p. Emphasis in original.
7. Bluemner, introduction to *Oscar Florianus Bluemner.* Emphasis in original.

23.

Landscape without Words, 1927

Oil on board
22 × 16 3/16 in. (55.3 × 41.1 cm)
Gift of Mari and James A. Michener
1991.190

Provenance: An Intimate Gallery, New York; Henry F. Bent, New York; James L. Davis, Hampton Falls, New Hampshire; purchased by James Michener from Parke-Bernet Galleries, New York, 1966; long-term loan to The University of Texas at Austin, 1968–1991
Signed lower right "Florian"
Inscribed verso "'Landscape without Words' Oscar Bluemner 1927"

Derek Boshier

b. Portsmouth, England, 1937

w. Somerset, England, 1953–1957; London (frequent trips overseas), 1959–1979; Houston, 1980–1992; Somerset, England, 1992–1997; Los Angeles, 1997–present

English-born artist Derek Boshier painted *Religious Visitor* (1985, plate 24) during his twelve-year residence in Texas between 1980 and 1992. His work from this period often drew on regional motifs and associations, such as cowboys, the city skyline, oil rigs, and astronauts. For its part, *Religious Visitor* explores religious fanaticism—a subject that Boshier addressed in subsequent works as well—with an eye, in this case, to its specifically American manifestations.

Painted in the thick impasto technique and rough expressionistic style typical of his work from the 1980s, *Religious Visitor* depicts a lone man wearing a black tuxedo, a bishop's hat, and a swastika armband. He holds red poppies and a black cross in the shape of the letters "TV" in his hands. Inspired by a Mexican mask owned by Boshier, the man's broad grin and white face were intended to accentuate his overly zealous personality.[1] In content as well as style, *Religious Visitor* recalls Day of the Dead artifacts characteristic of Mexican American culture in the Southwest, including some areas of Texas. The Gothic-inspired architectural setting further emphasizes the religious tone of the work, while the state of ruin, the black crows (common symbols of bad luck), the swarming green waters, and the deserted church all contribute to its desolate mood. *Religious Visitor* alludes to world wars, religious extremism, and popular culture in general, and to televangelism in particular. In fact, televangelism in the United States advanced into an empire of superstars during the 1970s and 1980s. This phenomenon provided the perfect confluence of power and media spectacle that so often serves as Boshier's subject matter and as the target of his critiques.

Boshier addressed themes of religious and political fanaticism, intolerance, and the abuse of power in other works from the 1980s, such as *False Patriots* (1984) and *KKK* (1982). *False Patriots* depicts a cardinal and a businessman holding a bundle of rods, symbols of fascist authority. Whereas the painting draws parallels between religious and corporate power, *KKK* caustically links the Klan with cowboy culture (the three letters of the title appear in the form of red cowboy boots). Both works are biting commentaries on controversial subjects, although *False Patriots,* like *Religious Visitor,* is more universal in its references.

Boshier's paintings developed a devoted following and appeared in several important exhibitions of local and/or regional artists. In 1983 they were included in *Images of Texas* at the Archer M. Huntington Art Gallery (now the Blanton Museum of Art). *Southern Fictions,* an exhibition held at the Contemporary Arts Museum, Houston, that same year, explored the interest in Gothic narrative among regional artists, including Boshier. Two years later, *Fresh Paint* at the Museum of Fine Arts, Houston, showcased work by Houston-based painters, Boshier among them; even though it did not satisfactorily define a Houston aesthetic, it did fuel a growing self-consciousness in the local art scene.[2] The 1986 exhibition *Texas Time Machine* at the Cullen Center in Houston situated Boshier's ironic cowboy paintings, perhaps at a stretch, within a tradition of Texas-based painting, characterized by mythmaking, narration, vivid color, and references to Hispanic culture.

Boshier's ironic and humorous attitude, his attention to topical social, political, and cultural subjects, as well as his engagement with the negative aspects of advertising have been evident in his work since the 1960s. These qualities are also characteristic of British Pop art, a movement that Boshier became associated with while studying at the Royal College of Art in London, which he attended from 1959 to 1962. Stimulated by the work of Marshall McLuhan and Vance Packard, analysts of media and consumer culture, Boshier and his colleagues David Hockney, R. B. Kitaj, Allen Jones, Peter Phillips, and Patrick Caulfield appropriated and recontextualized sources from the mass media.

As Pop art found acceptance in the mainstream, Boshier changed his approach and adopted a style of hard-edge geometric abstraction. Throughout the 1970s, he experimented with film, photography, drawing, collage, constructions, books, posters, record covers, and installations. After leaving Houston in 1992, Boshier lived in England for four years, and then moved to Los Angeles in 1997, where he taught at the California Institute of the Arts for two years and still resides today. His work from this period incorporates local iconography, such as freeways, architecture, art collectors, and Hollywood figures, into an accessible Pop idiom. Boshier continues to mine everyday life, the social and political environment, and popular culture as source material for his art, which he delivers with wit and irony.[3]

Mariani Lefas-Tetenes

Notes

1. Derek Boshier, correspondence with the author, July 10, 2004.
2. Jamey Gambrell, "Art Capital of the Third Coast," *Art in America* 75 (April 1987): 188.
3. For further information on Boshier, see *Derek Boshier, Texas Works* (London: Institute of Contemporary Arts, 1982), and Lynn Herbert and Marti Mayo, *Derek Boshier: The Texas Years* (Houston: Contemporary Arts Museum, 1995).

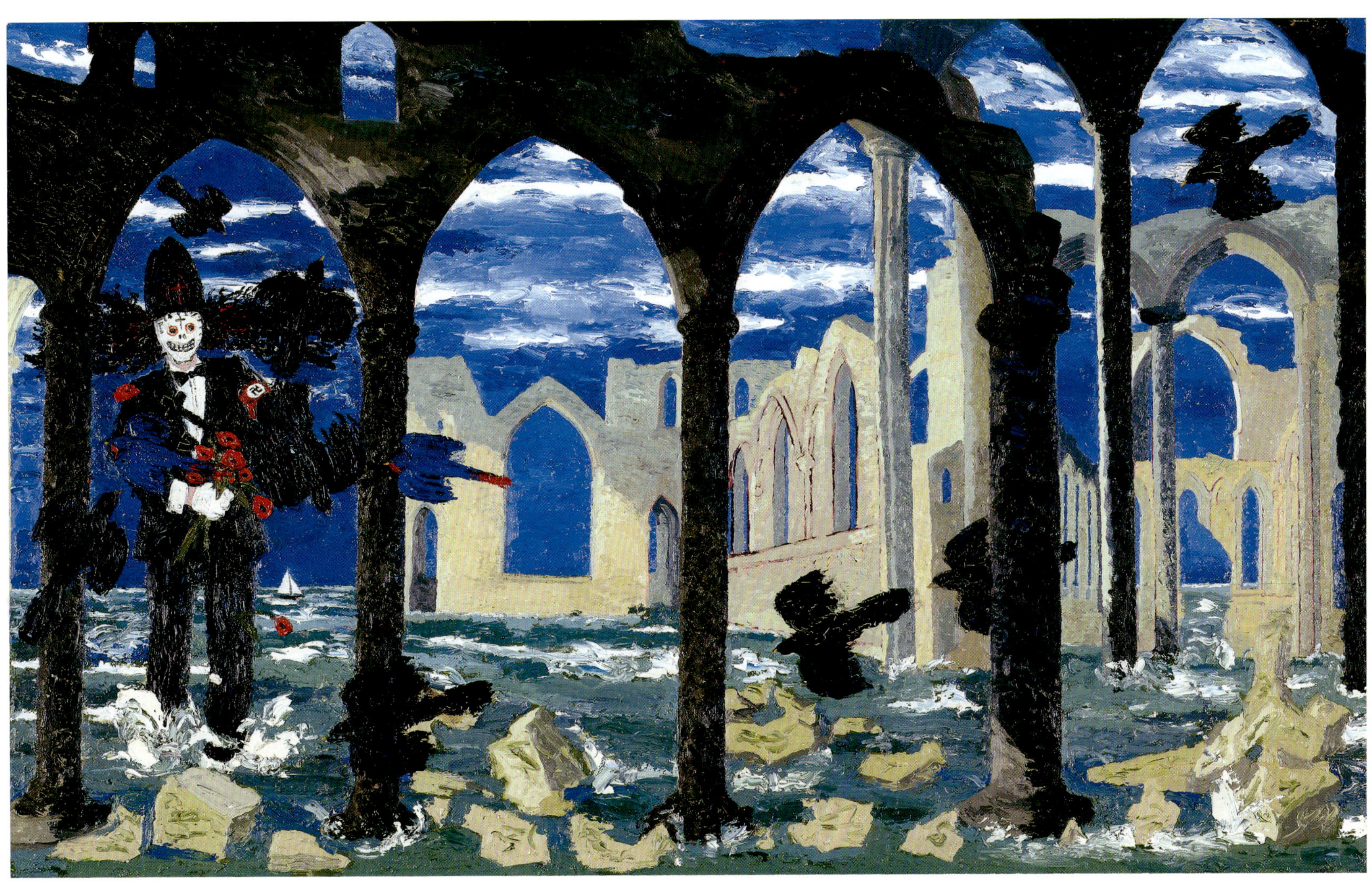

24.

Religious Visitor, 1985

Oil on canvas
88 × 138 in. (223.5 × 350.5 cm)
Gift of the Artist
1993.6
Signed verso "Derek Boshier"
Inscribed verso "'Religious Visitor' / 88 × 138¾ inches / 1985 / oil on canvas"

Charles Burchfield

Ashtabula Harbor, Ohio, 1893–West Seneca, New York, 1967

w. Cleveland, 1912–1916; Salem, Ohio, 1916–1922; Buffalo, 1922–1925; Gardenville, New York, 1925–1967

"Visionary," "romantic realist," twentieth-century "Victorian," "American Scene" painter—these contradictory, yet appropriate, terms have been used to describe the idiosyncratic art and outlook of Charles Burchfield, who lived and worked for most of his life in Gardenville, New York, a suburb of Buffalo.[1] Like Henry David Thoreau, one of the naturalist writers whom he deeply admired, Burchfield traveled extensively in his immediate environment, drawing artistic inspiration from local scenery.[2] Despite his considerable powers of visual observation and description, Burchfield often subordinated these to expressive concerns by infusing his paintings (predominantly watercolors) with romantic spirituality, subjective mood, and personal memory. "It is the romantic side of the real world that I try to portray," Burchfield wrote in 1940.[3]

Such concerns first emerged in Burchfield's many visions of Salem, Ohio, the small town of his youth, where he moved at the age of five with his mother and siblings after the death of his father. That early loss and displacement help explain the artist's enduring preoccupation with old houses and a childlike sense of wonder at the spiritual mystery of nature—themes evoked in *Old House and Spruce Trees* (1951–1960, plate 25). Burchfield's frequent return to such themes suggests that his work was, in some respects, a lifelong pursuit of reenchantment with the world after his family's early personal tragedy. At the same time, his paintings also responded to the broader dislocations of modernity.[4]

Burchfield's artistic career roughly divides into three phases. The first—marked by his development of a unique brand of fantastic naturalism—began when he enrolled at the Cleveland School of Art in 1912. While studying in Cleveland, Burchfield immersed himself in Asian art and philosophy, nature writings by Thoreau and John Burroughs, and the ideas of Friedrich Nietzsche, among others. In 1916 Burchfield spent six weeks in Manhattan, where he met several artists, critics, and dealers. After returning to Salem, he began to paint small, imaginative watercolors of local houses and scenery, often using agitated or repeated forms, arbitrary hues, and other visual metaphors for sounds in nature. In addition to reflecting Burchfield's lifelong love of music (especially that of Jan Sibelius), these works bring to mind modernist abstractions by Arthur Dove as well as illustrations by Aubrey Beardsley, John Tenniel, and Daniel Carter Beard. Yet they also embody Burchfield's own distinctive vision, which he codified in a manuscript entitled "Conventions for Abstract Thoughts" and illustrated with sketches symbolizing ominous mental concepts and psychological states such as "Fear," "Dangerous Brooding," "Melancholy," "Morbidness," and "Fascination of Evil."[5]

The second phase of Burchfield's career—characterized by greater realism and a growing reputation—began in 1922, when he moved to Buffalo. Despite the new responsibilities of work, marriage, and parenthood, Burchfield remained very active artistically. Regular exhibitions and sales in New York culminated in a solo show at The Museum of Modern Art (1930) and the purchase of several of his works by Abby Aldrich Rockefeller beginning in 1935. Adopting a more straightforward realism, Burchfield also painted on a grander scale, using a muted palette suited to the grim urban, industrial, and suburban scenery of Buffalo that now provided his subject matter. These works invite comparison with Regionalist painting and the work of Edward Hopper, whom he befriended in 1928. Burchfield never embraced the strident xenophobia sometimes associated with the American Scene movement, but he did admire the Nordic "nationalist spirit" of Sibelius's *Finlandia*. In 1935 nativist art critic Thomas Craven praised Burchfield in a *Harper's Magazine* article entitled "Our Art Becomes American."[6]

The third and final phase of Burchfield's career began in 1943, when he abruptly abandoned realism and revived his youthful romanticism, perhaps partly in response to the horrors of World War II. Works from this period imbued his early visionary style with a new monumentality that also obliquely addressed evolving avant-garde concerns, specifically the apocalyptic, psychological, mythical, and spiritual dimensions of New York School abstraction.[7]

Old House and Spruce Trees belongs to this last phase of Burchfield's career. The work reinvigorates Burchfield's visionary romanticism by returning to early themes and techniques: the old house, trees, flowers, the star, and bird (here an owl), all depicted with a combination of vibrant animism and moody expressionism. Unlike his interwar realist paintings, *Old House and Spruce Trees* exhibits looser, less precise brushwork. Yet the palette remains subdued, except for the vivid pink and yellow flowers in the foreground. While reminiscent of Burchfield's first Salem pictures, the setting is undetermined, giving the work universal significance. The house looks less anthropomorphic than others executed in this vein, but it does retain a metaphysical aura thanks to the mysterious owl perched on the chimney, the vines hanging heavily over one window, and the peculiar highlighting along its left edge and roofline. Indeed, the house aptly, if unintentionally, illustrates Sigmund Freud's psychological theory of the uncanny or *unheimlich* (literally "unhomely"), referring to repressed emotions and images that return to conscious memory in altered (and often unsettling) form.

A similar uncanny glow encircles the trees in the neighboring forest, infusing them with spiritual energy. This effect is accentuated by the upward "Gothic" reach of the V-shaped branches and the twinkling star at the top center—symbols of Nordic Christianity familiar to Burchfield.[8] The hopeful, uplifting quality intimated in these elements is counteracted, however, by the menacing darkness of the silhouetted trees, which outline sinister eye shapes that recall the abstract symbols of "Insanity" and "Morbidness" in Burchfield's "Conventions." Moreover, given Burchfield's penchant for arboreal identification, the tree in the left foreground, looking old and haggard with its gray trunk and

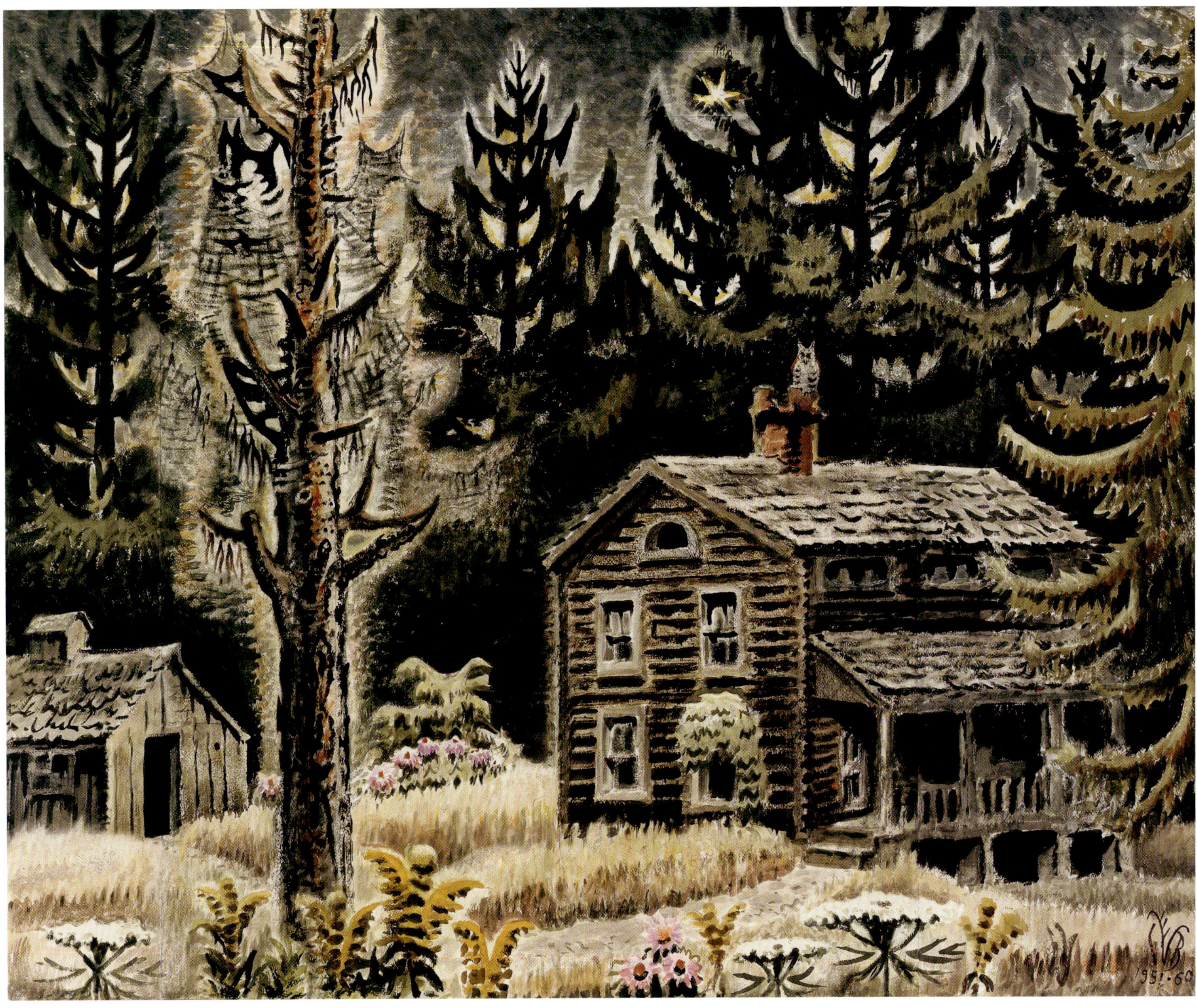

broken limbs, may stand metaphorically for the aging artist himself.[9] Completed in 1960, when the painter was nearly seventy, *Old House and Spruce Trees* arguably constitutes one of Burchfield's more autobiographical works, powerfully summarizing personal themes that were central to his identity and art.

Alan C. Braddock

Notes

1. On Burchfield, including instances of these terms, see John I. H. Baur, *Charles Burchfield* (New York: Whitney Museum of American Art and Macmillan, 1956); Nannette V. Maciejunes and Michael D. Hall, *The Paintings of Charles Burchfield: North by Midwest* (New York: Harry N. Abrams, in association with the Columbus Museum of Art, 1997).
2. On Burchfield and Thoreau, see Maciejunes and Hall, 44.
3. Burchfield to Frank K. M. Rehn, October 2, 1940, quoted in *Charles Burchfield's Journals: The Poetry of Place*, ed. J. Benjamin Townsend (Albany: State University of New York Press, 1993), 452.
4. Nannette V. Maciejunes and Norine S. Hendricks, "Charles Burchfield's Painted Memories," *Magazine Antiques* 151 (March 1997): 458–69.
5. Baur, 27–31.
6. Maciejunes and Hall, 24–37, 269.
7. Maciejunes and Hall, 120, 129.
8. Maciejunes and Hall, 114.
9. Maciejunes and Hall, 121–23.

25.

Old House and Spruce Trees, 1951–1960

Watercolor on paper
44⅝ × 53¾ in. (113.4 × 136.6 cm)
Gift of Mari and James A. Michener
1991.199

Provenance: Purchased by James Michener from Frank Rehn Gallery, New York, 1962; long-term loan to The University of Texas at Austin, 1968–1991
Signed lower right "CB 1951–60"

Jerry Bywaters

Paris, Texas, 1906–Dallas, 1989
w. Dallas, 1922–1927; France–Spain, 1927; Mexico City–New York, 1928; Dallas, 1929–1989

An irrepressible force in his native state of Texas, Jerry Bywaters enjoyed a long, multifaceted career as an artist, writer, critic, teacher, arts administrator, and museum director.[1] Bywaters is best remembered for his participation in the Dallas Nine, an enterprising group of young painters who were active during the 1930s and who helped establish a regional identity for Texas art.[2] At a time when scenes of the state's treasured bluebonnets, painted in the pastel colors and broken brushwork of Impressionism, still dominated Texas painting, the Dallas Nine defined a regional aesthetic within the larger context of American Scene painting.

In 1936 Bywaters asserted that "each art era of the past could contribute its part to the formation of an initial technical vocabulary, but this vocabulary must be modified under the impact of new experiences in the particular environment of Texas and the Southwest."[3] *Oil Field Girls* (1940, plate 26), painted just four years later, epitomizes this credo. It also became Bywaters's most popular work, the one painting so closely identified with the artist that the *Dallas Morning News* reproduced it in his obituary in 1989.[4]

Born in 1906 in Paris, Texas, Bywaters displayed an early interest in art. At Southern Methodist University he studied art and literature, graduating in 1926 with a degree in comparative literature. In June 1927 he embarked on a painting trip to Europe, returning to Dallas that fall to study briefly at the newly founded Dallas Art Institute. A seminal event in Bywaters's early development was his encounter with Diego Rivera in March 1928 in Mexico City, where Rivera was executing murals for the government education building. Rivera's ideology transformed Bywaters's thinking about the role of art in society, as evidenced by his declaration that "Diego Rivera has taught me a lesson I had not learned elsewhere in Europe or America. I know now that art, to be significant, must be a reflection of life; that it must be understandable to the layman; and that it must be part of a people's thought."[5] In 1928 Bywaters enrolled in classes at the Art Students League of New York, where one of his instructors, John Sloan, encouraged him to paint his native region, and after only three months at the League, Bywaters returned to Dallas to commence his career as a professional artist.

By the late 1930s Bywaters had become widely known throughout the Southwest and was highly regarded within Dallas art circles. It was around this time that he conceived *Oil Field Girls,* which belongs to a group of canvases that portray distinct human types posed against the vast Texas landscape, such as *Sharecropper* (1937).

In *Oil Field Girls* Bywaters presents two women standing by the side of the road with suitcases in hand. Behind them is a landscape cluttered with ramshackle buildings, abandoned tires, hand-lettered road signs, and dozens of oil derricks, one of which produces a greasy plume of smoke that zigzags across the sky. Bywaters used a somber palette to describe the bleakness of the hardscrabble terrain, enlivening it with vivid contrasts, such as the touches of bright red paint on the road signs and the women's clothing. The strong Texas light endows the scene with a vibrant clarity. The result is a powerful evocation of the physical life force of two women set against the squalid disorder and desolation of the booming Texas oil industry.

The women, both heavily made-up and overdressed in tight, form-fitting outfits that accentuate their figures, are most likely prostitutes. The slightly younger of the two sports a pair of stylish cowboy boots, while the older woman displays more overt signs of her profession with an ankle bracelet and high heels. Bywaters told his biographer, Francine Carraro, that the idea for the composition sprang from a Neiman-Marcus fashion advertisement and that his wife's friends served as models.[6] Though he endowed these sturdy, over-life-sized women with stature, he made them appear as comic figures, as Amazons towering above their pitiful surroundings. The women's eccentric forms owe something to Bywaters's knowledge of El Greco's expressive distortion of the human figure. Writing about another work from the same year as *Oil Field Girls,* Bywaters commented, "It seems to me that an element of caricature (or exaggeration) is necessary in securing a perceptive portrait, and certainly El Greco demonstrated the point."[7] His portrayal of these two women is a wry commentary on their position in society. Standing in the middle of nowhere, determined to go somewhere, these dolled-up Amazons are out-of-place. They may be looking for adventure or they may have been forced to leave town.

The painting's narrative implies that they are ready to hitch a ride to a more glamorous spot far away from the heat, dust, and grime of an oil field.[8] In this respect, Bywaters's "girls" have much in common with the distinctive American types portrayed in Hollywood films of the 1930s: brash, ambitious characters like those played by Barbara Stanwyck in *Baby Face* (1933) and *Gambling Lady* (1934). As Carraro pointed out, in *Oil Field Girls* Bywaters was "equat[ing] the profit and pollution of the oil business with prostitution. With this combination of raw realism and gentle humor, Bywaters was able to embrace simultaneously both the myth of the Texas independent spirit and the reality of everyday life."[9]

Though part satire, *Oil Field Girls* reflects Bywaters's sensitivity to the plight of these women. While they appear to have no assets other than their looks and no future but life on the road, they may also envision a better existence for themselves and possess the gumption to go after it. Like Honoré Daumier, an artist he greatly admired, Bywaters offers a penetrating social commentary beneath a comic veneer.

Rebecca E. Lawton

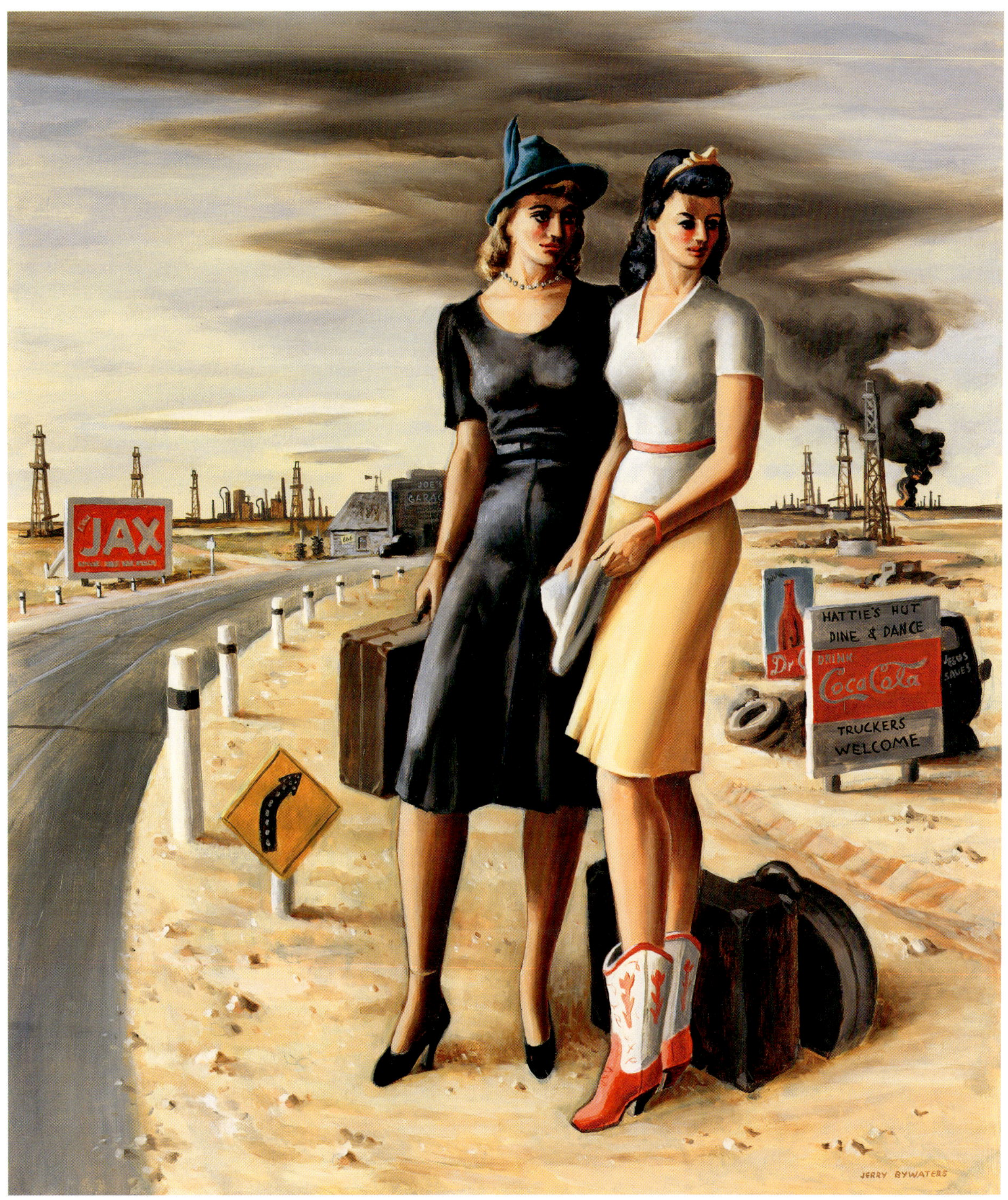

Notes

1. Francine Carraro, quoted in "1930s-era Texas artist Jerry Bywaters dead at 82," *Austin American-Statesman*, March 8, 1989. Bywaters Bio File, Amon Carter Museum Library, Fort Worth, Texas.
2. For a history of the Dallas Nine, see Rick Stewart, *Lone Star Regionalism: The Dallas Nine and Their Circle* (Austin: Texas Monthly Press, 1985).
3. Jerry Bywaters, "The New Texas Painters," *Southwest Review* 21 (spring 1936): 336.
4. Janet Kutner, "Dallas Arts Figure Jerry Bywaters Dies," *Dallas Morning News*, March 8, 1989: 12A.
5. Gerald [Jerry] Bywaters, "Diego Rivera and Mexican Popular Art," *Southwest Review* 8 (July 1928): 480.
6. Francine Carraro, *A Regionalist Rediscovered: A Biography of Jerry Bywaters* (Ph.D diss., University of Texas at Austin, 1989), 357, n. 58.
7. Jerry Bywaters, "Notes," in *A Retrospective Exhibition: Jerry Bywaters* (Dallas: Owen Arts Center, Southern Methodist University, 1976), 20.
8. Francine Carraro, *Oil Patch Dreams: Images of the Petroleum Industry in American Art* (Beaumont, Tex.: The Art Museum of Southeast Texas, 1998), 23.
9. Carraro, *A Regionalist Rediscovered*, 189.

26.

Oil Field Girls, 1940

Oil on board
30 x 25 in. (75.3 x 62.2 cm)
Michener Acquisitions Fund
1984.1

Provenance: Purchased from the artist, 1984
Signed lower right "Jerry Bywaters"

William Merritt Chase

Williamsburg, Indiana, 1849–New York, 1916

w. New York, 1869–1871; Munich, 1871–1877; New York (summers in Long Island, New York, 1891–1902), 1878–1902; Philadelphia, 1896–1903; Philadelphia–New York–Europe, 1903–1909; New York–Europe, 1909–1916

William Merritt Chase was born in Williamsburg, Indiana, in 1849 and traveled to New York when he was twenty to study at the National Academy of Design.[1] In 1871, following the advice of fellow artist John Mulvaney, Chase left for Munich, where he remained for six years, studying at the Royal Academy. After his return to the United States in 1878, he rapidly gained recognition, soon becoming known as one of the most important and prolific painters of the day. Chase was a dynamic advocate of American art, an important art instructor, and an active participant in many artist organizations, including the Society of American Artists, the American Society of Painters in Pastel, and The Ten, a group of American Impressionists who exhibited together.

Over the course of his thirty-eight-year career as an instructor, Chase trained many artists at a number of institutions, including the Art Students League, New York, and the Pennsylvania Academy of the Fine Arts, Philadelphia. Chase also taught private lessons at the Tenth Street Studio Building, New York, the Shinnecock Summer School of Art on Long Island, and the Chase School of Art, New York (also known as the New York School of Art). His students included such noted artists as Charles Demuth, Georgia O'Keeffe, Charles Sheeler, and Joseph Stella.

Chase's early work centered primarily on the still-life, but following his studies in Germany, he also pursued subjects such as genre, landscape, and portraiture. Chase eventually became one of the leading American portraitists of his day, rivaled only by John Singer Sargent. Up through the mid-1910s, Chase painted portraits of a significant number of academics, commissioned from a wide range of institutions. In 1912 he won the Proctor Portrait Prize of the National Academy of Design, which may have been an important factor in Chase gaining these academic commissions. The Blanton's portrait of Thomas Ulvan Taylor, who was a founder and the first dean of The University of Texas College of Engineering, was commissioned in 1913 by the College of Engineering and a group of alumni to celebrate the twenty-fifth anniversary of the dean's appointment (plate 27). The portrait was unveiled and presented to the university at a ceremony in 1914.

Chase's portrait style, as seen in *Portrait of Dean Thomas U. Taylor,* is indebted to the Munich School's use of expressive brushwork, its preference for a darkened, somber palette, and its respect for the Old Master tradition, particularly as exemplified by Spanish painter Diego Velázquez and Dutch painter Frans Hals. The painting also recalls the portrait tradition of American painters Thomas Eakins and Robert Henri, who themselves looked to Velázquez and Hals for inspiration. While critical assessment of Chase's paintings has frequently centered on his European influences, his contemporaries often lauded what they saw as its thoroughly American spirit. Chase's peers praised his successful blending of bravura brushwork and his forthright depiction of his sitters.[2]

In the portrait of Dean Taylor, rich earth tones dominate the canvas, enhancing the stately portrayal of the sitter. The gleam of Dean Taylor's watch chain echoes the rims of his glasses, which offers relief from the otherwise sober palette. Flourishes of the brush are signature elements in Chase's paintings. The artist frequently painted without the aid of a preliminary sketch and was known to work rapidly, sometimes completing a painting in as little as an hour. Chase's technique demonstrates at once his virtuoso skill and his philosophy that quick execution was necessary to capture a vital and spontaneous likeness. Dean Taylor's cursorily sketched hands illustrate the artist's enduring commitment to the primacy of technique as an expressive element in a composition.

Chase portrayed his subject as a dignified and learned man, as signified by the inclusion of a book. Dean Taylor appears distant, even timeless, a formality typical of the artist's commissioned portraits of men from the 1910s. (In his images of women, on the other hand, Chase often presented his sitters in more relaxed poses and with a greater sense of spontaneity and personality.) At the same time, however, Chase infused this portrait with a touch of casualness, as seen in the way Dean Taylor holds his book open with his finger and slightly turns his body in the chair.

Although Chase continued to receive recognition and accolades late in his career, by the time this portrait was painted he no longer represented the progressive strain in American art. Indeed, his work was deemed conservative and even old-fashioned. Following the Armory Show of 1913, America's first major introduction to American and European modernism, Chase's painting style began to appear outdated.

At the time of his death in 1916, critics recognized Chase's cosmopolitan style, his enduring promotion of American art, and his impressive teaching career as noteworthy achievements, yet his importance has been widely acknowledged only in recent decades. Today he is regarded as a major figure in the canon of nineteenth- and early twentieth-century art, and his *Portrait of Dean Thomas U. Taylor* is a noteworthy example of his portrait style.

Kathleen V. Jameson

Notes

1. For additional information on Chase, see Katharine Metcalf Roof, *The Life and Art of William Merritt Chase* (New York: Scribner's Sons, 1917); Ronald G. Pisano, *William Merritt Chase* (New York: Watson-Guptill Publications, 1979); *A Leading Spirit in American Art: William Merritt Chase, 1849–1916* (Seattle: Henry Art Gallery, University of Washington, 1983); and Keith L. Bryant, Jr., *William Merritt Chase: A Genteel Bohemian* (Columbia and London: University of Missouri Press, 1991).
2. See Mariana Griswold Van Rensselaer, "William Merritt Chase: First Article," *American Art Review* (January 1881): 95.

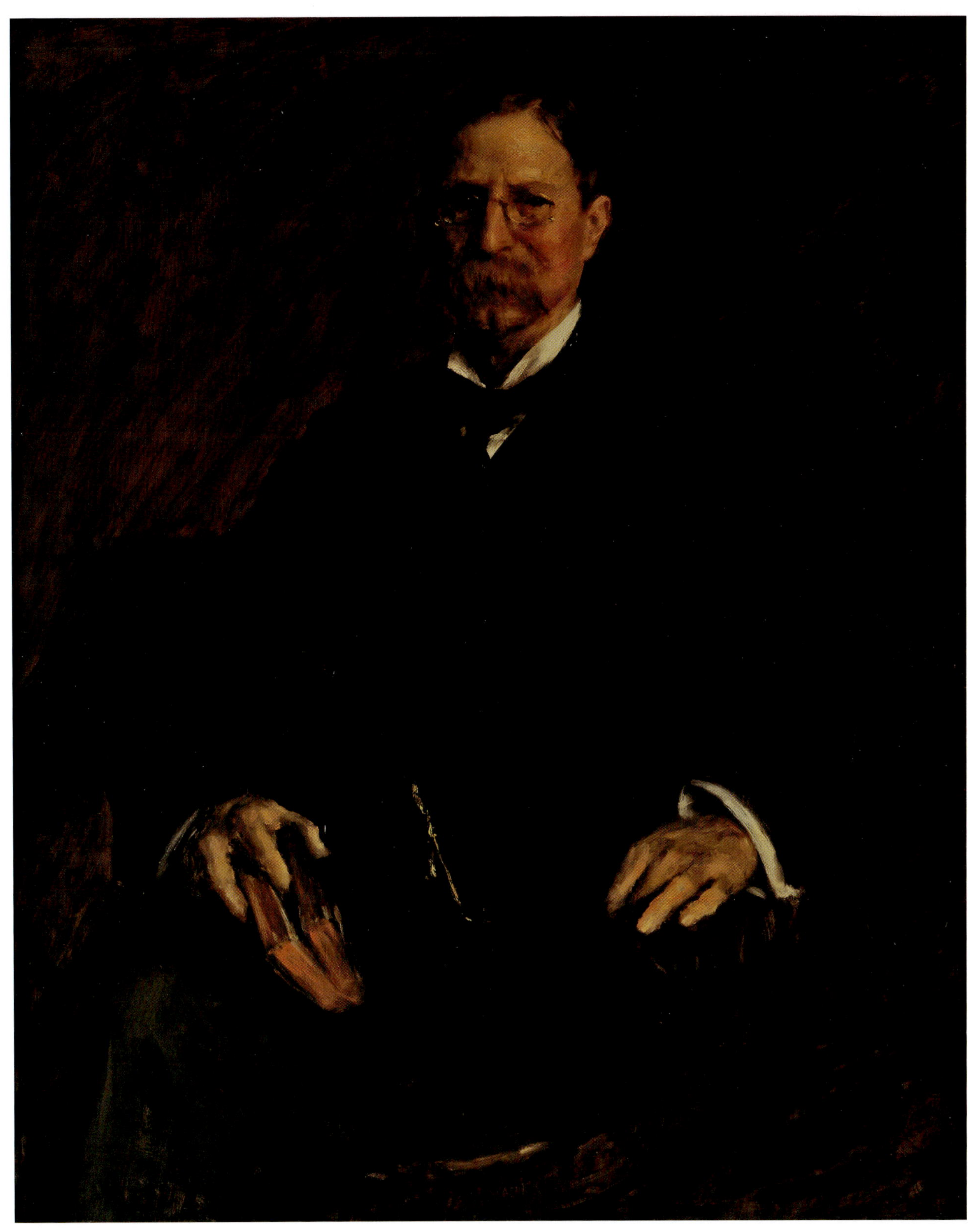

27.

Portrait of Dean Thomas U. Taylor, 1914

Oil on canvas
45 3/16 × 35 5/8 in. (114.8 × 90.5 cm)
Gift of Alumni, College of Engineering, The University of Texas at Austin, 1914
1987.34

Provenance: Commissioned by the College of Engineering and its alumni, The University of Texas at Austin, 1913; transferred from the College of Engineering, 1987
Inscribed verso "Prof T. U. Taylor, Painted by Wm M Chase, New York, 1914"

Anne Chu

b. New York, 1959
w. Philadelphia, 1982–1985; New York, 1985–present

Anne Chu's subversive engagement with art history extends from Chinese funerary statues to the paintings of Diego Velázquez and modern sculpture. Chu taps into a multitude of artistic traditions, often combining them in a single work, but she veers away from a unified distillation of her sources, interpreting freely instead. Born in New York in 1959, Chu received a BFA from the Philadelphia College of Art in 1982 and her MFA from Columbia University in 1985. She lives and works in New York and has shown widely in the United States and Europe.

Castle Number One (2001, plate 28) exemplifies the artist's interest in a diverse array of artistic conventions. The work consists of a wooden castlelike structure with a parapet set somewhat precariously on a hillside. This reference to medieval culture is complicated by the concomitant reference to Chinese landscape painting, signaled by the work's miniature stature and its evocation of an alternate reality. Chu further upsets the timeline by placing the structure on a thoroughly modern-looking base that alludes to the austere, geometric forms of Minimalist sculpture. As *Castle Number One* suggests, Chu actively and creatively mines art history, but in a way that is idiosyncratic, even irreverent, and executed with an eye for rupture rather than historical accuracy. Her series of anthropomorphic bears from the mid-1990s, for instance, draws loosely on the life-size terra-cotta soldiers found in a third century BC tomb near Xi'an, China, while her subsequent works depicting court ladies, goddesses, and warriors reinterpret ceramic funerary sculptures from the Tang Dynasty. Much like *Castle Number One,* these works tend to juxtapose rather than harmonize disparate historical styles, periods, and motifs.

The appropriation of medieval culture and Chinese art in *Castle Number One* is typical of Chu's sculpture, as is its intentionally provisional appearance. Here the artist exposes the sculpture's seams at a material level. The screws that hold the work together are visible to the viewer; so too is the interior of the plinth, thanks to its three translucent sides and one open side. While the facade view of the castle's parapet is carved in detail, the side and back views are less finished, the lower wall of the castle retaining the grain of the wood. The work's only color occurs in a resin-coated area of pale blue and white paint that roughly coats the contoured terrain of a section of the mountainside and castle. Together these details establish a tension between material surface and content, painting and sculpture.

Castle Number One also displays a tension between abstraction and representation, a relationship Chu first explored in 1999 in a series of low-lying wooden landscapes placed directly on the ground. There she turned landscapes into objects by detaching them from each other and from any larger context and by disassociating color from realistic description. Although *Castle Number One* might seem more representational than these earlier landscapes, Chu allows its manifestly abstract qualities, from the Minimalist base to the unfinished sections to the seemingly arbitrary application of paint, to eclipse, at times, its recognizable subject matter.

Chu's fascination with confusing the boundaries between abstraction and representation is accompanied by an equally pervasive interest in merging sculpture and painting. She thinks of sculpture as a painted form and is interested in "the fusion of painting and sculpture so that the painting in the sculpture is intrinsic to the form . . . not decorating it."[1] Chu has also shown sculptures and paintings that relate thematically, often to explore representational shifts across media, as in a 2000 exhibition where she raised the semiabstract landscape forms from 1999 onto workbench-style platforms and displayed them alongside watercolor landscapes. These particular sculptural works reinterpreted the tradition of Chinese scholar's rocks (small rocks seen to possess intrinsic aesthetic value and collected for the purposes of meditation and contemplation) as well as Chinese jade or bamboo mountain sculptures, which were originally conceived as microcosms of the universe or as subjective evocations of the spirit of the landscape.[2]

Chu continues to explore the expressive potential inherent in reinterpreting traditional idioms in her more recent life-sized wood, yarn, and cloth marionettes that are simultaneously frightening and comic. Her large hanging landscapes signal a new direction in her efforts to investigate that genre's boundaries. As these works suggest, Chu embraces hybridity as it relates to every aspect of her work—from media, materials, scale, and sources to subject matter and meaning. At once playful, evocative, and mysterious, Chu's work exploits the disjunctive relationships between medium and image to reveal both how the artistic past informs the artistic present and how the present can inform the past.[3]

Mariani Lefas-Tetenes

Notes

1. Anne Chu, artist's statement, from a press release for an exhibition at Victoria Miro Gallery, London, May 2001, Blanton Museum of Art Archives, The University of Texas at Austin.
2. Holland Cotter, "Anne Chu," *New York Times*, January 7, 2000, sec. E, p. 43.
3. For further information on Chu, see Bonnie Clearwater, *Anne Chu* (North Miami, Fla.: Museum of Contemporary Art, 2005).

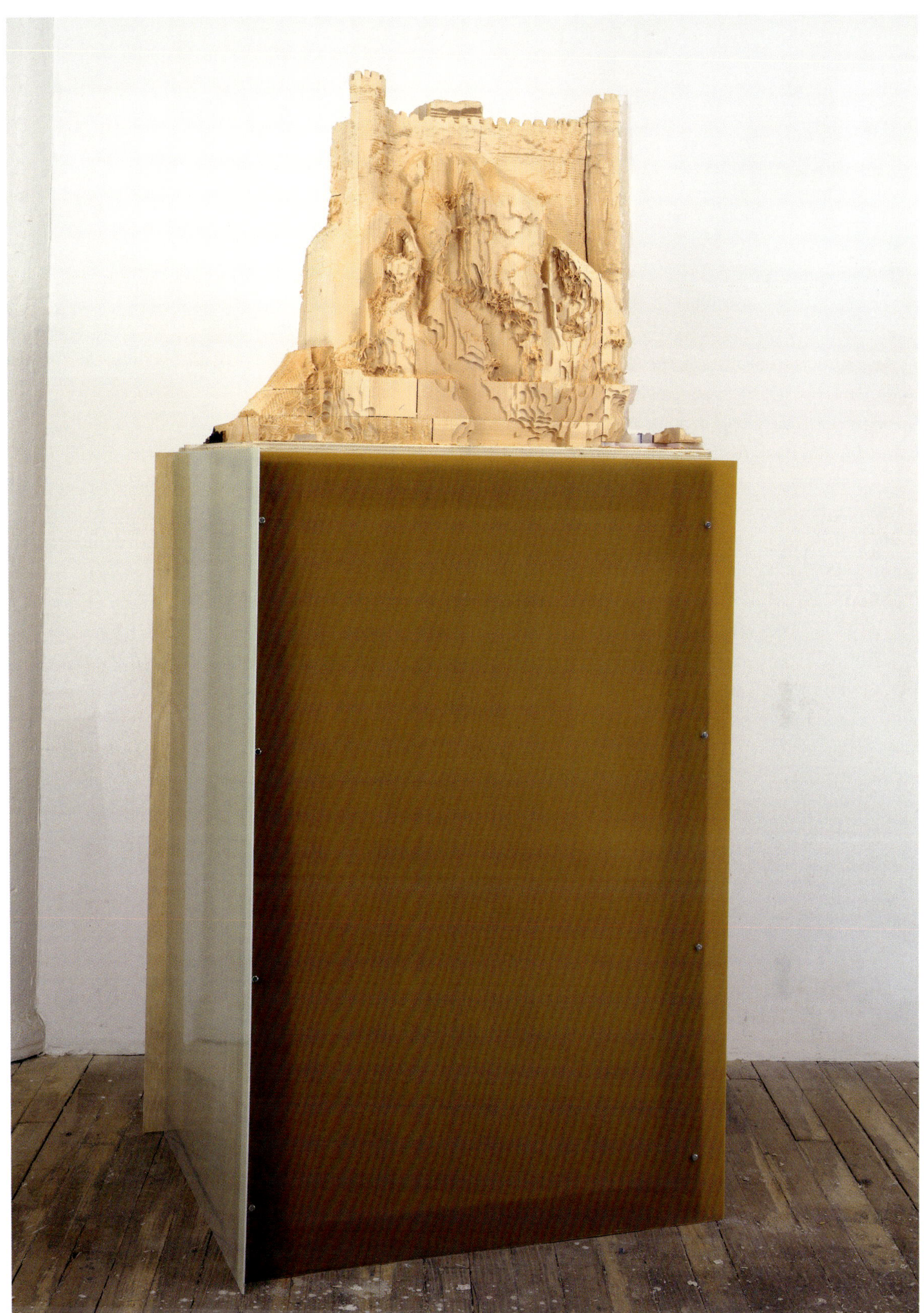

28.

Castle Number One, 2001

Painted wood and resin with fiberglass and wood base
98 × 69 × 63 in. (248.9 × 175.3 × 160 cm)
Partial and pledged gift of Jeanne and Michael Klein
T2001.2

Provenance: Purchased at the request of the museum by Jeanne and Michael Klein from Victoria Miro Gallery, London, 2001

Mary Corse

b. Berkeley, California, 1945

w. Santa Barbara, California, 1963; Los Angeles, 1964–late 1960s; New York, late 1960s; Los Angeles, 1970–present

The work of Mary Corse, who has lived and worked in southern California almost her entire career, is distinguished by its sensitivity to the visual effects of light. Corse received an undergraduate degree in fine art from the University of California, Santa Barbara, and then pursued graduate studies at the Chouinard Art Institute (now California Institute of the Arts) in Los Angeles. By 1964, while studying in Los Angeles, Corse had become preoccupied with light, an interest that manifested itself in her white paintings on shaped canvases as well as her eight-foot-high white columns. Soon thereafter, she began experimenting with light boxes suspended or placed on pedestals, eventually using hollow shells that, with wiring and interior lamps, resembled luminous slabs. Her broad creative inspirations included Tibetan Buddhism, the work of Barnett Newman, the dot paintings of Larry Poons, and Robert Irwin's disc paintings.

Untitled (1969, plate 29) is an early example of the signature White Light paintings that Corse initially undertook in 1968 and continued to produce throughout much of her career. Irregular brushstrokes in varying directions animate the static format of this square canvas, which is divided into twenty-five different sections, as do the tiny reflecting glass microspheres (materials used on highway signs) that Corse incorporated into the pigment.[1] Equally essential to the perceptual experience are the three 300-watt reflector floodlights that the artist stipulated be set at specific angles, distances, and heights from the canvas during its installation.[2] The floodlights tilt toward the center of the painting, producing a brightly lit surface with ephemeral rainbows, ambient space, and other varied visual effects.

Untitled exemplifies the artist's ongoing investigation of the visual properties of light in largely monochromatic paintings, an approach that links Corse to Southern California artists Irwin and James Turrell, who pioneered the use of light and space as media and evinced a more general interest in the "perfection of surface, reflection, refraction, transparency, dematerialization, [and] de-objectification."[3] Indeed, by 1971 critics had placed Corse's work within the broader context of the Light and Space Movement, which formed one strand of West Coast Minimalism. Corse was also favorably contextualized with an emerging generation of Southern California artists who were exploring a range of approaches to art making. This relationship was formalized in two exhibitions in the early 1970s, one at the Los Angeles County Museum of Art in 1971, the other at the Pasadena Museum of Art in 1972.[4] The critical reception of Corse's work was mixed. Some described it as jazzy and cerebral,[5] while others characterized it as "sugar-coated, fairy-sprinkled Robert Rymans."[6] Like this latter critic, authors sometimes took note of Corse's tendency toward seductive prettiness, a viewpoint that may have partially derived from a traditionally masculine reading of Minimalism, whose canon has only recently been expanded to include artists such as Agnes Martin, Jo Baer, and Corse, among others.

In the early 1970s Corse introduced a new element into her White Light paintings—deep beveled stretcher bars that had the appearance of floating planes. She also began painting small squares in the corners, reasserting the shaped canvas and uniting painting with the three-dimensional object. Corse turned to new materials in the 1970s, cutting and coating metal as another means to reflect and dissolve the form of the object. She also experimented with thin squares of black or colored acrylic or metal and worked with glazed ceramic tile, which entailed constructing a kiln to fabricate unusually large square tiles to fit her grid format. Following her use of metallic glazes, she created earthen tiles with uneven surfaces cast from impressions of rocks and fired with black glaze.

Corse made her first Black Light paintings, which date to 1983, with the same microspheres as the White Light paintings of the early 1970s, but she employed black canvases to generate a glittery look, which inspired critics to refer to them as glamorized Ad Reinhardt paintings.[7] In 1987 Corse produced her first Grey Light painting, and, just a short time later, she created a small series of gray paintings that introduced red paint on the borders as well as square shapes on the edges. Using a range of approaches and canvases of varying shapes and sizes, Corse continued to create ambitious, experimental art throughout the late 1980s and 1990s.

Having reinvigorated the monochromatic tradition as practiced by artists like Ryman and Reinhardt, Corse exemplifies the contributions of women artists to postwar art in general and to Light and Space Art of the 1960s. Pioneering and experimental, her work investigates ways of harnessing the intangible sensations of light and space.

Mariani Lefas-Tetenes

Notes

1. Leah Ollman, "'Selections I' Prods the Mind, Not the Spirit" *Los Angeles Times*, February 11, 1988, 1.
2. Mary Corse to Richard Hirsch, August 29, 1970, Blanton Museum of Art Archives, The University of Texas at Austin.
3. Elizabeth C. Baker, "Los Angeles, 1971," *Artnews* 70 (September 1971): 30.
4. These exhibitions were the Los Angeles County Museum of Art's 1971 *24 Los Angeles Artists* and the Pasadena Art Museum's 1972 *15 Los Angeles Artists*.
5. Peter Plagens, "The Decline and Rise of Younger Los Angeles Art," *Artforum* 10 (May 1972): 81.
6. Joseph Masheck, exhibition review, *Artforum* 10 (June 1972): 82.
7. Lilly Wei, "Mary Corse at ACE," *Art in America* 84 (June 1996): 100.

29.

Untitled, 1969

Acrylic with reflecting crystals on canvas
108⅝ x 108⅝ in. (275 x 276 cm)
Gift of Mari and James A. Michener
1979.25

Provenance: Purchased by James Michener from Goldowsky Gallery, New York, 1970; loan to The University of Texas at Austin, 1970–1979

Alan Cote

b. Windham Center, Connecticut, 1937

w. Boston, 1955–1960; Europe, 1961–1964; New York, 1965–late 1990s; Port Ewen, New York, late 1990s–present day

In the late 1960s and early 1970s, after many years of training in the visual arts, Alan Cote achieved recognition for his series of abstract paintings featuring scattered bars of intense color distributed across the surface of large-scale, shaped canvases.[1] While several artists, ranging from Frank Stella to Larry Zox, experimented with the shaped canvas in the 1960s, Cote's bar paintings are distinctive for their combination of size and declarative color, for their systematic approach to composition, and for their sense of movement and activity.

Tocqueville (1969, plate 30) exemplifies Cote's effort to create associations within the composition and to activate space beyond the confines of the canvas edge. The painting is comprised of long, thin bars in a multitude of colors on an asymmetrical, trapezoidal support. The ends of the bars are either beveled or straight. (Cote began to bevel the edges of his multicolored bars in the late 1960s, giving them the appearance of pieces of paper chopped off with scissors, which in turn suggested the "disintegration of pre-existing configurations."[2]) While these bars generally flow from top to bottom, right to left, the artist introduced tension by varying their colors, lengths, edges, and orientation. Some bars descend at an angle; others are placed almost vertically. The edges of the canvas abruptly cut off several bars, allowing the viewer to infer a space beyond the painting.

Despite its energetic, slightly chaotic impression, *Tocqueville* was planned systematically in several stages, as were all of Cote's bar paintings from this period. After building the stretcher, the artist painted a dark ground. He then made small-scale drawings using modular units to represent the bars, adjusting them until he was satisfied with their arrangement. He followed these with further studies to determine color combinations. Finally, Cote marked the positions of the bars on the canvas using tape and applied the preselected colors.[3]

The work's title refers to Alexis de Tocqueville, the nineteenth-century French political thinker and historian who examined the social habits and means of association in the early American republic in such texts as *Democracy in America* (1835–1840). Cote read de Tocqueville's writings in the late 1960s at the height of the Vietnam War. He titled the Blanton's painting after the author in an effort to counter the characterizations of lightweight decorativeness sometimes directed against abstract painting. Cote's use of a black background and his programmatic approach to painting underscore this desire to create a work that expressed the 'weightiness' and seriousness of de Tocqueville's ideas.[4] On a structural level, moreover, the interaction of the bars suggests the author's notion of the networks of association that form civil society.

Cote's first successful solo exhibition—held in late 1970 at Reese Palley Gallery, one of the first galleries to open in the emerging Soho area—featured his bar paintings.[5] In his exhibition review, Robert Pincus-Witten situated Cote, along with Stella, Larry Poons, and Edward Avedisian, within a group of artists linked by their explorations into the expressive possibilities of color, form, and composition. (Cote, in fact, had attended the School of the Museum of Fine Arts, Boston, with both Poons and Avedisian.) Pincus-Witten also connected Cote's works to early twentieth-century painting, describing them as "a chromatic restatement, on a monumental scale, of the maze-like functioning of the edge in the Hermetic Cubist paintings of Picasso and Braque in the period of 1910–12, an idiom transferred into the 'plus and minus' compositions of Mondrian of 1913."[6]

By 1973 Cote had stopped making his commercially successful bar paintings. He moved away from the hard-edged clarity, brilliant colors, and irregularly shaped canvases that had been such constant features in his early work, instead using rectangular canvases and creating textured surfaces with paint applied in thick globs. His approach to painting became less systematic, more organic and intuitive.[7] These works from the mid-1970s, vaguely reminiscent of Clyfford Still's paintings, contain forms that the viewer can perceive alternatively as irregular shapes or spatial voids.[8] Cote changed his style again in the late 1980s, embracing nature-inspired imagery and monumental scale.

More recently, Cote has been drawn to the possibilities of conjoining two separate panels so that they converse with one another, simultaneously encouraging the viewer's active participation.[9] This work continues Cote's earlier efforts, evident in *Tocqueville,* to energize the composition and to establish some continuity between the painting and the space around it. Despite this similarity, however, such paintings are not only more serene than *Tocqueville,* their surfaces reveal traces of the artist's increasingly intuitive decision-making process as well.[10] Cote still paints actively today, just as he continues to investigate the dynamic interactions of forms, colors, and formats.

Mariani Lefas-Tetenes

Notes

1. Cote attended the School of the Museum of Fine Arts, Boston, from 1955 to 1960 and later studied in Europe from 1961 to 1964 on a scholarship, visiting Berlin, Paris, Italy, and Greece.
2. J.G., exhibition review, *Artnews* 69 (December 1970): 14.
3. Alan Cote, conversation with the author, June 2, 2005.
4. Cote, conversation with the author.
5. The artist's work from this exhibition also appeared on the cover of *Arts Magazine* 45 (December 1970/January 1971).
6. Robert Pincus-Witten, exhibition review, *Artforum* 9 (March 1971): 62.
7. Cote, conversation with the author.
8. Exhibition review, *Arts Magazine* 48 (December 1973): 60.
9. Cote, conversation with the author.
10. Lydia Davis, *Alan Cote, Recent Paintings* (Poughkeepsie, N.Y.: Marist College Art Gallery, 2002), n.p.

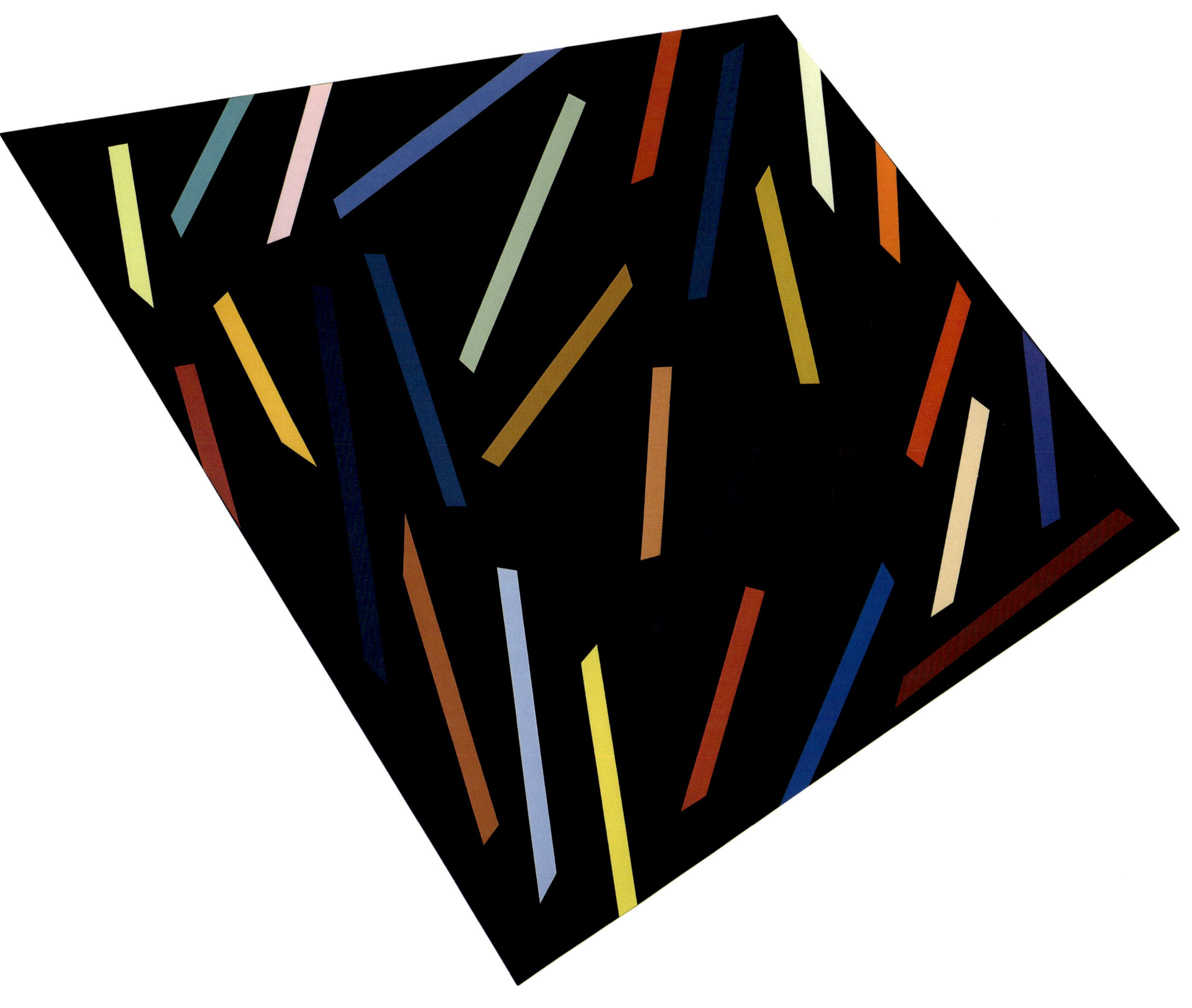

30.

Tocqueville, 1969

Acrylic on canvas
100 × 120 in. (254 × 304.8 cm)
Gift of Mari and James A. Michener
1979.26

Provenance: Purchased by James Michener from the artist, 1969
Inscribed verso, lower left "Alan Cote 1-69"

Konrad Cramer

Würtzburg, Germany, 1888–Woodstock, New York, 1963
w. Munich–Karlsruhe, Germany, 1906–1911; New York–Rock City, New York, 1911–1963

Improvisation Number 2 (1913, plate 31) belongs to an early and important series of pure abstractions that Konrad Cramer executed soon after he immigrated to the United States from his native Germany in late 1911. In part an homage to Wassily Kandinsky, the series represents Cramer's investigation into the possibilities of nonrepresentational art. As he later recalled, "In the beginning, I consciously broke away from painting 'reality' in order to explore the extent to which communication between painter and beholder could be maintained when painting became more and more abstract."[1] Recognized as one of the first artists to create abstract paintings in the United States, Cramer also played a role in disseminating knowledge of European avant-garde art to a wide circle of American modernists before the Armory Show of 1913.

Born in Würtzburg, Germany, in 1888 to an artistic family, Cramer studied at the conservative Karlsruhe Academy of Fine Arts from 1906 to 1909. He established a studio in Karlsruhe in 1910 but spent considerable time in Munich, a more stimulating environment for exploring new techniques and styles. In Munich Cramer became familiar with the work of vanguard artists such as Kandinsky and Franz Marc, who exhibited with the *Neue Künstlervereinigung München* (the New Artists' Association).[2] At the time, Kandinsky had nearly completed his treatise on non-objective painting, *Concerning the Spiritual in Art* (published in January 1912), and although the paintings he exhibited remained based in representation, they reflected a transition toward abstraction. There is no evidence to confirm that Cramer actually met Kandinsky, but he visited Marc's studio in March 1911, just as Marc and Kandinsky were planning the almanac *Der Blaue Reiter (The Blue Rider)*. This almanac promoted their radical ideas about the "inner sound" of colors and the correspondence between form and the "principle of internal necessity, which springs from the soul."[3] Cramer left Germany before the almanac appeared in print, two months prior to the opening of the first *Der Blaue Reiter* show in December 1911, which included Kandinsky's early non-objective paintings. Nonetheless, Cramer knew enough about their new aesthetic ideas to transmit his enthusiasm for them to artists in the United States.

Cramer and his American wife, the artist Florence Ballin, whom he had met in Munich, arrived in the United States in the fall of 1911 and settled in Rock City, an area just north of Woodstock, New York, where the Art Students League held its summer classes. The paintings Cramer executed soon after his arrival demonstrate how thoroughly he had absorbed the tenets of German Expressionism. The broad, simplified forms, vivid colors, and heavy outlines of the small gouache *Boat in River* (c. 1911), for example, mirror paintings by Kandinsky's close colleague Gabriele Münter. Cramer's rejection of naturalism also reveals an affinity for the paintings of Marc, who similarly used color as an expressive vehicle.

Cramer's initial foray into pure abstraction was guided primarily by Kandinsky's theoretical writing on art and aesthetics. The evolution of his Improvisation series of 1912–1913 owes much to Kandinsky's essay "Über die Formfrage" ("On the Problem of Form"), which appeared in *Der Blaue Reiter*. Rejecting natural forms, Kandinsky instead advocated using lines, shapes, colors, and planes. By extending the vocabulary employed in painting to forms that were divorced from objective reality, Kandinsky believed that artists could more easily attain the spiritual properties that lay at the heart of modern painting. While some of Cramer's Improvisations retain references to the landscape, others, such as the Blanton's *Improvisation Number 2*, are completely nonrepresentational and therefore remarkably progressive for their early date. Cramer's choice of palette for *Improvisation Number 2*—consisting of tans and light yellows, light and dark blues, reds, and lavenders—suggests a close adherence to Kandinsky's ideas about the symbolic importance of colors and their ability to evoke sounds. "Color itself offers contrapuntal possibilities and, when combined with design, may lead to the great pictorial counterpoint, where also painting achieves composition, and where pure art is in the service of the divine," Kandinsky once wrote.[4]

The Improvisation paintings also reflect Cramer's interest in the principles of Cubism. As one art historian commented of *Improvisation Number 2*, for instance, it "contains heavy diagonal lines, striated shading and a substructure derived from Cubism."[5] Cramer likely read an excerpt about Cubism from *Concerning the Spiritual in Art* in the July 1912 issue of the American publication, *Camera Work*. Here Kandinsky describes Picasso's Cubism "as a logical road to an annihilation of the material, not by analysis, but by a kind of taking to pieces of each single part and a constructive laying out of them as a picture."[6] This passage is particularly illuminating in light of Cramer's spatial arrangement of elements in *Improvisation Number 2*. Using fragmented, overlapping planes, Cramer seems to have structured the painting according to Kandinsky's color theories as well as his characterization of Cubism as a "laying out" of parts. Without one dominant plane to create a sense of perspective, the elements collide with one another, imparting a sense of formal turmoil and struggle.

Cramer exhibited six of the Improvisations, including *Improvisation Number 2*, at the MacDowell Club in New York in November 1913 alongside abstractions by Cramer's Woodstock colleague, Andrew Dasburg. The *New York Times* art critic was unimpressed with both artists' work, summarily dismissing Cramer's paintings as "exercises skillfully practiced" and labeling Dasburg's "quite meaningless as art."[7] Such criticism did not deter Cramer from continuing his experiments with abstraction, yet his struggle to come to grips with nonrepresentational art did not sustain his interest after the late 1910s. He later explained, "When the point of contact with the beholder is lost entirely, the painting itself seemed to become sterile."[8]

Rebecca E. Lawton

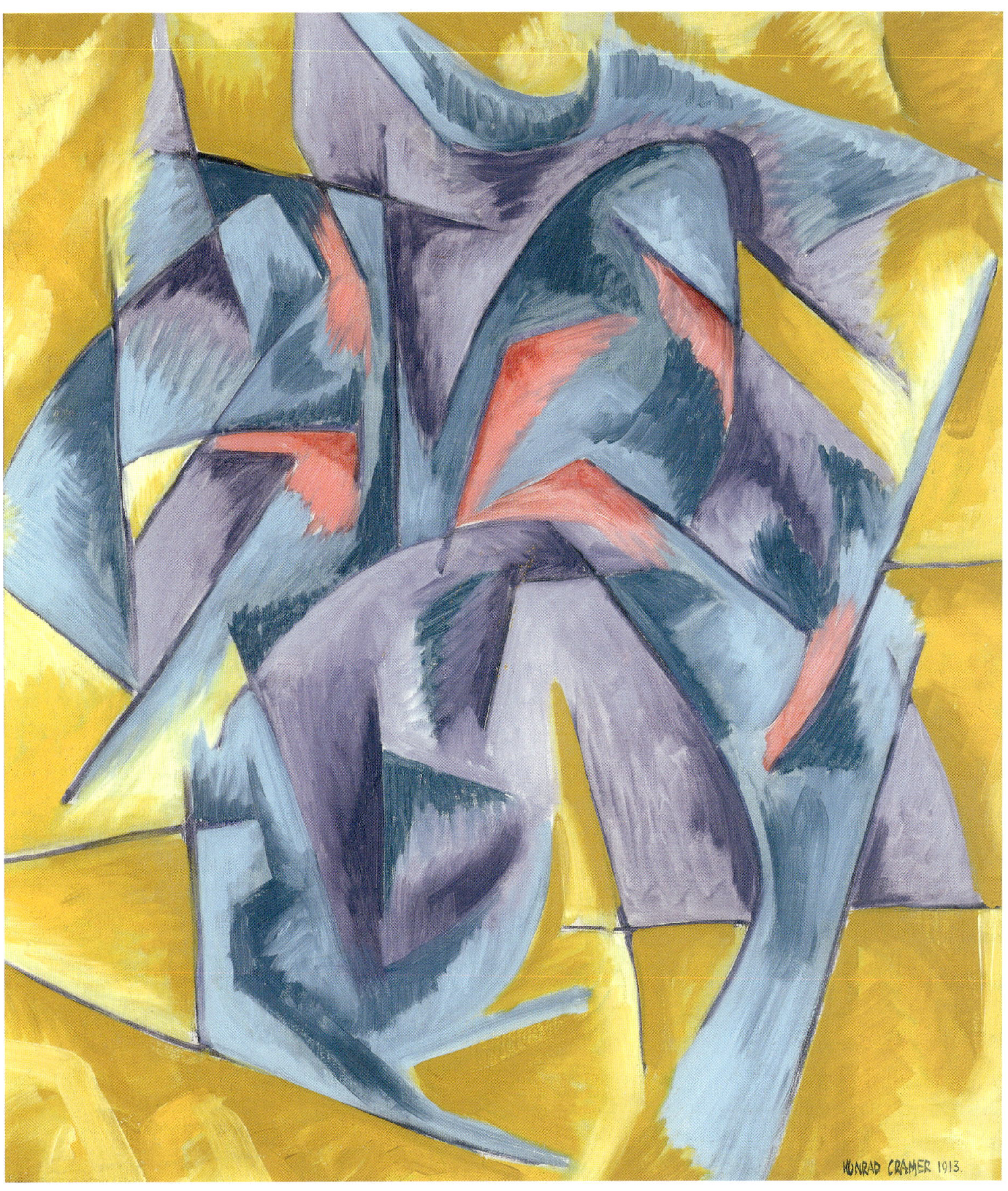

Notes

1. See Gail Levin, "Konrad Cramer: Link from the German to the American Avant-Garde," in Tom Wolf and Franklin Riehlman, *Konrad Cramer, A Retrospective* (Annandale-on-Hudson, N.Y.: Edith C. Blum Institute, Bard College, 1981), 9.
2. Levin believes that Cramer would have seen the group's highly important second exhibition held in September 1910, which included not only examples of advanced German painting but Cubist works by Pablo Picasso and Georges Braque as well (Levin, 6).
3. Wassily Kandinsky, *Concerning the Spiritual in Art* (New York, 1947), 75, as quoted in Peter Selz, *German Expressionist Painting* (Berkeley, Los Angeles, London: University of California Press, 1974), 204.
4. Kandinsky, 51–52, as quoted in Selz, 230.
5. Levin, 8.
6. Cramer met the photographer Alfred Stieglitz, who edited and published *Camera Work*, in 1911, shortly after he arrived in the United States. Cramer's wife's diary records that they read Gertrude Stein's article on Matisse and Picasso published in the August 1912 issue (Levin, 7). It is likely that they read *Camera Work* regularly and would have seen the excerpt from *Concerning the Spiritual in Art*. [Wassily] Kandinsky, "Extracts from *The Spiritual in Art*," *Camera Work*, no. 39 (July 1912): 34.
7. "Art Notes," *New York Times*, November 19, 1913, 8.
8. As quoted in Levin, 9.

31.

Improvisation Number 2, 1913

Oil on canvas
27 9/16 × 23 5/8 in. (70 × 60 cm)
Michener Acquisitions Fund
P1969.11.1

Provenance: Purchased from Zabriskie Gallery, New York, 1969
Signed lower right "Konrad Cramer 1913"

Stuart Davis

Philadelphia, 1892–New York, 1964

w. New York, 1909–1923; New Mexico, 1923; New York (trip to Paris, 1928 and summers in Gloucester, Massachusetts, 1915–1934), 1923–1964

Born in Philadelphia in 1892 and raised in New Jersey, Stuart Davis began his formal art training in 1909 when he left high school and entered Robert Henri's progressive art school in New York. From Henri's "Ashcan" sensibilities, Davis learned the importance of reacting to visual sensations in his surroundings. Although Davis valued such an approach to art making, he found Henri's tendency to emphasize subject matter over formal issues confining. The 1913 Armory Show solidified this viewpoint for the young artist. In response to the works he saw there, Davis transformed his artistic production from one based on illustration to one grounded in concepts.

The time Davis spent working in the coastal town of Gloucester, Massachusetts, was also critical to his artistic development. Initially encouraged by his close friend, John Sloan, Davis visited Gloucester annually from 1915 to 1934, and he continued to incorporate his impressions of this locale into his art throughout the remainder of his career.[1] Davis learned from the Armory Show and from his time in Gloucester that his art, rather than illustrating a single encounter with his surroundings, should represent his accumulated mental and perceptual experiences of them. This understanding was important because it encouraged Davis to think about the implications of perception in his art making. By considering his artistic production to be more than a reflection of what he saw, Davis realized that his experience of the world around him in the present was relative to his experience of that world in the past and future. The artist later explained: "We do not simply reflect the things we see, like a mirror, but we compare them, in our ideas and emotions, with things we have seen before and with things we hope to see."[2]

A trip Davis made to New Mexico in the summer and fall of 1923, accompanied by his brother, Wyatt, and John and Dolly Sloan, solidified these ideas. Davis greatly anticipated seeing the New Mexican landscape firsthand; like Gloucester, it had come highly recommended by Sloan. Unlike many of his colleagues, however, and contrary to his experience in Gloucester, Davis ultimately decided that the desert setting of New Mexico held more ethnographic than artistic interest for him: "I don't think you could do much work there except in a literal way, because the place is always there in such a dominating way. You always have to look at it."[3] Despite these frustrations, Davis painted a number of works during his stay in New Mexico, including the Blanton's *Landscape* (1923, plate 32). The majority of these works reflect a "literal" or illustrative approach to art making rather than a conceptual one. *Landscape,* for instance, is very much about "place," with its emphasis on the land and the objects it contains.

Davis's Egg Beater series of 1927 and 1928 represents a profound shift in his artistic production. In these paintings, instead of finding his subject matter in the world around him, the artist invented his own geometric forms inspired by the shapes and colors of still-life arrangements. Davis felt that by abstracting the objects in these compositions he was better able to create visual equivalents for sensations and experiences common in the modern world. But despite the success of his Egg Beater paintings, Davis was not entirely satisfied. He found that the works did not adequately convey the "immediate" or "accidental" associations that accompany everyday perceptions. He determined, therefore, that his art making process as a whole needed to be rethought in reference to his personal interactions with his surroundings.

Lawn and Sky (1931, plate 33) responds to Davis's desire to incorporate his perceptions of his surroundings into his art. Davis most likely based *Lawn and Sky* on an actual view of Gloucester, since he spent most of his time painting both there and in New York during the 1930s.[4] In general, scholars overlook this work in favor of the artist's later, more vibrantly colored abstract paintings. John Lane, for example, deemed the visual contrasts in *Lawn and Sky* to be lacking "a consistent sense of direction [that] was accompanied by an absence of substantial

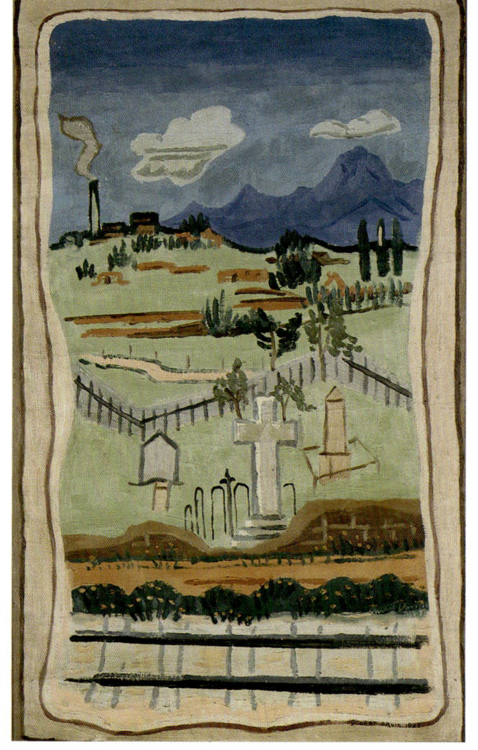

32.
Landscape, 1923
Oil on canvas
35 11/16 × 21 5/8 in. (91 × 55 cm)
Gift of Mari and James A. Michener
G1968.42P

Provenance: Purchased by James Michener from Parke-Bernet Galleries, 1965
Signed lower right "Stuart Davis 1923"

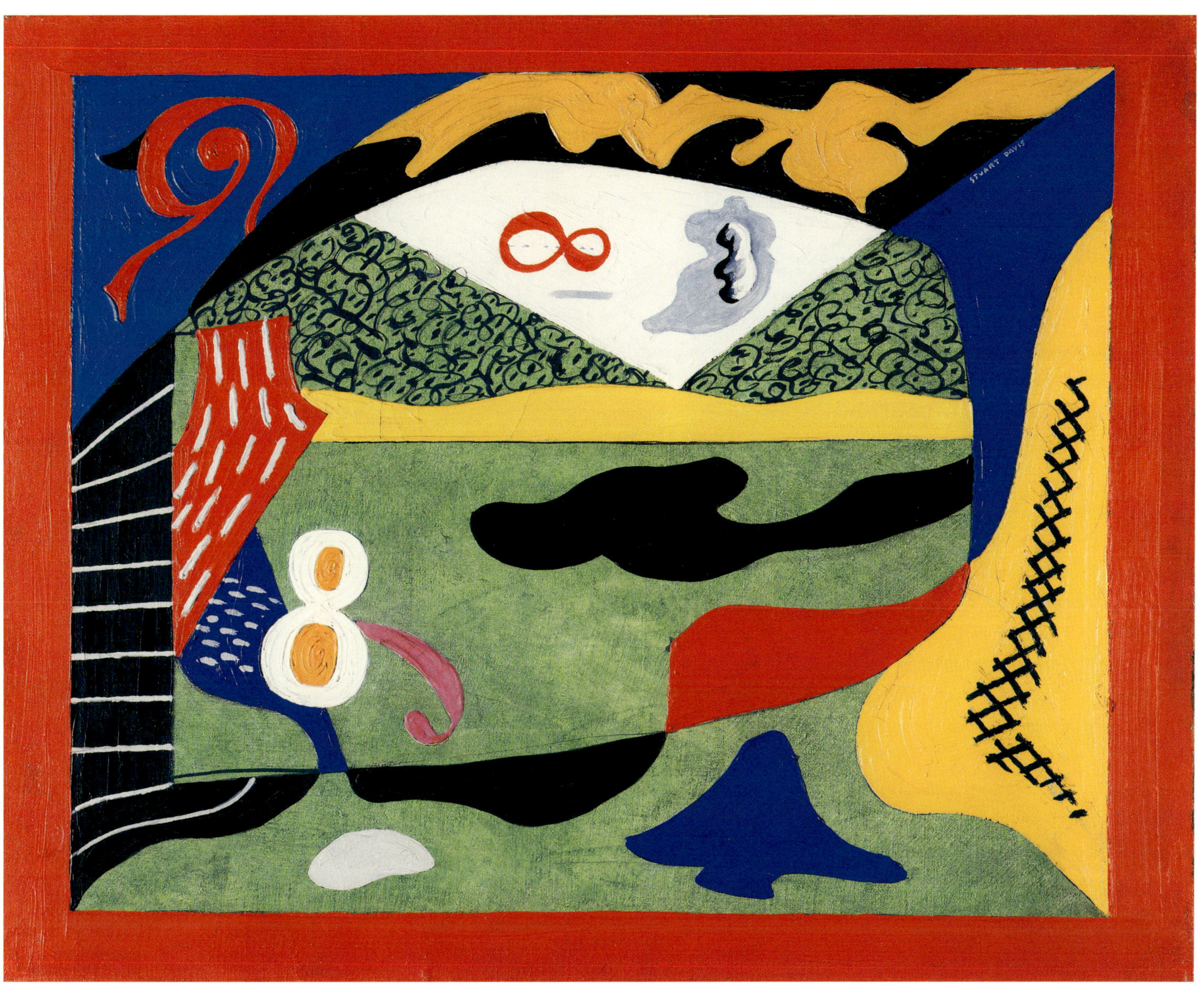

theoretical counterpoint in the years just following [Davis's] return from France."[5] While Lane correctly described *Lawn and Sky* as bereft of visual unity, one can also argue that the painting's discord was deliberate. It is through juxtaposition that Davis organized the space of his picture and came to terms with the problem of translating the instantaneous act of seeing into paint.

Davis had in common with the Cubists and other modernists his approach to art as a means of exploring perception. What makes *Lawn and Sky* different from the work of his contemporaries, however, was his use of superposition to simultaneously depict two views of the same landscape. By placing one view on top of the other, Davis created an ambiguity that forces his viewers to make sense of the represented scenes. He also used the disjunction produced by layered views to demonstrate that seeing is not a passive activity but rather one that requires effort to keep the multiple scenes in focus. In other words, by superimposing concurrent views in *Lawn and Sky,* Davis revealed to viewers the visual inconsistencies, reactions, and adjustments that constantly accompany their perceptions of the world, reawakening in them a sensitivity to how seeing works and, in particular, how seeing functions moment to moment.

Erina Duganne

33.

Lawn and Sky, 1931

Oil on canvas
18⅝ × 22⅝ in. (47.3 × 57.5 cm)
Gift of Mari and James A. Michener
1991.205

Provenance: Purchased by James Michener from Downtown Gallery, New York, 1962; long-term loan to The University of Texas at Austin, 1968–1991
Signed upper right "Stuart Davis"

Notes

1. Davis speaks about the importance of Gloucester to his art making in "Autobiography," reprinted in Diane Kelder, ed., *Stuart Davis,* Documentary Monographs in Modern Art (New York, Washington, D.C., and London: Praeger Publishers, 1971), 25.
2. Stuart Davis, "Mural for Studio B, WNYC (working notes)," 1939, reprinted in Kelder, 92.
3. James Johnson Sweeney, *Stuart Davis* (New York: The Museum of Modern Art, 1945), 15.
4. William Agee believes that Davis derived *Lawn and Sky* from his 1916 *Gloucester Landscape (Backyard View),* which depicts a view of the lawn as seen from the back of the house that Davis lived in during his stay in Gloucester (William Agee, telephone interview with the author, April 2, 1997).
5. John R. Lane, *Stuart Davis: Art and Art Theory* (New York: The Brooklyn Museum, 1978), 21. Lane maintains that Davis's paintings *Egg Beater No. 5, Mandolin and Saw,* and *New York–Paris No. 3* all illustrate the same lack of visual consistency as *Lawn and Sky.*

Manierre Dawson

Chicago, 1887–Ludington, Michigan, 1969

w. Chicago, 1909–1910; Europe, 1910; Chicago (frequent trips to New York) 1910–1914; Ludington, 1914–1969

An early American modernist, Manierre Dawson is best known for his experiments with abstract painting, in particular for a series he began in 1910 of Cubist interpretations of Old Master and contemporary avant-garde works. Dawson's *Woman in Brown* (1912, plate 34) is one such Cubist "transliteration," and it demonstrates his keen understanding of formal structure.[1] It also points to broader issues, like the influence of European modernism on early twentieth-century American painting.

Dawson was born in Chicago in 1887 to a middle-class family. Although he began to draw and paint at a young age, his father encouraged him to pursue engineering instead of art, so he enrolled at the Armour Institute of Technology. After graduating in 1909, he joined the Chicago architectural firm of Holabird and Roche. Dawson continued to paint in his spare time, often small, abstract landscapes on cardboard or canvas. The majority of his paintings reveal a fascination with the underlying structure of objects, the result of his training as a draftsman and his careful study of the work of Paul Cézanne.

In the summer of 1910 Holabird and Roche granted Dawson an extended leave of absence to travel to Europe and study architecture. While in Europe, he also studied painting, especially that of the Old Masters and contemporary avant-garde. The three weeks Dawson spent in Paris made the greatest impact on his work. He visited Ambrose Vollard's gallery on rue Laffitte, where he likely viewed some of Cézanne's paintings, and met Gertrude Stein at one of her salons at 27 rue de Fleurus.[2] Dawson was elated when Stein bought one of his paintings for 200 francs (his first sale), and he recorded the meeting in his journal. Although he does not mention Stein's important collection of modern art, it no doubt made a lasting impression on the artist. Indeed, scholars have identified Pablo Picasso's 1906 portrait of Stein, a work that was hanging in her apartment at the time of Dawson's visit, as the main source of inspiration for *Woman in Brown*.[3]

The similarities between the Dawson and Picasso paintings are striking. Dawson, for instance, retained the basic composition of the Picasso, in which the female figure leans forward in a stuffed, high-backed chair, her hands and arms resting on her thighs. Dawson also reproduced Picasso's neutral, earthy palette, a hallmark of Analytical Cubism. Unlike Picasso's more realistic portrait, however, *Woman in Brown* is reduced to geometric forms. Curvilinear and elliptical shapes are flattened and multiplied to create a barely identifiable head, torso, and lap. To make matters even more confusing, the eyes and nose have been extracted from the face and set floating in the air to the left of the figure. Dawson likely painted *Woman in Brown* as a tribute both to Stein and Picasso. The series of Cubist transliterations to which it belongs, painted after his return to Chicago in late 1910, includes reinterpretations of paintings by Titian and Jan Vermeer among others.[4]

Upon his return from Europe in late 1910, Dawson visited New York with a letter of introduction to Arthur Davies. Davies was impressed with Dawson's paintings and invited him to submit work to the Armory Show of 1913. Dawson was the only Chicago-based artist to participate in the exhibition; his painting *Wharf Under Mountain* hung in the Cubist Room.[5] The Armory Show made quite an impact on Dawson, who expressed admiration for the artists and works in the exhibition. As he wrote in his journal, "The whole show is producing in me a great excitement. It is an eye opener because I had begun to think of my own works as an exception. But there I am, knowing now that many are thinking and expressing the same ideas that I am growing into."[6] Dawson even bought two works from the Armory Show: one of Marcel Duchamp's studies for *Nude Descending a Staircase* (1912) and a painting by Amadeo de Souza-Cardoso, further evidence of his attraction to art concerned primarily with form and structure. In the winter of 1913 Davies again invited Dawson to participate in an exhibition he was planning titled *The Fourteen,* which was to feature work by American avant-garde artists.

Between the Armory Show and *The Fourteen,* Dawson gave up his career as an architectural draftsman to pursue painting. Perhaps in an effort to distance himself from the negative reviews of modern art by Chicago art critics, he decided to spend most of 1914 at his family's summer home in Ludington, Michigan, where he planned to work in the fruit orchards and focus on painting in the off-season. Dawson soon met a local woman, whom he married the following year. Because of these new responsibilities and the increasing difficulty of ordering painting supplies from Chicago, Dawson essentially gave up painting by 1920. Although he worked briefly with sculpture in the 1950s, he never received the critical attention he had earlier in his career, nor did he renew his contacts with other modernist artists.

Dawson's short career brought him much success between 1909 and 1914, the years he was most active as an artist. Isolated from the burgeoning art scene in New York, his style developed apart from the support and patronage of the modernist movement as a whole. Yet Dawson's paintings, some of the earliest examples of abstract art in the United States, still stand as landmarks in the history of modernism.

Sarah Holian

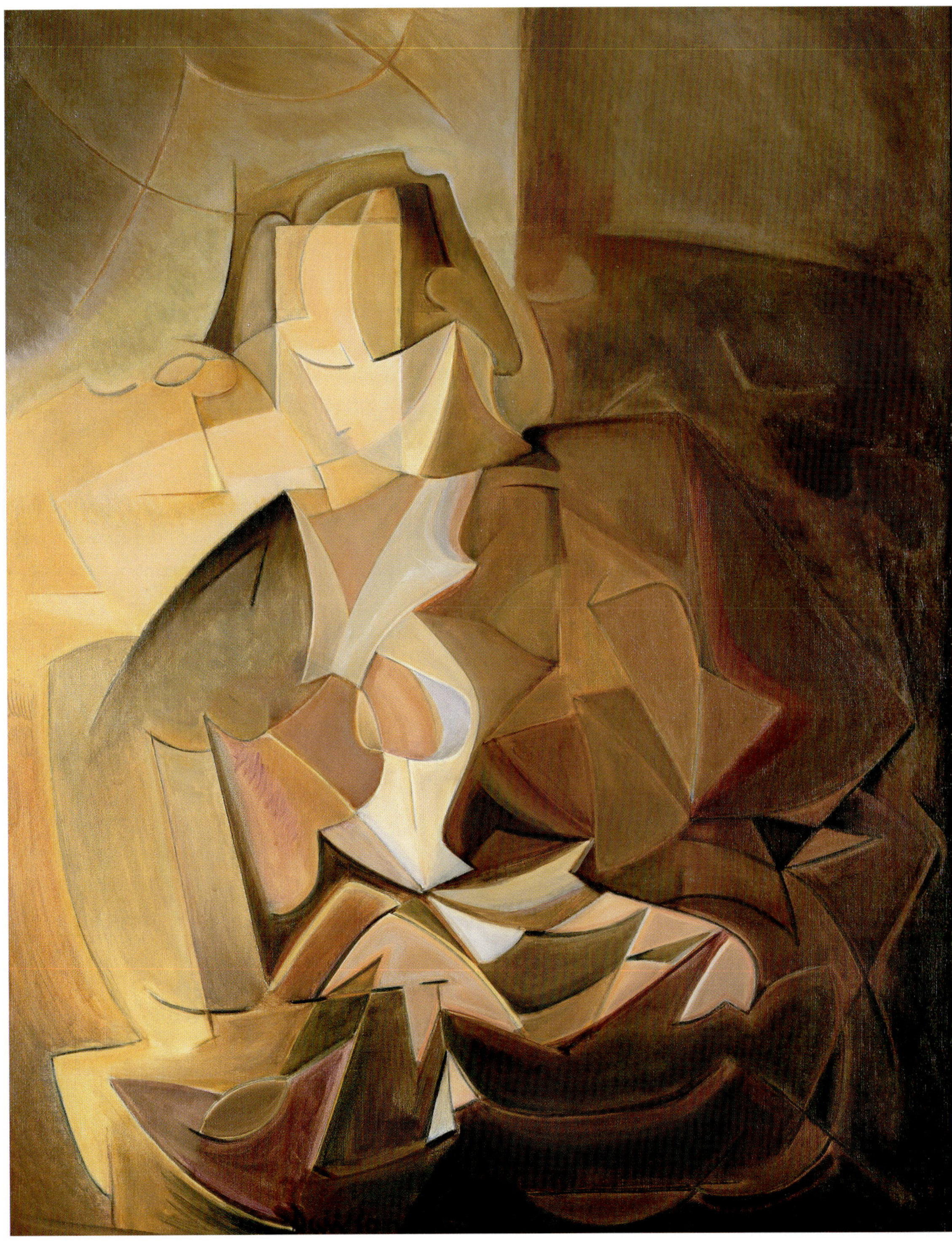

Notes

1. Mary Mathews Gedo used this term to describe these paintings in her article "Modernizing the Masters: Manierre Dawson's Cubist Transliterations," *Arts Magazine* 55 (April 1981): 135–45.
2. Kenneth Hey, "Manierre Dawson: A Fix on the Phantoms of the Imagination," *Archives of American Art Journal* 14, no. 4 (1974): 8.
3. Earl A. Powell III, "Manierre Dawson's 'Woman in Brown,'" *Arts Magazine* 51 (September 1976): 76–77. Powell was the first scholar to establish Picasso's portrait of Stein as the source for Dawson's *Woman in Brown*. Gedo discusses Picasso's influence in Dawson's work, including *Woman in Brown*, and raises questions as to when Dawson decided to sketch and paint the image in her article "The Secret Idol: Manierre Dawson and Pablo Picasso," *Arts Magazine* 56 (December 1981): 116–24.
4. Gedo, "Modernizing the Masters," 135–45. Gedo, at length, identifies sources for a number of Dawson's Cubist paintings.
5. Hey, 9.
6. Hey, 9, 12 (n. 10). Dawson's journal is unpublished and now held at the Ringling Museum of Art in Sarasota, Florida. The dates of the journal entries with notes to the Armory Show are March 25 and 27, 1913.

34.

Woman in Brown, c. 1912

Oil on canvas
36 × 28 in. (92 × 71 cm)
Michener Acquisitions Fund
P1969.12.1

Provenance: Purchased from Robert Schoelkopf Gallery, New York, 1969
Signed lower left of center "Dawson"

Peter Dean

Berlin, 1934–New York, 1993
w. New York, 1959–1993; New York–Columbia County, New York, 1977–1993

Peter Dean's dense and strident narrative paintings express his outrage over the violence and chaos of world events. Born in Berlin in 1934, Dean experienced the brutality of the Nazi regime firsthand when his Jewish parents were forced to flee Germany with their two children in 1938. The family eventually settled in New York, where Dean's father encouraged his artistic inclinations by taking him to museums and concerts and giving him private art lessons. These lessons, however, served mainly to reinforce Dean's distinctly antiauthoritarian attitude toward formal instruction. As he said of his decision to study geology at the University of Wisconsin, "Geology isn't like other sciences. It can't be, because geological formations break all the rules. . . . The only thing as free as doing geology is being an artist."[1]

After living in the western United States and Brazil and working as a mining engineer during the 1950s, Dean gradually made the transition to a career as an artist. He took night classes at City College in New York with the French painter André Girard. The latter introduced him to the Fauves, the German Expressionists, and James Ensor, all of whom exerted a profound influence on the development of Dean's work. Throughout the 1960s Dean painted in a figurative style, placing him at odds with Post-Painterly Abstraction and Minimalism, the two reigning artistic movements in New York at the time. In 1969 he became a member of the Rhino Horn group, which included Benny Andrews, among others. Rhino Horn was committed to an expressionistic yet figurative painting style and to subject matter that combined magical, dreamlike imagery with sociopolitical commentary. The group described its intentions as follows:

> *Our Art is involved with life; it is concerned with humanity, with emotion. We will not listen to explanations from or about the technically-minded artist of yesterday. Just as Abstract Expressionism—the art of the fifties—was superseded by pop, op, hard-edge, minimal, and color-field—the art of the sixties—so now, a humanistic art, will characterize the seventies.*[2]

Dean's interest in social commentary peaked in 1980, the same year he served on a grand jury that decided the cases of thirty-two murders in one month. This experience inspired Dean's Little Murders series, which gradually evolved from depictions of anonymous crimes into scenes of the assassinations of such notable historical figures as Abraham Lincoln, Malcolm X, and John Lennon. According to Dean, "The murder of John Kennedy was the beginning of violence for my generation," insofar as it corresponded to public awareness of the travesties of the Vietnam War, the backlash against civil rights protestors and antiwar demonstrators, and the string of assassinations of prominent political and cultural leaders of which Kennedy's was just the first.[3] *Dallas Chaos* (1981, plate 35) and *Dallas Chaos II* (1982, plate 36) belong to the Little Murders series. The paintings depict the tragic assassination of President Kennedy and the shooting of presumed assassin Lee Harvey Oswald by gangster Jack Ruby that followed. Both works were bold commentaries on the violence of contemporary mass culture.

The composition in *Dallas Chaos* is tightly packed with figures—claustrophobic, even. Surrounding Kennedy, his face splattered with blood, are numerous policemen and Secret Servicemen, whose distorted physiognomies recall the characters in a George Grosz montage. Although they presumably are trying to protect Kennedy, they seem either ineffectual or unperturbed. What is more, with their guns drawn, it is impossible to determine for certain if these men are threatening the president or protecting him. Suddenly, the line between villains and heroes becomes blurred—everyone is complicit, everyone is to blame, both for Kennedy's death and for the media spectacle that ensued, Dean seems to suggest. In the background are four American flags, a reference, perhaps, to the heated nationalism that helped bring the United States to the brink of nuclear war with Russia in the early 1960s. The

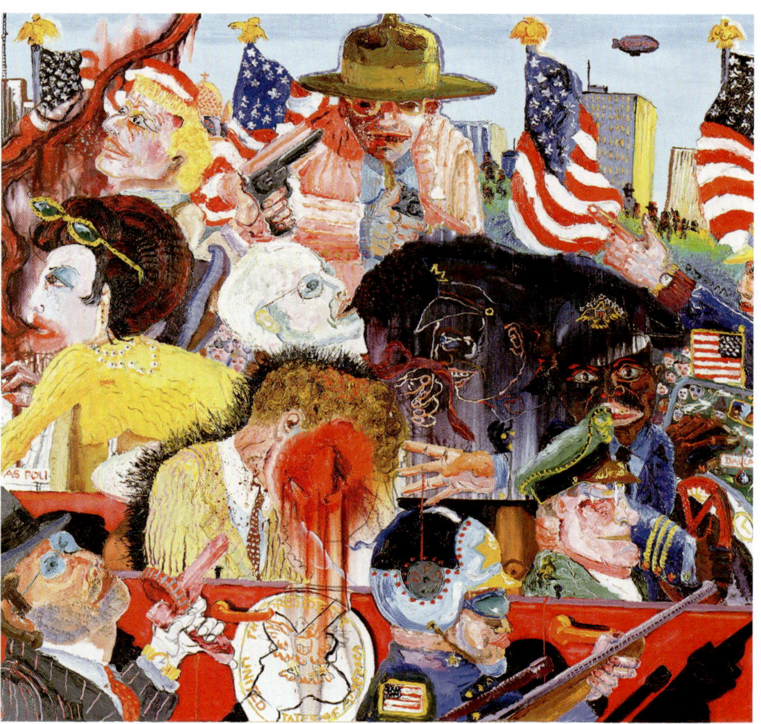

35.
Dallas Chaos, 1981
Oil on canvas
68 × 72 in. (172.7 × 183.4 cm)
Gift of Lorraine Dean and Gregory Dean
1994.38
Inscribed verso "Dallas Chaos oil 68 × 72 1981 PETER DEAN" in dark brown paint

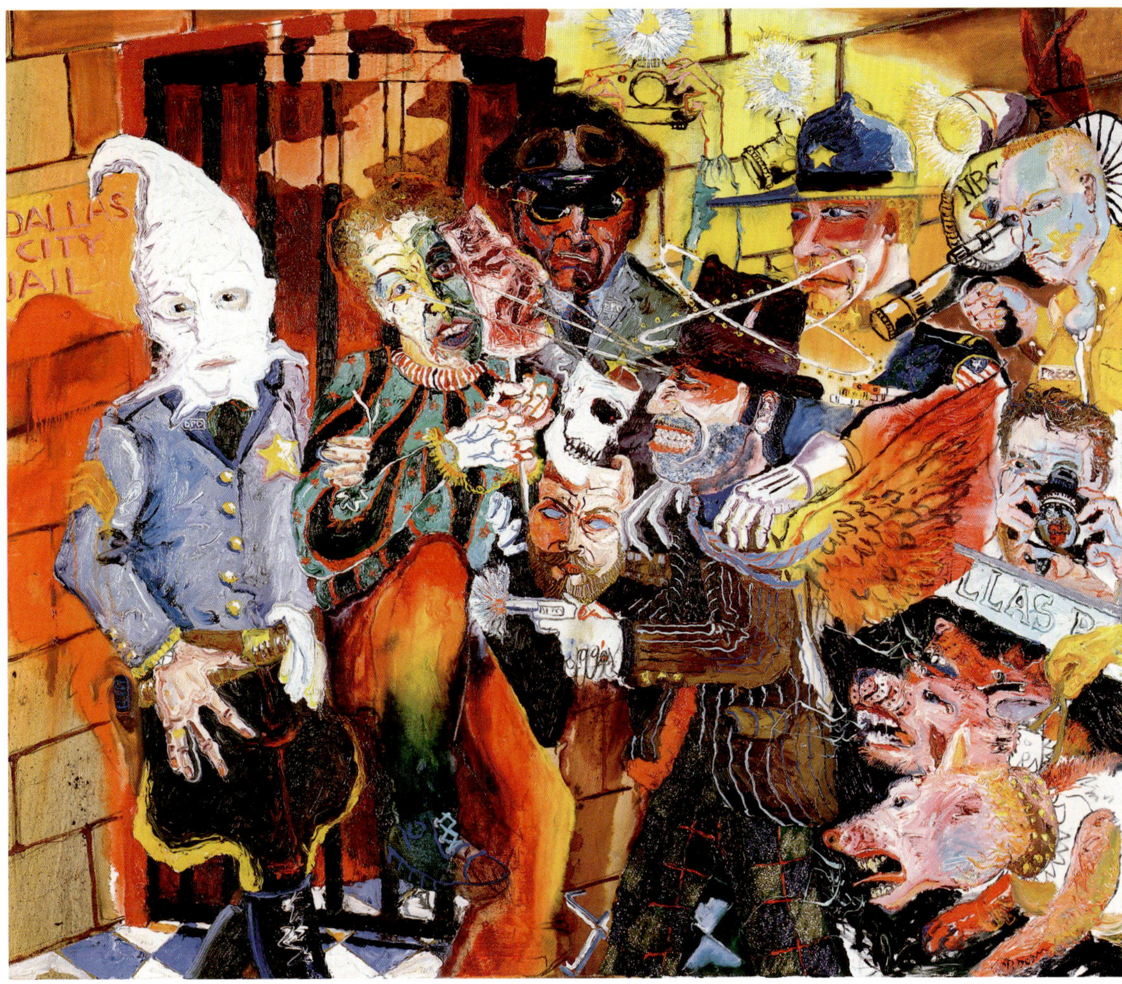

36.

Dallas Chaos II, 1982

Oil on canvas
84 × 96 in. (212.3 × 244 cm)
Gift of Lorraine Dean and Gregory Dean
1994.39
Inscribed verso "Dallas Chaos II oil 1982 84 × 96 PETER DEAN" in dark brown paint

colors used in the painting are bright and garish, underscoring the sense of dread communicated by the painting's content.

Dallas Chaos II is even more overwrought than *Dallas Chaos.* It offers a closer view of an image many Americans remember seeing played out live on their television sets—a real-time murder that was so shocking it is indelibly etched in the nation's memory. Here Jack Ruby, portrayed as the scowling villain from a Hollywood Western, shoots Lee Harvey Oswald, who is dressed as a clown. A death's head mask hovers in front of Oswald's face, while the walls of the Dallas City Jail appear to be dripping with blood. The reporters in the background contribute to the violence in their own way, the claustrophobic leer of their camera shots just as violent and predatory as the shots from Ruby's gun. The barking police dogs have the faces of pigs—a derogatory reference to the police who resemble Klansmen or clowns with their white faces and hats. In *Dallas Chaos II* Dean holds the horrors of the narrative image in perfect tension with the over-the-top expressionism of his painting style. The seeming chaos of the composition is belied by the extraordinarily tight organization of its underlying structure. Moreover, the work's surface is a veritable encyclopedia of expressive painterly techniques. In some areas, Dean incised the thick pigment with thin lines, a technique called *sgrafitto* that is hundreds of years old, while in other areas, he added modern commercial glitter to the medium, accentuating the carnivalesque atmosphere of the charged scene.

Dean's assassination paintings, along with his works portraying Native Americans and Sandanista rebels, do not glorify violence but rather explore the human psyche and employ indignation and empathy in order to expose acts of injustice. Such pronounced idealism combined with an unapologetically virtuosic painting technique are the hallmarks of Dean's production.

Erin Aldana

Notes

1. Lucy Lippard, "Builder on the Edge of a Chaotic World," in *Peter Dean: A Retrospective* (New York: Alternative Museum, 1990), 7.
2. Quoted in Sam Hunter, "Peter Dean's Mystical Theater," in *The Apocalyptic Vision: Four Artists* (New York: Gallerie Bellman, 1983), 3.
3. Quoted in Laura Stewart, "The Paintings of Peter Dean," in *The Apocalyptic Vision*, 13.

Jim Dine

b. Cincinnati, Ohio, 1935

w. New York, 1958–1968; London, 1967–1971; Putney, Vermont, 1971–1985; New York–Washington, Connecticut, 1985–present

In his early assemblage painting, *Four Coats* (1961, plate 37), Jim Dine combines Abstract Expressionist brushwork with Pop art's ironic engagement with everyday objects. Though at first glance *Four Coats* could be taken for an abstract painting, on closer inspection one can see that the four vertical panels' heavy gestural brushwork and abstract patterning evoke the thick weaves of wool, tweed, and other coat fabrics. Cuts and folds in the heavily painted canvas create overlapping edges, and four rows of actual buttons—disorientingly out of scale with the weave of the fabrics—are attached to the surface of the painting. Although he was inspired by the spontaneous, visceral quality of Abstract Expressionist painting, Dine disliked the movement's lofty individualism. Accordingly, he strove to combine the physical energy of action painting with a focus on the subject matter of everyday life. Asserting that his work did not seek to destroy Abstract Expressionism but to move beyond it in the "natural course of things," Dine said in 1963, "I tie myself to Abstract Expressionism like fathers and sons."[1]

Dine was born in 1935 in Ohio and studied art at the Cincinnati Arts Academy, the School of the Museum of Fine Arts, Boston, and Ohio University, where he received his BFA. In 1958 Dine moved to New York and within the year began to participate in art events at the Judson Gallery, performing Happenings and exhibiting with artists such as Claes Oldenburg, Tom Wesselmann, and George Segal. Like these artists, Dine was interested in exploring the intersections of art and everyday life. His paintings of this period commonly depict and sometimes actually include such everyday consumer items as hatchets, lawnmowers, and children's bedroom lamps. With its pieced and folded canvas and real buttons, *Four Coats* is an early example of Dine's use of assemblage in his paintings.

Clothing and domestic objects figure prominently in much of Dine's work from the 1960s to the present, particularly in his series of robe paintings. He began these shortly after *Four Coats,* in 1964, and has continued to produce them to the present day. As the title of one such painting, *Double Isometric Self-Portrait (Serape)* (1964), suggests, the robe motif captured Dine's interest as a way to create a kind of self-portrait. The idea came from a bathrobe advertisement in the *New York Times*: Dine said of the ad, "There was nobody in the robe, but when I saw it, it looked like me."[2] Though often critically linked to Pop art because of his focus on consumer culture and quotidian objects, Dine's emphasis on his personal relationship to subject matter distinguishes him from the Pop artists. As he commented in 1963, "I don't deal exclusively with the popular image. I'm more concerned with it as a part of my landscape . . . the artistic landscape, the artist's vocabulary, the artist's dictionary."[3]

A lifelong experimental approach to art has led Dine to explore new media and to adopt new styles and techniques throughout his career. In addition to assemblage paintings such as *Four Coats,* Dine has created still-lifes, representational drawings, prints, ceramics, large-scale installations, and performance works using such varied materials as oils, ink, charcoal, found objects, and his own body. In recent years his work reflects an increasing interest in carefully executed line and refined, painterly effects. Despite his varied styles, mediums, and ideas, Dine's abiding interest in the humanity of things, in objects as a "vocabulary of feelings,"[4] has allowed him to explore "the thing I was most interested in . . . that is, my interior self as a landscape or as a subject matter for everything."[5]

Karen C. Gonzalez

Notes

1. Quoted in G. R. Swenson, "What Is Pop Art?" *Artnews* 62 (November 1963): 25.
2. Quoted in "Poet of the Personal," *Time* 9 (March 1970): 50.
3. Quoted in Swenson, 25.
4. Quoted in John Gruen, "Jim Dine and the Life of Objects," *Artnews* 76 (September 1977): 38.
5. Quoted in Barbaralee Diamonstein, "Jim Dine," *Inside New York's Art World* (New York: Rizzoli, 1979), 99.

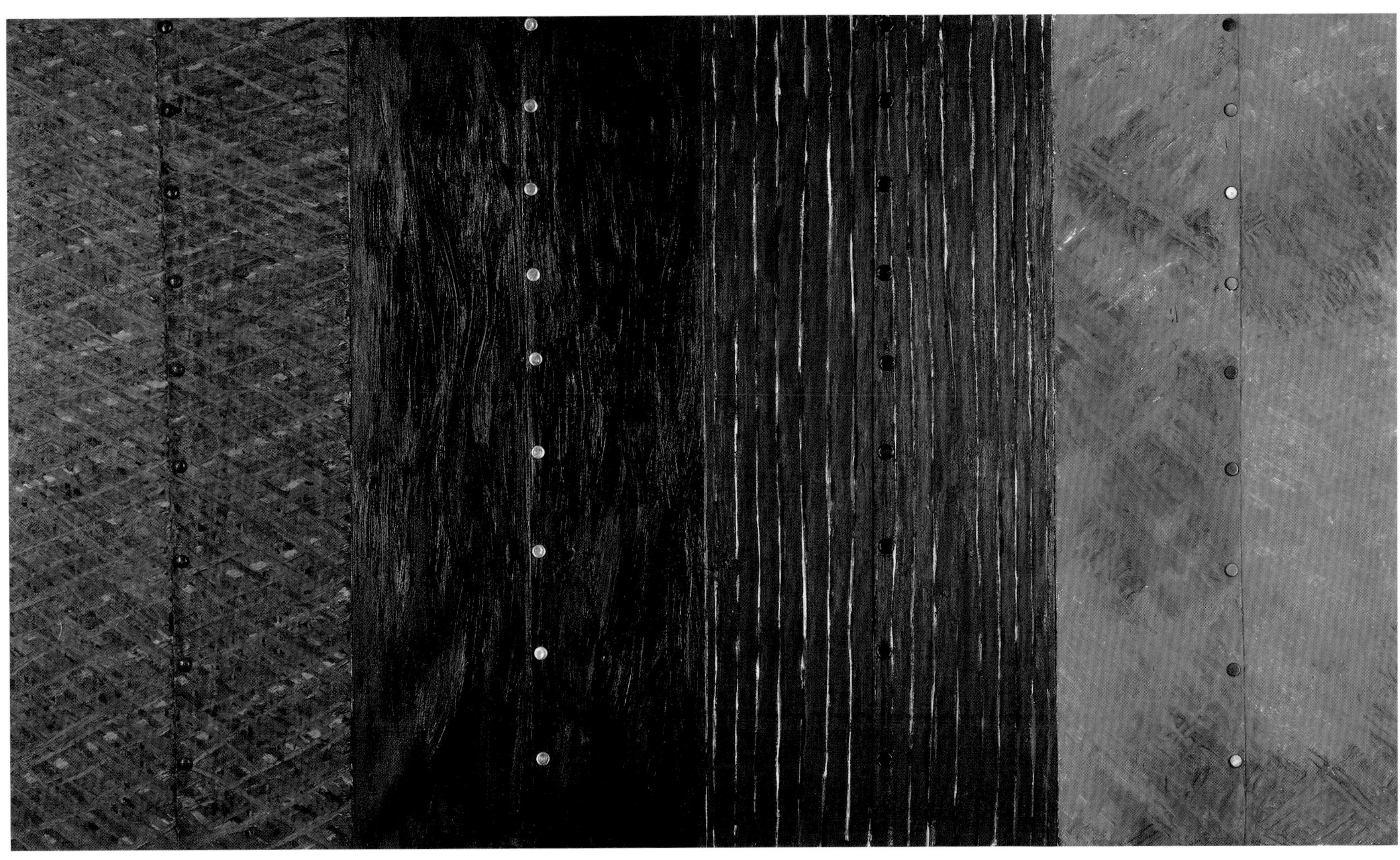

37.

Four Coats, 1961

Oil and collage on canvas
72 × 120⅝ in. (183.9 × 306.4 cm)
Gift of Mari and James A. Michener
1991.207

Provenance: Purchased by James Michener from Martha Jackson Gallery, New York, 1968; long-term loan to The University of Texas Austin, 1968–1991
Inscribed verso "Jim Dine Four Coats"

Arthur Garfield Dove

Canandaigua, New York, 1880–Centerport, New York, 1946

w. New York, 1903–1908; France, 1908–1909; Westport, Connecticut, 1910–1921; Long Island, New York, 1921–1932; Geneva, New York, 1933–1938; Centerport, New York, 1938–1946

In 1926 Waldo Frank wrote that Arthur Dove "belongs to the true tradition of American art . . . with his fathers, among whom are Ryder, Thoreau, Melville."[1] Dove cultivated this notion of the quintessential American artist as one who is connected transcendentally to nature with such romantic assertions as, "I can claim no background except perhaps the woods, running streams, hunting, fishing, etc."[2] Yet this was not simply pretense; Dove truly believed that living in nature was fundamental to his existence and to his art making. His oeuvre includes pastels, assemblages, and paintings that have earned him recognition as one of the first abstract artists in the United States. The Blanton's paintings, *Barge, Trees, Silver Ball* (1930, plate 38) and *Good Breeze* (1931, plate 39), date to the most prolific stage in Dove's career and are excellent examples of his brand of abstraction, which he called "extraction" because it was always rooted in nature.[3]

Born in 1880 in Canandaigua and raised in Geneva, New York, Dove attended Hobart College (now Hobart and William Smith Colleges) and Cornell University. After earning a bachelor's degree from Cornell in 1903, Dove embarked on a successful career as an illustrator for such periodicals as *Cosmopolitan, Pearson's,* and *Life*.[4] From 1910 until 1921 Dove lived with his first wife, Florence, and son, Bill, on a farm in Westport, Connecticut. In 1921 he began living on a houseboat with Helen "Reds" Torr, a fellow painter who would become his second wife in 1932. Dove asserted in a 1929 letter to his friend and dealer Alfred Stieglitz, "If we have no boat, I miss something of the storms and weather that seem to give me more."[5] Accordingly, *Good Breeze* and *Barge, Trees, Silver Ball* feature views of boats under an expansive sky, elements that Dove considered vital to his artistic inspiration.

Throughout his career, Dove sought to create paintings that do not simply represent nature but symbolize its power and vitality. As he wrote in 1933, "To make it breathe as does the rest of nature it must have a basic rhythm."[6] Dove captured this "basic rhythm" in *Good Breeze* and *Barge, Trees, Silver Ball,* both of which are animated by his signature "force lines," concentric bands of subtly shifting colors that radiate out from a particular form. The Italian Futurist painters, including Umberto Boccioni, had used the term "force lines" to describe the underlying vibratory nature of the universe, which they sought to capture in their paintings. In so doing, they responded to such nineteenth-century scientific discoveries as the X-ray, radioactivity, and the electromagnetic field.[7] Dove shared both their interest in occultism and their impulse to render invisible forces visible through color and brushstroke.[8] His own conception of the universe was influenced as much by Eastern religions, theosophy, and American transcendentalism as it was contemporary science.[9]

Good Breeze debuted under the title *Breezy Day* in 1932 in Dove's one-man show at Stieglitz's gallery, An American Place. Dove based the paintings in that exhibition on "the different conditions of each day."[10] For its part, *Good Breeze* captures the effect of a pleasantly forceful wind on a sailboat. The vibrant, yellow boat with its billowing sails dominates the center of the canvas. The boat glows and projects its brightness onto the foliage directly behind it, which responds by conforming to the shape of the boat. The rippling waves that fill the foreground establish an undulating pattern that echoes in the distant land and sky. Together these repeated shapes create a formal relationship between the land, water, sky, and boat. Dove thus achieved a dynamic continuity between each element in the landscape, reflecting the symbiosis that he believed characterized his relationship with his surroundings. Using force lines to animate the surface of the canvas, Dove created a rhythm that leads the viewer's eye from bottom to top, foreground to background. Within those bands of blue and green, one can observe remnants of Dove's brushstrokes, which radiate like waves of energy off the canvas.

Like *Good Breeze, Barge, Trees, Silver Ball* depicts a boat floating on the water, though in this painting the water exists below the picture plane. The silver ball is a composite of the moon and the light it emits, saturating the night sky. Dove used silver metallic paint for the force lines around the moon, which reflect light off the surface of the painting

38.
Barge, Trees, Silver Ball, 1930
Oil and silver paint on beaverboard
23 × 33 in. (59 × 83 cm)
Gift of Mari and James A. Michener
G1968.44
Provenance: Purchased by James Michener from Downtown Gallery, New York, 1962
Signed lower right corner "Dove"

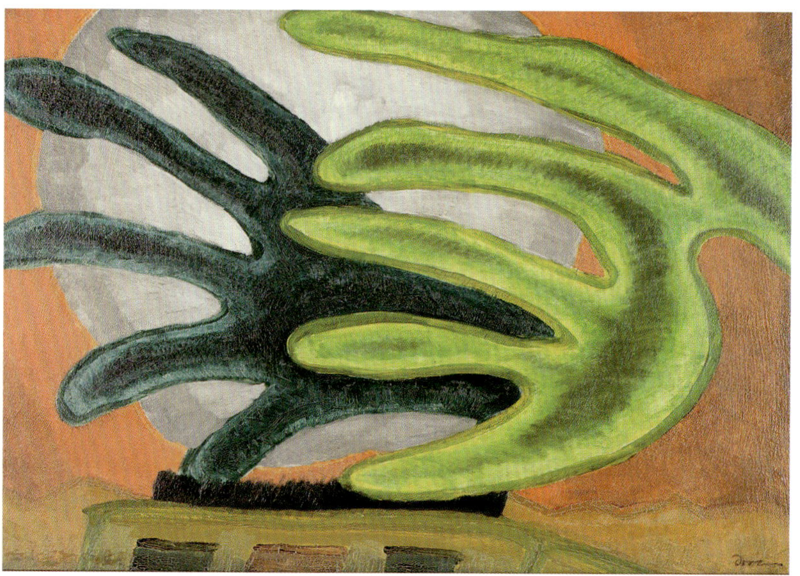

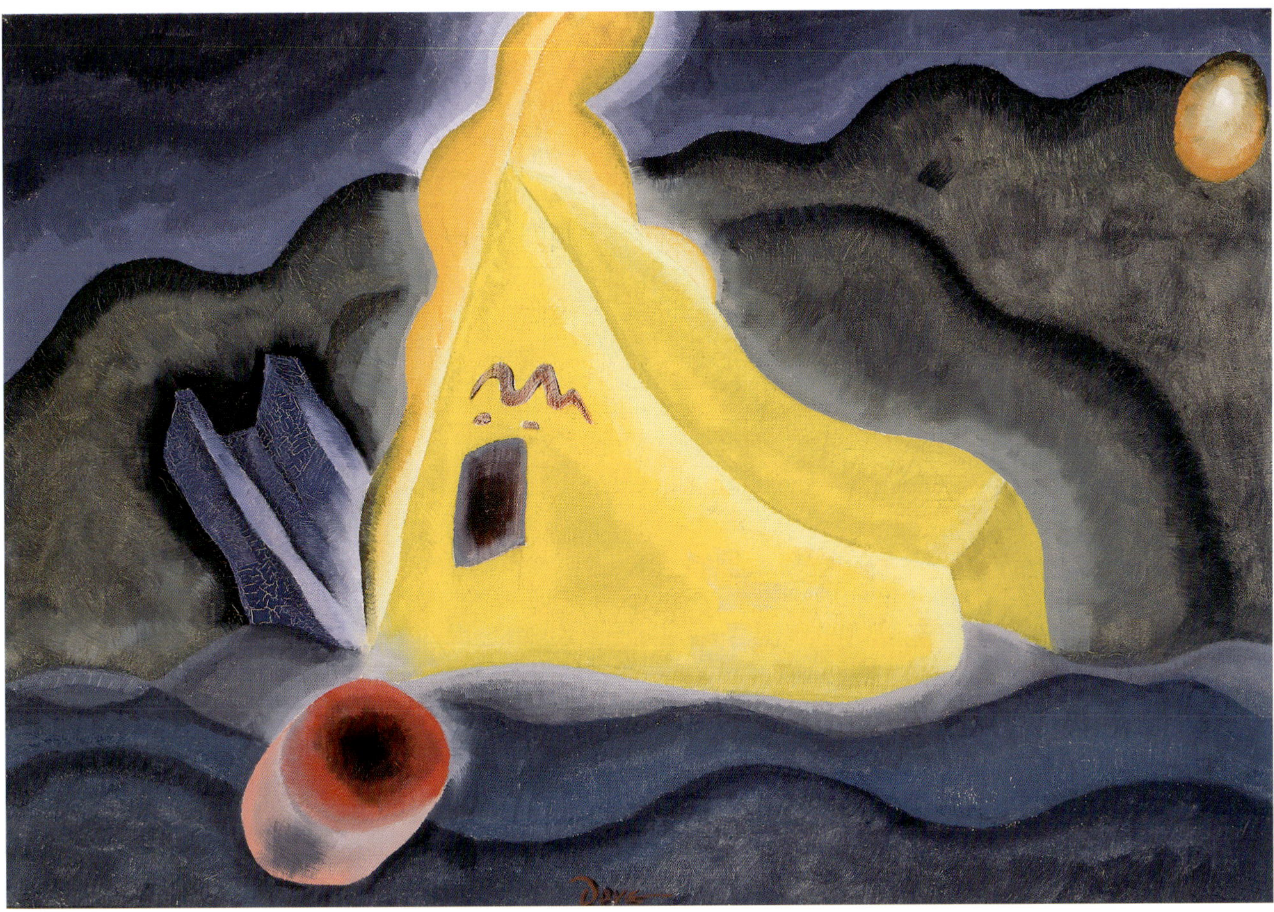

39.
Good Breeze, 1931
Oil on canvas
19 11/16 × 27 9/16 in. (50 × 70 cm)
Gift of Mari and James A. Michener
G1968.45P

Provenance: Purchased by James Michener from Downtown Gallery, New York, 1962
Signed lower center "Dove"

and add to its luminosity. The hues of silver surrounding the moon darken as they move outward. In turn Dove rendered the sky in shades of red that darken as they increase in distance from this illusionary light source. Here he energized nature by anthropomorphizing the limbs of the trees so that they seem to reach out to connect earth and sky. Such communion between the heavens and earth is precisely what Dove sought in many of his paintings of this era, including *Moon* (1935), in which a tree dramatically fuses with the moon.

As a core member of the circle of artists surrounding Stieglitz's galleries that included John Marin and Georgia O'Keeffe, Dove occupies a central place in the development of American modernism. Thanks to Stieglitz's encouragement and the patronage of Duncan Phillips, Dove was able to realize his goal of working as an artist outside the bustle of New York. He also benefited from discussions and correspondence among his Stieglitz circle colleagues that exposed him to contemporary art theory, literature, science, and philosophy. Stieglitz's journal *Camera Work* (1902–1917) was an early forum for many of the issues that would prove important for Dove in subsequent decades. It featured essays by philosopher Henri Bergson and an excerpt from painter Wassily Kandinsky's *Concerning the Spiritual in Art*. Dove found Bergson's theories, particularly his emphasis on intuition, quite compelling, as he did Kandinsky's argument for the spiritual as the basis for art.[11] Dove believed that both paintings and nature were reflections of his inner feelings, writing, "paintings are mirrors, so is nature,"[12] a remark that seems to prefigure Jackson Pollock's famous adage, "I am nature." Like the Abstract Expressionists of the 1940s and 1950s, who turned their attention inward, mining the personal and collective unconscious to create large, nonrepresentational paintings, Dove fostered an intuitive, subjective relationship with his surroundings that resulted in expressive paintings of nature, which, though small in size, are vast and emotive in effect.[13]

Lara Kuykendall

Notes

1. Waldo Frank, "The Art of Arthur Dove," *New Republic*, January 27, 1926, 269–70.
2. Arthur Dove, autobiographical statement, c. 1930, Arthur and Helen Torr Dove Papers, Archives of American Art, roll 4682, frame 172.
3. Sherrye Cohn, *Arthur Dove: Nature as Symbol* (Ann Arbor, Mich.: UMI Research Press, 1985): 14.
4. For more on Dove's work as an illustrator, see Barbara D. Gallati, "Arthur G. Dove as Illustrator," *Archives of American Art Journal* 21, no. 2 (1981): 13–22.
5. Arthur Dove to Alfred Stieglitz, c. May 20, 1929, in Ann Lee Morgan, *Dear Stieglitz, Dear Dove* (Newark, N.J.: University of Delaware Press, 1988): 174.
6. Arthur Dove to Elizabeth McCausland, May 21, 1933, quoted in Roxana Barry, "Foreword," in Ann Lee Morgan, *Arthur Dove: Life and Work with a Catalogue Raisonné* (Newark, N.J.: University of Delaware Press, 1984): n.p.
7. Cohn, 33–35.
8. On Futurism, occultism, and physics, see the work of Linda Dalrymple Henderson, including "Vibratory Modernism: Boccioni, Kupka, and the Ether of Space," in Bruce Clarke and Linda Dalrymple Henderson, *From Energy to Information: Representation in Science and Technology, Art, and Literature* (Stanford, Calif.: Stanford University Press, 2002): 126–49.
9. Cohn, 45–57.
10. Arthur Dove to Alfred Stieglitz, January 7, 1932, in Morgan, 234–35.
11. Dove created a "suggested interview" in which he wrote, "What do you mean by abstraction? Intuition, not analysis . . . Bergson's *Introduction to Metaphysics* is very clear on this subject." Arthur and Helen Torr Dove Papers, Archives of American Art, roll 4682, frame 109. Also quoted in Cohn, 45. See also Sue Davidson Lowe, *Stieglitz: A Memoir/Biography* (New York: Farrar Straus Giroux, 1983): 210, 212.
12. Dove's writings, quoted in Cohn, 1.
13. For a discussion of the relationship between Dove's art and Abstract Expressionism, see Helen A. Harrison, "Arthur G. Dove and the Origins of Abstract Expressionism," *American Art* 12 (spring 1998): 66–83.

Philip Evergood

New York, 1901–Southbury, Connecticut, 1973

w. London, 1921–1923; New York, 1923–1924; Paris, 1924–1926; New York, 1926–1935 (frequent trips to Europe); Long Island, New York, 1935–1952; Southbury, Connecticut, 1952–1963; Bridgeport, Connecticut, 1963–1973

Philip Evergood was committed to creating art that exposed and protested social injustice. Varied and unconventional in his approach to art and in the way he lived, Evergood was an artist whose work resists easy classification.

Evergood was born in New York as Philip Blashki to an Australian father and an English mother. Influences from both sides of his family shaped Evergood's identity; his father was a dedicated painter, while his mother insisted on educating him in England, both of which had profound consequences for the young artist. In 1909, at the age of eight, Evergood sailed for England to attend a succession of schools that included Eton, Cambridge, and the University of London, where he entered the Slade School of Art in 1921. At Slade Evergood gravitated toward a traditional approach, emphasizing skills such as draftsmanship and the use of conventional subject matter drawn from the Bible and mythology. Friends, however, introduced him to more modern and progressive art, including the works of Vincent van Gogh and Paul Gauguin.

After receiving a certificate from Slade in 1923, a stint at the Art Students League in New York landed Evergood under the tutelage of George Luks, who impressed him with the observation that one must live life before painting it.[1] Evergood also frequented studio sessions at the Educational Alliance, which was founded to provide poor immigrants with opportunities and attracted social progressives and established artists like Robert Henri, who critiqued student work. Through this progressive organization Evergood developed long-lasting friendships with other artists, including Chaim Gross and Moses Soyer.

For most of the 1920s and early 1930s, Evergood moved freely between Europe and the United States, absorbing ideas and art from both sides of the Atlantic. In between trips to Paris and Spain, where he studied the work of Diego Velásquez, Francisco Goya, and El Greco, Evergood had his first solo exhibition in New York in 1926. He permanently settled in New York in 1931 and married Julia Cross, a dancer.

Evergood's arrival back in the United States coincided with the Great Depression. Like many artists in the 1930s, Evergood was a participant in New Deal art projects, which mitigated his impoverished state. As a Social Realist, his artistic concerns extended beyond himself to include society at large. Indeed, the purpose of his art was to elicit strong emotional responses from viewers and prompt them to take action to improve society. Evergood was also socially active in organizations such as the American Artists Congress, the Artists' Committee of Action, and the Artists' Union, and he participated in the "219" protests of WPA layoffs in 1936.

Painted during the height of the Depression, *Dance Marathon* (1934, plate 40) depicts an entertainment fad that swept the country in the 1920s and had become a seamy symbol of desperation by the 1930s. Couples entered dance marathons as much for the food and shelter as for the promotional prize money. Rules differed, but contestants danced twenty-four hours a day with short hourly breaks until one by one they dropped out from exhaustion. The last couple standing was the prizewinner. While the selection of a subject from American popular culture ties Evergood to Urban Realism and the American Scene painters, his expressive style reflects an affinity for European Expressionists such as Van Gogh and Max Beckmann.

Dance Marathon initially appears to be a confused jumble of figures. Upon closer examination, however, the painting's compositional logic emerges. The heads and torsos of the largest pair of figures are situated at the hub of a "wheel." Their lower extremities, as well as the other couples, form the wheel's rim. Circular motifs are repeated in the weblike pattern of the floorboards and the rail enclosure. Here the unending nature of the circle suggests infinite misery, the web implies entrapment, and the rail refers to a circus or rodeo, equating the dancers with performing animals. Evergood's use of masklike faces and garish, clashing colors further dehumanizes the dancers but only in an effort to lay bare their degradation by dance marathons specifically and society in general.

From three corners of the canvas, the cropped hands and forearms of a man, woman, and skeleton extend into the composition. The skeletal hand proffering cash is a jarring element of fantasy that underscores the desperation of the dancers, while the crude male and female hands indicate the pure debasement of the spectators. Evergood's treatment of the cigar chomping man at the far left mirrors the type of biting social commentary typical of Beckmann. Like Beckmann, Evergood employs dark outlines and rough features, which are seen here in the raw yellow, geometric zigzags of the man's hair and gross face that convey vulgarity. By placing three glowing light fixtures and a clock in the background of the composition, Evergood is likely paying homage to Van Gogh's *The Night Café* (1888), another work that used nondescriptive color and form to expose human passions and failings.[2]

Building on both American and European antecedents, Evergood combined realism, fantasy, and expressionism to craft his powerful indictment of a society that dehumanized the poor for a perverted form of entertainment.

Feay Shellman Coleman

Notes

1. Kendall Taylor, *Philip Evergood: Never Separate from the Heart* (London and Toronto: Associated University Presses, 1987), 63.
2. Susan Lou Tocker Sternberg, *Philip Evergood's Dance Marathon* (master's thesis, The University of Texas at Austin, 1984), 25–26.

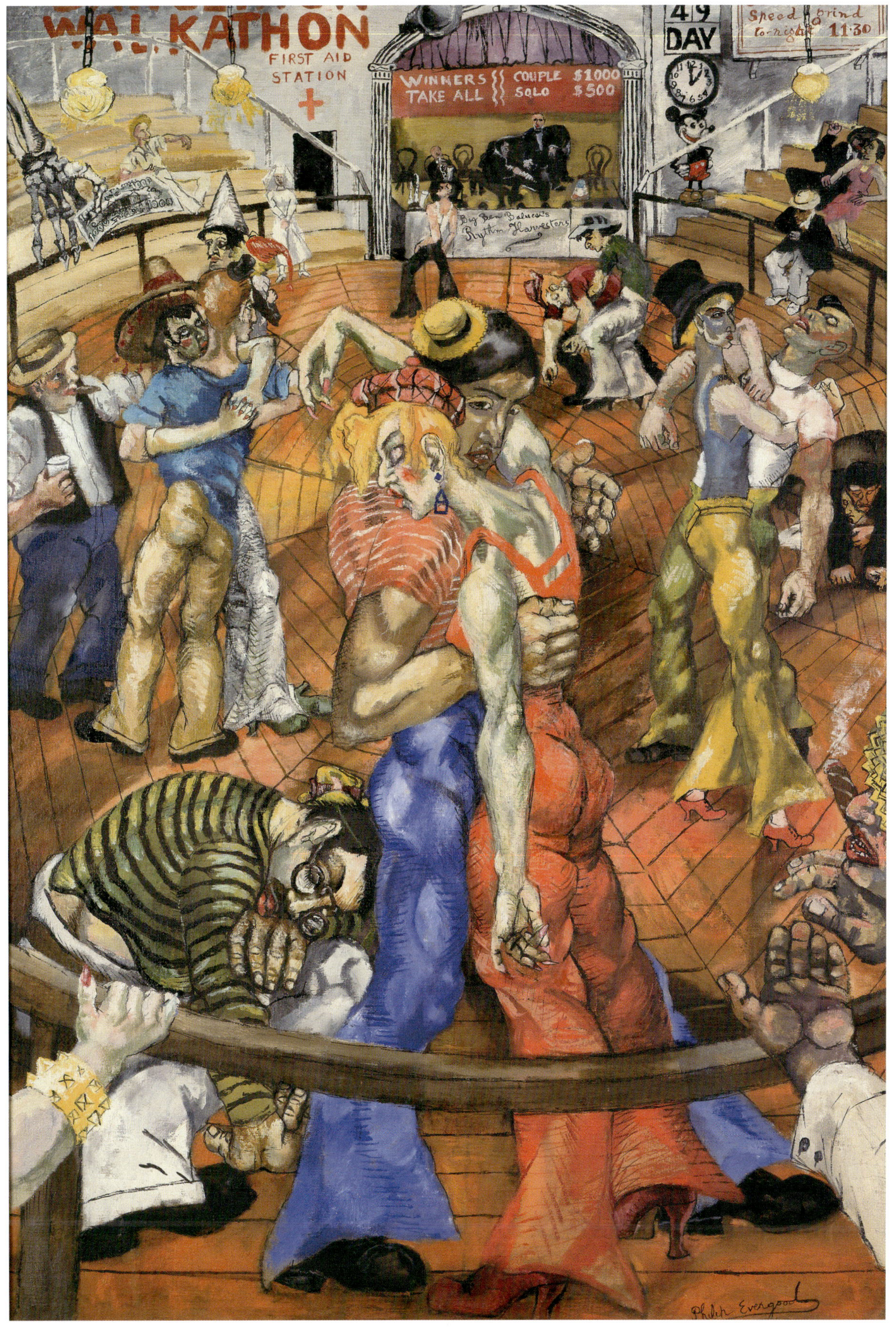

40.

Dance Marathon, 1934

Oil on canvas
60 × 40 in. (152.6 × 101.7 cm)
Gift of Mari and James A. Michener
1991.210

Provenance: Terry Dintenfass Collection; purchased by James Michener from ACA Gallery, New York, 1962; long-term loan to The University of Texas at Austin, 1968–1991
Signed lower right "Philip Evergood"

John Ferren

Pendleton, Oregon, 1905–Easthampton, New York, 1970
w. Paris, 1931–1938; New York, 1938–1970

John Ferren, who began his career as a sculptor, was born in Pendleton, Oregon, in 1905. While living in California in 1926, he learned to cast plaster and carve tombstones. Ferren studied at the Sorbonne in Paris and later took courses at the Universities of Florence, Italy, and Salamanca, Spain. A 1929 exhibition of the work of Henri Matisse held in Munich, which he visited with Hans Hofmann, prompted Ferren's rapid change in media from sculpture to painting.

The title of Ferren's *A Rose for Gertrude Stein* (1962, plate 41) is likely a reference to the American author's famous aphorism, "a rose is a rose is a rose." Ferren met fellow American Gertrude Stein while living and working in Paris from 1931 to 1938. During this period, he associated with members of the Parisian avant-garde, and his marriage to the daughter of a Spanish artist solidified his relationships with other European artists. He exhibited with Wassily Kandinsky, Alberto Giacometti, and Jean Hélion, among others, and between 1936 and 1937, he worked as an assistant on Pablo Picasso's mural *Guernica*. Ferren also spent time investigating color relationships, basing his inquiries on the theories of Johann Wolfgang von Goethe. He wrote a manifesto with Hélion and Georges Vantongerloo that criticized the Surrealists for focusing on literature instead of modern art. Despite his official opposition to Surrealism, Ferren was friendly with Max Ernst and André Breton and also created book illustrations for Surrealist poets.

While in France, Ferren aligned himself more closely with French artists than with other American expatriates, particularly through his association with the Abstraction-Création group. Stein herself described Ferren (in characteristically elliptical fashion) in her book *Everybody's Autobiography* of 1937: "He is the only American painter foreign painters in Paris consider as a painter and whose painting interests them."[1]

After his return to the United States in 1938, Ferren joined the American Abstract Artists but left the organization only two years later. He found a more comfortable niche with the Abstract Expressionists, socializing at the now-famous Cedar Tavern and Waldorf Cafeteria, and serving as director of the "Club," a group that developed out of this informal collective in 1955. In the mid-1950s Ferren began incorporating figurative elements suggestive of flowers, vases, windows, or doors into his work, though he still remained committed to exploring abstraction.

Ferren was one of the first Abstract Expressionist artists to experiment with symmetrical compositions, and his canvases often combine gestural brushstrokes with geometric abstraction. For instance, while the calligraphic brushwork of *A Rose for Gertrude Stein* exemplifies the spontaneous handling of paint of the Abstract Expressionists, Ferren simultaneously imposed a geometrical structure on the composition. He confined the loose, colorful strokes of paint to the red ground at the center of the canvas, which is circumscribed by a pink border. Ferren explored this type of composition in numerous other works, where a central mass of high-keyed, thickly applied brushstrokes matches the shape of the canvas. In the late 1960s he moved away from the gestural qualities of Abstract Expressionism and returned to the simplified geometry, clear contours, and color typical of his hard-edged abstractions of the 1930s.

Ferren's return to stylistic austerity can be attributed partially to his appointment as the first artist-in-residence in the federal program Artist Specialists Abroad. In 1963 he spent a year in Beirut, later traveling through the Middle East and India. The architecture Ferren encountered during his travels, notably the mosques of Isfahan, Iran, inspired the paintings he created in subsequent years. In addition to the symmetry, distinctive arch forms, and broad planes of color of the Isfahan mosques, Ferren also adopted central mandorla shapes. The Blanton's *Orange, Blue, Green* (1969, not illustrated), which features a modified double almond at its center, exemplifies his paintings from the late 1960s.

Ferren's embrace of Islamic influences reflects a lifelong interest in religion and spirituality. As a young man, he identified with an animistic philosophy that linked humanity with nature, which in turn led him to Taoism and Zen Buddhism. His exposure to Islam during an extended stay in Lebanon gave him an appreciation of that faith as well. Ferren explicitly linked religion and art. He believed that art contained the power to reveal meaning beyond superficial appearances, observing in an early diary entry, "abstract art is religiously the manifestation of God to man."[2]

Ferren enjoyed critical success throughout his career, exhibiting regularly in group and solo shows until the end of his life. In 1969, the same year he painted *Orange, Blue, Green*, Ferren had solo exhibitions at the A. M. Saks Gallery in New York and the Parrish Museum in Southampton, New York. He also distinguished himself as a teacher at Queens College in New York, where he taught for many years and was instrumental in developing the school's fine arts curriculum. The artist's long career includes work in media other than painting: in addition to returning to sculpture at different points in his life, Ferren occasionally practiced textile design as well.

R. Sarah Richardson

Notes

1. Gertrude Stein, quoted in "American Abroad," *Time*, August 29, 1938, 29.
2. Quoted in Craig Bailey, *Ferren: A Retrospective* (New York: The Graduate School and University Center of the City University of New York, 1979), 7.

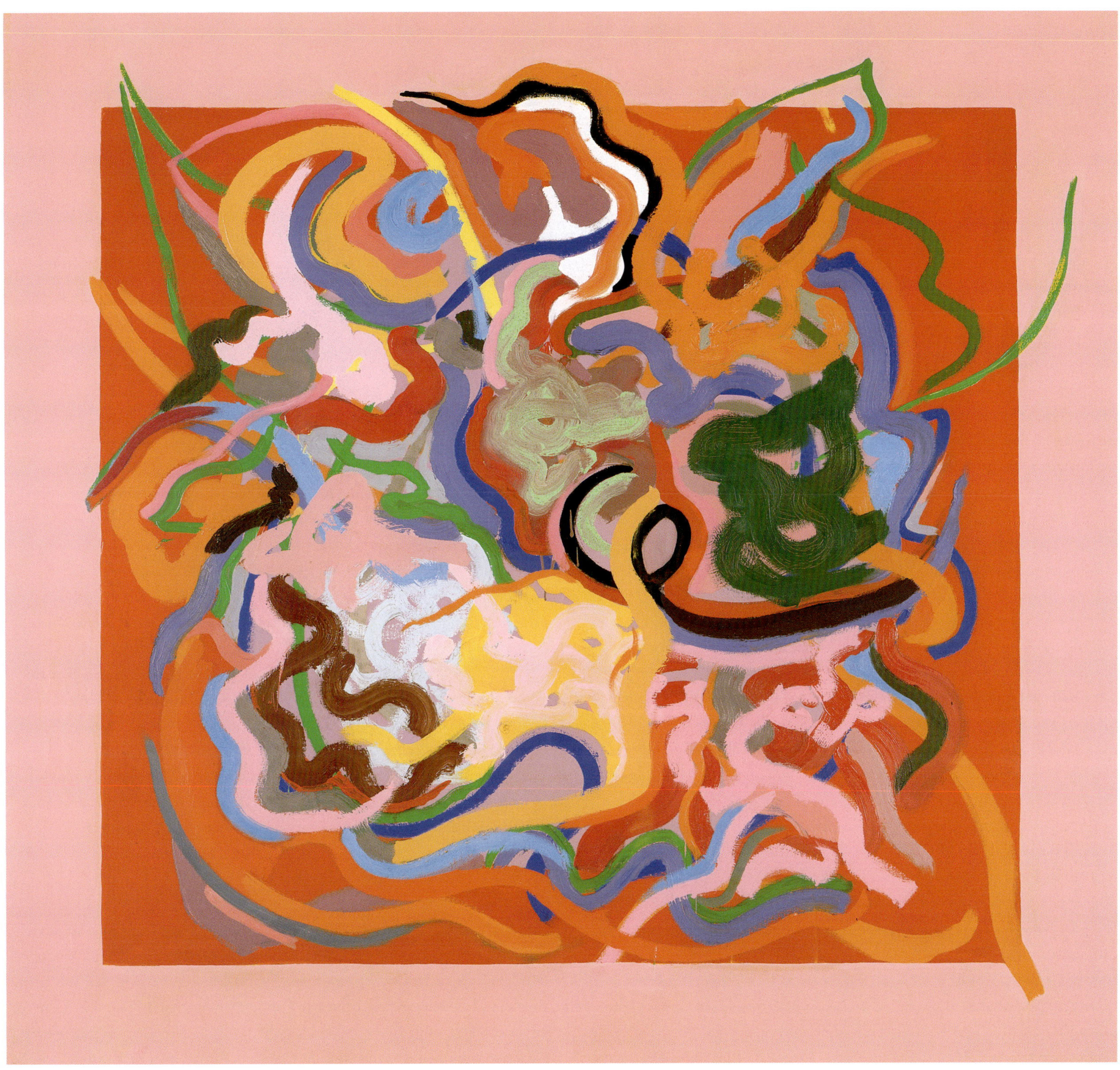

41.

A Rose for Gertrude Stein, 1962

Oil on canvas
71 × 76 in. (180 × 194 cm)
Gift of Mari and James A. Michener
G1968.51

Provenance: Purchased by James Michener from Rose Fried Gallery, New York, 1963
Inscribed verso, upper right "John Ferren 1962"
Inscribed verso, upper left "A Rose for Gertrude Stein"

Vernon Fisher

b. Fort Worth, 1943

w. Champaign-Urbana, Illinois, 1967–1969; Sherman, Texas, 1969–1978; Fort Worth, 1978–present

Evidence of Houdini's Return (1994, plate 42) is a blackboard painting by Texas-based Conceptual artist Vernon Fisher. An accumulative layering of disparate images and writing, it is exemplary of his approach. Since the 1970s Fisher has created mixed media works and installations that address issues of abstraction, verisimilitude, and interpretation by citing commonplace subjects drawn from popular culture or his personal experiences and written notes.

Evidence of Houdini's Return refers to professional magician Harry Houdini's efforts in the first decades of the twentieth century to debunk spiritualist claims about the afterlife, specifically by arranging to contact his wife after his death (contact that Houdini knew could never be substantiated). Although proclaimed as the leading illusionist of his day, Houdini nevertheless posited the rationalism of science as superior to the deceptions of spiritualism. Fisher appropriated this American icon's story as a way of commenting on broader artistic debates about the nature of illusionism. In fact, Fisher's own ironic and questioning approach to art making finds a perfect counterpart in Houdini's skeptical attitude toward the psychics and mediums of his day. But whereas Houdini used his magical training to expose frauds who had fooled scientists,[1] Fisher presents a more nuanced perspective on his subject in *Evidence of Houdini's Return*.

This is a complex, fascinating work whose individual elements function sometimes against and sometimes in concert with one another, generating a heady internal dialogue about scientific discourse and the nature of representation. By introducing several images of the human body and superimposing upon them boxlike forms, Fisher recalls Houdini's sensational escape acts from glass and steel cabinets. The artist's depictions of these body parts, as well as the ruler and the numbers that appear alongside them, reference scientific diagrams and anatomical studies, a representational mode that Fisher has incorporated into his blackboard paintings since at least 1995. While such details might suggest that the artist is privileging science, in fact, the story is far more complicated, for Fisher smudged many of these same marks and images. This action not only invests *Evidence of Houdini's Return* with a provisional, ephemeral appearance, it has the effect of nullifying the clarity of these objective, quantitative, and scientific modes of representation. In so doing, Fisher incapacitates them, rendering them only so useful, only so accurate, at the same time that he calls into question their operative value. He thus subverts the language of objectivity and science even as he relies on it.

Evidence of Houdini's Return also indicates Fisher's interest in the ontological character of art. More specifically, it demonstrates the fluidity between what is real and what is representation, largely by combining real objects—the piece of wood and the faded photograph (culled from Fisher's massive archive)[2]—with several types of representational systems, from written words and numbers to drawn images, photographs, and trompe l'oeil motifs (such as the beaker filled with milk, from the top of which poke the ears of Mickey Mouse). While Houdini thought that all illusions could be exposed, Fisher demonstrates the appeal of visual illusionism while simultaneously acknowledging that representations cannot adequately capture reality's slippery nature.

Punctuated as it is with both clearly rendered and obscure elements, *Evidence of Houdini's Return* resembles the unstructured, free-flowing nature of memory. Indeed, Fisher has always been fascinated by stories, especially those moments when stories digress and dissolve. This interest manifests itself in *Evidence of Houdini's Return* as a plethora of visual and textual ingredients that can be assembled to form several different interpretations. Fisher's refusal to pin down meaning, in addition to his combination of diverse sources and media and his embrace of shifting representational styles, demonstrates parallels with postmodernism, which revolves around an acceptance of fragmentation and contradiction with regards to the formal structure and meaning of a work of art.

Fisher's work can be contextualized within several major strains of modern and contemporary art. Both Cy Twombly and Jean-Michel Basquiat used the blackboard as a surface, albeit to radically different ends. Fisher's layering of images and text recalls Jasper Johns's ironic mixed media works that interrogate the nature of reality and art,[3] while his humorous, colloquial approach to language resembles that of Ed Ruscha, who influenced the artist early in his career.[4] Ultimately, however, Fisher's assimilation of these artistic inspirations is filtered through his own daily experiences and observations.

Widely acclaimed, his art frequently exhibited in prestigious venues, Fisher continues to be innovative and influential. In 1990 he was the first Texas-based artist to have a solo exhibition at The Museum of Modern Art in New York, and in 2000 he was featured in the Whitney Biennial. Fisher has taught at the University of North Texas in Denton since 1978. In 1992 he was awarded the College Art Association's Award for Distinguished Teaching of Art. Fisher's more recent Zombie paintings consist of abstract color-fields to which hyperrealistic cast and painted flies have been attached. This series sustains his exploration of disparate systems of representation as a way to comment on the complex, multifaceted nature of reality.

Mariani Lefas-Tetenes

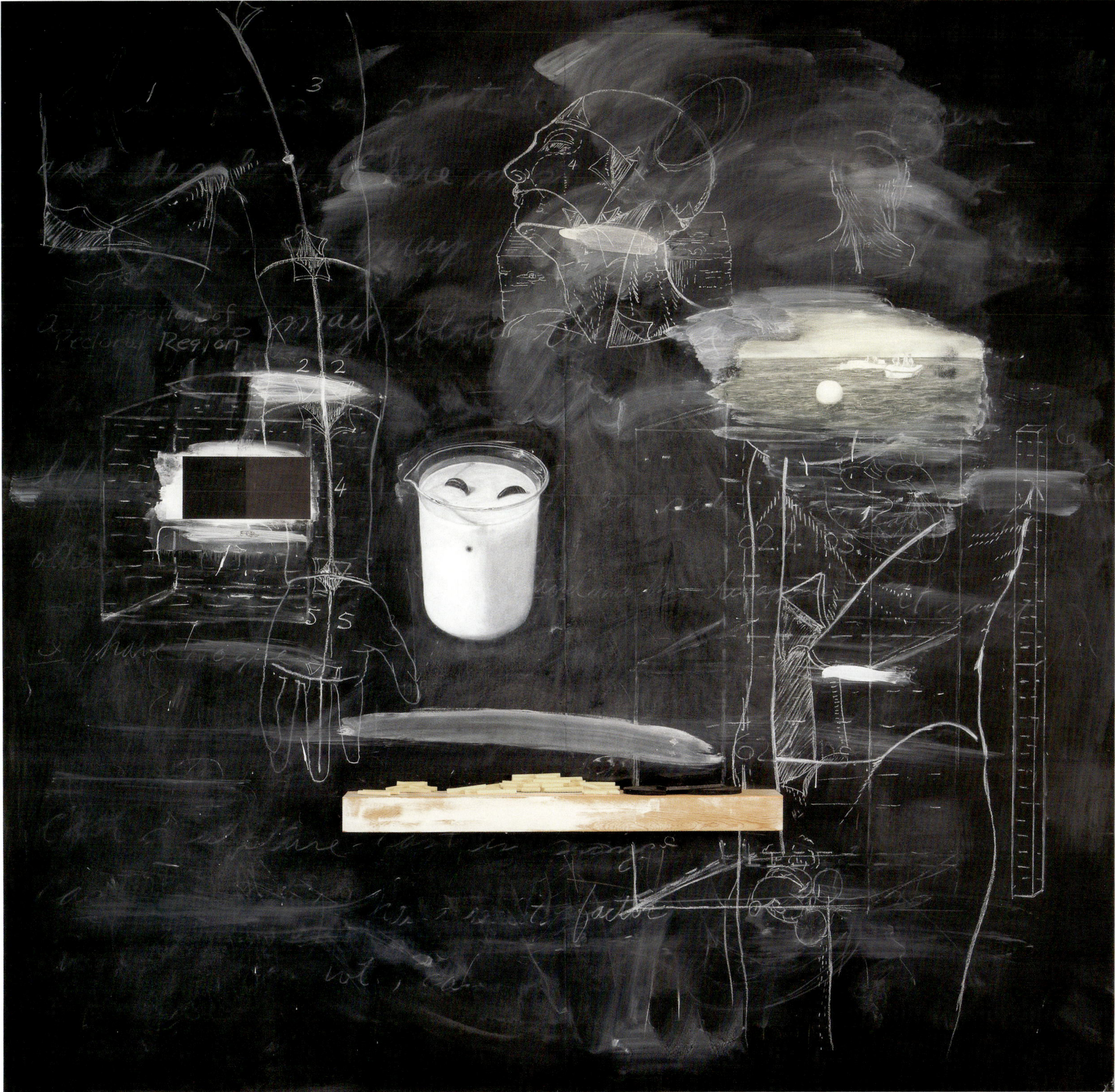

Notes

1. Available at http://en.wikipedia.org/wiki/Harry_Houdini [June 11, 2005].
2. Valerie Loupe Olsen, *Vernon Fisher's File 00* (Houston: The Glassell School of Art of the Museum of Fine Arts, Houston, 2000), 11.
3. Susan Freudenheim, exhibition review, *Art in America* 71 (March 1983): 165.
4. Emily T. Robinson, in a discussion of Fisher's *Basutoland* (1989), in the collection of the Art Museum, Arizona State University, available at asuartmuseums.asu.edu/collections/contemporary/fisher1.htm [June 11, 2005].

42.

Evidence of Houdini's Return, 1994

Oil, blackboard slating, wood, and mixed media
93 × 93 × 10 in. (236.2 × 236.2 × 25.4 cm)
Purchase through the Michener Acquisitions Fund and with support from Linda Pace
2001.94

Provenance: Hiram Butler Gallery, Houston; Milagros Contemporary Art, San Antonio; Linda Pace, San Antonio; Finesilver Gallery, San Antonio; Purchased from Finesilver Gallery, 2001

Helen Frankenthaler

b. New York, 1928

w. Bennington, Vermont, 1945–1949; New York–Provincetown, Massachusetts, 1949–1969; New York, 1969–1974; New York–Stamford, Connecticut (frequent trips to Europe), 1974–present

We can see why Helen Frankenthaler entitled this particular painting *Over the Circle* (1961, plate 43): an expansive black form, a large, fiery orange form, and smaller yellow forms hover—leap, even—over a sizeable circle drawn in one stroke with thinned black paint. Not every abstract painting bears such a demonstrable relationship to its title. Perhaps more so than the title, however, the painting itself is revelatory, insofar as it recounts the tale (or records the process) of its own making. In 1952 Frankenthaler developed an approach that entailed staining the canvas with paint as it lay on the floor. While she was painting, she would often step into, onto, and around the canvas. The circle near the bottom edge of *Over the Circle* marks the spot where Frankenthaler positioned herself as she created the work, and it is in this same circle that she chose to place her signature.

Frankenthaler's staining technique promotes fluidity and other distinctive painterly effects. For some parts of *Over the Circle,* the artist applied and manipulated thinned paint with a brush, allowing it to splatter in the process. In the orange and black areas, she poured paint onto the canvas, where it seeped into the receptive surface of the support. The subtle halos around the black and orange forms, through which the canvas's texture remains visible, are the result of fibers wicking away the wet paint. Critics often invoke organic metaphors when describing Frankenthaler's paintings and the process used to create them. For instance, if we think of the surface of *Over the Circle* as skin, the artist has effectively tattooed it with forms of lyrical beauty. While these loose, stained forms are typical of her work, *Over the Circle* departs from Frankenthaler's later paintings in that large portions of the support remain exposed. Sections of raw canvas interact and contrast with areas of color, creating interplay between positive and negative zones.

Frankenthaler's training as a painter began as a teenager, when she studied with noted Mexican artist Rufino Tamayo at the Dalton School in New York. She then attended Bennington College in Vermont, where she studied with Paul Feeley. After graduating in 1949, she returned to New York and continued her training at the Art Students League. The year 1950 was an especially momentous one for Frankenthaler. That summer she began studying with Hans Hofmann, the celebrated abstract painter and teacher, in Provincetown, Massachusetts. In the fall she saw Jackson Pollock's landmark show of drip paintings at the Betty Parsons Gallery, in New York, and befriended the influential art critic Clement Greenberg—two events that would prove of crucial importance to the development of her art and career.

Frankenthaler developed her signature stain technique, as is often noted, by both borrowing and departing from Pollock's drip method. A 1952 painting entitled *Mountains and Sea* remains a pivotal work because it is the first one she created using the staining process. Here she controlled the play of paint not only through her manner of application, but by lifting and pulling the edges of the canvas. This innovative approach, also evinced nine years later in *Over the Circle,* had a significant impact on other artists. Greenberg credited a visit to Frankenthaler's studio, for instance, as the cause of Morris Louis's abrupt adoption of pouring and staining.[1]

Frankenthaler emerged into an art scene populated by some of the most celebrated painters of the twentieth century: Pollock, Willem de Kooning, Adolph Gottlieb, Lee Krasner, Robert Motherwell (to whom Frankenthaler was married from 1958 to 1971), and Barnett Newman, to name but a few. She was one of the only women associated with the so-called "second generation" of Abstract Expressionist painters, prompting scholars and critics to compare her work to that of her female contemporaries, Joan Mitchell and Grace Hartigan (a comparison that Frankenthaler neither denied nor embraced).[2] This comparison thins when the criterion is technique, and some critics in the 1950s and 1960s noted the differences between the three artists, not the similarities.[3] Frankenthaler prefers that her work be appreciated for itself, neither because of nor despite the fact that she is a woman. To this day, she continues to pursue her own painterly and lyrical artistic aesthetic, as she has done since the beginning of her long and distinguished career.

Justine Price

Notes

1. Clement Greenberg, "Louis and Noland," in John O'Brian, ed., *Clement Greenberg: The Collected Essays and Criticism,* vol. 4 (Chicago: University of Chicago Press, 1993), 96. Originally published in *Art International* 4 (May 1960).
2. For examples of comparisons between Frankenthaler's paintings and those of Joan Mitchell and Grace Hartigan, see "Laurels for Lady Artists: Women Artists in Ascendance," *Life,* May 13, 1957, 74–78; "The Vocal Girls," *Time,* May 2, 1960, 74; and Jean Lipman and Cleve Gray, "The Amazing Inventiveness of Women Painters," *Cosmopolitan* 151 (October 1960): 62–66.
3. For example, see Eleanor C. Munro, "The Found Generation," *Artnews* 60 (November/December 1960): 38–39ff.

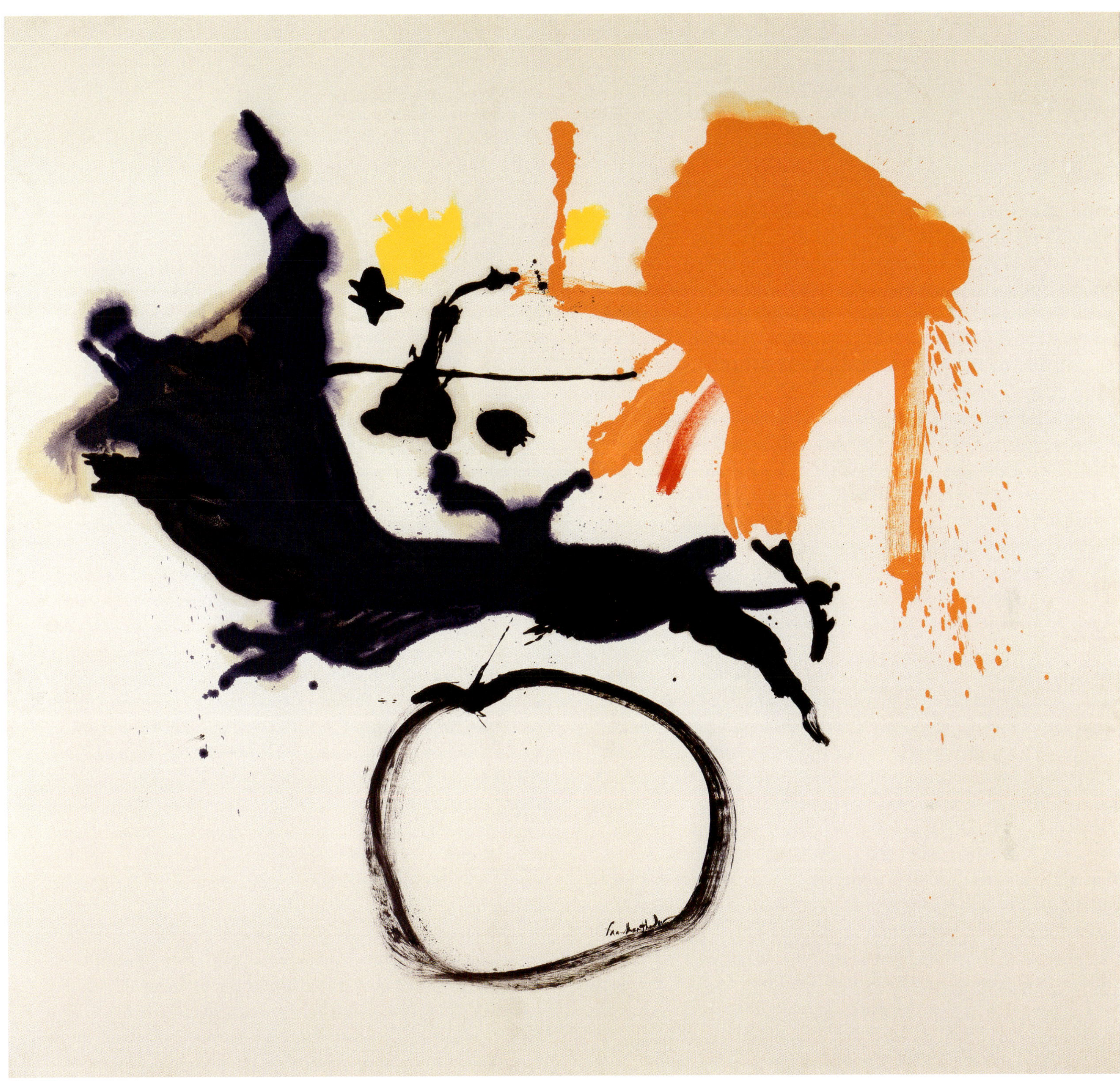

43.

Over the Circle, 1961

Oil on canvas
84 1/8 × 87 7/16 in. (213.8 × 222.1 cm)
Gift of Mari and James A. Michener
1991.213

Provenance: Purchased by James Michener from André Emmerich Gallery, New York, 1962; long-term loan to The University of Texas at Austin, 1968–1991
Signed lower center "Frankenthaler"

Ellen Gallagher

b. 1965, Providence, Rhode Island

w. Boston, 1988–1992; Skowhegan, Maine, 1993; Provincetown, Massachusetts, 1995–1997; New York, 1997–2000; New York–Rotterdam, the Netherlands, 2000–present

Ellen Gallagher's work combines extraordinary visual beauty and subtlety with a socially engaged artistic stance, using this contrast to subvert ideas about the distance between aesthetics and politics. Moreover, Gallagher interrogates accepted critical ideas about the opposition between the formal purity and sophistication of modernism and the more prosaic, issue-oriented approach of postmodernism.

Gallagher was born in Providence, Rhode Island, and attended Oberlin College in Ohio from 1982 to 1984, the School of the Museum of Fine Arts in Boston in 1992, and the Skowhegan School of Art in Maine in 1993. The artist had her first solo exhibition in 1992 at Akin Gallery in Boston, and burst onto the national art scene with her appearance at the 1995 Whitney Biennial and her exhibition the following year at Mary Boone Gallery in New York. Gallagher has traveled extensively, and currently splits her time between Rotterdam and New York.

Gallagher's work concerns in large part the fluidity of language, signs, and identities. Both formally and thematically, it oscillates between different modes and forms of expression. At first view, for instance, many of her large paintings, including the Blanton's *Untitled* (2000, plate 44), appear to be simple, spare abstractions. Gallagher's use of earthy, shallow pinks and beiges has prompted many critics to compare her work to that of Agnes Martin, an influence the artist readily acknowledges. Although *Untitled* is more purely black and white, its blockish areas of tone do bring to mind "hard-edge" abstraction and Minimalism. Upon closer approach, however, specific forms begin to appear within the painting's textilelike surface and geometric shapes. These forms turn out to be patterns of lines and dots that resolve into cartoonlike illustrations of fat, bulbous lips and a few bugged-out eyes (the latter embedded in the solid area of black paint). Images such as these, as well as the locks of curly hair that appear in many of Gallagher's other works, are derogatory shorthand for African American facial features that the artist appropriated from the imagery of black minstrel shows.

Gallagher places the pattern of faces in many of her works in a framework of lined, schoolchildren's paper. In so doing, she transforms the modernist grid from an autonomous pictorial structure into a surface upon which cultural identity is both taught and learned. The fact that in *Untitled* the paper (not lined in this case) is placed on the surface of the canvas further emphasizes this idea of the work of art as a kind of screen where the signs of race and gender are negotiated, instead of a neutral space, free of prior meaning. Gallagher has pointed to her involvement in these negotiations, saying of black minstrelsy, "I was . . . interested in the language around those images. The language as a site. It was like a real place between a body."[1] This complex statement reveals her awareness of the work of theorists like Michel Foucault, for whom language is not an objective or neutral conveyer of previous meanings, but rather the producer of meanings and thus the site of a battle for its control.

Gallagher's practice reveals the way in which apparently abstract, autonomous artistic marks are a part of this battle, especially when we compare her work to aspects of the modernist tradition to which she makes visible reference.[2] For instance, when seen at a distance, *Untitled* possesses all of the geometric elegance and formal purity of Minimalism. Minimalist painters like Frank Stella wanted their work to be free of narrative, symbolism, surface texture, and formal complexity so that it could be perceived by the viewer completely and instantly. Stella famously described this approach by saying, "What you see is what you see." In such a way, his work is the logical extension of the modernist principle of the isolation of the brushstroke as an independent, nonreferential entity.

The simple geometrical forms that comprise *Untitled* suggest a connection to this aspect of Minimalist painting, but only when viewed from a distance. Upon closer approach, they become recognizable forms that serve to undercut the non-narrative, disengaged basis of the Minimalist style and modernism in general. Gallagher reinvests individual marks with layered social content, which acts as an almost alien presence within the structure of an apparently abstract work of art. In this way, her work denies any distinction between political and nonpolitical art and implies that all mark making is always already invested with social content. Gallagher thus critiques modernism even as she appears to participate in its visual language, and her marks suggest, *contra* Stella, that what you see is never completely what you see and that even seemingly abstract, apolitical art is wrapped up in the economy of sign and identity.

This practice also places Gallagher in a complex and sometimes contradictory relationship with other aspects of the modernist artistic tradition. Her use of optical mixture for instance, ties her to a line of artists that includes Diego Velázquez, Eugène Delacroix, Claude Monet, and Georges Seurat, who also created work through the building up of small, separate strokes of paint that coalesce into recognizable forms when viewed from a certain distance. To paint in this manner, in the first place, is in part a demonstration of artistic virtuosity, which Gallagher carries off with skill in *Untitled*. This is crucial, because it undermines the long-held critical assumption that politically engaged art cannot be simultaneously beautiful and formally sophisticated and subtle.

Part of the radicality of *Untitled*, and Gallagher's work overall, is the questioning of the absolute relationship between form and meaning. The slight variations in the stereotyped facial features that comprise *Untitled*, as well as the constantly shifting and changing of signs and identities in general, suggest that racial signifiers are not fixed and given, but are instead contingent, mutable, and, by extension, available

44.

Untitled, 2000

Ink, acrylic, and graphite on paper on canvas
78 × 68 inches (198 × 173 cm)
Partial and pledged gift of Jeanne and Michael Klein
T2000.1

Provenance: Purchased at the request of the museum by Jeanne and Michael Klein from Anthony d'Offay Gallery, London, 2000

for appropriation and subversion. This process parallels the use of black face by lower-class immigrants in the twentieth century, about which Gallagher has said, "So the same language that dehumanizes, the same disembodiment—the lips and the eyes—as it becomes chaotically used by other immigrants, it can be dangerous."[3] Rather than simply accepting and recirculating cultural stereotypes and visual codes, Gallagher critiques them, while also denying the opposition between art and politics. In the process, she creates a model for artistic practice that is also, in the best sense, dangerous.

Leo Costello

Notes

1. Ellen Gallagher, "Ellen Gallagher with Peter Halley," interview by Peter Halley, *Index* (July/August 1997): 10.
2. In a number of later works, Gallagher further explored these questions by creating collages using images from black photography magazines.
3. Gallagher, 10.

Paul Georges

Portland, Oregon, 1923–Normandy, France, 2002

w. Provincetown, Massachusetts, 1947; France, 1949–1952; New York (summers in Sagaponack, Long Island, 1962–1977), 1952–1977; Sagaponack, Long Island–Waltham, Massachusetts–Pomfret, Connecticut, 1977–1984; Isigny-sur-Mer, France–New York, 1985–2002

In the 1950s and 1960s noted critics such as Frank O'Hara and Fairfield Porter placed Paul Georges among the leading modernist figurative painters of the day.[1] Georges explored a variety of genres, including allegory, landscape, self-portraits, and the nude, combining classical realist painting with a technique indebted to Abstract Expressionism.

Born in Portland, Oregon, in 1923, Georges served as an army radio operator in the Pacific during World War II. After his discharge from the military, he pursued a degree in business administration at the University of Oregon, but soon thereafter developed an interest in painting and began working with artist Jack Wilkinson. After graduating in 1947, Georges studied with noted colorist and Abstract Expressionist Hans Hofmann at his school in Provincetown, Massachusetts. There he became acquainted with fellow students Larry Rivers, Wolf Kahn, and Jane Freilicher, among other noted figurative painters. Two years later Georges moved to Paris, where he studied with Ferdinand Léger and furthered his education in European modernism by exploring various painting styles and techniques, all of which greatly influenced the development of his work. Georges was an avid student of art history as well, and he looked to such Renaissance and Baroque painters as Diego Velázquez, Pieter Brueghel the Elder, and Rembrandt van Rijn for inspiration.

Reflecting these diverse influences, Georges's paintings contain classical as well as modernist elements. On the one hand, the artist's bravura style, at once realist and painterly, is influenced by the Old Masters, while on the other it involves the (distinctly modern) manipulation of space and the subversion of one-point perspective. The latter alternately expands and flattens the picture plane, creating the visual tension or "push-pull" promoted by Hofmann. Although the figures he depicts are recognizable as such, they are in fact composites of various points of view—a technique Georges borrowed directly from Cubism. For Georges the depiction of the figure, particularly the nude, was a question of form, one that he approached with care and deliberation. As he stated,

> *Devious means are required to render her if one wants to show a nude truly. She must be free in space, she must belong to it, she must relate to it. If one thinks of her as an object all is lost, if one does not think of her as an object all is lost. There is the same contradiction in painting of this kind as there is in woman herself. If one paints the relations one does not have the essence, and if one paints the thing the essence eludes you.*[2]

In the late 1940s Georges began a series of paintings that depict himself in the studio alongside nude models, as in *Self-Portrait Standing with Seated Model* (1964–1965, plate 45). This portrait joins his work to a long tradition of depicting the artist at work in his studio, usually in the company of a model or models, a tradition reaching back to Johannes Vermeer, Gustave Courbet, and Thomas Eakins, to name only a few. The Blanton's painting belongs to a particular subcategory of that genre. Unlike Courbet's *The Painter's Studio* (1855), for instance, where the artist proposes himself as romantic and heroic, Georges portrays himself in an unidealized manner that is reminiscent of the more straightforward representations of artists in such paintings as Vermeer's *The Artist's Studio* (c. 1665–1666) and Eakins's *William Rush Carving His Allegorical Figure of the Schuylkill* (1877).

Here the artist places his stocky frame in the center of the canvas and a seated female nude at the far right. The space of the painting is oddly shallow and collapsed, which accentuates the unrealistic difference in scale between the two main figures: the model resembles a giant, while in contrast the artist (a large man in actuality) is portrayed as if he were only about five feet tall. There is little interaction between the two. The model faces the artist, but the artist gazes out of the scene in the direction of the viewer. The artist's body even sways slightly away from the nude woman, divesting the painting of any erotic tension, although the brush that Georges holds in his hand possibly signifies both masculine virility and the act of artistic creation.

While Georges and his model are the focus of the painting, other, more expressionistically rendered figures seem to emerge from the composition. A nude figure seen from the back, his or her arm stretching upward, appears to float between the two main figures; a loosely depicted torso and leg surface at the right edge of the canvas. It is possible that Georges has situated himself and his model in front of another painting, perhaps one of the artist's many large-scale political or mythological murals.

Georges's brushstrokes are varied, ranging from the long, loose ones in the background, which evoke his Abstract Expressionist roots, to the more deliberate ones that comprise the two primary figures. The impetuous brushwork in the background serves to heighten the work's sense of immediacy. This is accentuated by the artist's outward gaze, which pulls the viewer into the intimate space of his studio.

Throughout his career, Georges strove to execute canvases with an innovative combination of classical and modern techniques. That he would willfully adopt a figurative style at the height of abstraction underscores his individuality as well as his commitment to the genre. Georges fashioned a complex approach to art that synthesized aspects of concurrent trends and provided an inimitably contemporary perspective on a traditional subject, the human form.

Jennifer Jankauskas

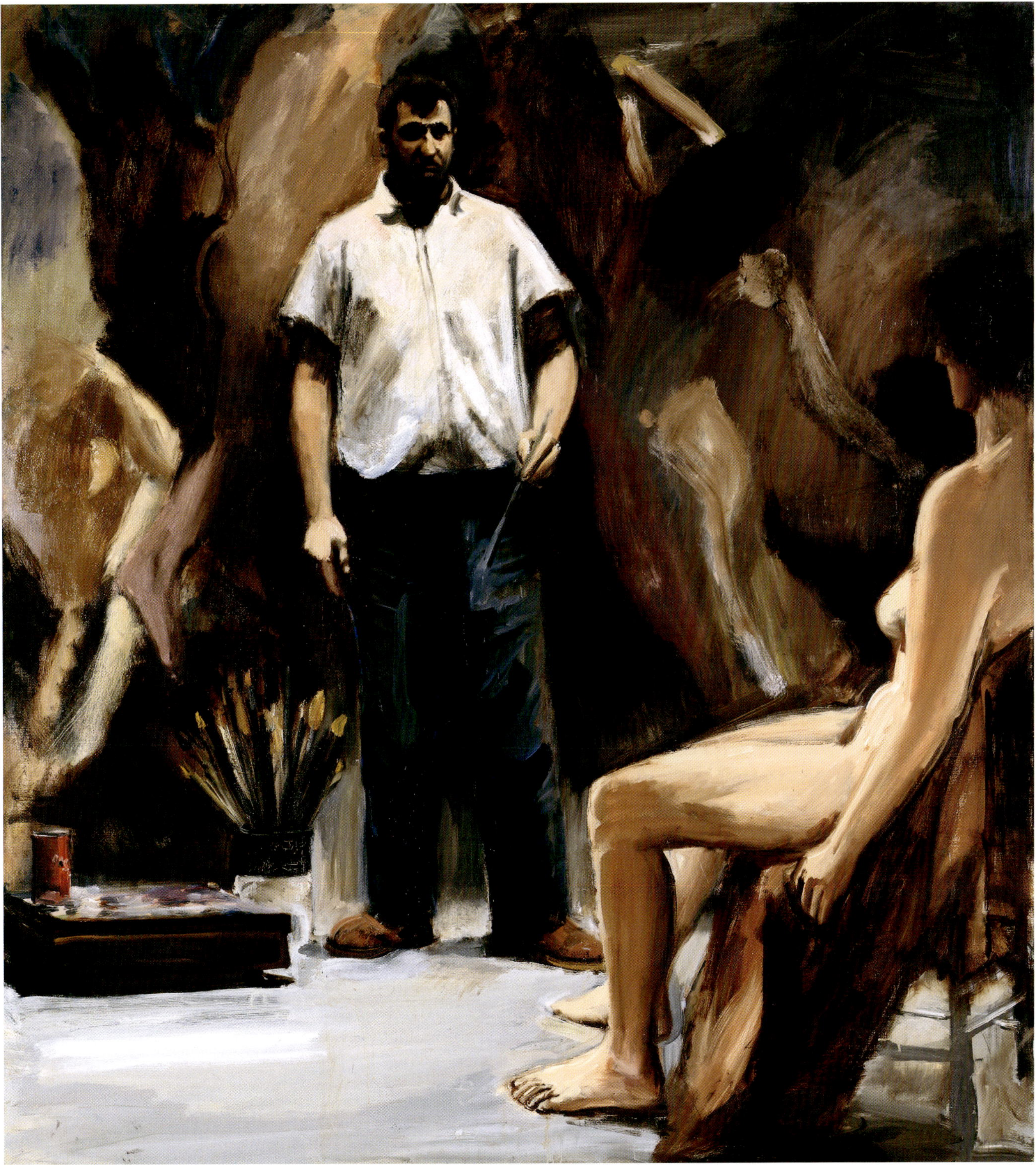

Notes

1. Frank O'Hara, "Paul Georges," *Artnews* 53 (November 1954): 61; Fairfield Porter, "Art, Georges: The Nature of the Artistic Tradition," *The Nation*, February 11, 1961, 128, reprinted in Fairfield Porter, *Art in Its Own Terms: Selected Criticism 1935–1975*, ed. Rackstraw Downes (New York: Taplinger, 1979), 130.
2. Paul Georges, "A Painter Looks at a) The Nude, b) Corot," *Artnews* 55 (November 1956): 40.

45.

Self-Portrait Standing with Seated Model, 1964–1965

Oil on canvas
82 × 72 in. (208.7 × 183 cm)
Gift of Mari and James A. Michener
1991.217

Provenance: Purchased by James Michener from Allan Frumkin Gallery, New York, 1965
Inscribed verso, upper right on stretcher bar "Georges Self Portrait"

Sam Gilliam

b. Tupelo, Mississippi, 1933
w. Louisville, Kentucky, 1952–1956, 1958–1961; Washington, D.C., 1962–present

In the late 1960s Sam Gilliam earned a place in American art history by liberating the painted canvas from the stretcher and draping it in architectural environments. He created suspended paintings by pouring paint directly onto raw canvas on the floor; he then hung the canvases from ceilings or suspended them over impromptu armatures so that gravity affected the final images (figure 9, page 410). These works defy conventional definitions of painting and emphasize the relationship between form and process.

The suspended canvases emerged out of Gilliam's involvement with Color Field painting. In 1961 Gilliam received an MA in fine arts from the University of Louisville, where he created expressionist figurative paintings. The following year he moved to Washington, D.C., and soon became part of the Washington Color School. By the time Gilliam arrived in Washington in 1962, Morris Louis had recently died and Kenneth Noland had already moved to New York, but widespread recognition of the Washington Color School was only beginning. There he met Tom Downing, Howard Mehring, and Gene Davis. Downing introduced him to the principles and techniques of color painting and converted him to abstraction.[1] Initially, Gilliam produced hard-edged paintings with flat areas of color, but by the mid-1960s he had moved to more active and gestural means of paint application: pouring, staining, splashing, tilting, folding.

Gilliam's work with suspended canvases attracted major commissions for permanent public works beginning with *Triple Variant* for the John Russell Federal Building in Atlanta in 1979. *Triple Variant* comprises three elements: a delicately stained and eccentrically perforated draped canvas wall hanging and, resting on the floor, a long aluminum beam and a large irregular rock. The need to work in more permanent wall-based formats, the constraints of specific sites, and his desire to maintain the flexibility and energy of the suspended paintings led Gilliam to experiment with media and composition. The importance of geometry became increasingly apparent in his public commissions.

Like David Smith, Gilliam believes that no essential difference exists between painting and sculpture, and he notes that his own paintings have always leaned toward sculpture.[2] He observes that his work "is based on the fact that the framework of the painting is in real space."[3] This holds true for his suspended canvases, his wall-based assemblages for public spaces, and his other art forms.

Concurrently with his monumental public commissions, Gilliam created more modestly scaled works that sometimes parallel and sometimes diverge from his larger works. In his studio work of the mid-1970s, he returned to flat canvases. Some of the stained canvases he cut up, rearranged, and collaged back together. Soon he began applying acrylic paint thickly in places, sparingly in others, and then manipulating it with a rake or broom so that the paint fell into grooves and the color settled in strata. In the late 1970s Gilliam moved to shaped canvases with increasingly complex internal structures. These evolved into his constructed paintings of the 1980s, a period when the artist created work in both two and three dimensions.

The three-dimensional Pantheon series displays a complex, irregular profile and internal patterns that carry on a dialogue with the edges of the work. The center of *Pantheon II* (1983, plate 46) is collaged out of brightly colored segments of circles and polygons of thickly impastoed canvas that evoke a patchwork quilt. It is bracketed by enamel-coated geometric shapes whose sleek, straight-edged arcs and angles contrast with the handmade character of the center. Some of the enameled forms snuggle up to the canvas; others cantilever over or project from it. The discrete areas of rough pigment and glossy enamel include solid colors, mottled monochromes, and multiple hues.

Gilliam first exhibited *Pantheon II* in his solo show *Another Kind of Jazz* at the Monique Knowlton Gallery in New York in 1985. The artist notes that jazz has inspired many abstract painters, including Stuart Davis and Piet Mondrian, who both started listening to boogie woogie before World War II. He recalls that when he first came to Washington in the early 1960s, the Color Field painters used to attend jazz concerts together.[4] Jazz informs the configuration and composition of *Pantheon II* as well as other works from the same series. The way that Gilliam keeps the profile of the series constant while altering the internal arrangements parallels the structure and improvisation of jazz. As one critic noted, "the musical connotations of this mode of working are clearly intentional."[5] Shapes, textures, and colors reappear, subtly altered, across the surface of the work, establishing internal rhymes and rhythms. Hence *Pantheon II,* like many of Gilliam's best works, maintains "a delicate balance between improvisation and structure—a sense of chaos controlled."[6]

Nancy Deffebach

Notes

1. William Wilson, "Abstractionist with Concrete Concerns," *Los Angeles Times,* December 24, 1990.
2. Sam Gilliam, "Solids and Veils," interview with Annie Gawlak, *Art Journal* 50 (spring 1991): 10–11; and Gilliam, as quoted by Wilson.
3. Gilliam, 10.
4. Chris Waddington, "Putting Paint Before Politics," *Times-Picayune* [New Orleans], October 11, 1994.
5. Eleanor Heartney, "Old Masters of Abstraction Meet the Eighties," *New Art Examiner* 12 (April 1985): 33.
6. Walter Hopps made this often-cited observation about Gilliam's work in 1976, seven years before the artist created *Pantheon II.* I repeat his words here because they epitomize the essence of Gilliam's method and style. Walter Hopps, "Introduction," in *Sam Gilliam: Paintings and Works on Paper* (Louisville, Ky.: J. B. Speed Art Museum, 1976), n.p.

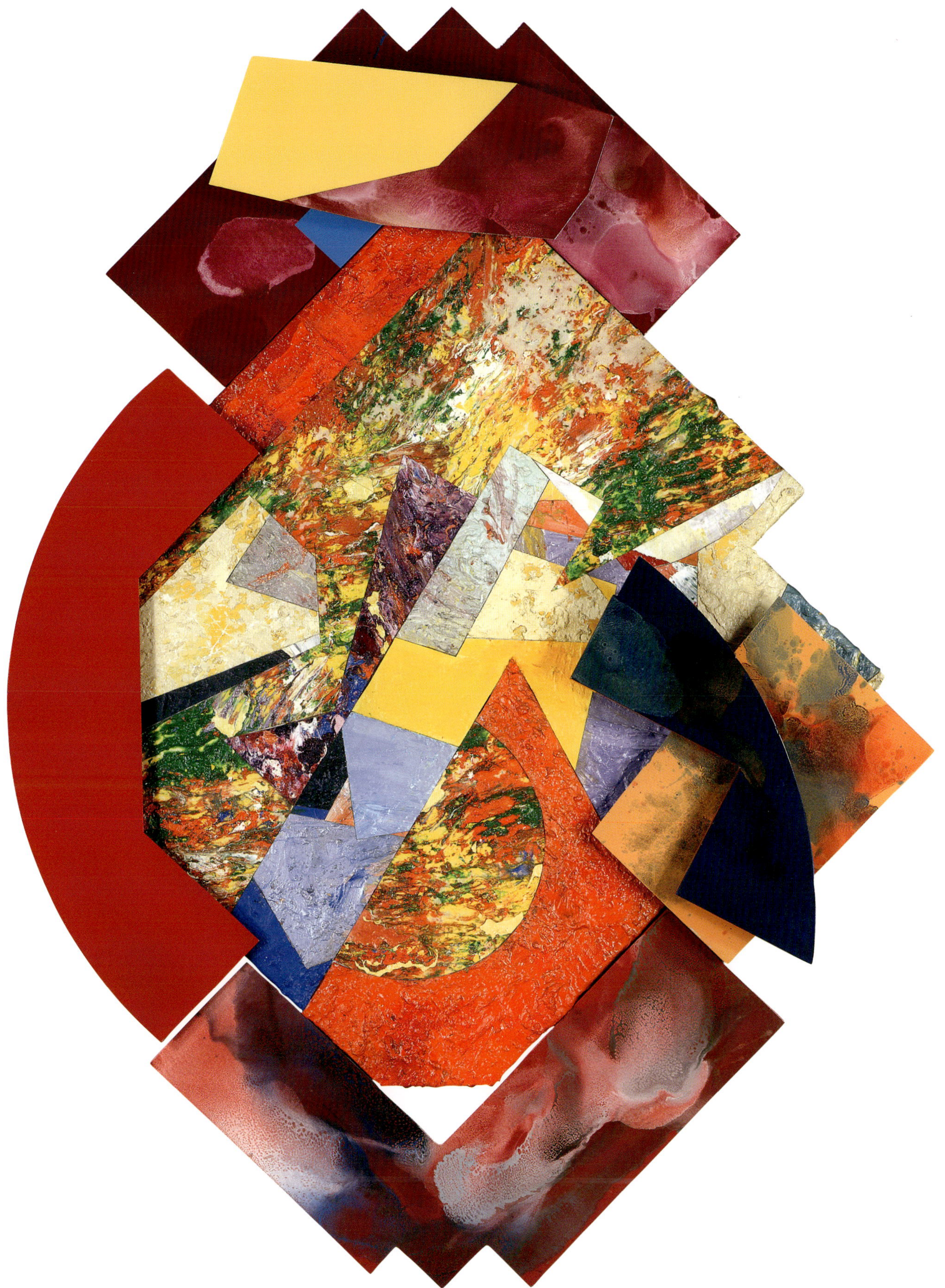

46.

Pantheon II, 1983

Acrylic on canvas and polyurethane enamel on aluminum
77 × 44 × 6 in. (195.6 × 111.8 × 15.2 cm)
Archer M. Huntington Museum Fund
1985.35

Provenance: Purchased from Monique Knowlton Gallery, New York, 1985

Michael Goldberg

b. New York, 1924

w. New York, 1940–1980; New York–Siena, Italy, 1980–present

Often designated a second-generation Abstract Expressionist, Michael Goldberg attained artistic maturity at a time when Abstract Expressionists such as Willem de Kooning and Jackson Pollock were transforming the artistic landscape, making New York the major art capital of the world, and paving the way for younger artists to experiment with abstraction. In an environment rich with creative activity and intellectual discourse, Goldberg emerged as a committed abstract painter, gaining recognition for the vigorous physicality of his brushwork.

Goldberg began studying art at Hans Hofmann's influential School of Fine Arts when he was seventeen. He recalled that "the professionalism there and the contact it afforded with the European avant-garde gave one the feeling that everybody was accessible."[1] The advent of World War II put his artistic instruction on hold. After serving as a first sergeant in North Africa and Burma, he was discharged in 1946, and in 1948 he resumed his studies with Hofmann.[2] Though appreciative of Hofmann's tutelage, Goldberg credits de Kooning as one of his greatest sources of inspiration: "The biggest visual influence I had besides Kandinsky was de Kooning. . . . De Kooning offered a way to use Cubism and fuse it with a kind of expressionist content, rather Abstract Expressionist content, which to people like me was very liberating."[3]

The status of the second generation as a successful heir to the Abstract Expressionist movement was established by 1951. That year a group of first-generation artists organized a large survey of vanguard art, an exhibition that came to be known as the "Ninth Street Show." Of the sixty-one artists represented, at least thirteen were of the second generation, including Goldberg. The show attracted a great deal of attention, confirming the position of younger painters within the New York School.[4]

Two years after the "Ninth Street Show," Goldberg had his first solo exhibition at the Tibor de Nagy Gallery in New York, in September 1953. By 1956 he was living near the studios of de Kooning and Milton Resnick, and began showing with Martha Jackson, a prominent New York dealer who also represented Alfred Leslie, Sam Francis, and Joan Mitchell. Goldberg's circle of acquaintances widened to include poet Frank O'Hara, who was also a curator at The Museum of Modern Art. O'Hara wrote a poem about Goldberg's work, and their friendship led to a collaboration on a book of poetry and silk screens called *Odes* in 1960.[5]

Early in his career, Goldberg worked from a live model, experimenting with different styles and creating cubist-inspired works. In 1957, the year before creating *Split Level* (1958, plate 47) and *Dune House II* (1958, plate 48), he developed an interest in houses and facades. At this point, he ceased to create representational work and began to examine dichotomies between structure and formlessness and between two- and three-dimensionality. Influenced by Wassily Kandinsky's landscapes, Goldberg used architectural forms to examine man's relationship to nature, considering in particular how a building is physically situated in its environment.[6] *Split Level* and *Dune House II* share a few similar features—most importantly, their titles both conjure up associations with architecture, while their large scale provided Goldberg with the space to explore the notion of architectonic structure in relation to the canvas support.

A rough approximation of a square dominates the composition of *Split Level*. Inside the square, the paint, in murky shades of black, green, orange, and red, is weighty and thick. The strokes in this area are abbreviated, in contrast to the looser brushwork on the outer edges of the canvas that consist of broad swathes of white mixed with shades of gray, brown, and yellow. The manner in which the square shape rests on a flat, horizontal plane suggests a dwelling anchored to a landscape. Scale contributes to the painting's effect. Viewers, engulfed by the immensity of the painting, may feel a sense of expansiveness.

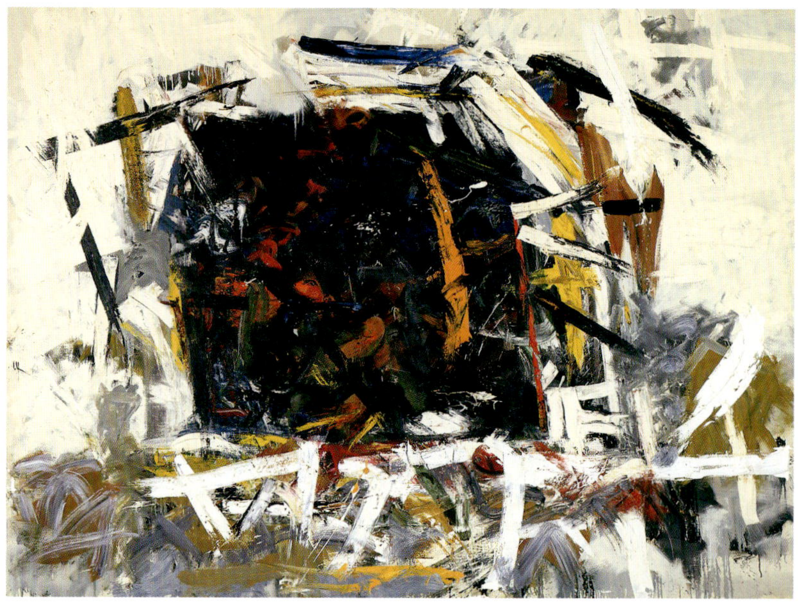

47.

Split Level, 1958

Oil on canvas

87⅛ × 115½ in. (221.4 × 268 cm)

Gift of Mari and James A. Michener

1991.221

Provenance: Purchased by James Michener from Martha Jackson Gallery, New York, 1962; long-term loan to The University of Texas at Austin, 1968–1991

Inscribed verso, upper right "Split Level 113 × 87"

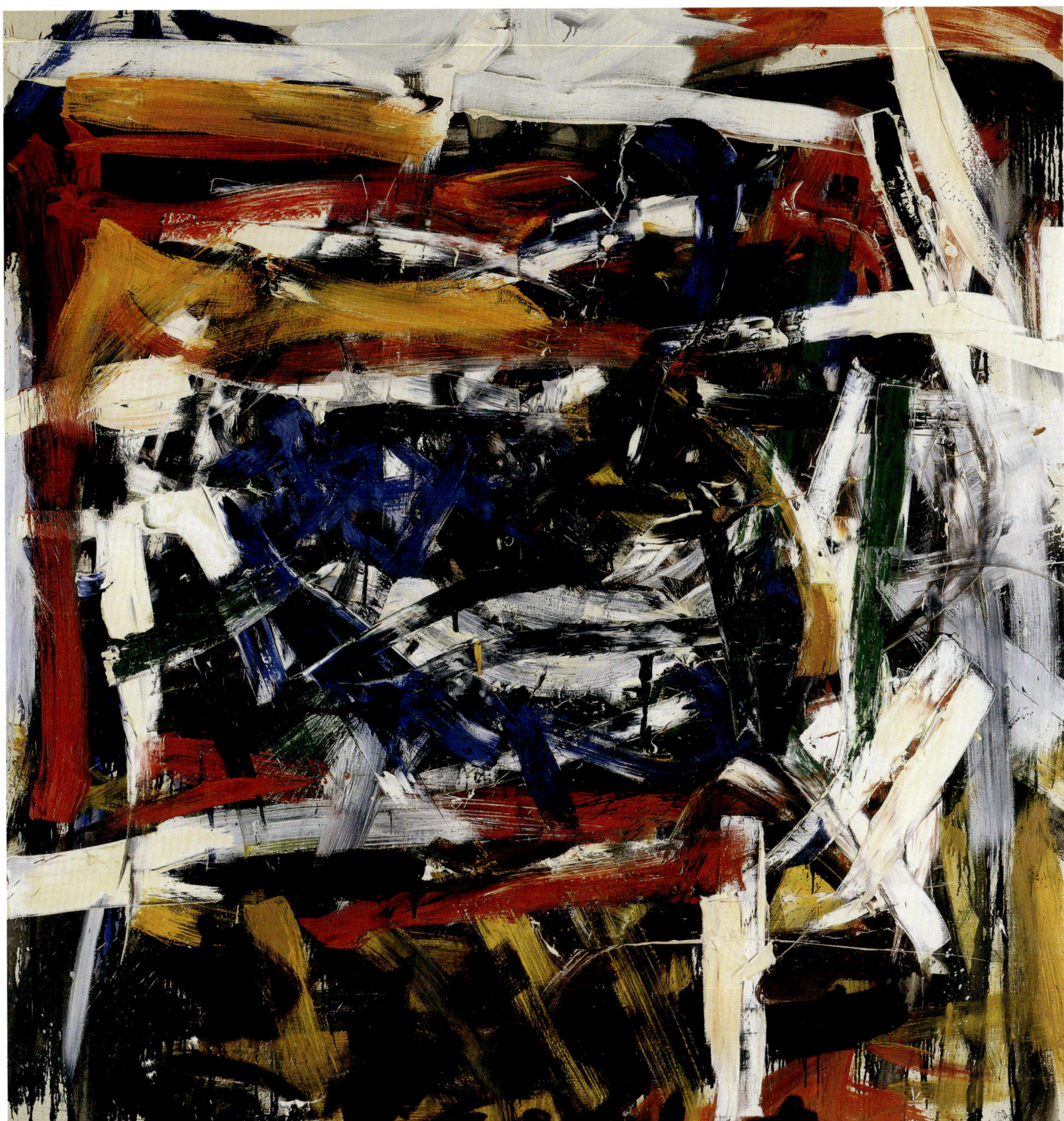

48.

Dune House II, 1958

Oil on canvas
86¾ × 80⅛ in. (220.4 × 203.5 cm)
Gift of Mari and James A. Michener
1991.220

Provenance: Purchased by James Michener from Martha Jackson Gallery, New York, 1962; long-term loan to The University of Texas at Austin, 1968–1991
Signed verso, upper right "M. Goldberg '58"

Dune House II is executed with greater gestural abandon than *Split Level*. The palette is a bold mixture of blue, black, orange, red, and green balanced by bursts of white. As in *Split Level*, the brushstrokes seem to radiate out from and rotate around a central axis, creating a dynamic centrifugal composition. *Dune House II* probably owes its turbulent atmosphere to Goldberg's technique of working "wet into wet," which involves applying additional layers of oil paint to the canvas before the others have dried. By keeping the surface of the canvas alive or pliable as he worked, Goldberg was able to mix colors on the canvas, allowing him to make aesthetic decisions more instinctually.

Since the late 1950s, Goldberg has experimented with a variety of styles, creating geometrically structured paintings in metallic hues, and, more recently, employing an oil stick for calligraphic effect. Yet he remains close to his roots in the New York School. Goldberg was, and is, devoted to abstraction. "For me, the concept of abstract painting is still the primary visual challenge of our time," he said during a 2001 interview. "It might get harder and harder to make an abstract image that's believable, but I think that just makes the challenge greater."[7]

Claire Barliant

Notes

1. Stephen Westfall, "Then and Now: Six of the New York School Look Back," *Art in America* 73 (June 1985): 117.
2. Hunter Drohojowska-Philp, "A Life in the Abstract," *Los Angeles Times*, March 15, 1998.
3. Ellen Lee Klein, "All Kinds of Rational Questions: An Interview with Michael Goldberg," *Arts Magazine* 59 (February 1985): 81.
4. Klein, 259.
5. Drohojowska-Philp.
6. Drohojowska-Philp.
7. Saul Ostrow, "Interview with Michael Goldberg," in *Michael Goldberg: Over the Moon: Paintings 2000–2002* (Los Angeles: Manny Silverman Gallery, 2003), n.p.

Leon Golub

Chicago, 1922–New York, 2004

w. Chicago, 1950–1956; Italy, 1956–1957; Bloomington, Indiana, 1957–1959; Paris, 1959–1964; New York, 1964–2004

Early in his career, Leon Golub decided two things: first, that art had to be aesthetic as well as ethical in nature; second, that figurative painting was the only means by which this criterion could be met. From the 1960s on, Golub's arsenal of images—wealthy entrepreneurs, mercenaries, and victims of war, to name only a few—unwaveringly exposed the mechanisms of power and violence shaping contemporary life in a style every bit as painterly as that of the preceding generation. To create work such as this at the height of the critical hegemony of Abstract Expressionism was not without its risks. Even though the art world did not completely neglect him, Golub worked decidedly against the grain for most of his career.

In 1960 Golub painted *Seated Boxer I* (plate 49). There is little hint here of the overtly political work to come. Both sumptuous and repellent, chaotic and minutely precise, the canvas deals with art's most sanctified theme, the human body—except that what Golub has put on display is an incomplete body made up of ill-formed parts, not so much depicted as reconstituted in the canvas' heavily worked surface. The thick notches of coarse and roiled paint add up to a structure that is coherent largely on account of its juxtaposition against a light blue background. Beyond this, the eye mostly discerns featurelessness itself: a partially eroded head indissolubly bound to an athletic yet obstinately lifeless torso, truncated legs, and only one arm, half-formed. The sitting figure pushes close to the edge of the canvas and is delimited by it. Indeed, the space of the painting is so dense, the framing so forced, that one automatically takes a step back before moving closer.

Born in Chicago in 1922, Golub enrolled at the Art Institute of Chicago in 1946, four years after acquiring his undergraduate degree in art history at the University of Chicago. While attending the Institute, Golub played a decisive role in the formation of the annual *Momentum* exhibitions of the late 1940s and early 1950s. These were student-led shows that attracted a number of significant figures from New York as attendees and jurors, including Jackson Pollock, Clement Greenberg, Betty Parsons, and Ad Reinhardt. Throughout the 1950s Golub's paintings unfolded into groups of thematically related works—figures of priests, shamans, and sphinxes dominate. In 1954 the artist was selected for the prestigious *Young American Painters* exhibition at the Guggenheim Museum, and he had his first solo show at New York's Artists Gallery that same year. Then came the impetus for a change in style and subject matter that would occupy him at least through the close of the decade: with the financial backing of a private patron, Golub moved to Italy, spending the summer months of 1956 on the island of Ischia, near Naples.

In Italy Golub discovered classical sculpture and Greek tragedy. During brief trips to Naples, he roamed the large collection of Greek and Roman sculpture at the city's museum. "What the museum had mostly . . . were these late Roman sculptures and plaster casts," Golub recalled. "Now, you might say they were ugly and gross. There was no technique, no refinement. Proportions all out of whack. They were grotesque . . . but in a way grand."[1] The first work to come from this experience was *Orestes* (1956), a nearly full-length figure based loosely on the sculptural fragments Golub saw in Naples and Florence. As the paintings from this period multiplied, Golub's handling became looser, the traces of making and the implications of violence—physical as well as mental—more apparent. After a brief stint at Indiana University following his return home a year later, Golub moved to Paris in the ultimately futile hope of forging a network of gallery connections. It was there that he painted *Seated Boxer I*.

Based on a photograph of a Roman copy of a Hellenistic bronze sculpture of a boxer, Golub's painting is concerned less with fidelity to the source than with providing a psychic equivalent of its crumbling state. "It seems to me that some of the most beautiful things that exist are just pieces of things," Golub stated in a 1968 interview. "When you come across a Greek fragment, it's very beautiful because this thing still has traces of its original perfection. It's a wonderful kind of feeling in the piece itself. I don't think I'd like it as much had I seen it in its original state. Let's say it's been hurt."[2] To find beauty in the fragmented or in the fragment itself is a quintessentially modernist trope. What is immediately striking, however, is the extent to which *Seated Boxer I* forecloses the possibility of "original perfection," instead foregrounding the absolute abjectness of the human subject.

The work's surface—it was painted flat on the floor—is almost uniformly charted. The pigment is spread around the canvas with deliberation, the colors forming strata in ways that accentuate their harsh tonalities rather than easing them. Just before moving to Italy, Golub began using a lacquer varnish called Dev-o-lac. In earlier works, he physically damaged his canvases by slicing, burning, and tearing them, but with varnish, he realized, he could achieve many of the same effects without altering the support. *Seated Boxer I* consists of up to ten coats of Dev-o-Lac. Golub coated it with paint solvent that he then scraped off, applied again, and scraped off again, until the painting looked as eroded and wounded as the cast on which it was based. The image is understood to be willfully and metaphorically hemmed in, cropped, cut off, attacked.

Meaning literally resides on the surface of *Seated Boxer I*, where the threat of a loss of wholeness is made physically manifest, a sign of the wider disruption of connection and empathy universally lamented in the twentieth century. As Golub makes clear through his choice of subject matter, this is a fragmentation that, though revealing the trauma of contemporary life, reaches back to the decadent undercurrents of classicism.

Patrick Tomlin

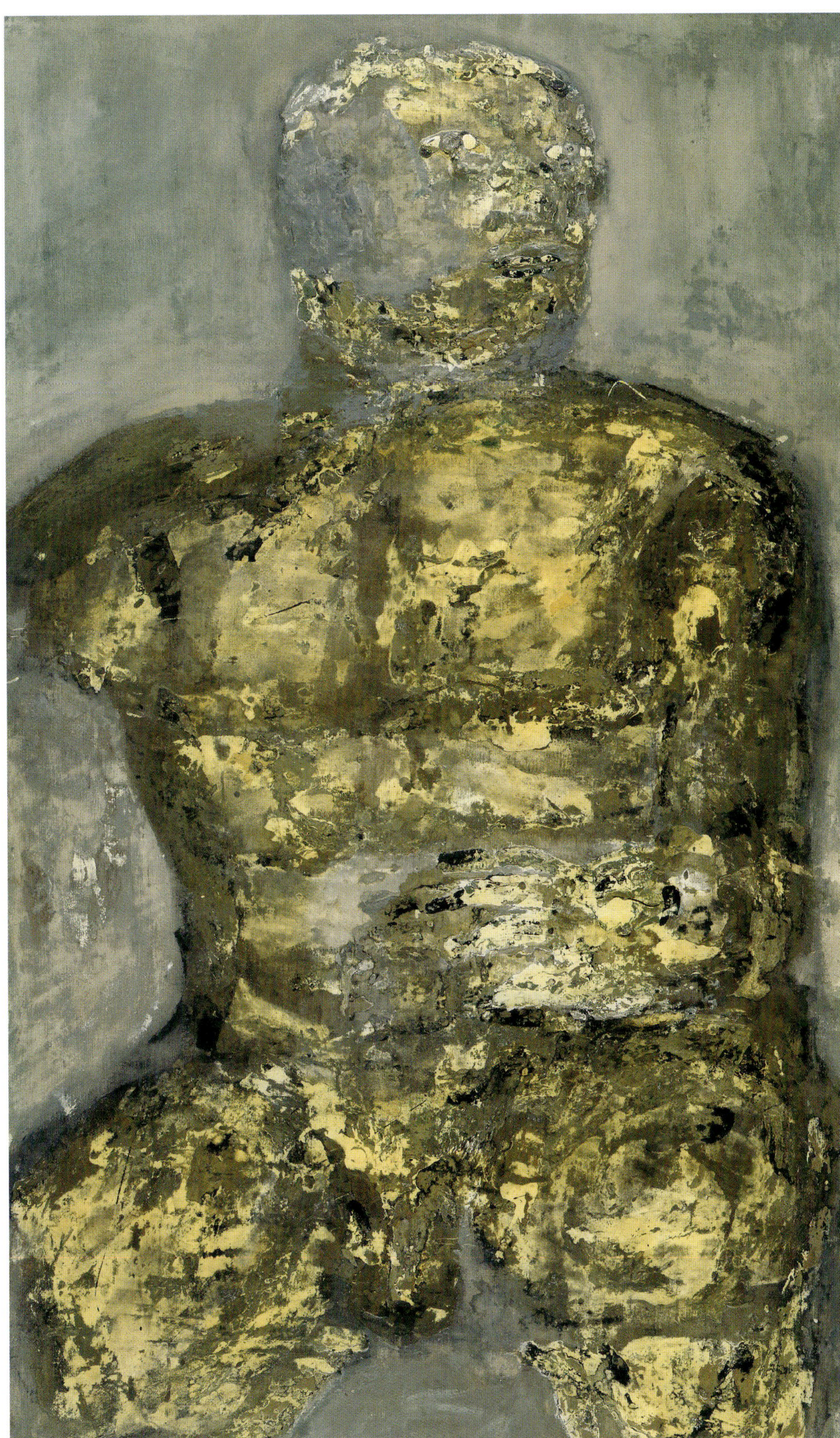

49.
Seated Boxer I, 1960

Lacquer and acrylic on canvas
82 × 48 in. (206 × 119 cm)
Gift of Mari and James A. Michener
1991.222

Provenance: Purchased by James Michener from Allan Frumkin Gallery, New York, 1965; long-term loan to The University of Texas at Austin, 1968–1991
Signed at bottom "Golub"

Notes

1. Quoted in Gerald Marzorati, "Leon Golub's Mean Streets," *Artnews* 84 (February 1985): 82.
2. Leon Golub, interview with Irving Sandler (unpublished typescript of tape recorded interview), October 28, 1968. Quoted in Ned Rifkin and Lynn Gumpert, "On Power and Vulnerability: The Art of Leon Golub," in *Golub* (New York: The New Museum of Contemporary Art, 1984), 14.

Arshile Gorky

Khorkom, Armenia (Turkey), 1904–Sherman, Connecticut, 1948
w. New York, 1925–1942; New York–Sherman, Connecticut, 1942–1948

Although scholars sometimes have disagreed about how to classify Arshile Gorky, they widely acknowledge that he was a principal figure in the New York School and that his knowledge of the European Cubist and Surrealist traditions was widely influential.[1] The events that Gorky experienced and the personal relationships he formed during his short and difficult life had a profound impact on his artistic production. The dramatic changes in his style, as seen in the two paintings in the Blanton's collection, were linked to contemporary events as well as childhood memories. The first, *Composition with Vegetables* (c. 1928, plate 50), exemplifies Gorky's early work from New York and demonstrates his interest in European modernism. The second, *The Dialogue of the Edge (Study for Dark Green)* (c. 1946, plate 51), an example of his distinctive mature style, is a late work from the period of illness and depression that preceded the artist's suicide in 1948.

Gorky, whose original name was Vosdanik Adoian, was born in Khorkom, Armenia, near Lake Van, in an area that is now part of Turkey. He experienced a turbulent youth after his father left Armenia for the United States. He grew up with his mother and sisters in the ancient towns around Lake Van until the family was forced to flee to eastern Armenia to escape Turkish persecution in 1915. His mother died of starvation shortly after they arrived in the Armenian capital, Yerevan, and the Adoian children joined their father in Watertown, Massachusetts, in 1920. The family later settled in Providence, Rhode Island, where Gorky studied art briefly before moving to New York in 1925.[2]

Gorky's move to New York was a symbolic new beginning, as he adopted his new name and committed himself fully to his artistic development.[3] Initially, European painting—especially that of Paul Cézanne, Pablo Picasso, Georges Braque, and Wassily Kandinsky—heavily influenced his work. His interest in Cézanne and Picasso is particularly clear in early still-lifes such as *Composition with Vegetables.* In *Composition,* fruits and a pitcher are set against a series of flat planes of white, red, pink, and gray and framed by the brown table and blue wall. The tilted tabletop derives from Gorky's earlier explorations of Cézanne's style, but the flat planes used to enclose the still-life stem from his interest in the Synthetic Cubism of Picasso and Braque.[4] The interplay of contrasting and harmonizing tonalities created by the assortment of rounded objects in an array of saturated hues, on the other hand, attests to an affinity for and a skillful building of color relationships that was Gorky's own.

In the succeeding years, Gorky continued to draw upon the work of other contemporary artists, notably Surrealists such as Max Ernst, Giorgio de Chirico, and Salvador Dalí, as well as sources as diverse as the Italian Renaissance painter Paolo Uccello and the Armenian illuminated manuscripts he had seen in his youth. In the 1930s, turning again to Picasso and Cubism, Gorky executed a series of family portraits inspired by Picasso's early figurative work and the more abstract compositions of Henry Moore, Ernst, and de Chirico. Later in the decade, he also experimented with biomorphic abstractions similar to those of Surrealist Joan Miró.

By the early 1940s Gorky's work acquired an increasingly melancholic tone. He seemed to return more frequently to subjects from his childhood in Armenia, and he often reminisced about how the American countryside, which he visited with his new wife, Agnes, and their daughter, Maro, reminded him of places he had been as a young boy. Gorky seemed fortified by these reminders of home, so much so that the family eventually moved to Sherman, Connecticut.[5]

In his mature paintings of the mid-1940s, Gorky introduced biomorphic forms and calligraphic lines. He also placed a strong emphasis on color, frequently incorporating subtle washes, drips, and heavy impasto while removing layers of paint and reworking the surfaces multiple times. Like many artists in the New York School, Gorky

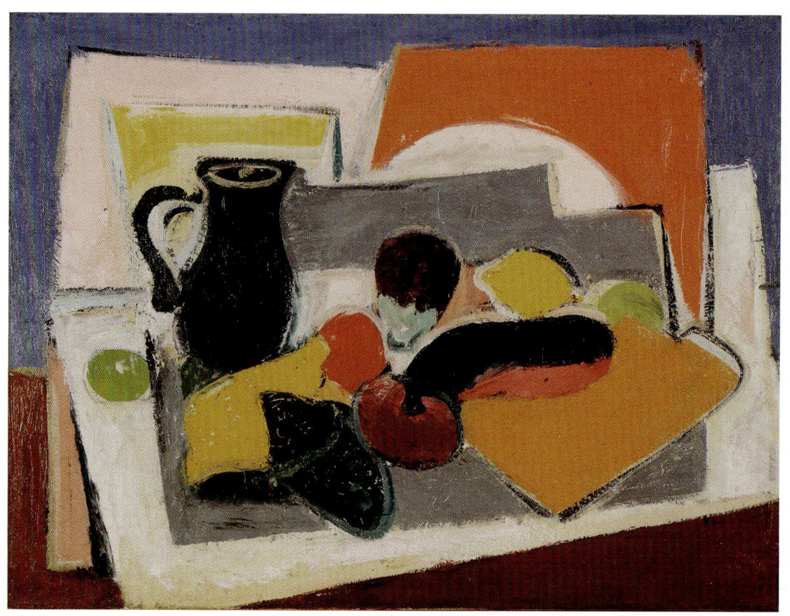

50.
Composition with Vegetables, c. 1928
Oil on canvas
28 × 36 in. (71.3 × 91.6 cm)
Gift of Albert Erskine to the Mari and James A. Michener Collection
G1974.6

Provenance: Bernard David; Collection La France Institute, Philadelphia; Miami Museum of Modern Art, Miami; Parke-Bernet Galleries, New York, 1962; Mrs. Victor Leventritt, 1962; Albert Erskine, c. 1974
Inscribed verso "1924"

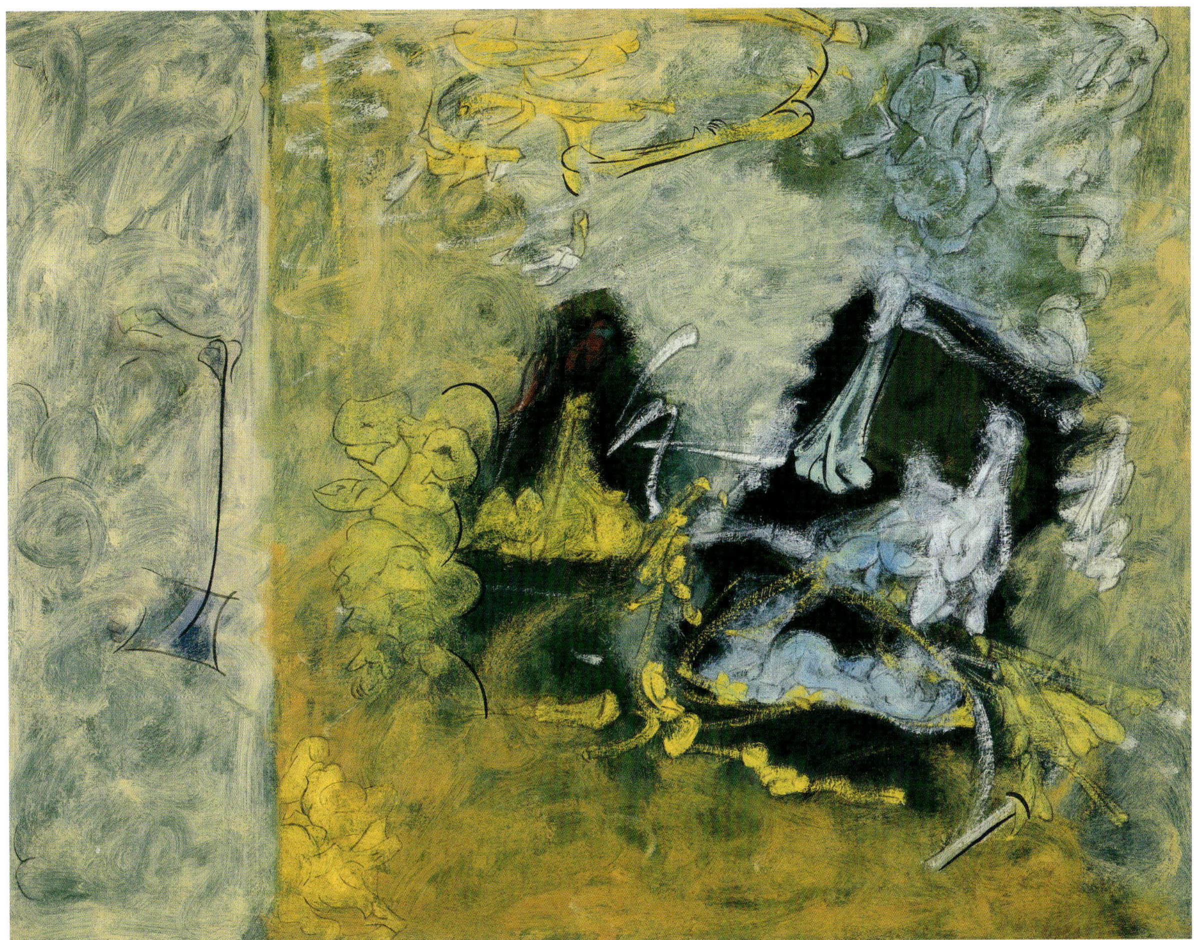

51.
The Dialogue of the Edge (Study for Dark Green), c. 1946
Oil on canvas
$32\frac{1}{8} \times 41\frac{1}{8}$ in. (81.5 x 104.4 cm)
Gift of Mari and James A. Michener
1991.223

Provenance: The estate of the artist; Paul Kantor Gallery, Beverly Hills, California; William Janss, Palm Desert, California; Sidney Janis Gallery, New York; purchased by James Michener from Parke-Bernet Galleries, New York, 1965; long-term loan to The University of Texas at Austin, 1968–1991
Inscribed verso "study for dark green ptg./ authentic Gorky ptg./ Agnes Gorky Phillips"

expressed a strong interest in Surrealism and adopted the stylistic and compositional traits of some Surrealist artists, while distancing himself from their emphasis on psychoanalysis. Gorky's Surrealist-inspired juxtapositions of disparate objects and forms located in ambiguous spaces became one of the signatures of his later career.[6] The Surrealists eagerly embraced these works, yet Gorky never truly associated himself with the movement and was even quite critical of it at times.[7]

Painted during a period of extreme personal trauma, *The Dialogue of the Edge* exemplifies Gorky's mature style. In January 1946 his studio burned, destroying virtually all his recent work, and one month later he underwent surgery for cancer. Gorky drew and painted prolifically in the succeeding months, creating some of his greatest works. *Dialogue* vividly illustrates the almost frantic lines and heavy layering of intense colors that were characteristic of this period, and several areas of the composition reveal the artist's intense scrubbing and scraping of the canvas surface. His free handling of paint and obsessive concern for the surface of the canvas tie this piece to the burgeoning Abstract Expressionist movement. The work was probably among the hundreds of drawings and studies Gorky created during the summer of 1946, which he spent in Virginia at his in-laws' farm.

The image is also one of a series of studies for *Dark Green Painting* (c. 1948), but it bears little resemblance to the final work. Gorky replaced the cool blues and pale gold of *Dialogue* with a broader palette, and the color green, which permeates the study's underpainting, became the dominant hue in the final version. In addition, the skeletal, biomorphic forms in *Dialogue,* which appear to be emerging from the viscous paint to move laboriously across the painting's multilayered surface, disappear completely in *Dark Green Painting.* Every stroke on this study seems to reflect Gorky's anxiety and uncertainty after the stresses of early 1946. *Dialogue,* like many other works completed during that difficult year, has a subdued palette, a darkly morbid or sinister tone, and a sparse composition. The final painting shares the openness of the study, but reflects the calmer atmosphere of Gorky's life in the relatively peaceful months of early 1948, before his tragic car accident and subsequent suicide later that year. The works together demonstrate the interrelation between Gorky's complex, intense emotional life and his artistic production in this incredibly important period of his brief career.

Kayaneh T. Wood

Notes

1. William Rubin, "The New York School," *Art International* 2 (March/April 1958): 25.
2. Melvin P. Lader, *Gorky* (New York: Abbeville Press, 1985), 11–13.
3. Gorky changed his name from Vosdanik Adoian in 1924. Although the inspiration for his new name is not completely clear, it seems that he took the last name from the Russian writer Maxim Gorky (a nickname from the Russian word for "bitter"). The first name is possibly an amalgam of various Armenian surnames, as well as the name Achilles. See Nouritza Matossian, *Black Angel: The Life of Arshile Gorky* (Woodstock, N.Y.: Overlook Press, 2000), 125–32.
4. Diane Waldman, *Arshile Gorky, 1904–1948: A Retrospective* (New York: Harry N. Abrams, 1981), 24.
5. Lader, 71.
6. Waldman, 29–30.
7. Waldman, 83–85.

April Gornik

b. Cleveland, 1953

w. Cleveland, 1971–1975; Halifax, Nova Scotia, 1976; New York, 1976–present

Landscape painter April Gornik works from memory and dreams, photographs and firsthand experience to create representations of nature that are eerily familiar yet intentionally unrealistic. She uses landscape to explore personal truths and to expand upon intuitive perceptions about her surroundings, both real and imagined. "Landscape," she said, "is my vocabulary for thinking about the world."[1]

Born in Cleveland, Gornik showed an early talent for drawing.[2] In 1971 she entered the Cleveland Institute of Art and eventually transferred to the Nova Scotia College of Art and Design in Halifax. At NSCAD Gornik encountered the prevalent discourses about Conceptual art, post-structuralism, feminism, and Marxism. Taught that painting was "dead," Gornik's conceptual work centered on how images respond to language and how to illustrate semiotic and structuralist texts.[3] She met her future husband, Neo-Expressionist painter Eric Fischl, while studying at NSCAD, and he encouraged Gornik in her experiments with painting. After graduating, Gornik made her first trip to Europe, where she encountered Jan Vermeer's *View of Delft* (1660–1661), a painting she credits with subconsciously influencing her understanding of the way exterior and interior spaces can function within depictions of the landscape.[4] When she returned to Halifax, Gornik embraced landscape painting, though not without some trepidation, as it contradicted much of her academic training. However, she eventually decided that the landscape genre complemented her overall artistic vision, and ever since then it has fueled all her work.

The timing of Gornik's shift to representing landscapes coincided with a growing interest in painting and the rise of Neo-Expressionism in the 1980s. After being dominated for years by Minimalism and abstraction, both figuration and painting returned to the art world with renewed force, as signaled by the Whitney Museum of American Art's exhibition *New Image Painting* of 1978. Neo-Expressionist painter Julian Schnabel had his first show with the prestigious Mary Boone Gallery in 1979, followed by painter David Salle in 1981. Fischl showed there in 1984, six years after he and Gornik had moved to New York. Gornik began having solo exhibitions in 1981 at the Edward Thorp Gallery in Soho and was subsequently invited to participate in the 1984 Venice Biennale and the 1989 Whitney Biennial.[5]

Though the zeal for Neo-Expressionism and figurative painting eventually waned, Gornik's work has remained markedly consistent since the 1980s. The artist begins each painting with an image that she considers a "cipher" for the inner workings of her unconscious, something to which she relates on a personal level. She then photographs the image, usually a landscape, and does extensive sketching from the photograph. The final work, however, can only be finished through the act of painting. "It takes painting the image to finally reach what is spiritually and psychologically compelling about it. It's painting that contains it," she said.[6] Gornik is less interested in accurately conveying the objective, topographical features of the landscapes she depicts than in portraying the emotional content she finds already latent within a particular scene. To this end, she embraces some degree of abstraction and dispenses with those artistic conventions used to suggest depth and perspectival recession.

In *Divided Sky* (1983, plate 52), a bank of ominous thunderclouds hovers over a craggy, uneven hillside and a lush green valley. The sun, which is either in the process of rising or setting, contrasts the sky's stormy intensity with a sense of regeneration and bright optimism. There are no figures in the image, lending *Divided Sky* an ambiguous scale. "The grandeur in my work, I hope, is more open-ended, more about the size of human spirit as it inhabits a place," Gornik noted. "The viewer can feel the same scale as the place itself rather than identifying with another human presence depicted in it."[7] Additionally, Gornik used loose, sketchy brushstrokes to suggest the individual elements of sky, clouds, and landscapes, reducing each part of the environment to the essentials of color and form. The physicality of the space inside the painting, its humidity, temperature, and air, are what Gornik hopes the viewer will intuit while experiencing the work.[8]

Critics have compared Gornik's paintings to those by Caspar David Friedrich, Albert Pinkham Ryder, the artists affiliated with the Hudson River School, as well as Surrealist painters Giorgio de Chirico and René Magritte. Gornik herself encourages comparison to a group of American painters called the Luminists, who were active between 1848 and 1876. Like Gornik, these painters juxtaposed nature's fleeting, stormy moods with seemingly contemplative or dreamlike moments.

Regarding each finished painting as a "momentary resolution of [her] place in the universe," Gornik strives to accomplish more than the mere depiction of nature as it appears to the eye.[9] Her paintings consistently represent the sensation of place, rather than place itself, and mine the poetic implications of natural environments, whether fictional or factual.

Laura A. Lindenberger

Notes

1. Quoted in Eleanor Heartney, "April Gornik's Stormy Weather," *Artnews* 88 (May 1989): 120.
2. Heartney, 122.
3. Heartney, 122.
4. Heartney, 122.
5. Heartney, 121.
6. April Gornik, "Conversation," interview by Dede Young, in *April Gornik: Paintings and Drawings* (New York: Hudson Hills Press, 2004), 36.
7. Gornik, 40.
8. Gornik, 40.
9. Gornik, 45.

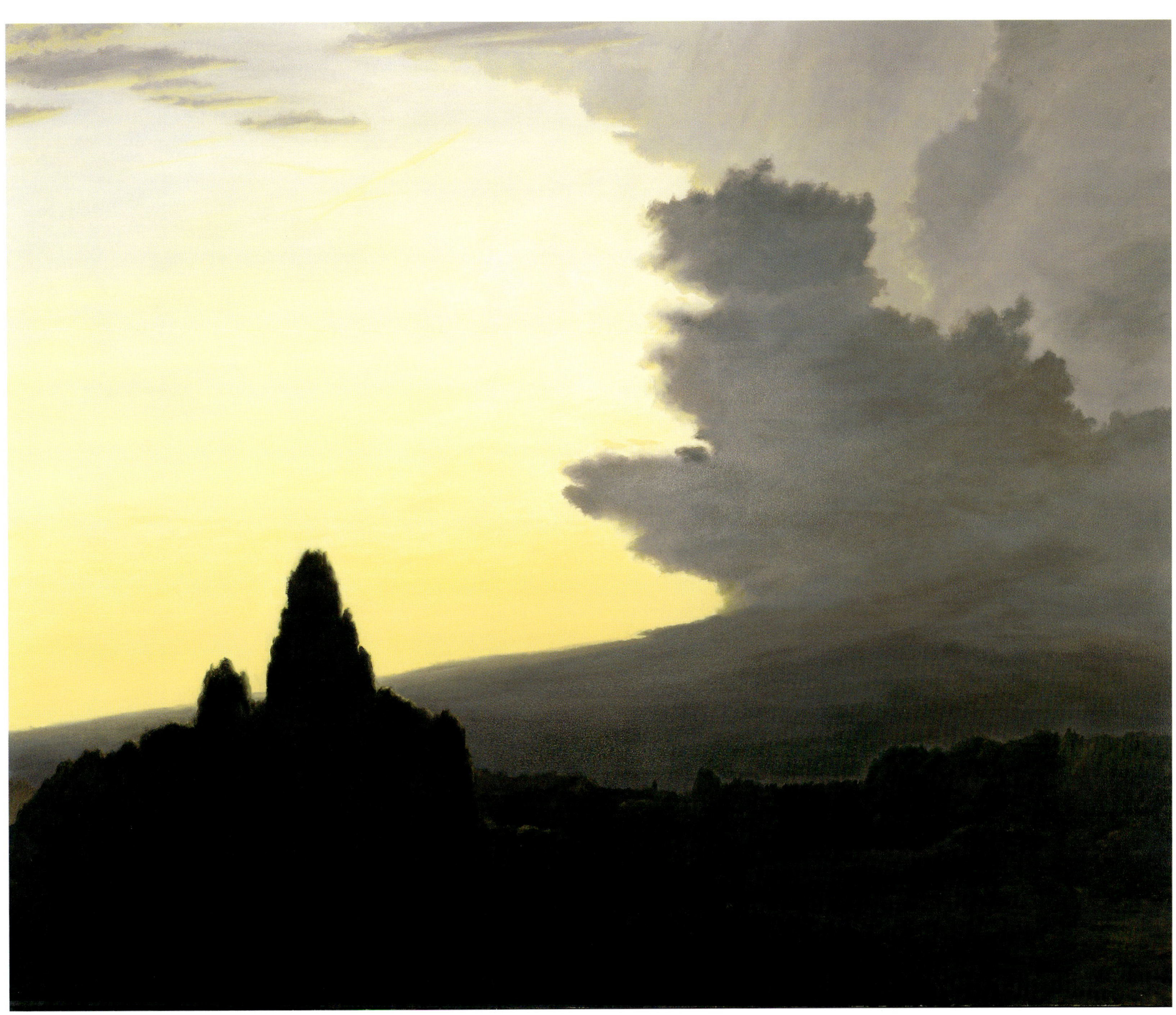

52.
Divided Sky, 1983

Oil on canvas
72 × 85 in. (183 × 215.9 cm)
Gift of Mr. and Mrs. Jack Herring
1984.48

Provenance: Purchased by Mr. and Mrs. Jack Herring for the museum from Edward Thorp Gallery, New York, 1984

Adolph Gottlieb

New York, 1903–Easthampton, New York, 1974

w. New York, 1920–1921; France–Germany, 1921–1922; New York, 1923–1937; Tucson, Arizona, 1937–1938; New York, 1939–1959; New York–Easthampton, New York, 1959–1974

As a member of the group known as the Abstract Expressionists, Adolph Gottlieb is a central figure in the history of twentieth-century American art. While creating paintings of remarkable stylistic diversity over the course of a forty-year career, Gottlieb helped to define the goals of Abstract Expressionism, giving lasting theoretical and visual form to the concerns of a generation of American artists. *Cadmium Red Above Black* (1959, plate 53) is a powerful example of a group of abstractions that he referred to as Bursts, which have become Gottlieb's most recognizable images.

Born near Tompkins Square in Manhattan in 1903 to parents who had emigrated from Hungary, Gottlieb studied art with John Sloan and Robert Henri at the Art Students League and Cooper Union. He traveled in Europe from 1921–1922, mounting his first one-person show in New York in 1930. After spending much of the next decade working for the WPA Federal Art Project and living in Arizona between 1937 and 1938, Gottlieb returned to New York in 1939. Over the next three years, his work evolved rapidly in response to the momentous events of World War II. Gottlieb, along with a number of other artists, including Mark Rothko, rejected both non-objective painting and Social Realism as empty, academic styles that lacked the metaphysical weight necessary to speak to the traumatic events of the twentieth century. These artists simultaneously came under the influence of exiled Surrealist artists such as Max Ernst, André Breton, and Matta. In Surrealist techniques, and in Sigmund Freud and Carl Jung's explorations of the dynamic subconscious, they found both a means of digging into individual and collective psychic motivations and the appropriate artistic vocabulary to express feelings of crisis.

The Abstract Expressionists were particularly attracted to ancient and prehistoric depictions of mythic themes, which they felt expressed elemental aspects of human nature that transcended cultural boundaries. Writing in 1943, Gottlieb and Rothko said, "Since art is timeless, the significant rendition of a symbol, no matter how archaic, has as full validity today as the archaic symbol had then."[1] Two years earlier Gottlieb had begun a series of paintings called Pictographs, in which he assembled images, objects, and symbols within a roughly drawn rectangular grid. Gottlieb carefully avoided assigning any specific meanings or values to these forms, allowing them to function instead as ambiguous but intense explorations of fundamental aspects of human existence: birth, death, love, sex, fear, and evil.[2]

One of Gottlieb's methods for communicating ambiguity was the establishment of dialectical relationships, both thematic and visual. A number of paintings from the late 1940s and 1950s, for instance, refer to "man" and "woman" and employ formal oppositions to explore the links between the sexes as well as their separate, distanced status.[3] Beginning in 1951 with the series he called Imaginary Landscapes, Gottlieb let this interest in dualism inform the very structure of his paintings.

As radical and distinct from his earlier paintings as they may initially appear, the Bursts, begun in 1957, have their roots in the Pictographs and Imaginary Landscapes. *Cadmium Red Above Black,* for instance, preserves the two-part format of the Imaginary Landscapes, with an ovoid red form looming over a frenetic conglomeration of black paint strokes. It also duplicates the expansive, open space of Gottlieb's earlier work, which seems to have stemmed in part from his memories of a visit to the Arizona desert in the late 1930s.[4] In the Bursts, however, Gottlieb distilled his formal means to an absolute minimum. This economy allowed him to focus on the dynamics of duality, expressed now not with symbols and metaphors, but with the contrast of strong visual elements in a large-scale format. In this way, *Cadmium Red Above Black* realizes Gottlieb and Rothko's ambition as stated in 1943: "We favor the simple expression of the complex thought. We are for the large shape because it has the impact of the unequivocal."[5] Some of the titles of the early Bursts, such as *Blast I* (1957), seem to make reference to the elemental force and terrifying power of nuclear explosions, but typically Gottlieb sought to eschew any such direct reference.[6] The communicative power of the paintings lies instead in the subtle variation of form, tone, and texture.

It is precisely this relationship between forms that is crucial to understanding the Bursts. A number of authors have described Gottlieb's juxtapositions and oppositions of forms in terms of synthesis.[7] The extraordinary quality of *Cadmium Red Above Black,* however, seems to reside more in its lack of resolution. For as much as the red and black forms are related to each other by overall size, oblong shape, and proportion to the canvas as a whole, they are markedly, stubbornly different. The red shape at top is languid, slightly transparent, and announces its presence on the flat surface of the canvas. If it can be said to imply motion, it is only a slow, oozing crawl. Although equally powerful in intensity as the red, the mass of black paint strokes below is dynamic and turbid, seemingly moving in all directions at once. The two forms, then, are not synthesized so much as they are bound by mutual difference.

Cadmium Red Above Black does not represent a complementary, harmonized vision of yin and yang but instead a dynamic, elemental tension. For Gottlieb this tension expressed the experience of modern man. "Different times," he famously wrote in 1949, "require different images. Today when our aspirations have been reduced to a desperate attempt to escape from evil, and times are out of joint, our obsessive, subterranean and pictographic images are the expression of the neurosis which is our reality."[8] The Bursts are one of the most powerful statements of that reality, monumental emblems not only to the awful sublimity of modern life, but testaments to the ambition of a generation of artists who faced it.

Leo Costello

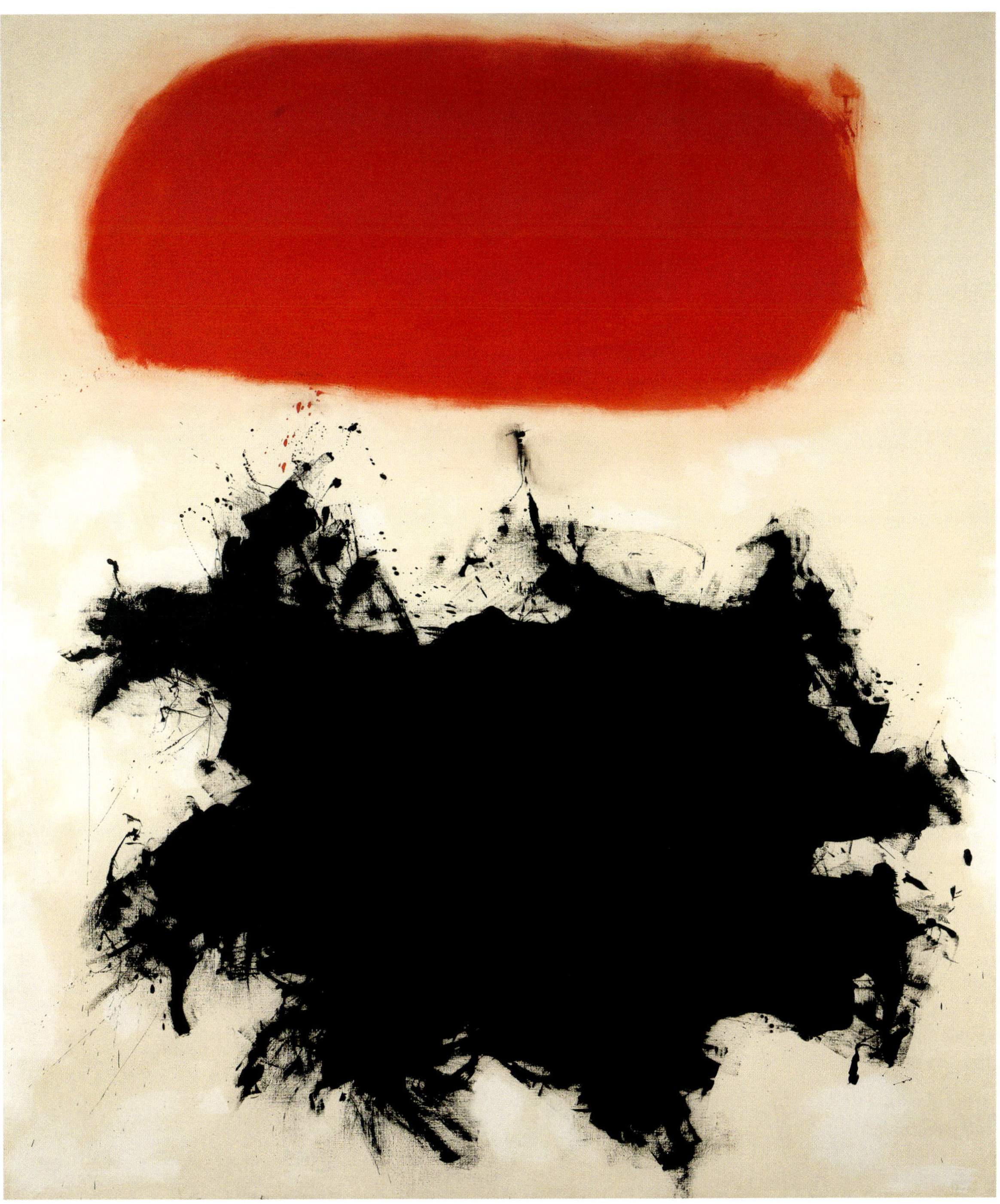

NOTES

1. Adolph Gottlieb and Mark Rothko, "Statement," *New York Times*, June 13, 1943, 9.
2. Gottlieb later explained, "And when all of these images and symbols were combined, they could not be read like a rebus. There was no connection of one to the other. And, however, by the strange juxtaposition that occurred, a new kind of significance stemmed from this juxtaposition." Quoted in Jeanne Siegel, "Adolph Gottlieb: Two Views," *Arts Magazine* 42 (February 1968): 30.
3. Mary Davis has discussed Gottlieb's frequent oppositions of different modes of expression as well as the formal styles of abstraction and Surrealism. See "The Pictographs of Adolph Gottlieb: A Synthesis of the Subjective and the Rational," *Arts Magazine* 52 (November 1977): 141–47.
4. See Joanne Stuhr, ed., *Adolph Gottlieb and the West* (Tucson, Ariz.: Tucson Museum of Art, 1999).
5. Gottlieb and Rothko, 9.
6. Harry Rand, "Adolph Gottlieb in Context," *Arts Magazine* 51 (February 1977): 129. Of the strictly nonrepresentational quality of his forms, Gottlieb once said, "I never use nature as a starting point, I never abstract from nature, I never consciously think of nature when I paint." Quoted in Martin Friedman, *Adolph Gottlieb* (Minneapolis: Walker Art Center, 1963), n.p.
7. As Friedman wrote, "Dualism is the pervasive theme of Gottlieb's art, and his painting is the eloquent resolution of conflicting forces and emotions." Friedman, n.p.
8. Adolph Gottlieb, "Ideas of Art," *The Tiger's Eye* 1 (June 1949): 52.

53.

Cadmium Red Above Black, 1959

Oil on canvas
108 1/16 × 90 1/16 in. (274.4 × 228.7 cm)
Gift of Mari and James A. Michener
1991.224

Provenance: Purchased by James Michener from Sidney Janis Gallery, New York, 1962; long-term loan to The University of Texas at Austin, 1968–1991

William Gropper

New York, 1897–1977
w. San Francisco, 1912–1913; New York (trip to Europe, 1948–1950), 1913–1977

Point of Order (1960, plate 54) by William Gropper, the noted social satirist, is typical of his politicized subject matter and depictions of establishment power over the masses. The painting is based on an autobiographical event in which the artist's left-wing tendencies landed him in a similar courtroom.

Gropper experienced injustice, prejudice, and corruption from early in life, and these conditions consistently recur as themes in his art. Born in a New York ghetto, he was confronted by the harsh reality of impoverished circumstances and began working in a sweatshop at the age of fourteen. Soon thereafter, he attended the Ferrer School, where he studied with George Bellows and Robert Henri and was exposed to their realist approach and to the school's liberal social doctrine. Gropper worked as an illustrator for the *New York Tribune, The Rebel Worker,* and *The New Masses,* among other newspapers, and became known as an "American Daumier" for his characterizations.[1] He favored depictions of the struggles of the lower and working classes against the dominant social order and found inspiration in the biting satirical images of George Grosz. Gropper's caustic social commentaries earned him a WPA mural commission in the 1930s and a Guggenheim Fellowship in 1937. During World War II, he lampooned the Axis alliance of Germany, Italy, and Japan in cartoons; after the war, he traveled to Central and Eastern Europe to experience the devastation firsthand and remained for two years.[2]

Gropper relied on certain artistic sources at different points in his career. He took inspiration from Cubism during the early 1920s but turned toward realism by the end of the decade, which linked him to the broad movement known as Social Realism. Initially cartoonish, his style gradually evolved to include richer colors and more fully realized figures and scenes. Drawing and draftsmanship played a key role in Gropper's art, often serving as the basis for his paintings and as a means for working out compositional ideas, as with *Point of Order,* which was preceded by numerous sketches.

Like many left-wing artists in the 1950s, a period of virulent anti-Communism, Gropper was subpoenaed to testify before the McCarthy hearings in 1953. He was accused of subverting the government when he mailed his personalized map of the United States (which was based on folklore and folk heroes) to American information offices abroad.[3] Gropper chose to retaliate in paint. The result was *Point of Order,* which derisively depicts dull and bloated politicians clothed in sumptuous suits that reflect their lucrative positions and entitlement. The diagonal structure of the composition, from the angle of the desks to the outstretched arm of the politician on the right, creates a sense of dynamism, while the body language of the other politicians, and by extension their rhetoric, appear weak and effectual. *Point of Order* has an antecedent in another painting titled *The Senate* (1935). Gropper had firsthand knowledge of this subject, since the journal *Vanity Fair* sent him on multiple occasions to Washington, D.C., to sketch the Senate while it was in session.[4]

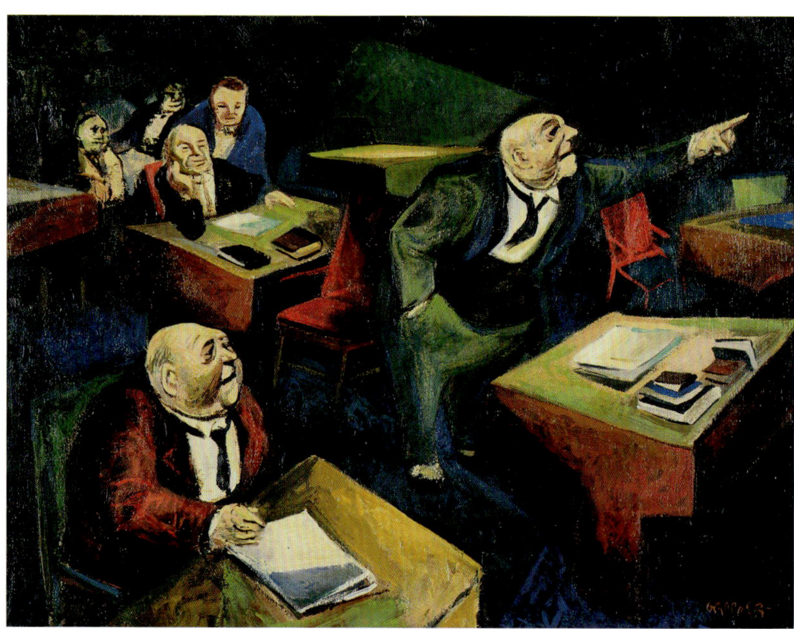

54.
Point of Order, 1960
Oil on canvas
22 1/16 × 28 1/8 in. (56.1 × 71.5 cm)
Gift of Mari and James A. Michener
1991.228

Provenance: Purchased by James Michener from ACA Galleries, New York, 1962; long-term loan to The University of Texas at Austin, 1968–1991
Signed lower right "Gropper"

Eschewing the contemporary vogue for abstraction, Gropper remained committed to depicting political and social themes, such as McCarthyism, police brutality, and the commercialization of art, well into the 1960s.

Ann Clifton

Notes

1. Frederick S. Wight, *Milestones of American Painting in Our Century* (New York: Chanticleer Press, 1949), 80.
2. Louis Lozowick, *William Gropper* (Philadelphia: Art Alliance Press, 1983), 52.
3. Lozowick, 53.
4. Lozowick, 48–49.

Philip Guston

Montreal, Canada, 1913–Woodstock, New York, 1980

w. New York, 1935–1941; Iowa City, Iowa, 1941–1945; St. Louis, 1945–1947; Europe, 1948; New York–Woodstock, New York (trips to Europe, 1960, 1970, and 1971), 1948–1980

Philip Guston is perhaps best known for his unexpected transition in the late 1960s from gestural abstraction to emphatic, cartoonlike figuration. While his paintings of the previous decades were protean and unique, they were not cutting edge but instead paralleled contemporary developments in art. Ultimately, it was his extraordinary figurative work of the late 1960s and 1970s—produced during a time when most ambitious artists considered figuration passé—that secured Guston a special niche in the history of art.

Guston was born in Montreal into a family of Russian Jewish immigrants but grew up in Los Angeles, where he befriended Jackson Pollock at the Manual Arts High School. Throughout the 1930s he painted murals under the auspices of public institutions, most importantly the WPA Federal Art Project. Guston's socially committed wall paintings, which represented such subjects as the Ku Klux Klan and labor, were inspired by his acquaintance with the Mexican muralists and, more decisively, by his intense study of the work of Pablo Picasso, Giorgio de Chirico, and Italian masters like Piero della Francesca. In the 1940s he returned to the creation of easel paintings, many of which depict children engaged in mock wars and combine the perspectival architectural rendering of Renaissance art with the flattened, compressed space of Cubism. Guston's work became increasingly abstract toward the end of the 1940s, when the paintings of his friends Pollock, Willem de Kooning, and Mark Rothko had already heralded the birth of the revolutionary New York School. In 1951 Guston began to develop his idiosyncratic version of Abstract Expressionism, using short, thick brushstrokes in an animated, lattice-like field at the center of the canvas. The delicate balance of deliberation, structure, and agitation in Guston's early abstract paintings, as well as their relatively small format, distinguish his work of this period from the larger-scale paintings of his Abstract Expressionist colleagues.

In the mid-1950s Guston's paintings began to exhibit fewer but broader and more dramatically painted brushstrokes that sometimes consolidated into semi-identifiable forms. In *The Alchemist* (1960, plate 55) condensed red, blue, and black shapes emerge from a predominantly blue and white background of gesticulatory, layered paint. As reported by his friend H. Harvard Arnason, Guston chose the title because the blue, egglike form near the upper right corner had emerged of its own accord and dominated the work "in an almost magical way."[1] The painting elicits a wealth of potential meanings, evoking perhaps the alchemist's preoccupation with the transmutation of base matter into precious, enlightening substances, or the alchemical symbolism of the egg as the self-contained primordial matter that leads to creation. Guston reflected frequently on the nature of meaningful artistic creation and reveled in the alteration of paint or "colored dirt"[2] into something profound and mysterious. He insisted that he did not preconceive an image before he began painting, instead allowing both abstract and suggestive forms to emerge during the creative process.

The tension between abstract form and incipient meaning became increasingly urgent for Guston in the second half of the 1960s. As more concrete semblances appeared in his paintings and drawings, the artist believed that he was close to tearing "the last mask" away.[3] His 1970 exhibition at the Marlborough Gallery in New York showed what was behind the mask: crude and darkly comical yet exquisitely painted Ku Klux Klan figures, ropes, empty frames, severed legs, light bulbs, clocks, books, disembodied heads, and, a few years later, floods and desolate landscapes. The juxtaposition of grotesque images as well as the formal clarity and stark outlines—reminiscent of the cartoons Guston made as a youngster and the caricatures he drew from 1950 onward—gives these works a narrative quality. Yet there is no storyline, and the elusive and fragmentary imagery evokes an incoherent string of associations, at once disturbing and intriguing.

The initial reception of Guston's new, irreverent paintings was primarily hostile: "It was as though I had left the Church; I was excommunicated for a while," Guston remembered eight years later.[4] A number of people like de Kooning and Harold Rosenberg, however, immediately recognized the importance of Guston's transition to the forgotten realm of images, understanding that the artist's breakthrough was a defiant act of freedom. And freedom was precisely what Guston had sought for many years, sensing that abstraction had backpedaled into dogma. As early as 1960 Guston wrote: "There is something ridiculous and miserly in the myth we inherit from abstract art—that painting is autonomous, pure and for itself. . . . But painting is 'impure.' We are image-makers and image-ridden."[5]

The images in Guston's paintings often are rooted in the artist's own experiences, but their implications far exceed the personal. The recurrence of ropes, for instance, is most likely related to his father's suicide in the early 1920s, and the repeated appearance of hooded figures in his work of the 1930s is undoubtedly linked to the Klansmen who were so prominent in Los Angeles around 1930. But the import of these images reaches much further. The hooded creatures in the artist's late work, even when they are depicted in the act of painting or discussing art, appear to personify nothing less than the evil that afflicts all of humanity. In 1978 Guston articulated the complexity of the hood-bearing characters, which he referred to as self-portraits:

> *In the new series of 'hoods' my attempt was really not to illustrate, to do pictures of the KKK, as I had done earlier. The idea of evil fascinated me, and rather like Isaac Babel who had joined the Cossacks [an anti-Semitic regiment of the Russian Red Army], lived with them and written stories*

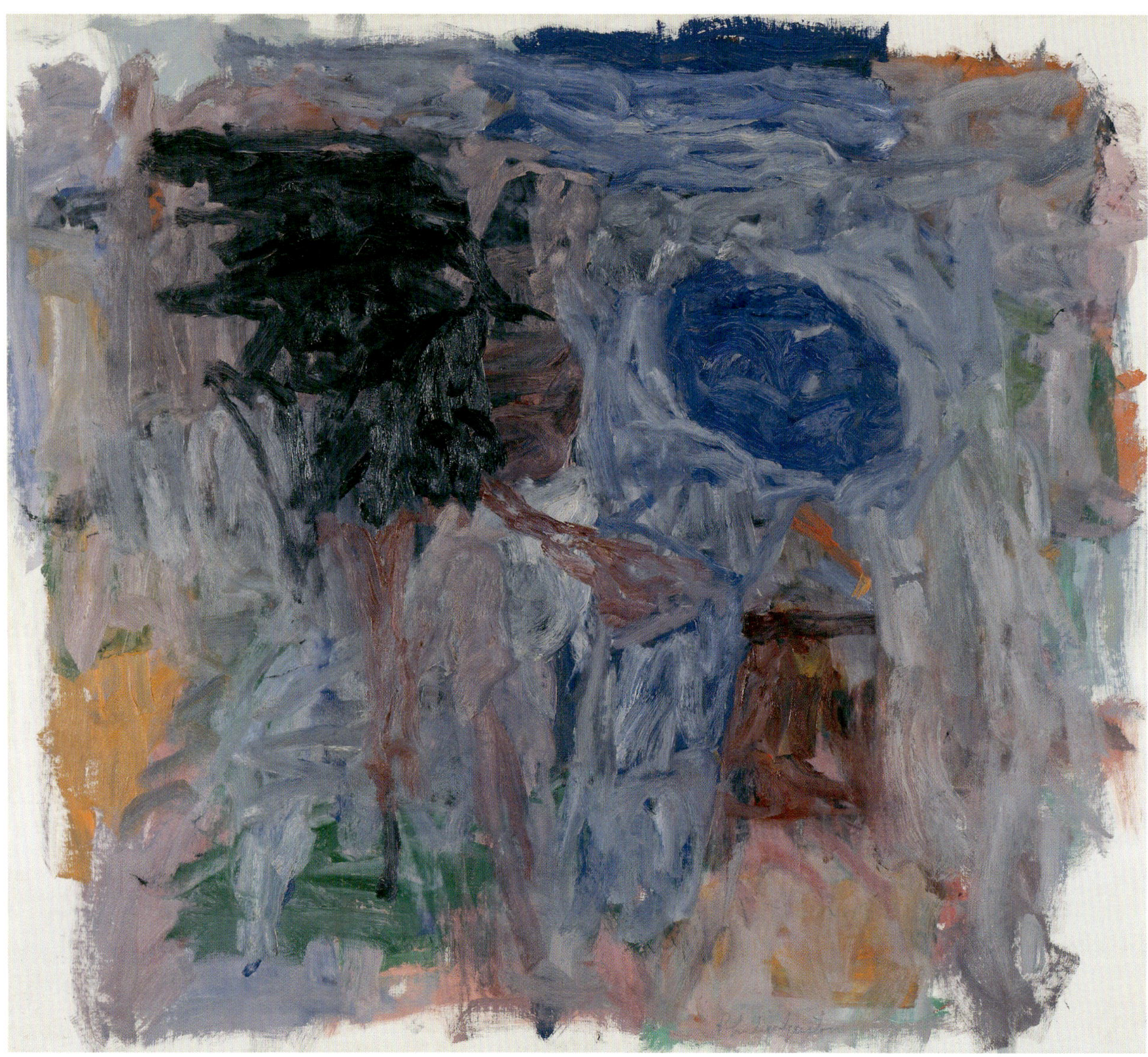

55.
The Alchemist, 1960
Oil on canvas
61 × 67 in. (155 × 171 cm)
Gift of Mari and James A. Michener
G1968.69

Provenance: Purchased by James Michener from Sidney Janis Gallery, New York, 1962
Signed lower right "Philip Guston"

> *about them, I almost tried to imagine that I was living with the Klan. What would it be like to be evil?*[6]

It was no coincidence that these provocative images began to inhabit Guston's works around 1968. As the Vietnam War and the brutally oppressed demonstrations against it escalated, the artist asked himself: "What kind of a man am I, sitting at home reading magazines, going into frustrated fury about everything—and then going into my studio to adjust a *red to a blue*?"[7] While autonomous abstraction had lost its pertinence for the artist, the anxiety-laden images in his paintings from the late 1960s and 1970s proved sufficiently powerful to embody the world's sorrows. Their bold, simple compositions, along with their humor, only increase the impact and strangeness of these works.

The paintings Guston made in the last few years of his life raise the specter of genocide and desolation most poignantly, even if the style and figures remain unmistakably witty. Dismembered legs dominate many of these works, sometimes isolated and centered, as in *Two Legs* (1976, plate 56), but more frequently tangled and piled up in red, barren landscapes that evoke the desolate settings described by T. S. Eliot, Samuel Beckett, and Franz Kafka, authors whose work Guston much admired. The meaning of the macabre leg images is, again, ambiguous, but in addition to associations such as holocaustal mass graves and the bony legs and bulging shoes found in Disney animation, they call to mind the artist's brother, who in the early 1930s died of gangrene after his legs were crushed in a car accident. An equally plausible source is the partly autobiographical story "My First Goose" by one of the artist's favorite authors, Isaac Babel. The story's Jewish narrator Liutov, after counterintuitively killing an old lady's goose to gain respect from the Cossack soldiers, goes to sleep with his new comrades, his legs "intermingled" with theirs for warmth. This story must have resonated strongly for Guston, who—relentlessly self-critical—saw no clear distinction between criminal and victim and had earlier visualized himself socializing with the very Klansmen he so detested.

The disturbing paintings from the 1970s express Guston's belief that art should enlighten the viewer by evoking doubt and suffering. To Guston the idea that the art we need most leads to discomfort was not contrary to the notion that such art is an antidote to violence and one of the very few means of surviving a disconsolate life. After Augusto Pinochet's coup of Chile in 1973, Guston wrote: "Our whole lives (since I can remember) are made up of the most extreme cruelties of holocausts. We are the witnesses of hell. When I think of the victims it is unbearable. To paint, to write, to teach in the most dedicated

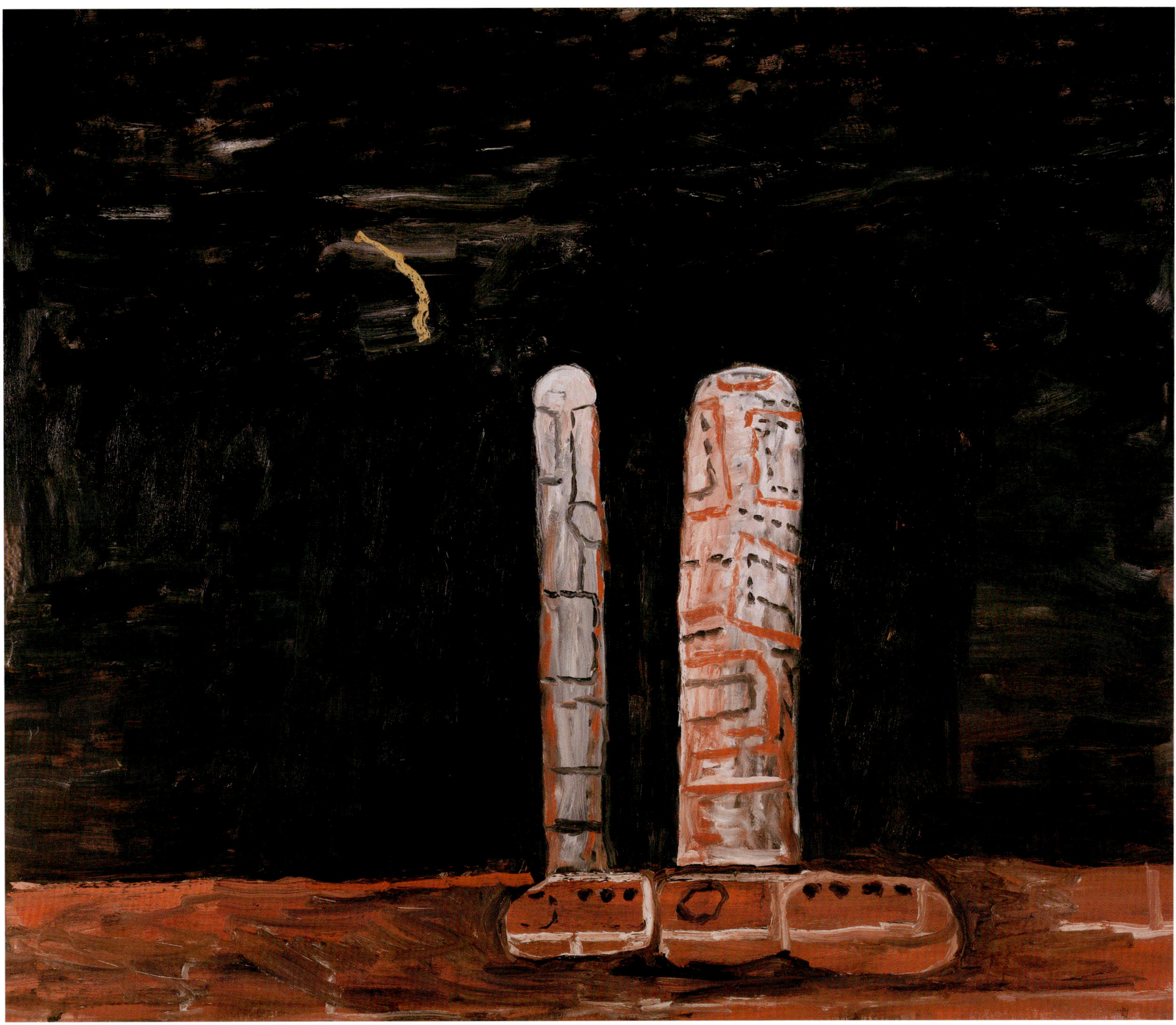

sincere way is the most intimate affirmation of creative life we possess in these despairing years."[8]

Mette Gieskes

Notes

1. H.H. Arnason, *Philip Guston* (New York: Solomon R. Guggenheim Museum, 1962), 36.
2. Quoted in Dore Ashton, *A Critical Study of Philip Guston* (Berkeley, Los Angeles, and Oxford: University of California Press, 1976), 5.
3. Ashton, 127.
4. Philip Guston, "Philip Guston Talking," in Nicholas Serota, ed., *Philip Guston: Paintings 1969–1980* (London: Whitechapel Art Gallery, 1982), 53.
5. Quoted in Michael Auping, ed., *Philip Guston Retrospective* (Fort Worth, Tex.: Modern Art Museum of Fort Worth, 2003), 37.
6. Guston, 52.
7. Quoted in Jerry Talmer, "Creation Is for Beauty Parlors," *New York Post*, April 9, 1977, 22.
8. Quoted in Ashton, 177.

56.

Two Legs, 1976

Oil on linen canvas
80 × 92 in. (203.2 × 233.8 cm)
Bequest of Musa Guston
1992.283
Signed and inscribed verso "Philip Guston, 'Two Legs' 1976, 80 × 92 inches, oil on canvas"

Trenton Doyle Hancock

b. Oklahoma City, 1974

w. Commerce, Texas, 1994–1997; Philadelphia, 1997–2000; Houston, 2000–present

Biblical is a word not often employed when describing a contemporary artist's body of work, especially an artist born in 1974. But Trenton Doyle Hancock's art is full of parables similar to those told in the Old Testament that illuminate and struggle with the essential questions of the human condition. His paintings, drawings, and fictional stories are truly larger-than-life and also full of life. They encompass history, life and death, the struggle between good and evil, love, sex, authority, divine intervention, righteousness, spirituality, and moral relativism, with some prophesy thrown in for good measure. And, in the telling of his tales, Hancock creates a visual world that is visceral as well psychological and spiritual. His invented universe serves as a system of organization, a schematic where imaginary stories and characters can play out their fates.

Raised in Paris, Texas, a small town 100 miles northeast of Dallas, Hancock began drawing at an early age and developed in nascent form some of the unique characters that now populate his paintings, drawings, and prints. Even at this early stage, his artwork had a visual richness and complexity that was informed by his experiences as an African American boy growing up in a predominantly Anglo Texas town. The artist often explains his process as one of re-creating his childhood, examining his own personal battles on the journey toward self-discovery and self-assurance. Since childhood, Hancock has collected action figures, children's toys, board games, and movies—images and tales that inform his visual lexicon.

While an undergraduate at East Texas State University (now Texas A&M University) in Commerce, Hancock studied with artists Lee Baxter Davis and Michael Miller, who nurtured his investigation into cartoon imagery and its ability to slip between high and low art. Moreover, they gave him the freedom to be the storyteller he longed to be. While attending school, he drew cartoons for the college newspaper and discovered and followed the work of nationally recognized "underground" comic artist Gary Panter who, paradoxically, also attended the same university over twenty years before.

Hancock's mythology began to emerge during this period, first through the image of Coon, a hefty, black and white striped, orb-shaped figure who often serves as an alter ego for the artist himself. Later, while in graduate school at the Tyler School of Art, the characters of Torpedo Boy, Painter, Loid, and an assortment of creatures known as the Vegans began to appear in his visual narratives, most of them set in a sumptuous yet ominous forest. By this time Coon had transformed into the universal everyman, Mound, a half-human, half-plant mutant that spawned several succeeding generations of Mounds. In Hancock's cosmology, the Mounds are sacred and therefore supernatural creatures under constant attack by those who wish to wrestle away their strength and authority. The artist identifies their primary enemies as the Vegans, who he describes as a band of vicious rebels, perhaps suggesting his disdain for self-righteous behavior. Each new work by Hancock contributes to the saga of the Mounds, portraying the birth, life, death, afterlife, and even the dream states of these misshapen yet endearing creatures. The evolving story is simultaneously grotesque, beautiful, weird, and poignant.

In *Painter and Loid Struggle for Soul Control* (2001, plate 57), Hancock depicts the moment after the demise of the first Mound, a figure the artist often refers to as The Legend, and the conflict that then takes place for possession of his soul. This battle explodes between Painter, Hancock's nurturer, who is visually signified by abstract strokes of vibrant colors, and Loid, the omniscient father figure, who is symbolized by mysterious black or white text collaged onto the canvas.

Although much of the story is prescribed by the artist, Hancock encourages viewer participation. He intentionally allows the bottom edge of the canvas to drape across the floor, creating a theatrical space in which the viewer is literally and figuratively thrust into the mythic drama. Influenced by earlier painting styles, especially Abstract Expressionism, Hancock pushes and pulls the viewer's eye across the canvas through his orchestration of images, forms, colors, collage elements, and text. Ultimately, the viewer's gaze arrives at the lower right corner of the composition, where The Legend sinks in horror, bubblegum pink mounds of meat oozing from his bulbous, striped body as his life wanes. With a large expanse of exposed canvas at the lower left, the entire painting has a haunting presence, a metaphorical double for the ethereal soul being released. This disturbing and soulful image is intended to prompt contemplation of hope, loss, despair, and even the promise of an afterlife.

Representing the true psychic culmination of The Legend's story, *Painter and Loid Struggle for Soul Control* signals the beginning of his apotheosis in Hancock's mythology. Just as the prophet Moses died before entering the promised land, so too, Hancock implies, does The Legend meets his earthly demise before fulfilling his true potential. The soul becomes the future and the promise is no longer literal, but mystical. This operatic scene between Painter, Loid, and The Legend's recently departed soul represents the epic struggle between good and evil. Balancing moral dilemmas with wit and an inspired sense of language and color, Hancock's work creates a painterly space with an intense psychological dimension.

Currently producing an artist's book to be published in winter 2006, Hancock will continue the telling of his saga in yet another format. Incorporating new visual material and text, this book will be a unique transformation of the graphic novel form in which Hancock manipulates color, pattern, and language to create new characters, develop sub-plots, and convey symbolic meaning.[1]

Sue Graze

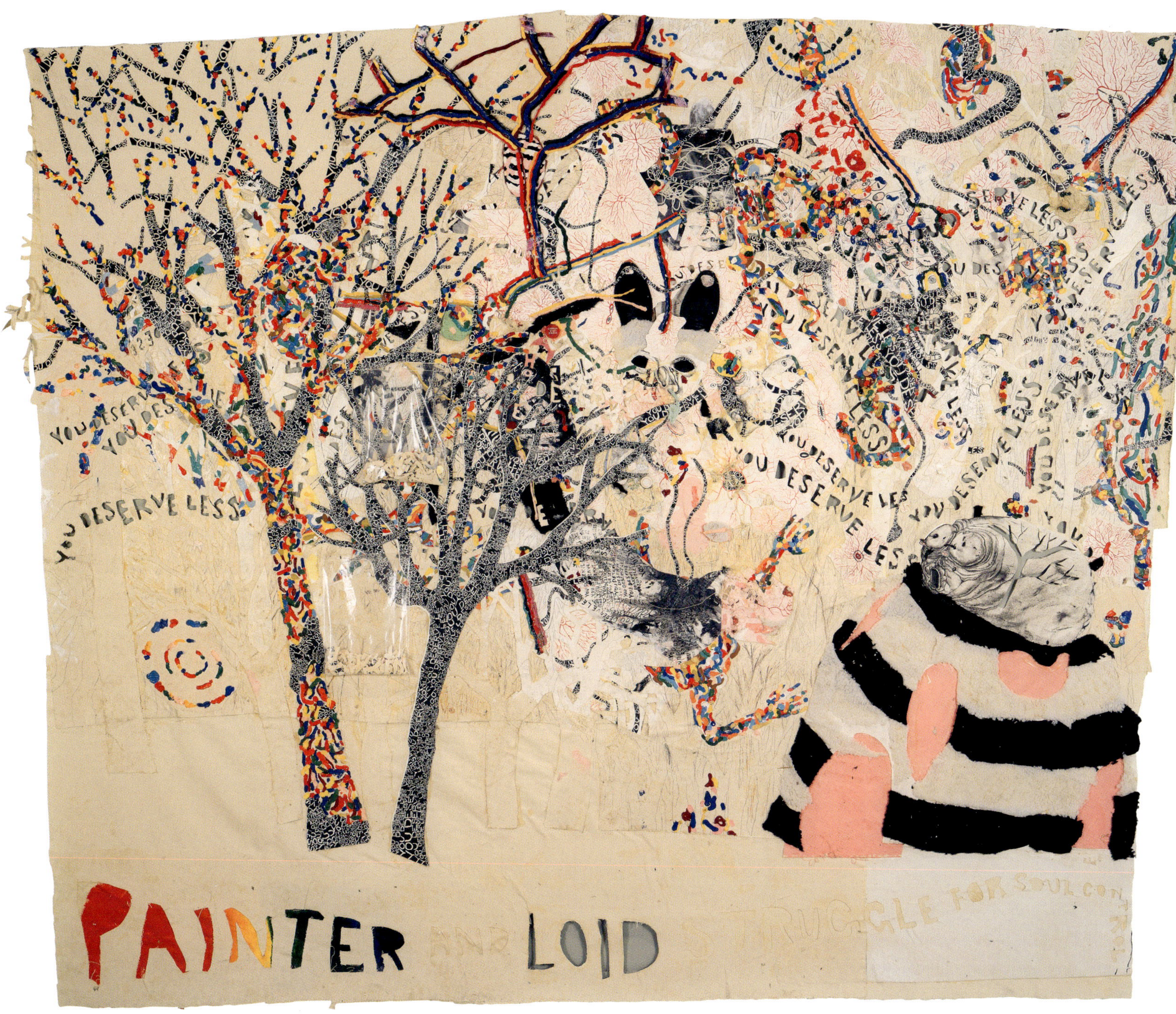

Note

1. For further information on Hancock, see Lynn M. Herbert, *Trenton Doyle Hancock: The Life and Death of #1* (Houston: Contemporary Arts Museum, 2001); Nancy Princenthal, "Trenton Doyle Hancock: Full Immersion," *Art in America* 91 (June 2003): 114–15, 143; Laura Smith, "Like a Bunny Attacking Your Jugular," *Swingset* no. 5 (2004): 41–45; and Susan Sollins, ed. *Art 21: Art in the Twenty-First Century* 2 (New York: Harry N. Abrams, 2003).

57.

Painter and Loid Struggle for Soul Control, 2001

Mixed media on canvas
102⅞ × 119⅛ in. (261.6 × 302.3 cm)
Partial and pledged gift of Jeanne and Michael Klein
T2001.3

Provenance: Purchased by Jeanne and Michael Klein for the museum at the artist's studio through James Cohan Gallery, New York, 2001

Rachel Harrison

b. New York, 1966
w. Brooklyn, New York, 1989–present

Brooklyn-based artist Rachel Harrison effects thrilling collisions between the abstract and the anthropomorphic, between sculpture, video, and photography, and between the handcrafted and the mass-produced. Harrison's works most often take the form of discrete sculptures, but occasionally they sprawl outward and sideways, occupying space like installations. Narratives and cultural references abound in these eclectic works. What links them conceptually is Harrison's fascination with the overlapping fields of visual, popular, and consumer culture in the late twentieth and early twenty-first centuries.

Harrison received her BA in fine arts from Wesleyan University, although she did not begin to create art until 1989, as she was nearing completion of her degree. That same year, she moved back to New York, where she was born and raised, and started to refine the formal and thematic vocabulary that she would employ in her work of the 1990s.

From the beginning of her career, Harrison has striven to make the act of looking exciting. Her work is full of false starts and surprises—rarely are things what they seem upon first glance. In the process of dramatizing our encounter with the art object, moreover, Harrison elicits acute self-consciousness on the part of the viewer, sensitizing her to the conditions and mechanics of spectatorship. The viewer, compelled to circumnavigate Harrison's sculptures and installations in order to see them in their entirety, and faced with completely different views and elements at any given moment, arrives at an awareness of how interpretation fluctuates depending on the position of the body relative to the work at hand and of the essential fluidity of interpretation in general.

Buddha with Wall (2004, plate 58) is exemplary in this regard. Blocking our access to (and thus, initially at least, our awareness of) a crucial component of the work is a leaning wood structure covered in cement and white and gold acrylic paint. Insistently frontal, definitely handmade, a little gaudy, and imbued with an emphatic materiality, the identity of this structure generates some uncertainty: it reads either as a wall or as a painting. The question as to why it rests on the floor remains unanswered, too, until the viewer, tempted by a tantalizing glimpse of something just on the other side, rounds the corner and encounters not only the structure's exposed bracing but a large statue of a jovial Buddha. An experience comprised of equal parts anticipation, confusion, and pleasure commences as the viewer orbits the sculpture and teases out the relationship between what appears in front and in back. Careful attention to the design on the leaning structure, for instance, reveals formal affinities with the statue that it shields: what was once merely a curved line incised into cement comes to resemble, in fact, the Buddha's round belly or his beaded necklace. And, indeed, this pattern is based on a series of drawings Harrison made, in a nod to Marcel Duchamp, titled Buddha Descending a Staircase.

Another conspicuous feature of Harrison's work is its self-consciousness with regard to previous artistic traditions. Harrison is keenly aware of the position she occupies as an artist working at the end of the twentieth century and the beginning of the twenty-first. By extension, she seems on occasion to narrate her own (art) history by acknowledging the artists whose work has informed and created the conditions of possibility for her own. Yet it is even more than this, for Harrison approaches what we might think of as her genealogy with considerable sophistication, responding to it in a singular, innovative, and dialectical fashion.

These were some of the stakes in Harrison's 2004 exhibition at Greene Naftali Gallery, which featured a group of works, *Buddha with Wall* included, that engaged such artists as Duchamp, Andy Warhol, and Cindy Sherman.[1] Duchamp, Warhol, and Sherman produced quite disparate bodies of work, but the technique of appropriation links them to one another and to Harrison. "What I get from Pop is the importance of recycling," Harrison said. "Maybe it's more Duchamp than Warhol, but it's hard to think of one without the other."[2] For her part, Harrison recycles found photographs and objects. She tends to target readymade materials that are common and mass-produced, like cans of peas or ceramic figurines. These constitute a different category (or class) of consumption from that generally understood to occur in a gallery or museum, and they are for that very reason provocative and "loaded,"[3] something that holds equally true for the statue in *Buddha with Wall*.

Salvaged by the artist from a now defunct storefront church in Brooklyn, the Buddha statue encapsulates numerous contradictions—contradictions that Harrison is more interested in activating, even exacerbating, than in resolving definitively. The primary contradiction concerns its status as an object in the world: manufactured on an assembly line, but then painted by hand, the statue signals the collapse of categorical distinctions between anonymous homogeneity and personalized intervention, and, perhaps most importantly, between consumer kitsch and objects of religious contemplation. Depending on the viewer, this statue might represent either the trivialization of spirituality or the manifestation of an authentic spiritual impulse. But what Harrison would like us to consider, I think, is that it is both at the same time. Indeed, one has only to recall the temporary altars, with their profusion of artificial flowers and plastic gods and saints, erected on the sides of roads or in the nooks and crannies of homes and restaurants to realize just how precarious the boundaries that once insulated religion from industry have become. To a large extent, commerce now facilitates faith, which is also to say that it facilitates the mobility and dispersion of faith. Propped up on a plywood base and protected by a wood structure, the Buddha in *Buddha with Wall* might be understood to occupy his own provisional shrine.[4]

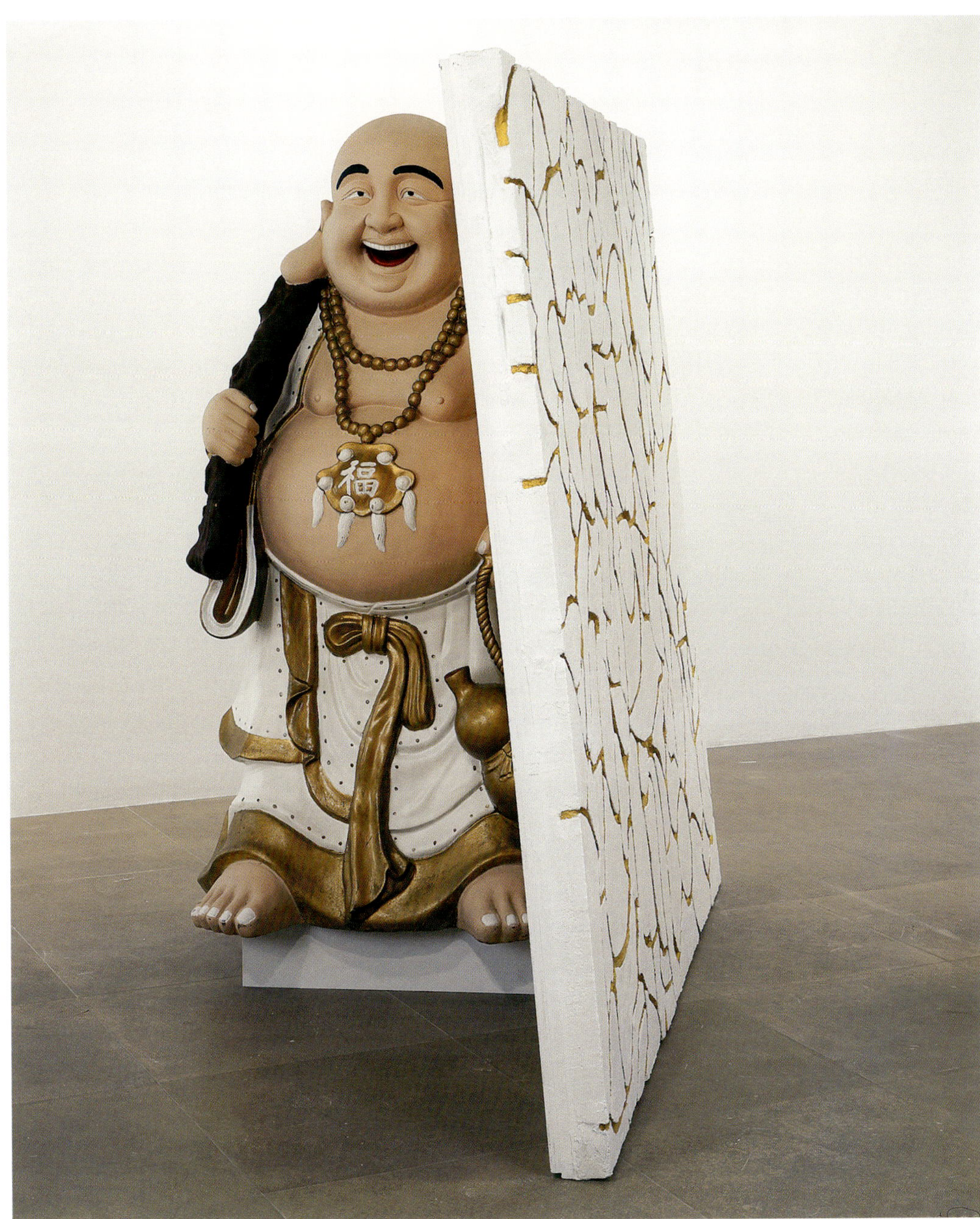

58.

Buddha with Wall, 2004

Wood, Styrofoam, white Portland cement, Parex adhesive, acrylic paint, and plastic statue on plywood base
80 x 82 x 40 in. (203.2 x 208.3 x 101.6 cm)
Partial and pledged gift of Jeanne and Michael Klein
T2005.1.1/2–2/2

Provenance: Purchased at the request of the museum by Jeanne and Michael Klein from Greene Naftali Gallery, New York, 2004

However, this shrine also alludes to the museum, insofar as museums were for centuries regarded as temples of art. Indeed, Harrison described the structure that leans against the Buddha statue as a surrogate for the museum wall and, more broadly still, for "the site of art, the system we don't look at."[5] As this comment implies, Harrison considers the museum an institution deserving of some necessary demythologizing. Many of her sculptures and installations interrogate the economic, physical, and institutional structures that support and confer value on works of art, while others deliberately parody curatorial (and commercial) methods of display, thereby "opening a zone of indistinction between displaying [themselves] and displaying things."[6]

Harrison's intent is communicated as much by the formal and structural components of her works as it is by their subject matter. For the artist, shape, color, and material themselves constitute conceptual strategies.[7] Ultimately, this is what distinguishes Harrison's sculptures and installations from conventional institutional critique—that, and the manner in which they assiduously avoid pedantry and didacticism, and wholeheartedly revel in play, ambiguity, and humor.

Kelly Baum

Notes

1. Harrison also acknowledges important affinities with artists Cady Noland and Haim Steinback.
2. Rachel Harrison, "Empire State," *Artforum* 43 (October 2004): 147.
3. Rachel Harrison, telephone conversation with the author, September 12, 2005.
4. As Harrison commented in our telephone conversation, the relationship between the statue and the wall—the manner in which the wall protects or shields the Buddha, who holds the branch of a tree in his arm—also triggers a narrative specific to the Buddhist tradition, according to which the Buddha is said to have attained enlightenment while meditating for several days underneath the Bodhi tree.
5. Rachel Harrison, email conversation with the author, September 8, 2005.
6. John Kelsey, "Rachel Harrison," *Artforum* 43 (November 2004): 225.
7. Harrison, telephone conversation with the author.

Marsden Hartley

Lewiston, Maine, 1877–Ellsworth, Maine, 1943

w. New York–Maine, 1899–1907; Boston, 1907–1909; New York, 1909–1912; Paris–Berlin, 1912–1916; New York–Taos, New Mexico–Gloucester, Massachusetts, 1917–1921; Europe, 1921–1929; traveling overseas, 1930–1937; Maine, 1937–1943

Maine native Marsden Hartley began his training as an artist at the New York School of Art in 1899. The American painter William Merritt Chase founded the school (it was known then as the Chase School) in 1896, and it quickly became the most important American art school of the time. In his early years, Hartley focused on painting the landscape of his home state, seeking divinity in nature's forms, much like Walt Whitman, whose poems he avidly read. Hartley also took inspiration from the atmospheric, dark landscapes of the late nineteenth-century visionary painter Albert Pinkham Ryder. Ryder worked in an expressive style that embodied Hartley's own desire to depict the psychology of a landscape rather than literally transcribing its form.

In his effort to create landscapes that went beyond mere representation, Hartley noted in a letter from c. 1910, "I do not sketch much these days for I work almost wholly from the imagination—making pictures entirely from this point of view using the mountains only as backgrounds for ideas. . . . I do not allow myself to work from nature much, but from my memory of it."[1] As he abandoned representation and turned inward for inspiration, Hartley found the creative process to be slow and difficult.

In 1910 Hartley joined a circle of artists known as the Stieglitz circle. Alfred Stieglitz was a progressive photographer and art dealer based in New York who became Hartley's mentor and advocate. Through Stieglitz and exhibitions held at his gallery, 291, Hartley was exposed to the art of European modernists such as Henri Matisse, Pablo Picasso, Georges Braque, and Paul Cézanne, all of whom made a lasting impression on the young artist. Hartley also enthusiastically studied Wassily Kandinsky's 1911 treatise, *On the Spiritual in Art*, which advocated personal expression rather than representation in art. Financed by Stieglitz, Hartley traveled to Europe for the first time in 1912. In Berlin the powerful and highly masculine military culture pervading the city became a major source of inspiration for him, and he quickly began incorporating aspects of this culture into a series of symbolic abstractions.

Following World War I, and in need of a stable source of income, Hartley accepted a teaching job in Taos, New Mexico, where a colony of artists was flourishing around Mabel Dodge Luhan. Although immediately awed by the dramatic southwestern landscape, Hartley was disappointed by the community of artists in Taos, describing it as "the stupidest place I ever fell into . . . a society of cheap artists from Chicago and New York."[2] Hartley became transfixed, however, by the ceremonies and costumes of the native people and the vivid topography of the red desert landscape. Unfamiliar with such vast stretches of land, he grappled with its physical monumentality in a series of pastels and small oil sketches in which he tried "copying nature as faithfully as possible."[3] Working first in a realistic manner, Hartley hoped to communicate a spiritual vision of America that he felt had been lacking in his earlier work. He believed that the spiritual depth he wished to capture could not be achieved with symbolism, and six years' devotion to abstraction left him searching for a new style. The landscapes Hartley completed while in New Mexico reflect his evolving sensibilities as he mined aspects of Cubism, abstraction, and even Expressionism.

In 1919 Hartley left New Mexico for New York. Upon his arrival, he began a group of paintings based on his numerous sketches of the New Mexico landscape and on his memories of his experiences there. These paintings accentuate the natural sculptural quality and sensuality of the mountain contours; the terrain appears as a series of modulated, overlapping forms, creating the illusion of spatial recession not found in his earlier work. Hartley's remoteness from New Mexico offered him fresh insight into its exceptional features, which he had not been able to represent when working in proximity to them. Though some authors find connections between these landscapes and Hartley's experience as a homosexual living in an unforgiving time, these particular paintings speak more of his emotional commitment to creating a new style of American painting achieved through introspection and not just from formal studies.[4]

In 1921 Hartley returned to Europe and began another group of landscapes inspired by the southwestern terrain. These he titled New Mexico Recollections. He created this extended series of highly stylized landscapes, which includes the Blanton's *New Mexico Recollection #12* (1922–1923, plate 59), over a period of more than three years. Hartley described them as "not pictures thank god—but paintings."[5] He had finally achieved the emotional and psychological depth for which he had been searching. The topography and atmosphere of the Southwest left an indelible impression on him, as manifested in the paintings' sweeping colors and solid forms that pierce the horizon.

Hartley spent much of the 1920s and 1930s visiting various places in the United States and beyond, eventually returning to Maine in 1937. At this time, he essentially abandoned landscapes in favor of figurative themes. Nonetheless, his approach to subject matter remained the same. In the Blanton's *Girl with a Kitten* (1943, not illustrated), which exemplifies Hartley's late portraits, he attempted to capture the essence of his sitter in much the same way he had sought to depict the essence of his landscapes.

Hartley was a deeply philosophical individual who enriched his paintings with an infusion of emotions and elements drawn from his personal experiences. In this way, his landscapes are never just depictions of mountains and earth: each reflects the artist's desires, fears, and needs.

Lea Cline

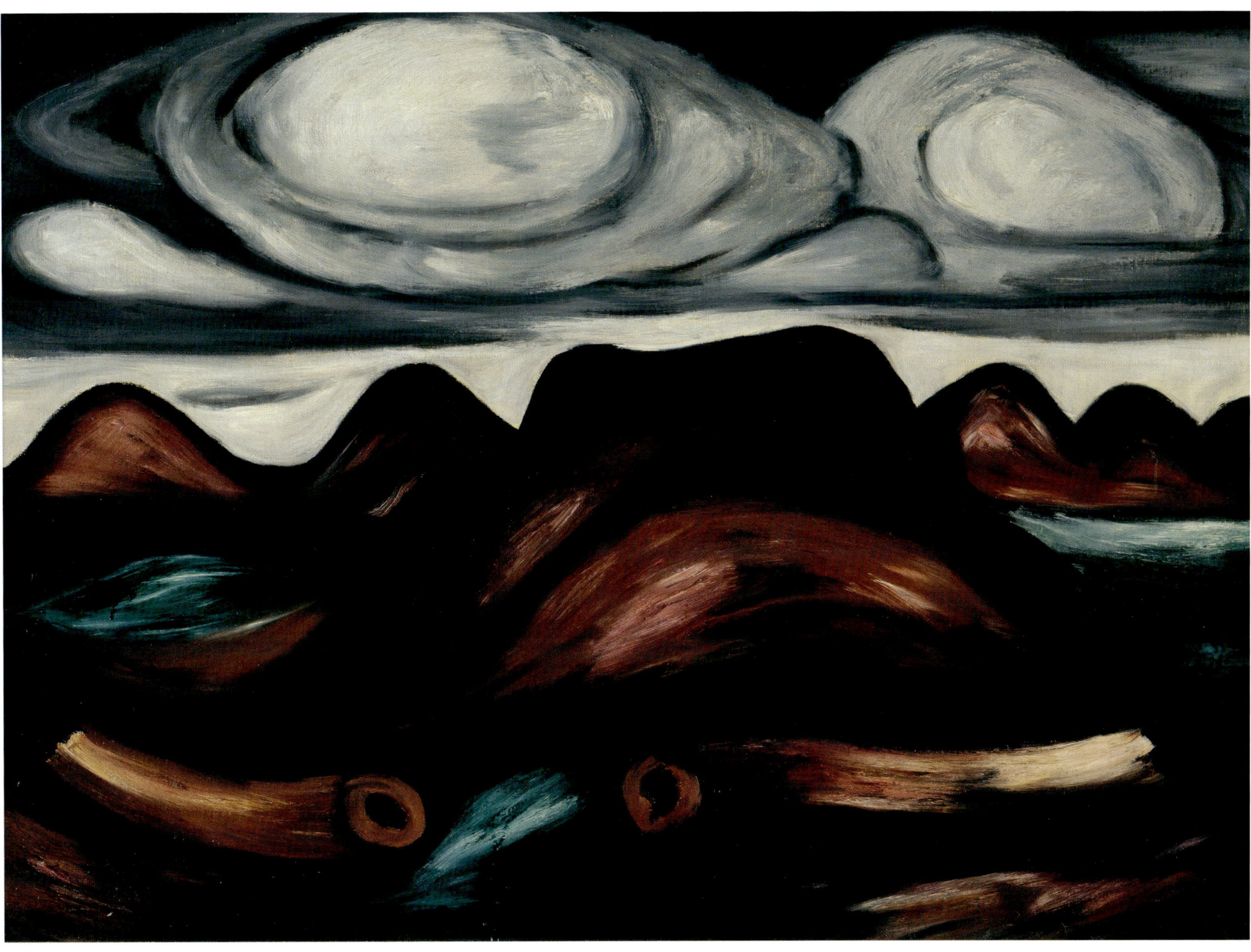

Notes

1. Quoted in Townsend Ludington, *Marsden Hartley: The Biography of an American Artist* (Boston: Little, Brown, 1992), 66.
2. Marsden Hartley to Harriet Monroe, August 22, 1918, quoted in Barbara Haskell, *Marsden Hartley* (New York: Whitney Museum of American Art, in association with New York University Press, 1980), 58.
3. Stephen May, "Searching for the Sublime: Marsden Hartley in New Mexico and Mexico," *Southwest Art* 128 (January 1999): 59.
4. For further information on the connection between Hartley's sexual orientation and his artwork, see Bruce Robertson, *Marsden Hartley* (New York: Abrams in association with the National Museum of American Art, Smithsonian Institution, 1995).
5. Ludington, 161.

59.

New Mexico Recollection #12, 1922–1923

Oil on canvas
30⅛ x 40⅛ in. (76.6 x 101.7 cm)
Gift of Mari and James A. Michener
1991.232

Provenance: Purchased by James Michener from Babcock Galleries, New York, 1959; long-term loan to The University of Texas at Austin, 1968–1991

Joseph Havel

b. Minneapolis, 1954

w. Minneapolis, 1972–1976; University Park, Pennsylvania, 1977–1979; Sherman, Texas, 1979–1991; Houston, 1991–present

Joseph Havel strives to maintain balance between the formal and conceptual aspects of his art. Havel's respect for the integrity of his materials, coupled with his technical expertise, results in sculptures of beauty and complexity.

Havel received an undergraduate degree in fine arts in 1976 from the University of Minnesota and a master's degree in 1979 from Pennsylvania State University. He moved to Texas later that year to join the faculty of Austin College in Sherman. In 1991 he relocated to Houston to become associate director of the Glassell School of Art at The Museum of Fine Arts, Houston, where he currently serves as director. In the 1990s Havel began to gain national recognition and was invited to participate in the 1994 exhibition series *Twentieth-Century American Sculpture at the White House* and the 2000 Whitney Biennial.[1]

Havel's work has its roots in the art of assemblage, particularly as it was practiced by the Dadaists and Surrealists, whose frequent use of humor and irony Havel has also adopted. Using found objects and materials that often reference domesticity, such as mens' shirts, labels, lampshades, and chairs, the sculptor creates lyrical compositions that are abstract but that also suggest narrative readings. Best known for his work in bronze, Havel has investigated a wide range of media, including mixed-media constructions, ceramics, drawing, and photography. He began casting bronze in 1987 after receiving a fellowship from the National Endowment for the Arts.

In *Exhaling Pearls* (1993, plate 60) Havel cast the delicate forms of two Japanese paper lanterns and a rope found at the Houston ship channel to create a quixotic, almost mischievous sculpture.[2] The lower lantern appears simultaneously to expand and collapse under the weight of the elements above it. The rope rises out of the lower lantern, reaching upward to embrace the upper lantern, and suggests hands, gnarled tree roots, or a serpentine figure twisting in space. While the upper lantern appears to be supported by the rope, Havel cleverly implies the impossibility of the lower lantern actually holding up the rope in the first place. Furthermore, he exploits the expressive use of gesture and line in three dimensions, foregrounding the interaction between positive and negative space, as seen in the manner by which the rope's ends function much like drawn lines on a sheet of paper.

Here Havel's intent was to construct a sculpture of heroic proportions in the tradition of monumental public sculpture, thus making bronze the logical material of choice. Bronze also allowed the artist to create a formally complex vertical structure that appears to propel itself into the sky. The direct wax casting technique, moreover, permitted Havel to translate found objects into bronze in minute detail, producing an astonishing variety of textural surfaces that range from the semblance of thin paper on the Japanese lanterns to the frayed ends of the rope.

Exhaling Pearls also reflects Havel's enduring fascination with embracing and fostering contradiction. For instance, the inconsistencies in scale, balance, weight, gravity, and engineering are typical of his sculptures, where the casting process confers on once soft, malleable materials a tough durability, allowing them to perform in ways contrary to their nature. This, as well as Havel's penchant for incorporating everyday objects that one would expect to find in the home or in a shipyard, for instance, rather than in a museum sculpture garden, disturbs the formality and solemnity typically associated with monumental outdoor sculpture. Havel's works are both serious and ironic and always imbued with a vulnerability (evidenced in *Exhaling Pearls* by the seeming precariousness of its structure) that, despite the authority implied by their scale and materials, makes them inherently accessible.

The title of *Exhaling Pearls* extends this play. The formal suggestion of the figure, coupled with the narrative associations of luxury, sex, "pearls of wisdom," and the action of breathing, result in endless interpretive connections and disconnections. The title also evokes the weightlessness of breath, a connotation reinforced by the sense of an impossibly floating ball, a forever-upright rope that does not collapse as it should, and the delicate paper lantern upon which everything rests: *Exhaling Pearls* is rooted and rootless.

Havel has argued that his work addresses the difference between contradiction and conflict, wherein contradiction allows for a dialogue between opposing themes or positions. Indeed, like many of his other sculptures, *Exhaling Pearls* embodies an inherent tension between strength and delicacy, stability and instability, stasis and movement, being and transformation, and balance and asymmetry. Havel's sculptures are "verbs" rather than "nouns," to use his own terminology: works that capture singular moments in the process of transformation. Havel renders this transitory quality in bronze, a signifier of permanence, to create elegant sculptures that are both monumental and intimate, formal and conceptual, and stirringly profound in their range of associative possibilities.

Kathleen V. Jameson

Notes

1. For more on Havel, see Peter Doroshenko and David Pagel, *Joseph Havel* (Huntington Beach, Calif.: Huntington Beach Art Center, 1996); *Joseph Havel: Weather* (Dallas: Barry Whistler Gallery, 1997); Alison de Lima Greene, *Texas: 150 Works from The Museum of Fine Arts, Houston* (Houston: The Museum of Fine Arts, Houston, 2000); and Marisa C. Sánchez, "Non-Places: An Interview with Joe Havel," *Artlies,* no. 44 (fall 2004): 40–41.
2. Harry Geffert at Green Mountain Studio and Garden in Crowley, Texas, cast *Exhaling Pearls.* He cast the rope and lanterns using different alloys in order to give the rope greater tensile strength. *Exhaling Pearls* is part of what Havel calls a "unique edition," wherein a group of works are formally related, and may even share cast forms, but the individual works remain distinct through "flexible elements" that vary from sculpture to sculpture. *Exhaling Pearls* is the third and final large-scale sculpture in a series; the other two sculptures are located in a private collection and at The Museum of Fine Arts, Houston.

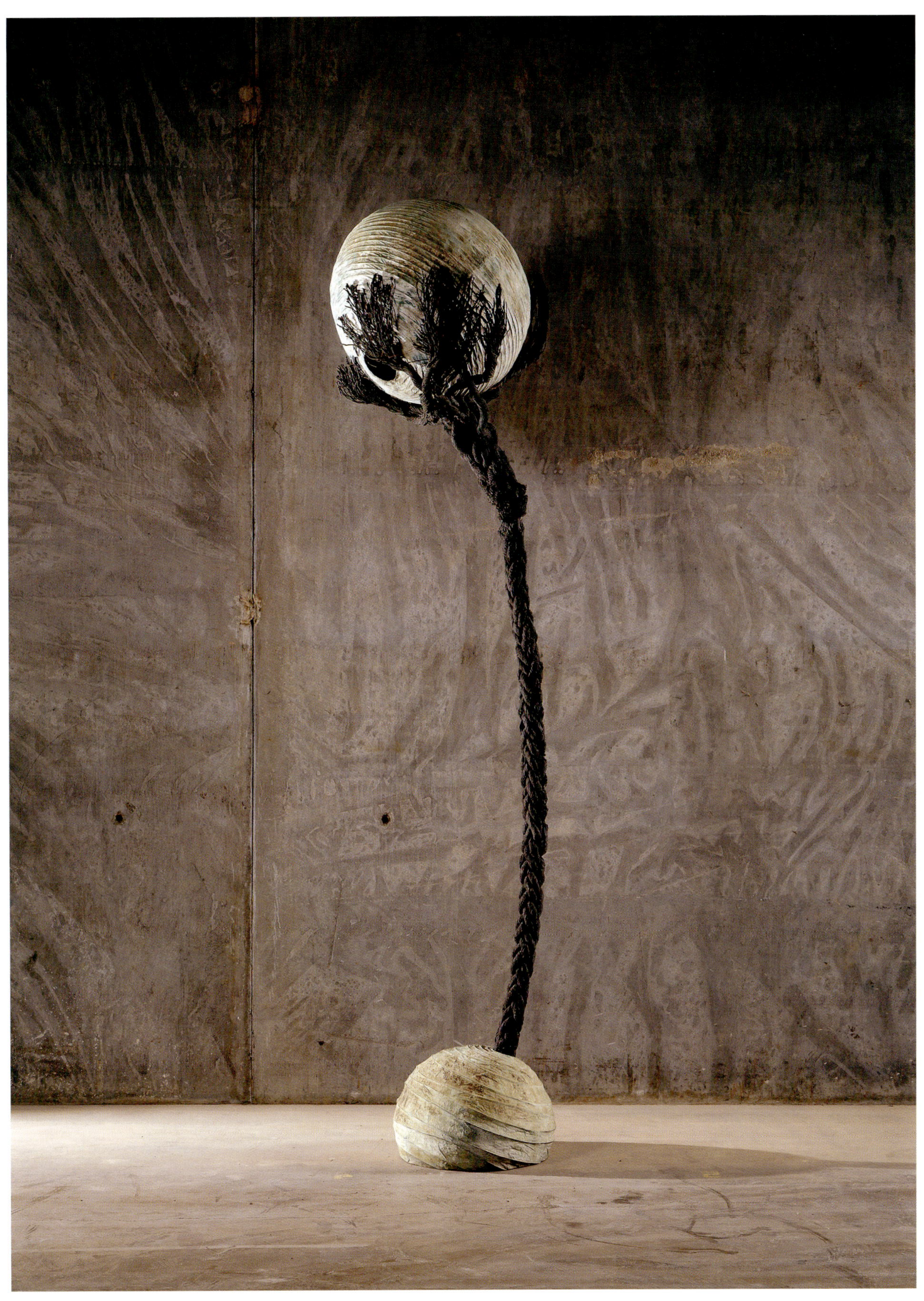

60.
Exhaling Pearls, 1993

Patinated bronze
130 × 55 × 33 in. (330.2 × 139.7 × 83.8 cm)
Gift of Jack S. Blanton and Family
2002.2869

Al Held

New York–Todi, Italy, 2005

w. Paris, 1950–1952; New York, 1953–1962; New York–New Haven, Connecticut (summers in Boiceville, New York), 1962–1980; Boiceville–Perugia, Italy–Todi, Italy, 1980–2005

Al Held is one of a number of painters who redefined abstraction in the wake of Abstract Expressionism. Untitled (1961, plate 61) belongs to a pivotal moment in his career, when Held had recently transitioned from the gestural style characteristic of his early paintings to the geometric abstractions that exemplify his work of the early to mid-1960s. Bold, vibrant, and animated, paintings such as Untitled generate a sense of spirited play between colors and forms.

Held was born in Brooklyn in 1928. After serving two years in the Navy, he returned to New York in 1947, where he participated in Folksay, a left-wing political organization comprised of writers, artists, musicians, and activists. With aid from the GI Bill, he enrolled in the Art Students League in 1948. During this time, he produced Social Realist paintings, although an encounter with Jackson Pollock's drip paintings at The Museum of Modern Art in New York in 1949 tested his commitment to the genre. In 1950, with his remaining GI Bill funds, Held moved to Paris. There he studied with sculptor Ossip Zadkine at the Académie de la Grand Chaumière and joined a lively expatriate community that included painters Ellsworth Kelly, Joan Mitchell, Milton Resnick, Sam Francis, Norman Bluhm, Jules Olitski, and Kenneth Noland and sculptor George Sugarman, who would become a lifelong friend.[1] It was not until he moved to Paris that Held abandoned figurative painting definitively.

Held returned to New York in 1953. By 1956 he was frequenting the Club and the Cedar Bar and participating actively in an artistic community whose members lived, worked, and/or exhibited on the Lower East Side. East Tenth Street represented the hub of this community: it was home to Willem de Kooning's and Philip Guston's studios, for instance, as well as the Brata Gallery, an artist cooperative founded by Nicholas and John Krushenick with help from Held and Sugarman.

Held's first solo exhibition in New York, at the Poindexter Gallery in 1959, showcased his distinctive variant of European and Abstract Expressionism: dense, turbulent paintings with heavily encrusted surfaces, thick layers of impasto, and a palette comprised of somber, earthen tones. In 1960, however, Held made a decisive shift. With the aim of "formaliz[ing] abstract expressionism,"[2] "mak[ing] something more definite, more definitive,"[3] as the artist put it, he began to assemble geometric forms painted in an array of bold, vibrant hues into tight, interlocking patterns. These compositions are considerably more disciplined than those of Held's earlier work. The geometric shapes that comprise them might touch and abut one another, but their boundaries, and by extension their identities, remain distinct. Likewise, the colors in Held's paintings coincide exactly with the geometric forms they encompass. Despite Held's embrace of "clarity, order, and structure,"[4] however, a work such as Untitled is neither inert nor mechanical. Indeed, if anything, the painting communicates a sense of exuberance thanks to its eccentric, irregular geometries, its asymmetrical composition, its bright, intense colors, and its active figure/ground relationships.

Although discrepancies in scale and shape exist between the geometric forms that comprise Untitled, they are balanced by the artist's adept use of color, which allows even the tiniest constituent part, like the yellow wedge at the far right, to be just as effective and affective as the large white field adjacent to it. Here Held achieves unity within variation, just as elsewhere he achieves animation within stability. And these are only a few of the contradictions that enliven Held's "geometric" paintings. Although they lack the irregular brushstrokes and variations in texture of his earlier, more gestural paintings, for instance, their surfaces are nonetheless thick and heavy, some covered with over a hundred layers of paint. At times, bumps and ridges interrupt the general uniformity of a painting's surface, remnants of its prior incarnation. The palpable materiality of even Held's most austere paintings testifies to his laborious working method. Typically, the artist started with a general idea or premise, which he then developed in a series of exploratory drawings. From that point forward, he relied almost exclusively on intuition and improvisation. After "drawing" the geometric shapes onto the canvas by hand, he repeatedly tested, adjusted, and refined his compositions, an approach facilitated by his use of Liquitex, a fast-drying acrylic paint.

Over the course of the 1960s, Held's canvases grew in scale, some achieving mural-sized proportions. They also gradually began to substitute for geometric shapes letters of the alphabet, but letters so distorted, whether through magnification, cropping, or disorientation, they continued to read as abstract forms. Although it does not bear the distinctive title of Held's letter paintings (such as *The Big A* of 1962), Untitled seems to anticipate works like these. The artist divided the painting into two vertical registers, one of which is dominated by a field of white paint whose shape approximates the letter "K." As with his letter paintings, moreover, this shape/letter strains against the edges of the canvas, confirming Held's interest, expressed as early as 1959, in reaching "outward toward the spectator."[5] The artist likewise activated the space between Untitled and the spectator through spatial ambiguity and vivid colors, which appear to alternately project and recede back onto the planar surface of the canvas.

By the early 1960s Held was attracting considerable critical attention. Along with work by artists such as Kelly, Noland, Frank Stella, and Ray Parker, his paintings were featured in the groundbreaking exhibition *Towards a New Abstraction* at The Jewish Museum in 1963. This represented one of the first attempts to scrutinize the new (and extremely diverse) modes of abstraction that emerged as alternatives to Abstract Expressionism in the late 1950s and early 1960s.[6] Clement Greenberg likewise included Held's paintings in *Post-Painterly Abstraction* in 1964, as did Lawrence Alloway in his 1966 exhibition *Systemic Painting*.

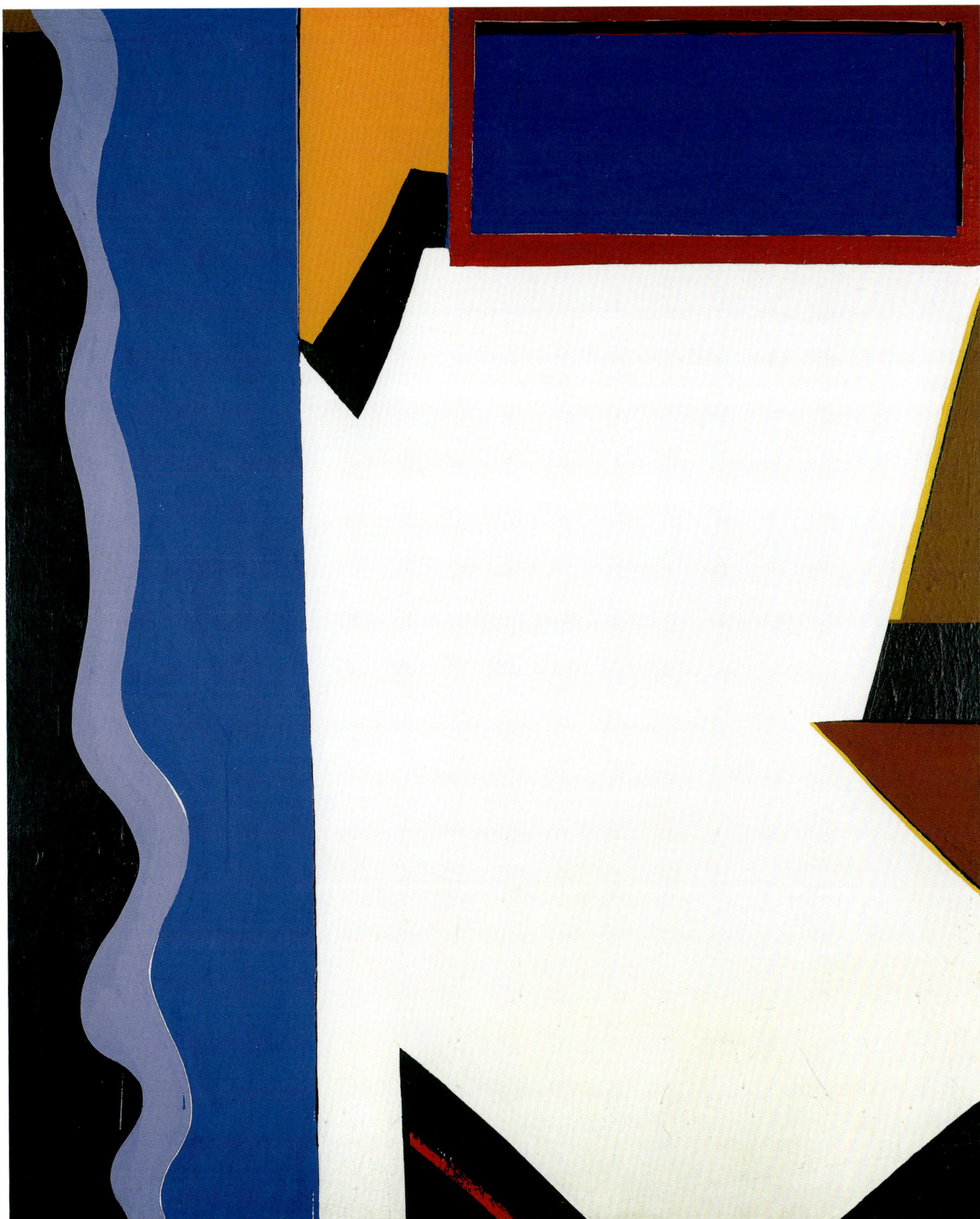

61.

Untitled, 1961

Acrylic resin on linen
90 × 72 in. (230 × 183 cm)
Gift of Mari and James A. Michener
1991.234

Provenance: Purchased by James Michener from the artist's studio through Poindexter Gallery, New York, 1962; long-term loan to The University of Texas at Austin, 1968–1991

In 1962 Held was appointed to the faculty of the Yale University School of Art. In the late 1960s and then again in the late 1970s, his work underwent other dramatic shifts. But these shifts in some respects were anticipated by his earlier work, particularly its facility at generating complex spatial and/or chromatic relationships as well as its interest in closing the space that separates viewers and paintings. Held remained committed to experimenting with the possibilities and parameters of abstract painting until the very end of his career.

Kelly Baum

Notes

1. Sugarman's sculptures and Held's painting from the early to mid-1960s demonstrate intriguing parallels, among them an interest in the physicality of materials, vibrant colors, and irregular geometry. See Cary Levine, "Al Held and George Sugarman at Washburn," *Art in America* 91 (June 2003): 121.
2. Dore Ashton, "Al Held: New Spatial Experiences," *Studio International* 168 (November 1964): 211.
3. Quoted in Corinne Robins, "Six Artists and the New Extended Vision," *Arts Magazine* 39 (September/October 1965): 23.
4. Al Held, "The '60s in Abstract: 13 Statements and An Essay," interviews with Maurice Poirier and Jane Necol, *Art in America* 71 (October 1983): 124.
5. Quoted in Irving Sandler, *Al Held 1959–1961* (New York: Robert Miller Gallery, 1980), n.p.
6. However, Held took issue with those who made categorical distinctions between the "new" abstraction and the New York School. If any line was to be drawn, Held maintained, it was between the "new" abstraction and the critical discourse that had crystallized around Abstract Expressionism, particularly that of Harold Rosenberg, which Held believed had misinterpreted, particularly with regard to process, the very work it sought to explain. See "The New Abstraction: A Discussion Conducted by Bruce Glaser," *Art International* 10 (February 1966): 42.

Robert Henri

Cincinnati, 1865–New York, 1929

w. Philadelphia, 1886–1888; Paris, 1888–1891; Philadelphia, 1891–1895; Europe–United States, 1895–1900; New York (frequent trips to Europe and throughout the United States), 1900–1929

Robert Henri, one of the most influential American artists of the early twentieth century, is noted as a portrait painter and inspiring teacher to many accomplished artists, including George Bellows, Edward Hopper, and Stuart Davis. He is recognized most often, however, for his leading role in the organization of the groundbreaking exhibition of The Eight, held in 1908 at the Macbeth Galleries in New York, which proclaimed the introduction of a new progressive style of realism. Henri initially established his reputation with landscapes before he decided to concentrate on portraiture. Though he has been associated with the Ashcan School and the movement of urban realism, he in fact produced relatively few city scenes.

Henri was born in Cincinnati and spent his youth in Cozad, Nebraska, until his family resettled in Atlantic City, New Jersey. In 1886 he entered the Pennsylvania Academy of the Fine Arts, studying with noted realists Thomas Anshutz and Thomas Hovenden and Impressionist Robert Vonnoh. He left in 1888 to travel abroad and continue his studies in Paris at the Académie Julian with William-Adolphe Bouguereau and Tony Robert-Fleury until 1891, when he gained entry into the elite École des Beaux-Arts. However, he remained there only a short time before returning to the United States, where he resumed study at the Pennsylvania Academy. Henri made additional extended trips to Europe over the course of that decade to study the work of Édouard Manet and the Old Masters, in particular Diego Velázquez, Francisco Goya, Rembrandt van Rijn, and Frans Hals. These studies greatly impacted the course of his development.

After returning from Europe in 1900, Henri settled in New York and rented a studio in the Sherwood Building on Sixth Avenue and 57th Street. He taught for much of his life at various institutions including the New York School of Art and the Art Students League. In the early 1900s he painted New York street scenes, including several of the area around his studio. Of the few urban scenes Henri produced, he favored depictions of the city's waterways, especially views of Blackwell's Island (now known as Roosevelt Island) located off 59th Street on the East River. *East River Snow (Blackwell's Island)* (1900, plate 62) is typical of the approximately fifteen such views Henri painted.[1]

Henri described the scene in *East River Snow* in his record book: "Cold, gray, winter most, river chocked with ice. 3 canal boats right corner (yellow note) snow all over."[2] In his painting, patches of snow and ice provide a stark contrast to the subtle array of hues in the somber sky. Henri favored winter and snow scenes and probably influenced some of his students and colleagues, including Bellows, Rockwell Kent, Carl Sprinchorn, and Ernest Lawson, who were also attracted to such themes. Henri's compositions typically differ from others' representations, however, in the notably bleak and blustery atmospheric effects they depict. Henri executed a smaller version of the Blanton's painting, *Blackwell's Island, East River* (1900), which shows nearly the same view, though with only one canal boat visible at the lower right. Of the two, John Sloan selected Henri's *East River Snow* for inclusion in the 1931 Memorial Exhibition held in honor of his close friend at the Metropolitan Museum of Art.

Although Henri primarily painted portraits after about 1902, he did occasionally create views of the city and its waterways as a more personal means of expression. He wryly observed of this decision:

> *[I] regretted there was but one of me, for as I said, if there were two, I could then paint both the people and the landscape. As it is, there being but one of me, I spend six to eight hours a day in actual painting and the rest of the time getting ready for the work . . . and in my passage to and from the studio where I paint people, I see most beautiful landscape* [sic] *under rare effects slide by. And this is a true loss to me for I have the feeling, and had considerable experience, in painting landscape.*[3]

Henri soon became widely recognized for his ability to rapidly capture not just the visual characteristics but also the essential spirit of his subjects. Unlike most portrait painters, Henri painted few commissioned works, instead seeking out various "types" that he encountered during peripatetic travels throughout the United States. He spent considerable time in Maine and the Southwest, and in Europe, where his preferred destinations were Spain, Holland, and Ireland.

Henri had a particularly sympathetic response to the people and culture of Spain. He visited the country on several extended excursions between 1906 and 1912, and again in 1923–1924. His chosen subjects included many depictions of the less fortunate, such as peasants, gypsies, and beggars; he also portrayed entertainers, such as singers, toreadors, and dancers, along with others who engaged his attention. The portraits Henri painted in Spain in 1912 include, besides the Blanton's *The Old Model (Old Spanish Woman)* (c. 1912, plate 63), *Spanish Shepherd*, *Blind Singers*, and *Blind Spanish Singer*. In these works, Henri responded to the melancholy strain commonly associated with the Spanish character. Critics often accused him of painting commonplace or ugly subjects, to which he responded: "The subject can be as it may, beautiful or ugly. The beauty of a work of art is in the work itself."[4]

Henri painted *The Old Model* in Madrid. The model, whose name he did not note in his record book, transmits a persuasive and gripping presence, an attribute common among the sitters Henri painted on this trip. As he noted in a letter to his mother, "There are some wild looking gypsies and some children—these are not laughing Dutch children to do here—there is a more dramatic strain in these people."[5] Although he did paint some comely subjects, Henri's objective, as can be observed in this work, was to penetrate the superficial layers of a sitter's personality in an effort to capture the essence of his or her

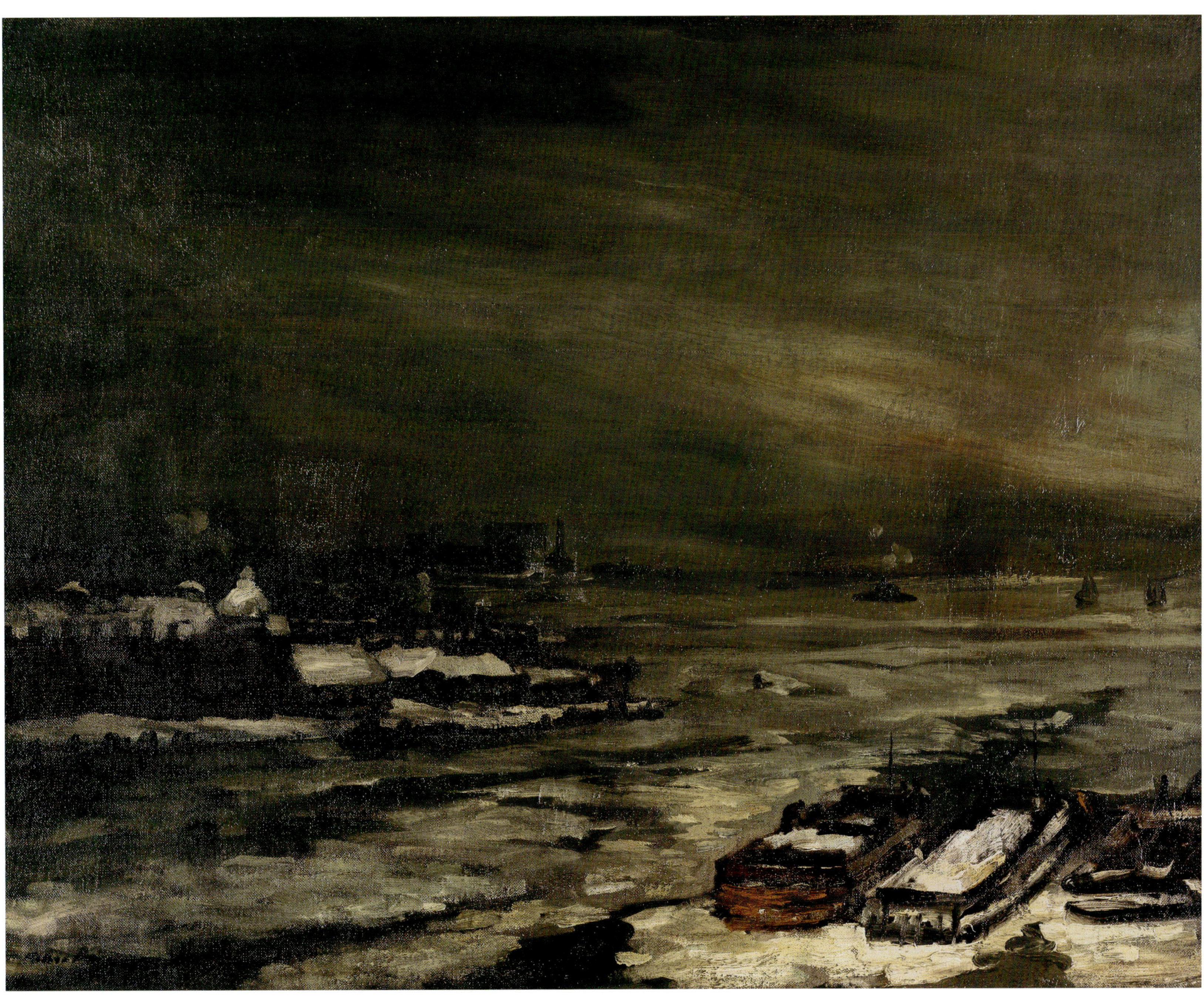

62.

East River Snow (Blackwell's Island), 1900

Oil on canvas
25¼ × 32¹⁄₁₆ in. (64.2 × 81.4 cm)
Gift of Mari and James A. Michener
1991.236

Provenance: Purchased by James Michener from Hirschl & Adler, New York, 1962; long-term loan to The University of Texas at Austin, 1968–1991
Signed lower left "Robert Henri"

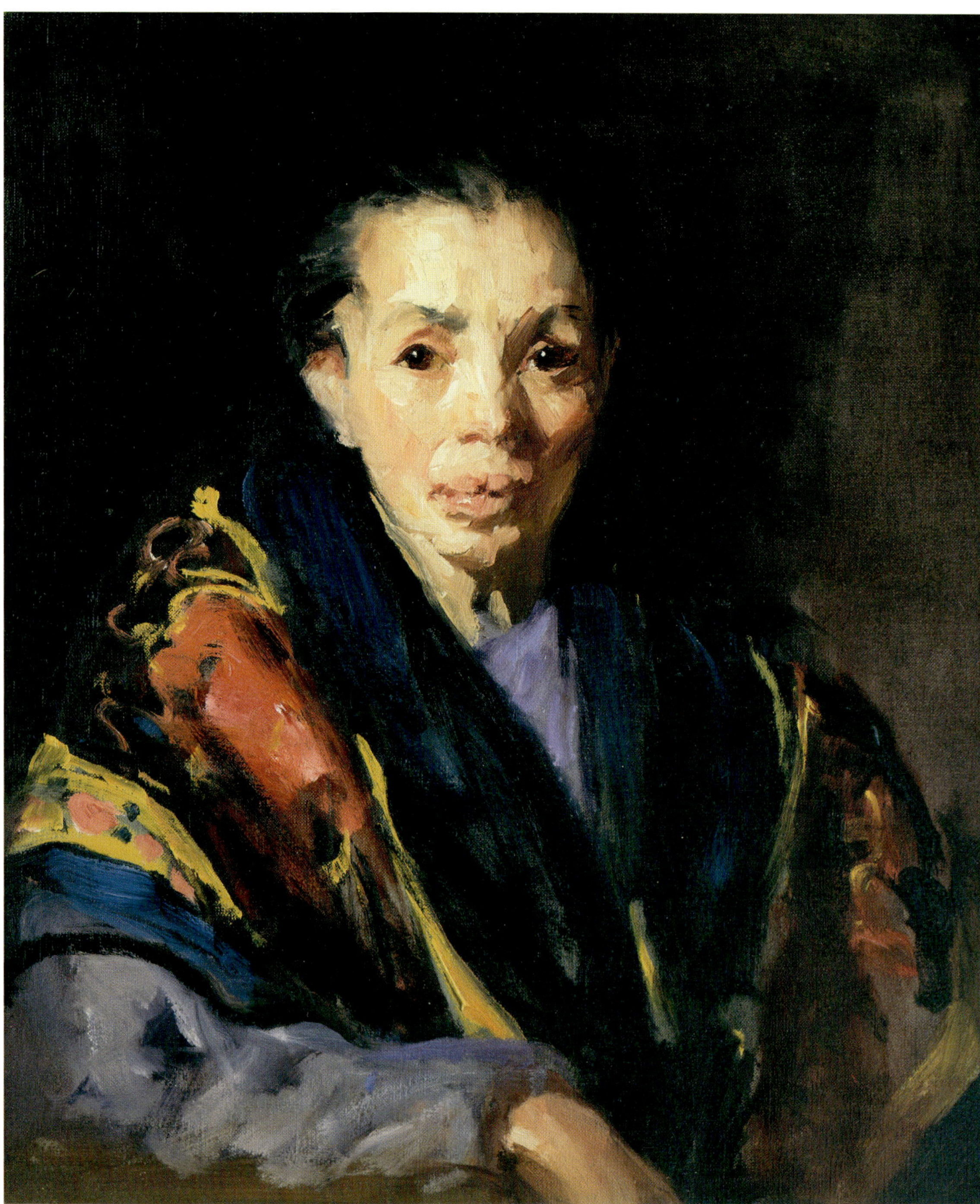

63.
The Old Model (Old Spanish Woman), c. 1912
Oil on canvas
24 × 20¹⁄₁₆ in. (60.9 × 51 cm)
Gift of Mari and James A. Michener
1991.237
Provenance: Purchased by James Michener from Hirschl & Adler, New York, 1962; long-term loan to The University of Texas at Austin, 1968–1991
Inscribed verso, upper center "131 H"

character. The models who especially piqued his interest were those who evoked a resonant chord within him:

> *The people I like to paint are "my people," whoever they may be, wherever they may exist, the people through whom dignity of life is manifest, that is who are in some way expressing themselves naturally along the lines nature intended for them. My people may be old or young, rich or poor. . . . But wherever I find them . . . my interest is awakened and my impulse immediately is to tell about them through my own language—drawing and painting in color.*[6]

Over the course of his career, Henri won many prizes for his art; in addition to painting prolifically, he organized numerous important exhibitions, wrote essays, and maintained an extensive correspondence. He remained active and was a productive painter of portraits, especially of children, into his final years.

Valerie Ann Leeds

Notes

1. Robert Henri, Artist's Record Book, Estate of Robert Henri.
2. Henri, Artist's Record Book.
3. Robert Henri, in Margery Ryerson, ed., *The Art Spirit* (1923; reprint, New York: Harper and Row, 1984), 115.
4. Henri, *The Art Spirit*, 166.
5. Henri to his mother, August 9, 1912, Henri Papers, Beinecke Rare Book and Manuscript Library, Yale University, New Haven, Conn.
6. Robert Henri "'My People:' By Robert Henri," *The Craftsman* 26 (February 1915): 459.

Arturo Herrera

b. Caracas, Venezuela, 1959

w. Tulsa, Oklahoma, 1978–1982; Chicago, 1990–1998; New York, 1998–2003; Berlin, 2003–present

Fragments of recognizable Disney characters—Snow White's distinctive coiffure, the characteristic tuft of Donald Duck's posterior—populate much of Arturo Herrera's work, from the collages to the installations. Such elements are seamlessly joined together in surprising and unexpected configurations. As the eye oscillates between the disparate fragments, the viewing dynamic provokes a rhizomic array of associations and sensations. The titles, suggestive fragments from common parlance, expand rather than limit interpretation, opening the works up to multiple significations, multiple meanings. In all, there are no definitive readings of Herrera's works since they are always in a state of becoming, activated in dialogue with the viewer.

A native of Caracas, Venezuela, Herrera received a BFA in 1982 from the University of Tulsa and an MFA from the University of Illinois in 1992. According to artist and critic Pablo Helguera, Herrera is part of the new generation of conceptualists coming out of Chicago. These artists are characterized by "the tendency to favor works with strong psychological content; the idea of innovating formal questions, though without breaking the dialogue with pop art; and the fascination with naïve and eccentric art."[1]

Herrera's earliest works are comprised of cuttings from children's coloring books, intermingled with painting and drawing.[2] These compositions operate as hybrids, not only in terms of their material and content, but also with regard to their art historical references.[3] Pasting together fragments of preprinted matter is an approach that dates back to the early twentieth-century collages of Pablo Picasso and Georges Braque, while the use of mass-produced imagery—in this case, the common visual language of popular children's illustrations—links the constructions to Pop art practices. With the aid of an Exacto blade, Herrera reveals the inherently abstract qualities of his source materials, transforming a dwarf's stocking-clad foot or floppy hat into a biomorphic abstraction that calls to mind the paintings of Joan Miró or the sculptures of Jean Arp. At the same time, the incorporation of paint drips and splatters relates this body of work to aleatory compositional strategies and Abstract Expressionist explorations of the emotive capacities of paint. The themes and ideas explored in these early collages continue to actively inform Herrera's work.

Herrera's cut-felt pieces, which he began producing in 1998, blur the boundaries between traditional media categories.[4] These sensuous works are part painting, part collage, and part installation. A chance ink spill or paint drip typically serves as the starting point. Herrera then modifies and adjusts it to achieve the form he seeks. Using felt as pure pigment, Herrera cuts the desired shape from a single sheet of fabric and affixes it to a wall. In his application of formal manipulation and deliberate precision, the artist enacts a revision of Abstract Expressionism's gestural spontaneity. At the same time, Herrera's choice of material brings to mind the 1960s avant-garde practices of artists such as Robert Morris and Joseph Beuys, who used felt to quite different ends.[5]

The tangled lines of Herrera's felt piece *One Time* (2001, plate 64) evoke multiple associations, from a skein of paint drips lifted from a Jackson Pollock canvas to a mess of bodily fluids. The work's apparent lack of specificity prompts the viewer to make his or her own connections, and it is the individual viewer's train of thoughts and emotions that Herrera aims to generate through his practice. Curator Hamza Walker has compared the experience to taking a Rorschach inkblot test, where one is prompted to freely associate and, in so doing, tap into subconscious memories.[6]

Herrera's *Night Before Last* (2002, plate 65) is a grid of sixteen framed drawings. Acting as a matrix of sorts, it documents earlier variations on a formal theme, while also serving as a study for a later series of large-scale, cut-paper silhouettes.[7] Working in series, according to Herrera, allows him to "investigate different angles and positions both conceptually and emotionally in the piece."[8] *Night Before Last* demonstrates the fruits of such investigations. The artist created its sixteen drawings from eight source images overlaid with varying permutations of paint drips. A formal logic underlies the production and presentation of the drawings, with a central drip formation linking them all together. Variations of the formation recur in each image, as well as in other works, such as Herrera's installation *When Alone Again* (2001) at the UCLA Hammer Museum. Each framed drawing is comprised of a dyad: the same source image obfuscated by different drip patterns. Each dyad has a partner: there are eight solid and eight outline versions. The two sets are arranged in a formally balanced grid, achieved without recourse to rigid symmetry. The overall layout prompts the viewer to jump from drawing to drawing, in no particular order, searching for the pairs as well as possible clues to the source imagery.

Herrera said, "in my work there is always editing and removing from the original source."[9] In *Night Before Last* he first obscured a children's illustration with a layer of paint drips, then reduced it to one medium (from preprinted matter and paint to graphite), and finally abstracted to an outline. Each step removed a level of detail, making it increasingly difficult to parse the components comprising the drawing. Throughout the abstracting process, however, Herrera maintained a connection to the source materials. This allowed him to provide an entry point for the viewer without dictating a specific reading. In *Night Before Last* the viewer may pick out a musical note, a soapy scrubbing brush, or a wooden floor, but she would be hard pressed to identify the specific source imagery. For some viewers, the particular combination of association and obfuscation might prompt the recall of "Whistle While You Work," with the classic sing-song tune eliciting a web of thoughts and memories detached from a specific message or narrative.

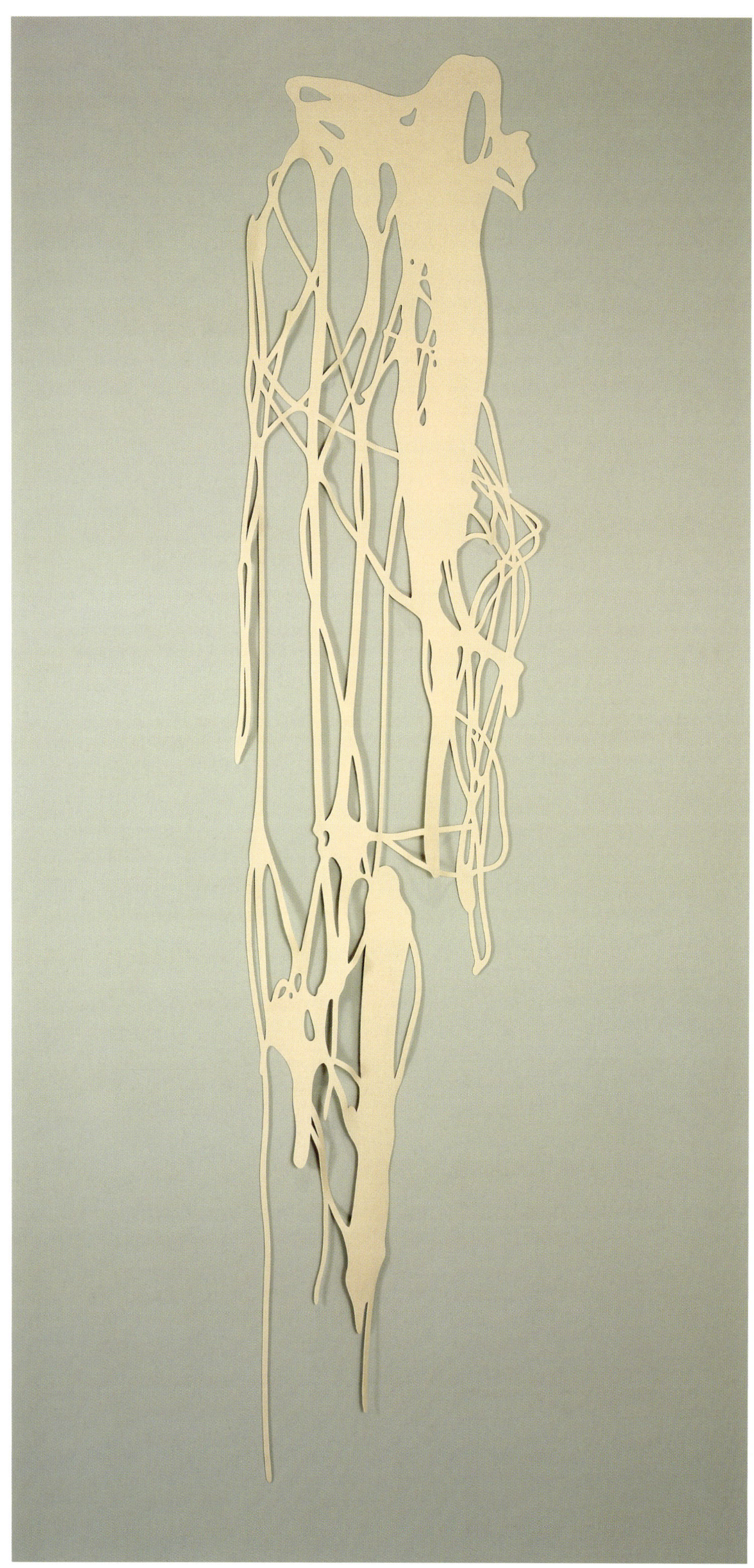

64.

One Time, 2001

Wool felt

96 × 20 in. (243.7 × 50.7 cm)

Partial and pledged gift of Jeanne and Michael Klein

T2001.4

Provenance: Purchased at the request of the museum by Jeanne and Michael Klein from Marvelli Gallery, New York, 2001

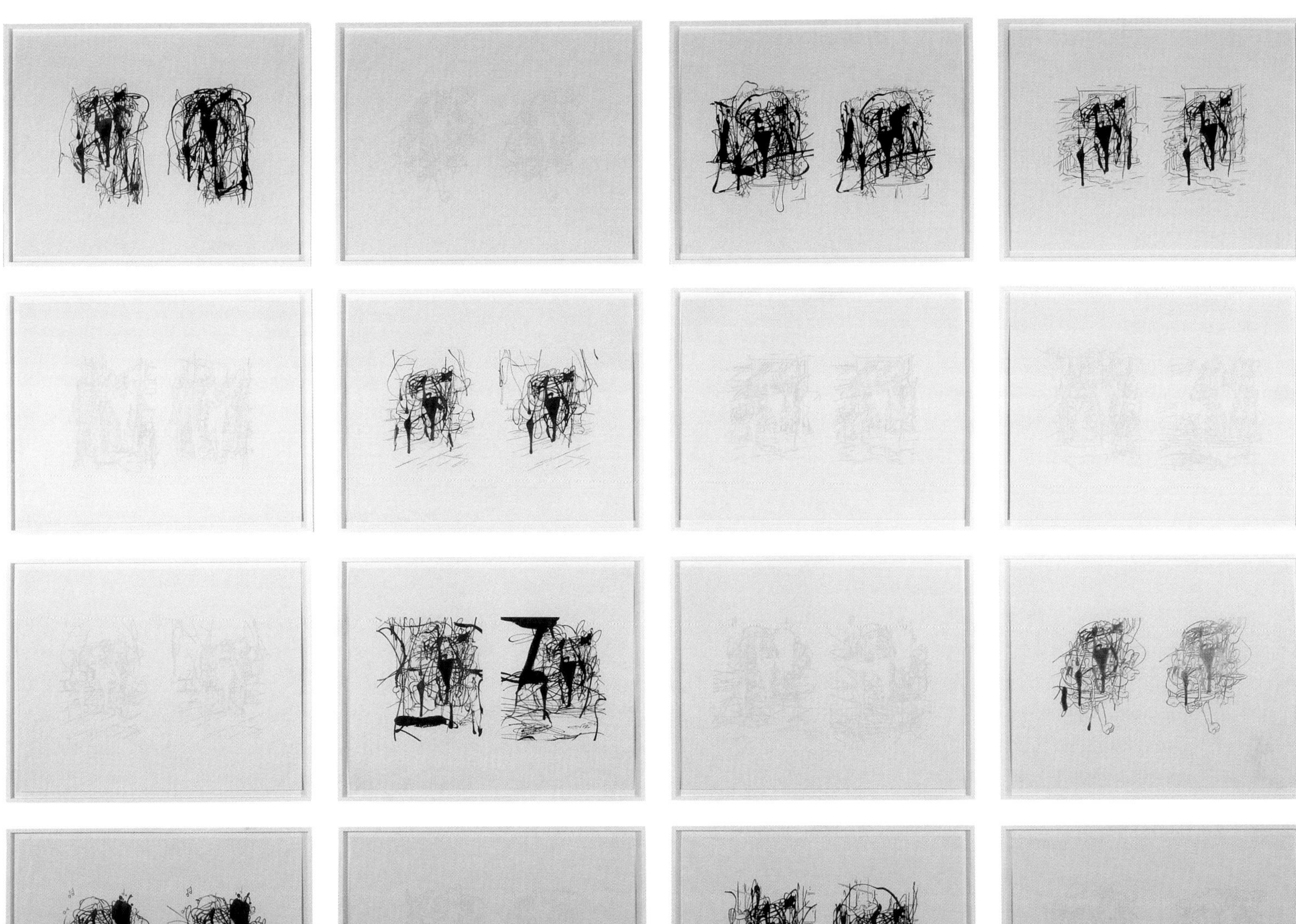

The open-ended quality of Herrera's work can be unsettling, reflecting as it does flux and uncertainty. It destabilizes the traditional subject-object relationship and refuses to be fixed into a concretely knowable thing, outside and separate from the viewer. It is precisely this condition of Herrera's work that makes it so alluring, however. The shifting combinations of emotions, memories, and thoughts that it elicits create it afresh at each viewing. The collage or painting thus extends, repeatedly realizing itself in a sort of hybrid space of the imagination.

Amy Dove

65.
Night Before Last, 2002
Graphite on paper
Overall: 68⅞ × 99 in. (175 × 251.5 cm)
Each: 19 × 24 in. (48.26 × 60.96 cm)
Partial and pledged gift of Jeanne and Michael Klein
T2003.3.1/16–16/16

Provenance: Purchased by Jeanne and Michael Klein for the museum from Brent Sikkema Gallery, New York, 2002

Notes

1. Pablo Helguera, "Arturo Herrera: The Edges of the Invisible," *Art Nexus*, no. 33 (August/October 1999): 49.
2. Carolyn Christov-Bakargiev, *Arturo Herrera* (Los Angeles: UCLA Hammer Museum, 2001), n.p.
3. Arturo Herrera, telephone conversation with the author, January 11, 2005.
4. Julie Rodrigues Widholm, "Arturo Herrera," in *Life Death Love Hate Pleasure Pain: Selections from the Museum of Contemporary Art, Chicago, Collection* (Chicago: Museum of Contemporary Art, Chicago, 2002), 302.
5. Morris incorporated gravity in the production of his "anti-form" felt works, while Beuys used the material for symbolic purposes.
6. Hamza Walker, "Arturo Herrera: A Gentle Trauma," *Renaissance Society at the University of Chicago Newsletter* (January 1998): 3.
7. Herrera produced a total of sixteen cut-paper works after the drawings, each in a different color and measuring approximately 50 inches tall. Michael Jenkins, telephone conversation with the author, December 15, 2004.
8. Herrera, telephone conversation with the author.
9. Herrera, telephone conversation with the author.

Oliver Herring

b. Heidelberg, Germany, 1964
w. Oxford, England, 1985–1988; Brooklyn, New York, 1990–present

German-born, New York–based artist Oliver Herring once described his work succinctly as "Minimal means for maximum impact."[1] This "impact" derives largely from Herring's innovative, even counterintuitive approach to media. He routinely coaxes wood, Mylar, Scotch tape, video, and photography to contradict or perform against their nature, always to mesmerizing effect. Herring also employs both time and the human body as expressive platforms, handling them as materials to be manipulated and transformed like any other.

Originally trained as an abstract painter, Herring received an MFA from Hunter College in New York in 1991. That same year, the playwright and performance artist Ethyl Eichelberger committed suicide after learning that he had contracted AIDS. Herring rather abruptly abandoned painting and began to knit—first as a meditative endeavor, but then more consciously as a form of artistic practice. These two impulses coincided in Herring's first knit piece in 1991, which served both as a jubilant memorial to Eichelberger and as a commentary on the passage of time.[2] Instead of the more conventional yarn, however, Herring employed Scotch tape, whose transparency and ability to reflect light generated the impression of fragility and insubstantiality, belying the work's actual, three-dimensional form. The artist's sensitivity to both the physical and symbolic properties of materials characterizes his work to this day.

Herring continued to create knit pieces throughout the 1990s using silver Mylar, scotch tape, or wood reinforced with wire armatures. Initially, these pieces represented coats, blankets, beds, chairs, and other objects that implied the presence of an (absent) human body. In the late 1990s Herring began to invest what were becoming increasingly complex sculptural tableaus with a temporal component—or the illusion of one, at least. With the aid of video stills, he depicted the body at successive moments in the act of standing, falling, or rocking by synthesizing (or knitting together) different yet partial views of the same figure. These sculptures were static, but they nonetheless implied motion in the manner of Étienne-Jules Marey's stop-motion photographs from the late nineteenth century or Marcel Duchamp's *Nude Descending a Staircase* (1912).[3] In works like *Double Rocker* (1999), sculpture and photography intersected in Herring's work for the first time, anticipating sculptures such as *Patrick* (2004, plate 66).

In 1998 Herring adopted video, not as a tool, as he had done with his sculptures, but rather as one of his primary media. Herring's videos rebuff the primary advantage afforded by the medium—temporal continuity—and continue to employ (somewhat perversely) sequential, stop-motion techniques. The artist compares this, his incremental approach to video, to the process of creating paintings or sculptures: "I try to exploit the stop-motion vehicle to basically paint one still life at a time or construct one sculpture at a time."[4] Later, Herring splices together these discrete segments of video footage (or still-lives or sculptures) to generate the illusion of movement. In many of his videos, human bodies appear to fly, somersault, climb, dive, and jump against backdrops comprised of abstract forms or rudimentary galactic and landscape motifs.[5] (One critic compared Herring's videos, with their peculiar mixture of whimsy and melancholy, to the early films of Charlie Chaplin and Buster Keaton.)[6] However, these same videos just as often disavow the illusion of movement. Herring severs the conventional relationship between video and representation in other ways as well, either by incorporating abstract design elements or using human actors to produce (paradoxically) abstract passages that read solely on a two-dimensional plane.

While these earlier projects combine elements from different media and genres, they tend to do so on a purely conceptual or technical level. In 2004 Herring would take the next step and literally fuse sculpture and photography, an experiment that resulted in the hybrids *Patrick* and *Gloria* (2004).[7] The genesis of *Patrick* is complex and fascinating. In 2004 Herring photographed a man named Patrick over the course of several weeks, recording every detail of his hair, skin, face, and body. He then created a foam-core sculpture that duplicated Patrick's proportions and original pose, which was based on Auguste Rodin's pensive *The Thinker* (1881). After dissecting the photographs into small pieces, Herring attached them to the appropriate part of the sculpture so that each fragment corresponded to the very section of flesh, the very strand of hair, the very eyelash that it represented. (The photograph of the bridge of Patrick's nose, for instance, rests just there, on the bridge of *Patrick*'s nose.) In this way, Herring might be said to have returned the model's flesh to his body. Matching the parts of Patrick's body depicted in the images with those fashioned out of foam-core allowed the artist to almost exactly synchronize photography and sculpture. Just as importantly, it achieved the near perfect coincidence of materials and subject matter—more precisely, of representation with its referent.

The work is "near perfect" insofar as Herring deliberately refused to complete the illusion—the seams of the photographs are still visible to the viewer. However, this stutter, this disruption in the illusion, by no means detracts from the work's powerful effect. Indeed, if anything, it exaggerates it. This effect might be best described as the uncanny, what Sigmund Freud described as the bewilderment—discomfort even—generated by our encounter with objects that manifest qualities of the animate and inanimate simultaneously. Put another way, while the correlation between media and content in *Patrick* creates the sensation that what we are observing might not just be the replica of a man, but possibly the man himself, those gaps in between the photographs and the tension they establish between part and whole, as well as the plastic box in which *Patrick* has been confined, alert us to its artificiality. And it is precisely this friction between the organic and inorganic that is responsible for the work's palpable uncanniness.

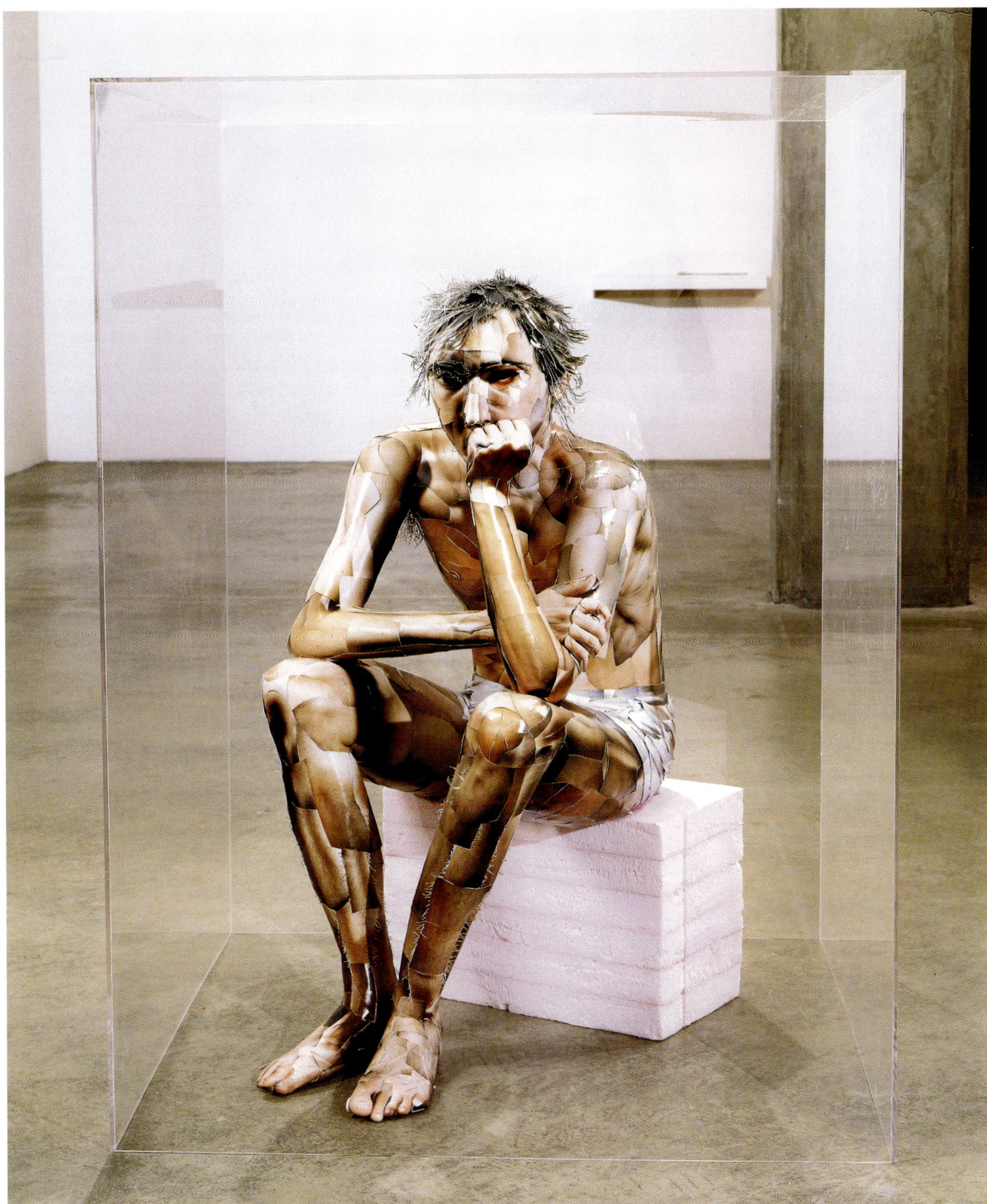

66.

Patrick, 2004

Foam core, museum board, digital C-print photographs, and polystyrene
42 × 18 × 27½ in. (106.7 × 45.7 × 69.9 cm)
Partial and pledged gift of Jeanne and Michael Klein
T2005.2

Provenance: Purchased at the request of the museum by Jeanne and Michael Klein from Max Protetch Gallery, New York, 2004

Patrick also reflects Herring's enduring preoccupation with intimacy, but intimacy manifested less in the actual objects or videos he produces than in his working methods, which depend on collaboration as much as they insist on intimacy. To parse and then reassemble the body of another, this speaks to the artist's quixotic desire, which is most certainly our own desire as well, to forge meaningful connections with other human beings, the opportunities for which seem less and less abundant thanks to the increasing intercession of media and computer technology into our everyday lives. Ultimately, then, *Patrick* represents the fulfillment of a wish.

Kelly Baum

Notes

1. Quoted in Kristin Chambers, *Oliver Herring: Sleepless Nights* (Cleveland: Cleveland Center for Contemporary Art, 2001), 32.
2. For more information on this work and on the knitting process, see "Oliver Herring in Conversation with Kristin Chambers," in *Oliver Herring*, 7–9.
3. Janet Koplos, "Stitches in Time," *Art in America* 91 (January 2003): 96.
4. "Oliver Herring in Conversation with Kristin Chambers," in *Oliver Herring*, 14.
5. For more information on Herring's videos, see Elisabeth Kley, "Everyday Miracles," *Performing Arts Journal* 74 (May 2003): 77–81.
6. Koplos, 98.
7. *Patrick* and *Gloria* were exhibited at Max Protetch Gallery in New York in fall 2004. In addition to the original photographs from which Patrick and Gloria were crafted (or what remained of them, at least), the exhibition included the video *Trucks* (2004), the photo-based sculpture *Birdseye View of the Theater Below* (2004), and the photo installation *Do Two Monologues Make a Dialogue?* (2004), among other works.

Charles Hinman

b. Syracuse, New York, 1932
w. New York, 1955–1991; Athens, Georgia, 1991–1994; New York, 1994–present

Charles Hinman has worked at the vanguard of geometric, abstract painting since the 1960s. His three-dimensional constructions have expanded the exploration of the shaped canvas initiated by Ellsworth Kelly in the 1950s and developed by Frank Stella in the 1960s. However, Hinman's playfulness and early interest in movement, color, and the sensuousness of surfaces and materials reveal a different approach to art making than that prescribed by Minimalism's more rigorous adherents.

Hinman received a BFA from Syracuse University in 1955. He also attended the Art Students League in New York, where he studied with Morris Kantor and met fellow students Lee Bontecou and James Rosenquist. After serving two years in the Army, Hinman taught mechanical drawing at the Staten Island Academy from 1960 to 1962 and carpentry at the Woodmere Academy on Long Island soon thereafter. Both jobs required that he learn basic drawing and construction skills, which would soon contribute to the development of his artistic practice. While working on Staten Island, Hinman and Rosenquist shared the studio vacated by Agnes Martin on Coenties Slip in Lower Manhattan, where the views, affordable rents, and plentiful lofts attracted such artists as Kelly, Robert Indiana, Jack Youngerman, and Cy Twombly.

In 1963, after moving to his own storefront studio on 95th Street, Hinman made his first breakthrough. Using his mechanical drawing and carpentry skills, he began to approach art making as if he were a craftsman building an object. To his first exhibition at Sidney Janis Gallery in May 1964 (with Arakawa, Robert Irwin, Robert Whitman, and Norman Ives) Hinman contributed panels held together with hinges and ropes. The position and orientation of these early constructions were determined primarily by gravity.

Hinman's November 1964 solo exhibition at Richard Feigen Gallery presented a series of eccentric, three-dimensional curved constructions. To create such works, Hinman first produced charcoal studies in which he established volumetric relationships. He then made line drawings that served as blueprints, including essential information about angle, distance, and scale. In the process of making the wood armatures for his constructions, Hinman further adjusted the type and degree of projection in order to take into account the shadows cast onto the wall. Around these wood armatures he stretched canvas and applied layers of flat saturated colors that alternately accentuated or downplayed the constructions' buoyancy and three-dimensionality. Donald Judd, who reviewed the show in which these works appeared, was critical of what he saw as their internal contradictions and ambiguities: "Sometimes the painting implies more projection and sometimes less; the actuality and the painting don't always agree and the effect is strange."[1] As Hinman later noted, however, his work deliberately rejected many of the same characteristics that Judd promoted:

> The Minimal tendency came along right when I was starting and it really threw me. My work was about everything that Judd was against. His idea was about neatness and blankness and the inert, and from the beginning, my paintings were about movement and color and the sensual achieved through materials.[2]

In 1968 Hinman's decision to focus on the sides and back of his shaped canvases, while simultaneously retaining an intact frontal view, thereby defying the assumption that the shaped canvas disrupted the traditional two-dimensional picture plane, earned him the epithet "mannerist."[3] By 1972 critics described Hinman's interpretation of space as "baroque" because of his synthesization of Constructivist ideas, his reliance on primary colors (a recent development), and his romantic ornamental values.[4]

Surface Volume Hybrid (1973, plate 67) continued Hinman's earlier investigations into the relationship of two-dimensional planes and physical space. The reference to "hybridity" in the title hints at the work's multiple nature, since this three-dimensional, shaped canvas is neither painting nor sculpture, or rather both simultaneously. *Surface Volume Hybrid* is divided into two separate parts, each one comprised of geometric shapes like trapezoids and parallelograms. These two pieces join along a white grey border in the center, but this is the only point at which they meet: gaps in the shape of elongated triangles appear in two areas, providing a glimpse of the wall behind the construction. The work's asymmetry lends it a dynamic quality that Hinman's use of oblique angles, eccentric geometries, and bold color combinations such as yellow and black exaggerates. Together these characteristics keep the distinction between surface and volume, two- and three-dimensionality, and painting and sculpture in play.

In 1975 Hinman made a formal departure by hanging three-dimensional, jigsaw-shaped white paintings on white walls, works that were partly inspired by Russian Suprematist investigations.[5] Here the dented or internally curved planes of Hinman's canvases, as well as their overlapping forms, introduce shadows that reveal the works' three-dimensionality, but this is somewhat disguised by the elimination of chromatic elements.[6] Phyllis Derfner praised this subtle strategy as a way of articulating sculptural qualities through shape rather than color.[7]

In the late 1970s Hinman further explored spatial concepts using handmade paper formed into sculpted molds. He continues to make and exhibit works that engage with and expand the boundaries of geometric abstract painting, while simultaneously teaching at the Art Students League in New York.[8]

Mariani Lefas-Tetenes

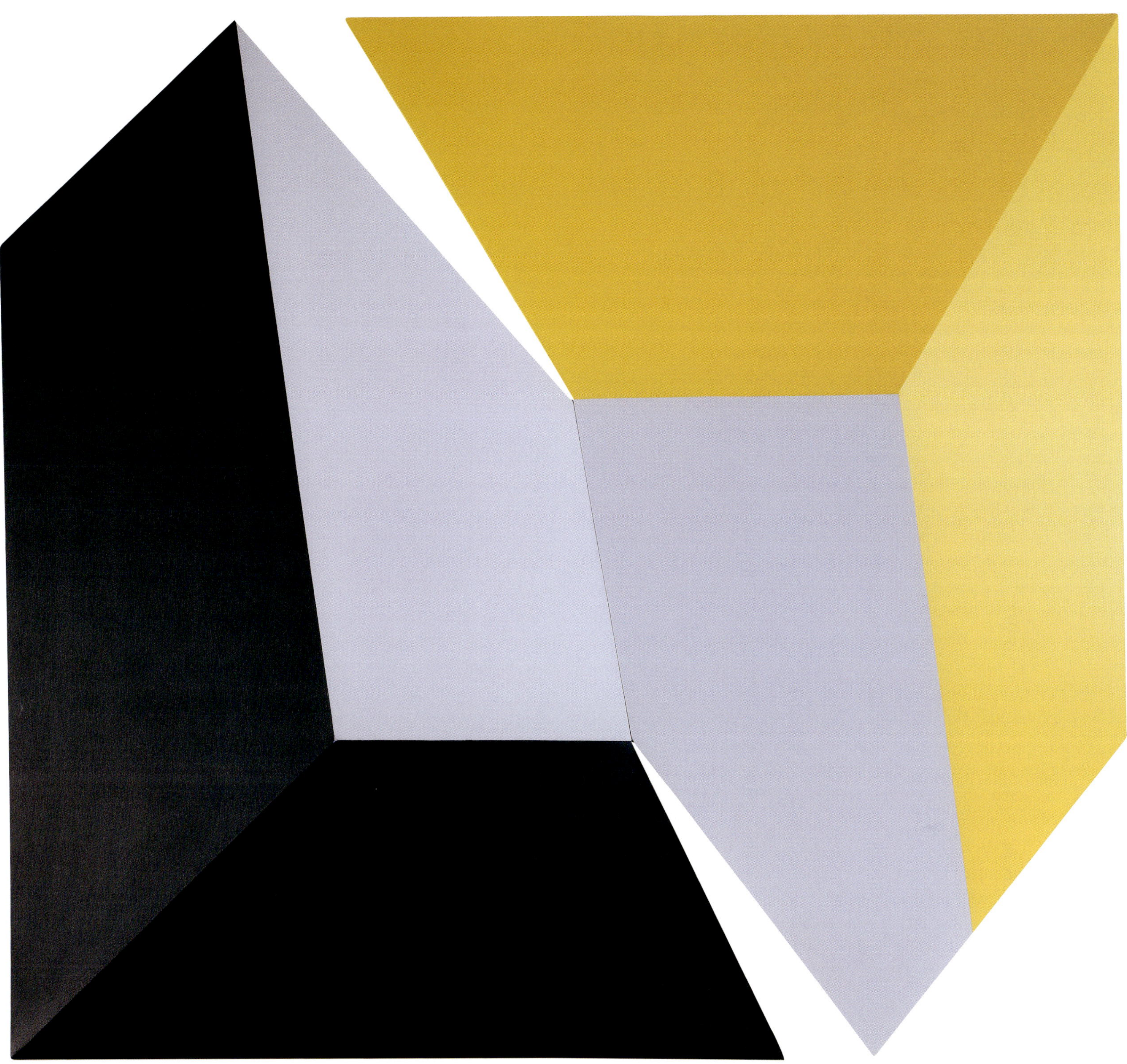

Notes

1. Donald Judd, exhibition review, *Arts Magazine* 39 (January 1965): 59.
2. Corinne Robins, "Charles Hinman," in *Charles Hinman, Current Works* (Syracuse, N.Y.: Everson Museum of Art, 1980), 13.
3. Charles Giuliano, exhibition review, *Arts Magazine* 42 (December 1967): 59.
4. R. C. Kennedy, exhibition review, *Art International* 15 (April 1971): 36.
5. Robins, 16. Donald Kuspit also refers to Hinman's debt to Malevich. See Donald Kuspit, *Charles Hinman: Recent Work* (Raleigh, N.C.: North and South Galleries, University Student Center, North Carolina State University, 1990), 16.
6. Roberta J. M. Olsen, exhibition review, *Arts Magazine* 49 (April 1975): 24
7. Phyllis Derfner, exhibition review, *Art International* 19 (April 1975): 63.
8. Hinman's previous teaching positions include Princeton University and the University of Georgia, Athens, where he was the Lamar Dodd Chair.

67.

Surface Volume Hybrid, 1973

Acrylic on canvas
98 × 92 × 10 in. (249 × 234 × 25.5 cm)
Gift of Janice Bireline Hinman in tribute to Professor John Wheeler, Department of Physics, The University of Texas at Austin
1981.91

Hans Hofmann

Weissenberg, Bavaria, 1880–New York, 1966

w. Munich, 1898–1904; Paris, 1904–1914; Munich, 1914–1930; Berkeley, California, 1930–1931; New York (summers in Provincetown, Massachusetts), 1932–1966

Through both practice and pedagogy Hans Hofmann played a vital role in the development of twentieth-century American painting. Born in 1880 in Weissenberg, Germany, Hofmann had begun a career in the Bavarian department of public works by age sixteen. He invented several devices, including a sensitized light bulb, an electromagnetic comptometer (similar to an early accounting machine), and a radar device for ships.[1] His inventions, though not directly relevant to art, reflect his lifelong concern with problem solving through formal means.

In the late 1890s, against his father's will, Hofmann began to study art. He moved to Paris, where he remained from 1904 to 1914, a pivotal time in the European cultural scene. While residing there, he met Pablo Picasso, Georges Braque, Henri Matisse, Fernand Léger, and Robert Delaunay. The work of these artists, as well as Paul Cézanne and Piet Mondrian, remained paramount to Hofmann's teaching and practice. He often quoted Cézanne's view that everything in nature could be seen in terms of the cylinder, the sphere, and the cone. To this formula Hofmann added the cube and the square, the result of his exposure to and synthesis of Cubism.

Hofmann was visiting Germany when the war broke out in 1914; unable to return to France, he opened his first art school in Munich the following year. Many students traveled there to study with him, including four artists represented in the Blanton's collection: Carl Holty, Ludwig Sander, Alfred Jensen, and Louise Nevelson. In 1930 and 1931, as Germany became increasingly hostile to artists, Hofmann went to California to teach at the University of California, Berkeley. He remained in the States and moved to New York, teaching first at the relatively conservative Art Students League before opening the Hans Hofmann School of Fine Arts in 1933. Two years later, he opened a second school in Provincetown, Massachusetts. Possessed of a teaching style that was charismatic and persuasive, but not controlling, Hofmann taught artists whose developing works differed dramatically from his own. His ideas and his example inspired the careers of such varied artists as Robert Beauchamp, Helen Frankenthaler, Milton Resnick, and Larry Rivers.

Hofmann's contention, made in a series of lectures between 1938 and 1939, that the School of Paris painters derived their chief inspiration from the medium in which they worked—or, put another way, that painting's primary subject is itself rather than some external reference—formatively affected the art critic Clement Greenberg as well.[2] Even Greenberg's later insistence on "flatness" in Modernist painting bears kinship with Hofmann's pedagogical dicta about abolishing traditional linear perspective.

In a notorious encounter with Jackson Pollock, Hofmann once told the much younger artist that he was mistaken for working by heart and not from nature, prompting Pollock's legendary reply, "I am nature." Hofmann—fully committed to abstract painting—believed nature was the sole source of the creative impulse, regardless of whether an artist worked from memory, fantasy, or a more literal source. For Hofmann, translating nature into the two-dimensional form of painting involved a spiritual process akin to the German metaphysical tradition. He frequently invoked the *plastic* quality of painting, by which he meant not only its actual, physical plasticity, but also the formative energy inherent in the act of creation.[3] In his late period, he came to believe that color was the key element of form and plasticity. Hofmann is most closely associated with the theory of "push-pull." According to this system of force and counterforce, each mark or color placed on the painting's surface affects every other element and generates the illusion of depth.[4] "Push-pull" denies the tyrannical vanishing point of Renaissance perspective by creating depth through purely formal relationships.

In 1958, at the age of 78, Hofmann began a new period in his life and work, closing both of his art schools to dedicate himself full-time

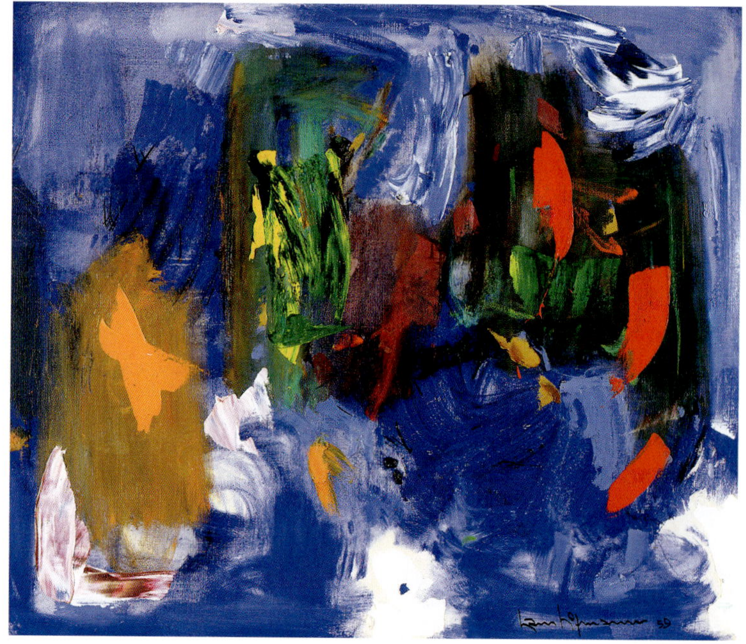

68.

X Orange, 1959

Oil on canvas
52 x 60¾ in. (33.1 x 154.3 cm)
Gift of Mari and James A. Michener
1991.240

Provenance: Purchased by James Michener from Samuel Kootz Gallery, New York, 1961; long-term loan to The University of Texas at Austin, 1968–1991
Signed lower right corner "hans hofmann 59"

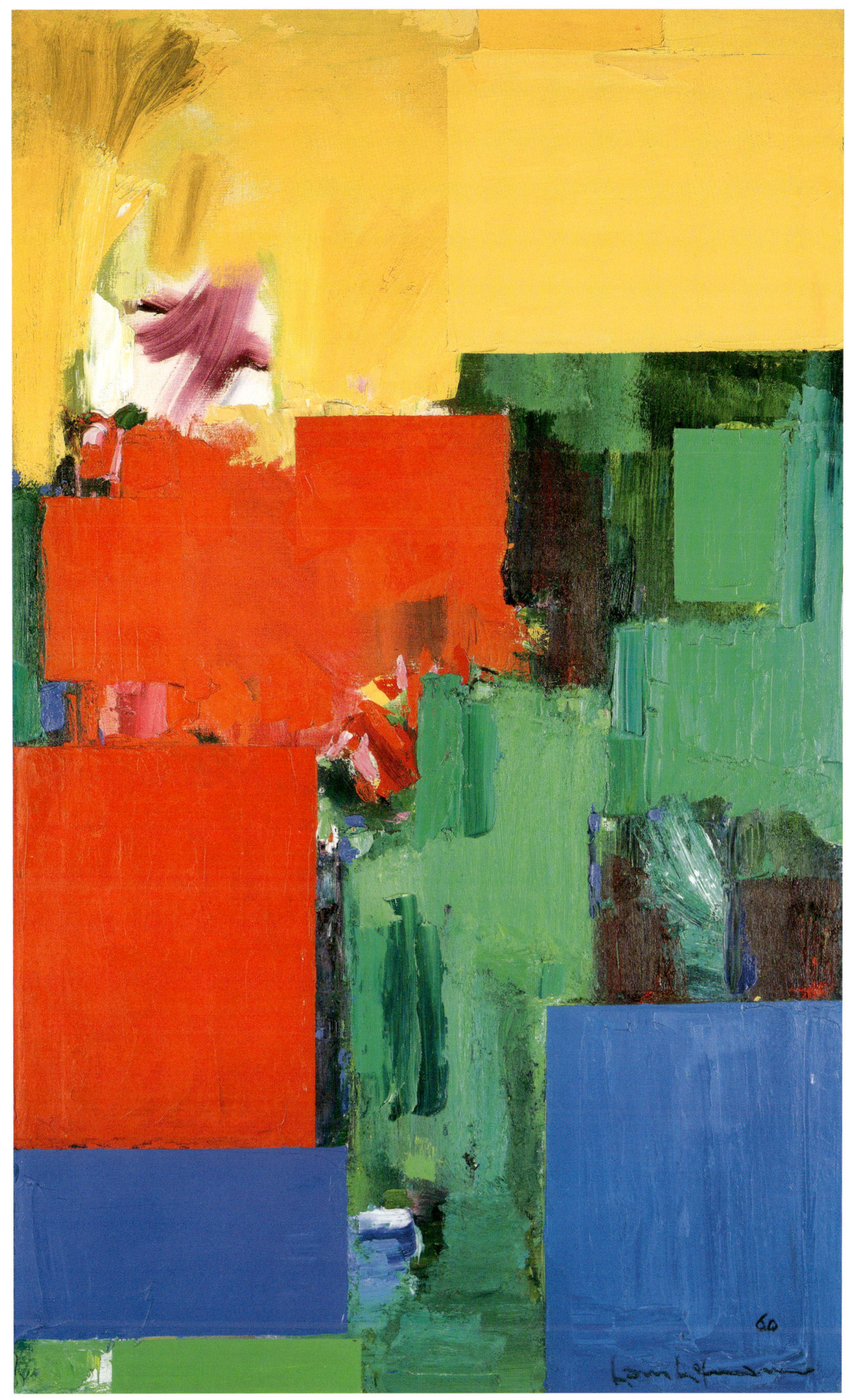

69.

Elysium, 1960

Oil on canvas
84 × 50 in. (214.9 × 127.7 cm)
Gift of Mari and James A. Michener
1991.239

Provenance: Purchased by James Michener from Samuel Kootz Gallery, New York, 1962; long-term loan to The University of Texas at Austin, 1968–1991
Signed lower right corner "hans hofmann 60"

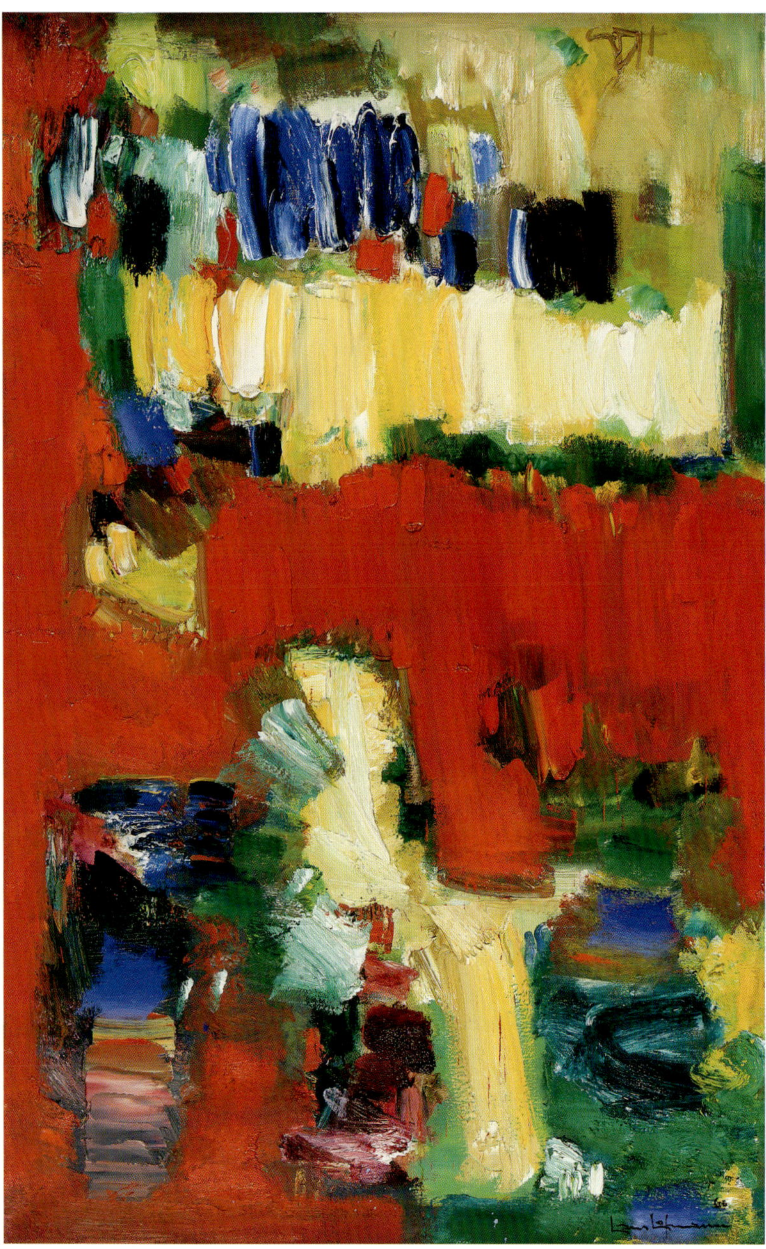

70.

Cascade, 1960

Oil on canvas
84 × 52 in. (214.7 × 132.2 cm)
Gift of Mari and James A. Michener
1991.238

Provenance: Purchased by James Michener from Samuel Kootz Gallery, New York, 1962; long-term loan to The University of Texas at Austin, 1968–1991
Signed lower right corner "hans hofmann 60"

to painting. His three works in the Blanton's collection belong to this productive and creative period. Each one represents an experimental approach to abstraction. Hofmann's *X Orange* (1959, plate 68) restates his longtime admiration for Fauvist landscape in wholly abstract terms. Centralized passages of red, green, yellow, and orange are set within a turbulent blue that wavers between figure and ground. Dense and painterly with a vertical emphasis offset by a countering diagonal, *Cascade* (1960, plate 70) reveals the artist's hand, visible in areas marked delicately by the tip of the paintbrush and elsewhere in thickly applied deposits of pigment. It is as if Hofmann set himself the task of using staccato brushstrokes to achieve maximum movement and vibrancy.

Made the same year as *Cascade, Elysium* (1960, plate 69) is painted in a completely different dialect, and embodies the essence of push-pull through color, form, and paint handling. Each rectangle, painted with a distinct hue and texture, floats in front of a varied and expressionistic background. Large passages that explore the nuances of green (a secondary color) show their origins in the primary colors blue (below) and yellow (above) while complementing the adjacent red. Thickly impastoed sections contrast with thin patches of bare, gessoed surface. When James Michener asked Hofmann which painting would best complete the group of three, the artist steered him toward the freshly painted *Elysium*: "It's where old artists go when they die. It's . . . very clean and simple—only a nest of squares, but they tell everything."[4]

Katie Robinson Edwards

Notes

1. Cynthia Goodman, *Hans Hofmann* (New York, Abbeville Press, 1986), 15.
2. Compare Hofmann's statements to ideas developed by Clement Greenberg in "Avant-Garde and Kitsch," 1939, section I, reprinted in John O'Brian, ed., *Clement Greenberg: The Collected Essays and Criticism*, vol. 1 (Chicago: University of Chicago Press, 1986), 9.
3. On "plastic," see William C. Seitz, *Hans Hofmann* (New York: The Museum of Modern Art, 1963), 54. Hofmann's use of "plastic" also reveals his strong kinship with Mondrian's theories.
4. Hans Hofmann, "The Search for the Real in the Visual Arts," in Sara T. Weeks and Bartless H. Hayes, eds., *Search for the Real*, rev. ed. (Cambridge, Mass.: MIT Press, 1977), 78. Paraphrased in Cynthia Goodman, "Hans Hofmann as a Teacher," *Arts Magazine* 53 (April 1979): 123.
5. James A. Michener, "Why I Collect Art," *Reader's Digest* (May 1970): 152.

Benito Huerta

b. Corpus Christi, Texas, 1952

w. Houston, 1970–1975; Las Cruces, New Mexico, 1976–1978; San Francisco, 1978–1980; New York, 1980; Houston, 1981–1997; Arlington, Texas, 1997–present

A serious engagement with popular culture is evident in the work of artist Benito Huerta. *Brave New World* (2000/2001, plate 71), an attention-grabbing watercolor, reads like a billboard advertising a barrage of obscenities or a stream-of-consciousness rant. Referencing European and Mexican artistic traditions, Huerta mines a range of visual sources including Catholicism, art history, current events, folk art, and mass culture. This marriage of high art and so-called "low art" can be seen in such works as *Exile Off Main Street* (1999), a reinterpretation of Pablo Picasso's *Les Demoiselles d'Avignon* (1909) executed on black velvet. In other surprising works, Huerta reinvented the Modernist grid and transformed pinups into abstract compositions.

Huerta studied art at the University of Houston and New Mexico State University. He currently is active not only as an artist, but as a teacher, writer, and curator as well. Huerta is a cofounding editor and board member of the Texas art magazine *ARTL!ES* and a professor at the University of Texas, Arlington, where he also serves as director of the University Art Gallery. He has curated exhibitions around the country and is involved with public art commissions throughout Texas. His generous efforts to promote his regional artistic community are ceaseless.

Brave New World, with its Pop sensibility, word play, and sharp wit, exemplifies the artist's tendency to fuse high and low. The critic Lucy Lippard observed that Huerta attempts to "reconcile the humor and political perversity of *rasquachismo* [an irreverent form of expression that combines recycled materials, kitsch, and found fragments] with the formalist framework of Jasper Johns or Al Held. . . . Without abandoning the baroque intensity of Chicano culture, Huerta's images are evolving into a kind of linear language hidden within textures and behind other images."[1]

In Huerta's hands, words are both volatile and evasive, as seen in *Brave New World*, where the vulgarity of the expletives is undercut by the elegance of their presentation. By superimposing his jarring obscenities on top of one another, Huerta effectively abstracts them. Exquisitely hand-rendered, the words appear in recognizable typefaces on a pale blue ground. This results in an image that is at once decorative and provocative, whereby the contradictions between the language and its patterned and colorful depiction generate unavoidable tension. Executed with the precision of commercial typography, *Brave New World* simultaneously mocks censorship and parodies the crassness of advertising.

The title refers to Aldous Huxley's *Brave New World*, a classic satirical book about a future dystopia plagued by numbing consumerism and totalitarianism. According to Huerta, his own *Brave New World* explores how our current historical moment echoes the future as predicted by Huxley: "The watercolor is a variation of a painting with the same title, completed in 1993, that dealt with the idea that as our society progresses culturally and technologically, we are devolving socially."[2] Emblematic of his varied production, *Brave New World* demonstrates Huerta's talent for fusing political commentary with formal exploration.

Katherine Roeder

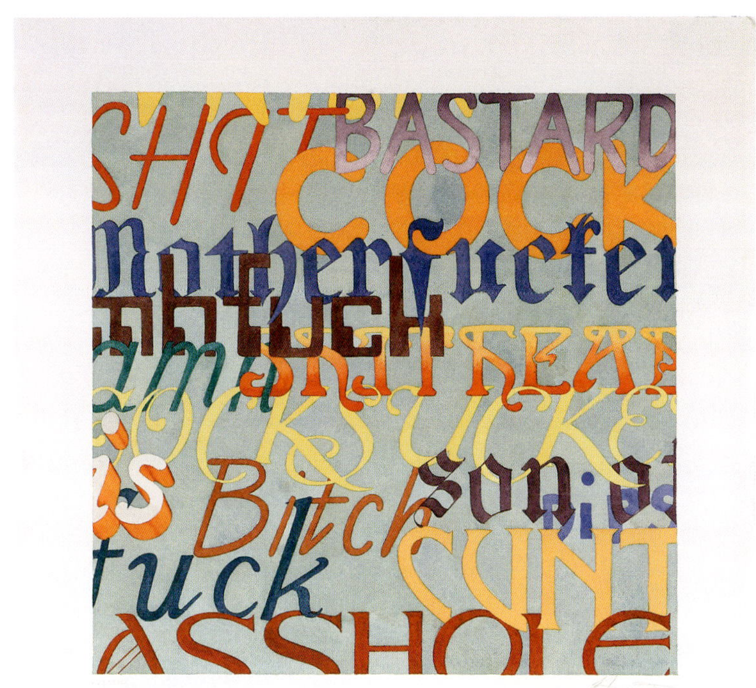

71.

Brave New World, 2000/2001

Watercolor on paper
30 x 22 in. (76.2 x 55.9 cm)
Purchase with support from the Blanton Contemporary Circle
2003.134

Provenance: Purchased from d berman gallery, Austin, 2003
Signed lower right "Benito Huerta" in pencil
Inscribed lower left "2000"

Notes

1. Lucy R. Lippard, *Mixed Blessings: New Art in a Multicultural America* (New York: Pantheon Books, 1990), 225.
2. Benito Huerta, email interview with the author, January 27, 2005. See also Susie Kalil, *Soundings: Benito Huerta, 1991–2005* (Corpus Christi, Tex.: The Art Museum of South Texas, 2005).

Robert Indiana

b. New Castle, Indiana, 1928

w. Chicago, 1949–1953; Europe, 1953; New York, 1954–1978; Vinalhaven, Maine, 1978–present

In *Highball on the Redball Manifest* (1963, plate 72), Robert Indiana critiques the American dream of progress and material success through autobiographical references to his past, his present, and his hopes for the future. The painting depicts a stylized steam locomotive viewed head-on. Emblazoned on its grill are the words "highball on the redball manifest," railroad parlance for "all clear for a fast express." The "25" painted in the center refers to the address of Indiana's studio at the time, 25 Coeties Slip in southern Manhattan, where he lived in the early 1960s. According to Indiana, the phrase, in conjunction with the number, refer to the sense of success he felt in 1963 as his career accelerated.[1] *Highball on the Redball Manifest* also alludes to an element of his family history: Indiana's grandfather, Fred Clark, worked for the Pennsylvania Railroad as a locomotive engineer. The locomotive in the painting, one of Indiana's rare representations of technology, represents his ambivalent relationship with progress. The engine hurtles toward an unknown destination, bearing an optimistic slogan; yet by the time Indiana painted it, the steam engine—and thus the locomotive engineer—were already technologically outmoded. In combining his grandfather's obsolete past with his own optimism for the future, Indiana questions both his own and America's belief in social and personal progress.

When he painted *Highball on the Redball Manifest,* Indiana was living among a community of New York–based artists that included Jack Youngerman, Agnes Martin, and Ellsworth Kelly. These artists strongly influenced his painting style, particularly Kelly, who became Indiana's early mentor. Kelly exposed Indiana to the hard edges, saturated color, and smooth, uninflected brushwork that would become hallmarks of both artists' work and that are clearly evident in *Highball on the Redball Manifest.*[2]

In New York, Indiana became fascinated by the visual culture of the street, particularly the streamlined visual and verbal vocabulary of commercial signs. He said, "There are more signs than trees in America. There are more signs than leaves. So I think of myself as a painter of the American landscape."[3] Indiana's reduction of the locomotive in *Highball on the Redball Manifest* to simple geometrical elements reflects the influence of the compelling visual language of commercial graphic design. In 1960 he introduced another signlike element into his paintings: words stenciled onto the canvas with a set of old commercial stencils that he discovered in his Coeties Slip warehouse-turned apartment.[4] He employed these stencils in *Highball on the Redball Manifest* and in many other paintings from this period. For Indiana, the use of text was a breakthrough that allowed him to explore language as both a graphic and semiotic element in his work.

Historically, Indiana is often grouped with the Pop art movement. He exhibited with his contemporaries and friends Roy Lichtenstein and Andy Warhol, with whom he shared an interest in the techniques of commercial art and in images derived from mass culture. However, Indiana occupies an uneasy place in the movement; his artistic vocabulary of signs and icons is more autobiographical, and more literary, than that of his contemporaries. In a 2003 interview he called himself the "least Pop of the Pop artists . . . I was a Pop artist simply by association, not by design."[5]

Indiana wrote that *Highball on the Redball Manifest* is among his favorite paintings.[6] It was the last one he completed before beginning his well-known *LOVE* sculptures, which have occupied the artist to the present day.

Karen C. Gonzalez

Notes

1. See "Note on *Highball on the Redball Manifest,*" January 25, 1974, in Earl A. Powell III, *James A. Michener Collection: Twentieth Century American Painting* (Austin: University Art Museum, University of Texas at Austin, 1977), 173.
2. Patricia McDonnell, *Dictated By Life: Marsden Hartley's German Paintings and Robert Indiana's Hartley Elegies* (Minneapolis: University of Minnesota Frederick R. Weisman Art Museum, 1995), 62.
3. Robert Indiana, "Vital Signs," interview by Deborah Solomon, *New York Times*, December 1, 2002.
4. Susan Ryan, *Robert Indiana: Figures of Speech* (New Haven, Conn.: Yale University Press, 2000), 135.
5. Robert Indiana, "Robert Indiana," interview by Francine Koslow Miller, *Tema Celeste,* no. 95 (January/February 2003): 71.
6. Robert Indiana, "Letter to Richard T. Hirsch," June 30, 1969, Blanton Museum of Art Archives, The University of Texas at Austin.

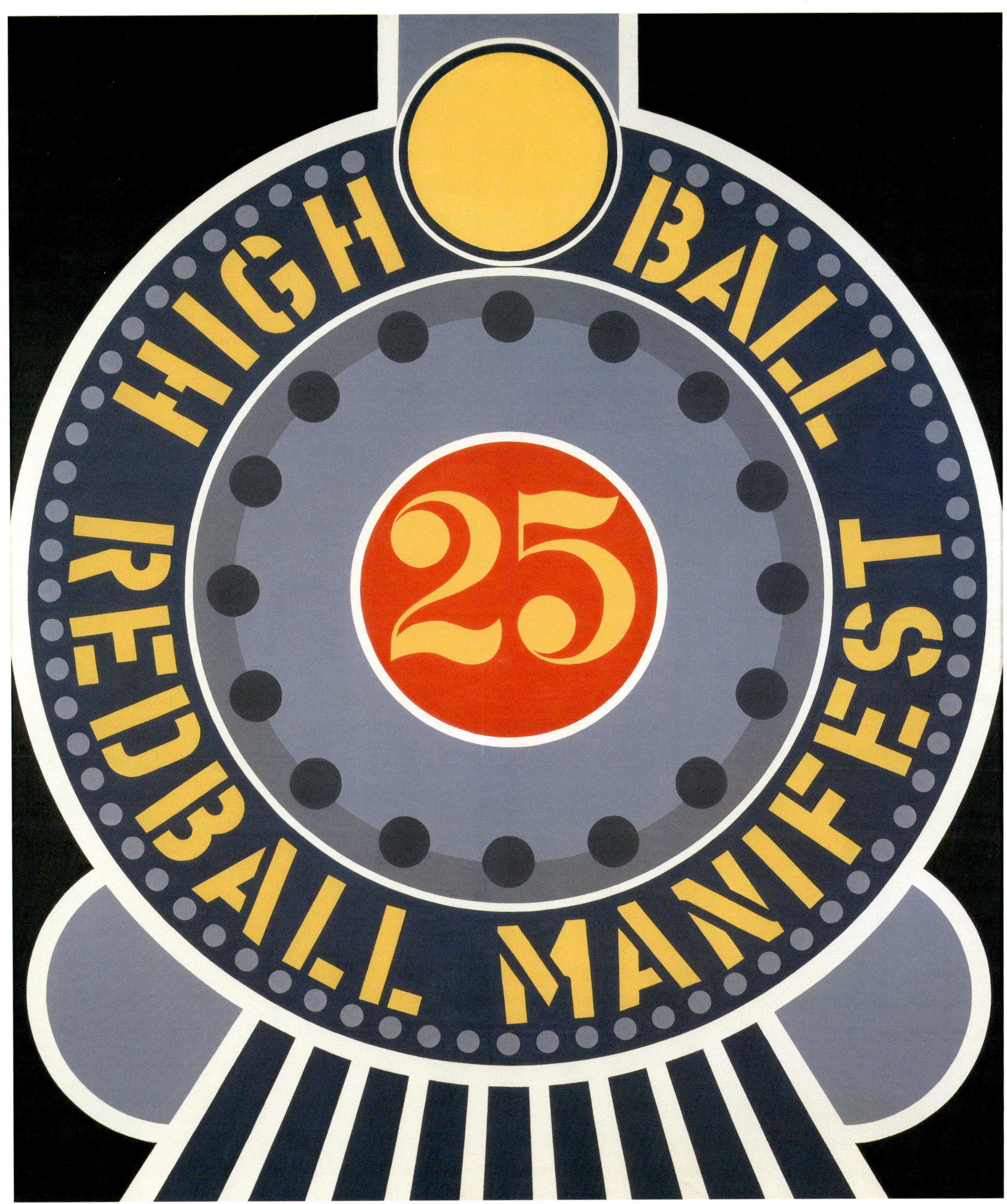

72.

Highball on the Redball Manifest, 1963

Oil on canvas
60 × 50 in. (152.5 × 127 cm)
Gift of Mari and James A. Michener
1991.243

Provenance: Purchased by James Michener from Stable Gallery, New York, 1963; long-term loan to The University of Texas at Austin, 1968–1991

Emily Jacir

b. Amman, Jordan, 1970

w. Irving, Texas, 1988–1992; Memphis, Tennessee, 1992–1994; Bethlehem, Palestine, 1994; Dallas, 1994–1996; Snowmass, Colorado, 1996–1997; Paris, 1997–1998; Ramallah, Palestine–New York, 1999–present

from Texas with love (2002, plate 73) is deceptively simple. It is comprised of a sixty-minute video made in Texas as well as an accompanying soundtrack offered on headphones. The video footage depicts the more or less banal, uneventful west Texas landscape, where long open roads carve out most of the giant state. But this is precisely the point. Upon reading Jacir's description of the video installation and her provided play list, one immediately understands the acutely painful reversal of fortune alluded to here. To accentuate the halting immobility of the Palestinian people in occupied territories, Jacir set up an imaginary action: she asked a group of Palestinians to choose a song they would listen to if they could drive, uninterrupted by checkpoints, for one hour. The songs given to Jacir make up an unlikely compilation of American and Arab tunes, old and new, ranging from popular Arab divas such as Umm Kathoum, Warda, and Fairuz, to the Algerian hero of Rai music, Cheb Khaled, to American soul and pop stars such as James Brown, Madonna, and the Indigo Girls. The viewer is then invited to select his or her own song from the provided play list and watch the road as if seated in the driver's side of the car.

By setting up this effective transaction of displacing one body for another, Jacir insists on the personal and emotional impact of, as well as the physical limitations caused by, the Israeli occupation. The ordinary quality of the image of the open road serves to emphasize how the occupation disrupts the most banal aspects of Palestinian life—not just the big issues of nationhood, identity, and continuity, but daily actions such as going to a wedding reception, to work, or to school. Given the glut of news reports focusing on the Israeli/Palestinian conflict, one of the thorniest issues from the last century until today, Jacir has chosen to present images in the form of photographs and video footage that elicit sympathy for the familiar, in an everyday context. Her decision to produce *from Texas with love* in Texas also suggests considerations regarding the geopolitical relationship between these three territories.

A later work that could be considered a companion piece to *from Texas with love* is *Crossing Surda* (2003). Here the artist hid a video camera in her bag and crossed the Surda checkpoint from Ramallah to attend Birzeit University, a typical commute that many Palestinians are forced to undertake through a checkpoint manned by Israeli soldiers. Delays, intimidation, bad weather, and frustration are evident from the perspective of the camera's lens placed at her waist. *Crossing Surda* is more straightforward and perhaps more of a social realist document than *from Texas with love,* which the artist has described as activating the pathos of longing and unrequited desire: "The piece is about being in a place so incredible and beautiful and being able to drive freely and to listen to music, and at the same time wanting to cry, because this cannot happen back home."[1]

In another significant work from 2003 entitled *Where We Come From,* Jacir literally placed herself "in another's shoes." Here she enacted a "proxy" rite that involved returning to places and people otherwise off-limits to certain immobilized Palestinians suffering from nostalgia and dislocation. Again engaging her community in a directive, she asked for instructions to do something wishful on their behalf in a Palestinian territory to which she could gain entry using her American passport. The "favors" asked of Jacir were poignantly quotidian: "play soccer with a boy from the territories," "walk the streets of Nazareth," "kiss and hug my mother for me," "go to Haifa at dawn and light a candle for the Palestinians." Each favor delivered to and from family members and friends constituted, for Jacir, a political act in its own right.

Jacir was born in Amman, Jordan, in 1970, although different sources have mistakenly listed her birthplace as Bethlehem, Ramallah, Houston, Palestine, and Saudi Arabia. She has lived in Saudi Arabia and in Texas, amongst other places, but she now resides in Ramallah and New York. Always on the move, she stated, "the ability to actually experience such freedom in other countries is a painful marker and reminder of the impossibility of experiencing such a basic human right in Palestine."[2] Having attended art schools in the United States, including the Whitney Independent Study Program in New York, Jacir was catalyzed by debates regarding the role of politics in art, the agency of activism, the practice of site-specific and community projects, as well as the discourse surrounding identity politics and postcolonial thought (especially as expressed in the writing of Edward Said) that pervaded graduate institutions in the 1990s. This generation of artists struggled with the hubris of the politically driven art practice of their predecessors, such as Hans Haacke, Alfredo Jaar, and Jochen Gerz, realizing more down-to-earth, less programmatic projects.[3]

Perhaps the most relevant precedent for Jacir is the Palestinian artist Mona Hatoum. In the 1980s Hatoum, who was educated in London, enlisted her own plight of exile and familial estrangement as a source for potent works in video, sculptural installation, and performance, adopting the voice and aesthetics of the "colonizer" in order to express political dissent. Jacir furthers this project, but complicates it by rendering transparent her own dual personality: a Palestinian in exile as well as an American artist with international mobility and freedoms. In this self-conscious mode, she embodies, rather than represents, the inherent contradictions of this political quagmire.

Regine Basha

Notes

1. Stella Rollig, et al., *Belongings: Works 1998–2003* (Wien: Folio Verlag, 2004), 18.
2. Emily Jacir, interview, available at www.ucr.com [February 15, 2005].
3. Community engagement and relational aesthetics beyond the gallery space, where the viewer or participant becomes an integral part of the completion of meaning and value of a work—a practice common in the 1970s—became a more mainstream activity in the 1990s with figures such as Rirkrit Tiravanija and Thomas Hirshhorn.

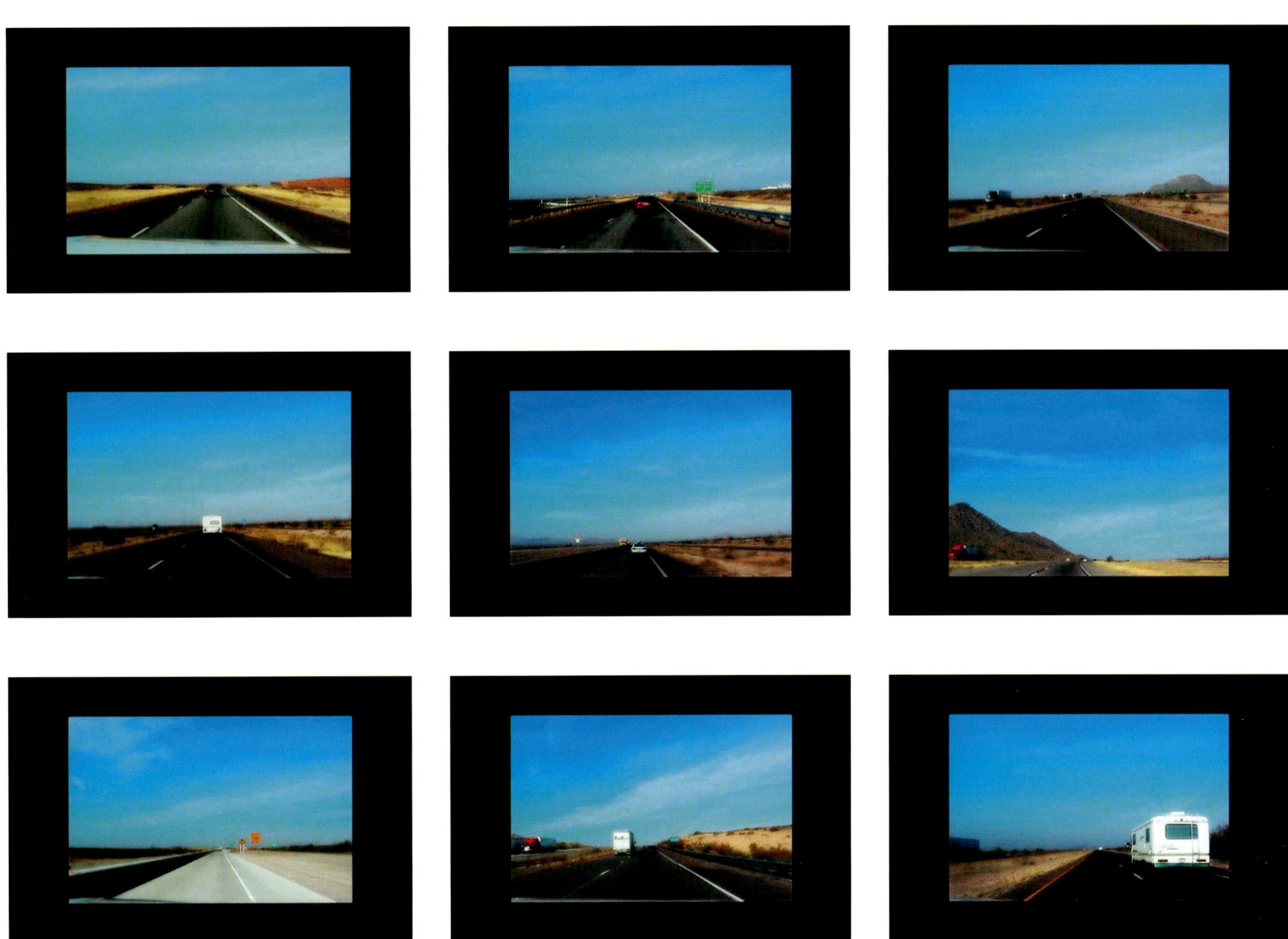

73.
from Texas with love [installation details], 2002

Video installation; DVD and MP3 with 51 songs (60 minutes)
Edition 2/7
Partial and pledged gift of Jeanne and Michael Klein
T2005.3

Provenance: Commissioned by Marfa Studio of Arts, 2001; purchased at the request of the museum by Jeanne and Michael Klein from Alexander and Bonin, New York, 2005

Alfred Jensen

Guatemala City, 1903– Glen Ridge, New Jersey, 1981

w. San Diego, California, 1925; Munich, 1926–1928; Europe–North Africa, 1929–1951; New York, 1951–1972; Glen Ridge, New Jersey, 1972–1981

Alfred Jensen occupies a place in the history of twentieth-century art alongside artists such as Sonia and Robert Delaunay, Wassily Kandinsky, and Josef Albers as one of the most searching interrogators of color and color theory. *Aurora, Per III: Daily Color Progression* (1961, plate 75) and *Mayan Temple, Per II: Palenque* (1962, plate 76) are emblematic of Jensen's mature style: both feature small patches of richly textured, intense colors arranged in geometric patterns, which are the expression of Jensen's view of man's position within an overarching, all-embracing structure of a physical and mystical universe.

Jensen was born in Guatemala to a Danish father and French-Polish mother. He initially went to school in Europe before moving back to the United States to begin his art education, returning again to the Old World in 1926 to study painting at Hans Hofmann's school in Munich. Here his interest in bold color combinations certainly must have been nourished. Traveling as a companion and adviser to Sadie May Adler, a wealthy fellow student of Hofmann's, Jensen spent much of the next fifteen years in Europe, often going to Paris, where he associated with such artists as Pablo Picasso, Joan Miró, Alberto Giacometti, and Henri Matisse. After Adler's death in 1951, Jensen moved to New York to begin painting full-time, and he had his first one-person exhibition there a year later at the John Heller Gallery.

Already deeply concerned with color theory by the early 1950s, Jensen created a number of color diagrams to record his thoughts and test relationships between hues. Mark Rothko, with whom Jensen was close in these years, saw the studies and remarked that they "have a beauty. You ought to do something more with them."[1] Jensen eventually followed Rothko's advice, and beginning in 1957 his diagrams evolved into paintings with bright, primary colors that were arranged in various patterns and grids and often accompanied by handwritten symbols, letters, and numerical sequences. Of the diagrams Jensen later said, "I was unconsciously doing my style for ten years but I didn't know a painting could look that way."[2] Jensen's theoretical concern with color had already led him some years earlier to closely examine and test the precepts of Johanne Wolfgang Goethe's treatise on the subject. The artist once claimed, "I read *Zür Farberlehre [Color Theory]* once a year until I understood it—25 years later."[3] For Jensen, Goethe's treatise offered a means of putting color to work, allowing it to function actively by structuring a painting rather than simply describing tonal values.

This was crucial because, like Piet Mondrian before him, Jensen's use of color and geometry can only be understood within the context of a passionate and rigorous philosophy. Just as Mondrian's grid was based in his study of theosophy and sought to express a belief in the presence of universal connections existing in the natural world, so too must Jensen's abstractions be seen as visual manifestations of larger forces and energies in the universe. His preoccupation with such relationships led him to engage in diverse historical studies, ranging from Chinese philosophy to Greek art to astronomy, geometry, and number theory. In particular, he was guided by a pervasive interest in the presence of structuring dualities and harmonizing opposites in the universe. Important to Jensen in this regard was the work of the nineteenth-century English philosopher Michael Faraday and his conception of "fields." Faraday wrote, "I do not perceive in any part of space, whether . . . vacant or filled with matter, anything but forces and the lines in which they are exerted."[4] It is this sense

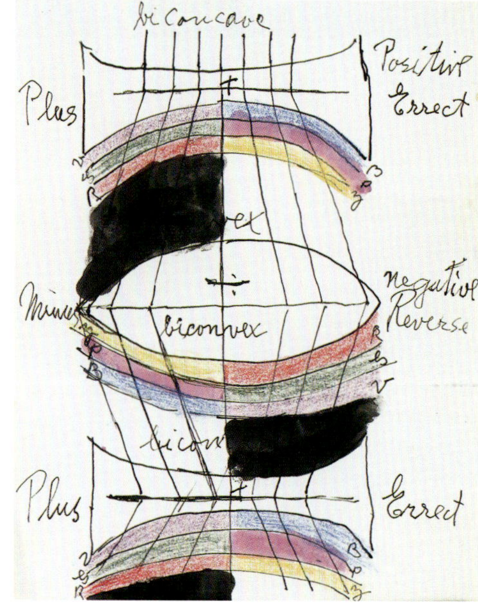

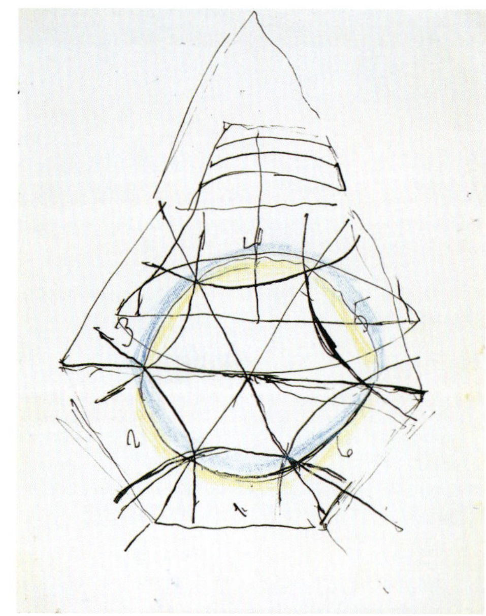

74.
Diagram of the Study for Aurora, Per III: Daily Color Progression (Sun and Moon), 1961–1962

India ink, crayon, and watercolor on paper (doublesided)
11 × 8½ in. (28 × 21.6 cm)
Gift of Mari and James A. Michener
G1968.134

Provenance: Gift of the artist to James Michener, 1961–1962

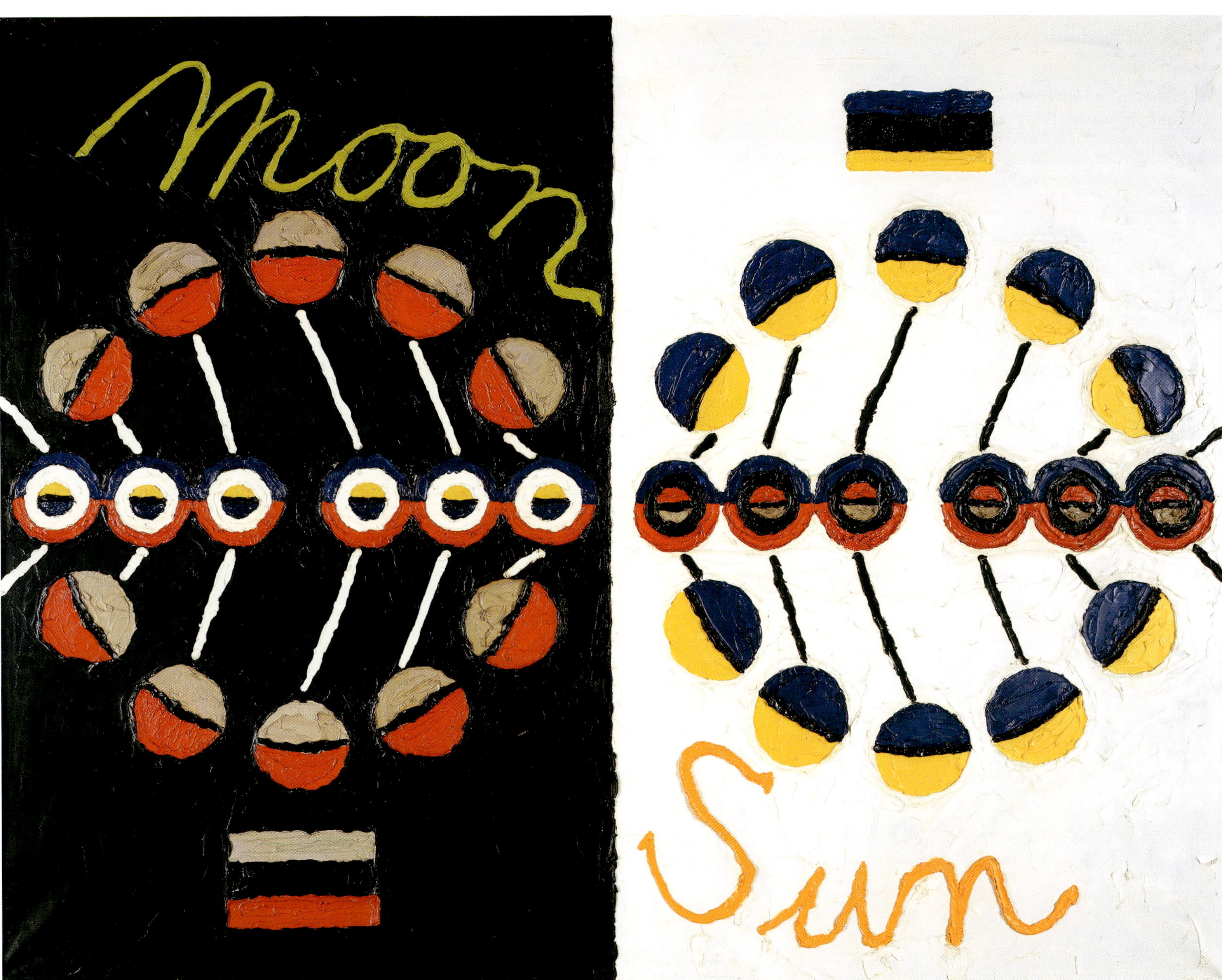

75.

Aurora, Per III: Daily Color Progression, 1961

Oil on canvas
54 × 68 in. (137.2 × 173.3 cm)
Gift of Mari and James A. Michener
G1968.83

Provenance: Purchased by James Michener from the artist, New York, 1962
Inscribed verso "Mural comprising six panels Title: 'Aurora.' Title: Per III 'Daily Color Progression' Size 54" × 68" Painted in 1961 by Alfred Jensen"

of an energy-rich, dynamic universe that has informed much of Jensen's work.

The choices of colors and patterns in *Aurora, Per III* and *Mayan Temple, Per II* articulate different aspects of Jensen's philosophy. In the case of *Aurora, Per III,* named for the Greek goddess of the dawn, Jensen arranged the colors according to Goethe's discussion of hot and cool values.[5] The cool tones, such as blue and violet, are placed above the hotter red and yellow. The resulting combination of semicircles creates an orb, itself part of a larger sphere, suggesting the formation of celestial bodies through the combination of opposing forces and energy. Jensen further joins opposite values by using a black field in one half of the picture and a white field in the other to represent the light environments of the moon and sun respectively.[6] Finally, Jensen unites the painting, containing its various dualities within a balanced, harmonious whole by means of a rotational symmetry that suggests the revolving motion and circular paths of moons and planets.

Mayan Temple, Per II, one of a series of six paintings on this theme, stems from Jensen's study of Mayan culture and cosmology. As Jensen wrote, "The color's distribution order is patterned after the Mayan concept of Polar Star worship and religion."[7] The painting's title refers to the temple at Palenque in modern day Mexico. All the colors and their positions in relation to one another replicate that temple's physical plan, which was oriented, according to Jensen, around the path of the north star in the night sky. He executed this work on commission for James Michener, who shared Jensen's fascination with Mayan culture and architecture. The two had met, in fact, while Michener was at work on a book about Guatemala, Jensen's birthplace, in 1961–1962. The artist's enthusiasm for the subject led him to turn the work into a series.

Careful observation of both *Aurora, Per III* and *Mayan Temple, Per II* reveals an insistent painted materiality that is one of the most remarkable aspects of Jensen's work. The surfaces of his paintings are lushly treated, with dabs of paint, often applied directly from the tube, rising from the canvas in a thick impasto. The playful, joyous exuberance of Jensen's pigments gives his work a sensuousness and immediacy that contrasts with its studied intellectualism. As artist Paul Brach pointed out, his paintings also possess an "earthbound and almost primitive" quality, precisely because they so frankly declare themselves to be material objects.[8]

Thus for all of the theoretical complexity of Jensen's paintings, they are filled with the sense of wonder and even ecstasy that the painter sought to convey in his dynamic combinations of color and form. Like so many other artists of the last century, Jensen reacted to the growing industrialism, commercialism, and secularism of Western society by seeking to create an art that allowed artist and viewer to place themselves in relation to a larger spiritual framework. These theories, finally, had a deeply personal relevance for Jensen, who saw philosophy, geometry, astronomy, and art as means of expressing the elemental forces that tie people to each other and to the vast cosmos that surrounds them.[9] The passion with which Jensen applied pigment to canvas is an unmistakable sign of the emotional immediacy of that project.

Leo Costello

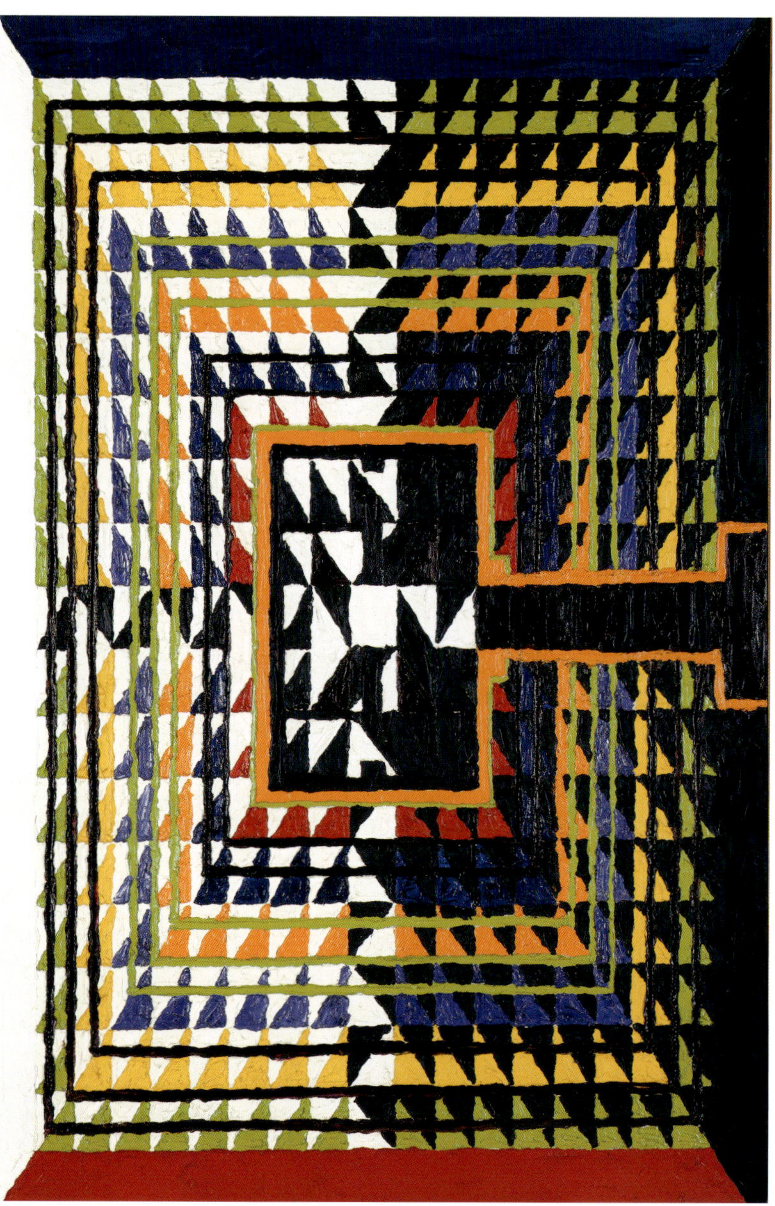

76.

Mayan Temple, Per II: Palenque, 1962

Oil on canvas
76 × 50 in. (193.1 × 127 cm)
Gift of Mari and James A. Michener
G1968.84

Provenance: Commissioned by James Michener and purchased from the artist, New York, 1962
Inscribed upper left "A Series of six panels comprising Title: 'Mayan Temple.' Per II: 'Palenque' Size 76" × 50" painted by Alfred Jensen Feb–May, 1962"

Notes

1. Quoted in Philip Herrera, "Obituary," *Art in America* 69 (summer 1981): 19.
2. Quoted in Linda Cathcart, "Paintings and Diagrams from the Years 1957–1977," in *Alfred Jensen: Paintings and Diagrams from the Years 1957–1977* (Buffalo, N.Y.: Albright-Knox Art Gallery, 1978), 6.
3. Quoted in Herrera, 19.
4. Quoted in Donald Kuspit, "Alfred Jensen: Systems Mystagogue," *Artforum* 16 (April 1978): 41.
5. Alfred Jensen to James Michener, June 27, 1962, Blanton Museum of Art Archives, The University of Texas at Austin.
6. Jensen to Michener.
7. Jensen to Michener.
8. Paul Brach, "Alfred Jensen and the Abstract Absolute," *Art in America* 66 (May/June 1978): 75.
9. Kuspit, 40–41.

Luis A. Jiménez, Jr.

b. El Paso, 1940

w. Austin (trip to Mexico City, 1964), 1960–1966; New York, 1966–1972; El Paso–Hondo, New Mexico, 1972–1984; Hondo (spring semesters in Houston since 1995), 1984–present

Luis Jiménez is known primarily for his monumental figurative fiberglass sculptures that address themes of personal and collective experience and the history of the American West. His work is brightly colored and brash, qualities it shares with other persuasive works by Chicano artists who emerged in the 1960s. However, the stylistic tendencies of Pop art, the predominant artistic language when the artist was beginning his practice, also influenced Jiménez, as did the historical movement of Regionalism, with its ambitions to capture the specificities of place in works of art.

Jiménez's father was a sign maker in El Paso who specialized in "spectaculars" or signs with neon lights and moving parts. Jiménez worked in his father's shop as a young boy, and by his early teens, he had learned how to weld and spray paint. Throughout his youth, his parents noticed and encouraged his artistic ability, taking him to Mexico City to see the work of the Mexican muralists Diego Rivera, David Alfaro Siqueiros, and José Clemente Orozco, among others. Jiménez attended The University of Texas at Austin, first majoring in architecture, then fine arts. His early sculptures were abstract and made from traditional materials such as wood and stone. After graduating from UT in 1964, Jiménez traveled to Mexico City, where he worked with the sculptor Francisco Zuñiga before deciding to move to New York to pursue a career as an artist.

During the mid-1960s Jiménez made the transition from working in wood to constructing sculptures in fiberglass, a material used to make customized car bodies and amusement park decorations. Other artists, including Billy Al Bengston, Craig Kauffman, and Judy Chicago in the Los Angeles area, were also working in fiberglass at this time. They emphasized the medium's slick, flawless surface, and their work, according to critics, exhibited a "finish fetish."[1] Casting them from large-scale molds, Jiménez coated his sculptures in brightly colored urethane paints and clear resin, which gave them an almost fluid appearance. For subject matter, he drew from both personal experiences and popular culture. His sculpture *American Dream* (1969) depicts a nude blonde woman locked in a sexual embrace with a Volkswagen Beetle, a subject reminiscent of both Pop artist Tom Wesselmann's paintings and mythological themes in art history, such as Leda and the Swan. At this time, Jiménez also explored more politically charged themes, as in *Man on Fire* (1969), which references Cuauhtémoc, a figure from Mexican history whom the Mexican muralists (particularly Siqueiros) appropriated as a heroic image of the indigenous Mexican. This sculpture fuses a straining male figure with bright yellow red flames and makes an oblique reference to the Chicano political movement that was gaining momentum in the late 1960s.

After spending six formative years in New York, Jiménez returned to the Southwest permanently, settling in Texas and New Mexico. While an artist-in-residence at the Roswell Art Center, he began a series of sculptures that examined the history of the Old West by revealing the moral ambiguities underneath the romantic mythology of cowboys and Indians. One work from this series, *Progress I* (1974), represents an Indian on the back of a buffalo. The Indian is attempting to kill the animal, even as his own body is pierced and twisted by the force of their collision. The contorted shapes of other animals, skulls, and ghostly figures evoke not only a sense of heroic struggle for survival but also the systematic slaughter of wild bison, wolves, and Native Americans during western expansion.

Jiménez continued to represent his revisionist history of the American West with his first public commission (by the City of Houston), *Vaquero* (1981). The sculpture depicts a Mexican cowboy riding a bucking Appaloosa—a highly charged image referring to both classic equestrian sculpture and the work of American artist Frederic Remington,

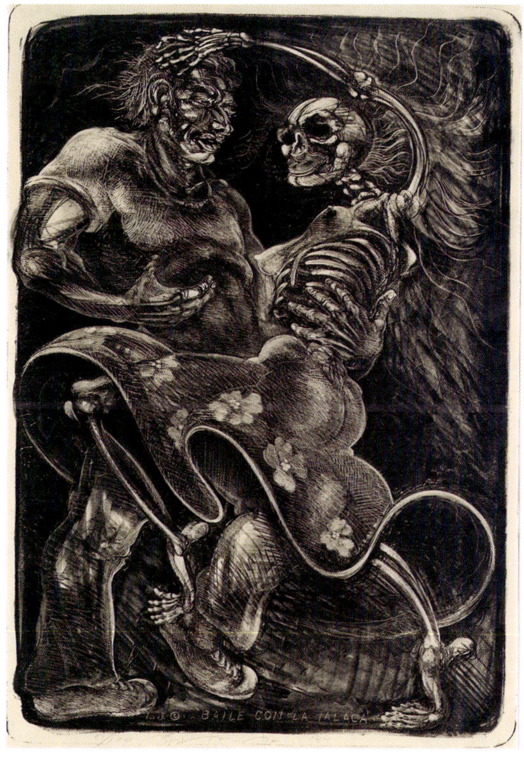

77.
Baile con la talaca [Dance with the Skeleton], 1984

Lithograph
Edition 81/100
39⅛ × 26⅞ in. (99.3 × 68.2 cm)
Archer M. Huntington Museum Fund
1985.79

Provenance: Purchased from the artist, 1985
Signed lower corner "81/100 Luis Jiménez Jr. '84" in pencil
Inscribed lower corner "L.J. © 'BAILE CON LA TALACA'" in stone

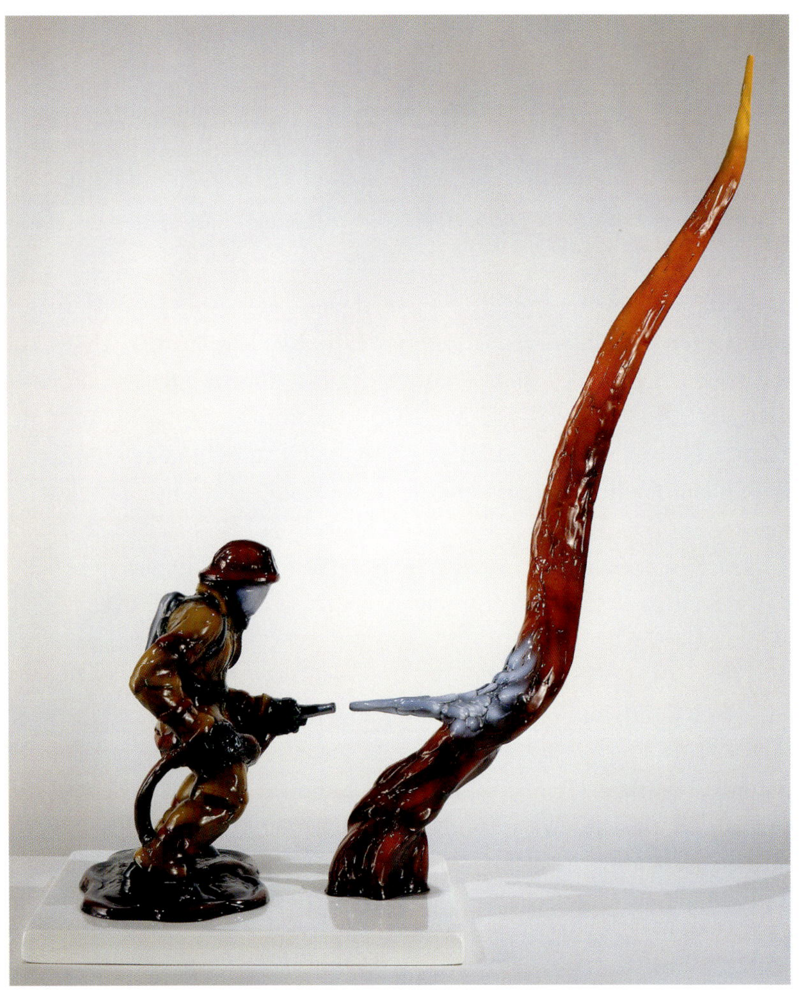

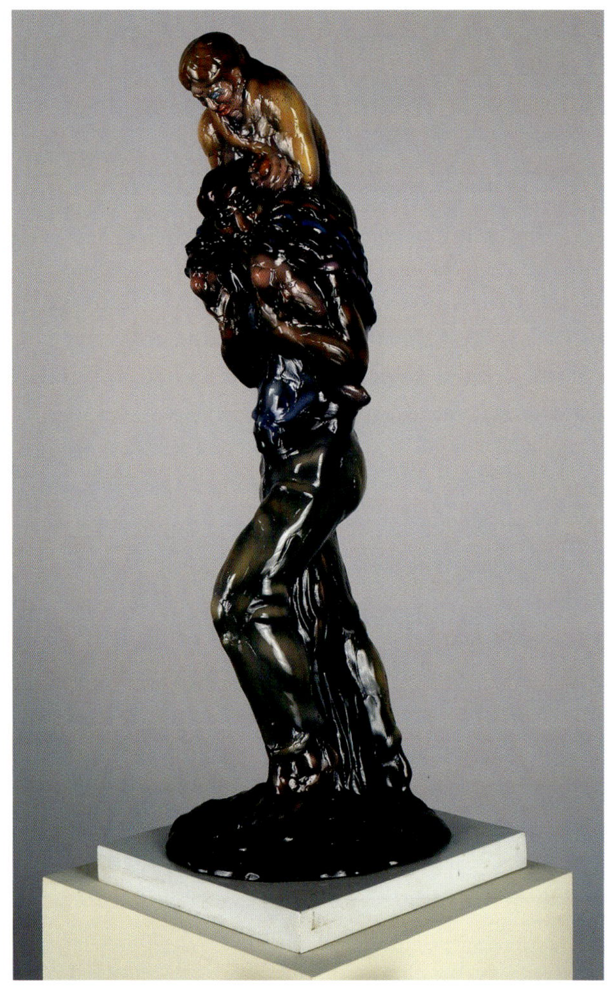

78.
Fire Man, 1996–1997

Painted fiberglass
Edition 5/10
41½ × 34 × 14 in. (105.4 × 86.4 × 35.6 cm)
Purchase through the generosity of the Blanton Contemporary Circle and the Archer M. Huntington Museum Fund
2001.7
Signed on base "Luis Jiménez"
Inscribed on base "5/10" in black marker or paint
Inscribed on base "Fire Man/'96" ("'97" added in black marker or paint)

Provenance: Purchased from Moody Gallery, Houston, 2001

79.
Border Crossing, 1987

Painted fiberglass
Edition 3/10
32½ × 11½ × 9½ in. (82.5 × 29.2 × 24.1 cm)
Gift of Jeanne and Michael Klein, 2005
2005.20
Signed on base "L.J. 3/10" in ink
Inscribed on base "L Jiménez 87" in raised letters

simultaneously revealing the history of conquest that lay behind one of the most treasured American icons. As the artist explained,

> *The* Vaquero *piece is a tribute to the Mexican origins of the American cowboy, a statement about Texas, and also about the Mexican community within Texas. If you think of words connected with cowboys, like rodeo, corral, remuda, lariat, those words are all Spanish. The cowboy was a Mexican invention. . . . It wasn't John Wayne who was the original cowboy. That's the myth.*[2]

Vaquero underscores the fact that the territory of the American Southwest was acquired through war with Mexico and that the cowboy, long a symbol of the independent and individualist American spirit, is actually of Mexican origin.

The site originally intended for *Vaquero* was Tranquility Park in Houston, located near City Hall. Local officials expressed apprehension about a sculpture of a gun-wielding Mexican occupying such a prominent site, so it was moved to Moody Park, in a predominately Hispanic neighborhood. However, even in this location the sculpture continued to generate controversy: critics argued that it was a reminder of riots and gang violence.[3] Jiménez often produces his sculptures in small editions, and a later copy of *Vaquero* was temporarily installed on the UT campus in 1989 as part of the exhibition *A Century of Sculpture in Texas, 1889–1989*, organized by the Blanton Museum (then the Archer M. Huntington Art Gallery).[4]

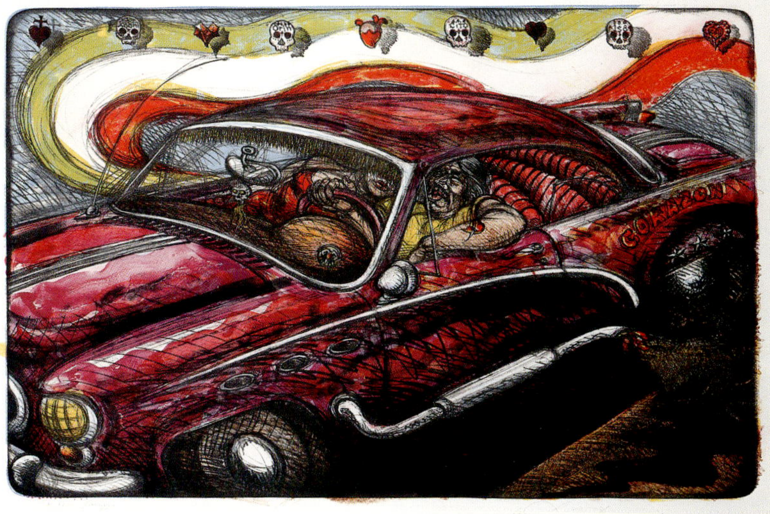

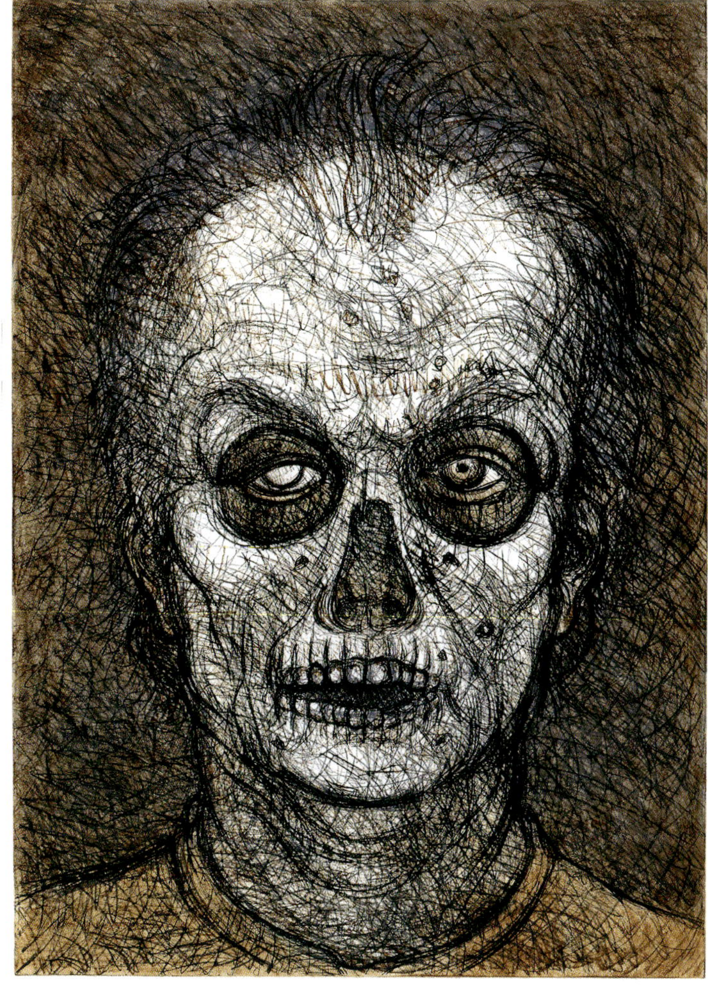

80.
Untitled (Low Rider), 1994
Lithograph
29½ × 41¾ in. (75 × 106 cm)
Gift of Mona and Ken Hale
2001.88
Signed lower right "©Luis Jiménez '94" in pencil
Inscribed lower left "KJH Imp." in pencil

81.
Self-Portrait, 1996
Soft-ground etching with aquatint
Edition 16/50
45 × 32 in. (114.3 × 81.3 cm)
Gift of Jill Wilkinson
2001.61
Signed lower right "Luis Jiménez"

Jiménez explored themes of personal and collective experience in other well-known works, such as *Border Crossing* (1989, plate 79). Here a Hispanic man, his head bowed and the muscles of his columnar body bulging, supports both a woman and a baby on his shoulders as he prepares to wade across the Rio Grande River. An event in the lives of Jiménez's father and grandmother inspired the sculpture, but the work also pays homage to every immigrant who has attempted to cross the border, risking deportation, and even death, in the process.

By creating sympathetic images of honky-tonks, sodbusters, and steelworkers, Jiménez eventually developed a reputation as an artist who championed the working class. In 1996 a group of firefighters in Cleveland, Ohio, selected him to design a memorial to their fallen coworkers, and they financed the work by deducting money from their paychecks. The *Fire Man* sculpture in the Blanton's collection (1996–1997, plate 78) is a maquette for this larger monument, which depicts the focused body of a fireman in direct opposition to an elongated tongue of flame—a Promethean image that speaks to both endurance, persistence, and the human will to control.[5] Yet here the use of fire is more complicated: it is both a part of the fireman's body and his foe.

As part of his process of developing proposals for public commissions, Jiménez often completes a number of drawings, lithographs, and smaller-scale maquettes before making his edition of the finished work. He considers each iteration of the original idea a fully realized work of art, and within each medium, he shows extraordinary skill and sensitivity, his ability to render in both two- and three-dimensions seemingly effortless. Jiménez's work combines aspects of Chicano, Pop, Western, and public art, but it also extends the boundaries of these genres with an element of satire that reexamines the myths of US history, simultaneously incorporating the experiences of those whose stories traditionally have been excluded.

In 1998 UT Austin honored Jiménez as a distinguished alumnus. To mark that occasion, two of his sculptures were temporarily installed outside The Performing Arts Center (the site of the award ceremonies). It is a longtime hope of the University to one day acquire a major outdoor sculpture by Jiménez to permanently display on its campus as part of the Blanton's collection.

Erin Aldana

Notes

1. Charles Dee Mitchell, "A Baroque Populism," *Art in America* 87 (March 1999): 101. For more on the use of fiberglass by artists in the Los Angeles area, see Laura Meyer, "From Finish Fetish to Feminism: Judy Chicago's *Dinner Party* in California Art History," in Amelia Jones, ed., *Sexual Politics: Judy Chicago's Dinner Party in Feminist Art History* (Berkeley and Los Angeles: University of California Press, 1996), 46–52.
2. Luis Jiménez, "Signs: A Conversation with Luis Jiménez," interview by Amy Baker Sandback, *Artforum* 23 (September 1984): 84.
3. Mitchell, 103.
4. For more information on this exhibition, see Patricia D. Hendricks and Becky Duval Reese, *A Century of Sculpture in Texas, 1889–1989* (Austin: The University of Texas at Austin, 1989).
5. Camille Flores-Turney, "Howl: The Artwork of Luis Jiménez," in *Howl: The Artwork of Luis Jiménez* (Santa Fe, N.Mex.: New Mexico Magazine, 1997), 50.

Lester F. Johnson

b. Minneapolis, 1919

w. Chicago, Illinois, 1942–1947; New York, 1947–1966; New Haven, Connecticut, 1964–1989; Milford, Connecticut/Easthampton, New York, 1966–present

Lester Johnson is a painter whose work defies categorization. Although associated with the New York School, Johnson gained note as one of a group of artists who rebelled against some of the tenets of Abstract Expressionism while simultaneously incorporating others into their work. Indeed, Johnson's paintings generally combine figurative subjects with loose, impetuous brushwork.

Born in Minneapolis in 1919, Johnson was inspired to study art at an early age when he found several books on Post-Impressionist artists Vincent van Gogh and Paul Gauguin in his hometown library. After high school, he found work as a framer at the Cosmopolitan Art Company before attending the Minneapolis Institute of Art, the St. Paul Art School, and the School of the Art Institute of Chicago. In 1947, at the height of Abstract Expressionism, Johnson moved to New York. There he began associating with artists of the New York School, such as Willem de Kooning and Jackson Pollock, and frequenting the famed Cedar Bar. In addition to attending classes at Hans Hofmann's school, Johnson shared studios with both Larry Rivers and Philip Pearlstein. These friendships facilitated his admittance into a variety of artistic circles, immersing him in a dynamic atmosphere of new ideas and artistic exchange.[1] Initially concerned with abstraction and gestural painting, Johnson soon shifted to concentrate on figurative subjects. As he recalled:

> *I thought it very quickly became a cliché, . . . it was too easy, they could make the drips, the gestures—it was so beautiful and everybody loved them but they were empty. I was into human content so I used it, and I found it a very, very exciting thing to do. I did a lot of paintings at the time where you can hardly see the figure, but it's there.*[2]

The forceful, abstracted heads in Johnson's early paintings gradually evolved into monumental and stylized single and multiple figurative subjects placed in urban settings. The artist is especially identified with a series of images of men in suits and bowler hats. Much of his work was dedicated to exploring both the human condition and the frenetic atmosphere of the city, which he observed from the window of his studio in the Bowery.

Johnson sought to represent man's existential struggle in post–World War II American society. His works, particularly the early paintings, are infused with a rawness, energy, and aggression that often evoke violence. Process oriented, Johnson built up his canvases with thick paint then scraped it away, sometimes scarring the surface by scumbling and gouging the paint with the end of a brush. Johnson called himself an "action painter with content,"[3] clearly feeling a kinship to the Abstract Expressionists, especially Pollock, but unwilling to abandon recognizable subject matter.

In 1953 Johnson began a series of paintings of flat, mask-like heads whose large scale relative to the size of the canvas convey a sense of claustrophobia and enclosure. The works are rendered in a somber earth-toned palette of brown, green, midnight blue, and black. Johnson created his own paints by using a grinding mill to combine pigment, oil, and beeswax, lending the paintings a uniquely textural appearance.

Studio Interior (1962, plate 82) belongs to this series. Here Johnson compressed three frontal heads resembling sculptural busts into a horizontal composition. He used a murky green color with ocher undertones that rises from the depths of an infinite black background. The heads bear uniformly grim expressions and are devoid of identifying characteristics. Archetypal in nature, Johnson's figures symbolize the Everyman and attempt to encapsulate the universality of human experience and emotions. Centered in the canvas is the most fully realized head; it is attached to a torso, offering solidity and balance. Flanking this central figure are similarly rendered heads. The one on the right is confined in a box as if peering through a window or represented in another picture, while the other is depicted with brighter, more intense tones. The vertical brushstrokes invoke a primal, visceral energy, as if the artist had attacked the canvas with his brush.

Johnson's commitment to the figure as a vehicle for exploring the human condition led the artist to distance himself from the practices and philosophies of Abstract Expressionism. He forged his own path and garnered the respect of his peers, becoming one of the leading figurative painters of his day. Johnson's paintings can be seen to anticipate the Neo-Expressionist movement that flourished in the 1980s and that likewise merged content with a gestural painting style. Like the Neo-Expressionists, Johnson explored the emotional underpinnings of contemporary urban life in an effort to illustrate the alienation, uncertainty, and turbulence underlying human existence.

Jennifer Jankauskas

Notes

1. These included the Eighth Street Club, the Hansa Gallery Group, and the Tenth Street Co-op movement.
2. Lester Johnson quoted in Bruce Chernow, "Lester Johnson: In New York and P-town," *Provincetown Arts*, January 1, 1996.
3. Lester Johnson, from remarks at a Club Panel, January 24, 1958, quoted in Irving Sander, *The New York School: The Painters and Sculptors of the Fifties* (New York: Harper & Row, 1978), 126.

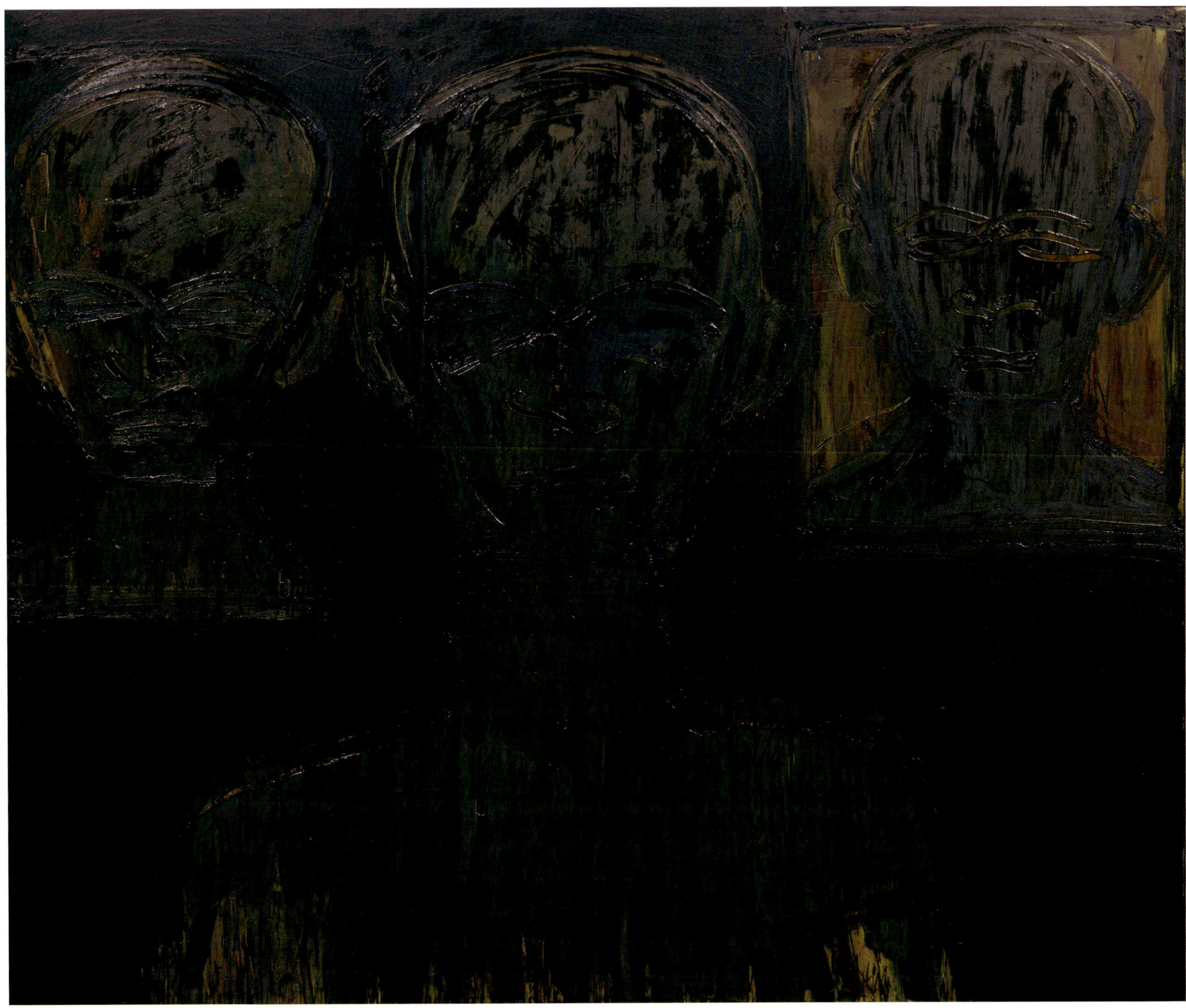

82.

Studio Interior, 1962

Oil on canvas
68¼ × 80 in. (173.4 × 203.3 cm)
Gift of Mari and James A. Michener
1991.245

Provenance: Purchased by James Michener from Martha Jackson Gallery, New York, 1962; long-term loan to The University of Texas at Austin, 1968–1991
Signed verso, upper left "Lester Johnson 1962"

Raymond Jonson

Chariton, Iowa, 1891–Albuquerque, New Mexico, 1982

w. Portland, Oregon, 1909–1910; Chicago, 1910–1924; Santa Fe, New Mexico, 1924–1950; Albuquerque, New Mexico, 1950–1982

Recognized as one of the most important non-objective artists of the American Southwest, Raymond Jonson is also remembered for his leading role in the creation of the influential Transcendental Painting Group, founded in 1938. Although Jonson began his career working in a naturalistic style, after the mid-1920s he turned to creating paintings free from nature or objective representation. His shift toward abstract art was gradual and occurred over the course of years of study and reflection. The writings of Wassily Kandinsky, which he read in translation in 1921, inspired Jonson to adopt a more creative and intuitive approach to making art. Kandinsky also reinforced his growing awareness that a work of art was an entity in its own right and existed beyond empirical reality. Jonson theorized that a painting could "stand as the expression of an emotion, the abstract spiritual ego of the individual . . . that indispensable something which deals with the spirit."[1]

Jonson's introduction to the landscape of the southwestern United States occurred during a summer visit to Santa Fe, New Mexico, in 1922. This visit would prove to have important consequences for his artistic development. Jonson was intrigued by the physical characteristics of the southwestern environment and moved to Santa Fe permanently in 1924. The region's intense light, rugged topographical contours, and wide open vistas struck an emotional cord within him, instigating a search for a new formal language with which to express his vision. He worked intensively, making countless sketches from nature that he later subjected to rigorous theoretical analysis in the studio. Jonson's breakthrough came in the mid-1920s with a cycle of paintings titled Earth Rhythms, in which he reduced the landscape to solid, geometrical components that he repeated throughout the canvas, thereby establishing a sense of rhythmic order.

By the end of the decade, Jonson moved further away from representation. He turned to abstract symbols and began working in serial sequence more consistently. In 1929 he commenced the Digit series, choosing an Arabic number, zero through nine, as a point of departure. The following year, he initiated a series of twenty-six paintings titled Variations on a Rhythm, which were based on the letters of the alphabet. Using the graphic characteristics of a particular letter, Jonson allowed its distinctive shape to dictate the painting's structural format, as in the Blanton's *Variations on a Rhythm—G* (1931, plate 83). By repeating the letter with varied manipulations, the artist achieved an innovative and more pure level of abstraction removed from emotional experience. Unlike the Digit series, where numbers embody human characteristics and color functions symbolically, in the Variations series the letters are highly schematized and color operates as an element of design. In both series, Jonson meticulously finished the surfaces, composing them of precisely crafted brushstrokes that create variegated patterns and textures. His preference for luminous colors recalls the colored filters he used while working as a lighting designer for the Chicago Little Theatre.[2] Indeed, in conception *Variations on a Rhythm—G* exhibits a stagelike quality that more than likely owes a debt to Jonson's firsthand knowledge of set design.

Rebecca E. Lawton

Notes

1. Quoted in Ed Garman, *The Art of Raymond Jonson, Painter* (Albuquerque, N.Mex.: University of New Mexico Press, 1976), 55–56. For further information on Jonson, see Nicolai Cikovsky, Jr., *Raymond Jonson (1891–1982): Pioneer Modernist of New Mexico* (New York: Berry-Hill Galleries, 1986), and Van Deren Coke, ed., *Raymond Jonson: A Retrospective Exhibition* (Albuquerque, N.Mex.: The University of New Mexico Press, 1964).
2. See Garman, 25–33. Tiska Blankenship also discusses the relationship between Jonson's paintings and his work as a lighting and set designer for the Chicago Little Theatre from 1913 to 1917 in *The Raymond Jonson Centennial Retrospective* (Albuquerque, N.Mex.: University of New Mexico Art Museum, 1991), n.p.

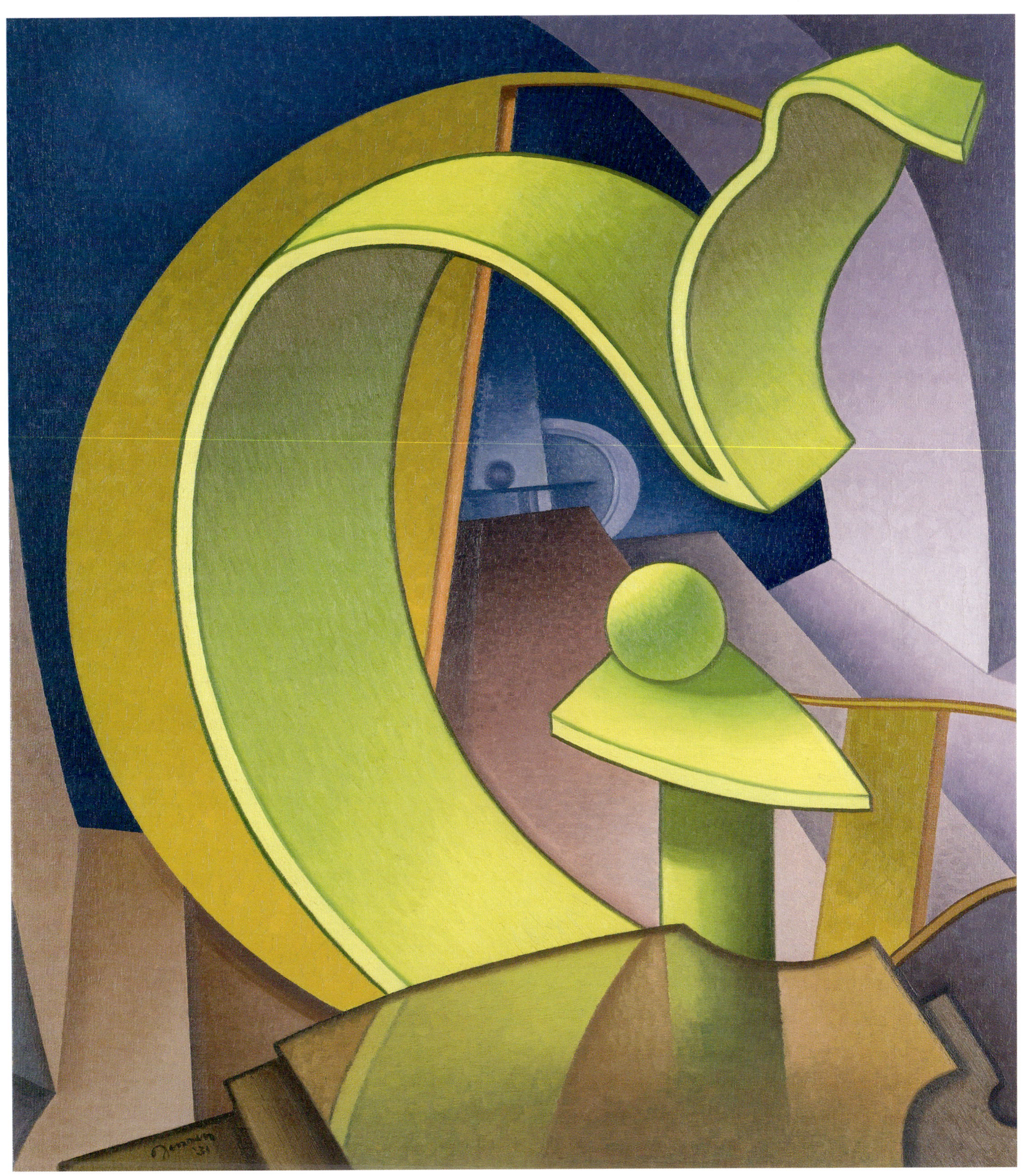

83.

Variations on a Rhythm—G, 1931

Oil on canvas
38⅛ × 33 in. (96.8 × 83.8 cm)
Gift of Thomas Gilcrease Foundation
1981.54
Signed lower left "Jonson '31"
Inscribed verso "Variations on a Rhythm—G 1931 Oil on canvas"
Signed lower left "By Raymond Jonson size—33" wide × 38" high"

Ellsworth Kelly

b. Newburgh, New York, 1923

w. New York, 1941–1943; Boston, 1946–1948; Paris, 1948–1954; New York, 1954–1970; Spencertown, New York, 1970–present

Ellsworth Kelly's work is characterized by the singular and enduring pursuit of ideas and strategies that the artist first began to develop in the late 1940s.[1] His large-scale monochrome panels of distinctive, heraldic shapes are well known, as are his numerous two panel paintings.[2] Within the artist's oeuvre, *High Yellow* (1960, plate 84) is relatively atypical, due both to its three-color palette and its suggestion of an abstracted landscape. Though his work usually is derived from a specific referent, that referent is rarely apparent in the final painting. Such subtleties have long characterized Kelly's practice, but they were largely misunderstood early in his career. Only recently, as the specifics of his background and training have been considered in greater depth, has Kelly gained recognition as a major twentieth-century artist.

Born in Newburgh, New York, in 1923, Kelly began his studies at the Pratt Institute in Brooklyn (1941–1942). He visited Europe for the first time during his service in the United States Army, from 1943 to 1945. Upon his release, Kelly enrolled in the School of the Museum of Fine Arts, Boston. As part of the school's relatively classical training, he copied paintings in the museum's collection, becoming versed in the techniques of the Old Masters. The school was also characterized by a focus on German Expressionism, and Max Beckmann, a guest there in 1948, left a lasting impression on Kelly. When the young artist decided to travel to Paris later that year, he claimed that his entire "modern art baggage" consisted of Beckmann, Paul Klee, and Pablo Picasso.[3]

Once in France, the figurative portraiture that dominated Kelly's Boston period gave way to abstraction. Kelly looked to a variety of sources in search of a new direction: Byzantine mosaics and manuscripts, Romanesque architecture, and the physical environs of Paris and other locales in France. Though he frequented museums and met with several contemporary artists, including Alexander Calder, Joan Miró, and Francis Picabia, he never associated with a particular movement or group. In 1949 he created a painting that represented a significant breakthrough in his practice, *Window, Museum of Modern Art, Paris*. Despite being somewhat smaller in scale, it is an accurate replica of the object in question, consisting of two joined rectangular canvases—the upper painted white and the lower, set back slightly, painted gray—and a black wooden framework indicating the glazing bars. In asserting its status as an object occupying space rather than mimetically representing depth, the piece broke with the Renaissance-derived notion of painting as a window onto the world.

Subsequently, Kelly decided that painting as he understood it was finished. He wrote, "Everywhere I looked, everything I saw became something to be made, and it had to be exactly as it was, with nothing added. It was a new freedom: there was no longer the need to compose. The subject was there already made, and I could take from everything."[4] Here Kelly draws attention to the strategy of the "transfer," whereby a composition or motif observed—not created—by the artist is transferred to the canvas in a fairly direct manner.[5] The smooth, flawless application of paint that characterizes the artist's paintings from 1950 on relates to this notion of the direct transfer, whereby subjective mediation is minimized. Kelly was very drawn to the idea of the "already made," and he searched for other methods to obviate his role in composing. Meeting John Cage in 1949 and Jean Arp in 1950 encouraged Kelly's exploration of aleatory strategies, and both his collages, guided by the laws of chance, and automatic drawings served as the source of a number of paintings from this period. *Colors for a Large Wall* (1951), a pivotal piece, grew out of this sort of experimentation. Its large scale and use of separate panels for different colors are features that would characterize the artist's work for years to come.[6]

In 1954 Kelly moved to New York, and in this new setting the focus of his work shifted. In France he had been occupied with discovering strategies; in New York he exploited the potential of his findings. The paintings from the mid-1950s and early 1960s are characterized by a focus on mass and color and a renewed interest in the curve. Within two years of arriving in New York, Kelly began showing at Betty Parsons Gallery. Critics did not know what to make of him. Some linked him to Constructivism, de Stijl, or the Bauhaus, not recognizing the distinctive features of his approach.[7] Others erroneously grouped him with the "hard edge" painters and the Minimalists.[8] Because Kelly never identified with a particular movement or group, misreadings are ubiquitous in the early literature.

High Yellow made its debut in the exhibition *American Abstract Expressionists and Imagists,* organized by the Guggenheim Museum in 1961. The show paired paintings by key Abstract Expressionists with the work of younger, emerging artists, arguing that the newer paintings demonstrated a trend toward "greater simplicity, clarity, and power of expressive means."[9] *High Yellow*'s combination of heraldic form, flat color, and seamlessly applied paint stood out among the works in the exhibition. Indivisible from their tightly interlocked forms, the three areas of equally intense color—yellow ovoid, blue encasement, and green rectangle—exert pressure against each other and create an expressive force that is largely independent of any possible subject matter. Although *New York Times* critic Stuart Preston found the show's premise poorly conceived, he considered Kelly's work exemplary of new directions in abstract painting.[10]

Though *High Yellow,* in its suggestion of an abstracted landscape, is relatively unique in the artist's oeuvre, it reminds us of one of the most significant aspects of the artist's practice: Kelly never engages in pure abstraction, rather his work is always grounded in observable phenomena.

Amy Dove

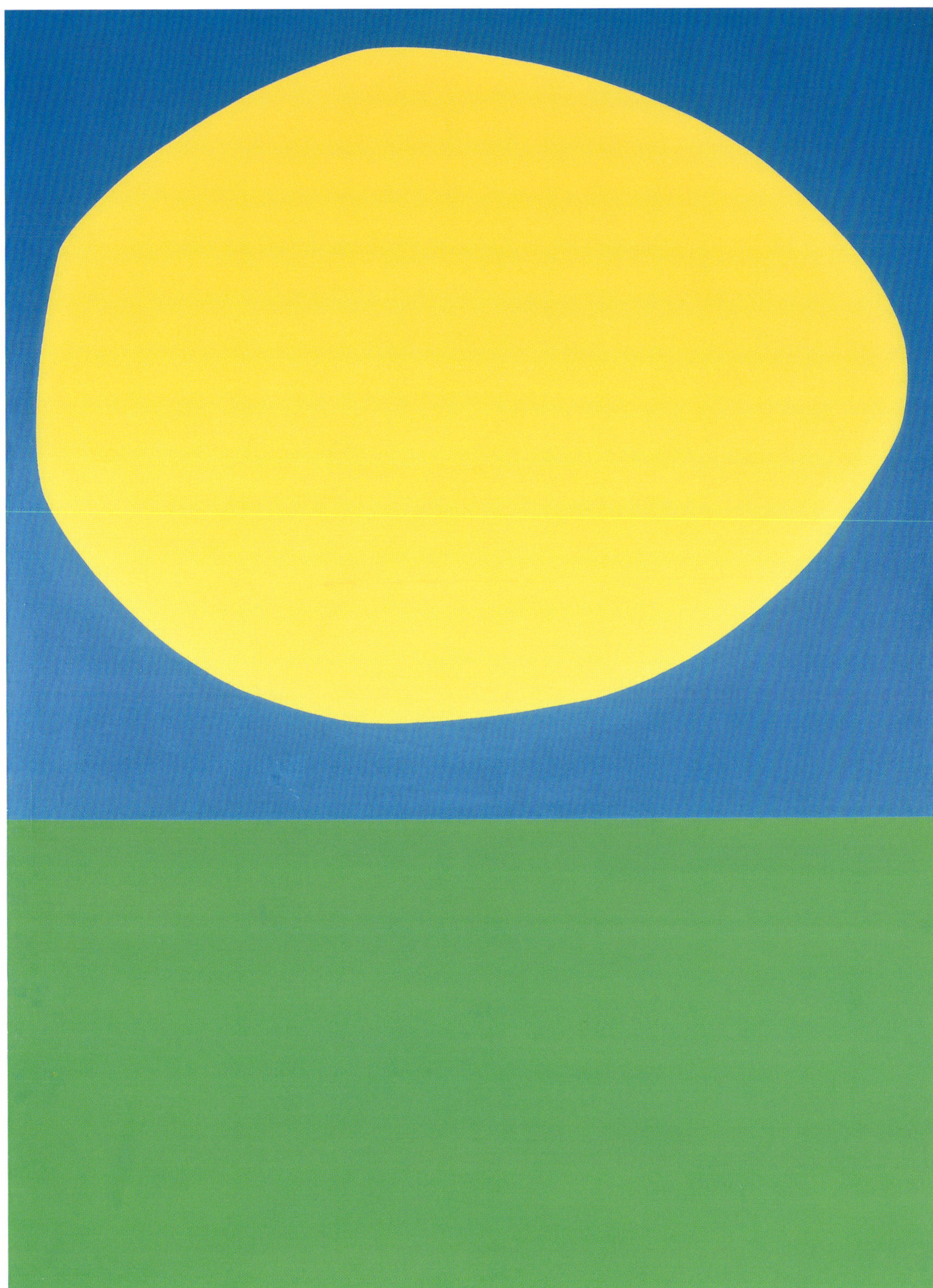

84.
High Yellow, 1960

Oil on canvas
81 × 58 in. (204.6 × 146.8 cm)
Gift of Mari and James A. Michener
1991.246

Provenance: Purchased by James Michener from Betty Parsons Gallery, New York, 1961; long-term loan to The University of Texas at Austin, 1968–1991
Inscribed verso "Kelly 60"

Notes

1. See Diane Waldman, "Ellsworth Kelly," in *Ellsworth Kelly: A Retrospective* (New York: The Solomon R. Guggenheim Foundation, 1996), 11.
2. See Lawrence Alloway's discussion of heraldry in Kelly's work, "Heraldry and Sculpture: Ellsworth Kelly," *Art International* 6 (April 1962): 52–53.
3. Yve-Alain Bois, "Ellsworth Kelly in France: Anti-Composition in Its Many Guises," in *Ellsworth Kelly: The Years in France, 1948–1954* (Washington, D.C.: National Gallery of Art, 1992), 16.
4. Ellsworth Kelly, "Notes from 1969," in *Ellsworth Kelly: Painting and Sculptures, 1963–1979* (Amsterdam: Stedelijk Museum, 1979), 30.
5. Bois, "Ellsworth Kelly in France," 14.
6. For more information, see Yve-Alain Bois, "Kelly's *Trouvailles:* Findings in France," in *Ellsworth Kelly: The Early Drawings, 1948–1955* (Cambridge, Mass.: Harvard University Art Museums, 1999), 26.
7. See, for example, Barbara Butler, "Ellsworth Kelly," *Arts Magazine* 30 (June 1956): 52, and Parker Tyler, "Ellsworth Kelly," *Artnews* 55 (summer 1956): 51.
8. See John Coplans's "John McLaughlin: Hard Edge and American Painting," *Artforum* 2 (January 1964): 28–31, and Bois, "Ellsworth Kelly in France," 10.
9. H. H. Arnason, *American Abstract Expressionists and Imagists* (New York: The Solomon R. Guggenheim Museum, 1961), 24.
10. According to Preston, identifying continuity instead of caesura as a framework for the exhibition effectively dulled the contributions of all included. See Preston, "All Unquiet on the Wide Abstract Expressionist Front," *New York Times*, October 15, 1961, X17.

Byron Kim

b. La Jolla, California, 1961
w. Skowhegan, Maine, 1986; Brooklyn, New York, 1987–present

When Piet Mondrian reduced painting to its elemental components, he intended to access the truth of the medium. His canvases of perpendicular black lines and red, yellow, and blue rectangles were based on an assumption underlying all non-objective abstraction: that there can exist an arrangement of color, line, and form that is pure, nonreferential, and universally meaningful. While this assumption spawned a diverse field of practices, it was bound to a particular worldview that is, perhaps, no longer tenable. The idealized and fixed forms of Plato have given way to the series of Gilles Deleuze and the archaeologies of Michel Foucault. Contemporary artist Byron Kim's brand of abstraction reflects this conceptual shift. His work demonstrates that color, and by extension abstraction, does not exist in a pure state but rather is always already embedded in a web of references and associations.

Though sometimes discussed within the context of 1990s "identity art," Kim's practice is considerably more nuanced. The artist's engagement with the abstraction of Ad Reinhardt, Mark Rothko, Brice Marden, and others allows for a subtler and more complex meditation on issues of ethnicity and power relations. Kim is a conceptualist at heart, the product of his study of art and literature at Yale University and of his further education at the Skowhegan School of Painting and Sculpture. Curator Eugenie Tsai remarked, "Like other artists of his generation, for example his friends Janine Antoni and Glenn Ligon, Kim infuses the anonymous abstract language of sixties Minimalism with personal and political content."[1] *Emmett at Twelve Months* (1994), for example, is a grid of twenty-five panels. The work is made legible as a portrait of the artist's son through its title and legends, such as "Bottom of Foot," "Under Big Toe," "Rim of Nostril," identifying the color of each panel as a referent for a particular region of the boy's body.[2] *Emmett* deliberately operates in a liminal space between representation and abstraction.

For several years, Kim's practice focused principally on color and how it operates. In his Koryŏ Green Glaze series from the mid-1990s, for instance, the artist considered the question of whether color can be beautiful and inherently perceived as such, or only in relation to something else, such as the value attached to Korean Kory dynasty (918–1392) pottery.[3] He provocatively explored the intersection of memory and sentiments attached to certain colors in *46 Halsey Drive, Wallingford, CT 06492* (1995), for which Kim asked his mother, father, and sister to select from a chart the specific shade of their family home. Each chose a slightly different pink, and the resulting painting is a palimpsest-like layering of color.[4] Privileging color's associative aspects dovetails with current theories of how our brains process stimuli. When confronted with an unknown—whether a sound, smell, or visual image—the tendency is to connect it to something already known.

Kim began *Synecdoche* in 1991, recording on separate panels the skin color of friends and family.[5] The work engages in a bit of double-entendre, playing on the Modernist focus on the surface, or as Marden referred to it, the "skin" of painting. The title refers to the figure of speech in which a small component part stands in for a/the larger whole. In this case, each panel refers to a specific person, and in the aggregate—*Synecdoche* now contains well over 300 oil paintings—the panels function as a group portrait. By reducing the complexity of his subjects to a single characteristic, *Synecdoche* foregrounds color's capacity to be politically charged. The work immediately brings to mind the pervasive practice of racial stereotyping, whereby a person's skin color stands in for a full set of unjustified preconceptions.

Like the larger work to which it belongs, the Blanton's *Synecdoche* (1991/1998, plate 85) is a grid of monochromatic panels, each the size of a standard headshot and ranging in tone from beige to dark brown, accompanied by a key of names. The format simultaneously resembles the paradigmatic Minimalist grid and a school yearbook. The panels represent the skin colors of nineteen students and one security officer on The University of Texas at Austin campus. It was commissioned by the Blanton Museum in the wake of the 1996 Hopwood decision, a federal court ruling that banned the use of affirmative action as a recruitment tool at the university. *Synecdoche* serves as a time capsule of sorts, a snapshot of the racial demographics of the university population (as determined by skin color rather than ethnicity). Given the context of its making, Kim's piece opens up a larger discussion, synecdochically raising the issue of affirmative action and the history of race relations in Austin specifically and the United States in general.

Kim breaks down painting to its elemental components, and his analysis yields a result different from that of Mondrian. Said Kim, "Purity in abstraction is an anachronism."[6] Rather than striving for Mondrian's truth in painting or the spiritualism of Rothko and other Color Field painters, Kim's abstraction is associative and referential. With a concerted focus on color, his oeuvre directly challenges the "what you see is what you see" claim of artists such as Reinhardt and Frank Stella. For him, abstraction operates on many levels, from aesthetic and linguistic to cultural and personal. Kim's approach expresses a worldview that embraces complexity. As such, his work enables the viewer to discover his or her own truth in painting.

Amy Dove

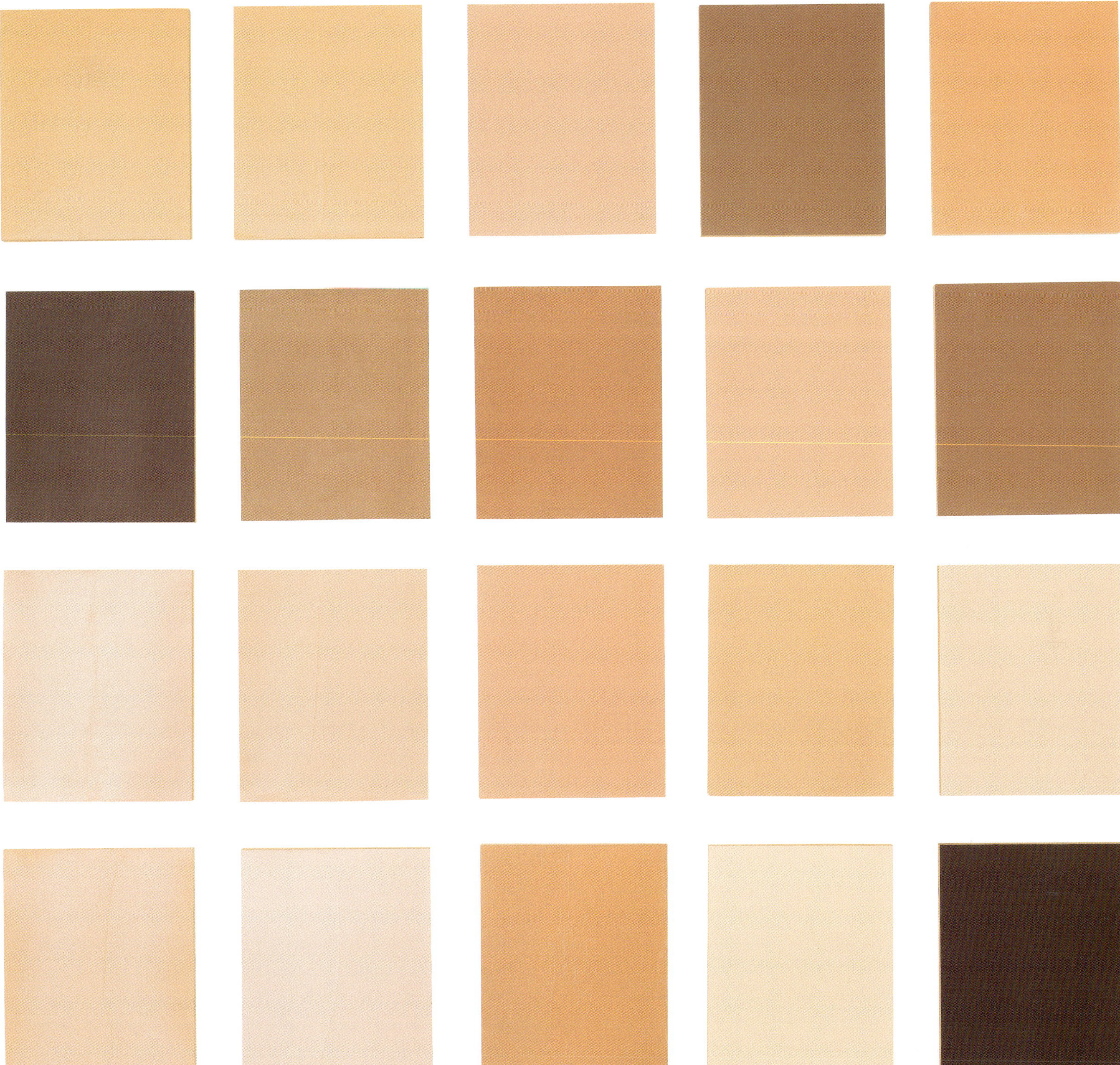

Notes

1. Eugenie Tsai, "Between Heaven and Earth," in *Byron Kim: Threshold 1990–2004* (Berkeley, Calif.: University of California Press, 2004), 18.
2. Andrea Miller-Keller, *Byron Kim/Matrix 125* (Hartford, Conn.: Wadsworth Atheneum, 1994), n.p.
3. Kim said, "There is a consensus among Koreans that the various greens, blues, and greys produced by Koryŏ potters are unsurpassed in their beauty. Why is such significance attached to these colors? The answer to this question is complex and cannot be limited to aesthetics." Phyllis Rosenzweig, *Byron Kim: Grey-Green* (Washington, D.C.: Smithsonian Institution, 1996), n.p.
4. Susan Krane, *Tampering (Artists and Abstraction Today)* (Atlanta: High Museum of Art, 1996), n.p.
5. Miller-Keller, n.p.
6. Byron Kim, "Ad and Me," *Flash Art*, no. 172 (October 1993): 122.

85.

Synecdoche, 1991/1998

Oil and wax on twenty wood panels
Overall: 46 × 48 in. (116.9 × 122 cm)
Each panel: 10 × 8 in. (25.5 × 20.4 cm)
Michener Acquisitions Fund
1998.77

Provenance: Commissioned by the museum and purchased from Max Protetch Gallery, New York, 1998
Signed verso with names of each person represented and date on each panel

Franz Kline

Wilkes-Barre, Pennsylvania, 1910–New York, 1962

w. Boston, 1931–1935; London, 1936–1938; New York, 1938–1962

Known for his large, enigmatic abstract paintings, Franz Kline was one of the leading artists of the New York School, which also included Jackson Pollock, Mark Rothko, and Arshile Gorky, among others. Having aligned himself with the New York School, Kline was subsequently influenced by Cubism and the work of Gorky in particular; yet he did not necessarily move through a strict Cubist-Surrealist phase, like the other Abstract Expressionists.[1] Instead, he abandoned the representational subjects of his work from the 1940s and turned somewhat abruptly to abstraction, which he distinguished as his own through his gestural, animated brushwork and angular compositions. This shift from representation to abstraction culminated in Kline's first solo show at the Charles Egan Gallery in New York in 1950, a landmark exhibition that became a milestone for the artist, marking a major development in his career and signifying the beginning of his mature style.

Kline grew up in Wilkes-Barre, Pennsylvania, one of the many industrial, coal-mining towns of the Lehigh Valley. Two years after his father, a saloon owner, committed suicide in 1917, Kline attended Girard College, a boarding school in Philadelphia for fatherless boys. Six years later, when his mother remarried, he returned home to complete high school. Kline's early forays into pen and ink drawings and cartooning led him to pursue formal academic training in art. In 1931 he enrolled at Boston University and attended classes at the Boston Art Students League, where he studied illustration with John H. Crosman and was encouraged by illustrator John Richard Flanagan to pursue a career in commercial art. Kline traveled to London in 1935 to continue his art studies, initially drawing works in museums as well as scenes of urban life and eventually attending Heatherley's School of Fine Arts.

Kline returned to the United States in 1938 and settled in New York, where he remained until his death. In 1946 he created what he called his "first abstract painting"[2]—a small oil on masonite titled *The Dancer* (1946). As he worked toward his mature style, Kline found inspiration in Bradley Walker Tomlin's calligraphic abstractions and Willem de Kooning's black and white abstractions.[3] Of greater importance, according to Elaine de Kooning, was the occasion in 1948 or 1949 when he saw his enlarged drawings projected onto a wall in de Kooning's studio.[4] Kline realized that, with the aid of a projector, he could sustain the economy of his studies in large-scale paintings without losing the spontaneous and raw quality of his gestural brushwork. More specifically, as Harry Gaugh pointed out, the artist discovered that "black and white could stand alone at the scale of a painting rather than a drawing."[5] These events motivated Kline to begin producing what would become the mainstay of his oeuvre: large-scale black and white abstract paintings.[6] Such works brought him critical recognition as well. They were included in *Talent 1950*, an exhibition organized by Clement Greenberg and Meyer Schapiro, securing Kline a prominent role in the New York School.

Throughout the 1950s Kline maintained what had become his signature palette of black and white, sometimes incorporating a small amount of additional color. He also produced color abstractions such as the white, black, blue, green, and red *Lester* (1959), and the red and black *Red Painting* (1961). These paintings borrow many of the same formal and technical strategies employed in the black and white paintings, strategies Kline continued to refine over the course of the 1950s and early 1960s, as evidenced in *Black and White No. 2* (1960, plate 86).

Completed two years before his untimely death, the asymmetrically balanced *Black and White No. 2* epitomizes Kline's classic style and his ability to perpetuate a style of painting that maintains an enduring sense of spontaneity. A bold, thick stroke of black paint, which the artist applied with a house painter's brush, anchors the right side of the canvas; it is paired with a thinner stroke of black paint to the left of center that veers up from the irregular horizontal bar across the middle of the canvas. A much broader gesture in black paint anchors the lower left portion of the canvas, adhering to the edge as if it continues beyond the frame. The grid that results from the intersection of these marks calls to mind the work of Piet Mondrian. In contradistinction to the mute anonymity of Mondrian's paintings, however, *Black and White No. 2* maintains the appearance of immediacy, with its gestural qualities acting as indices of the artist's personal touch.

Kline's painted lines have often been associated with calligraphy, but he dismissed such interpretations: "The oriental idea of space is an infinite space; it is not painted space . . . calligraphy is writing, and I'm not writing."[7] Moreover, the artist's large brushstrokes in black and white give neither color a hierarchical advantage. Kline's paintings are not black *on* white. The white areas, inconsistent in tone throughout, do not recede as a ground upon which to paint. Opaque, layered spaces, they remain on the surface, creating an integral relationship with the neighboring black. Kline's compositions maintain this cohesive tension, enabling his gestures to dominate the picture plane.

True to the Abstract Expressionist aesthetic, the scale of Kline's paintings becomes a physical quality that seeks heroic potential, yielding traces of the artist's action in and over time. There is an incredible tension that lingers in Kline's work between the static and dynamic, the simple and complex. These enduring elements enable his paintings to sustain their impact into the present.

Jennifer Davy

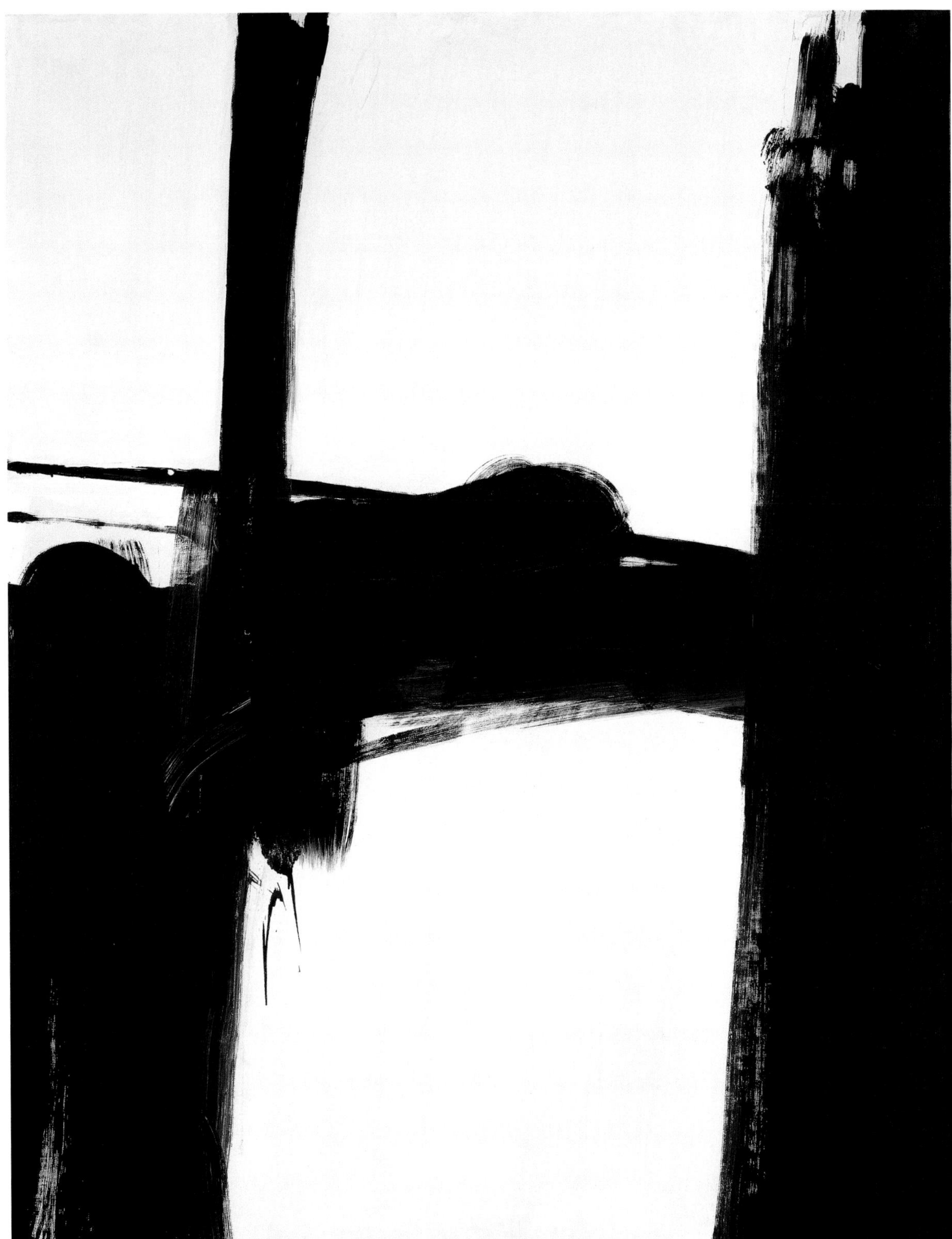

Notes

1. Arthur C. Danto, "Franz Kline," in *The Madonna of the Future* (New York: Farrar, Straus and Giroux, 2000), 114–22.
2. Harry F. Gaugh, *The Vital Gesture: Franz Kline* (New York: Abbeville Press, 1985), 81.
3. Gaugh, 81.
4. Elaine de Kooning, "Franz Kline: Painter of His Own Life," *Artnews* 61 (November 1962): 67–68.
5. Gaugh, 84–85.
6. De Kooning, 67–68.
7. Franz Kline, interview by Katharine Kuh, in *The Artist's Voice* (New York: Harper and Row, 1962), 144. According to Gaugh, "William C. Seitz observed in 1955 that Kline had 'staked everything on single units of black-and-white calligraphy.'" He also refers to Clement Greenberg's cursory reference and subsequent explanation of Kline's work in terms of calligraphy (18).

86.

Black and White No. 2, 1960

Oil on canvas
80¼ x 61 in. (203.9 x 155 cm)
Gift of Mari and James A. Michener
1991.248

Provenance: Purchased by James Michener from the artist, New York, 1961; long-term loan to The University of Texas at Austin, 1968–1991
Signed verso "Kline '60"

Yasuo Kuniyoshi

Okayama, Japan, 1889–Woodstock, New York, 1953

w. Los Angeles, 1906–1910; New York (summers in Ogunquit, Maine, and trips to Europe, 1925 and 1928), 1910–1928; New York, 1929–1953

Continuously well received by critics since his first solo exhibition at the Daniel Gallery in New York in 1922, Yasuo Kuniyoshi remains an important figure in the history of early American modernism. *Waitresses from the Sparhawk* (1924–1925, plate 87) exemplifies Kuniyoshi's mature period and represents his ability to synthesize Japanese art, European modernism, and American folk art into a conservative yet modern style impossible to categorize using conventional art historical terms.

Kuniyoshi was born in Okayama, Japan, in 1889. During his early teens, he attended a technical school, where he studied weaving, dyeing, and textile design. He traveled to the United States in 1906, not realizing that he would remain there permanently and would visit Japan only once more in 1931.[1] Upon arriving on the West Coast, Kuniyoshi settled in Los Angeles and enrolled in the Los Angeles School of Art and Design. He moved to New York in 1910, but due to financial troubles relocated upstate in 1913, finding work at a hotel. Kuniyoshi returned the following year and enrolled in the Independent School under the direction of modernist Homer Boss. In 1916 he transferred to the Art Students League, where he studied with Kenneth Hayes Miller. After exhibiting at the Society of Independent Artists in 1917, he was introduced to his first patron, Hamilton Easter Field.

Field was responsible for giving Kuniyoshi a living space and studio in Brooklyn as well as a summer residence in Ogunquit, Maine, where Field and sculptor Robert Laurent had founded the Thurnscoe School of Modern Art in 1909. Kuniyoshi spent many productive summers in Ogunquit during the late 1910s and early 1920s, and the rugged Maine landscape provided inspiration for much of the work he created during this time, including *Waitresses from the Sparhawk*. Similar to other paintings from the same period, the landscape in *Waitresses* is colored in rich, earthy tones of ochre and sienna. The mysterious browns and grays in the clouds, along with the sharp, angular background, create an abstract landscape that reflects Kuniyoshi's familiarity with Paul Cézanne, while the flatness and two-dimensionality can be attributed to his and his colleagues' interest in Japanese prints.

Kuniyoshi's selection of subject matter in *Waitresses* (the Sparhawk was a popular resort in Ogunquit, Maine) is not surprising considering his past experience working at hotels. The two figures wearing French maid's uniforms in the foreground are employees at the resort. They are in the process of leaving work, their arms linked in an intimate gesture of friendship that contrasts with the barren, inhospitable landscape around them. Such images of women occur frequently in Kuniyoshi's oeuvre, and specific representations of female friendship are found in such works as *Sisters* (1920) and *Sisters Frightened by a Whale* (1923). Depicted with a naïve simplicity often found in American folk art, the two women in *Waitresses* challenge Western standards of female beauty. They have full, rounded faces with large almond eyes and miniature mouths. The relatively large mass of their bodies is balanced precariously on tiny feet. The waitresses' bulging calves and forearms lend them a slightly masculine appearance. These types of stylized features would remain typical of Kuniyoshi's figures throughout much of the 1920s.

Kuniyoshi's work changed dramatically after his second trip to Europe in 1928. He began to create more complex compositions, sometimes using abstract forms, and expanded his palette to include brilliant oranges, reds, and blues. In addition to landscapes and still-lifes, he continued to paint women, but they tended to conform more closely to Western standards of female beauty. In 1929 Kuniyoshi's work was included in The Museum of Modern Art's exhibition *Nineteen Living Americans,* but this led critics to debate whether he was actually an American. Kuniyoshi responded by stating, "I have worked and lived here since a boy. My art training and education have come from American schools and American soil. I am just as much an American in my approach and thinking as the next fellow."[2] In 1933 he began to teach at his alma mater, the Art Students League. The 1930s also marked the beginning of his involvement with left-wing organizations dedicated to the social and economic problems facing artists. Kuniyoshi was a founding member of the American Artists' Congress in 1935 and was elected president of Artists' Equity in 1947.

World War II was an especially difficult period for Kuniyoshi. Following the attack on Pearl Harbor, he was declared an enemy alien because of his Japanese heritage. Yet he was able to avoid many of the restrictions placed on other Japanese Americans by participating in activities directed against the Japanese government, such as broadcasting antiwar messages via radio to Japan and drawing posters that depicted Japanese war atrocities for the Office of War Information. Kuniyoshi supported the United States, but he did not endorse its discrimination against other Japanese Americans, and in 1946 he organized a fundraiser to benefit those being held in American internment camps.[3] Nonetheless, his professional acclaim only increased as his peers continued to champion his work and career throughout the 1940s. Kuniyoshi was honored in 1948 with a retrospective at the Whitney Museum of American Art. This was the first retrospective ever awarded to a living American artist, and it marked an important moment in the defense of Kuniyoshi as an American.

Kuniyoshi applied for United States citizenship in late 1952, the first year it became available to Japanese immigrants, but he passed away before the paperwork was completed. Though he never attained the legal status of a United States citizen, Kuniyoshi always characterized himself as an American, and today many consider him to be one of the most important early American modernists.

Sarah Holian

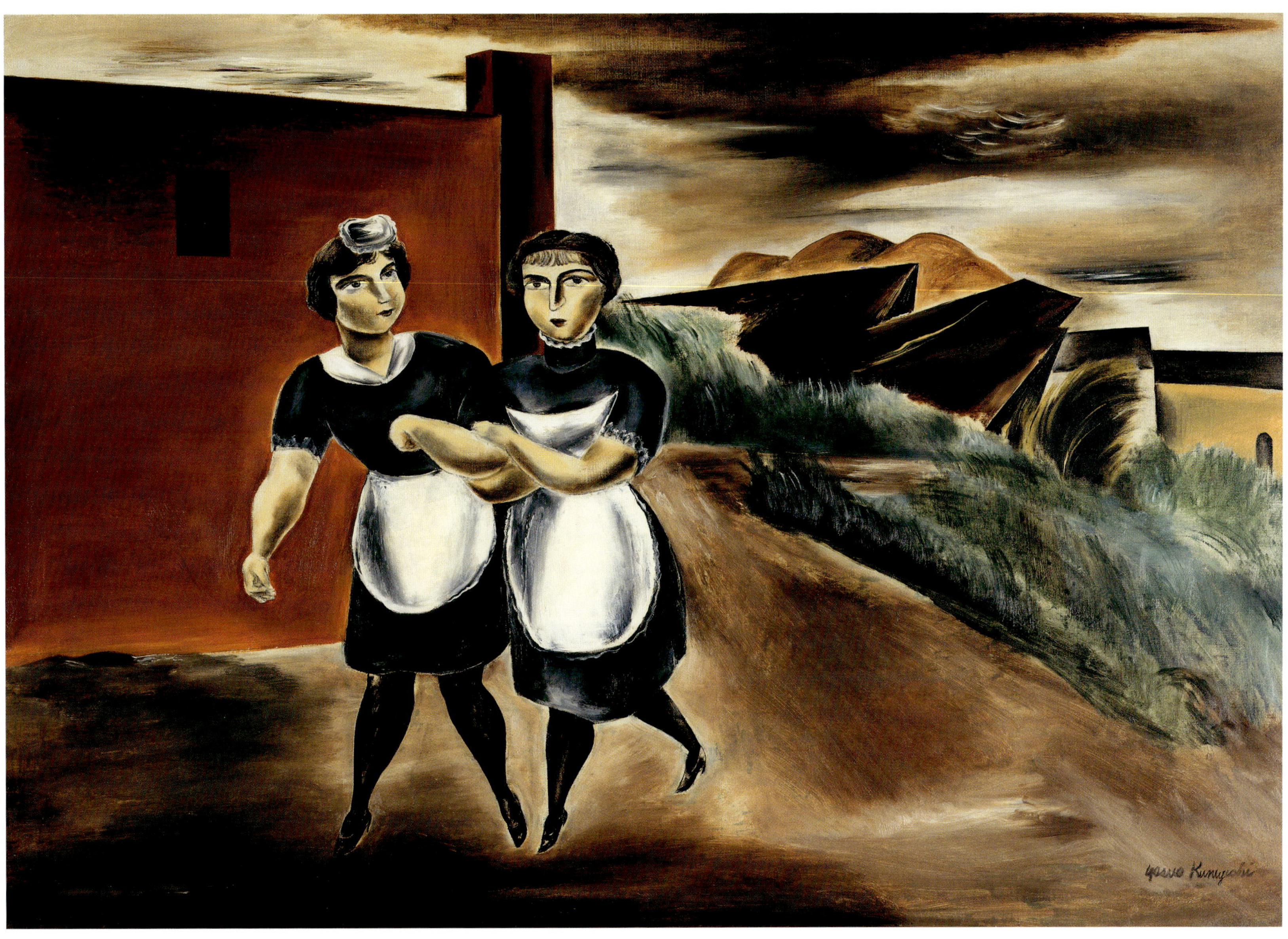

Notes

1. Yasuo Kuniyoshi, "East to West," *Magazine of Art* 33 (February 1940): 72.
2. Quoted in Lloyd Goodrich, *Yasuo Kuniyoshi: Retrospective Exhibition, March 27 to May 9, 1948* (New York: Whitney Museum of American Art, 1948), 35–36. The original source for the quote is Kuniyoshi's article, "East to West."
3. Tom Wolf, "The War Years," in Lloyd Goodrich, ed., *Yasuo Kuniyoshi* (New York: Whitney Museum of American Art, 1986), n.p.

87.

Waitresses from the Sparhawk, 1924–1925

Oil on canvas
29 × 41 in. (74.7 × 105.5 cm)
Gift of Mari and James A. Michener
1991.252

Provenance: Purchased by James Michener from Downtown Gallery, New York, 1961; long-term loan to The University of Texas at Austin, 1968–1991
Signed lower right corner "Yasuo Kuniyoshi"

Yayoi Kusama

b. Matsumoto City, Japan, 1929
w. Seattle, Washington, 1957; New York, 1958–1972; Tokyo, 1972–present

Yayoi Kusama arrived in the United States from Japan in 1957, bringing with her more than a thousand small paintings (plates 88–90) on paper, including the eleven in the Blanton Museum's collection. Delicate abstractions produced from watercolor, ink, and paint, Kusama's early images, such as *Horizontal Love* (1953, plate 88), often feature radically simplified forms on dark monochromatic backgrounds that highlight her use of dense, repetitive patterns made from cell-like clusters. These paintings offer a dichotomy of readings that work closely together, appearing as both microscopic biological images and as celestial views of deep space.

Intimate and strangely compulsive, Kusama's early works suggest a very personal approach to art making. Her choice of repeated configurations of dots and fluctuating nets, often in seemingly boundless compositions, is the product of an obsessive-compulsive impulse that fuels her creative output. As a child, she suffered visions of proliferating patterns that seemed to spread over herself and her surroundings:

> *One day I was looking at the red flower patterns of the tablecloth on a table, and when I looked up I saw the same pattern covering the ceiling, the window and the walls, and finally all over the room, my body and the universe. I felt as if I had begun to self-obliterate, to revolve in the infinity of endless time and the absoluteness of space, and be reduced to nothingness.*[1]

The need for "self-obliteration" through the accumulation of repeated elements would ultimately lead Kusama to construct immense, mural-sized Infinity Net paintings; sculptures completely engulfed by soft, stuffed phallic forms; and enclosed mirrored environments that reflect *ad infinitum*. Throughout Kusama's career, one can witness her consistent use of a single element endlessly multiplied until it is effectively obliterated and abstracted, a technique that can also be traced through the works in the Museum's collection.

While her condition drives the idiosyncratic nature of her work, Kusama was keenly aware of contemporary trends in art and eager to participate in gallery exhibitions. Although she received some art-school training and successfully exhibited her early watercolors, Kusama's nontraditional approach to art, as well as her overt ambitiousness, caused her to seek out an artistic milieu more suitable for her needs than the predominantly conservative art traditions in Japan.[2]

Kusama's motifs drew the attention of European and American artists who were themselves exploring repeated patterns, infinite space, and optical effects. Her work was first introduced to European artists via *Monochrome Malerei*, a 1960 German exhibition highlighting the common use of a monochrome palette in the activities of the postwar European avant-garde. Kusama's inclusion in this show launched her decade-long association with European artistic collectives such as the German-based Zero group and its Dutch offshoot Nul.

Between 1958, the year she moved to New York, and 1968, when she began to focus on performance, Kusama produced a body of work that anticipated subsequent artistic developments in the United States. She arrived at a time when painting was undergoing a radical shift away from the subjective, gestural works of Abstract Expressionism toward the cool, reductive aesthetic of Minimalism. In fact, Kusama's earliest critical supporters included Donald Judd and Frank Stella, both of whom collected her Infinity Net paintings. In a 1959 review, Judd praised Kusama as an "original painter" whose use of repetitive interlacing lines and monochromatic coloring created an effect that he admired as being "both complex and simple," a standard that Judd would apply to his own artistic endeavors.[3] By no means limited to painting and sculpture, Kusama's obsessive use of repeated imagery also carried over into her assemblages. Stickers, egg crates, macaroni, and hand-sewn, stuffed fabric are just some of the everyday materials

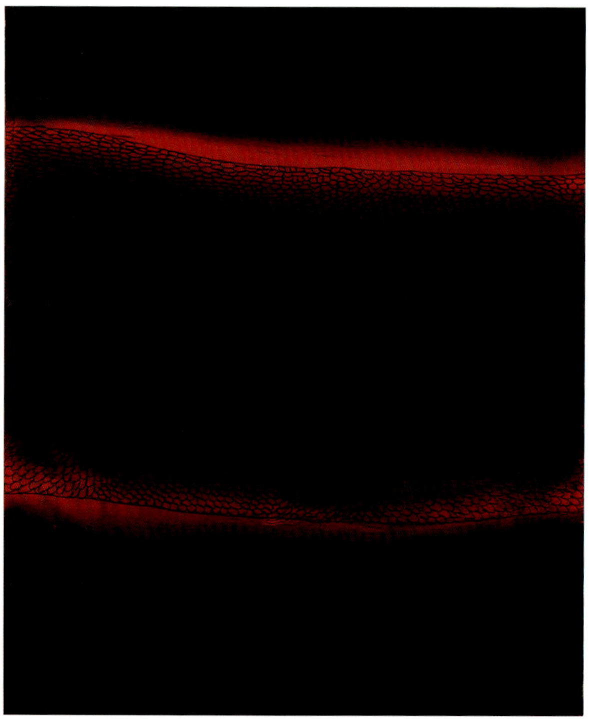

88.
Horizontal Love, 1953
Spray enamel and ink on paper
16¼ × 13⅛ in. (41.3 × 33.4 cm)
Gift of the Center for International Contemporary Arts; Emanuel and Charlotte Levine Collection
1992.267

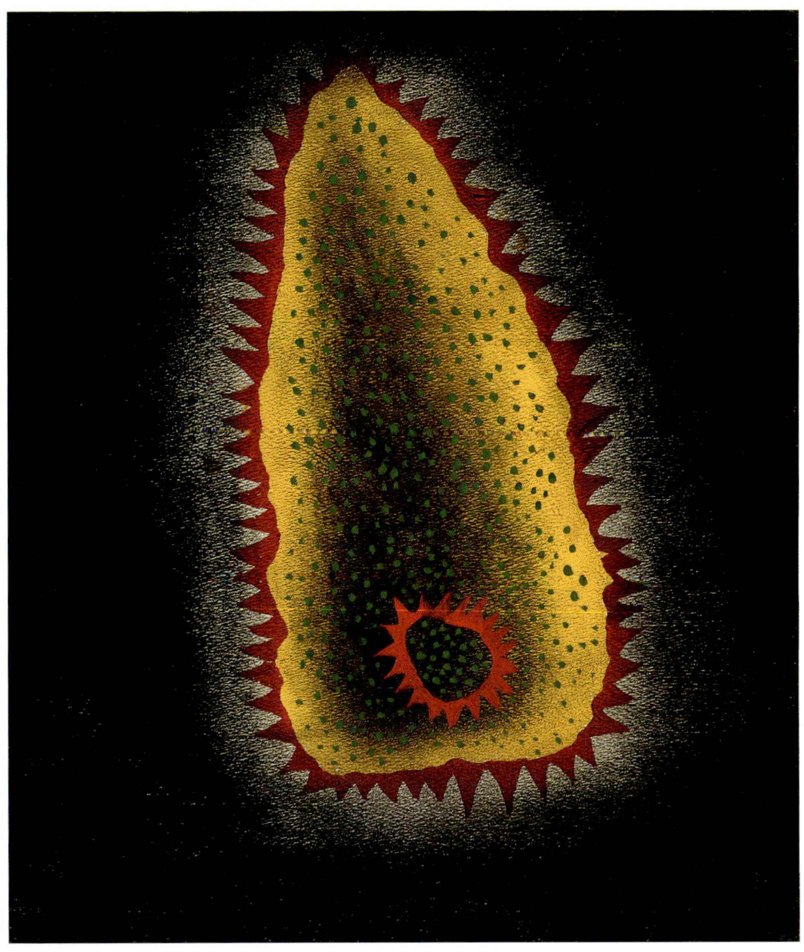

89.
The Woman, 1953
Pastel, aqueous tempera, and acrylic paint on paper
17⅞ × 15 in. (45.4 × 38.2 cm)
Gift of the Center for International Contemporary Arts;
Emanuel and Charlotte Levine Collection
1992.277

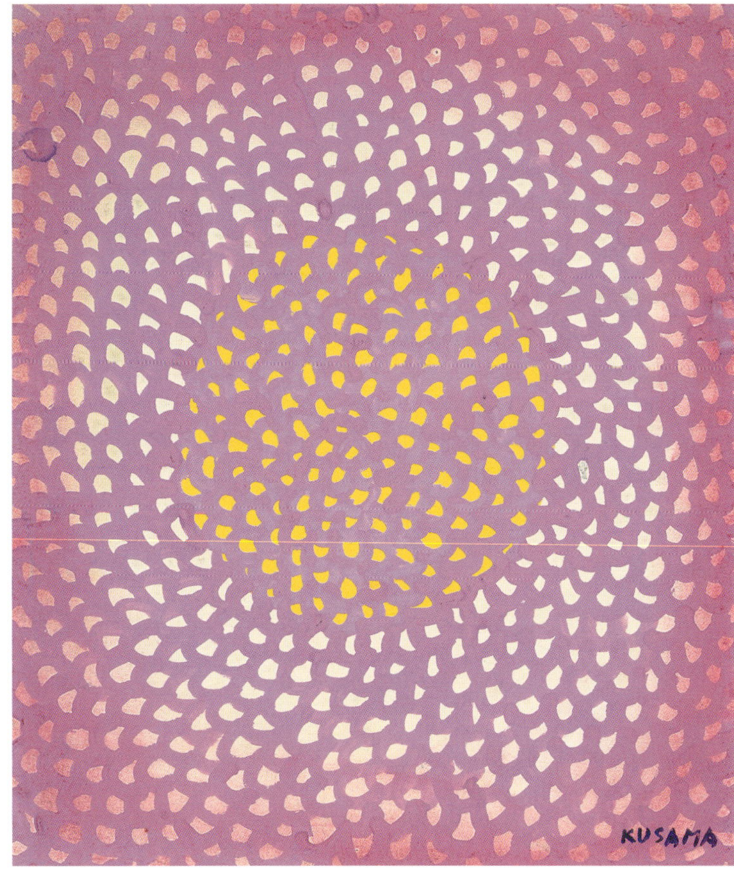

90.
Nets (K.L.M.), 1957
Pastel and aqueous tempera on paper
15¼ × 12 13/16 in. (38.8 × 32.5 cm)
Gift of the Center for International Contemporary Arts;
Emanuel and Charlotte Levine Collection
1992.271

that cover the surfaces of her Accumulation works, of which *No. 62 A.A.A.* (1962, plate 91) is one example. Made of square cardboard egg cartons, the sort used for bulk egg deliveries in the 1960s and readily found in street garbage, *No. 62. A.A.A.* is also Kusama's closest expression of a Minimalist aesthetic.[4] The egg cartons effectively establish a serial grid relief of multiple concave hemispheres.

Yet Kusama's use of urban detritus in *No. 62 A.A.A.*, including the cotton stuffing salvaged from a discarded mattress, pushes the piece beyond the pure, reductionist form of its material toward a more Pop interest in consumer items. Her soft sculptures and sticker collages of the early 1960s anticipate the three-dimensional works of Claes Oldenburg and the serial imagery of Andy Warhol. At the same time, her inclusion in Lucy Lippard's 1966 anthology of New York Pop artists, as well as her participation in important exhibitions at the Green Gallery, locate her firmly within the tradition of Pop art.

By the end of the 1960s, as Kusama moved away from painting, sculpture, and environments toward a propensity for performance, her working methods acquired the taint of sensationalism. She became infamous for promoting her nude Happenings and eventually lost the critical support that she had achieved earlier in her career. Kusama returned to Japan in the early 1970s.

Despite her foothold in the New York art scene, as a Japanese woman Kusama remained an outsider, an important factor that led to her work being virtually forgotten in the United States until the 1990s. It was not until 1982, when she had a solo exhibition at the Fuji Television Gallery in Tokyo, that she entered a new period of success. This led to the eventual critical reexamination of her career, as well as a renaissance in her artistic production.[5] After having worked primarily with sculptural forms since returning to Japan, Kusama began painting again in the mid-1980s, creating single or multiple panel two-color acrylic paintings with allover patterns. Typical of her work during this period is *Sprouting (The Transmigration of the Soul)* (1987, plate 92), which depicts interconnected spermlike forms swimming against a green sea. As Alexandra Munroe pointed out, the main difference between this work and her earlier Infinity Net paintings is the use of a dark, high-contrast background color that creates the illusion of deep space.[6] With backgrounds such as this one, Kusama returned to the notion of infinite space

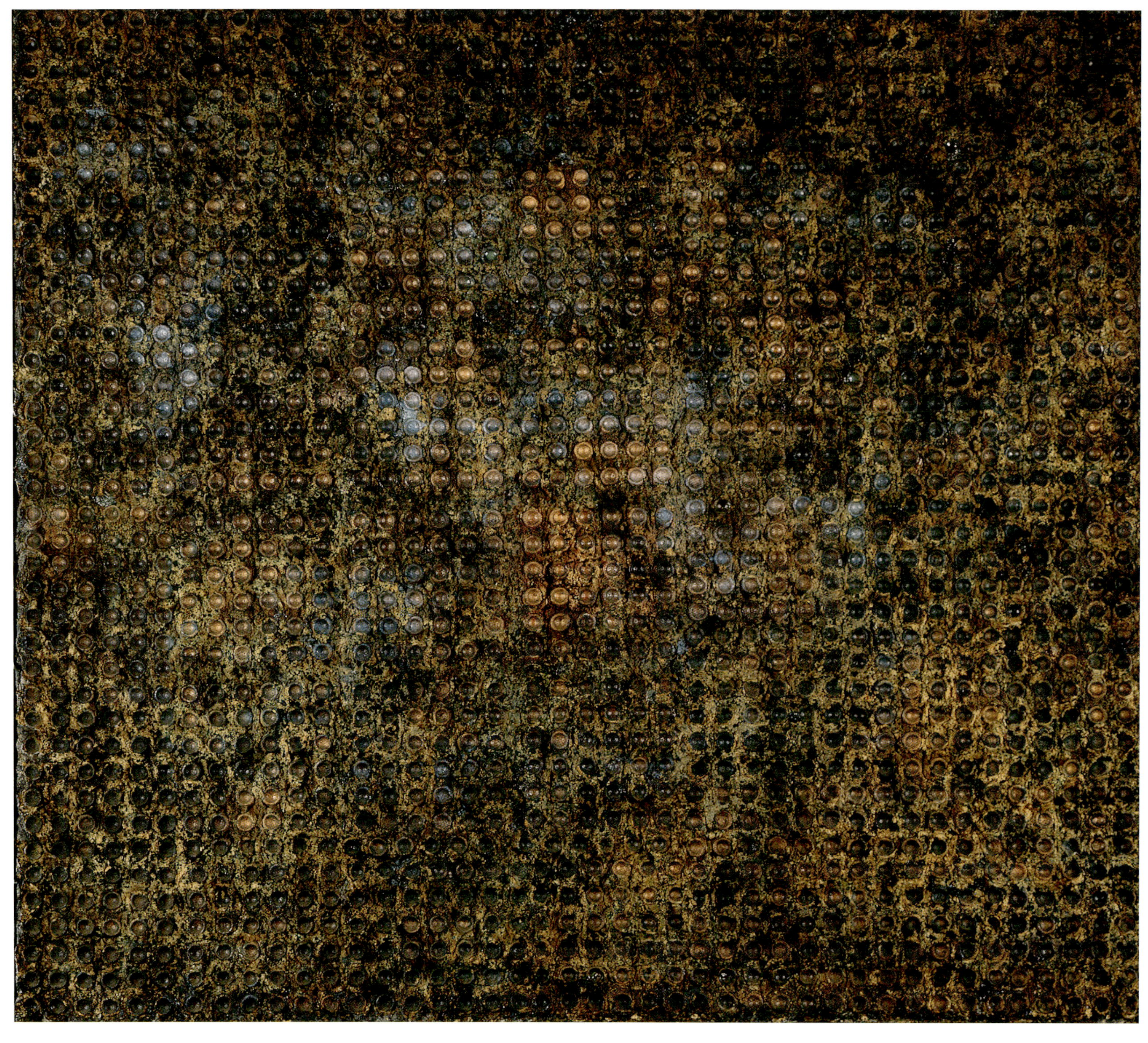

91.

No. 62. A.A.A., 1962

Paint, mattress stuffing, and cardboard egg crates on canvas
70 × 80 in. (178 × 202 cm)
Gift of the Center for International Contemporary Arts; Emanuel and Charlotte Levine Collection
1992.272

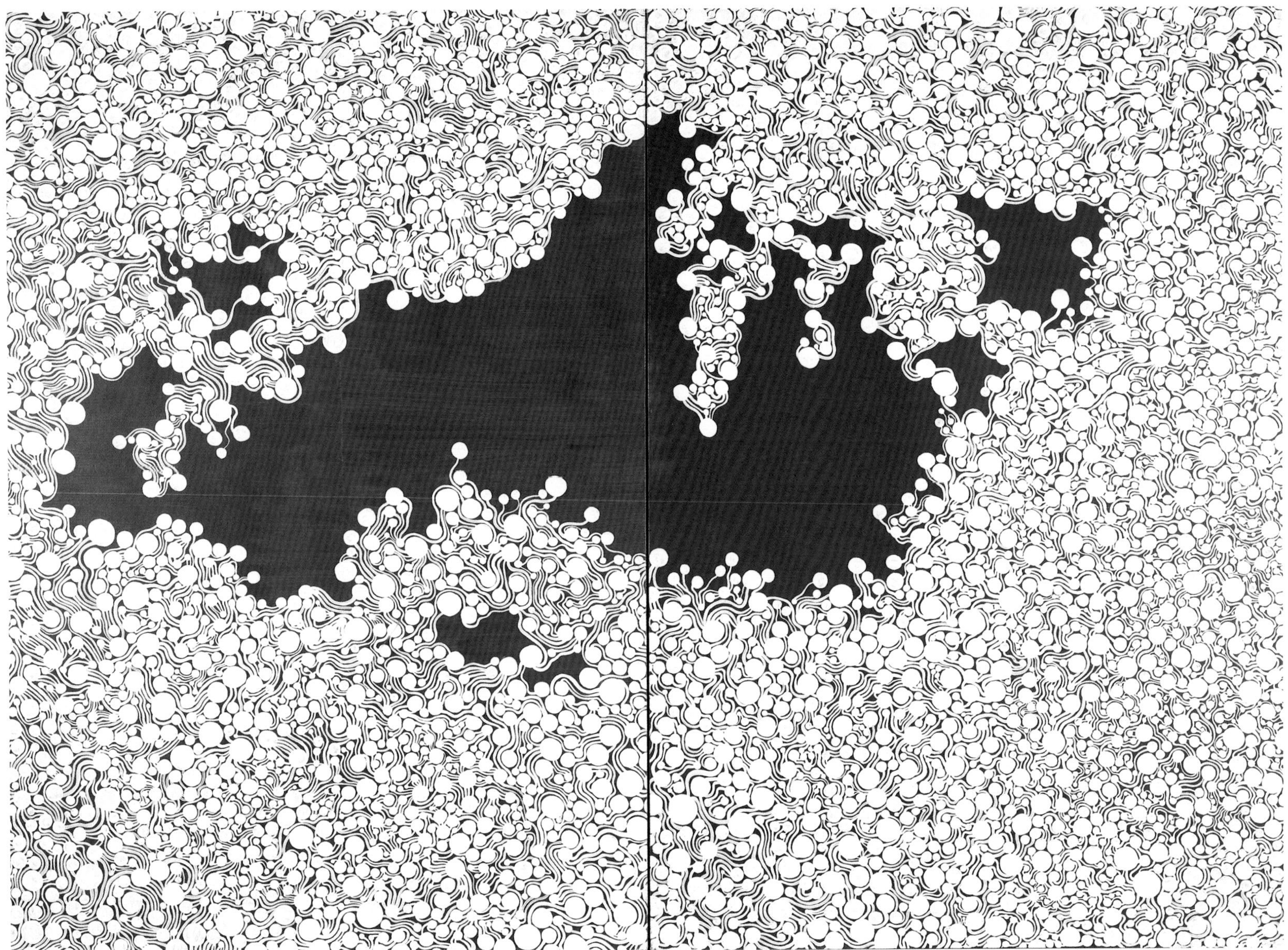

exemplified by the soft black backgrounds of her paintings on paper from the 1950s.

In many ways, Kusama's work mirrors the paradoxes of her life: it is at once intensely personal, yet at the same time desperately public. On the one hand, Kusama sought recognition as a great artist working in a visual vocabulary directly related to the most current artistic explorations of the day. She participated in the major international avant-garde movements that emerged in the late 1950s and 1960s, sharing key formal elements with European and American artists: pattern, seriality, and noncomposition. Despite these stylistic affinities and relationships, however, her work resists all "isms," maintaining her independent artistic vision and the individualistic, compulsive need that drives it. At the beginning of the twenty-first century, Kusama stands as one of Japan's most famous contemporary artists, actively creating and exhibiting, with her work being shown in historical Modernist contexts as well as vital contemporary venues.

Stephanie Hanor

92.

Sprouting (The Transmigration of the Soul), 1987

Acrylic on canvas
Overall (diptych): 152⅜ x 102 in. (387.1 x 260.4 cm)
Gift of the Center for International Contemporary Arts
1992.274.1/2–2/2

Notes

1. Yayoi Kusama, "*Waga tamashii no henreki to tanaki*" ("Odyssey of My Struggling Soul"), *Geijutsu seikatsu (Art and Life)* (November 1975), quoted in Alexandra Munroe, "Obsession, Fantasy and Outrage: The Art of Yayoi Kusama," in *Yayoi Kusama: A Retrospective* (New York: Center for International Contemporary Arts, 1989), 14.
2. Kusama received one year of formal art education at the Kyoto School of Arts and Crafts in 1948. She experimented with both *Nihonga* (Japanese-style) and *yoga* (Western-style) painting before committing herself to more personal and avant-garde techniques. See Kusama, "Odyssey of My Struggling Soul."
3. Donald Judd, "Reviews and Previews: New Names This Month," *Artnews* 58 (October 1959): 17.
4. Munroe, 21.
5. Feminist interpretations of Kusama's work, for instance, began pointing to the importance of the body, gender roles, and personal identity in her art, as well as her friendships with women artists such as Eva Hesse and Carolee Schneemann. See Whitney Chawick, ed., *Mirror Images: Women, Surrealism and Self-Representation* (Cambridge, Mass.: The MIT Press, 1998); and Dana Friis-Hansen, "Yayoi Kusama's Feminism," *Art and Text*, no. 49 (September 1994): 48–55.
6. Munroe, 34.

Annette Lawrence

b. Rockville Center, New York, 1965

w. West Hartford, Connecticut, 1982–1986; Morgantown, West Virginia, 1988; Baltimore, 1988–1990; Houston, 1991–1994; Skowhegan, Maine, 1996; Denton, Texas, 1996–present

Annette Lawrence submits the quotidian details of her day-to-day existence to close examination. Out of this intense scrutiny she has created a body of work that functions as an archive, with each drawing or installation representing a unique system of coding and transcribing life's fleeting moments. Every artistic decision Lawrence makes, from the forms she uses to her means of representation, relates to a larger project: asserting her presence in time and space.

The link between writing and drawing is a strong one for Lawrence, who sees both practices as methods of recording personal and global events. She began keeping a journal in 1982 as part of an assignment in a freshman foundations course at the University of Hartford in Connecticut.[1] For a time, when asked to give a presentation on her work, Lawrence would prepare by pulling her journals from the preceding ten years and including in her speech the entries she had written exactly one, two, three, or more years earlier.[2]

In her drawings, Lawrence has explored different methods of time-keeping, such as the Mayan and Roman calendars, as well as her own menstrual cycle. Stemming from this desire to encode ephemeral phenomena into pictorial language, she has also long been interested in incorporating musical notation into her work. In a sense, this is exactly what musical notation does—as a set of predetermined instructions, it preserves and formalizes an otherwise transitory performance that fluctuates according to the whims of the musicians who interpret it. In 2000 Lawrence stumbled upon her third-grade music notebook in the piano bench at her parents' house, where it had been stored for more than twenty-five years. She recalled that the "hand-drawn notation in the notebook embodied the visual quality I was looking for."[3]

The Blanton's *Theory #1* (2001, not illustrated) and *Theory #2* (2001, plate 93), two of a series of nine mixed-media drawings on brown butcher paper, the artist's preferred surface, include elements from this same notebook. Thin vertical lines, rendered in graphite, extend out from the center of the drawings toward both their right and left sides. The lines in the center are clustered together, but the distance between them expands near the edges. They would seem to mimic the technique of hatching, where parallel lines are employed to generate the illusion of relief or three-dimensionality. In the case of *Theory #1* and *Theory #2*, these hatch marks suggest an open notebook whose two pages dip inward toward the spine, creating a pocket of shadow that gradually disperses as the pages are exposed to light. Over this design Lawrence painted a number of circles and ovals in white, sienna, and black ink: some solid, some merely outlines.

Lawrence employed a process she deems "mechanical" to execute the *Theory* drawings.[4] She first drew an exact copy of a page of music as it appeared in her third-grade notebook, then photographed the drawing. She projected a slide of the drawing onto a wall and photographed it from a severe angle, sometimes lying on the floor in front of it. Using sienna, white, and indigo acrylic, Lawrence then redrew each successive composition on a piece of paper to create the three layers of her drawing. The accumulation of individual and grouped circles, ovals, and lines in *Theory #1* and *Theory #2* is thus an imaginative and deliberately imperfect re-creation of those in her composition notebook.

Apart from her drawings, Lawrence is also known for her site-specific installations, many fabricated from ordinary postal string. These dramatic pieces occupy the space of the gallery and recall a variety of acts and devices, from Marcel Duchamp's invasive use of string in an exhibition held in New York in 1942 to the wires that enclose boxing rings. A recent work by Lawrence involving all the string employed in her previous installations was shown at "testsite," an experimental venue for art located in Austin. At once archival, commemorative, and mysterious, the sculpture was composed of ninety-five balls of string attached to a wall with clear packing tape and organized into four arcs that evoked the shape of a spiral. It was accompanied by an audio poem by Annette DiMeo Carlozzi entitled "Ninety-Five," a thoughtful response that captured the nature of the artist's work: "A counting game provokes memory/and history waits, embodied, still."[5]

Lawrence became interested in installation art in 1989, when she saw the exhibition *Art is a Verb* while completing her MFA at the Maryland Institute College of Art in Baltimore.[6] The artist credited this show, which featured the work of thirteen prominent artists, including David Hammons and Adrian Piper, with having a lasting impact: "To be immersed in a group of African American artists doing installation art was really meaningful to me."[7] Lawrence found particular inspiration in Hammons's work, and took to heart his decision to maintain an outsider status in relation to the art world.[8] An early installation piece by Lawrence entitled *Rock Writing* (1992) recalls the polemical messages about racism and identity conveyed in much of Hammons's work. Created during the race riots that broke out in Los Angeles in the wake of the Rodney King verdict, *Rock Writing* consists of a six-foot-long bed of white limestone rocks in which the artist embedded pitch-black lava rocks that spell out the phrase: "They Must Don't Know Who We Are."

Lawrence, who has taught at the School of Visual Arts at the University of North Texas in Denton since 1996, continues to make work that is engaged with sociopolitical concerns but that projects such issues through a highly personalized lens. Her unique perspective and refined sensibility manifest themselves in the subtle variations of *Theory #1* and *Theory #2*.

Claire Barliant

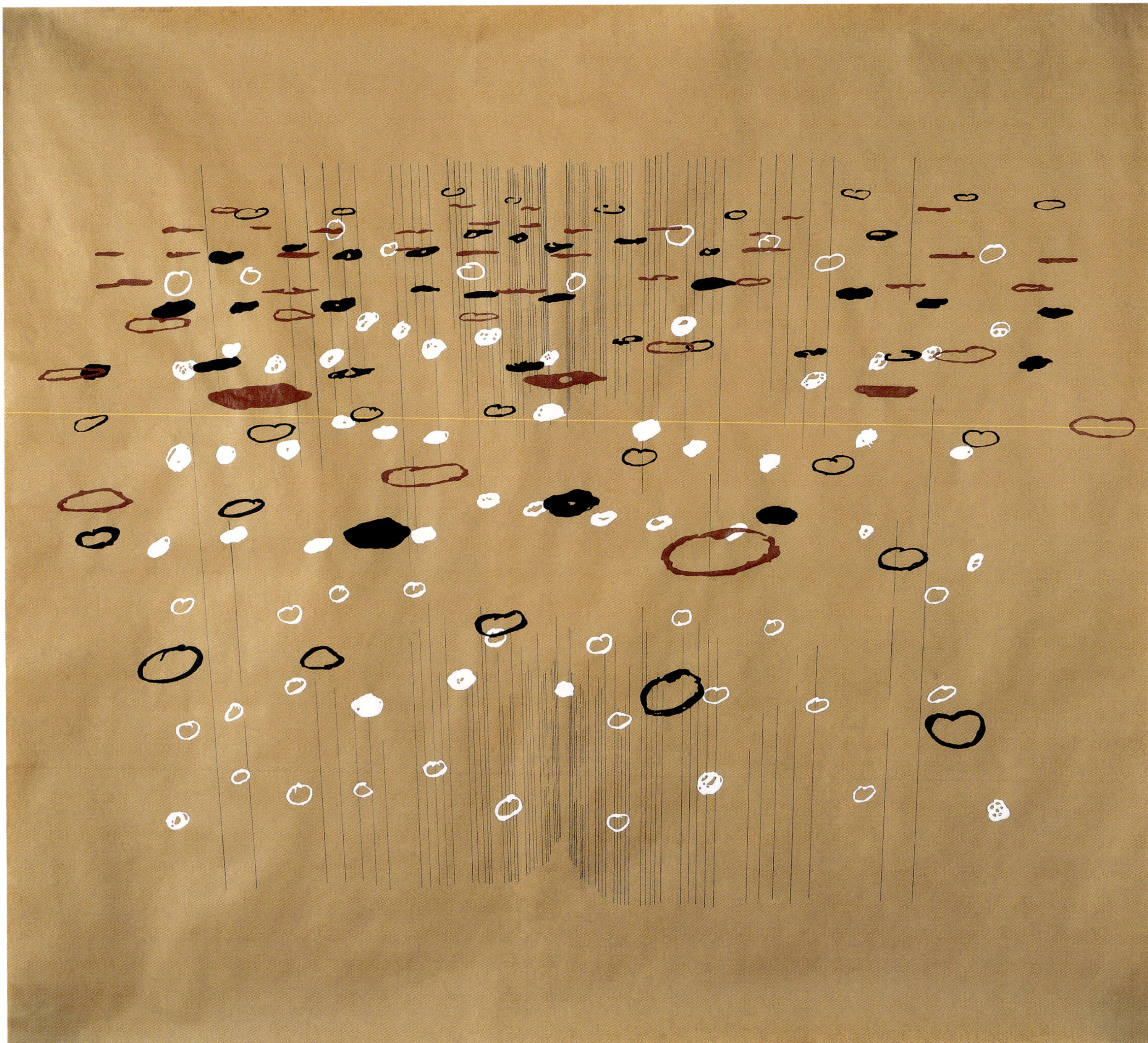

Notes

1. Annette Lawrence, telephone conversation with the author, November 1, 2004.
2. Lawrence, telephone conversation with the author.
3. Valerie Loupe Olsen, *Annette Lawrence: Theory* (Houston: The Glassell School of Art, 2002), 15.
4. Lawrence, telephone conversation with author.
5. Annette DiMeo Carlozzi, "Ninety-Five," available at http://www.fluentcollab.org/testsite/project.php?id=39§ion=archives [October 18, 2004].
6. The exhibition was organized by Lowery Stokes Sims and Leslie King-Hammond at the Maryland Institute College of Art. It later traveled to New York as a two-part installation at the Metropolitan Life Gallery and The Studio Museum in Harlem.
7. Lawrence, telephone conversation with the author.
8. Lawrence, telephone conversation with the author.

93.

Theory #2, 2001

Acrylic, ink, and graphite on paper
$43\frac{1}{2} \times 48\frac{1}{16}$ in. (110.5 × 122 cm)
Purchase through the generosity of the Blanton Contemporary Circle
2002.2804

Provenance: Purchased from Arthur Roger Gallery, New Orleans, 2002

Jacob Lawrence

Atlantic City, New Jersey, 1917–Seattle, 2000
w. New York, 1930–1970; Seattle, 1970–2000

Created when Jacob Lawrence was seventeen, *The Eviction* (1935, plate 94) is one of his earliest surviving paintings.[1] Given its early date, it is remarkably representative of his mature work in style and theme. Lawrence had moved to Harlem around 1930, when he was about thirteen years old, and the neighborhood's dynamic environment became a source of great interest to him visually and intellectually. *The Eviction* depicts life in Harlem, a theme to which the artist returned throughout his career.

During the 1920s Harlem was a thriving center of black culture that attracted intellectuals and artists from all over the world. There such diverse and significant figures rose to fame as novelist Zora Neale Hurston, poet Langston Hughes, singer Marion Anderson, pianist "Jelly Roll" Morton, painter Hale Woodruff, and sculptor Augusta Savage. Beginning in 1929 and continuing into the next decade, Harlem was severely impacted by the Great Depression. While many black intellectuals remained, living conditions declined due to overcrowding, poverty, scarcity of food, and frequent evictions.[2] This is the historical context to which *The Eviction* belongs and responds.

Soon after Lawrence arrived in Harlem, his mother enrolled him in after-school care at Utopia House, where he participated in an art program run by the painter Charles Alston.[3] From 1932 to 1934, he took classes with Alston at the Harlem Art Workshop at the 135th Street Public Library. Between 1934 and 1937, he continued to study with Alston and began to work informally with Henry Bannarn at the WPA Harlem Arts Workshop at 306 West 141st Street. Lawrence rented space from Bannarn at the workshop and probably painted *The Eviction* there.[4] During this period, "306" was an intellectual and social center, thus giving Lawrence the opportunity to meet established artists, writers, dancers, and musicians. He attributed his motivation and "desire to be an artist to . . . the black community and certain people within it, like Augusta Savage and [the poet] Claude McKay."[5] Through books at the Harlem Art Workshop, Lawrence also became familiar with the work of Francisco Goya, Pieter Bruegel, George Grosz, Käthe Kollwitz, and the Mexican muralists. "We were interested in these artists because of their social commentary," he later recalled.[6]

The Eviction depicts an irate white landlord threatening a family with light brown complexions seated on the stoop of their former tenement. Their furniture has been dumped in the street. Two children cling to their mother while their overalls-clad father raises his hand in an imploring gesture. The landlord lifts his cane as if to strike him, at the same time pointing accusingly at him with the other hand. His gestures, combined with his cane, create a strong sweeping diagonal, which is further extended by the tenant's outstretched hand. The men's hands almost meet, and the short distance between their fingers ironically recalls the similarly charged space between those of God and Adam in Michelangelo's *The Creation of Adam* in the Sistine Chapel. Like most of Lawrence's work of the next few years, *The Eviction* is painted in the water-based medium of gouache using somber tones, in this case primarily earth and neutral tones in low values, contained within flat, hard-edged areas of local color. Isolated light accents draw the viewer's eye to key narrative elements: the faces, hands, cane, clothing, and bed frame.

Over the course of his sixty-five-year career, Lawrence sympathetically recorded the history and culture of African Americans using a visual language indebted to modernist art. He is best known for his narrative series documenting aspects of the history and struggles of blacks in the New World. The first of these, the Toussaint L'Ouverture series of 1937–1938, chronicles the life of the Haitian slave who, in the late eighteenth and early nineteenth centuries, liberated his country from French rule and founded the Republic of Haiti. Between 1939 and 1940, Lawrence created series dedicated to Frederick Douglass and Harriet Tubman, American abolitionists who lived around the time of the Civil War. The Frederick Douglass series presents the life of the Maryland slave who escaped servitude and rose to greatness as an abolitionist writer, editor, publisher, and diplomat. The Harriet Tubman series tells the story of her flight from slavery, her trek north, and her work to direct over 300 slaves through the refuge network of the underground railroad. Lawrence's Migration of the Negro series (1940–1941) documents the exodus of blacks from the South, their journeys to urban centers in the North, and the situations they faced upon arrival. The Harlem series (1942–1943) presents thirty genre scenes of life in Harlem that rework some of Lawrence's childhood memories, including street scenes directly related to *The Eviction*. The artist's serial works, all based on substantial research, are exceptional in their emphasis on content and finely crafted narratives. Each image, accompanied by a caption, forms a link in a discrete narrative unit with a beginning, middle, and end.

During the Civil Rights Movement of the 1960s, Lawrence protested contemporary racial injustice. Individual works address school integration, interracial marriage, police brutality, and interfaith solidarity. Taken together, Lawrence's art provides a compelling portrait of African American experiences in the United States.

Nancy Deffebach

Notes

1. Lawrence dated *The Eviction* in the lower right corner. However, in a 1984 letter to Tammy Gest, Lawrence wrote that "'THE EVICTION' was either executed in 1935 or 1936," and he added that it was "one of my earliest figurative works. . . . The significance of the two different dates is not recalled." *The Eviction* is the first work reproduced in Lawrence's catalogue raisonné, one of only two paintings from 1935. Jacob Lawrence to Tammy Gest, December 2, 1984, Blanton Museum of Art Archives, The University of Texas at Austin; Peter T. Nesbett and Michelle DuBois, *Jacob Lawrence: Paintings, Drawings, and Murals (1935–1999): A Catalogue Raisonné* (Seattle and London: University of Washington Press, 2000), 20.
2. Ellen Harkins Wheat, *Jacob Lawrence, American Painter* (Seattle: University of Washington Press, 1986), 27.

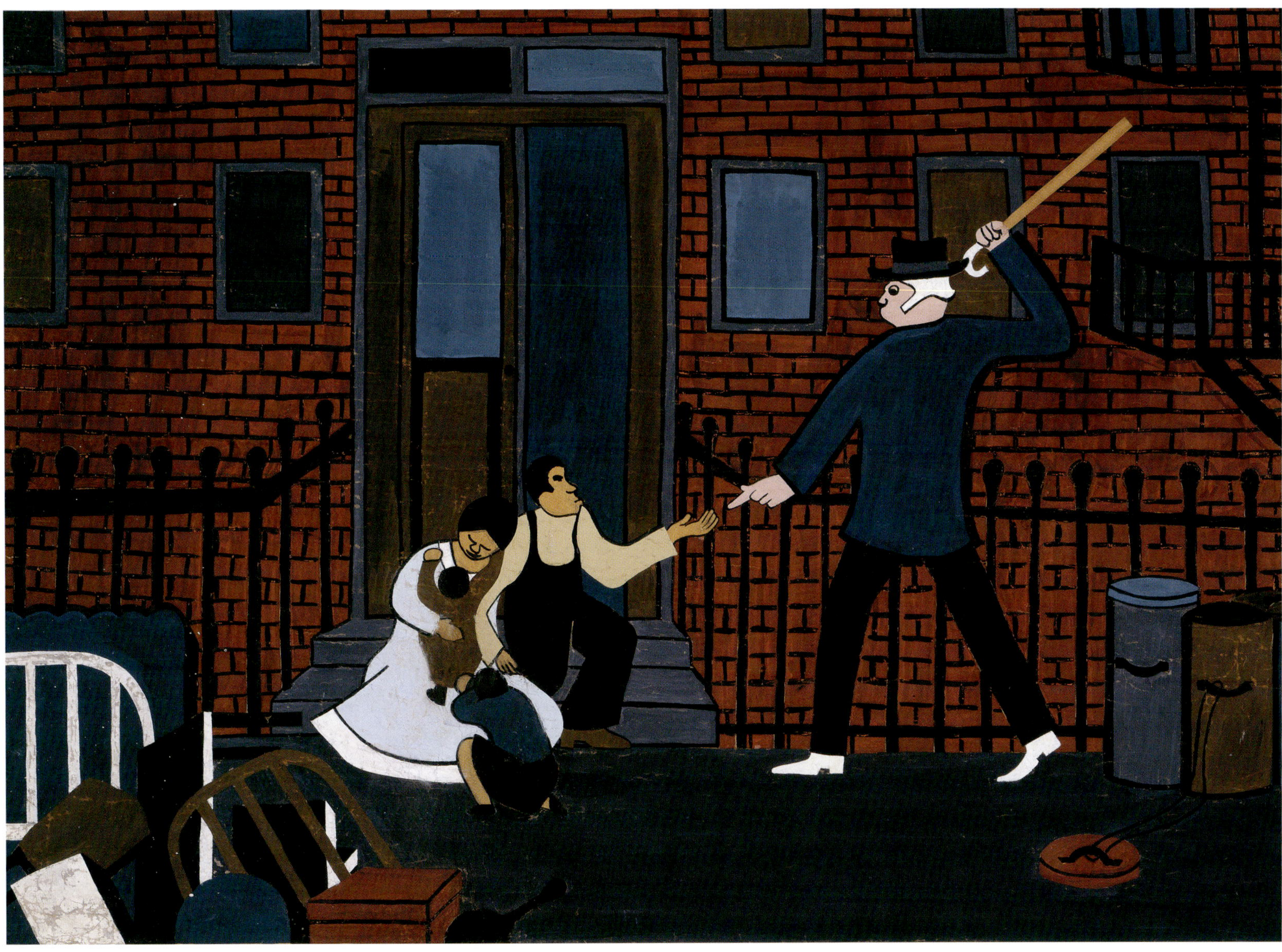

3. At Utopia House, Lawrence first made geometrical designs and papier mâche masks; later, he began cutting up boxes to make stage sets and triptychs that reflected his own experience. "I built street scenes inside corrugated boxes," he recalled, "taking them to familiar spots in the street and painting houses and scenes on them, recreating as best I could a three-dimensional image of those spots." These street scenes could be considered predecessors to *The Eviction*. Elton Fax, *Seventeen Black Artists* (New York: Dodd, Mead, 1971), 149.
4. Lawrence wrote that *The Eviction* "was most likely painted in [sculptor] Henry Bannarn's studio." The address written on the back of *The Eviction* was Lawrence's home address at the time the work was created. Lawrence to Gest; Wheat, 194.
5. Lawrence, quoted in Clarence Major, "Jacob Lawrence, Expressionist," *The Black Scholar* 9 (November 1977): 23.
6. Lawrence, quoted in Wheat, 36.

94.

The Eviction, 1935

Gouache and collage on paper
28 × 38⅜ in. (71.1 × 97.5 cm)
Michener Acquisitions Fund
P1969.12.2

Provenance: Purchased from Robert Schoelkopf Gallery, New York, 1969
Signed lower right corner "Lawrence 35"
Inscribed verso "by JL / 142 West 143rd N.Y.C. 1/22/36."

Alfred Leslie

b. New York, 1927
w. New York, 1946–present

Alfred Leslie's work encompasses almost every type of artistic enterprise. In the 1950s Leslie was known variously as an avant-garde artist, filmmaker, painter, model, musician, poet, and even a gymnast. A peripheral member of the core group of Beat poets, he collaborated on the making of the independent film *Pull My Daisy* (1959), which was directed by Robert Frank and featured narration by Jack Kerouac. *Pull My Daisy* also includes performances by Beat luminaries Allen Ginsberg and Gregory Corso, gallerist Richard Bellamy, artists Larry Rivers and Alice Neel, and other individuals disaffected by bourgeois Eisenhower-era values.

In addition to his place in this late 1950s and 1960s countercultural movement, Leslie also enjoyed the more elite artistic credibility afforded him as a favored member of the so-called "second generation" Abstract Expressionists. In addition to Leslie, this group included Joan Mitchell, Ray Parker, and others who expanded and redefined the boundaries of gestural abstraction as their predecessors Jackson Pollock and Willem de Kooning had practiced it. Leslie's colleague and fellow painter Grace Hartigan wrote of his work in 1959:

> *Alfred Leslie's paintings are strong because he knows how to be weak. They are beautiful because they triumph over ugliness. In all of Leslie's work his gentleness pursues his power relentlessly and unforgivingly. . . . In the expression of my generation, which turns to irony on one hand and rhetoric on the other, it is infinitely moving to come upon true and controlled passion.*[1]

Leslie's seemingly contradictory impulses toward both fervent expression and controlled composition dictated the style of his abstract paintings from the 1950s up to the early 1960s.

Painted in 1961, just one year before he abandoned abstraction in favor of monumental figurative painting and prints (plate 95), *The Red Side* (plate 96) occupies an important transitional moment in Leslie's artistic pursuits. It shows the artist experimenting with abstract composition by juxtaposing free-form gestural splashes of paint with colored geometric forms, creating an almost Cubist impression of planes colliding in space. James Michener purchased *The Red Side* at the artist's studio in late 1961. Immediately prior to the purchase, it was included in the highly influential and expansive exhibition *American Abstract Expressionists and Imagists* at the Guggenheim Museum, which showcased work by action painters, geometric abstractionists, and the burgeoning Minimalists. In his introductory essay for the catalogue, curator H. H. Arnason praised Leslie's ability to successfully balance gestural and geometric forms, thereby raising "the whole question of the expressive implications of geometric abstraction."[2]

The Red Side also exemplifies what one critic described as Leslie's "collage principle"—that is, his tendency to approach painting in the manner of a collage, pilfering, recontextualizing, and juxtaposing seemingly disparate painterly elements, from controlled lines and nearly transparent layers of pigment to thick brushstrokes and haphazardly applied paint drips, in a single work.[3] Here Leslie synthesized a variety of styles and sources whose origins lie with Abstract Expressionism. *The Red Side* reflects his assimilation of the gestural style of de Kooning as well as the thick impasto and visual pull of Hans Hofmann's squares. In addition, it references the characteristic "zip" or sharp vertical line that cuts across the large chromatic fields in Barnett Newman's monumental canvases from the 1950s and 1960s.[4]

Leslie attended the Art Students League and New York University, where he studied under Tony Smith and William Baziotes. A frequent participant in discussions at the Cedar Bar in the late 1940s, he first gained acclaim as an exhibiting artist in Meyer Schapiro and Clement Greenberg's *New Talent* exhibition at the Samuel Kootz Gallery in 1949. He held his first solo exhibition at Tibor de Nagy Gallery in New York in 1952, and five years later, in 1959, his work appeared in *Sixteen Americans* at The Museum of Modern Art. In 1960 Leslie

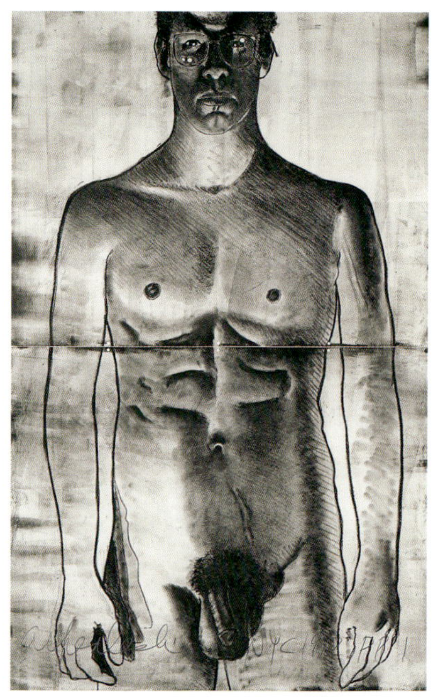

95.
Hugh, 1992
Softground etching from two plates
Edition of 20; printer's proof, 1/5
Sheet: 70 1/16 × 45 9/16 in. (178 × 115.7 cm)
Gift of Bill Hall
1994.20
Signed bottom "Alfred Leslie NYC 1992 PPI" in graphite

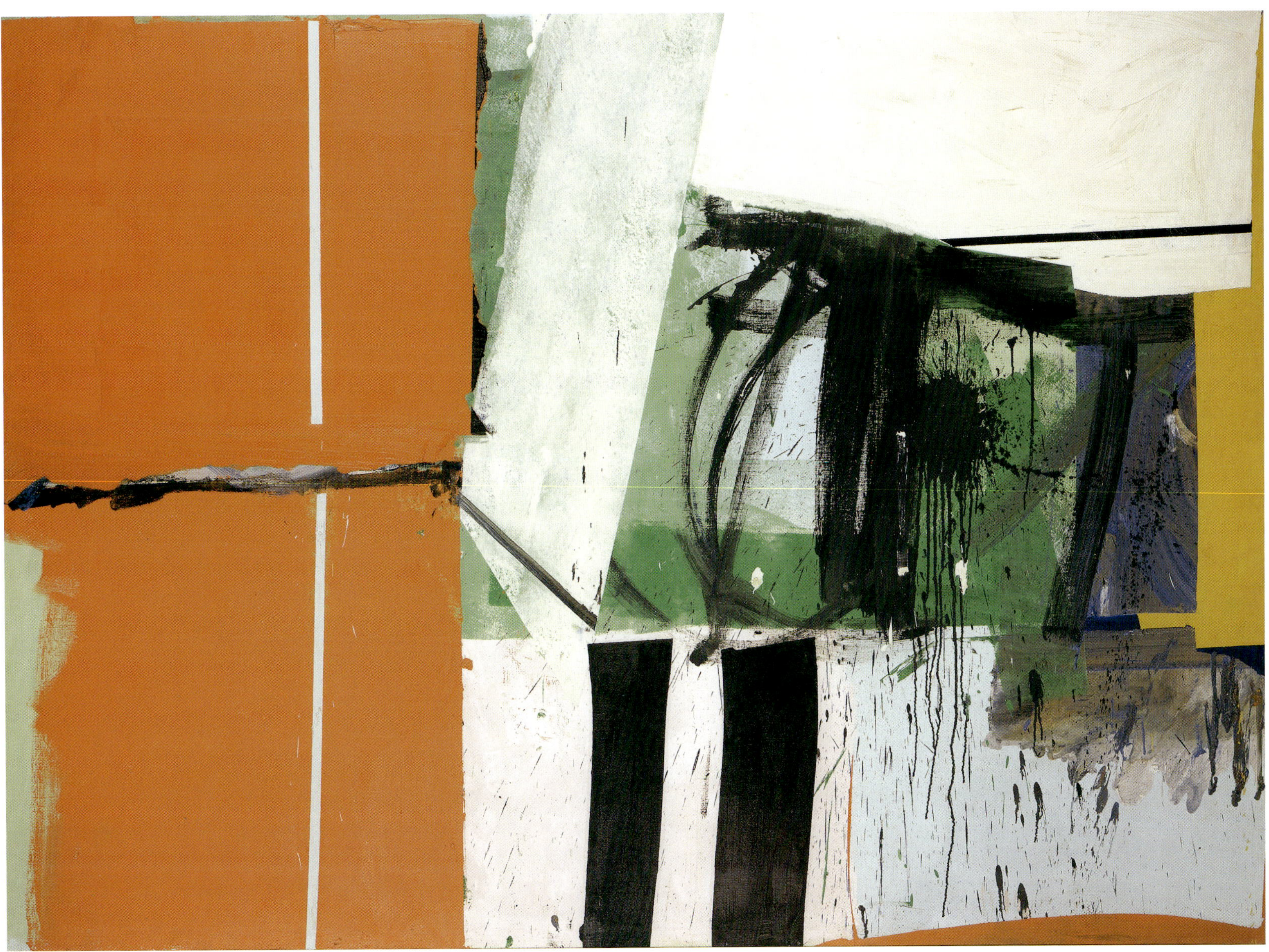

began to pursue several publishing ventures. He created silk-screened print illustrations for a set of poetry published by Tiber Press and edited a literary review titled *The Hasty Papers*, which included submissions by writers and poets like Kerouac, Ginsberg, Jean-Paul Sartre, Frank O'Hara, and William Carlos Williams. In 1966, shortly before his retrospective at the Whitney Museum of American Art was to open, a fire destroyed Leslie's studio and all of its contents, including many important paintings and film masters from the 1950s and early 1960s.

The same critic who identified Leslie's "collage principle" once described his paintings as simultaneously "elegant and raw, painterly, exuberant and personal."[5] With diverse adjectives like these at play, it should come as little surprise to learn that the painter whose work graced the hallowed halls of The Museum of Modern Art and the Guggenheim also participated in the raucous, spontaneous, and sometimes crude anarchism of the downtown Beat poets. For his part, Leslie embraced his stubborn irreducibility and his polymathic sensibility, recently referring to himself as an "octopussarian."[6]

Melissa Warak

96.

The Red Side, 1961

Oil and collage on canvas
78 × 104⅛ in. (198.2 × 264.5 cm)
Gift of Mari and James A. Michener
1991.253

Provenance: Purchased by James Michener from the artist, 1961; long-term loan to The University of Texas at Austin, 1968–1991
Inscribed verso, upper right "The Red Side, 1961 / Alfred Leslie 6'6" × 8'8¼" / New York City 940 Bwy"

Notes

1. Quoted in Dorothy Miller, ed., *Sixteen Americans* (New York: The Museum of Modern Art, 1959), 34.
2. H.H. Arnason, "Introduction," in *American Abstract Expressionists and Imagists* (New York: The Solomon R. Guggenheim Foundation, 1961), 29.
3. I.H.S., exhibition review, *Artnews* 61 (April 1962): 13.
4. Newman's *Vir Heroicus Sublimus* (1950–1951), which makes characteristic use of the "zip," resurfaced in a 1959 exhibition at Bennington College in Vermont.
5. I.H.S., 13.
6. R.C. Baker, "The Octopussarian Drugstore Cowboy," *Village Voice*, November 30, 2004, 30. For more information on Leslie, see Richard Kalina, "The Right Moves: Alfred Leslie in the Fifties," *Art in America* 92 (April 2005): 130–33.

Norman Lewis

New York, 1909–1979
w. New York (trip to Europe and North Africa, 1957), 1933–1979

Norman Lewis had been struggling for a decade with the problem of how to render his relationship to the world in an abstract as opposed to a literal manner when, one morning in the mid-1950s while fishing off the coast of Long Island, he noticed how the fog blurred the distinction between water and sky. From the fog's ability "to obscure outlines and reveal essences," Lewis realized the incredible aesthetic potential of natural phenomena.[1] *La Puerto del Sol* (plate 97), painted in 1958 and perhaps inspired by a trip to Spain the preceding year, belongs to this period in which Lewis turned to nature as a means of expressing his subjective feelings. The work consists of loosely drawn strokes of primarily violet, rust, and black paint that burst through a thinly applied overlay of yellow. While the patterns of color resemble crowds of "little figures," a common motif in paintings by Lewis, the title, which translates as "The Port of the Sun," alludes to the artist's personal recollection of the way darkness penetrates the light.

Born and raised in Harlem, Lewis's artistic career began in the 1930s when he befriended the sculptor Augusta Savage, one of the most influential artists living in Harlem at that time. Allowing Lewis access to her studio, Savage provided him with a model to follow and a place where he could work and meet other artists. Among those the young artist met was the painter Charles Alston, whose studio housed the "306 Group," an informal collective of African American artists, poets, dancers, and writers who met regularly to exchange ideas and discuss contemporary events. Lewis soon joined the group and actively participated in debates over the responsibility of African Americans to create works of art that heightened awareness of cultural and political issues within their racial community. Lewis's paintings from the 1930s were greatly influenced by these discussions. They rely on a figurative style influenced by Social Realism and primarily depict street scenes and the everyday lives of black workers and families.

By the mid-1940s Lewis began to question the ability of art to produce social change, stating in his 1949 application for a Guggenheim Foundation fellowship:

> *For many years I, too, struggled single-mindedly to express social conflict through my painting. However, I gradually came to realize that certain things are true: the development of one's aesthetic abilities suffers by such emphasis; the content of truly creative work must be inherently aesthetic or the work becomes merely another form of illustration; therefore the goal of the artist must be aesthetic development and, in a universal sense, to make in his own way some contribution to culture.*[2]

In an effort to break free from social commentary, Lewis began to incorporate abstraction and stylization into his work. In particular, he found inspiration in the aesthetic inclinations of the emerging Abstract Expressionists, some of whom he had befriended during his involvement with the government-sponsored WPA Federal Art Project in the 1930s. While his new approach to art making shared commonalities with the Abstract Expressionists, crucial differences remained.

In his "Abstract Expressionist" works, Lewis used soft, delicate brushstrokes to produce fragile compositions of lacelike imagery.[3] These serene paintings, many of which focused on the artist's relationship to the spaciousness of nature, differed considerably from the aggressive slashing and splashing approach used by Willem de Kooning and Jackson Pollock. His frequent references to the natural world and human forms, even in his strictly non-objective paintings, as well as his evocative titles, which often alluded to an African or French heritage, also separated Lewis from the group. Such references tied his work too closely to his subjectivity as an African American, as Ann Gibson suggested:

> *Lewis chose subject matter and methods that were at the forefront of avant-garde modernist production, but that used the visual forms of modernist art, sometimes in combination with his titles, to represent his singularity as a black man.*[4]

Even though the Abstract Expressionists never rejected Lewis solely on the basis of his race, in the end his attempt to locate the universality of Abstract Expressionism within the particularities of his racial and cultural experience alienated him from the group.

Race also played an implicit role in Lewis's feelings of marginalization in the art world. By 1960, the same year the Blanton acquired *La Puerto del Sol,* Lewis had exhibited his work in nine solo shows at the Willard Gallery.[5] Since few galleries represented African American artists, Lewis assumed that the prestigious support of Marion Willard—who also represented Mark Tobey, David Smith, and Lyonel Feininger—would launch his career. The positive reviews that his paintings received and the fact that one work, *Migrating Birds,* was awarded the popular prize at the Carnegie Institute's Pittsburgh International Exhibition in 1955 further encouraged Lewis. Yet, when few buyers purchased his paintings, he became aware of the racial prejudice permeating the art world.[6]

Lewis initially thought that hard work and a good dealer would bring him well-earned recognition in the art world. By the time he recognized the false idealism of such beliefs, he had lost too much self-confidence to find another gallery. Lewis turned to teaching in an effort to foster the talents of young students before they, too, were disillusioned by racial discrimination. In spite of these setbacks, he continued to paint until his sudden death in 1979. While it is impossible to ascribe his relative obscurity to any single cause, in recent years scholars have begun to note his contribution to American abstract art, and Lewis is finally being given the recognition that eluded him during his lifetime.

Erina Duganne

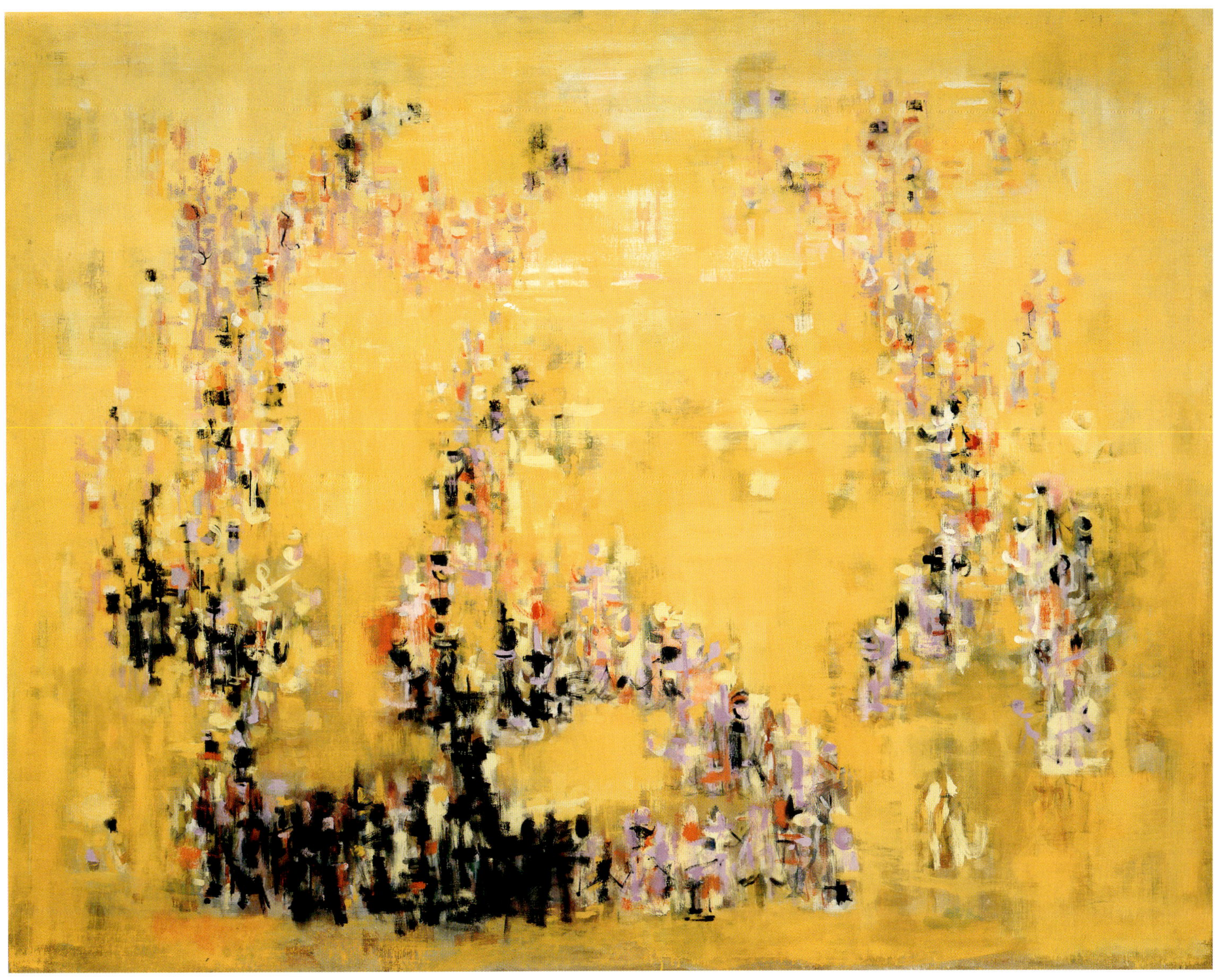

Notes

1. Naomi Vine, "Norman Lewis at Berman/Daferner," *Art in America* 82 (September 1994): 115.
2. Norman Lewis, *Norman Lewis: From the Harlem Renaissance to Abstraction* (New York: Kenkeleba Gallery, 1989), 65.
3. See *A Dictionary of Abstract Painting* (London: Methuen and Co., 1958), 209.
4. Ann Gibson, "Diaspora and Ritual: Norman Lewis's Civil Rights Paintings," *Third Text,* no. 45 (winter 1989/1990): 33.
5. Although James Michener purchased a large number of the twentieth-century American works in the museum's collection, he is not responsible for the acquisition of *La Puerto del Sol*. The painting was acquired by the Longview Foundation, an organization that provided funds to institutions to purchase works of art chosen by the foundation's Arts Selection Committee—whose members included Adolph Gottlieb, Hans Hofmann, and Meyer Schapiro. In 1960, the Longview Foundation found The University of Texas at Austin an excellent candidate for their grant and provided the university, which was planning a new art museum, the means to acquire significant modern paintings and sculptures by artists who had not yet received the financial or professional recognition they deserved.
6. Lewis speaks about his relationship with the Willard Gallery in an interview with Henri Ghent, July 14, 1968, Oral History Program, Archives of American Art, Smithsonian Institution, Washington, D.C. See also Harry Henderson, "Norman Lewis: The Making of a Black Abstract Expressionist, His Achievements and His Neglect," *International Review of African American Art* 13 (1996): 58–64.

97.

La Puerto del Sol, 1958

Oil on linen canvas
51¼ × 63¾ in. (130.2 × 161.9 cm)
Gift of the Longview Foundation, Inc.
G1960.10

Glenn Ligon

b. New York, 1960

w. Providence, Rhode Island, 1980; Middletown, Connecticut, 1980–1982; Brooklyn, New York, 1982–present

More than twenty years into his artistic career, Glenn Ligon remains concerned with issues surrounding identity and the inscrutability of language and images. *Untitled (Hands/Stranger in the Village)* (1999, plate 98) demonstrates this and other characteristics of Ligon's oeuvre, especially the palpable tension it generates between the strategies of Conceptual art, specifically the interrogation of words and their meanings, and the attention to materials that is the hallmark of formalist practices.

Ligon was born in New York in 1960. His childhood home was in the South Bronx, but as an elementary school student he began attending a private school on the Upper West Side of Manhattan. The distance he traveled was both physical and psychological. One world was working class and black, the other upper-middle class and white. The first implied stasis, and the second promised access and opportunity. The movement between these two worlds fostered in Ligon a sense of "profound separation" that would put him in the unique position of being an insider and outsider simultaneously.[1] Having one foot in and one foot out of several different identity categories offers Ligon a curious perspective that permeates his work.

Ligon enrolled at the Rhode Island School of Design in 1980 and finished his undergraduate degree at Wesleyan University in 1982. A few years later, in 1985, he participated in the Whitney Museum Independent Studies Program. No doubt, participation in this program helped the artist hone the critical and formal language that he employs when thinking about, making, and discussing his work. Ligon's career took off when he was featured in the Whitney Biennials of 1991 and 1993. The 1993 Biennial is significant for having formalized a trend known as identity-politics art.

Ligon is best known for his works from the early 1990s in which he appropriated text and then stenciled the words in black pigment on a white ground. The pieces derive their subjects and titles from poignant quotes excerpted from writings by authors such as Zora Neale Hurston, Ralph Ellison, and Mary Shelley. The first two lines of text are almost always legible, for Ligon wants the viewer to read the quote and understand its meaning. However, as the words repeat, they become increasingly difficult to decipher because the pigment builds up, obscuring the letters. The words do not disintegrate so much as they aggregate. In this way, Ligon renders void the ability of words to have significance. Decidedly conceptualist, this strategy forces viewers to work to fathom meaning at the same time that it undermines trust in communication.

Untitled is very much in keeping with Ligon's earlier text-based work. It takes its words from James Baldwin's 1953 essay, "Stranger in the Village," in which the author recalls the time he spent in a Swiss village with his Swiss lover and meditates on what those experiences had to say about race relations in the United States. The quote is taken from the last paragraph of the essay and reads, "The time has come to realize that this interracial drama acted out on the American continent has not only created a new black man, it has created a new white man, too." Unlike his earlier works, the passage in *Untitled* is layered onto the mottled grey and black ground of a photographic image that Ligon appropriated from the news media. Here the text is exceedingly difficult to read, but it is still relevant as it refers to the complexities of the author's life. Baldwin was a stranger in the Swiss village because he was American and black, but he was also a stranger in a larger sense because he was poor in a society that despises poverty, intelligent in an environment where educational opportunities were limited, black in racist America, and gay in a society that did not tolerate homosexuality. Ligon relates to the strangeness about which Baldwin wrote because of certain shared common experiences.

Ligon's use of Baldwin's words has more significance than mere identification, however. Rather, by employing the critical strategy of juxtaposition, the artist uses the passage to bring new meanings to bear on a particular event: the Million Man March/Day of Absence of 1995. The image onto which Ligon superimposed the quote depicts attendees of the March raising their hands in a pledge to protect and uphold the family. The March was a mass, peaceful demonstration organized by Louis Farrakhan, leader of the Nation of Islam. Mounted at the National Mall in Washington, D.C., the March gathered together African American men to advocate atonement and fellowship, support family values and black-owned businesses, and counter negative images of black people in general and black men in particular. While the goals of the March were altruistic, it operated from a platform of exclusion. The organizers requested that black women show their support by remaining absent from the event. The March, concentrating as it did on a traditional view of men as (presumably heterosexual) fathers and family providers, also barred participation by gay African American men. That the uplift of one group of African Americans would depend upon the prohibition of so many others is the strangeness to which Ligon points in *Untitled*.

A gay black man, Ligon approached the March with skepticism and ambivalence, both of which are evident in the form that *Untitled* takes. For instance, the photographic image suggests throngs of men because of its focus on a multitude of hands, but the hands are severed from their particular owners, lending the image an uncanny discomfort. The disembodied hands serve to remind viewers of the sometimes problematic relationship of group identity to individual identity and the uncomfortable compromises between the two that one is often forced to make.

Ligon's use of an abrasive granular substance that he refers to as "coal dust" is also meaningful. As he once said, he was "drawn to it because of all the contradictory readings it engenders. Worthless. Waste. Black. Beautiful. Shiny. Reflective."[2] The artist uses the material

to critique racial hierarchy in the United States by pointing to some of the many vilifying and exoticizing terms that are applied to black people. The accumulation of this industrial by-product, together with the purposefully messy silkscreen, produces different hues of blackness and renders text and image nearly unrecognizable. That, after all, is Ligon's aim in *Untitled:* to show the variety in blackness and emphasize the impossibility of language to communicate meaning effectively or completely.

Cherise Smith

Notes

1. Glenn Ligon, *Glenn Ligon: Stranger* (New York: Studio Museum in Harlem, 2001), 23.
2. Ligon, 27.

98.

Untitled (Hands/Stranger in the Village), 1999

Silkscreen, coal dust, glue on paper mounted on linen
40⅝ × 45 in. (103.5 × 114.8 cm)
Michener Acquisitions Fund
2000.29

Provenance: Purchased from Brent Sikkema Gallery, New York, 2000
Inscribed verso, upper right "G. Ligon, 1999" in marker

Ken Little

b. Canyon, Texas, 1947

w. Lubbock, Texas, 1966–1970; Salt Lake City, Utah, 1970–1972; Missoula, Montana, 1974–1978; Davis, California, 1979–1980; Norman, Oklahoma, 1980–1985; New York, 1985–1988; San Antonio, 1988–present

Ken Little employs unconventional materials to create sculptures with strong visual impact and complex metaphorical associations. Born in West Texas, Little currently lives in San Antonio, where he heads the sculpture program at The University of Texas at San Antonio and is an advocate for emerging Texas-based artists. After completing an undergraduate degree in art at Texas Tech University in 1970, he attended the University of Utah, in Salt Lake City, where he received an MFA in 1972. Initially focusing on ceramics, Little found inspiration in the work of artists who were involved with chance and other aleatory techniques, such as Joseph Beuys and Eva Hesse. His encounter with the work of these artists led him to allow the natural properties of wet clay to determine the final form of his ceramic pieces.

Little developed his own distinctive style through the encouragement of ceramicists Rudy Autio and Robert Arneson, whom he met while teaching at the University of Montana in 1974 and the University of California, Davis, in 1979. Arneson was closely identified with "dude ranch dada," or California Funk art, as well as a certain brand of deadpan humor and social commentary that was an important part of the West Coast aesthetic. Little's work of the mid- to late 1970s was characterized by precisely this aesthetic. The shattered dishes embedded in the clay sculptures he produced during this time anticipate his departure from ceramics and his embrace of other forms of art making, especially assemblage.

Little's work took a significant turn in 1980, when he began to make bronze animal sculptures cast from molds made of leather shoes and belts. Around the same time, the artist began to experiment with taxidermy models. He realized that old, discarded shoes fit the models surprising well, and he commenced a series of shoe-covered animal figures, a body of work that includes *Monitor* (1982, plate 99). Little manipulated the surfaces of these sculptures and infused them with a painterly expressiveness. His recycling of leather, moreover, raises issues about consumerism and waste, in much the same way as the broken dishes in his earlier work allude to the disillusionment with domestic happiness.

In *Monitor,* a wolf stands on a base that assumes the form of a boat; its front paw is raised as if in a pose of submission, and its body is entirely covered by a "coat" comprised of leather shoes, as is the outer shell of the boat. Little created a companion piece to *Monitor,* titled *Merrimac* (1982), in which a boar rests on top of what appears to be a boat. The sculptures reference the first two ironclad ships to engage in battle, an event that took place during the Civil War in 1862. Monitor was the name of the Union ship, while Merrimac was the name of the Confederate ship.[1] After each ship had been pummeled with cannonballs for several hours, the encounter was judged to be a standoff. According to writer Susan Caldwell, Little saw this battle and the sculptures inspired by it as "symbolic of the pointlessness, the absurdity of war."[2]

Delighted with visual puns and double-entendres, Little has lately taken to papering large-scale hollow human figures with dollar bills featuring the visage of George Washington. As he cycles through various media, Little invariably returns to a theme that haunts his work: the idea that a mask—whether protective, in the case of the shoes, or potentially destructive, in the case of the dollar bills—conceals the true self. As the artist said, "I work and live in a cycle. . . . That is, I seem to reach the same or similar position over and over. To visually think about it is a lot like visualizing an old 33-1/3 vinyl record. The grooves circle the core, beginning large and long in the first years. Getting older, the grooves get tighter and tighter, passing through the same rhythm, a little different each time."[3]

Claire Barliant

Notes

1. Susan Havens Caldwell, *Ken Dawson Little* (San Francisco: Quay Gallery, 1983), 21.
2. Caldwell, 21.
3. Ken Little, quoted by Kathleen Whitney, "Introduction: Pygmalion and Pinocchio," in *Ken Little: Little Changes* (San Antonio: Southwest School of Art & Craft: 2003), 21.

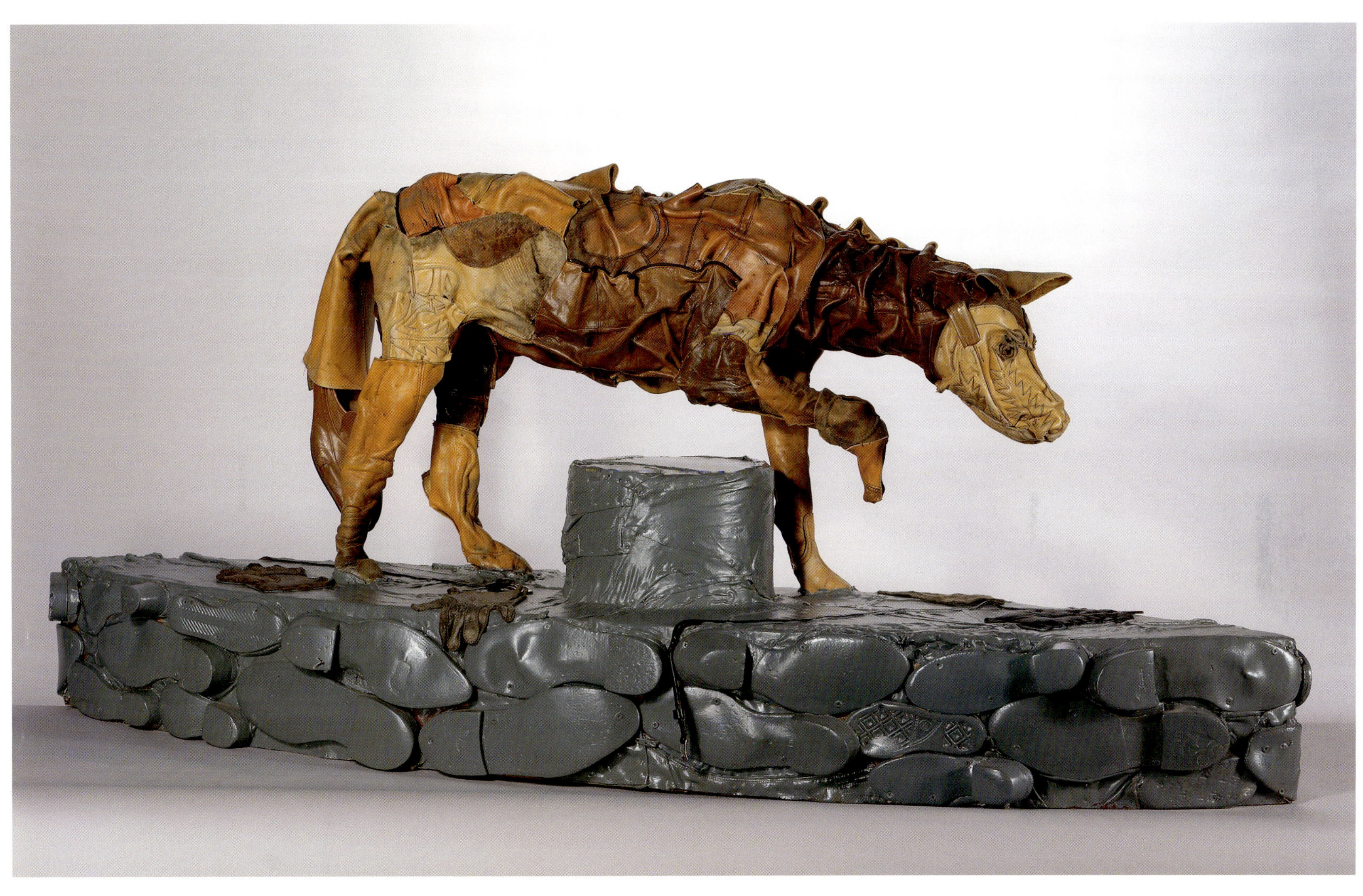

99.
Monitor, 1982

Mixed media with leather shoes
34 × 76 × 23 in. (86.36 × 193.04 × 58.42 cm)
Gift of the Artist
1998.112

Provenance: Ken Little, San Antonio

Bert Long, Jr.

b. Houston, 1940

w. Los Angeles, 1968–1972; Las Vegas, 1975; Houston, 1977–1990; Rome, 1990–1991; Houston–Berzocana, Spain, 1992–present

Houston native Bert Long began to make art at age thirty-five while working professionally as a restaurant chef. A self-taught artist, Long recalled that his training consisted of "sit[ting] down in the Houston museum and library and look[ing], and read[ing] every art book and magazine that I could get my hands on."[1] In his efforts to teach himself to become an artist, Long was encouraged and championed by artist James Surls, a leader in the Houston arts community, which had a strong network of support for Texas-based artists. Long built a notable place for himself within this community, educating others about art, becoming a vocal advocate for his fellow artists, and participating in a wide range of cultural activities, all while developing a substantial body of mature work.[2]

In the 1980s Long began to create carved ice sculptures that were monumental yet ephemeral community gifts. He revealed these works, conceived as extended performances, over the course of a day's passage. Using a loud chainsaw to carve massive blocks of colored ice located on a public site, the artist would shape and arrange the blocks, creating an abstract composition at which audiences marveled. Long is one of the relatively few artists to consider ice sculpture a serious art form and to mine it for its artistic potential. In a 2005 exhibition at the Contemporary Arts Museum, Houston, curator Valerie Cassel Oliver considered Long's ice sculptures in the context of work by three generations of African American artists grappling with the heritage of Conceptual art.[3] In addition to his ice sculptures, Long created a body of paintings in the 1980s for which he received the prestigious Rome Prize. This allowed him to live and work at the American Academy of Rome from 1990 to 1991.

Perseverance (1985, plate 100) is characteristic of the works that earned Long the Rome Prize. Grounded securely in the history of assemblage as practiced by modern and vernacular artists, it addresses the artist's personal experiences.[4] A strip of vivid blue filled with torn bits of money divides the surface of the canvas vertically into abstract and figurative halves. A self-portrait of the bearded and bespectacled artist fills one side of the canvas while a chromatic abstraction, dominated by primary colors, fills the other. For Long, this tension between figuration and abstraction speaks directly to the fate of African American artists. He pointed out that the division in the middle of the painting confronts "the great divide in the art world, between those folks like me and those things that sell in the art world, like Abstract Expressionism, art by white men."[5] Two small paintbrushes, each wrapped in money and collaged into *Perseverance*, symbolize Long's search for financial and critical artistic success at this juncture in his career. The vibrant, handmade frame that the artist constructed for the work hints at the artist's interest in three-dimensional form.

Along with dreams and visions, a constant return to autobiography characterizes Long's art. "Art is about life," he said, revealing the personal and narrative structures that unify his diverse oeuvre. "And my art is just about that—about my life."[6] Rendered with the rough handling typical of the Expressionist tradition, the self-portrait in *Perseverance* shows a disembodied head, its beard and hair disheveled to depict the artist as a "mad genius," but only in order to deflate that stereotype.

Concerned with assuring that his contributions will be remembered and understood, Long continuously documents the personal history alluded to in paintings such as *Perseverance*. He has assembled something known as "Bert's Book," an encyclopedic accounting of virtually all his art, exhibitions, and reviews; it constitutes multiple volumes and weighs several pounds.[7] In conversation, moreover, Long repeatedly reveals the narratives that undergird his artworks and add layers of meaning to their imagery. These narratives constitute a sort of performance akin to those associated with his ice sculptures. They also indicate the degree to which Long's "art and . . . stories become complete (and complex) narratives capable of conveying their individual meanings only when presented in tandem, so that the verbal and visual half-texts together form a satisfying whole."[8]

In 1980 Long founded *ArtScene*, Houston's first art newspaper. He continues to maintain an important presence within the arts communities of Houston and beyond, ever willing to talk about art and to serve as an informal mentor to others. As an artist who seeks to challenge stereotypes while educating others about art, Long insists, "my quest is just to persevere."[9]

James Housefield

Notes

1. Bert Long, Jr., telephone conversation with the author, July 11, 2005.
2. Long's status as a self-taught artist and his use of assemblage invite comparison with larger vernacular traditions. As Lowery Stokes Sims noted, "For African American artists the relationship to self-taught or folk art provides a direct link with ancestral identities and traditions." See Sims, "Self-Taught and Trained Artists: An Evolving Relationship," in William Arnett and Paul Arnett, eds., *Souls Grown Deep: African American Vernacular Art of the South*, vol. 2 (Atlanta: Tinwood Books, 2001), 92. For Long, these traditions coexist alongside a history of art that includes the painters of seventeenth-century Holland and modern France.
3. Valerie Cassel Oliver, *Double Consciousness: Black Conceptual Art Since 1970* (Houston: Contemporary Arts Museum, Houston, 2005). Each of Long's monumental ice sculptures is accompanied by a suite of studies—works on paper charting the conceptual and physical development of that sculpture. He made his first ice sculpture in 1980 in Galveston, Texas.
4. Elements of assemblage that recur in Long's work recall the blurring of painting and sculpture as celebrated by The Museum of Modern Art's exhibition *The Art of Assemblage* as well as vernacular and African American assemblage traditions. On the African roots of African American assemblage, see Robert Farris Thompson, *Flash of the Spirit: African and Afro-American Art and Philosophy* (New York: Random House, 1983); on the MoMA exhibition, see William Seitz, *The Art of Assemblage* (New York: The Museum of Modern Art, 1961).
5. Long, telephone conversation with the author.
6. Long, telephone conversation with the author.
7. "Bert's Book" is nearly legendary among curators and the younger artists for whom it serves as an example. The artist periodically deposits copies with museums that own his works, including the Blanton.
8. Roger Manley, "Half-Told Tales: Some Thoughts on African-American Self-Taught Art as Narrative," in Arnett and Arnett, vol. 1, 362.
9. Manley, 362.

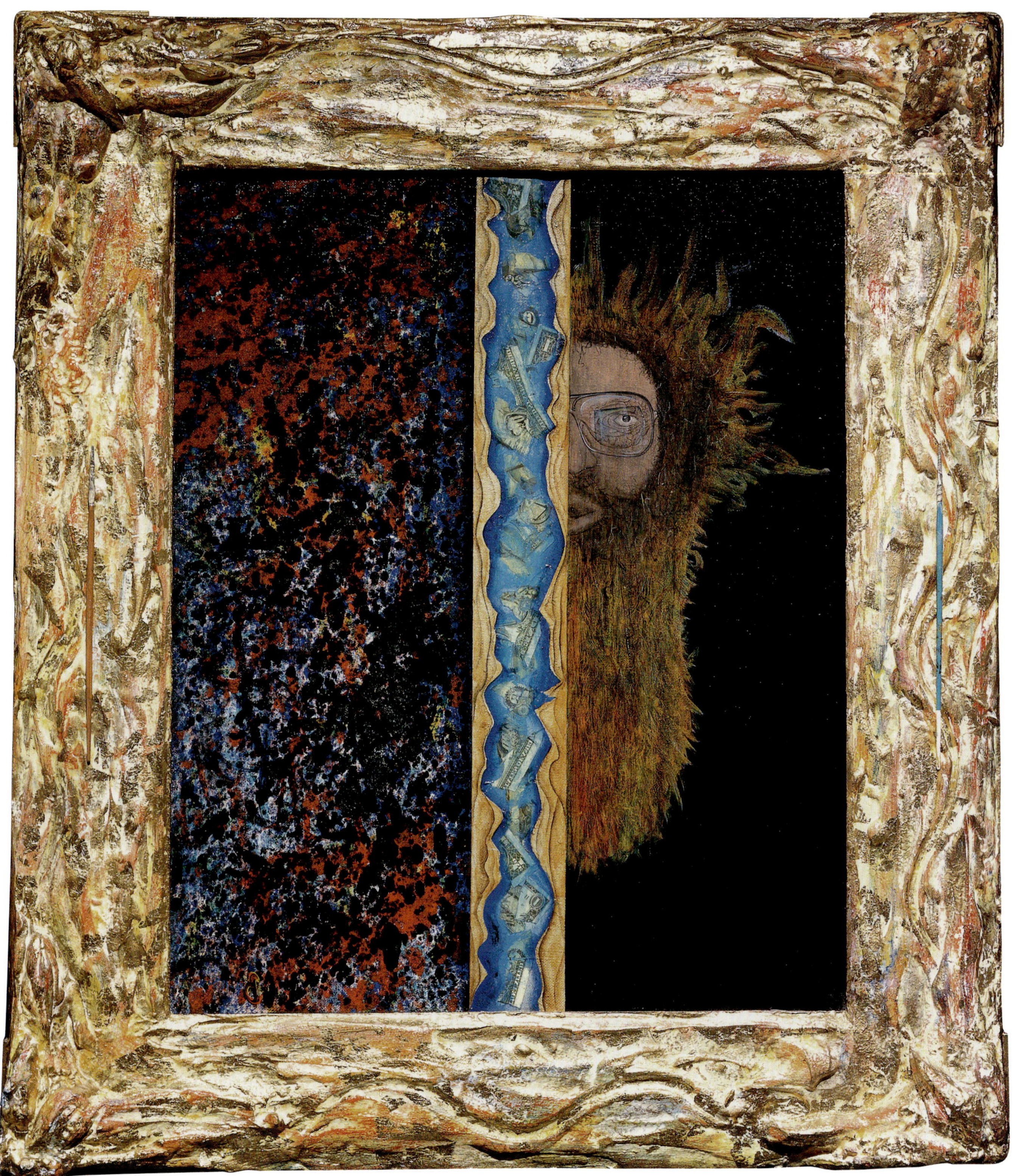

100.

Perseverance, 1985

Acrylic, hydrostone, and collage on canvas
29 15/16 × 24 1/4 in. (76 × 61.6 cm)
Gift of Nadine Cochran Vickery
1986.289

Provenance: Purchased by Nadine Cochran Vickery from Hiram Butler Gallery, Houston, 1985
Inscribed lower right "B 9-18 '85"
Inscribed verso, upper center on stretcher "BL0198" in black paint
Inscribed verso, on canvas "BL0198 / Bert / 9-18 85" and "PRESEVERANC" [sic] in black paint

Morris Louis

Baltimore, 1912–Washington, D.C., 1962

w. Baltimore, 1927–1936; New York, 1936–1940; Baltimore, 1940–1952; Washington, D.C., 1952–1962

Born to Russian immigrants in Baltimore in 1912, Morris Louis Bernstein graduated from the Maryland Institute of Fine and Applied Arts at age nineteen.[1] He devoted his entire life to painting, despite pressure from his family to pursue careers in medicine and pharmacy. Although Louis achieved recognition during his lifetime, critical and financial success eluded him until the last five years of his life.

In the 1930s Louis lived in New York, where he worked for the Easel Division of the Federal Art Project, made frequent visits to The Museum of Modern Art, and participated in his first group exhibition in 1937 at the A.C.A. Gallery on 8th Street. He returned to Baltimore in the early 1940s and married Marcella Siegel in 1947. Together they bought a house in Washington, D.C., converting the modest dining room into the studio Louis would use for the rest of his life.

In 1952 Louis began teaching at the Washington Workshop Center for the Arts. He befriended a fellow teacher, Kenneth Noland, who introduced him to the influential New York critic, Clement Greenberg. A pivotal moment in Louis's career occurred during a trip to New York in 1953 when Greenberg took Louis and Noland to the studio of Helen Frankenthaler. Like many artists in the 1950s, Frankenthaler was coming to terms with the formal lessons of Abstract Expressionist painting. Taking inspiration from Jackson Pollock's practice of painting on unprimed canvases, she began to thin her pigments so that they soaked more thoroughly into the canvas. The two Washington-based artists were deeply affected by Frankenthaler's approach. Louis later commented that her work served as "a bridge between Pollock and what was possible."[2]

Inspired by Frankenthaler's example, Louis developed his own method of stain painting using a brand of acrylic resin called Magna. Typically, he would pour paint directly onto the support and then fold, tip, and tilt the canvas so as to direct the pigment down or across the surface, leaving a swath of color in its wake. Stain painting causes the pigment to integrate more fully with the canvas' weave, thereby uniting color and support. Greenberg championed Louis's work and established a critical position that lauded the way staining both flattened and emphasized the surface of a painting.[3] Though Louis remained in contact with Greenberg and regularly visited New York, he was a reclusive, solitary man who preferred the relative isolation of Washington. Aside from teaching art, he spent most of his time painting alone in his studio.

Louis rigorously culled his prodigious output, destroying hundreds of paintings as he assessed his production. Although he rarely titled his works, historians tend to categorize them into four different groups. The first three are comprised of enormous canvases that share formal characteristics. The Veils (1954) as well as the larger Veils II from 1957–1959, have broad swaths of overlapping stains, often somber in color. The Florals (1959–1960) are brighter in hue with poured designs that radiate out from the center of the canvas. The Unfurleds (1959–1960) leave the center bare but include narrow stripes traveling diagonally down either side of the canvas.

The Blanton's *Water-Shot* (1961, plate 101) belongs to Louis's last series, the Stripes, begun the same year. Though still large in scale, these canvases are smaller and more controlled than the paintings in the other three groups. Louis employed the same technique of emphasizing the individual color pours as he had in the Unfurleds, but here the stripes cling together, forming neatly aligned parallels in the center of the canvas. One end of the stripes is cropped from the painting, but the other end shows rounded and dripped tails. These were created when the paint Louis was pouring dripped backwards over the fold at the top of the temporary canvas stretcher.[4] He used only nine colors, ranging from bright yellow to somber green, to form the primary stripes, but at least nineteen more stripes were created through the proximity and bleeding of pigments, a typical outcome of his technique. Indeed, close observation of *Water-Shot* reveals stained ghost images alongside the forest green stripe at the far left, while the navy blue and mustard yellow stripes in the center have merged slightly, creating a muted blue green in between.

Water Shot is among many of Louis's works whose correct orientation has been disputed. The artist preferred the clean edge along the bottom, with drips at the top. However, when they were first exhibited, Louis was persuaded to hang some with the tails along the bottom. The Blanton's research upholds Louis's original intent, which also reflects the dominant direction of the paint flow.[5]

Louis's very last paintings include some painted on the diagonal, suggesting that he was about to enter a new phase of his career, but he died rather suddenly at age 49. Although his career was cut short, Louis's passionate exploration of painting showed a way to move beyond Abstract Expressionism and into a new, more pure approach to formalist painting.

Katie Robinson Edwards

Notes

1. By 1938 Morris Louis had officially changed his name.
2. The original source of this oft-quoted remark is Gerald Nordland, *The Washington Color Painters* (Washington, D.C.: Washington Gallery of Modern Art, 1965), 12.
3. Greenberg adamantly positioned these artists and others as bonafide heirs to the Abstract Expressionist painters, grouping their work under the title "Post Painterly Abstraction." An important exhibition of works selected by Greenberg was mounted in 1964, two years after Louis's death. See Clement Greenberg, *Post Painterly Abstraction* (Los Angeles: Los Angeles County Museum of Art, 1964).
4. By the latter part of the series, however, Louis's technique had changed from this earlier "backflow" method.
5. Diane Upright, *Morris Louis, The Complete Paintings: A Catalogue Raisonné* (New York: Harry N. Abrams, 1985), 45, 47.

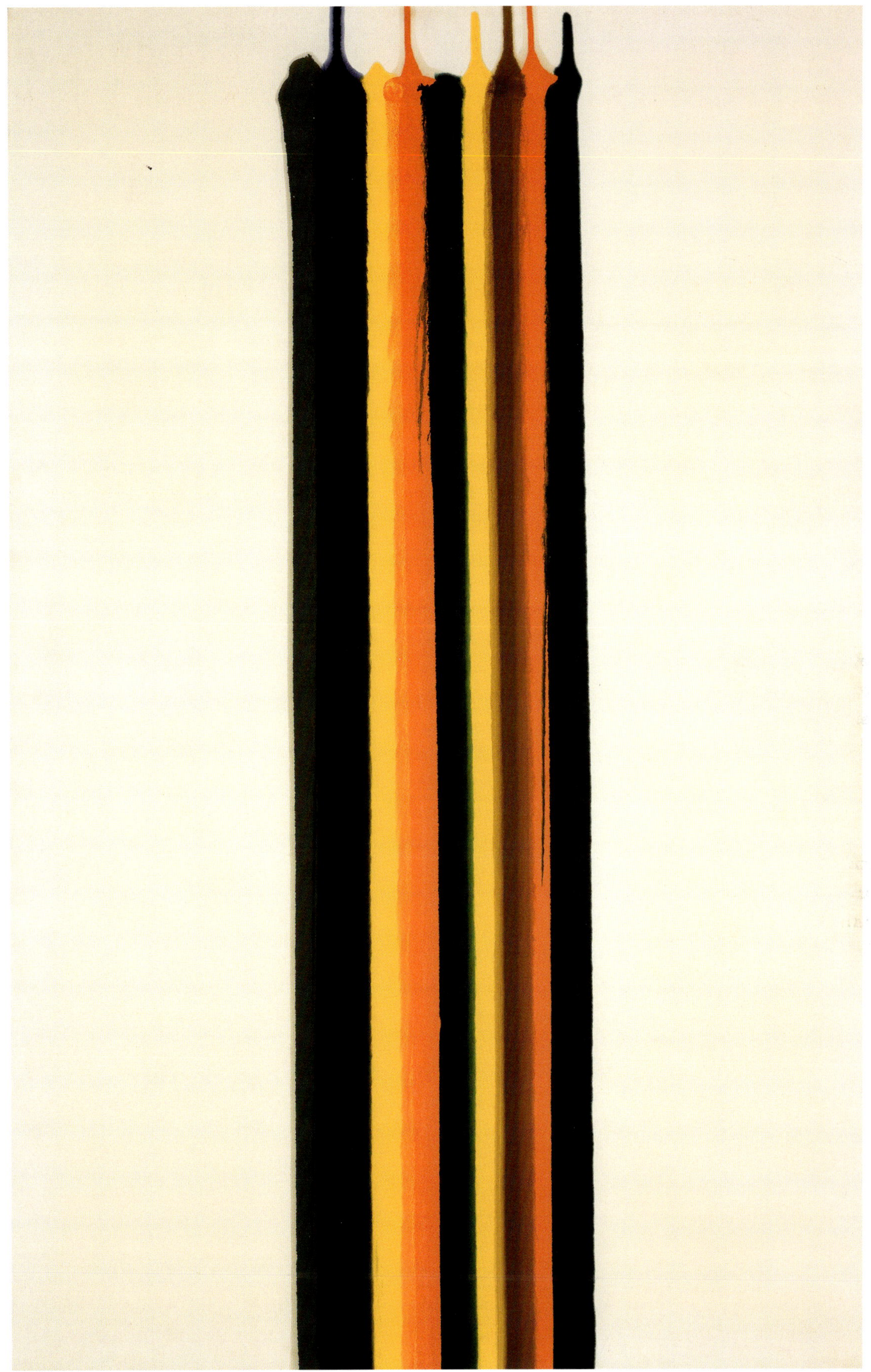

101.

Water-Shot, 1961

Acrylic on unsized canvas
84½ × 53¼ in. (214.7 × 135.3 cm)
Gift of Mari and James A. Michener
1991.257

Provenance: Purchased by James Michener from André Emmerich Gallery, New York, 1962; long-term loan to The University of Texas at Austin, 1968–1991

Lee Lozano

Newark, New Jersey, 1930–Dallas, 1999
w. Chicago, 1948–1960; New York, 1960–1972

Lee Lozano's work traverses many of the major tendencies influencing the art of the 1960s. Beginning around 1961, Lozano was making messy, figurative paintings containing sexually fraught imagery, but by mid-decade she was producing closely painted, monumental depictions of tools and hardware. These paintings were followed in the late 1960s by a series of abstract works that investigated the intersections of science, representation, and duration in painting. In conjunction with her later painting practice, Lozano also produced numerous conceptual, performance-based pieces that combined radical self-examination with a critique of the institutions and social dynamics of the 1960s art world. The progressively critical stance expressed by this work led her to abandon the art world altogether by 1972. While the breadth of her practice and the intensity of her commitment made her a major figure during the late 1960s, her work was subsequently nearly completely forgotten until a spate of retrospective exhibitions in the late 1990s reawakened interest in her remarkable career.[1]

Lozano was born Lenore Knaster in Newark, New Jersey, in 1930. She attended the University of Chicago between 1948 and 1951, and received her BA there before enrolling in the MFA program at the Art Institute of Chicago in 1956. That same year, she married architect Adrian Lozano. After completing her fine arts degree in 1960, she traveled in Europe for several months and then returned to the United States to relocate to New York, where she made her career until moving to Dallas in 1972.

Lozano's work of the early 1960s can be read as an aggressive challenge to the Pop painting conventions of the period. In contrast to depictions of the immaculate and sexualized female body in domestic settings, such as Tom Wesselman's Great American Nude series, Lozano began her career by making messy, gestural paintings that present the body as the site of hygienic intervention—pimples are popped, nose hair is plucked, and breasts are juxtaposed with a toothbrush dripping with toothpaste. Other images represent body parts that have morphed into genitalia, and guns and tools that take the form of charged sexual symbols. Hand tools such as hammers, wrenches, and clamps held a particular fascination for Lozano. Far more than simple inanimate objects, these tools became menacing, anthropomorphized entities in a number of untitled works made between 1961 and 1963. The first major shift in Lozano's style and execution occurred around this time, as exemplified by the clean lines, shallow space and meticulously applied surface of *Ream* (1964, plate 102).

Ream is one of the first paintings to signal Lozano's increasing interest in abstraction. Images of the body or anthropomorphically inflected objects are no longer present; the tools portrayed in these works represent a focusing of her visual imagination into an encounter with a single, monumental form. Yet the sexuality and menace present in her earlier work has not disappeared but now operates in another register. Because Lozano has depicted the carpenter's tool that is the apparent subject of this painting in such a way that it completely fills the visual field of the canvas, space is radically flattened and color has been reduced to the grays and blues of cold, hard steel. Accompanying these visual aspects is a title suggestive of both verbal and physical aggression that is more direct in its impact than the titles used for her other works of the mid-1960s, such as *Peel* (1964), *Slide* (1965), and *Clash* (1965). The play between noun and verb, abstraction and realism in these paintings indicates Lozano's increasing fascination with the relationship between language and imagery during this period.

Reflecting an interest in combining illusionism with the vocabulary of Minimalism, Lozano's work of the late 1960s features raked and finely textured surfaces that are visually responsive to the exhibition context and the movement of the viewer. This attention to surface, along with an emphasis on treating the painting as an object, led Lozano to shape and alter her canvases, as she did in *Stroke* (1967–1970, plate 103). In this two-panel piece, Lozano carefully perforated the canvas to create a pattern of ovals, which draws attention to the surface and also adds the effect of light as it penetrates the support. A note written at the bottom of *Study for holes in* Stroke *(dark half)* (1970, plate 104) reveals that Lozano intended the painting to be hung so that it casts shadows on the wall behind it, its perforations creating an illuminated design essential to the light/dark contrasts of the piece.

During the late 1960s, while Lozano was critiquing the conventions of abstract art through works such as *Stroke,* she began a major series of canvases dubbed the "wave paintings." With a wide, thick-bristled brush and ferrous oxide paint, she obsessively repeated waveforms to create a textured surface that caught and reflected light in a way that seemed to both describe and demonstrate its natural properties. Following this intense period of work, Lozano began making conceptual pieces, which now exist only as "write-ups" of scenarios as recorded in her many notebooks. *General Strike Piece* (1969, plate 105) stands as one of the most significant of these works to the extent that it reveals the radical commitment at the heart of Lozano's practice and announces the beginning of her self-imposed exile from the art world.[2]

According to the conditions of the piece, Lozano began to withdraw her work from shows and to refrain from attending openings and social functions and visiting museums. Her intention in doing so was to further her goal of "total personal and public revolution." By partaking in the commingling of art and activism that occurred in the late 1960s, *General Strike Piece* also resonates with other famous avant-garde refusals, such as Marcel Duchamp's declaration in 1923 that he had given up art for chess. Yet the degree of Lozano's disenchantment with the cultural scene as expressed in *General Strike Piece* is emphasized by the fact that she shortly thereafter conceived *Dropout Piece.* She began the execution of this, her final work, in the summer of

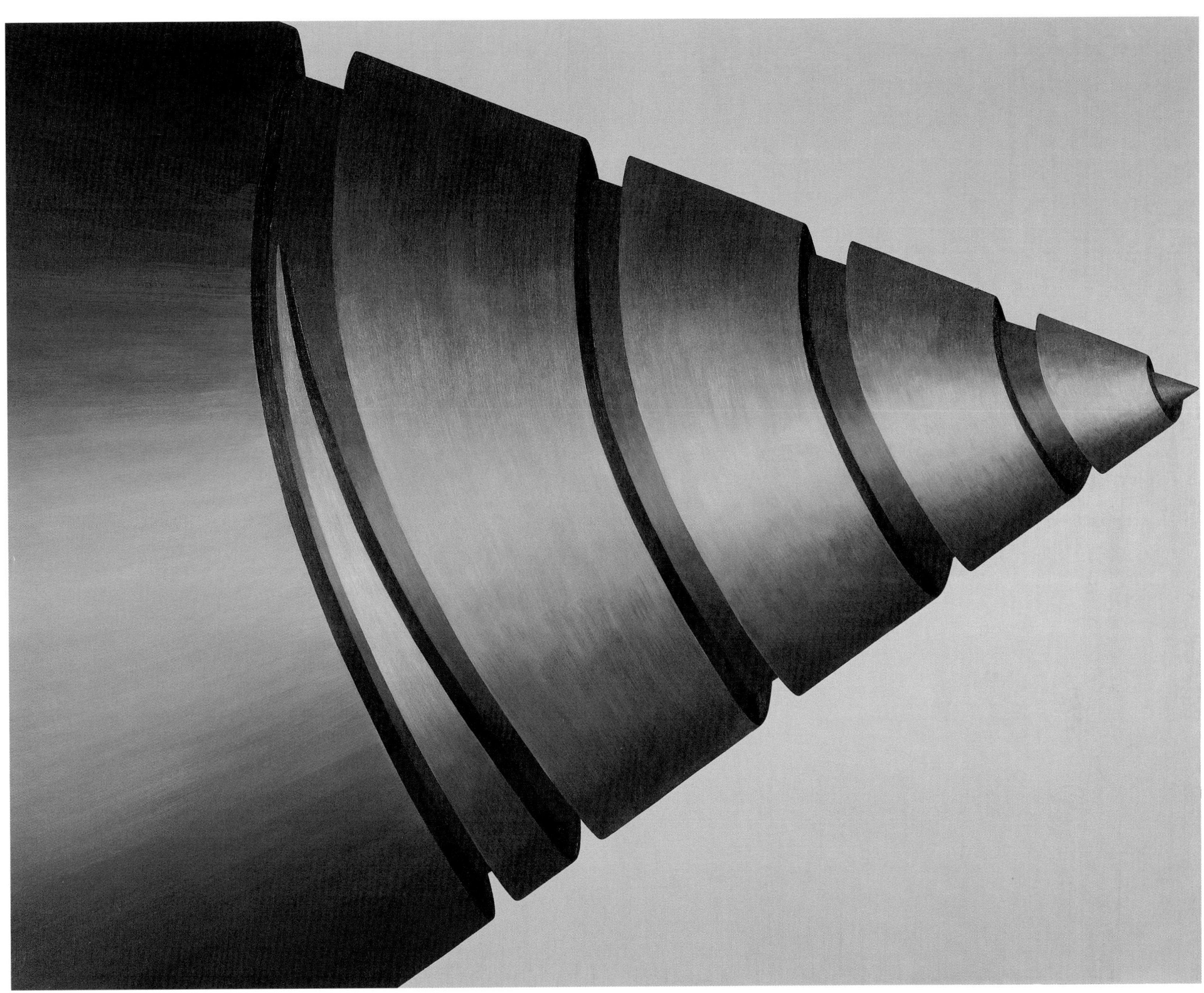

102.

Ream, 1964

Oil on canvas
$78\frac{3}{8} \times 96\frac{1}{16}$ in. (199 × 244 cm)
Gift of Mari and James A. Michener
G1968.92

Provenance: Purchased by James Michener from the artist through Richard Bellamy, New York, 1964
Inscribed verso, upper left "lee lozano '64"

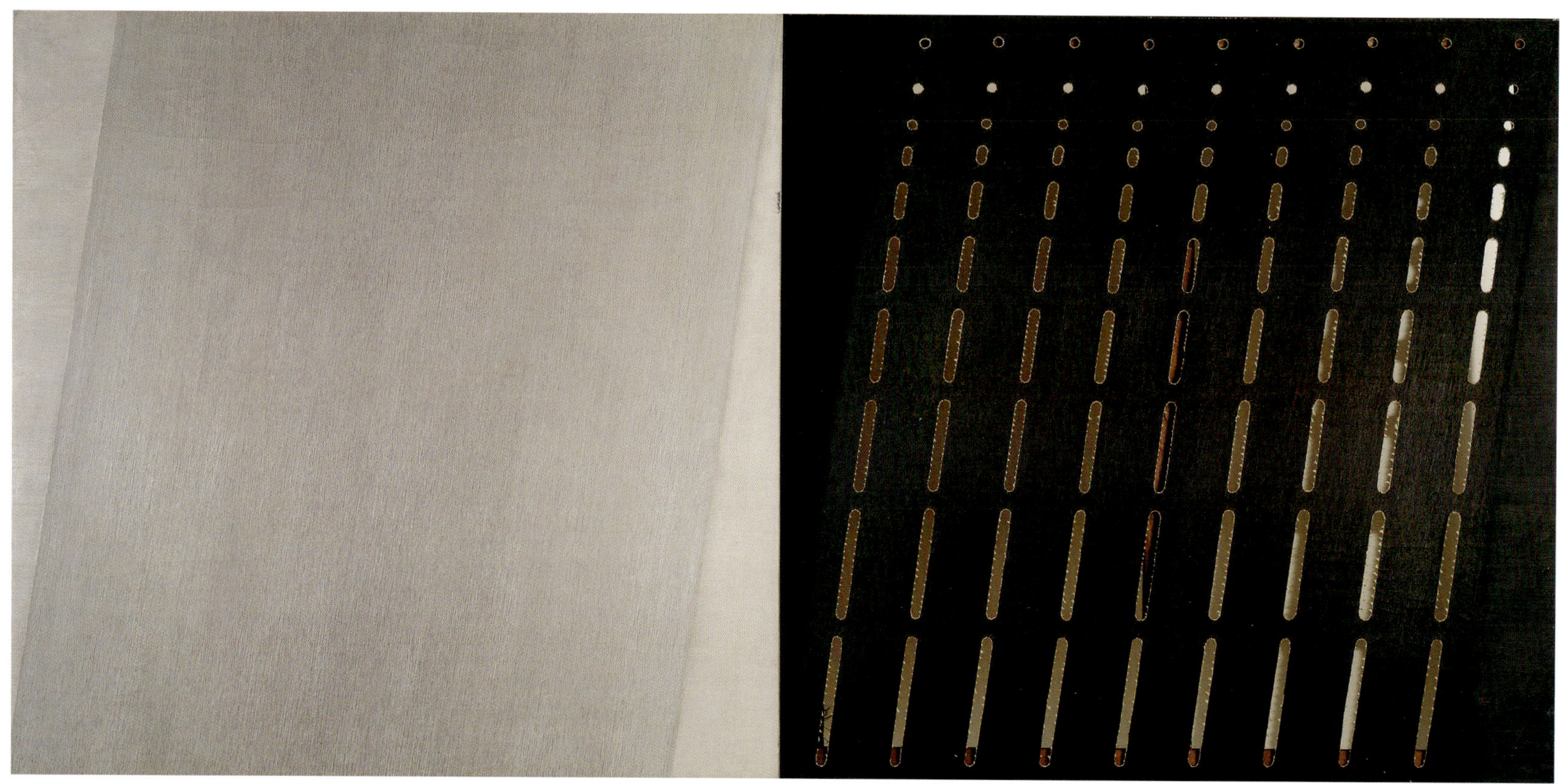

103.

Stroke, 1967–1970

Oil on canvas (two panels)
Each panel: 42 × 42 in. (106.68 × 106.68 cm)
Purchase through the generosity of The Judith Rothschild Foundation and the Michener Acquisitions Fund
2001.82

Provenance: Purchased from Van Liere Fine Art, New York, 2001

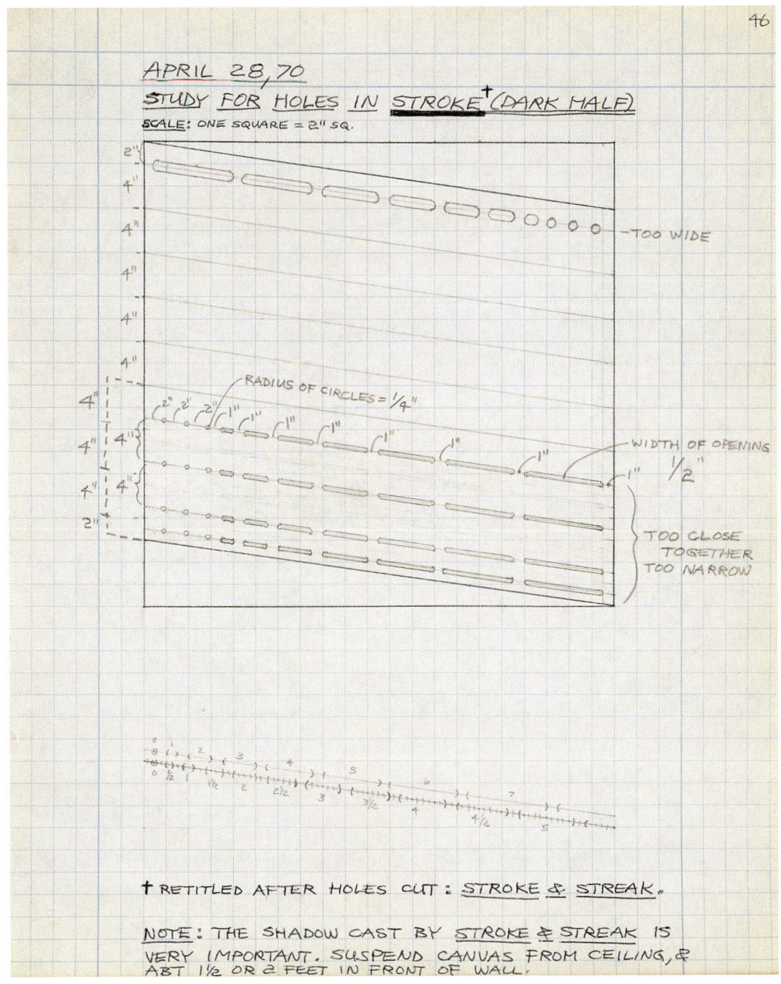

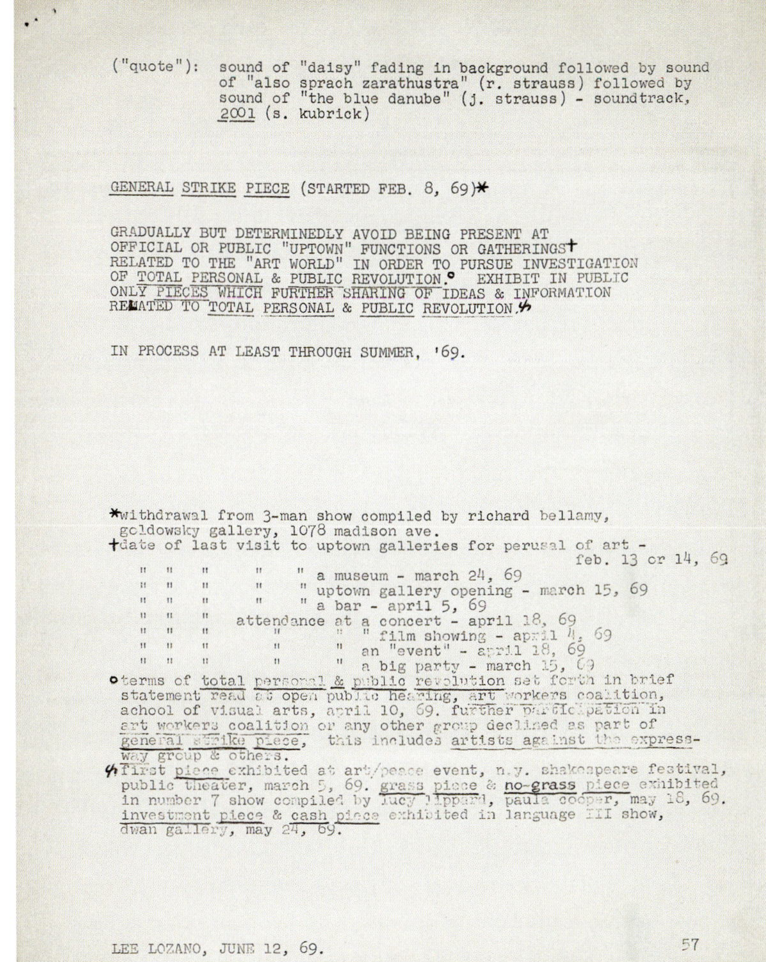

("quote"): sound of "daisy" fading in background followed by sound of "also sprach zarathustra" (r. strauss) followed by sound of "the blue danube" (j. strauss) - soundtrack, 2001 (s. kubrick)

GENERAL STRIKE PIECE (STARTED FEB. 8, 69)*

GRADUALLY BUT DETERMINEDLY AVOID BEING PRESENT AT OFFICIAL OR PUBLIC "UPTOWN" FUNCTIONS OR GATHERINGS† RELATED TO THE "ART WORLD" IN ORDER TO PURSUE INVESTIGATION OF TOTAL PERSONAL & PUBLIC REVOLUTION.° EXHIBIT IN PUBLIC ONLY PIECES WHICH FURTHER SHARING OF IDEAS & INFORMATION RELATED TO TOTAL PERSONAL & PUBLIC REVOLUTION.%

IN PROCESS AT LEAST THROUGH SUMMER, '69.

*withdrawal from 3-man show compiled by richard bellamy, goldowsky gallery, 1078 madison ave.
†date of last visit to uptown galleries for perusal of art - feb. 13 or 14, 69
" " " " " a museum - march 24, 69
" " " " " uptown gallery opening - march 15, 69
" " " " " a bar - april 5, 69
" " " attendance at a concert - april 18, 69
" " " " " " film showing - april 4, 69
" " " " " an "event" - april 18, 69
" " " " " a big party - march 15, 69
°terms of total personal & public revolution set forth in brief statement read at open public hearing, art workers coalition, school of visual arts, april 10, 69. further participation in art workers coalition or any other group declined as part of general strike piece, this includes artists against the expressway group & others.
%first piece exhibited at art/peace event, n.y. shakespeare festival, public theater, march 5, 69. grass piece & no-grass piece exhibited in number 7 show compiled by lucy lippard, paula cooper, may 18, 69. investment piece & cash piece exhibited in language III show, dwan gallery, may 24, 69.

LEE LOZANO, JUNE 12, 69. 57

1971 with what she called a boycott of women, in which she refused to speak or interact with any woman. Initially developed as a month-long activity, Lozano continued this practice even after she left New York in 1972 and moved to Dallas, where she lived until her death in 1999. This final gesture, whatever its ultimate consequences for Lozano, underscores the combination of self-examination and formal experimentation evident in every stage of her work.[3]

Ken Allan

Notes

1. The recent solo exhibitions of her work include *Lee Lozano: Drawn from Life, 1961–1971*, P.S. 1 Contemporary Art Center, Long Island, New York, 2004; *A Wave Painting and Some Drawings*, Van Liere Fine Art, New York, 2000; *Lee Lozano/Matrix 135*, Wadsworth Atheneum, Hartford, Connecticut, 1998; *Early '60s*, Mitchell Algus Gallery, New York, 1998; *Tool Paintings*, Rosen & van Liere, New York, 1998; and *Minimalism*, Margarete Roeder Gallery, New York, 1998.
2. This version of *General Strike Piece* is from the June 1969 issue of *0–9*, an alternative publication edited by Vito Acconci. A handwritten version exists in the Wadsworth Athenaeum.
3. For more information on Lozano, see Eleanor Heartney, "The Return of a Rebel," *Art in America* 87 (May 1999): 146–49; Helen Molesworth, "Tune In, Turn On, Drop Out: The Rejection of Lee Lozano," *Art Journal* 61 (winter 2002): 64–71; and Katy Siegel, "Making Waves," *Artforum* 40 (October 2001): 120–27.

104.

Study for holes in Stroke *(dark half)*, 1970

Graphite and pen on graph paper
11 x 9 in. (28 x 22.7 cm)
Gift of Jaap van Liere
2001.49

105.

General Strike Piece, 1969

Offset on paper
11 x 9 in. (28 x 22.7 cm)
Gift of Jaap van Liere
2001.48

Sven Lukin

b. Riga, Latvia, 1934
w. New York, 1958–present

Lawrence Alloway's catalogue essay for the Guggenheim Museum's 1964 exhibition, *The Shaped Canvas,* which included the work of Sven Lukin among others, begins with the blunt statement, "A shaped canvas is not a sculpture." To prevent any possible confusion, Alloway continued, "It may be three-dimensional, in that it carries projections or is opened up, but it retains connections with the paintings we are accustomed to, flat right-angled planes on the wall."[1] Neither overtly polemical nor even particularly argumentative, this pronouncement nevertheless carried significant implications at the time. By claiming the shaped canvas for painting rather than sculpture (or, more importantly, anything in between), Alloway was taking sides in a debate concerning the boundaries between the individual arts, which became one of the defining issues of American art of the 1960s.

Lukin's involvement in this debate began shortly before he produced *Untitled II* (plate 106) in 1961. Born in Riga, Latvia, in 1934, the artist emigrated from Germany to the United States in 1949. After studying architecture at the University of Pennsylvania in the mid-1950s, he moved to New York in 1958 and began to focus on painting. His paintings of the late 1950s were strongly influenced by the work of Mark Rothko and Ad Reinhardt, but in 1960 he started to experiment with shaping and adding sculptural elements to his canvases. During the following year, Lukin developed a format he would use to make a number of works, including *Untitled II,* that might be described as painting-reliefs. This format consisted of a rectangular canvas bisected vertically or horizontally by a laminated wooden beam that curved forward at one or both ends.[2] Stretched over a shaped plywood frame, the canvas too curved forward on the top and bottom or on the sides. Onto these unconventionally configured canvases Lukin painted curvilinear hard-edge shapes, often bilaterally symmetrical, in dark colors on a light-colored ground or on the unprimed canvas. Aware of the inevitable comparison of this work to Ellsworth Kelly's contemporaneous hard-edge paintings, Lukin did not deny his debt to them. However, while Kelly's abstract forms always had a referent in the natural world, Lukin maintained that his were determined solely by the structure of his paintings: "I tried hard to stay away from Hard-Edge finality and definition. I didn't want it, and fought against it. But the canvas's forms would not take the indefiniteness of soft-edged areas of color."[3] Lukin would continue to produce reliefs like these for several years, but by the mid-1960s he had already adopted a new format in which smaller square or rectangular canvases were attached to the surface of a larger primary canvas.

Frank Stella, one of the other artists included in Alloway's exhibition, began his own investigation of the shaped canvas around the same time as Lukin, but the results he obtained were very different. In 1959 Stella completed a series of black stripe paintings in which the pattern of the stripes, starting at the edge and moving concentrically toward the painting's center (or vice versa), reiterated the shape of the rectangular canvas. The width of the stripes corresponded roughly to the depth of the canvas' stretcher, which was deeper than usual, so that the painting's "image" derived from its structure—a scheme Modernist art critic Michael Fried called "deductive structure."[4] Several subsequent series of more idiosyncratically shaped paintings executed in metallic paint were even more successful than the black paintings at eliminating spatial illusionism and dispelling the notion that the images might refer to anything else. These were important issues for Stella, who adopted the shaped canvas in order to confront problems intrinsic to painting. The artist and critic Donald Judd, however, valued Stella's paintings, which he referred to approvingly as "slabs," for their objectlike quality, not for their self-referentiality.[5] For Judd, these paintings were instrumental in prompting the transition from painting to what he called "specific objects," a broad category of three-dimensional work—in which he included Lukin's—that was "neither painting nor sculpture."[6] Unlike Fried and Alloway, Judd was not convinced that art needed to fit into predetermined categories, and he saw the shaped canvas as the catalyst for the new three-dimensional work for which he became an advocate.

Not coincidentally, Judd himself had simultaneously developed a relief form with a kind of cornice at the top and bottom that closely resembled the structure of *Untitled II.* The principal difference between the two was that Judd abandoned the canvas support altogether in favor of painted plywood and galvanized iron or aluminum. Although Lukin's work became increasingly sculptural during the late 1960s, eventually engaging not only with the floor but with more of the space in front of the wall as well, he appears to have been less interested in moving into "actual" space, as Judd would say, or in giving up painting. As Lukin admitted, "I liked the wall behind them, they need the wall. It establishes their background, their boundaries, it is their environment."[7] In some ways, Lukin's shaped canvases of the 1960s might be said to constitute a kind of middle term between Stella's paintings and Judd's reliefs. His interest in painting is manifest, but it is combined with a desire to invest the work with a more assertive physical presence. "I wanted them to have more the quality of *things,*" Lukin wrote, so they would "relate to a person, to exist physically in the same space, along with his body, the room, the wall, the floor."[8] Along with the shaped canvases of artists like Charles Hinman, Neil Williams, and Richard Smith, as well as Stella, Lukin's work was implicated in the dispute that took place primarily in New York art galleries and the pages of *Artforum* magazine during the 1960s over the autonomy of the art object. And, while Lukin might have agreed with Alloway's contention that a shaped canvas was not a sculpture, he would not have denied that it was an object.

Mary Leclère

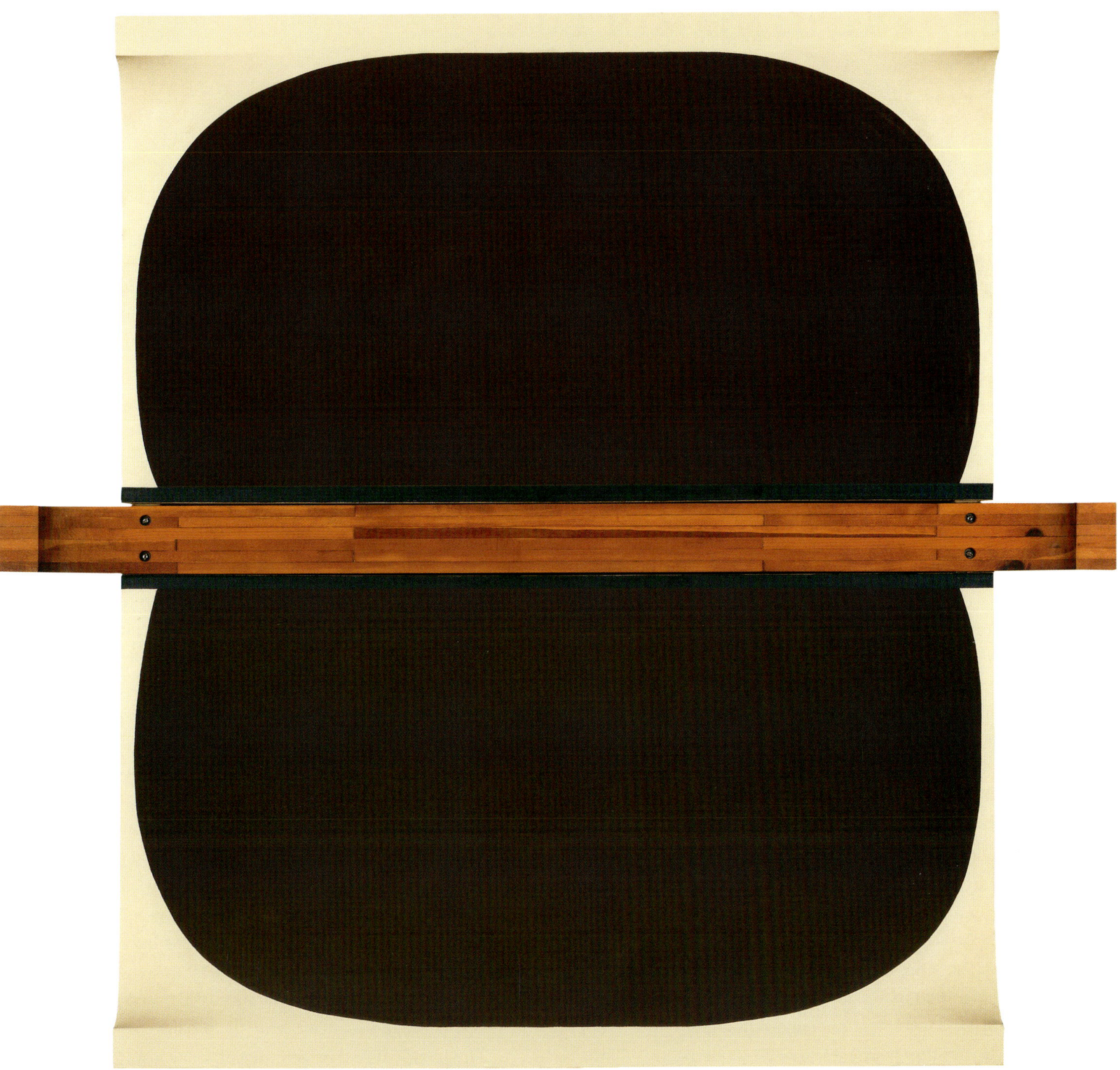

Notes

1. Lawrence Alloway, "Introduction," *The Shaped Canvas* (New York: The Solomon R. Guggenheim Museum, 1964), n.p.
2. Lukin soon abandoned the wooden beams because, he said, "With their grains exposed, they were too rustic—and it would have been a crime to paint them." Quoted in Elizabeth C. Baker, "Solid Anti-Geometry," *Artnews* 65 (March 1966): 75.
3. Quoted in Baker, 75.
4. Michael Fried, "Introduction," *Three American Painters: Kenneth Noland Jules Olitski Frank Stella* (Cambridge, Mass.: Fogg Art Museum, 1965), 40ff.
5. Donald Judd, "Local History," *Arts Yearbook* 7 (1964), reprinted in *Complete Writings 1959–1975* (Halifax, Canada: Nova Scotia College of Art and Design, 1975), 153. See also Donald Judd, quoted in Bruce Glaser, "Questions to Stella and Judd," *Artnews* 65 (September 1966), reprinted in Gregory Battcock, ed., *Minimal Art: A Critical Anthology* (Berkeley: University of California Press, 1995), 162.
6. Donald Judd, "Specific Objects," *Arts Yearbook* 8 (1965), reprinted in *Complete Writings 1959–1975*, 181.
7. Quoted in Baker, 75.
8. Quoted in Baker, 74.

106.

Untitled II, 1961

Oil on canvas and wood construction
73 × 76 in. (184.2 × 193.1 cm)
Gift of Mari and James A. Michener
1991.258

Provenance: Purchased by James Michener from Martha Jackson Gallery, New York, 1962; long-term loan to The University of Texas Austin, 1968–1991

George Benjamin Luks

b. Williamsport, Pennsylvania, 1867–New York, 1933

w. Philadelphia, 1883–1885; Europe, 1880s–1890s; Philadelphia, 1894–1895; New York (trips to Nova Scotia, Pennsylvania, and the Berkshires), 1896–1933

George Luks, a brash and rebellious personality, was part of a revolution in American art at the beginning of the twentieth century that advanced a new approach to realism. Independent in his artistic outlook, he first aligned himself with four other Philadelphia artists, Robert Henri, William Glackens, John Sloan, and Everett Shinn; after moving to New York, they joined with Maurice Prendergast, Arthur B. Davies, and Ernest Lawson to form a group known as The Eight. Luks is best known for his association with this group, but he had a varied and productive career that extended far beyond it as well.

Luks was born in Williamsport, Pennsylvania, and began studying art at the Pennsylvania Academy of the Fine Arts in 1884, but he remained for only a short time. He traveled to Europe in 1889 and enrolled at the Düsseldorf Academy of Fine Arts. Soon thereafter, Luks left for Paris and London to study the Old Masters, and on this and subsequent European sojourns, he was captivated by the work of August Renoir, Rembrandt van Rijn, Diego Velázquez, Francisco Goya, and, most importantly, Frans Hals. In 1894 Luks settled in Philadelphia, where he shared an apartment with his colleague Shinn and began working as an illustrator at the Philadelphia Press. The two artists soon became acquainted with Glackens, Sloan, and Henri. Luks worked at several Philadelphia journals and, in 1895, traveled on assignment as a war correspondent to Cuba. In 1896 he moved to New York, where he began contributing illustrations to the *New York World* and working as a cartoonist. By 1902 he had fully committed himself to painting and had gained representation at the prestigious Macbeth Galleries in New York.

Luks's rough subject matter and unrefined technical approach, especially evident in his early style, did not garner him popularity. When the National Academy of Design 1907 annual exhibition jury rejected his work, Luks, along with other young progressive painters, found a champion in an outraged Henri, one of the exhibition's jury members. The following year, Henri organized an exhibition of The Eight at the Macbeth Galleries to protest the rigid criteria of the Academy's annual shows.

Luks's relocation from downtown to upper Manhattan in 1913 coincided with his increasing interest in landscape scenes and the watercolor medium. Dynamic and temperamental, Luks was an exuberant character prone to erratic behavior. Nevertheless, colleagues highly respected him for his mastery as a painter, and the mainstream art world gave him greater acceptance and recognition over the course of the decade, during which he won a number of major awards. He also became an art instructor, first at the Art Students League, where he began teaching in 1920, and subsequently at his own art school.

Elsie (1930, plate 107) is one of a group of sophisticated female portraits produced during the 1920s and 1930s that represents a pointed departure from Luks's earlier and better-known gritty, urban genre subjects, such as *The Spielers* (1905), *The Wrestlers* (1905), or *Woman with Macaws* (1907). Painted toward the end of his career, *Elsie* depicts an intense young female model, Elsie Dore, whose identity we know only from the provenance of the portrait. Luks had a particular faculty for capturing the essential character of a sitter, an achievement he refined in his early work as a reporter-illustrator. *Elsie* is an exceptional characterization, exhibiting many of the signature traits of Luks's late style, as the influence of the European Old Masters receded and his own individual approach emerged. Conceived and executed rapidly with animated strokes that define areas of light and shadow, the overall composition exhibits a fluid technique wherein the artist streamlined details in favor of a broad painterly interpretation. The portrait has a certain formality that is unusual for Luks, though the circumstances that inspired the portrait are not known. The sitter appears reticent in her expression with a slightly downturned chin that causes her to look up shyly, but she may just have been uncomfortable as a model. Luks rarely included additional elements in his portraits. In the Blanton's painting, however, he added two vessels for visual interest—a goblet on the table to Dore's right and a copperware pitcher that she holds in her hands.

One curator characterized Luks's artistic development during this late period as that of "a strong personality working its way through the difficulties of an exacting medium to the expression of a depth of sympathy with the subject rare among artists of any time."[1] Luks's ability to capture all types of subjects coalesced in his later years, as can be seen in the portrait of Dore, whose physical presence seems to resonate from the canvas. As James Huneker, the noted critic and supporter of Luks, wrote, his portraits can "leap from the bare canvas into being. . . . The most admirable qualities of Luks [are] humor, technical audacity, solid modeling, vital color, sweet sentiment, and a searching humanity . . . all combined."[2] Huneker could indeed be describing the portrait of Dore.

Valerie Ann Leeds

Notes

1. Elisabeth Luther Cary, *George Luks* (New York: Whitney Museum of American Art, 1931), 9. See this text for more biographical information on the artist.
2. James Huneker, "New Portraits by Luks," *New York Sun* (February 23, 1921): magazine section, 9.

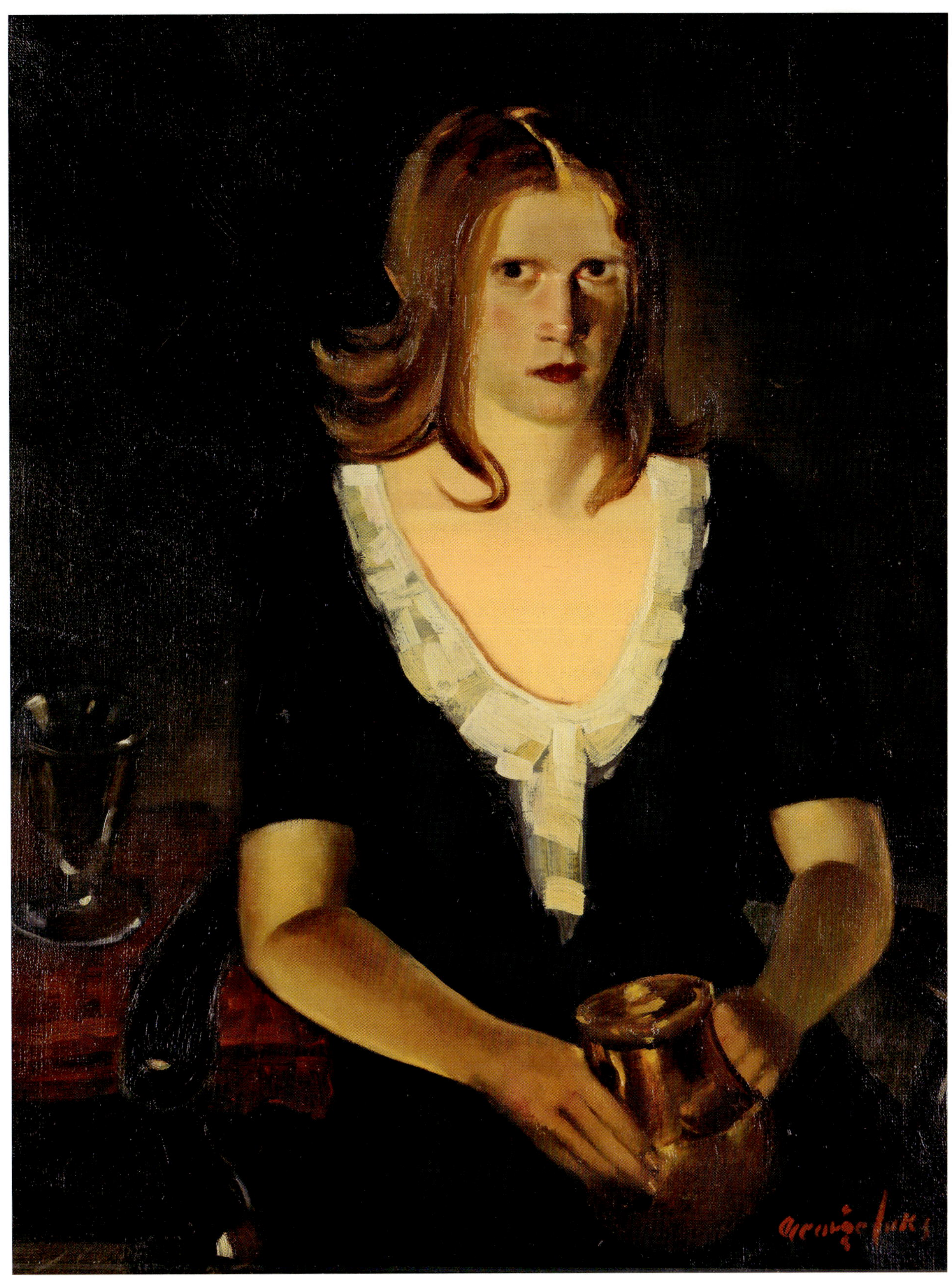

107.

Elsie, 1930

Oil on canvas
40 × 30 in. (102.3 × 77 cm)
Gift of Mari and James A. Michener
1991.259

Provenance: Elsie Dore; Vose Gallery, Boston; Milch Galleries, New York; Kraushaar Galleries, New York; purchased by James Michener from Kraushaar Galleries through Midtown Galleries, New York, 1961; long-term loan to The University of Texas at Austin, 1968–1991
Signed lower right "George Luks"

Stanton Macdonald-Wright

Charlottesville, Virginia, 1890–Pacific Palisades, California, 1973

w. Los Angeles, 1906–1908; Paris, 1909–1913; New York–Europe, 1913–1915; New York, 1915–1918; Los Angeles (frequent trips to Japan), 1918–1973

Born in Charlottesville, Virginia, and raised in California, Stanton Macdonald-Wright commenced his artistic education in 1906 at the Art Students League in Los Angeles with Warren T. Hedges, a former colleague of Robert Henri from the New York Art Students League.[1] In 1909 Macdonald-Wright traveled to Paris and studied at the Sorbonne, the École des Beaux-Arts, and the Académies Colarossi and Julian. While in Paris, he encountered the work of Joseph Mallord William Turner, Paul Cézanne, Auguste Renoir, Pablo Picasso, and Henri Matisse, each of whom provided him with models for his later explorations of light, color, form, and space.

Macdonald-Wright met fellow artist Morgan Russell in 1911 in Paris, and shortly thereafter they began to formulate a system of painting based on color harmonies, which they termed Synchromism (meaning "with color").[2] Other artists in Paris, such as Robert and Sonia Delaunay, concurrently and independently were exploring similar principles of abstraction. Both Synchromism and the Delaunay's Orphism were rooted in color theories popularized by late nineteenth-century Neo-Impressionist painters Georges Seurat and Paul Signac. Synchromism also appears to have been inspired by theorist Hardesty Maratta, who had previously originated an approach to color using premixed paints and a set palette with color harmonies closely aligned to ideas in Western music.

Macdonald-Wright and Russell exhibited together as "Synchromists" in Munich and Paris in 1913 and in New York the following year. While they only showed jointly under the rubric of Synchromism for a brief period, both men continued to investigate for many years the color principles they first laid out in the early 1910s. Russell completed his last Synchromist painting in 1930, while Macdonald-Wright continued to work in this vein for the rest of his career.

Macdonald-Wright produced his most successful work after 1914, when he temporarily discarded the human figure and turned to completely abstract paintings. He revisited representational subject matter, however, only two years later, in 1916. That same year, the Forum Exhibition of Modern American Painters at the Anderson Galleries in New York exhibited his work, along with that of Russell, John Marin, and others. The following year, Alfred Stieglitz gave Macdonald-Wright his first solo show at his New York gallery, 291. By 1918, the date of *Synchromy in Purple Minor* (plate 108), Macdonald-Wright had successfully combined Cubist fragmentation and color theory, resulting in some of his strongest paintings, many of which were exhibited at 291 and the Daniel Gallery, another New York gallery noted for showing contemporary American art.

Drawing on the lessons of Cubism, Macdonald-Wright and Russell created a system of spatial and formal construction based on color sequences. Synchromism differed from both Cubism and Orphism, however, in its emphasis on representing space and volume with color alone. The use of color as the means of rendering sculptural form is particularly evident in *Synchromy in Purple Minor,* where intense shades of blue, fuchsia, green, and orange convey a sense of three-dimensionality in the female figure. The combination of blue purple and yellow orange intensifies the illusion of depth, insofar as the cool colors appear to recede and the warm colors appear to advance. *Synchromy in Purple Minor* is an exceptional example of Macdonald-Wright's use of color to convey luminosity as well. Because the eye perceives gradations of color as radiant nuances of light, the painting seems to glow from within.

As an important element of Synchromism, Macdonald-Wright and Russell also developed specifically delineated color sequences or harmonies based on their correspondence to musical scales.[3] In this way, the color wheel or spectrum could be employed as a kind of melody. Indeed, the title of *Synchromy in Purple Minor* suggests a synesthetic relationship between sound and color, referencing Macdonald-Wright's lifelong interest in music.

Macdonald-Wright, more so than Russell, remained committed to the figure as a central element in his work, often referencing sculptural sources such as Michelangelo's *Pietà* (c. 1498), as is evident in *Synchromy in Purple Minor.* Although it initially appears to be composed of planar elements, the figure in this painting assumes a curvilinear form with flowing hair and a serpentine outline common in Michelangelo's sculptures.

In 1918 Macdonald-Wright left New York for Los Angeles, where he resided until his death in 1973. During this period, he continued his experiments with color and served as director of the Southern California WPA Federal Art Project and as an adviser for the Western region of the Federal Art Project. In the 1930s he developed an interest in Eastern art and philosophy, and traveled to Japan for the first time in 1937. During the last decades of his life, Macdonald-Wright spent several months each year in a Zen monastery in Kyoto. He taught art history and Asian philosophy at the University of California, Los Angeles, beginning in 1942.

By the time Macdonald-Wright returned to California in 1918, awareness of Synchromism had dissipated. His contribution to American modernism remained largely obscured until 1967, when an exhibition at the Smithsonian Institution, Washington, D.C., revived interest in and garnered recognition for the pseudoscientific approach originated by Macdonald-Wright and Russell. A 2001 retrospective of MacDonald-Wright's work at the North Carolina Museum of Art cemented his place in the history of twentieth-century American art. As a result, works such as *Synchromy in Purple Minor* are now considered masterpieces of interwar American modernism.

Kathleen V. Jameson

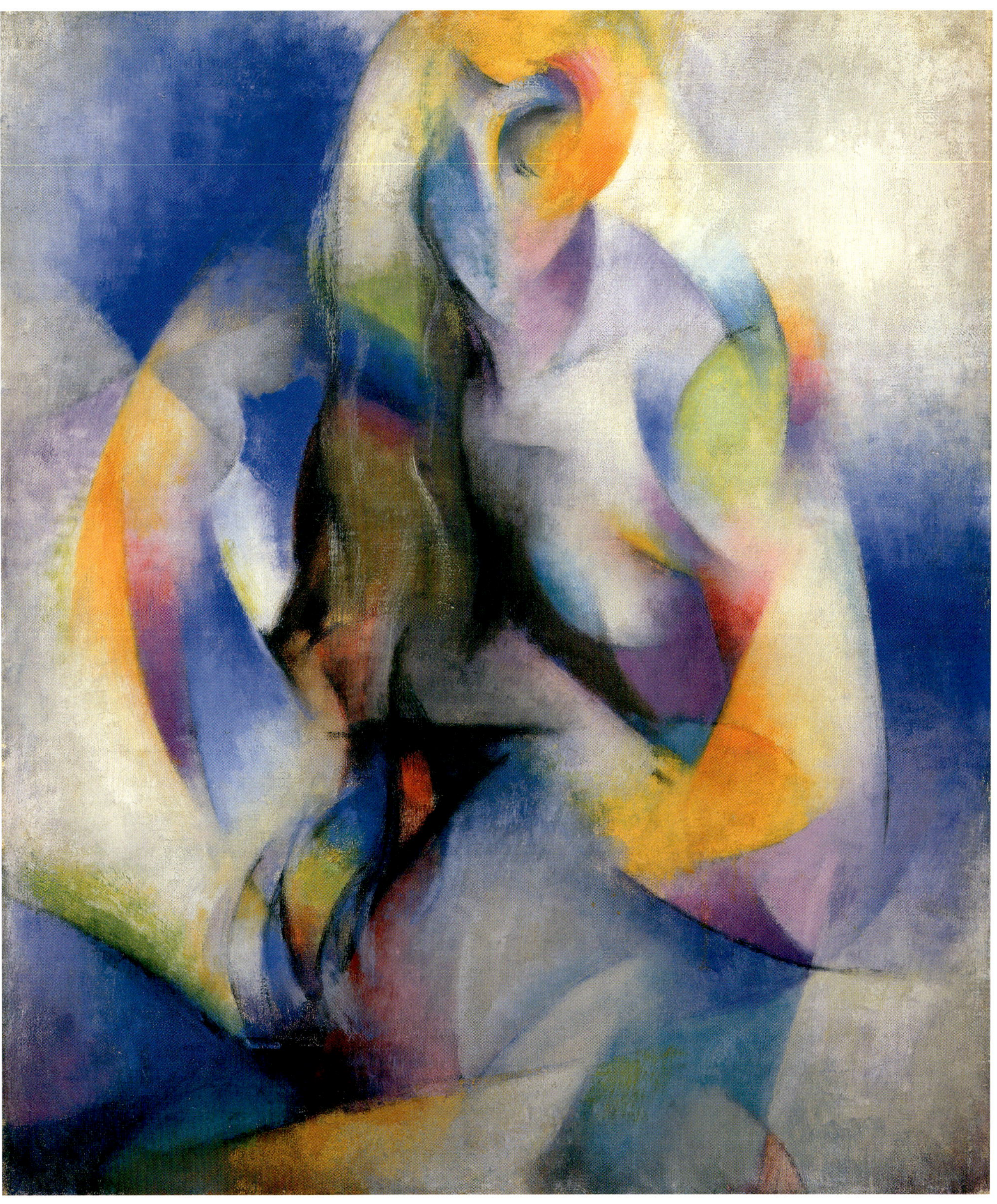

Notes

1. For further information on Stanton Macdonald-Wright, see *Stanton Macdonald-Wright: A Retrospective Exhibition, 1911–1970* (Los Angeles: The UCLA Art Galleries/The Grunwald Graphic Arts Foundation, 1970); Gail Levin, *Synchromism and American Color Abstraction, 1910–1925* (New York: George Braziller in association with the Whitney Museum of American Art, 1978); and Will South, *Color, Myth, and Music: Stanton Macdonald-Wright and Synchromism* (Raleigh, N.C.: North Carolina Museum of Art, 2001).
2. The art critic Willard Huntington Wright, Macdonald-Wright's brother, outlined the principles of Synchromism in two books: *Modern Painting: Its Tendency and Meaning* (New York: John Lane, 1915) and *The Future of Painting* (New York: Huebsch, 1923).
3. Macdonald-Wright described this system in depth in his *Treatise on Color* (Los Angeles: privately printed, 1924).

108.

Synchromy in Purple Minor, 1918

Oil on canvas
24 × 20$\frac{1}{16}$ in. (61 × 51 cm)
Michener Acquisitions Fund
P1970.16.1

Provenance: Daniel Gallery, New York; Hugh Henry Breckenridge, Washington, Pennsylvania, 1918; William Temple, Philadelphia, Pennsylvania, 1937; M. Knoedler & Company, New York, 1968; purchased from M. Knoedler & Company, 1970
Inscribed verso, upper center "Synchromy in Purple Minor/ S. Macdonald-Wright 1918"

Conrad Marca-Relli

Boston, 1913–Parma, Italy, 2000

w. New York (trips to Rome, 1948 and 1951, and Mexico, 1952), 1930–1953; Easthampton, New York–Sarasota, Florida–Ibiza, Spain (trip to Rome, 1957), 1953–1988; New Jersey, 1988–1997; Parma, Italy, 1997–2000

Conrad Marca-Relli studied at The Cooper Union in New York City (1930), was employed by the Works Progress Administration/ Federal Art Project (1935–1938), and exhibited regularly during the 1950s with the Abstract Expressionists in New York. Several of the latter—including Willem de Kooning, Jackson Pollock, and Franz Kline—were his friends (Pollock was his neighbor at Springs, near Easthampton, Long Island, from 1953 until the latter's death in 1956). A large and important work, *Conversion* (1958, plate 109) exemplifies an especially dynamic period of formal experimentation during the late 1950s, when Marca-Relli's visual language gravitated away from figuration toward greater abstraction.

Despite his connections to the American avant-garde, Marca-Relli's career unfolded in a wider, more international context than that of the Abstract Expressionists. Unlike most artists of the New York School, Marca-Relli traveled overseas many times, mostly to Europe. The son of an international correspondent, he spent his childhood traveling between Boston and Italy until the age of thirteen, when his family settled in New York. After serving in World War II, Marca-Relli oscillated back and forth between New York and Europe, living occasionally in Rome, where he drew inspiration from its ancient and Renaissance traditions as well as its modern and contemporary culture. Although Marca-Relli's work is not widely represented in European collections, it has been included in numerous exhibitions abroad. In 1996 the artist moved to Parma, Italy, where he died in 2000.

Evidence of an international perspective emerges in many aspects of Marca-Relli's work. His postwar Roman cityscapes of 1948–1949, for example, with their haunting voids and uncanny architecture, bring to mind the metaphysical spaces of Giorgio de Chirico and the surrealist topographies of Yves Tanguy.[1] They also parallel postwar Italian cinematic perceptions of urban space and social anxiety, as seen in such neorealist films as Roberto Rossellini's *Open City* (1945) and Vittorio De Sica's *The Bicycle Thief* (1948). Marca-Relli's figural abstractions of the mid-1950s closely relate to New York School works by Arshile Gorky and de Kooning, especially the latter's Woman series, but they also suggest an awareness of currents in European postwar Expressionism (Tachisme, L'Art Informel, Art Brut, and CoBrA).

Marca-Relli's *Conversion* is not a conventional easel painting but instead consists of variously painted and cut fragments of different fabrics—fine-weight linen, muslin, coarsely woven canvas—assembled and glued onto a plain-weave, medium-weight cotton canvas support. As such, the work powerfully exemplifies Marca-Relli's signature artistic contribution: the rigorous integration (or reconfiguration) of Abstract Expressionism with collage, resulting in paintings that approach three-dimensional *bas relief.* Invented by the Cubists, Pablo Picasso and Georges Braque, around 1912, collage is often considered the paradigmatic modernist medium because its fragmentary effects helped inaugurate a critical exploration of artistic form and illusion that contributed greatly to the unraveling of classical representation. According to the influential American art critic Clement Greenberg, who championed the Abstract Expressionists as heirs to Cubism, "The collage medium has played a pivotal role in twentieth-century painting and sculpture, and it is the most succinct and direct single clue to the aesthetic of genuinely modern art."[2]

During a 1953 trip to Mexico, where Marca-Relli admired the colors and geometric abstractions of adobe architecture, he reportedly ran out of paint and resorted to creating works by cutting, gluing, and assembling pieces of canvas and other fabrics.[3] That felicitous technical experiment offered him a new method for achieving richly varied effects of line, contour, form, texture, and spatial composition, while reinterpreting prevailing notions of gesture in painting. Whereas Pollock used sticks, turkey basters, and other implements to produce his dramatic drip or "action" paintings of 1947–1950, Marca-Relli employed scissors to cut and compose canvas and other fabrics, upon which he dripped and brushed additional colors. As he once observed, "Going beyond the figures of traditional painting through collage has enabled me to reach a 'painting' which is always fresh, a composition which year after year is always visibly active. Collage allows me to achieve purity of action, I can continuously experiment 'in the painting,' a thousand times over."[4]

In a manner not unlike that of Pollock, who spoke of being "in" his paintings, Marca-Relli infused *Conversion* with a dynamic, allover sense of visible action and pictorial-spatial complexity. This he achieved through jarring juxtapositions of painted and cut fabrics, arrayed with an explosion of brushed and dripped colors: vermilion, lavender, maroon, orange, magenta, purple, olive, turquoise, and white. Its composition brings to mind de Kooning's *Excavation* (1950), but the palette and disruptive drama of its collaged elements seem closer to Pollock's *Out of the Web* (1949), in which areas of canvas have been cut and scraped away, leaving lacunae in the visual field that create a similar optical vibration.

Despite the parallels to de Kooning and Pollock, *Conversion* and Marca-Relli's other collage paintings of the 1950s cannot simply be assimilated to Abstract Expressionism, but must instead be viewed in a broader context, especially given the currency of related techniques among European artists of the period. One such artist was Henri Matisse, whose celebrated series of brightly colored cutouts appeared in the late 1940s. Others were Alberto Burri and Lucio Fontana, Italian and Italian Argentine artists respectively who, like Marca-Relli (an Italian American), rigorously interrogated traditional easel painting, in their cases by literally perforating its physical support, burning materials with blow torches, and introducing metals along with other heterogeneous elements.[5] Nor should we underestimate the importance

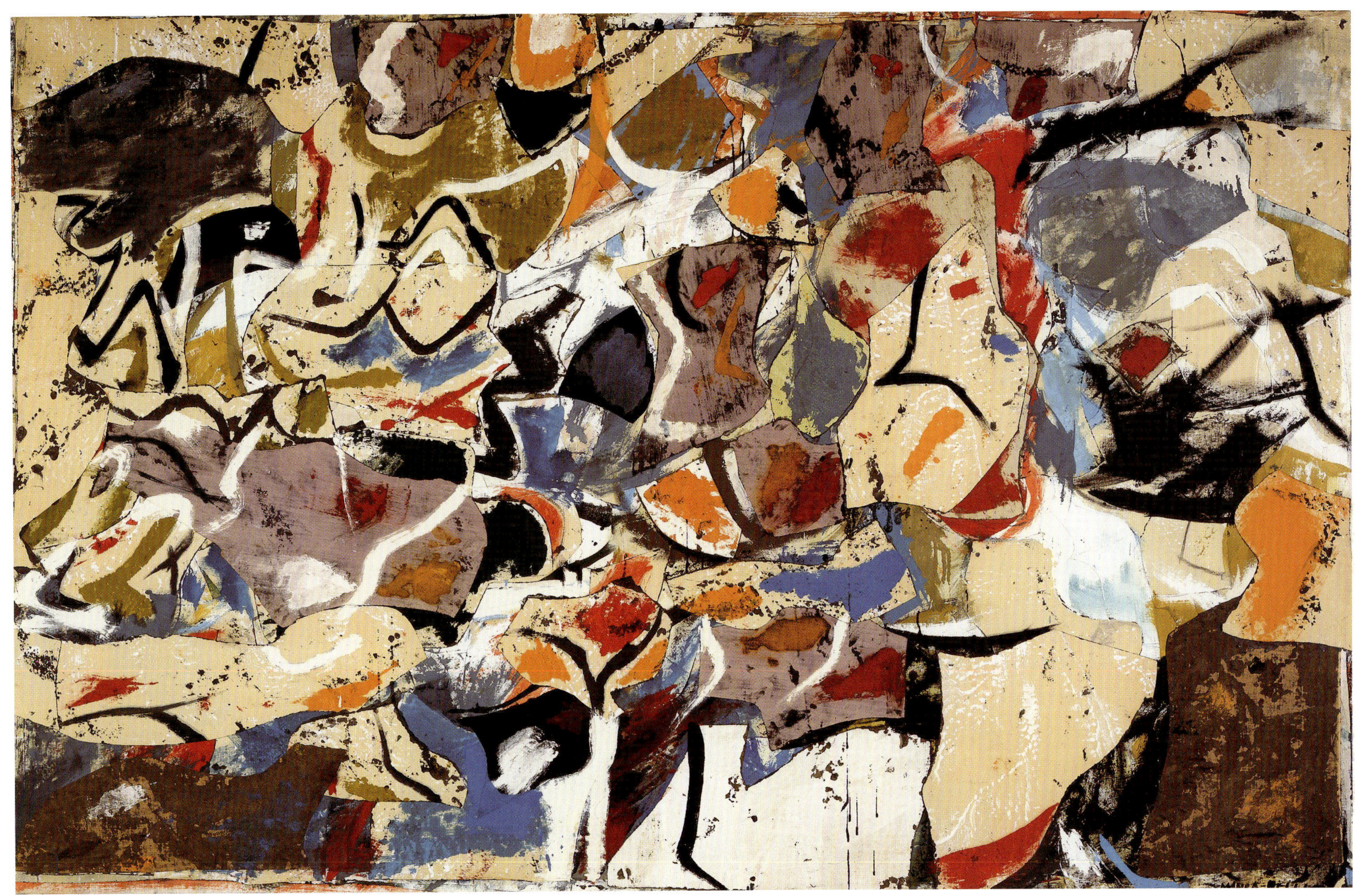

of Marca-Relli's peripatetic existence for understanding the fragmentary effects of collage in *Conversion*. Such effects proceed from a productive sense of displacement residing at the core of his Euroamerican artistic selfhood.[6] In a statement recalling his many travels and asserting a desire to avoid "nationality" in his art, Marca-Relli observed, "I freed myself as a person, and also in my art which I wanted to keep as open as possible so as to avoid becoming an absolutist."[7]

Alan C. Braddock

109.

The Conversion, 1958

Oil and collage on canvas
57 7/8 × 87 in. (147 × 221 cm)
Gift of Mari and James A. Michener
G1968.94

Provenance: Purchased by James Michener from Mr. and Mrs. Samuel Kootz, 1962
Signed lower right "Marca-Relli"

Notes

1. H. H. Arnason, *Marca-Relli* (New York: Harry N. Abrams, Inc., 1963), 2.
2. Clement Greenberg, "Review of the Exhibition *Collage*," in John O'Brian, ed., *Clement Greenberg: The Collected Essays and Criticism*, vol. 2 (Chicago: University of Chicago Press, 1986), 259–60.
3. Arnason, *Marca-Relli*, 5–6. Arnason suggests that collage was "an idea towards which his paintings had been unconsciously tending for several years."
4. Quoted in Luca Massimo Barbero, ed., *Conrad Marca-Relli* (Milan: Electa, 1998), 19.
5. On Burri and Fontana, see Yve-Alain Bois and Rosalind Krauss, *Formless: A User's Guide* (New York: Zone Books, 1997).
6. The multipart modular sculptures of Isamu Noguchi, a Japanese American (Nisei) artist who traveled extensively abroad in the same years, derives from a similar sense of productive displacement. Amy Lyford, "Noguchi, Sculptural Abstraction, and the Politics of Japanese Internment," *Art Bulletin* 85 (March 2003): 137–51.
7. Quoted in Barbero, ed., *Conrad Marca-Relli*, 17.

Fabian Marcaccio

b. Rosario de Santa Fe, Argentina, 1963
w. New York, 1986–present

Fabian Marcaccio admits that his paintings are so layered and mutable that they read "almost like a kaleidoscope."[1] Mimicking the dizzying complexities of contemporary life, he makes extraordinarily dense and dynamic works of art as analogues to the flux, speed, cacophony, and intensity of daily experience. Marcaccio's over-the-top hybrids combine elements of painting, printmaking and digitizing techniques, and Internet-derived photographs, along with aspects of theoretical architecture and allusions to science fiction, cyber-politics, and social theory. These sophisticated but nevertheless jarring expressions defy the usual logics of how we look at paintings and challenge every assumption about what we expect to find within seemingly static works of art.

Trained in philosophy in his native Argentina, Marcaccio moved to New York after college to pursue a painting career with the aid of an Exxon Foundation fellowship. He supported himself at first as an artist's assistant, working for fellow Argentineans Liliana Porter and Osvaldo Romberg,[2] and also studied with esteemed artist and master printer Bob Blackburn at the Printmaking Workshop. Those experiences helped fuel the young artist's voracious appetite for technical innovation and conceptual breadth. His multidisciplinary and collaborative approach to painting, which has grown ever more exuberant over the past twenty years,[3] stems in part from his polymathic enthusiasm for new theories and possibilities. But the influence of Marcaccio's upbringing in South America is also key to understanding the scope of his artistic ambitions, for there, artists are expected to serve not only as aesthetic forecasters but also as public intellectuals, political activists, and philosophers engaged with all the issues of the day.

Based in New York but operating internationally, Marcaccio has earned an impressive exhibition record since the early 1990s for ambitious works that push painting to perform in ways contrary to painterly convention. Casting painting in relationship to "linguistic, poetic, political, philosophical, formal, and spatial experiences,"[4] Marcaccio elevates its function from that of a flat, illusionistic art form to a platform for the discussion of ideas and experiences, and stakes a claim for the relevance—indeed, the urgency—of painting as a necessary discourse of modern life. Noting this redoubtable commitment, one critic said that an exhibition of Marcaccio's work is like "a cyclone of ideas on subjects ranging from the progress of modernist painting to the nexus of high finance and international terrorism."[5]

Marcaccio's earliest paintings, like *Subject and-and-and-object* (1991), explore abstraction as a remnant of utopian belief systems now stripped of their absolute meaning and function.[6] Picturing simulated brushstrokes as somewhat naïve characters having grand adventures, he bids his Candide-like marks to perform subversive acts—slipping out of their grids, off their supports, and across the wall, escaping, as it were, from their predetermined destinies as ordered gestures. And if the strokes' restless pseudovelocity seems the starring act, the support soon takes its turn in the limelight. Figure/ground—and object/subject—relationships turn topsy-turvy as the very weave of the canvas becomes active, threads unraveling, neat horizontal and vertical alignments melting into chaos.

By the mid-1990s, pushing the boundaries of scale, dimension, and the framing edge with heir-to-Cubist collage techniques that conjoin a plethora of unexpected materials, Marcaccio devised wildly theatrical presentations that transform corners, traverse rooms, or burst out of buildings. At the same time, he developed an extensive index of signs and symbols, a veritable alphabet of recurring forms recalling commercial logos, swastikas, hammers and sickles, and other national insignias and emblems of religious faith and dogma. Interrupting the dance of warp, weft, and facture with strategically placed moments from this forest of signs, he layered even more visual information onto flexible supports in the form of photographic-transfer fragments—pictures of mass gatherings, political demonstrations, and other communal public events, as well as snippets of found pornographic imagery. By 1997 his surfaces were saturated, teeming with incident that careens wildly from doodle to documentation. Macro to micro and back again, Marcaccio's discrete clusters of imagery, like little theaters of activity, spread viruslike across the panoramic expanse of his works.

More evocative of simultaneity than any Futurist painting ever could have hoped to be, Marcaccio's dense networks of narrative break new artistic ground. Rauschenbergian in their capacity to incorporate multiple materials and techniques, akin to Jessica Stockholder in their antic, improvisational energy, but willfully eschewing the grace of both, these works embody a wild embrace of dystopian fantasy. Marcaccio's "paintants," or mutant paintings, as he calls them, operate as both a report on the status quo and a projection of the future. They merge the conceptual platforms of advertising, propaganda, and art even as their physical forms morph from painting to sculpture to architecture and environment.

In the Blanton's *Total Paintant* (plate 110), commissioned for the museum's 1999 painting exhibition, *Negotiating Small Truths,* constellations of enhanced and invented images suggest a vibrant, contaminated universe whose complex systems interact in unpredictable ways. Marcaccio's every artistic urge is to complicate; the work's excesses of form and information are impossible to clarify or summarize. *Total Paintant* behaves as if it were a time-based animation, forcibly pulsing out from the wall at irregular intervals, disparate vignettes screaming for attention. Marcaccio once said that he is not creating "action painting, but action viewing,"[7] and indeed, the work coerces the viewer, who struggles to read disjunctive parts in relation to one another—moving in front of it, from side to side, from near and far, every attempt at linear cohesion foiled. Time, space, distinctions between public and private, between individual and collective experience, all merge or perhaps tumble together in a heady mix of two-, three-, and four-dimensional inquiry.

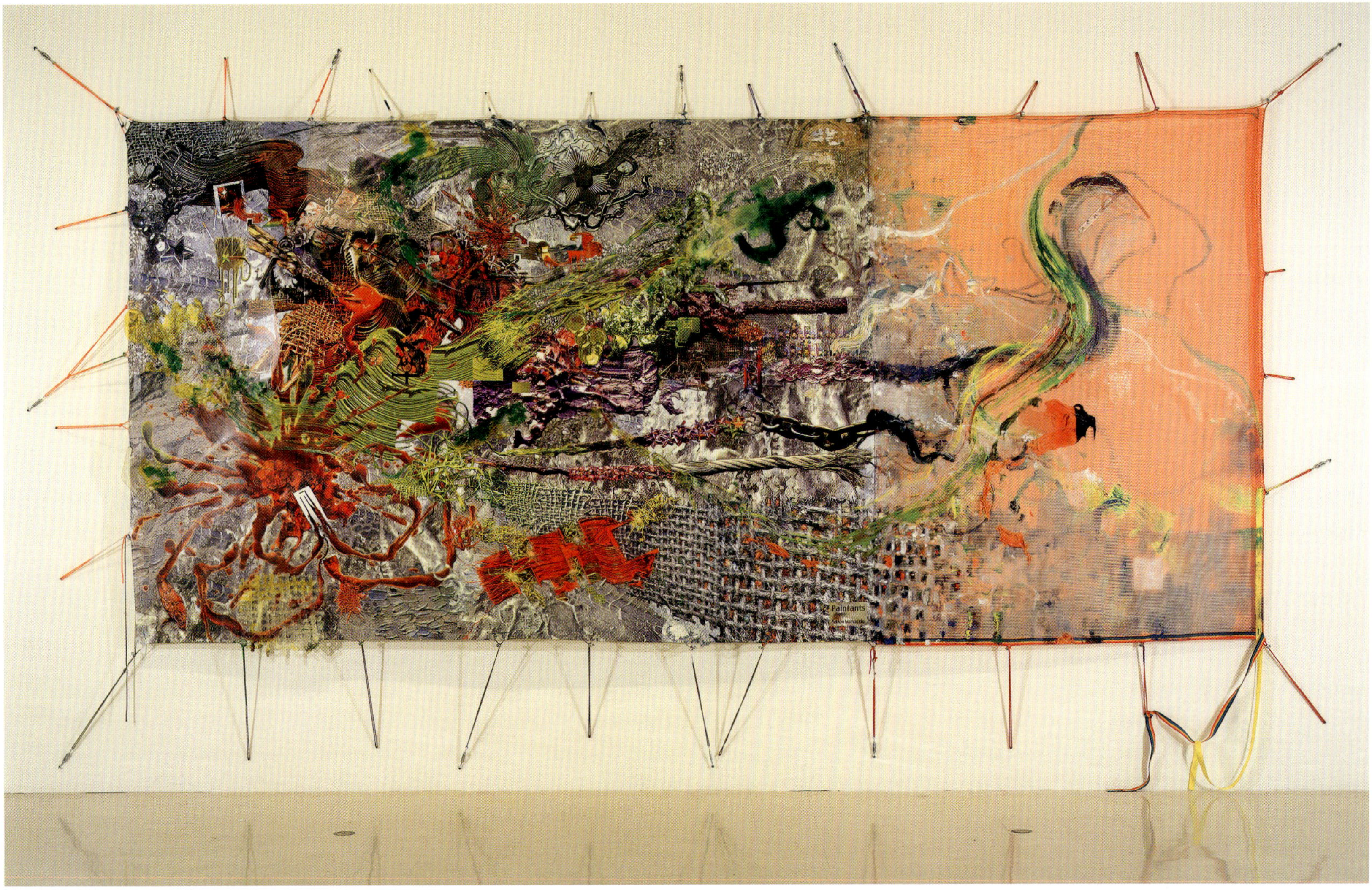

Marcaccio's works overturn the traditional conventions of Modernist painting by representing dematerialized imagery on exaggeratedly materialistic structural supports. Championing the boldness of painting as a choice today, embracing its artifice and contradictions as valid conditions for experimentation, his "paintants" offer passionate proposals about the slippery nature of multiple and conflicting truths.

Annette DiMeo Carlozzi

Notes

1. Fabian Marcaccio, interview with the author, artist's studio, New York, May 6, 1999.
2. For an excellent analysis of Marcaccio's work in relation to that of two more senior Argentinean artists, see Ines Katzenstein, "Noe, Porter, Marcaccio: In Praise of Complexity," in Gabriel Perez-Barreiro, ed., *Blanton Museum of Art: Latin American Collection* (Austin: Blanton Museum of Art, The University of Texas at Austin, 2006), 59–67.
3. Marcaccio has collaborated with artists in other disciplines on numerous occasions, including projects with architects Greg Lynn at the Wexner Center, Columbus, Ohio, and Galia Salomonoff at Artists Space, New York, and with musician Claudio Baroni at the Metronome in Barcelona and the National Gallery of Ontario.
4. Marcaccio, interview with the author.
5. Nancy Princenthal, "Fabian Marcaccio: Paintant's Progress," *Art in America* 91 (January 2003): 63.
6. For extravagantly illustrated surveys of Marcaccio's works, see *Fabian Marcaccio: With-ject Spain* (Madrid: Galeria Salvador Diaz, 1998) and *Fabian Marcaccio: Paintant Stories* (Stuttgart, Germany: Wurttembergischer Kunstverein, 2000).
7. Marcaccio, interview with the author.

110.

Total Paintant, 1999

GO inks on Tyvek, oil and acrylic paint, silicone, poli-optics on aluminum structure
100 × 240 in. (254 × 609.6 cm)
Michener Acquisitions Fund
1999.89

Provenance: Commissioned by the museum and purchased from Gorney, Bravin + Lee, New York, 1999

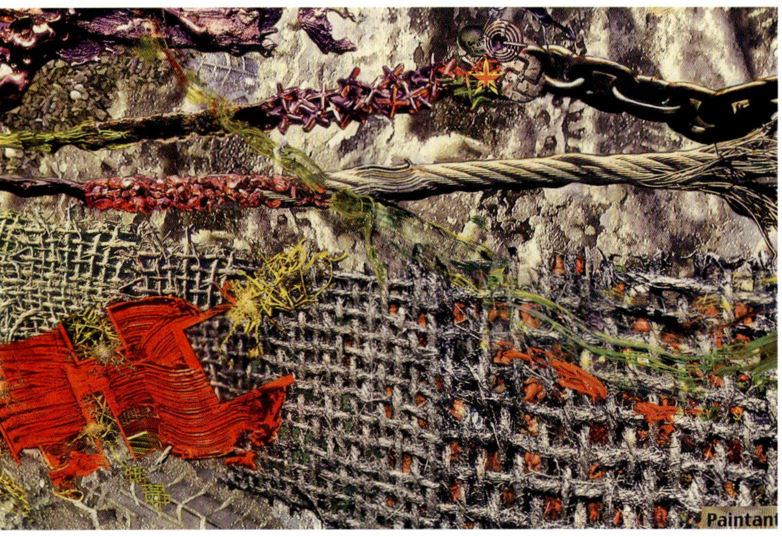

Brice Marden

b. Briarcliff Manor, New York, 1938

w. New Haven, Connecticut, 1961–1963; Paris, 1963; New York (frequent trips to Greece and Asia), 1963–present

In 1964 Brice Marden was working as a guard at the Jewish Museum when it mounted a retrospective of work by Jasper Johns. The young artist was impressed by the harmony of surface and subject in Johns's paintings of flags and targets and equally intrigued by his encaustic medium, a blend of pigment with heated beeswax. Marden, who had completed his MFA at Yale the year before, was growing frustrated with the reflective properties of oil paint. Johns's technique provided an antidote, and at the suggestion of a friend, Marden began adding beeswax to his oils. The mixture, prepared on a hot plate in his studio, lent a palpable opacity to the paintings he went on to produce.

The technical execution of *Fave* (1968–1969, plate 111), which was part of the artist's mid-career retrospective at the Guggenheim Museum in 1975, emphasizes the materiality of its waxy oil. Marden layered paint onto the canvas with a knife and spatula, laboriously scraping away and reapplying. "The form itself is static, but there's a dynamic going [on] within it," he commented about some of his later works, and this description applies equally well to *Fave*.[1] Beeswax imbues the surface with a matte patina, but subtle traces of Marden's process slowly reveal themselves—evidence of an underlayer here, a particularly tactile stroke there. Although the painting is insistently nonillusionistic, Marden named as an influence on his palette two doyens of the still-life and the portrait, Francisco Goya and Francisco de Zubarán. Zurbarán's dramatic light especially moved Marden, and *Fave*'s complementary panels, one a muted gray and the other a creamy beige, emanate a luminous glow reminiscent of the Spanish Baroque master.

Marden was born in Briarcliff Manor, New York, in 1938. He came of age in an American art world still feeling the hegemonic effects of Abstract Expressionist painting. The structural constraints and reductivist austerities of the new Minimalism seemed to harness the frenetic, vivid tonalities of postwar painting. Marden recalls heated conversations—with, among others, Carl Andre, Patti Smith, and Bob Dylan—at New York bars such as Max's Kansas City in the 1960s. The topics of the day were heady ones: was painting an object or an image, was the medium itself moribund, was illusionism ever permissible? Like many Minimalists, Marden worked with predetermined formal constraints, or what he termed "Spartan limitations."[2] As a student at Yale, he divided his paintings into grids, and he began painting diptychs in 1965 and triptychs in 1968. In his monochromatic canvases of the early 1960s, Marden often marked a line near the bottom edge of the support below which he would not paint (drops fell below the line, a residue of the painting's facture). Like works by Frank Stella and Donald Judd, *Fave* exhibits a near-perfect union of image with plane, surface with support.

Yet Marden's methodical structures were in the service of an evocative subjectivity, one inherited from Abstract Expressionism and often absent in highly self-referential Minimalist works. "Within these strict confines, confines which I have painted myself into and intend to explore with no regrets, I try to give the viewer something to which he will react subjectively," he wrote in his MFA thesis. He added, "I believe these are highly emotional paintings not to be admired for any technical or intellectual reason but to be felt."[3] Marden imparted a subjective dimension to works that appear resolutely objective by occasionally basing their dimensions on human measurements (including those of friends and his wife), and, unlike many Minimalists—chief among them Judd and Robert Morris—he remained committed to the medium of painting.

The mid-1980s, a propitious moment for figurative painting, signaled a change of direction for the artist. While working on a commission of stained glass windows for a chapel in Basel, Switzerland, between 1978 and 1985, Marden was forced to confront (in the windows' lead frames) the form of the diagonal. He moved away from bi- and tripartite pictorial organizations, and, inspired by the calligraphic, gestural marks in Chinese scrolls and landscape paintings (seen on travels in the Far East), he began covering his canvases with lyrical matrices of ribbonlike lines. Although they represented a departure from his earlier work, these looping skeins—sensuous, finely modulated topographies, ever chary of color—manifest the formal constants that are a hallmark not only of *Fave* but of Marden's long career.

Lisa Pasquariello

Notes

1. Brice Marden, "An Interview with Brice Marden," interview by John Yau, in Eva Keller and Regula Malin, eds., *Brice Marden* (Zurich: Daros Collection, 2003), 48.
2. Quoted in Marden, 48.
3. Marden, 59.

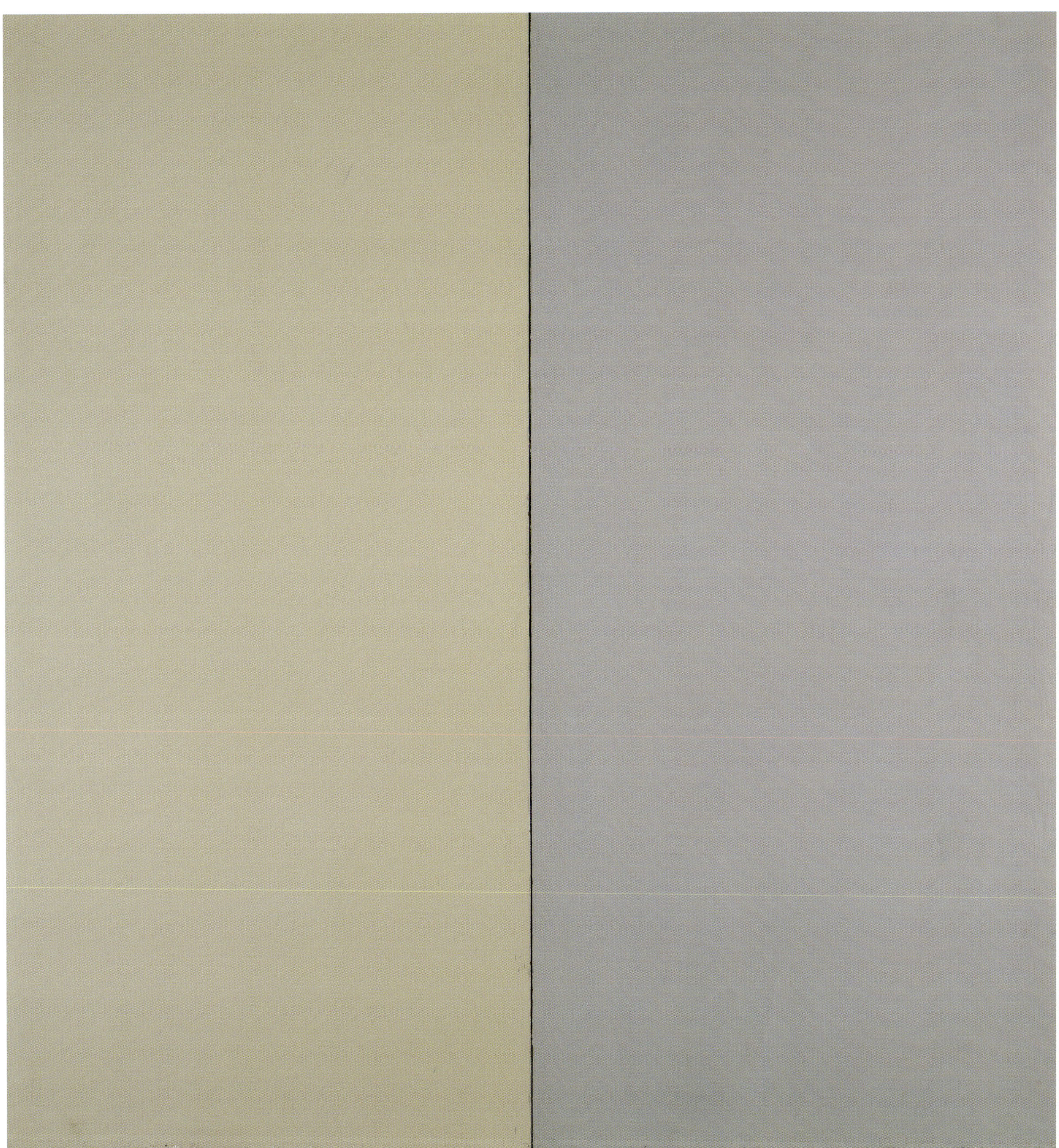

111.

Fave, 1968–1969

Oil and beeswax on canvas
72¼ × 66$^{3}/_{16}$ in. (184 × 168 cm)
Gift of Mari and James A. Michener
1979.30

Provenance: Purchased by James Michener from the artist, 1969
Inscribed verso, upper left "Fave / 72 × 66" / 1968–69 / B. MARDEN"

John Marin

Rutherford, New Jersey, 1870–Cape Split, Maine, 1953

w. Philadelphia, 1899–1901; New York, 1902–1904; Paris, 1905–1910; New York, 1910–1916; Cliffside, New Jersey (summers in Maine, 1914–1953, and frequent trips to the Adirondacks, the Berkshires, Canada, and Taos, New Mexico, 1912–1953), 1916–1953

Maine was a place of great importance to the painter John Marin, and it inspired a significant body of work within his oeuvre. The photographer Paul Strand, a friend of Marin, described the special meaning Maine had for the artist and his particular affinity for depicting it: "This is Maine and nowhere else. We are made to experience something which is our own, as nothing which has grown up in Europe can be our own."[1] Marin first visited Maine in 1914 and spent each summer there until his death in 1953. Although he painted cityscapes and landscapes, his representations of the sea, many of which were inspired by the Maine coast, allowed the artist greater freedom to explore the inherent properties of paint, color, and light using a naturalistic vocabulary.

According to Marin's biographer, a 1947 family fishing trip to Maine in an old lobster boat inspired *Movement: Sea, Ultramarine and Green; Sky, Cerulean and Grey* (1947, plate 113).[2] Marin depicted the scene from an unusual and even exhilarating point of view, placing the viewer in close proximity to the dramatic swells battering the side of the boat. Although the perspective is ambiguous and the space flattened, Marin successfully conveyed the fluid movement of the water and a feeling of the tumultuous energy of the sea. The confrontation between boat and sea perhaps symbolizes the struggle between man and nature and the cycle of life and death.

Born in Rutherford, New Jersey, in 1870, Marin began experimenting with watercolor while working as an architectural draftsman.[3] He trained at the prestigious Pennsylvania Academy of the Fine Arts in Philadelphia from 1899 to 1901, studying with Thomas Anshutz and Hugh Henry Breckenridge. He also studied at the Art Students League from 1902 until 1904, before leaving for Paris in 1905. In Paris he attended the Académie Julian and saw the avant-garde art of the Fauves and Cubists. Marin absorbed ideas from these progressive European modernists, although he denied their impact on his own development.[4] He sought to establish his independence as an artist and was determined to define a new form of American modernism distinct from European traditions. As Strand observed, Marin's "work attests frankly to an unusual recognition on his part that he is rooted in this American continent."[5]

Marin became an important member of the stable of artists assembled by noted photographer and dealer Alfred Stieglitz. He first met other members of the Stieglitz circle, including Edward Steichen and Max Weber, while living in Paris. Along with Steichen, Weber, and Alfred H. Maurer, Marin formed The New Society of American Artists in Paris in 1908. The following year Stieglitz held an exhibition of Marin's and Maurer's work at his New York gallery 291. Marin had his first one-person show at 291 in 1910, while his first retrospective exhibition took place at The Museum of Modern Art in New York in 1936. By 1947, the year he painted *Movement*, Marin was firmly established as a living master.

While principally known as a watercolorist (plate 112), Marin began to experiment with oil paint in the 1930s, culminating in works such as *Movement*, which belongs to the last phase of the artist's career. Critics received Marin's oils with little enthusiasm as compared to his watercolors, which initially established his reputation. One sympathetic critic, Jerome Mellquist, however, sought to defend Marin's use of oil in his seascapes: "When he uses oils for the sea, some strong dark feeling—such as he had so much in the early twenties, but sterner—rushes into them and makes them grey, terrible, almost overhanging. In a peculiar and necessary way Marin's work in this medium has reinforced the man of the earlier watercolors."[6] In *Movement*, the artist left

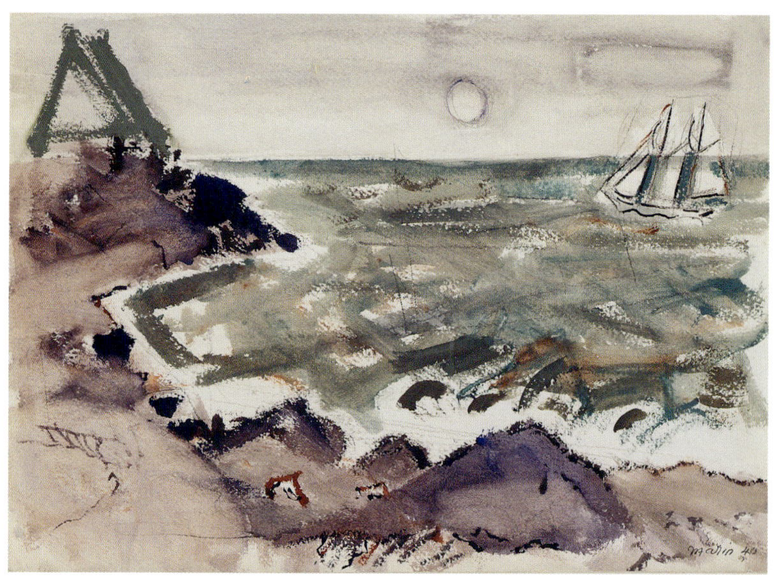

112.

Green Sea, Rocks and Boat, Cape Split, Maine, 1940

Watercolor
15 3/16 × 20 3/8 in. (38.6 × 52.4 cm)
Gift of Mari and James A. Michener
1991.261

Provenance: Purchased by James Michener from Downtown Gallery, New York, 1961; long-term loan to The University of Texas at Austin, 1968–1991
Signed lower right "Marin 40"

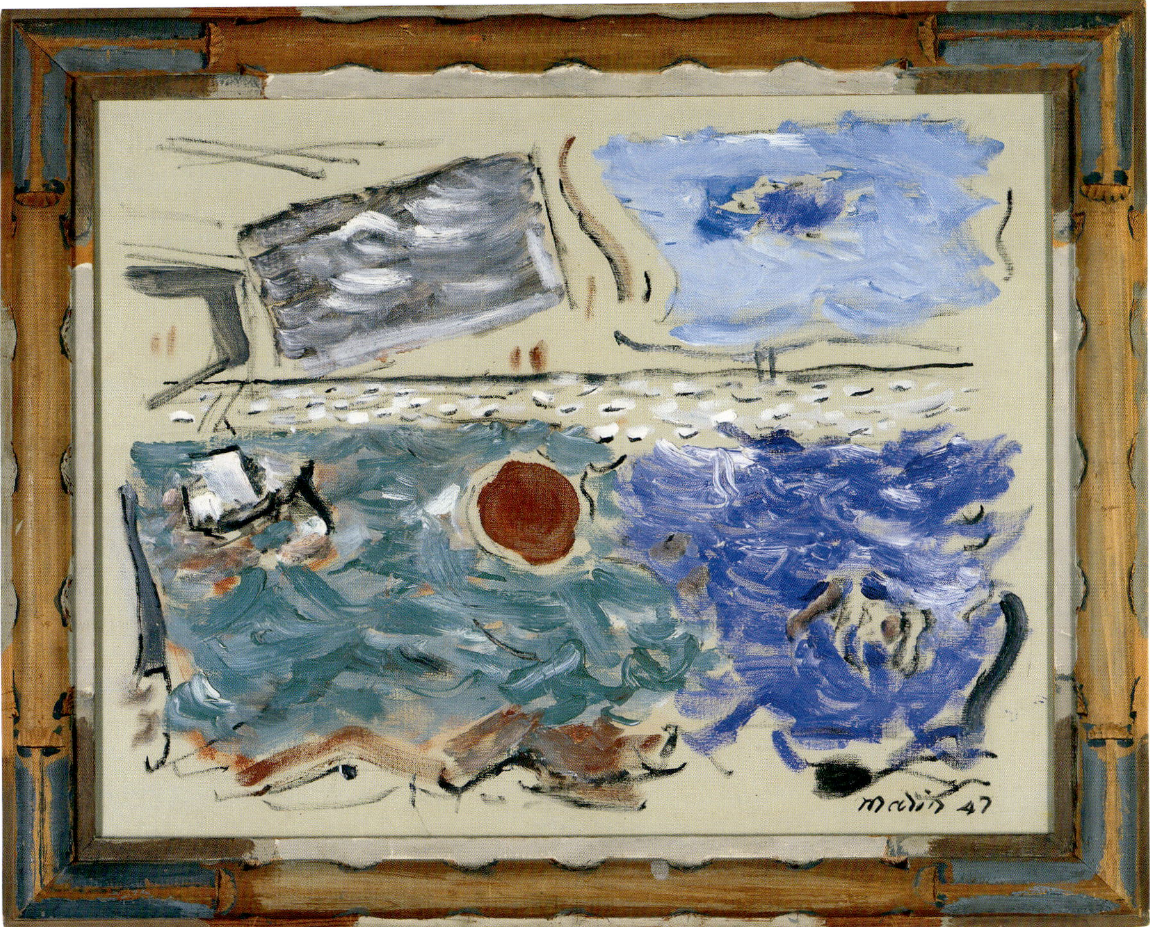

113.
Movement: Sea, Ultramarine and Green; Sky, Cerulean and Grey, 1947

Oil on canvas
21 5/8 × 27 5/8 in. (55 × 70 cm)
Gift of Mari and James A. Michener
1991.262

Provenance: Purchased by James Michener from Downtown Gallery, New York, 1961; long-term loan to The University of Texas at Austin, 1968–1991
Signed lower right "Marin 47"

exposed patches of primed canvas that alternate with areas of pigment of varying thicknesses, thereby exploiting the interplay of negative and positive space and of recognizable and fragmented visual elements. Through these devices, Marin communicates the concept of catching and interpreting a momentary glimpse of landscape and atmosphere. His working method combined plein air painting with studio work. While in the midst of painting, Marin had a habit of turning the canvas upside down to judge its overall compositional balance. As in the case of *Movement*, he also periodically extended his compositions out to the frames themselves, which he sometimes painted and carved so that they functioned as integral elements of the paintings.[7]

In *Movement*, Marin strove to render the effects of light and atmosphere, reflecting his early interest in Impressionism. Yet his depiction of the seascape is not a mere transcription, but rather a personal, expressive interpretation of nature. Like Paul Cézanne, whose work Stieglitz showed at 291 in 1911, Marin transformed the observed scene into an exploration of form and color. While Marin's seascape approaches abstraction, there remains a solid connection between the referent and its representation. The title alludes to the movement of the sea as well as the equivalence between music, nature, and color, an idea that Marin fostered throughout his career. In a catalogue for his 1913 exhibition at 291, for instance, he described the forces in nature that he sought to capture in his paintings using terms that call to mind a symphony: "While . . . these powers are at work pushing, pulling, sideways, downwards, upwards, I can hear the sound of their strife and there is great music being played."[8] Marin first employed the word "movement" in his titles in a group of watercolors from 1917, which may relate to Marsden Hartley's Movement series from 1916–1917. Describing the series to which the Blanton's work belongs, Marin asserted, "Using paint *as* paint is different from using paint to paint a picture. I'm calling my pictures this year 'Movements in Paint' and not movements of boat, sea, or sky, because in these new paintings, although I use objects, I am representing paint first of all, and not the motif primarily."[9]

Kathleen V. Jameson

Notes

1. Quoted in "American Water Colors at the Brooklyn Museum," *The Arts* I–II (December 1921): 152.
2. MacKinley Helm, *John Marin* (Boston: Pellegrini & Cudahy in association with The Institute of Contemporary Art, Boston, 1948), 101.
3. For further information on John Marin, see Sheldon Reich, *John Marin: A Stylistic Analysis and Catalogue Raisonné* (Tucson, Ariz.: University of Arizona Press, 1970); Ruth E. Fine, *John Marin* (Washington, D.C.: National Gallery of Art; New York: Abbeville Press, 1990); and Sam Hunter, *Expression and Meaning: The Marine Paintings of John Marin* (West Palm Beach, Fla.: Eaton Fine Art, 1998).
4. For a discussion of this issue, see Reich, 14–15, wherein the author notes that Marin himself and members of the Stieglitz circle were primarily responsible for perpetuating the idea that Marin was unaffected by European art.
5. Quoted in "American Water Colors at the Brooklyn Museum," 151.
6. Quoted in Reich, 222.
7. See Herbert J. Seligmann, "Frames with Reference to Marin," *It Must Be Said*, no. 3 (January 1934): n.p. Marin began exploring the idea of framing his compositions internally in works from the early 1920s. In these Marin painted frames directly on the supports.
8. *Camera Work*, no. 42–43 (April–July 1913): 18.
9. Helm, 101.

Reginald Marsh

Paris, 1898–Dorset, Vermont, 1954
w. New York, 1920–1925; Europe, 1925–1926; New York (trip to Europe, 1929), 1927–1954

Known at the height of his career as the "Hogarth of Manhattan," Reginald Marsh was an urban realist whose paintings and drawings resonate as impressionistic snapshots of their time.[1] Marsh chronicled urban existence during the Great Depression of the 1930s, one of the most socially troubled periods in American history; yet, unlike other Social Realist paintings of the day, Marsh's work did not include overt didactic content.

Marsh was born in Paris in 1898 but only lived there for two years before his family moved to suburban Nutley, New Jersey. His parents were painters who raised him within a small community of artists and writers.[2] In 1916, having entered Yale University, he honed his skills in drawing and caricature as an illustrator for *The Yale Record*. Marsh moved to New York in 1920 and spent a decade illustrating for the *Daily News* and *The New Yorker*. In 1925–1926 he traveled to Europe, where he made copies of works by Old Masters such as Titian, Peter Paul Rubens, Rembrandt van Rijn, and Eugène Delacroix. During this time abroad, he became thoroughly engrossed in the art of printmaking, which in turn informed his paintings and drawings of the 1930s, in particular their use of cross-hatching and other etching techniques to create the illusion of depth.

From 1927 to 1928 Marsh studied with the Ashcan School painters George Luks and John Sloan as well as his primary mentor, Kenneth Hayes Miller, at the Art Students League in New York. Although impressed by Marsh's drawing skill, Miller urged the younger artist to translate his images into paintings.[3] He also encouraged Marsh to secure his own studio. Accordingly, Marsh established one on Fourteenth Street on Union Square in 1929, after another extended trip to Europe. This studio offered him a venue from which to observe the people and places of downtown Manhattan. Also in 1929, under the advice of the American Regionalist painter Thomas Hart Benton, Marsh began experimenting with egg tempera, a medium that allowed him to incorporate heavy neutral tones as well as bright bursts of color into his works.

Painted just two years later, in 1931, *Chatham Square* (plate 114) depicts a maze of urban architecture that engulfs a group of people on a busy corner of Division Street, on Manhattan's Lower East Side. Marsh utilized strong vertical lines that give an impression of an infinite urban structure with no visible peak. Men in overcoats chat in front of rows of shop windows that display various wares and goods. Marsh illuminates his figures with lights from the shops' interiors, which cast an eerie glow and highlight the pointed dichotomy between ongoing commerce and those suffering from the depressed economy. His interest in printmaking is most evident in the rendering of the central figure, where crosshatched lines emerge from under layers of tempera. Marsh cut this figure from another painting and collaged it onto the surface of *Chatham Square* with gesso.

Within a palette of neutral browns, Marsh employed red and purple to highlight details in the painting. He also drew attention to the disparities of social class through the careful delineation of these same details: from the woman's fashionable kitten-heeled shoes, indicative of a certain level of prosperity, to the homeless man's aged craggy face, rumpled coat, and worn shoes. In the stores, wealth and beauty abound; on the street, poverty and privation rule the day.

Chatham Square, located near New York's Bowery and City Hall, was one of Marsh's regular observation spots, and the inspiration for this work was surely one of his almost daily sketching outings. As Marsh historian Edward Laning observed of the artist's routine:

> *He was dedicated; he was always working. After the day in his studio on Union Square was over, he walked the short distance to his apartment on Fifteenth Street and spent the evening at his etching press. And when the work in the studio faltered, he put a sketchbook in his pocket, picked up a couple of artist's fountain pens and set out on a sketching trip. He would walk along Fourteenth Street and take the Third Avenue El to Chatham Square or the Bowery.*[4]

Marsh loved New York and lived there until the end of his life. He died suddenly while on a weekend trip to Vermont in 1954. The Blanton's *Chatham Square* exemplifies the artist's unique ability to render reality and add human interest while presenting an image of day-to-day activity in 1930s New York.

Melissa Warak

Notes

1. Anonymous, "Half-day in the Studio of Reginald Marsh, Virile Painter of the American Scene," *American Artist*, no. 5 (June 1941): 5.
2. Lloyd Goodrich, "Reginald Marsh, Painter of New York in its Wildest Profusion," *American Artist*, no. 19 (September 1955): 19.
3. F. A. Blossom, "Reginald Marsh as a Painter," *Creative Art* (April 1933): 262.
4. Edward Laning, *The Sketchbooks of Reginald Marsh* (Greenwich, Conn.: New York Graphic Society, 1973), 14.

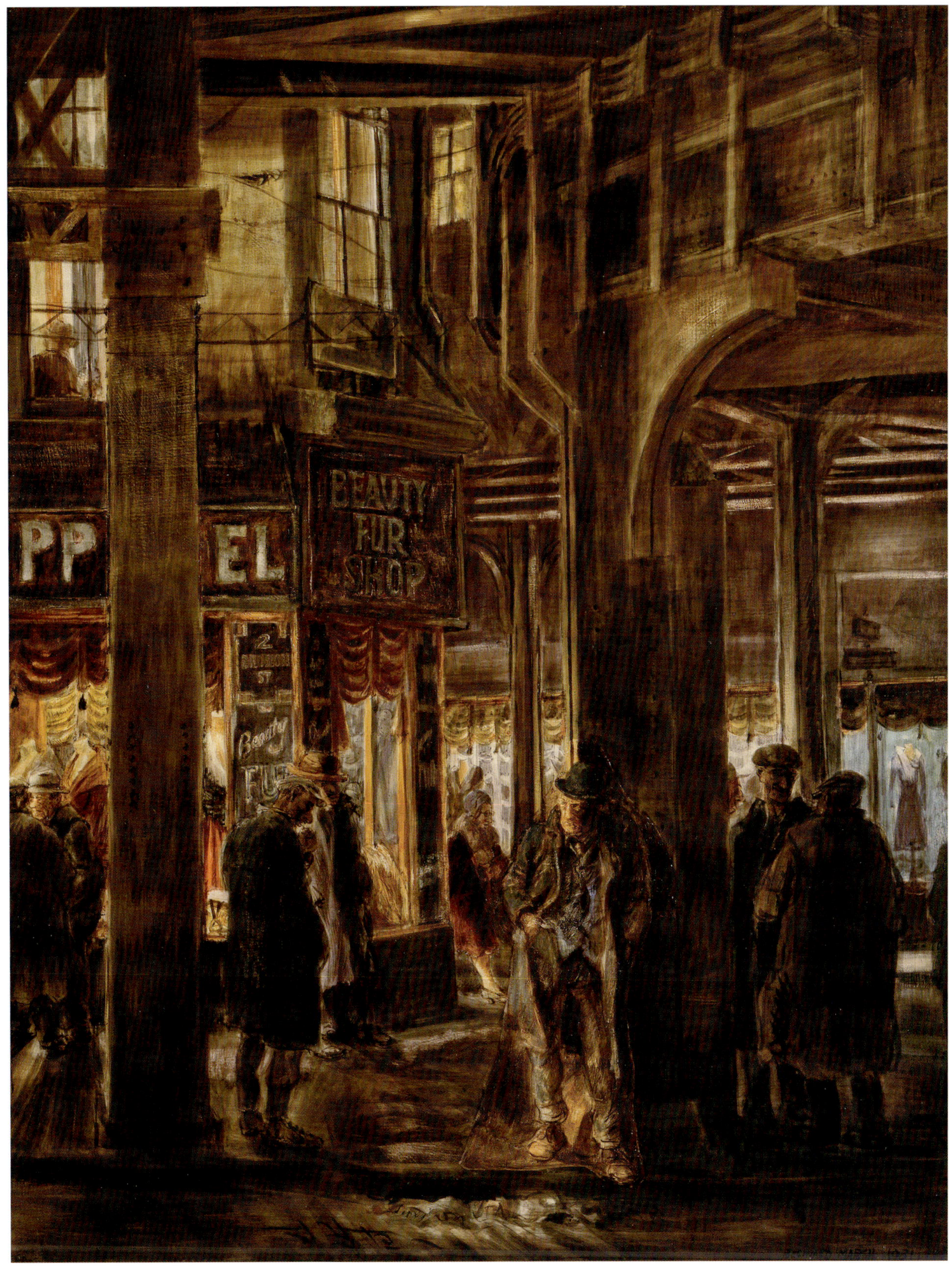

114.

Chatham Square, 1931

Tempera and collaged canvas on board
47¼ × 35¼ in. (120.1 × 89.6 cm)
Gift of Mari and James A. Michener
1991.263

Provenance: Purchased by James Michener from the estate of the artist through the Frank Rehn Gallery, New York, 1961; long-term loan to The University of Texas at Austin, 1968–1991
Signed lower right "Reginald Marsh 1931"

Howard Mehring

Washington, D.C., 1931–1978

w. Washington, D.C., 1953–1961; Europe, 1961–1966; Washington, D.C., 1966–1968; Europe, 1968; Washington, D.C., 1969–1978

Howard Mehring was the youngest member of a group of artists, including Kenneth Noland, Morris Louis, Sam Gilliam, Tom Downing, and Gene Davis, known as the Washington Color Painters. Along with a common geographical location and moment in time, the Washington Color Painters shared an interest in extending the canon of abstraction that had been established by their predecessors, the Abstract Expressionists. Some critics and artists question the veracity of grouping these artists together—after all, Louis and Davis met only a few times casually, and by the time these artists could be identified stylistically as a movement, around 1961–1962, Noland had moved to New York and Louis was deceased. Nevertheless, stylistic similarities, related technical experimentation, and critical responses to their work unite the artists historically. In 1965 Gerald Nordland, director of the now defunct Washington Gallery of Modern Art, organized a traveling exhibition entitled *The Washington Color Painters.*[1]

Mehring was born in Washington, D.C., in 1931 and lived there his entire life. After attending Wilson Teachers College, he won a full scholarship to Catholic University, where he met and studied with Noland. He earned an MFA in 1955 and had his first solo show two years later at the Sculptors Studio. During this time, he met and later shared a studio with Downing, another student of Noland. The excitement of working to create a new form of abstraction, which Mehring and his cohorts believed could be achieved through color, defines Mehring's early artistic career. As with most artists of his generation, he vehemently defended abstraction, once observing, "the eye sees nature in a literal way, but the ears do not hear sounds in nature in quite the same manner. The ear will accept the fact that music is not an imitation of nature, but the eye still insists on a representation of what it has seen."[2]

An early work by Helen Frankenthaler entitled *Mountains and Sea* (1952) particularly influenced the development of the Washington Color Painters. Louis and Noland saw the work in Frankenthaler's studio on a trip to New York with Clement Greenberg in the spring of 1953. The stained, not brushed, areas of pale color with which Frankenthaler saturated the unprimed canvas opened up a world of possibilities for Noland, Louis, and, eventually, other Washington Color Painters. As Louis said of Frankenthaler, "She was a bridge between Pollock and what was possible."[3] Greenberg, too, exerted influence over the group, making numerous trips to Washington and supporting the artists with studio visits, critiques, and published articles.

Noland, in particular, was instrumental in keeping the Washington artists abreast of critical developments in New York, the epicenter of the art world in the United States in the late 1950s. This had a monumental impact on Mehring's own search to find a style that not only built on the achievements of the Abstract Expressionists, especially Jackson Pollock, but moved beyond them. Considering that Mehring's early experimentation with color and space was based on theory, it is interesting that a main ingredient for achieving his goal was a technical, not a critical, development. In 1948 Leonard Bocour had developed Magna paint, an acrylic-based pigment which, when thinned with turpentine and applied directly to an unprimed canvas, seeped directly into the weave of the cloth. Following the lead of Frankenthaler, Mehring and his colleagues used Magna paint to integrate color into and across the canvas.

Painting after Monet (1959, plate 115), with its stippled, soaked markings and edge-to-edge composition, is from a series considered Mehring's breakthrough work. The subtle contrast between high key and subdued tones conveys a floating sensation of color while creating a pulsating, shallow space. Music played an important role in Mehring's approach to abstract painting. His comment on Bach's

115.
Painting after Monet, 1959

Acrylic on canvas
57⅜ × 43½ in. (145.7 × 110.5 cm)
Michener Acquisitions Fund
P1970.15.2

Provenance: Purchased from A. M. Sachs Gallery, New York, 1970
Inscribed lower right "Howard Mehring 1959 'Painting after Monet'"

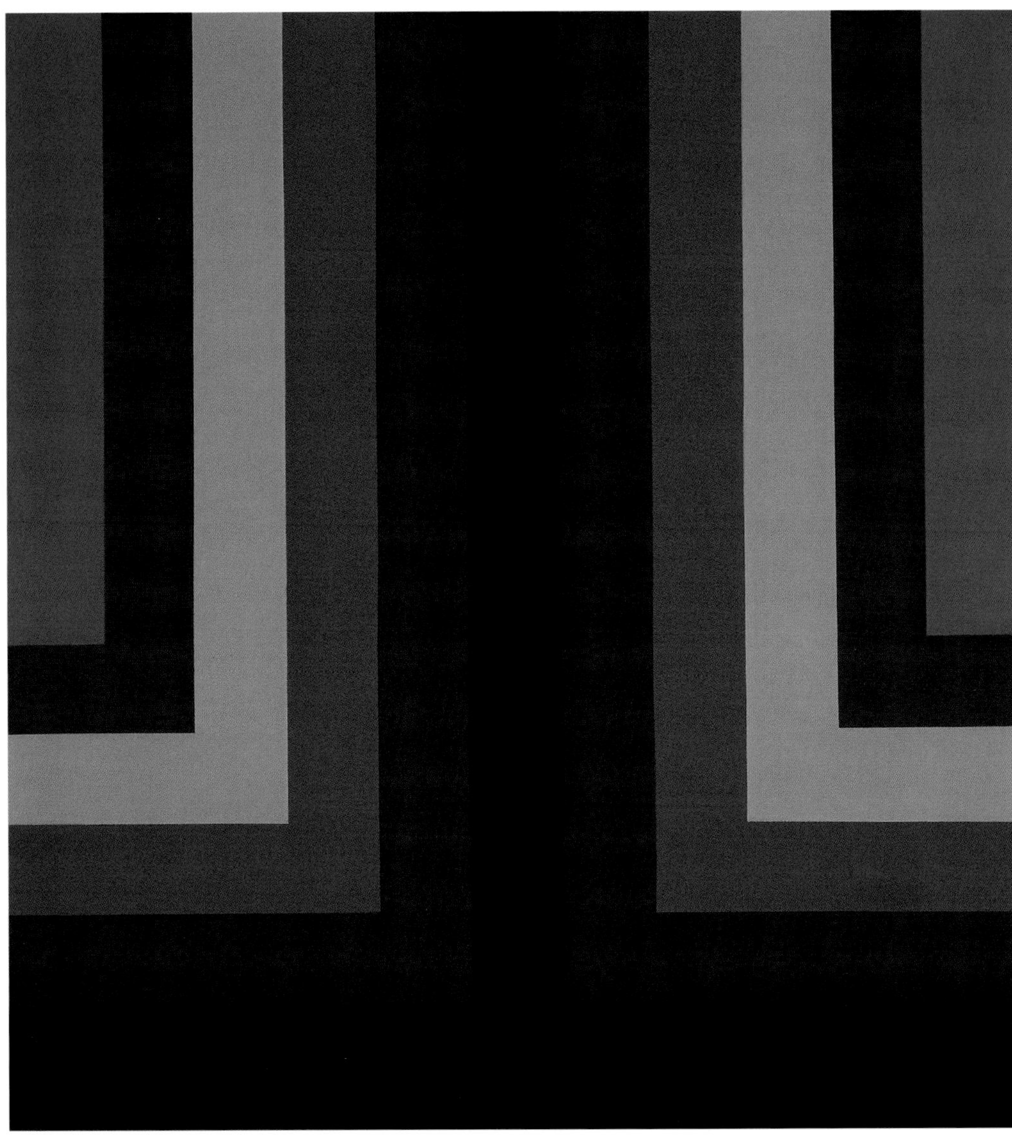

116.

Element of Blue, 1965

Acrylic on canvas
51 3/16 × 46 1/16 in. (130 × 117 cm)
Gift of Mari and James A. Michener
G1968.96

Provenance: Purchased by James Michener from A. M. Sachs Gallery, New York, 1966
Inscribed verso, upper center "'Element of Blue' 1965 Howard Mehring"

fugues—"What struck me is the way the notes floated and yet had a pull of gravity"—could also be a poetic description of *Painting after Monet,* which effects a subtle push/pull of color against color.[4] As his work developed, Mehring, probably influenced by Greenberg, wanted his paintings to have more definition than the free floating, overall abstraction of the early works. To achieve this goal, he initially painted canvases with his signature stippling, then cut and taped them together in geometric forms. These forms provided an enclosure for the dappled hues, much like Noland's targets, which were both recognizable shapes and containers for color. Mehring eventually abandoned the stippling and cutting and progressively moved toward a less painterly style, adopting hard-edged forms such as the inverted "T" (and in other cases "Z") found in *Element of Blue* (1965, plate 116).

By 1964 Mehring was garnering national recognition. Greenberg included three of Mehring's works from 1963, *Double Black, Double Red,* and *The Key,* in the groundbreaking 1964 exhibition, *Post Painterly Abstraction,* at the Los Angeles County Museum of Art. The following year Mehring's paintings appeared in *The Washington Color Painters* exhibition. His 1966 exhibition at A. M. Sachs Gallery in New York was a huge success. All the paintings sold, many to the most prestigious museums and collectors in the country. James Michener purchased *Element of Blue* from this exhibition, giving it to The University of Texas at Austin just two years later.

Around 1968, in a development that still leaves art historians mystified, Mehring—who in the preceding few years had had the good fortune to experience heights of success most artists never know—stopped painting. Although he participated in exhibitions, spoke with curators and critics about his work, and made small-scale drawings, he never returned to the studio. Nordland noted in 1990, "Perhaps the most mercurial and elusive of the Washington Color Painters, Mehring took his public leave of us, as an artist, long before his early death in 1978."[5] As a favorite son from the nation's Capitol, Mehring was honored with a retrospective at the Corcoran Gallery of Art in 1977.

Sue Scott

Notes

1. Leslie Judd Ahlander, "An Artist Speaks: Howard Mehring," *Washington Post,* September 2, 1962. The exhibition also included the work of Paul Reed.
2. Quoted in Jane Livingston, *Howard Mehring: A Retrospective Exhibition* (Washington, D.C.: Corcoran Gallery of Art, 1977), 66.
3. This remark originally appeared in Gerald Nordland, *The Washington Color Painters* (Washington, D.C.: Washington Gallery of Modern Art, 1965), 12.
4. Quoted in Livingston, 66.
5. Quoted in Livingston, 66.

Ana Mendieta

Havana, Cuba, 1948–New York, 1985

w. Iowa City, Iowa (summers in Mexico, 1971–1978), 1967–1978; New York–Iowa City, 1978–1980; New York (frequent trips to Cuba–Mexico), 1978–1983; Rome–Europe, 1983–1985

Ana Mendieta's life and art are surrounded by debate, mythmaking, and controversy.[1] During her lifetime and since her death, critics have pigeonholed Mendieta into various movements and ideologies, including feminism, Conceptualism, postmodernism, and identity politics, among others.

The highly personal nature of Mendieta's art has led some scholars to interpret it in terms of biography. Due to the primacy the artist placed on the female form, in part the result of her use of her own body as a principle vehicle of expression, some have viewed Mendieta's work primarily as a feminist enterprise. Although she embraced many early feminist approaches, particularly goddess-centered imagery, Mendieta sought to extend her art beyond strictly feminist interpretations, desiring instead to address universal themes. She also came to criticize her feminist colleagues for excluding women of color. For that matter, her status as a Latina artist placed Mendieta in the position of an outsider, leading some critics to assess her work strictly in terms of her ethnicity. While this view fits in well with contemporary postmodernist multiculturalism, it neglects Mendieta's erudite integration and refutation of Western historical and contemporary art and theory. Indeed, the difficulty in characterizing her work is a compelling testament to its complexity and enduring power.

Mendieta and her sister were forced to leave Cuba in 1961. They arrived in the United States under the auspices of Operation Pedro Pan, an anti-Castro, Catholic-based program designed to relocate Cuban children; the experience left both sisters feeling displaced and longing for family and home. After living in a series of foster homes in Iowa, Mendieta attended the University of Iowa, graduating with a BFA in 1969. The following year, she enrolled in Iowa's groundbreaking Intermedia Program, then under the direction of Hans Breder, where she met experimental Conceptual and feminist critics and artists, especially those who used performance and the body as integral elements in their aesthetic production. Breder and Mendieta began to travel to Mexico; the young artist drew on the spiritual, iconographic, and cultural traditions she encountered there, finding a sense of belonging that had been lacking in Iowa.

Even in her earliest work, Mendieta explored issues such as death, resurrection, and absence through the vehicle of the female body, using organic materials in ritualistic performances. By 1973 she had embraced the natural landscape both formally and conceptually as an integral element of her work, which she described as "earth/body art," an amalgamation of Earth art, Body art, and Performance art. While many artists of the period were exploring these practices, Mendieta's engagement with nature can be differentiated by its lack of domineering intervention and her apparent desire to merge with the landscape through aesthetic means. In addition, her focus on the body appears less concerned with the specificity of self and more centered on the universality of the human form. Finally, Mendieta's "performances" were most often conducted in remote locations without an audience and later communicated through documentary materials such as photographs, slides, and films.

In her best-known series, the Siluetas [Silhouettes], Mendieta used flowers, water, fire, gunpowder, stones, mud, sand, and grass to fashion images of her own body that evoked its absence and presence simultaneously. She constructed an iconography of longing and spirituality

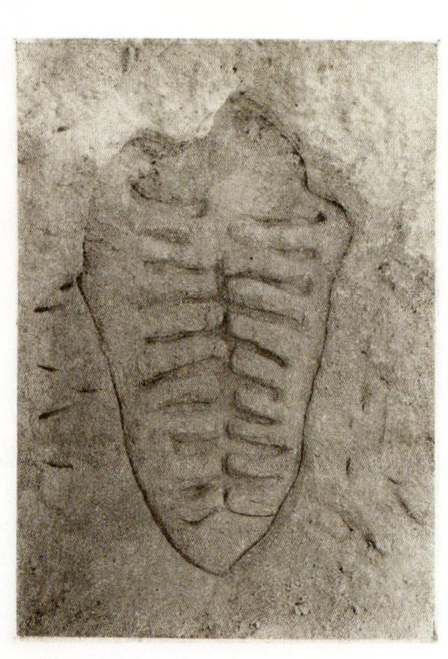

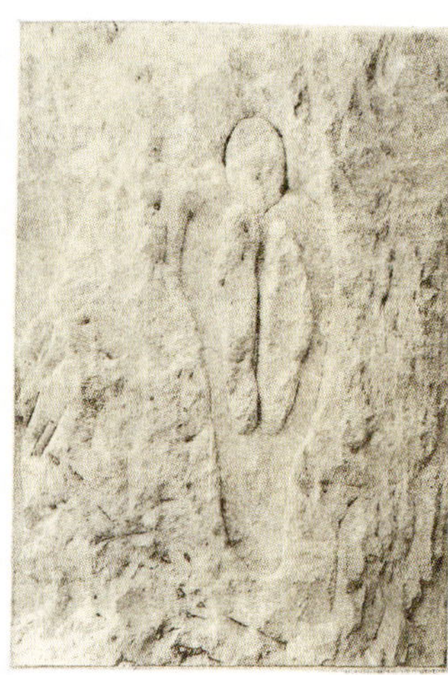

117.
Itiba Cahubaba II (Old Mother Blood), from the Rupestrian Sculptures series, 1981/1983

Photo etching on Chine collé mounted on Arches cover paper
10 × 7 in. (25.2 × 18.3 cm)
Purchase through the generosity of The Judith Rothschild Foundation and the Michener Acquisitions Fund
1999.65

Provenance: Purchased from the Estate of the Artist and Galerie Lelong, New York, 1999

118.
Atabey (Mother of the Waters), from the Rupestrian Sculptures series, 1981/1983

Photo etching on Chine collé mounted on Arches cover paper
10 × 7 in. (25.5 × 18.3 cm)
Purchase through the generosity of The Judith Rothschild Foundation and the Michener Acquisitions Fund
1999.62

Provenance: Purchased from the Estate of the Artist and Galerie Lelong, New York, 1999

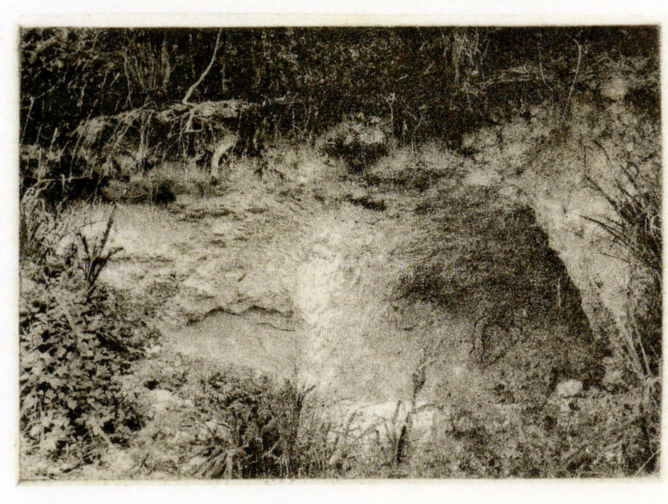

119.
Cueva del Aguila (Eagle's Cave), from the Rupestrian Sculptures series, 1981/1983

Photo etching on Chine collé mounted on Arches cover paper
7 x 10 in. (18 x 25.2 cm)
Purchase through the generosity of The Judith Rothschild Foundation and the Michener Acquisitions Fund
1999.63

Provenance: Purchased from the Estate of the Artist and Galerie Lelong, New York, 1999

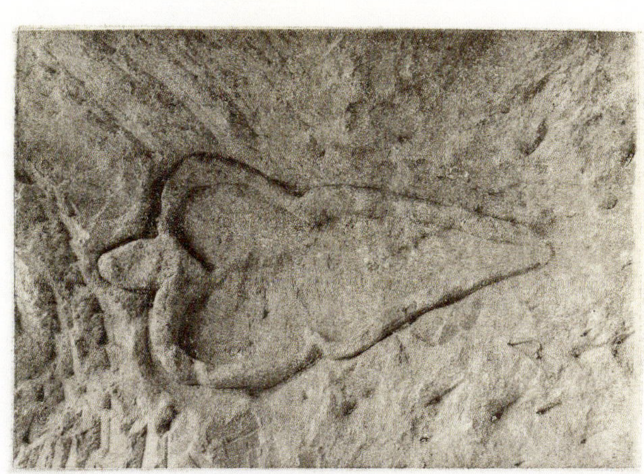

120.
Untitled, State II, from the Rupestrian Sculptures series, 1981/1983

Photo etching on Chine collé mounted on Arches cover paper
7 x 10 in. (17.9 x 25.2 cm)
Purchase through the generosity of The Judith Rothschild Foundation and the Michener Acquisitions Fund
1999.67

Provenance: Purchased from the Estate of the Artist and Galerie Lelong, New York, 1999

through a combination of earth-goddess imagery and a highly personal, intimate approach.

Mendieta returned to Cuba for the first time in 1980. The following year she executed the Rupestrian Sculptures or *Esculturas rupestres* (*rupestre* means "carved rock"). Mendienta carved the sculptures into the walls of caves at Las Escaleras de Jaruco, Jaruco State Park, near Havana. She embellished them with paint and then documented them with photography.[2] While their imagery relates to her interest in female-centered iconography, Mendieta's primary reference was to the mythology and culture of the Taíno and Ciboney Indians, displaced groups indigenous to Cuba and the Greater Antilles.[3] Distilled to essential forms, these sculptures evoke ancient petroglyphs and fertility sculptures. Mendieta recalled that her interest in "primitive" cultures, as she termed them, began as a young girl in Cuba. She wrote, "It seems as if these cultures are provided with an inner knowledge, a closeness to natural resources. And it is this knowledge which gives reality to the images they have created. This sense of magic, knowledge and power found in primitive art has influenced my personal attitude toward art-making."[4]

Site-specific works such as the Rupestrian Sculptures depend on photo documentation because of their transitory nature. However, Mendieta conceived of the series of photo etchings in the Blanton's collection (1981/1983, plates 117–122) as both an integral part of the project and an independent endeavor. She received a grant from the New York State Council on the Arts to produce a limited edition book of photo etchings based on photographs of the sculptures as a means of "revealing [the] elusive works" she had carved in Cuba.[5] Unfortunately, the project was left unfinished due to Mendieta's untimely death in 1985.[6]

In 1982, after returning from Cuba to New York, Mendieta began creating images on leaves and bark by such means as drawing and scratching, a practice she continued while living in Rome on a fellowship at the American Academy. The ephemeral nature of these works and their inherent fragility locates them firmly within her oeuvre. Untitled (c. 1984, plate 123) illustrates the artist's continued interest in employing ancient female forms to express universal ideas; the swirling lines she used to delineate the figure, for example, appear in a number of works, including ones from

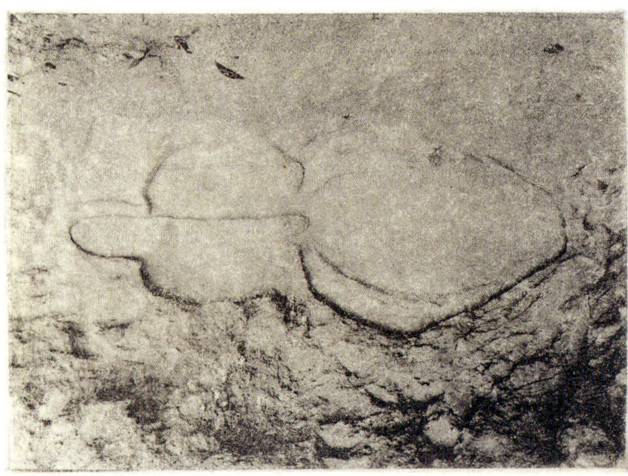

121.

Iyare (Mother), from the Rupestrian Sculptures series, 1981/1983

Photo etching on Chine collé mounted on Arches cover paper
7 × 10 in. (17.9 × 25.2 cm)
Purchase through the generosity of The Judith Rothschild Foundation and the Michener Acquisitions Fund
1999.66

Provenance: Purchased from the Estate of the Artist and Galerie Lelong, New York, 1999

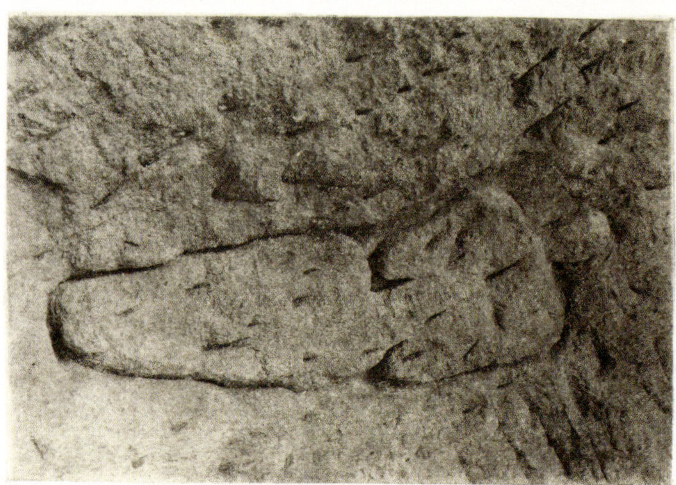

122.

Guabancex (Goddess of the Wind), from the Rupestrian Sculptures series, 1981/1983

Photo etching on Chine collé mounted on Arches cover paper
7 × 10 in. (18.1 × 25.5 cm)
Purchase through the generosity of The Judith Rothschild Foundation and the Michener Acquisitions Fund
1999.64

Provenance: Purchased from the Estate of the Artist and Galerie Lelong, New York, 1999

the Rupestrian Sculptures series. In Untitled, however, Mendieta further abstracted her iconography with a greater simplicity of line, suggesting that she had distilled the image to its most fundamental elements.

Mendieta's art continues to resonate strongly with diverse audiences because she addressed an astounding array of issues, including feminism, postcolonialism, globalism, and identity, in a deeply complex and moving body of work. Her awareness of art historical and sociopolitical connections, along with the force of her art, establishes Mendieta as one of the most significant artists of her generation.

Kathleen V. Jameson

Notes

1. For further information on Ana Mendieta, see Bonnie Clearwater, ed., *Ana Mendieta: A Book of Works* (Miami Beach, Fla.: Grassfield Press, 1993); Michael Duncan, "Tracing Mendieta," *Art in America* 87 (April 1999): 110–13, 154; and Olga M. Viso, *Ana Mendieta: Earth Body: Sculpture and Performance, 1972–1985* (Washington, D.C.: Hirshhorn Museum and Sculpture Garden, 2004).
2. The A.I.R. Gallery in New York, which was operated by and exhibited work by women only, exhibited the photographs later that year. Mendieta became a member in 1978.
3. The titles of the works in the Rupestrian Sculptures series refer to Taínan goddesses.
4. Quoted in Clearwater, 41.
5. Quoted in Clearwater, 41. Mendieta proposed twelve photo etchings for the book but changed the number to ten. Norma Jean de Vico printed five sets of the photo etchings prior to Mendieta's death. Artists Luis Camnitzer and Liliana Porter printed the rest of the edition of twenty in 1993. All of the photo etchings from the Rupestrian Sculptures series, along with related archival documents, were published posthumously in *Ana Mendieta: A Book of Works,* edited by Bonnie Clearwater. The Blanton's set of prints is incomplete as the museum purchased the last remaining works from the lifetime edition.
6. Mendieta died in 1985, falling from a window of an apartment that she shared with her husband, Carl Andre, a prominent Minimalist sculptor. Her death, the subsequent arrest of Andre, and his acquittal triggered a fissure in the art and feminist communities.

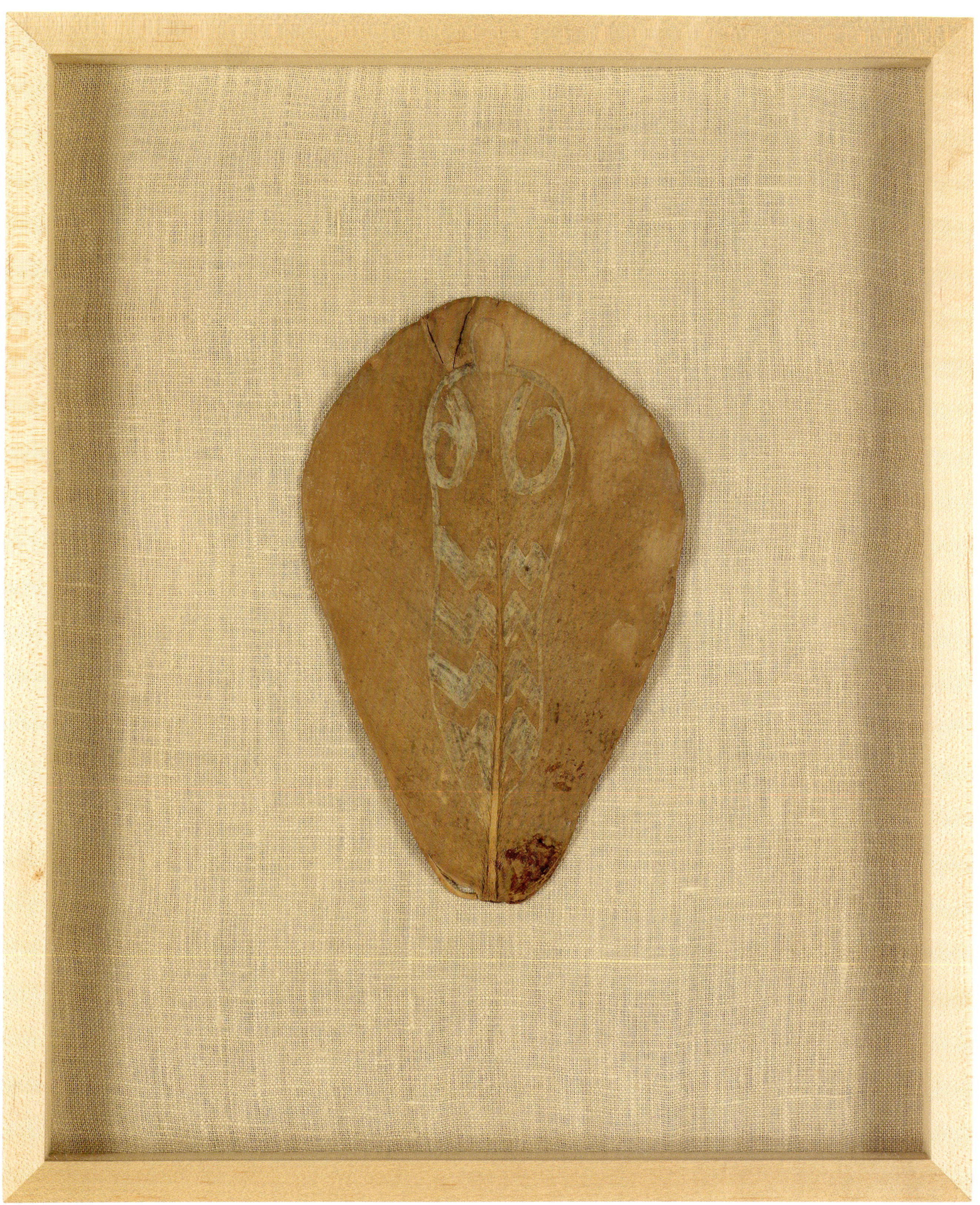

123.

Untitled, c. 1984

Drawing on leaf
7 5/16 × 4 1/2 in. (18.5 × 11.5 cm)
Purchase through the generosity of The Judith Rothschild Foundation and the Michener Acquisitions Fund
1999.68

Provenance: Purchased from the Estate of the Artist and Galerie Lelong, New York, 1999

Eleanore Mikus

b. Detroit, 1927

w. New York–Denver, Colorado–Rahway, New Jersey, 1960–1973; London, 1973–1977; New York, 1977–1979; Ithaca, New York, 1979–present

Tablet 164 (1967–1968, plate 124) belongs to Eleanore Mikus's Tablets series, a group of monochromatic paintings (either white, grey, or black) created between 1960 and 1968. This series represents the culmination of nearly a decade of artistic experimentation that coincided with Mikus's residence in New York.

Born in Detroit in 1927, Mikus received her BFA in 1957 and her MA in art history from the University of Denver in 1967. She settled in Rahway, New Jersey, in 1959 to study art at the Art Students League, New York University, and the New York Art Institute. Soon thereafter, Mikus became an active participant the New York art scene, displaying her work at galleries and in group exhibitions at the Whitney Museum of American Art and The Museum of Modern Art.[1]

In the early 1960s Mikus adopted monochromatic abstraction as a response to what she and other artists, including Agnes Martin, Robert Ryman, and Ad Reinhardt, perceived as the slickness and cynicism of Pop art and the highly personal gestures of Abstract Expressionism.[2] Around this same time, she began working with paint as a sculptural medium, "building" her paintings by adding plywood, cardboard, epoxy, fiberglass, and folded paper to the support.[3] Mikus simplified her process in the mid-1960s. She began to coat canvas and wood surfaces with resin in an effort to paint and model the material simultaneously. To these surfaces she applied layers of acrylic paint, oil paint, or epoxy—often sanded and buffed to a sheen. The process used to make each work was similar, yet the results were always unique; the paintings vary in size and visual effect.[4]

Tablet 164 exemplifies Mikus's second stage of experimentation, when greater nuance and more highly finished surfaces replaced the rough textures of her earlier works. The raised surface of *Tablet 164* evokes the Minimalist grids favored by Martin and Reinhardt, but rather than appearing as a palimpsest as in Martin's work, or as an a priori structure as in Reinhardt's, Mikus's grid seems to float up from beneath the support, suggesting an archaeological or geological presence that may be in the process of either disappearing or emerging. What is more, Mikus elevated the surface of *Tablet 164* just enough to create shadows. In this way, its visual attributes, such as the interplay of light and dark and the variations in depth, are generated by the physical qualities of the painting itself, as opposed to formal techniques that merely create the illusion of such qualities.

Mikus's work has been compared to that of Louise Nevelson for its subtle effects in three dimensions. Both artists exhibited at the Pace Gallery in New York, and a work by Mikus now owned by The Museum of Modern Art was purchased by Nevelson for the collection in 1964. Although the two artists employed different media, they shared an aesthetic based on simplicity and pristine elegance. Nevelson's sculptures are composed of found objects, often architectural remnants, harmonized by a monochromatic palette of white, black, or gold. Quiet and compelling, the compressed forms of these works cultivate similar relationships between light and shadow as those found in Mikus's paintings.

While sharing with Minimalist painting a lack of recognizable "content" or imagery, the roughly formed remnants of the grid underlying *Tablet 164* have emotive, ambiguous, and tactile characteristics that are more suggestive of the "process art" of sculptor Eva Hesse. These characteristics are also associated with Zen Buddhism, a body of philosophical and spiritual teachings that influenced a young generation of artists in the 1960s.[5] Arguably, unpretentious works such as *Tablet 164* offer a metaphor for the practice of self-reflection ascribed to Zen Buddhism. Mikus herself wrote that she aimed for "a simplicity, and a oneness achieved through nonaggression, acceptance and understanding."[6]

Mikus's Tablets series also drew inspiration from sources outside mainstream (Western) artistic discourse. For example, the monochromatic paintings of Japanese and Chinese artists from the 8th century played a significant role in the development of Mikus's technique and were the subject of her master's thesis in art history. Mikus admired in particular the 8th-century Chinese painter Wang Wei for his ability to "simplify the objective images of the world and replace them with ideal images, which through his prolonged meditation, were free of nonessentials."[7]

Following the completion of her Tablets series in 1968, Mikus radically changed direction, creating Neo-Expressionist paintings that contain recognizable subject matter and are rendered in crude, childlike brushstrokes. These are often compared to paintings by her contemporaries Philip Guston and Alfred Leslie, as well as those by European artists Jean Dubuffet and Paul Klee. It was around this same time, in the early 1970s, that Mikus left New York to teach, first in London and then at Cornell University in Ithaca, New York (where she is now professor emeritus). In the early 1980s, she returned to monochromatic works, experimenting with folded sheets of paper and vellum to achieve geometric patterns with the same subtle qualities as her earlier relief tablets.

Jennifer Barrett

Notes

1. Judith Bernstock and Robert Hobbs, *Eleanore Mikus: Shadows of the Real* (Ithaca, N.Y.: Groton House, 1991), 26.
2. Eleanor Heartney, "Eleanore Mikus at Claudia Carr and Mitchell Algus," *Art in America* 87 (May 1999): 154. Bernstock and Hobbs, 15. Ad Reinhardt, Louise Nevelson, and Andy Warhol have received specific mention in writings about Mikus's life and work.
3. Mikus and Reinhardt met after Reinhardt saw Mikus's work at the Whitney Museum of American Art in 1961. Press Release, Mitchell Algus Gallery, New York, September 2003; also available at http://www.mitchellalgus.com/pr/mikus03.html [May 14, 2004].
4. Bernstock and Hobbs, 16.
5. Bernstock and Hobbs, 15–16.
6. Quoted from the artist's notes in Bernstock and Hobbs, 20.
7. Quoted from the artist's notes in Bernstock and Hobbs, 22.

124.
Tablet 164, 1967–1968
Epoxy resin on fiberglass
51¾ × 30 × 2 in. (131.4 × 76.2 × 5 cm)
Gift of Gabrielle Burns, courtesy the Artist and Mitchell Algus Gallery
2004.107
Signed verso "E. Mikus 1967–68" in black paint

Melissa Miller

b. Houston, 1951

w. Austin, 1969–1971; Houston, 1971; Albuquerque, New Mexico, 1971–1974; Austin, 1975–present

As a child, Melissa Miller spent a great deal of time on her paternal grandfather's ranch in Flatonia, Texas (a town between Austin and Houston), and at her maternal grandparents' home in the mountains of New Mexico. These formative experiences introduced her to the wonders of the natural world and the animals that populate it, subjects that would become central to her artistic practice. In 1969 Miller enrolled at The University of Texas at Austin before attending the Master of Fine Arts School of Houston (now the Alfred C. Glassell School of Art). Beginning in 1971, she studied at the University of New Mexico in Albuquerque and with Gabriel Laderman, a realist painter, at the Yale Summer School of Music and Art. She received her BFA from UNM in 1974.

Having attended college at a time when Abstract Expressionists dominated painting programs, Miller learned to compose and construct paintings by intuitively building up marks and colors directly on the canvas, and by responding to the visceral quality of the paint. As she once observed of her early landscapes, "They emphasized my love of active surface and gesture, and my interest in the abstract qualities of the medium itself."[1]

Upon returning to Texas in 1975, Miller began painting landscapes populated with animals, a topic that would continue to absorb her interest for close to thirty years. She conceived of these early animal depictions as "portraits," but by the mid-1980s, instead of focusing on a single protagonist, Miller multiplied the actors in large-scale tour de forces. *Zebras and Hyenas* (1985, plate 125) shares the vivid palette and expressionistic brushstrokes of such early work. Here Miller portrays the moment after a pack of hyenas has driven a herd of zebras into motion. As they disperse, the zebras' stripes merge into a dynamic optical field. Of the artistic challenges posed by the painting's subject matter, Miller said:

> *I'm interested in the many complexities of relationships, power, and survival, that was the thematic impetus for this work. However, composition, color, and marks play an equal role in the construct of all my paintings. Of the many predator/prey conflicts I could have chosen to portray, the idea of juxtaposing the stripes of zebras and the spots of hyenas intrigued me. Combined with expressive brushstrokes, the painting became almost abstract. Keeping track of all those moving patterns was difficult and fun at the same time.*[2]

By using bright yellows in the foreground (earth) and background (sky), the artist contorts the space of the picture plane. A distant mountain range anchors the receding landscape, so that the upper and lower edges of the canvas seem to occupy the same pictorial space. The fiery orange-gold color of the sky and landscape enhances the drama of the scene, as does the point of view and the direction of the zebras' dispersal, which place the viewer directly in the line of the stampede. At the same time, the composition, suggestive of a classical relief or frieze with its tightly interwoven forms, lends the painting a degree of stability, maintaining unity and coherence within a field fraught with activity.

While it may be tempting to group Miller with her contemporaries, the Neo-Expressionists, because of her use of saturated color, evident brushwork, and representational subject matter, she declines this affiliation.[3] For inspiration, she looks to a wide variety of sources, including Persian miniatures, folk art, Japanese prints and scrolls, and the European Old Masters.[4] A lifetime student of art history, Miller has acknowledged that these influences bind her to a tradition and allow her to explore the relationship between past and present.[5]

Through richly allegorical animal paintings, Miller has explored complex conceits such as environmental crisis, predator and prey, temptation and deception and, later, themes of transformation. The artist said of her approach:

> *Thematically, I wish my paintings to depict the many facets and layers of life and survival, of which I am a constant and curious observer. My abstract concerns demand that the painting be treated, while in process, as a changing, living organism, and that the brushstrokes themselves ultimately serve as both form and content.*[6]

Miller continues to experiment with compositional strategies, using shifts in scale and spatial organization to construct scenes that contain elements of the factual and the fabulous. The artist also remains interested in the interaction of animals on a micro- and macrocosmic scale. Her recent work reflects on the introduction of exotic game onto Texas ranches in the 1950s, and explores the unlikely contact between native and non-native species, another evocative painterly topic. In *Farm* (2002), for instance, emus live among cows, and jackrabbits exist in harmony with llamas. She has replaced the dramatic and violent scene of intra-species conflict in *Zebras and Hyenas* with one equally staged, yet gently unfolding.

Charlotte Cousins

Notes

1. Quoted in Barbara Rose and Susie Kalil, *Fresh Paint: The Houston School* (Houston: Texas Monthly Press, 1985), 154.
2. Melissa Miller, email correspondence with Annette Carlozzi, August 17, 2005.
3. Katherine Gregor, "Melissa Miller's Animal Kingdom," *Artnews* 85 (December 1986): 108.
4. Gregor, 113–14. A few other sources among the many influences she cites include: the nineteenth-century artist Tsukioka Yoshitoshi's *One Hundred Aspects of the Moon*, Sir Edwin Landseer's animal allegories, Paolo Uccello's composition of space, and Charles Burchfield's regional landscapes.
5. Melissa Miller, conversations with the author, February 2004.
6. Quoted in Annette Carlozzi, *50 Texas Artists* (San Francisco: Chronicle Books, 1986), 67.

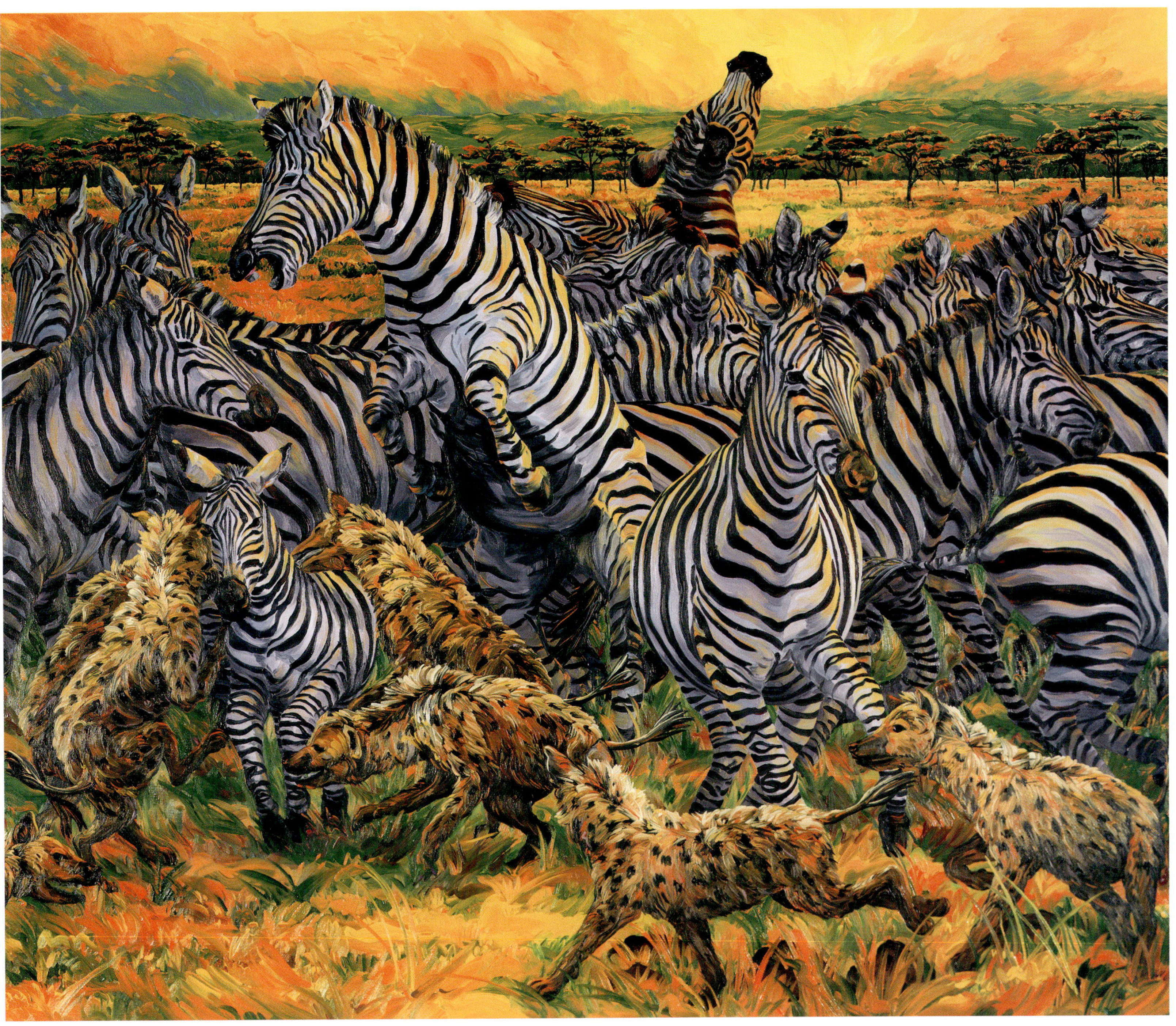

125.

Zebras and Hyenas, 1985

Oil on linen on canvas
73⅝ × 84⅞ in. (183.7 × 213.1 cm)
Michener Acquisitions Fund
1985.169

Provenance: Purchased from Texas Gallery, Houston, 1985
Signed lower right "Miller"

Joan Mitchell

Chicago, 1926–Paris, 1992

w. Chicago (frequent trips to Mexico), 1944–1947; Europe, 1948–1949; New York, 1950–1955; Paris–New York, 1955–1959; Paris (summer in Easthampton, New York, 1960), 1960–1967; Vétheuil, France, 1968–1992

Joan Mitchell remains known as a "painter's painter."[1] Her work is most closely identified with large, abstract, and vibrant oils, her medium of choice. In the 1960s and 1970s, when Pop art, Minimalism, and hard-edge painting styles dominated the art scene, Mitchell resisted those tendencies; challenging classifications, she sardonically observed: "Pop art, op art, flop art, and slop art. I fall into the last two categories."[2] She also refused such labels as "Second Generation Abstract Expressionist," "Abstract Impressionist," and "woman painter." All of these terms apply to Mitchell in one way or another, but as with all generalities, the fit is imperfect.

Mitchell was born in 1926 to an affluent Chicago family. Her father was a successful doctor and her mother a poetry editor, and she grew up in an artistic atmosphere peopled by writers and poets, including Edna St. Vincent Millay, T. S. Eliot, and Dylan Thomas. Mitchell attended Smith College and trained as a painter at the School of the Art Institute of Chicago. She was particularly close to her maternal grandfather, who made his fortune as a steel engineer and from whom she received an inheritance, which enabled her to pursue her artistic goals free from financial struggle. In 1947 Mitchell moved to New York briefly to study with Hans Hofmann. She traveled through Europe on an extended fellowship between 1948 and 1949. In 1950 she returned to New York, where she studied art history at Columbia University and French at New York University. In the summer of 1955 Mitchell met Jean-Paul Riopelle, the Canadian artist, who would be her companion until 1979. Thereafter, she began dividing her time between New York and Paris, deciding to move there permanently in 1959, although she rented a cottage on Easthampton, Long Island, during the summer of 1960. Despite living abroad, Mitchell continued to exhibit in New York, maintaining a studio on St. Mark's Place in the heart of New York's East Village.

The most productive years of Mitchell's career were spent in France, first in Paris and later in Vétheuil, a small town outside Paris where she acquired the house that Claude Monet, the celebrated Impressionist painter, had made his home several generations earlier. There she found inspiration in the surrounding landscape. If the Impressionists, as the writer Émile Zola famously declared, painted "nature seen through a temperament,"[3] Mitchell painted landscapes as seen through the filter of her memory. In general, she described her works as "remembered landscapes" that "become transformed" through the act of painting.[4]

Rock Bottom (1960–1961, plate 126), which Mitchell first exhibited at the Stable Gallery in New York in 1961, then showed in *Forty Artists under Forty* at the Whitney Museum of American Art in 1962, is representative of her work from the early 1960s. Mitchell once described *Rock Bottom* as a "very violent painting."[5] Her assessment is borne out by the manner in which she applied the pigment, occasionally thinned with turpentine, to create a thick impasto that evokes the sea crashing upon coastal rocks. Although it appears casual, perhaps even reckless, this technique is actually practiced with deliberation. As Mitchell asserted in 1957: "The freedom in my work is quite controlled."[6] In the case of *Rock Bottom,* a central "figure" comprised of deep shades of aubergine, cornflower blue, rose red, and ochre hovers over a "ground" of whites and light creams. This central mass of color meets the viewer at eye level before moving down and out across the canvas. The composition cultivates a taut relationship between the central forms and the looser, more playful areas at the canvas's edges. Toward the lower part of the composition, which is filled with streaks of cadmium red, the forms almost completely dissolve. Mitchell deliberately chose not to interfere with the chance movements of paint, except at the lower right-hand corner. Here she overpainted the drips using a brush loaded with cadmium white.

Mitchell fulfilled the myth of the postwar American painter in some ways and ran contrary to it in others. She made the decision to leave New York and move to France in the late 1950s—just as New York was gaining prominence as a center of avant-garde artistic production and, by many accounts, was eclipsing Paris as the international center of the art world.[7] Mitchell was unique amongst her generation of fellow painters in that she maintained a highly visible presence on both sides of the Atlantic. When she died in 1992, she left behind a singular body of work, recognized for its originality and self-assured mastery. Mitchell's paintings, true to form, remain compelling—difficult, even—and unrepentantly so.

Justine Price

Notes

1. For example, see Douglas Davis, "The Painter's Painter," *Newsweek*, May 13, 1974, 108.
2. Quoted in Judith E. Bernstock, *Joan Mitchell* (New York: Hudson Hills Press, in association with the Herbert F. Johnson Museum of Art, Cornell University, 1988), 57.
3. Émile Zola, *Correspondance*, vol. 2 (Montréal: Presses de l'Université de Montréal; Paris: Editions du Centre National de la Recherche Scientifique, 1978), 375.
4. Quoted in *Forty Artists Under Forty: From the Collection of the Whitney Museum of American Art* (New York: Circulated by the American Federation of Arts, 1962), n.p.
5. Joan Mitchell, interview with Judith E. Bernstock, June–July 1986, as quoted in Linda Nochlin, "Joan Mitchell: A Rage to Paint," in Jane Livingston, ed., *The Paintings of Joan Mitchell* (New York: Whitney Museum of American Art; Berkeley: University of California Press, 2002), 49.
6. Quoted in Irving Sandler, "Joan Mitchell Paints a Picture," *Artnews* 56 (October 1957): 47.
7. For example, see Serge Guilbaut, *How New York Stole the Idea of Modern Art: Abstract Expressionism, Freedom, and the Cold War,* trans. Arthur Goldhammer (Chicago: University of Chicago Press, 1983).

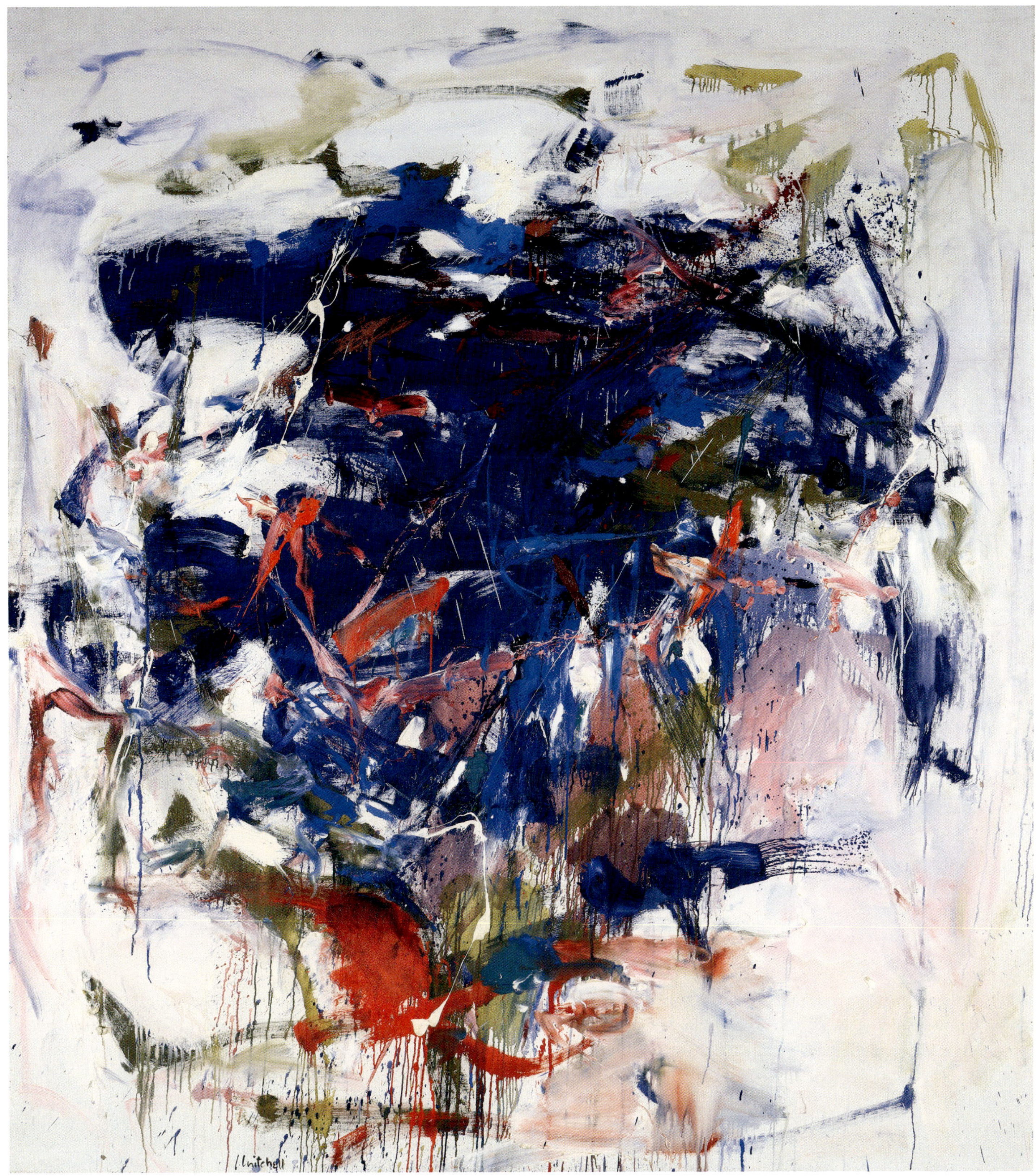

126.

Rock Bottom, 1960–1961

Oil on canvas
78 × 68 in. (198.2 × 172.8 cm)
Gift of Mari and James A. Michener
1991.276

Provenance: Purchased by James Michener from Stable Gallery, New York, 1961; long-term loan to The University of Texas at Austin, 1968–1991
Signed lower left "Mitchell"

Jesús Moroles

b. Corpus Christi, Texas, 1950

w. Denton, Texas, 1976–1978; El Paso, 1978–1979; Pietrasanta, Italy, 1979–1980; Rockport, Texas–Cerrillos, New Mexico, 1981–present

Jesús Moroles creates granite sculpture for both indoor and outdoor settings. He prefers granite because it is an exceptionally hard "living stone" that is pushed up from the center of the earth.[1] Moroles recalls that when he first began working in granite "it was so consuming that I got lost in it. . . . I realized that I had found something that was actually fighting back and resisting. I really liked that struggle."[2]

The Blanton's *Spirit Inner Column* (1994, plate 127) is a rectangular monolith of pink granite with an S-shaped inner core revealed by parallel horizontal incisions in the stone. Although bilaterally symmetrical, *Spirit Inner Column* possesses a distinct front and back: the incisions are cut deep into the stone on three sides of the upper portion of the work, while the serpentine shape is flush with the surface of the back. The highly polished areas of the front and back contrast with the rough stone of the sides and inner column. The extensive amount of stone that Moroles cut away, as well as the dynamic grace of the curving inner column, convey a quality of lightness that belies the substantial nature of the sculpture's size and medium.

Moroles refers to the parallel cantilevered platforms of *Spirit Inner Column* and related works as mesas or tables, a term used to describe the flat mountains of New Mexico. The Blanton's sculpture belongs to his Female series, which he began in 1984.[3] Moroles explains that for him "*spirit* . . . means curves."[4] He created this series in conjunction with another series, exemplified by *Las Mesas Zig Zag #2* (1985) and *Zig Zag Las Mesas* (1986), which contain a zigzagged inner core that suggests the more angular forms of the male body.

Moroles's work often challenges the physical properties of stone. The cantilevered mesas of *Spirit Inner Column* push the tensile strength of granite to its limits. In the late 1980s Moroles began literally weaving granite. The monumental warp and weft of works like *Granite Weaving* (1995) and *Granite Weaving Playscape* (1996) address the themes of mutuality and coexistence. The artist explained, "The granite weavings are done in rows. I made strands of granite yarn; if you pull one out it falls apart like fabric."[5]

Moroles grew up in Dallas and studied sculpture and industrial arts at North Texas State University, where he initially created abstract sculpture in bronze, ceramic, and wood.[6] During his senior year, he switched to stone: limestone, marble, serpentine, and, ultimately, granite. After graduation in 1978, he worked for a year as an assistant to the figurative sculptor Luis Jiménez in El Paso. Moroles spent the following year in Europe, first and primarily in Pietrasanta, Italy, near the marble quarries of Carrara, where he experimented with different styles of sculpture, and then in Paris, where he visited museums and studied the stonework of medieval cathedrals, especially Notre Dame. Moroles admires the sculpture of Isamu Noguchi, Eduardo Chillida, Pablo Picasso, and Constantin Brancusi and considers Noguchi a particularly strong influence on his work. "Because of him," he noted, "I am able to do stone carving and still be considered a contemporary artist."[7]

One of the salient characteristics of Moroles's work is the combination of raw and worked stone, a theme he identified early in his career. On one of his last days in Pietrasanta, he climbed Altissimo, "the mountain where Michelangelo would get his white marble."[8] Moroles set off on his journey early, passing through the last villages on the way to the summit before daybreak. Just when he reached the peak, there was an explosion; later he learned that it was a dynamite blast announcing the Day of the Carvers. As Moroles descended the mountain, he realized that the steps he was treading had been "foot carved" from hundreds of years of people choosing the same route. The center of the stones had been worn smooth by shoes rubbing the same spots, while the sides remained rough with grass growing over the edges. Because it was still early, dew on the stones made them translucent. For Moroles, these steps, which combined unworked stone, stone that had been touched by man, and growing vegetation, epitomized the balance, harmony, and coexistence between people and nature that he wanted to show in his work.

One of the ways Moroles achieves a balance between raw and worked stone is by *tearing* the granite, a quarrying technique he has adopted, which allows the natural breaking points of the stone to determine the direction of the sculpture's final form.[9] In almost all of Moroles's work, including the Blanton's *Spirit Inner Column*, completely unworked areas of rough stone remain, contrasting in color and texture with highly polished surfaces. Usually Moroles draws directly on the stone before carving, which is done with a saw instead of a chisel, another technique that contributes to the distinctive appearance of his sculpture.

Moroles's work is exhibited internationally, and he often receives commissions to create large-scale public sculptures, such as those recently situated throughout China. Since 1982 he has worked from a studio in Rockport, Texas, where he currently employs a crew of approximately a dozen assistants, some of whom are members of his family. He also occasionally works in Cerrillos, New Mexico, and in 1996 he opened a multidisciplinary cultural center there that hosts an artist-in-residence program designed to bring artists from other countries to New Mexico and to promote the international exchange of ideas among artists.

Nancy Deffebach

Notes

1. Andrew Simons, "Art Set in Stone," *Denver Post*, March 12, 1998. The article reviews an exhibition that included the Blanton's *Spirit Inner Column*.
2. Jesús Moroles, "Jesús Moroles: A Conversation with Jesús Moroles," interview by R. William McCarter, available at http://www.artsednet.getty.edu/ArtsEdNet/Resources/Moroles/interview.html [November 20, 2000].

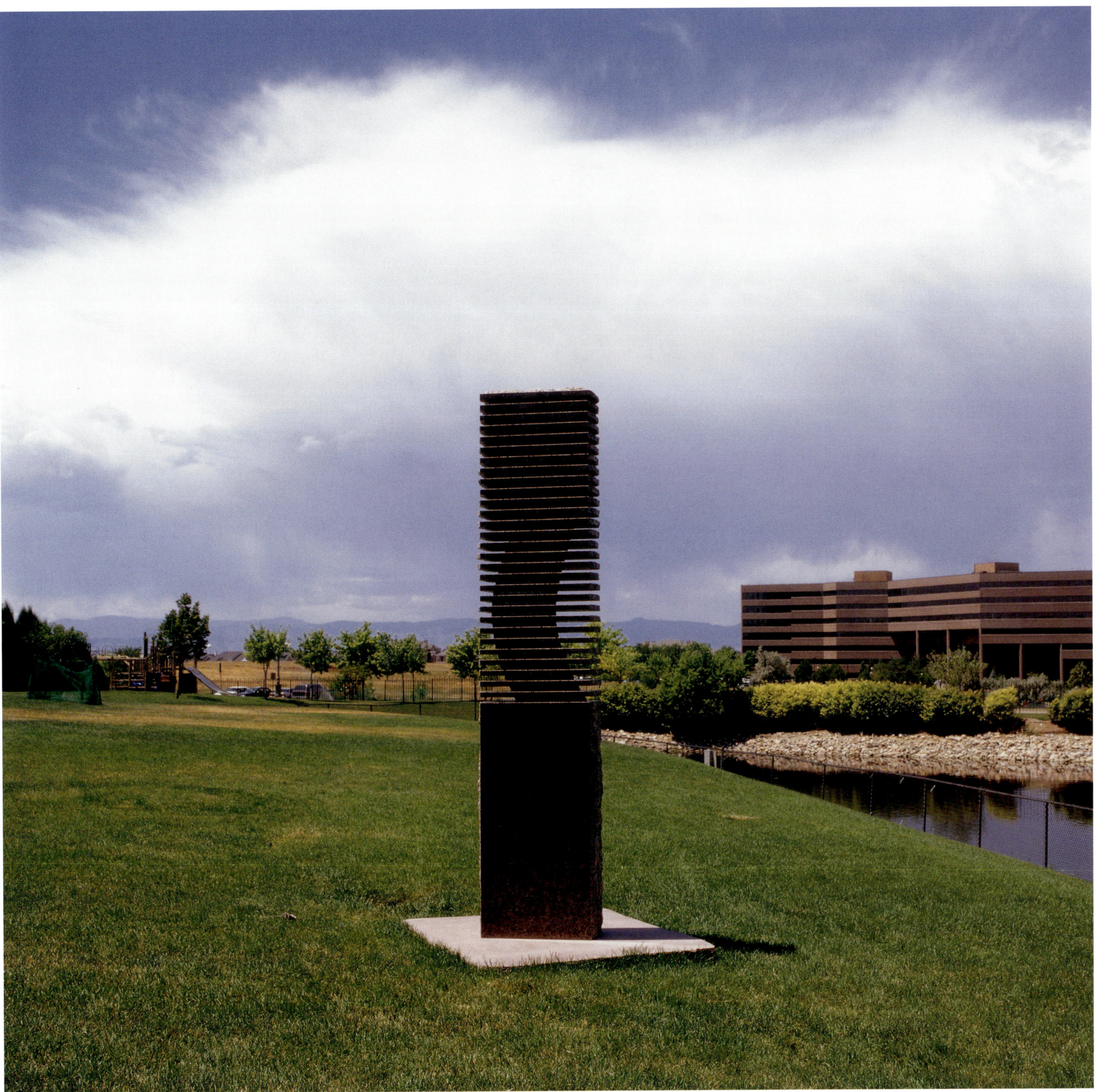

3. The first work in the series was *Spirit Inner Column* (1984) in the collection of Mr. and Mrs. Alan Rudy of Houston, Texas.
4. Jesús Moroles, interview with the author, Rockport, Texas, May 25, 2000.
5. Kathleen McCloud, "Jesús Moroles: Taking Sculpture for Granite," *New Mexican* [Santa Fe], July 19, 1996.
6. As a teenager Moroles created figurative paintings and drawings and ran his own silkscreen business.
7. Moroles, interview with the author.
8. Moroles, "Jesús Moroles: A Conversation with Jesús Moroles."
9. "Tearing" is a quarrying technique in which holes are drilled into the stone and pressure is applied in order to extract large boulders from the quarry.

127.

Spirit Inner Column, 1994

Texas pink granite
106 × 22½ × 10⅜ in. (269.2 × 57.2 × 26.4 cm)
Purchase as a gift of Mary and Jack Bartholow
1999.23

Provenance: Purchased by Mary and Jack Bartholow for the museum from the artist, 1998

Robert Motherwell

Aberdeen, Washington, 1915–Provincetown, Massachusetts, 1991

w. Palo Alto, California, 1932–1937; Cambridge, Massachusetts, 1937–1938; Paris, 1938–1940; New York (summers in Easthampton, New York, and Provincetown, and trips to Spain and France, 1958, and Italy, 1960), 1940–1970; New York–Greenwich, Connecticut, 1970–1991

Robert Motherwell was the youngest and most formally educated of the Abstract Expressionists. He earned an undergraduate degree in philosophy from Stanford University in 1937. During a year at Oxford, he began a thesis on the writings of Eugène Delacroix and traveled extensively in Europe. Motherwell studied philosophy at Harvard University before deciding to move to New York in 1940. There he enrolled at Columbia University to study art history under the prominent scholar Meyer Schapiro, who encouraged him to pursue painting and introduced him to the Surrealist artists who had immigrated to New York from war-torn Europe. In 1941, through the Surrealist artist Matta, Motherwell met William Baziotes, Jackson Pollock, and other young American artists who would become associated with the New York School. He had his first exhibition at Peggy Guggenheim's influential gallery, Art of this Century, just two years later.

Motherwell was one of the few American artists admitted into the close-knit group of exiled Surrealists. Thanks in large part to his fluency in French, he quickly became a bridge between the Surrealists and the younger New York artists, to whom he transmitted Surrealist ideas and techniques.[1] These artists developed a particular interest in the Surrealist technique of psychic automatism—a stream of conscious, free-association method of drawing that allowed them to express their innermost thoughts, memories, and desires more directly than with methods of symbolic representation.[2] However, Motherwell and his friends eventually abandoned psychic automatism because they felt it did not allow for deliberate artistic decision-making.

More than any other artist of his generation, Motherwell remained engaged with the art and literature of European modernists such as Guillaume Apollinaire, Stéphane Mallarmé, Piet Mondrian, and the Dada poets.[3] He shared many formal concerns with these earlier modernists, but as with other Abstract Expressionists, his primary concern was to communicate his subjective experience—a concern that echoed Jean-Paul Sartre's philosophy of Existentialism and implied the necessity of making ethical choices. In the late 1940s Motherwell and art critic/poet Harold Rosenberg coedited a short-lived magazine, *Possibilities,* that synthesized Existentialism and a certain strain of Marxism and emphasized the idea that art proceeded directly from the artist's identity. As Rosenberg wrote in an essay on Arshile Gorky, "In art of our time, the identity of the artist is a paramount theme. The concept of art as creation brings the artist literally into the picture. The process by which the work comes into being often constitutes the content of the work; the artist's activities furnish its 'plot.'"[4] This interpretation of the artistic process stood in contradistinction to the views of prominent art critic Clement Greenberg, who focused instead on formal concerns and the two-dimensionality of painting. These polarities are evident in reviews of Motherwell's 1961 exhibition at the Janis Gallery, where the Blanton's *Painting* (1960, plate 128) debuted. One review provided strictly formal descriptions of his paintings, while another addressed their autobiographical aspects, calling Motherwell "the most personal of the New York artists."[5]

Motherwell also shared many views on the artistic process with French poet Mallarmé. Like Mallarmé, Motherwell believed that the most significant aspect of art was the process by which it was created, not the finished object or the image depicted. By the same token, he intended the title of the Blanton's *Painting* as a verb rather than a noun. As he explained in a 1974 letter, "It is a picture of what a painter does uniquely, at least to my way of thinking."[6]

Motherwell uses a limited color scheme in *Painting.* The work exhibits a subdued range of earth tones, including a large area of ochre in the composition's center, which is surrounded by drips of black paint, and an ominous black band at the far right. The forms, which one reviewer described as "obese and ungainly" and "suggestive of the soft underbelly of being,"[7] give *Painting* an organic quality, as does Motherwell's handling of paint. The artist applied pigment in a seemingly haphazard manner with smears, smudges, and splatters evocative of an immediate creative force that he purposefully sought in all his paintings.

Although *Painting* is an eccentric and not altogether successful work, Motherwell secured his place in history with two major accomplishments. He was responsible, in part, for exposing the young artists of the New York School to a new mode of expression—psychic automatism—thus setting off the experiments of postwar abstraction. Moreover, Motherwell's masterful suite of Elegies to the Spanish Republic, an epic series begun in 1949 and continued into the 1970s, demonstrate how abstraction can also be read as an eloquent commentary on the human condition.

Valerie Hellstein

Notes

1. Stephanie Terenzio, ed., *The Collected Writings of Robert Motherwell* (New York: Oxford University Press, 1992), 113.
2. Stephen Polcari, *Abstract Expressionism and the Modern Experience* (New York: Cambridge University Press, 1991), 359.
3. Motherwell edited the series Documents of Modern Art, which published English translations of writings by major modernists.
4. Quoted in Brian Winkenweder, "Art History, Sartre and Identity in Rosenberg's America," *Art Criticism* 13, no. 2 (1998): 85.
5. D. J., "Robert Motherwell," *Arts Magazine* 35 (May 1961): 84, and Irving Sandler, "Robert Motherwell," *Art International* 5 (June 1961): 44.
6. Robert Motherwell to Michael Danoff, January 28, 1974, Blanton Museum of Art Archives, The University of Texas at Austin.
7. Sandler, 44.

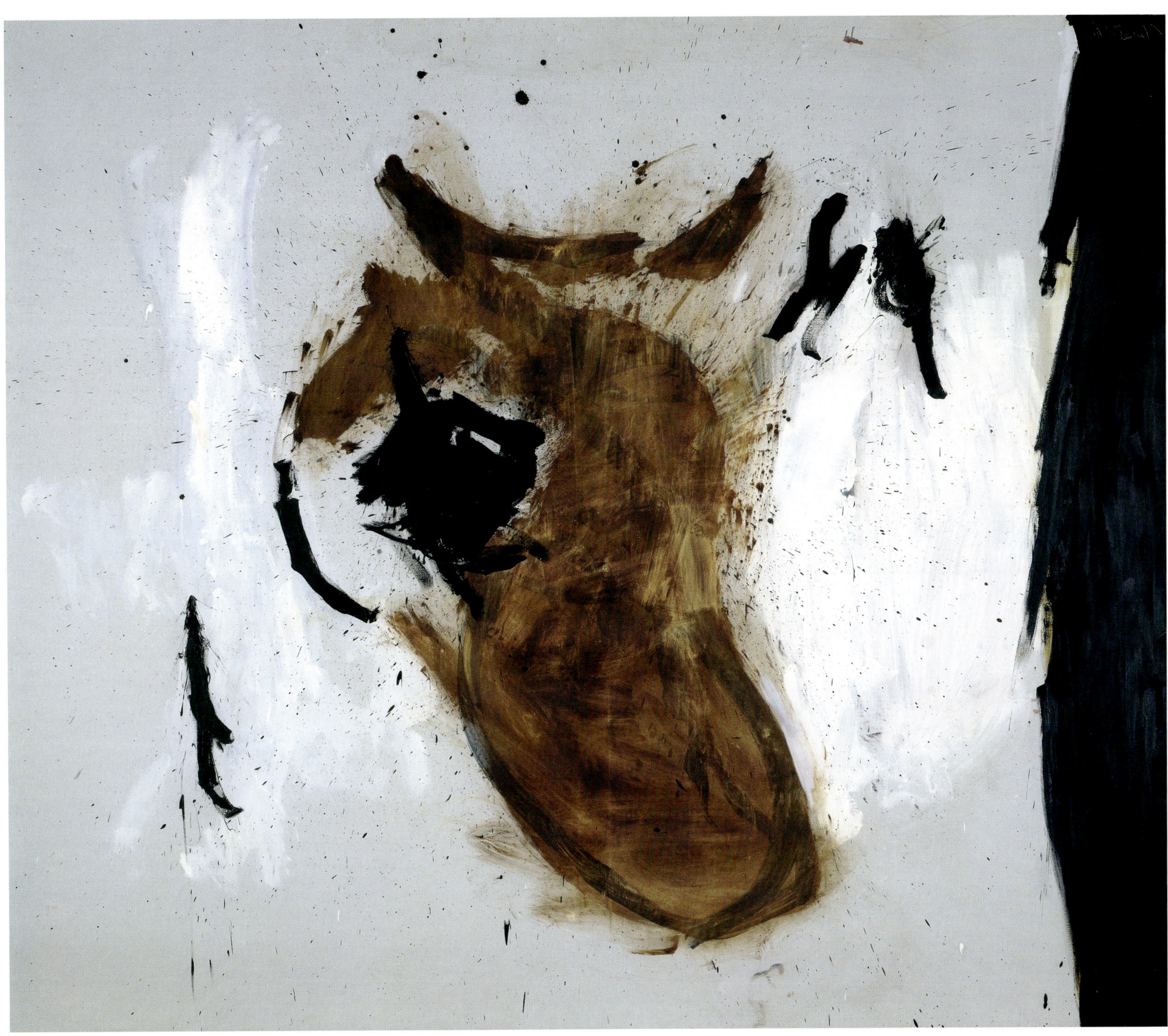

128.

Painting, 1960

Oil on canvas
83 × 96 in. (213 × 244 cm)
Gift of Mari and James A. Michener
G1968.99

Provenance: Purchased by James Michener from Sidney Janis Gallery, New York, 1961

Celia Alvarez Muñoz

b. El Paso, 1937

w. Arlington, Texas, 1975–1977; Arlington–Denton, Texas, 1977–1982; Arlington, 1982–present

Celia Alvarez Muñoz explores familial nostalgia as well as the elasticity of language and memory in works that cross media boundaries. Weaving together the personal and political, she questions the ways that we perceive and present ourselves, using the artifice of photography to prove her point. Muñoz often adopts the voice of a child to make clever, sometimes even perverse observations about the porous boundaries between fiction and fact, truths and lies. Truth, the artist seems to suggest, is a human construction.

Born in El Paso, Texas, in 1937, Muñoz worked both as a fashion illustrator for a department store and as an art educator during the 1960s and 1970s. She was forty years old when she enrolled in graduate school at the University of North Texas in Denton in 1977. It was there that she realized her deep-seated fascination with words and her "inherent feel for semantics and syntax, and for being a formal imagist."[1] As a graduate student, Muñoz began to experiment with pairing texts and images, especially photographs. The narrative-based work of Mexican printmaker José Guadalupe Posada, the mixed-media projects of her professor, Vernon Fisher, and the conceptual photography of Duane Michals exerted a profound influence on her work, as did the photographic montages of Barbara Kruger and the language-based art of Jenny Holzer.[2] Like Muñoz, Holzer and Kruger create subversive, complex, conceptually layered works, but whereas those by Holzer and Kruger address issues of power, gender, and social conditioning, those by Muñoz are intimately tied to memory, place, and knowledge.

Made between 1980 and 1985, the Enlightenment series is a collection of ten works, each comprised of separate pages that together function like an unbound book. Each of the ten works presents a short story. Combining staged photographs with text written in the voice of Muñoz's remembered childhood self, these stories recount specific experiences in the artist's transition from childhood to adulthood. In their direct and conversational prose, they subtly note the role that family wisdom, religion, and myth played in mediating that transition.

In *Enlightenment #4: Which Came First?* (1982, plate 129), Muñoz weaves a narrative that deftly addresses the multiple possibilities for misinterpretation that exist in bilingual communities. More specifically, the work recounts two experiences that overlapped historically and psychologically: the difficulty Muñoz faced conjugating the verb "to lay" and her struggle to understand the mechanics of sexual reproduction as a young girl growing up on the Texas/Mexico border.

Five separate pages make up *Which Came First.* At the top of each page, Muñoz presents one or two photographs of eggs resting against a yolk yellow background. Below the photographs are typed sentences that reminisce about how "Learning to speak English and understanding chickens were the hardest things for me during the primary grades," as one of them reads. Underneath these lines of typed text Muñoz pasted slips of paper from what appears to be a child's grammar notebook. Each sentence, written out in careful, pencil-drawn cursive letters, is an exercise in conjugation: "The chicken will lay an egg tomorrow. . . . The chicken has laid an egg already." Here sexual and linguistic confusion collide, the latter reinforcing and exacerbating the former, with altogether witty results. As a child, Muñoz would wait for hours hoping to see a chicken lay an egg through its mouth, which is how her grandmother explained the reproductive process to her. Eventually, however, she realized the truth. "The chicken lies everyday," Muñoz wrote on the final panel of *Which Came First.* Punning on the words *lying* and *laying,* the artist points to her grandmother's lie and, in pointing, alludes to the fact that she now has mastered the intricacies of language and the subtleties of reproduction. Ultimately, *Which Came First* borrows elements of Muñoz's biography to comment on the nature of language, specifically the role that it plays in actively constructing, as opposed to merely passively transmitting, knowledge. Although he was writing about a later body of work, the comments of critic Robert L. Pincus hold true for *Which Came First:* "Muñoz's words and pictures have the terse feel of parable—surface simplicity, rich implications."[3]

As much as they represent her attempts to understand the world in terms of family, personal history, and community dynamics, Muñoz's projects also explore Mexican American identity as manifest in bilingual wordplay and storytelling while simultaneously touching upon the universal quest for self-awareness and enlightenment. Throughout her work, Muñoz strikes a delicate balance between the personal and the collective, the private and the public, the specific and the general. Said Muñoz: "These topics are everyone's questions and examinations about a very basic fact: our tragic human condition—of being vulnerable and yet cocky, or ignorant and yet arrogant, knowing and disguising it."[4]

Since the 1980s Muñoz has moved from book works such as the Enlightenment series to larger format images and site-specific installation projects. These include a lyrical commission for the Historic Civic Center River Link Project in San Antonio; a collaboration with Mexican architect Ricardo Legorreta on the design for the Latino Cultural Center of Dallas; and a photographic residency at Blue Star Art Space in San Antonio. Despite changes in scale and media, however, her projects continue to prod the distinctions between stories and histories, myths and truths, in an effort to flesh out how we understand (and occasionally misunderstand) our relationship to the world around us. As Muñoz said, "The question is, then, what's real or invented?"[5]

Laura A. Lindenberger

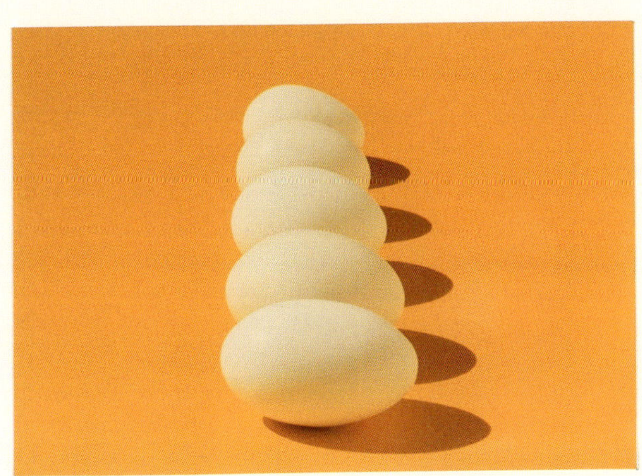

Learning to speak English and understanding chickens were the hardest things for me during the primary grades.

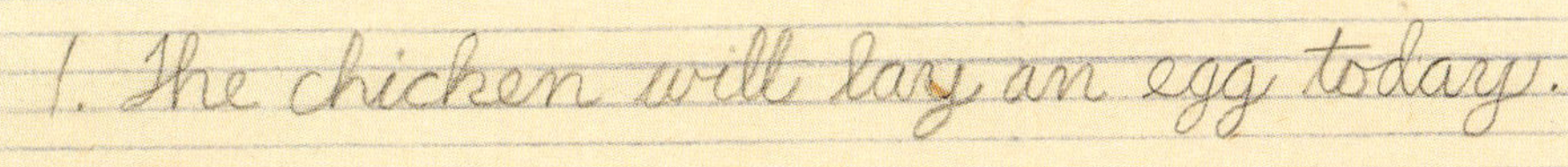

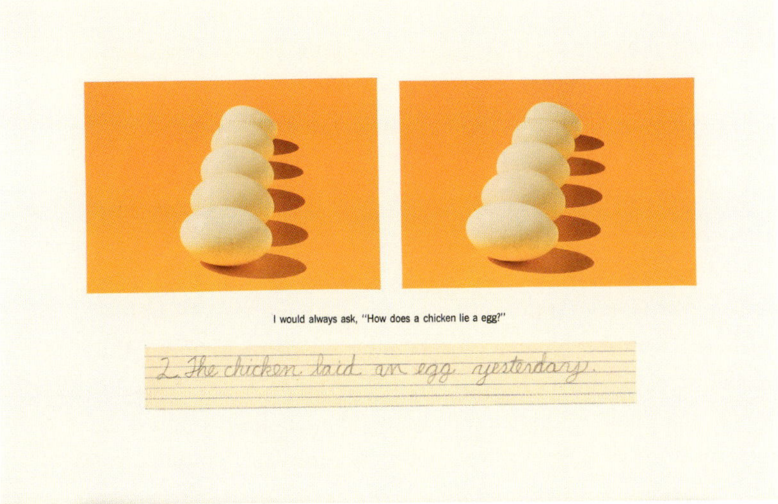

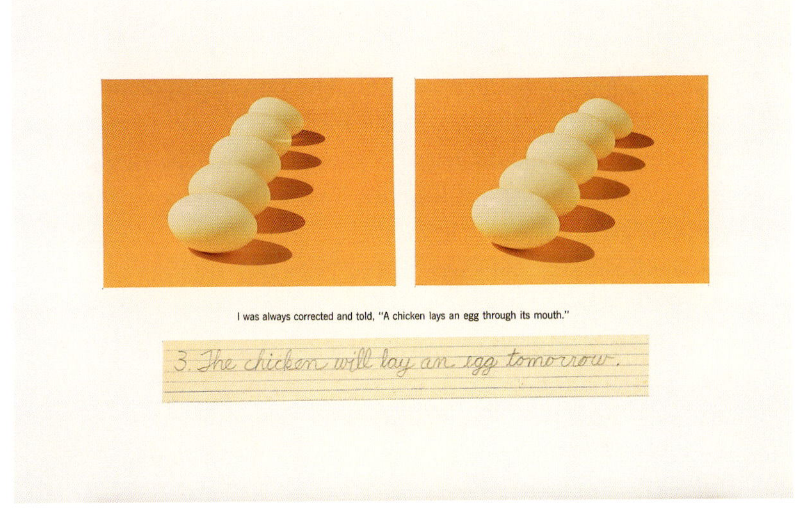

Notes

1. Celia Alvarez Muñoz, "An Interview with Celia Alvarez Muñoz," interview by Benito Huerta, in *Stories Your Mother Never Told You* (Arlington, Tex.: The Gallery at UTA, 2002), 19.
2. Annette DiMeo Carlozzi, "Truth and Consequences," in *Stories Your Mother Never Told You*, 9.
3. Robert L. Pincus, "Celia Alvarez Muñoz at the Museum of Contemporary Art," *Art in America* 79 (December 1991): 125.
4. Muñoz, 18.
5. Muñoz, 17.

129.

Enlightenment #4: Which Came First? [details], 1982

Five color photographs, letterpress on rag paper, and graphite on Gekkeikan Homespun paper in curly maple box
Edition 5/10
Each sheet: 12 × 19 in. (30.5 × 48.3 cm)
Box: 1½ × 22¼ × 15 in. (3.8 × 56.5 × 38.1 cm)
Purchase through the generosity of the Blanton Contemporary Circle
2004.163.1/8–8/8

Provenance: Purchased from the artist, 2004

Wangechi Mutu

b. Nairobi, Kenya, 1972

w. Wales, 1988–1991; New York, 1992–1998; New Haven, Connecticut, 1998–2000; Brooklyn, New York, 2000–present

Kenyan born, Brooklyn-based artist Wangechi Mutu holds advanced degrees in both studio art and cultural anthropology, and the breadth of these interests is readily decipherable in her art—an oeuvre that includes video, installation, and two-dimensional mixed-media works.[1] To create her mixed media works on Mylar, Mutu quarries fashion magazines, *National Geographic*, books on aerial photography, and pornography with equal voracity. In doing so, she repeatedly takes the ethnographic no-no of the "other" to freakish visual extremes, but only so as to question how we view those different from ourselves. Mutu's images wed horror and beauty in ways that evokes multiple allegories—some historical, some cultural, some personal—and play them out across the tender landscape of feminine flesh.

Mutu's work speaks of ritualized body modifications and uneasy cultural collisions, injecting extreme violence into beauty, much like the disturbing union of technology and sex in J. G. Ballard's classic underground novel, *Crash* (1973). The artist inflicts traumatic impressions on the skin of the women she depicts—alterations that critique fetishized aspects of physical beauty like pillowy, bee-stung lips, impossibly perfect breasts, and lanky, almost pubescent extremities. Disarticulated limbs float atop distorted satellite imagery, oftentimes depicting aerial journeys across the African continent.[2] Violent splatters of dark ink erupt where inner and outer worlds might otherwise overlap. The sum of these parts creates a severely distorted yet oddly salacious outline of the female form.

Ethnicity, gender roles, place, beauty, and time: these notions are all culturally defined. For women in the West, the self-cannibalizing pursuit of physical perfection reigns supreme. Beauty ideals propagated by the famous and the affluent are an illusion; likewise, Mutu's women are surgically assembled. Individual parts are carefully chosen to approximate the size and shape of the limbs they stand in for. This, as well as the fact that the collages are practically seamless, creates an illusion of wholeness, an organicity that is quickly betrayed upon closer inspection, heightening the works' uncanny quality.

Once assembled, Mutu's distorted figures have as much to do with notions of beauty as with how such notions vary from culture to culture. Her creatures are made monstrously voluptuous by the exaggeration of certain features, in particular the lips and necks. Alterations are made with a precise hand, allowing the exotic ethnicity of her subjects to bleed through, surreptitiously exposed in the bridge of the nose, the haunted, almond-shaped eyes, the full mouth, and the subtle but shapely curve of the body.

In the Blanton's two works, both created in 2004, Mutu inserts yet another layer of complexity, exposing the role of figurative imagery as a sort of historical iconography of imperialism. The artist mines the conventions of Western portraiture, a practice in which the sitter's head, neck, and shoulders communicate the entirety of his or her bearing, character, and social status. In these instances, Mutu depicts two women: one in profile, the other in a three-quarters pose. Both mimic the posture of a society lady sitting for a portrait. Layering washes of color and collage, the artist creates two culturally hybridized and physically amalgamated images of varying brutality.

Both pieces explore a familiar sort of formal fracture; as in most of Mutu's works on Mylar, these women are partially assembled from readymade imagery. In *Untitled* (plate 131), Mutu substitutes an aerial landscape for a woman's chest, the breasts conspicuously bare and nipples protruding. Legs and a partial torso appropriated from fashion magazines or erotica form the woman's mouth and the lower portion of her face. These limbs are romanticized, rosy-colored, and glossy; still, they seem alien due to the reptilian texture applied to the woman's face and neck, where ink and acrylic splotches also resemble open sores.

The woman's neck is elongated and her eye narrowed and somewhat wary. An out-of-scale black child rides atop her head, forming an outlandish albeit ornamental circlet. Fluid spurts violently from the same area as if from a recent trauma. Its spray pattern makes the child's position and expression all the more suspect, intimate yet potentially injurious. During her 2004 residency at ArtPace, in San Antonio, Mutu drew a parallel between the violence depicted in her work and the genocidal carnage that tore Rwanda apart in 1994. Ethnic differences fueled by the preferential treatment of Tutsis over Hutus under colonial rule literally pitted neighbor against neighbor. This relationship was reflected in the intimate way in which the majority of some 800,000 people were slaughtered: by machetes, clubs, and sticks.[3] Vanquishers must be extremely close to their prey when using such weapons, close enough to look them in the eyes.

Mutu's second work (plate 130) is less overtly violent, but the presence of severed limbs and a significant splatter pattern reveal that this, too, does not depict a bloodless battle. Mutu rendered the work in a similar palette of dark brown and cream, applied in the same almost reptilian and scalelike manner. Shapely body parts suggest various facial structures, although these limbs seem more abjectly pornographic than those used in the previous image: the legs of a woman, spread-eagled with a hand resting between them, form the nose; the back of the head and neck are actually an arm and breast. Equally eroticized is the extremely large mouth, candied and slick with pink gloss, as if culled from a cosmetics advertisement.

A plume of honey-blonde hair protruding from the forehead puts a last, bizarre touch on the image and seems ornamental despite its odd placement. This element is questionable, both aesthetically and conceptually. Its addition makes the woman seem less human, beastly even, while also suggesting the uneasy hybridization of Western and African identities. Consider again the social connotations

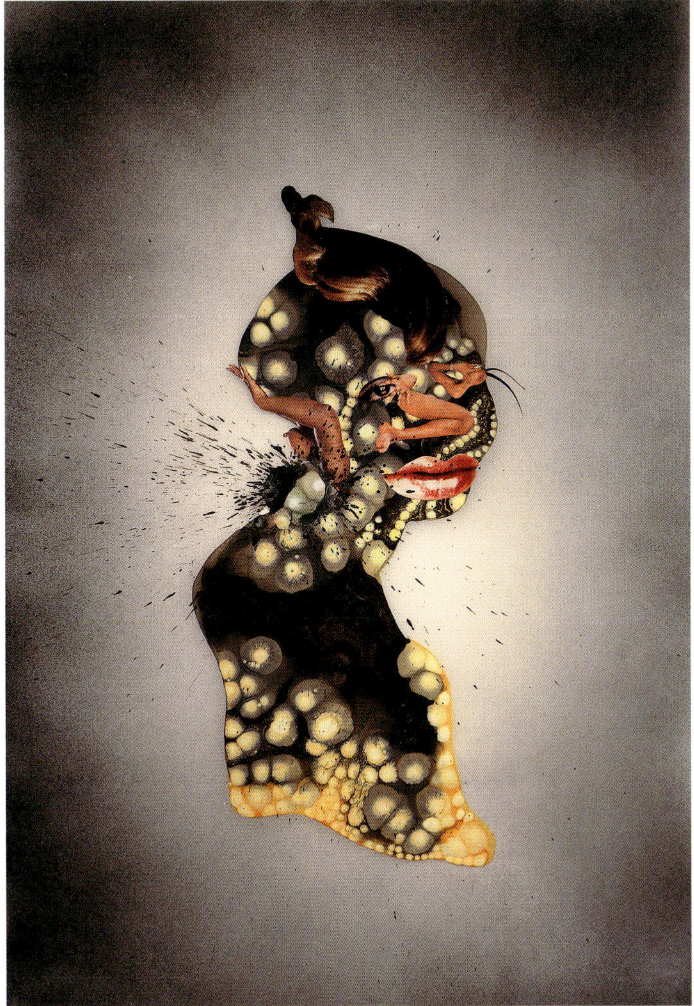

130.
Untitled, 2004
Ink, acrylic, collage, and mixed media on Mylar
36 15/16 × 25 1/2 in. (93.9 × 64.7 cm)
Partial and pledged gift of Jeanne and Michael Klein
T2005.4
Provenance: Purchased at the request of the museum by Jeanne and Michael Klein from Susanne Vielmetter Los Angeles Projects, 2005
Signed lower right "Wangechi Mutu"

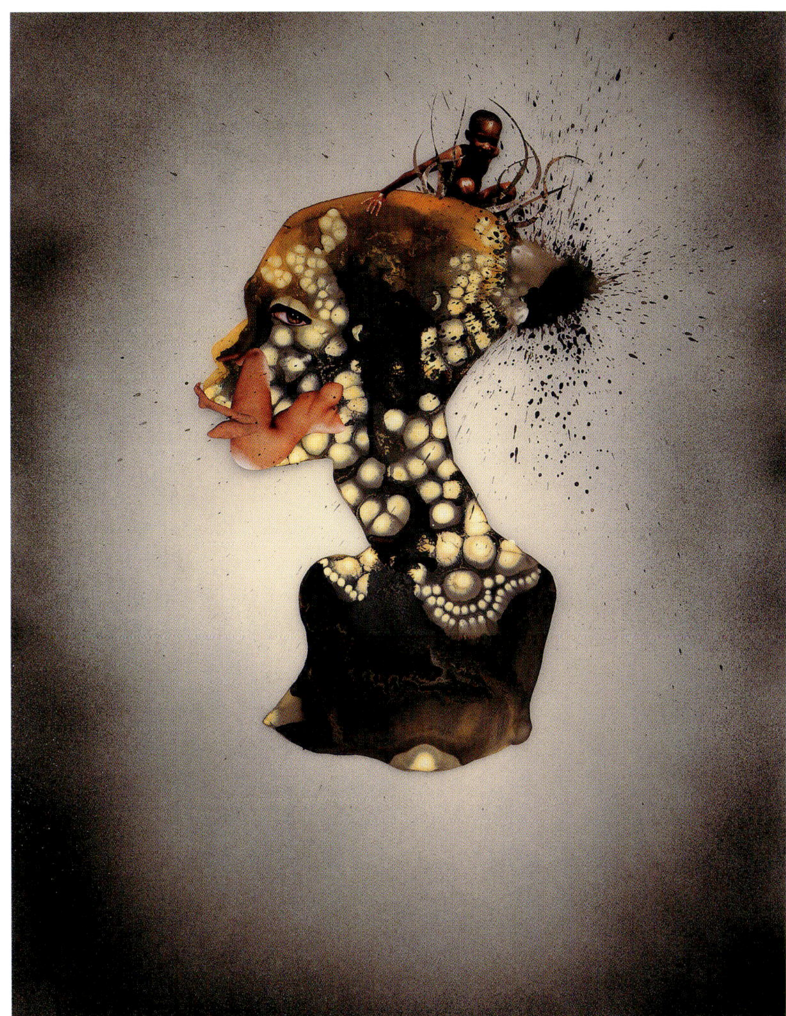

131.
Untitled, 2004
Ink, acrylic, collage, and mixed media on Mylar
36 × 27 1/4 in. (91.4 × 69.2 cm)
Partial and pledged gift of Jeanne and Michael Klein
T2005.5
Provenance: Purchased at the request of the museum by Jeanne and Michael Klein from Susanne Vielmetter Los Angeles Projects, 2005
Signed lower right "Wangechi Mutu"

of the portrait, a staple of polite Western society that reflects wealth, beauty, power, privilege, and taste.

Historical images of the indigenous populations of Africa, Asia, the Pacific, and the Americas emphasized something quite the contrary: squalid living conditions, ritual dress, tattoos, and unusual body modifications—in essence, the inferiority embedded in *otherness*. Although their appearance opened a new chapter in anthropological history, for the people they depicted, these images represented a rupture: the point in which cultural agency transferred from the native population to the colonial authorities.

This was a quiet battle waged across the continent of Africa for centuries, and Mutu's scarred creatures wear their wounds as both ornaments and lesions. However, if iconographic depiction still plays any role in establishing authority—in the confirming, denying, or transference of power—perhaps this work also speaks to the possible disintegration of traditional Western power structures in a critique that operates on the overlapping fronts of gender and race. Through works such as those in the Blanton's collection, Mutu speaks without omitting the painful, all the while making the battle seem startlingly beautiful.

Anjali Gupta

Notes

1. Mutu studied in Wales before moving to the United States to attend Cooper Union in New York, where she received a BFA in 1996, and Yale University, where she received her MFA in 2000.
2. Information available at http://archive.blackvoices.com/articles/qa/ar20030305mutu.asp [April 28, 2005]. For additional information on Mutu, see Merrily Kerr, "Extreme Makeovers," *Art on Paper* 8 (July–August 2004): 28–29; Sonaya Murray, "Africaine," *NKA: Journal of Contemporary African Art*, no. 16–17 (fall–winter 2002): 88–93; and Carmela Ciuraru, "Cutting Remarks," *Artnews* 103 (November 2004): 116–17.
3. Information available at http://news.bbc.co.uk/1/hi/in_depth/africa/2004/rwanda/default.stm [April 28, 2005].

Alice Neel

Merion, Pennsylvania, 1900–New York, 1984

w. Philadelphia, 1921–1925; Havana, Cuba, 1926–1927; New York, 1927–1930; Philadelphia, 1930–1932; New York (trips to Europe, 1965, and Mexico and Europe, 1969), 1932–1984

Alice Neel is best known for the distinctive and compelling portraits that she painted throughout her long career. Whether celebrities or unknown children, the artist depicted her subjects with equal respect for their dignity and personal histories. Neel's portraits are deeply human as well as humane, penetrating beneath superficial likeness to reveal the inner spirit of her sitters. "Like Chichikov of Gogol's novel *Dead Souls,* I am a collector of souls," she famously wrote.[1] It is tempting to read her portraits as "conversations" between the artist and her sitters, since painting allowed Neel to understand as well as record her subjects and to overcome her sense of alienation by connecting with other people.[2]

Born and raised in Pennsylvania, Neel attended the Philadelphia School of Design for Women and committed herself to becoming an artist at a relatively young age. Loss and difficulty marked her personal life. Neel's first child, a daughter, died of diphtheria in 1927, and her second child, also a girl, was taken from her three years later by her husband, Carlos Enríquez. Distraught, she suffered a nervous breakdown and was hospitalized for a year. Neel moved to Greenwich Village in 1932 and soon became politically and socially active, briefly enlisting in the Communist Party. Her works from this period often reflect her socially conscious position. In 1938 Neel moved to Spanish Harlem and found subjects in her new surroundings, painting from models as well as from memory. During the Depression, from 1935 to 1943, she supported herself by working for the WPA Federal Art Project.[3]

Neel struggled to earn a living as an artist, painting in relative obscurity and with little financial or critical support for decades. Her lack of recognition can be attributed to the fact that she adhered to a figurative practice during the 1940s and 1950s when, under the sway of the influential critic Clement Greenberg, Abstract Expressionism dominated the New York art world. As Neel explained of her contrary position, "I am not against abstraction and feel in fact that every good work has abstract elements . . . but I was convinced that people and also psychological truths were important."[4]

Even though she went largely unnoticed by the public, Neel established a reputation in avant-garde circles and befriended many of the artists, critics, and writers of the day. Often these same individuals served as her sitters, as in the portraits of the young sculptor *Robert Smithson* (1962), the art historian *Meyer Schapiro* (1947 and 1983), and the artist *Faith Ringgold* (1977). Notably, Neel played the mother figure in the avant-garde Beat film, "Pull My Daisy" (1959), directed by Robert Frank and narrated by writer Jack Kerouac.

Although she worked within a portrait tradition that includes Anthony Van Dyck, Sir Joshua Reynolds, and John Singer Sargent, among others, Neel eschewed the idealizing and flattering manner used by these artists to represent their subjects. Indeed, she preferred the term "figure painting" or "painting of people" to "portrait" because of the conventions it typically implied.[5] Rather than depicting sitters realistically, Neel often emphasized particular characteristics or gestures to create a sense of their psychological state and personality. Her works can be shocking for their intimacy and unflinching depiction of the ravages of time and lived experience upon the body. Through her unidealized nudes and sympathetic depictions of countercultural icons, Neel challenged social stigmas regarding sexuality and race.

David Bourdon and Gregory Battcock (1970, plate 132) represents two gay men—a couple—sitting next to one another. Battcock, a critic and artist, published a number of critical anthologies on subjects including Minimalism, Performance Art, and American cinema. Bourdon was also a well-known New York–based critic, serving as a correspondent for *The Village Voice* and *Life* magazine in the 1960s and publishing monographs on Christo and Jeanne-Claude, Alexander Calder, and Andy Warhol. In the painting, the unshaven Battcock, dressed in underwear and a pair of red socks, averts his gaze. In contrast, Bourdon is elegantly attired in a brown suit and tie, his elongated fingers draped over the chair arm. Neel frequently depicted subjects in her home and repeatedly used recognizable props and furniture, as in the blue and white striped chair seen here.

David Bourdon and Gregory Battcock is an exceptional example of Neel's work, exuding a sense of immediacy and freshness. "I want it to spring right out of the canvas," she once said of her art.[6] To achieve this end, Neel varied the application of paint, using strong expressionistic brushstrokes to define the background and foreground space while leaving areas of canvas near the bottom edge open and "unfinished." Her masterful use of color is evident in the sitters' faces and hands, which are comprised of pink, blue, green, violet, and yellow as well as more conventional flesh tones, and in the ultramarine blue outlining their bodies. The artist created tension within the picture plane by dividing the composition in half; the lower zone is painted with warm reds and oranges, the upper with chilly blues. Neel maintained the sense of contrast between the two subjects beyond their apparel; even as they are turning toward one another, their gazes do not intersect and their chairs occupy different spatial planes. As one writer noted, "It is a devastatingly unnerving portrait of a relationship that has gone irrevocably wrong."[7] Not for the first time, Neel had intuited a breakup and prophesized it on canvas.

Neel finally gained critical recognition late in life, and in 1974 the Whitney Museum of American art honored her with a retrospective. Since her death in 1984, appreciation of her paintings has continued to rise, culminating in a retrospective at the Philadelphia Museum of Art in 2000. The artist is now acknowledged as one of the foremost painters and portraitists of her generation.

Charlotte Cousins

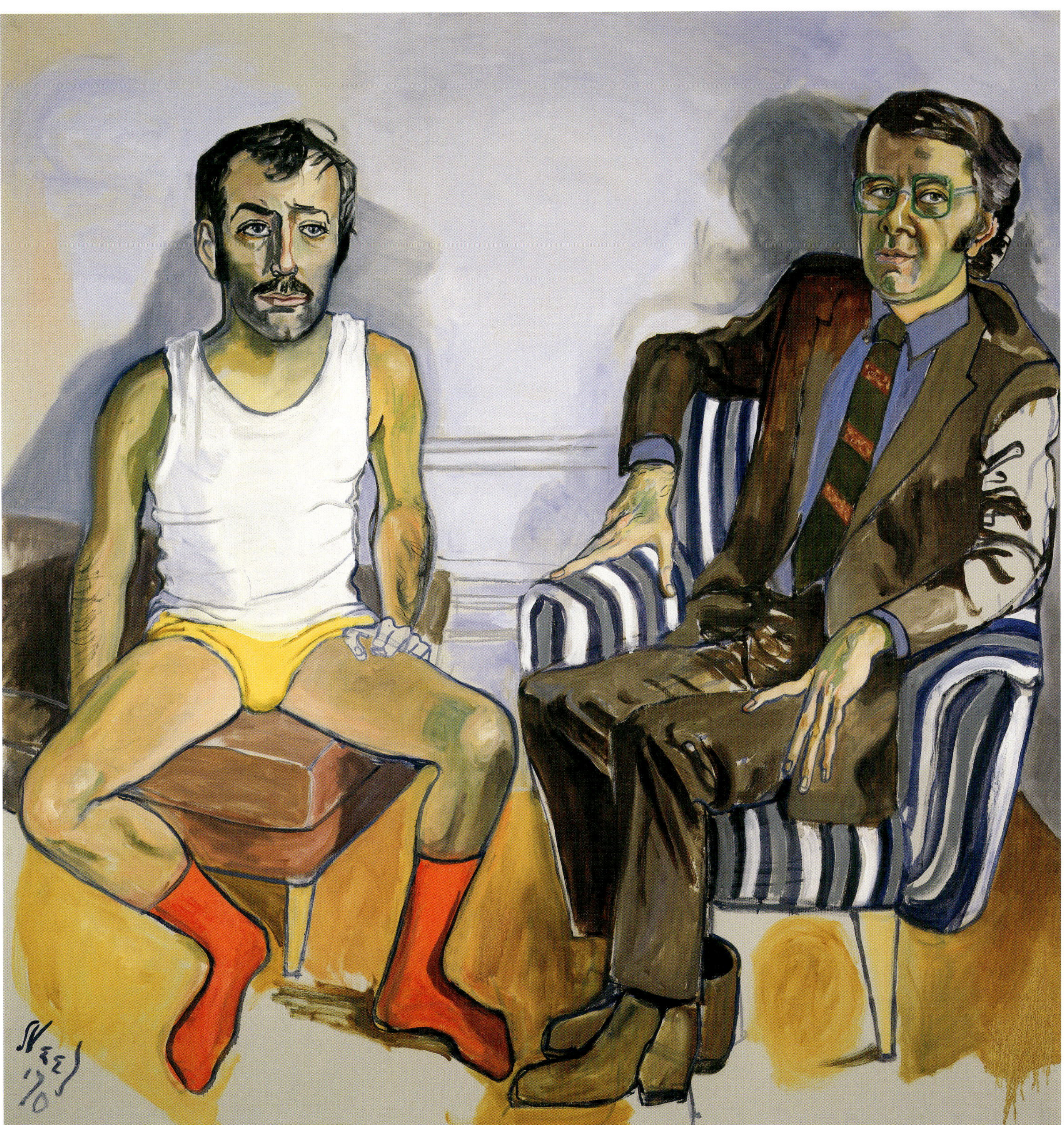

Notes

1. Alice Neel, "Alice Neel," *Art International* 12 (May 15, 1968): 48.
2. Judith Higgins, "Alice Neel and the Human Comedy," *Artnews* 83 (October 1984): 72.
3. Alice Neel, "Interview with Alice Neel," interview by Frederick Ted Castle, in *Alice Neel: Paintings since 1970* (Philadelphia: Pennsylvania Academy of the Arts, 1985), n.p. Reprinted from the October 1983 issue of *Artforum*. Neel explained, "You see, I did [sketched] all the neighborhoods of New York for the WPA. I would go out into the street and make a little sketch and just write the names of the colors in it and then go home and paint it from memory. I did a huge body of work."
4. Quoted in Higgins, 72.
5. Higgins, 72.
6. Quoted in Higgins, 77.
7. Richard Flood, "Gentlemen Callers: Alice Neel and the Art World," in Ann Temkin, ed., *Alice Neel* (New York: Harry N. Abrams, 2000), 59.

132.

David Bourdon and Gregory Battcock, 1970

Oil on canvas
59¾ × 56 in. (151.8 × 142.2 cm)
Archer M. Huntington Museum Fund
1983.13

Provenance: Purchased from Graham Gallery, New York, 1982
Signed lower left "Neel '70"

Louise Nevelson

Pereyaslav, Russia, 1899–New York, 1988
w. New York, 1920–1931; Munich, 1931; New York, 1932–1988

In 1959 Dorothy Miller, then curator of Paintings and Sculpture at The Museum of Modern Art in New York, invited Louise Nevelson to contribute to the upcoming exhibition *Sixteen Americans.* Up to this point in her career, Nevelson had built her reputation on the color black, both in stand-alone sculptures and in her environment *Moon Garden + One,* shown in 1958. "She didn't bother to say yes or no," Miller remembered. "She just said, 'Dear, we'll do a white show . . . Don't tell anybody, it'll be a surprise.'"[1] Later that year, the installation *Dawn's Wedding Feast* made its debut to an enthusiastic, if somewhat bemused, reception.

Dawn's Presence—Two Columns (1969–1975, plate 133) was not present at that feast, but photographs of the installation, along with this work's title and monochromatic palette, testify to a familial relationship.[2] In fact, much of *Dawn's Wedding Feast* exists now only in photographs; Nevelson broke up the larger pieces, only to subsequently resurrect them in the form of other works—a frequent practice on her part.

According to critics such as Hilton Kramer, Robert Rosenblum, and Sidney Tillim, Nevelson's environments were the sculptural equivalents of Abstract Expressionist painting, which dominated the New York art world in the mid-1950s.[3] These environments, comprised of wall units and freestanding columns, combine the surface complexity and energy of Jackson Pollock's carefully controlled drips and splatters with the brooding mystery evoked by Mark Rothko's floating color fields or Clyfford Still's thickly impastoed, cataclysmic compositions. Likewise, Nevelson's environments evoke complex, visceral responses in the viewer—in part because they so assertively occupy space as a result both of their scale and the minimal intrusion of a base.[4]

Born Leah Berliawsky in 1899 in Russia, Nevelson, her older brother, and their mother immigrated to the United States in 1905 to join her father, who had settled three years earlier in Rockland, Maine. In 1920 she moved to New York with her husband, Charles Nevelson, and began to dabble in singing and acting (about a decade later, she would also explore modern dance), nurturing the theatrical sensibility that would later inform her sculptural installations. Nevelson began the serious study of art in 1929, when she enrolled in classes at the Art Students League. Beginning in the autumn of 1931, she spent about ten months in Europe and studied briefly in Hans Hofmann's school in Munich.

By the early 1930s Nevelson was turning with increasing interest to sculpture. Her early efforts were largely figural and executed in clay and plaster. By the 1940s she had begun to experiment with wood, a medium considered rather old-fashioned and quaint at the time; Nevelson herself thought of wood as "closer to the feminine" than the metal favored by her male contemporaries, like David Smith and Alexander Calder.[5] From the beginning, she worked with discarded scraps, free and abundant during the war years. She would subject these scraps to a process of "translation" and "transformation," as she described it,[6] saturating them with black paint by dipping them directly into the pigment, then combining them with other scraps to form a new whole. (Nevelson considered black her trademark; she always returned to it after working with white and, less successfully, gold paint.)[7] Scraps allowed her to work intuitively, to fit pieces together like a puzzle, as in *Dawn's Presence—Two Columns.* As Kramer noted, Nevelson's work arose in large part out of the Cubist wood constructions of Pablo Picasso, Jacques Lipchitz, and Henri Laurens, who likewise applied the practice of collage to sculpture, a practice involving appropriation from, rather than representation of, reality.[8] Nevelson also discovered affinities with the Surrealists, whose work had been shown at Julien Levy's New York gallery since the early 1930s. It is likely that she saw The Museum of Modern Art's landmark 1936 exhibition *Fantastic Art, Dada, Surrealism* as well, responding to "its theatricality, its emphasis on the unconscious, and its reverence for the rich associations of the found object."[9]

Nevelson first exhibited *Dawn's Presence—Two Columns* as part of a larger work, *Dawn's Presence—Two,* at Pace Gallery in New York in 1976. This installation was composed of seven or eight discrete sculptures, most of them columns or towers that were loosely arranged.[10] That earlier arrangement created an architectural impression, and, indeed, Nevelson often drew inspiration from Manhattan, which she viewed as an immense and ever-changing sculpture. The same year she showed *Dawn's Presence—Two,* she asserted, "All I need is to feel New York coming through the wall."[11]

Dawn's Presence—Two Columns, however, seems less architectonic than totemic, conveying an oracular presence, as if it were the guardian of hidden knowledge. The sculpture's vertical thrust is offset by the smaller, horizontal components of the column to the left, the bowed slats at midpoint, and the two small stacked triangles just above them. The three circles of the foremost column balance these linear elements, establishing a cyclical counterweight to the sculpture's vertical and horizontal lines. The bowed slats suggest, by only the slightest segments of their arcs, other horizontally aligned circles protruding into the viewer's space, creating an echo of the foremost column's circles. In the context of the sculpture as a whole, these are more than mere formal elements. Indeed, Nevelson has an uncanny gift for evoking other realms and dimensions using only the tossed-off scraps and debris of our familiar world.

In her wood sculptures, Nevelson brought together elements from three influential movements of the twentieth century, combining the surprising juxtapositions of Cubist collage with the intuitive invention of Surrealism and the emotional and phenomenological force of Abstract Expressionism. Nevelson's creations are presences the viewer

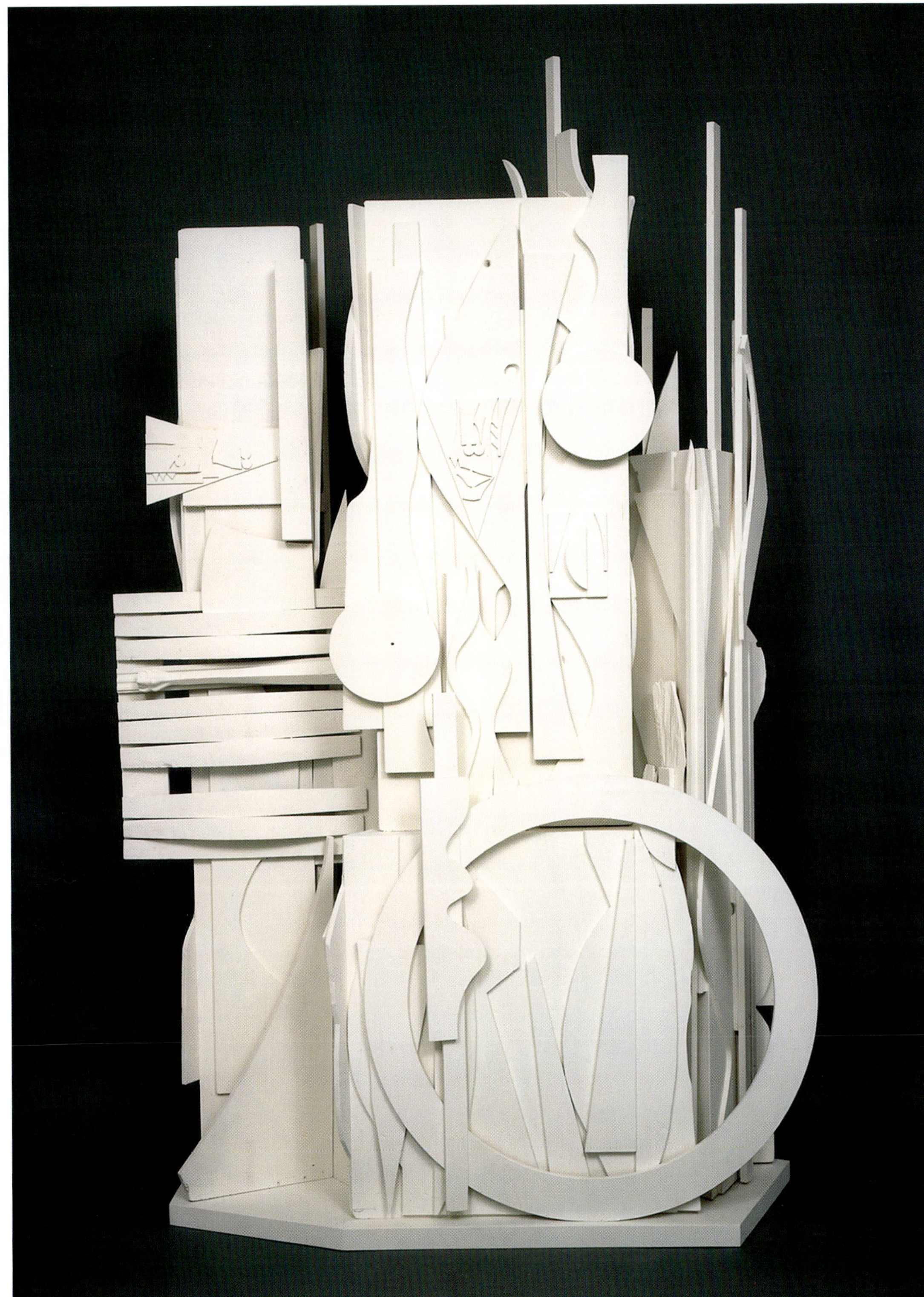

133.
Dawn's Presence—Two Columns, 1969–1975

Painted wood
116 × 70 9/16 × 31 in. (294.6 × 179.2 × 78.7 cm)
Purchase as a gift in memory of Laura Lee Scurlock Blanton by her children
2005.1

Provenance: Purchased from PaceWildenstein Gallery, New York, 2005

feels as much as sees, engages with rather than simply regards. The magic by which she conjured such strange beauty and power from such humble materials proves her to be one of the most original sculptors of the last half of the twentieth century, and perhaps the most inimitable.

John Devine

Notes

1. Quoted in Laurie Lisle, *Louise Nevelson: A Passionate Life* (New York: Summit Books, 1990), 220.
2. For photographs of *Dawn's Wedding Feast,* see Jean Lipman, *Nevelson's World* (New York: Whitney Museum of American Art, 1983), 116–18, and Edward Albee, *Louise Nevelson: Atmospheres and Environments* (New York: Clarkson Potter and Whitney Museum of American Art, 1980), 102–127, 187–88.
3. See Lisle, 210–11, and Arnold Glimcher, *Louise Nevelson* (New York: Praeger Publishers, 1972), 86.
4. See, for example, Hilton Kramer, "The Sculpture of Louise Nevelson," *Arts* 32 (June 1958): 29.
5. Diana MacKown, ed., *Dawns + Dusks: Taped Conversations with Diana MacKown* (New York: Charles Scribner's Sons, 1976), quoted in Lisle, 130.
6. *Louise Nevelson: Sculpture 1957–1987* (New York: PaceWildenstein Gallery, 1997), 24.
7. MacKown, 145.
8. Kramer, 27.
9. Lisle, 140.
10. For a photograph of *Dawn's Presence—Two,* see Lipman, 126.
11. Quoted in John Russell, "Despite Serious Ills, City Keeps Chin Up," *New York Times,* July 5, 1976, 17; quoted in Lisle, 282.

Kenneth Noland

b. Asheville, North Carolina, 1924

w. Asheville, North Carolina, 1946–1948; Paris, 1948–1949; Washington, D.C., 1949–1961; New York, 1961–1962; Vermont, 1962–2002; mid-coast Maine, 2002–present

Kenneth Noland's paintings served as a crucial bridge between the work of the New York School of the 1950s and the more austere forms of abstraction prevalent the 1960s. Noland studied at Black Mountain College in North Carolina between 1946 and 1948 with financial assistance from the GI Bill. Departing from what was then the dominant aesthetic, represented by Abstract Expressionists like Jackson Pollock and Willem de Kooning, Noland's instructors, Josef Albers and Ilya Bolotowsky, emphasized geometric abstraction and the constructivist sensibilities of the Bauhaus and Piet Mondrian's Neo-Plasticism. Noland traveled to Paris twice between 1948 and 1949 before settling in Washington, D.C., where he associated with what came to be known as the Washington Color Painters, a group that included such artists as Morris Louis, Leon Berkowitz, Sam Gilliam, and Gene Davis.

In the early 1950s Noland met three individuals who would go on to exert tremendous influence on his artistic development: Louis, Helen Frankenthaler, and the prominent art critic Clement Greenberg. Noland returned to Black Mountain College, where he heard Greenberg deliver a lecture on Abstract Expressionism, in the summer of 1950. Just two years later, while teaching at the Washington Workshop Center, he developed a close working relationship with fellow instructor Louis. When he and Louis visited New York in April 1953, Greenberg took them to meet Frankenthaler, who introduced them to the possibilities of staining paint into unprimed canvas, a technique that allowed color to fuse, quite literally, with the support. Although critics sometimes have referred to Noland as a Color Field painter, Greenberg coined the term "Post-Painterly Abstraction" in 1964 to describe the unique position that Noland, along with Louis and Frankenthaler, occupied between gestural and geometric painting.[1]

In the years following his fortuitous encounter with Frankenthaler, Noland experimented with the staining technique but continued to paint in the biomorphic, more gestural style that had characterized his work in the early 1950s.[2] Eventually, though, he synthesized this diverse array of approaches, simultaneously streamlining his formal vocabulary, to create his first body of mature work, a series of Circle paintings begun in 1958 and originally exhibited at French and Company in 1959.[3] *Split Spectrum* (plate 134), painted in 1961 at the height of his Circle series, is almost six feet square, a scale deliberately cued to the height of Noland's own body.[4] The painting is comprised of ten concentric rings that radiate out from the center of the canvas, their sequence echoing the order in which they were painted. Anchored by a solid core of dark rust, the rings alternate between sometimes pale, sometimes vivid colors and patches of bare canvas, where the rings are implied more so than demonstrated. (Here, as elsewhere, the absence of paint plays as active a role in Noland's composition as its presence.) The variations in hue, value, and intensity, from the bright red and somber ochre of the inner rings to the delicate lavender, brilliant yellow, and cool blue of the outer rings, generate a gentle, pulsating rhythm. As Noland once observed, "I do open paintings. I like lightness, airiness, and the way color pulsates."[5]

Color is only one of the ways that Noland animated the otherwise staid targetlike motif, striking a delicate balance between uniformity and spontaneity, deliberation and chance. Although the target's internal geometry might seem to demand it, Noland chose not to delineate the rings in pencil first (no marks are visible on the canvas), so subtle irregularities in width and spacing exist.[6] Nor did he go to extraordinary lengths to discipline the rings' soft, blurry edges, the unpredictable effects of acrylic paint thinned with turpentine soaking into and spreading across unprimed canvas.[7] In this respect, *Split Spectrum* exemplifies Noland's efforts to synchronize process and product. "We wanted the appearance to be the result of the process of making it—not necessarily to look like a gesture, but to be the result of real handling," he asserted.[8]

Split Spectrum demonstrates another important aspect of Noland's practice. In an attempt to subsume form to the imperatives of color, the artist relied on neutral, nonreferential, ready-made compositional motifs like the target—what Michael Fried referred to as literal, versus depicted, shapes. This had the effect of foregrounding the subtle chromatic relationships established by and in his paintings.[9] Changes to format or composition, as well as shifts from one series to the next, signaled a desire on Noland's part to "ge[t] the color to do different things."[10]

In 1963 Noland commenced a new series, what are known as his Chevron paintings, probably to do just that. These dynamic, often asymmetrical compositions strain against the edges of the canvas, some appearing to protrude into or extend out of the support. On occasion, Noland would change either the orientation or the shape of a canvas so that its edges reiterated—complied with, as it were—the chevron pattern embedded in the composition. This experiment in establishing a logical reciprocity between support and motif links the Chevron paintings to Frank Stella's work of the late 1950s and early 1960s, a connection acknowledged by Fried.[11]

Early in his career, Noland strove to identify a painting style that, while by no means mute or reticent, expressed itself with an economy of means. "There's getting to . . . an essential level of expressiveness, a precise way of saying something rather than a complicated way," Noland once said.[12] Despite the Minimalist tendencies inherent in his pictorial language, however, he actively mined the ability of color to "convey a total range of mood and expression" independent of "descriptive or literary" associations, as seen in *Split Spectrum*.[13] Noland likewise evinced great sensitivity to the optical properties of colors, to the differences in weight, density, transparency, value, and

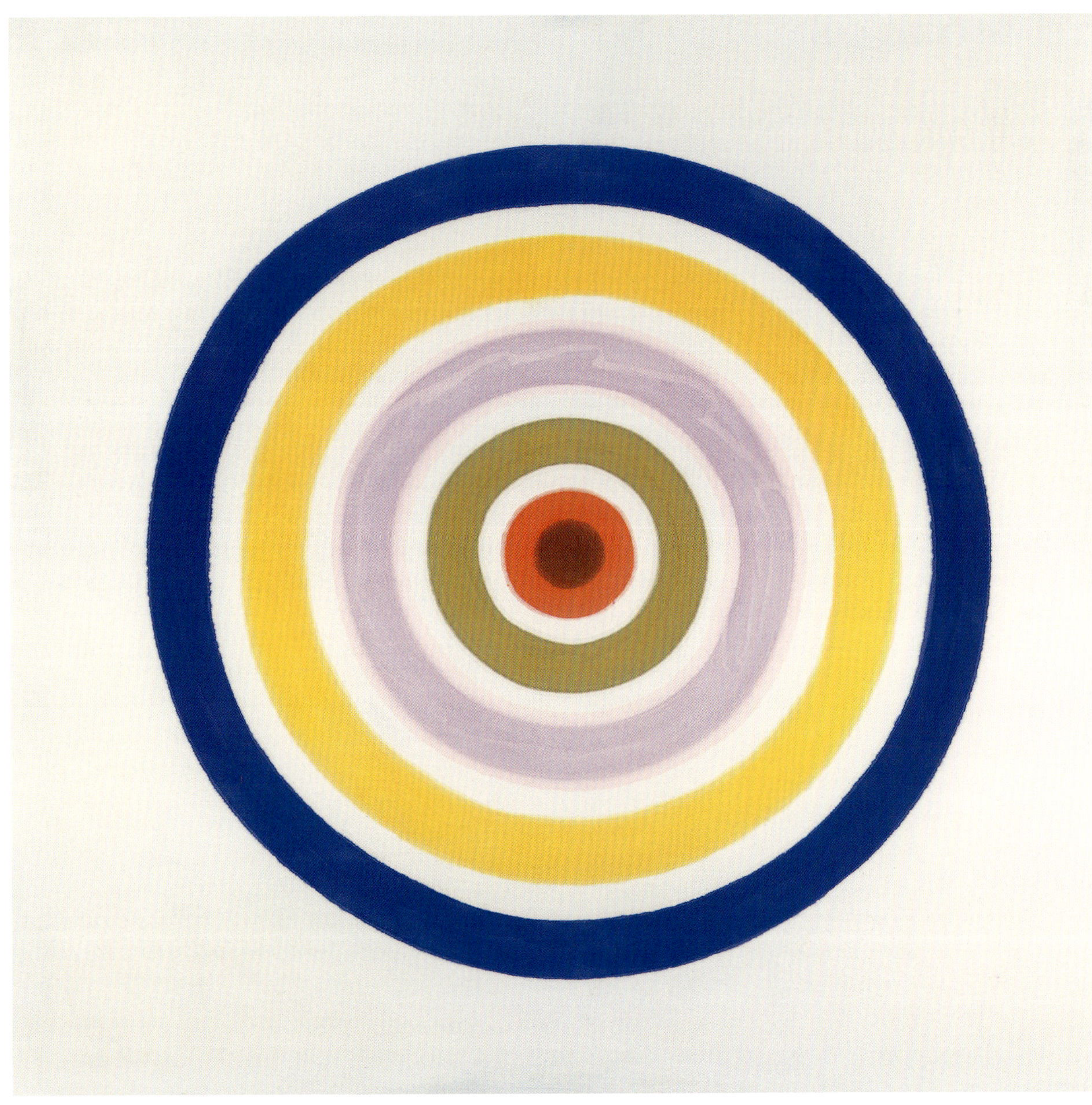

134.
Split Spectrum, 1961
Acrylic on unsized canvas
70 x 70 in. (177.6 x 177.6 cm)
Gift of Mari and James A. Michener
1991.280

Provenance: Purchased by James Michener from Andre Emmerich Gallery, New York, 1961; long-term loan to The University of Texas at Austin, 1962–1991

contrast that separate one color from another. This, along with his experimental approach to structure and composition, helped instigate important shifts in abstract painting in the 1960s.

Kelly Baum

Notes

1. Greenberg included all three painters in an exhibition of contemporary American and Canadian art at the Los Angeles County Museum of Art in 1964. See Clement Greenberg, *Post Painterly Abstraction* (Los Angeles: Los Angeles County Museum of Art, 1964). Michael Fried, one of Greenberg's followers, included Noland in a 1965 exhibition titled *Three American Painters.* Fried adhered closely to the tenets of Greenbergian Modernism but placed particular emphasis on the concept of opticality, which he believed was exemplified by Noland's paintings, among others. See Michael Fried, *Three American Painters: Kenneth Noland, Jules Olitski, Frank Stella* (Cambridge, Mass.: Fogg Art Museum, 1965). See also Fried's 1967 endorsement of opticality, which doubled as his rebuke to Minimalism, "Art and Objecthood." Excerpted in Charles Harrison and Paul Wood, eds., *Art in Theory, 1900–2000: An Anthology of Changing Ideas,* new ed. (Malden, Mass.: Blackwell Publishers, 2003), 835–46.
2. On this transitional period, see William C. Agee, *Kenneth Noland: The Circle Paintings 1956–1963* (Houston: The Museum of Fine Arts, Houston, 1993), 21–27.
3. Noland completed his first Circle painting in 1956 and a few more in 1957–1958, but he created the majority between 1958 and 1963. Approximately 175 paintings comprise this series. See Agee, 14.
4. Kenneth Noland, excerpt from "Color, Format and Abstract Art: An Interview with Kenneth Noland by Diane Waldman [1977]," in Kristine Stiles and Peter Selz, eds., *Theories and Documents of Contemporary Art: A Sourcebook of Artists' Writings* (Berkeley, Calif.: University of California Press, 1996), 98.
5. Quoted in Kenworth Moffett, *Kenneth Noland* (New York: Harry N. Abrams, 1977), 51.
6. Although no pencil marks are visible on this canvas, Noland was known to draw the rings beforehand using either plates or a string compass. He rarely used sketches; instead, he chose his colors intuitively and applied them to the canvas freehand with brushes. Noland described his process as "one-shot painting," because he refused to change or correct the composition afterwards (see Agee, 15, 21–22, 37).
7. According to Agee, by 1959 Noland was using exclusively Magna, an acrylic resin paint manufactured by Leonard Bocour, to create his Circle paintings (14).
8. Quoted in Moffett, 39.
9. Michael Fried, from "Shape as Form: Frank Stella's New Paintings," in Harrison and Wood, 795.
10. Noland, 97–98.
11. See Fried, 793–94. However, Fried also points out that, while Noland "has shaped his pictures," his "chief concern throughout his career has been with color—or, rather, with feeling through color—and not with structure . . . it is precisely his deep and impassioned commitment to making color yield major painting that has compelled him to discover structures in which the shape of the support is acknowledged lucidly and explicitly enough to compel conviction" (795).
12. Noland, 94.
13. Noland, 97.

David Novros

b. Los Angeles, 1941

w. Norfolk, Connecticut, summer 1961; Los Angeles, 1962–1963; Europe, 1963; New York (with frequent trips to New Mexico, Los Angeles, and London, 1964–1990), 1964–present

David Novros achieved early recognition as one of a seminal group of abstract painters of the 1960s and 1970s. However, his decision some three decades ago to produce murals rather than portable paintings and to limit his participation in the commercial gallery system has led to the unfortunate marginalization of his profile in the contemporary art world. Nevertheless, he remains admired and respected by artists and critics. Following his second solo show in New York, critic Emily Wasserman identified him "as a major young talent who has just begun to live up to the promise and originality of his earlier work."[1] Indeed, his work has been included in most major exhibitions of abstraction, such as *Systemic Painting* at the Guggenheim Museum (1966) and, most recently, *A Minimal Future? Art as Object 1958–1968* at the Museum of Contemporary Art in Los Angeles (2004). In Texas, Novros's paintings are in the collections of the Dallas Museum of Art, the Modern Art Museum of Fort Worth, the Museum of Fine Arts, Houston, and the Menil Collection in Houston. The Blanton Museum boasts one of the most extensive holdings of his work in any public collection.

Born in Los Angeles in 1941, Novros grew up in the Los Angeles suburb Van Nuys. He attended the University of Southern California, where he studied with painter James Jarvaise, whose energetic abstract landscapes were included in the groundbreaking *Sixteen Americans* at The Museum of Modern Art in 1959. In 1961 Novros attended the prestigious Yale Summer School of Art and Music, where he met such notable contemporaries as Brice Marden, Chuck Close, and Vija Celmins.

After graduating from college in 1963, Novros traveled in Europe, making pilgrimages to the great medieval sites of Ravenna, Assisi, Granada, and Moissac. The mosaics and frescoes he encountered stimulated his future concern with "painting-in-place." Other influences on his early work include pre-Columbian architectural motifs and the painted patterns of Native American pottery.

In 1964 Novros moved to New York, where he soon developed an association with the group of artists whose work would come to be collectively known as Minimalism. While comprising various media, ideologies, and techniques, their art shared an emphasis on the work of art as an object rather than a representation of some other thing and on the use of new and specifically industrial materials not commonly associated with sculpture and easel painting. In an essay published in 1965, Donald Judd, Novros's friend, carefully articulated the differences between what he called "specific objects" and traditional paintings or sculptures.[2] The shaped canvas, introduced by Frank Stella in 1960, also blurred the line between painting and sculpture and emphasized painting's architectural presence on the wall and in the viewing space.

The two earliest works by Novros in the Blanton's collection, *4:24* (1965, plate 135) and *4:32* (1965, not illustrated), each include four canvas panels that form an irregular but straight-edged silhouette that maintains a dynamic relationship with the wall. Painted with sprayed acrylic, *4:24* is a rich ultramarine blue, while *4:32* is reddish brown with a slight metallic sheen due to the mixture of aluminum powder in the paint. The titles reflect the number of individual panels (four) and the total number of sides (twenty-four or thirty-two) of all the canvases in each painting.[3] Alluding to symmetry, the works divide in the center to create mirror images comprising two panels each. Their eccentric forms allow the walls on which they hang to be incorporated into the works, and, vice versa, the paintings become part of the walls. In a 1980 interview Novros stated:

> *I thought that making an independent, physical entity out of the painting was a way for a painter to reclaim some of the control that has been lost, a control over architectural context, a control over the spiritual context. This was an essentially moral basis. I doubt that many of the people who were painting "shaped canvases" shared that basis.*[4]

Although the architectural implications of his work are reminiscent of Robert Mangold's *Walls* and *Areas* (1965–1967), Novros's paintings differ in their emphasis on color and light. In this sense, he is a painter rather than an object maker.

Novros first exhibited his work, including *4:32*, in 1966 at Park Place, a cooperative gallery in New York founded by Mark di Suvero and other artists from San Francisco.[5] Primarily financed by gallerist Virginia Dwan and collector Patrick Lannan, Park Place was run by and for artists. At her gallery in Los Angeles in the fall of 1966, Dwan showed Novros's next series of works: large complexes of attenuated rectangles reminiscent of pre-Columbian designs. Novros painted these works white and sprayed them with Murano, an iridescent pigment that causes the reflected, pearlescent colors to shift with the movement of the spectator.

A major shift occurred in Novros's work of 1967. He replaced the irregular silhouettes of the canvas paintings with multiple right-angular fiberglass shapes. Sitting closer to the wall, the inch-thick fiberglass supports are therefore identified more with it than were the bulky canvases. The right angle also responds to the rectilinear architecture of gallery spaces. Untitled (1967, plate 136) consists of six fiberglass sections painted in warm jewel-like tones with a different shade of Murano applied to each section. The coloristic variations of the painting unfold temporally as one walks in front of its seventeen-foot length.

According to the artist, he did not so much "return to the rectangle" in the late 1960s as "add rectangles to the right angle."[6] The additional element is first seen in drawings such as Untitled (1968, plate 137). In this drawing, free-floating, upside-down L-shapes are juxtaposed with a sectioned rectangle containing several right angles. Novros's

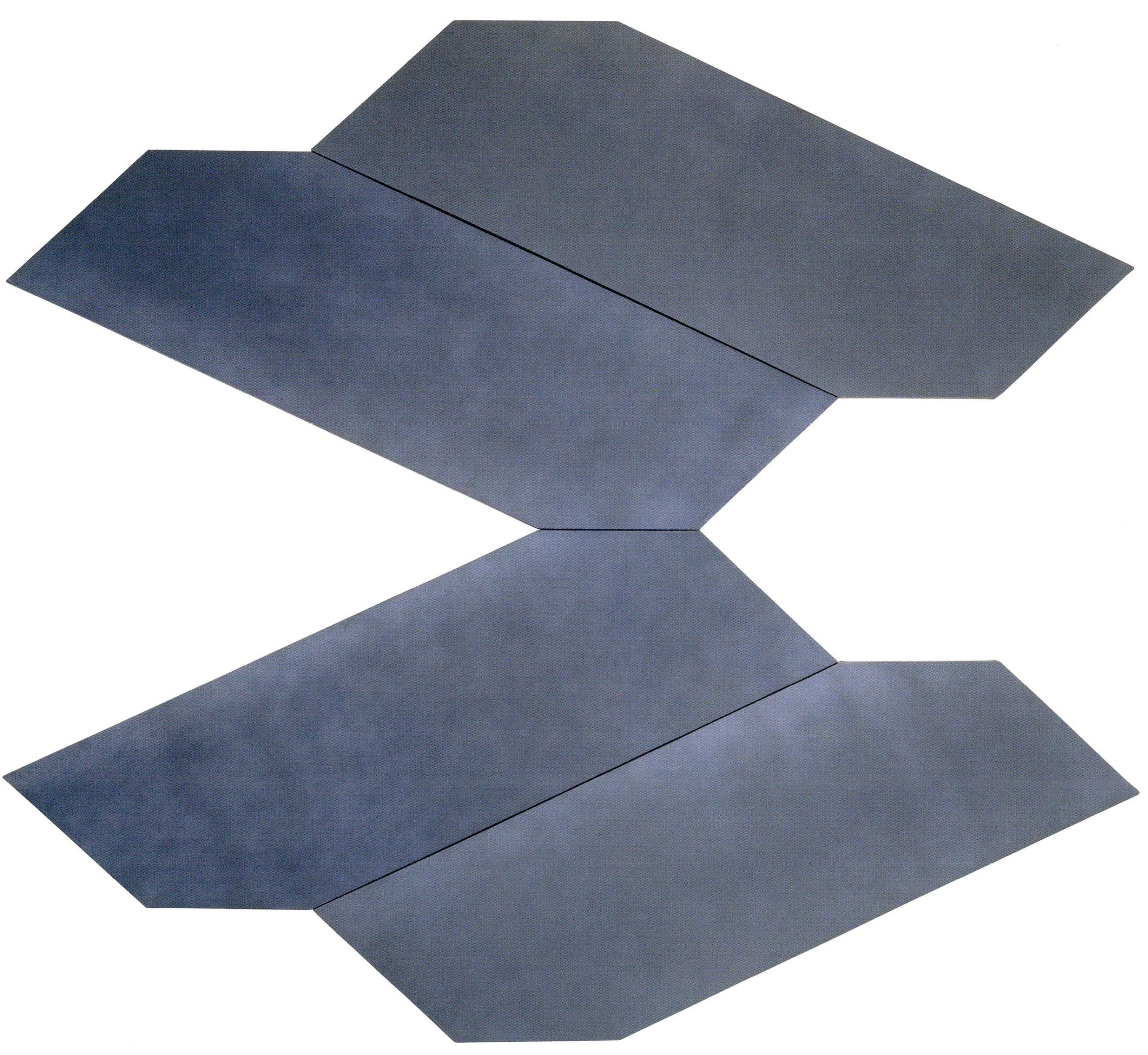

135.

4:24, 1965

Acrylic on canvas, four parts
Overall: 92½ × 100½ × 1⅝ in. (235 × 255.3 × 4.13 cm)
Gift of the Lannan Foundation, courtesy the Artist
1999.97.1–4

Provenance: Purchased by the Lannan Foundation from Park Place Gallery, New York, 1966

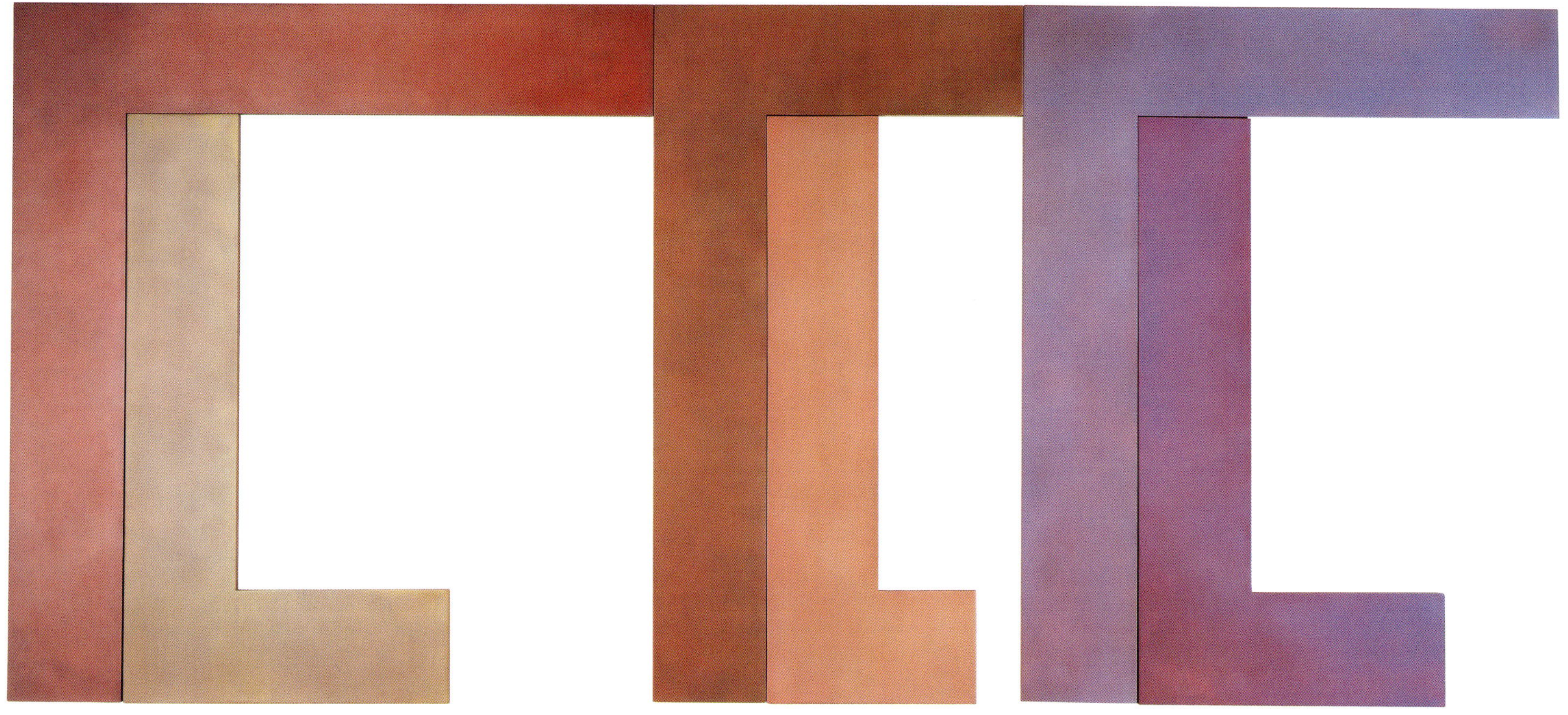

136.
Untitled, 1967

Lacquer on fiberglass, six parts
Overall: 87 × 204 in. (221 × 518.2 cm)
Gift of the Lannan Foundation, courtesy the Artist
1999.99

Provenance: Purchased by the Lannan Foundation from Bykert Gallery, New York, 1968

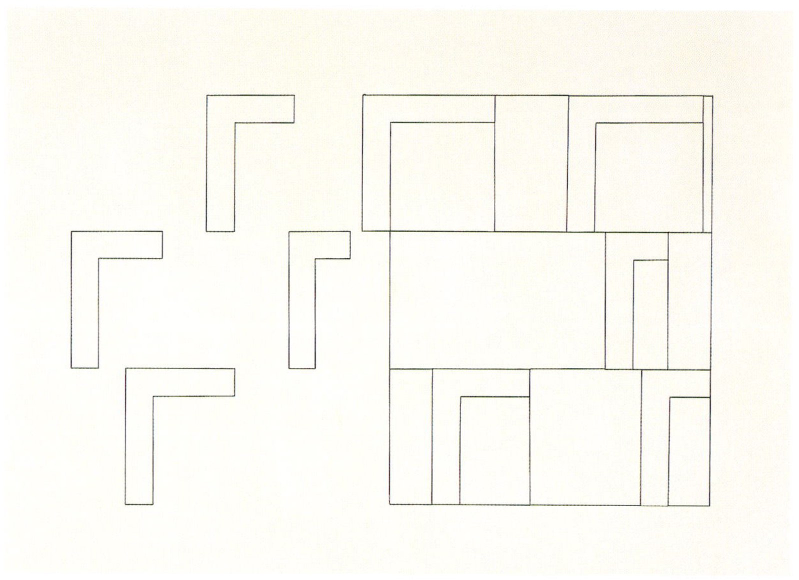

137.
Untitled, 1968

Ink on paper
22½ × 30 in. (57.15 × 76.2 cm)
Gift of the Lannan Foundation, courtesy the Artist
1999.100

Provenance: Purchased by the Lannan Foundation from the artist, 1968

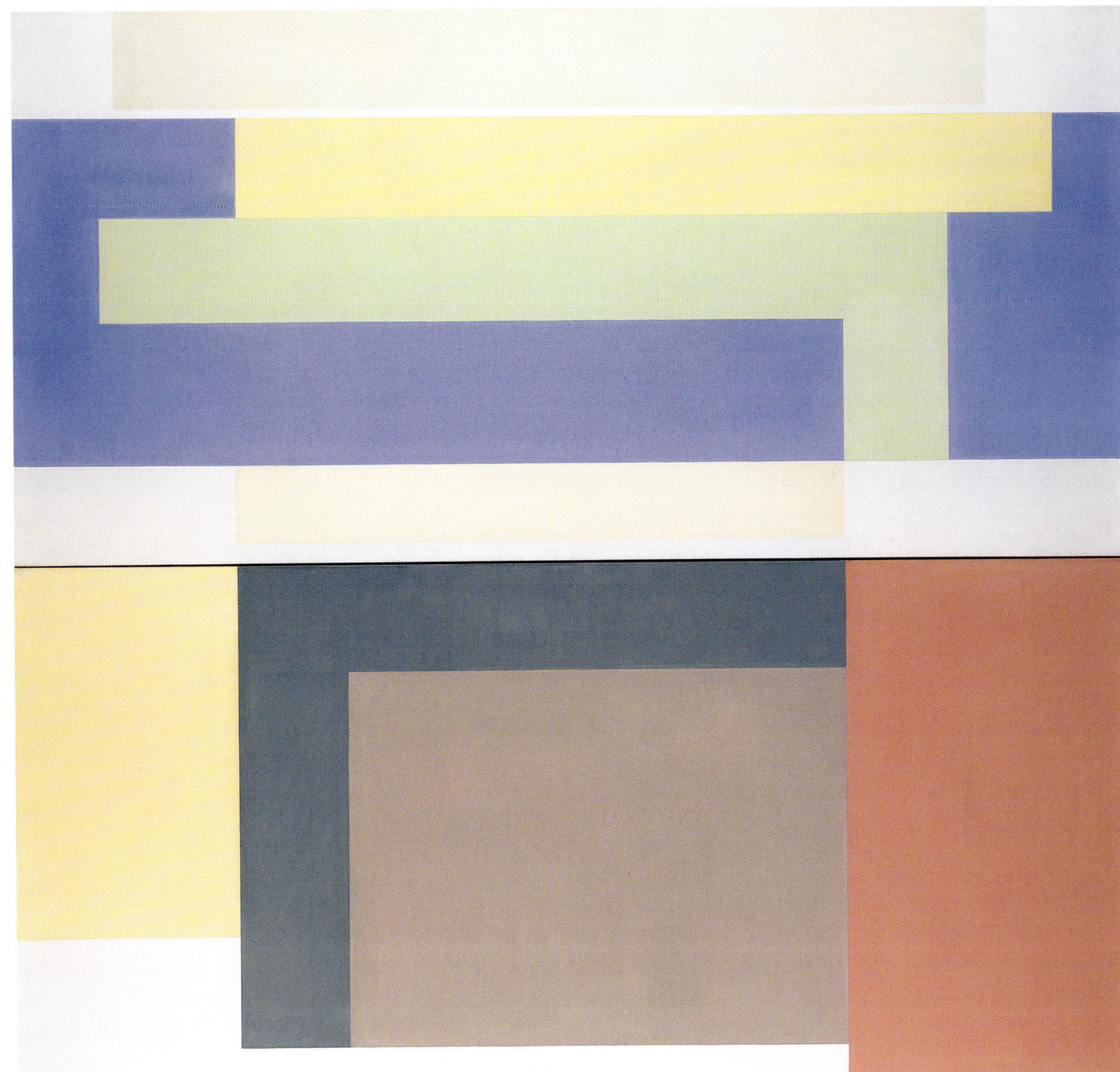

138.
Untitled (diptych), 1973
Oil on canvas
Overall: 77 × 84 in. (195.6 × 213.4 cm)
Gift of Christophe de Menil
2001.40
Provenance: Long-term loan from Christophe de Menil to The University of Texas at Austin, 1992–2001

rectangular paintings of the 1970s remain multipaneled and inclusive of the right angle form. Painted in Barranca, New Mexico, Untitled (diptych) of 1973 (plate 138) contains the softer, more complex hues favored by the artist in that decade. Its opacity and large scale reflect his growing interest in mural painting, a practice that he began with a fresco in Judd's building in New York in 1970.

When unable to complete a painting-in-place, Novros pursued the next best thing, such as the series of three freestanding painted canvas "rooms" exhibited in *Marden, Novros, Rothko* at Rice University in 1975. He followed this with a 1976 fresco for the Pennzoil Place building in Houston.[7] Novros painted other frescoes including those at The Museum of Modern Art in 1972 (no longer extant); the Gooch Auditorium at the University of Texas Health Science Center at Dallas in 1977; and the Old Federal Courthouse in Miami in 1984 (no longer extant). In the last decade, Novros has focused on private commissions.

Throughout his career Novros's vision has remained constant. From his earliest association with Park Place, he has eschewed the commercial art world, since it "allow[s] a system of markets (galleries, auction houses, universities, publishers, etc.) to determine that which is worth saving and that which is expendable."[8] From the irregular mirror images to the right angles, the multipaneled rectangles, and the murals, Novros has progressed from the dynamic, angular images of the 1960s to work that embraces both the ancient fresco tradition and a contemporary focus on the integration of painting and space.

Frances Colpitt

Notes

1. Emily Wasserman, "Richard Van Buren, David Novros, Charles Ross: Three Californians in New York," *Artforum* 6 (summer 1968): 35.
2. Donald Judd, "Specific Objects," in *Complete Writings: 1959–1975* (Halifax: Nova Scotia College of Art and Design, 1975), 181–89.
3. In homage to Novros, Brice Marden titled one of his rectangular paintings of 1966 *4:1 (for David Novros)*.
4. David Novros, interview with the author, New York, November 17, 1980.
5. For further information on Park Place Gallery, see Linda Henderson's essay, "Dean Fleming, Ed Ruda, and the Park Place Gallery: Spatial Complexity and the 'Fourth Dimension' in 1960s New York," in this catalogue.
6. David Novros, telephone conversation with the author, February 20, 2004.
7. This fresco was recently relocated to the Museum of Fine Arts, Houston.
8. David Novros, "Death, Ownership, and Public Art" (lecture delivered at the American Institute for Conservation Annual Meeting, Miami, 2002), author's archive.

Jules Olitski

b. Snovsk, Russia (Shchors, Ukraine), 1922

w. New York, 1940–1942; Paris, 1949–1950; New York, 1950–1963; Bennington, Vermont, 1963–1967; New York, 1967–present

It would be very difficult to separate the reputation of Jules Olitski from that of Modernist painting as a whole. Along with Kenneth Noland, Morris Louis, and Helen Frankenthaler, Olitski played a key role in the creation of Color Field painting in the mid-1960s. Influential critics such as Clement Greenberg, Michael Fried, and Rosalind Krauss identified the work of these artists as the culmination of a history of Modernist painting that had begun with the work of Édouard Manet. For Greenberg and others in the 1960s, this history focused on the essential qualities of painting as a medium, most importantly the arrangement of colors on a flat surface without any obligation to the description of forms or values from the natural world. While Greenberg admired Abstract Expressionists like Jackson Pollock for their disavowal of figuration and their refusal to create any illusion of three-dimensional space, the critic also lamented the vestiges of subject matter and spiritualism that lingered in much of their work. Olitski, on the other hand, made pigment and surface, rather than ideas or emotions, the exclusive subjects of his paintings, so that Greenberg was able to champion Olitski's work as the next step in the progression of Modernist painting.

Olitski was born in Snovsk, Russia, and immigrated to the United States with his mother and grandmother following the execution of his father in 1923. Growing up in New York, he showed an early aptitude for drawing and was impressed by the work of Old Masters such as Rembrandt van Rijn as well as the art he saw at the Guggenheim Museum. After serving in World War II, Olitski went to Paris on the GI Bill and returned to New York to earn a BA and MA from New York University in 1952 and 1954, respectively.

In his work from the late 1950s and early 1960s, Olitski allowed the particular qualities of colors, whether the advancing tones of reds or the receding tones of blue, to determine spatial relationships within the picture without creating the illusion of three-dimensionality.[1] This suggests an affinity to Ellsworth Kelly's abstractions of the same period, which are likewise concerned with the visual interaction of expansive fields of color as a structuring element in the composition. However, Olitski's thickly painted canvases from this period remained closer to the gestural tradition of Abstract Expressionism, even while they shunned its sources in the Surrealist exploration of the subconscious.

Olitski's interest in eliminating all visible form and linear structure led him to the decision sometime in 1961 to apply paint to unprimed canvas so that it seeped into and stained the fabric, thereby fusing with the painting's surface. By this frank acknowledgment of the support, Olitski's work pointed to the central Modernist issue of flatness. At the same time, he generated extraordinarily subtle effects of color with finely calibrated modulations of tone and texture. Indeed, part of Olitski's reputation rests on his ability to liberate color from line, completing in some senses a process begun by the Impressionists and carried forward by Russian painter Wassily Kandinsky.

Olitski's decision in early 1965 to switch to paint applied by spray gun allowed him to further explore the effects of color and resulted in some of his most important contributions to Modernist painting.[2] By producing areas of increased intensity of hue and with minutely varied mixing of pigments, his spray paintings imbued the colors themselves with a remarkable sense of depth without violating the flatness of the surface onto which they were applied.[3] In this way, Olitski achieved something akin to the extraordinary tension between the second and third dimensions created in Paul Cézanne's depictions of Mont Sainte-Victoire from the 1880s into the early 1900s. For her part, Krauss compared Olitski's paintings from the 1960s to Claude Monet's *Water Lilies* (1890s–1910), arguing that their variations in tone suggest opaque surfaces tilting away from the viewer like those of Monet's images of his garden pond.[4] The spray-gun technique employed by Olitski, which builds form through minute dots, also connects to the interest in optical mixture shared by nineteenth-century artists such as Monet, John Constable, Eugène Delacroix, and Georges Seurat.

The Blanton's *Green Rose* (plate 139) occupies a remarkable place within Oltiski's development. The artist started the painting (then titled *Red Rose*) in 1964, just before the spray technique became central to his work, and dramatically reworked it in 1968, changing the dominant tone to a blue green common in his spray paintings. Little remains of the original work except for the stained pastel tones at the upper left. Olitski created the flowing transitions within the area of blue green by scraping the surface of the canvas. The effect this technique produces can be distinguished from the more abrupt transition seen in the only sprayed passage in the painting, which borders the raw canvas at the upper right. The areas of contrasting color appear to work independently both of the other tones, including the dominant green blue, and of any intimation of structuring linearity. Some of the areas of color seem to overlap, while others touch, but they do so without recourse to any overarching system or hierarchy. At the same time, the long strip at the bottom of *Green Rose,* which recurs throughout Olitski's spray paintings, seems to displace drawing, acting as a frame around color rather than as a structuring element within, or prior to, color.[5]

To continue to describe Olitski's work in terms of Modernism may seem to accept too willingly Greenberg's formalism, ignoring postmodern critiques of the exclusionary nature of that critic's focus on formal quality and pictorial sophistication. It is perhaps enough to note that Olitski himself, intelligent and self-aware, was very much engaged in the tradition of Modernism to which Greenberg connected him, and to be aware that we need not take these as the only valid criteria for successful art, as Greenberg would have it. That said, Olitski's best works, such as *Green Rose,* offer many of the pleasures of painting

that postmodernism denies, with its sometimes overstated skepticism of beauty and transcendent experience. Olitski's lush colors and subtle formal harmonies appear to exist in a realm entirely their own. They create a place not outside the everyday world but rather a sanctuary within it.

Leo Costello

Notes

1. Rosalind Krauss, *Jules Olitski: Recent Paintings* (Philadelphia: Institute for Contemporary Art, 1968), 8.
2. See Michael Fried, *Jules Olitski: Paintings 1963–1967* (Washington, D.C.: Corcoran Gallery of Art, 1967) and Michael Fried, *Three American Painters: Kenneth Noland, Jules Olitski, Frank Stella* (Cambridge, Mass.: Fogg Art Museum, 1967). Both essays are reproduced in Michael Fried, *Art and Objecthood: Essays and Reviews* (Chicago and London: The University of Chicago Press, 1998).
3. Clement Greenberg, "Introduction to the Work of Jules Olitski at the Venice Biennale," in *Modernism with a Vengeance, 1957–1959*, vol. 4 of *Clement Greenberg: The Collected Essays and Criticism*, ed. John O'Brian (Chicago: University of Chicago Press, 1993), 230.
4. Krauss, 1–4.
5. Fried, *Art and Objecthood*, 137–38.

139.

Green Rose, 1964/1968

Acrylic on canvas
81½ x 117⁵⁄₁₆ in. (207 x 298 cm)
Gift of Mari and James A. Michener
G1968.106

Provenance: Purchased by James Michener from Goldowsky Gallery, New York, 1968
Inscribed verso, upper center "1964 Jules Olitski"

Robyn O'Neil

b. Omaha, Nebraska, 1977

w. Commerce, Texas, 1997–2000; Chicago, 2000–2001; Dallas, 2001–2002; Houston, 2002–present

The process was painstaking: over the course of three months, while in residence at ArtPace in San Antonio in 2003, Robyn O'Neil used only paper and mechanical pencils to craft an alternate universe whose expansive size, meticulous detail, and disturbing subject matter exert a forceful impact on the viewer. Here a mountainous winter landscape serves as the stage for an apocalyptic narrative titled *Everything that stands will be at odds with its neighbor, and everything that falls will perish without grace* (2003, plate 140). Slightly overweight men in identical sweatsuits run, crawl, and fall seemingly without purpose or direction, while World War II airplanes descend from the ominous thunderclouds above. The sensation of dread that pervades the drawing is underscored by its composition and tripartite format, loosely based on Hieronymous Bosch's altarpiece *The Garden of Earthly Delights* (c. 1504), as well as its title, whose cadence and tone recall Old Testament prophesies of impending social and spiritual disaster.[1]

Scattered throughout the landscape is a cast of animals, mostly elk, although visible in the foreground is a miniature schnauzer whose presence here defies explanation. In keeping with the work's absurdist undercurrent, several of the animals lie dead on the ground, the victims of unseen violence, but many seem surprisingly self-composed. The poise and dignity of the animals stands in pointed contrast to the men, who either respond inappropriately or nonproductively to the chaotic events that unfold around them (a few smile, some engage in group calisthenics) or lose their faculties altogether. No longer in control of their bodies or minds, these men raise disturbing questions about human agency, infallibility, and self-determination.

What is more, the animals have been rendered with an eye to verisimilitude that the men have not—a calculated discrepancy on O'Neil's part. The musculature of the animals is supple and lissome, thanks in large part to her skill at generating the illusion of three-dimensional relief through contrasts between light and dark. In the case of the men, the mimetic details with which O'Neil has endowed them are ultimately overwhelmed by the awkwardness of their gestures and gaits. These physical attributes serve to dehumanize them, literally as well as metaphorically, in the eyes of the viewer. As O'Neil said, "I am constantly trying to show that humans are the species most unclear of their place, most uncomfortable on this land."

The tension O'Neil generates between realism and abstraction extends to other aspects of the drawing as well. For instance, the work is punctuated by large areas of empty, uneventful space whose manifest flatness contradicts the illusion of perspectival recession established elsewhere in the drawing.[2] That these open spaces are meant to represent snow does little to mitigate their abstract dimension, for they lack modeling or articulation of any kind. What is more, despite her scrupulous attention to detail elsewhere—created in part by consulting books on mammals, aeronautics, and meteorology—O'Neil took considerable liberty with some of the trees, fashioning creative hybrids like "The Even-Sided Limb Tree" or "The 'Weeping' Evergreen."

Prior to creating *Everything that stands,* O'Neil worked on a much smaller scale.[3] She described these earlier drawings, most of which featured the same men found in *Everything that stands,* as well as the occasional dinosaur, as "short poems, or even sentences or chapters in a book." *Everything that stands* was the "novel" to these excerpts, the metanarrative encompassing all the narrative strands embedded in her previous work. Indeed, it was only while she was making *Everything that stands* that O'Neil realized the broader symbolic import of the subject matter she had been depicting. "The epic story [about war, death, love, and mourning] came out because in the large scale I was able to show so many men within one picture plane and then I could see it was more complex than renderings of two people relating or not-relating to one another," she recalled.

O'Neil is one of many artists who began to embrace drawing with renewed enthusiasm in the late 1990s. *Drawing Now: Eight Propositions* was one of the first exhibitions to thoroughly examine this trend (and in so doing did much to formalize it as a trend). The works showcased in *Drawing Now* did not constitute "drawing as usual," however. Indeed, as curator Laura Hoptman pointed out, the "return to drawing" among contemporary artists such as Julie Mehretu and Matthew Ritchie involved a radical reassessment of its terms, parameters, and ambitions. First and foremost, Hoptman claimed, drawing is today "attached less to process than to finished product"[4] insofar as its subject matter is imagined or proposed *before* being realized on paper, an approach Yve-Alain Bois has described as "projective."[5]

Although similarly product-oriented, O'Neil's work did not appear in that particular exhibition, but this drawing, *Everything that stands,* was included in the 2004 Whitney Biennial, which explored the pervasive fascination among contemporary artists with low-tech materials and techniques, drawing included.[6] This particular impulse, the curators speculated, represented a loss of faith in the ability of technology to effect "positive global change" as well as a deliberate rejection of the high production values prevalent in art of the 1990s.[7] O'Neil characterized the attraction of drawing in similar terms. Originally trained as an abstract painter, she decided to adopt drawing as her primary medium while attending the University of Illinois. This decision constituted nothing less than an act of rebellion for a student whose graduate program was dominated by the imperatives of conceptual art. More importantly, perhaps, O'Neil "wanted to discuss what it felt like to be a human on this earth in a very direct way. . . . I didn't want the distraction of words, of a keypad, of an electrical plug, of color. Drawings . . . seemed to be the perfect solution for these rather humble and elemental needs."

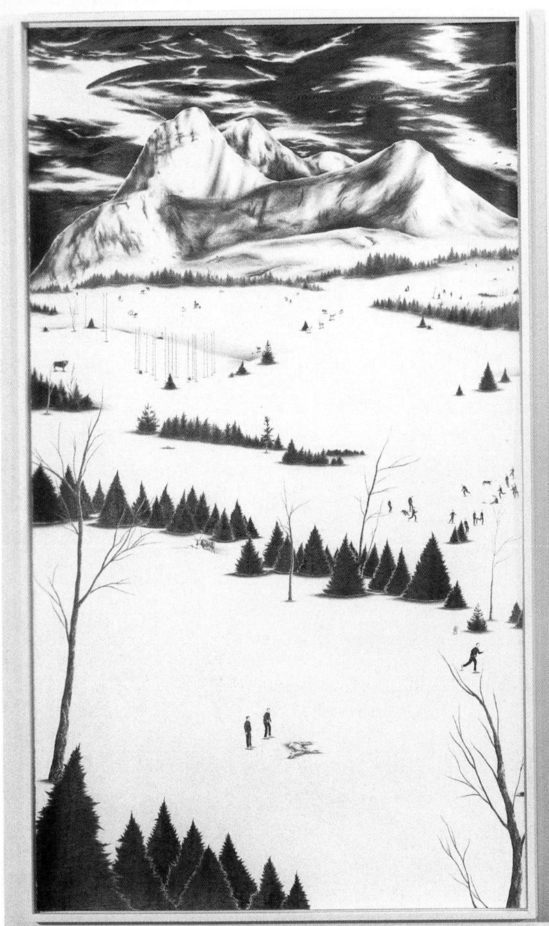
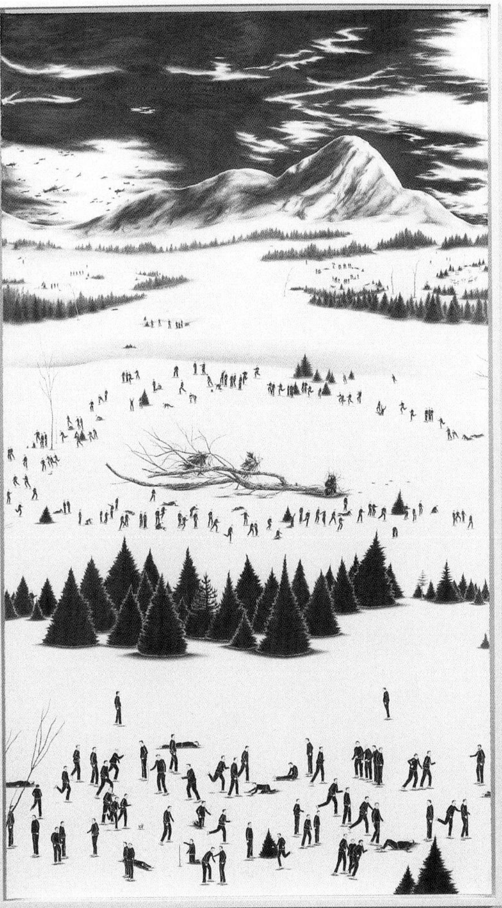
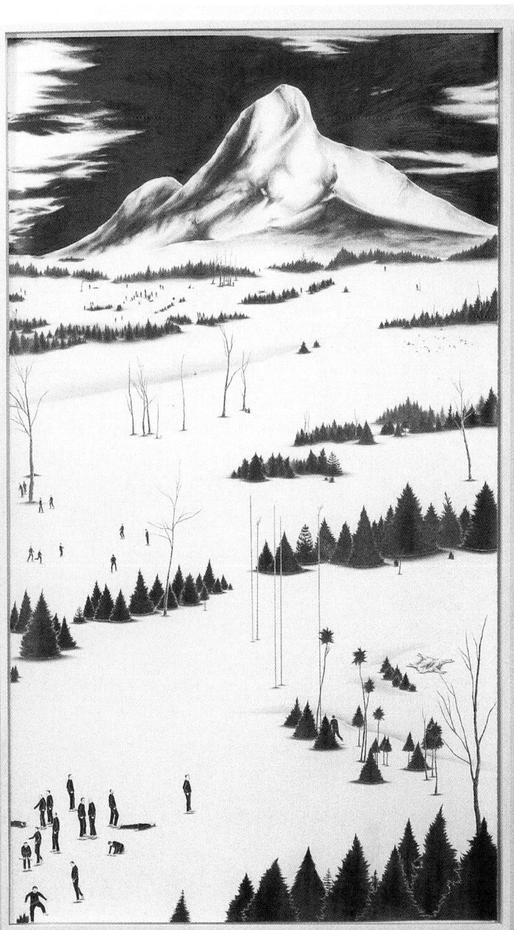

According to one of the curators of the 2004 Biennial, O'Neil's work exemplified another broad trend in contemporary art, what she described as an interest in constructing "alternative worlds [that] embrace the absurd chaos of our existence," thereby providing "a prismatic view" of an "increasingly dangerous and alien" reality.[8] *Everything that stands* might thus be understood as an oblique commentary on the current historical moment. It exaggerates, to considerable effect, the feelings of fear, anxiety, and trepidation that have accompanied the social, political, and economic crises of the last several years. This, in combination with the tension it generates between reality and fantasy, the believable and implausible, accounts for much of the drawing's powerful effect.

Kelly Baum

140.
Everything that stands will be at odds with its neighbor, and everything that falls will perish without grace, 2003
Graphite on paper
91¾ × 150⅜ in. (233 × 382 cm)
Partial and pledged gift of Jeanne and Michael Klein
T2004.2.1/3–3/3

Provenance: Commissioned by ArtPace, San Antonio, 2003; purchased by Jeanne and Michael Klein for the museum from Inman Gallery, Houston, 2003

Notes

1. In this respect, the work also reflects O'Neil's many sources of inspiration, from the epic fiction of Marcel Proust to horror movies, the films of Ingmar Bergman, true crime stories, and the television show "Unsolved Mysteries." Robyn O'Neil, email conversation with the author, July 19, 2005. All the quotations by O'Neil that follow are from this conversation.
2. The large amount of empty space in this work signals O'Neil's predilection for "economy," an aesthetic approach inspired in part by her memory of Ben Kingsley's production of Samuel Beckett's play, *Waiting for Godot*.
3. O'Neil now alternates between large and small formats.
4. Laura Hoptman, *Drawing Now: Eight Propositions* (New York: The Museum of Modern Art, 2002), 167.
5. Quoted in Hoptman, 15. Process-based drawing was more prevalent in the 1960s and 1970s. For more information, see Cornelia H. Butler and Pamela M. Lee, *Afterimage: Drawing through Process* (Los Angeles: Museum of Contemporary Art; Cambridge, Mass.: MIT Press, 1999).
6. As for her working method, O'Neil does not create sketches for her drawings, but she does prepare beforehand by writing a story, one often inspired by a sentence from a book or something sad she overheard in public. As she said, "It is usually language that inspires my drawings."
7. Chrissie Iles, Shamim M. Momin, and Debra Singer, *Whitney Biennial 2004* (New York: Whitney Museum of American Art, 2004), 15. On the appeal of drawing to contemporary artists, see also Catherine de Zegher's intriguing essay, "Drawn to You," in this same catalogue.
8. Shamim M. Momin, "Beneath the Remains: What Magic in Myth?" in *Whitney Biennial 2004*, 39.

Carl Ostendarp

b. Amherst, Massachusetts, 1961

w. Boston, 1979–1983; New York (part-time residence in New Haven, Connecticut, 1994–1996), 1983–2000; New York–Ithaca, New York, 2000–present

Carl Ostendarp challenges the traditions of late Modernist abstraction with a personal visual language that is at once playful and serious. As painter David Reed recently commented, "Ostendarp's paintings have the clarity, directness, and power of the best of painting culture, as well as the complexity and humor that results from active engagement with popular culture."[1] Ostendarp created *Still Further South* (1990, plate 141), an early hybridized foam painting, during a period of intense productivity that proved crucial to the formation of his early reputation and the direction of his later career. Indeed, the artist continues to expand upon the ideas, forms, and apparent contradictions that motivated the creation of *Still Further South*.

Ostendarp completed his BFA in 1983 at Boston University's School of Fine Arts, where a notoriously academic curriculum steeped in figurative painting prevailed. In 1996 he earned his MFA from Yale University, where he studied under renowned artists such as Mel Bochner and his classmates included Ann Hamilton, Maya Lin, and Jessica Stockholder. Ostendarp's abstractions offer a parallel world to the figurative paintings of his Yale colleagues John Currin and Lisa Yuskavage. Like them, Ostendarp pushes the bounds of propriety and sobriety. Whereas Currin and Yuskavage question the figurative tradition through their embrace of popular culture and knowing references to art history, Ostendarp subverts the traditions of Modernist abstraction.

Ostendarp made *Still Further South* for the 1990 exhibition *Update 90* at White Columns, where the artist had had his first New York solo exhibition the year before.[2] The artist sprayed urethane foam (a material sold in hardware stores as an insulating sealant) onto a linen support and then covered it with oil paint. Rather than planning beforehand, Ostendarp capitulated to chance and allowed the "material [to] do its own drawing," as he put it.[3] The billowing flow of painted foam that results spills over the top of the panel, encroaching upon the geometric purity of the mint green square below. Furthermore, the palpable physicality of the foam contrasts with the purely optical qualities of the accompanying monochrome.[4] According to the artist, he was exploring the strategies of piling and accretion employed by Jackson Pollock, Robert Smithson, and a variety of process-based artists, such as Robert Morris and Lynda Benglis.[5]

Ostendarp discovered the material used to make *Still Further South* when he was working odd jobs, including construction. With this industrial urethane foam, Ostendarp was not only able to endow his paintings with sculptural qualities, he was able to create layers of paint quickly, often in as little as five minutes, as opposed to the five months it took him to produce his earlier paintings, on which he applied layers of pigment in the manner of Milton Resnick.[6] The dynamic interplay between two and three dimensions in foam paintings such as *Still Further South* ultimately led Ostendarp to make painted sculpture.

One might think of Ostendarp's foam paintings as creative misinterpretations of Abstraction Expressionism, as exaggerated versions of the gestural brushwork found in the paintings of Pollock and Franz Kline. As if squeezed from an immense tube of paint, these biomorphic "brushstrokes" equally recall intestines and the process of digestion, juxtaposing the scatological with the serious aims of Modernist abstraction. Ostendarp's fusion of these realms of apparent contradiction verge on caricature, and are reminiscent of the work of Ad Reinhardt, who occasionally merged his serious investigation of abstraction with the tools of comic narrative. Viewers trained to see a language of formalist abstraction or deeply personal expression may find themselves instead contemplating the vulgar materiality of Ostendarp's foam paintings.

These works take their titles from the tales of Edgar Allan Poe, the heavy metal songs of Black Sabbath, and the poetry of Samuel Taylor Coleridge. Ostendarp borrowed the words "Still Further South" from the long subtitle of Poe's novel *The Narrative of Arthur Gordon Pym* (although they might also refer to the implied downward motion of the foam, which appears capable of movement despite its solidity).[7] As scholar Harold Beaver noted, in this novel by Poe "all is paradox . . . What begins as a practical joke turns all experience (social and natural) upside down till the whole universe is revealed as a metaphysical hoax."[8] With his foam paintings, Ostendarp similarly sought to reveal "hoaxes" perpetrated within Modernism's critical heritage. He said it was as if

> *you had the feeling that the Abstract Expressionists had been found out, that they had this narrative element, and you couldn't trust the criticism [that characterized it as being about flatness or "Action Painting"]. These paintings function the way those stories do. They function as though to say "you're not going to believe what I'm going to tell you."*[9]

Ostendarp's use of quick-drying and self-forming foam asks viewers to question, by extension, the New York School's supposed access to the sublime through the materiality of paint as well as the tenets of Greenbergian formalism.

At five feet square, *Still Further South* moves beyond the scale of easel painting into the realm of objecthood. "I think what has gotten lost in painting since [the time of Barnett Newman and the Abstract Expressionists] is this issue of scale," Ostendarp told critic David Clarkson. He continued, "I'm interested in this 'life-sized' quality, where the image edge and the object edge are the same, where you're dealing with a real thing in the world."[10] At a scale comparable to that of the human body, these sculptural paintings command our attention, in part because they compete to occupy the same space as our bodies.

Works like *Still Further South* display Ostendarp's engaged understanding and humorous, sometimes subversive reinterpretation of the

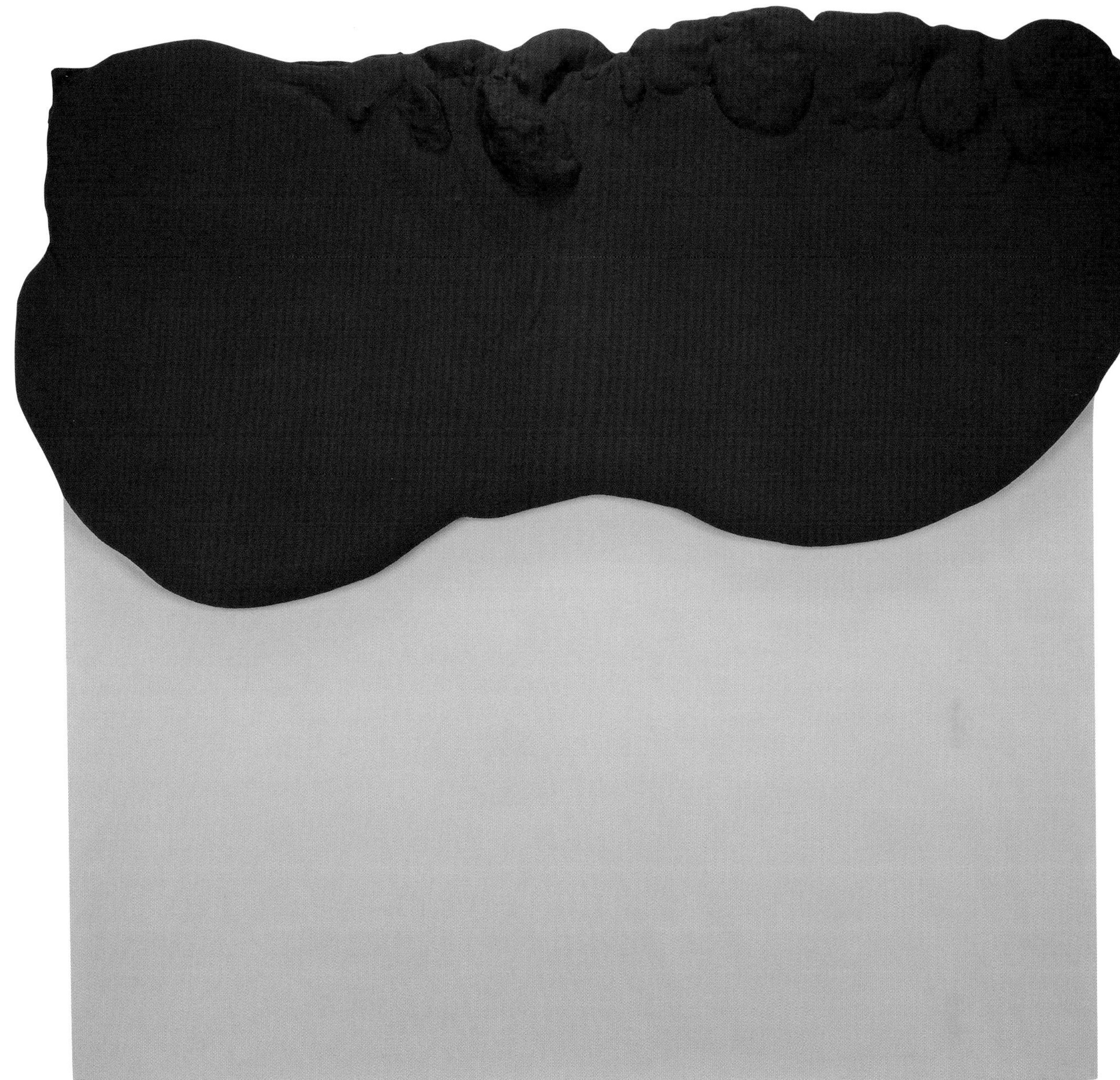

141.
Still Further South, 1990
Oil, foam urethane on linen over board
60 × 60 in. (152.6 × 152.6 cm)
Gift of Nancy and Robert Mollers
1999.84

traditions of Modernist abstraction. Above all, the artist seeks to create works that confound the viewer's expectations. "What was missing" from art in the 1990s, Ostendarp recalled, "was thinking . . . of the way that art . . . could be uncanny."[11] Like Poe, but with oil paint and urethane foam, whose strong material presence disguises what is in actuality an absence of weight and mass, Ostendarp uses his art to remind us that things may not be quite what they seem. *Still Further South* promotes the possibility that strange, unforeseen experiences lurk beyond Modernism's rational surface.

James Housefield

Notes

1. David Reed, *Carl Ostendarp: 189 Drawings* (Ridgefield, Conn.: The Aldrich Museum of Art, 2003), n.p.
2. Carl Ostendarp, telephone conversation with the author, July 4, 2005.
3. Ostendarp, telephone conversation with the author.
4. Ostendarp, telephone conversation with the author.
5. Ostendarp, telephone conversation with the author.
6. Ostendarp, telephone conversation with the author.
7. Harold Beaver, "Introduction" in Edgar Allan Poe, *The Narrative of Arthur Gordon Pym of Nantucket*, Harold Beaver, ed. (New York: Penguin Books, 1975). As Beaver noted, when published in 1838, the title page bore the full title of Poe's novel from which Ostendarp adapted this title: "The Narrative of Arthur Gordon Pym of Nantucket. Comprising the details of a mutiny and atrocious butchery on board the American brig Grampus, on her way to the South Seas, in the month of June, 1827. With an account of the recapture of the vessel by the survivers [*sic*]; their shipwreck and subsequent horrible sufferings from famine; their deliverance by means of the British schooner Jane Guy; the brief cruise of this latter vessel in the antarctic ocean; her capture, and the massacre of her crew among a group of islands in the eighty-fourth parallel of southern latitude; together with the incredible adventures and discoveries *still farther south* to which that distressing calamity gave rise" [emphasis is the author's], (41).
8. Beaver, 21.
9. Ostendarp, telephone conversation with the author.
10. Carl Ostendarp, "Carl Ostendarp," interview by David Clarkson, *Flash Art*, no. 171 (summer 1993): 106.
11. Ostendarp, telephone conversation with the author.

Ray Parker

Beresford, South Dakota, 1922–New York, 1990
w. Iowa City, Iowa, 1940–1948; Minneapolis, 1948–1951; New York, 1951–1990

As a member of the so-called second generation Abstract Expressionists, New Abstractionists, or Post-Painterly Abstractionists, Ray Parker was engaged in reshaping the goals and methods of abstraction pioneered by painters such as Mark Rothko and Jackson Pollock. By the late 1950s, the influence of Abstract Expressionism could be detected not only in its large number of practitioners, but in the diverse range of styles reacting against and responding to it.[1] Rather than creating brushy, gestural paintings and relying on the subconscious mind to generate content, young abstract painters like Parker, Ellsworth Kelly, Morris Louis, Kenneth Noland, and Jules Olitski sought to simplify the form, color, and pictorial space of their pictures and to ground their studio practice in a rigorous intellectual approach. As Parker said in 1966, "What I was and still am concerned about is that an artist regard himself as intelligent and aware and not take quite such a romantic attitude toward his process as was the case in many of the Abstract Expressionist paintings."[2]

Born in 1922 in South Dakota, Parker worked as a radio operator in the Merchant Marines during World War II. In 1948, he received his BA in art history and his MFA in painting from the University of Iowa. In the mid-1950s Parker developed a method of painting that restricted shapes, forms, and colors to their essentials but allowed for spontaneity; he applied this process to his paintings most systematically between 1959 and 1962. In these years, he reduced the number of forms to two, three, or four generally oval or oblong shapes that he grouped in post-and-lintel or other parallel and ninety-degree arrangements. The edges of these forms appear soft or torn. Parker rarely mixed paints and was particularly attentive to the texture, density, and saturation of color.[3] He applied pure color to canvas stapled to the wall, spreading and smearing paint, often directly from the tube or with rags, until he achieved "not so much the right shape as the right volume of color and paint," as Ken Johnson wrote.[4]

Parker's use of this improvisational technique relates to his earlier experience as a jazz musician.[5] He often referred to work that was progressing smoothly as "swinging" and emphasized the experimental nature of his practice: "My work is done all at once, without the opportunity to make any changes or corrections in the painting. It's like jazz in that sense."[6] Unlike most painters, Parker defined the size and proportions of the wooden stretcher at the end of his process, only after he finished painting the canvas.

Despite his attention to the framing edges of these "simple paintings," as he referred to them, Parker believed that "it was not the interaction of colors, between one spot and another, in the canvas that was important. It was the distinctiveness, the identity of the color."[7] For Parker, areas of color existed without relation to one another: he wrote that in his paintings "simple spots of color . . . came into being all by themselves and were not interdependent in any way. If I had a canvas with two colors in it, I thought that each of them was individually self-sufficient."[8]

While Untitled (1959, plate 143) embodies the strict reduction and measured clarity of the "simple paintings," Untitled (1970, plate 142) exemplifies Parker's subsequent embrace of a wider variety of shapes and colors. In his paintings of the late 1960s and early 1970s, Parker made the edges of his forms noticeably sharper and smoother and blended colors rather than applying them as unmixed pigments. He also moved away from his familiar elongated oval to approach the rectangular. Untitled (1970) retains the light background field of the earlier paintings, but other works from this period experiment with colored grounds. Ultimately, these explorations led Parker to a significant stylistic evolution. He began to incorporate drawing into his paintings, combining line and organic shape in an approach that recalls Henri Matisse's cutouts of the 1950s.

While his later work did not receive the same degree of critical attention as his earlier paintings, Parker remained influential in the art world throughout his life, particularly as a teacher at Hunter College in New York, where he taught generations of young artists from 1955 until his retirement in 1989.

Karen C. Gonzalez

142.
Untitled, 1970
Acrylic on canvas
22 × 30 in. (55.93 × 76.2 cm)
Gift of Buffie Johnson
1985.163

Notes

1. See Barbara Rose, "The Second Generation: Academy and Breakthrough," *Artforum* 5 (September 1966): 53–62, and Bruce Glaser, "The New Abstraction," *Art International* (February 1966): 41–45. Several exhibitions attempted to explain and categorize this proliferation of responses to and reactions against Abstract Expressionism. Exhibitions such as *Towards a New Abstraction* at The Jewish Museum in 1963 and Clement Greenberg's *Post-Painterly Abstraction* at the Los Angeles County Museum of Art in 1964, both of which included Parker's works, yielded a variety of names for this trend, including New Abstraction and Post-Painterly Abstraction.
2. Quoted in Glaser, 42.
3. Irving Sandler, *The New York School: The Painters and Sculptors of the Fifties* (New York: Harper & Row, 1978), 255.
4. Ken Johnson, "Ray Parker: Painterly Sensualist," *Art in America* 79 (March 1991): 126.
5. Gerald Nordland, *Ray Parker* (Washington, D.C.: Washington Gallery of Modern Art, 1966), 8.
6. Jon Hutton, "Dialogue: Conversations with Ray Parker and Doug Ohlson," *Arts Magazine* 56 (April 1982): 128.
7. Hutton, 128.
8. Quoted in Glaser, 43.

143.

Untitled, 1959

Oil on canvas
70 × 88 in. (177.9 × 223.6 cm)
Gift of Mari and James A. Michener
1991.283

Provenance: Purchased by James Michener from Samuel Kootz Gallery, New York, 1961

Philip Pearlstein

b. Pittsburgh, 1924

w. Pittsburgh, 1947–1949; New York (extended trip to Italy, 1958), 1949–present

Philip Pearlstein is best known as the painter of languid, mostly impersonal nudes. Indeed, the considerable volume of his output concerned with the naked human body over the past five decades has obscured the fact that his initial turn to the figure in the late 1950s was hard fought and radical in its implications. At a time when the gestural fields of Abstract Expressionism had supplanted figurative painting, the very notion of depicting the nude seemed untenable to most artists. Figurative painting, let alone realism of any sort, was anathema to high Modernism's pursuit of flatness and disembodied opticality. The often dogmatic support of abstract painting by American critics made Pearlstein's decision to concentrate on the intricacies of the human form—a decision from which he has never wavered—all the more remarkable.

Pearlstein began to draw from the studio model in 1958 and to paint from it in 1962, in part because he found the body's curves to inherently contain elements of abstraction. "A moralistic ban has been placed on spatial illusionism. But it is an arbitrary ban. The flatness of the picture plane is no more a truth than was the flatness of the world before Columbus," he argued in the early 1960s.[1] Pearlstein strove to balance exacting observation of his models with an economy of means and a formal handling that might stand on its own in terms of expressive capability.[2] He was also attentive to the various external forces structuring his compositions, such as the slightly incongruous viewpoints produced by separate viewings of the model and the presence of the canvas edge as a constant if arbitrary framing device. Manipulation of these formal components produced an abstract quality in his works that extended the tradition of figurative painting while simultaneously staking a claim on the tenets of mid-twentieth-century Modernist abstraction.

Painted in 1964, the Blanton's *Two Nudes* (plate 144) displays this concern with both abstraction and figuration. Pearlstein recorded the poise and bearing of two nude females with photographic fidelity, but these women are made strangely unfamiliar by his attentiveness to the complex mechanics of articulating the three-dimensional human body, with its seemingly infinite inventory of movements and gestures, across the two-dimensional surface of the canvas. The artist obviously ignored Western conventions for depicting the figure; the striking absence of faces gives the torsos, arms, and legs a declarative independence that facial expressions would otherwise forestall. Pearlstein also paid meticulous attention to the rendering of shadows cast by stark lighting positioned above and to the left of the models. The dark tones give density to his figures, but they take on an angular, calligraphic presence that nearly upstages the illusionism of the painting. If one expects the simple act of juxtaposing two nudes to provoke a narrative, disappointment awaits. The only story to be found in *Two Nudes* resides in the interaction of intangible light and solid form, flesh and fabric.

The strangeness of *Two Nudes* also comes from the apparent contingency of its composition. Pearlstein often determines the scale in his paintings through the isolation of an eye-catching feature of the posing model—a grasping hand or thrust leg—which then serves as the composition's point of origin. From that initial detail, the artist proceeds to paint to the edge of the canvas. In *Two Nudes*, Pearlstein placed the two figures in the immediate foreground of the picture; coupled with his partial cropping of the sitting model's head, they seem to push uncomfortably close to the edge of the picture plane, as if on the verge of spilling out into the viewer's own space. The painting's perspective, placed slightly above but still within the intimate physical space inhabited by the women, coincides with the artist's location, or perhaps with that of an unseen third model. For all its intimacy, however, neither woman is able to return the viewer's scrutiny or communicate a sense of identity. Faced with the nearly headless body of one model and the coolly factual recording of the backside of the second, the painting, like its subjects, seems strikingly mute and self-contained.

Art historian Matthew Baigell argued that Pearlstein has produced "some of the most disturbing and truthful images in modern life, a self-portrait of a generation."[3] With their cropped and awkward bodies, their lack of faces and eyes, Baigell claims that Pearlstein's physically incomplete subjects embody—quite literally—the spiritual deficiency marking the period to which they belong. By paying equal attention to the pattern of fabric as to the tendons in their arms and the mass of their breasts, the artist reduces his subjects to mere *things*. His figures seem emotionally vacant and lifeless. Pearlstein answered this charge by claiming, "The meaning of the figure in its particular situation has no interest for me. I refuse to be an amature [*sic*] psychoanalyst, or novelist. I would prefer to be thought of as a sort of stilled-action choreographer."[4]

If *Two Nudes* forecloses any possibility for psychoanalytic interpretation, the painting nevertheless creates an erotic dimension through the formal tension Pearlstein choreographed between the female figures. The women seem on the cusp of making contact in multiple places: the big toe of one nearly grazes the forearm of the other; the hand of the sitting model almost—but not quite—touches the auburn-haired head whose shape it mimics; the jutting bent knees of each seem engaged in conversation, on the verge of connecting. This subtle play of perpetually delayed communication, perhaps more than the evident nudity of the women, lends a slightly sexualized undercurrent to the painting.

Attention to the procedures and conventions of representation blur the categories of "figurative" and "abstract" in Pearlstein's paintings. It is that same attentive eye that imbues the flesh of his figures with a pictorial dynamism and sense of mystery.

Patrick Tomlin

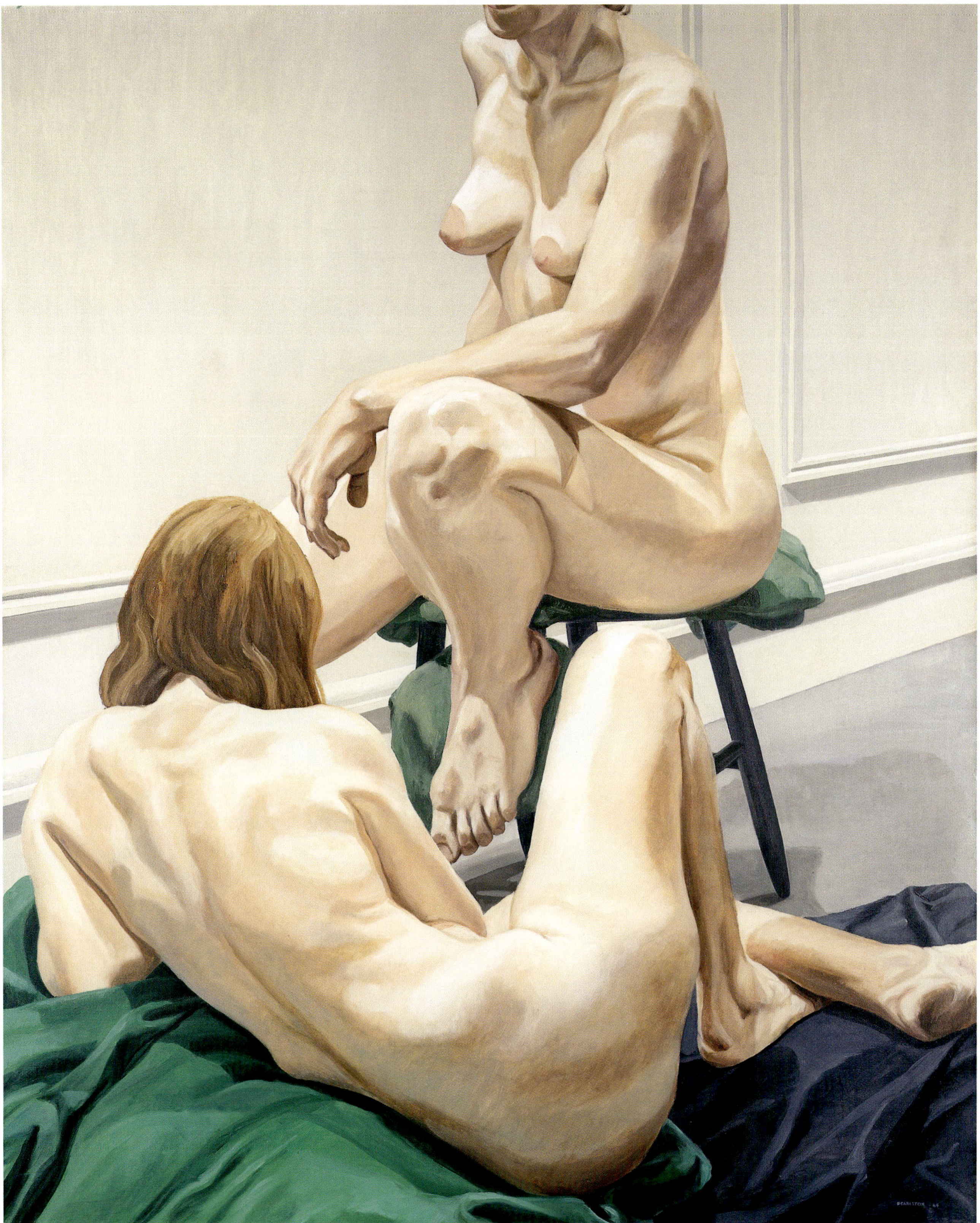

Notes

1. Philip Pearlstein, "Figure Paintings Today Are Not Made in Heaven," *Artnews* 61 (summer 1962): 39.
2. Philip Pearlstein, "The Artist's Involvement with Nature" (lecture delivered at an Artists Club panel, New York, March 15, 1957), as quoted in *Philip Pearlstein, a Retrospective* (New York, London: Alpine Fine Arts Collection, 1983), 17.
3. Matthew Baigell, "Pearlstein's People," *Art Criticism* 1 (spring 1979): 3.
4. Philip Pearlstein, "A Statement," *Philip Pearlstein, the human figure* (London: Gimpel Fils, 1975), n.p.

144.

Two Nudes, 1964

Oil on canvas
76 × 60 in. (193.1 × 152.6 cm)
Gift of Mari and James A. Michener
1991.285

Provenance: Purchased by James Michener from Allan Frumkin Gallery, New York, 1964; long-term loan to The University of Texas at Austin, 1968–1991
Signed lower right "Pearlstein 64"

Irene Rice Pereira

b. Boston, 1902–Marbella, Spain, 1971

w. New York, 1927–1931; Europe and Africa, 1931–1932; New York (frequent trips to Italy, 1960s and 1970s), 1932–1970

Irene Rice Pereira developed a rich and distinctive artistic practice over the course of her forty-year career. Continually pushing the boundaries of her own knowledge, she embraced artistic as well as conceptual experimentation, and her work often defied contemporary trends. Pereira began studying art at the Art Students League in the late 1920s, and after traveling extensively, she established a studio in New York with her husband, artist Humberto Pereira. Although she had already begun to read authors such as Immanuel Kant, George Santayana, and Oswald Spengler, her early work, which consisted largely of landscapes, some with still-life elements, did not yet reflect her broad philosophical interests. By 1933 Pereira had her first one-person exhibition at ACA Gallery in New York, and in 1936 she began teaching at the new Design Laboratory in New York as one of its founding faculty members. Around the same time, she began to focus on nautical and machine imagery, perhaps influenced by Fernand Léger and by the American Precisionists.[1]

By the late 1930s and early 1940s, Pereira's work became increasingly abstract, though it still derived from recognizable imagery, as did most abstract paintings and sculptures at the time. It was also during this period that her study of science and philosophy gradually began to manifest itself in her paintings. Pereira's readings included Kant's ideas on order and self-awareness, Spengler's theories about the forces that drive culture and history, and C. Howard Hinton's visionary ideas on the fourth dimension and the relationship between "primitive consciousness and spatial awareness."[2] As a teacher, Pereira incorporated numerous artists' theories into her courses, particularly those of Laszlo Moholy-Nagy and other émigrés from the German Bauhaus. Eventually, she began writing texts outlining her own art theory.

Inspired in part by Moholy-Nagy, Pereira began to experiment with various media, leading some critics at the time to credit her with being on the cutting edge of artistic production.[3] She incorporated unusual materials into her paintings: resins, casein, parchment, silver and gold leaf, gesso, marble dust, and glass, among other things. Some of Pereira's most unique and innovative paintings developed out of her experiments with polarized glass, phosphorescent paint, and plastics. She would often paint directly on glass plates that she then mounted with space between them, allowing light to enter and exit the plates from different angles, thereby creating dramatic and ephemeral optical effects.[4] As she experimented with these methods and materials, Pereira developed her ideas about space and dimensionality in painting, one of the central themes of her art philosophy.

Pereira was also fascinated by the way light and color can create the illusion of motion. This aspect of her practice was considered a significant precursor to the Op art movement of the 1960s, although her work appeared in only one Op art exhibition, *Whence Op?*, at the Heckscher Museum in Huntington, New York.[5] Pereira's experiments with light eventually led to her informal study of optics.[6] She considered the ideas about science and optics that her generation explored to be rivaled only by those of the Renaissance in terms of their potential to change human perception of the universe and space. Just as Renaissance artists illustrated three dimensions on two-dimensional surfaces using linear perspective, Pereira hoped that her work would be able to illustrate multiple dimensions within a two- or three-dimensional object.[7]

In the mid-1950s Pereira began to cultivate a new set of visual motifs that she viewed as being symbolically, cosmically, and spatially connected to both landscape and the universe. To create them she constructed layered planes on the canvas surface, each one representing a different dimension of space and earth, such as islands, lakes, and the ether. Periscope-shaped forms and other geometric shapes, loosely based on the nautical and landscape themes from her work of the 1930s, served to connect these various planes (or dimensions). The formal and spatial relationships that Pereira had explored earlier through the play of light and shadow in her glass paintings she now was generating in two dimensions through the strategic placement of planes of color and intersecting forms.

The One (1960, plate 145) exemplifies this approach, which Pereira continued to employ for the last fifteen years of her career. The blue, yellow green, and turquoise horizontal bands in the background emulate such elements as sky, water, and landscape. The broken horizontal lines that appear in all three zones evoke images of waves or rippling water, an interpretation supported by the blues and greens that Pereira used, although in other works from this period she incorporated a much wider range of colors. Superimposed on top of the bands are the floating, periscope-shaped forms that represent planes of light and space. The title of the piece refers to the means by which humans can perceive, and conceptually unite, the concrete, tangible world with the infinite universe and all its dimensions.[8] Paintings like *The One* allowed Pereira to fully realize her philosophical and artistic goals and create a body of work unique for its time.

Kayaneh T. Wood

Notes

1. Karen A. Bearor, *Irene Rice Pereira: Her Paintings and Philosophy* (Austin: University of Texas Press, 1993), 31.
2. Bearor, *Irene Rice Pereira*, 10–12, 17. On the relationship between Pereira and the fourth dimension, see also Linda Dalrymple Henderson, *The Fourth Dimension and Non-Euclidean Geometry in Modern Art* (Princeton, N.J.: Princeton University Press, 1983).
3. Elizabeth McCausland, "Alchemy and the Artist: I. Rice Pereira," *Art in America* 35 (July 1947): 177.
4. Therese Schwartz, "Demystifying Pereira," *Art in America* 67 (October 1979): 118.
5. Bearor, *Irene Rice Pereira*, 227.
6. Bearor, *Irene Rice Pereira*, 123.
7. Bearor, *Irene Rice Pereira*, 133.
8. Karen A. Bearor, "Rice Pereira's *The One*," *Archer M. Huntington Art Gallery Newsletter* (fall 1984): 5.

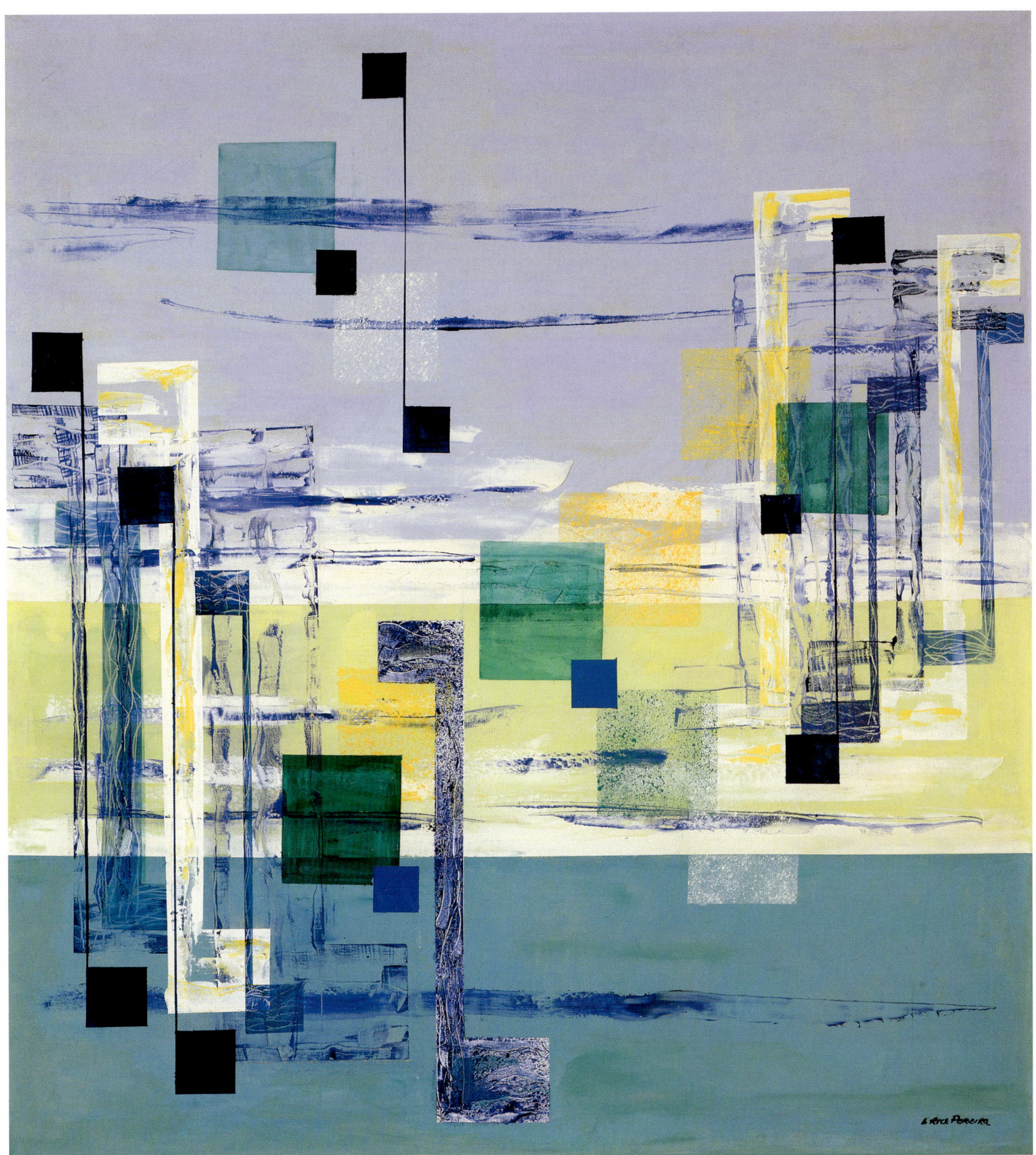

145.

The One, 1960

Oil on canvas
56 × 50¼ in. (142.3 × 127.7 cm)
Gift of Mari and James A. Michener
1991.309

Provenance: Purchased by James Michener from Midtown Galleries, New York, 1961; long-term loan to The University of Texas at Austin, 1968–1991
Signed lower right "I. Rice Pereira"

John Pomara

b. Dallas, 1952

w. Commerce, Texas, 1974–1979; New York, 1979–1984; Dallas, 1984–present

For Dallas-based artist John Pomara, the handmade and the mechanically reproduced are not necessarily mutually exclusive categories. Pomara combines traditional artistic techniques, such as painting, with newer image technologies, including photocopying and scanning, to create works of art that intentionally confuse the boundaries between the two. *Deadline No. 2* (2001, plate 146), for example, is part of a series of paintings inspired by "paint-droppings" that spilled onto Pomara's studio floor—accidental drips at once referencing and ridiculing that most revered Abstract Expressionist gestural mark. Seeing aesthetic potential in these leftover abject dribbles of paint, the artist began to salvage and experiment with them. First, he traced the drips, then he dragged the tracings over the lens of a photocopy machine, deliberately blurring the copy. Pomara repeated the process with the resulting photocopied sheets, progressively distorting the image until satisfied with the outcome. He then scanned the images, enlarging small sections, and printed them on a cheap printer before finally translating the image back into paint. Typically understood as a technology of replication, the Xerox machine here becomes a method to alter, deform—and ultimately to generate—the image.

With its slick veneer and modern materials (enamel paint on aluminum panel), *Deadline No. 2* has the aura of an industrial object. Because he used a squeegee to drag wet paint across the panel, Pomara divested the work of brushstrokes and other signs of his own hand. This intentional distortion of the painted image continues the act of blurring begun with the photocopier, carrying the viewer yet further from the original image. In *Deadline No. 2* horizontal bands of color traverse a vertical black ground. Red and white lines streak across the smooth black surface of the painting, sometimes resolving into torpedo-shaped patterns. These marks bring to mind the residual traces of visual stimuli, of something moving too quickly to be registered by the eye, like a bug or moth flitting across one's field of vision. However, if these striations of paint suggest the limitations of human vision, they also point to its augmentation and acceleration through technology, a process that theorists such as Paul Virilio argue characterizes contemporary visual culture.[1] After all, Pomara literally used such technologies to generate and manipulate the forms in his paintings, employing a photocopier and computer to produce specific visual effects. Citing Virilio's influence on his work, Pomara stated:

> *TV and media allowed us to see from a distance; and now new technology allows us to act at a distance, with 'touch' at a distance a possibility. That idea interests me. In working with drip patterns that I manipulate on copy machines then scan into the computer and manipulate more, my hand works with and through these machines, removed from direct touch.*[2]

Yet if for Virilio such "vision machines," which include cinema, digital technologies, and new virtual reality machines, are largely about efficiency and totality, Pomara implicitly questions this assumption, using technology to interrupt and impede our ability to see the image. He welcomes—indeed invites—the distortions that result from these technologies, using the photocopier and scanner to blur and alter rather than merely reproduce the image. Furthermore, his work is based on an alternation between the mediation of our senses by machines and the immediacy of the artist's hand. He stated, "I think painting is tied to intimacy and that of the hand making it."[3] Indeed, Pomara's project is to see just how abstracted that intimate gesture can become and still retain a memory of human presence.

Pomara's paintings might be thought of as "pictures" in Douglas Crimp's sense of the word. Crimp coined the term in his 1977 exhibition of that same title to refer to a new type of image that challenged the medium specificity of painting. Unlike traditional categories, "picture" is nonspecific and impure, exploiting "new media" such as photography, film, and performance, as well as conventional media such as painting, drawing, and sculpture.[4] Pomara saw the landmark *Pictures* exhibition, which included work by Troy Brauntuch, Jack Goldstein, Sherrie Levine, Robert Longo, and Philip Smith, while living in New York as a young artist just out of graduate school. In its original usage by Crimp, the term "picture" referred mainly to work that incorporated recognizable images, but it usefully applies to Pomara's abstractions as well, which stem from a similar impulse to mix up categories of artistic medium with those of visual culture.

Thomas Lawson's provocative 1981 essay "Last Exit: Painting" also influenced Pomara, with its call for a new set of criteria for radical appropriation strategies.[5] Reading this essay, Pomara realized, "I could no longer paint the way I was painting. Abstraction couldn't be about modernist purity anymore."[6] If the gestural mark had signified the purity of painting in Jackson Pollock's time, Pomara's version of this mark instead insists on painting's inseparability from a larger cultural field. Indeed, his work investigates the meaning of abstraction in the information age—an age in which the painterly mark is always already contaminated, always referring outside itself to a broader experience of visual culture. Pomara acknowledges, for example, that his color palette was influenced by Jean Luc Godard's film *Contempt* (1963) as well as by Taiwanese filmmaker Wong Kar-Wai, who directed *Chungking Express* (1994) and *In the Mood for Love* (2000). Pomara's work thus suggests that not only have new technologies expanded the formal vocabulary available to artists, they have demanded new approaches to understanding the relationship between form and content as well.

Gwen Allen

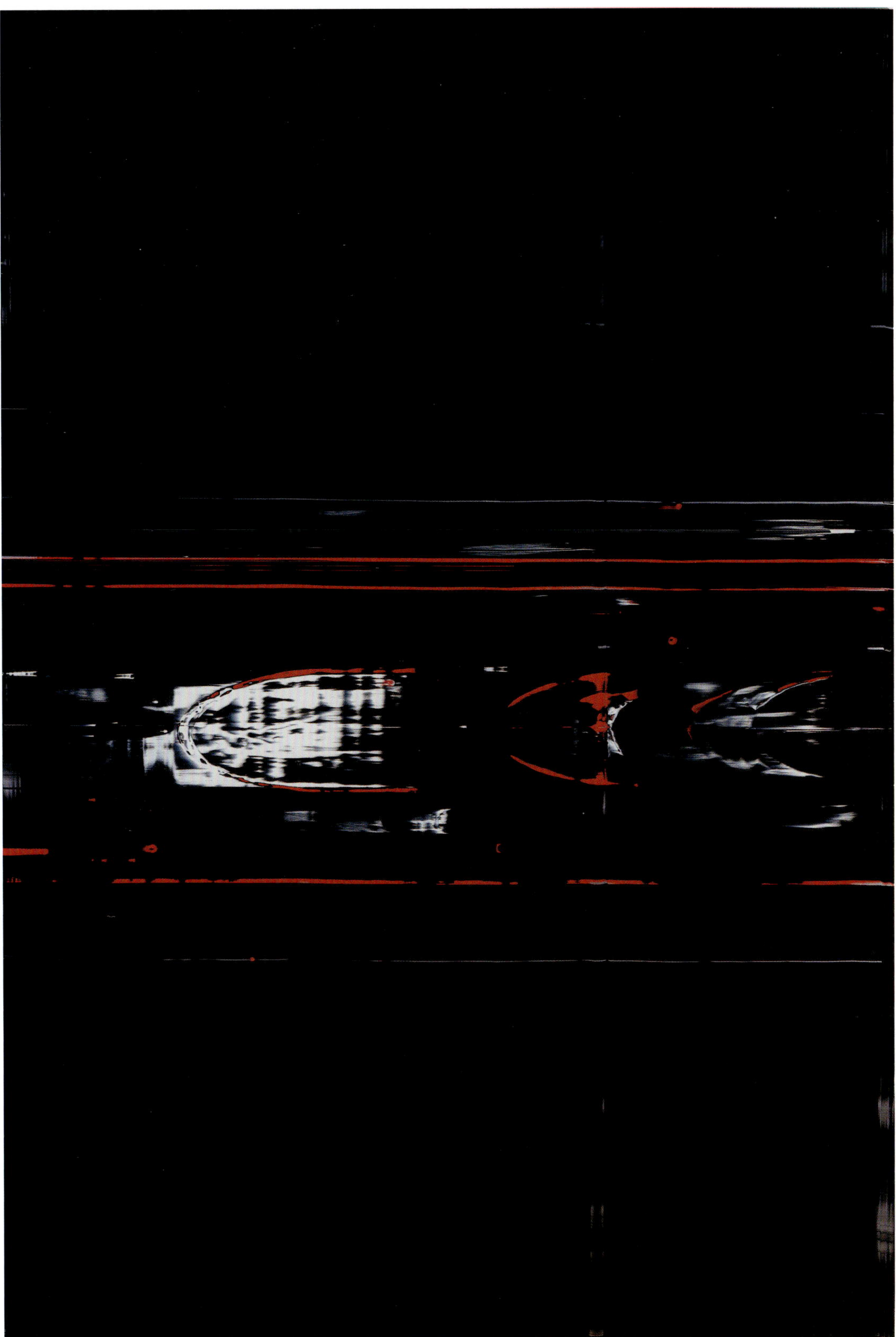

Notes

1. Paul Virilio, *The Vision Machine* (Bloomington, Ind.: Indiana University Press, 1994).
2. John Pomara, "Speed and Intimacy," interview by Annette DiMeo Carlozzi, *Artlies*, no. 31 (summer 2001): 11.
3. John Pomara, interview by Suzanne Weaver, in *Concentrations 39: John Pomara* (Dallas: Dallas Museum of Art, 2001), n.p.
4. Douglas Crimp, *Pictures* (New York: Artists Space, 1977). For a revised version of this essay, see Douglas Crimp, "Pictures," *October*, no. 8 (spring 1979): 75–88.
5. Thomas Lawson, "Last Exit: Painting," *Artforum* 20 (October 1981): 40–47.
6. Pomara, interview by Suzanne Weaver, n.p.

146.

Deadline No. 2, 2001

Oil enamel on aluminum
72 × 48 in. (182.88 × 121.92 cm)
Michener Acquisitions Fund
2001.97

Provenance: Purchased from Barry Whistler Gallery, Dallas, 2001

David Reed

b. San Diego, California, 1946

w. New York, 1966–1967; Portland, Oregon–southwestern United States, 1967–1968; New York–southwestern United States, 1968–1971; New York (frequent trips to Europe), 1971–present

Informed at once by a deep knowledge of the history of painting and a keen awareness of the visual influences of mass culture, David Reed's work is hauntingly familiar to both the eye and the body. It operates at the intersection of a number of different discourses relative to the practice of painting, drawing upon the visual devices of more culturally dominant media such as film and photography, as well as inherited traditions such as baroque painting. The seductive quality of Reed's paintings, however, belies the complex experience they offer, which derives from the artist's sustained investigation into the nature of representation. A member of the generation of artists who remained committed to painting during its much discussed "crisis" of the 1980s, Reed has emerged as one of the most important American artists working today.

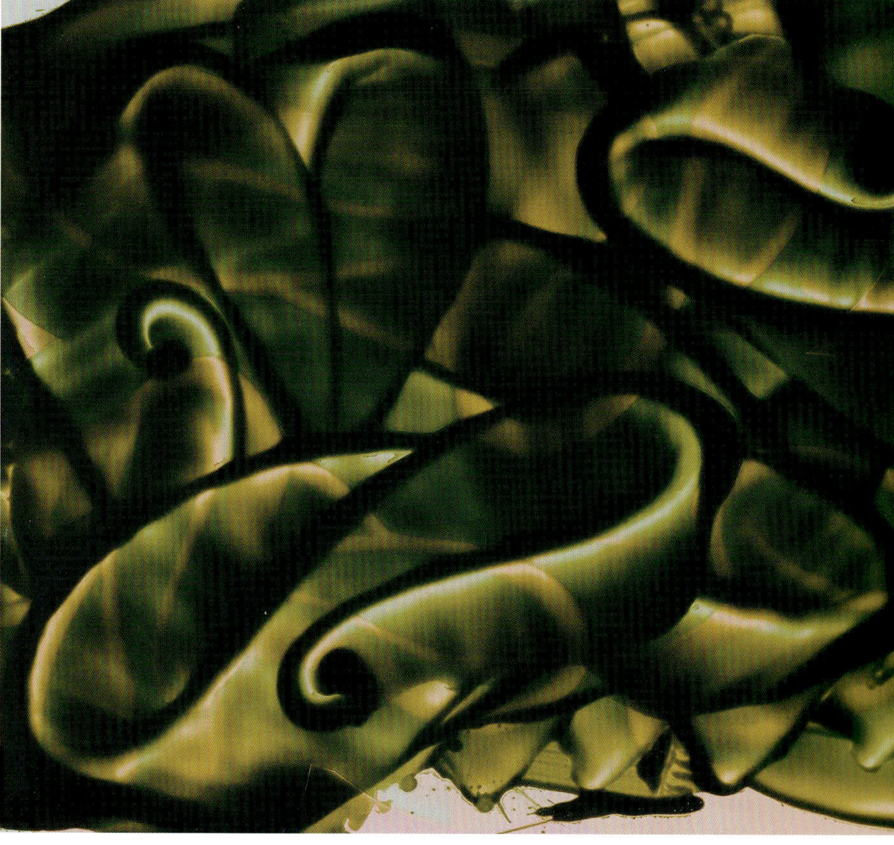

Originally from San Diego, Reed received a BA from Reed College in Oregon in 1968. While attending college, he also studied at the New York Studio School with Milton Resnick and Philip Guston and the Skowhegan School of Painting and Sculpture in Maine. Reed credits his college painting teacher, Willard Midgette, with convincing him not to become a doctor and with giving him the impetus to study art by, among other things, introducing him to the painting of Peter Paul Rubens. Reed began painting figuratively but then turned to landscape after recognizing an affinity between the abstract paintings of Jackson Pollock and the spaces of the American West.

In the late 1960s and early 1970s, Reed painted in the desert, often just off the highway in Monument Valley. There he developed a sense of space that he would continue to explore when he began making abstract work after settling in New York in 1971. In these "brushmark" paintings, as he called them, Reed allowed the limitations of his physical relationship to the canvas to structure the work. Combining signature elements of process art and Minimalism, each painting consists of a series of parallel, horizontal brushstrokes, the length of which was determined by the reach of Reed's arm from a single point in front of the canvas. The repetitive horizontality of the gesture is related to his fascination with the space and geography of the Western landscape. Horizontality, in fact, would become one of the most significant features of Reed's work, allowing him to use abstraction to address a range of formal and thematic issues. The "brushmark" paintings also clearly reveal the process by which they were made. They are predicated on the transparency of the painted mark read as a trace or record of an action in time.

#476 (2001, plate 147) reflects the shift that has defined Reed's subsequent work. Beginning around 1980, the artist redirected his interest from the transparency of the painted gesture to the illusionism of a mark that effaces the process of its own making. In *#476*, the large, ribbonlike forms are modeled in such a way that they resemble brushstrokes or folds of paint applied with a palette knife. They invite the viewer to re-create the sequence in which they were painted. But the way the work is constructed serves to defeat any such effort by the viewer. The layering of different kinds of painterly line within the shallow space of the image and the two-part composition indicate that this is a painting not to be read simply as a series of marks but as a picture *about* the painted mark. Moreover, the curling, pointed ends of these depicted brushstrokes do not exist as textured elements of built-up paint wherein we have been trained to seek the hand of the artist. Instead, they only emphasize the quality of the illusion created on the smooth, sanded surface of the painting. Reed further complicates the play between surface and illusion in *#476* by suggesting that the very pigment of these bold, heavily outlined brushstrokes paradoxically contains another seemingly arbitrary pattern of green and yellow marks that are continuous across the complex folds of the composition. Throughout his career, Reed has developed a variety of techniques to heighten the impact of such effects, from working with glazes and transparent gels to sanding and abrading the surface of the painting itself.

Reed's work has some affinity with earlier pictures that engage the legacy of gestural painting, such as Roy Lichtenstein's "brushstroke" paintings of the mid-1960s and Robert Rauschenberg's *Factum I* and *II*

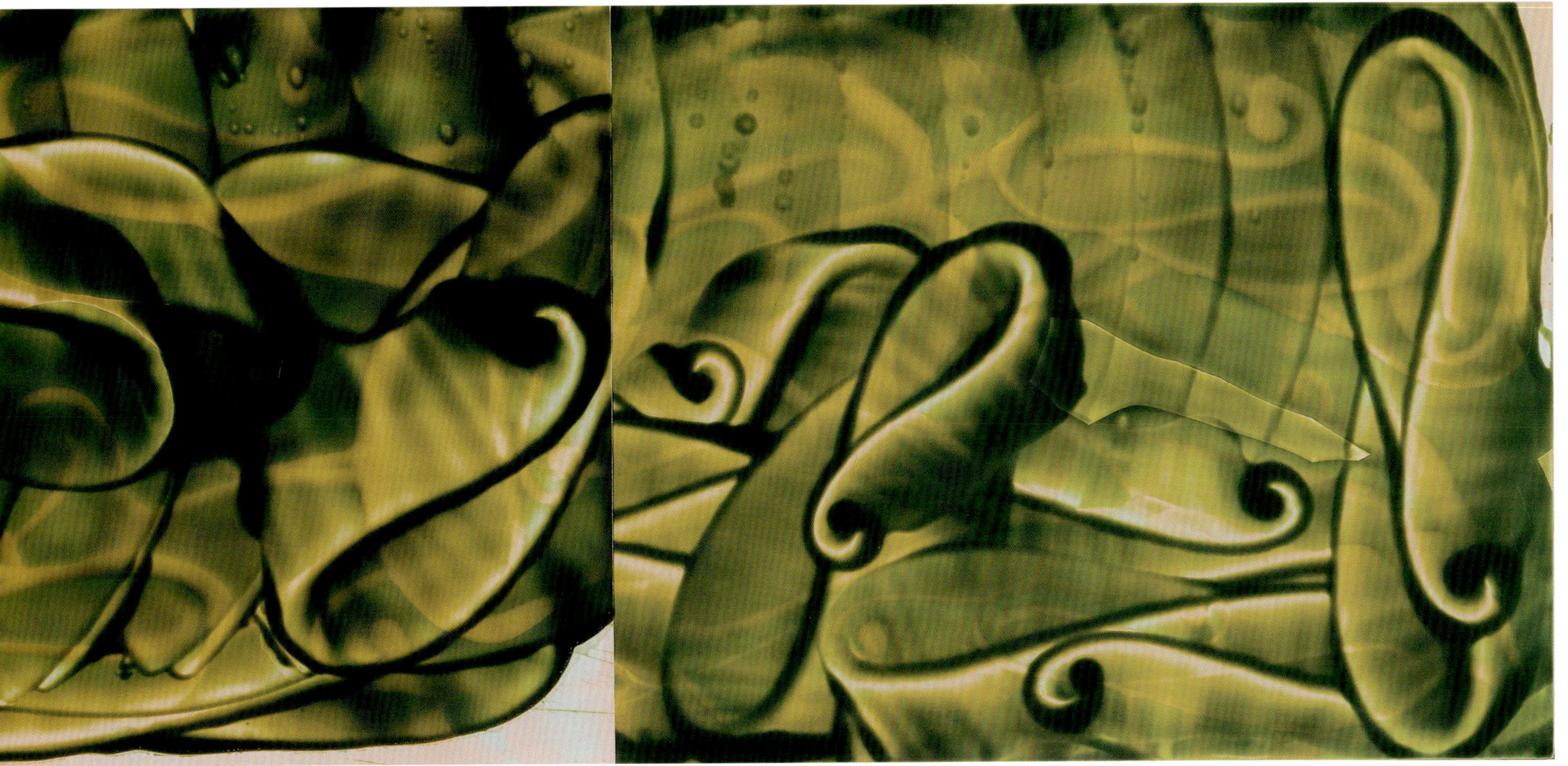

(1957). Like Gerhard Richter and Sigmar Polke, however, Reed has dedicated his practice to the reinvention of abstract painting for the contemporary moment in a more sustained way, although with very different results than these German artists. His rich visual vocabulary contains the sensuous materiality of the Baroque, the saturated colors of Cibachrome photography, and the horizontal format of Cinemascope film. One of the ways that Reed unites these various influences is through the use of light. He explained this quality of his painting, remarking that

> *during the Renaissance and baroque periods they had a wonderful religious light that always came from above. Now we have a technological light, the light of a TV or movie screen, which is directionless—homogeneous across the screen—and increases the intensity of every color. Since we see this light on or through machines, it seems beyond the human, even immortal. To that extent it's similar to the divine light in the older paintings.*[1]

Reed's use of this "technological light" in *#476* serves to illuminate a whole series of oppositions central to his practice: the play between opacity and transparency, materiality and dissolution, spontaneity and repetition, and clarity and deception. His ability to make these oppositions legible on both a literal level and as metaphors for larger conflicts within our present cultural moment vindicates Reed's claims for the continued vitality of abstract painting.

Ken Allan

147.
***#476*, 2001**

Oil and alkyd on linen
$34\frac{3}{16} \times 110\frac{1}{4}$ in. (86.9 × 280.1 cm)
Michener Acquisitions Fund
2002.2836

Provenance: Purchased from Max Protetch Gallery, New York, 2002

Note

1. David Reed, "David Reed interviewed by Stephen Ellis," in Lucinda Barnes, Miyoshi Barosh, William S. Bartman, Rodney Sappington, eds., *Between Artists: 12 Contemporary American Artists Interview 12 Contemporary American Artists* (Los Angeles: A.R.T. Press, 1996), 192. For more information on Reed, see Elizabeth Armstrong, et al., *David Reed Paintings: Motion Pictures* (San Diego: Museum of Contemporary Art, 1998); Konrad Bitterli, et al., *David Reed: You Look Good in Blue* (Nürnberg: Verlag für moderne Kunst, 2005); and Richard Shiff, et al., *David Reed—Leave Yourself Behind: Paintings and Special Projects 1967–2005* (Wichita, Kansas: Ulrich Museum of Art, 2005).

Milton Resnick

Bratslav, Ukraine, 1917–New York, 2004
w. New York, 1932–1940; Paris, 1946–1948; New York (extended stays in New Mexico), 1948–2004

Despite his active involvement in the beginnings of the New York School, some critics erroneously grouped Milton Resnick with the second generation Abstract Expressionists because of the late date of his first one-person exhibition in 1955. The three paintings in the Blanton's collection, *Bo-Bo* (1957, plate 148), *Sovereign* (1959, plate 149), and *The Winds Crossing and Later* (1963, plate 150), illuminate his position within the New York School while offering unique insights into the evolution of his career. Resnick's work endures as a testament to his influential role in American Modernism after World War II.

Resnick immigrated to the United States from the Ukraine with his family at the age of five. As a teenager, he attended the American Artist's School, where he befriended fellow aspiring artist Ad Reinhardt. Like many artists at the end of the 1930s, Resnick participated in the WPA Federal Art Project. He also served in the army between 1940 and 1945 and lived in Paris between 1946 and 1948, setting him apart from many of the New York School artists.[1] After leaving Paris, Resnick returned to New York and began painting in an abstract manner. Along with Reinhardt, Willem de Kooning, and Franz Kline, he formed the Eighth Street Club in 1948, which became a weekly forum for young artists and critics concerned with issues of aesthetics and artistic practice.[2]

Stylistically, *Bo-Bo,* the earliest of the Blanton's three paintings, recalls the work of de Kooning. In fact, critics such as Thomas Hess likened Resnick to de Kooning, who also tended to delineate space and the boundaries between spaces with painterly edges as opposed to exact outlines.[3] Resnick denied that de Kooning influenced him, however.[4] He also refused to affiliate himself with any one artistic movement despite his close association with the Abstract Expressionists and the parallels between his own early work and theirs.

In *Bo-Bo,* a seemingly haphazard arrangement of brushstrokes suggests a kind of gestural violence, while the colors and directional force of the painterly marks create a sense of overall balance within the composition.[5] One critic noted the "conversational" nature of Resnick's working method, especially in early works like *Bo-Bo*: "Each gesture of Resnick's is an intuitively calibrated response to the previous mark and a question posed to the mark that follows."[6]

Unlike *Bo-Bo,* which Resnick composed out of large, gestural strokes, *Sovereign* and *The Winds Crossing and Later* exhibit thousands of tiny marks that at first glance appear nearly monochromatic. In fact, Resnick filled both paintings with varied hues. In *Sovereign,* red, blue, green, yellow, and hints of purple abound, while in *The Winds Crossing and Later* instances of green, white, blue, and orange are mixed in with the predominant ochre color. Layers of pigment cover the surfaces of both paintings; colors are buried within and under other colors, some completely invisible.[7] Perhaps counterintuitively, Resnick believed that this process of building up the surfaces of his paintings was subtractive rather than additive: as unwanted images emerged, he eliminated them by over-painting.[8] The result is a dense, allover surface that appears impenetrable and infinite, as if it extends beyond the edges of the canvas or is a fragment of a larger whole.[9] Both thickly painted compositions extend the principles of the Abstract Expressionist gesture in a new direction.

Resnick's method of layering paint creates the illusion of both depth and light. Because he used oil instead of acrylic paints, he was able to build up colors without muddying the hues, producing a luminous effect on the painting's surface.[10] One art critic astutely observed of Resnick's work that "the more one looks the more one sees, the more differences there are, and, at the same time, the more onenesses, the more light . . . What may first suggest only vast fields of texture soon turns into palimpsests."[11] Resnick continued to explore the allover surface apparent in *Sovereign* and *The Winds Crossing and Later* throughout the remainder of his career, even when he returned to figuration toward the end of his life.

Resnick asserted a strong presence in the art world not only through his paintings but through teaching and lecturing as well. He worked at various schools throughout New York, California, Wisconsin, and Maine, helping shape the next generation of painters, including David Reed. In the late 1960s and early 1970s, he gave a series of challenging talks at the New York Studio School, in which he related his experience of what it means to be an artist.[12] Resnick was never given full credit for the vital role he played in postwar American painting, a situation instigated by Hess's dismissal of him as a mere follower of de Kooning in his 1955 review. Resnick disdained art world politics anyway, and he succeeded in alienating many of the period's prominent critics, among them Hess, Harold Rosenberg, and Clement Greenberg. Despite facing personal as well as professional adversity, Resnick remained committed to his painting practice, and perhaps because of the lack of critical and scholarly recognition, he was able to explore the process of painting without concerning himself with the fashions of the art world.

Valerie Hellstein

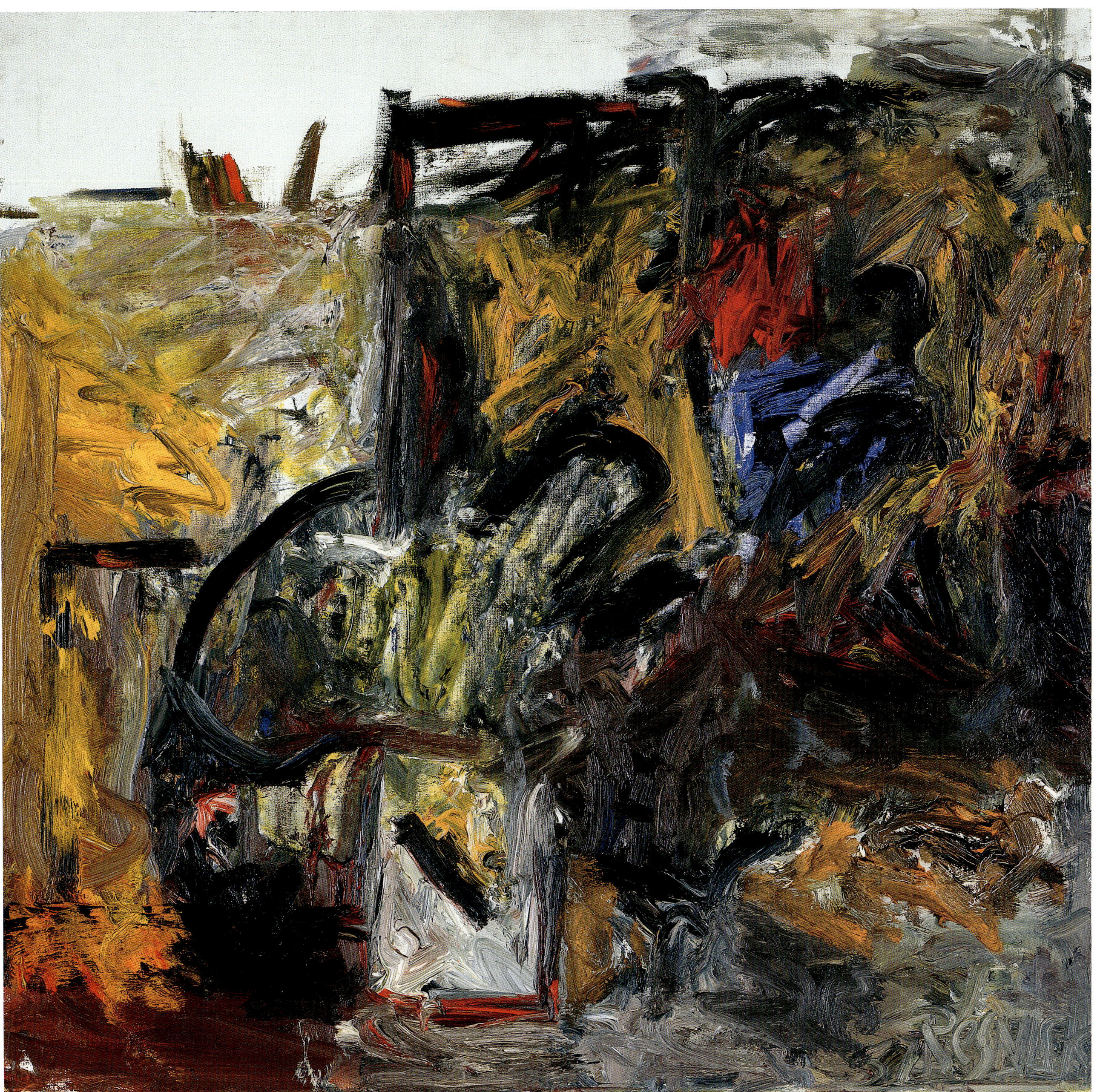

148.

Bo-Bo, 1957

Oil on canvas
38 × 38 in. (96 × 96 cm)
Gift of Mari and James A. Michener
1991.312

Provenance: Purchased by James Michener from Parke-Bernet Galleries, New York, 1965
Signed lower right "57 Resnick"

149.

Sovereign, 1959

Oil on paper mounted on stretched canvas
$75\frac{7}{8} \times 43\frac{3}{8}$ in. (192.8 × 110.2 cm)
Gift of Robert A. Ellison, Jr.
1995.115

150.

The Winds Crossing and Later, 1963

Oil on canvas
68⅛ x 50 in. (173 x 128 cm)
Gift of Mari and James A. Michener
G1968.113P

Provenance: Purchased by James Michener from Parke-Bernet Galleries, New York, 1965
Signed verso "M. Resnick, 1963"

Notes

1. Linda L. Cathcart, *Milton Resnick: Paintings 1945–1985* (Houston: Contemporary Arts Museum, 1985): 77.
2. Cathcart, 6–7; and Hiram Carruthers Butler, "Downtown in the Fifties," *Horizon* 24 (June 1981): 15.
3. Thomas B. Hess, *Willem de Kooning* (New York: George Braziller, 1959), 31.
4. Resnick stated: "I am not the follower of Monet, I am not an admirer of de Kooning. I am not an action painter. I am not an Abstract Expressionist. I am not any younger than anybody or older." (Quoted in Cathcart, 83.)
5. Resnick may even have created the surface texture by manipulating the pigment with his hands.
6. Stephen Westfall, *Milton Resnick: Paintings 1957–1960* (New York: Robert Miller Gallery, 1988), n.p.
7. In later pieces from the 1960s and 1970s, Resnick used so much paint that some of his canvases weighed as much as 450 pounds. See Corinne Robins, "Milton Resnick," *Arts Magazine* 52 (September 1977): 2.
8. See Cathcart, 7; and Henry Hopkins, "Introduction," in *Milton Resnick: Selected Large Paintings* (Fort Worth, Tex.: Fort Worth Art Center-Museum, 1971), n.p.
9. Donald Judd once described the surfaces of Resnick's canvases as "continuous." D[onald] J[udd], "Milton Resnick [Wise]," *Arts Magazine* 34 (March 1960): 54–55.
10. See Nancy Ellison, "The New Work in Roswell," in *Milton Resnick: Selected Large Paintings*.
11. L. C., "Milton Resnick [Wise]," *Artnews* 62 (February 1964): 8.
12. For transcripts of the lecture, see Geoffrey Dorfman, ed., *Out of the Picture: Milton Resnick and the New York School* (New York: Midmarch Press, 2002).

Larry Rivers

New York, 1923–Southampton, New York, 2002

w. New York (summers in Provincetown, Massachusetts), 1947–1948; Paris–Italy, 1950; New York (summers in Southampton, New York, and frequent trips to Europe and Africa, late 1950s and 1960s), 1951–2002

Dead Veteran (1961, plate 151) belongs to a series of paintings and small oil sketches whose subject matter Larry Rivers derived from photographs commemorating the last two surviving Civil War veterans. In particular, Rivers studied a photograph reproduced in the January 11, 1960 issue of *Life* magazine that depicted the veteran Walter Williams lying in his coffin with a marine guard. The nostalgic quality of this image, as well as its ability to arouse emotion and sympathy, greatly captivated Rivers. However, he did not simply use the picture to create a narrative painting or to suggest melancholy or regret. As an intimate source of personal history and a ready-made representation of reality, the photograph provided Rivers with a vehicle to fuse the subjective gestural language of the Abstract Expressionists with the mass-produced subject matter of the emerging Pop artists. By inserting the photograph into the context of a personally inflected oil painting, Rivers challenged the separation of art and life endorsed by the Abstract Expressionists and created an image that is both rich in painterly substance and infused with sentimentality and psychological complexity.

Rivers began his artistic career as a musician, not a painter. A talented jazz saxophonist while still in high school, he earned his living during the late 1930s and early 1940s playing in professional jazz bands. In 1945, while playing at a resort in Maine, he met the aspiring artist Jane Freilicher, who encouraged him to paint. A year later, he rented a modest studio in New York and, at the suggestion of his neighbor, the painter Nell Blaine, he enrolled in Hans Hofmann's school of painting. Hofmann taught his students to appreciate the formal features of their compositions, including scale, weight, and texture. Rivers valued this emphasis on form, yet he never abandoned his interest in representation. As *Dead Veteran* attests, he instead sought to find a means of reconciling Hofmann's emphasis on abstract form with his own penchant for figurative subject matter. The first pictures that Rivers produced using this approach shared a stylistic affinity with Pierre Bonnard, whose 1948 retrospective at The Museum of Modern Art made a lasting impression on the young artist, as did Willem de Kooning, whom Rivers met that same year. In the end, Rivers transcended the influence of both artists to create his own personal idiom that incorporated complex reinterpretations of history painting, an innovative use of materials and media, and a willingness to occupy contradictory positions.

Early in his career, Rivers made a favorable impression on a number of New York critics. In 1949 Clement Greenberg lavished praise on the artist's Bonnard-inspired canvases, and he included Rivers's paintings in the prestigious *Talent 50* exhibition, organized with Meyer Schapiro at the Samuel Kootz Gallery the following year. By the late 1950s, however, the same critics had become openly hostile toward his work. Beginning in 1953, with his monumental *Washington Crossing the Delaware,* Rivers developed an increasingly sardonic approach to painting, synthesizing the historical and personal in a manner that evoked both amusement and irreverence.[1] Rivers explained his reasons for choosing this iconic episode in American history:

> *I wanted to make a work of art that included some aspects of national life. . . . Washington Crossing the Delaware was always the dopiest, funniest thing in American life. Year after year, as a kid in school, you see these amateurish plays that are completely absurd but you know they represent patriotism—love of country, so here I am choosing something that everybody has this funny duality about.*[2]

By appropriating a subject familiar even to school children, Rivers believed that he could render the content of his work invisible and thereby enable it to function on ideographic terms, not unlike pure form in abstract painting. Art critics, including Greenberg, considered such work "anti-art," and by the late 1950s, they had dismissed Rivers's paintings as offensive and distasteful.

Negative reactions such as these provided Rivers with the incentive to become even more reactionary: "I was energetic and egomaniacal and . . . cocky and angry enough to want to do something that no one in the New York art world could doubt was disgusting, dead and absurd."[3] Throughout the 1960s and 1970s, he continued to offend the art world with his irreverent appropriation of themes and imagery from the work of past masters and his use of banal and often vulgar subject matter. For example, in 1964 he made two free-hand copies of Jacques-Louis David's *Napoleon in His Study* (1812), which he brazenly titled *The Greatest Homosexual* and *The Second Greatest Homosexual*. Rivers also challenged established moral standards by incorporating sexually explicit subject matter into his work.

In the late 1970s and early 1980s, Rivers became increasingly introspective and embarked upon a series of exceptionally large canvases called Golden Oldies. In these, he recreated and recapitulated themes and subjects from the preceding twenty-five years. As he had with the photographs of the last Civil War veterans, the artist embraced the nostalgic and sentimental qualities evoked by the juxtaposition of his earlier compositions and his latest experimentations with different styles and media.

Rivers explored more serious themes in the 1980s and 1990s, including the Holocaust, Nazi occupation, and slavery. Throughout this period, his designation as a "bad boy" continued to flourish. When his memoir, *What Did I Do? The Unauthorized Autobiography,* was published in 1993, it infuriated a number of people, including many women whose intimate secrets Rivers openly divulged. In spite of these criticisms, the book, with its lurid and frequently exaggerated claims, represents Rivers's ongoing effort since paintings like *Dead Veteran* to break down the boundaries between art and life.

Erina Duganne

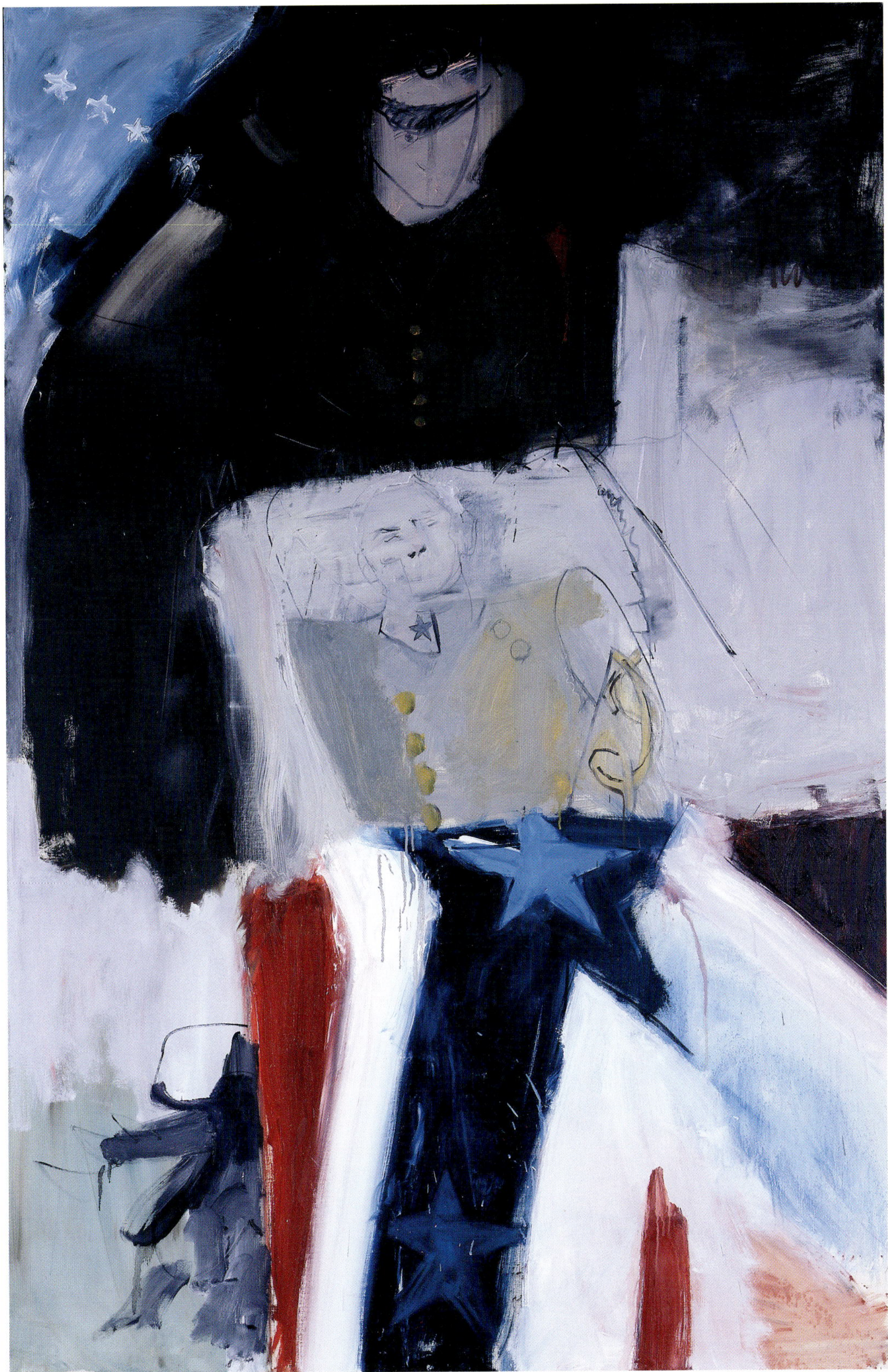

Notes

1. Rivers based his *Washington Crossing the Delaware* on Emmanuel Leutze's 1851 painting of the same name.
2. Quoted in Sam Hunter, *Larry Rivers* (New York: Rizzoli International Publications, 1989), 16.
3. Larry Rivers, "A discussion of the work of Larry Rivers," *Artnews* 60 (March 1961): 54.

151.

Dead Veteran, 1961

Oil on canvas
81 x 52 in. (205.8 x 132.2 cm)
Gift of Mari and James A. Michener
1991.317

Provenance: Purchased by James Michener from Martha Jackson Gallery, New York, 1962; long-term loan to The University of Texas at Austin, 1968–1991

Dario Robleto

b. San Antonio, 1972
w. San Antonio, 1991–1993; El Paso, Texas, 1993–1996; San Antonio, 1996–present

The work of Dario Robleto can be approached from many angles, each offering the viewer/reader multiple layers and trajectories into its overall meaning. As these variables are intended to collide simultaneously and without hierarchy, it is a challenge for the writer to delineate them all. Robleto's diverse research and extensive production methods draw upon the history of American roots music, current scientific inquiry, battle history, race issues, alchemical processes, and phenomenological thought. Yet, as a visual artist who emerged in the 1990s, Robleto asserts that his artistic evolution is first and foremost intertwined with the rise of DJ culture, in particular the practice of electronic "sampling" and its approach to history. "Sampling is a world view," he stated, referring to the constructive value of mining history by mixing the past and present to create the future.[1] Robleto's fascination with the history of music production has led him to realize much of his work as a musician would create a record album.[2]

The work of a serious DJ, according to Robleto, investigates, mines, and freely borrows elements from previous songs, including the emotions they elicit and their capacity to transport the listener to other eras through their respective genres, such as R&B, New Wave, and Grunge. In philosophical terms, the DJ offers a way out of the historical trap—a means to renew the past that is creatively and willfully productive, as opposed to deconstructive and analytical. This method has played a significant role in much of the art and music of the 1990s, which reinterpreted the electronic fluidity made possible by the proliferation of digital production through decisively handmade, "lo-tech" processes, an activity that Robleto heralded in the mid-1990s.[3]

Although Robleto's work is first experienced on a visual level as object-based sculpture, it is only completed on a conceptual basis by its neighboring text, in the form of a museum label. This text provides the key to the inner workings of the sculpture, the weighted history of its evolution, and the expanded auratic value that the artist has invested in it. Comprehension of the work at hand involves intimate knowledge of the sensorial and historical properties of the objects' own ingredients, such as bone dust from every bone in the human body, melted bullet lead from every American war, melted vinyl phonograph records (Billie Holiday, Bob Dylan), and black cherry wine tonic fortified with a variety of herbs and compounds. Thus the work, masquerading as a readymade, actually functions as a site for a series of past events and a proposal for future transmogrification.

Of significance to Robleto's development is the technique of appropriation, especially as artists such as Sherrie Levine and Richard Prince practiced it in the late 1980s. Working mainly with two-dimensional images, these artists openly appropriated the symbols of power, aura, and meaning from other value-laden sources, a post-structuralist tactic aimed at questioning those sources' supposedly inherent truth-value. This led to artists adopting an increasingly ironic posture in their work from the 1990s. Robleto, on the other hand, chose to distance himself from commentary and irony and push the act of appropriation toward extremely sincere ends, stating: "What does it say about a culture when to be sincere is a radical position?"[4]

The generative question behind nearly all of Robleto's work is: *What if?* As a scientist in a laboratory might conjecture, the artist sets himself the task of asking art to solve a problem. Robleto seems to be interested in creating intersections where leaps of faith and the scientific process might actually corroborate and contaminate one another. Often he seeks to create "an alternate route through history" by fusing mutually exclusive bodies of thought and engendering hybrid and progressively potent new alternatives.[5] For instance, the elements Robleto brought together in *Hippies and a Ouija Board (Everyone Needs to Cling to Something)* (2003, plate 152), part of his Southern Bacteria 2 trilogy, combine both compatible and conflicting histories in order to unlock what the artist hoped would be a "healing." The primary question here is: what would a hippie from the 1960s need today to heal the ailments from which he might be suffering?

For this problem, the artist imagined a turn-of-the-century company, one that would sell medicinal tonics door-to-door. The tonics, encased in individually marked bottles, each contain specific solutions for such ailments as rheumatism, psychedelic flashbacks, depression, osteoporosis, nostalgia, lack of hope, and other imagined aged-hippie syndromes of the body and spirit. Beneath the bottles, placed in a nearly hidden part of the suitcase, 45-rpm records (cast in prehistoric whale bone dust—as if to echo from a very deep, remote belly) of artists such as Jimi Hendrix, Patti Smith, Bob Dylan, and The Beatles are provided for aural and moral support. The Ouija board is offered for continual contact with the dead.

The company name, Lomax & Cleaver, which appears on the case and bottles and reappears in other works as well, is one that the artist went to great lengths to invent. It refers to two historical figures who unwittingly become collaborators in the healing process: John Lomax, a folklorist and archivist who conducted the first field recordings of Southern Blues music, and Eldridge Cleaver, a Black Panther whose politics included concerted revenge against the white man. Both are practices that Robleto believes led to the commercial exploitation of black culture.[6] In suggesting the collapse of these two fundamentally opposed figures of history, ethical questions regarding race and the history of black music production are unpacked and reshuffled. Asking *What if?* Robleto draws the viewer's attention to history as effervescent and open-ended, and stresses the continual need to pursue and remix its unanswered questions.

Regine Basha

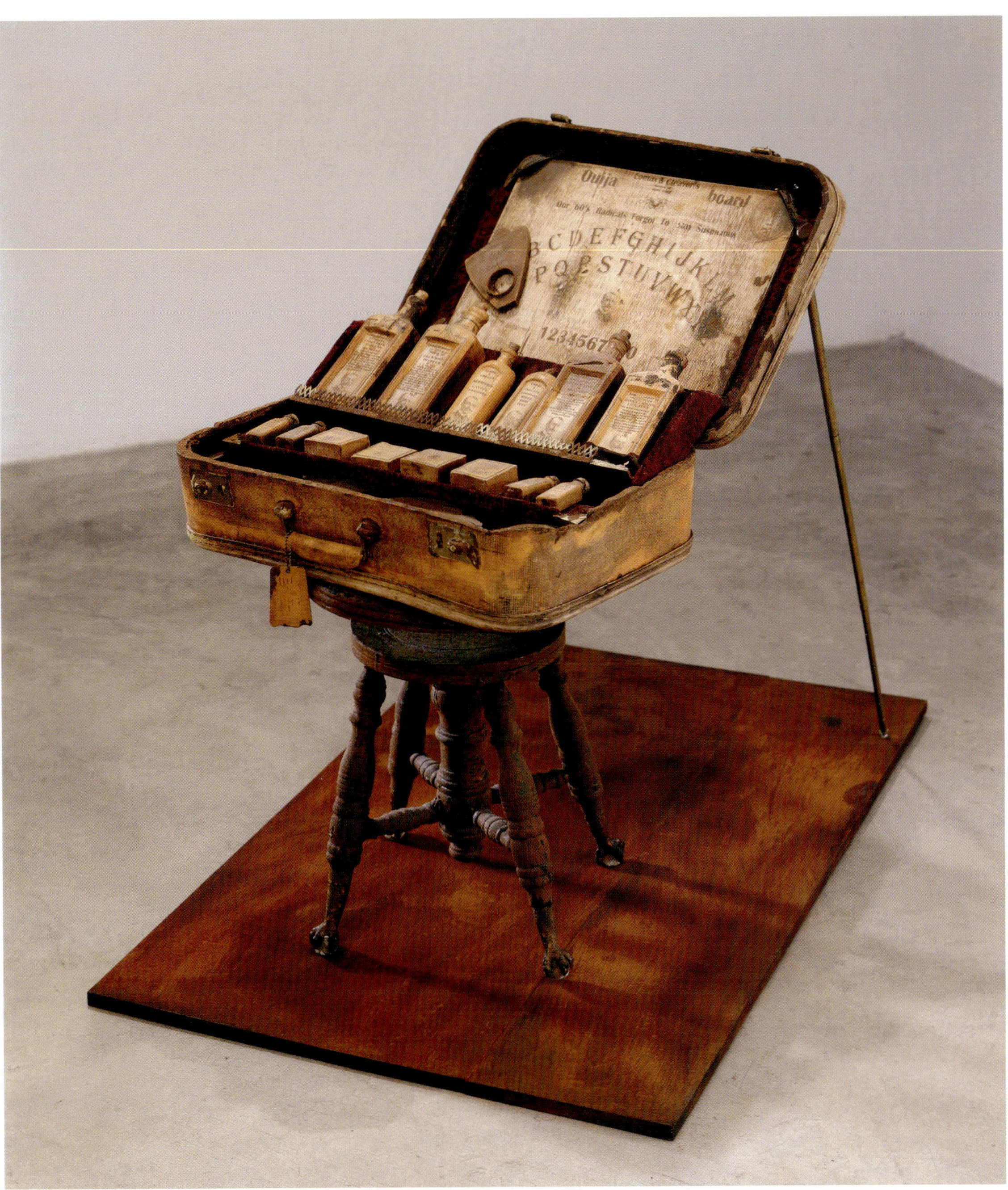

Notes

1. Dario Robleto, conversation with the author, Austin, October 3, 2005.
2. Many works are billed as the 'b side' to other works.
3. Robleto worked as a DJ for many years. Many of the artists he admires, including Christian Marclay, have also been DJs and have allowed this practice to color their processes of making sculpture and installation art.
4. Joe Holley, "Conceptual Artist as Mad Scientist," *New York Times*, April 13, 2003.
5. Dario Robleto, conversation with the author, San Antonio, January 9, 2005.
6. Robleto, conversation with the author.

152.

Hippies and a Ouija Board (Everyone Needs to Cling to Something), 2003–2004

Suitcase: cast and carved dehydrated bone calcium and bone dust from every bone in the body, microcrystalline cellulose, cold cast iron and brass, rust, antique syringe, crushed velvet, leather, thread, water extendable resin, typeset

Ouija board, bottles and medicines: cast and carved dehydrated bone calcium and bone dust from every bone in the body, typeset, home-brewed moonshine (potato-derived alcohol), home-made wine health tonics (water, sugar, fermented black cherries, yeast, gelatin, tartaric acid, pectinase, sulfur dioxide, oak flavoring, fortified with: 100-year-old hemlock oil, Devil's Claw, witch hazel bark, swamp root, powdered rhubarb, pleurisy root, belladonna root, white pine tar, coal tar, dandelion, sarsaparilla, mandrake, mullein, scullcap, cramp bark, elder, ginseng, horny goat weed, tansy, sugar of lead, mercury with chalk and tin-oxide, calcium, potassium, creatine, zinc, iron, nickel, copper, boron, vitamin K, crushed amino acids, home-cultured antibiotics, chromium, magnesium, colostrum, ironized yeast, ground pituitary gland, ground wisdom teeth, ground sea horse, shark cartilage, coral calcium, iodine, and castor oil)

Records: various 1960s 45-rpm records cast in prehistoric whalebone dust, typeset

42 × 23 × 19 in. (106.7 × 58.4 × 48.3 cm)

Purchase through the generosity of The Brown Foundation, the Michener Acquisitions Fund, and the Blanton Contemporary Circle

2004.182

Provenance: Purchased from Acme Gallery, Los Angeles, 2004

Peter Rostovsky

b. St. Petersburg, Russia, 1970
w. Ithaca, New York, 1991–1995; Brooklyn, New York, 1995–present

Russian-born, Brooklyn-based artist Peter Rostovsky manufactures situations in which antediluvian and contemporary worldviews collide, effecting a sort of visual eulogy of the human condition. The artist studied at Cooper Union Art School, Parsons School of Design, and Cornell University and is an alumnus of the Whitney Museum's Independent Study Program. His stiff, hyperrealistic works, such as those from the Epiphany Model series, function as a collective homage to, and a poignant deconstruction of, classical notions of the sublime, specifically modern man's intellectually irreconcilable relationship with the natural world. In this respect, the artist could be considered a slightly cynical postmodern illusionist.

Rostovsky produces consistently hallucinatory works, be they paintings, sculptures, or hybridized pendant objects. He places great emphasis on artificiality in hue, form, and perspective, enhancing the rift between human beings and nature. In the hybrid painting/sculpture *Epiphany Model 5: Expedition* (2004, plate 153), to date, the most recent work in the Epiphany Model series, Rostovsky finalizes this act of separation. He renders his human subjects, two climbers, as a discrete sculpture on a pedestal gazing at a picturesque landscape of stately, ice-capped blue mountains mounted on the wall a few feet away. Both figures wear climbing gear, and they appear atop what looks to be a mountain summit. The landscape before them is vast, generalized, and sweeping. The figures and mountaintop, amalgams of paint, Super-Sculpey, and other materials, are comparatively tiny and festooned in meticulous detail. This disparity in scale and specificity sets the stage for an existential drama played out in the empty space between the climbers' perch and the daunting mountain chain that spreads before them in the distance.

If *Epiphany Model 5* indeed depicts an attempt to confront nature, Rostovsky's subjects are faced with the truly celestial grandeur of their failure. Such an interpretation dovetails with traditional notions of the sublime as outlined by Edmund Burke in *A Philosophical Inquiry into the Origin of Our Ideas of the Sublime and Beautiful* (1757). Burke portrayed encounters with the sublime as awe inspiring, even terrifying experiences, and if viewed from behind the pedestal, this reading of *Epiphany Model 5* is appropriate. The men appear miniscule, dwarfed by the landscape and frozen in the stance individuals might assume after having surrendered their free will.

When viewed from the side or in front of the pedestal, however, the work takes a decisive philosophical turn. From these perspectives, the spectator suddenly gains access to visual cues that complicate what once appeared to be a straightforward encounter with the sublime. Neither climber responds to the majestic landscape in ways that are characteristic of sublimity—that is, with some combination of wonder and trepidation, fright and acquiescence. One climber looks like he might be physically weary . . . or . . . is he just plain cocky? He is seated casually, his legs dangling over the edge of the summit like he does this sort of thing every day. The other figure stands at firm attention, arms crossed over his avalanche pole, as if contemplating the task set before him—of bridging the physical gap between himself and the distant landscape. *Epiphany Model 5*, then, is not a manifestation either of romanticism in the classical sense of being mesmerized by the sublime or of the *naissance* of a postmodern "rugged individual." On the contrary, the work is decidedly *un*romantic, despite the painting's affinity with the Romantic landscape tradition in terms of light, composition, and perspective.

The sculptural element of *Epiphany Model 5* speaks of a self-imposed distance on the part of the climbers—an intentional subjugation of nature that ultimately reduces its power. While the fractured physicality of the two-part piece could conceivably lament a dislocation between man and nature, relegating the climbers to the status of passive spectators, it also points to the innate and uniquely human arrogance that resides in any attempt to commune with or conquer something so obviously greater than ourselves.

Rostovsky uses a hybridized format and a similar mixed sentiment in several works with an equally high degree of success. For example, *Epiphany Model 4: The Meteor Shower* (2004) consists of a resin sculpture atop a pedestal—this time, a young man and woman on a hillside—placed directly in front of a painted landscape. Just as in *Epiphany Model 5*, the subjects reflect individuated responses. The couple seems disenchanted by the celestial spectacle before them; one could even surmise that they look downright bored.

The painted components of both *Epiphany Model 4* and *5* speak of a cinematic or photographic artificiality through the use of a hyperrealistic, almost garish palette. Shades of dreamy ultramarine and otherworldly cerulean blues dominate. These scenes, much like the physical

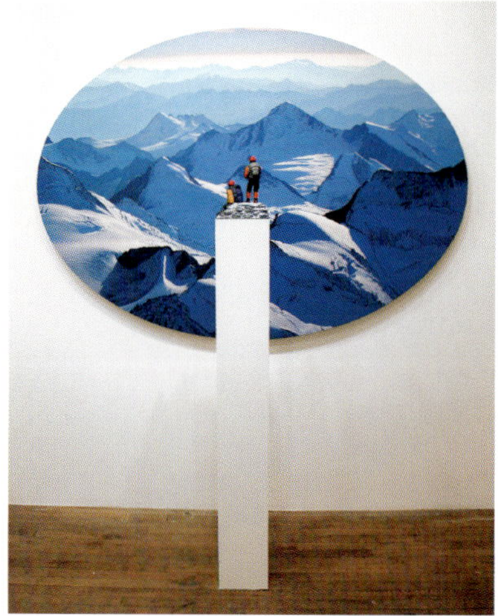

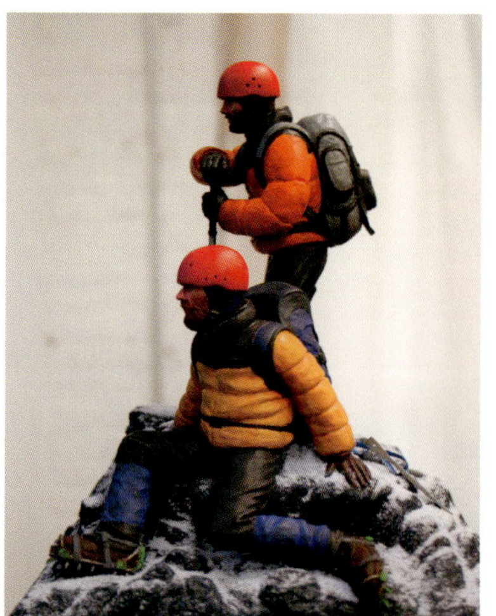

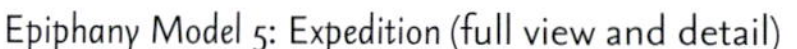

Epiphany Model 5: Expedition (full view and detail)

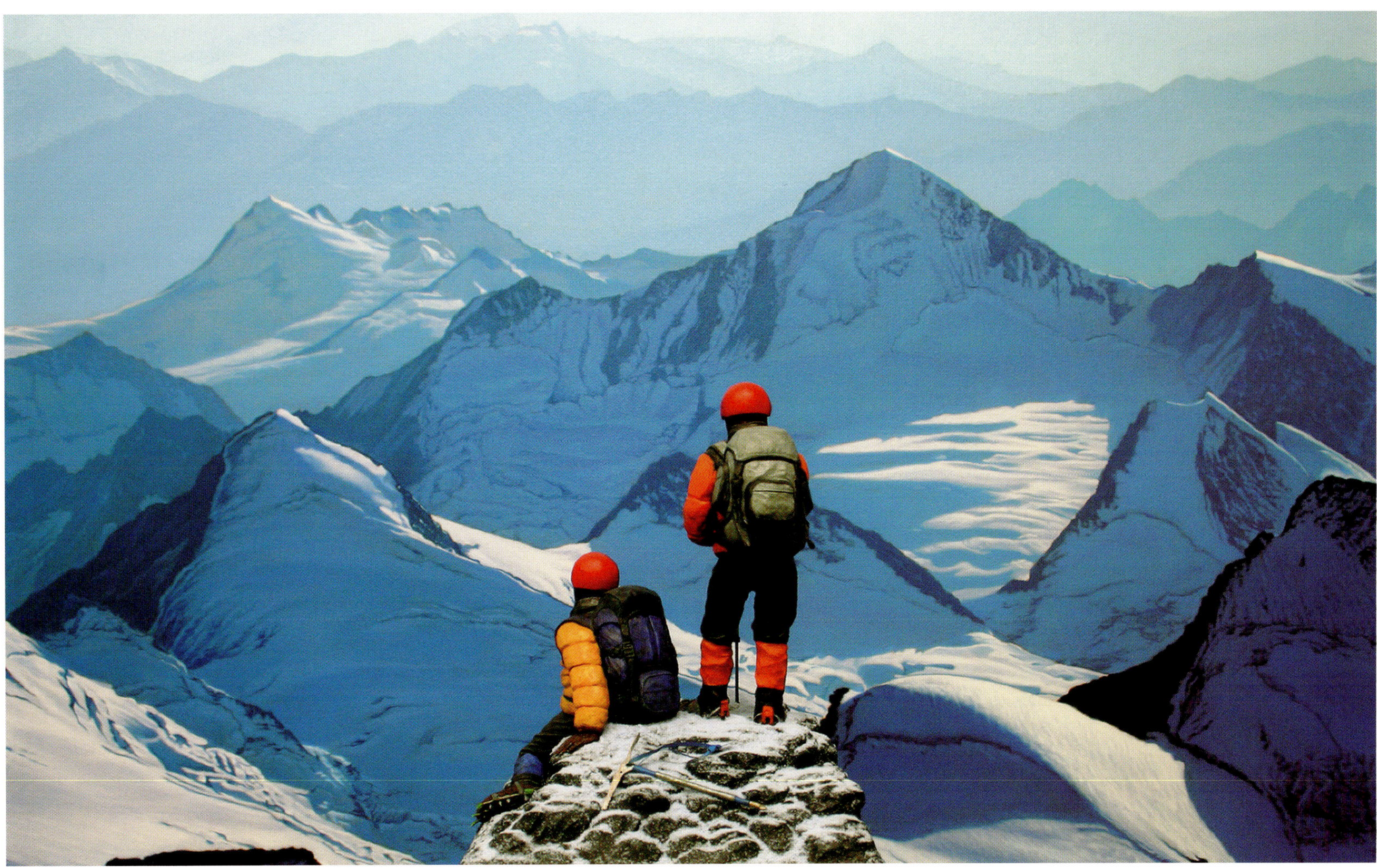

arrangement of the works, are very obviously mediated and constructed, almost synthetic. In actuality, the artist harvests his landscapes off the Internet, creating surreal panoramic impressions of locales that he himself has never seen firsthand. The conceptualization and process of Rostovsky's work has critical bearing on its impact: since his landscapes are illusory and, ultimately, unrepresentative, contemplation on the part of the viewer is all the more complex and potentially futile.

Rostovsky's image sourcing critiques the perceived immediacy of the landscape, a form of artistic expression traditionally considered spontaneous. This creates a parallel between painting and photography, which is, by its nature, more immediate than painting. Yet it is common knowledge that even in photography matters of framing, scale, angle, perspective, and format affect the end result, mediating subjectivity and experience. *Epiphany Model 5* is, to some extent, an indictment of the pervasiveness of the photographic in our society and the passive supplication with which images are received. We, like Rostovsky's climbers, no longer occupy the landscape much less participate in or interact with it. We simply consume it.[1]

Anjali Gupta

153.

Epiphany Model 5: Expedition [detail], 2004

Oil on canvas and Super-Sculpey, aluminum wire, wood, plastic, acrylic paint, and Styrofoam flakes with pigment
Painting: 52 × 72 in. (132 × 182.8 cm)
Sculpture and base: 62 × 7 × 7 in. (157.5 × 17.8 × 17.8 cm)
Partial and pledged gift of Jeanne and Michael Klein
T2005.6.1/2–2/2

Provenance: Commissioned and purchased at the request of the museum by Jeanne and Michael Klein from The Project, New York, 2004

Note

1. For additional information on Rostovsky, see Kelly Baum, "Peter Rostovsky," *Artlies*, no. 43 (summer 2004): 108; Holland Cotter, "Glenn Brown, Julie Mehretu, Peter Rostovsky," *New York Times*, June 23, 2000; and Michael Velliquette, "Notes on Peter Rostovsky," available at http://www.glasstire.com/reviews/sa/ArtPace_Rostovsky.htm [May 5, 2005].

Mark Rothko

Dvinsk, Russia [Daugavpils, Latvia], 1903–New York, 1970
w. New York, 1923–1970

For the first fifteen years of his career, Mark Rothko focused almost exclusively on figurative painting, but in 1940, the same year he changed his name from Rothkowitz to Rothko, he began to embrace abstraction. Inspired by ancient mythology and Surrealism's experiments with automatic drawing, Rothko's work entered a new phase that he described as his "symbolic style."[1] The Blanton's Untitled (1943, plate 154) is a representative example of this development in the artist's work.

In his "symbolic style" paintings, Rothko dismantled and reshaped the human body, separating it into parts reminiscent of classical sculptural fragments or transforming it into the biomorphic shapes seen in Untitled. These works also feature a flattening or compressing of pictorial depth, an approach that Rothko publicly endorsed in 1943 as one of his "aesthetic rules."[2] In both his paintings and words of this period, he expressed an increasing dissatisfaction with traditional modes of figural representation, though he continued to maintain the importance of the figure. "I belong to a generation that was preoccupied with the human figure and I studied it," remarked Rothko. "It was with utmost reluctance that I found it did not meet my needs."[3]

Untitled exemplifies the process of figural transformation in Rothko's work.[4] A small oil painting, it depicts several organic shapes that seem to flow through an airy or liquid landscape. The composition is divided into three horizontal regions—a hallmark of Rothko's work throughout his career—against which several biomorphic figure-shapes drift and interact. Three forms assert themselves as principal subjects. The first figure floating above center suggests a sphere whose curved mass has congealed into three or four upward-reaching bulbous head or limb shapes. In the bottom third of the canvas, below a turquoise wave, a secondary figure suggests an embryonic swimmer floating or tunneling through dripping root-forms. At the right appears the third subject, an upright turquoise figure with tentacles that reach downward and out toward the left. The other two subjects seem to be moving toward this third subject, whose role in connection to them is ambiguous: it might be a destination, a ferryman, or an obstacle. The energetic relationship between the painting's figural components hovers between rest and forward motion.

Rothko experimented with similar subjects in other "symbolic" works of the early 1940s, often selecting titles from mythology. While he was not then engaged in figurative painting in any traditional sense, the disembodied or transformed anatomies in "symbolic" paintings like Untitled are identifiable as referents to the human form. Rothko believed that the modern artist should embrace a broad approach to representing the figure: "The whole of man's experience becomes his model, and in that sense it can be said that all of art is a portrait of an idea."[5] Even as Rothko's works grew increasingly abstract, he nonetheless rejected descriptions that represented them in formal or abstract terms. In a 1943 radio address with Adolph Gottlieb, Rothko insisted: "Neither Mr. Gottlieb's painting nor mine should be considered abstract paintings. It is not their intention either to create or to emphasize a formal color-space arrangement."[6] Within a year of completing Untitled, Rothko and Gottlieb proclaimed: "There is no such thing as a good painting about nothing. We assert that the subject is crucial and only that subject matter is valid which is tragic and timeless. That is why we profess spiritual kinship with primitive and archaic art."[7]

By 1948 Rothko had abandoned representation entirely, expunged explicit references to subject matter by eliminating titles, and coined the term "multiform" to describe his new paintings. His works were now celebrated as pure abstractions remarkable for their bold use of color and their arrangement of organic forms.[8] In 1950 Rothko dedicated himself exclusively to the large-scale Color Field paintings that he would pursue with singular attention for the rest of his life. Yet even after abandoning all apparent vestiges of representation, he reasserted his long-standing allegiance to the human figure as his subject:

> *It was not that the figure had been removed, not that the figures had been swept away, but the symbols for the figures, and in turn the shapes in the later canvases, were new substitutes for the figures. . . . My new areas of color are things. I put them on the surface. They do not run to the edge, they stop before the edge. . . . These new shapes say . . . what the symbols said. . . . My present paintings are realistic.*[9]

The fame achieved by Rothko's Color Field style, which continues to be celebrated as a hallmark of Abstract Expressionism and the New York School, has tended to eclipse his earlier work. Close scrutiny of his art from the early 1940s, however, reveals a process of obsessive repetition and simplification that freed Rothko from an approach based on formal portrayal of the physical body, while simultaneously allowing him to continue to frame the dramatic realities that he believed the human figure contained. An understanding of the pivotal role of paintings such as Untitled offers insight into the relationship between the artist's early experimentations and his mature work.[10]

Rina Faletti

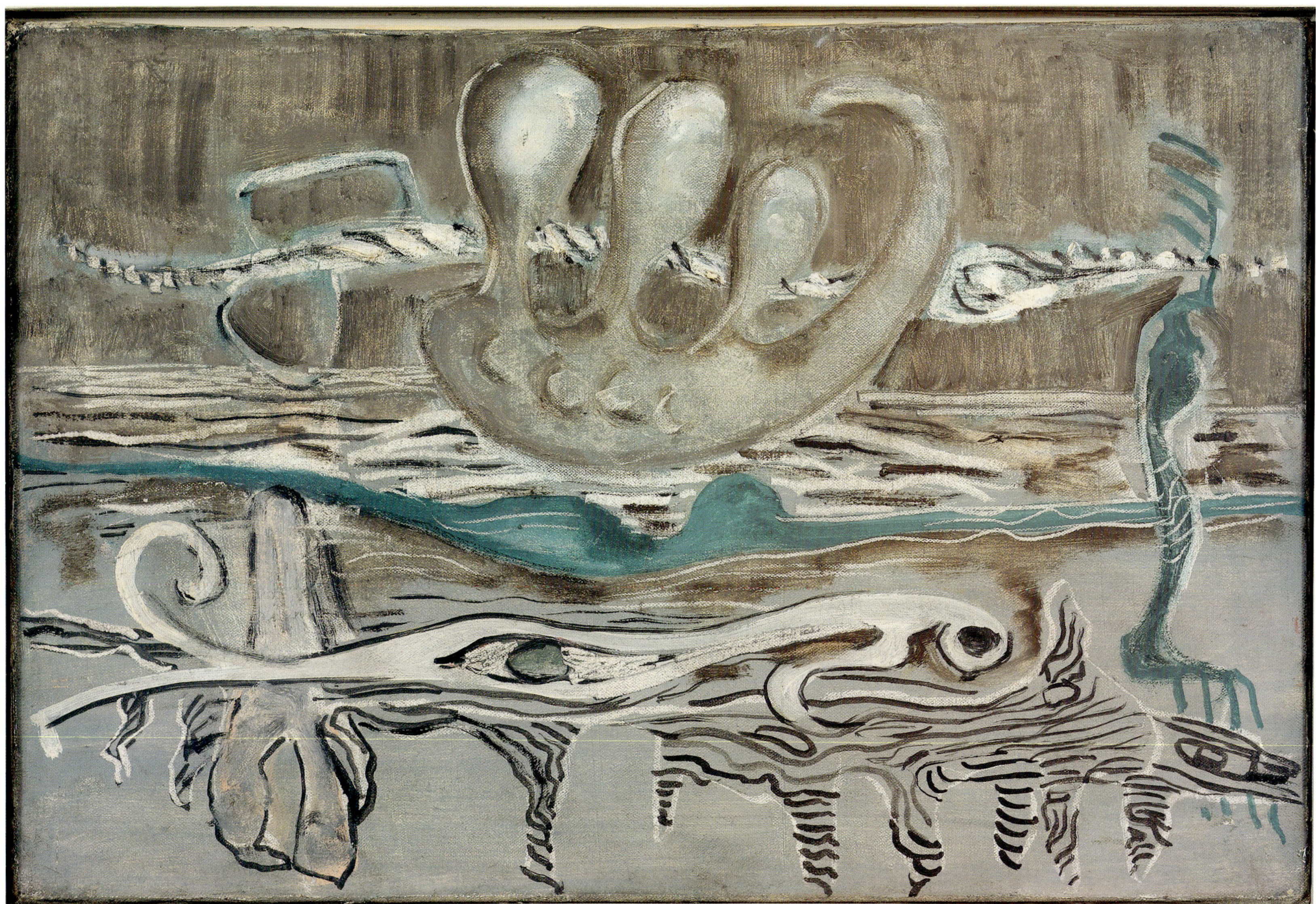

Notes

1. William Seitz, unpublished interview notes, January 22, 1952, Archives of American Art, Smithsonian Institution, Washington, D.C. Quoted in Bonnie Clearwater, "Selected Statements by Mark Rothko," in *Mark Rothko, 1903–1970* (London: Tate Gallery Publishing, 1996), 73.
2. "We wish to reassert the picture plane. We are for flat forms because they destroy illusion and reveal truth." Mark Rothko and Adolph Gottlieb, and partially drafted by Barnett Newman, "Letter to the Art Editor," *New York Times*, June 7, 1943. Quoted in Clearwater, 77.
3. Mark Rothko, transcription of a public lecture at the Pratt Institute, Brooklyn, October 27, 1958, Rothko Archive. Quoted in James E. B. Breslin, *Mark Rothko: A Biography* (Chicago: University of Chicago Press, 1993), 389–97.
4. For information about this work, see David Anfam, *Mark Rothko, Works on Canvas: Catalogue Raisonné* (New Haven: Yale University Press, 1998), 205.
5. Mark Rothko and Adolph Gottlieb, "The Portrait and the Modern Artist," typescript of a radio broadcast on "Art in New York," Radio WNYC, October 13, 1943. Reprinted in *Adolph Gottlieb: A Retrospective* (New York: The Arts Publisher, 1981), 170.
6. Rothko and Gottlieb, "The Portrait and the Modern Artist," in *Adolph Gottlieb: A Retrospective*, 171.
7. Rothko and Gottlieb, "Letter to the Art Editor," in Clearwater, 77–78.
8. For a discussion of the critical response to Rothko's stylistic shift to Color Field painting, see Anfam, 60. For a year-by-year comprehensive bibliography of Rothko criticism during the 1940s, see Anfam, 681–82.
9. William Seitz, unpublished interview notes, January 22, 1952, Archives of American Art, Smithsonian Institution, Washington, D.C. Quoted in Clearwater, 73.
10. I consider Untitled to be an experimental work, as it was never exhibited in Rothko's lifetime. Close study of the "symbolic" works reveals it to be a clear precursor to those he did exhibit. Compare it, for example, with nos. 217, 228, 237, and 246 in Anfam's catalogue raisonné.

154.

Untitled, 1943

Oil on canvas
12⅞ × 19 in. (33 × 48 cm)
Michener Acquisitions Fund
P1969.14.3

Provenance: Purchased by Donald O'Leary, New York, from the artist through Howard Putzel and Peggy Guggenheim, New York, c. 1945; James Robicheau, Newport, Rhode Island, c. 1963; John Stephan, New York and Rhode Island, c. 1963; Howard Wise Gallery, New York, 1963; purchased from Howard Wise Gallery, 1969
Signed verso, upper left "Mark Rothko"

Morgan Russell

New York, 1886–Broomall, Pennsylvania, 1953

w. Paris–Italy, 1906; New York–Paris, 1906–1909; Paris (frequent trips throughout France and Europe), 1909–1921; Paris–Aigremont, France (frequent trips throughout Europe), 1921–1946; Ardmore, Pennsylvania, 1946–1953

Morgan Russell and fellow American expatriate Stanton Macdonald-Wright developed a theory of painting known as Synchromism, which was based on progressive scientific color theories and on writings about color and music popular in contemporary intellectual circles. Synchromism proposed that color serve as the foundation of form and space and advocated using set color harmonies, similar to harmonies in Western music, an idea inspired by American color theorist Hardesty Maratta. Abstracted into faceted planes, Synchromist works often have a volumetric quality and are composed of bright, built-up layers of pigment.

Synchromism as an organized movement did not last long, though it was an important development in the history of early American modernism. Russell chose the term, meaning "with color," in 1912. He and Macdonald-Wright first exhibited together at Munich's Neuekunstsalon in June 1913. Later that year, they showed their work in Paris at the Galerie Bernheim-Jeune, a major venue for avant-garde art. Russell and Macdonald-Wright held their last joint exhibition in March 1914 at the Carroll Gallery in New York. Synchromism achieved wide exposure through the advocacy of Macdonald-Wright's brother, Willard Huntington Wright, an important art critic.

In the mid-1910s Russell began to employ a more representational style, as did many of his avant-garde counterparts. With a few further explorations into Synchromism, including his Eidos series of the 1920s, Russell would continue working in a representational manner through most of the rest of his career. These works, including *Purple and Red Still Life* (c. 1920, plate 155), reflect the enormous influence of Paul Cézanne on Russell. As an active member of avant-garde art circles, Russell had ample opportunity to learn about Cézanne, who he had firsthand knowledge of, having borrowed Leo Stein's Cézanne painting *Apples* (date unknown) in 1910.[1] Russell appreciated Cézanne's work, which he described as "wholes—solid and powerful without holes and rich and forceful in color and massive in form."[2] *Purple and Red Still Life* pays homage to the Post-Impressionist master in the placement of fruit on a folded white drapery. Furthermore, the distorted perspective and the thickly applied paint echo the work of the older artist. But Russell made the painting his own by eliminating the strong, dark outlines that Cézanne employed and by using a brighter palette that reflected his abiding interest in color contrasts. The white, yellow, and turquoise hues brighten the dominant reds and violets of the composition.

Born in New York to an architect father, Russell's early training was in architecture, though he had some initial instruction in the fine arts. A 1906 trip to Italy and Paris convinced Russell to pursue sculpture and painting. After his return to the United States, he studied painting at the New York School of Art with Robert Henri. He also studied sculpture with James Earle Fraser at the Art Students League, and on a return trip to Paris in 1909, he worked with Henri Matisse on a series of standing sculptures. From 1909 until 1946, Russell lived almost exclusively in France. The year 1920, to which *Purple and Red Still Life* dates, was a transitional period in the artist's personal life, since he had recently returned to Paris after spending a few years during and after the war in the south of France. He soon grew tired of urban living, however, and settled in a farmhouse in rural Aigremont, France. By summer 1921, Russell had almost completely isolated himself from the art world, though he continued to receive critical recognition for some time.

Russell became increasingly interested in creating representational scenes, including monumental figure studies that reflected his appreciation of classical, Renaissance, and Baroque art. He also explored religious subjects that predicted his conversion to Catholicism late in life. He regularly exhibited for the remainder of his career, but financial success proved elusive.

R. Sarah Richardson

Notes

1. Marilyn S. Kushner, *Morgan Russell* (Montclair, N.J.: Montclair Art Museum, 1990), 188.
2. Morgan Russell to Andrew Dasburg, October 27, 1910, Dasburg Papers, Washburn Gallery, New York. Quoted in Kushner, 17–18.

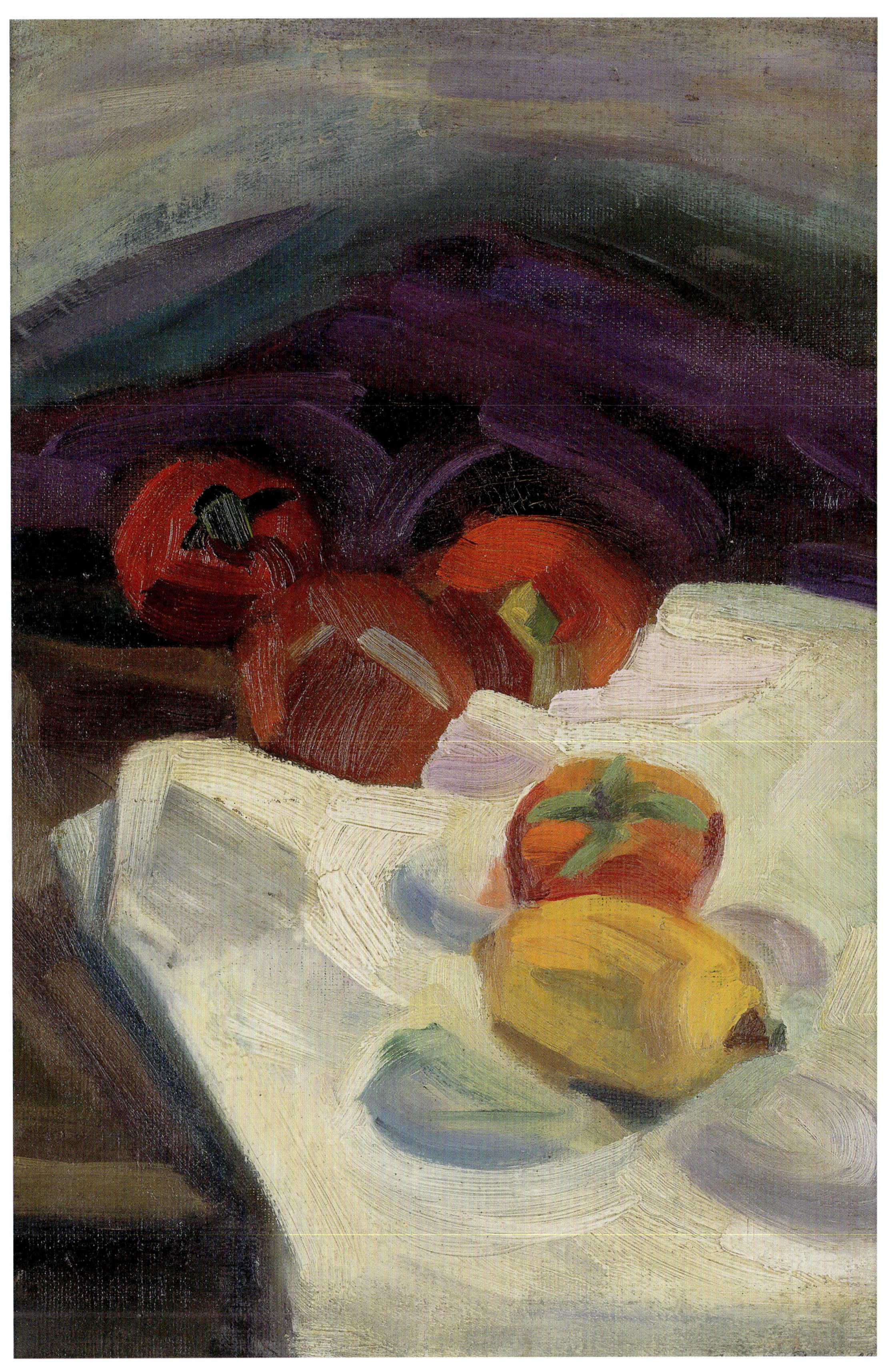

155.
Purple and Red Still Life, c. 1920

Oil on canvas
16 × 11 13/16 in. (41 × 28.4 cm)
Michener Acquisitions Fund
P1970.14.3

Provenance: Purchased from Robert Schoelkopf Gallery, New York, 1970
Signed lower right: Morgan Russell

Alan Saret

b. New York, 1944

w. New York, 1966–1971; India, 1971–1973; New York, 1973–1981; Harrison, Arkansas, 1981–present

When critic Emily Wasserman reviewed Alan Saret's first solo exhibition at the Bykert Gallery in New York in 1969, she described his work as "airy, energetic and lyrical."[1] While conceived and created over ten years later, *Autumn Cumulus* (1980, plate 156) demonstrates many of the same formal and aesthetic qualities as Saret's earlier work.

Saret attended Cornell University, where he completed his BA in architecture in 1966. He then moved to New York to study sculpture at Hunter College with Robert Morris, one of America's foremost Minimalist (and later Post-Minimalist) artists, receiving his MFA in 1968.

Saret shared concerns and strategies with a number of his contemporaries who came to prominence in the late 1960s and early 1970s, particularly Richard Serra, Eva Hesse, Robert Smithson, and Lynda Benglis. Collectively, the work of these artists was described by contemporary critics as "Post-Minimalist," a term that reflects an engagement with Minimalism's formal concerns coupled with a rejection of its philosophical rigidity. Post-Minimalist artists continued to experiment with industrial or nontraditional materials and to grapple with nonrepresentational, geometrically based forms, but they inflected these explorations with a focus on process, ambiguity, references to organic forms or substances, nature, and other philosophical and material diversions from Minimalist orthodoxy.

Although created after the height of Post-Minimalism, *Autumn Cumulus* exemplifies many of the formal tendencies specific to that movement, insofar as it transforms everyday, mass-produced materials into striking yet unimposing forms that refer to nature's own sculpture and palette. Here Saret curled and twisted together individual strands of lacquered copper wires. The wires are all of a similar hue, but changes in light and in the viewer's position produce subtle shifts in the work's fundamentally monochromatic "palette." *Autumn Cumulus* holds its form due to the tightness of the weave and the stiffness of the materials. Yet equal attention has been given to the space between the wires, which imparts to the piece a feeling of weightlessness and fragility. The airiness of *Autumn Cumulus* means that it has no central visual focus. Because it is composed around a cavity, Saret's work can be seen as a visual labyrinth that offers many points of entry.

With regard to the installation of his work, Saret's approach was both flexible and innovative. Not unlike the Minimalist sculptors who preceded him, Saret sought to redefine the manner in which sculpture (traditionally confined to a pedestal) might be displayed. *Autumn Cumulus,* for instance, can be hung on the wall like a painting, suspended from the ceiling, or placed directly on the floor. A change in position likewise effects a subtle alteration in the work's meaning, underscoring a different organic association. When hung on the wall or suspended from the ceiling, *Autumn Cumulus* evokes a cloud, with the wall and ceiling acting as its "sky." Indeed, the word "cumulus" implies a direct association between Saret's tangle of red wires and the way in which a cloud—a natural form composed entirely of gaseous particles—conveys at once a sense of lightness and density and hovers in a state between substance and nothingness. When placed on the floor, however, the work's tangled form suggests a tumbleweed, a coiled branch, or even a pile of leaves that has collected beneath a tree. In the case of the latter, the title "Autumn Cumulus" might be understood to allude to the work's reddish hue, a color associated with that season's foliage.

Autumn Cumulus represents the culmination of more than a decade of artistic experimentation. In the late 1960s Saret produced sculptures that highlighted his ability to combine architectonic structure, unconventional materials, and process. Works such as *Untitled (Folding Glade)* (1969–1970), *True Jungle: Canopy Forest* (1968), and *Mesh Makes Mountains* (1969) experimented with folding, curling, and draping inexpensive, industrial materials so that the resulting forms evoked both built and natural environments.[2] In an exhibition held at his downtown loft in 1970, Saret drew inspiration from the scale and formal qualities of materials associated with the building trade: panels of decorative tin, stainless steel mesh, cast iron architectural motifs, and draped sheets of rubber and cloth. His installation extended throughout the large loft space with the objects and materials placed on top of and alongside each other in unusual juxtapositions and often tenuous arrangements. Here Saret began to articulate his interest in rudimentary architecture and basic forms of shelter and containment.[3]

Saret went on to explore the theme of habitation in his 1975 *Ghosthouse,* a diaphanous teepeelike structure composed of a thin plastic membrane loosely draped over folded steel fencing.[4] He constructed *Ghosthouse* in Artpark in Lewiston, New York, and inhabited it for four months. The work reflected the influence of his early training as an architect and possibly the effects of his period of study with visionary architect Paolo Soleri, whose experimental community of Arcosanti was in the early stages of creation in 1975.[5] *Ghosthouse* also represented Saret's desire to display his work outside of traditional gallery and museum settings.[6] Indeed, by the late 1970s Saret had not only founded Spring Palace, an exhibition space and studio, he had established the foundation ALAEL, which was dedicated to "self-realization and enlightenment through art," and had spent three years residing in India.[7] These experiences in alternative living and alternative methods of displaying art reinforced his beliefs in art's spiritual and meditative qualities of art.[8]

By the time his work reappeared in commercial galleries in the early 1980s, Saret had begun to reembrace simple, industrial materials, but the results were often more intricate and self-contained than in his earlier pieces.[9] For his show at the Charles Cowles Gallery in 1980, he exhibited a series of seventeen wire sculptures, including *Autumn Cumulus.* One year later, the Whitney Museum of American Art

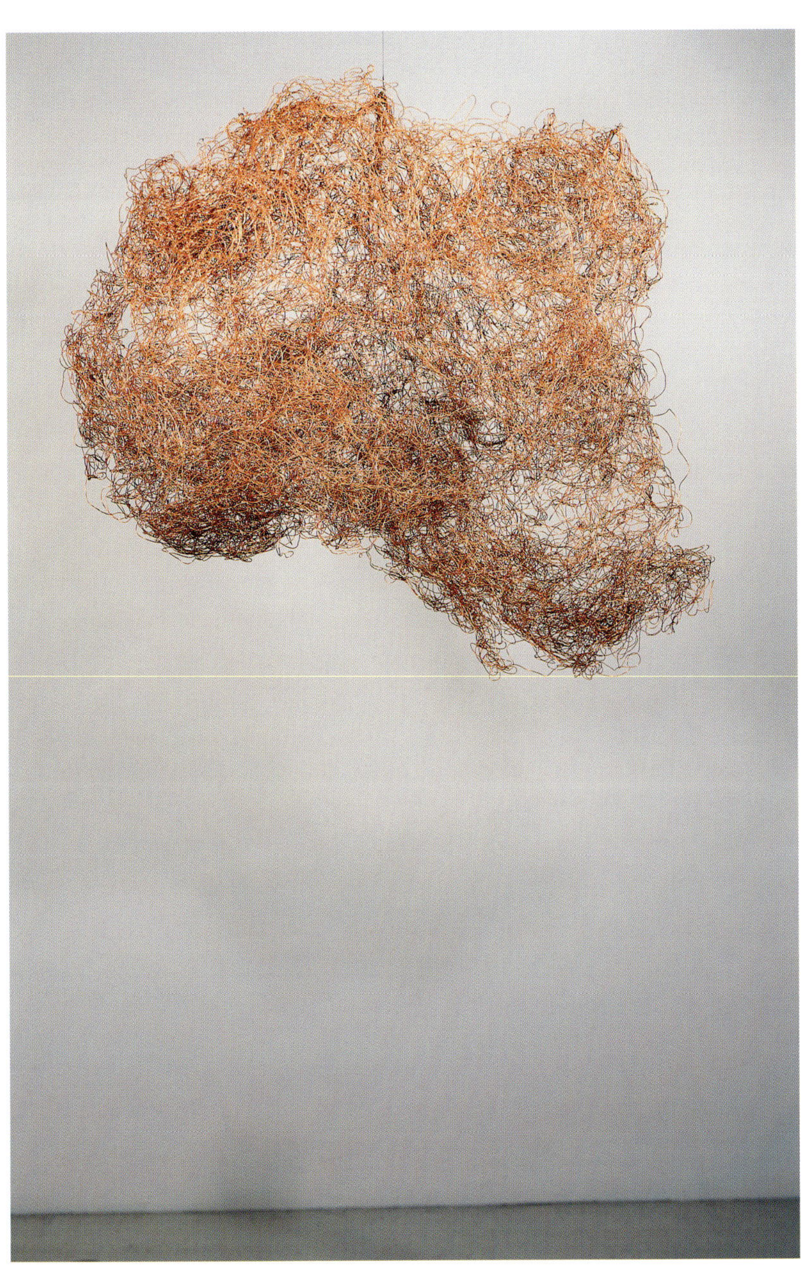

showcased twelve of Saret's sculptures in *Developments in Recent Sculpture*. This exhibition featured a wide range of Saret's work, showing his progression from the monumental and stationary wire mesh pieces of the 1960s to the more ephemeral works of the early 1980s. Saret was also selected for a "retrospective" of Post-Minimalist sculpture titled *The New Sculpture, 1965–1975: Between Geometry and Gesture*, which was held at the Whitney Museum in 1990.

While *Autumn Cumulus* seems to depart from the artist's interest in habitation, in reality the sculpture reflects many of the same concerns that informed *Ghosthouse*, in particular Saret's longstanding interest in exploring the structural nature of his medium—its ability to occupy, define, and alter space—while simultaneously eschewing that medium's materiality. Like *Ghosthouse, Autumn Cumulus* also demonstrates Saret's attempts at the "dispersal of structural matter."[10] As such, it exemplifies the type of experimentation that defined Saret's career and a generation of post-Minimalist artists.

Jennifer Barrett

Notes

1. Emily Wasserman, "Alan Saret," *Artforum* 7 (January 1969): 58.
2. Saret's art was included in the 1968 Whitney Biennial; in a 1969 solo exhibition at the Bykert Gallery, New York; and in the 1969 exhibition *9 in a Warehouse* at the Leo Castelli Gallery, New York. Saret chose not to be included in the Whitney's 1969 exhibition *Anti-Illusionism: Procedures/Materials* on the grounds that his work was still engaged with the creation of illusion—or at least with the desire to evoke associations. Saret's position thus separates him from many of his contemporaries whose concerns for process, materials, and concept defined their work as anti-illusionistic. For more on this, see Emily Wasserman, "Alan Saret's Studio Exhibition," *Artforum* 8 (March 1970): 62–63.
3. Wasserman, "Alan Saret's Studio Exhibition," 63.
4. Jonathon Crary, "Alan Saret," *Arts Magazine* 52 (September 1977): 4.
5. Crary, 4.
6. "Alan Saret at Charles Cowles," *Art in America* 68 (September 1980): 121.
7. Quoted in "Alan Saret," available at http://www.oberlin.edu/allenart/collection/saret_alan.html [May 1, 2004].
8. Crary, 4. For more information on Saret's exhibitions at alternative sites, see the exhibition review in *Artforum* 13 (summer 1975): 70.
9. Exhibition review, *Art in America* 68 (September 1980): 121; and Colin Gardner, "Alan Saret: Daniel Weinberg Gallery," *Artforum* 29 (March 1991): 138.
10. Crary, 4.

156.
Autumn Cumulus, 1980
Lacquered wire
48 × 40 × 36 in. (121.9 × 101.6 × 91.4 cm)
Archer M. Huntington Museum Fund
2004.108
Provenance: Purchased from James Cohan Gallery, New York, 2004

Peter Saul

b. San Francisco, 1934

w. San Francisco, 1950–1952; St. Louis, 1952–1956; the Netherlands, 1956–1958; Paris, 1958–1962; Rome, 1962–1964; Mill Valley, California, 1964–1975; Chappaqua, New York, 1975–1981; Austin, 1981–2000; Germantown, New York, 2000–present

It is difficult to imagine a subject too taboo for Peter Saul, known as the preeminent painter of the modern American grotesque. Above all, he is an artist who puts content before technique. As he once wrote, "Main thing I think about, artistically . . . is getting the 'idea' or the 'expressive idea' . . . out in front of the art supplies."[1] Defying the type of material-based formalism espoused by critics such as Clement Greenberg, as well as what he views as the high-mindedness of the discipline of art history and its canon, Saul seeks to address in painting what he deems it has thus far disregarded: the harsh realities of violence, perversion, vulgarity, and materialism in American society.

Born in San Francisco in 1934, Saul attended Stanford University and the California School of Fine Arts before studying art at Washington University in St. Louis, where he discovered the disturbing images of Max Beckmann and Francis Bacon. Saul lived in Europe from 1956 to 1964 and became a protégé of sorts to the Chilean painter Matta. In 1957, after having learned of Abstract Expressionism in the United States, he began experimenting with "sprinkling drips and loosening paint" in the manner of Jackson Pollock.[2] However, instead of working on canvas, he used popular images of sports cars and girls in bathing suits as supports.[3] By the early 1960s this technique had rendered Saul what he described as "the example of 'bad' pop art in many long articles about Roy Lichtenstein."[4] Dismayed by the critical reception of his combination of Pop art and abstract painting, Saul began to depict a vision of America gleaned from American magazines sold in Europe, such as *Life* and *Time*.[5] Drawing upon consumer culture and media propaganda, he commented critically on the middle class's laissez-faire attitude toward serious political issues. Saul's works from this period also echoed his growing interest in portraying crime, murder weapons, sexual deviation, and insanity, often using formal and design elements appropriated from advertising, filtered through his own brand of cartoonish dark comedy.

Saul painted *Criminal Being Executed* (1964, plate 157) in Rome and showed it at his 1964 exhibition at the Allan Frumkin Gallery in New York, where James Michener discovered it. The painting reflects several of the artist's predominant themes: crime and capital punishment, the irreverent appropriation of canonical works of modern art, and the Disney cartoon character, Donald Duck. In this image, Donald Duck plays the executioner to a large, amorphous, expressionless, and sexless figure labeled "CRIME," to whom Saul attaches the addendum "does not pay" in tiny lettering. Out of the duck's mouth come the slangy words: "you have to fry." Literalizing this sentence, the criminal complies by frying an atypical breakfast consisting of eggs, bacon, urine, poison, and a bullet. As is typical of his earlier style, *Criminal Being Executed* is flatly colored and possesses a sketchlike quality, unlike Saul's subsequent paintings, which employ precise, almost pointillistic color modeling.

Between 1962 and 1965 Saul painted many images depicting capital punishment, including *Sex Deviate Being Executed* (1964) and *Donald Duck Crucifixion* (1965). These are complex compositions featuring garish colors, twisted biomorphic figures, and execution apparatuses as jumbled machines. Saul's use of Donald Duck—who appears throughout his work as an everyman, an icon, and often an unwitting loser—is traceable back to his interest in the *cartoon noir* of *Mad Magazine* and the comic books that originated in 1950s underground culture.[6]

In the 1960s the issue of the death penalty was hotly contested in both the United States and Europe, with those seeking the abolition of the death penalty urging the courts to reconsider the constitutional validity of what they saw as a cruel and unusual punishment.[7] Saul often references timely political issues like the death penalty in his work but masks them with a deadly humor, making it difficult to discern his specific position or point of view. Indeed, for all the provocative, inflammatory qualities of his paintings, and despite his "contempt for authority, political or artistic,"[8] Saul is not a political activist (his contrarian nature does not lend itself to didacticism or propaganda); he prefers to convey his beliefs and convictions obliquely through his paintings.

Just as important as its subject matter is the manner in which Saul carefully orchestrated the viewer's response to *Criminal Being Executed*. He exaggerated the scene's shocking effects so as to stimulate the morbid curiosity of viewers, who find themselves repelled as well as fascinated by the execution. It seems Saul was intent on generating a situation where viewers are made aware of their own culpability, even own hypocrisy, in the face of endemic violence—denouncing brutality while simultaneously taking delight in it. As Ellen Johnson wrote in the catalogue for Saul's 1964 show at the Allan Frumkin Gallery:

> *Saul is not advocating a first-hand experience of perversion and murder (as the narrative of so many of his pictures testifies, he firmly believes that crime does not pay), but he does urge an honest awareness of their presence and of their dangerous appeal which makes the subject of crime such a commercial success in the entertainment field.*[9]

Over the succeeding decades, Saul continued to treat the theme of execution in works such as *John Wayne Gacy Being Executed* (1984) and *Jeffrey Dahmer* (1992), created while he was teaching at The University of Texas at Austin. Here, the humor is darker, the subjects more specific, and the images more disturbing than in *Criminal Being Executed*. As long as the public condemns crime on the one hand, but consumes it avidly in the mass media on the other, Saul's paintings will continue to resonate.

Melissa Warak

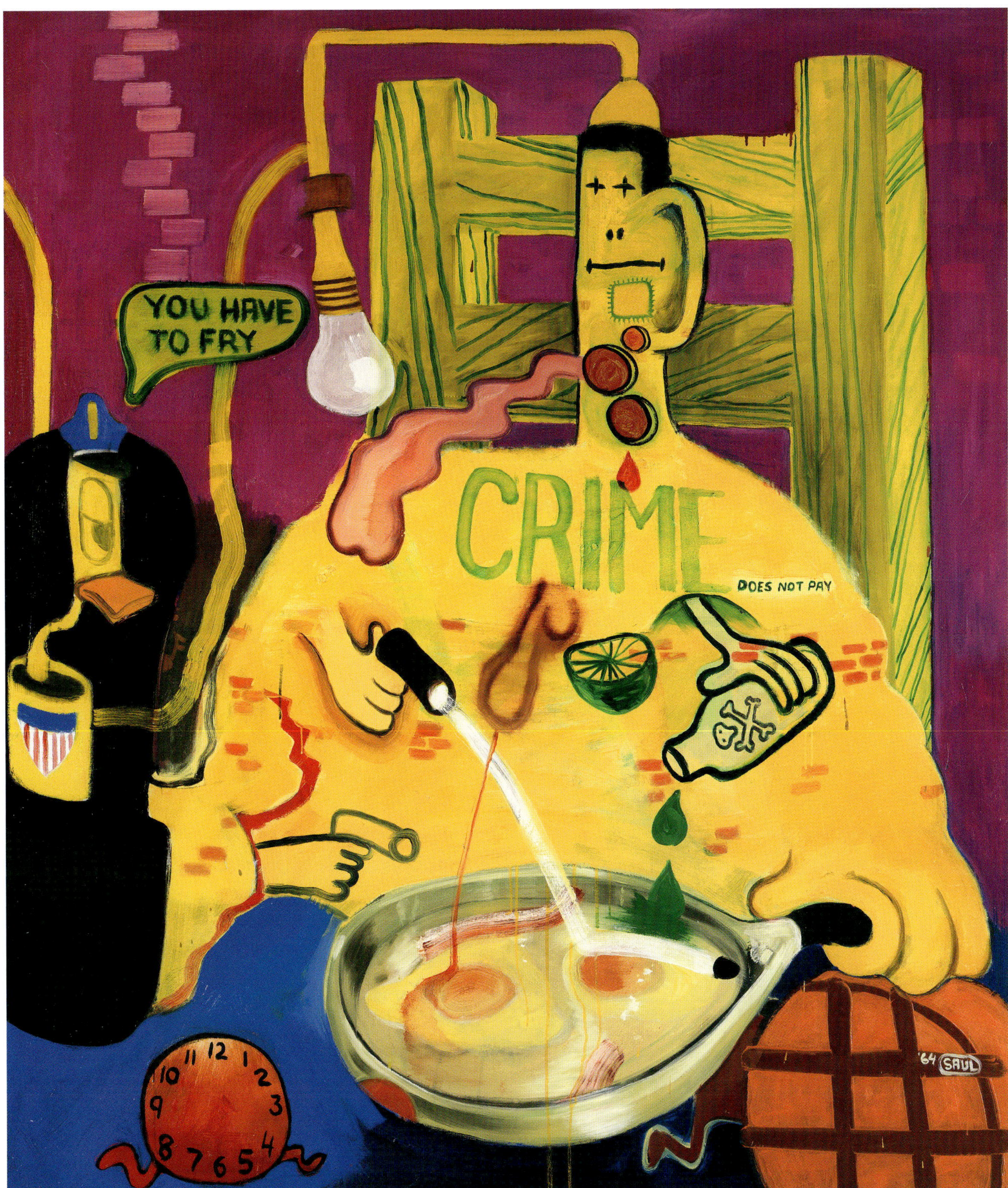

Notes

1. Quoted in Robert Storr, "The Peter Principle," in *Peter Saul* (Paris: Musée de l'Abbaye Sainte-Croix, Les Sables d'Olonne, 1999), 13.
2. Peter Saul, "Artist's Statement," in *Peter Saul* (Aspen, Colo.: Aspen Art Museum, 1989), n.p.
3. Saul, n.p.
4. Saul, n.p.
5. Ellen H. Johnson, *Recent Painting by Peter Saul* (New York: Allen Frumkin Gallery, 1964), n.p.
6. Storr, 37.
7. According to historian Michael Reggio, the death penalty came under scrutiny in the 1960s with the wide distribution of critical studies from England and Canada as well as films and memoirs detailing the ordeals of notable death row inmates. Michael Reggio, "History of the Death Penalty," in Laura E. Randa, ed., *Society's Final Solution: A History and Discussion of the Death Penalty* (Lanham, Md.: University Press of America, 1997), 8.
8. Saul, n.p.
9. Johnson, n.p.

157.

Criminal Being Executed, 1964

Oil on canvas
75 × 63⅛ in. (190.6 × 160.4 cm)
Gift of Mari and James A. Michener
1991.321

Provenance: Purchased by James Michener from Allan Frumkin Gallery, New York, 1964; long-term loan to The University of Texas at Austin, 1968–1991
Signed lower right "'64 SAUL" [name circled]

George Segal

New York, 1924–South Brunswick, New Jersey, 2000
w. New York–South Brunswick, New Jersey, 1941–2000

In a 1965 exhibition review, critic Robert Pincus-Witten described George Segal as "the wholly unanticipated heir" of Edward Hopper because of the similarities between his sculptures and the painter's scenes of lonely and isolated figures.[1] Two years later, Pincus-Witten gave a more extensive appraisal of the sculptor's early career in relation to Pop art, Abstract Expressionism, Minimalism, and Happenings, movements dominating the art discourse of the time.[2] Although his work as a painter and his transition to figural sculpture in the early 1960s defied easy categorization, what remained constant was Segal's interest in exploring the emotional depth found in private moments of contemplation and everyday routine.

Born to a Jewish immigrant family, Segal was raised in the Bronx at the height of the Depression. He attended the Pratt Institute and New York University from 1947 to 1949, working primarily in painting with some minor figural experiments in plaster through the late 1950s.[3] Between 1960 and 1962, however, Segal made a major break from his earlier work. Abandoning painting altogether, he began creating life-size sculptures of acquaintances from unpainted white plaster. He showed these new sculptures, which would become his best-known work, for the first time in 1962 at the Green Gallery in New York.[4] In the 1970s and early 1980s Segal made sculptures that addressed human suffering and current events, such as *The Holocaust* (1982), for the San Francisco Memorial to the *Six Million Victims of the Holocaust* at Lincoln Park, and *In Memory of May 4, 1970, Kent State: Abraham and Isaac* (1978) at Princeton University.

Like Andy Warhol, Robert Rauschenberg, and Jasper Johns, Segal incorporated commonplace objects into his work. His plaster casts of people, often set in tableaux of everyday life, include such elements as chairs, radiators, illuminated billboards, and bathroom fixtures. As a result, they were quickly classified as part of the Pop phenomenon. The quiet introspection of Segal's figures, however, distanced them from the cool satirical strains of Pop ideology. As Marco Livingstone noted of Segal's complex relationship to Pop art: "He had too great a concern for people living on the fringes of society to share in the celebration of material prosperity implicit in some Pop Art, but at the same time he had witnessed too much deprivation to wish to mock the desire for comfort and abundance."[5]

Because Segal created life-size tableaux with utilitarian objects, removed the pedestal from his sculptures, and occasionally incorporated film into his installations, his work has also been connected to the Happenings staged in the 1950s and 1960s by his friend and fellow artist Allan Kaprow. Indeed, Segal was very aware of Happenings, Performance art, and film, but his work remained sculptural rather than temporal: Segal's figures may be in the midst of an action, but they are stationary within the environments the artist built around them.[6]

Segal's unique method of casting required that he cover his models in sections with bandages soaked in a mixture of plaster of Paris and water. He would allow the bandages to set for almost an hour before removing them to finish drying, then he would piece them together. This was a slow and deliberate process that demanded personal contact as Segal touched and covered the model's body with wet strips of cloth. Each cast represents a specific individual who has been directly imprinted into the plaster. These individuals often remained anonymous: Segal's plaster cast portraits of his dealer, Sidney Janis, and art historian Meyer Schapiro are the only two identified by name.

Segal began painting his plaster sculptures in the late 1960s; *Blue Woman in Black Chair* (1981, plate 158) features his distinctive use of color. The sculpture depicts a woman, anonymous but individualized, sitting in a metal chair as if she had just woken up in the morning or was preparing to go to bed at night. The woman's eyes are closed, her body relaxed and comfortably weary. A garment draped casually over her slumped shoulders provides a modicum of protection and warmth, but it leaves her breasts, belly, and one leg exposed. This suggestion of physical vulnerability heightens the woman's seeming emotional vulnerability: she appears melancholy and withdrawn, as if the blue tint of her skin implied actual sadness. Looking at her in this private, fragile moment, one normally hidden from outside view, we become voyeurs. Segal used black, cobalt blue, and purple blue to heighten the visual impact and emotional tension of the work. The artist called himself a "closet colorist," noting that "color can be seductive, hallucinatory, depressing, disquieting, exhilarating. . . . [It] can be the rise and fall of my state of mind."[7] Late in his career, Segal returned to monochrome sculpture, this time black instead of white, but his instinct for color remained an integral part of his creative process.

Segal's depiction of the human condition, in the end, is what distinguishes his work from trends of the 1960s and 1970s and what reinforces the difficulty in successfully linking it to specific art movements. His entire oeuvre functions as a lifelong series of reflections on mortality.

Laura A. Lindenberger

Notes

1. Robert Pincus-Witten, "George Segal," *Artforum* 4 (December 1965): 51–53.
2. Robert Pincus-Witten, "George Segal as Realist," *Artforum* 5 (June 1967): 84–88.
3. Marco Livingstone, *George Segal Retrospective: Sculptures, Paintings, Drawings* (Montreal: Montreal Museum of Fine Arts, 1997), 16.
4. Pincus-Witten, "George Segal as Realist," 85.
5. Livingstone, 19.
6. Allan Kaprow, "Segal's Vital Mummies," *Artnews* 62 (February 1964): 33.
7. Quoted in Livingstone, 67.

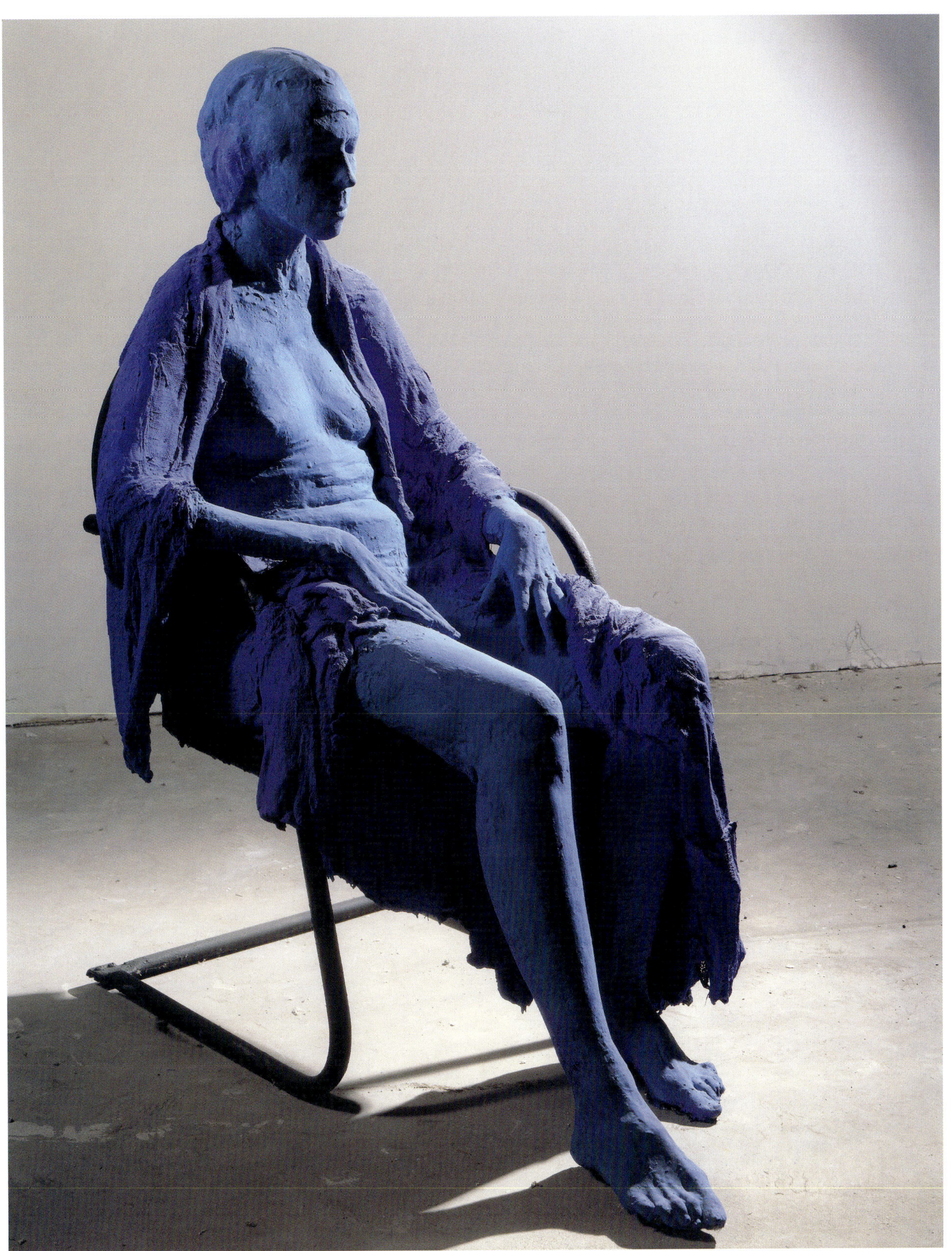

158.

Blue Woman in Black Chair, 1981

Painted plaster and metal
52 × 26 × 44 in. (132 × 66 × 111 cm)
Archer M. Huntington Museum Fund
1983.25

Provenance: Purchased from Sidney Janis Gallery, New York, 1983

Joan Semmel

b. New York, 1932

w. New York, 1950–1963; Spain, 1963–1970; New York, 1970–present

Joan Semmel's iconic female nudes emerged from and resonate with the concerns of the women's movement. When Semmel first encountered feminist ideas in New York in the early 1970s, she was a nontraditional art student—a single mother of two striving to complete her education, establish herself as a serious painter, and support herself and her children as an art teacher. Recently returned from Europe, where she had built a modest career as an Abstract Expressionist painter, Semmel embraced the movement's political activism by translating its central notion of empowerment into figurative, socially aware imagery that boldly departed from the prevailing Minimalist and Conceptual styles. Revisiting the centuries-old tradition of the female nude, she appropriated and subverted it, forging a new approach with a skillful mix of traditional realist and abstract painting techniques.

Semmel was drawn to art from a young age and attended New York's prestigious High School of Music and Art and The Cooper Union, where she studied with painters Nicholas Marsicano and Morris Kantor. She diverted from her studies early on, however, for marriage to a civil engineering student, leaving behind artistic challenges for a more conventional domestic life as a wife and mother in Queens. In the mid-1950s an extended period of illness and its long recuperation afforded her the opportunity to reexamine her path. When she was well, she recommenced her art studies, enrolling first at the Art Students League and then at the Pratt Institute, where she received her BFA in 1963. Later that year, her husband took an engineering position in Spain and the family relocated overseas. Divorced shortly thereafter, Semmel was left to support two children and create a professional life in the very conservative social environment of Franco's Spain. She drew upon her training as an Abstract Expressionist and, due to the popularity of that style abroad in those years, had some success exhibiting and selling her work in Spain and South America.[1]

In 1970 Semmel returned to New York, where the burgeoning women's movement immediately engaged her. Determined to improve the quality of life for herself and her children, she went back to school and earned an MFA from Pratt, which opened the door to teaching assignments at the Maryland Institute of Art and the Art School at the Brooklyn Museum.

A period of prolific production that has extended to this day began soon after Semmel's return to New York. From that time on, the artist has made paintings that offer a uniquely provocative and intimate view of female experience. In 1974 she began a series of nude self-portraits that merge the concerns of the post-Abstract Expressionist painting arena with feminist politics, adapting the almost exhausted vocabulary of the painted human form. These paintings explore what a woman sees, how she looks at herself, in details that are both self-evident and erotically allusive. At the core of all of Semmel's works is an implied critique of the "objectivity" of direct observation, as well as a willingness to expose both vulnerabilities and pleasures that are self-affirming for artist and audience alike.

Semmel's nude self-portraits present her reclining body, extending from the upper chest along the torso and limbs, in awkward repose—breasts, belly, legs, and arms are depicted in photorealistic detail, never glamorized or idealized. Picturing only the parts of the body that she can see, Semmel renders the figures headless, anonymous, giving literal and explicit form to the artist's perspective. Sometimes she portrays herself alone, at other times in prone relationship to male partners, whose bodies are also dispassionately drawn.

Within the dialogues of painting history, Semmel's works challenge the convention of a male artist's gaze on a passive female model. Within the feminist context of their making, they celebrate the sexual liberation of women whose actions are self-determining and heedless of social approval. Semmel presents the female body as a dynamic site, complex in its associations and functions. Essentially "first-person" representations, her images offer a rare experience of equivalence to the women who view them. They equate the body of the artist with the body of the viewer, and the space of the artwork with the space of the viewer, in ways not unlike those being explored by sculptors and abstract painters experimenting with Minimalism in the 1970s. Semmel's works precisely align her mastery of formal painting techniques with her desire for radical content. The artist said, "My intention was to present a confrontational view of the body rather than a voyeuristic one. I wanted the body to move out into the viewer's space and challenge the viewer. . . . By keeping the image large and up close the formal aspects are emphasized."[2]

Utilizing photographs she took of her own nude body as "sketches," Semmel cropped the images unexpectedly and employed steep foreshortening and exaggerated highlights and shadows in a formalist mix that recalls the paintings of her contemporary, Philip Pearlstein. But Semmel's work, because it clearly conveys the self as subject, has a high-pitched energy, an erotic tension, that is in direct contrast to Pearlstein's cool oeuvre. It aggressively claims a woman's body as her own subject matter, an artistic act that correlates exactly with the political actions of the feminist movement. Other artists, most notably Carolee Schneemann and Hannah Wilke, were making equally revolutionary statements in performance- and photo-based works concurrently; what remains unusual about Semmel's contribution is that it found persuasive equivalents in the framed canvas at a time when painting was deemed less urgent, compelling, and relevant as an art form.

Mythologies and Me (1976, plate 159) is one of Semmel's masterworks. An unusual three-paneled painting, it depicts three female nudes in wildly differing styles; their juxtaposition literalizes the title. The central panel shows Semmel's own view of her body, its monumental forms and the matter-of-fact intimacy of its presentation charged

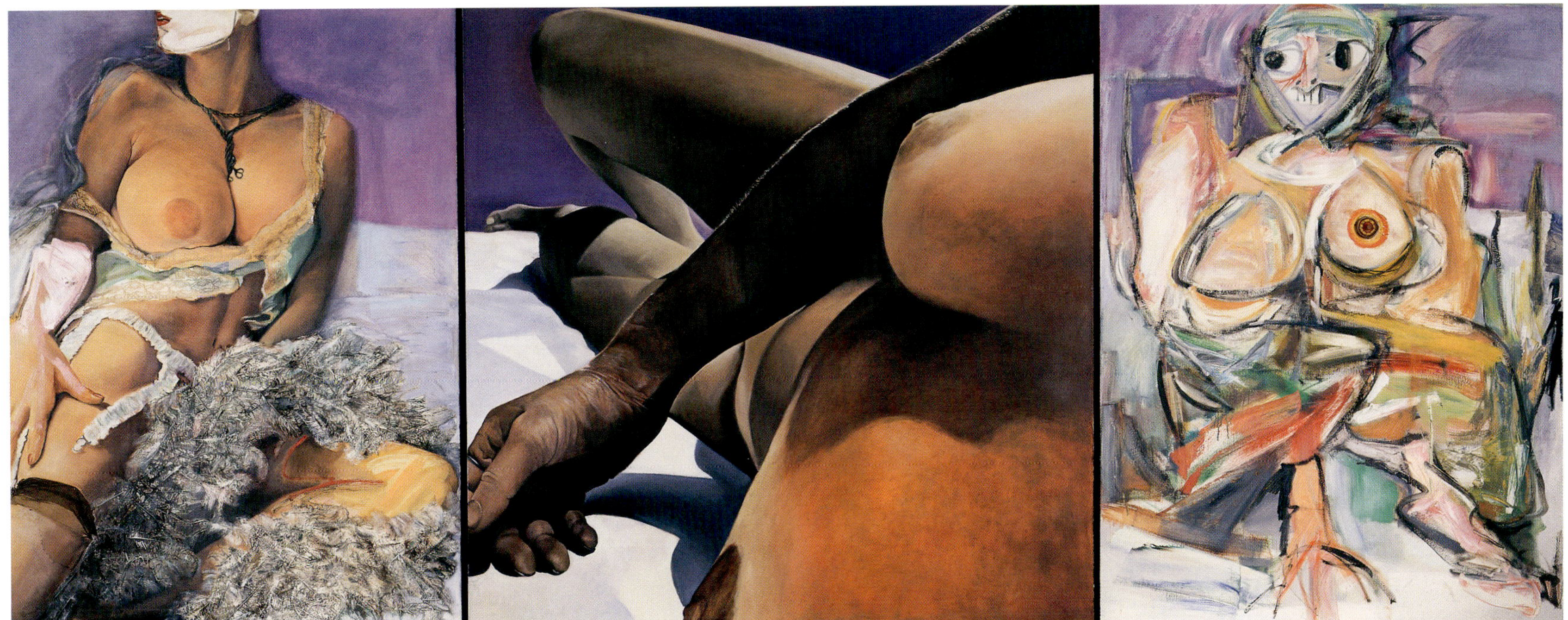

somewhat by painterly bravura. In contrast to the images flanking it, the legs of the self-portrait stretch discreetly away from the viewer toward the horizon line of the canvas, which appears, in all three panels, to suggest the edge of a bed. No object of desire, it is a landscape of human forms, its carefully articulated diagonals, mounds, and fields of skin finding their boldest expression in the flattening effects of gravity and the precise detailing of a sturdy hand that unfolds toward the viewer. Semmel constructed this central panel on a deeper stretcher so that it projects forward aggressively, asserting its presence in the viewer's space. To the left and right, each painted female form, smaller in scale and seen frontally, bears collaged elements, signals of an outside world whose attitudes toward women diminish them. On the left is Semmel's appropriation of a soft-core pornographic centerfold: the seductively posed fantasy woman, her breasts, fingernails, legs, and crotch more nuanced than her face, wears a real nylon stocking and lounges suggestively with an actual feather boa. To the right is a parody of Willem de Kooning's Woman series: a grotesque harpy rendered with violent gestures, her left breast adorned with a rubber nursing nipple, its concentric circles targetlike, the perfect send-up of male anxieties about female nurturing and sexual power. Even as Semmel fearlessly critiqued male fantasies and representations of women, she challenged the patriarchy of de Kooning, Jasper Johns, and others in the (male) pantheon of great modern painters.

Semmel's paintings have retained their enduring importance and originality, speaking in dialogue over the years with work by artists as varied as Cindy Sherman, Karen Finley, John Coplans, Jenny Saville, and Sam Taylor-Wood. Retired from a distinguished teaching career at Rutgers University, Semmel currently lives in New York and continues to paint. Her most recent work explores images of the aging female body and offers what critic Robert Berlind has called "an odd circuitry of vision and identity."[3]

Annette DiMeo Carlozzi

159.

Mythologies and Me, 1976

Oil and collage on canvas
60 × 148 in. (152.4 × 375.9 cm)
Gift of Buffie Johnson
1978.92
Signed verso, lower left of panel B "Joan Semmel '76"

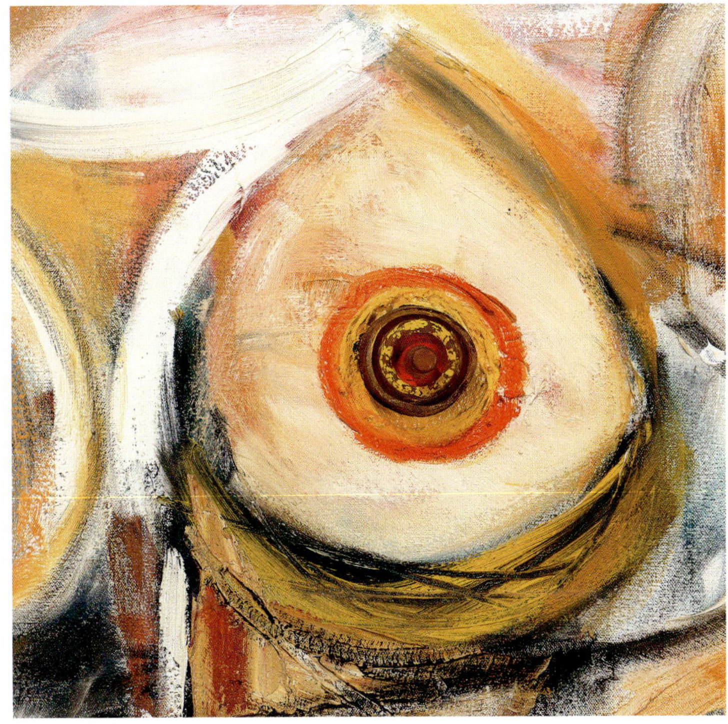

Notes

1. For more details on Semmel's biography, see Joan Marter, "Joan Semmel's Nudes: The Erotic Self and the Masquerade," *Woman's Art Journal* 16 (fall 1995/winter 1996): 24–28.
2. Joan Semmel, interview by Donald Goddard, in *Joan Semmel: Continuities* (Easthampton, N.Y.: Guild Hall Museum, 1998), 10.
3. Robert Berlind, "Joan Semmel at Mitchell Algus," *Art in America* 92 (January 2004): 102.

Ben Shahn

Kovno, Lithuania, 1898–New York, 1969

w. New York (trips to Europe and North Africa, 1924–1925 and 1927–1929), 1913–1935; travels throughout mid-Atlantic, midwestern, and southern United States, 1935–1938; Jersey Homesteads, New Jersey (trip to Japan, East Asia, and Southeast Asia, 1960), 1937–1969

From That Day On (1960, plate 160) is one in a series of paintings Ben Shahn based on a nuclear disaster that captured worldwide attention in 1954. A Japanese tuna trawler, *Lucky Dragon,* was caught in the radioactive fallout of a nuclear bomb that the United States exploded at sea as part of a test program conducted over several years near the Marshall Islands. *From That Day On* depicts one of the fishermen, Aikichi Kuboyama, who died several months after the disaster from radiation burns, blood poisoning, and liver damage.

The work is a late-career painting that exemplifies Shahn's lifelong dedication to the subject of violence and inequity inflicted on the innocent. In a 1968 interview he said: "I cannot separate art from life. Propaganda to me is a noble word. It means you believe something very strongly and you want other people to believe it; you want to propagate your faith. . . . [A]rt has always been used to propagate ideas and to persuade."[1]

This stance may have originated with Shahn's early experience in graphic and commercial art; he was apprenticed to a lithographer soon after immigrating with his family from Lithuania to the United States in 1909. He engaged in some fine art study at the Educational Alliance, the Art Students League, and the National Academy of Design, and in 1924 he traveled to Europe to view art and to paint. Upon his return to the United States, he actively set out to create his own style.

By 1930 Shahn had found his subject matter in victims of social and political injustice. That same year, he completed a portrait of Jewish sea captain Alfred Dreyfus who, in 1864, was wrongly convicted of treason. Over the next two years, Shahn gained fame for his well-known series The Passion of Sacco and Vanzetti, which commemorated the public outcry surrounding the 1927 execution of two Italian American radicals convicted of murder but widely believed to have been innocent.[2] In 1933 he created paintings that depicted the trial of labor leader Thomas J. Mooney, found guilty of bombings in San Francisco in 1916; perhaps helped by Shahn's artwork, Mooney was pardoned in 1939. After viewing this series, Diego Rivera, Mexican muralist and Communist Party supporter, selected Shahn as his assistant on *Man at the Crossroads,* the notorious Rockefeller Center mural destroyed after Rivera refused to erase a likeness of Lenin.

Shahn's empathy for those suffering from adversity also fueled his production as a WPA muralist and Farm Security Administration photographer. Working with other leading photographers—he shared a studio with Walker Evans—he chronicled the effects of the Great Depression in photographs and posters. By this time, Shahn had clarified his artistic mission; he believed there were only two kinds of subject matter: "the things you are very strongly for and the things you are very strongly against."[3] He had also discovered his personal connection with the plight of his subjects: "I had some curious sense of responsibility about it . . . [P]erhaps it was that I felt that I owed something more to the victim himself."[4] By the end of the 1930s, Shahn's artistic style had become as recognizable as his subject matter for its distinctive boldness of color, shape, and line.

Shahn aroused feelings of identification and outrage in his expressive Lucky Dragon series, of which the Blanton's *From That Day On* is one of the strongest pieces. Characterized by an exaggerated realism, apparent in oversimplified and disproportional limbs and features, the painting focuses on the figures' ashen skin, hollow gazes, and awkward poses. The artist's loose, open brushwork in the background and in the contrasting textile patterns of the figures' clothing creates a motion that propels the figures forward and moves the viewer's gaze continuously around the canvas until finally allowing it to rest on the painful simplicity and vulnerability of exposed skin. Rich reds and blues and overlapping textures contrast with flat skin tones; the gray blue hands and feet suggest physical pain and disfiguration, dramatizing the victims' innocence. The stiff pose of the cradled child, like that in Christian images of the Madonna and infant Christ, heightens Shahn's message.

In the upper left corner, level with Kuboyama's gaze, Shahn painted and incised a red dragon, a Japanese symbol for the sun. This stylized figure is a variation on a character that the artist had explored earlier in a series on a Chicago tenement fire disaster and in a set of allegorical paintings about Jewish life and history. The calligraphic motif, which Frances Pohl described as a "fire wreath," often incorporates a beast-like form resembling a wolf, lion, or dragon and symbolizes the destructive aspects of fire.[5] Shahn identified the "fire-wreath" in *From That Day On* as a dragon that warns of "the unspeakable tragedy toward which the world's people are moving."[6]

Shahn borrowed from many modernist traditions as he mounted his persuasive visual argument in *From That Day On.* The gestural underpainting and background brushwork is suggestive of the painterly abstraction of artists such as Mark Rothko, Willem de Kooning, Clyfford Still, and Helen Frankenthaler as well as the expressive representation of artists such as Richard Diebenkorn and Nathan Oliveira. The gestures of the victims and the allegorical nature of the painting call to mind Pablo Picasso's explorations of innocence and suffering in *Guernica* (1937) and *Charnel House* (1945). Not unlike Picasso, Shahn distorted body proportions and enlarged and simplified hands, feet, and facial features, seeking, in his own words, to depict "the emotional tone that surrounds disaster; you might call it the inner disaster."[7]

In 1961, one year after finishing the Lucky Dragon series, Shahn observed: "Whatever my basic promptings and urges may be, I am aware that the concern, the compassion for suffering—feeling it, formulating it—has been the constant attention of my work since I first picked up a paintbrush."[8]

Rina Faletti

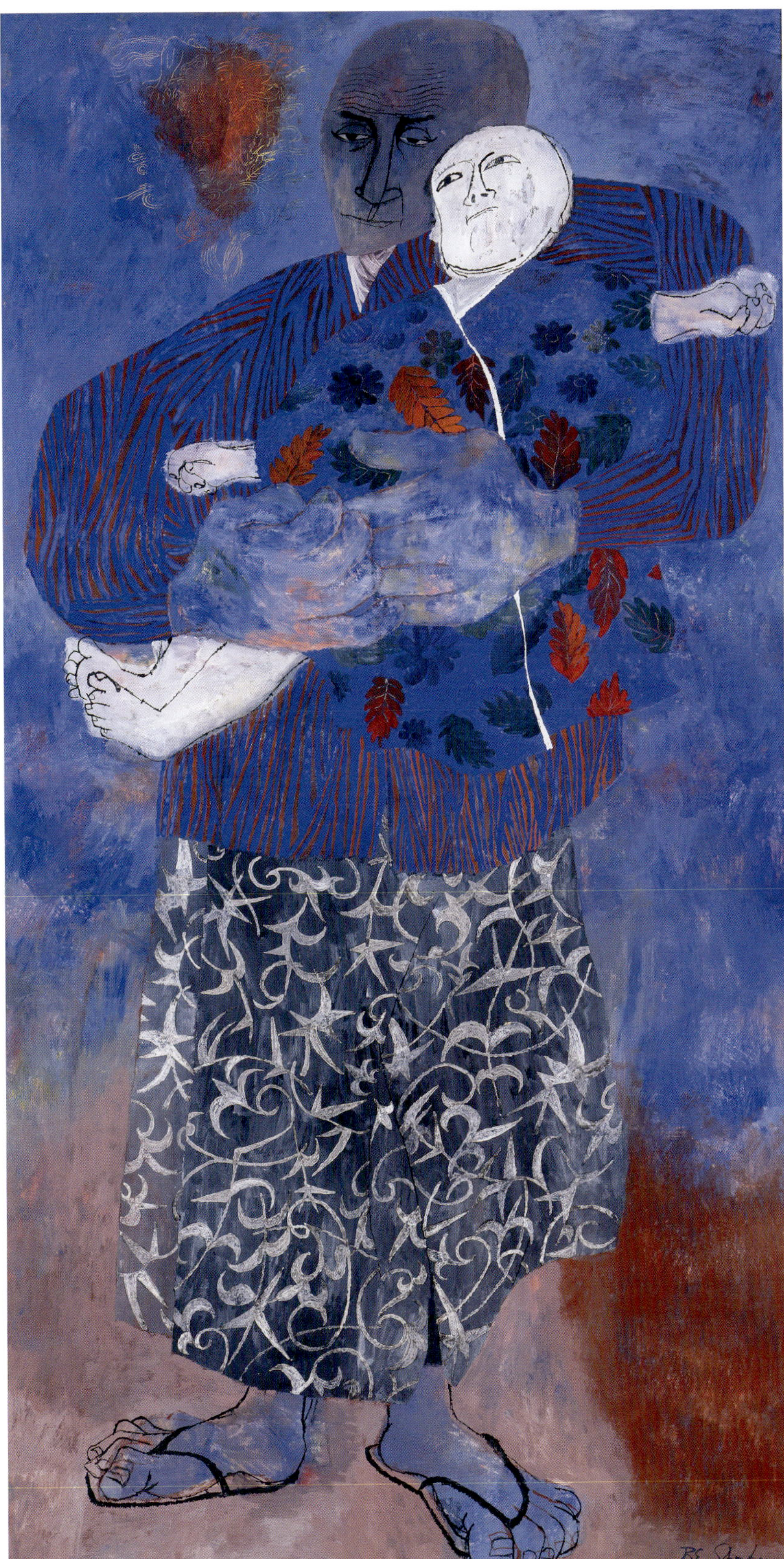

160.

From That Day On, 1960

Oil and tempera on canvas and board
71½ × 35⅜ in. (181.7 × 89.9 cm)
Gift of Mari and James A. Michener
1991.322

Provenance: Purchased by James A. Michener from the artist, through Downtown Gallery, New York, 1961; long-term loan to The University of Texas at Austin, 1968–1991
Signed lower right "Ben Shahn"

Notes

1. Quoted in Susan H. Edwards, "Ben Shahn: The Road South," *History of Photography* 19 (spring 1995): 14.
2. Diana L. Linden, "Ben Shahn," *Magazine Antiques* 150 (November 1996): 708–15.
3. Quoted in Edwards, 13.
4. Ben Shahn, "The Biography of a Painting," in *The Shape of Content* (Cambridge, Mass.: Harvard University Press, 1957), 28; quoted in Frances K. Pohl, "Allegory in the Work of Ben Shahn," in *Common Man, Mythic Vision: The Paintings of Ben Shahn* (Princeton, N.J.: Princeton University Press, 1998), 117.
5. See Pohl, 110–41. Shahn believed that the two fires he witnessed as a child motivated his work, as did the larger conflagrations of the Holocaust and nuclear warfare (Shahn, "Biography of a Painting," 29–30; quoted in Pohl, 117).
6. Ben Shahn, "Exhibition Preview: Shahn in Amsterdam," *Art in America* 49, no. 3 (1961): 62.
7. Shahn, "Biography of a Painting," 32; quoted in Pohl, 119.
8. Shahn, "Exhibition Preview," 62.

Joel Shapiro

b. New York, 1941
w. New York, 1967–present

When discussing Joel Shapiro's sculptures, commentators frequently resort to the word "ambiguity," and Untitled (1995–1997, plate 161) suggests why. Vaguely figural, the sculpture is suspended between abstraction and representation; it suggests a figure without depicting one outright. It appears to have arms and legs, but what the viewer may initially read as a thrust-out arm might also be read as a bowed and attenuated head. Seen from another side, the "figure" simply becomes a dynamic composition of ascending cubed rectangles, complicating a representational reading. This tension between abstraction and representation, in fact, defines Shapiro's career.

Born in New York in 1941, Shapiro exhibited an early interest in art, but at the urging of his parents, he attended the University of Colorado for two years and then completed a degree in premedical studies at New York University in 1964. He joined the Peace Corps in 1965 and spent the next two years in India, where he was profoundly affected by Indian sculpture and architecture. Determined to pursue a life in art, he returned to New York University in the fall of 1967 and received a graduate degree in the fine arts in 1969.

When Shapiro was studying art in the late 1960s, sculpture was largely defined by Minimalism. Artists like Donald Judd, Carl Andre, Robert Morris, Tony Smith, and Dan Flavin insisted that sculpture should reference nothing other than itself, that it should be concerned with space, mass, volume, form, and color alone. Rational and aloof, Minimalist sculpture was dedicated to mathematical rigor and precision. Shapiro came of age as an artist at the height of Minimalism, and his sculpture adopts some of the essential elements of Minimalism, particularly its emphasis on geometric abstraction.

Shapiro's work drew critical attention from the start. In 1969, the same year he graduated, Shapiro was included in *Anti-Illusion: Procedures/Materials* at the Whitney Museum of American Art, and a year later, he had his first New York solo show at Paula Cooper Gallery. His early work was devoted to experimenting with process and medium, but he soon moved into creating art with more psychological complexity, fashioning representational sculptures of houses, bridges, ladders, and animals. These works were of a diminutive scale and placed directly on the gallery floor, a strategy that ran parallel to, and commented upon, the Minimalists' own antipathy to the pedestal and platform. For the Minimalists, sculpture was not an object to be displayed apart from the viewer's world. Similarly, Shapiro's sculptures asserted their place in the gallery, but out of all proportion to their size. Occupying mere inches on the floor, they commanded a much larger space in the viewer's mind, in much the same way the density of a collapsed star warps the space around it. By the mid- to late 1970s Shapiro had found his way to the human figure and its greater possibilities for conceptual articulation.

That figure is never particularized. Shapiro works with the most ancient and universal stand-in for human representation: the stick figure. Indeed, his figurative sculptures are often quite literally constructed out of wood—even when he casts the finished figure in bronze, he deliberately leaves traces of the wood's grain visible, as he did with the Blanton's Untitled. The reason Shapiro works with the anonymous stick figure is related to the reason his sculptures are never titled: because he does not want to limit either the sculpture or the viewer to a specific interpretation. Shapiro's figures likewise arise from his emotional landscape; they are manifestations of their maker's psychological frame of mind as he was making them. The figure serves as something of a surrogate for the artist, "an embodiment of emotion,"[1] but not a single emotion. As Shapiro stated, "Emotional concerns drive my creative process but I don't think you can reduce the content of the work to some simple emotional state."[2]

Approached from one angle, Untitled is a rather jaunty piece, conveying energy and youthful enthusiasm; from another, the blocks of its construction suggest something more specific, an aspirational gesture, as if the figure were reaching upwards. Yet some ambiguity pervades that second angle: two of the blocks attached to the central block—one suggesting an arm raised toward the sky, the other a leg planted on the ground—preserve their identity as abstract shapes. Refusing to join smoothly, organically into the figure, they create hard right angles where they meet the primary beam, which is constructed of three more completely integrated blocks. At the same time that it aspires, physically and psychologically, the figure also seems to be falling apart, collapsing, perhaps, under the weight of those aspirations. The coexistence of these different readings—confidence, hope, disappointment—is quite deliberate on the part of the artist. As one commentator noted, "The states of feeling and being that are honored in Shapiro's sculptures do not exist in a hierarchical relationship to one another. Sadness, joy, depression, exhilaration, all coexist in a way that makes it clear they are all inescapable and valid."[3] The ambiguity in Shapiro's sculptures is the ambiguity of life.

John Devine

Notes

1. Martin Friedman, *Joel Shapiro: Sculpture* (Charleston, N.C. and San Antonio: Spoleto Festival and McNay Art Museum, 2000), 21.
2. Friedman, 14.
3. Michael Brenson, "Joel Shapiro and Figurative Sculpture," in Hendel Teicher, *Joel Shapiro: Sculpture and Drawings* (New York: Harry N. Abrams, 1998), 13.

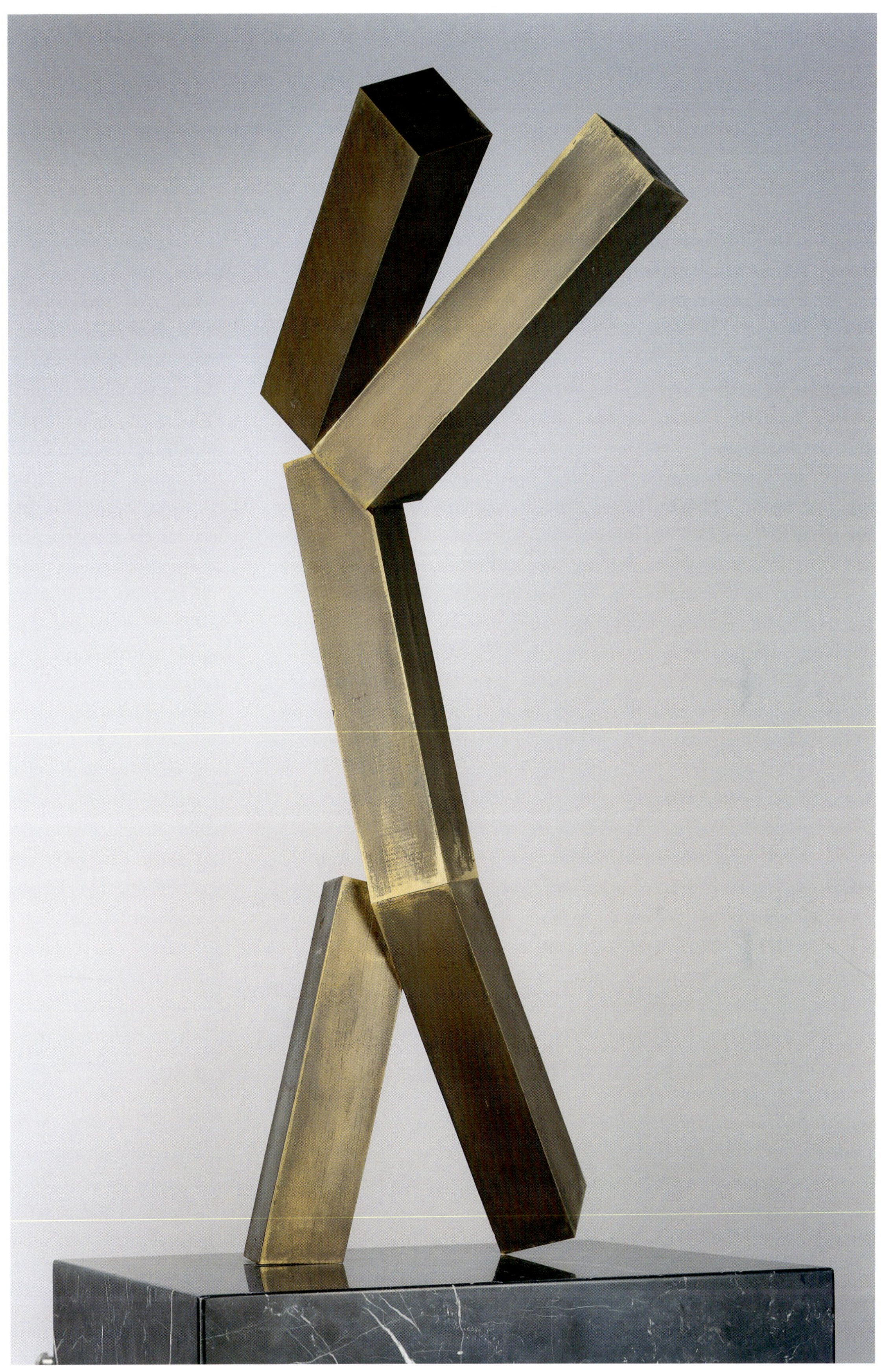

161.

Untitled, 1995–1997

Cast bronze with marble base
41¼ × 20 × 16 in. (104.8 × 50.8 × 40.6 cm)
Gift of Jack S. Blanton and Family
2002.2871

Provenance: Purchased from PaceWildenstein Gallery, New York, n.d.

Charles Sheeler

Philadelphia, 1883–Dobbs Ferry, New York, 1965

w. Philadelphia (frequent trips to Europe), 1903–1918; New York, 1919–1926; New York–South Salem, New York, 1926–1932; Ridgefield, Connecticut, 1932–1942; Irvington-on-Hudson, New York, 1942–1965

During a career spanning five decades, Charles Sheeler documented America's triumphant entry into the machine age with works that celebrate mechanized power and streamlined production.[1] Efficient factories, immense skyscrapers, and sophisticated machinery implied progress and recovery from the devastation of World War I. The position of the United States as the world's leading industrialized nation encouraged the romanticization of the machine as manifested in its forms, products, and environments. Against the historical backdrop of the machine age emerged the movement known as Precisionism. During the 1920s, the Precisionists combined elements of realism and Cubist abstraction to represent the industrial and urban landscape and advance them as the ultimate symbols of modernity. Often hailed as an exemplar of Precisionism, Sheeler produced a body of work that addressed ideas relating to structure, mathematical order, and the distillation of form.[2]

Sheeler commenced his art education at the Philadelphia School of Industrial Art as a student of applied design. Three years later, in 1903, he entered the Pennsylvania Academy of the Fine Arts, where he studied with William Merritt Chase. Initially an enthusiastic acolyte of Chase's artistic philosophy, Sheeler later broke with his teacher's traditional approach, which emphasized loose, impressionistic brushstrokes. At the Academy, he developed a close friendship with fellow student Morton Schamberg and, together with Chase and other students, they spent the summers of 1904 and 1905 in Europe studying Dutch and Spanish Old Master paintings. Three years later, Sheeler and Schamberg again traveled to Europe, where Sheeler had the opportunity to study Italian Renaissance painting, whose order and structure he found to be of great significance. During this same trip, the artists visited Paris. There Sheeler encountered the work of European modernists Pablo Picasso, Georges Braque, Paul Cézanne, and Henri Matisse, an experience that led him to adopt some of the tenets of Analytical Cubism.[3] Upon their return from Europe in 1910, the two artists obtained studios in the same Philadelphia building and rented a 1786 farmhouse in Bucks County, Pennsylvania. Weekend residence at the Doylestown farmhouse and his involvement in the surrounding community sparked a lifelong interest in rural life and traditional American craft objects, themes Sheeler assimilated into his work.

Schamberg died from influenza in 1918, and Sheeler moved to New York the following year, eventually giving up his lease on the Doylestown house. He was inducted into the city's lively literary and artistic circles, thanks in large part to his friendships with Marius de Zayas, Walter and Louise Arensberg, and Alfred Stieglitz. During this time, Sheeler also became acquainted with such notable figures as Marcel Duchamp, Paul Strand, William Carlos Williams, and Man Ray.

Sheeler began practicing photography as early as 1910 as a way to support himself financially. Initially, he expressed little interest in the creative potential of photography and limited himself to documenting projects for architectural firms and artwork shown at local galleries. A few years later, however, he befriended Stieglitz, a leading proponent of the then reigning mode of soft focus or "art" photography, who encouraged Sheeler to embrace his own personal vision. Nevertheless, Sheeler's preference for "straight" or clear-focus photography distanced him from Stieglitz, and eventually he began to associate less with art photographers and more with commercial photographers and photojournalists. Three years later, in 1926, the photographer Edward Steichen recruited Sheeler for the magazine *Condé Nast*. Sheeler produced fashion and celebrity portraits for the magazine and also contributed work to other well-known periodicals, including *Vogue* and *Vanity Fair.*

In addition to creating photographs that stand alone as images, Sheeler also employed photography as a source of subject matter and as a technical support for painting, creating work, including still-lifes, directly from photographs. Sheeler developed a technique he called "photographic blueprints," whereby he used photographs as compositional aids. With this method, he was able to compose paintings by looking through the lens of his camera, an innovation that enabled him to reduce the image to essential details and simultaneously increase its abstract, detached quality.

Despite his proclivity for subject matter associated with the machine age, Sheeler painted still-lifes, a genre associated with the organic and the natural environment, throughout his career. He created *Still Life* (1931, plate 162) during an especially productive and successful stage in his career, shortly after completing his highly acclaimed documentary series about the Ford Motor Company's River Rouge plant near Detroit. *Still Life* depicts a solitary vase containing a single yellow flower whose stamen and petal project forward in a graceful arc. Behind the flower a mysterious, expansive landscape appears. The velvety black form encasing the vase emphasizes both its pale colors and delicately rounded shape. Sheeler used similar geometric forms in his interior scenes from the early 1910s.

Although he practiced painting and photography, achieving success in both media, Sheeler sought recognition first and foremost as a painter. His choice of subject matter parallels his bifurcated artistic commitment. Sheeler repeatedly returned to seemingly opposite themes: the industrialized environments of modern urban life and rural architecture and its artifacts. However, whether representing Pennsylvania barns or sleekly mechanized factories, he delighted in his subjects' structural clarity, purity of form, and underlying order. Above all, Sheeler sought to depict the beauty of the everyday and to celebrate the ordinary objects and environments of American life.

Ann Marie Leimer

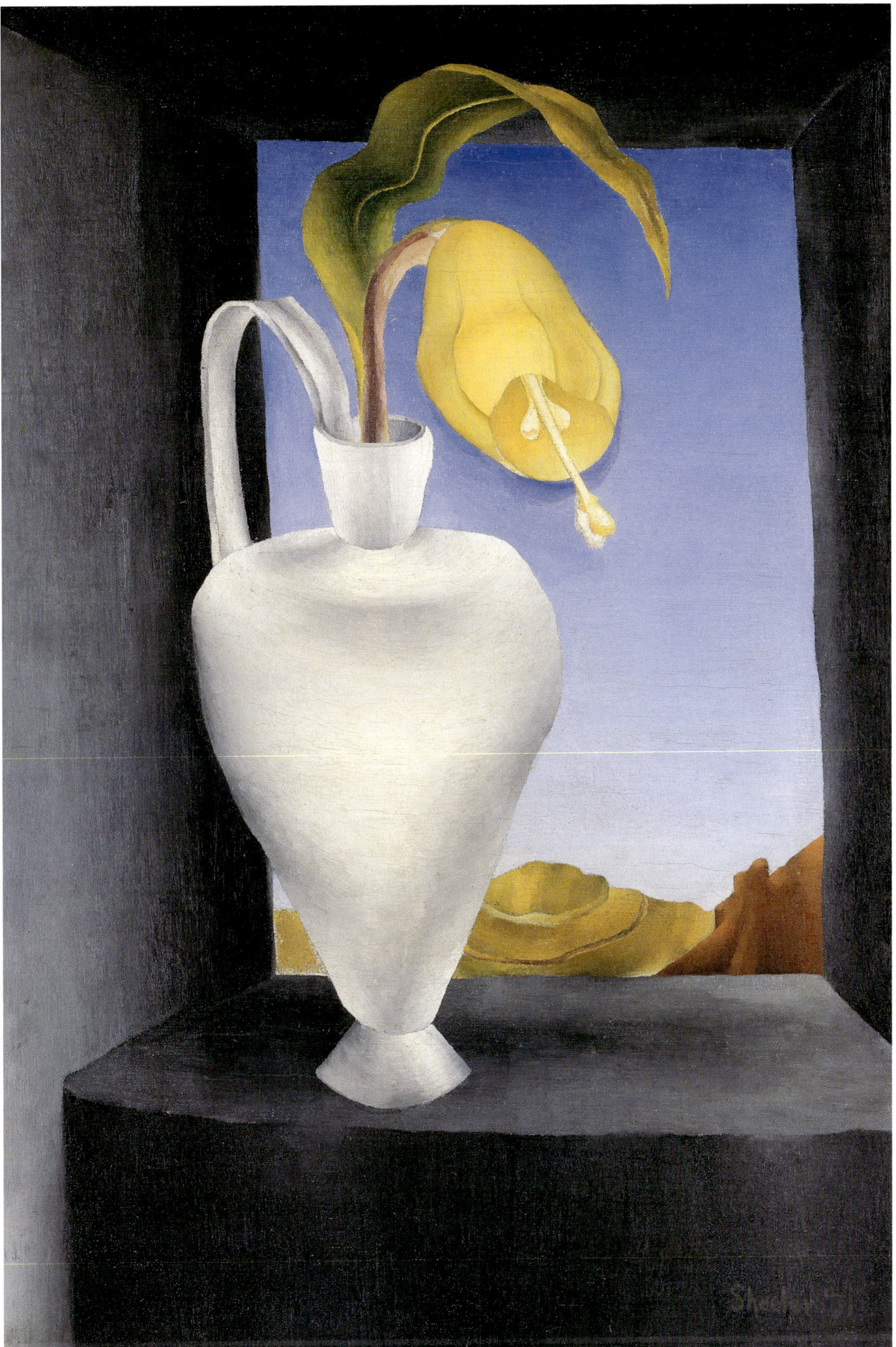

Notes

1. For more on Sheeler's career, see Karen Lucic, *Charles Sheeler and the Cult of the Machine* (London: Reaktion Books, 1991).
2. Rick Stewart, "Charles Sheeler, William Carlos Williams, and Precisionism: A Redefinition," *Arts Magazine* 58 (November 1983): 100–14.
3. Carol Troyen, "'From the eyes inward': Paintings and Drawings by Charles Sheeler," in Carol Troyen and Erica E. Hirshler, eds., *Charles Sheeler: Paintings and Drawings* (Boston: Little, Brown and Company, 1987), 4–7.

162.

Still Life, 1931

Oil on canvas
23 × 15¾ in. (58 × 40 cm)
Michener Acquisitions Fund
P1969.11.2

Provenance: Purchased from Zabriskie Gallery, New York, 1969
Signed lower right "Sheeler '31"

Shahzia Sikander

b. Lahore, Pakistan, 1969

w. Lahore, Pakistan, 1988–1992; Providence, Rhode Island, 1993–1995; Houston, 1995–1997; New York, 1998–present

Shahzia Sikander is in tune with the ambiguities and complexities of life in the twenty-first century. Since attending college, Sikander has worked primarily on miniature paintings loosely based upon the Mughal tradition—loose because they stray from standard Muslim iconography and blend such disparate elements as Hindu goddesses, Western motifs, and contemporary art historical references. Initially, this seems to be an impossible fusion. Given the tensions that exist between them, how is it feasible to resolve such polarities as Hindu and Muslim, tradition and experimentation, South Asian and Western identity? Yet Sikander does it, in large part because, as she said, "that is what sustains my work—this dichotomy of experience . . . creates . . . a sense of movement [that] help[s] to evolve a heightened sense of identity which is multilayered."[1] Sikander's multimedia installation *Intimacy* (2001, plate 163) reveals this duality with a twist.

Created during a two-month residency at ArtPace in San Antonio, *Intimacy* signaled a new direction in Sikander's art. For the first time, she worked with digital media, but not to make something new per se.[2] Instead, she used it as a way to revisit the body of work that she had created up to this point. With the help of computer technology, Sikander made digital reproductions of earlier paintings that she later wove together to fashion an ethereal montage.[3] The resulting video—a conglomeration of images of a woman with animals, floating Hindu goddesses, a young gymnast, Arabic calligraphy, allusions to Minimalism, and circular objects placed amongst a bevy of other forms—poses some challenges for the viewer. Sikander's highly detailed renderings generate a free-form narrative based upon visual associations. When juxtaposed and layered as they are in *Intimacy*, moreover, these interpretive strands seem to talk all at once, making any sort of translation daunting.[4]

Certainly the installation exacerbates this difficulty. *Intimacy* consists of two ten-foot by ten-foot walls placed parallel to one another and separated by only four feet. The walls create a claustrophobic viewing area for the two primary components of the installation. A drawing hangs on one of the walls. Embedded in the other is a monitor that displays the digital animation. The surfaces of the wall and screen are contiguous, while the screen itself has been encircled by a matte and frame that match those of the drawing, generating the illusion that the video has been mounted like a two-dimensional work of art. The video begins by "citing" the drawing on the opposite wall. Yet soon the image starts to morph, and subsequent motifs, many recycled from Sikander's earlier pieces, are added and subtracted. This has the effect not only of unfixing or animating what was once a static work of art, it also injects a temporal component that was not present in the original drawing.

The juxtaposition of different media and different types of pictorial expression creates an interesting tension—one similar to the "dichotomy of experience" that Sikander spoke about above. What is more, the physical constraints of the installation make it difficult to see both things at once. It is possible, yes, but this will give only partial views of the drawing and video. A close examination of either component means the viewer has to turn his or her back on the other half of the work. This is not a simple choice, but in many ways it mimics aspects of Sikander's life.

Sikander was born in 1969 to a middle-class Muslim family in Lahore, Pakistan. She studied at the National College of Art, where she decided to major in miniature painting and entered into an apprenticeship with Professor Bashir Ahmed. Despite the unpopularity of this discipline at the time, Sikander immersed herself fully in the various activities involved in painting miniatures: meticulously copying past works and putting endless hours in at the studio.[5] Soon she realized there was also tremendous room for experimentation. But she did not dispense with past precedent altogether. Indeed, each work Sikander produced set into motion a constant play between tradition and experimentation.

Sikander moved to the United States in 1993 to study at the Rhode Island School of Design. Occasionally, she ran into resistance from the faculty, whose expectations for her work differed from her own.[6] These experiences in graduate school caused Sikander to become more aware of her identity both as an artist and a Pakistani woman living in the United States. It also made her wary of becoming subject to ethnic preconceptions, as when she was repeatedly asked if she wore a veil like other women from predominantly Muslim countries.[7] The veil is perhaps Sikander's most noticeable motif. Not only does it occlude the faces of a number of women in her paintings, it also becomes a formal technique in her wall installations, where gestural images on tissue paper are layered in such a way as to partially obscure the adjoining depictions.

Part of Sikander's critical success is due to the social and cultural relevance of her work. The artist contributes in meaningful ways to our understanding of the experience of rootlessness endemic to the twenty-first century as well as to the social discourses surrounding globalization and immigration. *Intimacy* itself resonates with the historical moment in and for which it was created—a moment marked by the increasing hybridization of ethnic and racial identities—by bringing together many supposed contradictions into a mesmerizing whole. Yet none of this is simple, for Sikander's work does not lend itself to facile interpretations. In fact, its underlying ambiguity contributes much to what makes it so pertinent today. As Sikander puts it, her art is "more about raising questions than providing answers."[8]

Alexander Dumbadze

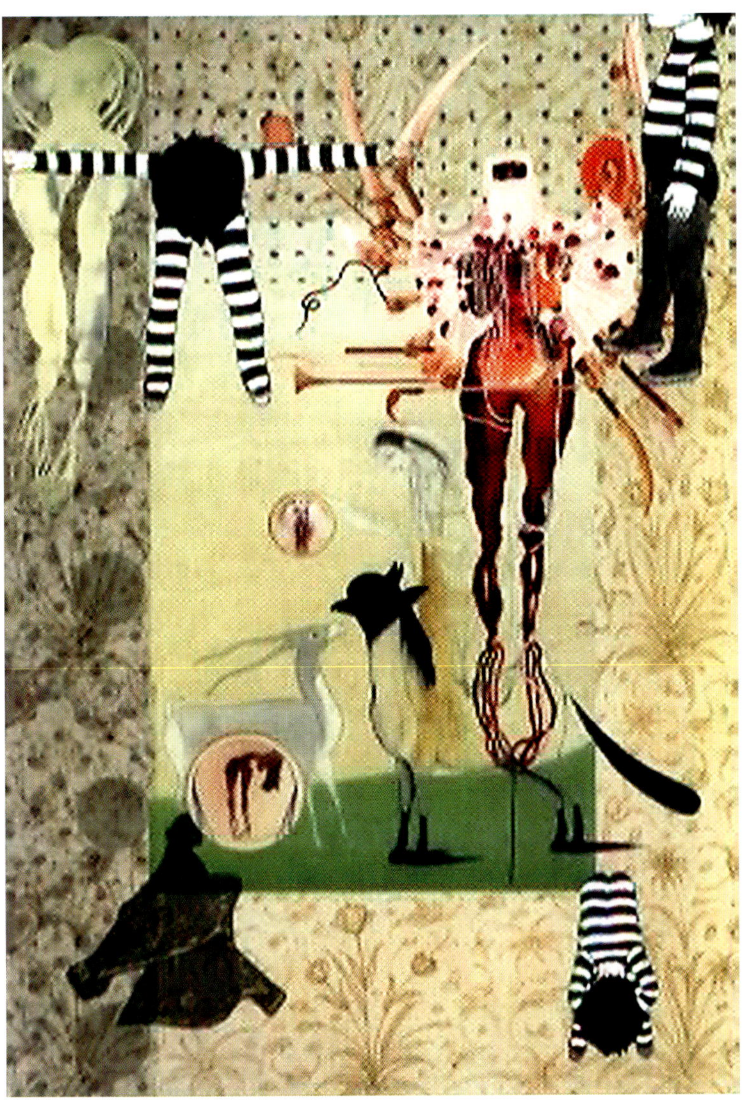

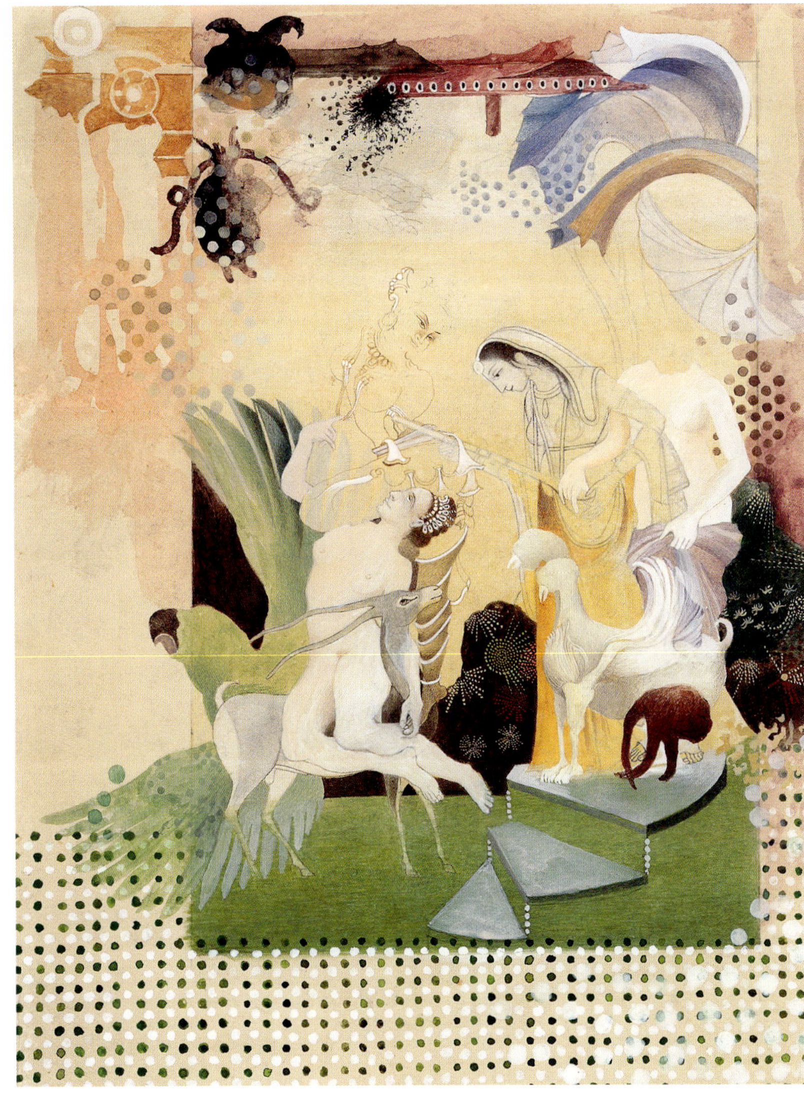

Notes

1. Quoted in Reena Jana, "Shahzia Sikander: Celebration of Femaleness," *Flash Art*, no. 199 (March/April 1998): 100.
2. For more on Sikander's work in digital media, see Ian Berry and Jessica Hough, *Opener 6: Shahzia Sikander: Nemesis* (Saratoga Springs, N.Y.: The Tang Teaching Museum and Art Gallery at Skidmore College, 2004).
3. Press release, March 15, 2001, ArtPace, San Antonio.
4. For an interesting discussion regarding the visual translation of Sikander's paintings in relation to Urdu and the tradition of poetry known as Ghazals, see Faisal Devji, "Translated Pleasures," in Hamza Walker, ed., *Shahzia Sikander* (Chicago: The Renaissance Society at the University of Chicago, 1998), 11–15.
5. Homi Bhabha, "Chillava Klatch: Shahzia Sikander Interviewed by Homi Bhabha," in Walker, 16–17.
6. Bhabha, 18.
7. Jana, 101.
8. Quoted in Bhabha, 20.

163.

Intimacy [details], 2001

Multimedia installation (animation on DVD and watercolor and dry pigment on wasli paper)
Dimensions variable
Partial and pledged gift of Jeanne and Michael Klein
T2001.1.1/2–2/2

Provenance: Commissioned by ArtPace, San Antonio, 2001; purchased by Jeanne and Michael Klein for the museum from Deitch Projects, New York, 2001

Amy Sillman

b. Highland Park, Illinois, 1955
w. Brooklyn, New York, 1975–present

Fluctuation, elasticity, flexibility: these qualities inform every aspect of Amy Sillman's paintings, from their conceptualization to their execution and installation. At the same time that they alternate effortlessly between different modes of representation, from abstract to figurative, so too do they combine an astonishing variety of marks and strokes. Sillman's paintings engage the eye as well as the mind: they not only imply stories replete with equal parts humor and pathos, they make oblique references to subjects such as literature, philosophy, music, and film.

Although she originally sought work as a Japanese interpreter, Sillman decided to pursue a BFA at the School of Visual Arts in New York, completing her degree in 1979. In the early 1990s she enrolled in the MFA program at Bard College, where she studied with painters Jonathan Borofsky, Elizabeth Murray, and Pat Steir until she graduated in 1995. Her paintings appeared in numerous solo and group exhibitions throughout the 1980s and 1990s, during which time she also codirected Four Walls, an artist-run space in Brooklyn. More recently, Sillman was included in the 2003 exhibition, *Comic Release: Negotiating Identity for a New Generation,* and the 2004 Whitney Biennial.[1]

Since 1979 Sillman's commitment to the medium of painting has been strong and unwavering. In 2003 critic Raphael Rubinstein identified Sillman as one of seven other New York–based painters who have, in his view, reinvigorated the practice of painting over the last several years. Sillman and these artists share not only considerable technical skill, according to Rubinstein, but an interest in layered, multifaceted subject matter and an informed engagement with previous artistic traditions.[2] For her part, Sillman has synthesized into her own unique vocabulary the work of Jean-Honoré Fragonard, Claude Monet, Philip Guston, Florine Stettheimer, and the Abstract Expressionists, among many others.

In her paintings from the 1980s, Sillman often incorporated letters and words, signaling an interest in language and writing that persists today. (The artist commented in a recent article, "I like the idea that I might be making up a foreign language, that to visit my work you have to come to a foreign country.")[3] Her paintings from the early 1990s, with their delicate and linear floral motifs reminiscent of William Morris's designs from the late nineteenth century, were more decorative in style. By 1993 Sillman's paintings also began to feature pendulous body parts and recognizable characters and animals that called to mind doodles and cartoons, as did the summary, notational manner in which they were rendered.

A Guggenheim Fellowship in 2001 allowed Sillman to take a leave of absence from Bard College, where she has been teaching since 1996, and spend the spring of 2002 in Austin. She was immediately inspired to create a series of paintings titled Letters from Texas, which she began in Texas and continued to produce after leaving the state. At once diaristic and epistolary, these paintings record the artist's response not only to the geographical and meteorological conditions of the state, in particular its vast sense of space and piercing light, but to the experiences (both real and imagined) that she had while living there.

Currently, the Letters from Texas series consists of thirty-four panels numbered two through thirty-five, four of which are in the Blanton's collection (plate 166).[4] Like the others, these four paintings communicate a sense of fluidity and spontaneity that belies the deliberation involved in their making. Sillman works slowly and intuitively, without using sketches, and often takes several months to complete a single painting. Evidence of her sensitivity to colors, pastels in particular, is in abundance here: various shades of yellow, orange, green, and pink, highlighted by dabs of fuchsia, blue, violet, and white, dominate the paintings.[5] A single figure or multiple figures—all communicating a sense of vulnerability, perhaps even resignation, mixed with a goofy awkwardness—appear in each of the four panels. Just as these figures are delineated with an economy of line, so too are the landscapes they inhabit not so much depicted as suggested.

Never content with a single stylistic approach, Sillman marshaled a variety of mark-making devices to her side. Short, punctuated strokes that mingle with drawn lines and passages of more gestural brushwork interrupt areas of blended and modulated colors, which create an almost atmospheric effect. Sillman added some layers of paint only to scrape them away, leaving behind gently scumbled surfaces and tantalizing glimpses of pentimenti. However, despite these disparities in style, considerable harmony characterizes Sillman's paintings. This derives not only from her skillful use of complementary colors, but from her facility at choreographing compositions and brushstrokes as well. As the eye traverses the paintings, marks gradually morph and evolve, absorbing at a certain point the identities of their neighbors. Related is the manner in which the different elements in Sillman's paintings seem to respond (formally, chromatically, physically, and even emotionally) to one another. For example, a kind of sympathy exists between certain elements in *Letters from Texas (21)* (plate 165): the dimpled abdomen of the bulbous figure at the bottom edge echoes, or is echoed by, the concave shape of the constellation of abbreviated brushstrokes above it. And just as the figure's belly cradles this constellation, so too does the constellation cradle a cluster of irregular, asymmetrical forms. There are stories to be assembled in these very aspects of Sillman's paintings. Put another way, the artist imbues every mark, form, or passage with its own peculiar "character" so that, no matter how nonreferential it might be, it nonetheless functions representationally, generating its own narrative associations apart from those that belong, strictly speaking, to subject matter.

Almost the entire Letters from Texas series was installed at the University of North Texas Art Gallery in Denton in 2004. Here the

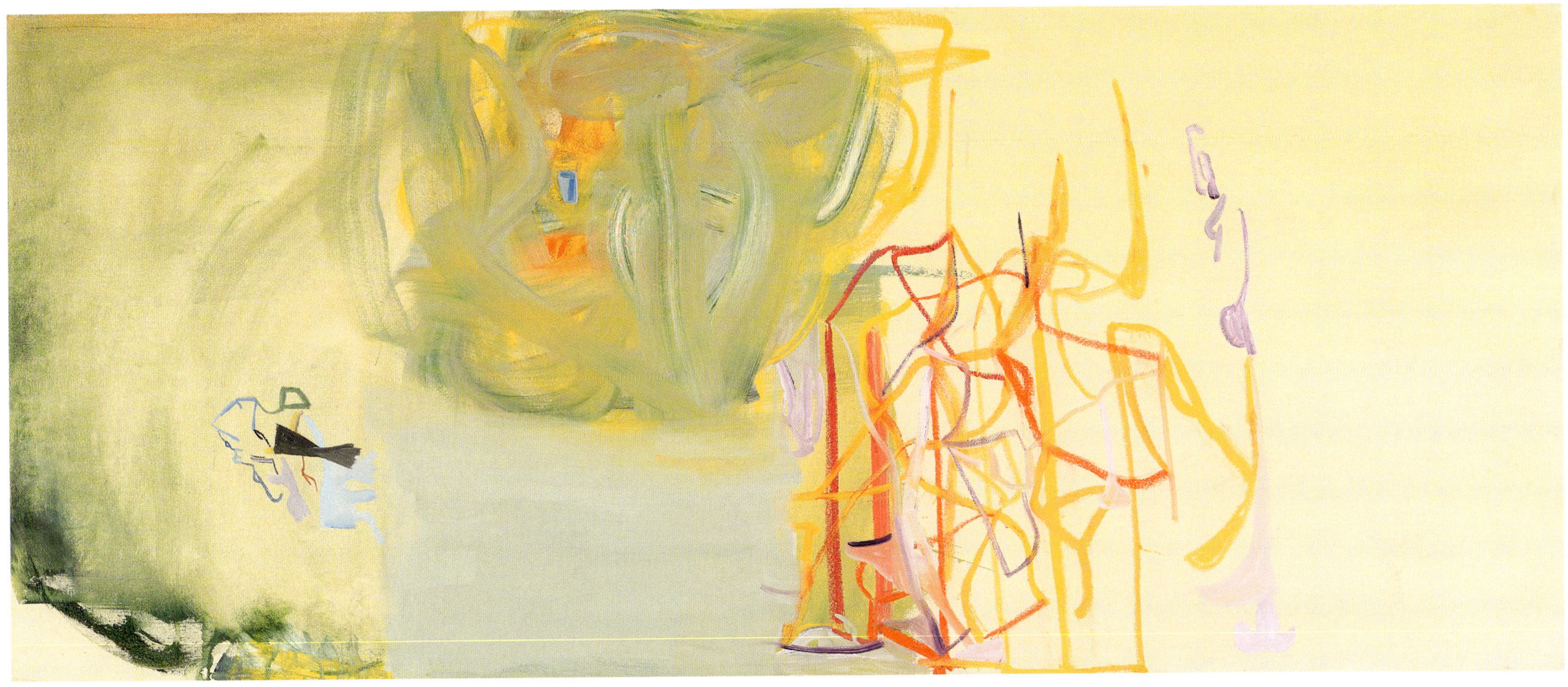

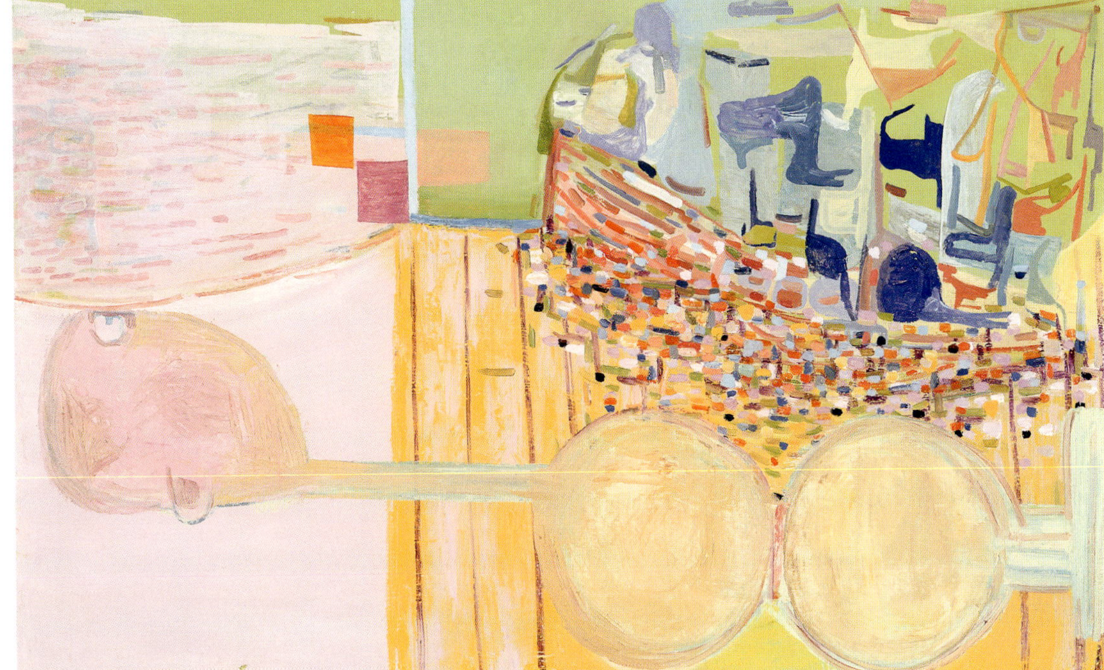

164.
Letters from Texas (22), 2003
Oil on canvas
26 × 60 in. (66 × 152.4 cm)
Partial and pledged gift of Jeanne and Michael Klein
T2003.2.3/4

165.
Letters from Texas (21), 2003
Oil on canvas
26 × 40 in. (66 × 101.6 cm)
Partial and pledged gift of Jeanne and Michael Klein
T2003.2.2/4

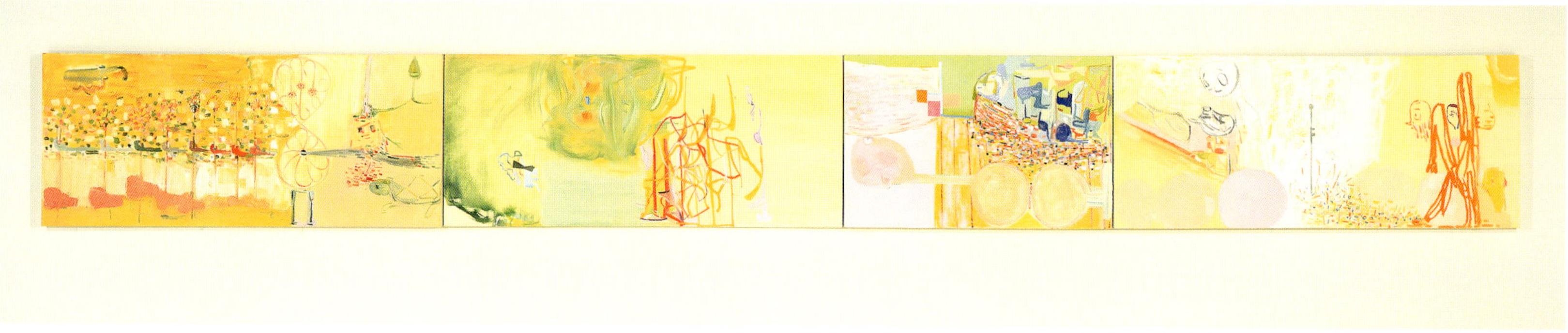

paintings, nestled next to one another and sometimes punctuated by smaller monochromatic panels, snaked around the gallery walls. Together they evoked the uninterrupted expanse of the Texas horizon, an association reinforced by the horizontal format of the panels as well as the multiple horizon lines embedded within individual paintings. The installation also generated a situation in which the process of looking mimicked that of reading: the viewer surveyed the paintings from left to right, her eyes moving in the same direction they would while perusing text on the pages of a book.

Despite what this linear presentation implied, however, Sillman's paintings—collections of disparate, fragmentary memories—do not resolve into a concrete, straightforward narrative. The viewer thus finds herself in the position of making (provisional) connections between different elements in a single work or connections across different works only to lose them again. There is pleasure in this kind of restless searching for meaning. Sillman herself described each painting as "a little timeframe," saying, "Things happen out of the picture, things happen in the picture and things happen after the picture."[6] We might add to this that things happen between pictures as well. What is more, whether installed in their entirety or in smaller groups, as in the Blanton's galleries, Sillman does not insist that the paintings be hung in any particular order. Complementing their fluid narrative structure, and literalizing the notion of free-association, therefore, is their equally flexible format. In this way, the artist establishes reciprocity between style, content, and installation, all of which are central to the work's underlying meaning.

Although very much about the practice of painting, Sillman's work also engages with the history of ideas while simultaneously mining her personal experiences. It constitutes what Sillman called a form of "contemporary painting that wants to be both full of ideas and painterly-ness." She continued, "I don't think there is a category. . . . It's a kind of abstract representation about language and image."[7]

Kelly Baum

166.

Letters from Texas (20, 21, 22, 23), 2003

Oil on canvas
Overall: 26 x 220 in. (66 x 558.8 cm)
Partial and pledged gift of Jeanne and Michael Klein
T2003.2.1/4–4/4

Provenance: Purchased at the request of the museum by Jeanne and Michael Klein from Brent Sikkema Gallery, New York, 2003

Notes

1. In the last several years, Sillman also has exhibited paintings produced collaboratively with artists David Humphrey and Elliot Green (collectively known as Team SHaG).
2. Raphael Rubinstein, "Eight Painters: New Work," *Art in America* 91 (November 2003): 130–41.
3. Quoted in Gail Gregg, "Streams of Consciousness," *Artnews* 100 (April 2001): 122.
4. These four paintings, along with twenty-four others from the Letters from Texas series, appeared in Sillman's 2003 solo exhibition *I am curious (yellow)* at Brent Sikkema Gallery in New York.
5. For an interesting discussion of Sillman's palette, see Helen Molesworth, "Pastels," in *Amy Sillman* (Hanover, New Hampshire: Jaffe-Friede & Strauss Galleries, Dartmouth College, 2002).
6. Quoted in Diana Block, *Amy Sillman: Horizon Line* (Denton, Tex.: University of North Texas Art Gallery, 2004). Sillman also compared the series as a whole to an "animated film"—more specifically, to a film that is animated by the viewer's presence. Amy Sillman, "Scattered Imagination," interview with Lyndsay Knecht, *North Texas Daily*, August 31, 2004.
7. Amy Sillman, "Sillman explores the 'deep structure' of painting," interview with Katie Van Syckle, *The Dartmouth*, November 2, 2002.

John Sloan

Lock Haven, Pennsylvania, 1871–Hanover, New Hampshire, 1951

w. Philadelphia, 1888–1904; New York (summers in Gloucester, Massachusetts, 1914–1918 and frequent trips to Santa Fe, 1919–1951), 1904–1951

Artist Aaron Bohrod, a former student of John Sloan, observed that the work of his teacher "needs no interpretation, no explanation—unless it be of a technical nature. It is a clear record of one artist's reaction to the visual experience of his life."[1] Sloan's talent for depicting the tangible world around him can be traced to his background as an illustrator and artist-reporter, which enabled him to capitalize on his natural ability to quickly encapsulate the essentials of a subject with the most economic means.

Born in Loch Haven, Pennsylvania, Sloan moved with his family to Philadelphia while he was still young. Largely self-schooled in art, Sloan first taught himself to etch and to make sketches, some of which he sold. His skillful and satirical caricatures soon gained notice, and he began work as an illustrator at the *Philadelphia Inquirer* in 1891. He attended an evening drawing class, taught by realist painter Thomas Anshutz, in 1892 at the Pennsylvania Academy of the Fine Arts. There Sloan met Robert Henri, who became an influential mentor to his early creative development as well as a close lifelong friend. The two soon befriended Everett Shinn, George Luks, and William Glackens, who were also Philadelphia residents and graphic artists.

This group, along with Maurice Prendergast, Ernest Lawson, and Arthur B. Davies, later joined together in 1908 to present a landmark exhibition known as The Eight. The group conceived of the show, which was instrumental in promoting a new mode of realist art with an urban orientation, as an alternative to the National Academy of Design's annual exhibition, with its conservative jury system that favored the staid academic art of the period. Sloan consistently involved himself in liberal causes and participated in independent exhibitions, including the 1910 Exhibition of Independent Artists, the 1913 Armory Show, and other exhibitions of the Society of Independent Artists. His liberal outlook had political implications as well; in 1909 he joined the Socialist Party and began working as an art editor for the socialist journal *The Masses,* an affiliation he continued until 1916. In his paintings, however, Sloan attempted to maintain an objective, apolitical stance.

Henri was instrumental in shaping Sloan's initial approach to working in oil. In 1909 he introduced Sloan to a new pseudoscientific method of painting advocated by theorist Hardesty Maratta, who devised a systematic approach based on the coordination of tonal relationships and harmonies in music that used a standardized palette. It was a technique that Sloan quickly adopted and continued to rely upon for the remainder of his life.

In 1913 Sloan sold his first painting to Dr. Albert Barnes, the wealthy Philadelphia industrialist and collector whom Glackens had known from his youth. However, he met with little critical or financial success until late in life and continued working as an illustrator until 1916. That same year, Sloan received his first solo exhibition at the Whitney Studio Club and secured his first gallery show at Kraushaar Galleries, an event that marked the beginning of a long-standing relationship. He also began teaching at the Art Students League in 1916, where he served as an inspiring instructor to many younger artists for more than two decades. In 1918 Sloan succeeded William Glackens as president of the Society of Independent Artists, a post he held for the remainder of his life, thereby solidifying his position as a significant force in progressive circles.

An event important to the development of Sloan's style was the 1913 Armory Show, where many Americans were introduced to the art of the European avant-garde. Sloan noted the effect it had on his own painting: "After I saw the Van Goghs at the Armory Show, there was a more conscious planning of the palettes."[2] Sloan painted *Carol with Blue Hair Ribbon* (1913, plate 167) soon after the Armory Show. The composition is one of a series of portraits of female models who boast bright red hair. He executed at least one other portrait, *Carol with Red Curls* (1913), of the same model in a similar pose.[3] Only the subject's first name, not her identity, is known, but she was likely a professional model as are the others depicted in the series. Some have suggested that Sloan chose these models because their red hair allowed him to experiment with more vivid juxtapositions of color. Indeed, the most striking quality of this series is its emphasis on color: Sloan used red purple and orange blue complements, the latter of which is seen in *Carol with Blue Hair Ribbon*. He also employed more exaggerated and visible brushwork, perhaps inspired by the modern art he saw at the Armory Show. Sloan's portraits of Carol heralded a new phase in his art, characterized by the more fully realized chromatic resonance evident in works from the following summer, when he began visiting the stimulating locale of Gloucester, Massachusetts.

After spending five summers in Gloucester, Sloan visited Santa Fe, New Mexico, at the suggestion of Henri in 1919. He ultimately became a fixture in that burgeoning artist colony, purchasing a house and spending a significant part of almost every year there until his death. By the late 1920s Sloan appeared to tire of the artistic conventions in which he had been working. Over the course of the ensuing years, he evolved an original technical approach to his art, focusing on a new plasticity, especially in figurative subjects and particularly in nudes that incorporated a richly textured surface patterning. This new style signaled a decided departure from the urban genre scenes that had defined his early reputation.

Valerie Ann Leeds

Notes

1. Aaron Bohrod, "On John Sloan," *College Art Journal* 10 (fall 1950): 3.
2. John Sloan, notes, as quoted in Roland Elzea, *John Sloan's Oil Paintings: A Catalogue Raisonné*, vol. I (Newark, Del.: University of Delaware Press, 1991), 23.
3. Elzea, 130–36.

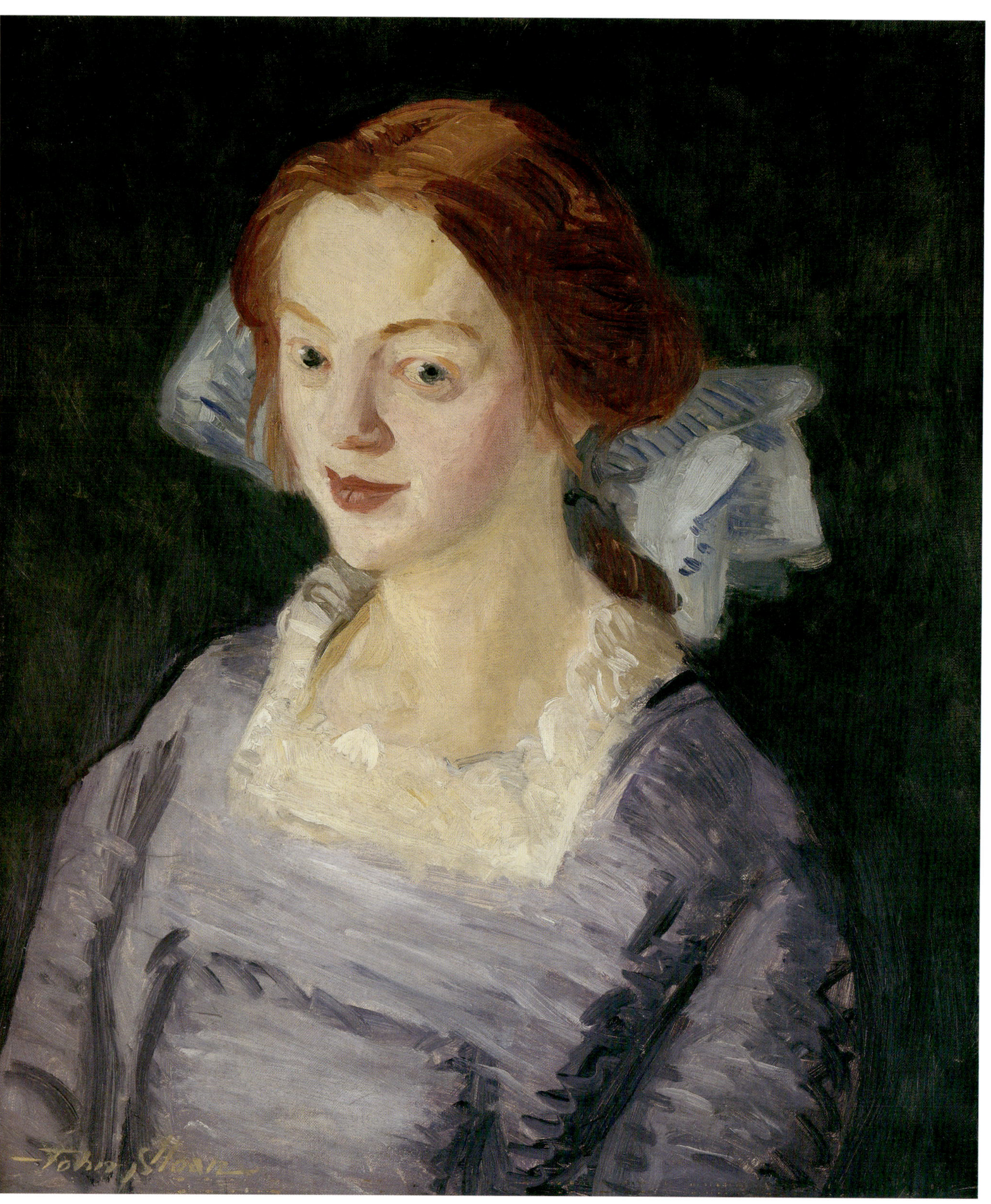

167.

Carol with Blue Hair Ribbon, 1913

Oil on canvas
24 × 20 in. (61 × 51 cm)
Gift of Mari and James A. Michener
G1968.120

Provenance: Marianna Sloan, c. 1945; private collector, c. 1956; Parke-Bernet Galleries, New York, 1965; purchased by James Michener from Parke-Bernet Galleries, 1965
Signed lower left "John Sloan"
Inscribed verso on stretcher "Carol with Blue Ribbon in Hair John Sloan"

Raphael Soyer

Borisoglebsk, Russia, 1899–New York, 1987
w. New York, 1916–1987

Raphael Soyer's *Transients* (1936, plate 168) is a New York scene that records the impact of the Depression at its height, a subject for which the artist is principally recognized. A dozen men sit in a flophouse, waiting to be assigned a bed; their haggard faces, sunken eyes, and slumped postures reflect the despair of their individual predicaments as well as the harsh conditions of life in the 1930s. The flattened pictorial space forces the group of disenfranchised men toward the viewer. Soyer's portraitlike depiction of each man stresses his individuality, whether young or old, while his subdued palette of browns and grays reinforces the painting's overall sense of despondency. Here, as elsewhere, the artist employed homeless people as his models, including Walter Broe, who appears in the left foreground and makes direct eye contact with the viewer.[1]

Along with such artists as Philip Evergood, Ben Shahn, and Reginald Marsh, Soyer is typically categorized as a Social Realist because his work from the 1930s focused on city life and revealed the sometimes seamy and hopeless situation of the less fortunate in American society. He is also associated with the Fourteenth Street School, which included Kenneth Hayes Miller, Isabel Bishop, and Marsh—artists whose studios on Fourteenth Street, in the heart of Manhattan's downtown commercial district, placed them in the midst of daily narratives of need and desire. Soyer's characteristic attention to particular detail and commitment to emotional truth evoke empathy for the human condition.

Raphael Soyer was a twin to brother Moses, also an artist; they were born in Borisoglebsk, Russia, and were the oldest of six children. The Soyer family immigrated to New York in 1913 when Raphael was fourteen. Raphael, Moses, and their younger brother, Isaac, all studied art at Cooper Union and the National Academy of Design in New York, Raphael from 1918 until 1922. In the early 1920s Raphael also studied with Guy Pène du Bois at the Art Students League, where he would later work as a teacher in the 1930s and early 1940s.

Throughout the 1920s Soyer embraced a variety of genres, from still-life and portraiture to the female nude and landscape. He often painted his own environment, producing reverent depictions of his family and middle-class Jewish life on the Lower East Side, as well as poignant scenes of people caught in quiet moments of introspection. Soyer had his first solo exhibition at the Daniel Gallery in New York in 1929—the same year of the stock-market crash and the onset of the Great Depression. That year also marked the beginning of Soyer's affiliation with the John Reed Club, a group of artists and writers (William Gropper among them) sympathetic to the Communist Party.[2] Soyer would remain a member until 1935, when the club disbanded and he joined the American Artists' Congress, which was likewise affiliated with the Communist Party but whose platform was more focused on combating the threat of Fascism.

Four years after joining the John Reed Club, Soyer's work underwent an important shift: he began to focus less on the urban and architectural elements that had dominated his earlier paintings and more on human figures, particularly homeless men, as seen in *Transients.* Soyer completed his first large-scale painting of the urban poor, *In the City Park,* in 1934. Art historian Samantha Baskind has attributed this change in Soyer's practice not only to his Jewish identity but to his embrace of Communism as well. As she argued, "Communism, and the social justice the party espoused, channeled Soyer's energies into his paintings of the homeless."[3] However, despite his membership in the John Reed Club, which he recalled as having helped him "to acquire a progressive world outlook," Soyer claims to have not allowed his political beliefs to "influence" his paintings. "My work never became politically slanted. I always painted only what I knew and saw around me. In the 1930's [*sic*] I painted many pictures of unemployed and homeless men, because I saw them everywhere," he said in his 1969 memoir *Self-Revealment*.[4]

In the 1940s Soyer found the streets of New York less artistically "accessible"[5] and took his art indoors, focusing on studio portraiture, as seen in *Portrait of a Girl (Cynthia Brown)* (1940–1949, plate 169) and *Girl in Stocking Cap* (1978, not illustrated), from late in his career. In these two paintings, Soyer used a dark and limited palette to depict the distinctive features of his two female models, each one conveying a sober, melancholy, and contemplative mood. Superficial beauty did not interest Soyer, who found that worthy subjects often revealed themselves in unsuspected places.

During the 1950s Soyer actively opposed Abstract Expressionism, the dominant mode of artistic expression at the time. He believed that Abstract Expressionism eliminated artistic standards and the need for well-honed artistic skills or talent. A lifelong realist, he remained committed to a traditional approach, without flattery or exaggeration, while his compositions were founded on direct observation. He painted a wide variety of individuals, some engaged in the activities of everyday urban life, such as disheveled workers, street people, derelicts, and others renowned for their talents, including dancers, actors, and friends and fellow artists Marsh, Arshile Gorky, Marsden Hartley, and Edward Hopper.

Soyer also executed self-portraits at various stages of his career and was even known to insert self-portraits surreptitiously into his genre scenes. The yawning man in the back right corner of *Transients,* for instance, is none other than Soyer himself, a moving symbol of the artist's empathetic identification with his subjects.[6]

Kelly Baum and Tiffany Rasco

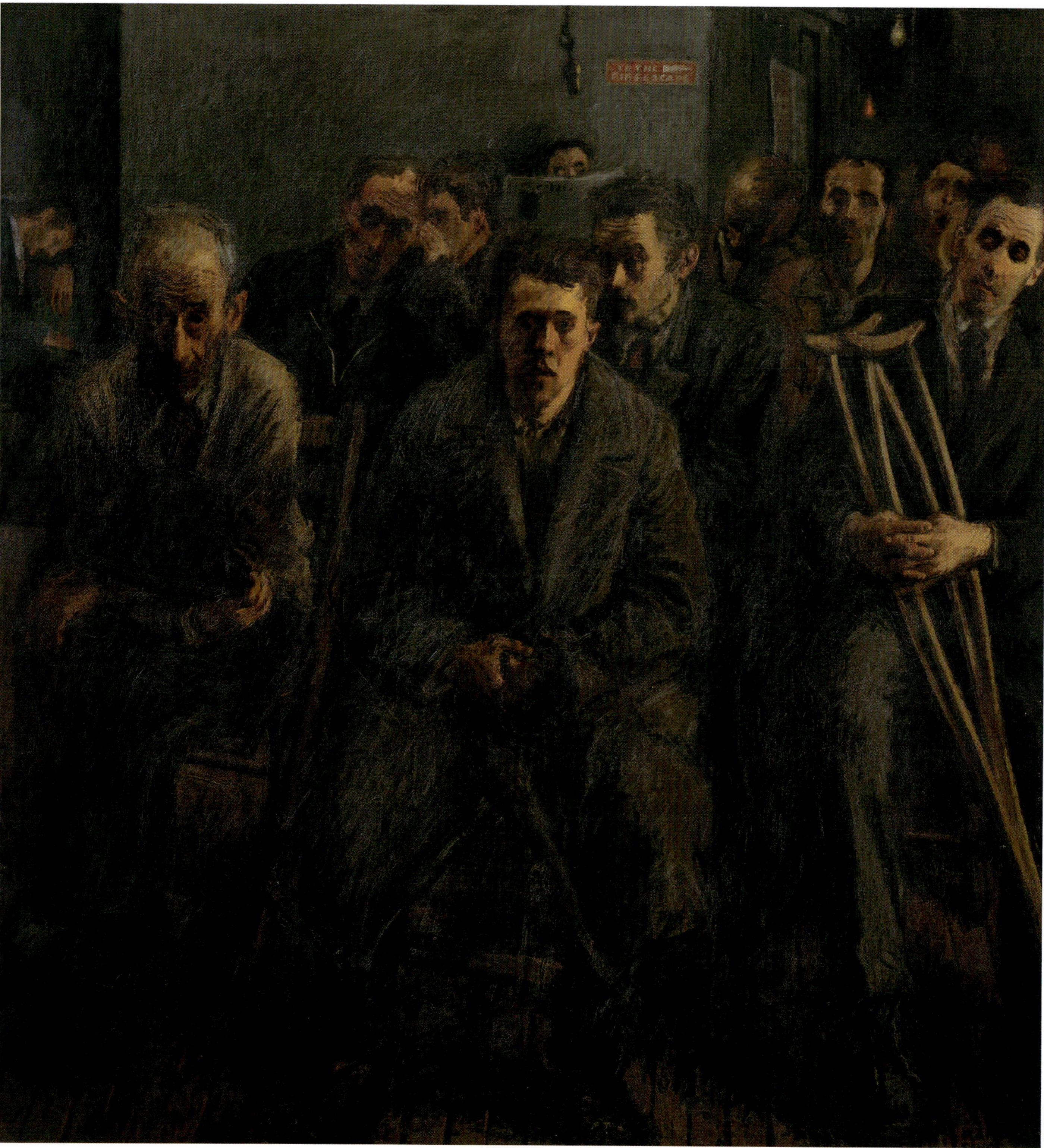

Notes

1. Samantha Baskind, *Raphael Soyer and the Search for Modern Jewish Art* (Chapel Hill, N.C.: The University of North Carolina Press, 2004), 79, 82. According to Baskind, Broe often modeled for Soyer for fifty cents a day. The two became close friends. Broe lived in and helped to maintain the artist's studio until he died, while Soyer introduced him to many of the other Fourteenth Street School painters, who likewise employed Broe as their model. In 1939 these painters organized a fundraiser for Broe at the Montross Gallery; the exhibition included *Transients*. See Baskind, 97.
2. Baskind, 80.
3. Baskind, 81.
4. Quoted in Baskind, 81.
5. Avis Berman, "Raphael Soyer at 80: 'Not painting would be like not breathing,'" *Artnews* 78 (December 1979): 42.
6. Baskind, 84.

168.

Transients, 1936

Oil on canvas
$37\frac{1}{2} \times 34\frac{1}{8}$ in. (95.3 × 86.7 cm)
Gift of Mari and James A. Michener
1991.324

Provenance: Purchased by James Michener from Midtown Galleries, New York, 1962; long-term loan to The University of Texas at Austin, 1968–1991
Signed lower right "Raphael Soyer, 193x"

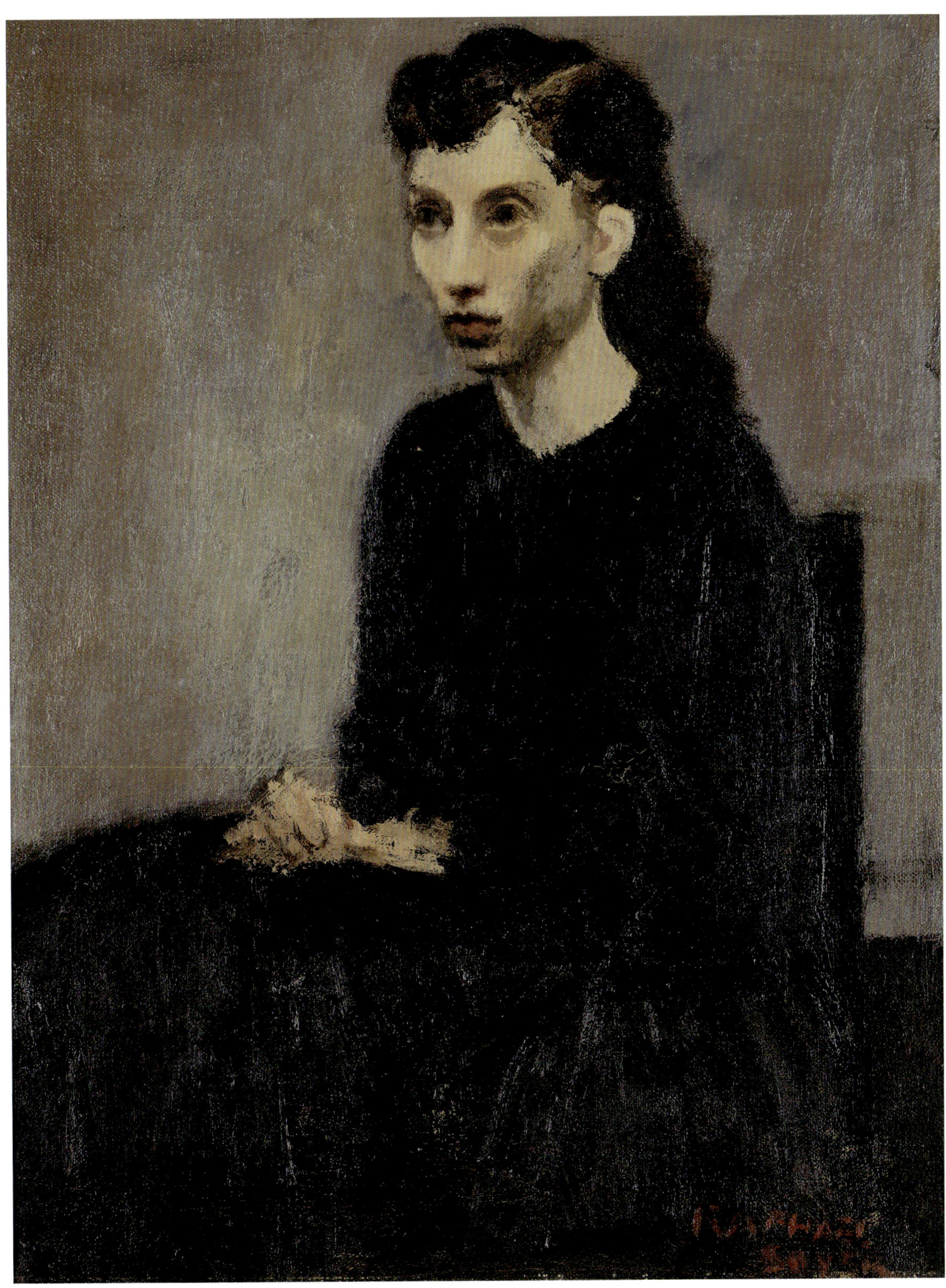

169.

Portrait of a Girl (Cynthia Brown), 1940–1949

Oil on canvas
16⅛ x 11 13/16 in. (41 x 30 cm)
Michener Acquisitions Fund
P1969.15.2

Provenance: Purchased from Parke-Bernet Galleries, New York, 1969
Signed lower right "Raphael Soyer"

Niles Spencer

Pawtucket, Rhode Island, 1893–Dingman's Ferry, Pennsylvania, 1952

w. Providence, Rhode Island (summers in Ogunquit, Maine), 1913–1915; New York, 1915–1917; Ogunquit (frequent trips to New York), 1917–1921; Europe, 1921–1922; New York (summers in Provincetown, Massachusetts, and trip to Europe, 1928–1929), 1923–1949; Dingman's Ferry, Pennsylvania–Sag Harbor, New York–New York, 1949–1952

Though his name is not widely recognized, Niles Spencer was one of the most dedicated practitioners of Precisionism, a modernist style of painting. Spencer rendered his reductive urban landscapes in subdued tones with stark and elegant simplicity, elevating the mundane and sometimes even dreary subject matter of buildings, factories, warehouses, or industrial equipment to a level of classical beauty that became the hallmark of his style.

Spencer received formal art training at the Rhode Island School of Design between 1913 and 1915 and also took summer classes with Charles Woodbury in Ogunquit, Maine. He then studied briefly with Kenneth Hayes Miller at the Art Students League and with Robert Henri and George Bellows at the Ferrer School, both in New York, from 1915 to 1916. Spencer initially employed the same deliberate and cerebral working methods as Miller, a realist painter. A 1921 trip to Europe, however, introduced him to the work of Paul Cézanne, Pablo Picasso, Juan Gris, and Georges Braque. This exposure profoundly impacted Spencer's development, providing him with the essential vocabulary that fueled his modernist exploration of form.

Spencer's work displays a thorough and intimate understanding of the paintings of Cézanne, whose lessons about abstracted form he assimilated into his own singular style. Spencer did not intend his paintings as transcriptions of nature but rather as vehicles of expression. As he remarked in 1941, "the deeper meaning of nature can only be captured in painting through disciplined form and design. The visual recognition is actually irrelevant. It may be there or not."[1] He often worked from several preparatory studies to construct images that achieved his desired tonal effects and formal arrangements.

Developing along a course parallel to that of his contemporaries Preston Dickinson and Charles Demuth, Spencer found particular inspiration in the work of Charles Sheeler, whose use of an exacting geometry greatly affected his own approach. An overview of Spencer's oeuvre reveals several discrete phases in which he successively employed a growing modernist syntax while his subject matter remained based in realism. His work of the 1920s and 1930s typically combines dense volumetric forms derived from architecture, industry, and nature. His late style, from the 1940s until his death, assumed an increasingly abstracted form, with flattened perspectives and somber colors.

Across the Tracks (1934, plate 170) shows Spencer's use of geometric form and compressed perspective but exhibits more definition than the work of his final years. Wendy Jeffers has astutely suggested that this composition is an amalgam of several scenes that the artist observed during his frequent train trips between Massachusetts and New York in the 1930s.[2] The painting suggests a composite view from the edge of a New England town, and it juxtaposes nature with industrial motifs such as the fenced-in lot, metal tanks, and adjacent road sign. The composition, devoid of any humanity or activity that would divert focus from its formal aspects, exemplifies Spencer's abstracted industrial images.

Spencer had his first solo show in 1925 at the prestigious Daniel Gallery in New York, a gallery that featured American art. He regularly exhibited in various group exhibitions over the succeeding two decades, but his next solo exhibition, at the Downtown Gallery, was not held until 1947. Spencer never achieved great popular or financial success during his lifetime; the subdued and cerebral nature of his art perhaps made it too inaccessible for a general audience, though his work was greatly appreciated within the artistic community of the time.

Valerie Ann Leeds

Notes

1. Richard B. Freeman, *Niles Spencer* (Lexington, Ky.: University of Kentucky Art Gallery, 1965), 11.
2. Wendy Jeffers, telephone conversation with the author, November 18, 2003. I wish to thank Jeffers for generously sharing with me her knowledge and insights about Spencer's work.

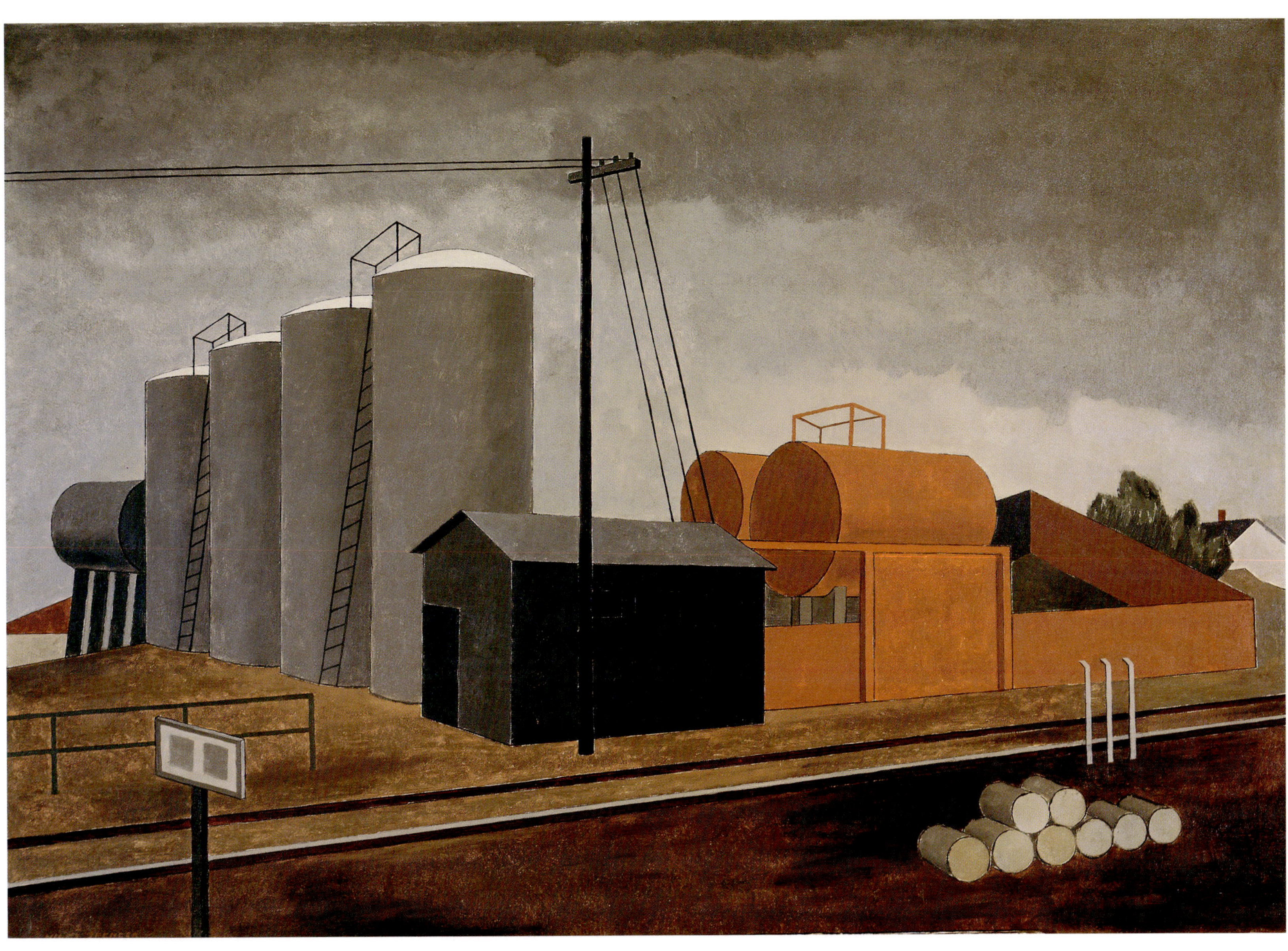

170.

Across the Tracks, 1934

Oil on canvas
36⅜ × 50³⁄₁₆ in. (81.5 × 104.4 cm)
Gift of Mari and James A. Michener
1991.327

Provenance: Purchased by James Michener from Downtown Gallery, New York, 1962; long-term loan to The University of Texas at Austin, 1968–1991
Signed lower left "Niles Spencer"

Gael Stack

b. Chicago, 1941
w. Champaign, Illinois, 1969–1970; Carbondale, Illinois, 1970–1972; Houston, 1973–present

Throughout her more than thirty-five-year career, Stack has combined linear, figurative images with written notations, creating a perplexing visual language that is vaguely familiar yet ultimately obscure. Just as Stack's paintings fuse visual and written forms of communication, they merge painting and drawing in a taut balance that is indivisible.

One can see these dynamics at work in the Blanton's *Untitled* (1989, plate 171). Fleshy and ghostly at the same time, Stack's protagonists are succinctly drawn in oil pastels atop a densely colored ground. In the left-hand panel, depicted in white, agitated lines, a Japanese mother holds a baby in her arms. To the right, represented with calm, confident lines, is a burly, oversized baby drawn from a Hieronymous Bosch painting. The outlines of these ghostly figures convey the weight and three-dimensionality of a body. Below the transparent drawings, both washy and thick, are painterly earth tones that locate Stack's main characters in space (albeit an indistinct, entirely abstract space). The illusion of depth thus created is subtle, something we sense rather than see.

The protagonists appear out of a swirl of paint as pockets of action. We glimpse only a moment of the private dramas they enact. Absorbed in themselves, they are grounded amidst the hurly-burly around them: peripheral fragments float in atmospheric space, as if supporting actors waiting offstage for their cue. Appearing across *Untitled,* we discover a seated monkey, a Japanese mask, a dog's head, and complicated, active marks reminiscent of flowers, vegetation, or other things to which we just cannot put a name. As in life, everything in the painting is in flux—aware of the past, involved in the present, impelled to move on. Through this temporal disruption and strange combination of images, Stack seeks to depict "the unspoken and the irrational," and to open up new ways for us to feel our way, rather than think our way, through the painting.[1]

Painted in mid-career, *Untitled* is a pivotal transitional work. One of Stack's first diptychs, it represents a move toward the scale and complex compositions for which she is best known today. *Untitled* introduces hallmarks of her later work, such as the profound influence of Japanese art, particularly from the twelfth to the fifteenth centuries, while still connecting to images from the Renaissance and Western medieval art.

Stack's paintings reflect her lifelong interest in language and visual art. These twin concerns blossomed as a fusion of image and word in the paintings she created as an undergraduate at the University of Illinois at Champaign-Urbana, following a short stint of secretarial work. Journalism was Stack's first major, but she quickly became disillusioned with it and began to pursue art in earnest. Her influences, which coincided with her first college sojourn at the beginning of what would become the tumultuous 1960s, included Abstract Expressionism and automatic writing.

Stack describes her academic career, which bridged the 1960s, as "beginning with the Twist and ending with the Rolling Stones." In 1969 she returned to college to finish her degrees. In addition to Andy Warhol's language of repetition, Stack explored ideas embodied in the works of avant-garde composer John Cage and the language systems created by authors James Joyce and Samuel Beckett. Joyce and Beckett focused on exploring the limitations of language and life, honing in on what the artist describes as "not knowing." Shorthand, a notation system that most viewers can recognize as language but that only secretaries can decipher, became a way for Stack to express this idea in visual terms, and she incorporated such marks into her late undergraduate paintings. Through shorthand, Stack began to translate systems of verbal language into a new visual language

Cage's work exerted perhaps the most profound influence on Stack. She was particularly struck by his experiments with splintered phrases, scrambled language, and interspersed story lines, his way of approaching life and music from a different, non-Western perspective. Cage also sought to escape deliberate choice, to incorporate the unpredictable, to use silence as an active element in the composition, and to produce the effect of simultaneity. Following Cage, Stack explored the effects of change and chance, simultaneity and unpredictability, in part by combining disparate images to create new symbols. One can readily see the multiple points of view, as well as the numerous time frames and historical contexts, that collide in the Blanton's *Untitled.* As the artist put it, "When you mix the past with the present, the past is evident—through symbol, or through traces in how you make the painting. The past has an implacable claim on the present."

Through visual and linguistic means, Stack's paintings embody ideas that reflect major artistic currents in the late twentieth century: the fragmentation of life and a subsequent search for meaning, as well as the necessity of audience participation in the completion of the artwork. The disassociation of imagery in Stack's paintings creates an undertow that draws us closer to the parts of life we experience, recognize, and know but cannot verbalize.

Madeline Irvine

Note

1. Gael Stack, telephone interviews with the author, January, March, and June 2005. All quotations that follow are from these interviews.

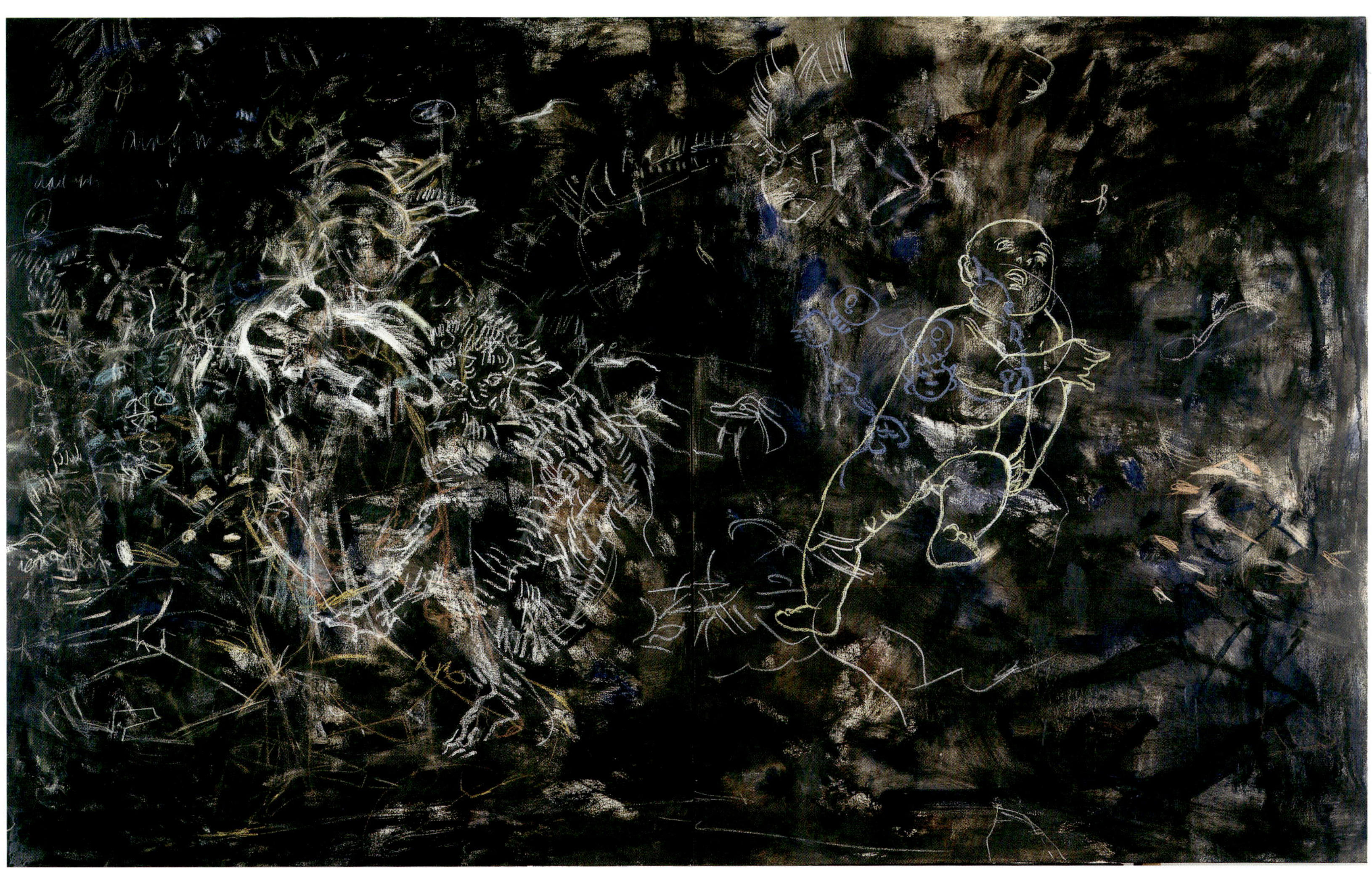

171.

Untitled, 1989

Oil on canvas
Overall: 60 × 96 in. (152.3 × 243.8 cm)
Gift of Jeanne and Michael Klein
2003.1.1/2–2/2

Provenance: Purchased by Jeanne and Michael Klein from Moody Gallery, Houston, n.d.

Lawrence Stafford

b. Kansas City, Missouri 1938

w. Kansas City, Missouri, 1960–1964; Chicago, 1964–1965; New York, 1965–1986; Dallas, 1986–present

Monumental in scale, abstract in form, and generous in its use of opulent color, Lawrence Stafford's *Untitled* (1968, plate 172) belongs to a strain of abstraction alternately referred to as "Abstract Illusionism" or "Lyrical Abstraction," which arose in the late 1960s. For his part, though, Stafford dismissed these labels, asserting that he belonged to an artistic circle—one that included such artists as Dan Christensen and Peter Ford Young—rather than a unified movement.[1] Optical and spatial illusionism intrigued these artists, who claimed that representational art was exhausted and anachronistic.

Stafford was born in Kansas City, Missouri, in 1938. He studied with Robert Barnes at the Kansas City Art Institute, and after graduating in 1964, he moved to Chicago. The following year, he relocated to New York, where he maintained a studio in the same building as Young and Ronnie Landfield. During the early part of his career, Stafford's paintings were highly sought after both in the United States and abroad. His first one-person show in 1969 at the Galerie Ricke in Cologne, Germany, sold out before opening night. The David Whitney Gallery gave Stafford his first one-person show in New York the following year.

Stafford once described *Untitled* as a work in which "strange spatial things [are] going on."[2] It consists of finely layered bands of pink, violet, yellow, orange, and green. Anchored by black and white, the colors mix on the surface and produce the illusion of spatial recession and projection. This fusion of color leaves the viewer unbalanced and disoriented; her attempt to focus on a single part of the painting is frustrated at every turn and ultimately proves to be a futile endeavor. The lack of optical precision in Stafford's work is reminiscent of a blurred photograph and calls to mind Gerhard Richter's photograph-inspired paintings of the 1960s. Following in the tradition of Abstract Expressionism, *Untitled* makes use of an allover composition; the painted forms fill the entire surface of the canvas, inviting scrutiny of every detail. Painted after a visit to Amsterdam, Stafford said that *Untitled* reflects "the energy . . . that [he] felt at that time,"[3] and that he intended "to create a very spiritual feeling, of something cosmic, eternal, color as content, no drips, and certainly not decorative."[4]

In 1964, while living in Chicago, Stafford began working with airbrushes, thereby removing his hand from the painting process. The technique he used to create *Untitled* involved propping the canvas against the wall and covering its every inch with airbrushed streams of paint, which he applied while walking back and forth in front of the painting. This method required a rhythmic approach that Stafford compared to the act of knitting a rug.[5] Shortly thereafter, he devised a different method of applying pigment, in which he stretched the canvas over a large horizontal cylinder. As the cylinder, powered by a motor, turned at a constant rate, he sprayed acrylic paint over the support. Stafford's painting techniques invite comparison to the innovations of Jackson Pollock and Morris Louis, who also embraced process and chance. While Pollock dripped and splattered paint across his canvases, Louis allowed gravity to control the direction of the pigment.

The so-called "New Informalists" and "Young Lyrical Painters" have received relatively modest attention in the decades since their debut. However, the works of Stafford, Christensen, Landfield, and Young represent a time when it seemed that anything was possible in painting.[6] Critics, for their part, were confident that these artists were about to spearhead the next great development in abstraction. Indeed, *Untitled*'s innovative optical effects and its sense of infinite, mysterious space, which the artist described as an effort to capture "the pattern and movement of the universe as a visual experience," remain unique achievements.[7] Stafford currently resides in Dallas, Texas, where he continues to produce colorful abstractions on glass and ceramic surfaces as well as works on paper.

Lara Kuykendall

Notes

1. Lawrence Stafford, interview with David Reed, Austin, May 5, 2001, Blanton Museum of Art Archives, The University of Texas at Austin.
2. Stafford, interview with Reed.
3. Stafford, interview with Reed.
4. Lawrence Stafford, correspondence with the author, May 20, 2004, Blanton Museum of Art Archives, The University of Texas at Austin.
5. Stafford, interview with Reed.
6. Carter Ratcliff, "The New Informalists," *Artnews* 68 (February 1970): 46–50; and Larry Aldrich, "Young Lyrical Painters," *Art in America* 57 (November 1969): 104–13.
7. Aldrich, 109.

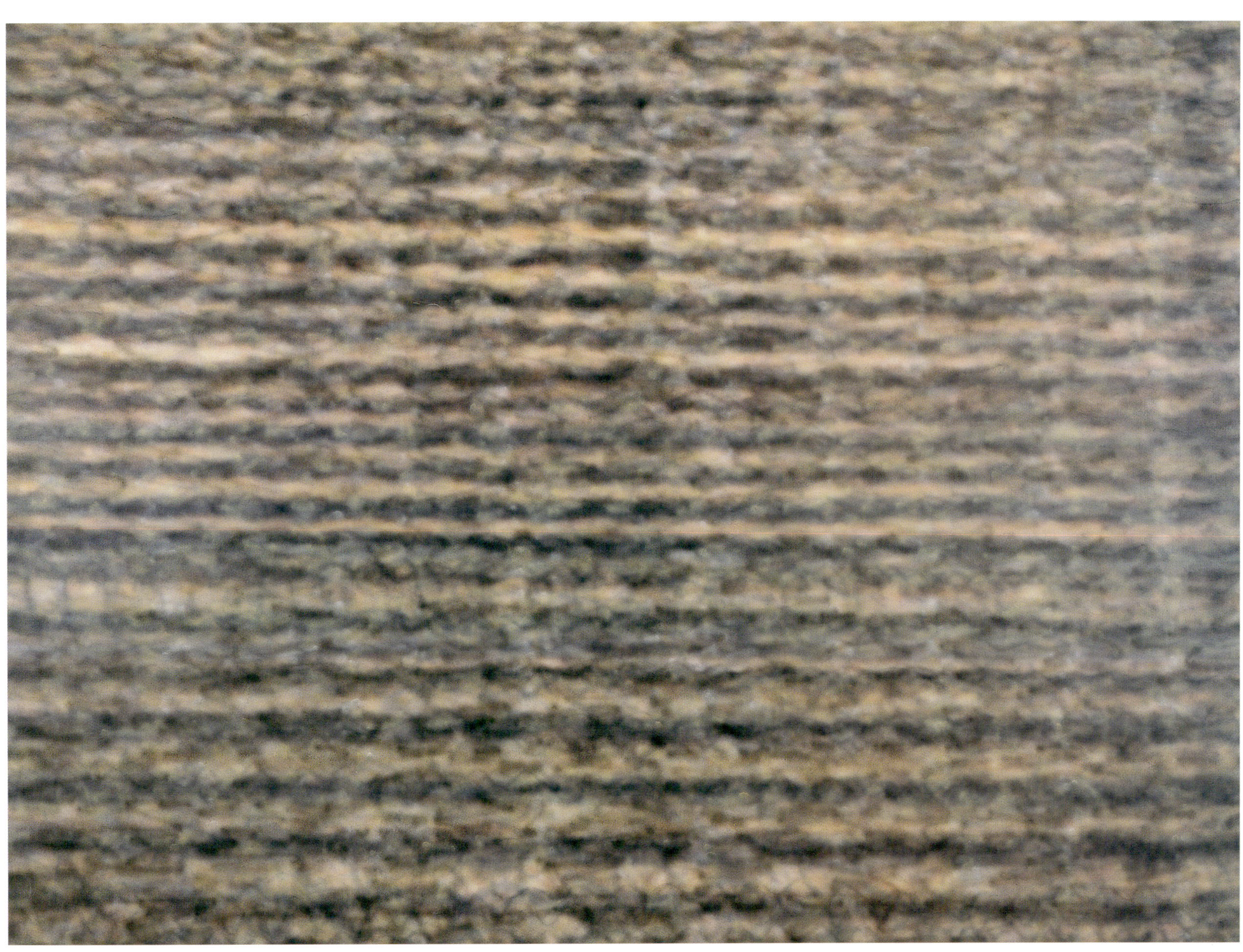

172.

Untitled, 1968

Sprayed acrylic on canvas
72 × 96 in. (183 × 244 cm)
Gift of Mari and James A. Michener
G1968.121

Provenance: Purchased by James Michener from the artist, through Richard Bellamy, New York, 1968
Signed verso, upper left "Lawrence Stafford 1968"

Harold Stevenson

b. Idabel, Oklahoma, 1929

w. New York, 1949–1959; Paris–New York–Oklahoma, 1959–present

Painted while the artist was living in Europe, Harold Stevenson's *The Arm of Don Juan* (1963, plate 173) is an expansive close-up of a male nude that stretches across two panels. This over-life-size homoerotic depiction of a man's torso creates a sensation of intimacy that it simultaneously disrupts. While the magnified representation allows viewers voyeuristically to inspect the details of the man's torso, the cropping of the composition denies them visual access to his entire body, most importantly his eyes and face. Employing techniques grounded in Old Master painting, Stevenson reinvigorated modern figurative painting through an innovative use of scale and the close-up.

Stevenson executed *The Arm of Don Juan* in a restricted palette of earth tones and with a considered use of light and shadow that endows the figure with the illusion of three-dimensionality. He further enhanced the work's realism by including details such as the individual wisps of hair on the subject's forearm. Stevenson found inspiration in the skilled proficiency of Renaissance painters like Michelangelo, who emphasized musculature through chiaroscuro and detailed draftsmanship.

In pursuing realist representation in the 1960s, Stevenson rebelled against the prevailing emphasis on abstraction, although his large-scale paintings do evoke the expansive compositions of the Abstract Expressionists. At the same time, it is difficult to categorize him with other figurative painters of that period, since his idealized figures depart from the blunt realism of artists like Philip Pearlstein.

Born in Idabel, Oklahoma, Stevenson received artistic training at the University of Oklahoma, Mexico City College, and the Art Students League in New York. Upon his arrival in New York in 1949, Stevenson gained representation at the Alexander Iolas Gallery and came into contact with Surrealist artists Max Ernst and René Magritte. He moved to Paris a decade later and soon commenced work on a series of monumental male nudes. He exhibited this series, along with a twenty-five-piece portrait of his lover, Lord Timothy Willoughby de Eresby, in 1962 at the Iris Clert Gallery in Paris under the title *Fantastic Sensuality*. In these works, Stevenson often fragmented the body into distinct compartments by splitting the composition into multiple canvases. When examined in isolation, the individual canvases verge on abstraction, which led one critic to compare their vast, unidentifiable expanses of color to Color Field painting.[1]

Although Stevenson clearly delights in paint and surface, the subject always remains paramount. The bullfighter, the actor, and the lover are all popular constructs of manhood that Stevenson portrays in his art, casting light on and disarming prevailing ideas about masculinity. The title of the Blanton's painting refers to the literary character "Don Juan," who was notorious for seducing women. Stevenson, however, transforms this archetypal sexual aggressor into a passive object of desire, thereby subverting the Western artistic tradition that typically represents women as the object of the gaze. Indeed, Stevenson's Don Juan, with his head notably absent, is unable to return the viewer's gaze, rendering him both powerless and anonymous.

In 1963 a critic referred to Stevenson's paintings of large-scale nudes as "skinscapes," an apt title for his atmospheric evocations of the body as a landscape.[2] The artist himself once said that he wanted his nudes "to be consumed as if in the dunes of the Sahara desert . . . to be as suffocating as a body can be in the night with someone under the bed sheets."[3] To this end, he employed close-ups and cropping so that his subjects' bodies press against the edges of the canvas. Stevenson, like the Abstract Expressionists, similarly enveloped the viewer within the vast expanse of his compositions.

For the past several decades, Stevenson has divided his time between Paris, New York, and Oklahoma, where he has maintained a studio since 1965. In the 1960s and 1970s he frequented the Factory and appeared in two of Andy Warhol's films, *Kiss* (1963) and *Heat* (1972). Warhol even made a film about Stevenson, released in 1964 and titled *Harold*. Stevenson's languorous *The New Adam* (1962), which features an over-life-size reclining male odalisque, may have inspired Warhol's *Sleep*, a film that obsessively documents a sleeping male nude over the course of several hours.[4] Warhol would later invoke Stevenson's art in *Torso* (1977), a series of silk screens that likewise depict large male and female nudes. Though some critics have labeled Stevenson a Pop artist, this description, likely the result of his association with Warhol, is misleading, since the fleshy eroticism of his nudes and his attention to traditional painting techniques is at stylistic odds with the detachment and commercial slickness of Pop art.

Stevenson's highly personal work offered an alternative to the dominant trends of the period: abstraction and Pop art. In terms of its bold subject matter, it was highly subversive, predating the 1969 Stonewall Riots and the official beginning of the Gay Rights Movement. Going against the grain, Stevenson transformed what some might consider a conventional figurative approach into a radical form of art making.

Katherine Roeder

Notes

1. Michael Duncan, "In the Flesh," *Art in America* 87 (April 1999): 132.
2. Exhibition review, *Artnews* 62 (December 1963): 16.
3. Duncan, 132.
4. John Giorno, the sleeping man in *Sleep*, described the film in terms reminiscent of Stevenson's paintings, "Andy got around homophobia by making the movie *Sleep* into an abstract painting: the body of a man as a field of light and shadow." John Giorno, *You Got to Burn to Shine* (New York: High Risk Books, 1994), 132–33.

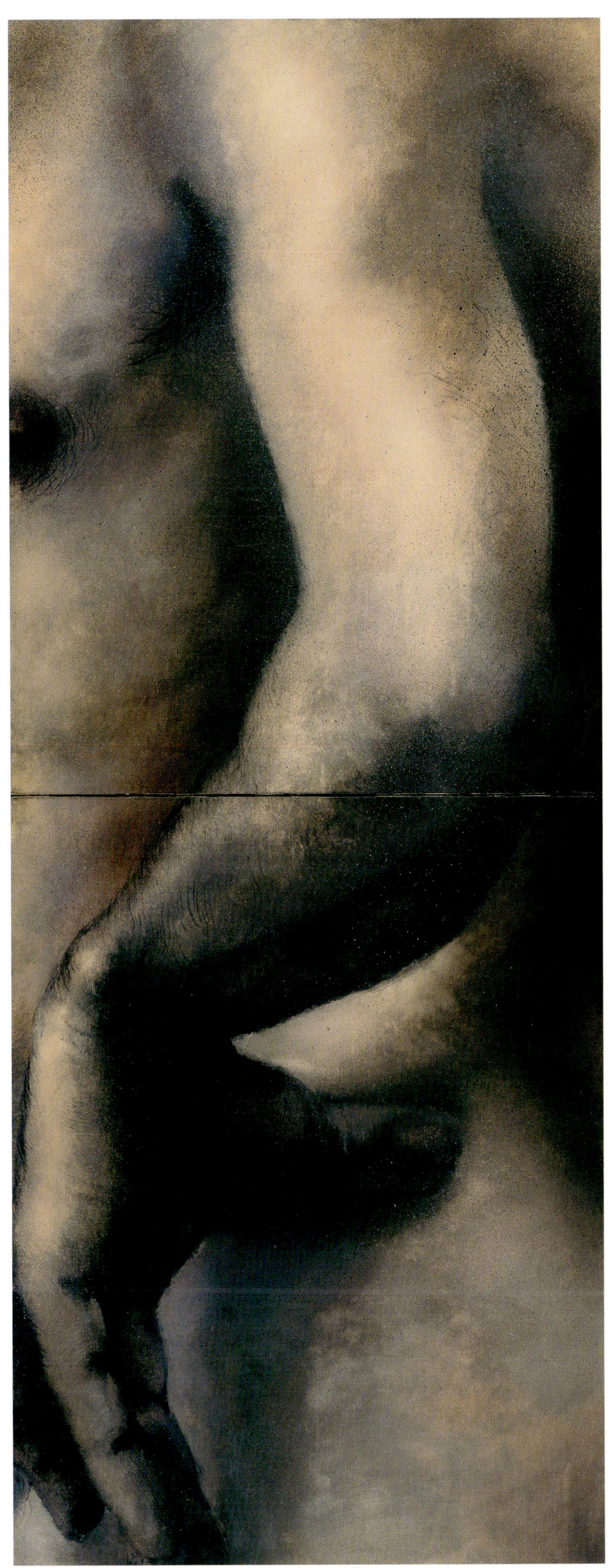

173.
The Arm of Don Juan, 1963
Oil on canvas
91 × 35 in. (231 × 89 cm)
Gift of Mari and James A. Michener
G1968.122

Provenance: Purchased by James Michener from Feigen-Herbert Gallery, New York, 1963
Signed verso, lower center "Harold Stevenson '63"

George Sugarman

New York, 1912–1999
w. Paris, 1951–1952; Europe, 1953–1954; New York, 1955–1999

George Sugarman was born in New York and educated at the City College of New York. Although he was an arts and crafts instructor under the WPA, he did not begin studying art until he was in his late thirties. In 1946 he enrolled in evening courses at The Museum of Modern Art. Inspired by this introduction, he decided to pursue the study of art in greater depth, so he departed for Paris in 1951 with support from the GI Bill. Sugarman studied in Paris with Ossip Zadkine, a painter and sculptor who worked in a Cubist style, but whose ideas Sugarman ultimately rejected as too limited and too dependent on an implied human figure. After a year in Zadkine's studio, the artist registered at the Académie de la Grande Chaumière, where he met Al Held, a lifelong friend and artistic colleague who engaged in similar explorations of form, color, and gestural impact.

In 1961, one year after his first solo exhibition, Sugarman's *Six Forms in Pine* (1959) won second prize at the Carnegie International, between Alberto Giacometti's wining submission and David Smith's sculpture. In many ways, *Six Forms in Pine* represented an ending for Sugarman. The artist soon abandoned the Cubist-inspired, unpainted, carved wood sculpture that he had been creating since the early 1950s and began to produce vibrant polychromed, laminated wood assemblages. These new works, more dynamic and emotionally charged than the earlier sculptures, represented an attempt on Sugarman's part to break definitively with European modernism, especially Cubism. At the same time, the artist wanted to avoid the pervasive influence of Abstract Expressionism, the dominant style in New York when he returned to the city in 1955. Inspired by the color theories of Stuart Davis, whose work came to prominence after a 1957 retrospective, Sugarman began to fashion multiple, brightly painted shapes in contrasting colors. By 1959 he was presenting work comprised of unique colored shapes with interchangeable parts. For Sugarman, color was integral to the conception of these works: rather than performing a decorative function, it reinforced the design and plastic quality of the sculpture.

Sugarman created *Two Reds and a Blue* (1961, plate 174) during his early color explorations. It is composed of diverse wood elements painted blue and two different shades of red, one intense and vibrant,

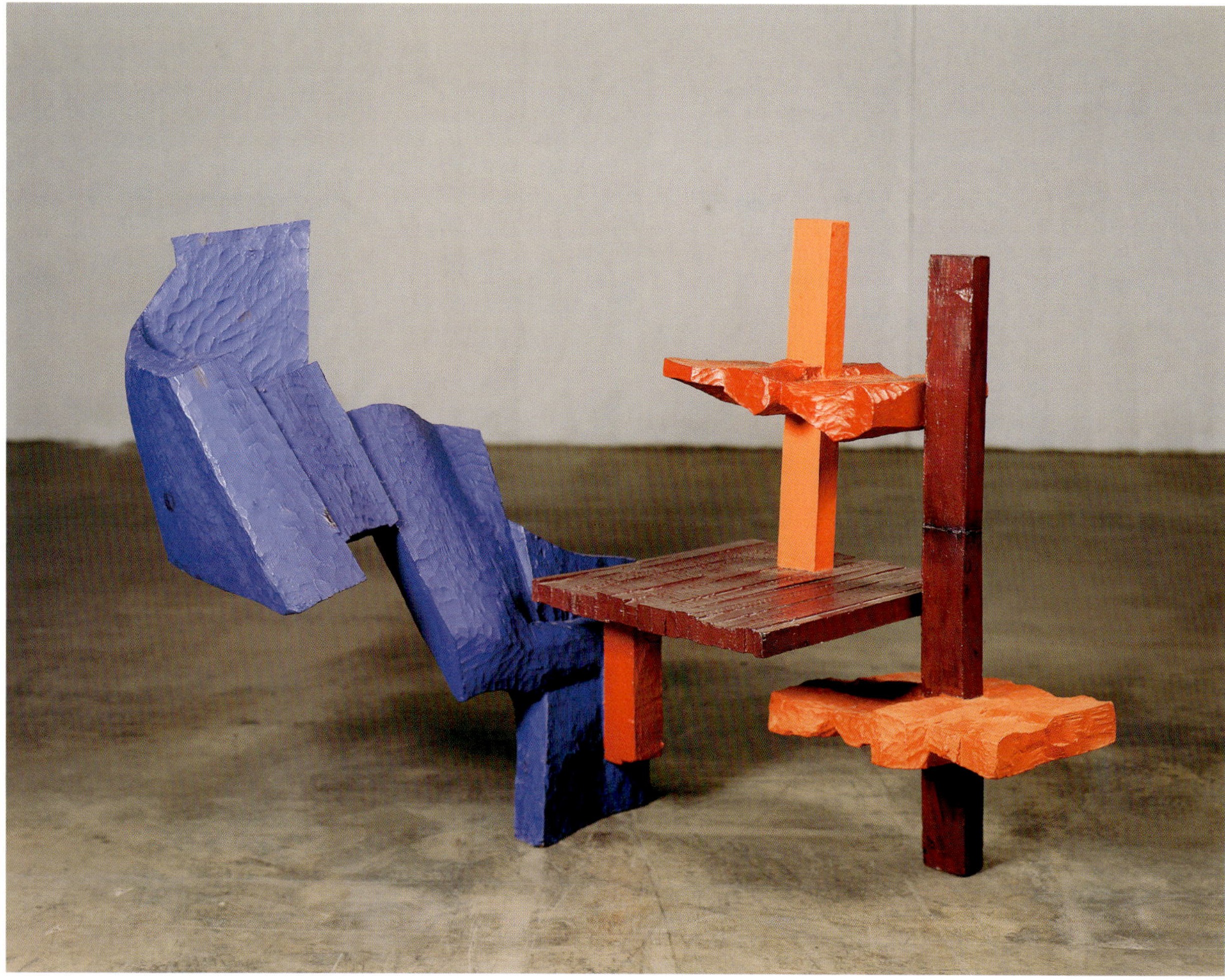

174.
Two Reds and a Blue, 1961
Polychromed wood
34 × 56 × 31 in. (86.4 × 142.2 × 78.7 cm)
Purchase through the generosity of Jack S. Blanton, Jeanne and Michael Klein, and The Judith Rothschild Foundation
2003.64

Provenance: Purchased from Joan T. Washburn Gallery, representing the estate of the artist, New York, 2003

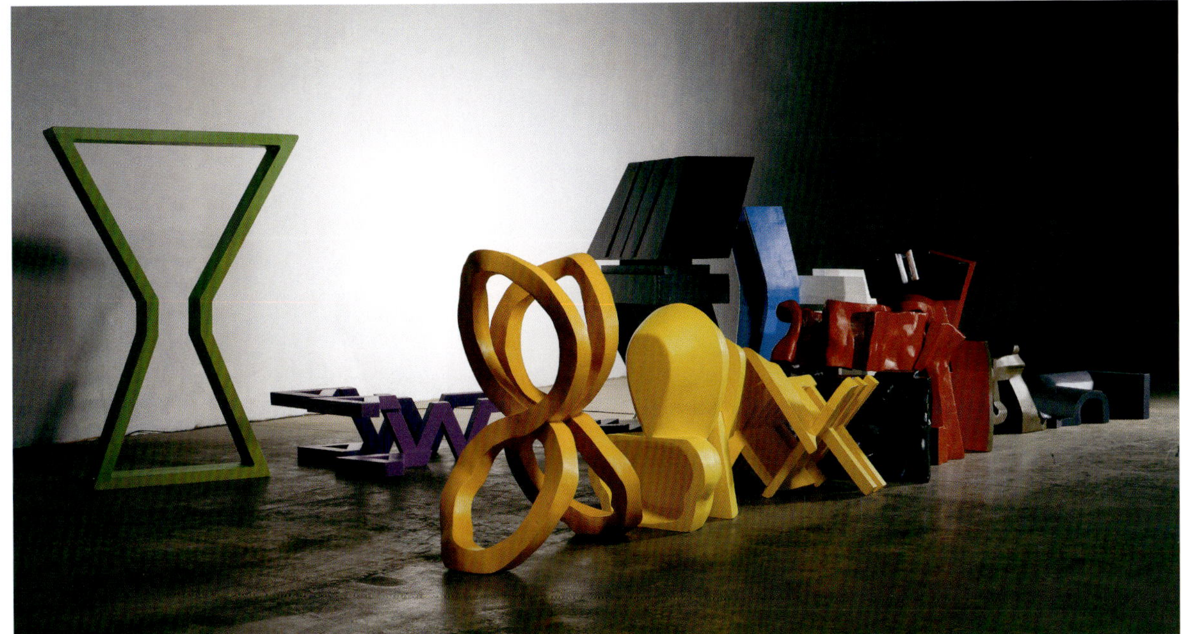

175.
Two in One, 1966
Polychromed wood installation of nineteen elements
97½ × 286 × 134 in. (247.6 × 726.4 × 340.4 cm)
Gift of the George Sugarman Foundation, Inc.
2003.154.1/19–19/19
Provenance: Collection of Arden Sugarman Eliopoulos

the other more brown and somber, which amplify the sculpture's nonsymmetrical formal arrangement. Its active engagement with space seems to reference the Hellenistic and Baroque art that Sugarman admired, such as Gianlorenzo Bernini's *Ecstasy of Saint Teresa* (1645–1652), which he knew from trips to Europe.

Like the Minimalist sculpture that it predated by a few years, *Two Reds and a Blue* lacks a pedestal. Sugarman considered the pedestal an antiquated contrivance that imposed a strict vertical orientation on sculpture. He elected instead to vary the work's orientation by employing vertical, horizontal, and diagonal elements. Each element is a different color and has a unique texture, ranging from rough to smooth. The nonlinearity and variation within forms, finishes, and tones emphasizes the fact that the sculpture, although static, appears to be made up of multiple, shifting volumes. In this manner, *Two Reds and a Blue* not only recalls the syncopated rhythms and atonal music found in modern jazz, a genre for which Sugarman had a particular appreciation, it challenges the concept of sculpture as a fully unified, balanced, and contained whole.

Sugarman's sculptures appeared in 1965 alongside works by Held and others in the exhibition *Concrete Expressionism*, a term coined by noted critic Irving Sandler.[1] Sandler observed that Sugarman and Held combined the geometric abstraction of Concrete art with "an assertive physicality and a sense of energy" as well as "a classicizing inclination —a will to clarity—which predisposes them to quasi-geometric structures, composed of exact planes of unmodulated color."[2]

In 1966 Sugarman created *Two in One* (plate 175), which critic Raphael Rubinstein described as "one of the most striking works of his career."[3] It consists of nineteen individual forms, each painted a different intense color. Once again eschewing the traditional pedestal, Sugarman dispersed the structures across the gallery floor, with some lying sideways and others resting upright. Rubinstein characterized the rounded, angular, curved, flattened, and occasionally interlocking forms as being "as abundant and various as the contents of a child's box of toys."[4]

Sugarman would continue to make polychromed, laminated wood sculpture throughout the 1960s. In the early 1970s he exchanged wood for painted aluminum and began producing wall reliefs and acrylic paintings. Today Sugarman is most closely identified with the outdoor public works that he created from the late 1960s until the end of his career. These metal sculptures are notable for their massive scale and intricately shaped, boldly colored forms that interact with the surrounding architecture and urban environment.

Throughout his career, Sugarman explored form and space using different media, scales, and configurations. This desire to mine the expressive potential of each structure in relationship to the space around it characterized all of Sugarman's sculptures, from his earliest works in wood to his monumental public commissions.

Jennifer Farrell

Notes

1. Irving Sandler, *Concrete Expressionism* (New York: New York University Art Collection, 1965), n.p.
2. Sandler, n.p.
3. Raphael Rubinstein, "A Polychrome Profusion," *Art in America* 87 (April 1999): 119.
4. Rubinstein, 119.

James Surls

b. Terrell, Texas, 1943

w. Bloomfield Hills, Michigan, c. 1967–1969; Dallas, 1969–1975; Houston–Splendora, Texas, 1982–1998; Basalt, Colorado, 1998–present

At first glance, it may seem odd that James Surls describes his whimsical wooden sculptures as self-portraits. Hovering somewhere between abstract forms and references to petals, tree branches, or eyes, his meandering, biomorphic sculptures speak of their close relationship to drawing, a medium that Surls has pursued alongside sculpture throughout his career. Indeed, Surls often refers to his sculptures as "drawings in space"[1] to describe the strong emphasis they place on continuity and line. As do his drawings, the sculptures have a weightless, animated quality about them that is deeply personal, bringing together the artist's lifelong interests in mystical symbolism, mathematical precision, and personal memory with a deep respect for the natural world.

Born and raised in a wooded area of east Texas, Surls has maintained close ties to nature throughout his life. His father was a carpenter who passed on the lessons of his trade to his son. From these lessons, Surls acquired an intimate understanding of the relationship between built form and natural materials. His interest in nature is related closely to a second unifying theme in his work: his belief that the qualities of a specific place shape an individual's spiritual, philosophical, and emotional connections to the world. As he described, "A person's art has to come from a place. You get comfortable in your terrain and you use that, you draw from it, conjure from it. I conjure from the earth, the woods. Even the violent part of it."[2]

Although Surls has lived in Michigan and currently resides in Colorado, his work has long been associated with Texas. After receiving an undergraduate degree in fine arts from Sam Houston State University in 1966, Surls went on to get a graduate degree from the prestigious Cranbrook Academy of Art in Michigan in 1969. He then returned to Texas, eventually purchasing thirty-two acres of land outside Houston in Splendora, Texas, where he and his wife, artist Charmaine Locke, lived and worked until 1995. Such forested terrain, reminiscent of his childhood home, has been a constant source of inspiration for Surls, teaching him daily lessons about the natural world's patterns of growth and decay. Surls is committed to protecting the environment, and he uses only naturally felled trees as material in order to ensure that the terrain will last for future generations.[3]

Surls's perception of the natural world as something both deeply integral to human life and magically distinct from it is evident in his 1989 sculpture *White Tipped Night Palm* (plate 176). Rife with motifs that have defined Surls's work throughout his career, the almost six-foot-high sculpture centers on an open-coil steel pipe whose stark industrial form contrasts with the rough-hewn, hand-carved oak petals that radiate from it in five-pronged branches. Playfully balanced on the tips of three of these petals, the large sculpture seems to float just above the ground, recalling Surls's parallel interest in creating suspended mobiles. Like a mobile, *White Tipped Night Palm* offers the viewer the opportunity to observe the form from different angles. Viewed along its length, the open spiral of the sculpture's steel core gives it a buoyant, organic feel. When viewed frontally, its rigid central organization becomes more apparent. The work appears less organic than mechanical from this perspective, suggesting the potential energy of an airplane propeller or paddle wheel at rest. As is true of most of his sculptures, *White Tipped Night Palm* shifts between allusions to natural and man-made forms.

Rather than describe his work as abstract, Surls prefers to think of it as a language where each form is rich with potential meanings. The motifs that recur in his sculpture, such as circles, spirals, and certain numbers like three, five, and seven, not only act in a formal capacity, they communicate symbolic values as well.[4] Surls's resistance to fixed meaning, however, prevents him from attaching any single significance to these motifs. As he observed, a circle might represent universality "unless it's around your ankles, as shackles, or handcuffs or you're chained to the dungeon wall. Then all of a sudden that business about union and the continuation and all of the symbolicness [*sic*] that we've put into that goes out the window."[5] Through shifts in scale and presentation, Surls embraces the complexity of meaning offered by the shapes and symbols he employs, often allowing contradictory impulses to coincide in the same piece.

Surls seeks to create accessible work that does not require formal art history training in order to be understood, although he cites a number of art historical influences. The artist has credited both folk art and modern art, in particular that of Alexander Calder and Joseph Cornell, with impacting his approach to sculpture.[6] He has praised folk artists for their sincerity and authenticity and twentieth-century movements like Surrealism for embracing chance and irrationality.[7] Surls's work can be interpreted as a reaction against the cold geometric forms of Minimalism, the movement that dominated the art world when he was in art school. He shares its interest in precision and mathematical structure, but in his hands, these elements take on a more metaphysical quality that suggests an underlying consistency with the structure of the universe.[8] Always seeking to reconcile contradictions, whether between nature and culture, dream and nightmare, or folk art and modernism, Surls offers a view of the world that is romantic without being sentimental, taking into account both the beauty and authority of the world around him.

Karen M. Rapp

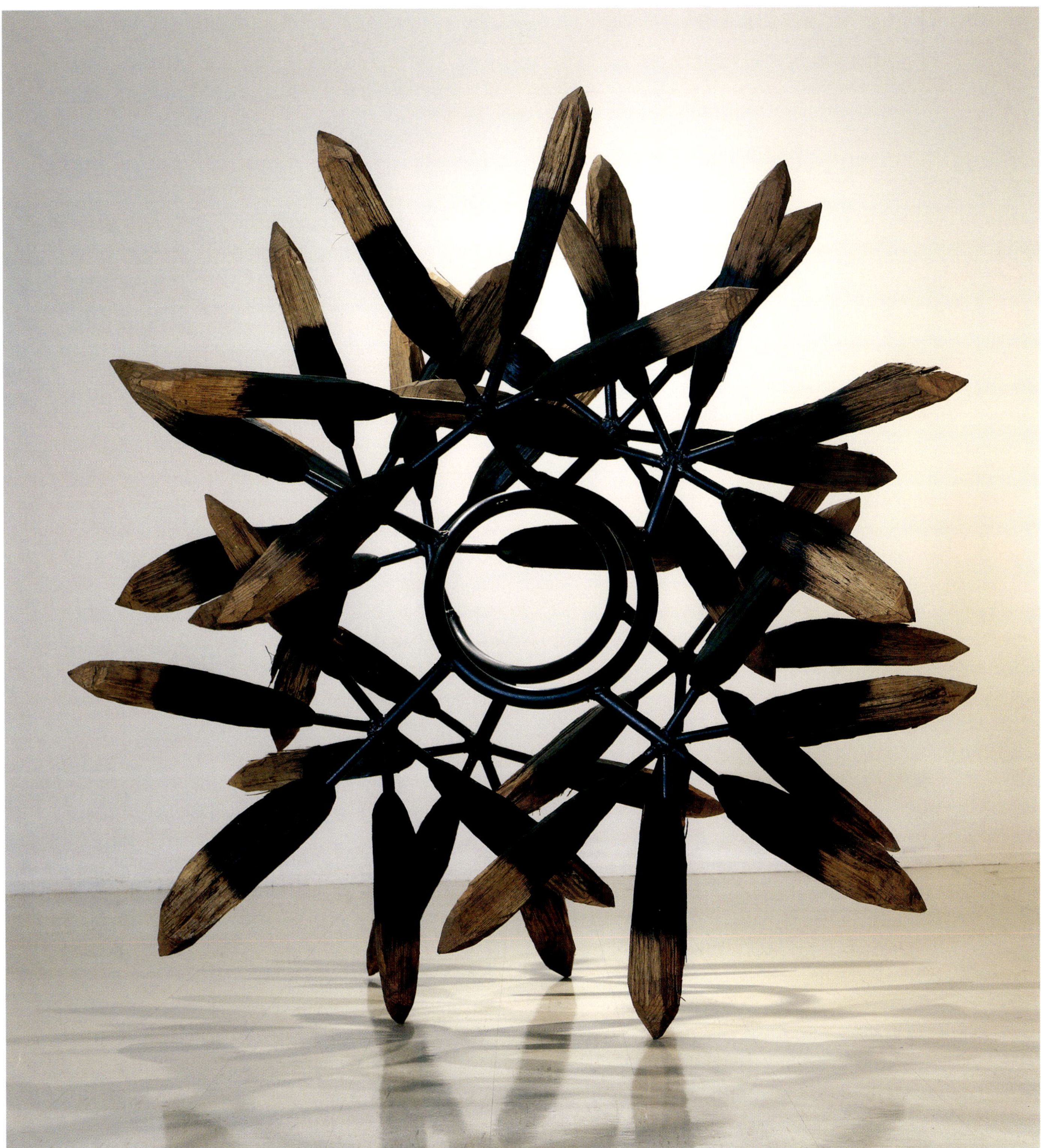

Notes

1. James Surls, "Interview with James Surls," interview by Sue Graze, in Sue Graze, *Visions: James Surls, 1974–1984* (Dallas: Dallas Museum of Art, 1984), 32.
2. Quoted in Robert Creeley, *Looking Out: James Surls, Sculpture, Drawing and Prints* (Honolulu: The Contemporary Museum, 1991), n.p.
3. Ellen Rosenbush Methner, "Deep in the Art of Texas," *Museum and Arts Houston* (August 1992): 28.
4. James Surls, "Interview—In the Studio with James Surls," interview by Gregory Warden, in *In the Meadows and Beyond: Recent Sculpture, Drawings, and Prints of James Surls* (Dallas: Meadows Museum of Art, Southern Methodist University, 2003), 153.
5. Surls, "Interview—In the Studio with James Surls," 153.
6. Mark Thistlethwaite, "An Art of the Eye and the I," in *In the Meadows and Beyond*, 46.
7. Thistlethwaite, 46.
8. Surls, "Interview with James Surls," 28.

176.

White Tipped Night Palm, 1989

Oak and steel
66 × 76 × 66 15/16 in. (167.6 × 193 × 170 cm)
Purchase as a gift of Mary and Jack Bartholow
1990.143

Provenance: Purchased from Hiram Butler Gallery, Houston, 1990

Sidney Tillim

Brooklyn, New York, 1925–New York, 2001

w. Syracuse, New York, 1946–1950; New York, 1950–1966; Bennington, Vermont, 1966–1993; New York, 1993–2001

By 1965, the year he painted *Work Jacket on Easel* (plate 177), Sidney Tillim already had achieved recognition as an artist, educator, and art critic. Tillim began writing for *Art Digest*, which later became *Arts Magazine*, in 1953. Criticism he published there and in *Artforum* demonstrates his knowledge of art history melded with a keen awareness of contemporary developments. Tillim's pithy reviews, some of the first to celebrate and analyze Pop art, appeared with those of Donald Judd and Vivien Raynor in *Arts Magazine*'s monthly "In the Galleries" column, joining his longer essays that included regular contributions to the "Month in Review" feature.[1]

With aid from the GI Bill, Tillim graduated in 1950 from Syracuse University, where his fellow students included Sol LeWitt. He pursued geometric abstraction both at Syracuse and in subsequent years, deliberately eschewing the gestural approach of Abstract Expressionism, the dominant style at the time. In 1958 Tillim once again defied the dominant trend in contemporary art—abstraction—and began to practice representational painting, depicting objects found in his studio. In contrast to the scope and complexity of his critical writing, his paintings of the 1960s are relatively modest, calling attention to the mundane and everyday.

In the Blanton's painting, a work jacket thrown over a tripod easel with casual abandon becomes a sculptural form in dialogue with the pitted surface of the wall and the textured density of an upholstered bench. Still-life paintings such as this one attend to objects that, though neither elevated nor monumental, signal the presence of unseen human actors. As Tillim later recalled, "I was very conscious of using insignificant things, drapery, a radio. An apple would have been saturated with history. It was pretty banal stuff. I was interested in spatial properties but, looking back, I see that the use of drapery was a surrogate for figurative action."[2] Following Tillim's logic, it becomes clear that each object in *Work Jacket on Easel* might stand in for a figure. Even the shadow cast by the blue jacket becomes a palpable element in dialogue with the green khaki trousers fallen upon the lilac upholstery of the stool.

Tillim sought an art that was grounded in art's history—that is, in the long tradition of representational art—while simultaneously relevant to contemporary life. "Since 1961 I have supported attempts to revive an art that in the context of modernism would be radically representational," Tillim wrote in 1969.[3] He continued, "There have been many 'new realisms' touted since that time, commencing with Pop art, but none have actually been engaged in what I think is the main business of any 'new realism'—the production of an authentic new episode in the history of representation."[4] He shared the attentive eye of the Photo Realist painters yet did not directly reproduce or transfer photographic images, as did many of those artists. Tillim's approach had more in common with that of his contemporary, Philip Pearlstein, whose realist canvases treated the live model and studio props as objects to be arranged in complex compositions.

Tillim abandoned writing in 1969 to focus his energies on painting and teaching at Bennington College in Vermont. He departed from the quiet realism of his mid-1960s work to paint figurative narratives that revived the language of history painting celebrated by art academies until the nineteenth century. However, Tillim's rough and occasionally awkward treatment of the human figure, his depiction of contemporary events, and his use of this "high" art tradition to represent scenes from popular culture distinguish these narratives from their predecessors. *Count Zinzendorf Spared by the Indians* (1972), Tillim's most famous modern history painting, adapted an early eighteenth-century story from the life of the founder of the Moravian Church to reflect on political concerns about the disenfranchisement of Native Americans in the early 1970s. Although its scale rivals that of nineteenth-century academic "machines," its deliberate awkwardness situates *Zinzendorf* within the modern tradition of expressionist figuration. By contrast, *Work Jacket on Easel* is an exercise in classically spare elegance in which a common jacket assumes the presence of a human figure.

Tillim returned to writing criticism in the late 1970s, by which time his interest in narrative placed him amid the broader artistic and cultural tendency known as postmodernism. His knowledge of the history of photomechanical reproduction enriched his return to abstract painting in the 1980s, yet he continued to paint in the figurative tradition inspired by history painting. Shortly before his death in 2001, Manhattan's Trans Hudson Gallery organized an exhibition of his recent narrative paintings that garnered critical acclaim. In these, Tillim adapted history painting techniques to images taken from the cinema or from tabloid news. "What makes the show so engaging," wrote Daniel Kunitz, "is the paradox offered by its means and thrust: the unrefined technique Tillim employs in painting these works belies the extremely sophisticated arguments about history and art that the show makes."[5] Tillim's awareness of the relationships between art history and artistic technique marked his criticism and his art alike.

James Housefield

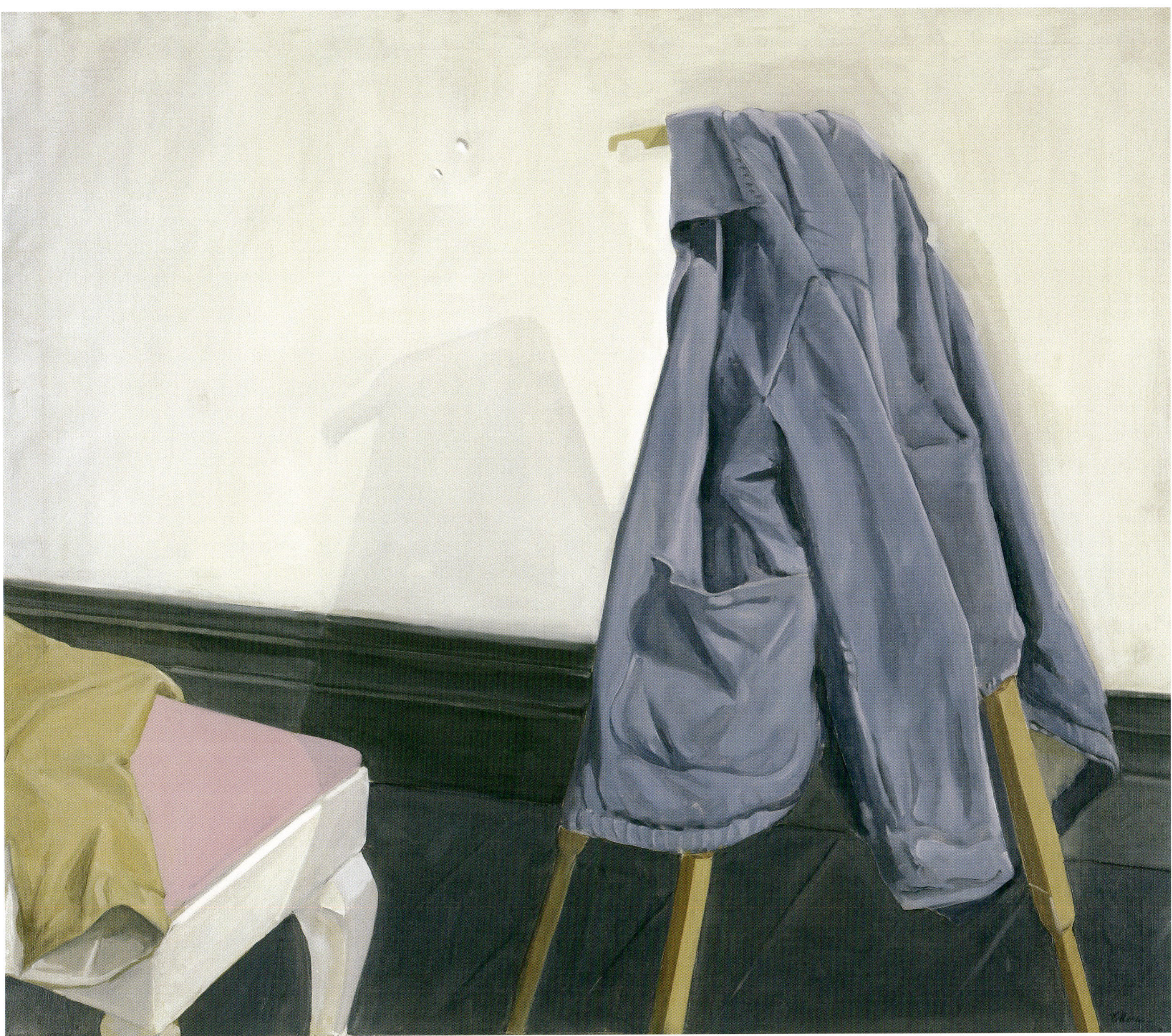

Notes

1. Tillim's essays and reviews for *Arts Magazine* grappled with the rise of Pop and challenged elements of that diverse movement, which he identified as Neo-Dada. "Despite what I, at least, believe are certain fundamental shortcomings in a basically transitional art, the Pop phenomenon has put the entire history of American art in a new perspective," Tillim summarized in *Artforum* of November 1965. In that essay, he pointed out that "My article on Pop Art (*Arts*, Feb. 1962), based largely on Oldenburg's wholly remarkable Store, was the first in this country and actually preceded the formal debut of the movement." Sidney Tillim, "Further Observations on the Pop Phenomenon," reprinted in Steven Madoff, ed., *Pop Art: A Critical History* (Berkeley and Los Angeles: University of California Press, 1997), 135–39. See also Tillim's review of the famed exhibition of Warhol's Brillo (and other) boxes at the Stable Gallery: "Andy Warhol," *Arts Magazine* 38 (September 1964): 62.
2. Sidney Tillim, "An Interview with Sidney Tillim," interview by Meyer Raphael Rubinstein and Daniel Weiner, *Arts Magazine* 62 (December 1987): 64–65.
3. Sidney Tillim, "A Variety of Realisms," *Artforum* 7 (summer 1969): 42.
4. Tillim, "A Variety of Realisms," 42.
5. Daniel Kunitz, "Sidney Tillim: Recent Paintings," *The New Criterion* 19 (June 2001): 54.

177.

Work Jacket on Easel, 1965

Oil on canvas
36 × 41 in. (91.5 × 104.2 cm)
Gift of Mari and James A. Michener
1991.332

Provenance: Purchased by James Michener from Robert Schoelkopf Gallery, New York, 1965; long-term loan to The University of Texas at Austin, 1968–1991
Signed lower right "Tillim"

Mark Todd

b. Leon, Iowa, 1950

w. Iowa City, Iowa, 1969–1976; Chicago, 1976–1978; San Marcos, Texas, 1978–present

Mark Todd is a visual artist and poet who integrates images and words in paintings, drawings, and books. He plays with the relationship between image and text, fragmenting and cropping both. Many of his visuals are highly abstract, but the texts add a narrative element that he intentionally disrupts and fractures. Paradoxically, Todd draws the audience into the narrative process through missing words, which tempt the viewer/reader to fill in the blanks. He is interested in the anxieties of human experience and writes that his work "reflects those little pieces of insanity we so cleverly disguise. . . . These 'stories' are never complete, but only fragments of something bigger than painting."[1]

Texture and text evocative of graffiti dominate the Blanton's *Things to Admit* (1986, plate 178). The thick impasto and scarred surface suggest a site where different sets of hands have surreptitiously marked, defaced, and reworked a wall. A large, loosely formed white square occupies the center of an otherwise nearly black canvas. A few scarcely coherent words and three abstract figures emerge from the surface. Two human silhouettes lean away from each other, suggesting alienation; gouged out of a black stain is a white line indicating a smaller figure. With considerable irony, Todd scratched the word "Heroes" into the dark gray surface of the border at the top of the painting. Also occupying the border, a slightly askew vertical black rectangle contains a handwritten, semicontinuous, stream-of-consciousness text that ends with the demand, "you need to admit everything." The text and title embody what the artist calls the suburban tragedy. "It is a confession, of sorts, of things a person would not like to face in their life."[2]

Things to Admit employs a format that Todd used for a decade: a square within a square with highly abstract human figures in the center and handwritten text in the wide margins. He arrived at the format by accident in February 1986. While working on a small drawing within a masked area at the center of a large piece of paper, a poem occurred to him, and he wrote it in the margin. Looking at the result, he liked the way the poem activated the margin and altered the space of the composition. The drawing—whose title, *claims to raise the dead,* was inspired by the poem—thus inadvertently became the prototype for an extended series of works and a vehicle for the union of text and image.[3]

Todd holds undergraduate and graduate degrees in printmaking from the University of Iowa, where he studied intaglio printmaking with Mauricio Lasansky and intermittently participated in the Iowa Writers Workshop. Although he has not made a single print since he completed his MFA, the practice and aesthetics of printmaking permeate his work in a variety of ways, including his preference for neutral colors, appreciation for the subtle range of tones within black, and tendency to apply paint as a stain or with a roller and to remove it with a screwdriver or rag, rather than manipulating it with a brush. He also believes that printmaking influenced his view of the picture plane as a two-dimensional surface. "When you print an intaglio print and that edge becomes embossed, it is first and foremost a two-dimensional plane. . . . I think that stamp never left my experience."[4]

Todd's work is perhaps even more influenced by poetry—especially the writings of Charles Bukowski and song lyrics—than by other art. There are, however, a handful of artists whose work he feels particularly attracted to and regards as influential: Oskar Kokoschka and Egon Schiele for the angst of their figures, Andy Warhol for his "caginess" and irony, Cy Twombly for his formal qualities and marks on paper, and Jean-Michel Basquiat for the abandon of his work and the beauty of his designs.

In the early 1990s Todd moved toward more straightforward narratives. Nevertheless, in his books of poetry, *Catfish Hens* (1999), *Ashe Motors* (2001), and *Possum Box* (2004), which he codesigned with David Shields, the poetry is enmeshed in the visuals in ways that defy conventional rules of typography.[5] Todd explained, "I am more interested in weaving the words through the visual, the texture of the page, and letting it become a part of that visual fabric, rather than having it sit on top of the visual."[6] In *Things to Admit* and his more recent books, Todd's dense layering of words and images forces the reader/viewer to decipher and interpret the work gradually.

Nancy Deffebach

Notes

1. Mark Todd, artist's statement for an exhibition at Foster Goldstrom Gallery, New York, October 1990, Blanton Museum of Art Archives, The University of Texas at Austin.
2. Mark Todd, interview with the author, San Marcos, Texas, March 31, 2000.
3. Todd writes, "The poem inspired the title for the drawing . . . and from then on it would always be the case." The drawing, *claims to raise the dead,* is in the artist's collection. Mark Todd, correspondence with the author, April 12, 2000.
4. Todd, interview with the author.
5. All three of these books were published by White Gas, San Marcos, Texas.
6. Todd, interview with the author.

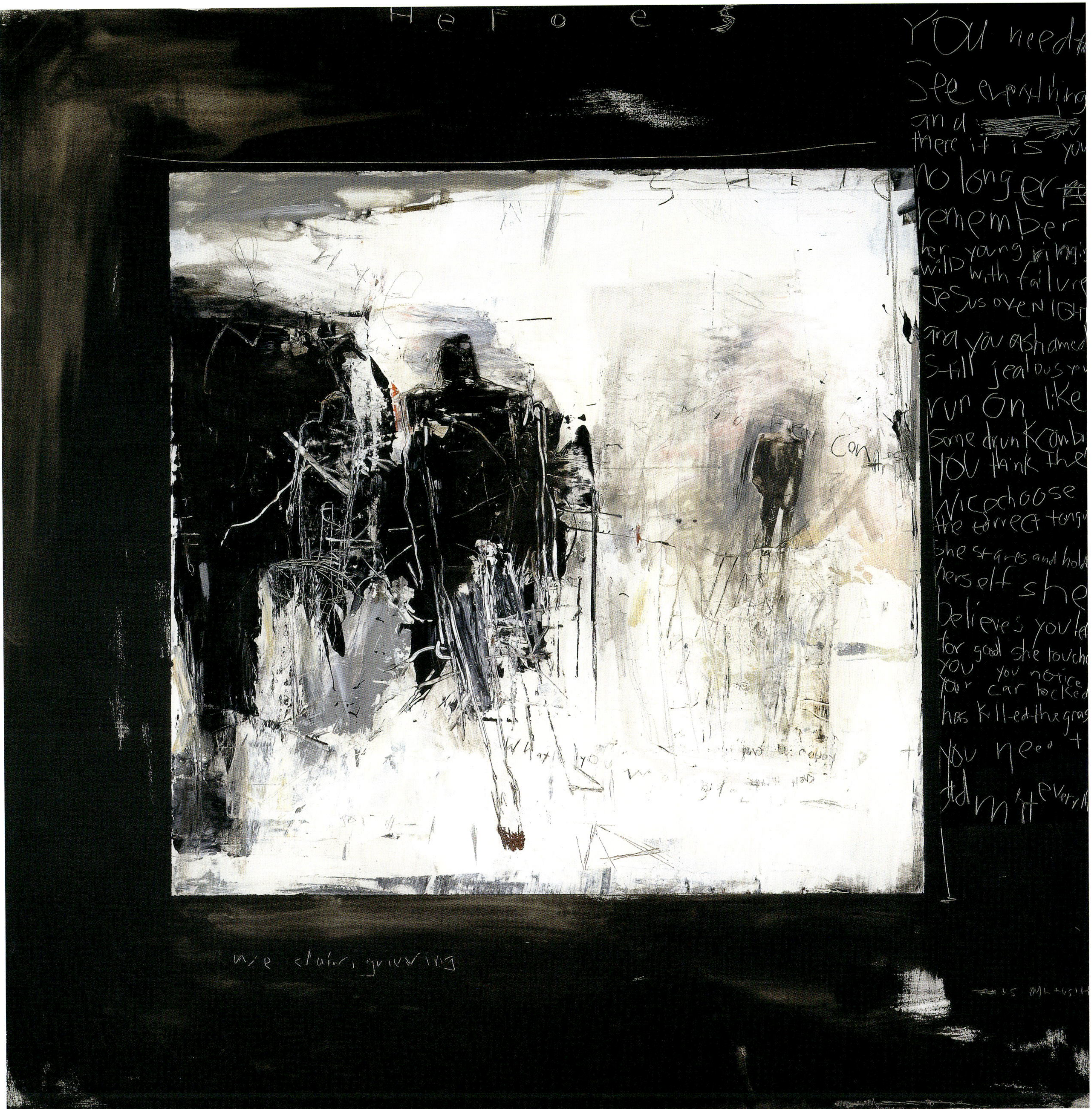

178.

Things to Admit, 1986

Gesso, acrylic paint, colored pencil, and china marker on canvas
72 × 70 1/16 in. (183 × 178 cm)
Michener Acquisitions Fund
1987.5

Provenance: Purchased from AIR Gallery, Austin, 1987

John Torreano

b. Flint, Michigan, 1941

w. Bloomfield Hills, Michigan, 1961–1963; Columbus, Ohio, 1964–1967; New York, 1968–present

I (plate 180) AND *UNIVERSE PAINTING* (plate 179), two works by John Torreano from 1968 and 1975, respectively, reflect the artist's belief that art is a process of communication between artist, artwork, and viewer. They also testify to Torreano's longstanding preoccupation with a particular set of formal issues: both *I* and *Universe Painting* are predicated on an interest in geometry as ornament and a vivid sense of color and surface. At the same time, they give viewers the opportunity to trace the development of Torreano's career between 1968 and 1975, when he refined certain theoretical principles and shifted media from painting to a hybridized form of painting and sculpture.

Torreano was born in Flint, Michigan, a small city near Detroit closely identified with the automotive industry in which his father worked. In 1961, after exhibiting his work locally, Torreano enrolled at the Cranbrook Academy of Art. He majored in painting and experimented with diverse media, including lithography and sculpture. After completing his undergraduate degree, he went on to earn an MFA at Ohio State University in 1967. Around the same time, he encountered the noted artist Richard Artschwager, who encouraged him to move to New York. Artschwager and Torreano were both creating representational paintings based on seemingly contradictory aesthetic practices, borrowing photo-based imagery, for instance, and then abstracting it through an excessively flat, two-dimensional painting style. They also were employing materials not generally associated with fine art: Artschwager made Formica sculptures of chairs, and Torreano began exploring the potential of glass jewels in the early 1970s. By combining abstraction with realism and traditional media with commercial materials, Torreano attempted to redefine the parameters of painting, a concern that has remained present throughout his career.

Soon after arriving in New York in 1968, Torreano created *I*, one in a series of round paintings from the late 1960s and the first painting he ever sold. James Michener purchased the work on the advice of Richard Bellamy, the former director of the Green Gallery in New York. *I* employs a resolutely flat, symmetrical allover design that recalls the serial and grid-based forms embraced by Minimalist artists Carl Andre, Donald Judd, Sol LeWitt, and Frank Stella. Torreano animated the inherent rigor and austerity of this structure by rendering the lines in brightly colored, contrasting tones that create a flickering effect in the eye. The exacting geometrical pattern, with its grid of intersecting vertical and horizontal lines, contrasts with both the round shape of the canvas and the plain white circle in its center. Torreano intended this circle to create the sensation of the painting literally being "opened" and its pictorial surface set into dialogue with the wall behind and around it. That this dialogue might also extend to the viewer is suggested by the title, a verbal pun on the words "eye" and "I" (as in me), as well as its physical form, which resembles an open eye.[1] The title serves to anthropomorphize the painting, as if *I* had the ability to return the viewer's gaze.

Torreano continued to explore abstraction and optical effects in a series called the Bulge paintings. Executed around 1969 and featured in the Whitney Biennial of that same year, the Bulge paintings are comprised of streaks, stains, and dots dispersed across the pictorial surface in a dynamic manner. They were so titled because their rectangular shape and rounded corners not only corresponded to the form of early television sets, they also created the illusion that the center of the canvas projected out into space, just as the screens on these same television sets had done. Torreano gradually simplified the surfaces of these works, eliminating everything but the dots. This "dot" motif would soon evolve into the jewels that he introduced into his next body of work in the early 1970s.

Jewels play an essential role in Torreano's *Universe Painting*, part of a series of one hundred spherical works, each covered in dozens of glass stones.[2] The Universe Paintings defy conventional categorization, drawing from the properties of both painting and sculpture but exactly

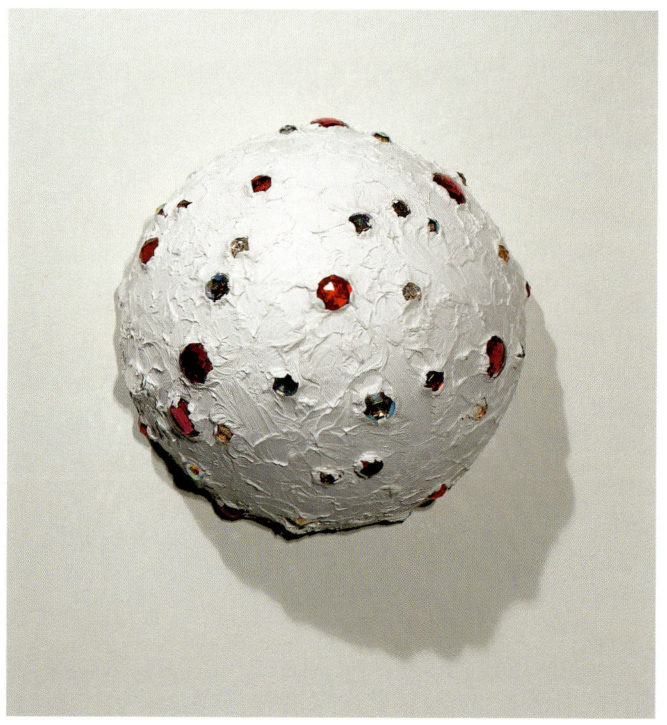

179.
Universe Painting, 1975
Oil, acrylic, and glass jewels on polyester sphere
9 in. diameter x 5 in. deep (22.86 x 12.7 cm)
Gift of David Reed
2003.136
Provenance: Gift of the artist to David Reed, c. 1976

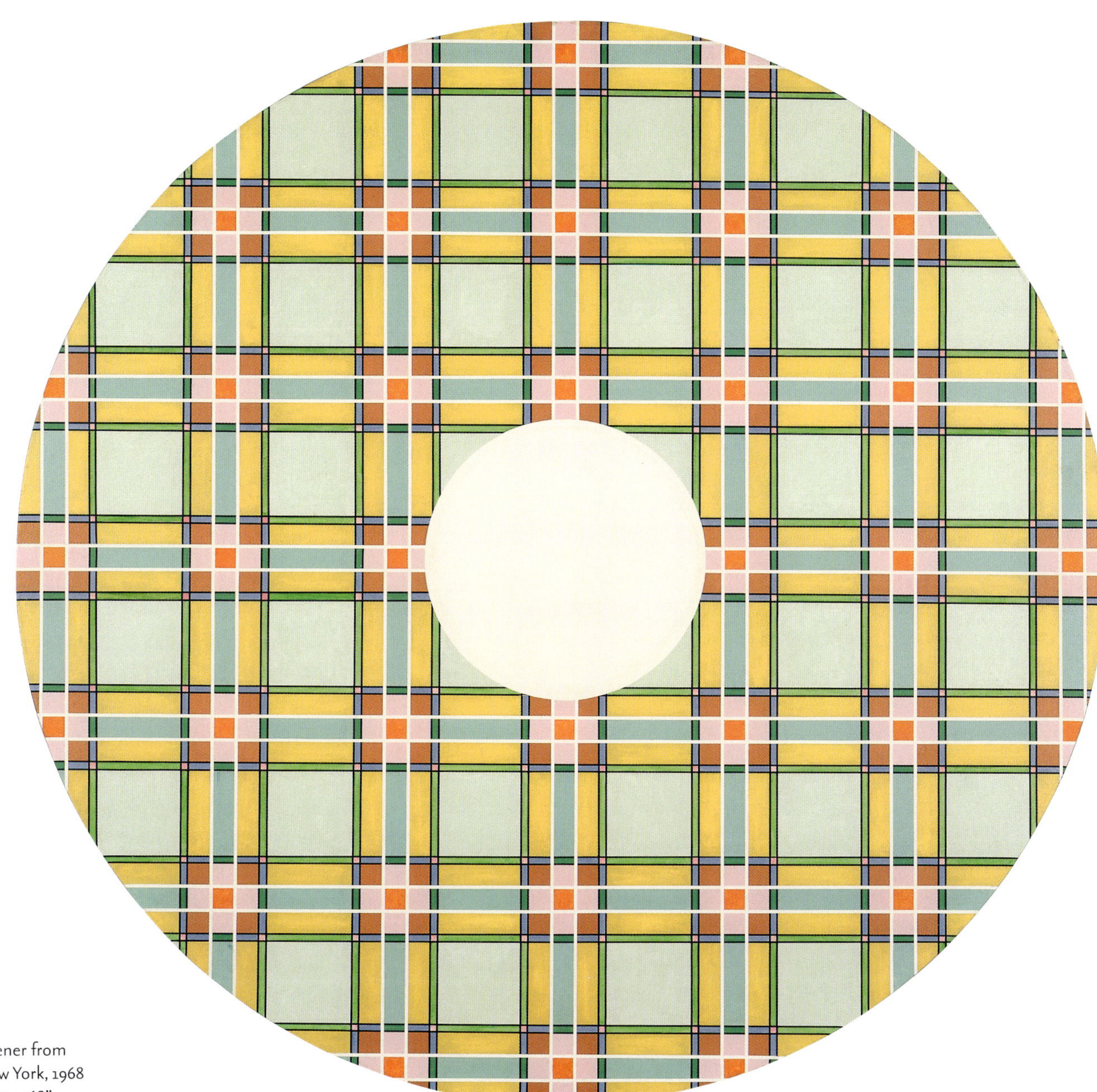

180.

I, 1968

Acrylic on canvas
78 in. diameter (198 cm)
Gift of Mari and James A. Michener
1979.31

Provenance: Purchased by James Michener from the artist, through Richard Bellamy, New York, 1968
Signed verso, upper right "John Torreano 1968"

adhering to the conventions of neither. Torreano intended the Universe Paintings to hang in groups from the ceiling or be mounted on the wall in imitation of a miniature cosmos. The jewels and spherical forms evoke galactic effects and the Big Bang theory, subjects that interested Torreano at the time. The half-hemispherical form of the Blanton's *Universe Painting* is covered by jagged strokes of icinglike paint whose sheer physicality defies conventional expectations of the purity, flatness, and self-referentiality so associated with the medium, at least as it was defined by art critic Clement Greenberg and his followers in the 1960s.[3] Faceted glass stones emerge from the thickly applied paint, sparkling in contrast to its dull, textured opacity. When the viewer approaches *Universe Painting*, she sees her distorted image reflected in these jewels. As a result, the work "particularize[s]" the viewer's location and fosters what Torreano called a "transaction" between art and viewer.[4]

Torreano continues to incorporate jewels in his works, which now include both furniture and sculpture. Since 1981 he has produced a series entitled Wall Gems—gem-encrusted wood sculptures that are either spherical or carved into the shape of jewels and that reference some of the ideas first explored in the Universe Paintings. Over the course of his long career, Torreano has created a variety of works that combine seemingly opposite qualities, such as beauty and humor, raw physicality and subtle delicacy, contemporaneity and timelessness.[5]

Jennifer Farrell

Notes

1. John Torreano, interview with David Reed, New York, 2001. Reed was a Luce scholar in the Department of American and Contemporary Art at the Blanton Museum of Art in 2000–2001. He conducted the interview as part of his research for his own essay published in this same catalogue (see pp. 244–45). A recording of the interview is in the Blanton Museum of Art Archives.
2. For a photograph of the Universe Paintings installed as a group, see Richard Armstrong and Richard Marshall, *Five Painters in New York* (New York: Whitney Museum of American Art, 1984), 86.
3. In his interview with Reed, Torreano described this body of work as an assault on the Modernist concept of the picture plane.
4. Torreano, interview with Reed.
5. For additional information on Torreano, see Prudence Carlson, *Torreano: Gems, Stars, and Perceptual Trackings* (Grand Rapids, Mich.: Grand Rapids Art Museum, 1988).

Richard Tuttle

b. Rahway, New Jersey, 1941

w. New York (trip to Paris, 1965), 1963–1988; New York–Abiquiu, New Mexico, 1988–present

Critics have characterized Richard Tuttle as spanning "the ill-defined boundary of Minimalism and Post-Minimalism" because he tends to reference "real-life objects" in his titles and employ "less austere materials" than the Minimalist artists.[1] However, generalizations do not adequately convey the diversity of his artistic production. The only constant is Tuttle's dedication to making art without prescribed rules and learning from his own practice.[2]

Tuttle had his first solo exhibition at Betty Parsons Gallery in New York in 1965 and his first major museum survey in 1975 at the Whitney Museum of American Art. The survey, which was organized by Marcia Tucker and included experimental works similar to *Light Pink Octagon* (1967, plate 181), was highly controversial. Critics such as Hilton Kramer took offense at Tuttle's spare reductive aesthetic because it seemed to deny the work of art its exalted status.[3] Yet this was in large part the artist's point. Tuttle's works are frequently small, fragile, modest, devoid of representational content, and, in a conventional sense, technically unrefined. Using line, edge, shadow, or color, they call attention to the spaces around them, between them, below them, and through them. As the artist once commented, "A lot of my work is about seeing, the chance to see what we don't ordinarily see."[4]

Tuttle exposes the possibilities and limitations of his materials, whether this involves installing his works at unexpected heights on the wall, situating them on the floor, or incorporating elements that lean or hang. He has been known to invest his art with a performative aspect as well, creating unique site-specific installations that are eventually dismantled. Unsurprisingly, then, Tuttle is not afraid of change, of changing his mind or changing his works even years after their inception. As he said, "I like anti-conservation: things passing away, nothing encumbering. People like something that lasts; I like something that vanishes."[5] This lack of stability over time and space plays an integral role in his practice and thinking.

Light Pink Octagon belongs to Tuttle's well-known series of cloth pastel octagonals made in 1967. To compose the work, the artist cut a piece of canvas into an irregular octagonal shape, hemmed both sides of each edge, and dyed it with pale pink Tintex fabric dye. The artwork may be placed at any height, pinned to the wall with small nails, or laid on the floor; it has no designated top or bottom, no front or back.[6] The surface remains crumpled, a result of the color staining process. These wrinkles contrast with the relative smoothness and concreteness of the support, simultaneously foregrounding the unevenly stained fabric. As an object, *Light Pink Octagon* draws attention to its support and the process by which it was created; at the same time, it suggests an unstable geometrical relationship with the exhibition space around it. Moreover, the irregular application of color and the hemmed sides affirm the status of *Light Pink Octagon* as a fashioned and manipulated object rather than a readymade in the tradition of Marcel Duchamp, even as Tuttle's use of everyday materials differentiates the work from conventional sculptural practice.

In the following year, 1968, Tuttle made more octagonals, this time from sheets of white paper. Lacking the visual play of color and textured surfaces of the earlier works, these delicate paper octagons seem to melt into the walls that support them. Tuttle explained, "I started out making thick wood pieces and they got thinner and thinner. They turned into cloth. And now I am doing paper."[7] He continued this dissolution of form and material with a new series of works in the early 1970s, each created from a single strand of wire nailed to the wall and then lit so that it cast shadows. Tellingly, Tuttle described these works as "drawings for three-dimensional structures in space," insofar as they hover between objects and descriptions of objects.[8] It is unclear, however, whether they represent the shape of an object from an aerial perspective or from a planar perspective, an ambiguity the artist intentionally preserves. In Tuttle's hands, therefore, "drawing," as it is embodied in his wire pieces as well as his cloth and paper octagonals, constitutes an exploration of potential forms in space—that is, of sculpture.

Tuttle has continued to challenge conventional conceptions of artistic production, creating a wide array of works, including artist books and sculptural floor drawings composed of diverse materials, a varied palette, and complex formal arrangements. The artist does not attempt to hide the material specificity of the substances he employs, whether bubble wrap, plywood, or mesh wire, nor does he exploit any culturally determined references that they might suggest. If there is any commonality to his materials, it is the nontraditional manner in which he chooses to use them. In effect, Tuttle's materials are no more than his (and the viewer's) experience of them. His work is often described as poetic for its seeming vulnerability and its evocation of the discarded and the castoff. His sensitivity to installation and space, in combination with his use of everyday materials and wide-ranging media, has had long-lasting effects on contemporary artists. In the summer of 2005, the San Francisco Museum of Modern Art organized a retrospective of Tuttle's work that was widely celebrated for its perceptive reappraisal of his distinctive achievements.

Charlotte Cousins

Notes

1. *The 20th Century Art Book* (London: Phaidon Press), 468. In her well-known article, "ABC Art," published in 1965, Barbara Rose characterized Tuttle as a "minimal" artist, grouping him with Ronald Bladen and Anne Truitt. However, at the time her conception of "minimal" was flexible enough to also include artists like Richard Artschwager and Andy Warhol. Barbara Rose, "ABC Art," *Art in America* 53 (October/November 1965): 58.
2. For an extended discussion on this interpretation, see Richard Shiff, "It Shows," in Madeleine Grynsztejn, ed., *Richard Tuttle: A Retrospective* (San Francisco: San Francisco Museum of Modern Art, 2005), 256–73.
3. See Robert Storr, "Touching Down Lightly," in Grynsztejn, ed., *Richard Tuttle*, 91–92.

4. Richard Tuttle, "Richard Tuttle, 19 February 1998," in Judith Olch Richards, ed., *Inside the Studio: Two Decades of Talks with Artists in New York* (New York: Independent Curators International, 2004), 192.
5. Richard Tuttle, "Community," quoted in *Richard Tuttle Portland Works* (Cologne: Galerie Karsten Greve; Boston: Thomas Segal Gallery, 1988), n.p.
6. Robert Pincus-Witten, "The Art of Richard Tuttle," *Artforum* 8 (February 1970): 62.
7. Quoted in Pincus-Witten, 65.
8. Richard Tuttle, quoted in Marcia Tucker, ed., *Richard Tuttle* (New York: Whitney Museum of American Art, 1975), 6.

181.

Light Pink Octagon, 1967

Canvas dyed with Tintex
56¾ × 53 in. (144.2 × 134.7 cm)
Gift of Mari and James A. Michener
1991.335

Provenance: Purchased by James Michener from Betty Parsons Gallery, New York, 1968; long-term loan to The University of Texas at Austin, 1968–1991

Jack Tworkov

Biala (Bielsko-Biala), Poland, 1900–Provincetown, Massachusetts, 1982

w. New York, 1920–1923; New York–Provincetown, Massachusetts (frequent trips to New Haven, Connecticut, 1963–1969), 1923–1982

Jack Tworkov was among the first wave of American artists to experiment with abstraction after World War II, and his development as a painter coincided with immense shifts in the national discourse about art during the 1940s and 1950s. By the late 1950s Tworkov was one of the leaders of the New York School. He later developed a highly personal approach to abstract painting based on the establishment of carefully planned geometric relationships within the picture plane.[1] Tworkov's primary interests throughout his career lay in abstracted shapes, the physicality of paint and the painting process, and the visual connections between color and form.

Tworkov studied art in Provincetown, Massachusetts, then in New York at the National Academy of Design and the Art Students League. Throughout the 1920s and 1930s he primarily painted still-lifes, genre scenes, and figures that were deeply influenced by Paul Cézanne, whose work he first encountered in a 1921 exhibition at the Brooklyn Museum. Tworkov recognized Cézanne's use of brushstrokes as structural elements in his paintings. He also intuited parallels between this approach to mark making and musical composition, a confluence he would eventually explore in paintings such as *To Stefan Wolpe* (1960, plate 182).[2] From 1935 to 1941, Tworkov worked in the easel division of the WPA Federal Art Project, where he met Willem de Kooning, with whom he would remain close friends through the early 1950s.[3]

During World War II, Tworkov stopped painting for three years to become a tool designer. When he reemerged as an artist in 1947 with a show at Charles Egan Gallery in New York, he returned to the mode of painting that he found most comfortable: still-lifes. Though aware of automatic painting and contemporaneous explorations of the unconscious in Dada and Surrealist circles, he chose not to exhibit his own experiments with these more personal, intuitive modes of expression.[4] In 1948 he showed twenty still-lifes and figure paintings at the Baltimore Museum of Art. In these works, Tworkov began to merge background and subject matter into one coherent visual structure, anticipating his more complete embrace of abstraction in the 1950s.[5]

An avid student of modern art, literature, and theater, Tworkov immersed himself in a community of like-minded avant-garde artists and thinkers based in New York. He was an active member of the Club, which held long, fervent discussions throughout the early 1950s first at an all-night cafeteria on Sixth Avenue and later at a loft on East Eighth Street. During these exchanges, the group codified a flexible aesthetic practice later termed Abstract Expressionism.[6] Although their work was quite varied and individual, what the Abstract Expressionists shared was the insistence that their paintings appear spontaneous and improvisational, even if their methods were, at times, quite deliberate. Furthermore, they worked on a more ambitious scale than earlier abstract painters. Artists like Tworkov, Jackson Pollock, and Franz Kline intended the resulting abstract paintings to be read as both radically new artistic processes and as metaphors for contemporary states of being.

Tworkov's work during the 1950s and early 1960s emphasizes assertive brushwork, thoughtfully conceived color relationships, and complex space, as seen in *To Stefan Wolpe*. Tworkov conceived this painting as the solution to a specific formal and chromatic problem: how to successfully employ the color green. In addition, he conceived the work as an homage to his friend, the experimental German American composer, Stefan Wolpe, who explored "irreconcilable opposites" in music during the 1960s in much the same way Tworkov welded movement and solidity, surface and depth, line and blocks of color in a single work.[7] In *To Stefan Wolpe,* Tworkov employed broad brushstrokes and layered colors to create a series of alternating vertical, horizontal, and diagonal elements. These elements form a taut composition that communicates the sensation of architectural stability while simultaneously accentuating the painting's underlying cadence and rhythm. Color might thus be said to function structurally as well as lyrically in *To Stefan Wolpe*. Writing about his painting style, Tworkov noted: "What I wanted was a simple structure dependent on drawing as a base on which the brushing, spontaneous and pulsating, gave a beat to the painting somewhat analogous to the beat in music. I wanted . . . a painting style in which planning does not exclude intuitive and sometimes random play."[8]

In the 1960s Tworkov shifted away from Abstract Expressionism toward a more ordered, geometric approach to painting. "I am tired of the artist's agonies, whether in painting or in poetry," he said of this change, alluding to the popular conception of the Abstract Expressionist artist as a tormented genius who mines his unconscious for creative inspiration.[9] Moreover, maintaining the appearance of improvisation and spontaneity had become a routine that Tworkov now wanted to avoid. In its place, he established a "system of limits" that allowed him to strictly choreograph how geometric shapes were deployed within his paintings. According to Tworkov, this system nonetheless made possible an infinite range of pictorial possibilities.

Though his style shifted significantly in the 1960s, Tworkov's motivation for painting remained the same: to explore the latent potential and unique character of every painting he envisioned. In 1958 Tworkov wrote, "My whole desire is to be as deeply in painting as possible without holding any prepared position, or maintaining any preconceived posture or attitude. To experience, not painting in general, but each particular picture as deeply as possible is my desire."[10]

Laura A. Lindenberger

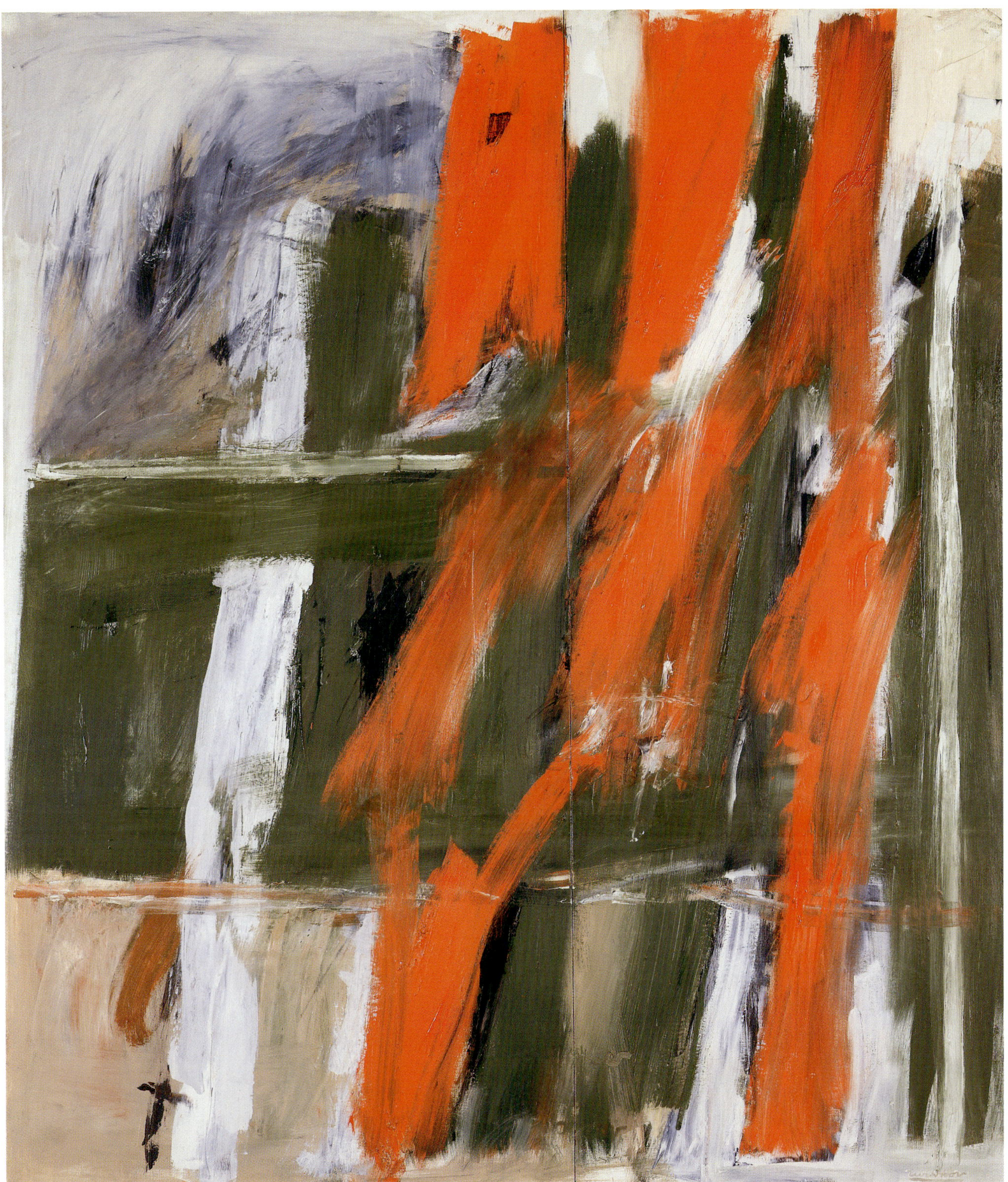

Notes

1. Jack Tworkov, "Tworkov: An Interview with Jack Tworkov," interview by Steven W. Kroeter, *Art in America* 70 (November 1982): 82.
2. Tworkov, "Tworkov: An Interview," 86.
3. Edward Bryant, *Jack Tworkov* (New York: Whitney Museum of American Art, 1964), 8.
4. Tworkov, "Tworkov: An Interview," 84.
5. Bryant, 10.
6. Bryant, 10.
7. Matthias Kriesberg, "A Composer Thinking Globally, Acting Locally," *New York Times*, May 26, 2002, 27.
8. Jack Tworkov, "Notes on My Painting," *Art in America* 61 (September/October 1973): 69.
9. Tworkov, "Tworkov: An Interview," 83.
10. Quoted in Bryant, 6.

182.

To Stefan Wolpe, 1960

Oil on canvas
Overall: 60 × 96 in. (226 × 191 cm)
Gift of Mari and James A. Michener
G1968.126

Provenance: Purchased by James Michener from Leo Castelli, New York, 1962
Signed lower right "Tworkov 60"

John Valadez

b. Los Angeles, 1951
w. Long Beach, California, 1972–1976; Los Angeles, 1976–present

The work of John Valadez operates in the gaps between photography and painting, Chicano and Anglo relations, art history and social history. Valadez grew up in Long Beach and Los Angeles, California, during the late 1960s and came of age as an artist at the height of the Chicano Movement *(el Movimiento)*. In an effort to create a particular community identity, artists associated with this Mexican American political group developed a shared set of imagery based on Mesoamerican iconography, contemporary struggle, collective memory, and modern urban experience. Unlike many of his colleagues, however, Valadez made a conscious decision to avoid using overt Chicano motifs in his art. He chose instead to create his own store of images based on the tense, sometimes violent experiences of Chicano life in the city and suburbs, often focusing on the awkward personal and social interactions of people from his childhood neighborhood, Boyle Heights.

Valadez studied art history and painting at East Los Angeles College and California State University, Long Beach, where he received his BFA in 1976. He cites as influences such artists as Salvador Dalí, John Sloan, Reginald Marsh, Carlos Almaraz, and the Mexican Social Realists.[1] Attempting to distance his work from any set methodology or art theory, Valadez described himself as a painter who combines realism with "visual subversion, emotional manipulation, and [attempts to] pierce that area of observation that transcends into memory."[2]

After graduating from California State University, Valadez collaborated with Almaraz and painter Barbara Carrasco on a mural for the premiere of *Zoot Suit,* Luis Valdez's musical. *Zoot Suit* was the first play written and produced by a Mexican American to appear on Broadway, and Valadez's participation in this project marks his role as a significant contributor to the arts of the Chicano Movement. Soon thereafter, Valadez painted his most recognized work, *The Broadway Mural* (1981), an eight-by-sixty-foot oil-on-canvas mural commissioned by the Victor Clothing Company for the interior of its Los Angeles store.

Adam and Eva Double Exposed (1991, plate 183) represents two figures awkwardly engaged in an act of physical intimacy and surrounded by an overabundance of suburban kitsch and clutter. Adam, in this case, is a middle-aged and middle-class balding Anglo man; his partner is a young Latina Eva. Valadez depicts the couple twice (at two different moments in time) and then superimposes the two images over one another, suggesting the photographic technique of double-exposure, which he alludes to in his title. On the far left side of the pastel, one Adam leans back into the cushions of an elaborately patterned couch and touches his partner's leg, looking directly at one of the two Evas, who in turn looks at the viewer with a large, open smile. A second Adam confronts the viewer's gaze with a slightly menacing expression. This Adam tightly grasps another Eva in his arms as she rigidly holds her eyes closed and opens her mouth in silent protest. Eva's purse has spilled open, revealing such accoutrements of femininity as lipstick, perfume, and sunglasses, as well as a disturbingly unexpected Kewpie doll that serves to emphasize her youth. The image is all the more charged because popular street slang uses the term "kewpie doll" to describe women of "loose morality." The scene's gaudy cheapness is underscored by the accumulation of signs and details, making the sexual tension and the possibility of violence almost tangible.[3]

In a pointed art historical comparison, Valadez includes a reproduction of both José Clemente Orozco's *Cortés and Malinche* (1926) and Albrecht Dürer's *Adam and Eve* (1504 engraving, 1507 painting) above the double-exposed Adam and Eva. Each image evokes a particular historical and religious narrative on conflicts caused by gender and race relations. According to Mexico's historical lore, Cortés and Malinche represent a conquering European Adam and an indigenous Mesoamerican Eve, whose offspring are the first *mestizos* (persons of mixed ethnic backgrounds). However, views on the nature and significance of their relationship vary widely: some believe Cortés claimed Malinche as his own and consigned her to an unhappy relationship despite her objections, while others see her as a willing partner in Europe's colonization of Mesoamerica. Associated with and blamed for the downfall of Mexico's native peoples, Malinche holds an uneasy place in legendary history similar to that of Eve, whose actions led to her and Adam's banishment from Eden in Christian belief. In this context, Valadez seems to point to Eva's betrayal of her people through her coupling with the Adam portrayed in the Blanton's work.

Valadez's attention to detail and his manipulation of photographic reality suggest his conceptual relationship to both photography and Photorealist painting of the 1970s. Yet the artist "does not draw or paint *from* the photograph, but *within* it."[4] Indeed, he uses camera-like reality to present an image in careful detail: the impact of his works comes directly from the tensions between the figures as photography might have captured them. In this way, without actually reproducing photographs, Valadez mimics both the aesthetic and the emotional logic of photography. Unlike the Photorealists, he avoids the "snapshot aesthetic"—that is, the appearance of having arrested time, plucking a single moment from a larger procession of moments. Instead, what Valadez pulls from the realistic image is its potential to represent psychological intensity and disturbing subject matter, as seen in his provocative *Adam and Eva Double Exposed*.

Laura A. Lindenberger

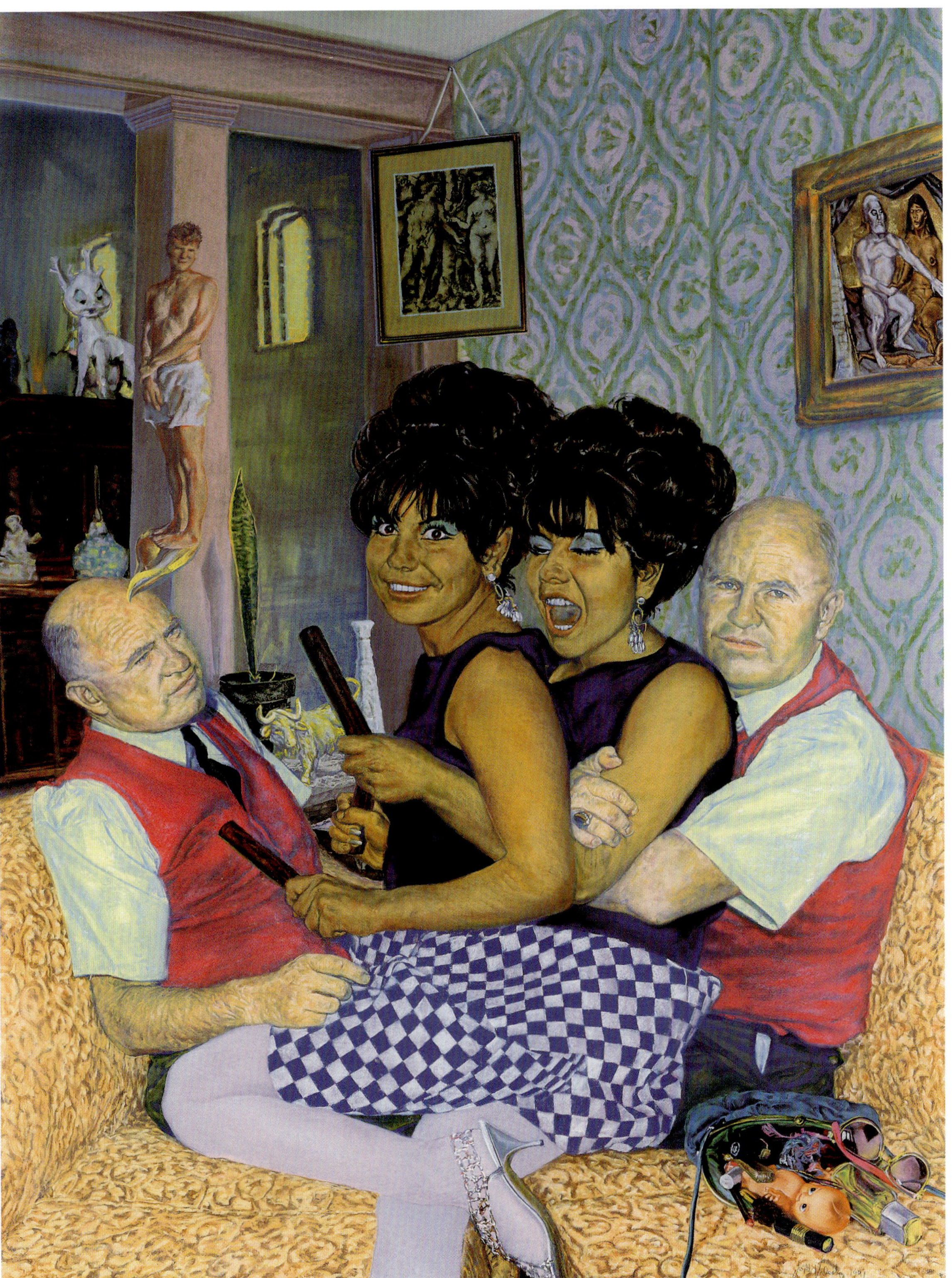

Notes

1. Victor Zamudio-Taylor, "Chicano Art," in Edward J. Sullivan, ed., *Latin American Art in the Twentieth Century* (London: Phaidon, 1996), 321.
2. Quoted in Gary D. Keller, ed., *Contemporary Chicana and Chicano Art: Artists, Works, Culture, and Education*, vol. 2 (Tempe, Ariz.: Bilingual Press/Editorial Bilingue, 2002), 286–87.
3. Zamudio-Taylor, 321.
4. Shifra Goldman, *John Valadez: A Decade of Dignity and Daring* (Santa Ana, Calif.: Rancho Santiago College Art Gallery, 1990), 3.

183.

Adam and Eva Double Exposed, 1991

Pastel on paper
68 × 50¼ in. (172.8 × 127.8 cm)
The 1994 Friends of the Archer M. Huntington Art Gallery Purchase
1994.14

Provenance: Purchased from Daniel Saxon Gallery, Los Angeles, 1994
Signed lower right "J.M. Valadez 1994" in pencil

Leo Villareal

b. Albuquerque, New Mexico, 1967
w. New Haven, Connecticut, 1986–1990; New York, 1990–present

Leo Villareal has established himself as a significant figure in New Media art with light sculptures like *Horizon 24* (2004, plate 184). Powered by microprocessors, animated by light emitting diodes (LEDs), and driven by a complex computer program, *Horizon 24* embodies Villareal's creative adaptation of omnipresent current technologies.

After completing his BA at Yale University, Villareal conducted research into virtual reality technologies at Paul Allen's Interval Research think tank in Palo Alto, California. He earned a Master of Professional Studies (MPS) degree from the Interactive Telecommunications Program at New York University's Tisch School of the Arts in 1994. Since that time he has consistently produced and exhibited work that explores the intersection of art, popular culture, and multimedia technologies. Mathematics and computer programming are among the tools with which Villareal fabricates his art. "I began programming when I was about fourteen," he recalled. "I program because that is what I need to do to make my art. I see the art and programming as completely integrated."[1]

Villareal reaches diverse audiences through a variety of interesting projects that bridge the realms of fine art and popular entertainment. In 1994 he displayed his first light sculpture, composed of thirteen strobe lights, at the Burning Man Festival in Black Rock Desert, Nevada. A few years later, he designed the light show for the 2001 concert tour of the recording artist Moby. Villareal's art projects refer to the light displays of raves, occasionally pairing sound with visuals. He even has collaborated with DJs and composers, including James Healey, John Eihenseer ("Jhno"), and other ambient-trance musicians. Villareal's art equally evokes historical predecessors: notably the light shows produced by Andy Warhol's Exploding Plastic Inevitable for the Velvet Underground in the late 1960s; the 1967 exhibition *Light/Motion/Space* at the Walker Art Center; the California-based light and space artists Robert Irwin and James Turrell; and Dan Flavin's fluorescent light sculptures.

Controlled by a computer that generates bursts of electrically powered light activity, *Horizon 24* consists of nine industrially manufactured light tubes made of frosted Plexiglas that are filled with 3,888 LEDs and attached to the wall in three parallel rows. The work's insistent horizontality recalls the horizontal elements of Piet Mondrian's harmonious modernist grids. Indeed, *Horizon 24* might lay claim to being a distant cousin of Mondrian's New York paintings, like *Broadway Boogie-Woogie* (1942–1943), that seem to oscillate with the energy of urban streets. Although Villareal's sculpture remains immobile, light courses through the nine tubes with such kinetic energy that the pace becomes, at times, frenetic.

In *Horizon 24*, Villareal creates a palette of hundreds of subtly distinct colors out of the raw material of red, green, and blue LEDs. Light sometimes passes through the tubes as pure white light, like the glow filling a fluorescent bulb when it is first illuminated. More often, though, the lights appear as other colors pulled from the spectrum (i.e., red, orange, yellow, magenta). Colors pop out and then recede suddenly in bursts of punctuated movement. Glowing balls of illuminated color pulse across the work horizontally as if the tubes contained the fireballs of Roman candles. *Horizon 24* bathes spectators in light and color, adding an ephemeral, ever changing, temporal element to the viewing experience.

When viewers and critics describe the experience of Villareal's light sculptures, they often allude to the neon lighting of Times Square, Las Vegas, or Tokyo. Others, however, displace these urban and industrial comparisons with the evocation of organic forms. Discussing Villareal's *Firmament* (2001), for example, Barbara Pollack commented that "though its effects were entirely synthetic, it was hard not to imagine fireworks, flashes of lightning, even fireflies, while watching this hypnotic light show."[2] The artist noted, "Our brains are coded to recognize patterned light, to match it to something we know," adding that "Sometimes a piece looks like a hive of bees or the shimmering surface of water."[3]

When Villareal and curator Alexander Gray exhibited *Horizon 24* at The Ballroom in Marfa, Texas, they mused about the work's relation to the changing light of West Texas, which the artist visited as a child and as an adult.[4] Indeed, the work's own internal cycles mimic natural cycles, specifically the rising and setting of the sun. It compresses this twenty-four-hour cycle into several minutes of activity choreographed by the microprocessors, which automatically start the program anew after each full display ends. In that sense, each display of light before the program repeats itself is like a day that melds seamlessly into the next.

If *Horizon 24* taps into the history of Romanticism and the representation of landscape, it does so in a decidedly technological way. Nature's lights are contained within tubes, powered by electricity, controlled by computer elements, and, ultimately, domesticated. Unlike the Marfa lights or the Aurora Borealis—phenomena that require specific geographical locations and meteorological conditions in order to be seen—the experience of *Horizon 24* requires only a pilgrimage to the museum.

James Housefield

Notes

1. Leo Villareal, "Immersed in Light," interview by Michael Hamilton, October 14, 2002, available at http://www.cultureflux.com/issues/10142002/immersed.html [September 3, 2005].
2. Barbara Pollack, "Digital Media: Ambient Art," *Art in America* 89 (November 2001): 57.
3. Villareal, "Immersed in Light."
4. Karen Bernstein, *Ballroom Marfa* (film) (Tamar Hacker, executive producer, Gallery HD; Karen Bernstein, producer/director; Mobilus Media, LLC, production company; all rights reserved by Gallery HD/Rainbow Media), 2004. *Horizon 24* was part of The Ballroom's inaugural exhibition, "Optimo," curated by Alexander Gray.

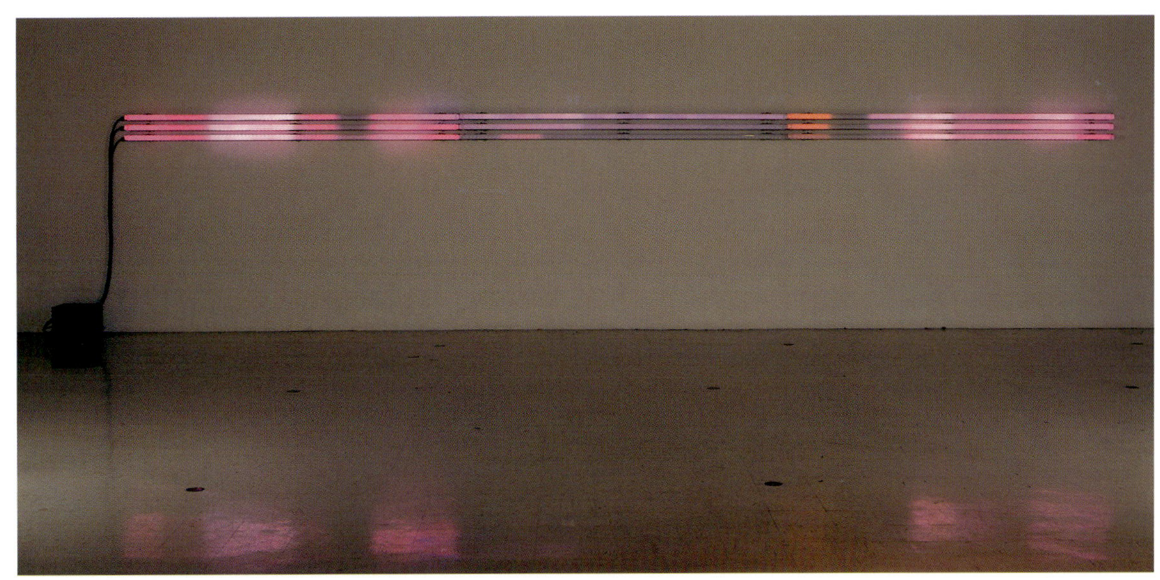

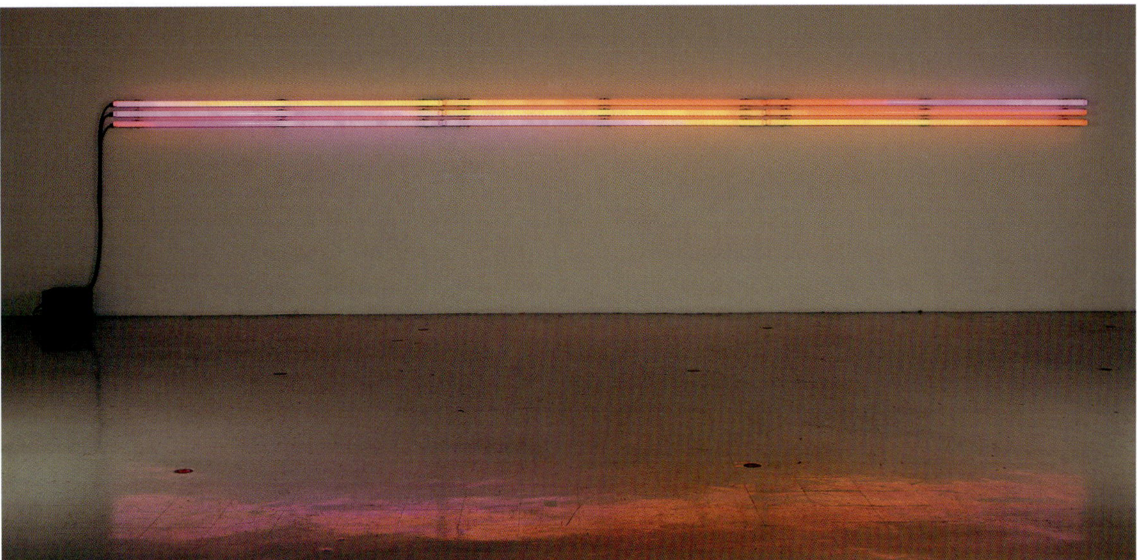

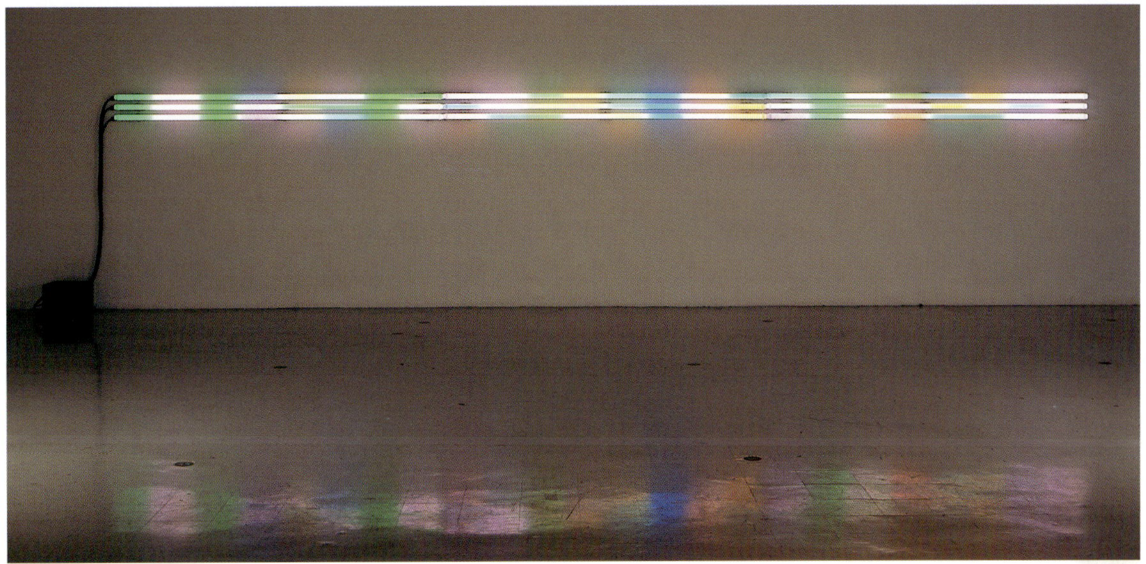

184.

Horizon 24, 2004

LED tubes, sequencer, hardware
11 15/16 × 288 in. (30.4 × 731.5 cm)
Purchase with funds provided by The Brown Foundation
2004.160

Provenance: Purchased from Sandra Gering Gallery, New York, 2004

Bill Viola

b. New York, 1951

w. Syracuse, New York, 1969–1973; Florence, Italy, 1974–1976; New York (frequent trips to Italy, Asia, Africa, and South Pacific), 1976–1980; Atsugi, Japan, 1980–1981; Long Beach, California (frequent trips abroad), 1981–present

One of the earliest practitioners of video art, Bill Viola mines the creative possibilities of video and, more recently, digital technology, while simultaneously deepening our understanding of subjects that range from perception and philosophy to religion and art history. In the early 1970s Viola attended one of the first new media programs in the country, at Syracuse University, where he began to experiment with the relatively new medium of video. The introduction of the Sony Portapak in 1965 made possible the rise of video art: for the first time, artists had access to relatively expedient, flexible, and inexpensive video equipment, which heretofore had been concentrated in the hands of large media corporations. As David Ross observed, "[Viola] was of the generation for whom, as John Baldassari said, video would be like a pencil."[1]

After leaving Syracuse University, Viola befriended such pioneers of video art as Peter Campus, Bruce Nauman, and Nam June Paik, as well as musician David Tudor and curator David Ross. Between 1974 and 1976 he worked as a technician at one of the first video art studios in Europe, Art/Tapes/22 in Florence, and immediately thereafter spent four years as an artist-in-residence at the WNET Thirteen Television Laboratory in New York. While serving as an artist-in-residence at Sony's Atsugi research laboratories in Japan between 1980 and 1981, Viola also embarked on an intensive period of study in Zen Buddhism. This interest in Eastern religion, and spirituality in general, has persisted: besides Zen Buddhism, Viola has explored such traditions as Christianity, Islamic Sufism, and religious mysticism. Beyond the influence they exert on specific works, these traditions also guide Viola in his quest to disclose symbolic meaning beyond the "world of appearances." As he commented, "One of the common threads in all these traditions . . . is the idea that everything in front of us right now is . . . only a surface—not the true reality. . . . [T]he task is to understand and master sensory experience . . . [to] penetrate through to the submerged connections underneath."[2]

Viola's early works were single-channel videos like *Cycles* (1973), but shortly thereafter, the artist began to create more complex, multipart works using video, sound, and sculptural components, as in *He Weeps For You* (1976). These evolved into installations like *The Crossing* (1996) and *Five Angles for the Millennium* (2001), which immerse viewers in images and sounds thanks to the darkened rooms in which they are displayed and the multiple screens onto which they are projected.[3] Frequently installed outside museum settings, Viola's videos parse such universal human experiences as birth, mortality, and the quest for enlightenment. Others probe themes—from transition and transformation to the underlying structure of the universe—common among the various religions Viola has studied. In addition to human actors and formal and iconographic elements borrowed from Eastern and Western artistic traditions, natural elements with powerful metaphoric connotations like fire and water also play a prominent role in his videos. Viola's work communicates directly, powerfully, and with a relative economy of means, despite the profundity of the subjects he treats (or perhaps because of it). These videos might unfold over time, like a narrative, but in effect they are more reminiscent of allegories—their communicative terrain is that of the symbol, not the story.

Anima (2000, plate 185) belongs to a series of videos created between 2000 and 2003 entitled The Passions, which explores the variety and complexity of human emotions. Viola embarked on the series a year and a half after serving as a guest scholar at the Getty Research Institute, where he participated in a yearlong seminar on "The Representation of the Passions." While in residence at the Getty, he read avidly on the subject, devouring texts by Henk van Os, Charles Le Brun, Charles Darwin, and others, in addition to visiting the museum's extensive collection of European art. These experiences, as well as his more recent "obsession" with medieval and early-Renaissance devotional images, formed much of the basis for The Passions in general and *Anima* specifically.[4] However, Viola's intention in *Anima* (whose title is Latin for "soul") never was to restage, much less upstage, the paintings that comprised these particular artistic traditions. Instead, the artist sought "to embody them, to inhabit them, to feel them breathe."[5] To this end, he hired actors to animate (albeit subtly, faintly) the static bodies that occupied such devotional images as Dieric Bouts's *Mater Dolorosa* (1470/1475) and Hans Memling's *The Virgin, St. John and the Holy Women* (c. 1475).

Using a high-speed 35-mm camera, Viola recorded three actors expressing a sequence of four different emotions, what he describes as the "primary emotions"—joy, sorrow, anger, and fear—in a single shot over the course of one minute.[6] He then transferred the film to high-resolution digital video, lending the images a pristine clarity that is further enhanced by the flat LCD screens on which they are displayed, and played the footage back in extreme slow motion, stretching it to eighty-two minutes.[7] The images thus resemble still photographs or small paintings more so than video footage.

Here Viola exploits the temporal flexibility of video (what he calls its "time-form") to considerable effect.[8] Indeed, to the extent that emotions themselves occur through time, to the extent that they too are transitory, the medium of video was ideally suited to his goal of capturing not discrete emotions but "an arc of intensity,"[9] "the passage of an emotional wave through a human being."[10] As Viola commented of The Passions series, "I was most interested in opening up the spaces *between* the emotions. I wanted to focus on gradual transitions—the idea of emotional expression as a continual fluid motion."[11] Ultimately, the synchronicity between content and technology that Viola established results in works that operate as seamless, indivisible wholes.

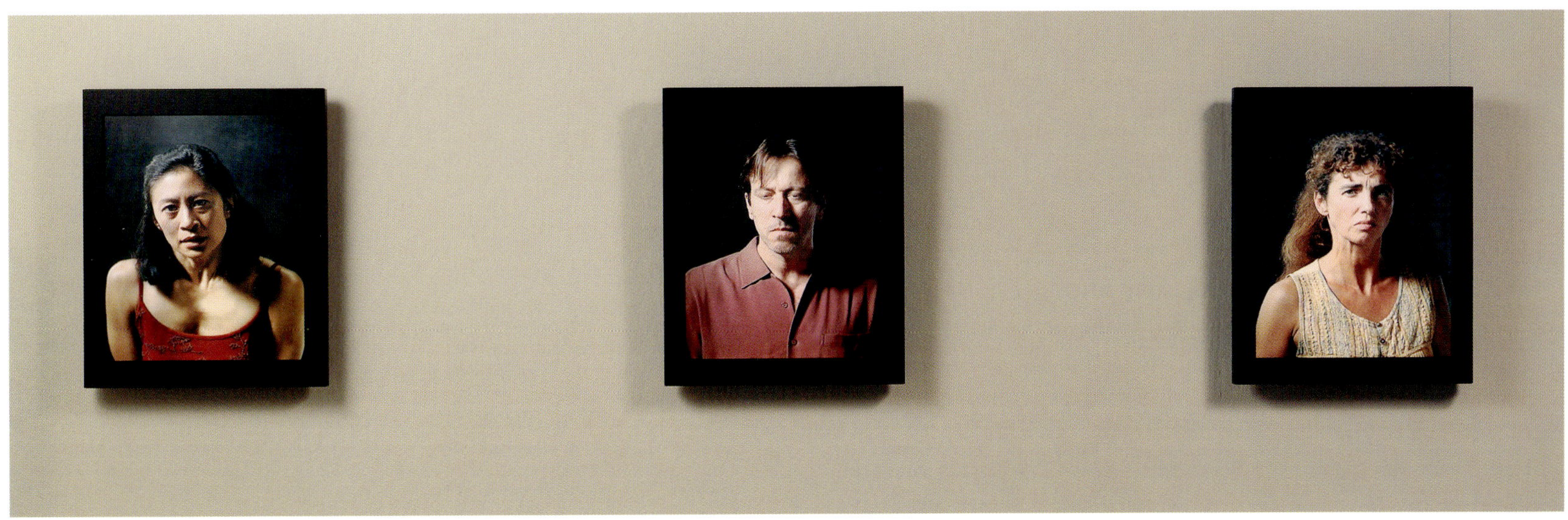

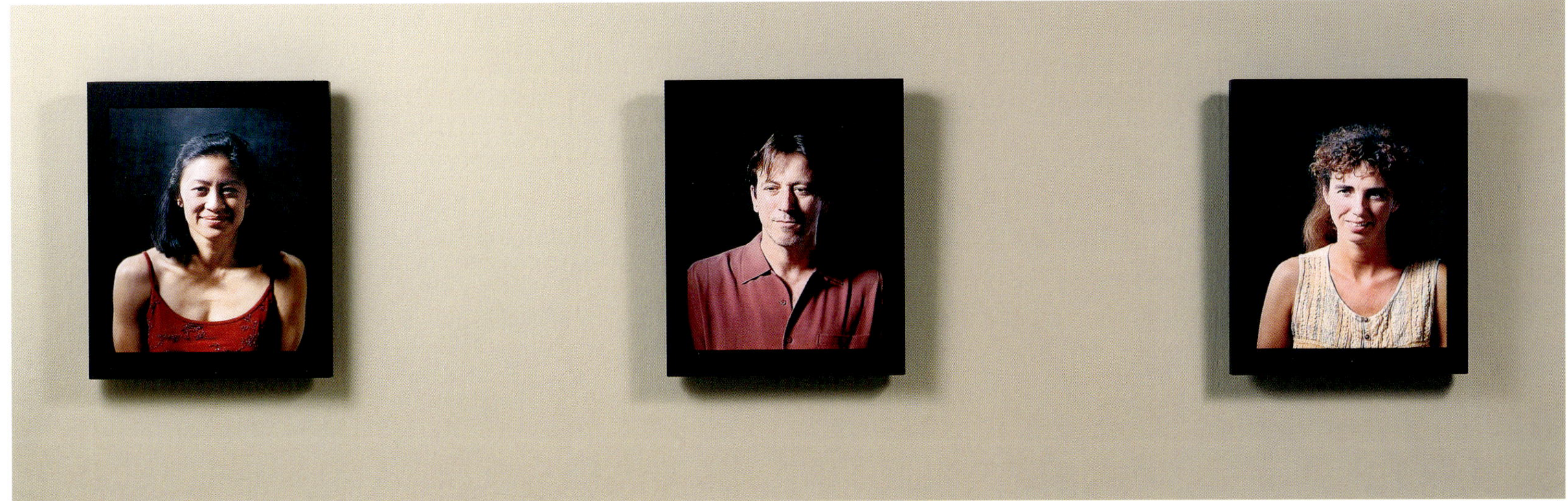

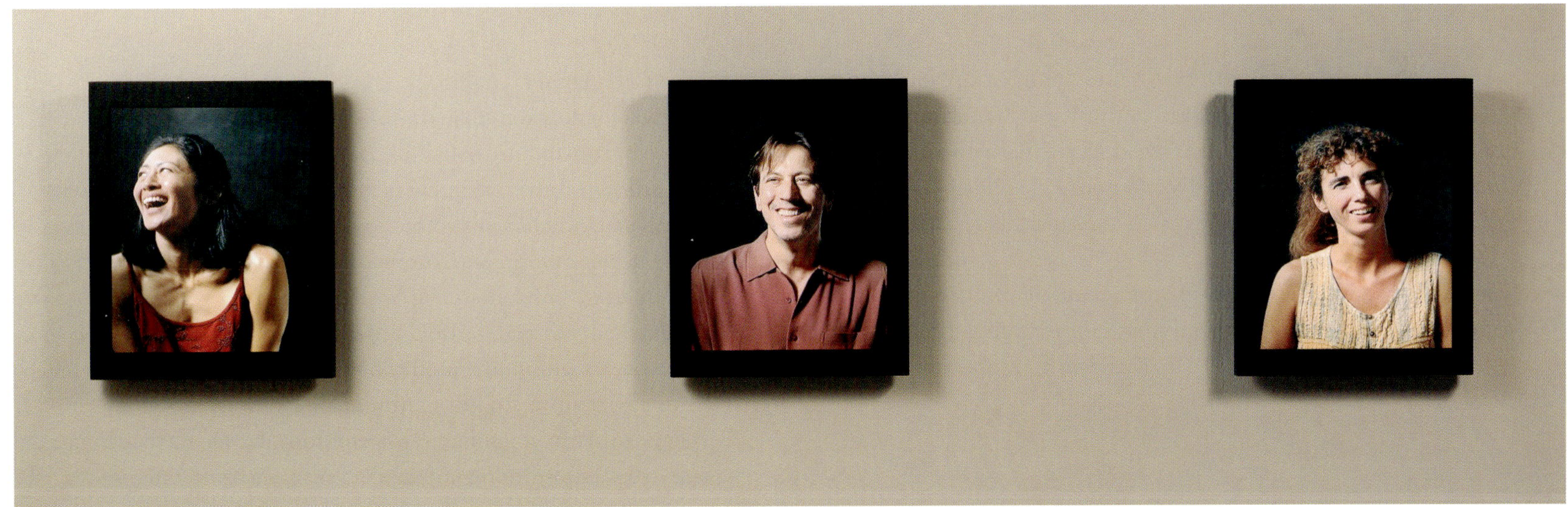

185.

Anima, 2000

Color video triptych on vertical LCD flat panels
Overall: 16¼ × 75 in. (41.28 × 190.5 cm)
2002 Gala Purchase Selection
2002.2841

Provenance: Purchased from James Cohan Gallery, New York, 2002

Viola's adept use of slow motion and close-ups, which capture subtleties otherwise invisible to the human eye, serves to amplify our powers of perception. We are invited to scrutinize infinitesimal adjustments in facial expression, to observe them in all their ecstatic, agonizing, furious, or terrifying permutations. Without sound, without back story, without any manifest motivation behind the cathartic displays taking place in front of us, our attention is riveted. Yet we are no mere voyeurs or anthropologists, for precisely what sensitizes our perception also stimulates our compassion. We do not look or observe with disinterest, we empathize and participate. In this way, "A kind of feedback loop [is] formed, a visceral/emotional circuit [has] been completed," as Viola once said.[12]

Viola's work is as ambitious in scope as it is profound in effect. Indeed, the artist has charged video with an important task: not only to prompt viewers to thoughtful reflection, but to enhance their perceptual, spiritual, and intellectual acuity as well. As Viola remarked, "It is useful for developing a deeper understanding, in a very personal, subjective, private way, of your own experience."[13]

Kelly Baum

Notes

1. David Ross, "The Self-Discovery Channel," *Artnews* 96 (November 1997): 206.
2. Bill Viola, "A Conversation: Hans Belting and Bill Viola," in John Walsh, ed., *Bill Viola: The Passions* (Los Angeles: J. Paul Getty Museum; London: National Gallery, 2003), 195.
3. For more information on Viola's work prior to 1997, see David A. Ross, *Bill Viola* (New York: Whitney Museum of American Art; New York and Paris: Flammarion, 1997) as well as Michael Duncan, "Bill Viola: Altered Perceptions," *Art in America* 86 (March 1998): 62–69, and Bill Viola, "Art at the End of the Optical Age," interview by Virginia Rutledge, *Art in America* 86 (March 1998): 70–76.
4. Viola, "A Conversation: Hans Belting and Bill Viola," 197.
5. Viola, "A Conversation: Hans Belting and Bill Viola," 199.
6. Viola, "A Conversation: Hans Belting and Bill Viola," 200.
7. More than likely, it was contact with devotional imagery that prompted Viola to work on a much smaller scale in *Anima* than he ever had before. The small screens on which the video footage is displayed (reminiscent of small religious altarpieces and manuscripts) not only heighten the sense of intimacy, they duplicate—intensify, even—the "spiritual power" of installations such as *The Crossing*.
8. Viola, "A Conversation: Hans Belting and Bill Viola," 199.
9. Quoted in Walsh, ed., *Bill Viola*, 36. "Arc of intensity" is performance artist Weba Garretson's phrase. Garretson coached Viola on how to direct his actors.
10. Viola, "A Conversation: Hans Belting and Bill Viola," 200.
11. Viola, "A Conversation: Hans Belting and Bill Viola," 200.
12. Viola, "A Conversation: Hans Belting and Bill Viola," 198.
13. Quoted in Walsh, ed., *Bill Viola*, 25.

Max Weber

Belostok, Russia (Bialystok, Poland), 1881–Great Neck, New York, 1961

w. New York, 1898–1905; Paris, 1905–1908; New York, 1909–1929; Great Neck, New York, 1929–1961

Max Weber was one of the earliest American artists to assimilate the tenets of European modernism and to introduce these ideas to artists in the United States. Weber was born in Belostok, Russia, in 1881. He immigrated to the United States ten years later with his mother, who settled in Brooklyn. From 1898 to 1900 Weber studied art under Arthur Wesley Dow at the Pratt Institute, and he traveled to Paris in 1905 to attend the Académie Julian as a student of Jean-Paul Laurens. While living in Paris, Weber encountered the work of the Fauves and other European moderns at the 1905, 1906, and 1907 Salons d'Automne. His exposure to these artists, especially the work of Paul Cézanne, was of great importance to the later development of his work.[1] In Paris Weber was also a regular presence at the salons of the expatriate patrons and collectors Gertrude and Leo Stein, through whom he met some of the leading members of the Parisian avant-garde. He befriended the primitivist painter Henri Rousseau, corresponded with Pablo Picasso, and organized a studio class with Henri Matisse in 1908.[2] It was Matisse who inspired Weber to incorporate the African sculpture exhibited at the Trocadéro Museum into his work. Significantly, these diverse influences, which Weber absorbed while living in Paris, did not manifest themselves fully in his paintings until he returned to New York in early 1909.

Shortly after Weber arrived back in New York, the photographer Edward Steichen introduced him to the art dealer, gallerist, and photographer Alfred Stieglitz. Stieglitz included Weber in an important group show at his New York gallery 291 in 1910 and gave him a solo show in 1911, effectively launching his career. Stieglitz also provided Weber with a forum to disseminate his ideas about modernism and non-Western art to a wider audience by publishing some of his writings in the influential journal, *Camera Work*.[3]

The 1910 issue of *Camera Work* included what would become Weber's most important contribution to American avant-garde theory, the essay "The Fourth Dimension from a Plastic Point of View."[4] Here Weber posited the notion of a spatial dimension that exists beyond the three-dimensional, physical world, perceivable only through the human senses.[5] As the first published definition of the fourth dimension, Weber's text is significant not just within an American context but internationally as well.[6] A series of paintings made in 1910 reflects his interest in representing the fourth dimension in art. The artist rendered his subjects as crystalline structures, reducing matter to what he considered its most basic geometric components and suggesting an extension of space beyond three dimensions.[7] Weber also began working in planes of color and representing his subjects from multiple

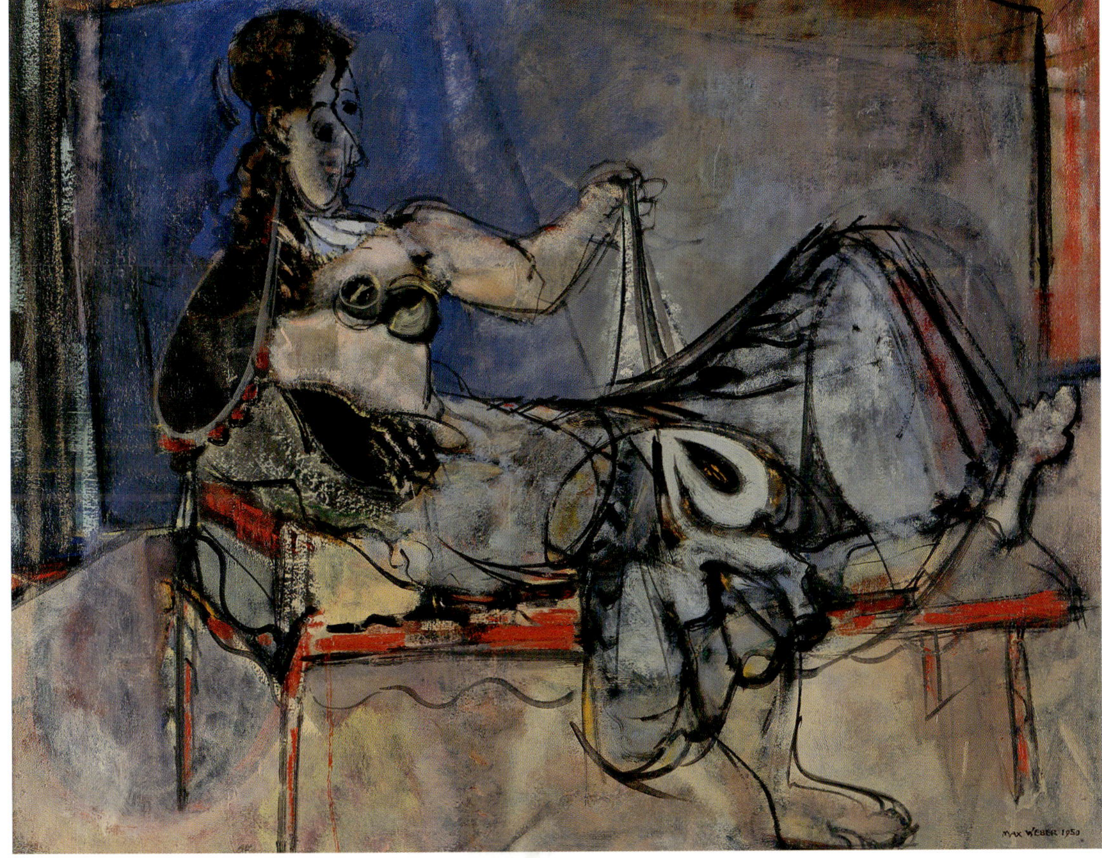

186.

Repose No. 2, 1950

Oil on canvas
31¼ x 40¼ in. (79 x 102 cm)
Gift of Mari and James A. Michener, 1991
1991.339

Provenance: Purchased by James Michener from Downtown Gallery, New York, 1962; long-term loan to The University of Texas at Austin, 1968–1991
Signed lower right corner "Max Weber 1950"

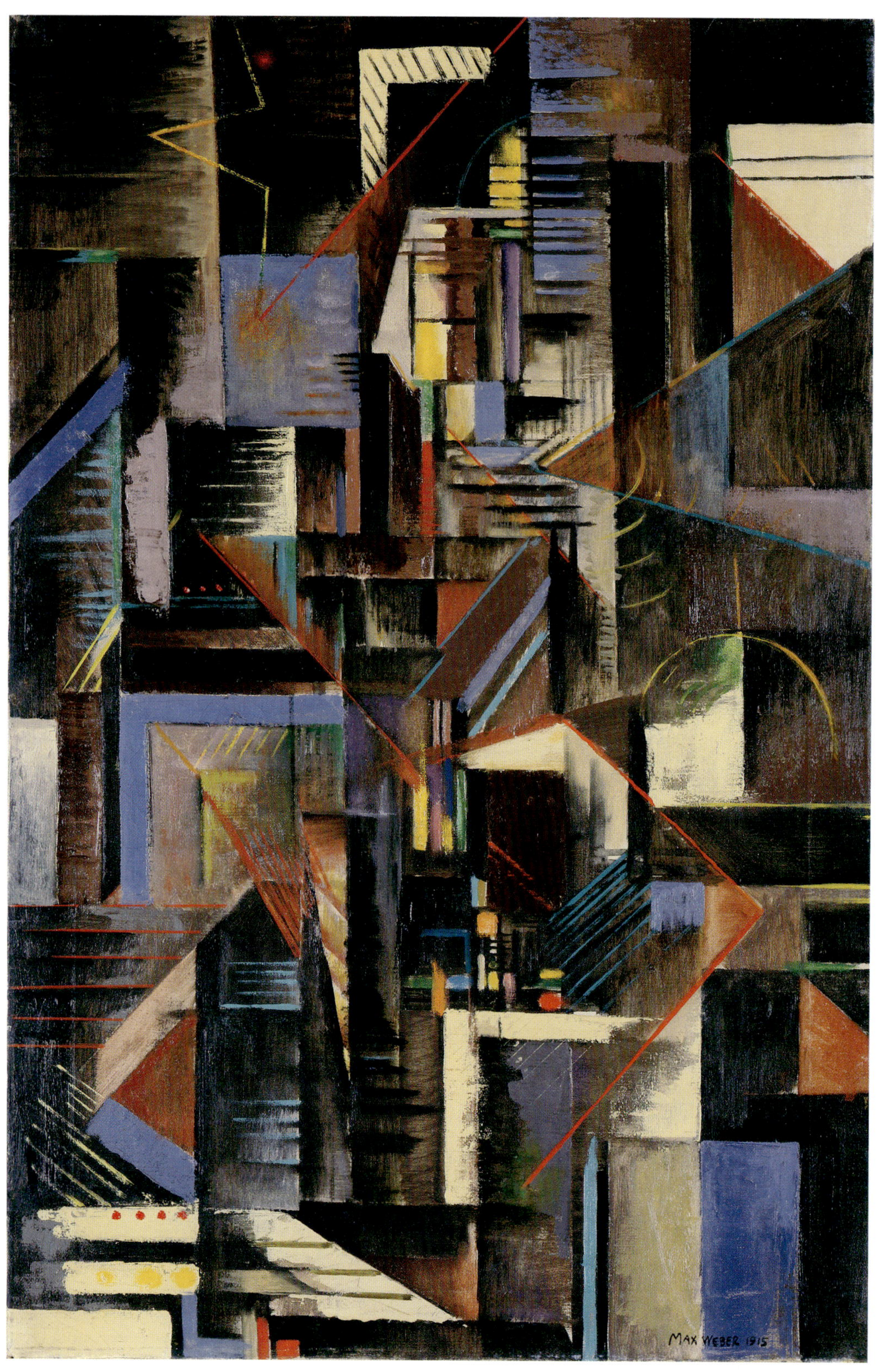

187.

New York at Night, 1915

Oil on canvas
33⅞ × 20¹⁄₁₆ in. (86 × 51 cm)
Gift of Mari and James A. Michener
1991.338

Provenance: Collection of the artist, 1933; A. P. Rosenburg and Co., Inc., New York, 1951; Downtown Gallery, New York, n.d.; purchased by James Michener from Downtown Gallery, New York, 1962; long-term loan to The University of Texas at Austin, 1968–1991
Signed lower right corner "Max Weber 1915"

perspectives, a technique inspired by Cézanne and used contemporaneously by the Puteaux or "Salon" Cubists.[8]

In the 1910s Weber embarked on an important group of works that were inspired by the vitality and monumental scale of New York, including the Blanton's *New York at Night* (1915, plate 187).[9] Here the artist defined space with strong, overlapping, and interpenetrating vertical planes intersected by diagonally oriented angles that signal both height and spatial recession, while slender, repeated parallel lines create the illusion of motion and reverberating sound. Commenting on these works later, Weber described the "electrically illumined contours of buildings, rising height upon height against the blackness of the sky now diffused, now interknotted, now interpierced by occasional shafts of colored light. Altogether—a web of colored geometric shapes, characteristic only of the Grand Canyons of New York at Night."[10]

Weber's approach in his city paintings, especially his use of sequential lines and shapes, evokes rapid motion and was likely informed by the work of the Italian Futurists. While Weber never actually saw any Futurist work, he read extensively about the movement and was familiar with its principles.[11] For Weber, modern transportation made rapid movement possible, and it was inextricably bound up with "the rapid pace and altered vision distinctive of the new century."[12]

By the end of the 1910s Weber's interest in science, new technology, and the metropolis had waned and was replaced by a renewed interest in the African sculpture he had seen in Paris, although his work from this period still reflects the impact of Picasso and Georges Braque's Analytical Cubism. In the 1920s, however, Weber modified his approach to the human figure, producing the thickly volumetric forms that appear in his work of the 1940s, when he began to paint scenes of Jewish life in New York. Weber ceased painting such themes after 1950, turning instead to the allegorical female figure.[13] The Blanton's *Repose No. 2* (1950, plate 186) is representative of that last decade of Weber's career. Here a woman reclines on a slender bench against a vaguely defined studio backdrop, leaning on her right hand while lifting her diaphanous gown with her left. The shifting perspective of the woman's face and lap are evidence of Weber's continued interest in the Cubist treatment of form, as are the alternately opaque and transparent areas of her torso and skirt. *Repose No. 2* demonstrates that Weber's late works remained heavily indebted to the European modernism that he had helped import to the United States earlier in the century.

Heather E. Mathews

Notes

1. Abraham A. Davidson, *Early American Modernist Painting, 1910–1935* (New York: Da Capo Press, 1994), 29.
2. Weber met Rousseau at the salon of Robert Delaunay's mother. See Susan Krane, "Introduction," in *Max Weber: The Cubist Decade 1910–1920* (Atlanta: High Museum of Art, 1992), 14.
3. Percy North, "Max Weber: The Cubist Decade," in *Max Weber: The Cubist Decade 1910–1920*, 21–47.
4. Max Weber, "The Fourth Dimension from a Plastic Point of View," *Camera Work*, no. 31 (July 1910): 25.
5. Weber encountered ideas about the fourth dimension in Paris, where it was a driving force behind much modernist thought and artistic production. Weber's essay preceded Albert Gleizes's and Jean Metzinger's discussion of the subject in *Du Cubisme*, written in 1911 and published in 1912, and Guillaume Apollinaire's 1913 *Les Peintres Cubistes*. In her book *The Fourth Dimension and Non-Euclidean Geometry in Modern Art* (Princeton: Princeton University Press, 1983), Linda Dalrymple Henderson notes that Weber and Apollinaire frequented the same circles in Paris and probably became familiar with the concept at around the same time (170). Henderson also argues that Weber introduced the idea of the fourth dimension to the artists of the Stieglitz Circle (180–81).
6. Henderson counts Weber's *Camera Work* article among "the most influential twentieth-century statements on art and the fourth dimension." See Linda Dalrymple Henderson, "Mysticism, Romanticism, and the Fourth Dimension," in *The Spiritual in Art: Abstract Painting 1890–1985* (Los Angeles: Los Angeles County Museum of Art, 1986), 219–37.
7. North, 24.
8. Henderson, 176.
9. While the Blanton Museum recognizes 1915 as *New York at Night*'s most probable date, in correspondence with the Museum, Stephanie Moye cites an inventory document provided by the artist for the American Art Research Council that lists the date as 1914. Stephanie Moye to Meredith D. Sutton, January 28, 1991, Blanton Museum of Art Archives, The University of Texas at Austin.
10. Quoted in Davidson, 33. Weber's sculptures of 1915 demonstrate another attempt by the artist to visualize four-dimensional space. See Roberta Tarbell, "Max Weber: The Cubist Decade, 1910–1920," *American Art Review* 5 (winter 1993): 132–38.
11. Dominic Ricciotti reports that Weber almost immediately responded to published news of the first Futurist show in Paris in February 1912 in his own work. See Ricciotti, "The Revolution in Urban Transport. Max Weber and Italian Futurism," *American Art Journal* (winter 1984): 46–64. At least one contemporary critic recognized that influence; see North, 25.
12. North, 37.
13. Matthew Baigell, "Max Weber's Jewish Paintings," *American Jewish History* 88 (September 2000): 341–60.

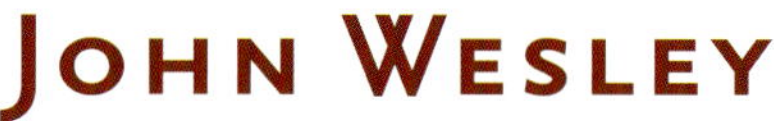

John Wesley

b. Los Angeles, 1928

w. Los Angeles, 1953–1960; New York, 1960–1974; New York–Conques, France, 1974–1996; Marfa, Texas–New York, 1982–1983; New York, 1996–present

John Wesley's paintings occupy a space somewhere on the outskirts of Pop art and Minimalism, projecting a myriad of popular sources and an amalgamation of differing styles. They synthesize the popular and commercial subject matter of Pop, the curtailed color palette and lack of expressive content of Minimalism, but also feature psychological dynamics and surreal figural combinations not usually seen in either Pop or Minimalist work.[1] When asked whether he considers his paintings cryptic or explicit, Wesley replied, "I like the idea of both at the same time."[2]

A self-taught artist, Wesley began painting while working as a blueprint illustrator for Northrop Aircraft in Los Angeles. After moving to New York in 1960 with painter Jo Baer, he befriended art critic and Minimalist sculptor Donald Judd, who quickly became one of his most vocal supporters. Much of Wesley's work from this period consists of pared down images of people and animals, decorative borders, and nude or semi-nude women in erotic and often peculiar positions and situations. Wesley's stylistic characteristics manifest themselves in his almost complete integration of images into a single plane, his reduced color scheme of unmodulated blues, pinks, reds, black, and white, and his use of black contour lines (a technique indebted to cartoons), which add to the appearance of two-dimensional flatness. The artist once stated that he prefers his works to resemble posters or banners rather than paintings.[3] In a 1963 review in *Arts Magazine*, Judd commented on the "cool, psychological oddness" of Wesley's paintings and on the ambiguity of his "nineteenth century" imagery—the artist's "main device," according to Judd.[4] At the end of the review, Judd teased out what he saw as Wesley's formal aesthetic:

> *The guise here is not appearances, but what some bumpkin made of appearances for some unartistic reason. This is a big difference and is interesting—it is sort of a meta-representation—but . . . the curious quality of Wesley's work would be better unconcealed, unadjusted, and unscaled to anything else.*[5]

Judd believed that Wesley's work intuited more psychological profundity than Pop art, which he thought merely borrowed commercial imagery for the sake of appearances alone. By stating that his paintings are best when not compared to anything else, Judd presciently summed up Wesley's career as an outsider Pop artist.

The representational ambiguity described by Judd, where an ostensibly light-hearted image has the ability to convey a deeper sense of ennui and alienation, is evident in the Blanton's *Annunciations* (1967, plate 188). Here Wesley depicted, in nonlinear order, one woman holding a newborn baby and, after her, five women in various stages of pregnancy. He placed each figure within a black panel, but, true to his style, the women's bodies violate the boundaries of the spaces in which they are confined, their feet and stomachs touching and sometimes overlapping the edges of the panels. The painting's title refers to Renaissance depictions of the Annunciation; however, the angel Gabriel is not present, nor is the Virgin Mary. Wesley's is a thoroughly modern adaptation of the biblical story, complete with the hairstyles and clothing popular among women in the 1960s.

Moreover, *Annunciations* lacks the erotic undercurrents so prevalent in Wesley's other works from this period, despite the inclusion of a lone nude figure in the earliest stages of pregnancy. Wesley based this fairly modest yet still somewhat flirtatious nude on a nude that appears in his painting *Pooh* of 1965. Here the children's cartoon character Winnie the Pooh stands behind the woman and holds a paw over her stomach, both obscuring any evident state of pregnancy and creating an unearthly sexual tension. Critic Peter Plagens aptly summarized the dilemma of examining paintings like *Annunciations* by stating, "The question that immediately arises . . . is not what does it mean?, but why did the artist paint it?"[6]

James Michener commissioned *Annunciations* after a visit to the Robert Elkon Gallery, where Wesley showed Michener one of his "painted objects," a four-by-four-foot square table with eight pregnant women adorning the top. As the artist recalled,

> *[Michener] saw this table and said he would really like it but he didn't want any sculpture in his collection. So he commissioned a painting, and I made a drawing of these pregnant girls into a large painting with [six] panels, all with pregnant women in them, except for the one who was holding a baby.*[7]

As with most of Wesley's paintings, it remains unclear why he selected the images originally painted on the tabletop—he generally remembers making choices based on either popular imagery or his own sense of caprice.[8]

The comic-inspired surreality of Wesley's paintings is often belied by their ability to foster a disturbing sense of emptiness. The pregnant women in the Blanton's work, for instance, seem to lack depth, both literally and figuratively. Stylistically, Wesley created a sense of perceptual flatness by using contour lines, eschewing shading and modeling, and paring down his palette to three solid colors. He generated the sensation of psychological shallowness by endowing the women with vacuous eyes, artificial smiles, and no signs of individual character or temperament. Their posed, affected stances, which Wesley probably borrowed from models in magazine advertisements (a favorite practice), serve to exacerbate the women's superficiality. In the end, he seems to poke fun—albeit subtly—at the feelings of joy experienced by expectant mothers, at least according to the advertising industry, and to question the cliché of their purity and happiness.

Critics have made much of Wesley's tendency to repeat female figures in the same work, as in his iconic *Brides* of 1966, which represents

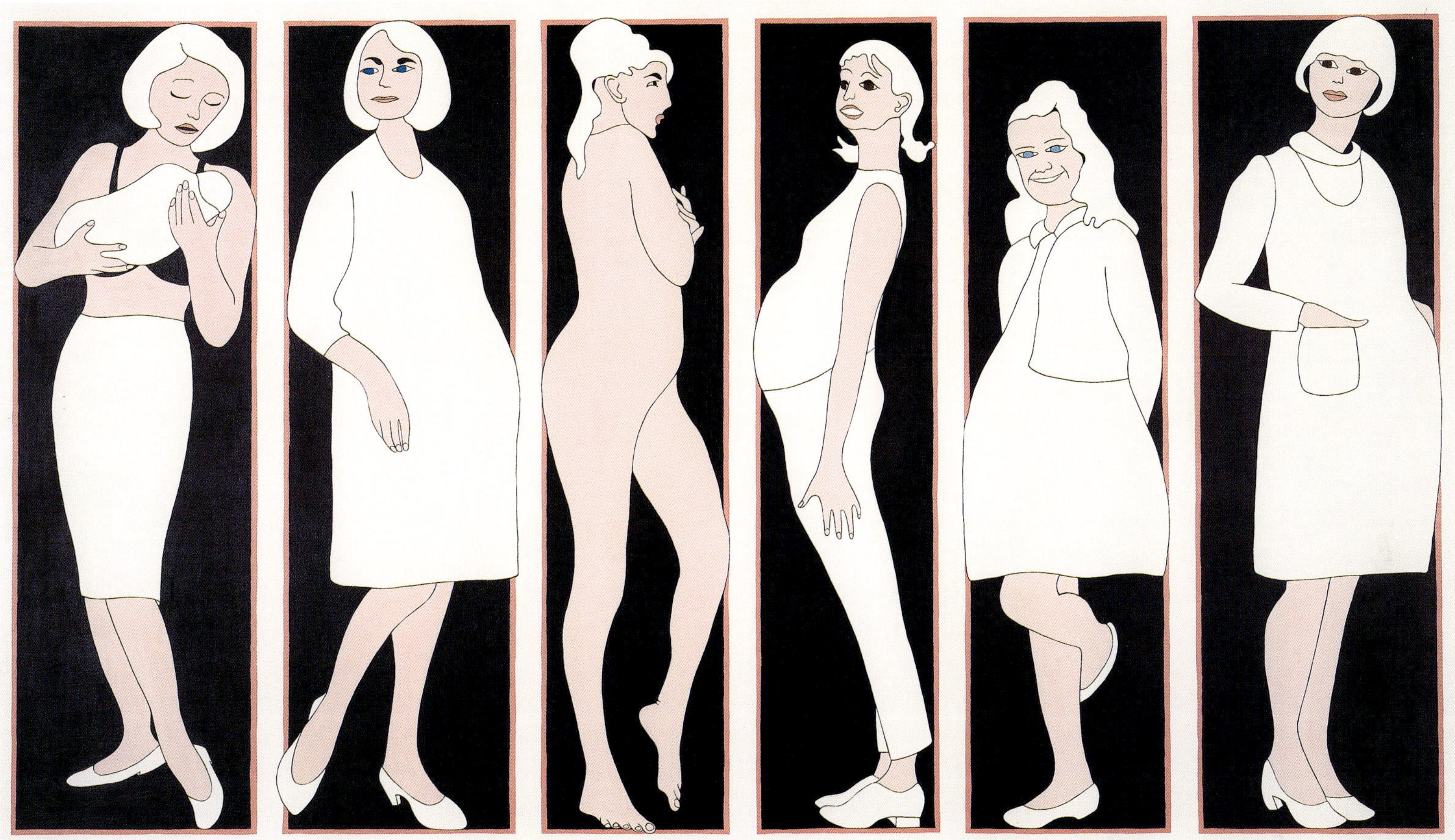

several identical and seemingly empty-headed brides standing above a fetal-positioned nude male. As Brian O'Doherty wrote, "If things get a little creepy, they are mitigated by charm and repetition. . . . [Wesley] uses repetition not to emphasize something, but to turn down the psychological heat."[9] Indeed, Wesley neutralized many of his *non sequitur* compositions by multiplying certain figures in fanciful patterns or creating decorative borders with recurring images. This Pop-like, light-hearted repetition has the effect of unifying otherwise disparate compositions and muting—but not eradicating—their psychological complexity. In *Annunciations,* Wesley's reiteration of posed pregnant women suggests both a narrative progression, as in a comic strip, and a world oversaturated by advertising images and the mass media. With these and other artistic devices at his disposal, Wesley tangled the sacrosanct ritual of pregnancy with impure commercial overtones to create images both familiar and quietly unsettling.

Melissa Warak

188.

Annunciations, 1967

Oil on canvas
46⅞ × 79¹⁵⁄₁₆ in. (119 × 203 cm)
Gift of Mari and James A. Michener
G1968.128

Provenance: Commissioned by James Michener and purchased from the artist, 1967
Inscribed verso, upper left "ANNUNCIATIONS John Wesley, 1967"

Notes

1. Through personal and professional relationships with the Minimalists, Wesley ostensibly absorbed some aspects of their aesthetic without feeling the need to create strictly Minimalist objects.
2. Quoted in Alanna Heiss, "Conversations with John Wesley," in Alanna Heiss, ed., *John Wesley: Paintings 1961–2000* (New York: P.S. 1 Contemporary Art Center, 2000), 23.
3. Heiss, "Conversations," 24.
4. Donald Judd, exhibition review, *Arts Magazine* 37 (April 1963): 51.
5. Judd, 51.
6. Peter Plagens, "John Wesley," *Artforum* 36 (May 1998): 141.
7. Quoted in Heiss, "Conversations," 26.
8. James Michener, "The Collector: An Informal Memoir," in Donald Goodall, ed., *The James A. Michener Collection: Twentieth Century American Painting* (Austin: The University of Texas at Austin, 1977), xv.
9. Brian O'Doherty, "Wesley's Hip-Pop," in Heiss, ed., *John Wesley: Paintings 1961–2000*.

Tom Wesselmann

b. Cincinnati, 1931–New York, 2004
w. Cincinnati, 1955–1956; New York, 1956–1963; New York–Wellfleet, Massachusetts, 1963–2004

Tom Wesselmann is heralded as one of the pioneers of the Pop movement for his singular utilization of imagery taken from advertising, popular culture, and the mass media, which he incorporated into stylized collages, still-lifes, and nudes. Pop artists such as Wesselmann, Andy Warhol, and James Rosenquist collapsed distinctions between high and low art and gave visual form to the consumerist vision of postwar culture, although disagreement exists as to whether their position with regard to the burgeoning consumer society of the 1960s was adulatory or satirical. Despite his alignment with Pop art, however, Wesselmann felt disconnected from the label because it connoted, in his mind at least, an overriding concern with subject matter at the expense of form, structure, and composition.[1]

Born in 1931 in Cincinnati, Wesselmann's interest in art and cartoons developed while briefly serving as an Army aerial photography interpreter in the early 1950s. After leaving the military, Wesselmann attended the University of Cincinnati on the GI Bill and completed his undergraduate degree in psychology in 1956. It was during this period that he began to take classes at the Art Academy in Cincinnati, where he encountered the gag cartoons of Sam Cobean. In 1956 Wesselmann moved to New York. That same year he enrolled at Cooper Union and studied with Alex Katz and Nicholas Marsicano, who pushed him to define his own unique style.

Wesselmann found inspiration not only in his teachers but in literature, especially the work of Samuel Beckett, Jack Kerouac, and Henry Miller, and in the art of Edward Hopper, Wassily Kandinsky, Henri Matisse, Amedeo Modigliani, Piet Mondrian, and the Abstract Expressionists, notably Willem de Kooning. Wesselmann briefly worked in an Abstract Expressionist style, but he soon abandoned it in favor of adapting objects from his surroundings—such as billboard scraps, magazine and newspaper fragments, photographs, and advertisements—and incorporating them into collages. In the early 1960s Wesselmann began to produce the large-scale figurative works for which he is best known today.

In 1961 Wesselmann commenced the Great American Nude series, a group of paintings devoted to the female body. It was a subject that he would revisit throughout his career using a palette of red, white, and blue. The works comprising this series often juxtapose elegantly delineated and intensely colored images of nude women with collage elements that Wesselmann incorporated into the backgrounds, such as found photographs and images culled from advertising. He flatly rendered and typically generalized, idealized, and abstracted the women's bodies, which have few distinguishing characteristics. While Wesselmann almost always included such isolated (and sexualized) body parts as lips, nipples, and the occasional glimpse of pubic hair, he seldom articulated the women's faces and eyes.

In 1962 Wesselmann began extracting the still-life elements that appeared in his nudes to create works that featured banal, mass-produced objects from everyday life. In these same still-lifes, the artist depicted domestic spaces with fabricated, painted, and simplified household objects placed on narrow kitchen shelves. *3-D Drawing 1964 (For Still Life No. 42)* of 1964 (plate 189) is among the more important of the shelf still-lifes because of the way it demonstrates Wesselmann's innovative propensity for blurring the line between two- and three-dimensional space and thereby blending sculpture with drawing. *3-D Drawing* relates to an assemblage painting titled *Still Life 42* and represents a varied combination of faux and real objects.[2] The real objects are a clock and a found picture frame molding. The faux objects, which include the beer bottles, orange, radio, and shelf, Wesselmann fashioned out of wood, composition board, and Formica. These tend to be realistic and convincing—the artist even went so far as to hit the orange with a ball-peen hammer in order to recreate the texture of its skin. After coating the materials with gesso and assembling them into a tableau, Wesselmann drew on their surfaces with charcoal so that his marks corresponded to the details and variations of light and dark that one would expect to find on the actual objects. Juxtaposing these sculptural elements with black and white drawing creates a powerful illusion that is heightened by the lack of color. The Carlsberg Beer bottle located on the left side of *3-D Drawing* represents something of an anomaly. Wesselmann rarely included specific brand names in his still-lifes from the mid-1960s. Indeed, it was around this same time that he began to reject brand familiarity for universally recognized imagery.[3]

While Wesselmann resisted the literal interpretation of his work, his choice of particular objects infers references to the domestic realm, to technological development, and to the consumer culture of postwar American suburbia. In addition, *3-D Drawing* evokes the more universal theme of the passage of time, signified by the inclusion of the clock and orange. In this exceptional three-dimensional drawing, Wesselmann captured aspects of American life in the 1960s without making recourse to critique or resorting to naïve optimism.

Jennifer Jankauskas

Notes

1. Tom Wessleman, quoted in Trevor J. Fairbrother, "Interview with Tom Wessleman/Slim Stealingworth," *Arts Magazine* 56 (May 1982): 136.
2. The artist did not remember if the drawing predates the painting or if he created it afterwards. The work does not function as a pure study as it is larger then the painting and came about as Wesselmann felt "it had to be made." See Thomas H. Garver, introduction, *Tom Wesselmann: Early Still Lifes: 1962–1964* (Balboa, Calif.: Newport Harbor Art Museum, 1970), n.p.
3. Garver, n.p.

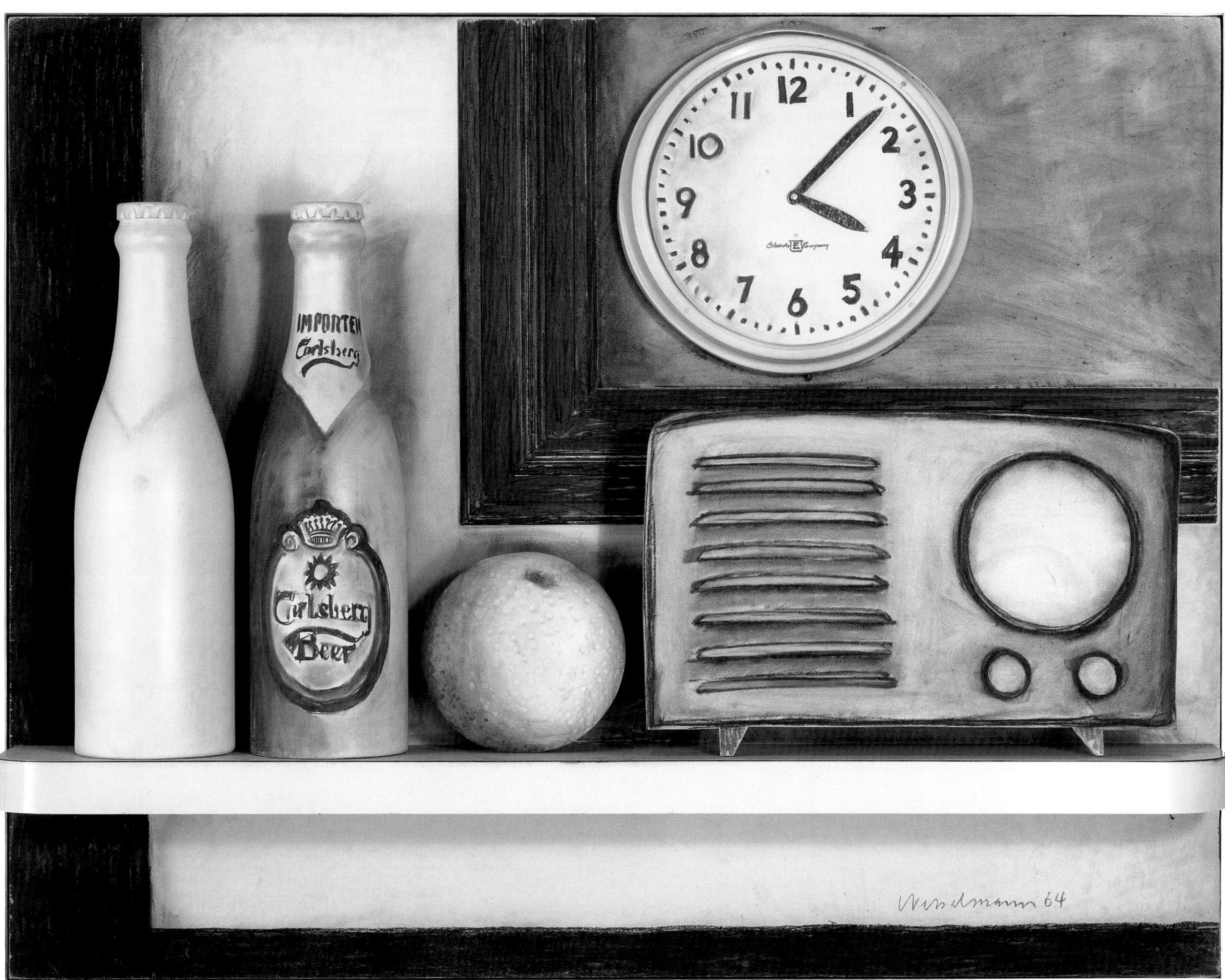

189.
3-D Drawing 1964 (For Still Life No. 42), 1964

Charcoal and gesso on wood and assemblage
48⅛ × 60 × 10 in. (122.3 × 152.5 × 25.5 cm)
Gift of Mari and James A. Michener
1991.340

Provenance: Purchased by James Michener from Green Gallery, New York, 1965; long-term loan to The University of Texas at Austin, 1968–1991
Signed lower right "Wesselmann 64"

Charmion von Wiegand

Chicago, 1896–New York, 1983
w. New York, 1926–1983

Charmion von Wiegand belonged to a group of innovative American artists, including Ilya Bolotowsky, Burgoyne Diller, and Carl Holty, who found their major source of inspiration in the work of Dutch abstractionist Piet Mondrian. Von Wiegand was born in Chicago in 1896. Her experiences in San Francisco's Chinatown, where she spent much of her childhood, would exert a powerful influence on her later artistic career. She attended secondary school in Berlin, where her father was stationed as a foreign correspondent for Hearst, and then went on to enroll at Barnard College and the Columbia University School of Journalism. Although she studied a variety of subjects, including Greek, Hebrew, art history, and world literature, von Wiegand never received an official degree and never formally studied studio art.[1] She entered psychoanalysis in 1926, and it was during one of her sessions that she realized she wanted to be an artist. For many years, von Wiegand pursued painting, but only as an avocation. Indeed, encouraged to purse a career in journalism by her father, she began working as the Moscow correspondent for Universal Capital Services, the Hearst newspaper chain, in 1926. Von Wiegand's early work consisted primarily of paintings of trees and landscapes.[2]

Von Wiegand visited the Soviet Union in 1932 and soon thereafter married Joseph Freeman, a writer and cofounder of the leftist journals *New Masses* and *The Partisan Review*. Both von Wiegand and Freeman were firm believers in Communism, but they became disillusioned with it after the Stalinist purges of 1936. At this time, there was no connection between her political beliefs and her artistic practice. However, she did believe that art had the potential to express the needs of all levels of society, not just the elite, and she expressed these ideas in her critical writings on art.[3]

In 1941 von Wiegand received a commission to write an article on an artist of her own choosing, and she selected Mondrian, who had moved to New York after his London studio was bombed in 1940. She was immediately attracted to Mondrian's merging of art and Theosophist teachings. Theosophy is a system of beliefs developed in the late nineteenth century that combines aspects of Tibetan Buddhism with European occultism through the writings of the Russian aristocrat, Madam Blavatsky. Theosophy greatly influenced Mondrian's work, particularly his theory of Neo-Plasticism, in which he abstracted and reduced all forms to rectilinear lines and shapes and all colors to red, yellow, and blue, plus the neutrals gray, black, and white, thereby attempting to achieve a utopian and spiritual form of artistic expression.

After meeting Mondrian, von Wiegand immersed herself in every aspect of his art and writing, even translating his essays into English. Their acquaintance ended in the fall of 1942 when Mondrian requested that she spend less time with him.[4] While much of von Wiegand's early work from the 1940s evinces the obvious influence of Mondrian in its reliance on rectilinear shapes, her studies of Eastern philosophy inspired her to move in a more personal direction. Her later work was still geometric but incorporated elements of collage and designs inspired by *mandalas* (Buddhist prayer diagrams) and Tantric diagrams.[5]

Von Wiegand's study of the spiritual aspect of geometric abstraction began in 1950 when she read *The Secret Doctrine,* a book by Madam Blavatsky that discussed the main principles of Theosophy. Realizing that Blavatsky had adapted much Theosophist color theory from similar ideas in Eastern religion, von Wiegand began to study Buddhism during the 1950s and converted to Buddhism in 1960.[6] Her interest in spirituality extended to non-Buddhist religions and cultures as well.

Throughout the late 1940s and early 1950s, von Wiegand worked in the vein of geometric abstraction, but she used a variety of colors and shapes that far exceeded Mondrian's. Von Wiegand also began to incorporate formal elements of specifically Buddhist origin into her paintings. The Blanton's *Offering to the Adi-Buddha Amoghasiddha* (1966–1967, plate 190) has many such forms: concentric circles divided into four parts, suggesting a mandala; a triangular altar; and a large central triangular shape, reminiscent of the shape of the seated Buddha, all of them painted in bright, prismatic colors. Amoghasiddha is a deity who helps others reach Enlightenment by manifesting himself in the form of teachers and guides. On either side of the altar are white triangles that suggest the shapes of *gtor ma,* small conical heaps of barley flour and butter that are an essential aspect of Tibetan ritual. In the center of the painting is a small dot—possibly a "seed-syllable"—that helps the devotee visualize the deity who is the focus of meditation. At the bottom of the painting is another small mandala containing the *visvavajra*—the double lightning bolt and symbol of Amoghasiddha. The shading of the colors in the mandala and the overlapping of shapes gives some suggestion of depth—a dramatic departure from the effects of strict Neo-Plasticism.[7]

Von Wiegand executed a number of works inspired by Buddhism, and she assimilated aspects of Buddhist symbolism to such a degree that her work was often associated with that of the Far East.[8] Yet she did not always adhere strictly to spiritual imagery, occasionally using shapes or colors that were of personal significance.[9] During the 1950s many Abstract Expressionist artists learned of Eastern philosophy through the writings of Carl Jung and incorporated aspects of this philosophy into their work. Von Wiegand pursued her interest in Buddhism independently, a trait that distinguishes her life and artistic production as a whole.

Erin Aldana

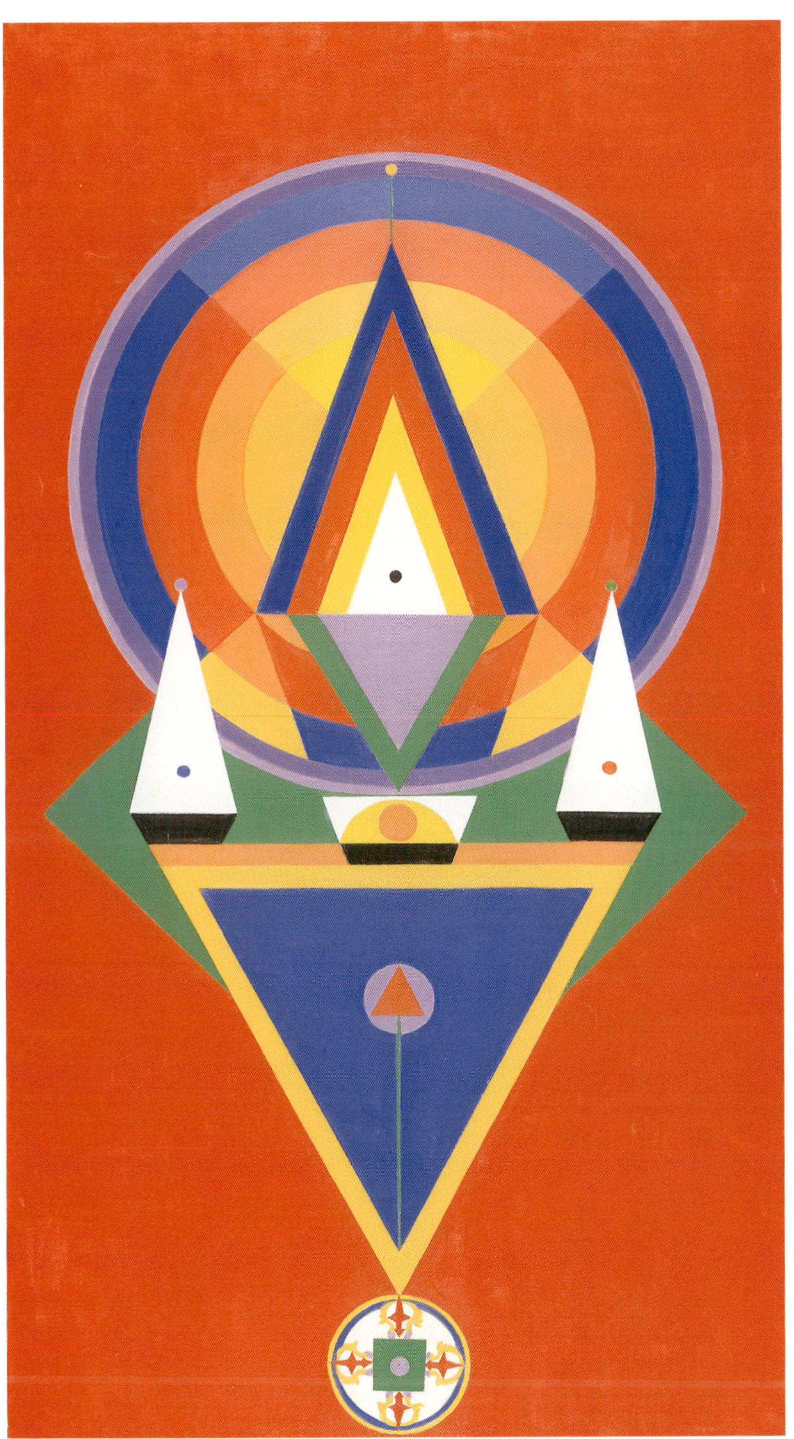

Notes

1. Susan C. Larsen, "Art Is a Bridge Between Heaven and Earth," *Charmion von Wiegand: Spirit & Form, Collages, 1946–1963* (New York: Michael Rosenfeld Gallery, 1998), 2.
2. Sandra Hagan Reynolds, "A Quest for the Spiritual: The Geometric Art of Charmion von Wiegand" (master's thesis, University of Texas at Austin, 1992), 5–6. Reynolds's research included von Wiegand's unpublished letters and personal journals and is an excellent source of information on the artist.
3. Reynolds, 7–10, 12.
4. Reynolds, 13–20, 29–31.
5. This progression is evident in von Wiegand's works included in the catalogue *Charmion von Wiegand: Her Art and Life* (Miami Beach, Fla.: The Bass Museum of Art, 1982), 9–39.
6. Reynolds, 37, 78.
7. Reynolds, 93–95.
8. Douglas MacAgy and Hsien Liang Koo both make this connection in their brief essays on von Wiegand. See *Charmion von Wiegand: Oils, Gouaches, Collages* (Austin: University Art Museum, 1969), n.p.
9. Reynolds, 43–48, 93–95.

190.

Offering to the Adi-Buddha, Amoghasiddha, 1966–1967

Oil on canvas
50 x 27 in. (127 x 69.01 cm)
Michener Acquisitions Fund
P1969.19.1

Provenance: Purchased from the artist, 1969

William T. Wiley

b. Bedford, Indiana, 1937

w. San Francisco, 1957–1962; Davis, California, 1962–1973; Woodacre, California, 1973–present

A large painting comprised of graphic charcoal trails, vibrant acrylic gestures, and flat patches of color, *Food Descending the Starecase* (1980, plate 191) presents many quintessential elements of California artist William Wiley's visual vocabulary.[1] The abstract and the representational coexist with ease as the painting's playful contours invite the viewer to explore an imaginative topography—an alchemical conceptual terrain populated with mischievous juxtapositions. Wiley's love of drawing is obvious and intoxicating. Within the charcoal skeins of *Food Descending the Starecase* lie myriad signs—some secretive and obsessively cryptic, others open and tantalizingly familiar. Bird heads, eyeballs, and telegraph poles dot the deceptively shallow space of Wiley's dense, surreal landscape, while meandering lines and colored threads of paint constitute the background.

Suggestions of a foreground begin at the bottom left corner of the canvas, where a human foot descends a green staircase marked with a black and white striped triangle. This simple motif, a favorite of Wiley's, is repeated four other times in the painting.[2] Like comets, these two-tone, triangular forms emit bright tails of paint, evoking phoenixlike energy. Propelling linear trajectories across the picture plane, they measure Wiley's dynamic space in dramatic and quasi-mathematical fashion. The bare foot appears again along the base of the painting, next to a small ladder, a tall drum, and a detailed shoe. A yellow line guides the curious procession from left to right, ending in a white "X" next to a male figure who, attended by a tiny horse, gazes upward toward the center of the canvas. The man's stare directs the viewer's eye past the triangle in the center of the composition to a flat oval of paint. Suggestive of a clear pool or hole, it is situated in a rocky landscape in the upper left of the painting, at the point where the background becomes the foreground in dizzying fashion.

Wiley's idiosyncratic symbols and mercurial space insinuate that multiple layers and diverse meanings exist in his paintings, prints, and sculpture. His elusive blend of reality and fantasy is consistent, longstanding, and well informed. Along with lifelong friends and fellow artists William Allan and Robert Hudson, in high school Wiley developed an interest in abstract painting, the creative investigation of everyday life through rituals and signs, and the work of European Surrealists Salvador Dalí, Giorgio de Chirico, and René Magritte.

During college in the late 1950s, influenced by teacher Frank Lobdell, Wiley borrowed his emerging style from the sophisticated currency of Abstract Expressionism. But although he gained the attention of important critics and curators, by the late 1960s he had become increasingly dissatisfied with the restrictions of pure abstraction.[3] During this period, while teaching in the fertile environment of the University of California at Davis, Wiley's contact with other artists, including Wayne Thiebaud and Robert Arneson, excited his interest in social concerns and in ideas associated with culture, history, and mythology.[4] Wiley stated: "The change for me, which happened in 1967, was that I wanted the work to reflect my consciousness—whether it was politics, or art, or the landscape or a coffee cup—I wanted it to be relevant to who I actually was, and I wanted to be able to use it to respond to anything in my life."[5] While indebted to abstraction, Wiley's subsequent style, now known as West Coast funk art or "Dude Ranch Dada," was overtly concerned with exploring autobiography and narrative.[6]

Titles such as *Wizdumb Bridge* (1969) mark Wiley's sense of humor and love of verbal puns. References to the work of artists such as Edouard Manet, Leonardo da Vinci, Alberto Giacometti, and Pieter Brueghel the Elder also inhabit many of his works. Indeed, Wiley makes his homage to Marcel Duchamp's *Nude Descending a Staircase* (1913) clear in his own painting, *Food Descending the Starecase,* both in the title and in the visual pun in the lower left of the work.[7] His erudite and quirky borrowings, often incongruous and no more than visual marginalia, illustrate Wiley's wit and understanding of the readymade as a technique as well as a philosophy.[8]

Sara-Jayne Parsons

Notes

1. Wiley received a BFA (1960) and an MFA (1962) in painting from the San Francisco Art Institute. From 1962 to 1973 he taught at the University of California, Davis, and the San Francisco Art Institute; his career was propelled when his work was included in the 1966 Whitney Biennial exhibition. Since the mid-1970s he has guest taught at various colleges. With numerous national and international solo and group exhibitions to his credit, Wiley continues to lecture, perform, and collaborate with other artists.
2. Wiley perceives the black and white form, based on a surveyor's measuring tool, as a powerful, rational symbol. The motif holds personal symbolism for him and has appeared in a number of his works over several decades. Graham W. J. Beal and John Perreault, *Wiley Territory* (Minneapolis: Walker Art Center, 1979), 25–27.
3. Critic and art historian Dore Ashton commented favorably on the young Wiley's work in a 1958 exhibition in New York, praising his originality, expressionist blur, and use of symbols. See Brenda Richardson, *William T. Wiley* (Berkeley, Calif.: University Art Museum, 1971), 8.
4. Thomas Albright, *Art in the San Francisco Bay Area, 1945–1980: An Illustrated History* (Berkeley, Calif.: University of California Press, 1985), 118.
5. William T. Wiley, "A Conversation with William T. Wiley," interview by Mary Hull Webster, *Artweek* 27 (March 1996): 28–29.
6. Albright, 120.
7. Marcel Duchamp's oil painting, *Nude Descending a Staircase,* received heavy criticism when exhibited at the Armory Show in New York in 1913. Critics derided Duchamp's dynamic attempt to reconcile Analytical Cubism with the representation of movement by presenting a figure through a series of dislocated planes. They also believed that the painting subverted traditional notions of what nudes should look like. It is, perhaps, no accident that Wiley's artistic awakening in the 1960s coincided with the rediscovery of Duchamp's intellectual approach to art making.
8. *Nothing Lost from the Original: William T. Wiley Looks at Art History* (San Francisco: Fine Arts Museums of San Francisco, 1996), 8.

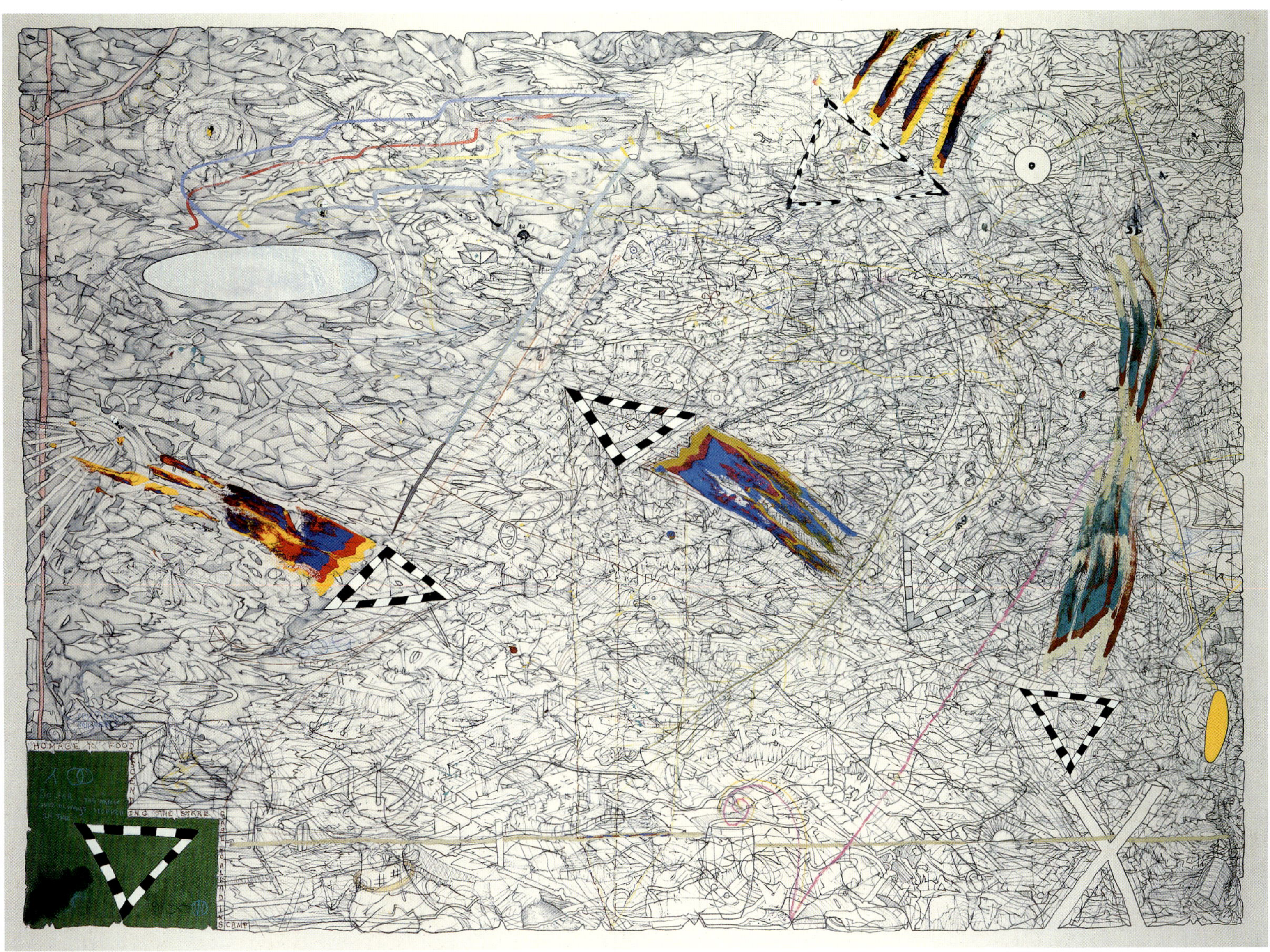

191.

Food Descending the Starecase, 1980

Charcoal and acrylic on canvas
86 3/16 × 113 1/8 in. (218.9 × 287.2 cm)
Archer M. Huntington Museum Fund
1983.1

Provenance: Purchased from Frumkin & Struve Gallery, Chicago, 1982
Inscribed lower left "19∞Ⓦ"

John Willenbecher

b. Macungie, Pennsylvania, 1936
w. New York, 1958–present

Paradox is the point of origin
Pattern becomes apparent
Paradox is the spark
Pattern attempts to make sense
Paradox is the mystery
Pattern engenders reassurance
Paradox is the point of ending
—John Willenbecher, 1974

John Willenbecher started creating mixed-media constructions in 1961, the same year he abandoned his studies in art history at New York University to embark on a career as an artist. In 1962 he produced a great variety of meticulously fabricated games reminiscent of the playful collaged boxes of Joseph Cornell, which Willenbecher had seen in William Seitz's exhibition, *Art of Assemblage*, at The Museum of Modern Art in 1961. Like *Unknown Game No. 2* (1962, plate 192), most of these games consist of found materials such as wooden balls, wire spokes, and targets or roulette wheels contained in recycled wooden receptacles. Painted numbers seem to indicate the score, while gilded, three-dimensional letters form strange words that add an extra layer of obscurity to the already unrecognizable, unplayable game.

Although the strongly metaphorical and associative character of his later works seems absent from the early assemblages, many of the themes Willenbecher began to explore around 1965 are already latent in the games. His miniature celestial constellations of the mid-1960s, the labyrinths of the late 1960s and early 1970s, as well as the ladders, bridges, and pyramids that appear in his work throughout the 1970s all conjure up metaphors of life and death. Like games, these forms have been used for centuries to symbolize not only the human need for structure and meaning in a chaotic, unpredictable world, but also the finite, uncertain course of life on earth and its relation to the seemingly infinite universe. Willenbecher has frequently expressed an interest in the dichotomy of change, paradox, and mystery on the one hand and invariability, pattern, and rational sense on the other.

In the 1960s and 1970s several artists besides Willenbecher mined the artistic potential of games and labyrinths, possibly in response to the increased application of probability and game theory in science, economics, and politics. Willenbecher's exploration of the symbolic and mystical dimensions of these forms, however, set him apart from his contemporaries, most of whom shunned all metaphor and spirituality, focusing exclusively on the structural and performative nature of games and mazes.

In the mid-1960s Willenbecher's lifelong fascination with astrology began to manifest itself in his work. With found objects like window frames and metal debris, the artist now gave visual form to the infinite universe, reinventing images of the cosmos in boxes and on panels. In *Spheremusic III* (1966, plate 193), a circle of nine metal balls with a tenth shiny ball at its core suggests the nine planets orbiting around the sun. This constellation is surrounded by another ring of twelve rainbow-colored balls that, like the nine metal balls, are suspended in the holes of a shallow black disk. A penumbral, lunar-shaped form painted in a scale of grey tones circumscribes the disk almost entirely. This miniature galaxy is set in a grey frame, which in turn is contained in a glass-covered black box.

The title presumably refers to the Pythagorean belief that the planets and stars were attached to a series of crystal spheres that each emitted particular musical notes while rotating around the earth. The numerical ratios of the resulting harmonious "music of the spheres" coincided, according to the Pythagoreans, with the mathematical principles that form the basis of the universe and all the natural phenomena and living creatures contained within it. In *Spheremusic III*, calculation and proportional harmony seem to govern compositional arrangement, tone, and color, while spatial complexity and reference to an unknown cosmos with abstruse laws invest the work with a sense of mystery and enigma.

Mette Gieskes

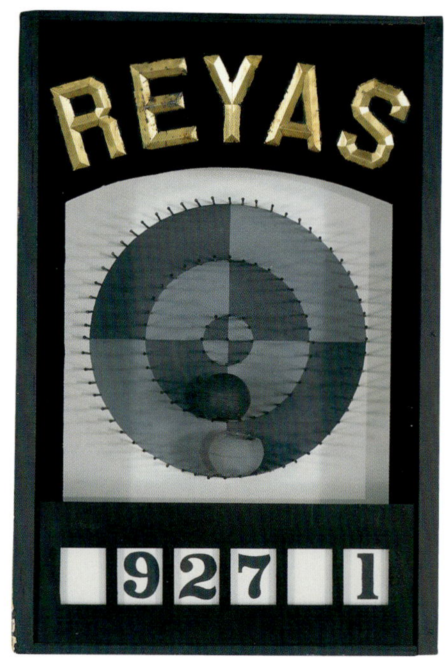

192.
Unknown Game No. 2, 1962
Tempera, gilt, wood, and glass construction
27 9/16 × 18 1/2 in. (70 × 47 cm)
Gift of Mari and James A. Michener
G1968.129

Provenance: Purchased by James Michener from Feigen-Herbert Gallery, New York, 1963

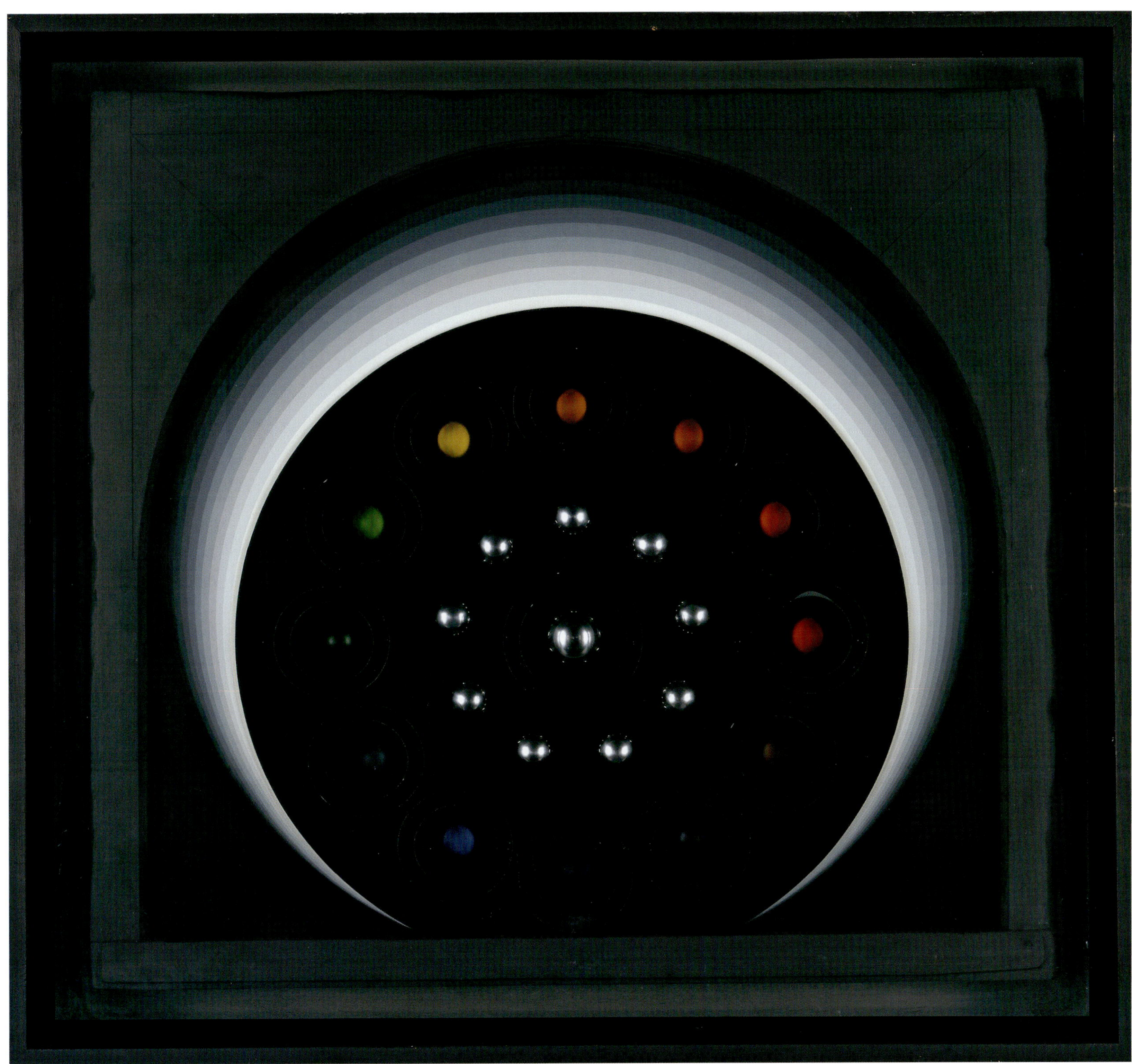

193.
Spheremusic III, 1966

Multimedia construction
41 × 44 in. (103 × 111 cm)
Gift of Mari and James A. Michener
G1968.130

Provenance: Purchased by James Michener from Richard Feigen Gallery, New York, 1967

Donald Roller Wilson

b. Houston, 1938
w. Fayetteville, Arkansas, 1967–present

The world of Donald Roller Wilson is full of hallucinatory scenarios rendered with a seamless realist technique reminiscent of such notable seventeenth-century Dutch painters as Jan Vermeer and Rembrandt van Rijn. Both Roller Wilson and his work could be described as eccentric in relation to current trends in contemporary art. Born in Houston in 1938, Roller Wilson received his MFA from Kansas State University in 1966. He currently lives and works in the Ozarks of Arkansas, where he settled in the 1960s after teaching at the University of Arkansas at Fayetteville. He has stated that he seeks to convey through his works the spirit he believes underlies all aspects of creation and with which human beings are rarely in touch.[1] Roller Wilson does so by creating paintings that are inhabited by an ever-evolving cast of characters of his own invention.

Painting in the dark with only a light fixture above his canvas, Roller Wilson insists on a controlled working environment with no outside distractions. He produces a physical template for each painting by constructing scenes in his studio, to which he adds items found in area junk stores and craft shows. When his characters are involved, he employs live models. Roller Wilson first prepares his canvas with gesso and three applications of white lead, which is then sanded and allowed to dry for one month between each application. After a six month curing period, he makes an underdrawing using oil colors and turpentine. Following another month of drying, Roller Wilson adds the overpainting, again using oil paint and turpentine; it is during this stage that the work assumes a rich coloration with fine detail. After an additional drying time of approximately one month, the surface of the painting is glazed with transparent colors and soluvar varnish.[2] Careful blending and multiple layers of varnish conceal the marks of the artist's hand and result in works with a high degree of verisimilitude.[3]

Mrs. Jenkins' Late Night Dinner in Her Room (While Out in the Hall Leading to Her Room, Her Small Friends Were Sleeping) (1984, plate 194) offers the viewer the kind of cryptically intriguing environment characteristic of most, if not all, of Roller Wilson's work. A sharply lit interior shows a vacated table with the remnants of what appears to be two individuals' meals; a man's hat rests on an adjacent table, and a roll of toilet paper lies unraveled in the lower right portion of the composition. While filled with the traces of recent use, the interior lacks any human or animal presence.

Perhaps in recognition of the difficulties facing the neophyte who encounters his layered universes, Roller Wilson usually provides a poetically configured wall label. In the case of the Blanton's painting, it reads:

Mrs. Jenkins' late-night dinner in her room. Alone
(While, out in the hall leading to her room, her small
friends were sleeping)

Mrs. Jenkins set her table
Made it look like two
Had dined together in her room last night

And in the morning—through her keyhole
Most who peeked inside
Had seen the plates but none had seen the light

And very few who saw caught on
For most were fooled—it seemed
And those who knew had tried to be polite

They knew that though she played her tricks
Down deep, she was inside
And, in the end, that she would be all right

Characteristically, Roller Wilson's text is more allusive and evocative than explanatory. An appreciative or curious viewer would be forced to explore his oeuvre more comprehensively to discover that the character of Mrs. Jenkins is the sister of another character, Mrs. White. Mrs. Jenkins moved from New York to Alabama 118 years ago and has never set foot beyond her home since, depending solely on her various (but here unseen) animal companions for news of the outside world. To Roller Wilson, she is "an imaginary figure which embodies an assorted collection of interpretations that I have about the ways a lot of people seem to be."[4]

Roller Wilson's practice of inscribing onto his works names that refer to both autobiographical and fictive entities adds another layer of complexity. Written on the recto of the Blanton's painting, "Bruce" and "Judy" refer to the owners of an early Roller Wilson work, "Judee" to his toy white poodle, and "Freeda" to his mother, while "Rabbit" is a nickname for his wife.[5] "Betty" (written on the left wall) refers to Betty Moody, owner of the Moody Gallery in Houston. The name "Cookie," which appears under the table, alludes to a precocious orangutan that makes repeated appearances in Roller Wilson's work.[6]

Although Roller Wilson's paintings may appear purely surrealistic, the artist intends a more mythic dimension for his work:

> *The more you seek to know the answers, the more you realize how much you don't know. As a result, you have to operate blindly on faith. More than anything, my work deals with that pointlessness. It takes all the arrogance out of everything you do when you know that God is so much bigger than you are. And yet everything you are and do and see is filled with God: the trees, the asphalt, and the people fighting over Aqua Net at Wal-Mart.*[7]

To this end, Mrs. Jenkins' bedroom is infused with the sharply etched yet quixotic reality of a dream world; a world that is physically

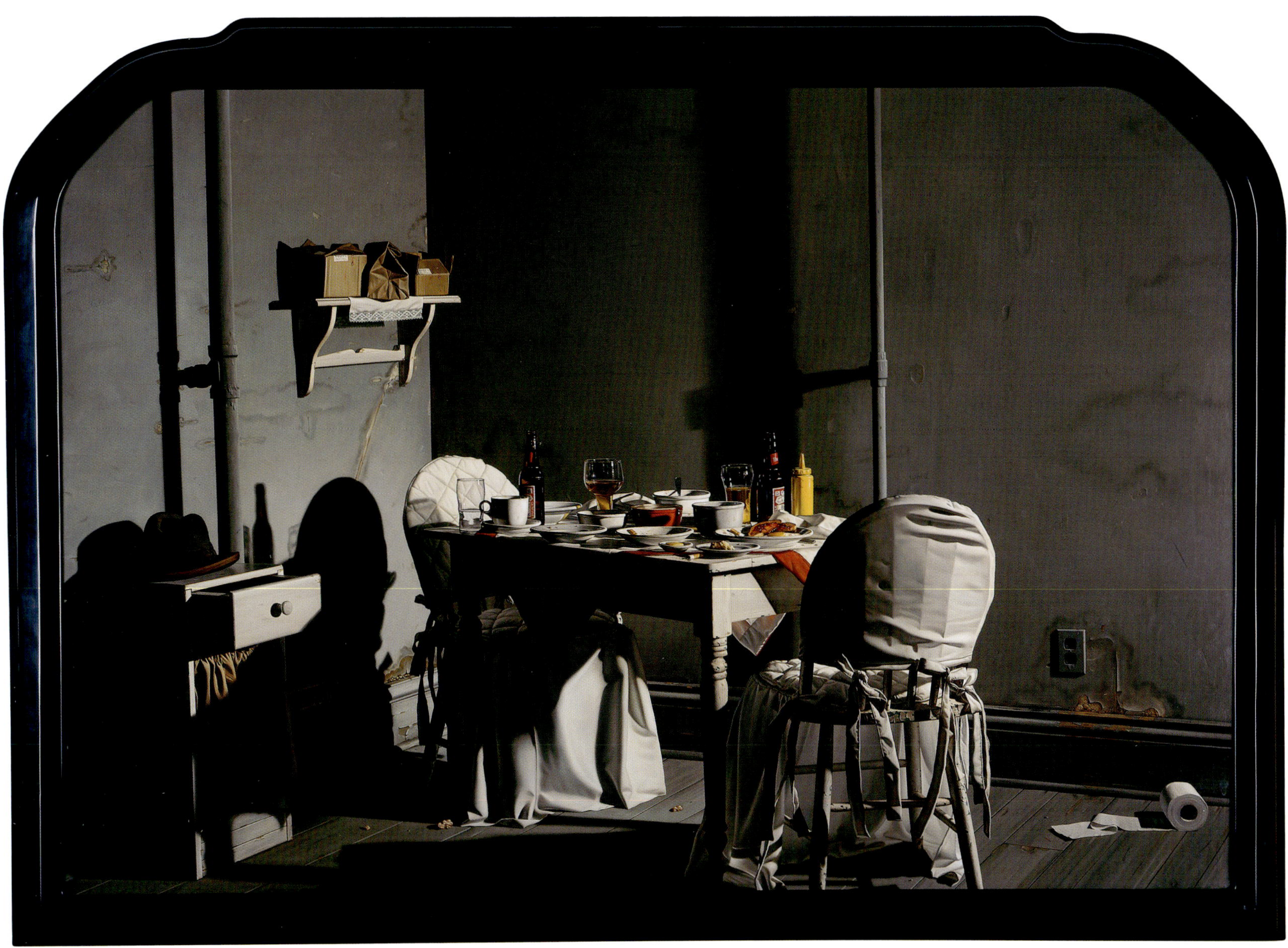

recognizable, yet whose hidden meaning remains maddeningly elusive. Roller Wilson has given viewers a glimpse into a secret, inexplicable dreamscape, one that he sees as imbued with a greater state of consciousness. To enter this universe, to share in its hidden meanings, the viewer must be willing to be immersed in its interpretive conundrums, to ask questions of the work and of themselves for which easy or obvious answers may not be forthcoming.

Charity Anderson

194.
Mrs. Jenkins' Late Night Dinner in Her Room (While Out in the Hall Leading to Her Room, Her Small Friends Were Sleeping), 1984

Oil on canvas
50 × 72 in. (127.5 × 182.9 cm)
The 1985 Friends of the Archer M. Huntington Art Gallery Purchase
1985.33

Provenance: Purchased from Holly Solomon Gallery, New York, 1985
Signed lower left "Donald Roller Wilson 1984/12-A 6:32 P.M. Saturday Evening, July 14"

Notes

1. Leigh A. Morse, *Donald Roller Wilson* (New York: Coe Kerr Gallery, 1987), n.p.
2. "Roller's Techniques," available at http://www.donaldrollerwilson.com/techniques.html [June 14, 2004].
3. Carl Little, "Donald Roller Wilson at Coe Kerr," *Art in America* 75 (June 1987): 154.
4. Charles Kauffman, "Huntington acquires 3 new paintings," *Austin American Statesman*, May 29, 1985.
5. Blanton Museum of Art Archives, The University of Texas at Austin.
6. A. M. Homes, "Donald Roller Wilson," *Artforum* 30 (January 1992): 102.
7. "Donald Roller Wilson," available at http://www.meyergalleries.com/scottsdale/bio/24.asp [November 15, 2004].

Dee Wolff

b. Springfield, Missouri, 1948
w. Houston, 1976–present

Since the mid-1970s Houston-based artist Dee Wolff has explored themes relating to humanity and consciousness through visual reinterpretations of Christian narratives and imagery. Ranging from large-scale paintings such as *Cry, What Shall I Cry?* (1985, not illustrated) to gouaches and drawings that can be held in the hands, like *Selah: Stations of the Cross (MacDowell set)* (1991, plates 195–196), Wolff's art integrates a unique mythology and personal iconography with traditional modes of religious expression.

Drawing on both her Roman Catholic upbringing and her training in Jungian philosophy at the Jung Center of Houston, Wolff explores the intersections between the individual and the universal, the subconscious and the conscious, and other dichotomies of human experience. The artist's extensive knowledge of a variety of Western and Eastern religious traditions underlies her efforts to transcend organized religion in her art and to identify the "common denominators of religion that unite us all in the same spirit."[1] Central to Wolff's elision of Christian and Jungian thought is her emphasis on the relation between "Christ's journey to death and man's inner journey to conscious realization of self."[2] For Wolff, this fundamental Christian narrative parallels and is symbolic of the psychological path toward individuation and the growth of self-knowledge, independence, and personal wisdom: "Each painting represents a moment of self-realization, insight, an epiphany, which is one person's own truth and also a universal truth."[3]

Over the past three decades, Wolff has explored the interplay between religion and psychology in her *Selah: Stations of the Cross* series. She has completed eighteen sets with this title, three of which belong to the Blanton Museum, and she is currently working on one additional set. A Hebrew word from Psalms, "selah" denotes a pause between the lines of a prayer; and, indeed, Wolff intends these works to provide a reflective yet participatory moment of silence for the viewer.

In the earliest of the three sets in the Blanton's collection, *Selah* (1980, not illustrated), Wolff abstracts each stop in the Stations of the Cross narrative, which describes the events surrounding the crucifixion of Jesus, into overlapping planes of color and gold leaf dominated by a central cross. The dynamic relationship between the crosses and the ambiguous background space recalls both Piet Mondrian's grids and Barnett Newman's weightier "zips." For Wolff, *Selah* represents a "psychic coming-together in time-space . . . these are conscious moments of joyful reunion-epiphanies."[4]

Whether in paintings or drawings, the artist values the "possibilities of chance" and works without preliminary plans: "If I approach paper with a preconceived idea, I cannot work."[5] Wolff also has created a constantly expanding visual language consisting of clusters of minute, detailed birds, angels, trees, and crosses, among other motifs. While many of these icons are infused with familiar cultural associations, Wolff believes that each viewer brings his or her own individual experiences to the work. The symbols she employs, then, are "open" symbols. As Wolff explained, "An open symbol holds intensely personal connotations, but yet, allows for open interpretation . . . that is, the experience of the viewer-participant allows communication with the symbol, dependent on his experience."[6]

Selah: Stations of the Cross (MacDowell set) and *Selah: Stations of the Cross* (1987, plates 197–198) contain a variety of such open symbols and also reflect Wolff's reduced yet decorative line and simple but intense palette. Both sets of gouaches are painted in bright, highly contrasting colors over a base layer of black paint. As Wolff said, "I

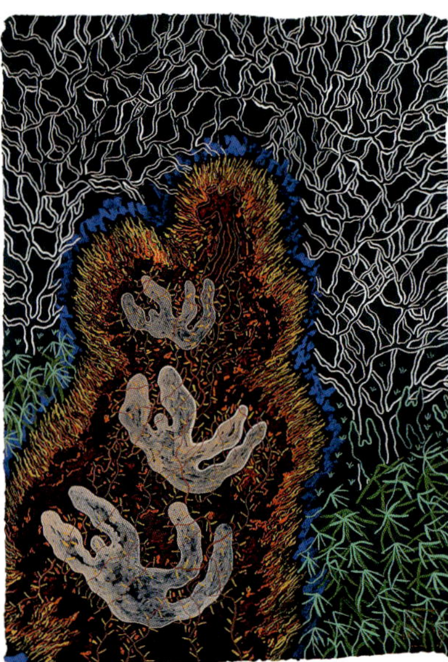

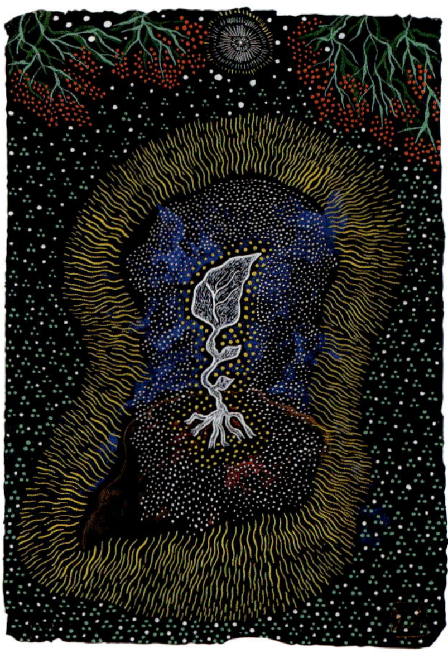

195.
Station IX—The Third Fall, from *Selah: Stations of the Cross (MacDowell set)*, 1991
Gouache on pondicherry paper
10 × 7 1/16 in. (25.4 × 17.9 cm)
Gift of the Artist
2002.2832.9/15
Inscribed verso, lower right "Station IX–The Third Fall," in black ink; "1991," in red ink

196.
Station XV—The Resurrection, from *Selah: Stations of the Cross (MacDowell set)*, 1991
Gouache on pondicherry paper
10 1/4 × 7 3/16 in. (26 × 18.2 cm)
Gift of the Artist
2002.2832.15/15
Signed bottom right "Dee I. Wolff," in pencil
Inscribed bottom edge "1991–Resurrection Stations Selah," in pencil
Inscribed verso, lower right "Station XV–The Resurrection–1991," in red ink

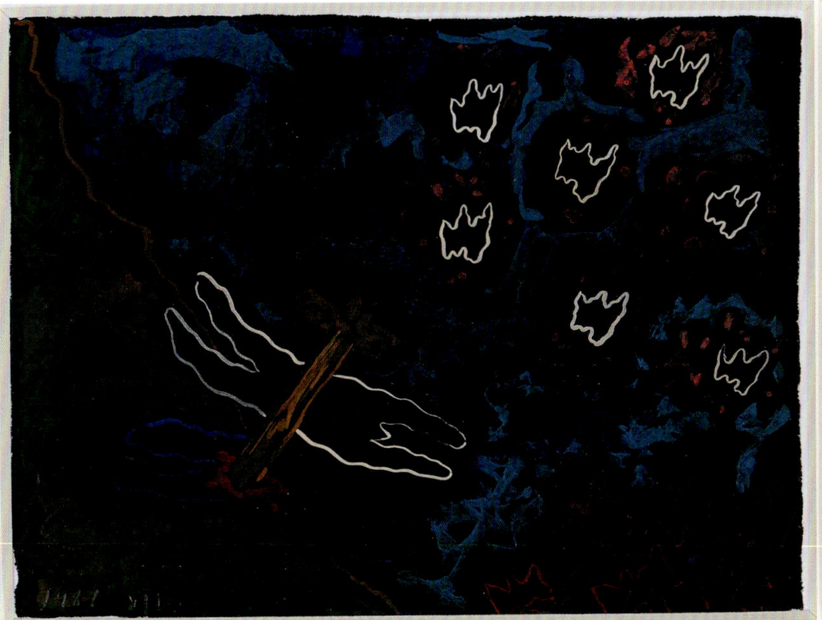

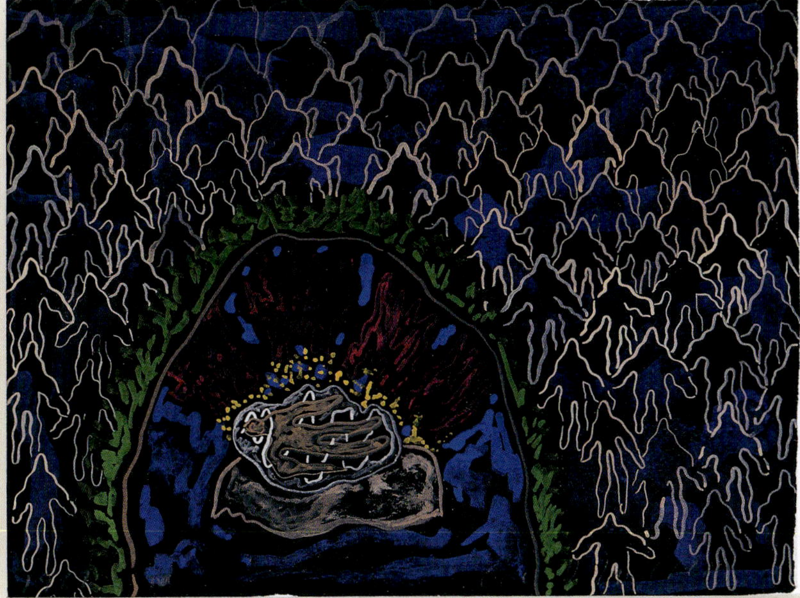

like to work dark and bring to the surface."[7] In the fifteen gouaches that make up *Selah: Stations of the Cross (MacDowell set)*, landscapes washed in bright blue, purple, and green emerge from fields of black, while the action of Wolff's narrative plays out between human figures and icons outlined in white. In the final frame of this 1991 series, *Station XV: The Resurrection*, a plantlike form stands on a raised ground beneath a yellow dawn, radiating force-lines of blue and green (plate 196). The small size of the *Selah* images references the holy cards of Wolff's childhood.[8]

The gouaches in *Selah: Stations of the Cross* also employ black backgrounds, out of which appear human forms and highly detailed plant life rendered in rich, fertile greens—a "life-affirming color" for Wolff.[9] The narrative and figural space of these panels is represented in a gestural, loose, and increasingly atmospheric style that recalls Wolff's large-scale painting *Cry, What Shall I Cry?* (1985, not illustrated). While not part of the *Selah: Stations of the Cross* series, this work explores similar religious and psychological themes and incorporates Wolff's personal iconography and detailed style, creating a densely populated visual field that encourages contemplation. Employing both abstract and representational approaches, and merging the media of drawing and painting, *Cry, What Shall I Cry?*, as well as the *Selah: Stations of the Cross* series, capture Wolff's delicate, complex investigation of the universal and individual power of religious narratives and the transcendent nature of everyday experience.

Karen C. Gonzalez

197.
Plate VII, from *Selah: Stations of the Cross*, 1987
Gouache on white wove paper
6 7/16 × 8 9/16 in. (16.3 × 21.7 cm)
Gift of the Artist
2002.2831.7/15
Signed lower right "Dee Wolff," in pencil
Inscribed lower left "1987–VII," in pencil

198.
Plate XIV, from *Selah: Stations of the Cross*, 1987
Gouache on white wove paper
6 1/4 × 8 3/8 in. (15.8 × 21.2 cm)
Gift of the Artist
2002.2831.14/15
Signed lower right "Dee Wolff," in pencil
Inscribed lower left "1987–XIV," in pencil

Notes

1. Dee Wolff, correspondence with the author, January 2004, Blanton Museum of Art Archives, The University of Texas at Austin.
2. Dee Wolff to Annette Carlozzi, March 15, 2002, Blanton Museum of Art Archives, The Univeristy of Texas at Austin.
3. Alison de Lima Greene, *Texas: 150 Works from the Museum of Fine Arts, Houston* (Houston: Museum of Fine Arts, 2000), 104.
4. Wolff, correspondence with the author.
5. Quoted in *Paperworks: An Exhibition of Texas Artists* (San Antonio: Witte Museum, 1979), 42.
6. Quoted in *Paperworks*, 42.
7. Quoted in Reine Hauser, exhibition review, *Artnews* 83 (November 1984): 89.
8. Wolff, correspondence with the author.
9. Wolff, correspondence with the author.

Robert Yarber

b. Dallas, 1948

w. New York, 1967–1971; New Orleans, 1971–1974; Dallas, 1975; Austin–San Francisco, 1976–1985; New York–University Park, Pennsylvania, 1985–present

Motel lobbies and bedrooms, glitzy casinos and fancy hotels, swimming pools, the night horizon of large cities, darkened movie theaters, and other sites of American leisure act as stages for personal dramas and erotic encounters in Robert Yarber's paintings. Since the early 1980s, Yarber has used these polished, glamorous locales to point to a dark and often desperate void in the souls of his cartoonish characters. Mingling lust with violence, Yarber's paintings are both foreboding and amusing, and, despite the seeming fulfillment of their desires, his characters are essentially lonely and haunted by boredom and emptiness.[1]

Yarber's early development as an artist coincided with a period of tumultuous change, both in the national political scene and in the artistic circles with which he was associated. He was born and raised in Dallas. His mother, a former child-actor and fashion model, and his father, who opened the first Holiday Inn in Dallas, typified the suburban, middle-class American experience of the 1950s, an experience that persistently informs Yarber's paintings. In Dallas in 1963, Yarber remembers seeing President Kennedy moments before his assassination—this traumatic event would stay with him for years.[2] In 1964, after visiting an exhibition of paintings by Francis Bacon, Piet Mondrian, Jean Dubuffet, and Max Beckmann, he began painting diners and restaurants in an expressionist (or what he called "visionary") style. Attracted by the bohemian scene in Dallas, Yarber read Jack Kerouac, Friedrich Nietzsche, and William Blake. He also spent hours at local movie theaters, sometimes watching as many as nine films a day. Altered states of perception and hallucination fascinated Yarber, as they did many young people of his generation. By the mid-1960s he had decided to pursue an eight-year "systematic disarrangement of the senses" in an effort to defy the conventions and expand the boundaries of his parents' reality.[3]

In 1967 Yarber moved to New York to attend art school at The Cooper Union. While there, he studied with Paul Georges, Rudolf Arnheim, Dore Ashton, and Hans Haacke. Invited to attend meetings of the Figurative Alliance because of his association with Georges, Yarber became part of a circle of painters who met weekly at Alfred Leslie's studio to debate art and politics as well as the roles of allegorical and figurative painting. He later noted that the palpable tension between proponents of figurative art and then-current explorations of Minimalism and Conceptual art enlivened these discussions (which included such artists as Sidney Tillim, Philip Pearlstein, and Alex Katz).[4] Despite his affiliation with the Figurative Alliance, Yarber was unsure of his commitment to realism, and he moved to New Orleans in 1971 to explore his own direction in painting, one unconstrained by the dichotomy between figurative painting and Minimalism/Conceptual art.[5]

While in New Orleans, Yarber created a series of sculptures, performances, and paintings of Mao Tse Tung. The Mao paintings, which he continued through 1975, anticipate aspects of his later style. Returning to Dallas for a short while, Yarber became involved in the budding Texas Funk School, which included Vernon Fisher and James Surls and juxtaposed Texas imagery with pop culture references. Fisher's Conceptual and narrative-based art contributed to the development of Yarber's hotel narratives, started in 1975. Before leaving Dallas for San Francisco, Yarber began *Apraxic Women* (1976), his first major painting to employ the swimming pool as a setting.[6] Interested in out-of-control behavior and influenced by philosopher Maurice Merleau-Ponty and literature on abnormal psychology, he investigated what he called "the apraxic body" or "the body incapable of performing purposeful activity."[7] Commencing with literal apraxia and painting a range of behaviors from catatonia to hyperkinesia, Yarber eventually began to incorporate dreamlike imagery and fantastic actions such as flying into his paintings. Flying and its correlate, falling, symbolize rapture and torment, the momentary ecstasy of falling in love while warning of the inevitable descent and impact of love's loss. Eros and Thanatos, love and death, constitute the major themes of Yarber's work.[8]

In *Triangle* (1983, plate 199), three figures stand at the intersection of two hotel hallways. The squat figures face each other with arms extended, forming three points of a triangle. The remainder of the hallway is empty and foreboding. Neon pink, blue, and green light from the windows spills across the generically patterned carpet like multicolored confetti, while the figures are alternately bathed in these gaudy colors or cast into inky shadow. As is typical of his approach, Yarber manipulates color and perspective to create a sense of vertigo. Here he positions the viewer so that she assumes the role of a voyeur or perhaps even a surveillance camera, observing the drama unfold from above.[9] As Ida Panicelli noted,

> *Yarber . . . will not let us escape the uncomfortable voyeurism of witnessing the most trite expression of love's sentimentality—the powerful transgression of the obscene. We find ourselves . . . living the same obsessions as the characters—the unrealizable desire for the other, the difficulty of commitment, a subtle and impalpable violence.*[10]

Yarber achieved considerable critical success in the 1980s. In 1984 he exhibited in the 41st Venice Biennale, and in 1985 he had his first solo exhibition at Sonnabend Gallery in New York. That same year, his work appeared at the Whitney Biennial. In 1987 a trip to Rio de Janeiro inspired him to create panoramic images. Since the 1980s, Yarber has continued to rework, refine, and elaborate thematic imagery similar to that found in *Triangle*. He not only investigates the intersection of the surreal and the quotidian, he depicts the eruption of private moments in public spaces and the enactment of our most intensely felt desires, fears, and emotions.[11]

Laura A. Lindenberger

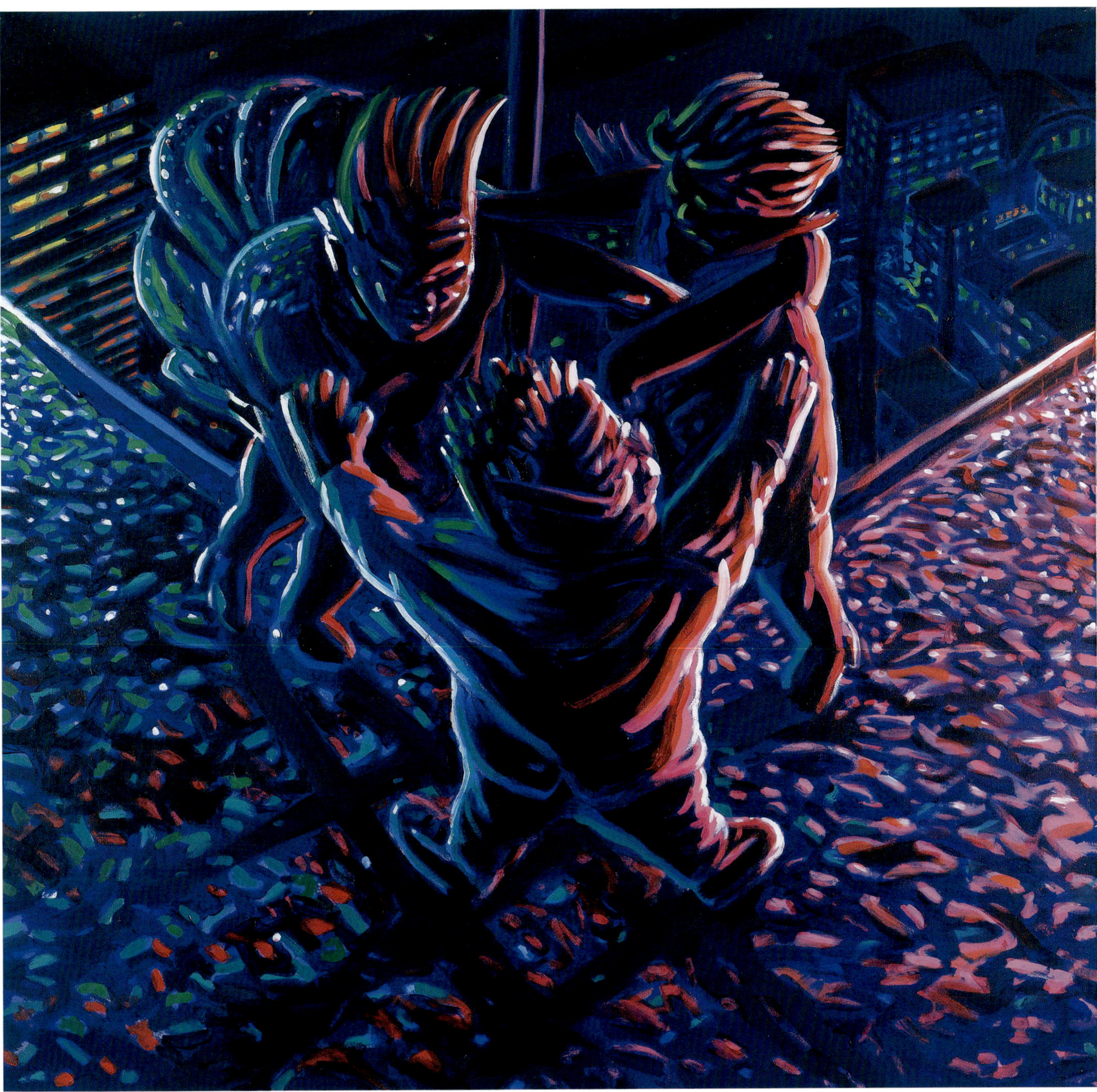

Notes

1. Eleanor Heartney, "Robert Yarber," *Artnews* 86 (November 1987): 191.
2. Sanford Sivitz Shaman, *Robert Yarber: Paintings, 1980–88* (University Park, Pa.: Palmer Museum of Art, Pennsylvania State University, 1989), 4.
3. Shaman, 7.
4. Shaman, 9.
5. Mary Haus, "Robert Yarber's Unbelievable Lightness of Being," *Artnews* 90 (January 1991): 137.
6. During this period Yarber also taught at The University of Texas at Austin.
7. Shaman, 20.
8. As Suzaan Boettger wrote, Yarber's "grand desires for union of self with Other, and of both with the Cosmos, are laden with fear, and with the flight of self from self-consciousness. They unite Eros and Thanatos. The motif projects a passionate desire to risk annihilation for these ecstatic unions—with self/other/cosmos—and the terror of doing so and crashing down to the very material ground below" ("Some Enchanted Evenings: The Paintings of Robert Yarber," *Arts Magazine* 62 [February 1988]: 71).
9. Robert Yarber, artist statement, in *New Work: New York/Outside New York* (New York: The New Museum of Contemporary Art, 1984), 55.
10. Ida Panicelli, untitled essay accompanying "A Rare Kind of Dread," an artist project by Robert Yarber in *Artforum* 29 (summer 1991): 29.
11. Suzaan Boettger, "Robert Yarber: Sonnabend Gallery," *Artforum* 24 (January 1986): 86.

199.

Triangle, 1983

Oil on canvas
65 × 65 in. (167 × 167 cm)
Michener Acquisitions Fund and the Archer M. Huntington Museum Fund
1984.80

Provenance: Purchased from Patrick Gallery, Austin, 1984

Peter Ford Young

b. Pittsburgh, 1940

w. New York, 1960–1969; traveled throughout Europe, the Middle East, and Latin America, 1969–1971; Bisbee, Arizona, 1971–present

Capitalist Masterpiece #26 (1968, plate 200) belongs to a series of large, colorful abstractions that Peter Ford Young began in 1963 and intended as a protest against the New York art world, which he considered "competitive, vapid, [and] fadish [*sic*]."[1] Young aimed his critique not only at the commercialism of the gallery system but at what he saw as the unimaginative and even conformist nature of the art being produced at that time. While working as a painter in New York in the 1960s, Young struggled to reconcile the creative impulse with the demands of the marketplace, grappling with the question, "How can an artist put his heart or soul into a work when he pretty surely knows that its collector is after self-importance and profit?"[2] Young satirized the gallery system in his ironically titled Capitalist Masterpiece series, which lived up to its name, capturing the attention of critics and collectors and earning him a degree of success.[3]

Young was born in 1940 and grew up in rural Pennsylvania and Santa Monica Canyon, California. Raised in a family that encouraged his interest in the arts, Young studied abstract painting with Russian émigré Ida Abbey during his early teens. When he was eighteen and traveling through Mexico, he met the poet George Oppen, who inspired him toward political activism. Young attended Pomona College in Claremont, California, before moving to New York, where he attended New York University, completing a bachelor's degree in art history in 1963.

Capitalist Masterpiece #26 is comprised of an intricate pattern of brightly colored, interlocking, abstract shapes that fill the entire canvas, much like a mosaic. Young created these shapes with the tip of a paintbrush handle, which he used to apply a series of dots to the surface of the canvas. The dots, whose colors range from blue and red to purple and green, call to mind gemstones, each one equal in size and distance from the other. This tightly controlled pattern lends the composition an evenness and precision, leading one critic to remark that Young's paintings "may be intoxicating but they are also marvels of discipline."[4] Indeed, the large scale of *Capitalist Masterpiece #26* envelops the viewer in an environment of seemingly infinite space, with the discrete, geometric dots creating the sensation of a pulsating rhythm. In addition to its social and political subtext, the Capitalist Masterpiece series also set out to depict the full spectrum of light. Eventually, Young concluded that "color is light and light is color,"[5] characterizing the environments of color in his paintings as optical sensations rather than depictions of concrete matter.

Young cites rock and roll, religion, and occultism among his interests, and as it did for many artists of the 1960s, the popular culture of the period exerted a profound impact on his outlook and his art. Additionally, he executed many of his paintings from that decade while smoking marijuana, which might partially account for their psychedelic colors and shapes.[6] For his part, Young believes the relationship between modern art and hallucinogenic drugs has been largely underestimated, going so far as to claim in 1970 that it was LSD that gave him the ability, as he put it, to "see the air."[7]

In the 1960s, Young belonged to a loose affiliation of artists known as the "Lyrical Abstractionists," which included Larry Poons, Lawrence Stafford, Ronnie Landfield, and Dan Christensen, among others. Young also shared a great deal with a more diverse group of artists, including Walter De Maria, Vito Acconci, and Richard Serra, who, like Young, found part of their motivation in a desire to denounce the commodification of artistic practice.

After living in New York for nine years and working in the same studio building as Stafford and Landfield, Young left the city in 1969, presumably out of frustration with the competition and commercialism of the art world. He then traveled throughout Europe, the Middle East, and Latin America, spending some time with the Boruca tribe in Costa Rica before settling in the western United States. In response to a 1970 questionnaire, Young wrote, "I've been making hand carved acrylic beads and have forsaken painting. I'm presently living near a mountain near Hurricane Utah."[8] Young currently lives and works in Bisbee, Arizona.

Lara Kuykendall

Notes

1. Peter Ford Young to Richard Hirsch, February 2, 1970, Blanton Museum of Art Archives, The University of Texas at Austin.
2. Young to Hirsch.
3. For example, see Ellen H. Johnson, "Peter Young: A Chronology of the Work," *Artforum* 9 (April 1971): 58–63.
4. Stephen Westfall, exhibition review, *Arts Magazine* 58 (June 1984): 38.
5. Quoted in Johnson, 61.
6. Johnson, 59.
7. Peter Ford Young, lecture delivered at Oberlin College, Ohio, November 23, 1970. Quoted in Johnson, 61.
8. Young to Hirsch.

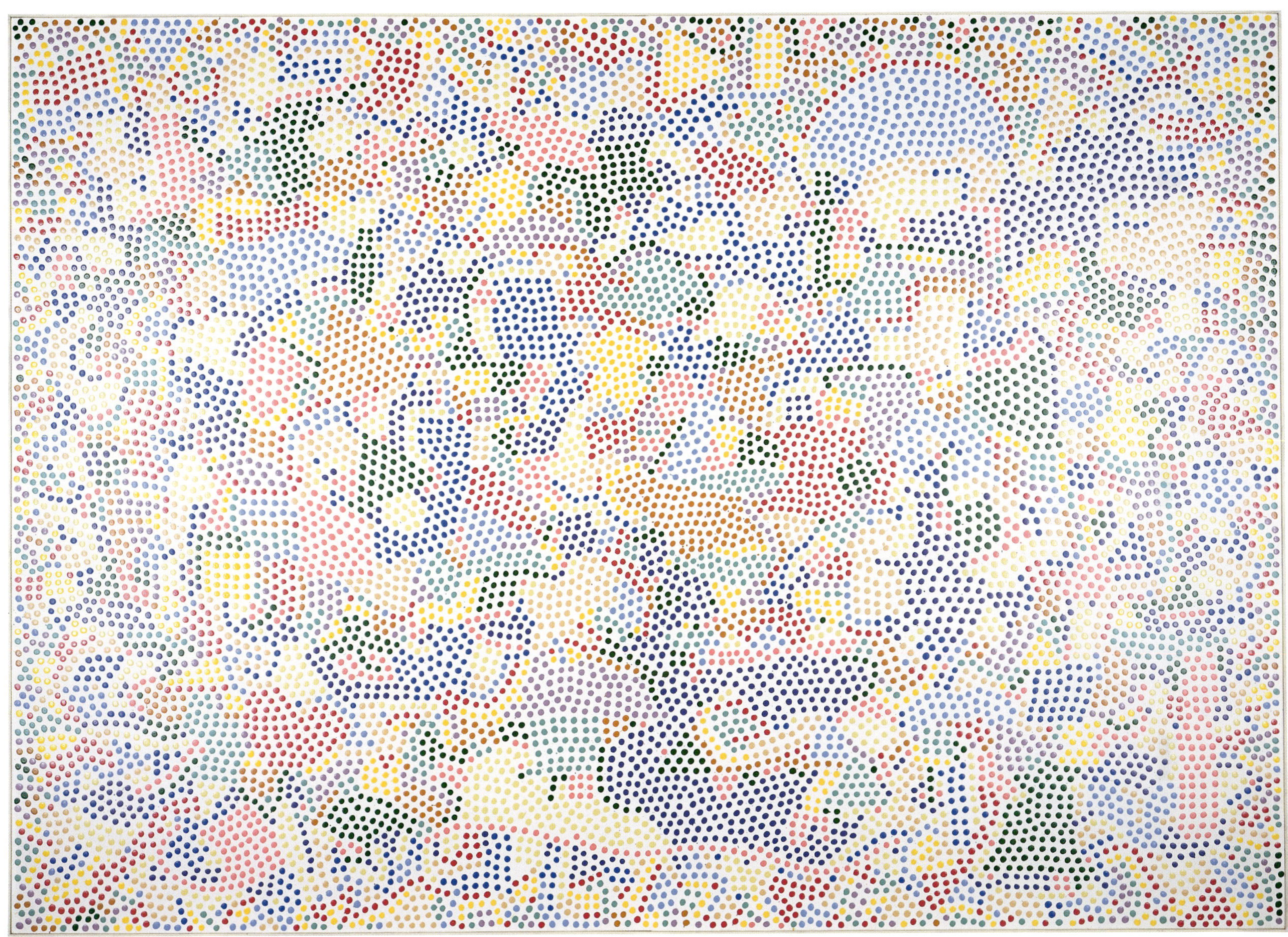

200.

Capitalist Masterpiece #26, 1968

Acrylic on canvas
96 × 132 in. (244 × 336 cm)
Gift of Mari and James A. Michener
G1968.133

Provenance: Purchased by James Michener through Richard Bellamy, New York, 1968
Signed verso, upper left "#26 1968 Peter Young"

Karl Zerbe

Berlin, 1903–Tallahassee, Florida, 1972

w. Munich, 1921–1924; Italy, 1924–1926; Munich, 1926–1934; Boston, 1935–1955; Tallahassee, Florida, 1955–1972

Historians generally characterize American art during and after World War II in terms of the ascendancy of Abstract Expressionism, but an often overlooked group known as the Boston Expressionists, led by Karl Zerbe, also attracted a great deal of critical success during this period. The Boston Expressionists experimented with new media and employed a figurative yet expressionistic style to communicate humanist themes. Zerbe himself is remembered primarily for his influence in the classroom and for helping to revive the technique of encaustic, contributions that have tended to overshadow his oeuvre. Critics unanimously applaud, however, his innovative use of media and composition, especially in his paintings from the 1940s.

Born in Berlin in 1903, Zerbe spent his childhood in Paris and Frankfurt and his teens in Munich. He initially decided to study chemistry, but in 1921 he turned his aspirations toward painting. Zerbe studied under Josef Ebers at the Debschitz School in Munich, where he was exposed to German Expressionism, and received a grant in 1924 that allowed him to study in Italy for two years. During this period, Zerbe also encountered a group of German artists affiliated with the *Neue Sachlichkeit* (New Objectivity) movement, which combined a realist style with social critique.[1]

When Zerbe returned to Munich in 1926, he earned critical praise and commercial success. Yet few of his early paintings still exist, since the Nazi Party labeled them "degenerate" and ordered them removed from official collections in the early 1930s. Charles Kuhn, then director of the Germanic Museum (now the Busch-Reisinger Museum) at Harvard University, who collected so-called "degenerate" art, invited Zerbe to present his first one-person show in the United States in 1934. After a brief visit to Germany in 1935, Zerbe returned to the Boston area and settled into a teaching position at the Fine Arts Guild in Cambridge. Two years later, he became head of the painting department at the Boston Museum School of Fine Arts, where he remained until 1955.

After his permanent immigration to the United States in 1935, Zerbe's style of painting changed dramatically. Previously, his interests had gravitated toward landscapes and still-lifes, which he rendered in either watercolor or gouache. Now he began to focus on portraits and allegories. At the same time, he drew upon his training as a chemist, experimenting with a wide variety of media including Duco enamel and encaustic. Used by the ancient Egyptians and Greeks, encaustic involved mixing powdered raw pigment into heated wax and applying it directly to the support. Zerbe was excited by this fast-drying method, since it permitted him to quickly build up layers of paint, thereby achieving a wide range of technical effects, from smooth, translucent finishes to heavy, grainy impasto. Encaustic also allowed for easy edits by simply reheating and melting the wax. Zerbe used encaustic throughout the 1940s, and it was his medium of choice for *Woman on Trapeze* (1946, plate 201). Because of its rapid drying time, encaustic was poorly suited to painting from life, so Zerbe often made preparatory sketches in pencil and watercolor before transposing the subject into encaustic, as he most likely did in this case.

Zerbe probably found inspiration for *Woman on Trapeze,* along with his other paintings of circus performers, during his brief travels with the Barnum and Bailey Circus in 1945.[2] In contrast to his often crowded allegorical paintings of the same time, here the female trapeze artist is the psychological and physical focus of the painting. The red ring of the stage and the red circle on the floor frame her body, while the vertical red stripe in the circus tent draws attention to her curious expression. Zerbe contrasts the deep red of the tent with the acidic green of both the trapeze artist's costume and the circular light directly above her head. Painted in thick encaustic, the green light lends an ominous tone to the painting. Zerbe's use of color to extract an emotional response from the viewer is typical of the German Expressionist paintings he looked to for inspiration. *Woman on Trapeze* is also noteworthy for its unusual perspective. Zerbe positioned the trapeze artist in mid-air, far above the audience below. She swings toward the viewer, who hovers even higher than she in dizzying but intimate proximity. Yet the viewer is excluded from the trapeze artist's personal thoughts, and the reason behind her satisfied grin ultimately remains a mystery.

Woman on Trapeze sold the first time it was exhibited, in 1946. That same year, it was included in *Sixty Americans Since 1800,* an exhibition organized by the State Department that traveled to Egypt and Europe. (By 1941 Zerbe had earned United States citizenship and married an American woman.) Appropriately, the United States used Zerbe, a refugee painter whom the Nazi regime fifteen years earlier had labeled "degenerate," to project an image of freedom abroad.

In 1949 Zerbe developed a severe allergy to encaustic, the medium that had defined his American career, so he began to paint using acrylics. He encouraged his students to continue to experiment with various techniques while maintaining a focus on humanistic expression, but discouraged them from visiting contemporary painting exhibitions in New York, with the exception of Willem de Kooning's.[3] In order to accommodate his health, Zerbe left Boston in 1955 for a post at Florida State University, where critical attention to his work declined. He retired from teaching in 1970 and passed away two years later. As a teacher, and especially in his revival of encaustic, Zerbe is acknowledged to have greatly influenced a younger generation of artists, including David Aronson, Bernard Chaet, and Jasper Johns.

Sarah Holian

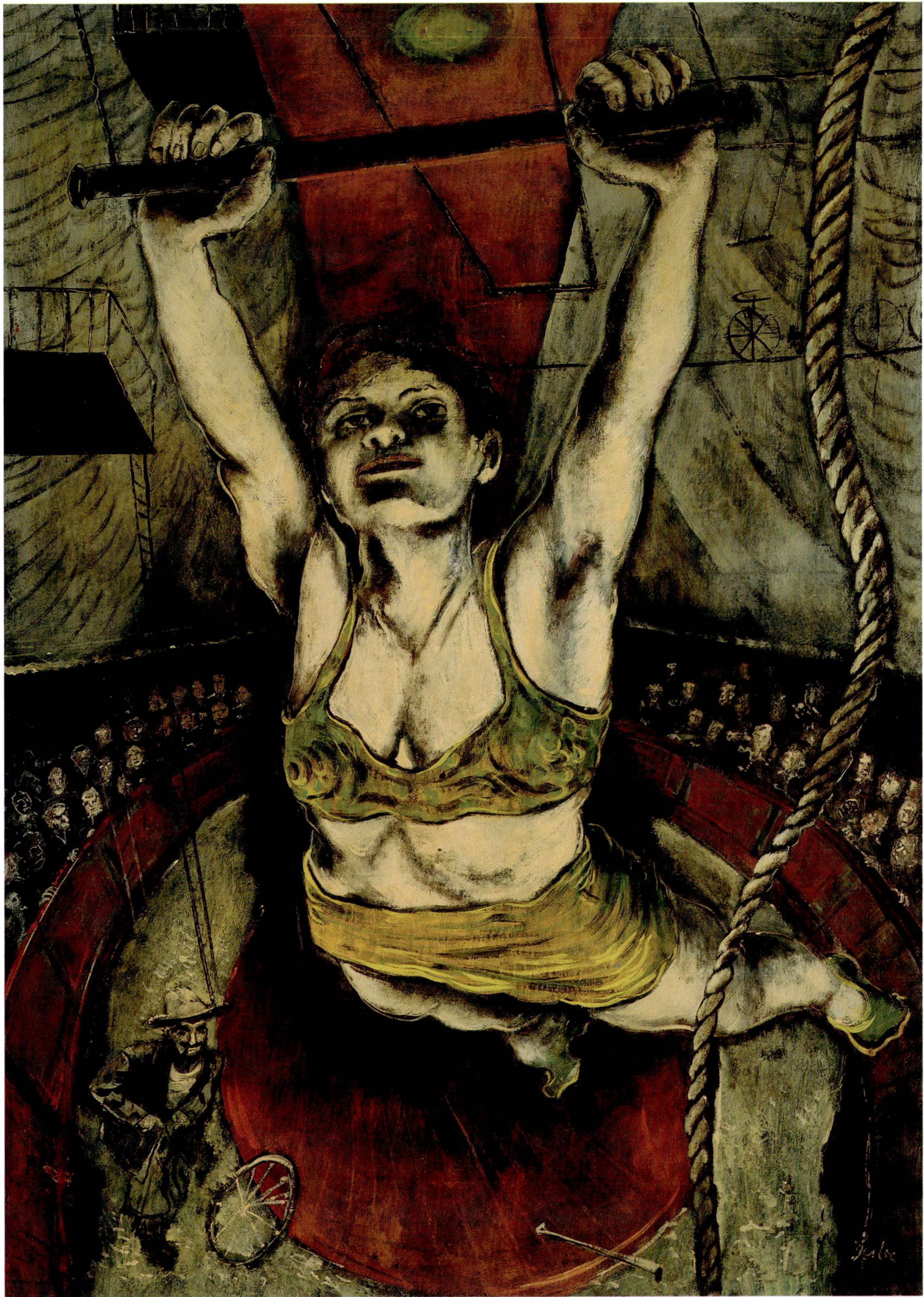

Notes

1. George Grosz, Otto Dix, Carl Hofer, and Max Beckmann were some of the New Objectivity artists with whom Zerbe was familiar.
2. Nicole Chism Griffin, "Circus Imagery in Karl Zerbe's *Woman on Trapeze*: Sources and Significance," unpublished essay, November 12, 1998, Blanton Museum of Art Archives, The University of Texas at Austin.
3. Bernard Chaet, "The Boston Expressionist School: A Painter's Recollections of the Forties," *Archives of American Art Journal* 20, no. 1 (1980): 25. For a broader discussion of Zerbe's teaching, see Pamela Edwards Allara, "The Humanist Vision: Expressionist Art in Boston: 1945–1985," in *Expressionism in Boston: 1945–1985* (Lincoln, Mass.: DeCordova Museum, 1986), 10–28.

201.

Woman on Trapeze, 1946

Oil and encaustic on canvas
53 × 37 in. (135 × 95 cm)
Michener Acquisitions Fund
P1969.7.6

Provenance: Downtown Gallery, New York, 1946; IBM Collection, Endicott, New York, 1946; Hirschl & Adler Galleries, New York, 1967; purchased from Hirschl & Adler Galleries, 1969
Signed lower right "Zerbe"

Marguerite Zorach

Santa Rosa, California, 1887–Robinhood, Maine, 1968

w. Paris–Europe, 1908–1911; Asia, 1911; New York, 1912–1923; New York–Robinhood, Maine, 1923–1968

William Zorach

Eurburg (Yurburkas) Lithuania, 1889–Bath, Maine, 1966

w. New York, 1902–1908; Paris, 1910–1911; Cleveland, 1911–1912; New York, 1912–1923; New York–Robinhood, Maine, 1923–1966

Marguerite Thompson painted *Rites of Spring—Olympic Offerings* (1909, plate 202) two years before she met her husband and creative collaborator, artist William Zorach. It was an exhilarating time for the curious and independent twenty-two-year-old, as she immersed herself in the cultural life of Paris. She visited galleries, took art courses, experimented with new styles of painting, and sought advice from some of the most important avant-garde literary and artistic figures of the day, including Pablo Picasso, Gertrude Stein, and Henri Matisse.

Marguerite had grown up comfortably in Fresno, California, and had excelled in art courses in high school. But it was not until 1908, when she first visited Paris with her aunt, that she was exposed to an environment in which she could thrive and develop the skills she needed to become a serious competitor in the international art world. Marguerite remained in Paris for the next four years. During the first two years, she took courses briefly at an academic art school and visited cities across Europe, but as she traveled, she grew increasingly disenchanted with academic painting.[1] Instead, her thoughts continually returned to the Fauvist and Cubist works she had seen at the Salon d'Automne in 1908, as well as her encounters with Picasso, Stein, Matisse, and others. In style and subject matter, *Rites of Spring* encapsulates the ideas that charged Marguerite's ambition and guided her painting during these early years, particularly her experimentation with the Fauvist juxtaposition of scorching colors to express emotion and her participation in the avant-garde revival of idyllic subject matter.

Marguerite's engagement with Matisse's theories of color and form are evident in the pyramidal arrangement of lavender-colored, faceless, mostly asexual figures gathering flowers amidst brilliant blue and red mountains. The figures' movements are fluid and graceful, their bodies supple and lissome. The carefully balanced colors and shapes create a sensation of joy that corresponds to Matisse's conviction that "Expression . . . does not reside in passion bursting from a human face or manifested by violent movement. The entire arrangement of my picture is expressive: the place occupied by the figures, the empty spaces around them, the proportions, all of that has its share."[2] Marguerite also employed a technique known as "cloisonnisme," from the French word for "partition," to outline the figures and fill them with solid color. The result recalls cloisonné enamelwork and stained glass and indicates her study of Gauguin, who had first used the painting technique in the 1880s.

The dreamlike landscape and blissful figures in *Rites of Spring* also position the painting within the mode of idyllic subject matter, which numerous avant-garde artists and writers chose to depict from the early 1890s to World War I. The Fauves, Matisse especially, whose painting *The Joy of Life* (1905–1906) perhaps best exemplifies the tradition, embraced this utopian imagery with particular enthusiasm. As Margaret Werth has demonstrated, such scenes of mythic communities gave modernist painters a vehicle through which to explore the complex workings of memory, fantasy, and anticipation. Utopia's transcendent image of the future was concerned not with nostalgia, but with a concentrated expectation of the future. *Rites of Spring* reveals Marguerite's confident participation with the Fauvists in this multifaceted dialogue. Specifically, its tranquil depiction of elegant figures who seem to have overcome the burden of individuality as they participate in a collective springtime ritual responds to Matisse, who wrote only a year earlier, "What I dream of is an art of balance, of purity, and tranquility, without any disquieting or preoccupying subject matter."[3] In her emulation and personalization of Matisse's ideas and subject matter, Marguerite demonstrated an ambition to compete with Paris's most accomplished avant-garde artists even as a student.

On the other side of the same canvas, Marguerite's husband, William Zorach, painted a portrait of their daughter, Dahlov, around 1920, more than a decade after the completion of *Rites of Spring.* At the time he created *Dahlov with a Baby Carriage* (plate 203), William was transitioning from a career devoted to painting to one of sculpture. He had trained as a painter at the National Academy of Design from 1908–1910 and in 1911 at the Académie de la Palette in Paris (along with Marguerite), where he absorbed new tendencies in modern painting, especially Post-Impressionism.[4] When he and Marguerite settled in New York in 1912, they became immersed in the world of modern art. Their investigation of new aesthetics expanded to include Cubism, a style that had intrigued William in Paris but that he did not fully embrace until after the Armory Show in 1913.[5] After arriving in New York, he also developed an intense appreciation for central African art and American folk art. In this portrait of Dahlov, the artist's interests in Cubism and American folk art converged to create a dynamic portrait riddled with internal contradictions.

The year of Dahlov's birth, 1917, marked William's initial foray into the medium of sculpture.[6] During the summer of that year, he began to explore woodblock printing. Working on a woodcut using panels extracted from the front of a bureau, William made a fully developed bas relief, which he titled *Waterfall.*[7] In the summer of 1918, his access to a kiln inspired him to explore further the modeling of three-dimensional figures. Similar to *Dahlov with Baby Carriage,* two sculptures that he made of his toddler daughter around the same time,

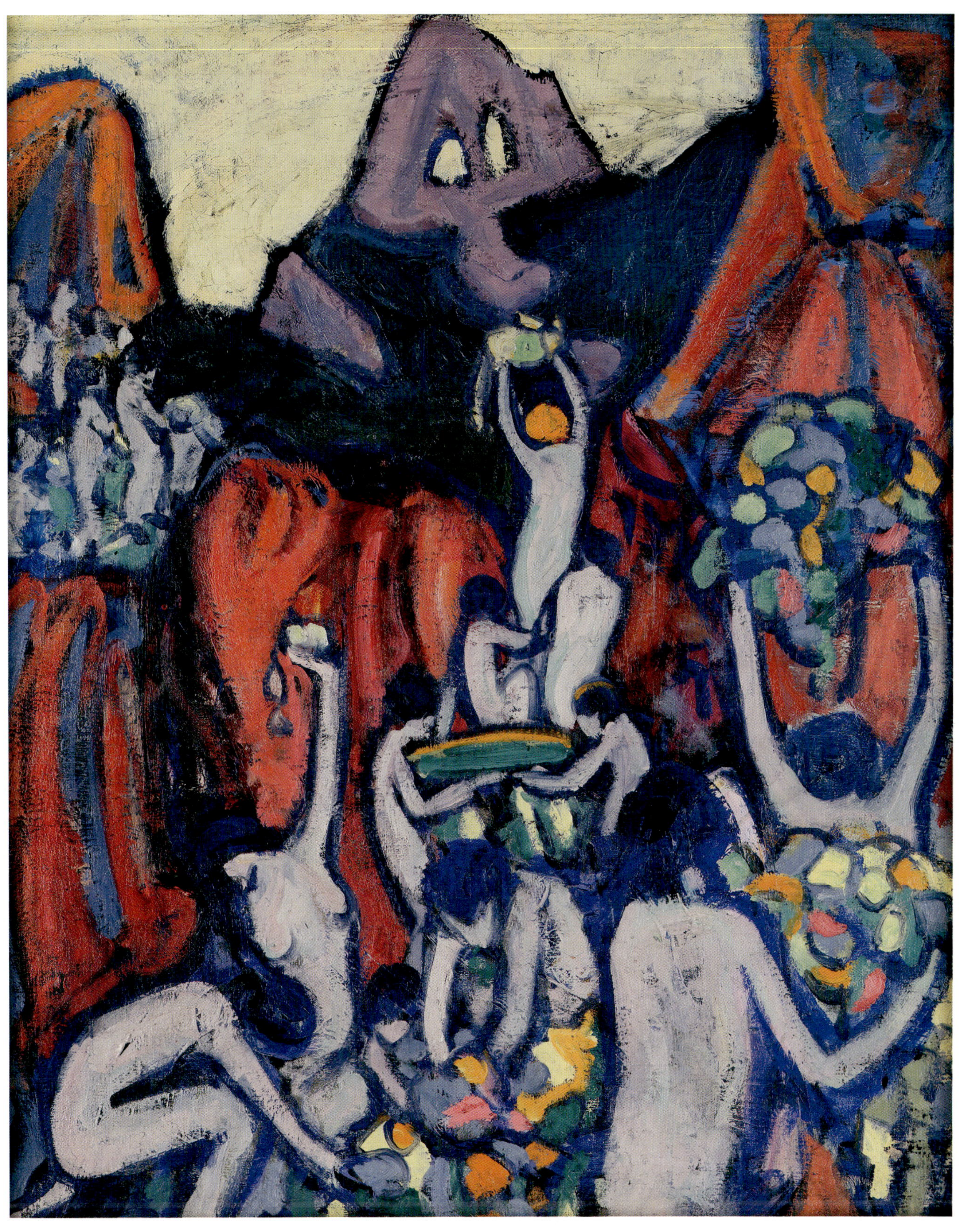

202. Marguerite Zorach
Rites of Spring—Olympic Offerings (recto), 1909

Oil on canvas
31 × 25 in. (78.2 × 63.5 cm)
Michener Acquisitions Fund
1985.74

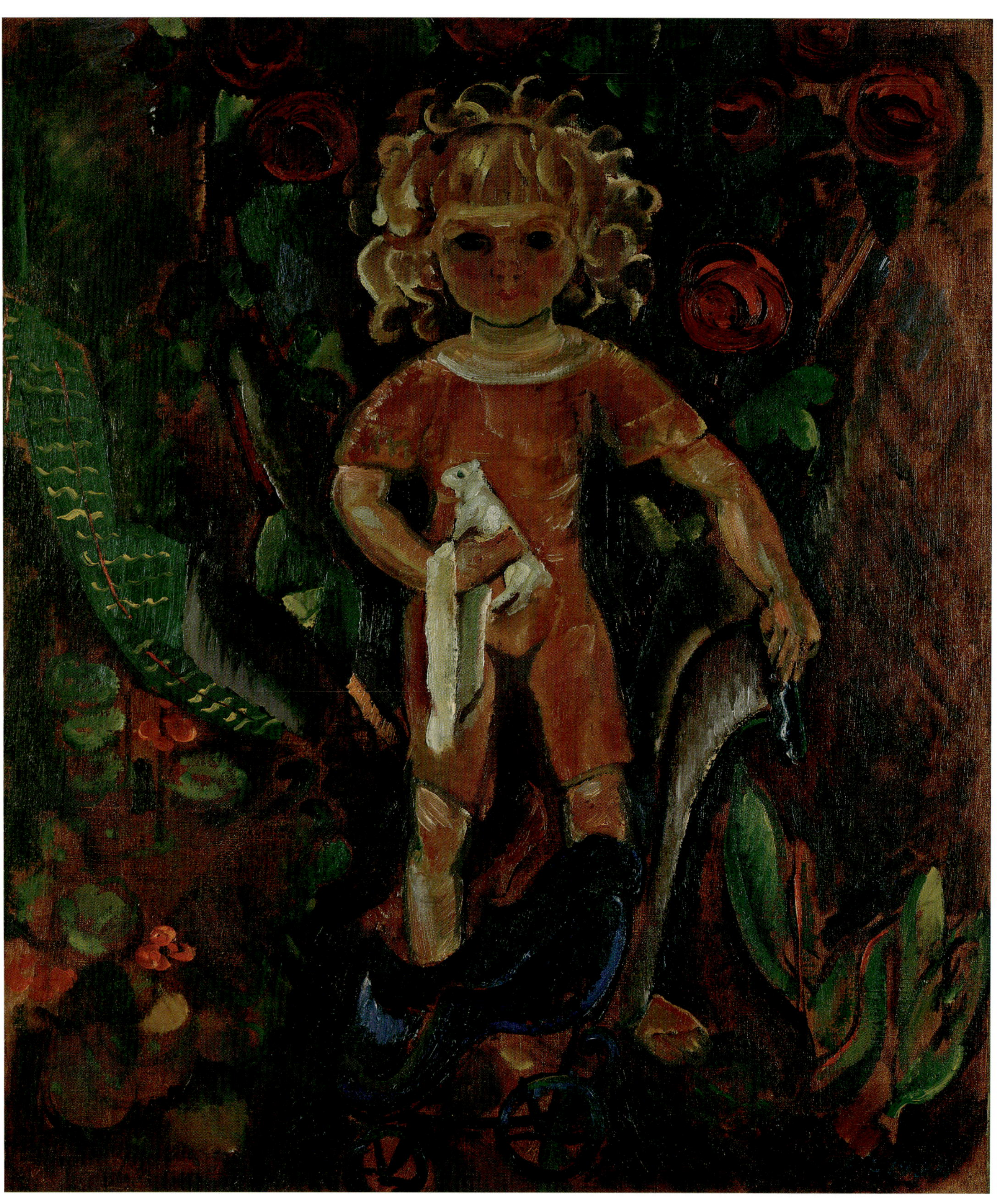

203. William Zorach

Dahlov with Baby Carriage (verso), c. 1920

Oil on canvas
30¾ × 25 in. (74.9 × 62.4 cm)
Michener Acquisitions Fund
1985.74
Signed lower right "Zorach 1920"

Provenance: Collection of the Zorach Family; purchased from Kraushaar Galleries, New York, 1985

First Steps (1918) and *Kiddie Kar* (1923), demonstrate the convergence of folk art and Cubism in his handling of objects and the human figure. *Dahlov with Baby Carriage* makes evident the artist's interest in juxtaposing rounded sculptural forms with flat surfaces. Set against the dark, earthy tones of an abstracted garden, Dahlov's colorful figure assumes an even greater animation and immediacy. Her arms and legs are clearly defined with outlines that recall woodblock printing, but unlike the effect of sharply delineated woodcuts, here the modeling creates the illusion of three-dimensionality. Zorach's handling of Dahlov's face, on the other hand, resulted in features that are flat and consist of simplified shapes reminiscent of American folk art.

As Roberta Tarbell pointed out, by 1916 the Zorachs had experimented with abstract, angular, Cubist forms as well as the geometrical shapes of central African sculptures.[8] In contrast to the fragmented forms that filled William's early paintings, however, those in both *Dahlov with Baby Carriage* and his early sculptures are generally organic and flowing. The link between his former Cubist-inspired paintings and his new, more cohesive style can be found in his handling of the baby carriage. Its exaggeratedly long, gray handle is an exception to and stands apart from the folk-inspired, flattened facial features and the well-proportioned sculptural curves of the child's figure. The handle of the carriage, with its abstracted and elongated form, is more akin to the Cubist works that characterize William's early career than it is to his later work. In its synthesis of all the styles available to him as a young modern artist working in New York, *Dahlov with a Baby Carriage* epitomizes a career devoted to experimentation.

The coexistence of Marguerite's ambitious *Rites of Spring*, painted at the beginning of her career, with William's portrait of Dahlov, created as he began to shift from a career as a painter to one as a sculptor, simultaneously captures each artist's individuality and shared drive to push their work to new and ever greater possibilities.

Dorothy Moss

Notes

1. Jessica Nicoll, "To Be Modern: The Origins of Marguerite and William Zorach's Creative Partnership, 1911–1922," in Jessica Skwire, ed., *Marguerite and William Zorach: Harmonies and Contrasts* (Portland, Oregon: Portland Museum of Art, 2001), 19.
2. Henri Matisse, quoted in Margaret Werth, *The Joy of Life: The Idyllic in French Art, circa 1930* (Berkeley, Calif.: University of California Press, 2002), 14.
3. Quoted in Werth, 222.
4. Nicoll, 20.
5. John I. H. Baur, *William Zorach* (New York: Whitney Museum of American Art with Frederick A. Praeger Publishers, 1959), 13.
6. Baur, 14.
7. Nicoll, 37.
8. Roberta K. Tarbell, "Life and Work: Marguerite and William Zorach in New York and Maine, 1922–1968" in Skwire, ed., 51.

NEW PERSPECTIVES ON AMERICAN ART: ARTISTS, CRITICS, AND ART HISTORIANS RESPOND TO THE COLLECTION

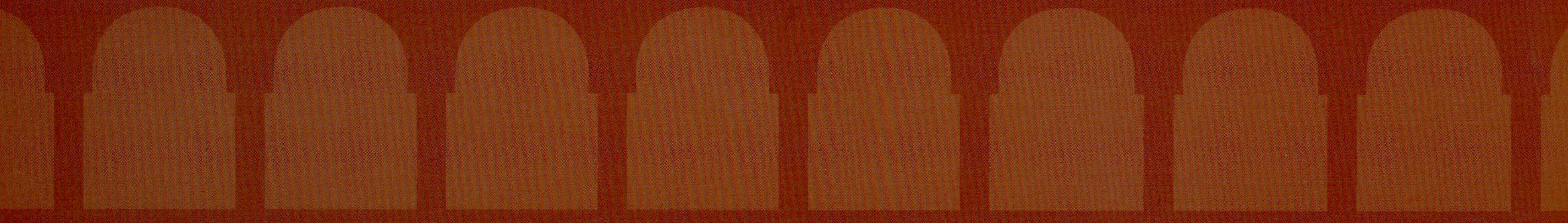

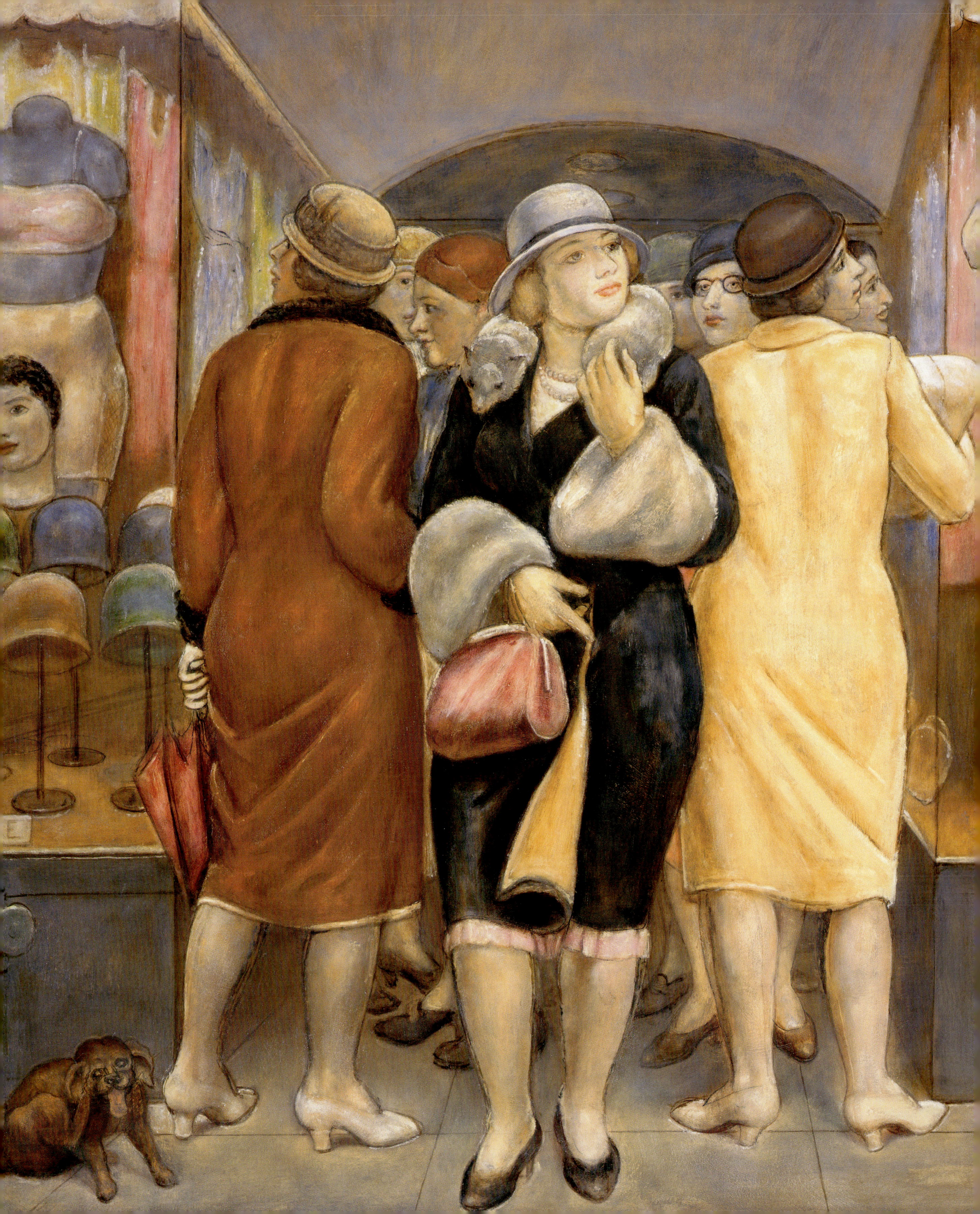

KENNETH HAYES MILLER'S VENUSES
WHY DO THEY SHOP?

Karal Ann Marling

Kenneth Hayes Miller's *Sidewalk Merchant* (1932/1948, figure 1) is one of the quirky treasures of the Michener Collection. Like the mysterious *Chatham Square* (1931, plate 114) by Miller's student Reginald Marsh, where Marsh imported the principal figure from another canvas, gluing it into place, research reveals that *Sidewalk Merchant* was substantially reworked by the artist. Whereas Marsh's urban subject matter clearly refers to the social interests of the Depression era, Miller's works—painted in the same streets, often before the same storefronts—seem less straightforward. Compared with the moody, sometimes exuberant work of his pupil and confidant, Miller's painting is curiously lacking in both movement and emotion. The difficulty of reading *Sidewalk Merchant* is compounded by the fact that it began life as a different composition—one that troubled the artist during both its creation and subsequent deconstruction.

The earliest published references to Miller's *Merchant* date the work to 1932, when the picture was called *Fourteenth Street*, or *In Fourteenth Street*.[1] One of the few major articles on Miller, written by Harry Salpeter and published in *Esquire* in October 1937, leans heavily on an interview Salpeter conducted with the artist, in which Miller discussed *In Fourteenth Street* and the process of painting it in minute detail, down to the leash on the dog and the corresponding folds in the garments. Milton Brown published a blurry photograph of *In Fourteenth Street* in his *American Painting From the Armory Show to the Depression* of the early 1950s. Brown's book, the bible for aspiring postwar Americanists, codified the existence of a Fourteenth Street School, "a revival of the Ash Can School" centered on New York's Union Square and led by the then recently deceased Miller by virtue of his prominence as a teacher. Brown had little empathy for Miller's work: he was "too prone to academicism, too concerned with theories and methods."[2] Yet by providing a glimpse of one of Miller's few large-scale canvases, Brown would help to sustain interest in the artist and in one of his key pictures—a picture that, by the time Brown published his book, had been changed into *Sidewalk Merchant*, disappearing thereafter into the storage vaults of the Rehn Gallery. "Miller did not sell many works during his lifetime," Virginia Zabriskie wrote in 1970 to the director of what became the Blanton Museum of Art. She continued, "Major paintings remain in the estate," which she then represented.[3]

Several years ago, while exploring the nether regions of the photograph collection in the University of Minnesota's Department of Art History, I came upon a huge cache of images of American paintings deposited with the slide curator sometime in the 1950s. None of the paperwork survives, but oral tradition has it that the photos came from the files of the *Magazine of Art* and its related family of journals. However it arrived in my hands, the cache does contain a sharp, fully readable

Kenneth Hayes Miller, *Sidewalk Merchant*, 1932/1948 (detail, figure 1)

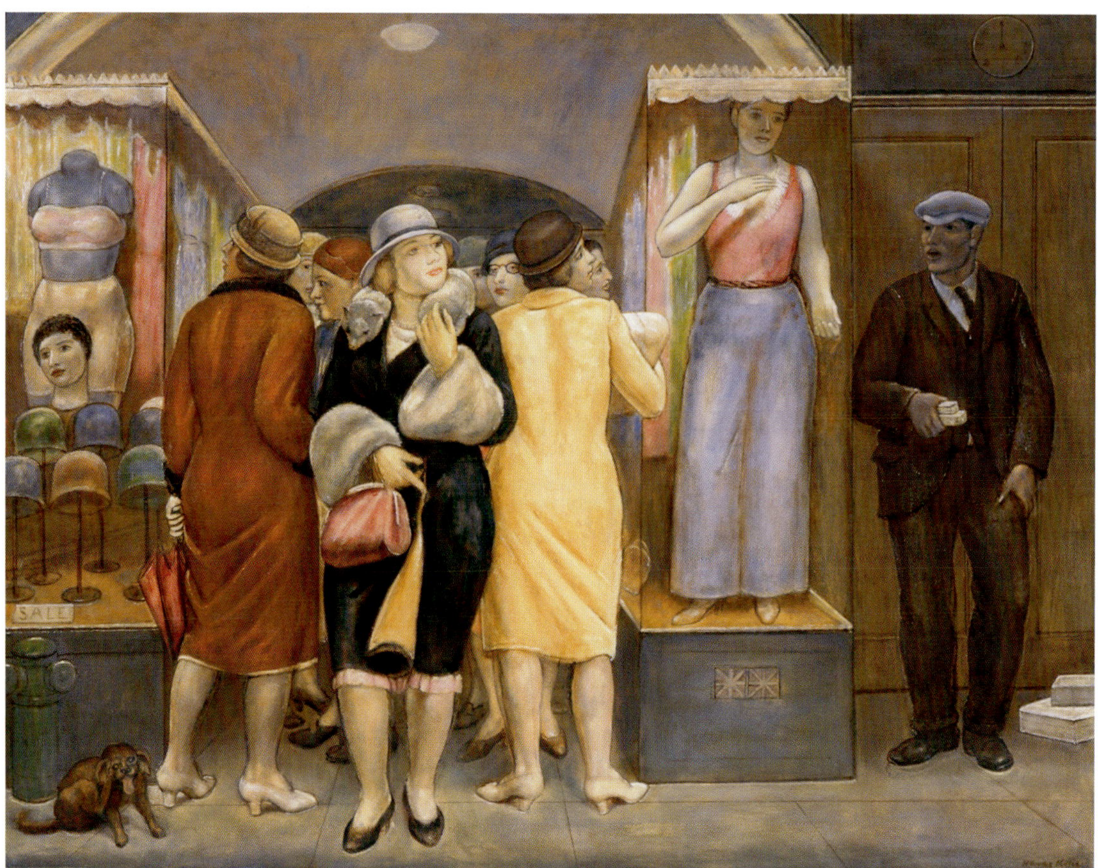

Figure 1. Kenneth Hayes Miller, *Sidewalk Merchant*, 1932/1948; oil on plywood, 36 × 45⅝ in.; Gift of Mari and James A. Michener, 1991.275

photograph of the work in question in its unaltered state. The photograph, taken by the Bogart Studio on East 23rd Street, is stamped with the name of the Frank Rehn Gallery. The glossy is identified on the reverse as "*In Fourteenth Street* by Kenneth Hayes Miller." Under that ink script is a faint pencil notation: "now *Sidewalk Merchant*."[4]

The photograph is especially helpful in deciphering the foreground detail almost lost in the blurry Brown reproduction. The second sidewalk square from the right edge of the frame, for example, is clearly signed "Hayes Miller '32." The fluttering objects on the pavement reveal themselves as leaves: the time is early autumn 1932, perhaps the worst moment in the deepening Depression, as Herbert Hoover and Franklin D. Roosevelt battled for the heart of America.

In the summer of 1932, at the climax of his work on a series of related pictures begun in the early 1920s, Miller's letters came to focus on a large painting that he was then developing, one on the subject of shopping. He referred to the work as his "shopping subject": this is the painting he initially would title *In Fourteenth Street*. By this point in his career, Miller had found etching better suited to his talents and decidedly less burdensome than painting: his usual practice was to draw or etch in the mornings and wrestle with the demon painting in the afternoons. In between, he indulged himself in a regular noontime walk around the 14th Street neighborhood, where he had maintained a studio since 1923.[5] "Every day at noon I go out and walk or stroll for 20 minutes to see the crowds out for lunch," he told a friend in 1925.[6] These walks gave him ample opportunities to observe such characters as he would include in his "shopping subject." In July 1929, for example, he noted that "short skirts and bare legs" were now the uniform of the day for the women in the bustling street below his windows.[7] But despite years of firsthand observation, the so-called "shopping subject" tormented Miller throughout the summer of 1932, perhaps because the large, multifigure composition was the most complex he had attempted to date: it included eight women, several mannequins or parts thereof, a man, a dog, and a series of tricky spatial recessions. "The shopping subject is developing," he wrote early that August, "But . . . it is a hard struggle." And again, two days later, after painting all morning and all afternoon, tormented by the need to make crucial artistic decisions soon: "The shopping subject draws toward some kind of completeness. The figures are nearly up to the finishing touches. The man lags a little. The architecture is still somewhat sketchy."[8]

On August 15, with the picture still on the easel and still not finished to his satisfaction, Salpeter came to call on Miller. It was almost certainly on this afternoon that the journalist took down the artist's detailed commentary on the formal elements of *In Fourteenth Street* and that, five years later, he would incorporate into his *Esquire* article. Perhaps the talking helped. Visiting friends showed no enthusiasm for the clutch of shoppers, which now demanded four hours of hard labor every day. "I am having the usual difficulty in satisfying myself with the latest painting," he confessed. "This shopping subject, as I expected, has proved to be particularly exacting. I shall perhaps start the frame this week."[9] Miller, haunted by doubt and uncertainty, called it quits on August 22.

Miller's uneasiness about the picture could only have been confirmed by the fact that this, a major work, did not sell, even after the art market began to recover from the Depression in the later 1930s. Nor were commentators and tastemakers interested enough to champion the canvas. *Art Digest* used a photo of *In Fourteenth Street* to illustrate

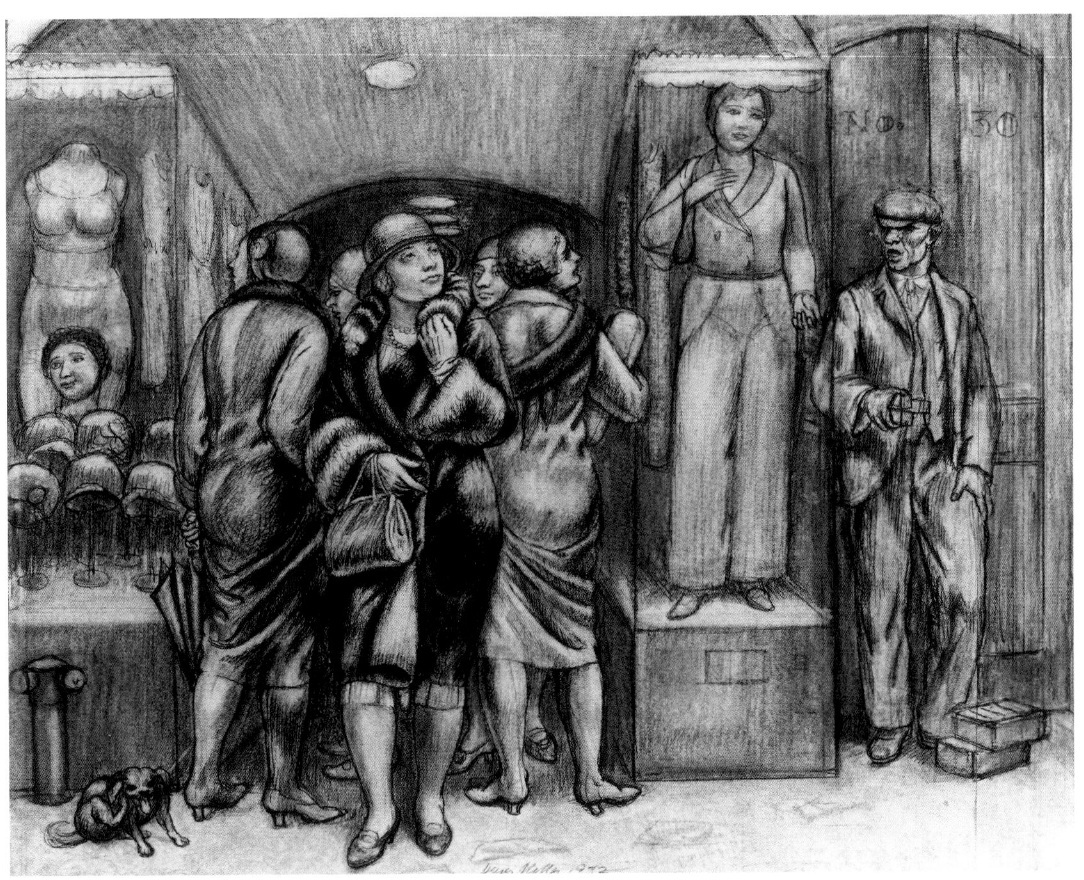

Figure 2. Kenneth Hayes Miller, *On Fourteenth Street*, 1932; ink and crayon on paper, 12 × 15 in.; Whitney Museum of American Art, New York; Purchase, 45.20

reaction to a Miller solo exhibition at the Rehn Gallery in 1935. The article was headed, "Critics Lose Some Enthusiasm for Miller" and quoted Margaret Breuning of the *New York Post,* who deplored the lack of feeling or real significance in the typical Miller work. "In fact, most of the canvases seem prodigious feats of organization," she observed, "integrating solid forms and sweeping rhythms into a final structure that is built up with architectural soundness. But in this fireworks of architectonics, emotional content seems to be left out, warmth or vitality of any kind."[10]

Whether Miller took such criticism to heart or whether the general indifference to the painting reinforced his own nagging dissatisfaction with it, the artist undertook a major revision of *In Fourteenth Street,* which is generally believed to have occurred around 1940. The accepted date of the reworking is based on the connoisseurship of Lincoln Rothschild, author of the 1974 monograph *To Keep Art Alive, The Effort of Kenneth Hayes Miller.* In 1973 Rothschild wrote to the owners of Miller works (including The University of Texas at Austin) seeking permission to reproduce them. At the museum's request, he offered an opinion on the proper dating of what was now entitled *Sidewalk Merchant.* "I judge 'Sidewalk Merchants' [*sic*] to be fairly late, probably toward the beginning of the period 1940–'45 in which Miller moved on from single shoppers and concise groups of three or four figures to more crowded and extensive street scenes," he told the researcher in charge of the picture, which was then undated in the records of the Michener Collection.[11] "The problem is complicated somewhat by the presence in works repainted at a later date of characteristics of the earlier stage," Rothschild admitted in closing.[12] Later, in his book on Miller, Rothschild elaborated on the issue of repaintings and reworkings especially common in the last years of the artist's life, a time "when his production flagged under pressures of physical distress and professional disappointment."[13] The caption beneath his reproduction of *Sidewalk Merchant* dates the picture to "c. 1940," with no mention of an earlier state.[14] Rothschild apparently did not know that the painting is a reworking of *In Fourteenth Street.* One final bit of evidence comes from a cryptic note in the curatorial files of the Whitney Museum, which owns an ink and crayon drawing entitled *On Fourteenth Street* (figure 2). The drawing, boldly signed and dated 1932 in the center foreground below the feet of one of the three would-be Graces window shopping among the hats and lingerie, may be a preparatory study for an etching, which often followed a painting in Miller's practice.[15] On the other hand, the Salpeter interview mentions a monotone cartoon for the painting and "after that five drawings in black and white, each one of which differed from the others in the working out of various details."[16] At several telling points, the details of the Whitney drawing do differ significantly from photographs of the original 1932 canvas: the emphasis on the genital region of the mannequins in the window is notably greater in the drawing, for instance, and the face of the one at the left, modeling a hat, is more lifelike, in the manner of Reginald Marsh, who delighted in confusing items of window display with the shoppers examining them. But more important still is the Whitney note uncovered by art historian Ellen Todd. Initialed R.I., it reads as follows: "Mr. Miller told me October 6, 1948 that he has repainted his 'In Fourteenth Street,' making minor changes. . . . He said the picture was originally painted in the 1930s. He is now going to call it 'Sidewalk Merchant.' It is 3' × 3'9"."[17]

If the Whitney note can be trusted—and the dimensions reported are close enough to the framed measurements of the Blanton's picture—

then the reworking was undertaken within the last four years of Miller's life (he died in 1952) and stands as a kind of testament to the importance of the work (and its failure) to the artist himself. "Can't repeat the past?" cries Gatsby in F. Scott Fitzgerald's great 1925 novel, "Why of course you can!"[18] Miller, who read the book in the summer of 1926, was not impressed: it was "less than I expected," he wrote.[19] But like Gatsby, he believed that he could change the past with a change of title and a few strokes of the brush.

The most significant, if not the most obvious, change comes at the far right edge of the composition, immediately behind the lone male figure. A somewhat critical and isolated observer of the teeming mass of women in the first version *(In Fourteenth Street),* he has become the titular hero of the second *(Sidewalk Merchant).* At the same time, the distinct compartment of space in which he stands—which was a paneled doorway leading to the upper stories atop the retail level—has become an elevator door, surmounted by an indicator dial pointing straight up: the car, it seems, is on the fifth floor. In the first version, the old-fashioned lettering on the door reads "No. 30," or the address of Miller's own studio on East 14th Street from 1928 to 1952. He too, in other words, is in *In Fourteenth Street,* along with the characters in the picture.

The shop itself is Lord's, a women's furnishings store that was located, in the 1930s, at 32 East 14th Street (just next door to Miller's studio entrance) according to the city directory.[20] And photographs of every building and block in the city, taken for purposes of taxation in 1941 and preserved in the New York Municipal Archives, clearly show that most if not all of the buildings on the block, including Miller's, were five stories tall with large studio or showroom windows above street level (figure 3).[21]

In light of the geographic specificity of *In Fourteenth Street,* it is tempting to conclude that the picture must be about Miller himself, the tenant at No. 30, observing shoppers as was his practice. The

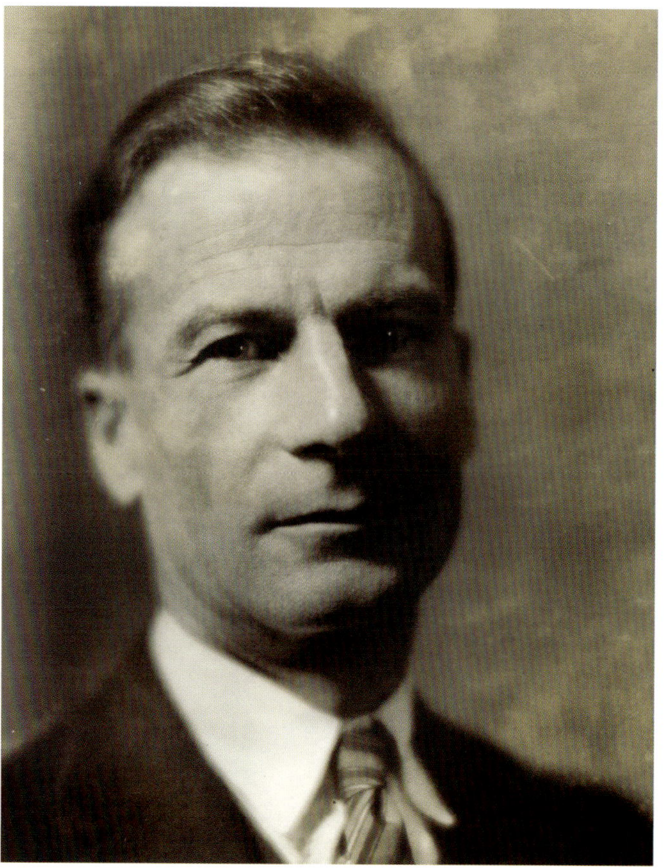

Figure 4. *Portrait of Kenneth Hayes Miller,* c. 1930s; photograph by Carlo Leonetti; Whitney Museum of American Art, Library, New York

saturnine appearance of the onlooker at the right is consistent with Miller's own: the frontispiece to Alan Burrough's sympathetic monograph, published in 1931 under the auspices of the Whitney Museum, shows the same severe, bony face and prominent nose (figure 4).[22] According to Burroughs and others, his manner matched his sharp, even forbidding appearance. During Miller's Wednesday afternoon salons in the 14th Street studio, he was taciturn, reserved, watchful: "a tall, gaunt man with a long cold nose [and] an air of quiet but very compelling authority."[23]

If the watcher is indeed Miller—a kind of modern-day Paris offering a candy bar or a package of cheap soap to the fairest of the three goddesses posing in *In Fourteenth Street*—his disguise is appropriate. Photographs of the Union Square neighborhood taken after the onset of the Great Depression consistently show vendors, usually lone men with a few boxes or a crate, creating instant streetcorner emporia on any vacant smidgen of pavement.[24] Neckties, socks, gadgets, wart cures, bits of coconut in the shell: all found their places at curbside.[25] Albert Halper's much-quoted 1933 novel *Union Square* specifically mentions the hawkers and the barkers with their song sheets, needlebooks, and bars of chocolate.[26] It also recalls that a class of sidewalk merchants in sympathy with radical causes often sold Communist-made goods among the Japanese toys and springless watches, including "Red" candy bars straight from Moscow.[27] Miller's political beliefs seem not to have colored his work, but the Whitney's sketch of (or for) the original painting shows barlike

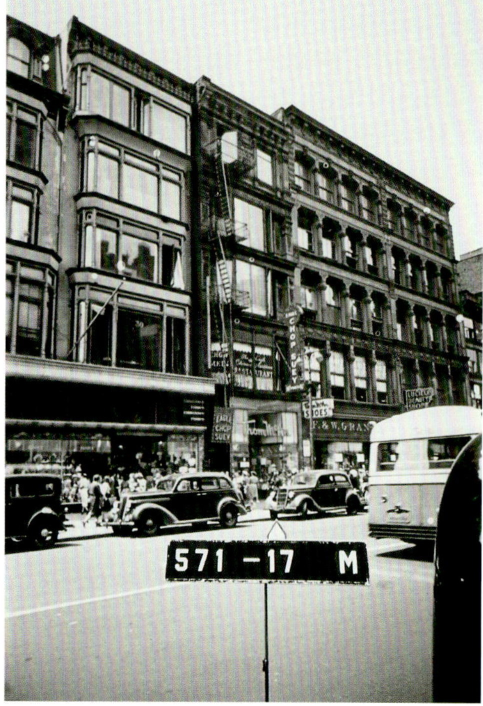

Figure 3. Fourteenth Street, New York, 1941

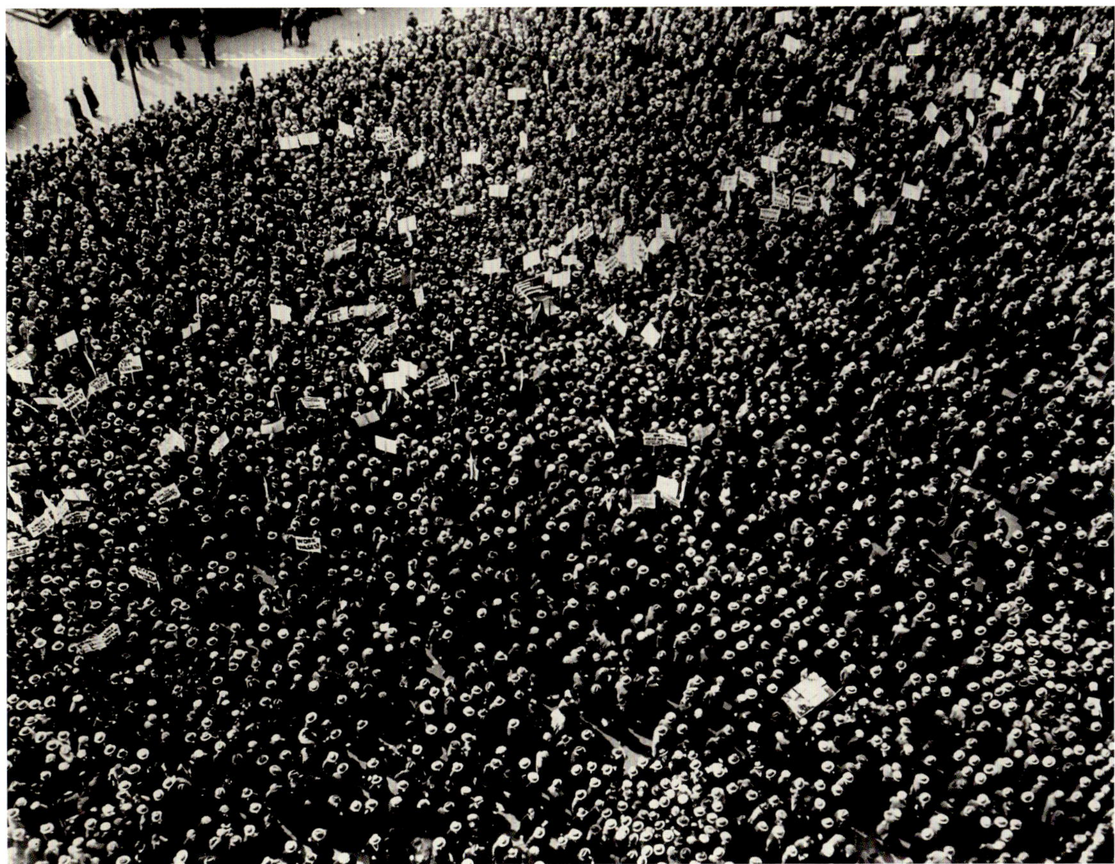

Figure 5. Sale day at S. Klein's, New York, 1920s–1930s

forms in the boxes in front of the man in the workman's cap. Miller, like Halper, saw those vendors of "Red" candy bars abroad in his neighborhood.

In the revised version of the painting, the "sidewalk merchant" is now the focus of the work. But the boxes of merchandise have been shoved aside (leaving the left leg of the salesman in an odd position) and his face, thanks to slight modifications in the contours and lighting, has been turned to confront the viewer of the picture more directly, as befits the titular subject of the canvas. He no longer seems so interested in the shoppers. Instead, he remains meditative and still before the elevator headed straight to the top. This is no longer the entrance to Miller's studio, identified by some banal street number, but the entrance to a conveyance headed for the world of art, high above the bustle of the street. In relinquishing its earlier burdens of geographic autobiography and figural classicism, the reworked painting acquires new baggage—an aura of regret for unsold paintings and a faltering reputation. If only the mistakes could be corrected. If only the legs were thinner. If only the folds of the coats and the swing of the leash were less obvious devices for binding the female group together with a pattern of rhythmic line. If only. . . . If only. . . . In the Salpeter interview, given toward the end of a long period of struggle and uncertainty, Miller was so sure that he was getting it right. "The leash of the Pekinese tied him into the body of the painting and . . . the creases in the women's dresses were plotted to lead the eye from and to the center, and . . . the dominant note was struck by the arc of the store front and the suggestion of depth beyond," he proudly proclaimed.[28] Items designed to assert a fictive recession on a flat canvas also echoed the shapes of ovular hats and cuffs, breasts and calves. Arc answered arc, except in the space that contains the watcher or the creator of it all. He is neatly boxed in a series of rectangles and sharp angles, circumscribed in a male precinct beyond the show windows.

FUR, FLESH, GODDESSES

The dog once wore a leash—to keep it from sniffing the hydrant, to keep it close to its mistress in the red coat with a matching umbrella that evokes the kind of blustery autumn day when one's best furs can finally come out of mothballs. Miller called the dog a "he," a tiny, silly thing, but male, uncouth, a scratcher, a panter, a furry captive, like a live version of the beguiling stoles and collars and cuffs. The visual analogy between the dog's face and that of the fur piece draped around the neck of the centermost shopper is unmistakable. The little gray fox, however, is perky, alert, and well behaved, a ladylike pet, a forest sister to the woman who fondly strokes its tail.

In the 1920s and 1930s, according to cultural historian Jenna Weissman Joselit, fur was a fashion necessity. "Fur-fur-fur: never was the temptation greater to sink your chin in its opulent folds than today," enthused a fashion editor in 1919.[29] Once the prerogative of the rich, fur was now available to the many, including the bargain-hungry shoppers in the Union Square area in search of the latest styles at the lowest prices—shoppers who were apt to turn sale days at S. Klein's into riots (figure 5). At those times, confessed a shopper's guide to Manhattan, "ropes are put around the curbing, trucks are overturned and the event is counted a failure without the breakage of one plate-glass window and an ambulance call."[30]

Even during the Depression, the fur piece remained precious as a status symbol, a token of America's material blessings still available to

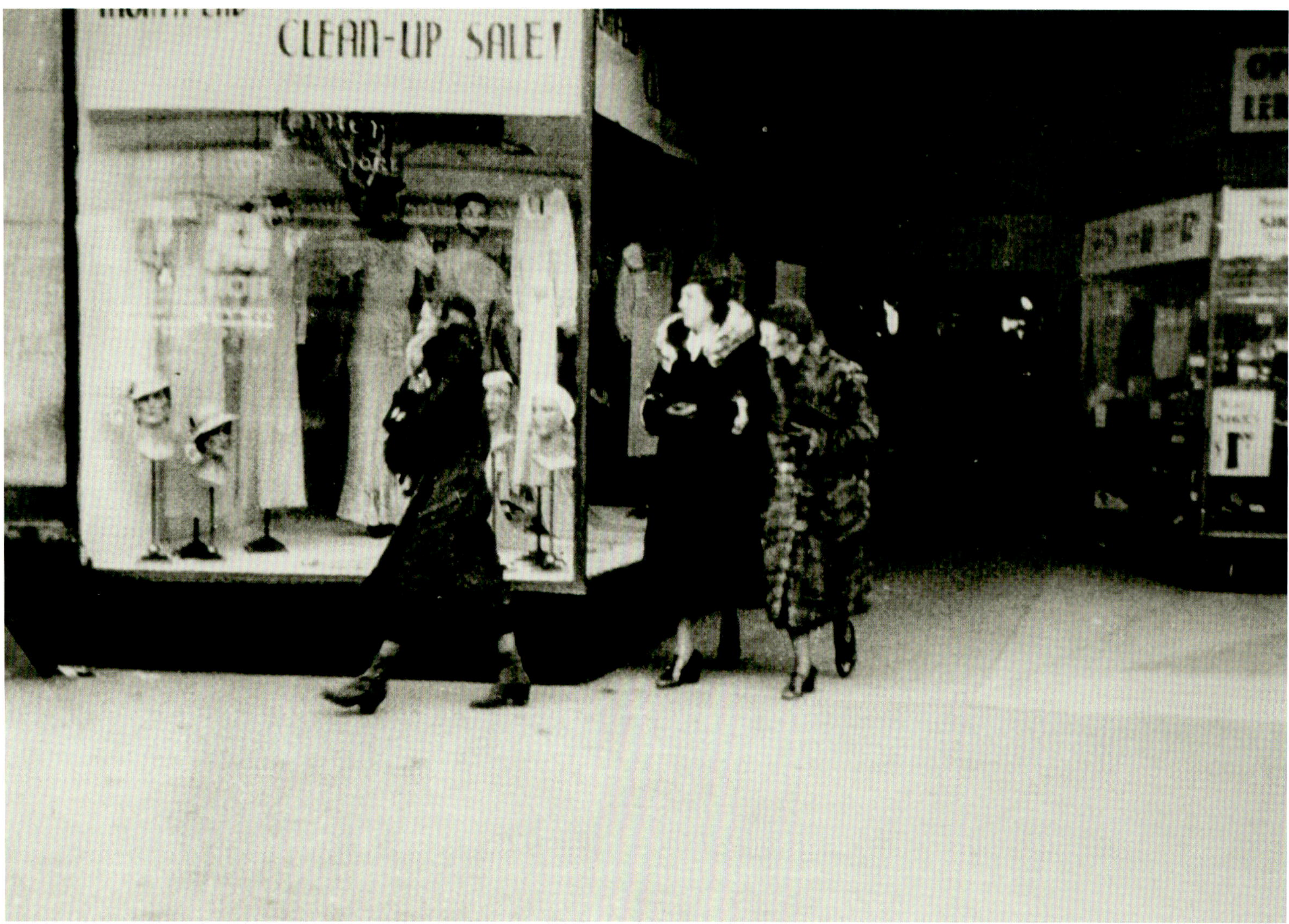

Figure 6. Women in furs next to mannequins, New York, 1920s–1930s

practically anyone willing to venture into the crowded shops around the Square (figure 6). There were summer furs, winter furs, and something called "coney," which was really rabbit dyed to look like fox or muskrat. The Sears catalog for 1932 offered heads-on Russian and Australian fox wraps for as little as $9.75, under a banner headline: "New York-To-You Fashion." Throughout the year when Miller labored over his painting, the pages of the *New York Times* were crowded with ads for "Fluffy Fox-like" scarves at bargain basement prices. Made of "thibetine," the fur of a Chinese goat "cleverly dyed to imitate blue fox," Wanamaker's sold them for a mere $9.75. Arnold Constable, on 5th Avenue, had genuine silver fox two-skin collars draped over coats that were knock-offs of Paris originals, all for $79. On 14th Street, of course, the prices were much lower.[31] Many garment factories economized by shipping their wool coats with narrow cuffs and no collars at all. Fur was more than a finishing touch. Why, it was an absolute, must-have item!

As the three fur-bearing shoppers stand there, in the passage between the shop windows at the center of the picture, it is apparent that they are posing like the women in the advertisements in order to show off a variety of garments from every elegant angle. The effect is of one shapely model pivoting slowly in space, from left to right, displaying all the possibilities of accessorizing a plain cloth coat. Is it last year's number—a little skimpy now, shorter than one might like, but elegantly lined in satin nonetheless and good for another season, with just the right scrap of fur tossed gracefully over one shoulder? The trio, too, is model-like in their impeccable blandness and sameness of facial features. Unlike the distinctive human types crammed like so many supporting actors into the rear of the entrance—the pale, the flushed, the fat, the lady with spectacles and too much lipstick—the faces of the three shoppers are almost identical to the plaster heads in the window: the same tilt of the head, the same carefully neutral expression. According to Ellen Todd, Miller never used live models.[32] His preference here was for the mannequins who quite properly inhabit the fashion parade in *Sidewalk Merchant*.

The mannequin is life at secondhand: to paint it is to copy a still-life, to make art of art or artifice. Although the scene ostensibly describes the vitality, vulgarity, and variousness of this place at the very heart of Gotham, the artist's static rendering of the central shoppers gives the impression of wooden and plaster figures assembled in the airless calm of the studio or in the artist's mind from mute, interchangeable parts. The shoppers are the merchandise. The mannequins are their own audience.

When questioned about *In Fourteenth Street* and its setting, Miller referred to Jean-Antoine Watteau and Peter Paul Rubens, who had used similar framing devices, albeit with antique architecture instead of store windows.[33] There is also a hint of deliberate archaism about the painting. The pajama-clad figure in the right-hand window could be a *kore*, a maiden from the Acropolis with her forearm extended as if to hold the garments of Athena, or to beckon us closer to the picture frame. As Rothschild was the first to observe, she points back toward a Golden Age lost beyond retrieval.[34] Can New York women in their cheap furs and flashy togs bear comparison with those of ages past, especially when they have been reduced to generalized solids, so many columnar limbs topped by the smooth, architectonic heads of plaster casts?

"I am not interested in subject matter of any particular kind," Miller would declare in a sort of manifesto written in 1944. "I touch contemporary life in themes relating to shopping, but what has absorbed me has always been simply the body."[35] At the same time, standardized bodies (and this is the strategy of the savvy window dresser) make costumes a source of greater interest. The use of contemporary garments is always a risky business for a painter: Regionalist Thomas Hart Benton—the master of observing modern fashion, makeup, and hairdos—risked making his work seem old-fashioned and quaint, or unmodern, to viewers approaching it from a distance of a mere seven years (the average fashion cycle). Benton had connections with Miller. He, too, lived in the Union Square area in the 1920s and early 1930s. A close friend of Marsh as well, who posed for one of the figures in his 1930 murals for the New School for Social Research, Benton even shared his formula for tempera painting on gesso with Miller.[36] Benton's revival of this Renaissance technique is another link to the art of the Old Masters who influenced his work. The plunging spaces of Tintoretto and the solemn attention to the mundane activities of daily life often embodied in Renaissance murals are also hallmarks of vintage Benton.[37] And like Miller, Benton referenced Western art's classical tradition in his works, placing classical and biblical figures in contemporary disguise.

Two of the major canvases of Benton's maturity refer openly to the iconography of the past. *Persephone* (1938–1939) shows the Greek goddess dozing amid the foliage of autumn and the harvest season, about to be led back into the underworld by the stealthy figure at the right (probably Benton himself). The other, *Susannah and the Elders* (1938), represents the biblical heroine taking a ritual bath somewhere in the Deep South as the elders spy on her like customers at a carnival peep show.[38] In both instances, contemporary details of costume and hairstyle make it obvious that these are American girls of the 1930s, reenacting the role of goddess or biblical heroine. They form a bond between Benton and the noble art of the past, between today's America and the glories of history. Of special importance in drawing these parallels are the vehemently contemporary high heels and other garments discarded in the grass in *Susannah and the Elders*. Susannah's white hat, for example, is a specific chapeau first seen by Benton on a 1932 sketching trip through the mountains of western Virginia, where he drew a Holy Roller camp meeting in the woods. Of great interest to him was the young girl who had risen from her place and pitched forward on the ground, moaning in ecstasy. In his autobiography, Benton made reference to his "Appalachian Oread" and her "little cheap but stylish hat," a detail used in two subsequent allusions in his work.[39]

Contemporary dress, the currency of 14th Street in 1932, thus makes a case for the existence of the eternal woman. Amid the calamities of the Great Depression, Miller's implicit allusions to art's age-old engagement with the female figure suggest an unbroken continuity between the Sears catalog and the sweep of human history. Depression or not, life goes on; a hat or a fur piece is a source of human delight whenever or wherever it may be found.

Grant Wood, the Iowa representative of Regionalism, had no ties to Miller or to Union Square: his world extended from Iowa City to Cedar Rapids and not much beyond. But he, too, was aware of the symbolic weight of modern costume as an indicator of class or status. *Appraisal* (1931) pits a woman from town against one from the farm in a tense battle of wits over the price of a chicken.[40] The town lady advertises her estrangement from the hardscrabble ethos of the barnyard by her clothing, a symphony in lush half-circles and curves, from her cloche hat to her fur collar, from her beaded bag to her own plump person. She is a consumer. The producer, by contrast, is as unfashionable as could be imagined, togged out in a home-knit cap and an old coat held closed by safety pins. Her side of the picture is spare and angular, from the spindly column on the front porch to the rickety fence in the center of the composition. The American past comes face to face with the present. Nature meets culture and is not altogether charmed by the encounter.

Miller's use of fashion was the issue on which his admirers and detractors most readily parted company. The artist's close friend Garet Garritt wrote one of the first articles on Miller for the *New Republic* in 1921, at the start of Miller's so-called fashion series. "Recently," Garritt stated, "he has painted the female figure in clothes, furs and fine millinery. . . . At a glance you might mistake one of these pictures for a striking popular magazine cover." But no, he continued. These are ironic images of humankind gilding the lily of God's creation. Or something more: "Is not the body clothed with flesh? Well, the flesh may be clothed with clothes and they are the same thing."[41] Alan Burroughs, later in the decade, also addressed the question of why a painter concerned with the "eternal verities" would take an interest in shoppers elbowing their way into bargain stores near Union Square. "Apparently," Burroughs reasoned, "he has been working toward the union of philosophic and physical exactness. He has been placing a hat of this season's style on the eternal shape which is a head."[42] Miller was the Masaccio of lower Manhattan.

By the time Miller died, however, such arguments (and the images that illustrated them) no longer dazzled; they were as passé as last season's millinery. In a cool review of the memorial show held at the Art Students League in 1953, Robert Coates of the *New Yorker* pooh-poohed the artist's "attempt to make Titian feel at home on Fourteenth Street and crowd Veronese into a department store."[43] Classical nudes gussied up in prewar finery held little interest for a

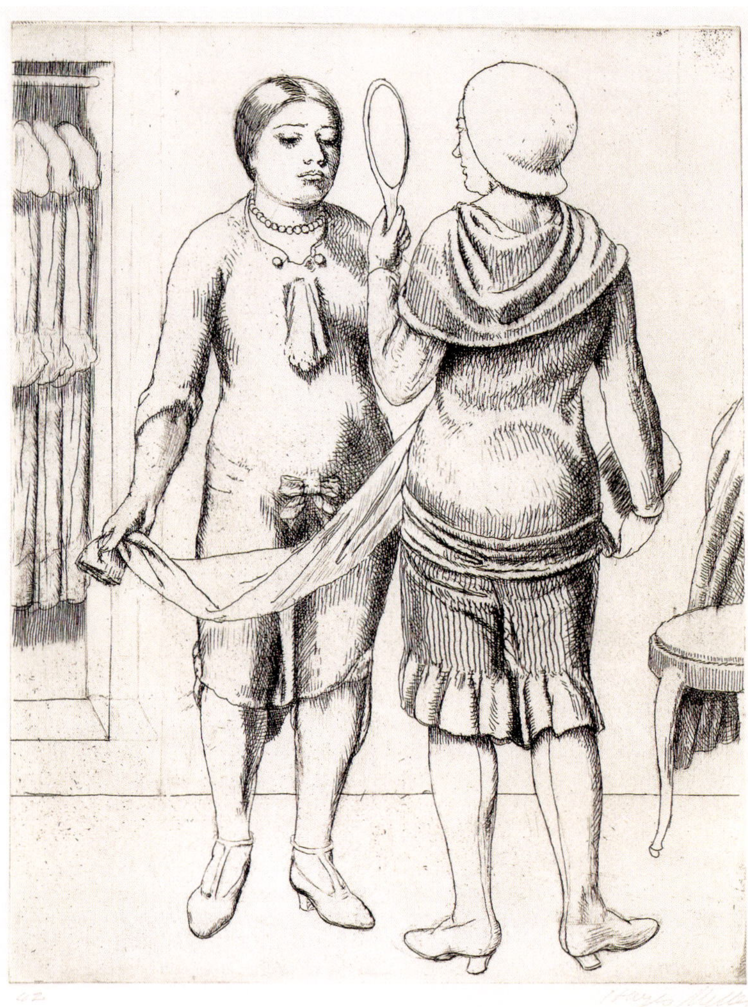

Figure 7. Kenneth Hayes Miller, *Two Women with Mirror*, 1930; etching, 11⅞ × 10⅛ in.; Gift of The Still Water Foundation, 1992.180

brave new world of suburban malls, pricey uptown boutiques, and Abstract Expressionism.

THE THEATRE OF SHOPPING

If historical continuities and the hats of grandma's day held little fascination for the 1950s—if Miller was "old hat" by the time of his death—today's audience brings yet another set of preoccupations and sensibilities to *Sidewalk Merchant*. Thanks to a vigorous preservation movement, it is impossible today to walk the streets that Miller walked without awareness of an historic district called "Ladies' Mile." A designated stretch of Fifth Avenue between Union Square and Madison Square west of Broadway, running roughly from 14th Street to 24th Street, the area has been the site of recent restoration in the overheated shopping climate of the 1990s.[44] Old retail spaces have been reclaimed in the guise of Barnes & Noble, Starbuck's, and the Gap.

Published in 1993, Ellen Todd's groundbreaking study of the art of the Fourteenth Street School is another byproduct of that decade's fascination with retailing. As she described them, Miller's shoppers seem to be the passive consumers of current theoretical literature, enthralled by the act of purchase, aquiver with desire stimulated by mercantile display. Yet this explanation of Miller's picture ignores the fact that Ladies' Mile was, as the name implies, a place especially for women, an historic refuge of sorts in which they were free to preen themselves, to inspect one another, and to dream of becoming that mannequin in the window (figure 7). It was a place where they could actively shape themselves. In other words, what went on here was more than a pig's dinner of buying and selling.

Beginning just after the Civil War, Ladies' Mile became a resort in which respectable women might walk unescorted and independent to enjoy the pleasures of convivial window shopping.[45] It was a public space uniquely receptive to the presence of women. Over time, the big stores began to creep northward following the carriage trade, leaving the Ladies' Mile to S. Klein's, discount hat shops, and second-floor showrooms for $9 fur pieces. But the area retained something of its traditional stature as a zone of freedom and self-transformation. In 1893 the *New York Sun* reported the case of a "handsome woman"—a lady dressed in diamond earrings and a black velvet cloak trimmed in fur—apprehended at the opera for theft; she was, in the colorful parlance of crime reporting, a "jewelry dip." What was meant to shock the reader, however, was the impossibility of telling a real lady from a dip if both were attired in sparklers and fur. Mrs. Astor and Annie Smith, age 32, dressmaker (a.k.a. Alice Cody or Dollie Reynolds) were, for all intents and purposes, indistinguishable.[46] Fashion and 14th Street were great social equalizers.

Here illusion and stagecraft became reality, too: "Theaters and emporiums coexisted amicably," according to a definitive new history of the city, "because each increasingly resembled the other."[47] Union Square had been the haunt of actors and chorus girls in the late nineteenth century. Napoleon Sarony posed them for photographs there in the 1870s, while restaurants like Delmonico's catered to their eccentric hours. In 1905, with Mary Pickford and the Gish sisters in starring roles, D. W. Griffith made his first one-reel movies for Biograph Pictures in a former mansion at 11 East 14th Street, just down the block from where Miller would have his studio.[48] The pungent mix of ladies, actors, respectable housewives disguised as movie stars, O. Henry shop girls who might be great ladies, Communists playing capitalists with boxes of chocolate bars, artists, and "dips" haunts Fourteenth Street still today. Its storefronts, where old wooden doors were gradually replaced by fancy brass-bound glass and plaster arches and elevators zooming skyward from the sidewalk, bear mute testimony to the layers of time and meaning embedded in Miller's painting. When the artist treated his figures as elemental, eternal women—as Venuses and *kores* and Graces—he merely tapped into the historical legacy of 14th Street, where he ponders in the shadows, like Paris or D. W. Griffith or Napoleon Sarony, ready to award a candy bar to the fairest of them all. If commercial culture is a game of illusion, a play stage for profit under glass, if the goal is to look just like the plaster figure in the window, then art, too, is a drama of resemblances, visual analogies, ruses, and outright lies. And sometimes the script becomes a little shopworn. The dog loses his leash. The lady loses her fur scarf to a light-fingered "dip." The salesman, in the end, loses faith in his role as critic and huckster.

Notes

1. Lincoln Rothschild, *To Keep Art Alive: The Effort of Kenneth Hayes Miller* (Philadelphia: Art Alliance Press, 1974), 100, notes that *In Fourteenth Street* was exhibited in January 1933, at the International Exhibition of the College Art Association, Worcester Art Museum, Massachusetts. Frank Rehn, Miller's dealer, also showed the work in his New York gallery in 1935. I am grateful to Leslie Brown for her meticulous work on the prehistory of *Sidewalk Merchant,* undertaken as a student at The University of Texas at Austin in a class taught by Professor John R. Clarke.
2. Milton W. Brown, *American Painting from the Armory Show to the Depression* (Princeton: Princeton University Press, 1955), 182. Brown began the book before World War II and finished the manuscript in 1953.
3. Virginia Zabriskie to Donald Goodall, September 29, 1970, Blanton Museum of Art Archives, The University of Texas at Austin. Because the Michener Collection had purchased *Sidewalk Merchant* in 1964 from the Midtown Galleries, Zabriskie may have believed the Blanton would be eager to acquire other Millers.
4. Miller file, photography archive, Department of Art History, University of Minnesota, Minneapolis.
5. Ellen Wiley Todd, *The "New Woman" Revised: Painting and Gender Politics on Fourteenth Street* (Los Angeles: University of California Press, 1993), 94.
6. Kenneth Hayes Miller Papers, July 30, 1925, Archives of American Art. Henceforth referred to as Miller Papers.
7. Miller Papers, July 5, 1929.
8. Miller Papers, August 9–11, 1932.
9. Miller Papers, August 15, 17, 22, 1932.
10. Margaret Breuning, quoted in "Critics Lose Some Enthusiasm for Miller," *Art Digest* (February 15, 1935): 8.
11. Elizabeth Roberts to Lincoln Rothschild, June 27, 1973, Blanton Museum of Art Archives, The University of Texas at Austin.
12. Lincoln Rothschild to Elizabeth Roberts, July 3, 1973, Blanton Museum of Art Archives, The University of Texas at Austin.
13. Rothschild, *To Keep Art Alive,* 95.
14. Rothschild, *To Keep Art Alive,* Fig. 99.
15. *City of Ambition: Artists and New York* (New York: Whitney Museum of American Art, 1996), 97, 139. Stephanie Hanor, former Assistant Curator of American and Contemporary Art at the Blanton Museum, kindly supplied this reference.
16. Harry Salpeter, "Kenneth Hayes Miller: Intellectual," *Esquire* (October 1937): 200.
17. Professor Todd originally shared this memo with Leslie Brown.
18. F. Scott Fitzgerald, *The Great Gatsby* (New York: Scribner Paperback, 1995), 116.
19. Miller Papers, August 3, 1926.
20. New York City Directory for 1933–1934, Local History and Genealogy Division, New York Public Library, New York.
21. Cassie Wilkins, a graduate student with whom I conducted a joint research project on the painting in the summer of 2001, found the photographs (571-17M and 571-20M) in the Municipal Archives, New York.
22. Alan Burroughs, *Kenneth Hayes Miller* (New York: Whitney Museum of American Art. 1931), frontispiece. The booklet was based on an article Burroughs (Marsh's brother-in-law) wrote for *Arts* in 1929.
23. Quoted in *East Side, West Side, All Around the Town* (Tucson: University of Arizona Museum of Art, 1969), 90.
24. See, for example, Andrew Herman, *Selling Pretzels,* undated photo (c. 1930) taken outside S. Klein's, now in the Museum of the City of New York.
25. "Commerce on the Curb," *The New York Woman* (October 7, 1936), 10, with photos by Jacobs and DePalma. See also Berenice Abbott, *Changing New York* (New York: New Press, 1997) and the local history collections of the New York Public Library (especially P. L. Speer's photo, "Coconut Vender at Union Square," June 5, 1933, taken across the street from Orbach's).
26. Quoted in Todd, 117.
27. Albert Halper, *Union Square* (New York: Viking, 1933), 181.
28. Salpeter, 199.
29. Jenna Weissman Joselit, *A Perfect Fit: Clothes, Character, and the Promise of America* (New York: Henry Holt, 2001), 149.
30. Gretta Palmer, *A Shopping Guide to New York* (New York: Robert M. McBride, 1930), 46. Leigh Rothke, who wrote an MA thesis on Miller under my direction at the University of Minnesota in 2001, kindly supplied this reference.
31. See advertisements in the *New York Times* for March 26, 1932, for example, and the Sears & Roebuck spring/summer catalog for 1932.
32. Todd, 165. During his first days in New York, in the 1890s (when he first lived briefly on 14th Street), Miller's letters reveal that he did use live models but he had largely discontinued the practice by the time he began his mature work.
33. Salpeter, 199.
34. Rothschild, *To Keep Art Alive,* 53–54.
35. Kenneth Hayes Miller to Grace Pagano, reprinted by Rothschild, *To Keep Art Alive,* 98.
36. Karal Ann Marling, *Tom Benton and His Drawings* (Columbia: University of Missouri Press, 1985), 13. Miller's letters show that Benton visited his studio as early as 1919 and supplied him with tips for applying gesso in 1929; Miller Papers, August 18, 1919; August 9, 13, 1929.
37. Marilyn Stokstad, "El Greco in the Ozarks," in *Benton's Bentons* (Lawrence, Kansas: Spencer Museum of Art, 1980), 32–48 points to other Benton borrowings.
38. See Matthew Baigell, *Thomas Hart Benton* (New York: Harry N. Abrams, 1973), 150–53 and Henry Adams, *Thomas Hart Benton: An American Original* (New York: Knopf, 1989), 284–88.
39. Marling, 58–66.
40. See Wanda M. Corn, *Grant Wood: The Regionalist Vision* (New Haven: Yale University Press, 1983), 80–81.
41. Garet Garritt, "The Painting of Hayes Miller," *New Republic* (July 27, 1921): 244–45.
42. Burroughs, 11–12.
43. Coates quoted in Rothschild, *To Keep Art Alive,* 49.
44. Joyce Mendelsohn, *Touring the Flatiron: Walks in Four Historic Neighborhoods* (New York: New York Landmarks Conservancy, 1998), 72–101.
45. See, for example, Edwin G. Burrows and Mike Wallace, *Gotham: A History of New York City to 1898* (New York: Oxford, 1999) and Hope Cook, "Ladies' Mile," *Seaport* (spring 1987): 13–19.
46. Untitled front-page article, *New York Sun,* December 5, 1893. See also Lori Landay, *Madcaps, Screwballs, and Con Women: The Female Trickster in American Culture* (Philadelphia: University of Pennsylvania Press, 1998).
47. Burrows and Wallace, 946.
48. Frank Beckman, "I Remember When," unidentified article filed under "East 14th Street" in the collection of the Museum of the City of New York.

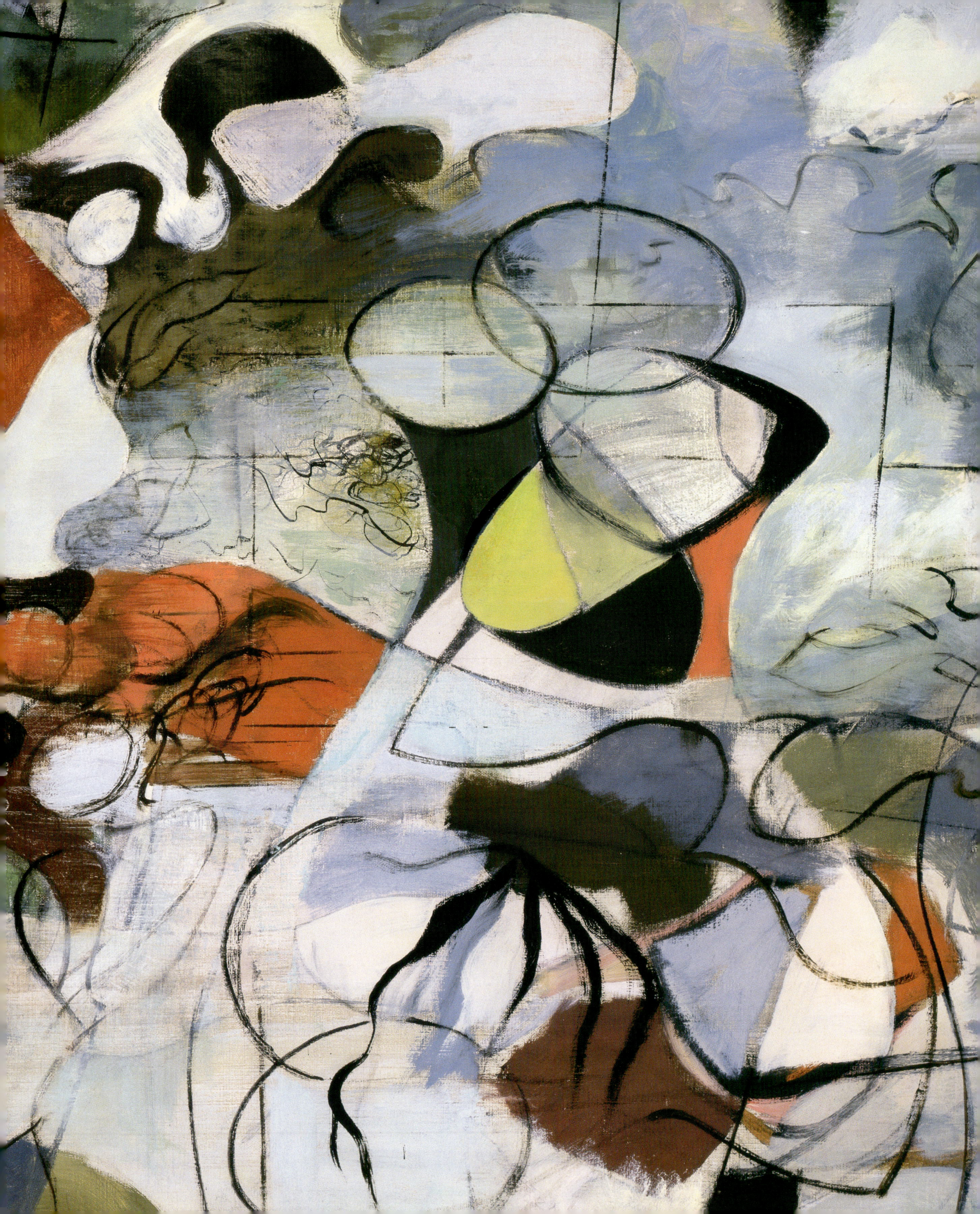

BRADLEY WALKER TOMLIN
WHO SAW THE WAY OUT

Dave Hickey

BRADLEY WALKER TOMLIN (1899–1953) is not much talked about today, and I think he should be. He is, in my view, responsible for three or four of the best paintings in the late twentieth century, and the consequences of Tomlin's aesthetic, although rarely acknowledged, are everywhere present in contemporary painting. The reasons for his de facto neglect, however, are not difficult to sort out. Tomlin lived and worked in a peculiar sort of cultural isolation, not so much before his time as above it, about three floors up. He died young, at fifty-three, not long after forging his mature painting style. He left a small oeuvre of paintings and virtually no machinery for perpetuating his public vogue. He left no trove of unseen work, no entourage of co-conspirators, no family or descendants, no fervent critical supporters, ardent collectors, passionate dealers, or enthusiastic followers—at least not at the time of his death. In truth Tomlin died with little more than the grudging respect of his peers in the practice of New York School painting, and that respect was granted less to his painting than his commitment to painting and his commitment to them, his peers in the practice. Hence Robert Motherwell's guarded, and pathologically condescending, tribute to him:

> *He loved painters and painting. This is the essential fact about him. In everything else, he was a dandy and a dilettante, at great ease in any social circumstance. One would have thought that he was the son of an Anglican bishop or a British general, he had an air—so that it would have surprised none of us if he indeed had been, though I realize now that he was his own construct, from the military moustache to the Brooks Brothers scarf. The gift he gave me, one Christmas, was a volume of English critics on T.S. Eliot. I gave him Joyce Cary's "The Horse's Mouth" in return, though at the time I was immersed in Celine. He liked me, because he regarded me as a gentleman, too; but he loved me, as he did Philip Guston and Jackson Pollock, because of a whole-hearted and perhaps reckless commitment on our parts—he never understood real despair—to painting and the acceptance of the existential consequences it brings about in one's life.*[1]

The subtext of Motherwell's damning faint praise is discerned easily here. Motherwell, the great painter, feels that he has done all he can. He has been friendly with Tomlin and behaved like a gentleman. He has given him Joyce Cary's bumptious parable as an antidote to T. S. Eliot's refinement. He has decided, on his own, that Celine's despair is beyond Tomlin's grasp, because Tomlin himself is a stylish construct, and, by extension, since style is the man, his paintings must be similarly "constructed" and lacking in artistic authenticity. Mostly Motherwell infers that

Bradley Walker Tomlin, *The Armor Must Change*, 1946 (detail, figure 4)

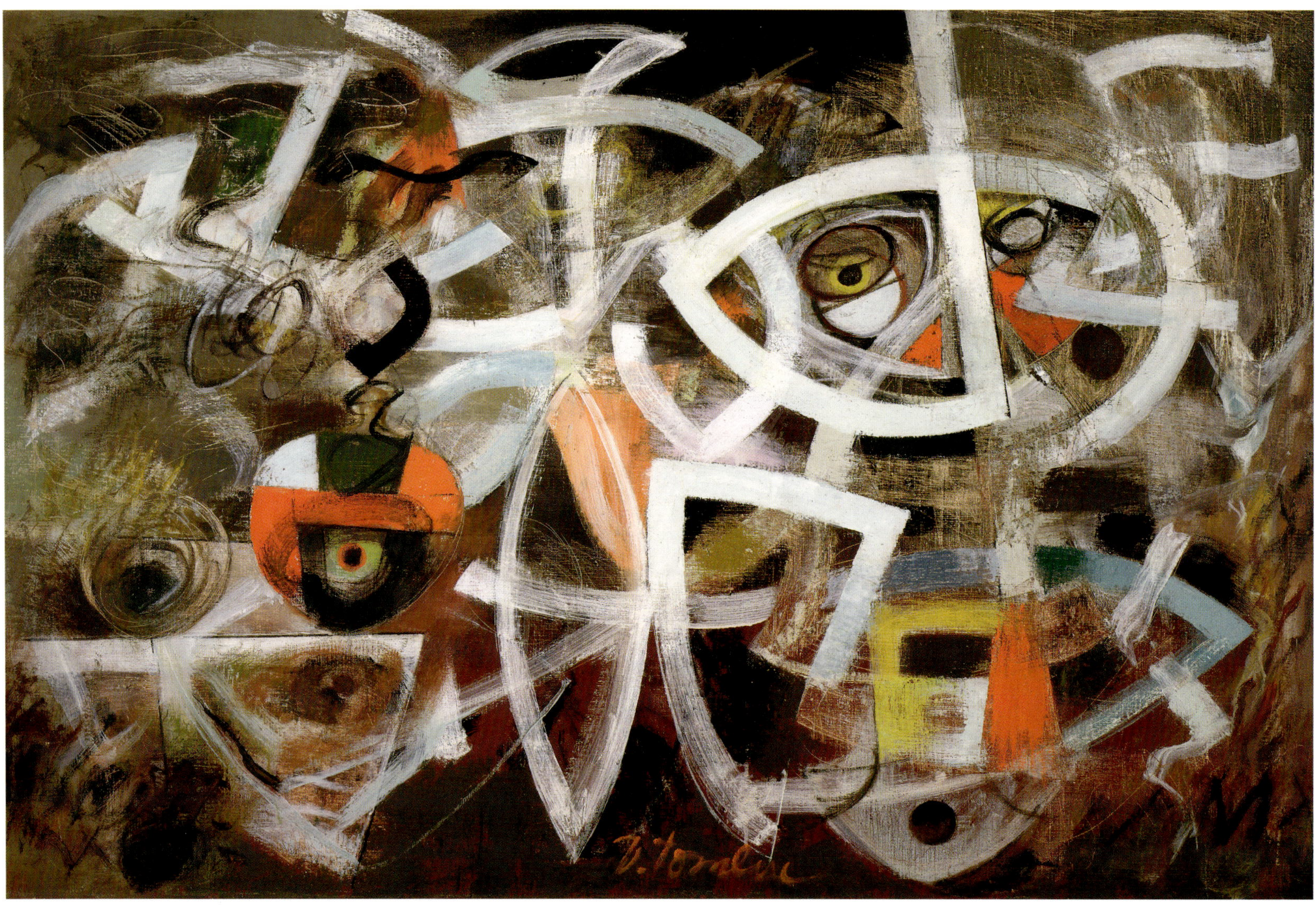

Figure 1. Bradley Walker Tomlin, *Maneuver for Position*, 1947; oil on canvas, 31 × 46 in.; National Gallery of Art, Robert and Jane Meyerhoff Collection, 1996.81.2; © Board of Trustees, National Gallery of Art, Washington, D.C.

Tomlin may have lived among the New York School, but he was never, truly, one of the group. In contemporary language Motherwell's encomium is a nice way of saying that Tomlin was a slick, dandified, Anglophile, homosexual climber whose paintings were facile confections, whose presence was only acceptable as a signifier of the group's generosity. In other words, Tomlin was a kind of pet who had no place in the company of "real" men with "real" artistic ambitions.

All of this, I hasten to note, is probably true in its own way. Certainly, without Tomlin, the New York School of painting presents itself to the world as a much more coherent enterprise. Although, if one does consider Tomlin's paintings as part of New York School practice, the group endeavor seems a much less local and parochial affair, since Tomlin's paintings offer a way out of the idiom's psychobabblicious mythology; they propose a way of painting about painting rather than painting about the act of painting and what that might mean to the painter. The key to this effect is evident in Tomlin's late, pictographic manner, which he freely appropriated from Adolph Gottlieb and put to his own ends. This manner allowed him to build paintings out of wide, brush-width geometric marks, each perfectly controlled, perfectly straight, or perfectly curved but still decidedly freehand. The slush and vibrato of the New York School mark is willfully suppressed, and Tomlin's new, cool, ordinary manner of marking has the effect of suppressing that mark's emotional urgency while celebrating its masterful spontaneity, as if the artist were quickly and deftly painting a pictograph of a painting, abstracting Abstract Expressionism into a bravura schematic, distancing the work from its presumed content by literalizing the dashing, graphic aplomb with which it is manufactured.

Considered in the context of the time, my point here should be obvious: Tomlin's late paintings are essentially images of images. His brush marks portray brush marks. His paintings, in a contemporary sense, are not even actively "painted." They are pictographs of paintings that exist at one remove from the urgency and intimacy to which most New York School paintings aspire. In this way Tomlin's late paintings prefigure the graphic distancing of Pop and Minimalist painting and prefigure the lesson of Roy Lichtenstein's Brushstroke paintings: that one may achieve the effect of expression through nonexpressive means. One can see this most clearly in Tomlin's last paintings, in which the brush mark had been shortened to an outsized impressionist daub and fields of these daubs have been laid over one another, each field in its own color. The effect is like a Pop/Pointillist abstraction rendered in the layered manner of Jackson Pollock, cooled by the willfulness of its means, and looking forward to the optical dynamics of Larry Poons, Bridget Riley, and a host of others.

The closest contemporary analogy for Tomlin's painting in the culture of the early fifties may be found in the music of cool jazz masters like Miles Davis who, at about this time, abandoned the cult of bebop spontaneity for a new brand of *sotto voce* yet energetic artifice that mimics spontaneity through nonspontaneous means. The effect of Davis's and Tomlin's sincere mimicry was to alter the whole atmosphere of postwar art without changing much beyond that atmosphere. Miles's music still sounds the way postwar jazz should sound; Tomlin's paintings look the way a New York School painting should look; yet each invites us to abandon our ideas about the supposed content of the way they sound or look by formalizing the fundamental building blocks of narrative and signification. They each propose, as Jacques Derrida does around this time, that "there is no meaning outside the text" beyond what we choose to find.

Davis's abstracted line will lead to Ornette Coleman, Don Cherry, and free jazz. Tomlin's abstracted line opens a path that will lead through Cy Twombly's *écriture* and Jasper Johns's cross-hatches to the flourishing of "synthetic abstraction" in the present moment. Thus in their bravura embrace of the graphic and their subtle abstraction of the spontaneous line, Tomlin's late paintings offer something that no other New York School paintings could: a way out of Motherwell's "real despair" and the ongoing cult of authenticity. In fact the attributes that Motherwell finds most wanting in Tomlin's life and art are the very attributes that serious painting will dispense with in the next decade. Thus of all the so-called Abstract Expressionists, Tomlin is the least "expressive" and the most premeditated—the least pretentious about what his paintings might "represent" and the most sophisticated in his performance of them. He aspires to elegance rather than sublimity, eloquence rather than angst, urbanity rather than sincerity; so in the end it is less Tomlin's painting than his sensibility that seems out of kilter in his moment and proves to be *après la lettre*.

A quick glance at Tomlin's painting in the Michener Collection reveals the difference that was always there in his art. *The Armor Must Change* (1946) is an accomplished transitional painting that immediately precedes Tomlin's mature manner. It has the physical size, worked surface, and atmospheric presence of an Arshile Gorky from about the same period. It even has a similar provenance, since Tomlin like Gorky felt the necessity of working his own way through the history of modern painting to reach his mature style. Everything else, however, is different. Tomlin's painting and Gorky's of this period are like utterances in the same accent but in two different languages. In Gorky's paintings of this time improvisational panache serves as his armor. The paintings derive their authority from the loose, be-bop disengagement of melody and harmony rendered by Gorky as line and color. Tomlin's armor, in *The Armor Must Change*, however, resides in the painting's covert orderliness, in its stable curves and prescient cool. Where the disengagement of line from color in a painting by Gorky seems to express a casual disinterest in matching one with the other, the disengagement of line and color in Tomlin's painting (when they are disengaged) is absolute and decisive. Tomlin's color is more defined and his line, as crisp as Francis Bacon's, bears real graphic authority. Even so Tomlin's painting feels as much like a performance as a painting by Gorky of this period, but with this caveat: Tomlin, as a performer, does not subscribe to the cult of innocence. He is neither ashamed of his urbanity nor embarrassed to leave evidence that he has, in fact, performed on the canvas's surface before this moment.

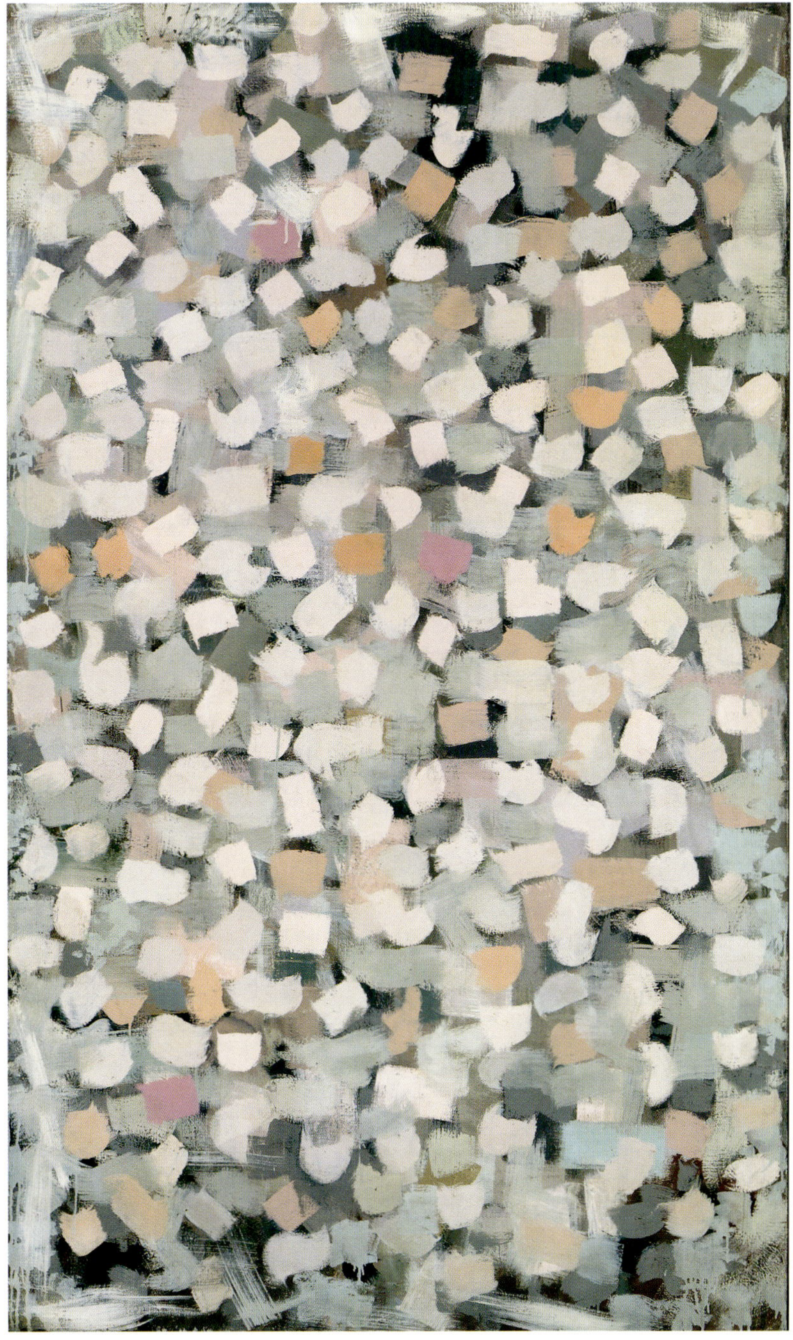

Figure 2. Bradley Walker Tomlin, *Number 1, 1952*, 1952; oil on canvas, 79 × 46 in.; Whitney Museum of American Art, New York; Purchase, with funds from Susan Morse Hilles, 73.12

All of the fugitive virtues that we attribute to Tomlin's paintings in their time would become commonplace in the subsequent decade. Tomlin's prescient embrace of the graphic, his abstraction of the line, and his ventures into the hot zone between the artistic and the

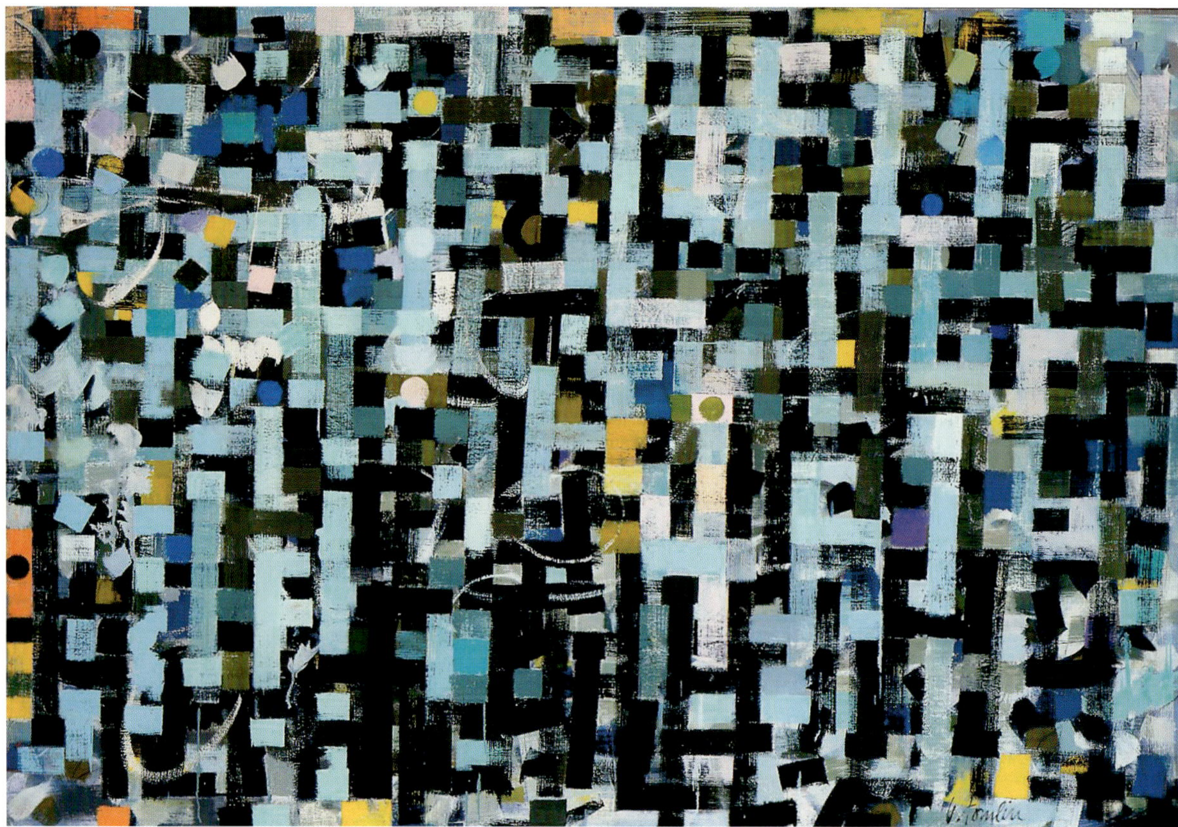

Figure 3. Bradley Walker Tomlin, *Number 10*, 1952–1953; oil on canvas, 72 × 102½ in.; Munson-Williams-Proctor Arts Institute, Museum of Art, Utica, New York, 53.217

commercial mark would provide the sixties with its prime signifiers. Urbanity, insouciance, impudence, sophistication, mastery, and premeditation would define that decade, so it goes without saying that Tomlin died too soon. The more interesting point is that the easy assimilation of cosmopolitan virtues into the American art world of the sixties derives, at least in part, from Andy Warhol's efforts to escape the fate that befell Tomlin's reputation. So the parallels between the two artists' careers are telling. Both Warhol and Tomlin were extravagant homosexuals from the working class provinces. They were both scholarship boys whose facility won them early success in the commercial art world of Manhattan, which predisposed the high art world against them. They both aspired to fame, elegance, and a brand of beaux arts legitimacy that was unfashionable in their times. They both dabbled in portraiture and mingled with high society. Both of their careers evolved slowly and in a similar trajectory, moving from success in commercial art, to success in the effete, "pseudo surrealist" milieu of chic eastside galleries, to success in the hardcore world of avant-garde painting where neither of them had much purchase or any extant constituency.

When we compare Warhol's success to Tomlin's relative failure, it becomes clear, I think, that Tomlin was doomed first by his isolation. He never found a world that matched his sensibility and his taste, as Warhol did in the Lower East Side poetry scene, because it wasn't there yet. Nor did he ever find an arena for his particular form of unpretentious integrity. Once he lost his innocence about the real agendas of New York School painting, he refused to feign belief in his paintings. He simply presumed that sophistication was a state to which one aspired—as one does, of course, anywhere but in America. Warhol, who was more tactical and knowing, evolved his own brand of faux innocence to protect himself—his own impenetrable passive armor—which is simply to say that Andy did some foolish things, but he never would have been so foolish as to give a book he loved to Donald Judd, as Tomlin did to Motherwell. The price Warhol paid for his feigned innocence, of course, was very real as well. He would never achieve the taut worldliness of Tomlin's best canvases, nor could he ever replicate the unfeigned courage and modesty of admitting, in America, that one has grown up and still has doubts.

"Does the artist," Tomlin wrote in a letter to critic Henry McBride, "find that the seemingly effortless structure, which he has evolved with total clarity, tends on repetition to escape him? That in spite of the production of masterpieces, art itself remains infinitely mysterious and that the work in progress is merely a kind of hall rack on which he has hung various nicely woven articles of clothing; jackets shabbily elegant, old hats battered to his image? Confronted by the cast of his own mind, he says it is at least mine. Yet the jacket he has slipped into binds slightly under the armpits. Umbrellas and old walking sticks clatter to the floor."[2]

Notes

1. Quoted in John I. H. Baur, *Bradley Walker Tomlin* (New York: Whitney Museum of American Art, 1957), 11.
2. Quoted in Baur, 17.

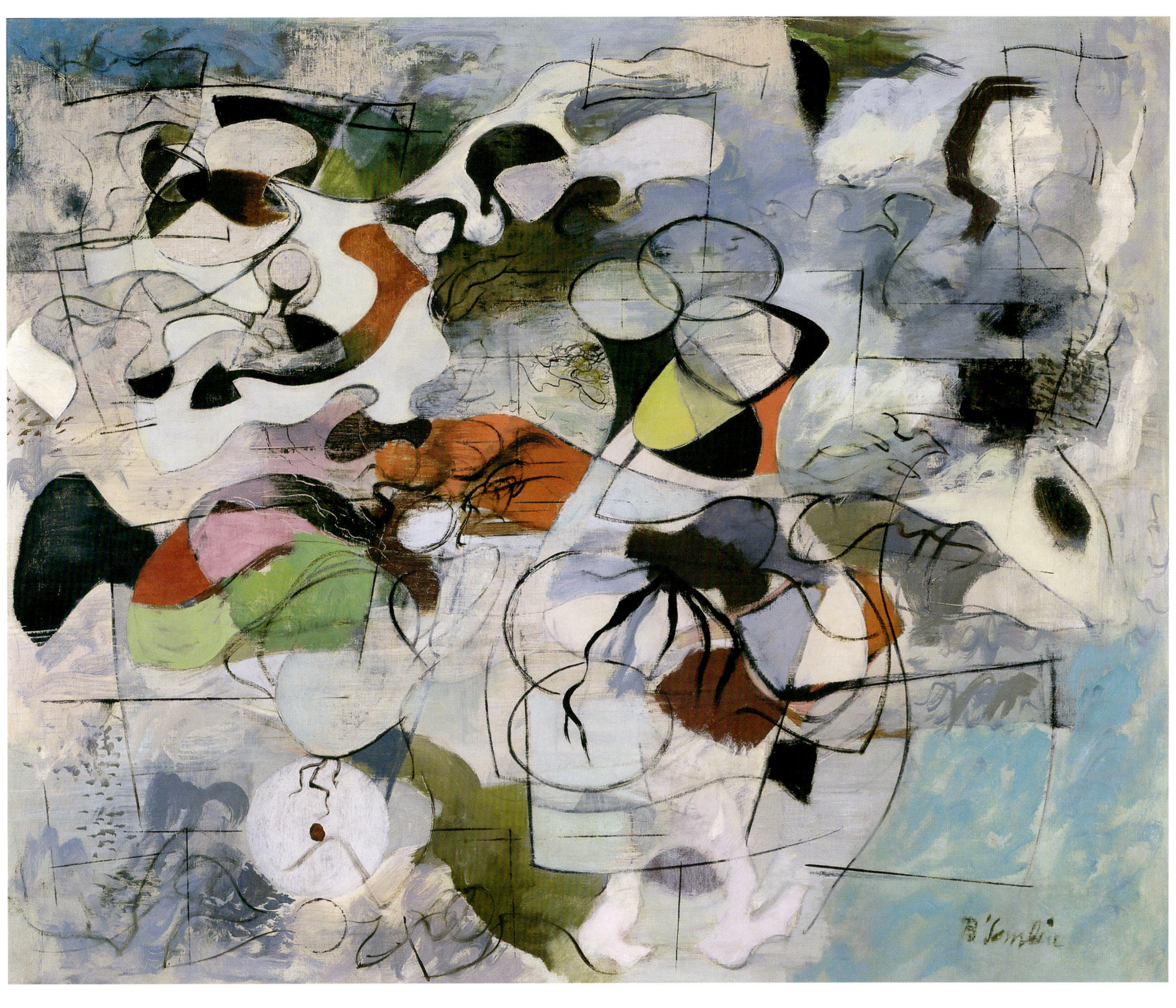

Figure 4. Bradley Walker Tomlin, *The Armor Must Change*, 1946; oil on canvas, 41⅛ × 49⅛ in.;
Gift of Mari and James A. Michener, G1968.124

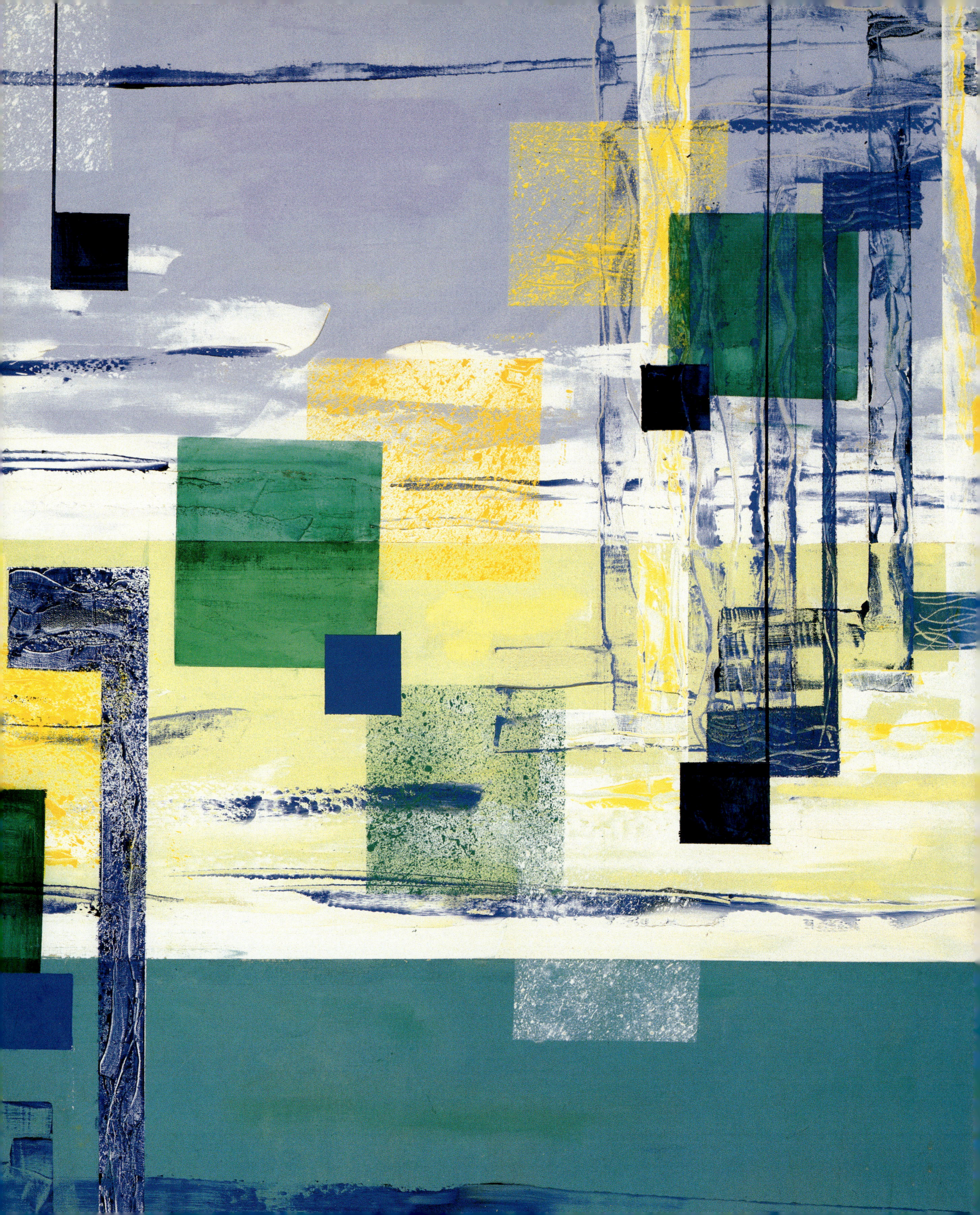

THE GOOD, THE BAD, AND THE UGLY

Robert Kushner

WHEN I VIEW THE CURATED SELECTION of twentieth-century American art from the Mari and James A. Michener Collection, it thrills me with its prescience: numerous excellent mid-century paintings bought the year they were painted, sometimes directly from the artists' studios; excellent choices of Social Realist and early modernist work; brilliant examples of Abstract Expressionism. I fully experience the excitement and foment of that heroic era of American painting when each year artists broke new ground as they continuously made new discoveries.

However, on visiting the racks, the out-of-sight area where the remainder of the collection—unedited, unprioritized—is stored, a slightly different picture emerges. Here we travel an aesthetic landscape that careens wildly from mountaintop to desolate desert with breathtaking rapidity. Rather than the fruits of a stellar curatorial temperament selecting one great work after another, we see the amassed successes and mistakes of Michener's collecting career—and they are surprisingly incongruous. I always have found patterns of collecting a fascinating and revealing journey. In this case, where the good is so good and the bad so puzzling, my curiosity was piqued.

The Michener Collection consists of 297 works of art, purchased over the years 1959–1975 and subsequently donated to The University of Texas at Austin. The works divide roughly into two historical groups. The earlier is an excellent collection of Ashcan School and Social Realist paintings, executed from roughly 1900 to 1940; the latter is an extensive collection of mid-century paintings purchased very close to the time of their making. For the purposes of this examination, I am leaving the earlier group aside for two reasons: 1) other scholars are addressing specific themes within this concentration; and 2) the period's historical distance from the 1960s, when Michener was collecting, gave him the advantage of hindsight.

Michener could trust his early love for Social Realism, which he had studied, tested, and reaffirmed. He could also take advantage of the mildly discredited, marginalized position this work held in the art world at that time to purchase very good paintings at reasonable prices. Michener had the good fortune of living next door to Alan Gruskin, the founder of Midtown Galleries, one of the bastions of Social Realist painting, and Edith Halpert of the Downtown Gallery counseled him well, as did others who were knowledgeable about early modernist art. With their advice and assistance, Michener acquired examples by most of the important figures in this area. Buying major works by Raphael Soyer, Yasuo Kuniyoshi (figure 1), George Luks, John Marin, and Marsden Hartley might have been considered an eccentric specialization at that time, but by 1961 these were painters of established historical importance. Looking back, we can all thank Michener for his healthy iconoclasm in assembling this part of his collection.

Irene Rice Pereira, *The One*, 1960 (detail, figure 9)

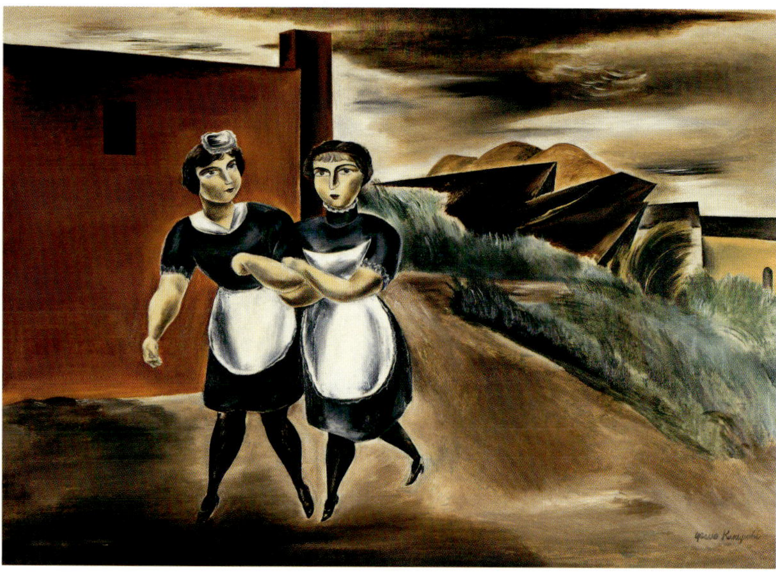

Figure 1. Yasuo Kuniyoshi, *Waitresses from the Sparhawk*, 1924–1925; oil on canvas, 29 7/16 × 41 9/16 in.; Gift of Mari and James A. Michener, 1991.252

For this overview, however, I will address only the work that Michener was purchasing at the time of its execution—that is, mid-century work, paintings produced from the late 1940s through the mid-1970s. Envisioning Michener's underlying strategy for doing so poses an interesting challenge.

Writing in 1977 in his introduction to the first catalogue of the collection, Michener revealed: "I became aware of my own aberration rather young, for I was an avid collector of stamps."[1] In contrast to a collector who might be drawn to historical depth and specialization, stamp collectors often develop a passion for acquiring and cataloguing a diverse selection of material. This pattern came to influence Michener in his approach to building a painting collection.

Michener studied art history in college. When he found himself in Japan soon after World War II, he began amassing a collection of six thousand Japanese woodcut prints, which he later donated to the Honolulu Academy of Arts (figure 2). Even at low prices, six thousand prints is a lot of prints, representing, for that time, a significant commitment in research, shopping, and money. Michener enjoyed the experience of buying Japanese prints in a severely depressed postwar market and, admittedly, there were overlooked treasures to be bought. A good scholar, he did his research well and was able to create a major, museum-quality collection. Michener wrote several books on the subject of collecting Japanese prints and by doing so "helped revive the field," with, as he put it, "the lamentable result that print collecting became so popular that I priced myself right out of the market" (x).

He expressly admired collector John G. Johnson of Philadelphia: "When his wealthier and better known contemporaries were collecting . . . first-rate Rembrandts and paying enormous prices for them, Johnson was quietly scanning the field of Sienese, Florentine, Venetian, North Italian, and Flemish painting and picking up hundreds of positive gems in fields that were being overlooked by the more conspicuous collectors. In the end he assembled what is now recognized as one of the top collections of minor Italian painting" (xvi).

It is interesting that Michener was not more admiring of the flamboyant and decisive Philadelphian, Alfred Barnes, who arguably built the finest collection of modernism in America—with kingly holdings of Henri Matisse, Paul Cézanne, and Pierre-Auguste Renoir. Rather, Michener wished to emulate Johnson, the quiet accumulator looking for high quality bargains in overlooked fields of collecting.

By the late 1950s Michener was an established, popular writer of colorful, fictionalized history. Then in his fifties, he had a surplus of money from selling the theatrical and film rights to several of his bestsellers, and he began to replicate his experience with Japanese prints by collecting heavily in American art.

Michener took pride in the catholicity of his taste, enjoying the juxtaposition of an abstract canvas with a carefully rendered realist painting. However, of all the styles he pursued, Abstract Expressionism was his greatest love. Michener clearly revealed where his instinctive aesthetic "home base" resided in this statement: "I find it easier to make up my mind about the purchase of an abstract painting than I do of a figurative one, probably because my judgment is more secure in the abstract field and certainly my sense of empathy" (xii).

Michener loved to visit the studios of the artists whose work he had an interest in acquiring. As a creative being himself, he must have felt energized and exhilarated by meeting and knowing famous as well as emerging artists and seeing their latest accomplishments in the intimacy of the studio. He often visited one studio as many as four or five times before finally selecting a painting for his collection.

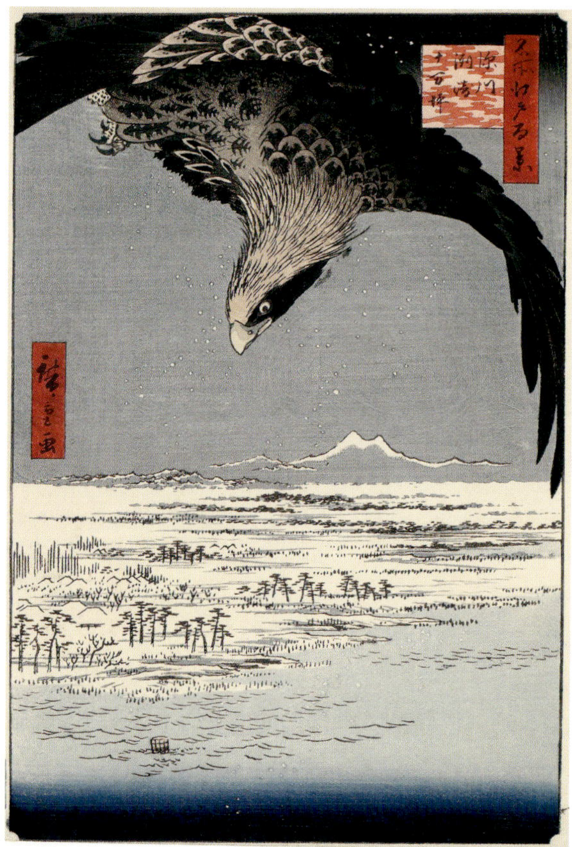

Figure 2. Utagawa Hiroshige, *Fukagawa Plain at Suzaki*, from the series *One Hundred Famous Views of Edo*, 1857; woodblock print, 14 × 9 in.; Honolulu Academy of Arts; Gift of James A. Michener, 1957 (13,903)

Michener also patronized the major dealers of his day, in whose galleries you could talk and listen as well as buy. At first Gruskin conducted a lot of the negotiations, but soon Michener began selecting and negotiating on his own. He acquired works from Sidney Janis, Martha Jackson, Sam Kootz, Leo Castelli, and others. With these contacts, he was right in the middle of everything that was new and interesting in the New York art world.

To understand the discrepancy between the hits and the misses of Michener's collecting, I began by looking at the Blanton's Michener files to determine who might have been advising him, suspecting that there might be an informed voice behind the curtain. At first I thought the legendary dealer and consultant Richard Bellamy might have been recommending the successful purchases, since many of them are recorded as having been made through Bellamy. However, when I looked through Michener's fastidious records, I found that the Bellamy recommendations were not necessarily of a higher quality. In fact, the case was occasionally quite the opposite. It seems that Michener made most of his successful selections on his own.

In this light, the quality quandary still remained unresolved. When we examine the mid-century part of the collection closely, very odd discrepancies—patterns in errors both of taste and judgment—begin to emerge. For example, Michener viewed the most important painting of his collection to be George McNeil's *Schwanda, the Bagpipe Player* (1962, figure 3), an adequate but somewhat generic Abstract Expressionist canvas. He wrote of it as "one of the loveliest paintings in this collection, and in time it may become known as one of the best" (xv). In a 1983 interview, he considered Miles Forst's *Two Doors* (1964) as one of his favorite paintings. Forst, even at the height of his recognition, was barely a major figure, and today he is on few curatorial rolodexes. Mari Michener, too, was closely involved in the formation of the collection. She steered her husband to select specific pieces, and she considered the haunting and tender *From That Day On* (1960, figure 4) by Ben Shahn to be her favorite painting.

Michener chose to form concentrations of work by two different artists over time. From among all his friends and acquaintances, he selected Carl Holty, a relatively unknown artist, and inexplicably acquired eight examples of his work (figure 5). He also collected four paintings by Robert Richenburg. I can only shrug and ask, "Why?" Comparing the prices paid, works by these two artists were not substantially less expensive than work by others that has fared better over the years. I wonder whether these two men had dynamic personalities that appealed to Michener. Perhaps they were great raconteurs? Another guess is that he loved to bet on the underdog. In his writing, he tended to concentrate on the overlooked but interesting corners of the world, and to pluck vivid epics out of obscurity. He may have hoped to do the same with Holty. Except for one problem: the Carl Holty story, or rather his body of artwork, is simply not very compelling.

Setting aside for the moment the question of Michener's fallibility, I decided to explore the general factors that appear to have motivated

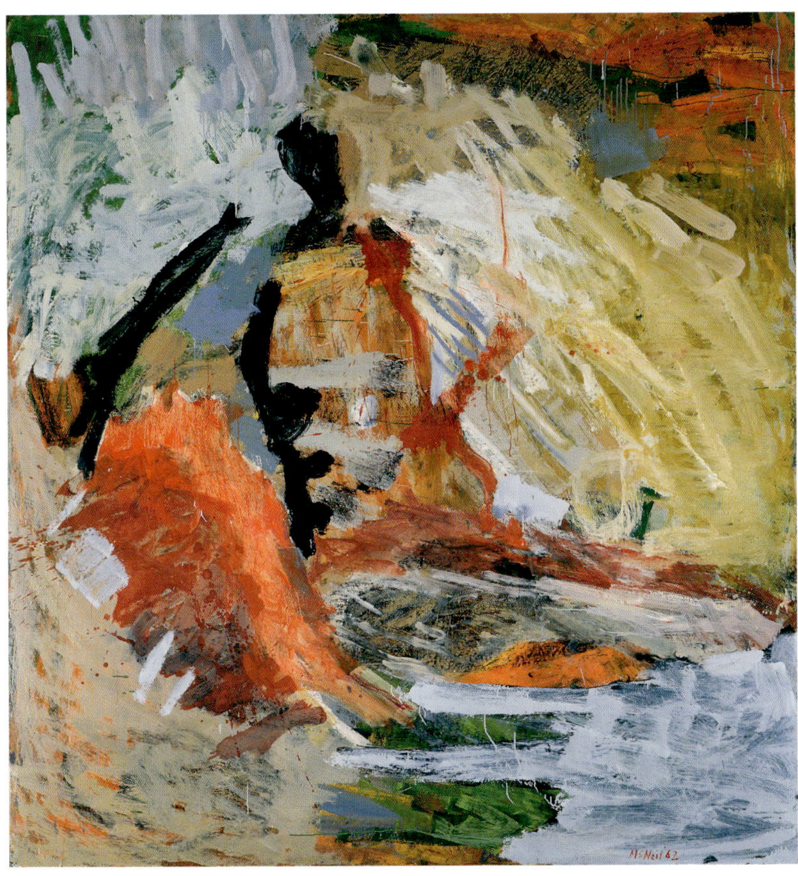

Figure 3. George McNeil, *Schwanda, the Bagpipe Player*, 1962; oil on canvas, 88 3/16 × 80 15/16 in.; Gift of Mari and James A. Michener, G1968.93

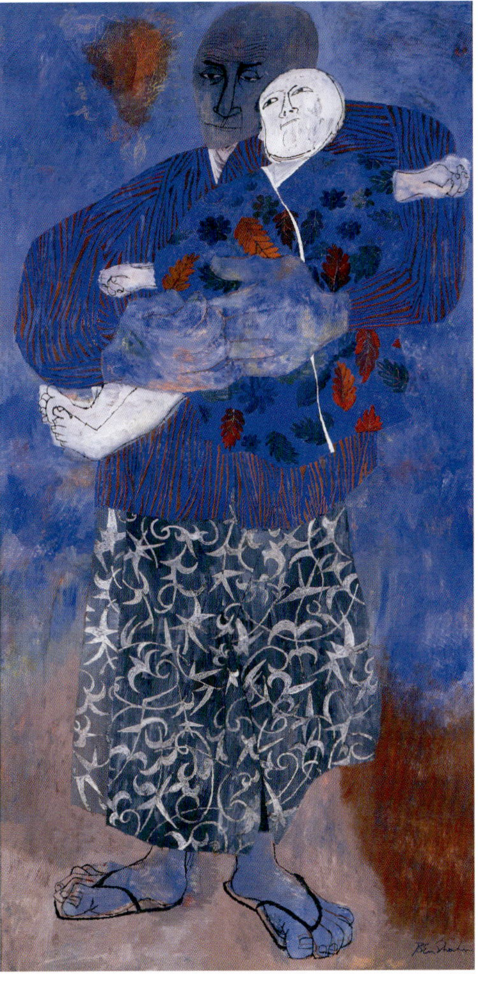

Figure 4. Ben Shahn, *From That Day On*, 1960; oil and tempera on canvas and board, 71 1/2 × 35 3/8 in.; Gift of Mari and James A. Michener, 1991.322

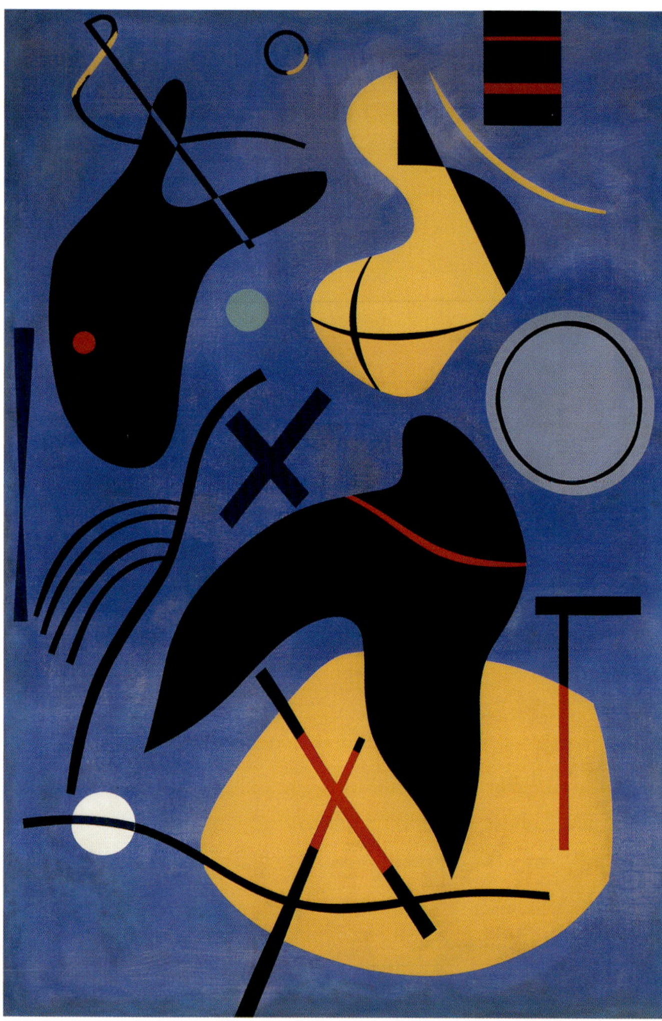

Figure 5. Carl Holty, *Circus Forms*, 1938; oil on Masonite, 59 13/16 × 39 3/4 in.; Gift of Mari and James A. Michener, G1968.75

his purchases. To address this, I looked at a summary of the collection as it was formed year by year. Immediately, certain patterns emerged that began to elucidate the overall contradictions of the collection.

Michener got off to a fast start. In 1961 he bought thirty-four works of art by artists ranging from Louis Eilshemius to Franz Kline. With the advantage of hindsight, one wonders why he didn't scrap the John Grillo, his first Holty, Sven Lukin, and all the Richenburgs when, for the same total amount of money, he could have purchased one good Willem de Kooning. He considered de Kooning or Jackson Pollock overpriced at roughly $30,000 for a good canvas! I suspect that in reality he found making such purchases unsporting. He was a gambler, and the stakes were potentially higher for the unknown or underrated than for the reigning kings of the art market. I imagine that he also enjoyed surprising his friends with the unexpected, instead of conforming to anticipated choices, and, besides, why not have six large canvases instead of just one? Despite all his insightfulness and generous qualities, I believe Michener had one glaring flaw as a truly discriminating collector: he loved bargains just a little too much. In his written introduction to the collection catalogue, Michener clearly stated his goal: "I would not be at all surprised if as many as one third of the paintings I acquired were finally consigned to some benevolent basement, and when that is done anyone looking only at those rejects would be entitled to say, 'whoever paid good money for them must have been out of his mind.' If only one third are judged to be mistakes, I would rest happy, for that would be a rather good average for someone who acquired paintings before the reputation of either the painter or the school was firmly established" (xviii). Keeping this expressly stated agenda in mind, let's look at Michener's patterns of acquisitions.

In 1961 Michener bought sixteen contemporary works and eighteen historical—just about half and half. He must have been like a kid in a candy shop. He could actually own a Hartley, a Kuniyoshi, and two Marins. In the mid-century field, he was buying Kline (figure 6), Joan Mitchell, Robert Motherwell, and Sam Francis—wise, educated, appropriately challenging selections. He understood and liked all of them. In 1962 he purchased sixty-nine more works ranging from Robert Beauchamp to William Glackens. Overnight, he had become a significant player in the contemporary art market, a role he must have relished. In these first two years of decisive collecting, Michener knew what he wanted.

In the next year, 1963, there was a shift of focus in the formation of the collection that would remain for the duration of the project: the ratio of old to new purchases drops. Twenty-three historical compared to forty-seven contemporary works. Michener's interest was now clearly in the new and untested. In this year, he was buying

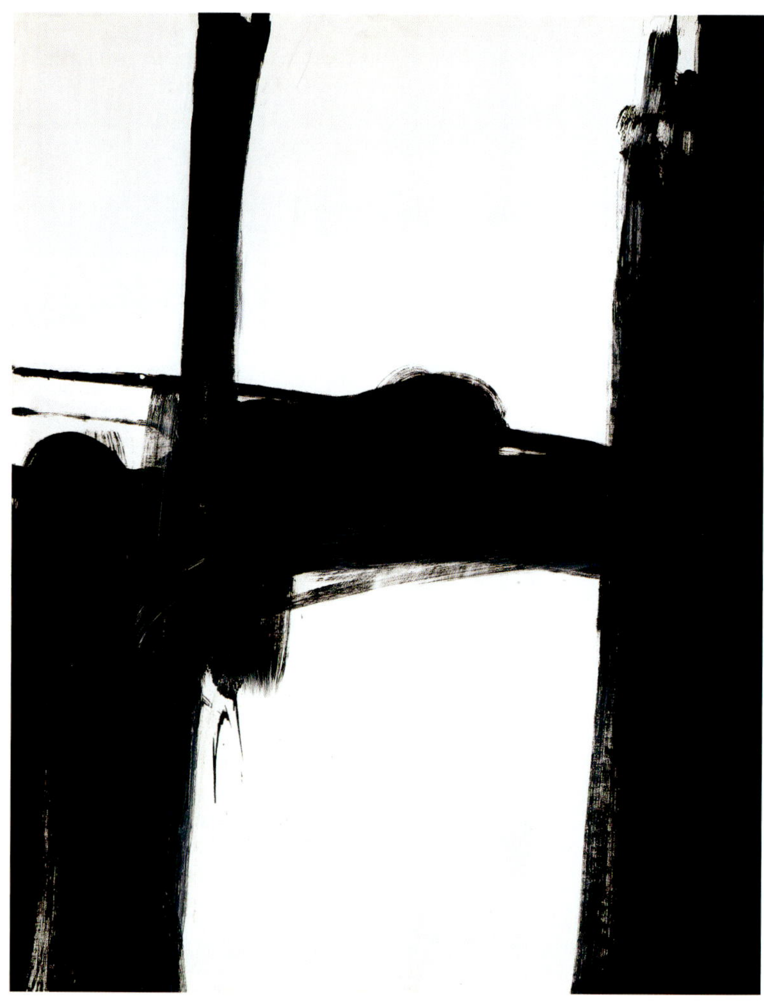

Figure 6. Franz Kline, *Black and White No. 2*, 1960; oil on canvas, 80 1/4 × 61 in.; Gift of Mari and James A. Michener, 1991.248; © 2005 The Franz Kline Estate/Artists Rights Society (ARS), New York

Hans Hofmann (figure 7), Jack Tworkov, Bradley Walker Tomlin, Theodoros Stamos, and Larry Rivers (figure 8). For the next thirteen years, this pattern of researching the new and assembling an overview collection of mid-century American art became the stated focus of his acquisitions.

Now, returning to Michener's "whoever paid good money for them must have been out of his mind," I would like to examine exactly what Michener bought year by year. Looking at the collection in this way, I have assigned his acquisitions a batting average: meaningful purchases in relation to total purchases for each year. I have made every effort to be generous. When there is an artist whose work I don't particularly like, such as Esteban Vicente, I consider it a good purchase if that artist has remained historically important. Likewise, if there is an artist such as Irene Rice Pereira (figure 9), whom I have always admired but whose work has not been shown in major museums for years, I also place her in the winners' column. But I think there is little doubt as to the low historical value of a monumental Lukin opus, for example. Someone else might divide things differently, so I have tried to give the collection the benefit of the doubt and to be both courteous and empathetic overall. However, as soon as I began to tally this analysis, the patterns of success and failure started to make their own kind of sense.

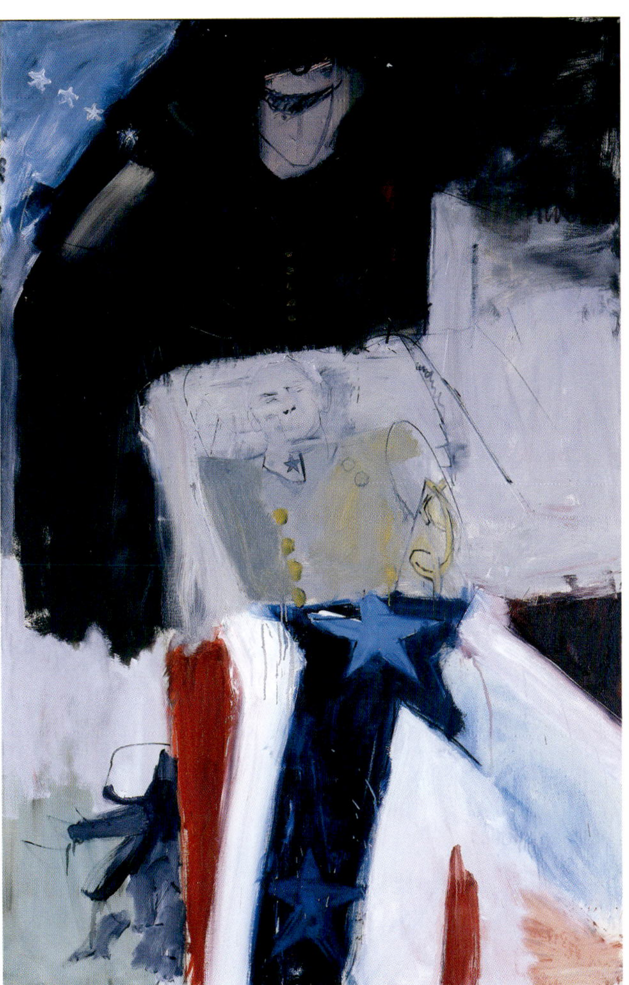

Figure 8. Larry Rivers, *Dead Veteran*, 1961; oil on canvas, 81 × 52 in.; Gift of Mari and James A. Michener, 1991.317

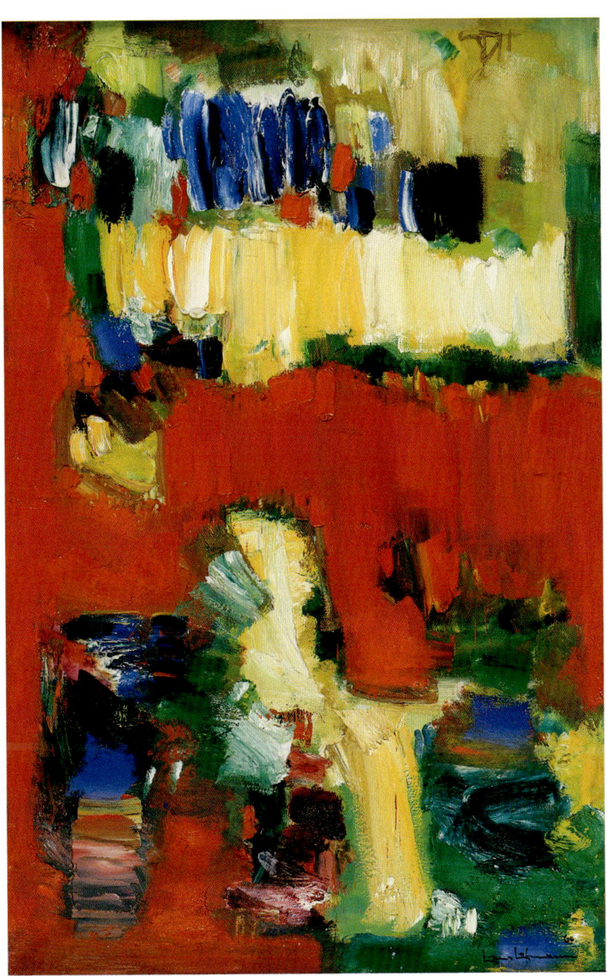

Figure 7. Hans Hofmann, *Cascade*, 1960; oil on canvas, 84½ × 52 in.; Gift of Mari and James A. Michener, 1991.238; © 2005 Estate of Hans Hofmann/Artists Rights Society (ARS), New York

With that disclaimer and its attendant potential for error, Michener's batting average for 1961 was an excellent .562, with nine hits out of sixteen contemporary at-bats.

For 1962 a similar .510, or twenty-four wins out of forty-seven contemporary purchases.

If we extend these averages over the next years, the batting averages unfortunately drop abruptly. For 1963 he purchased only fifteen contemporary works of art, with only three successes—resulting in a batting average of .170.

But then in 1964, a good season for Michener, he was back up there batting an estimable .500, in nine hits out of eighteen contemporary purchases.

For 1965 he came up with a .251—seven out of twenty-seven paintings.

For 1966 a discouraging .047—one out of twenty-three contemporary works.

For 1967 .100—two out of twenty contemporary paintings.

For 1968 it is .250—four out of sixteen contemporary purchases.

For 1969 .333—two out of a total of six contemporary works (and to his credit, this includes one of his stellar purchases: a Brice Marden painting bought directly from the studio [figure 10], the significance of which may have eluded Michener because he never mentions it in his general writing about the collection).

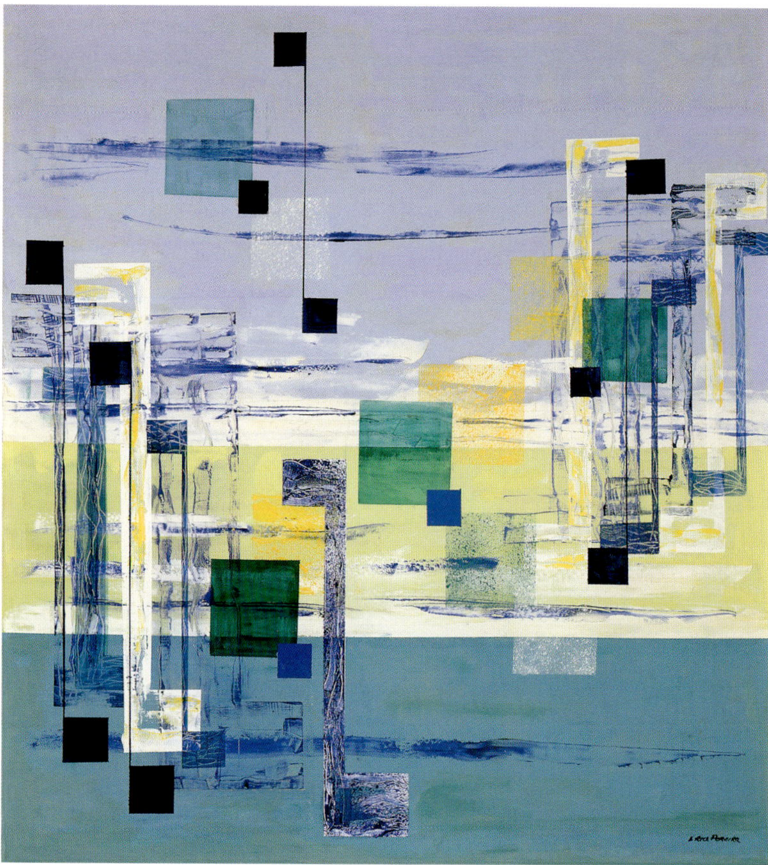

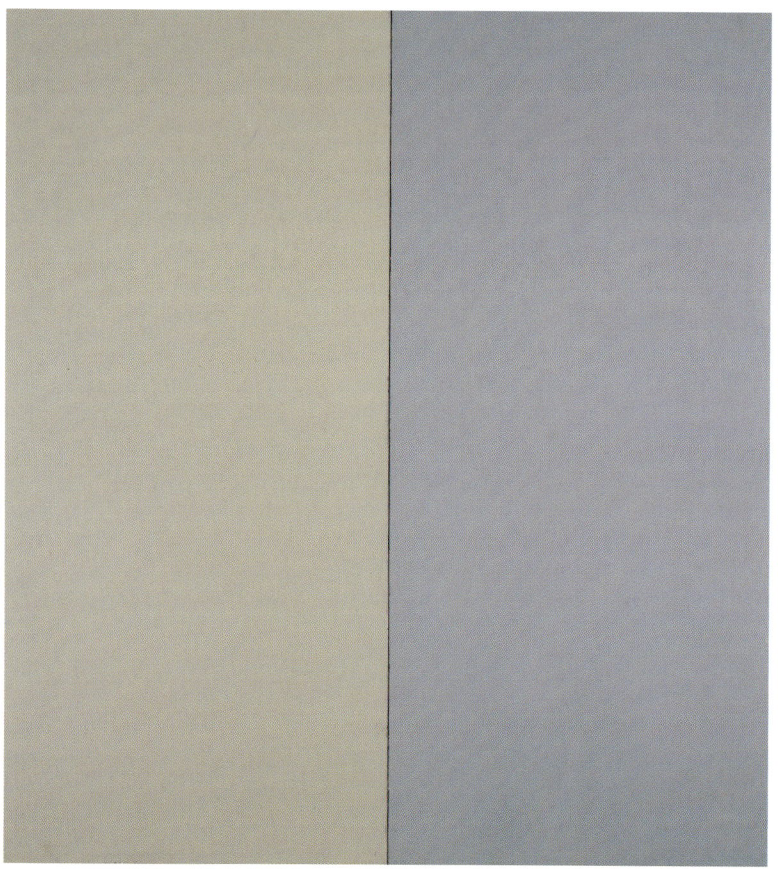

Figure 9. Irene Rice Pereira, *The One*, 1960; oil on canvas, 56 × 50¼ in.; Gift of Mari and James A. Michener, 1991.309

Figure 10. Brice Marden, *Fave*, 1968–1969; oil and beeswax on canvas, 72¼ × 66³⁄₁₆ in.; Gift of Mari and James A. Michener, 1979.30; © 2005 Brice Marden/Artists Rights Society (ARS), New York

For 1970–1973 there were few contemporary purchases with a resulting average of .000.

Putting these statistics together, Michener's lifetime average for picking contemporary painting was .319 or sixty-one successful hits out of 191 at-bats. Is this a good lifetime average or not? To obtain an answer, we would have to do a similar type of analysis for other major collections that have complete documentation. Given that Michener deaccessioned very little and donated the entire collection so shortly after its formation, eliminating the possibility of selling his less successful choices, this collection offers a unique opportunity for such evaluative analysis. I propose that this is a very good success rate overall. No collector can get it right 100 percent of the time when the works purchased are generally so new and untested. However, it also clearly explains why so many yard-sale drive-by paintings remain slumbering in the storage racks.

So what have we uncovered? A pattern where the success rate is at or above fifty percent for three years and then drops radically—as does the volume and price per painting. Why? Michener was collecting at a time of remarkably rapid change in the New York art scene. He clearly loved the Abstract Expressionists first and foremost. They were essentially his generation, their bold slashes curiously paralleling the bold strokes of his own writing style. How he must have enjoyed the vigor, high-keyed color, and rough, direct paint handling of their works. It is interesting to note that he chose three Hans Hofmann paintings to grace his dining room.

The Abstract Expressionists' contributions to postwar art were canonized and seemingly unshakable. Then, along came the unthinkable—a whole team of rapscallions in the late 1950s and early 1960s upsetting the proverbial apple cart. The spectrum is broad: the Neo-Dada group, the Pop artists, the Happening and installation artists, the Minimalists, even Conceptual art was beginning to emerge at this time. This work all seemed to burst into public awareness around 1962, and the agreed upon enemy was Abstract Expressionism. The art world was being turned upside down. Some collectors flew with the fevered excitement of those years. While we might wish that he had had the panache of Pop art collector extraordinaire Robert Skull, Michener was his own man and just didn't seem to like these new trends. He also could have chosen to stick to his guns and continue to acquire Abstract Expressionist works, which artists certainly still were producing well into the 1970s and beyond. However, he was trapped in his own self-appointed agenda—assembling a representative American collection of the best of the new—the problem being that he didn't especially like the newest.

Michener kept buying art but never tapped fully into the major movements of the 1960s. There is some Op art (a particularly good early Richard Anuszkiewicz). There is a surprising amount of color in most of the paintings that he selected, and the concentration of Color Field painting makes an interesting subset of the collection. There is only one West Coast expressionist painting, an Elmer Bischoff (figure 11), in a collection where a Richard Diebenkorn or David Parks would seem natural. Did he not know about this work? Perhaps he wanted to concentrate on developments in and around New York? The questions continue to expand.

When we look even more closely at the collection, we realize that we are missing many of the iconic artists of the 1960s. The most striking lacuna is the relative absence of Pop art, which was well within Michener's budget in the early 1960s. Given his circle of contacts, Michener had to have been aware of the Pop artists. He purchased a Tom Wesselmann still life—not a nude, an early Jim Dine, a Robert Indiana (figure 12), a Rivers, and a John Wesley. But nothing by any of the major players, whose work tended to be more challenging and acidic. My guess is that Michener may have found the self-conscious, ironic attitude toward contemporary culture of artists such as Jasper Johns, Robert Rauschenberg, Andy Warhol, Roy Lichtenstein, James Rosenquist, et al., too cynical. This work emerged vigorously at the time and was readily available, yet, for whatever reasons, Michener passed.

There is also very little Minimal art, with the exception of a Brice Marden, a Richard Tuttle, and a Tadaaki Kuwayama. I think that Michener tried to like this work as a reflection of contemporary taste but just couldn't abide the absence of an inflected painterly surface. On the other hand, it could be argued that most Minimal art was sculpture, a medium that had very little interest for Michener, a lover of painting first and foremost.

Looking at the bigger picture, I think that Michener might have bought just about all the names he wanted in those first few frenzied years. Perhaps the new art that he didn't really like as much as the style it was displacing called into serious question the confident bravado he exhibited in 1961 and 1962. The god-given superiority of Abstract Expressionism was no longer unquestioned, and Michener wanted to keep adding to the collection but just didn't know where to go.

I began this research with a mild suspicion of Michener's indiscriminate acquisitiveness, and a definite curiosity about the wild unevenness of his choices. There is something exhilarating about the close proximity of such highs and lows. In looking closer and reading Michener's notes and transcribed comments, I began to find sympathy for his abiding love of the artworks themselves and his admiration for the artists whom he befriended. With the paintings we examined, Michener was performing a high-wire version of collecting art right at the time it was being produced. He lacked the safety net of history to protect him, and the art world was changing fast. He wanted the impossible: to be both up to the minute and yet secure and comfortable in his established tastes.

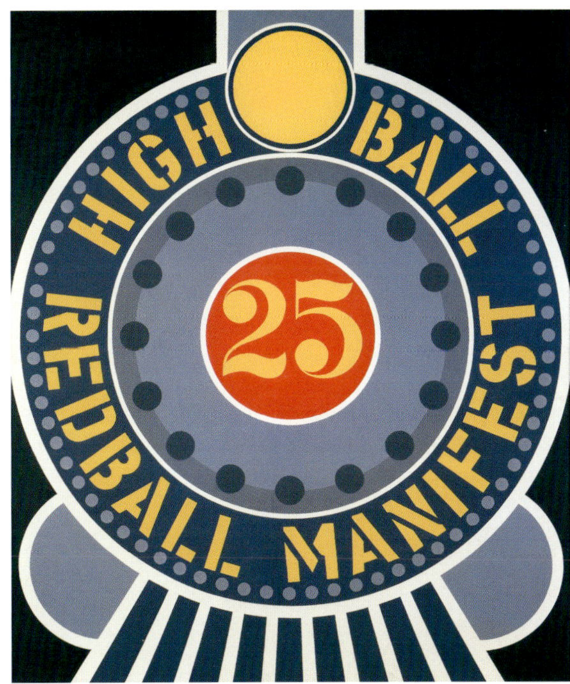

Figure 12. Robert Indiana, *Highball on the Redball Manifest*, 1963; oil on canvas, 60 × 50 in.; Gift of Mari and James A. Michener, 1991.243; © 2005 Morgan Art Foundation Ltd./Artists Rights Society (ARS), New York

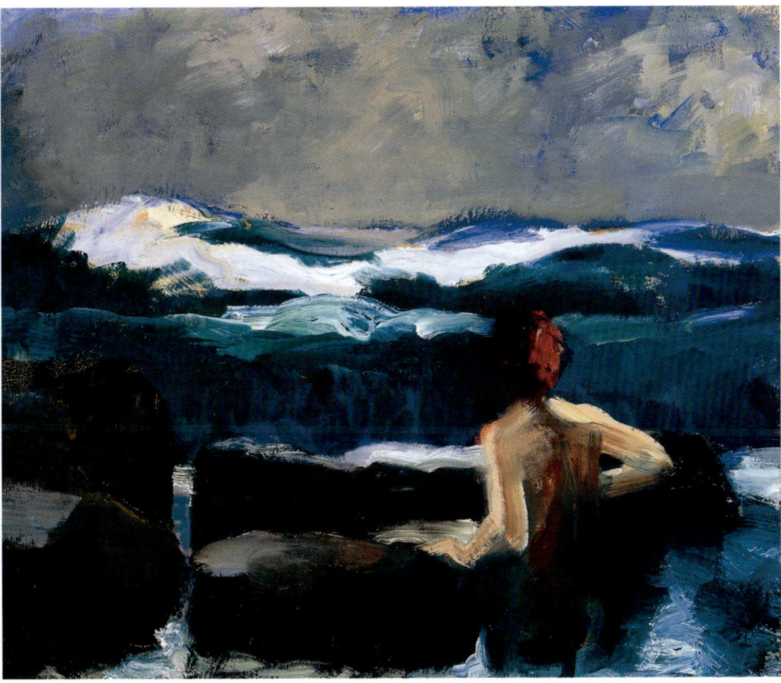

Figure 11. Elmer Bischoff, *Breakers*, 1963; oil on canvas, 61 × 70 in.; Gift of Mari and James A. Michener, G1968.33

Pursuing his goal of collecting the offbeat and underrecognized, Michener inadvertently provided us with two collections: a great survey of mid-century all-stars as well as an excellent time capsule of that period's B-list artists. His overall choices give us a vivid sense of the rough and ready, anything goes attitude of the 1960s, a glimpse of a more fertile and intimate art world than the one that exists today. In the end, Michener assembled an impressive collection that was justifiably a source of pride to him, as it is now to The University of Texas at Austin.

Perhaps his final success rate was lower than he would have liked to think it was. But it is not bad at all. For Michener, and for us as his audience, his process of collecting art as it was being made was a great adventure. To his credit, the high points, the successes, and the coups are an enduring testimony to his taste, perseverance, and panache.

Note

1. James Michener, "The Collector: An Informal Memoir," in *The James A. Michener Collection of Twentieth Century American Painting* (Austin: The University of Texas at Austin, 1977), ix. All subsequent quotations are from this introduction; the page numbers from which they were taken are indicated in parentheses after each quotation.

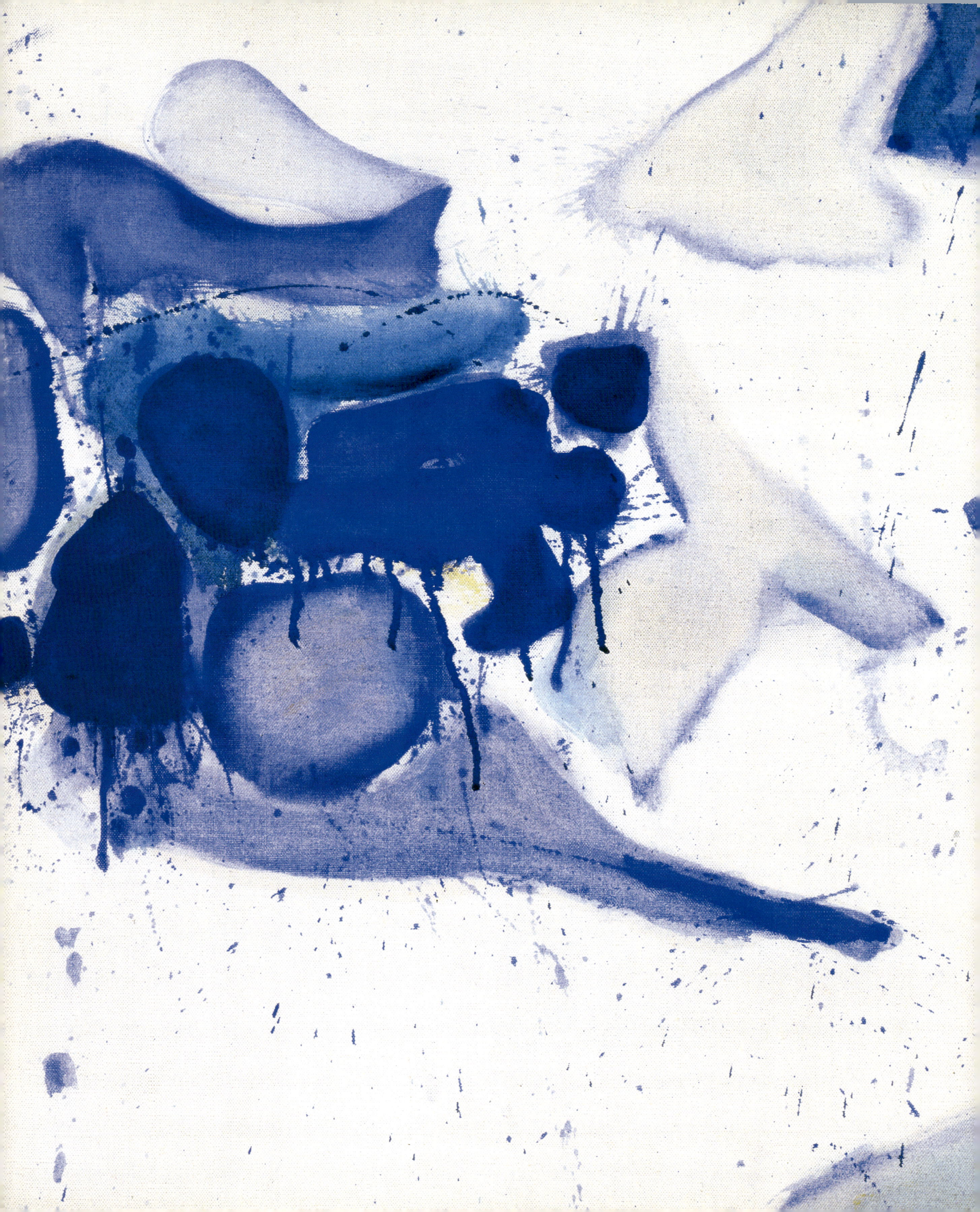

VIRTUOSITY IN CRISIS
NORMAN BLUHM, SAM FRANCIS, AND JOAN MITCHELL CIRCA 1960

Raphael Rubinstein

A GENERATION UNDER ATTACK

The trio of paintings from the Mari and James A. Michener Collection that I have chosen to focus on—*Apollo's Arc* by Norman Bluhm (figure 5), *Blue in Motion II* by Sam Francis (figure 7), and *Rock Bottom* by Joan Mitchell (figure 8)—all date to 1960, frequently characterized as a bad year for Abstract Expressionist artists such as these three American painters. Critics and art historians usually have categorized Bluhm, Francis, and Mitchell as "second generation Abstract Expressionists."[1] It's a label all of them disliked, for the obvious reason that it depicts them as being utterly dependent on the so-called first generation Abstract Expressionists such as Jackson Pollock and Willem de Kooning. Bluhm expressed another reason they rejected this tag (to no avail, as far as the public was concerned) in a 1985 interview: "The main thing should not be what you did at one time in your life, but how you moved through your full career. Everybody comes from somewhere—saw something, took off from something."[2]

In his standard history of the New York School, Irving Sandler, after chronicling the rise of the second generation of Abstract Expressionists, titled a crucial chapter "Circa 1960: A Change in Sensibility." By 1957 or 1958, Sandler observed, "some younger artists were becoming critical of gesture painting—not that of the pioneers but of the growing number of followers—and of the romantic rhetoric justifying it."[3] It was not only artists who were displaying signs of discontent. Sandler cited the infamous 1958 appearance of Alfred H. Barr, Jr. at the New York artists' discussion group known as the Club, during which The Museum of Modern Art director asked why younger artists weren't rebelling against Abstract Expressionism. (For this, abstract painter Michael Goldberg, a close friend of Bluhm and Mitchell, denounced him as a "grave digger."[4]) Ironically, Barr had just launched an exhibition, "The New American Painting," that was intended to demonstrate the "present triumph" of Abstract Expressionism. (The show, which included four mid-1950s paintings by Francis, toured eight European countries in 1958–1959.) However, following up on the sentiments he expressed at the Club, Barr soon embraced the work of Jasper Johns, buying three paintings for MoMA from the twenty-eight-year-old artist's first solo show, held at Leo Castelli Gallery. By placing the MoMA stamp of approval on the work of a young artist who diverged from Abstract Expressionism, Barr, unconsciously or not, helped to fulfill his own prophecy that it was time to move on.

Over the next couple of years, others joined Barr's call for a rejection of gestural abstraction, contributing further to the "change in sensibility" noted by Sandler. In the spring of 1960 an informal survey of the current scene by the magazine *Art in America* cited the opinion of New York art dealer Martha Jackson, who had shown

Sam Francis, *Blue in Motion II*, 1960 (detail, figure 7)

Francis (it was from her gallery that Michener would buy *Blue in Motion II* in 1961) and would also show Bluhm and Mitchell some years later. According to the article: "New trends foreseen by Martha Jackson who picks Jasper Johns, one of the Museum of Modern Art choices in 'Young Americans' show, as artist to watch. Miss Jackson believes abstract expressionism has gone as far as it can go."[5] The major exhibition *60 American Painters 1960: Abstract Expressionist Painting of the Fifties,* held at the Walker Art Center in Minneapolis, is an example of the continuing celebration of gestural abstraction (Bluhm, Francis, and Mitchell all had work in this show). It is telling, however, that the show lauded such art from a defensive position: the curator felt the need to devote much of his catalogue essay to dismissing the notion that "abstract expressionism or action painting is dead."[6]

Among those affected by the changing tide—and perhaps also helping to push it—was Clement Greenberg, once a firm supporter of Abstract Expressionism. When, in 1960, Greenberg revised an essay he'd published three years earlier on the evolution of Abstract Expressionism, he inserted a barbed attack on what he called "Tenth Street" painting (essentially de Kooning, Franz Kline, and the younger gestural painters who had learned from them). In its first appearance, in a 1957 issue of *Artnews* under the title "New York Painting Only Yesterday," the essay had been a triumphant appraisal of the abstract art Greenberg had helped lead to international prominence. He reminded his readers how, by 1940, "a number of relatively obscure American artists already possessed the fullest painting culture of their time."[7] But in 1960 he felt compelled to warn that although New York had "caught up" with Paris in the 1930s and 1940s, in the 1950s the city had been "falling behind itself" artistically. The reason for this lapse? The so-called Tenth Street painters' "implicit loyalty to what was an essentially French notion of 'good' painting."[8]

If, according to Greenberg, it was de Kooning and Kline who were dragging American painting back into provincialism, the good guys in 1960 were, among the older generation, Barnett Newman, Mark Rothko, and Clyfford Still, along with Morris Louis and Kenneth Noland, among the younger. The work of all five artists was notably free of expressionistic brushwork. That same year, the critic delivered a radio address on the US government-supported Voice of America radio network titled "Modernist Painting," which would become one of his most influential texts. It is here that Greenberg famously defined the "essence" of modernism as "the use of characteristic methods of a discipline to criticize the discipline itself, not in order to subvert it but in order to entrench it more firmly in its area of competence."[9] This notion formed the basis of Greenberg's argument for Color Field painting. Two years later, in a long critique called "After Abstract Expressionism," he got in another blow against gestural painting by insisting that "the only direction for high pictorial art in the near future" lay in the "repudiation of virtuosity in execution or handling."[10]

It's widely held that, for a long time now, artists and critics have rejected Greenberg and the brand of formalism he supported. Be that as it may—and the recent revival of Color Field painting suggests that it may not be—the effect of his dismissal of "Tenth Street" or "Second Generation" painters seems to have persisted. Art historian Caroline A. Jones's 1996 book *Machine in the Studio: Constructing the Postwar American Artist* is an example of this persistence. In her study, Jones contrasted a photo of Bluhm painting in his studio in 1961 with two of Frank Stella at work in 1959. In the image of Bluhm, taken by *Village Voice* photographer Fred McDarrah (and used on the cover of his 1961 book *The Artist's World in Pictures*), the painter stands on a ladder to apply a brushstroke to the top of the canvas (figure 1). Splatters of paint visible on the surrounding walls of the studio hint at the physicality of his process. In the photos of Stella, taken by his friend Hollis Framton, the artist stands or squats in front of his canvas—one of his Black paintings—methodically filling in the black stripes, like, said Jones, a housepainter. With barely concealed contempt, she described Bluhm as he appears in McDarrah's photo, which she did not reproduce in her book. She wrote of him as being "almost a parody of de Kooning, a manneristic exaggeration of the older generation's less self-conscious strokes. . . . The off-balance posture suggested 'trying to be an artist'—another of the things Stella would not do. For the housepainter, a loss of balance is disastrous, embarrassing, unprofessional. . . . The painter [in Hollis Framton's photo] is the picture of sobriety, and evidently a purveyor of a certain kind of monotonous but exacting labor."[11]

Although Jones didn't mention it and perhaps was unaware of the precedent, another commentator used this same photo of Bluhm twelve years earlier to draw a contrast with the previous artistic generation. In 1984 B. H. Friedman contributed an essay to the catalogue for *Action/Precision: The New Direction in New York, 1955–60,* a traveling exhibition of second generation Abstract Expressionist painting. Titled "Two Images, Two Moments in Art History," it compared McDarrah's shot of Bluhm with one of Hans Namuth's famous 1950 photographs of Jackson Pollock at work. Friedman, a novelist and critic who knew both Pollock and Bluhm, offered a different reading of the McDarrah photo. McDarrah took it, he pointed out, amid a booming art market:

> *Pollock has been dead for almost five years. The prices of his paintings have soared. Lifting those of other American abstractionists. By now art is 'in.' It's news. It's a media event, a happening. Every artist is being photographed—without anxiety. . . . Generations zip by. What used to span twenty or twenty-five years is now compressed into a decade or so. The second generation of Action or Gestural Painters . . . are being squeezed by time, compared constantly and invidiously with both previous and succeeding generations . . . [the photo] epitomizes the full and extreme development of truly confrontational Action Painting by a generation which has to some extent been lost.*[12]

What is it, one wonders, that makes this photograph of Bluhm so tempting a target for exegesis, that makes it such a convenient symbol of a generation? Is it the dramatic choreography, the precarious pose that Jones finds "self-conscious" and Friedman "confrontational"? Or is it that the photograph depicts something then rapidly vanishing from vanguard American art: a direct relationship between the work and the body of the artist? There's something a little ironic in the

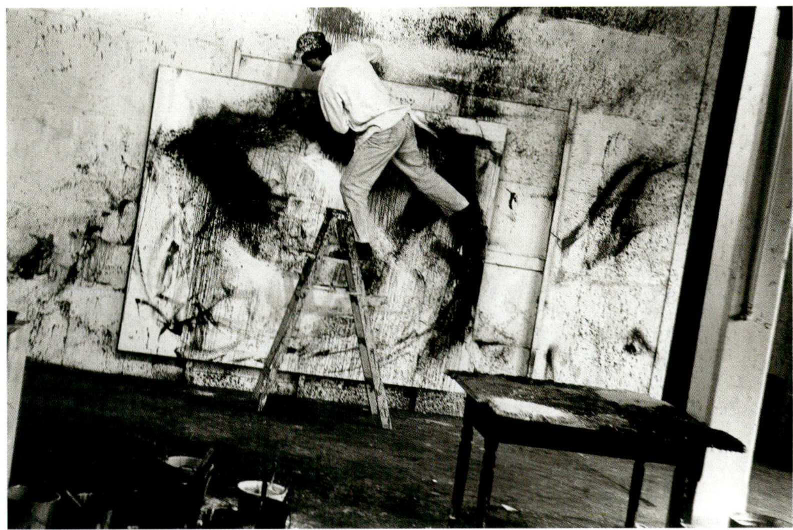

Figure 1. Fred W. McDarrah, Norman Bluhm in his Fourth Avenue Studio, February 22, 1961; Copyright © by Fred W. McDarrah

fact that Bluhm, whose subsequent career would be marked by an uncompromising individualism, should be recruited to represent his generation. But, indeed, he, Francis, Mitchell, and so many other painters were caught off-balance at the beginning of the 1960s, as the rich, nuanced, supple painting practice they had developed over the last decade fell out of fashion with an unexpected rapidity.

In *Machine in the Studio* Jones linked Stella's image of the artist as a sober executive or worker to Andy Warhol's Factory and to Robert Smithson's notion of "post-studio" art, all of which, she believes, reflected concurrent developments in American society. Biased though she may be against Bluhm's generation, Jones was right to take Framton's photographs as evidence of a sea change in artistic practice. A chasm was about to open up in contemporary art, with the development prophesied by Greenberg, the "repudiation of virtuosity," acting as a dividing wedge. When he came out against expressionistic abstraction, Greenberg was thinking of the Color Field painters he supported. But the rejection of "virtuosity" was equally evident in Pop art (Warhol wanting to be a machine) and Minimalism (Stella rejecting—for a couple of years, at least—what he termed "relational" painting), and this attitude essentially dominated much of American art for the next several decades. In "After Abstract Expressionism," pursuing the logic of his belief in the importance of "self-critical" art, Greenberg took his critique of virtuosity to the point where it seemed to provide an argument for the conceptually based art that was just around the corner. To his own question, "What is the ultimate source of value or quality in art?" he answered, "Not skill, training, or anything else having to do with execution or performance, but conception alone."[13]

In 1960, then, critical and institutional support for Abstract Expressionist painting was weakening (though there was a growing number of collectors, including, not least, James Michener, wanting to buy such work). At the same time, an entire generation of artists was about to emerge who would push gestural painting out of the spotlight in favor of Color Field, Neo-Dada, Minimalism, and Pop.

SOME TIME IN NEW YORK CITY

In 1960 Bluhm was thirty-nine, Francis was thirty-seven, and Mitchell was thirty-four. Of the many American painters who embraced abstraction in the wake of Abstract Expressionism, they were among the most successful. That year, Bluhm had his second solo show at Leo Castelli Gallery in New York; the year before, his work had been shown at Documenta II, the important international exhibition in Kassel, Germany, and at the Whitney Annual. Francis, who had also been in the 1959 Documenta, already had work in the collections of MoMA (two paintings) and the Guggenheim; a series of solo shows in Paris, Berne, London, New York, and Tokyo; and two major commissions for mural-scale paintings in New York and Basel. Mitchell had a record of solo New York shows, mostly at the Stable Gallery, going back to 1952. Also included in Documenta, her work had been shown at the Venice Biennale, the Whitney Museum, the Corcoran Biennial, and the Bienal de São Paolo. Influential critics in Paris, New York, and elsewhere were actively supporting the work of all three painters. Coming out of the 1950s, the decade which, to quote Sandler again, had seen the "triumph" of American painting, they appeared poised to assume commanding positions in American art, but the writing was already on the wall. Instead of being a prelude to ever wider acceptance, the year 1960 was perhaps the last moment when they would be able to paint with the feeling of being surrounded by a sympathetic art world. After this, their aesthetic positions would become increasingly embattled. Although one of them, Francis, who died in 1994, would continue to enjoy widespread recognition, Mitchell and Bluhm would spend the next decades in a kind of artistic exile. Mitchell, who died in 1992, would finally achieve considerable success in the last decade of her life, but Bluhm, who died in 1999, would never do so. This, however, wouldn't stop him from creating, in my opinion, the most significant, original body of work of the three of them, but that's another story, beyond the scope of this essay.[14]

* * * *

All three of the canvases considered in this essay were probably painted in or around New York.[15] This likelihood is worth noting if only because Francis, Mitchell, and Bluhm spent relatively little of their careers in New York. Francis only worked there for two years (1958–1960) and then intermittently. The Chicago-born Mitchell, who arrived in New York in 1950, began spending part of each year in France in 1955 and moved there permanently at the end of the decade, though she remained a frequent visitor to New York. As far as I can ascertain, *Rock Bottom* belongs to one of the last bodies of work—a group of paintings made on Long Island in the summer of 1960—Mitchell finished before moving to France. Bluhm spent the longest time in New York: 1956–1970, with a one-year hiatus in France in 1964–1965. Francis, Mitchell, and Bluhm made these paintings, thus, toward the end of the brief two-year period (1958–1960) when all three were active in New York.

Despite the brevity of their New York overlap, there were many points at which the lives and careers of these three artists crossed. At the beginning of the 1950s, Bluhm and Francis met in Paris, where they shared a studio for a short time (figure 2). Like many other members

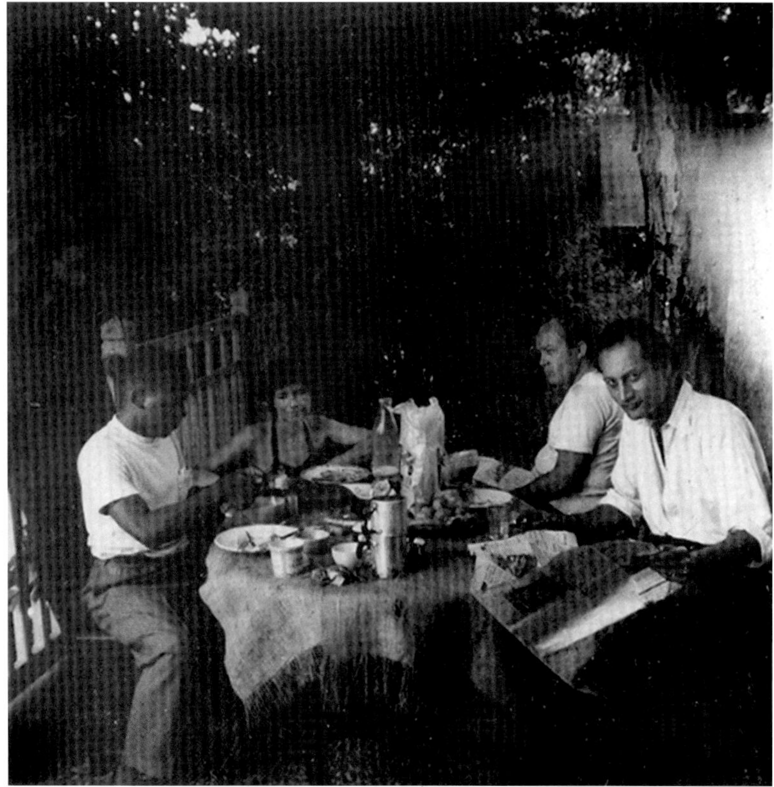

Figure 2. (l. to r.) Bill Rivers, Claude Souvrain, Sam Francis, and Norman Bluhm in Villefranche-sur-Mer, France, circa 1952; Private papers of Norman Bluhm, courtesy of his family

of the American expatriate community, they were taking advantage of their GI Bill benefits, which gave veterans a small monthly stipend if they were studying. Both men had served in the United States Army Air Force, Bluhm as a bomber pilot in North Africa and Europe, Francis as a pilot until he was injured in a crash during training in Arizona. Bluhm had arrived in Paris in 1947; Francis came in 1950. Their circle included French-Canadian painter Jean-Paul Riopelle (who would have a twenty-year-long romantic relationship with Mitchell), and US-born painters Shirley Jaffe and Kimber Smith. Both Bluhm and Francis became friends with the French critic Georges Duthuit, who was married to Henri Matisse's daughter, Marguerite, and through him became close to the Matisse family.

A rupture subsequently developed in Bluhm and Francis's friendship as a result of which, after their Paris days, they remained unreconciled for the rest of their lives. Bluhm and Mitchell, on the other hand, who both also happened to be Chicagoans by birth, stayed on friendly terms (figure 3). (There's also a marvelously evocative photograph taken of them with Franz Kline in the Cedar Bar in the late 1950s.) Francis and Mitchell first met in 1954, during a brief visit Francis made to New York. They met again in 1955 in Paris and continued to encounter each other in Paris and New York through the 1950s. When Francis arrived in New York in 1957, Mitchell organized a party at her St. Marks Place apartment to introduce him to the local art world. For many years, both painters showed at the same Parisian gallery, Jean Fournier.

Thus, among the 300 or so works in the Michener Collection, the three paintings that are the focus of this essay are linked not only stylistically and chronologically, but also by the network of friendships in which they were created.

NORMAN BLUHM: *APOLLO'S ARC*

It was in 1959, the year before *Apollo's Arc,* that Bluhm emerged as a stylistically individual painter with the completion of three large-scale canvases: *The Anvil, Chicago 1920,* and *Winter Nights*. Shortly after he returned to the US in 1956, Bluhm had begun moving away from the allover veils created by abbreviated strokes of saturated color that had characterized his work since 1953. The similarities between Bluhm's and Francis's paintings of 1952–1953 are striking, attaining a stylistic symbiosis that calls to mind the pervasive correspondences in the work of Picasso and Braque during the heyday of Cubism. Obviously, sharing a studio, which they did on the Boulevard Arago in Paris in 1952, brought them close artistically—perhaps too close.

In 1957 the poet James Schuyler reviewed for *Artnews* Bluhm's solo show at Castelli, held October 1–26 (figure 4). In the review, Schuyler broached the issue that plagued Bluhm and Francis in the 1950s and contributed to the break-up of their friendship. "His

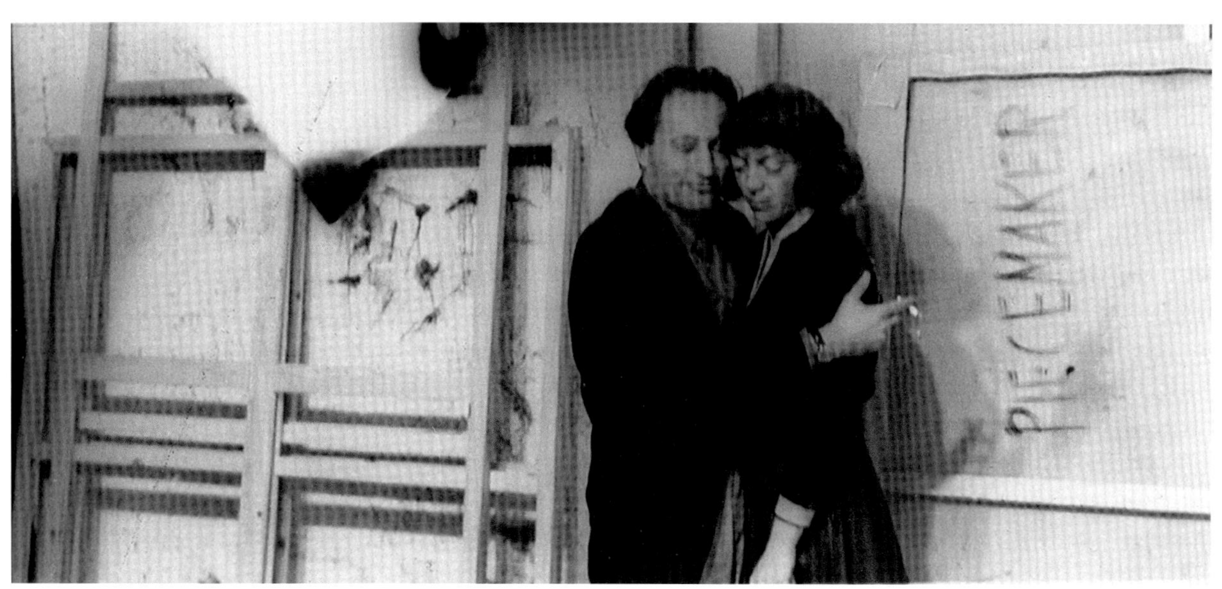

Figure 3. Norman Bluhm and Joan Mitchell in Bluhm's studio, New York, late 1950s; Private papers of Norman Bluhm, courtesy of his family

Figure 4. Norman Bluhm, *Jaded Silence*, 1957; oil on canvas, 71 × 79 in.; Worcester Art Museum

[Bluhm's] style superficially resembles that of Sam Francis," Schuyler wrote, "with whom he was associated in Paris, but Bluhm's expressivity, the quality of individual gesture and of the total gesture of the painting, most of all, subtlety and brilliance of color, make any question of who did what first beside the point."[16]

Both painters continued to work in the style they had forged together until about 1957 (figures 4 and 6), when they began, independently of each other, to rend the curtains of color, letting in more space. From that moment, they went on to develop in completely distinct directions, as can be seen by comparing *Apollo's Arc* (figure 5) and *Blue in Motion II* (figure 7). In contrast to the Francis's thinly painted, almost diaphanous forms, Bluhm worked with thick, jagged shapes built from quick slaps of a paint-loaded brush against the canvas. And in contrast to the traceries of blue dots in the Francis, Bluhm's paint runs in unstoppable rivulets and blankets the white areas with dense, omnidirectional splatters. Braiding together black, yellow, and white shapes, Bluhm created a kind of abstract contrapposto in which every form is twisted and truncated. Francis's forms, on the other hand, nuzzle and nudge each other; they seem to have gently separated into discrete groups, instead of battling for center stage, as Bluhm's forms appear to be doing.

Bluhm probably painted this canvas, which Michener bought from the Poindexter Gallery in 1962, in his New York studio at 333 Park Avenue South (the same studio in which McDarrah photographed him in 1961). The year had begun for the artist with his second, and last, show at Castelli from January 26–February 13.[17] Another notable event of 1960 was the creation of the Poem-Paintings, a series of collaborative works that Bluhm and poet Frank O'Hara made in October at 333 Park Avenue South. (Three years earlier, an O'Hara poem had been the inspiration for one of Mitchell's paintings, *To the Harbormaster* of 1957; the poet, who worked as a curator at The Museum of Modern Art, was a close friend of both artists.) Another work produced in that year is Alex Katz's painting *Portrait of Norman Bluhm*.[18]

Although the paintings in the Michener Collection don't show it (in addition to *Apollo's Arc*, Michener bought Bluhm's *Summer Steel*, 1961),[19] one of the innovations Bluhm helped bring to abstract painting at the end of the 1950s was the use of multiple panels in a single painting. Both *Chicago 1920* and *Winter Nights* are triptychs. While the older generation of abstract painters in New York—Pollock, de Kooning, Kline—had never worked with multiple panels, Bluhm, along with other young artists such as Ellsworth Kelly and Alfred Leslie, repeatedly turned to this format.[20] The reasons were partly practical. In Bluhm's case, it was the only way he could get large paintings out of his Park Avenue South studio. But the sudden return of this hitherto underused format invites speculation. It suggests, for one thing, a greater openness to the art of the past, in particular the multipanel paintings of the Italian Renaissance, as well as the precedent of the Japanese screen. In general, artists of Bluhm's age, many of whom had actually lived in Europe (unlike the Depression-bound painters of the preceding generation), were more willing to borrow from the European past in their mature work.[21] Interestingly, the advent of such multi-panel canvases also may have signified a more materialist approach to painting, opening the way for the painting-sculpture

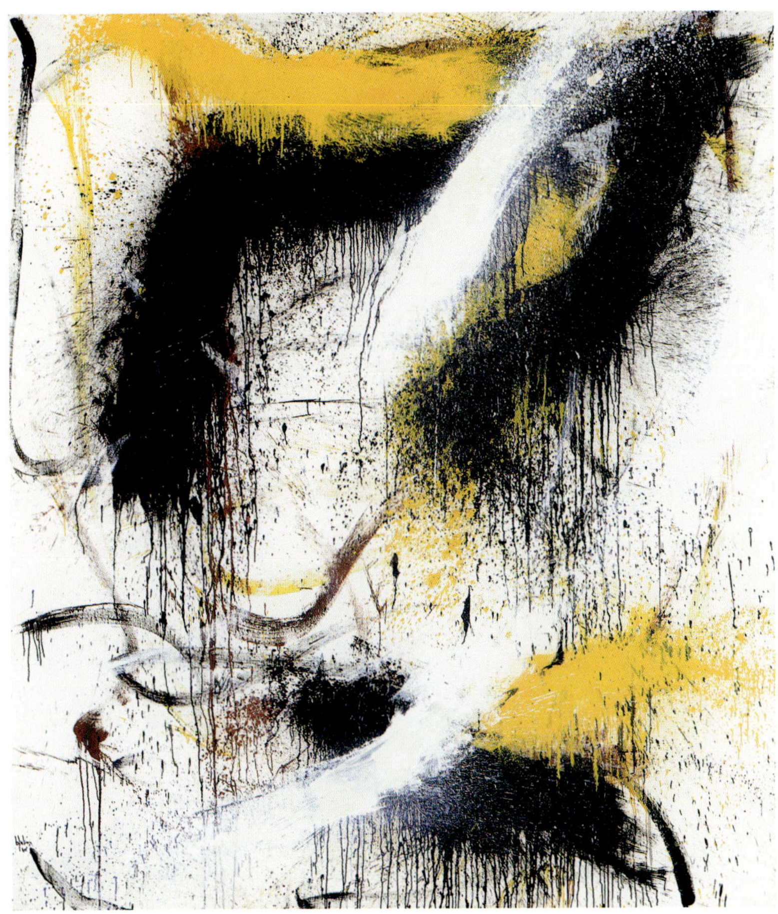

Figure 5. Norman Bluhm, *Apollo's Arc*, 1960; oil on canvas, 84¼ × 72 in.; Gift of Mari and James A. Michener, 1991.191

hybrids of Robert Rauschenberg's combines and Donald Judd's "specific objects."

In his later work, Bluhm unleashed the baroque figuration that was only hinted at in 1960, producing several decades' worth of amazing canvases that reconcile Abstract Expressionism with Baroque and Renaissance Italian painting. Although one couldn't easily have predicted this development from seeing *Apollo's Arc,* already a certain kind of tension was building. The forms in this painting seem barely to be contained by the edges of the canvas. Bluhm had little sympathy for the Neo-Dada of Johns and Rauschenberg, and even less for the rising Pop art style, but in his own way, he already may have been sharing some of the art world's growing dissatisfaction with the inherited assumptions attached to Abstract Expressionist painting. A year later, in 1961, Bluhm showed a massive new painting at the Graham Gallery in New York. Measuring 8 × 24 feet, this four-panel picture, *Oz,* employed an open, airy composition that was unprecedented for Bluhm; the contained energy visible in *Apollo's Arc* had exploded.

SAM FRANCIS: *BLUE IN MOTION II*

Francis spent most of 1959 and the beginning of 1960 in New York, where he had a studio at 940 Broadway. He was working on a large mural for the headquarters of Chase Manhattan Bank. An incessant traveler, he visited California and Japan at the time of his stay in New York as well as making a trip back to Paris. Probably painted during this time in New York, *Blue in Motion II* (figure 7) belongs to his Blue Balls series, which he began toward the end of 1959 and continued for two or three years.

In comparison to that used by Mitchell, and even by Bluhm, the paint Francis used for *Blue in Motion II* is extremely liquid. Indeed he treats paint more like ink or watercolor than traditional oil paint. Although its medium is identified as oil on canvas, I wonder if it doesn't also include some synthetic paint as well. Francis, who would later become well known for his use of acrylic paint, started mixing oils with synthetic paints in Paris in the 1950s.

Since the early 1950s, Francis had been composing with cellular units, first in allover patterns or veils, then, after 1955, in increasingly open arrangements where the forms separate into clusters (figure 6). This cellular quality contributes to the impression *Blue in Motion II* gives of showing a view through a microscope. We might be looking at tiny creatures or at blue-tinged blood cells. In later Blue Balls paintings, the forms become globular and even more cell-like. While these forms appear, pictorially, to reflect the title more aptly, the name of the series

Figure 6. Sam Francis, *Blue Black,* 1952; oil on canvas, 117 × 76¼ in.; Albright-Knox Art Gallery, Buffalo, New York; Gift of Seymour H. Knox, Jr., 1956; © 2005 Sam Francis Estate/Samuel L. Francis Foundation, California /Artists Rights Society (ARS), New York

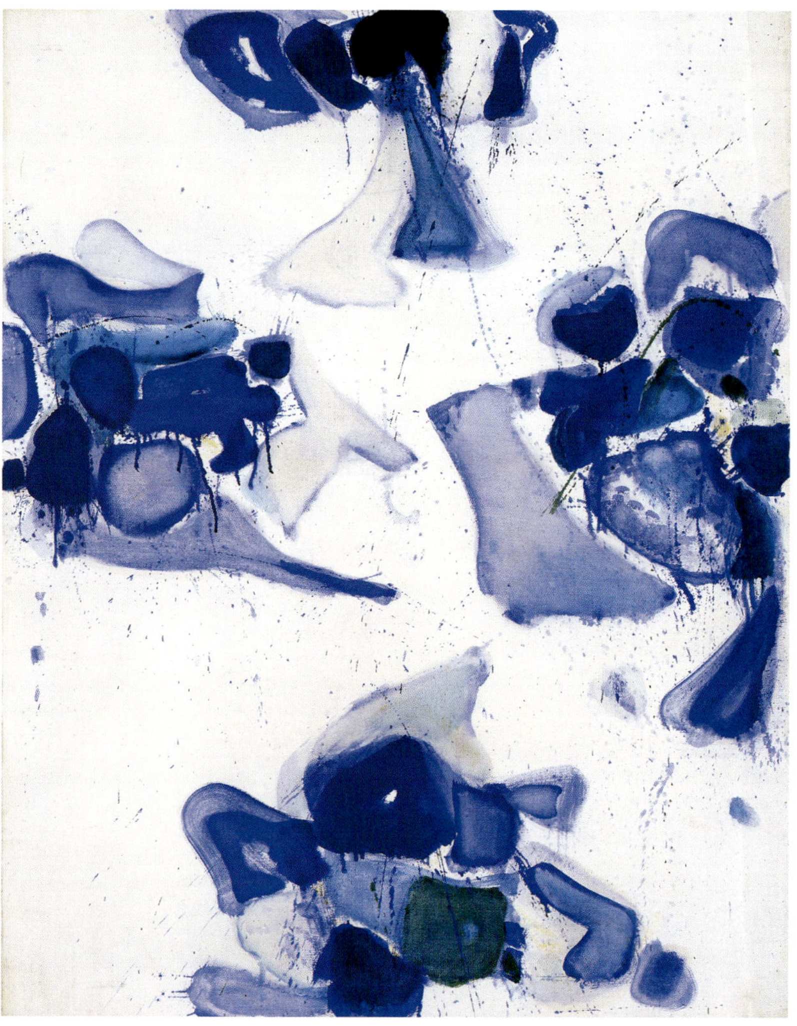

Figure 7. Sam Francis, *Blue in Motion II,* 1960; oil on canvas, 45½ × 35 in.; Gift of Mari and James A. Michener, 1991.211; © 2005 Sam Francis Estate/Samuel L. Francis Foundation, California /Artists Rights Society (ARS), New York

does double duty in its guise as a popular expression for male sexual frustration. In 1961 Francis was hospitalized in Switzerland with "urogenital tuberculosis." This threat to his testicles, and the accompanying anxiety about possible sterility, suggests another dimension to the biological aspect of the paintings and another layer of meaning to the name of the series. Although Francis began painting these testicular blue cells before his disease was diagnosed, the correspondence between the whimsical title he gave to the series and his incipient medical condition is especially interesting.[22]

Once he'd finished his mural commission, Francis didn't stay in New York, choosing instead to work in Japan and then California. This may have been, in part, because of a feeling of rejection by the New York art world. According to some of Francis's friends, Bluhm had poisoned the atmosphere by speaking badly of Francis to their shared painter and critic friends. One can't know what was said on any given night in the Cedar Bar, but judging from the 1957 James Schuyler review quoted above, it seems to have been Bluhm that had to defend himself from comparisons with the better-known Francis. Others attribute the cool reception of Francis's work to its divergence from New York–style gestural abstraction.[23] In any case, Francis seemed to have soon reconciled himself to his estrangement from New York. Once asked about his relation with the New York School, he responded, "I escaped by never being there, going to Paris, going to Tokyo, being a fugitive."[24]

Although Bluhm's and Francis's styles had diverged by 1960, one can't help noticing how much both *Apollo's Arc* and *Blue in Motion II* rely on diagonals: in Bluhm, through the torquing white, yellow, and dark green forms; in Francis, by means of the negative space defined by the clusters of irregular blue shapes hugging the four sides of the canvas. In later work, Francis would marginalize his colored elements to the point that the canvas becomes almost entirely filled with white space. Here, body and void remain more evenly balanced, although the transparency of these mutating blue cells (not yet devolved into "balls") suggests a confluence between figure and ground, almost as if the white ground were a clear amniotic fluid.

JOAN MITCHELL: *ROCK BOTTOM*

In the summer of 1959, Mitchell rented a studio at 10, rue Frémicourt in Paris's 15th arrondissement, where she began living with Jean-Paul Riopelle. She continued to make regular visits to New York, but, with the exception of the work made on Long Island in the summer of 1960, she painted only in France. As Mitchell and Riopelle were summering on Long Island, Bluhm was using Mitchell's Paris studio to paint.

The taffylike strands of blue and white paint cast around the central area of *Rock Bottom* (figure 8), which Michener bought from the Stable Gallery in 1961, begin showing up frequently in Mitchell's paintings around 1960. Prior to this, her mark making was almost always the result of the brush coming into direct contact with the canvas; after this, it resulted from paint being dribbled and spun from the brush. The immediate precedent for these thickened threads of paint is to be found not so much in Pollock's drip paintings as in the paintings of Riopelle, who had been using such snotty skeins of paint since the late 1940s, often in bramblelike clusters atop densely faceted grounds of paint laid on with a palette knife. A similar use of paint shows up in the work of the Paris-based, German painter and photographer Wols (Alfred Otto Wolfgang Schulze). In a review of Mitchell's first solo show in Paris, held the same year she painted *Rock Bottom,* French critic Pierre Schneider, who was a good friend of Bluhm's, wrote of her painting as being built from a series of "conflicting hesitations and mutually abolishing decisions." This marvelous formulation suggests the complex, infinitely nuanced process that goes into a painting like *Rock Bottom* and the fact that there is no prescribed way of looking at it. As with a landscape, each time one's eyes shift or refocus, the painting presents itself in a different aspect.

In the lower left of *Rock Bottom,* there's an area of pink and white that is almost rococo, while the lower right is emptied out in a way that suggests one of de Kooning's late canvases. In contrast to Bluhm and Francis, Mitchell never pursued figurative allusions. The basis of her work was always landscape, both as a complex of vegetation and as an arena for light. Mitchell once told an interviewer, "Light is something very special. It has nothing to do with white. Either you see it or you don't. De la Tour doesn't have light; Monet hasn't any light; Matisse, Goya, Chardin, van Gogh, Sam Francis, Kline have it for me. It has nothing to do with being the best painter at all." (Reading this, one wants to turn immediately to Francis's painting to see if light has a presence there, and indeed it does, in the play of blue-tinted translucency.) Speaking about *Rock Bottom* in 1986, Mitchell drew attention to the mood of the painting and also to the possibility of seeing in it

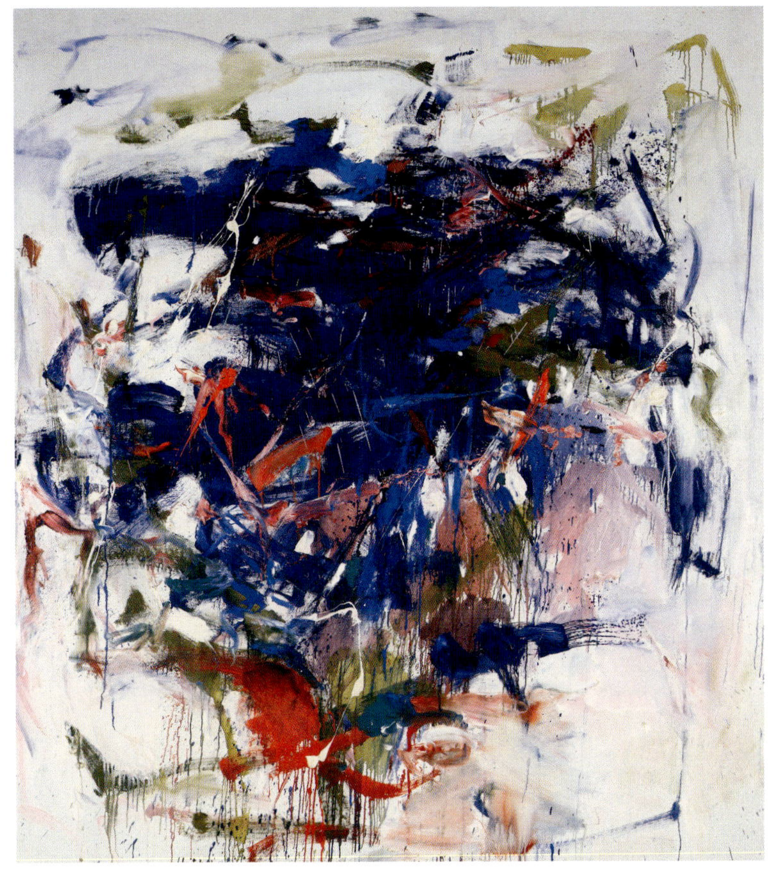

Figure 8. Joan Mitchell, *Rock Bottom*, 1960–1961; oil on canvas, 78 × 68 in.; Gift of Mari and James A. Michener, 1991.276

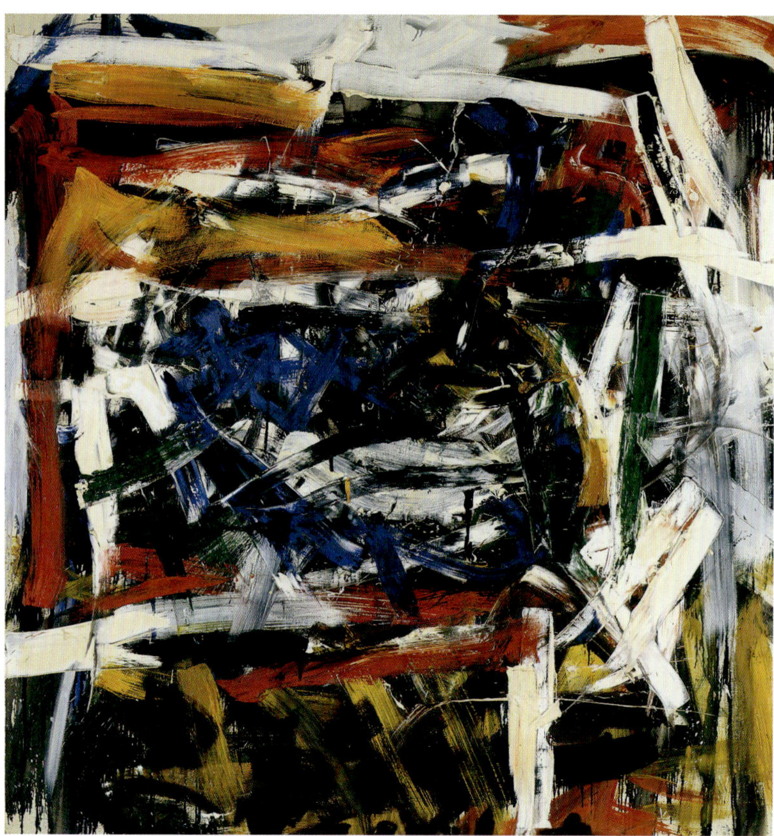

Figure 9. Michael Goldberg, *Dune House II*, 1958; oil on canvas, 86¾ × 80⅛ in.; Gift of Mari and James A. Michener, 1991.220

specific references to landscape. "It's a very violent painting, and you might say sea, rocks," she told author Judith Bernstock.[25]

While Riopelle was a more direct influence on her paint handling than Pollock, Mitchell's *Rock Bottom*, in which a rent seems to open up in the center of the painting, does recall Pollock's *The Deep* (1953), first shown in 1954 at Sidney Janis Gallery. It's an uncharacteristic painting for Pollock, with vigorous white-on-white brushstrokes surrounding a dark black and green gashlike area in the center of the composition. The most obvious difference is that, while Pollock's dark center, which some have termed vaginal, is a fissure, Mitchell's central tangle is more clearly positive space. There's another painting in the Michener Collection, Michael Goldberg's *Dune House II* (1958, figure 9), which also relies on vigorous brushwork to establish a central image. Actually, Mitchell, Francis, and Bluhm all built their paintings around a center—dense and clotted in Mitchell, open in Francis, contested in Bluhm. In noticing this similarity, one realizes how many other connections must exist between the oeuvres of these three artists and their closely intertwined careers. Perhaps in fifty or 100 years, some inquisitive curator will put together an exhibition examining Mitchell, Francis, and Bluhm in depth, tracing the crossovers, and the clashes, in their work. Given the current preoccupations of the art world, it's unlikely to happen much sooner. Until then, interested viewers will have to be satisfied with conjunctions of a smaller scale, such as the fascinating one offered by the Michener Collection.

Notes

1. As Lawrence Alloway pointed out in 1973, although Sam Francis's birthdate, 1923, put him in the "second generation," the fact that he developed early (according to Alloway, "his mature style was achieved by 1950") links him closely with "first generation" painters like Mark Rothko, who only solidified his style around 1949. See Lawrence Alloway, "Sam Francis: From Field to Arabesque," *Artforum* 11 (February 1973): 38.
2. "Then and Now: Six of the New York School Look Back," interviews by Stephen Westfall, *Art in America* 73 (June 1985): 116.
3. Irving Sandler, *The New York School: The Painters and Sculptors of the Fifties* (New York: Harper & Row, 1978), 292.
4. Sandler, 282.
5. Quoted in "Market Letter," *Art in America* 48 (spring 1960): 4. It's interesting to look at Michener's collecting activities in light of these developments. He bought the Francis and the Mitchell in 1961, the two Bluhms in 1962 and 1963, but steered clear of Neo-Dada, Minimalism and, for the most part, Pop art. His two forays into the Pop realm—Peter Saul's *Criminal Being Executed* (1964), bought the year it was made, and John Wesley's *Annunciations* (1967), purchased in 1968—are quite prescient, since Saul and Wesley are maverick artists whose work only gained wider recognition in the 1990s.
6. H.H. Arnason, "Abstract Expressionism in 1960," in *60 American Painters, 1960: Abstract Expressionist Painting of the Fifties* (Minneapolis: Walker Art Center, 1961), 11–23.
7. Clement Greenberg, "New York Painting Only Yesterday," *Artnews* 56 (Summer 1957), reprinted in John O'Brian, ed., *Clement Greenberg: The Collected Essays and Criticism,* vol. 4 (Chicago: University of Chicago Press, 1993), 22.
8. Clement Greenberg, "The Late Thirties in New York," *Art and Culture* (Boston: Beacon Press, 1961), 235. Here the revised essay carries two dates, 1957 and 1960.
9. Clement Greenberg, "Modernist Painting," Forum Lectures, Washington, D.C., Voice of America, 1960. Reprinted in O'Brian, 85.
10. Clement Greenberg, "After Abstract Expressionism," *Art International* 25 (October 1962). A slightly revised version is reprinted in O'Brian, 131. While Greenberg never wrote about Bluhm and Mitchell, no doubt associating them with the dreaded "Tenth Street," he approved of Francis's work. At the end of a 1960 article on Morris Louis and Kenneth Noland, Greenberg names them and Francis as "the only painters to have come up in American art since that 'first wave' who approach its level." See his "Louis and Noland," *Art International* 3 (May 1960), reprinted in O'Brian, 99–100. Greenberg also had good things to say about Francis in "After Abstract Expressionism." Noting the "crushing" influence of Barnett Newman, Mark Rothko, and Clyfford Still, he wrote that "the only younger artist who has yet been able to assert himself under it is Sam Francis" (133).
11. Caroline A. Jones, *Machine in the Studio: Constructing the Postwar American Artist* (Chicago and London: University of Chicago Press, 1996), 126–27.
12. B.H. Friedman, "Two Images, Two Moments in Art History," in Paul Schimmel, ed., *Action/Precision: The New Direction in New York, 1955–60* (Newport Beach, Calif.: Newport Harbor Art Museum, 1984), 49–52.
13. Clement Greenberg, "After Abstract Expressionism," in O'Brian, 132.
14. For more on Bluhm's later work, see James Harithas, Raphael Rubinstein, and Luigi Sansone, *Norman Bluhm* (Milan: Mazzotta, 2000); Raphael Rubinstein, "Bluhm's Day," *Art in America* 80 (October 1992): 136–41, 173; and Raphael Rubinstein, "Nine Lives of Painting," *Art in America* 86 (September 1998): 90–99.
15. In 1960 Bluhm's studio was in New York, and he probably painted *Apollo's Arc* there. However, since he spent the summer of that year in Paris where Mitchell had lent him her new studio, it's not impossible that he painted the canvas in Paris and shipped it back to New York. Mitchell herself was painting that summer in Easthampton, New York. Her Stable Gallery exhibition in the spring of 1961 in which *Rock Bottom* was first shown included works made in the US and France. In his preview of the show (*Arts Magazine* 35 [May 1961]: 13), Sandler wrote of "recent canvases, most of which were painted in Long Island last summer," as well as "a series of new works on their way over from Paris" which were "not available for preview." *Rock Bottom* was probably among the former paintings. The most peripatetic of the three, Francis spent several months in New York in the winter and spring of 1958. After extensive travels in Europe, Asia and the US, he rented a studio in New York in the beginning of 1959 and spent most of the following year and a half in the city. It was during this time that he started the Blue Balls series, of which *Blue in Motion II* is an early example. See the chronology complied by Debra Burchett-Lere in William C. Agee, *Sam Francis: Paintings 1947–1990* (Los Angeles: Museum of Contemporary Art, Los Angeles, 1999), 142–55.
16. James Schuyler, in Simon Pettet, ed., *Selected Art Writings* (Santa Rosa, Calif.: Black Sparrow Press, 1998), 199.
17. Bluhm was angered at twice coming into his solo show to find works by Jasper Johns and Robert Rauschenberg situated around the gallery. Dissatisfied with Castelli's excuse that collectors were avid for works by these artists, and realizing that his dealer no longer had any real commitment to his kind of painting, Bluhm left the gallery.
18. An article lauding the controversial return of figurative painting in the early 1960s included a reproduction of this painting. See Dorothy Gees Seckler, "Furor Over Figure," *Art in America* 49, no. 1 (1961): 99.
19. The reason Michener bought a second painting may have been his dissatisfaction with the first. In a tape-recorded account of his collecting activities, Michener complained about *Apollo's Arc:* "I did not like it too much when I got it and I went down to see Norman Bluhm to see if he would trade in for what I thought was a better. He was infuriated. I've never seen an artist so outraged. He said it was one of the best things he had done and there was nothing in his atelier that was any better and I should be happy with what I got. I have never liked the painting particularly and when I see it now, I still think that he had several much better in his shop and I think he made a mistake in not making the trade that I proposed, because it leaves a somewhat inferior painting in what may ultimately be a fairly important collection." Transcript of interview, 62, Blanton Museum of Art Archives, The University of Texas at Austin. In 1969 Bluhm told his side of the story to an interviewer from the Archives of American Art: "James Michener, the so-called writer, bought my painting from the Guggenheim. About two years later he called me. As a matter of fact, at nine o'clock in the morning the phone rang. I thought what the hell is someone calling me at nine in the morning for. 'Norman Bluhm?' 'Yes.' 'This is James Michener.' 'Hello.' 'I'd like to come up and see what you're doing. I hear they're terrific.' 'Okay, come up.' He must have been downstairs having a cup of coffee; he was up in about three seconds. So I showed him some paintings. He said, 'I like that one very much. How much is it?' I told him the price. He said, 'I'll tell you what I'll do. I'll give you back the one I bought and I'll take that one and I'll pay the difference.' I said, 'Look, you've got those shoes on your feet, haven't you? When you wear those shoes out do you bring them back to the shoe store and trade them in for a new pair of shoes? No thanks, fellow, I don't do things that way. If you want to buy a new painting buy a new painting.'" Norman Bluhm, tape-recorded interview by Paul Cummings, New York, October 23, 1969, Archives of American Art, Smithsonian Institution, Washington, D.C. Prior to Michener having seen it at Poindexter Galleries, the painting was included in the important 1961 exhibition "American Abstract Expressionists and Imagists" at the Solomon R. Guggenheim Museum.
20. Although the "first generation" Abstract Expressionists almost never worked on multiple panels, there was one major painter in the United States in the late 1940s who did: Max Beckmann. Notable multiple-panel paintings by Beckmann include *Departure* (1932–1933) and his two late paintings, *Beginnings* (1946–1949) and *The Argonauts* (1949–1950). MoMA acquired *Departure* in 1942, and thus it was available to be seen by New York painters during the 1950s.The museum showed another of Beckmann's triptychs, *Blind Man's Buff* (1944–1945), in 1947.
21. The European influence on New York abstraction of the late 1950s struck curator Paul Schimmel. In 1984 he observed of work by artists such as Bluhm and Mitchell that "it is important to recognize that the source for these paintings is not only American abstract expressionism but the French painting of Monet and Soutine and the work of Van Gogh and Mondrian, who were seen by the younger generation, more clearly than the first generation, as the true masters." Schimmel, *Action/Precision,* 27.
22. In fact Francis believed his art to be closely related to his experience of illness and hospitals. In 1985 he told a French interviewer, "My painting came through sickness. I left the hospital through painting. I suffered in my body in hospitals, for the first time right after the war, and it's because I was able to paint, to learn how to paint, that I was able to heal myself. [And the second time was] at the end of the 1950s when I had to leave Paris. I became very sick. With tuberculosis" (Sam Francis and Yves Michaud, *Entretiens* [Paris: Galerie Jean Fournier, 1985], 34). He further told of going to Switzerland for treatment: "I also occupied myself with painting, intentionally. Otherwise I wouldn't be here. Without painting, I never would have lived" (Francis and Michaud, 34).
23. See Priscilla Colt, "The Paintings of Sam Francis," *Art Journal* 22 (fall 1962): 7.
24. Francis and Michaud, 43.
25. Judith E. Bernstock, *Joan Mitchell* (New York: Hudson Hills, 1988), 57.

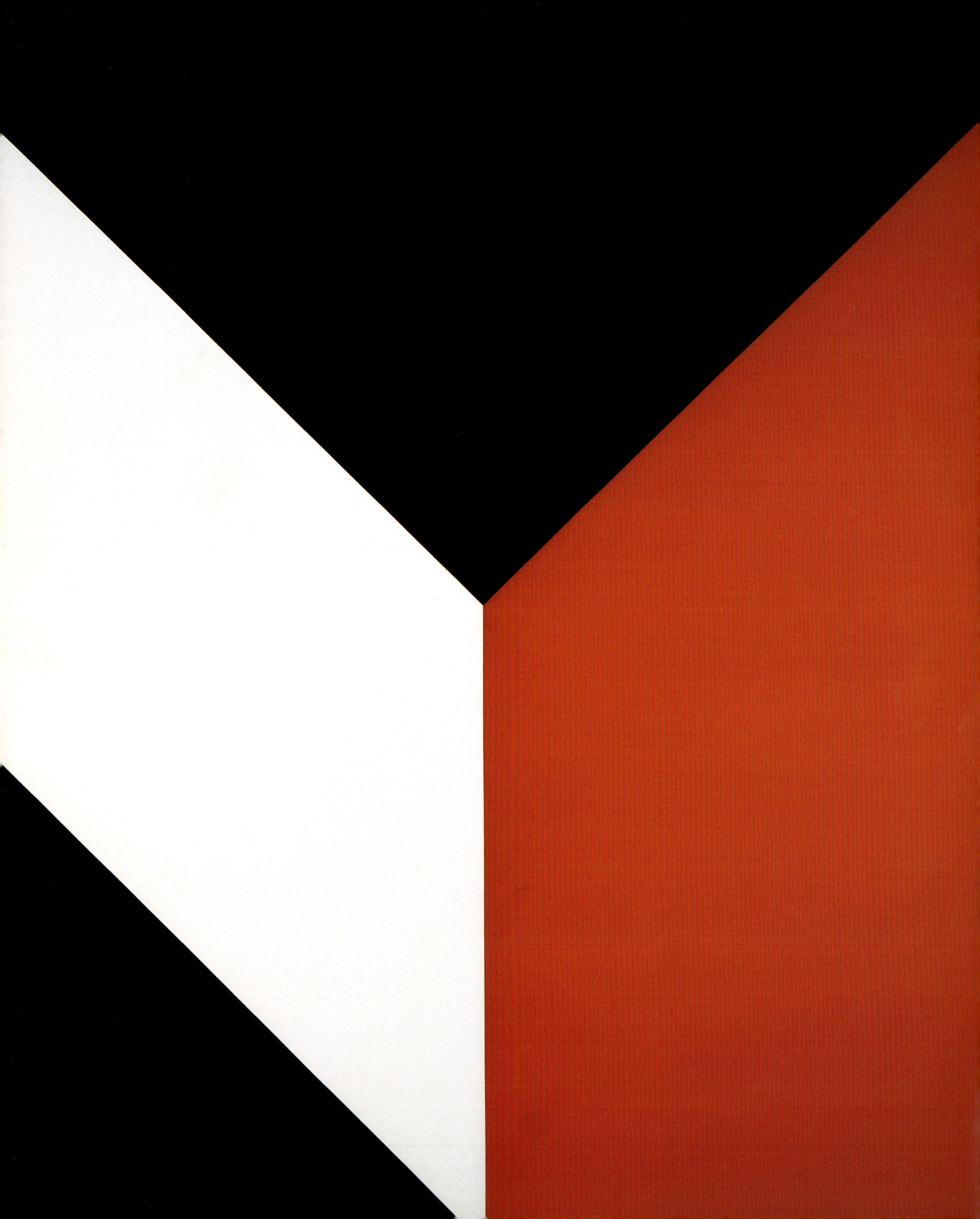

DEAN FLEMING, ED RUDA, AND THE PARK PLACE GALLERY

SPATIAL COMPLEXITY AND THE "FOURTH DIMENSION" IN 1960S NEW YORK

Linda Dalrymple Henderson

THREE PAINTINGS OF 1965–1966 in the Blanton's collection function as powerful catalysts for rethinking the history of American art of the 1960s as written to date. Dean Fleming's 1965 *Untitled* (figure 5) and *Snap Roll* (figure 6), both acquired in the 1960s, and Ed Ruda's 1966 *Reo Reo* (figure 9), a recent gift to the museum, are bold, intensely colored geometric abstractions that create paradoxical spatial effects at the same time that they acknowledge the literal surface of the canvas.[1] Characteristic of the work by the artists of the co-op Park Place Gallery in New York in the mid-1960s, Fleming's and Ruda's paintings document the group's commitment to exploring complex spaces that deny familiar readings as two- or three-dimensional. Such works had high visibility in this period, appearing, for example, in Lawrence Alloway's landmark *Systemic Painting* exhibition at the Guggenheim Museum in 1966. There Fleming and Ruda, along with fellow Park Place painter David Novros, showed works similar to those in the Blanton's collection.[2] Now reunited in Austin, Fleming's *Untitled* and *Snap Roll*, as well as Ruda's *Reo Reo*, attest convincingly to spatial complexity and ambiguity as vital avant-garde concerns that have been largely overlooked in art historical writing on the 1960s.

Ruda, a New Yorker, and Fleming, a Californian who moved to New York in 1961, first met in 1962. That fall the top floor of the five-story building Fleming rented at 79 Park Place became a communal gathering point for a group of his California friends who had migrated gradually to New York. Mark di Suvero had settled in the city in 1957, with Peter Forakis following later that same year. Fleming and Forakis had been fellow students at the California School of Fine Arts, and, once Fleming was in New York, he encouraged other of his former fellow students to join him in his building. Leo Valledor, Forrest Myers, and Tamara Melcher settled there during the course of 1962, and the friends began to share work informally on the fifth floor.[3] Ruda had met di Suvero in 1960 and joined the group, as did di Suvero's friends Tony Magar and Robert Grosvenor; the founders subsequently invited Novros to join in order to complete their roster of five sculptors and five painters (figure 1).[4]

After its informal origins in fall 1962, the Park Place Gallery opened officially as a cooperative gallery in mid-1963 and continued through spring 1964 in the Park Place location. When that building was slated for demolition, the group exhibited at Dan Graham's Daniels Gallery and at Noah Goldowsky Gallery during fall 1964 and spring 1965. By late 1965, with new backing from a group of collectors, the "Park Place Gallery of Art Research" opened in a new location at 542 West Broadway and operated there through summer 1967. Members of the group continued to exhibit together, however, through 1968, and many of the friendships formed in that era continue to the present day.[5]

Dean Fleming, *Snap Roll*, 1965 (detail, figure 6)

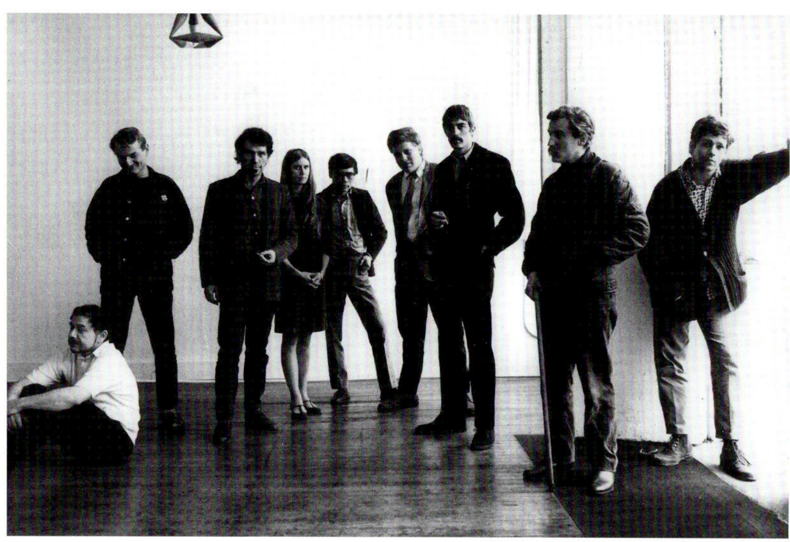

Figure 1. The Park Place Gallery Group, 1966 (l. to r.: Ed Ruda, Dean Fleming, Tony Magar, Tamara Melcher, Leo Valledor, Robert Grosvenor, Forrest Myers, Peter Forakis, David Novros)

Although Fleming and Ruda were nine years apart in age and from opposite coasts, they had a remarkable number of experiences and interests in common. Drawn to comics and cartooning in their youths (an activity Fleming, along with Forakis, pursued at Park Place as well), both painters subsequently arrived at their mature styles via Abstract Expressionism. Both did military service in the Pacific—Ruda in New Guinea and the Trobriand Islands during World War II, and Fleming in Korea and Japan during the Korean War—and both studied art on the GI Bill. Mexico held a strong attraction for the two artists, and their personal experiences of landscape—light and color for Fleming and space for Ruda—would inflect their mature geometric abstract styles (and titles). Although in recent years Fleming has turned wholeheartedly to landscape painting, while Ruda has continued to focus on abstraction, both are working once again in a gestural style. The pursuit of complexity and indeterminacy central to their Park Place works also remains key for both artists today.

Born in 1933, Fleming grew up in Santa Monica, California. He credits his later interest in geometry and grids in part to his father, an aeronautical engineer with training in architecture, who taught him to draw and letter precisely on graph paper as a child.[6] Furthermore, his father's collection of drawings and books—which included images by Bauhaus and Russian avant-garde artists such as the Suprematist painter Kazimir Malevich and the Constructivist El Lissitzky—exposed him to modernist geometric abstraction. Yet Fleming also responded to comics in the Sunday newspaper, and as a California teenager, he cartooned, surfed, and built hot rods. He briefly pursued aeronautical engineering at California Polytechnic State University in the early 1950s, and he remembers drawing abstract designs, including Necker-reversing "magic cubes," in the margins of his technical drawings.[7]

When he dropped out of college in 1952, Fleming was drafted and sent to Korea. There he discovered Korean and Japanese art as well as the Zen Buddhism that reinforced a spiritual quest he had already begun. This exposure to Asian art and thought, following upon visits to Mexico in the 1940s, was the first in a succession of encounters with various world cultures that would nourish his subsequent growth as an artist. Fleming's two years of Army service also solidified a growing anti-establishment social vision that would remain fundamental throughout his life.

Fleming returned from Korea in 1954 determined to become an artist; he then traveled to Mexico, where he absorbed the art of the Mexican muralists and Pre-Columbian art and enrolled for a time at Mexico City College.[8] From 1956 to 1959 he studied at the California School of Fine Arts (later the San Francisco Art Institute), where Elmer Bischoff headed the painting program and Frank Lobdell became his primary mentor in the West Coast variant of Abstract Expressionism. At Cal Fine Arts, Fleming also met his future Park Place compatriots Peter Forakis and Leo Valledor, with whom he participated in the Six Gallery, where Allen Ginsberg had given his first reading of "Howl" in 1955.[9] Through his studio mate, Manuel Neri, Fleming reconnected with Mark di Suvero, whom he had met briefly several years before. Working in the art school's library, he explored the world of art, from Tantric mandalas to the paintings of Hieronymus Bosch, Vincent van Gogh, Wassily Kandinsky, Piet Mondrian, and Willem de Kooning. In contact with Alan Watts and poet Gary Snyder, Fleming also continued his study of Zen Buddhism.[10] In a series of paintings titled *Bodhisatva on the Bridge* (1960, figure 2), he immersed himself in improvisatory gesture painting on the model of de Kooning.

After Fleming moved to New York in 1961, he gradually left his Abstract Expressionist phase behind, adopting a cooler, hard-edge style and, ultimately, returning to the geometric grids rooted in his youth as well as in Mondrian. During 1963–1964 Fleming taught at Carnegie Mellon, where his interest in Josef Albers's color theories resonated with the Bauhaus-oriented aesthetic of the Ulm School then dominant

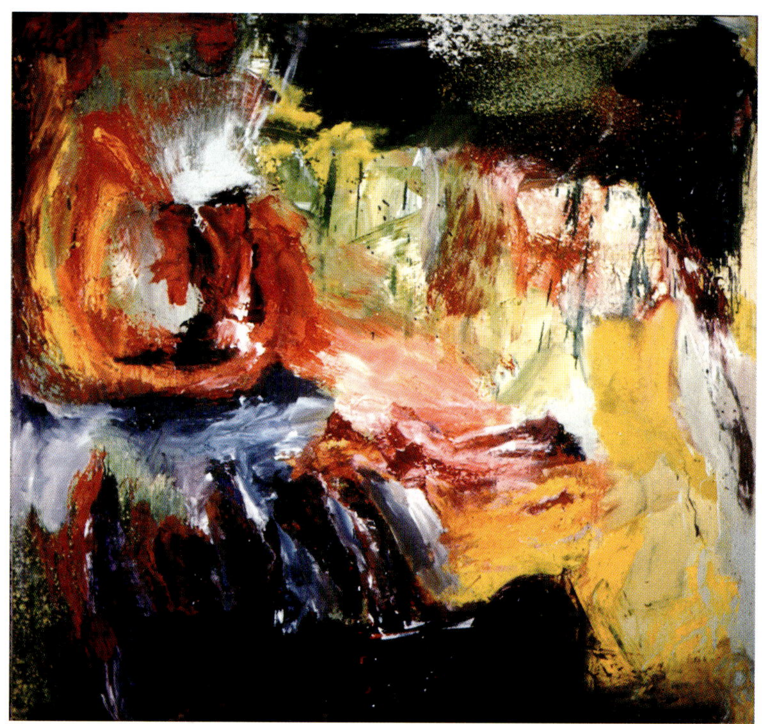

Figure 2. Dean Fleming, *Bodhisatva on the Bridge*, 1960; oil and acrylic on canvas, 72 × 72 in.; Private Collection, Oslo, Norway

at the university. Even more important for the emergence of his mature style of 1965, however, was the travel he undertook in 1964 to North Africa, Egypt, and Greece, which had a profound effect upon his developing sense of color and form. Following his encounter with the rich patterns and colors of Islamic art, Fleming not only began to bisect his gridded squares to form two or four triangles, he also adopted a palette rooted in Islamic art and "prismatic Mediterranean light," as in *Port Said* of 1964 (figure 3).[11]

Once Fleming returned to New York in late 1964, his palette brightened to highly saturated colors plus black and white, and he began to manipulate the vertical and horizontal dimensions of his X-divided modules. The result was a vertiginous spatial "warping" due to the stretching in size of the central squares or rectangles as they progressed toward the edges of paintings such as *Lime Line* of early 1965 (figure 4). Fleming subsequently explored the dynamic potential of the rhombus or parallelogram—the central white forms in *Untitled* (figure 5) and *Snap Roll* (figure 6)—in a group of paintings from spring 1965 that utilized rhomboids and trapezoids faceted into various-sized, irregular triangles.[12]

By mid-1965, however, Fleming had settled on the simplified elements of *Snap Roll* and *Untitled*. Here he used a paint roller and masking tape to create large, flat areas of high-keyed color, black, or white on canvases organized around two central points connected to the painting's edges. Aware from his youth of the phenomenon of Necker-reversing cubes, Fleming now utilized a central white rhombus or parallelogram as an ever-shifting fulcrum for contradictory spatial readings: the central form literally snaps back and forth, taking associated color areas with it.[13] Only Albers's *Structural Constellations* of the 1950s, which Fleming admired, provided a near-contemporary analogue for this bold defiance of the reigning formalist equation of modern painting and flatness propounded by Clement Greenberg in the 1950s and 1960s.[14]

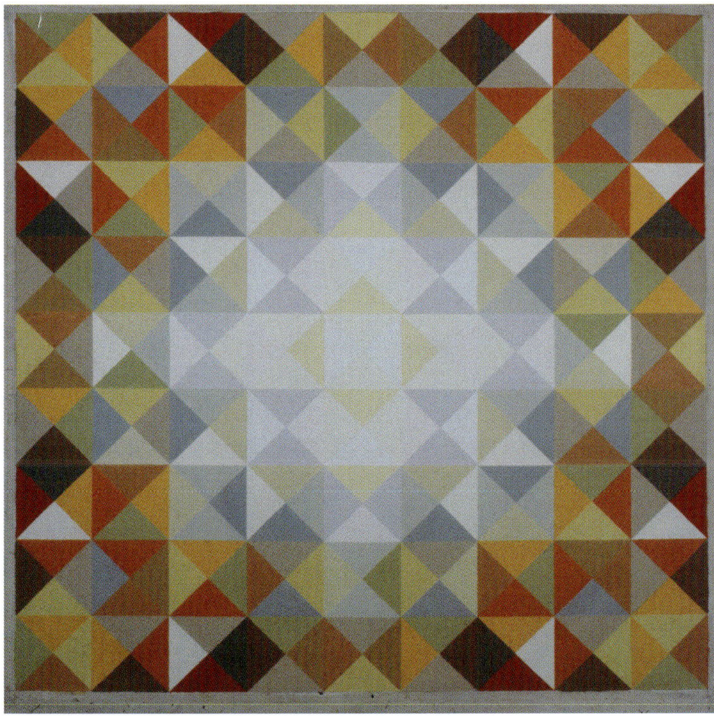

Figure 3. Dean Fleming, *Port Said*, 1964; acrylic on canvas, 58½ × 58½ in.; Collection of Linda Fleming

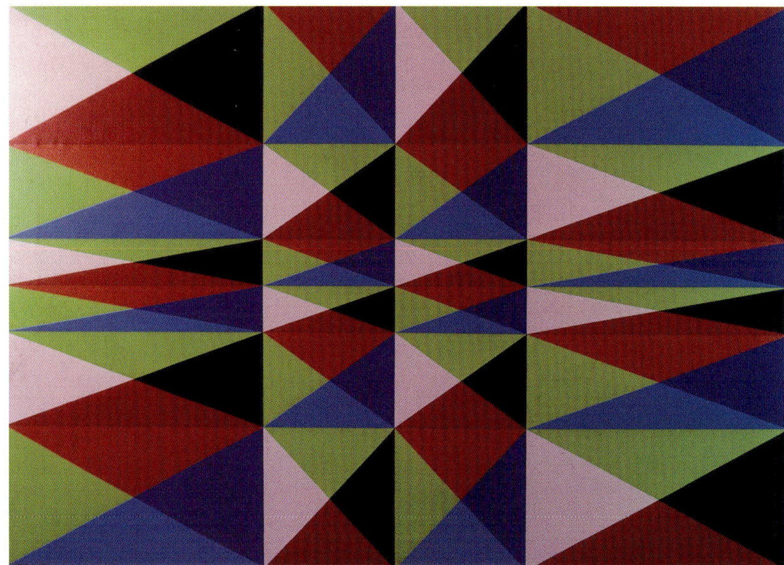

Figure 4. Dean Fleming, *Lime Line*, 1965; acrylic on canvas, 48 × 66 in.; Collection of the Artist

Creating a disorienting, paradoxical experience of spatial ambiguity and uncertainty was exactly Fleming's goal in paintings such as *Snap Roll* and *Untitled*. In 1959 Forakis had shared with him a copy of P. D. Ouspensky's 1911 *Tertium Organum*, which he had discovered in a 1957 sale of the books of San Francisco sculptor Adaline Kent at Cal Fine Arts.[15] Grounded in the early twentieth-century fascination with the possible existence of a suprasensible fourth dimension of space, Ouspensky—a mathematician and mystic—argued for the evolution of consciousness to a new level of "cosmic consciousness." In this state, the illusory world of three-dimensional existence would fall away as one experienced the "sensation of infinity" and true, four-dimensional reality. The "Tertium Organum" that Ouspensky proposed was a new system of alogical logic that would help free individuals from the false logic of the everyday world; hence, paradox and seemingly contradictory experiences could serve as steps toward liberating the mind in order to attain higher consciousness.[16]

As an art student, Fleming had embraced Kandinsky's *Concerning the Spiritual in Art* as well as Jungian psychology, and he found in Ouspensky and the fourth dimension a model for a spiritual, transformative mode of painting rooted in geometry.[17] Fleming also came to identify with Malevich when, as a reader of *Tertium Organum*, he sensed the parallels between certain of the Suprematist painter's statements and Ouspensky's focus on higher consciousness.[18] Fleming made his artistic intentions clear in the January 1965 text he published in the *Systemic Painting* catalogue: "The dominant subject of the painting is its effect on each individual viewer. . . . If an open viewer allows the reading to be in his own time, he can begin to receive an experience which separates from the work he sees and he can participate in the reversals of space and the apparent contradictions between stillness and sudden motion, weight and gravitationlessness."[19] Indeed, critic David Bourdon confirmed the constantly shifting perceptual effects of such

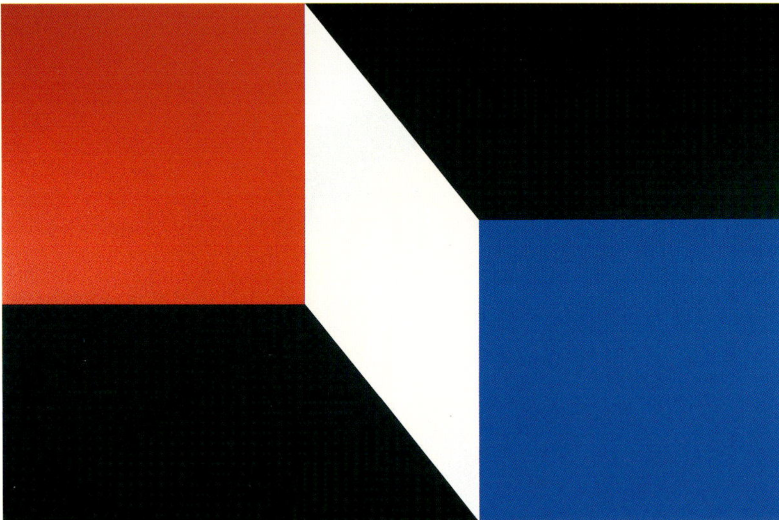

Figure 5. Dean Fleming, *Untitled*, 1965; acrylic on canvas, 66 × 99 3/16 in.; Gift of Art Research, Inc. and the Artist, G1966.4

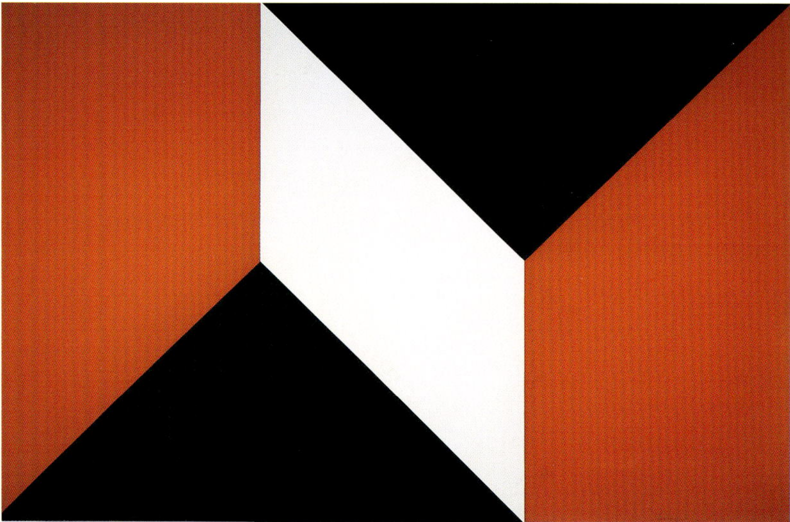

Figure 6. Dean Fleming, *Snap Roll*, 1965; acrylic on canvas, 65 3/4 × 99 5/8 in.; Gift of Mari and James A. Michener, G1968.54

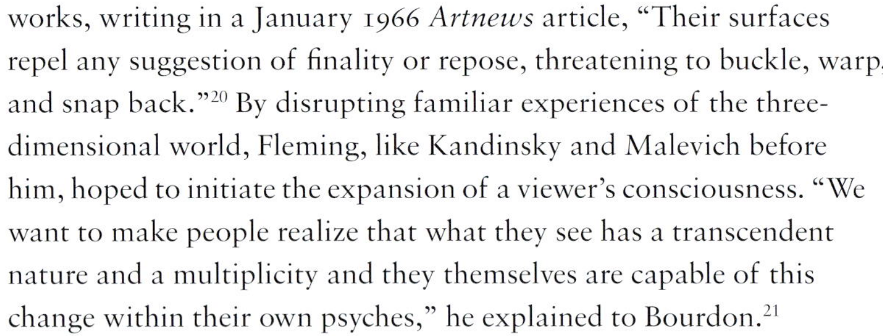

works, writing in a January 1966 *Artnews* article, "Their surfaces repel any suggestion of finality or repose, threatening to buckle, warp, and snap back."[20] By disrupting familiar experiences of the three-dimensional world, Fleming, like Kandinsky and Malevich before him, hoped to initiate the expansion of a viewer's consciousness. "We want to make people realize that what they see has a transcendent nature and a multiplicity and they themselves are capable of this change within their own psyches," he explained to Bourdon.[21]

Although Ed Ruda was immediately drawn to Fleming, Forakis, and others in their circle when they met in 1962, he never engaged the mystical "fourth dimension" of Ouspensky or Fleming's Kandinsky-like spiritual orientation. Instead, he found in the young Californians' "tough" geometric style and bold, paradoxical spaces a compelling alternative to the "abstract impressionism" he had been practicing in the circle of Milton Resnick.[22] Paintings such as *Untitled* (1963, figure 7) reflect both Ruda's past and future directions. Here clearly delineated, collagelike elements set in an irregularly curved field contrast with the area of atmospheric brushwork at the upper right, which recalls Ruda's connection to Resnick and, through him, to artists like Claude Monet and Pierre Bonnard.[23] Although Ruda included *Untitled* in his first Park Place show in December 1963, by then he had adopted the rectilinear geometry and high-keyed color that would result in large-scale canvases such as *Reo Reo* in 1966.

Born in the Bronx in 1924, Ruda began to draw by copying the comics he loved in his youth—from Krazy Kat to Alley Oop—then by creating cartoons of his own.[24] He graduated from the School of Agriculture of Cornell University with a major in biology in 1947. A stint in the Navy during 1942–1945, however, had interrupted his formal education and taken him to the South Pacific, where he carried out malaria control operations. Ruda made his first trip to Mexico after the war, retrieving samples of a type of blind fish and illustrating them for a professor's *Natural History* article.[25] Although Ruda took a few art courses at Cornell, he continued his study of painting, along with psychology and philosophy, at the New School for Social Research in 1947–1948. On the GI Bill, he also earned an MA in art education at Columbia Teacher's College during 1948–1949.[26] Ruda was thus in New York to observe at close range the emergence of Abstract Expressionism, seeing shows by de Kooning, Adolph Gottlieb, and Robert Motherwell, among others. In his own painting, he made studies after Georges Braque and Stuart Davis, and he has described his work of

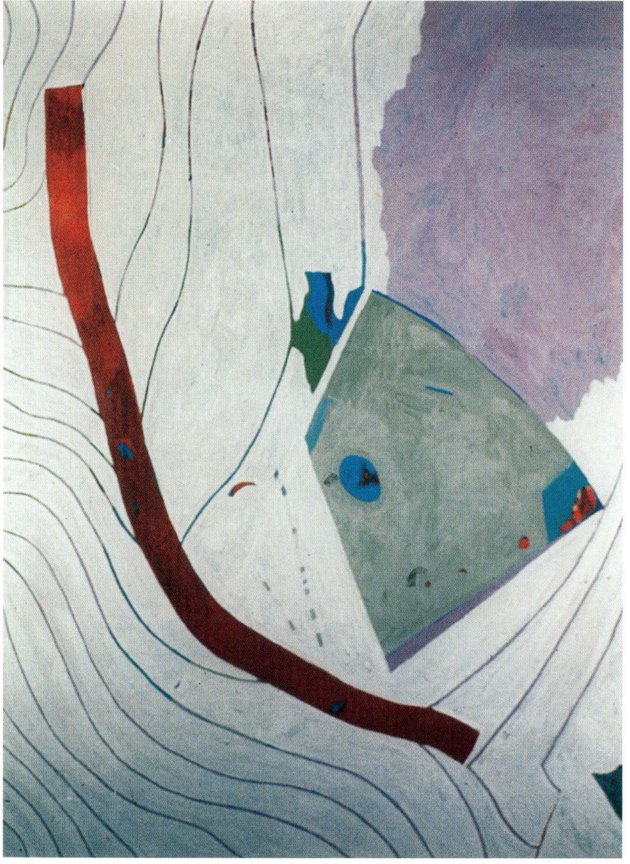

Figure 7. Edwin Ruda, *Untitled*, 1963; acrylic and aluminum paint on canvas, 84 × 60 in.; Collection of the Artist

this period as "little divided-up canvases that looked a little bit like Gottlieb" but with an increasing interest in "primal forms . . . subconscious forms, instinctive forms."[27]

With two years left on the GI Bill, Ruda decided to return to Mexico to study art in Mexico City and in San Miguel de Allende from 1949 to 1951. After teaching in El Paso between 1951 and 1954—at both Texas Western (now University of Texas at El Paso) and in a public school—Ruda earned an MFA at the University of Illinois. He then returned to Texas to teach at The University of Texas at Austin from 1956 to 1959.[28] The magnetism of New York was strong, however, and Ruda settled there early in 1960, gravitating to the Tenth Street gallery scene and the circle around Resnick. He also became a regular at the Club, the Abstract Expressionists' haunt, then in its final days. In Resnick's milieu, Ruda left behind figuration for a self-described "Bonnardian Impressionist" abstraction.[29]

If Ruda's *Untitled* of 1963 still carries a trace of that moment, it also reflects the types of painting that had begun to attract his attention, such as the hard-edge works of Ellsworth Kelly and the striped, shaped canvases of Frank Stella. Indeed, with its warped field delineated in aluminum paint, *Untitled* suggests a 1960 Stella stripe painting gone awry.[30] In contact with the Park Place artists, Ruda now adopted a geometric style and explored the use of shaped canvases. However, instead of matching shape and interior pattern like Stella, he created a deliberate tension between the exterior shape of the canvas (i.e., its status as a three-dimensional object) and a surface design with "multiple spaces going on."[31]

Following upon a number of such works in 1965, Ruda settled on the immediate precursors to the series to which *Reo Reo* belongs—paintings of inverted equilateral triangles evoked in the poster Ruda designed for his joint exhibition with Forakis in May 1966 (figure 8). Although the poster utilizes the same type of line segments (a contrasting outline and a pinched center), in Ruda's six-foot triangle paintings these linear elements radiate from the center of the triangle to bisect each angle.[32] The result is not only intense color pulses at the midpoints of the lines, like those of the poster, but also the potential shift of the entire form from two-dimensional to three-dimensional space—as if it were the top-down view of a tetrahedron. The poster actually offers the possibility of folding a tetrahedron, the geometrical form central to Forakis's sculptural response to Buckminster Fuller's "synergetic geometry."[33] For Fuller, the tetrahedron was the key to a physically modelable four-dimensional geometry, using 60-degree instead of 90-degree angles, and hence the four-sided tetrahedron, his basic building block, came to have strong associations with the geometrical fourth dimension at Park Place.[34] Evoking the topology that also fascinated the group, Ruda declared to the critic Bourdon, "We use an extremely flexible geometry because the space it implies can stretch, shrink, warp, twist, change position or become weightless."[35]

In contrast to the frontal extension of Ruda's triangle paintings, in the twenty-foot *Reo Reo* (figure 9) the spatial expansion occurs laterally, filling a viewer's perceptual field.[36] Ruda thinks of his painting in terms of "the possibilities of space related to the body," and once he had enlarged his canvases to engulf a viewer, he also was reminded of the vast spaces he had experienced in west Texas driving between

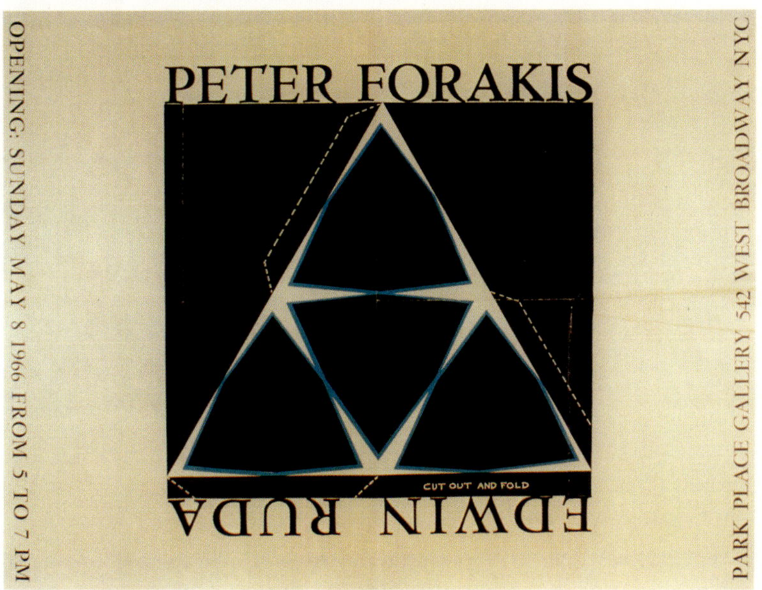

Figure 8. Edwin Ruda, Poster for Park Place exhibition, *Edwin Ruda/Peter Forakis*, May 1966

El Paso and Austin.[37] In *Reo Reo* an elongated, intensely colored diamond of orange bears complementary small blue diamonds at its tips as well as a dynamic network of crisscrossing yellow lines. As described by Bourdon, "the intersecting lines tend to distort in one's peripheral vision, assuming a literal velocity like the vibrations of a plucked string."[38] Color is even more central to the painting's effect, according to Ruda: "The way you range its intensities and values . . . can make the edge itself dissolve, giving the painting a multidimensional effect, a sort of action and interaction."[39] *Reo Reo* produces a disorienting effect in a viewer, as it defies familiar tools of measure and logic. Paradox is central for Ruda, as he declared in the *Systemic Painting* catalogue: "The subtle paradox is maddening, curious, and amusing."[40] That pursuit of logic-defying paradox and ambiguity is what brought his own painterly concerns most directly into line with Fleming's and Forakis's Ouspensky-based conception of the fourth dimension.[41]

Until the 2003 publication of Claudine Humblet's *La Nouvelle Abstraction Americaine 1950–1970*, the only major published records on the Park Place group were Bourdon's "E = MC² à Go-Go" article in *Artnews*, January 1966, and Ruda's November 1967 *Arts Magazine* chronicle, "Park Place 1963–67." Bourdon's essay, in particular, documents the group's engagement with the fourth dimension, an interest manifested most overtly in the *4D* exhibition they staged in February–March 1965 at the Daniels Gallery.[42] However, the title of Bourdon's essay points to the dominant public understanding of the term "fourth dimension" in this period—not as a spatial phenomenon, but as time in the space-time continuum of Albert Einstein's Relativity Theory. Di Suvero, in fact, was the only artist in the group with a deep allegiance to Relativity Theory and its focus on time and motion ("Space-time is the only way you can think since Einstein," he declared to Bourdon), although other artists often used words such as "time-line"

Figure 9. Edwin Ruda, *Reo Reo*, 1966; acrylic on canvas, 36 × 240 in.; Gift of the Artist, 2004.159

or, in Fleming's case, "motion," "velocity," and "dynamics."[43] Nonetheless, the commitment of Fleming and Forakis to both Ouspensky and Fuller meant that the geometrical, spatial fourth dimension was clearly a part of the group's thinking on the subject.

The possible existence of an unseen fourth dimension of space had been a central concern for many early twentieth-century artists—from the French Cubists and Marcel Duchamp to the Russian Suprematist Malevich and beyond. In the wake of the triumph of Relativity Theory after 1919, however, Einstein's new definition of the fourth dimension as time in the space-time continuum gradually replaced the highly popular spatial fourth dimension.[44] Thus, Forakis's chance discovery of the books of Ouspensky and Bragdon in San Francisco in 1957 represented a recovery of "ancient" wisdom largely lost from cultural memory. Indeed, one of the problems for the Park Place group was that the larger signification of the "fourth dimension" beyond Einsteinian space-time eluded the general public and many critics, just as its import for early modernism was almost completely forgotten. For example, only in February 1967 would Duchamp's extensive engagement with the spatial fourth dimension become known when the Cordier & Ekstrom Gallery published his notes on the subject in the deluxe *A l'infinitif* or *White Box*.[45] Although, as noted above, Fleming intuited Malevich's Ouspenskian orientation, art historians would recover the Russian painter's specific engagement with the fourth dimension only in the early 1970s. Often juxtaposed in the 1960s, usually as opposites, Duchamp and Malevich shared a concern with the fourth dimension—the leitmotif of Park Place—that no one suspected.[46]

Within Park Place, the multivalent "4D"—ranging from the geometry of Bragdon and Fuller, the mystical consciousness preached by Ouspensky, and science fiction usages to Einsteinian space-time—served as an effective, unifying watchword. If spatial complexity and paradoxical perceptual effects were the primary visual manifestation of the spatial fourth dimension at Park Place, members of the group also updated its meanings for the mid-twentieth century. Thus, just as Bourdon's "$E = MC^2$" title, along with his and certain artists' comments, augmented the Einsteinian implications of Park Place work, his listing of some of the group's "key terms" documents a specifically energy-oriented identity for the fourth dimension that was unique to the group.[47] In particular, phrases such as "four-dimensional color," "optic energy" [Ruda's term], and "eye-ibel (like decibel)," suggest the artists' goal of intensifying a viewer's visual experience to create a color energy equivalent to their dramatic effects of "space-warp."[48] Such completely new conceptions of color energy and space contributed as well to the use of "4D" at Park Place as a general, metaphorical sign for new possibilities—beyond the familiar, beyond logic, beyond current comprehension. And, in fact, the popular "fourth dimension" in the early twentieth century quickly had acquired that connotation as well. Such a visionary, optimistic belief in the future possibilities for art was fundamental to the founders of Park Place, and Robert Smithson captured its spirit when he wrote of the group in his June 1966 essay "Entropy and the New Monuments": "These artists face the possibility of other dimensions, with a new kind of sight."[49]

Smithson understood the geometrical side of the Park Place interest in the fourth dimension, since he was exploring the subject himself in works of the mid-1960s, including the *Enantiomorphic Chambers* of 1965. He actually had interacted with members of the group for several years and exhibited at the gallery in fall 1966.[50] Critics initially discussed Park Place members, as they did Smithson, in the context of the emerging "Minimalist" style, and Park Place invitational exhibitions included a number of future Minimalists, such as Sol LeWitt.[51] However, as Minimalism coalesced and became more restrictive, the complex space explored at Park Place violated its increasingly rigid focus on single gestalts or serial objects. And, although the 1966 *Systemic Painting* exhibition at the Guggenheim included Fleming and Ruda (and Novros), and Park Place sculptors Forakis, Myers, and Grosvenor showed in the 1966 *Primary Structures* exhibition, their work (apart from Novros's and Grosvenor's) in the end did not fit the Minimalist mold.[52]

Alloway's "systemic" paradigm was broader than either Greenbergian formalism or Minimalism, but ultimately, the flatness and determined rejection of spatial effects advocated by Greenberg and others came to dominate art world discourse. Writing in 1983, Al Held, a friend of the Park Place group, recalled the inordinate power of that paradigm in the 1960s: "It sounds ridiculous in 1983 to talk about the primacy of the flatness of the canvas. But this point was taken very seriously by very intelligent people, including most of the Minimalists. Actually, if you analyze the Minimalist rhetoric, it runs fairly parallel to Greenberg's thoughts."[53] Lucy Lippard, noting Albers's *Structural Constellations* as well as the Thiéry figure or Necker cubes from perceptual psychology, coined the term "perverse perspectives" in October 1966 to designate the "new and incongruous illusionism" she saw as the "structural answer to Op Art."[54] The artists she discussed in these terms included Fleming, Ruda, and fellow Park Place painters Valledor and Melcher—as well as Smithson, Stella, Larry Bell, Charles Hinman, Neil Williams, Will Insley, and Ron Davis. With its talk of "ambiguity," "formal dissonance," "logical illogicality," and dynamism, sections of Lippard's March 1967 "Perverse Perspectives" article might have served as the manifesto for a movement grounded in these issues.[55]

Lippard's category never took hold, however. Her use of the word "illusionism" may have been part of the problem, since "illusionism" had been the centerpiece of the critical backlash against "Op Art" in the wake of The Museum of Modern Art's *Responsive Eye* exhibition in 1965. Rosalind Krauss, for example, denounced most of the artists in the exhibition, including Bridget Riley, accusing them of creating the "illusion of a tactile object," "illusionistic projection," and "*trompe l'oeil* tactility."[56] However, as Richard Shiff recently argued in a cogent essay on Riley that critiques Krauss's position:

> *Illusion is a natural condition of vision, a physiological fact suited to study in* Scientific American *as much as to use in painting. . . . Whereas illusion has no history, illusionism does and is a fit subject for interpretive scholarship. . . . Illusion is real, what we experience at the very moment of looking; it does not substitute for another visual sensation. Illusionism removes us from reality; it refers to a type of real experience, now absent, that the viewer may or may not have had at some other time.*[57]

The critical war of words that conflated illusion and illusionism wrongly tainted too many artists in the mid-1960s.

Bourdon clearly was aware of the charge and sought to preempt such complaints about Park Place. "Their work does not depend on trompe l'oeil or illusions [read illusionism] of space, but rather on existent and genuine spatial ambiguities, some of which occur in time," he declared in "E = MC² à Go-Go."[58] In an era of heightened interest in perceptual psychology and fascination with visual illusion and paradox, it is remarkable that the dogmatic voices of Greenberg and his associates were so powerful that space could be denied to painting as a legitimate area of investigation. Only in 1981 would critic and historian Yve-Alain Bois begin to celebrate the work of Lissitzky for its "radical reversibility" based on axonometric or isometric projection—the very effect explored by Fleming, in particular, at Park Place.[59] However, in the mid-1960s Park Place simply did not fit the two primary molds—Minimalism and Greenbergian formalism—offered by critics and artist/theorists eager to define the territory of the avant-garde. As Fleming stated of Park Place, "It was impossible to identify what we were. That was our freedom."[60]

That freedom from classification went beyond the visual appearance of Park Place work. Rooted in the Six Gallery's fusion of painting and performance, Fleming and Forakis, for example, participated in the "Ergo Suits" "sculpture dance" activities of 1962–1963 (and later) with their friend Chuck Ginnever, bringing them into the milieu of Happenings and Fluxus.[61] If the iconoclastic spirit of Dada and Duchamp lay behind certain Park Place–related activities, the period's other touchstone, Malevich, was likewise a hero for members of the group. Fleming, in particular, focused on the Russian artist's quest for the infinite and its implication of transcending familiar dimensions.[62] Thus, Fleming's statements in the *Systemic Painting* catalogue position him closer to Kandinsky or Malevich than to his fellow exhibitors: "The subject of art is ultimately spiritual. . . . When basic forms and primary colors have the strength and velocity to communicate a new dimension, it is the spirit of our times an artist expresses rather than the fact."[63] Although less specifically spiritual, Ruda, too, envisioned a perceptual transformation in a viewer of his paintings: "How do you convert a still field into a vision that moves time, space, mind?" he queried in 1966.[64]

Fleming, Ruda, and other of their colleagues at Park Place were visionaries who saw art as a means to alter a viewer's psychic state, producing what Bourdon described as "a kind of drugless expansion of consciousness that one likes to think of as the aim of all art."[65] Indeed, although few extant art historical narratives of the period acknowledge this aspect of 1960s culture, the goals at Park Place were hardly out of keeping with the sensibility of the decade as described by Susan Sontag in 1965: "Art today is a new kind of instrument, an instrument for modifying consciousness and organizing new modes of sensibility."[66] Toward that end, music and synaesthesia played a key role at Park Place—both in the group's free jazz band, rooted in Forakis's earlier "No-Name Jazz" studio sessions, and in the experimental music concerts they staged by musicians such as Steve Reich and La Monte Young. Like the Six Gallery before it, Park Place represented "Painting [and sculpture], poetry, music knit together," as Fleming phrased it.[67]

Grounded in the counterculture of the 1960s and also sharing the concern of a number of artists about the growing commodification of art via the gallery system, Fleming left New York in 1967. He settled in southeastern Colorado, where he and friends cofounded the mountain community "Libre," and he built the Fuller dome in which he still paints today.[68] After the period of *Snap Roll* and *Untitled*, his paintings "came apart," as Fleming described them—first as groups of shaped enameled wood or steel panels in 1966–1967, and then as individual color elements placed in nature.[69] During the following decade, he continued to paint abstractly, but the expressionist brushwork of his early years came once again to the fore.

When Allen Ginsberg visited Libre in the 1970s, he told Fleming that "everyone is waiting for you to paint the mountains." Inspired since his time in Japan in the 1950s by Hokusai's series The Thirty-Six Views of Mt. Fuji, in 1984 Fleming commenced what has become a continuing, painterly communion with the landscape.[70] Works such as *Huerfano 10* of 1997 (figure 10) translate the view from his studio into a pulsating vision of nature as energy and process. Like his Park Place paintings, however, Fleming's landscapes also contain purposefully conflicting spatial cues. Here powerful, calligraphic brushstrokes continuously assert their two-dimensional presence, contradicting ideas of near and far and making a conventional, three-dimensional reading of the mountains impossible. Fleming has augmented, in recent years, his awareness of Ouspensky's (and Buddhism's) view of the world of three-dimensional appearances as *maya*, or as illusions to be transcended, through his embrace of Native American beliefs in the fundamental unity and interconnectedness of nature.[71] As Fleming explained in 2002, "Even though I am now working with mountains and trees, the way of looking, of reversals of space and meaning, are purely painting and tamper always with the 4D."[72]

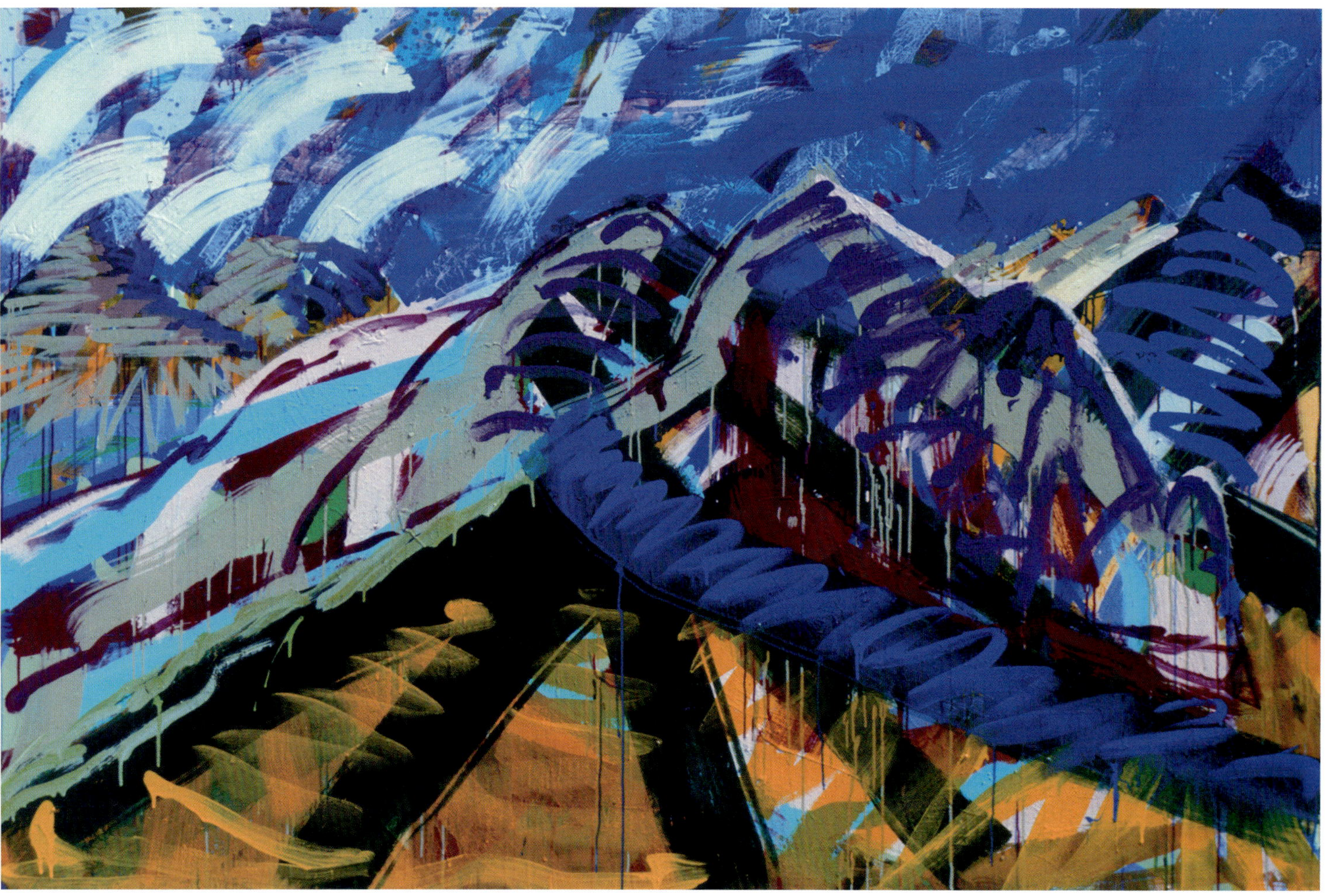

Figure 10. Dean Fleming, *Huerfano #10*, 1997; acrylic on canvas, 66 × 96 in.; Collection of the Artist

Ruda still paints in the Walker Street studio he first occupied in the early 1960s, near the original location of Park Place. Like Fleming, today he works in a more painterly mode, having first departed from the geometry of Park Place in his "band" paintings of the early 1970s.[73] *Azone* of 2003 (figure 11) is typical of his recent works, which combine freer drawing and atmospheric brushwork with more clearly defined forms. According to Ruda, "I am still fascinated by the notions of 'ambiguity' and 'paradox' which continue to haunt my paintings."[74] In *Azone,* for example, shapes and lines seem to overlap one another and then immediately confound any logical spatial relationships—as if this were a glimpse of some kind of four-dimensional weaving. Ruda's black half-circles can suggest depth, as does the black central shape in his 2001 painting *Ultimus,* which he titled when the finished painting reminded him of his experience in Mexico of throwing a stone into a cave mouth and never hearing it hit anything. At the same time, however, the clarity of such forms insistently positions them on the painting's surface.[75] In the 1980s Ruda found new support for his longstanding interest in paradoxical "indefiniteness" in Jacques Derrida's concept of "undecidability," which he encountered, along with the writings of Friedrich Nietzsche and others, when he returned to the New School for Social Research to audit philosophy courses in the 1980s.[76]

Fleming and Ruda, friends for more than forty years, thus have continued to share basic goals—whether sustained by the philosophy of Ouspensky (who had himself drawn on Nietzsche) or Derrida. Indeed, Fleming's 2002 discussion of his intention in the 1960s to creating paintings "where there was interchangeable figure and ground, where there was no figure and ground, where there was 'impossible' space and the observer would experience the spatial shift" applies to both his and Ruda's more recent paintings.[77] Equally relevant for the two artists is a recent declaration by Ruda that sums up both men's deep commitment to their art: "Painting is life."[78] Together once again as part of the Blanton's collection, Fleming's *Snap Roll* and *Untitled* and Ruda's *Reo Reo* stand as vital reflections of the rich and varied cultural moment that was the New York art world of the 1960s.

The spatial complexity of Fleming's and Ruda's paintings serves as a pointed reminder that the artistic milieu of New York in this period was far more complex than the rigid cataloguing of successive movements that current histories of the period would suggest. Indeed, art historians need to recover a larger picture of 1960s culture and artists' creative responses to it—from the impact of thinkers like Buckminster Fuller to new developments in perceptual psychology and the resurgence of interest in expanding perception and consciousness.[79] Members of the Park Place group were far "ahead of the curve" on the subject of Ouspensky, for example, who nourished early modernism and whose writings would attract considerable attention as part of the revival of mysticism and occultism in the 1960s and 1970s.[80] Their embrace of the

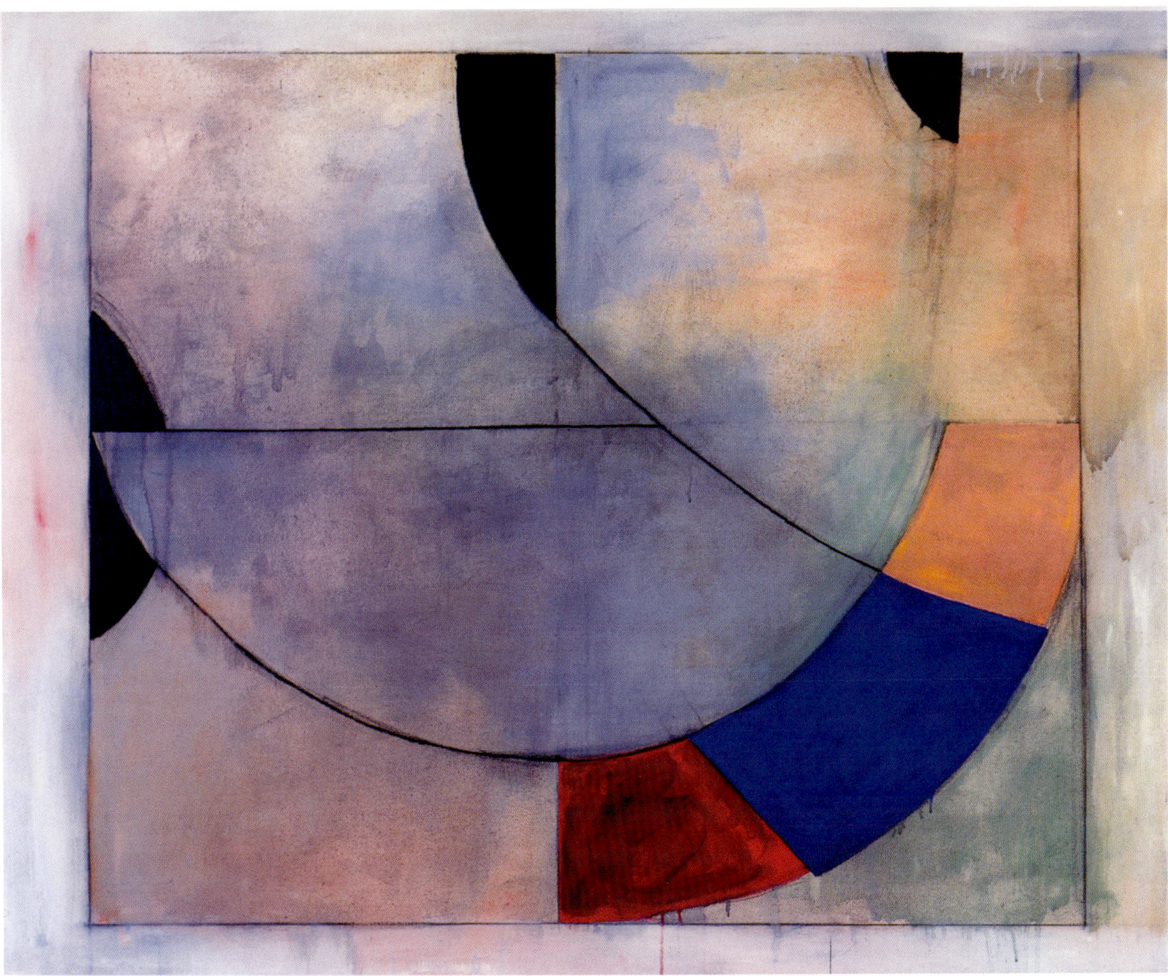

Figure 11. Edwin Ruda, *Azone*, 2003; acrylic and charcoal on canvas, 60 × 72 in.; Collection of the Artist

spatial fourth dimension, too, presaged the idea's gradual reemergence in public consciousness during the course of the 1970s and its subsequent return as a major cultural phenomenon by the end of the century, abetted by the emergence of cyberspace and multidimensional string theory in physics.[81]

Park Place represents a unique moment in the history of American art as well as in the history of the fourth dimension as a leitmotif of twentieth-century art. The pursuit by Fleming, Ruda, and others of newly complex and energetic forms of painting and sculpture in the name of the "4D" sets them apart from both their modernist predecessors and their contemporaries, especially formalist painters and Minimalists. In a refreshing approach to the period, critic Brian O'Doherty, who also had acknowledged the accomplishments of Park Place during the 1960s, described "cool" artistic expression via "paradox and contradiction" as "a major achievement of the best postwar American abstract painting."[82] Such positive valuation of paradox and contradiction, along with a recognition of the difference between perceptual illusion and the dreaded "illusionism," offers alternative criteria for evaluating 1960s art and allows us to see more clearly the significant contributions of Fleming, Ruda, and the Park Place Gallery in general.

NOTES

1. Fleming's *Untitled* came to The University of Texas in 1966 as a gift from Fleming and the Park Place Gallery of Art Research through Dallas collector and Park Place sponsor Betty Blake Guiberson. James Michener bought *Snap Roll* in 1967 and conveyed it to the museum in 1968.
2. For a view of the Guggenheim installation of Fleming's painting *2 V Dwan 2* (1965–1966), which resembles *Untitled* but is composed of three 99 × 66 inch panels, see James Meyer, *Minimalism: Art and Polemics in the Sixties* (New Haven, Conn.: Yale University Press, 2001), figure 118. Ruda exhibited *Here to Tucumcari*, a 3 × 20 foot work in the same series as *Reo Reo*. For these paintings, see Lawrence Alloway, *Systemic Painting* (New York: Solomon R. Guggenheim Museum, 1966), 32, 46. For Novros, who never focused specifically on space as did the others in the group, see the essay by Frances Colpitt in this catalogue.
3. Clarification of this history occurred in numerous interviews and telephone conversations between the author and Fleming, Ruda, and Forakis since early 2002. Claudine Humblet sets forth the basic chronology for each of these artists in her section "Les Sculpteurs et les peintres de 'Park Place,'" in *La Nouvelle Abstraction Américaine 1950–1970*, 3 vols. (Milan: Skira, 2003; Paris: Seuil, 2003), vol. 2: 1317–21, and vol. 3: 1683–1997. Further information on the group's history can be found in Dean Fleming, "Dean Fleming . . . The Life," in David Turner, *Dean Fleming: The Energy of Nature* (Colorado Springs, Colo.: Colorado Springs Fine Arts Center, 1998), 3–12.
4. For Ruda's account of Park Place's history, see Ed Ruda, "Park Place 1963–1967: Some Informal Notes in Retrospect," *Arts Magazine* 42 (November 1967): 30–33; and "Interview with Edwin Ruda . . . by Michael Chisholm," January 26, 1988, February 2, 1988, Archives of American Art, 87–95 (henceforth Ruda, AAA interview).
5. John Gibson initially managed the new gallery space on West Broadway; his assistant Paula Cooper later succeeded him. Financial backers of the gallery included Virginia Dwan, J. Patrick Lannan, Vera List, and Texas collectors Betty Guiberson and Clint Murchison. Member exhibitions at Park Place combined one painter and one sculptor in two-person shows; invitational shows included work by friends such as Ronald Bladen (a 1943 Cal Fine Arts graduate who had settled in New York in 1955), Chuck Ginnever (with whom di Suvero had driven to New York in 1957), Al Held, and younger, less-exhibited artists such as Sol LeWitt and Robert Smithson. See Ruda, "Park Place 1963–1967;" Fleming, "Dean Fleming," 5–6; and Robert Hobbs, *Robert Smithson: Sculpture* (Ithaca: Cornell University Press, 1981), 235. The *Park Place Group Show* at MIT in 1968 was the last time the group exhibited together as a whole.
6. Unless otherwise indicated, the biographical information herein is drawn from Fleming, "Dean Fleming," and Humblet, vol. 3, 1939–75. See also the vita and exhibition lists in *Dean Fleming: Paintings 1992–2004* (Sarasota, Fla.: Spotlight Graphics, 2004), 62–63.
7. Fleming clarified his early exposure to modernism in telephone conversations with the author in spring 2005, including May 26, 2005, in which he noted his abstract drawing in margins, including "magic cubes," as he terms them. Books such as Sigfried Giedion, *Space, Time and Architecture* (Cambridge, Mass.: Harvard University Press, 1941) and Laszlo Moholy-Nagy, *Vision in Motion* (Chicago: Paul Theobald, 1947) would have served to acquaint Fleming with modernist geometric design. His early introduction to the Russian avant-garde, in particular, was unusual since, apart from Alfred Barr's brief discussion in *Cubism and Abstract Art* (New York: The Museum of Modern Art, 1936), information on Malevich and Lissitzky first became generally available only in Camilla Gray, *The Great Experiment: Russian Art 1863–1922* (London: Thames and Hudson, 1962). An exception to this was a generously illustrated article on Lissitzky by war correspondent Ella Winter, who had managed to connect with Lissitzky's widow, Sophie. See Winter, "Lissitzky: A Revolutionary Out of Favor," *Artnews* 57 (April 1958), 28–31, 62–64, which Fleming probably saw in the library at Cal Fine Arts when he worked there.
8. Founded in 1940 as Mexico City College, the institution became a university in 1963 (Universidad de las Americas) and subsequently relocated to Puebla. Information available at http://www.udlap.mx/conoce/historia.html [June 13, 2005]. According to Fleming, Mexico City College was a popular destination for ex-soldiers continuing their educations on the GI Bill.
9. Dean Fleming, telephone interview with the author, February 2, 2002. On the Six Gallery and its poets, painters, and musicians, see Bruce Nixon, *Lyrical Vision: The 6 Gallery 1954–1957* (Davis, Calif.: Natsoulas Novelozo Gallery, 1990).
10. Dean Fleming, telephone interview with the author, February 2, 2002.
11. Fleming, "Dean Fleming," 6.
12. For these works, see Fleming, "Dean Fleming," 6, and Humblet, vol. 3, 1947–48.
13. Fleming's *Snap Roll* title alludes to the similarly dramatic shift that occurs in the very rapid "snap roll" maneuver in aerobatics (Dean Fleming, telephone interview with the author, March 30, 2005).
14. Dean Fleming, letter to the author, May 23, 2002; Dean Fleming, interview with the author, Libre, Colo., August 15, 2004. The classic Greenberg statement on this subject is "Modernist Painting" (1960), in John O'Brian, ed., *Clement Greenberg: The Collected Essays and Criticism*, vol. 4 (Chicago: University of Chicago Press, 1993), 85–94.
15. Fleming, telephone interview with the author, February 2, 2002; Peter Forakis, telephone interview with the author, December 14, 2001. Among the books of Kent, who had died that year, Forakis also found a copy of fourth dimension advocate Claude Bragdon's *The Frozen Fountain: Being Essays on Architecture and the Art of Design in Space* (New York: Alfred A. Knopf, 1932), which would serve as an important stimulus for his developing geometric sculpture.
16. See P.D. Ouspensky, *Tertium Organum: A Key to the Enigmas of the World*, trans. Nicholas Bessaraboff and Claude Bragdon (New York: Alfred A. Knopf, 1922); for "cosmic consciousness" and "sensation of infinity" as well as alogical logic, see chapter 21. On Ouspensky's philosophy, see also Linda Dalrymple Henderson, *The Fourth Dimension and Non-Euclidean Geometry in Modern Art* (Princeton, N.J.: Princeton University Press, 1983), 245–55; new ed. (Cambridge, Mass.: MIT Press, 2006).
17. Fleming, telephone interview with the author, February 2, 2002; Fleming, letter to the author, May 23, 2002. Kandinsky's 1911 text had been published as *Concerning the Spiritual in Art* in George Wittenborn's "Documents of Modern Art" series in 1947. Fleming also responded to the writings of G.I. Gurdjieff, who had become Ouspensky's mentor in the years after the publication of *Tertium Organum*, and attended meetings of the Gurdjieff Society in New York.
18. On Malevich's debt to Ouspensky, see Henderson, *Fourth Dimension*, chap. 5; see also n. 46 below, for the history of scholarship on this issue in the 1970s.
19. Dean Fleming, "Statement," in Alloway, *Systemic Painting*, 23.
20. David Bourdon, "E = MC² à Go-Go," *Artnews* 64 (January 1966): 58.
21. Dean Fleming, as quoted in Bourdon, 25.
22. Edwin Ruda, telephone interview with the author, February 20, 2002; Ruda, AAA interview, 93.
23. On his first visit to The Museum of Modern Art in 1946, Ruda was most impressed by Bonnard's paintings (AAA interview, 13). On Resnick, see, for example, Linda L. Cathcart, *Milton Resnick 1945–1985* (Houston: Contemporary Arts Museum, 1985). For Ruda's connections to Resnick, see n. 29 below.
24. The information that follows is drawn from Ruda's AAA interview; for cartoons, see AAA interview, 7, 14. For Ruda's career, see also Humblet, vol. 3, 1841–42; and Robert C. Morgan, "The Right Harmonic: The Paintings of Edwin Ruda," in *Edwin Ruda: Paintings and Studies* (London: Butler and Tanner, Ltd., 2004), n.p.
25. Ruda, AAA interview, 16–37.
26. Ruda, AAA interview, 43–51.
27. Ruda, AAA interview, 56; see also 52–54 on New York shows in the late 1940s.
28. See Ruda, AAA interview, 59–65 (study in Mexico), 66–78 (teaching in El Paso and Austin), and 72–75 (MFA study).
29. Ruda, AAA interview, 86; see also 79–82, 85–87 on Ruda's experiences in the Resnick circle.
30. Ruda's work reversed the Stella, of course, with lines painted rather than emerging as the interstices between wider painted stripes. For Stella's aluminum paintings, see, for example, William S. Rubin, *Frank Stella* (New York: The Museum of Modern Art, 1970), 47–63.
31. Ruda, AAA interview, 106; see also 105–108 for Ruda's clarification of his differences from Stella. For these works, see Humblet, vol. 3, 1846–49, where she also notes his debt to Lissitzky in *Round Up* of 1965 (1848).
32. See Humblet, vol. 3, 1850–56, for the triangle paintings.
33. For Forakis's sculpture, see Humblet, vol. 3, 1719–47, as well as Lawrence Alloway, "Peter Forakis Since 1960," *Artforum* 6 (January 1968): 25–29. Forakis first discussed his interest in Fuller in telephone interviews with the author, December 14 and 15, 2001.
34. See R. Buckminster Fuller, "Prevailing Conditions in the Arts" (1964), in *Utopia or Oblivion: The Prospects for Humanity* (New York: Bantam Books, 1969), 80–113. On Fuller's relevance for interest in the fourth dimension at Park Place, see the new introduction to Linda Henderson, "The Fourth Dimension 1950–2000: From Relativity's Dominance to the Digital Era and New Cosmologies," in *Fourth Dimension*, new ed., 2006.
35. Ruda, as quoted in Bourdon, 24; see also 25 for topology.
36. *Reo Reo* was originally titled *Yellow Crossing*, and its orange acrylic paint was brushed on over an initial layer of yellow. Ruda renamed the work for Park Place member Leo Valledor's son Rio at the time of Leo's death in 1989, changing the spelling to avoid associations with the Spanish word *river* (Edwin Ruda, telephone interviews with the author, November 27, 2004, April 17, 2005). Ruda nonetheless titled one of the same 1966 series of twenty-foot paintings *Around Big Bend*, connecting it more directly to Ruda's experience of west Texas in the 1950s; this is the painting Bourdon discusses in "E = MC²" (58). For other paintings in the series, see Humblet, vol. 3, 1858–59.
37. Edwin Ruda, interview with the author, New York, February 20, 2002. Ruda noted the importance of the expanse of Texas in a telephone interview with the author, November 27, 2004. He also discussed his attraction to "large barren spaces in both Mexico and the southwest United States" and his query, "Now, *how* do you paint that?," in AAA interview, 71. Ruda's future wife, Maria Antoinette Rogers, whom he had met in Mexico, was living in El Paso, and he drove there frequently from Austin. Once in New York with Ruda, Maria pursued an acting career and appeared in a number of the films of avant-garde filmmaker Jack Smith.
38. Bourdon, 58.
39. Edwin Ruda, as quoted in Corinne Robins, "Four Directions at Park Place," *Arts Magazine* 40 (June 1966): 24.
40. Edwin Ruda, "Statement," in Alloway, *Systemic Painting*, 25.
41. Edwin Ruda, interview with the author, New York, February 18, 2003.
42. See Humblet, vol. 3, 1943.
43. See Bourdon, 24–25; see also Fleming, "Statement," in Alloway, *Systemic Painting*, 23.
44. It was in 1919 that the first empirical test of Einstein's theory occurred, and he suddenly became an international celebrity. For the fate of the fourth dimension in the wake of Relativity's popularization, see Henderson, *Fourth Dimension;* see also Henderson, "Four-Dimensional Space or Space-Time?: The Emergence of the Cubism-Relativity Myth in New York in the 1940s," in Michele Emmer, ed., *The Visual Mind II* (Cambridge, Mass.: MIT Press, 2005), 349–98.
45. Apart from the 150 signed copies of the *White Box* of 1967, these notes became widely available only in 1973, with the publication of Michel Sanouillet and Elmer Peterson, eds., *Salt Seller: The Writings of Marcel Duchamp* (New York: Oxford University Press, 1973). The first full-scale study of the role of the fourth dimension in early twentieth-century art was the author's 1975 Yale University dissertation, which formed the basis for Henderson, *Fourth Dimension* (1983).
46. Barbara Rose, for example, contrasts Duchamp, "the rational Frenchman," to Malevich, "the poetic Slav," in "ABC Art," *Art in America* 53 (October/November 1965): 56–69. She did find, however, a quality of "renunciation" common to the two (58, 69). Art historians Charlotte Douglas, Susan Compton, and the author, working simultaneously in the early 1970s, established Malevich's fundamental debt to Ouspensky and the fourth dimension (see Henderson, *Fourth Dimension* [2006]).

47. See, for example, Bourdon, 25, 58–59, as well as the Fleming references at n. 43 above. Time and motion figured in Ouspensky's *Tertium Organum*—not as the fourth dimension itself, but rather as incompletely understood spatial phenomena (see, for example, Henderson, *Fourth Dimension* [1983], 250). Fleming's references to weightlessness (see at n. 19 above) parallel the belief of Ouspensky and others that freedom from gravity and familiar spatial orientation would be a step toward four-dimensional consciousness (see, for example, Henderson, *Fourth Dimension* [1983], 285–88). See Malevich's related statement in n. 62 below.

48. Bourdon, 24; for Ruda's use of "optic energy," see Edwin Ruda, "Artist's Statement," in Brian O'Doherty and Wayne Andersen, *Art '65: Lesser Known and Unknown Painters, Young American Sculpture—East to West* (Flushing Meadows, N.Y.: American Express Pavilion, New York World's Fair, 1965), 58.

49. Robert Smithson, "Entropy and the New Monuments," *Artforum* 5 (June 1966): 31. Fleming clarified the visionary belief in possibility as part of the meaning of the "4D" for the group at large in a telephone interview with the author, April 16, 2005. For the earlier history of this association, see Henderson, *Fourth Dimension* (2006).

50. For Smithson's comments on Park Place, see Smithson, 30–31. Smithson had met Forakis in the late 1950s, and the two shared a fabricator, with Forakis regularly driving them to that destination; the two also had long conversations at the Cedar Bar and all-night coffee shops (Peter Forakis, telephone interviews with the author, including December 15, 2001 and March 30, 2005). Smithson showed in a three-person show with Valledor and LeWitt at Park Place in fall 1966 (Hobbs, *Robert Smithson,* 235). On Smithson's engagement with the fourth dimension in the mid-1960s, see Henderson, *Fourth Dimension* (2006). On the *Enantiomorphic Chambers* in the context of Smithson's investigation of perception, see Ann Morris Reynolds, *Robert Smithson: Learning from New Jersey and Elsewhere* (Cambridge, Mass.: MIT Press, 2003), 59–72.

51. See previous note for LeWitt's exhibition.

52. For the *Primary Structures* exhibition (April 17–June 12, 1966), which was viewed as an important manifestation of Minimalism, see Meyer. Bourdon had already noted the Park Place view of Minimalism in his January 1966 "E = MC²": "The group as a whole is not very receptive to one of the most current recent manifestations, the widespread reductive tendency toward 'minimal' or 'ABC' art, as exemplified by Robert Morris, Donald Judd, and Carl Andre" (59). Nonetheless, John Perreault included Park Place members (Fleming, Ruda, Forakis, and Myers, along with Novros), like Smithson, in his essay "Union-Made: Report on a Phenomenon," *Arts Magazine* 41 (March 1967). This issue itself was titled *A Minimal Future?* and bore a Fuller design on the cover. That classification would come to seem increasingly inappropriate—as it was also for Smithson. Alloway had noted already the contrasts between Smithson's works and Minimalism in "Robert Smithson's Development," *Artforum* 11 (November 1973): 52–61. Ann Reynolds argues cogently against this categorization as well in *Robert Smithson*, 25–28, 243–44.

53. Al Held, "The '60s in Abstract: 13 Statements and an Essay," *Art in America* 71 (October 1983): 125.

54. See Lucy Lippard, "Perverse Perspectives," *Art International* 11 (March 1967): 28; and Lippard, "Rejective Art," *Art International* 9 (October 1966): 35, where Lippard introduced the phrase in a discussion of Smithson's *Enantiomorphic Chambers.* Both essays also appear in Lucy R. Lippard, *Changing: Essays on Art* (New York: E. P. Dutton, 1971), although "Rejective Art" is there assigned an incorrect date of September 1965.

55. See, for example, Lippard, "Perverse Perspectives," 29–30.

56. Rosalind Krauss, "Afterthoughts on 'Op,'" *Art International* 9 (June 1965): 75.

57. Richard Shiff, "Bridget Riley: The Edge of Animation," in Paul Moorhouse, ed., *Bridget Riley* (London: Tate Gallery, 2003), 82. Shiff continued, "The devices of illusionism change through history and from one culture to another. But illusion, where the link between perception and reason seems to snap, is built into the body, the human physiological medium." Reynolds analyzed the negative reaction to the *Responsive Eye* exhibition as well as Smithson's interest in perceptual illusion and ambiguity in *Robert Smithson,* chap. 1.

58. Bourdon, 24.

59. See Yve-Alain Bois, "Metamorphosis of Axonometry," *Daidalos* 1 (September 15, 1981): 40–56, in which he also cites Bragdon's celebration of "isometric perspective" in *The Frozen Fountain* (the book Forakis had found) and the "fundamental ambivalence" of Josef Albers's *Structural Constellations* (40–42, 56–57). See also Yve-Alain Bois, "El Lissitzky: Radical Reversibility," *Art in America* 76 (April 1988): 160–81.

60. Dean Fleming, telephone interview with the author, March 12, 2002.

61. On the Six Gallery's debt to Dada poetry and performance, see Nixon, *Lyrical Vision.* The "Ergo Suits" events also included artists Eva Hesse, Tom Doyle, Walter de Maria, and Allan Kaprow (Dean Fleming, interview with the author, Libre, Colo., August 14, 2004); see also *Charles Ginnever* (Santa Monica, Calif.: Dorothy Goldeen Gallery, 1987), 23–27, 140–45. Fleming and Forakis published art comics—Forakis's *Grope* of 1964 and 1966 and Fleming's *The Blown Mind* of 1966—that the critic Alloway celebrated. Alloway coined the term "Pop art" to signify his and his fellow British Independent Group members' embrace of all levels of contemporary culture. See, for example, Lawrence Alloway, "Pop Art: *The Words,"* in Lawrence Alloway, *Topics in American Art* (New York: W. W. Norton, 1975), 119–22. Alloway noted both Ergo Suits and the Fleming/Forakis comics as signs of "a link between popular culture and abstract artists." See Lawrence Alloway, "Chuck Ginnever: Space as a Continuum . . . ," *Artforum* 6 (September 1967): 39, n.3. Forakis exhibited with future Pop artist Robert Indiana at the Martha Jackson Gallery in 1962; he and di Suvero also showed in Jackson's 1960 *New Forms—New Media I* exhibition showcasing the emerging "Junk Culture"/Assemblage milieu in New York also chronicled by Alloway (Humblet, vol. 3, 1687, 1723, 1728; Alloway, "Chuck Ginnever," 39).

62. Barbara Rose quoted Malevich's important comment on infinity in "ABC Art" in fall 1965: "I have broken the blue boundary of color limits, come out into the white, beside me comrade—pilots swim in this infinity. I have established the semaphores of Suprematism" (69). Following the publication of Malevich's *The Non-Objective World* of 1927 (Chicago: Paul Theobald & Co., 1959), Robert L. Herbert made the "Suprematism" segment of that volume widely available in 1964 in his paperback anthology *Modern Artists on Art* (Englewood Cliffs, N.J.: Prentice-Hall, 1964). Yet the bulk of Malevich's writings (especially early texts) would not become available until the 1970s, when Troels Andersen's edited volumes appeared. James Lawrence has discussed the frequent misreading of Malevich in purely formalist terms in the 1960s and early 1970s, including by Donald Judd, in "False Positives: Malevich, MoMA, and Minimalism" (paper delivered at "Rethinking Malevich" conference, City University of New York, February 6–7, 2004; publication forthcoming).

63. Fleming, "Statement," in Alloway, *Systemic Painting,* 23.

64. Ruda, as quoted in Robins, "Four Directions," 24.

65. Bourdon, 25.

66. Susan Sontag, "One Culture and the New Sensibility," in *Against Interpretation and Other Essays* (New York: Farrar, Straus & Giroux, 1966), 296.

67. Fleming, telephone interviews with the author, February 2, 2002 and August 31, 2002.

68. Dean Fleming, letter to the author, February 4, 2002.

69. See Humblet, vol. 3, 1953–68; Fleming discussed the paintings' "coming apart" in "A Conversation with Painter Dean Fleming" (talk given at the Blanton Museum of Art, The University of Texas at Austin, October 6, 2004, in conjunction with the exhibition *Twister: Moving Through Color, 1965–1977*).

70. Dean Fleming, videotape interview by Monica Raynes, Libre, Colo., August 2002, author's archive. Dean Fleming, telephone interview with the author, October 3, 2004. On Fleming's landscapes, see also Henderson, "Dean Fleming and Nature in All Its Dimensions," in *Dean Fleming: Paintings 1992–2004*, 5–7.

71. See Henderson, "Dean Fleming," 7.

72. Dean Fleming, letter to the author, February 4, 2002.

73. See Humblet, vol. 3, 1870–72 for the "band" paintings; see 1873–87 for Ruda's subsequent works. See also *Edwin Ruda: Paintings and Studies.*

74. Edwin Ruda, correspondence with the author, July 14, 2001.

75. Ruda, telephone interview, November 27, 2004.

76. For "indefiniteness," see Ruda, AAA interview, 108; see 145 for "undecidability." See also Morgan, "Right Harmonic," in *Edwin Ruda: Paintings and Studies,* n.p. Ruda's goal of "undermin[ing] the polarity" (AAA interview, 108) is much like Ouspensky's and Fleming's emphasis on transcending "apparent contradictions" (see again n. 19, as well as Ouspensky, *Tertium Organum,* chap. 21).

77. Fleming, letter to the author, February 4, 2002.

78. Ruda, interview with the author, New York, February 20, 2002.

79. Using Smithson's extensive library as a guide, Ann Reynolds in *Robert Smithson* provides an excellent model for recovering knowledge of this cultural moment. The Fuller-inspired *Whole Earth Catalog,* published between 1968 and 1972, is a highly useful record of topics of prime concern in the mid-1960s through the early 1970s, including the growing interest in the mystical and occult.

80. Responding to this phenomenon, Random House in 1970 published Ouspensky's *Tertium Organum* as a paperback Vintage Book, with other of his works following subsequently. In 1969 E. P. Dutton issued a paperback edition of R. M. Bucke's *Cosmic Consciousness* of 1901, which had been an important source for Ouspensky himself and which the firm had kept in print since the early years of the century.

81. Artist Tony Robbin has been the primary painter to respond to the new visual insights into four-dimensional geometry and space made possible by computer graphics. The Blanton Museum's collection includes Robbin's *82-10* of 1982. Robbin emerged in the early 1970s as a central figure in the Pattern and Decoration movement, but it was the disjunctions between areas of pattern that increasingly interested him. By the mid-1970s he turned his attention wholeheartedly to complex space and, specifically, four-dimensional geometry as a mirror of the "protean" quality of contemporary experience. In *82-10* and other works of the early 1980s, Robbin laid down a richly colored background pattern of geometric shapes—squares, rhombuses, and trapezoids (some paired as hexagons)—that alternates constantly among contradictory three-dimensional readings. (Like Fleming, Robbin had been drawn to the Necker-reversing effects in Albers's *Structural Constellations,* which he encountered as a student of Al Held at Yale in the later 1960s.) Against this background Robbin painted the outlines of pairs of component cubes of the four-dimensional hypercube in perspective projection; to these painted lines he then added painted wire rods delineating the same projected pairs of cubes in slightly different positions. As a viewer moves in front of *82-10,* the background shifts dramatically, and the pairs of linear cubes (painted and actual) mutate as they do in four-dimensional rotation, producing an unprecedented degree of geometrical complexity. Thomas Banchoff's pioneering film *The Hypercube: Projections and Slicings* (1978) was an important source for Robbin, who subsequently mastered computer graphics programming himself. Topologist Scott Carter, while teaching at The University of Texas in the 1980s, saw Robbin's *82-10* and has credited the work with a breakthrough in his own understanding of four-dimensional space (Scott Carter, correspondence with the author, August 3, 2004). Carter is just one of the many mathematicians and physicists with whom Robbin has interacted; see Tony Robbin, *Fourfield: Computers, Art & the Fourth Dimension* (Boston: Bullfinch Press, 1992) and *Shadows of Reality: The Fourth Dimension and Projective Geometry in Cubism, Relativity, and Modern Thought* (New Haven, Conn.: Yale University Press, 2006). On Robbin's work as well as the recent resurgence of interest in the spatial fourth dimension, including among digital artists, see Henderson, *Fourth Dimension* (2006).

82. See Brian O'Doherty, *Dorothea Rockburne: A Personal Selection of Paintings 1968–1986* (New York: Xavier Fourcade, 1986), n.p. O'Doherty included Ruda, along with Valledor, in the 1965 exhibition *Art '65* for the New York World's Fair (see again n. 48).

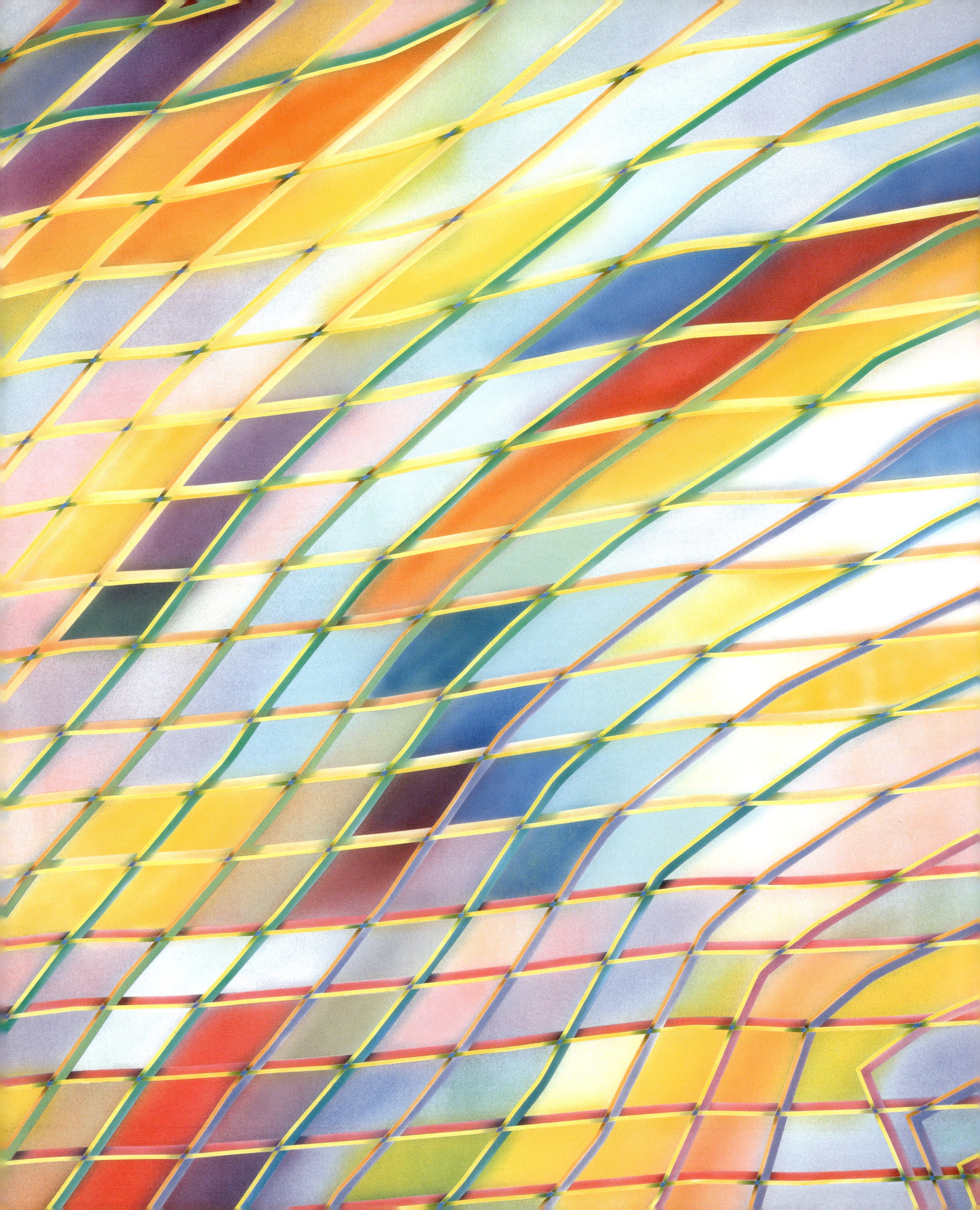

NEW YORK PAINTING CIRCA 1968
NOTES TOWARD THE MISSING HISTORY OF EXPERIMENTAL ABSTRACTION

David Reed

A GREAT DEAL OF CRITICAL ATTENTION has been paid to the fact that the late 1960s was an exciting and innovative time for art. In a relatively brief period, Pop, Minimalism, Conceptual art, language art, video and film works, sound works, Earthworks, performance, and Happenings were developing more or less simultaneously in New York. And yet, even though the experimental painting of this time had a relationship to these other forms of art, it has not been included in historical discussions of the period: art historians and curators have overlooked a crucial area of investigation. This may well be the reason that the situation in painting is muddled and confused, while the work of so many young artists involved with installation, film, and performance can be put into historical context. At this point, it is even difficult to come up with common terms and issues in discussions of painting. In this light, the period of the late 1960s and the 1970s can be viewed as a wound, a break in the history of painting that needs to be repaired if the medium is to develop with an articulated historical awareness. When its history has been repressed, how can current experimental painting be understood?

RICHARD BELLAMY

In an attempt to outline this missing history, I will write about twenty-three abstract paintings by twenty-two artists bought on the advice of Richard Bellamy for the Mari and James A. Michener Collection.[1] Rolf Ricke, a gallerist from Cologne who worked with some of the same artists, called Bellamy "the greatest art dealer of the twentieth century."[2] Bellamy, a unique and charismatic man, was known for his discriminating and innovative eye and his ability to discover artists who would go on to achieve great success and historical importance. In his legendary Green Gallery, which closed in 1965, he was the first to show the Pop artists Claes Oldenburg, George Segal, and James Rosenquist, as well as the Minimal artists Donald Judd, Robert Morris, and Dan Flavin, among many others. Bellamy's independent and opinionated voice was one of the most influential in the 1960s New York art world. Artists loved and respected him because they recognized how much he cared about art. I wish we had recordings of his conversations with James Michener. What did he say when he advised Michener to add these works to his collection?

All twenty-three paintings purchased under the advice of Bellamy were created in the five-year period between 1964 and 1969 and purchased for the Michener Collection between 1964 and 1970 (with the exception of the second painting by Dan Christensen, which Michener bought at auction in 1972). All of the paintings, except one, as far as I can tell, cost less than $1,000. (The Ralph Humphrey cost

Kenneth Showell, *Besped*, 1967 (detail, figure 4)

ARTIST	TITLE OF WORK	SIZE OF WORK	YEAR MADE	BORN	PURCHASED THROUGH
Baer, Jo	*Horizontals Tiered*	52 × 72" ea.	66	29	artist
Budd, David	*Gee-Bee Slipstream*	84⅜ × 90½"	64	27–91	Green Gallery
Canin, Martin	*Diptych #5 and #6*	56 × 112"	67	27	Goldowsky
Christensen, Dan (2)	Untitled	100 × 100"	Sept. 66	42	Goldowsky
	Untitled	100 × 100"	Nov. 66	42	Goldowsky
Conley, Steve	*Imperio II*	84¾ × 60"	66	37	Goldowsky
Corse, Mary	Untitled	108⅝ × 108⅝"	69	45	Goldowsky
Cote, Alan	*Tocqueville*	100 × 120"	69	37	artist
Diao, David	*Untitled*	87½ × 87½"	68	43	Bellamy
Humphrey, Ralph	*Untitled*	54¼ × 108¼"	68	32–90	Bykert
Lipsky, Pat	*Clear Music*	74½ × 112½"	69	41	artist
Lloyd, Elliot	*Untitled*	94¼ × 73¾"	68	37	Bellamy
Logemann, Jane	*Untitled*	54¼ × 54¼" ea.	69	42	Bellamy
Lozano, Lee	*Ream*	78⅜ × 96"	64	30–99	Bellamy
Marden, Brice	*Fave*	72¼ × 66¼"	68–69	38	artist
Pettet, William	Untitled	80 × 80"	67	42	Bellamy
Showell, Kenneth	*Besped*	108 × 90"	67	39–97	Bellamy
Stafford, Lawrence	*Untitled*	72 × 96"	68	38	Bellamy
Torreano, John	*I*	78" diameter	68	41	Bellamy
Tuttle, Richard	*Light Pink Octagon*	56¾ × 53"	67	41	Parsons
Williams, Neil	*Ship's Complement*	73 × 110¾"	64	34	Bellamy
Wofford, Philip	*H.C.E.*	93 × 76"	67	35	Bellamy
Young, Peter	*Capitalist Masterpiece #26*	96 × 132"	68	40	Bellamy

Figure 1. Abstract painters born after 1927 whose work James Michener purchased on the advice of Richard Bellamy between 1964 and 1972.

$1,600.) Only five of the twenty-two artists are women, which reflects the strong bias against women painters that existed in the 1960s—a bias that continues to this day.

TWO GENERATIONS

I find it useful to divide the artists whose work Bellamy advised Michener to buy into two generations—the first born around 1930 and the second born around 1940 (figure 1). Entering the art world at different moments and at different ages, these two generations had distinct experiences, though they shared similar concerns.

The three artists from the 1930s generation—Jo Baer (b. 1929), Ralph Humphrey (1932–1990), and Lee Lozano (1930–1999)—were especially important examples, even pioneers, for the younger artists. Michener added their work to the collection when they were in their mid- to late thirties, at which point their paintings were fairly well known. Each had exhibited in several shows that demonstrated their works' development. While their paintings are very different from one another, Baer, Humphrey, and Lozano all were caught historically between modernism and a subsequent moment, resulting in a compressed, complex maturation for each body of work. I would like to write a paragraph about each of these artists before addressing the younger painters and the characteristics of what I like to call experimental abstract painting.

Lee Lozano cannot be understood as just a painter; she must be considered in relation to performance, Conceptual, and language artists as well. Her work progressed with extreme intensity, seeming to cram the life's effort of a modernist painter into just a few years. In the early 1960s Lozano created a group of paintings focusing on body parts and internal/external perceptions that was informed by an awareness of sexual and gender politics. These painting are related in a striking way to the figurative paintings that Philip Guston started at the end of the 1960s. Lozano then moved into painting large images of tools, continuing to incorporate sexual and political references in an indirect way, after which time her work became more and more abstract, culminating in the series of Wave Paintings from 1967 to 1970. Lozano made

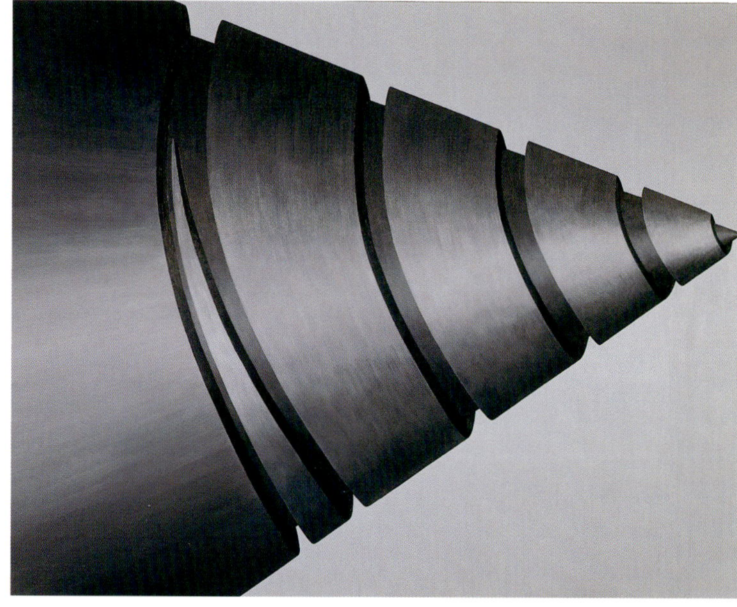

Figure 2. Lee Lozano, *Ream*, 1964; oil on canvas, 78⅜ × 96 in.; Gift of Mari and James A. Michener, G1968.92

Ream (1964, figure 2)—the painting in the Michener Collection of an oversized ream, a carpentry tool, which conveys a sensation of power with phallic connotations—at the moment of that change from tool imagery to abstraction. The movement of the pointed, triangular form slams so powerfully against the right side of the canvas that it creates an almost unbearable tension. It seems amazing that the force of this movement does not shatter the painting. Lozano insisted on finishing each painting in one sitting, repeatedly brushing paint—wet into wet—until she had built up the surface into a stringy, reflective relief. Because of this unusual surface, the values and even the hues change as one views the painting from different distances and angles, causing the forms to turn, move, and shift. The surface seems mechanical rather than handmade, and the cold gray has the mood of an industrial wasteland. I relate the color to the color and mood of Andy Warhol's contemporaneous disaster paintings.

During these years, Jo Baer was one of the few artists to have the courage and independence of mind to forcefully defend painting. In 1967 she wrote a letter to *Artforum* arguing against the criticisms of painting leveled by Donald Judd and Philip Leider. The painting in the Michener Collection, *Horizontals Tiered [Vertical Diptych]* (1966, figure 3), one of her classic works, is a stacked diptych. Each canvas has a narrow black border that starts slightly inside its outer edge. The centers of the two canvases are white, and inside the black border there are thinner grey/green bands that have a slightly more reflective surface. This grey/green is a very odd color that seems to turn the interior white into light and create a slight space inside the black borders. Despite its reductive geometric form, I do not think the painting can be considered Minimalist, since there is no sense of a whole. How can there be when there are two canvases? Everything is thrown into question by the doubling—nothing can remain in focus. In the early 1970s Baer often painted around the side edges of her canvases—an innovation that was very influential. The slight indentation of the black borders in *Horizontals Tiered [Vertical Diptych]*, which leaves a very narrow white band along the outer edge, seems to prefigure this later development in her work.

Ralph Humphrey's evolution is related to Baer's in that he also moved from making flat monochromes to variously shaped, three-dimensional paintings that project as much as a foot off the wall and are painted around the sides. Humphrey's work went through many different stages, and a major retrospective is needed to help understand its varied and multifaceted development. The Michener Collection's *Untitled* (1968, not illustrated) is a horizontal double square with rounded edges that is divided by eight vertical slices or slots into nine vertical sections. As in the painting by Baer, the colors produce a sense of light. (Light was one of Humphrey's major themes, although the surfaces of his canvases are even more sensitive than Baer's.) In the later 1970s Humphrey introduced playful figurative forms into his works, some depicting open windows and billowing curtains. I have often thought that I could feel the wind on my face, blowing out of these paintings.

* * * *

Figure 3. Jo Baer, *Horizontals Tiered [Vertical Diptych]*, 1966; oil and synthetic resin on canvas, each panel, 52 × 72 in.; Gift of Mari and James A. Michener, G1968.31

In contrast to his pattern with the artists from the 1930s generation, Michener bought the paintings of the 1940s generation of artists when they were very young (almost all were still in their twenties), often before or at the time of their first one-person shows. In many cases, Michener's purchase was their first major sale, and indeed, this is true of three of the six artists that I interviewed: David Diao, John Torreano, and Dan Christensen.[3] In this light, Bellamy's and Michener's studio visits must have been memorable events. Whether by his own initiative or at Michener's request, Bellamy must have made a point of taking Michener to the studios of unproven, unknown artists. Michener bought some of the paintings, such as those by Torreano, Christensen, Diao, Ken Showell, and William Pettet, so early in the artists' careers that they are examples of work that predate the paintings for which they became known. In other cases, Michener bought now-classic works, such as those by Alan Cote, Brice Marden, Richard Tuttle, Peter Young, Mary Corse, and Pat Lipsky. In view of the risks

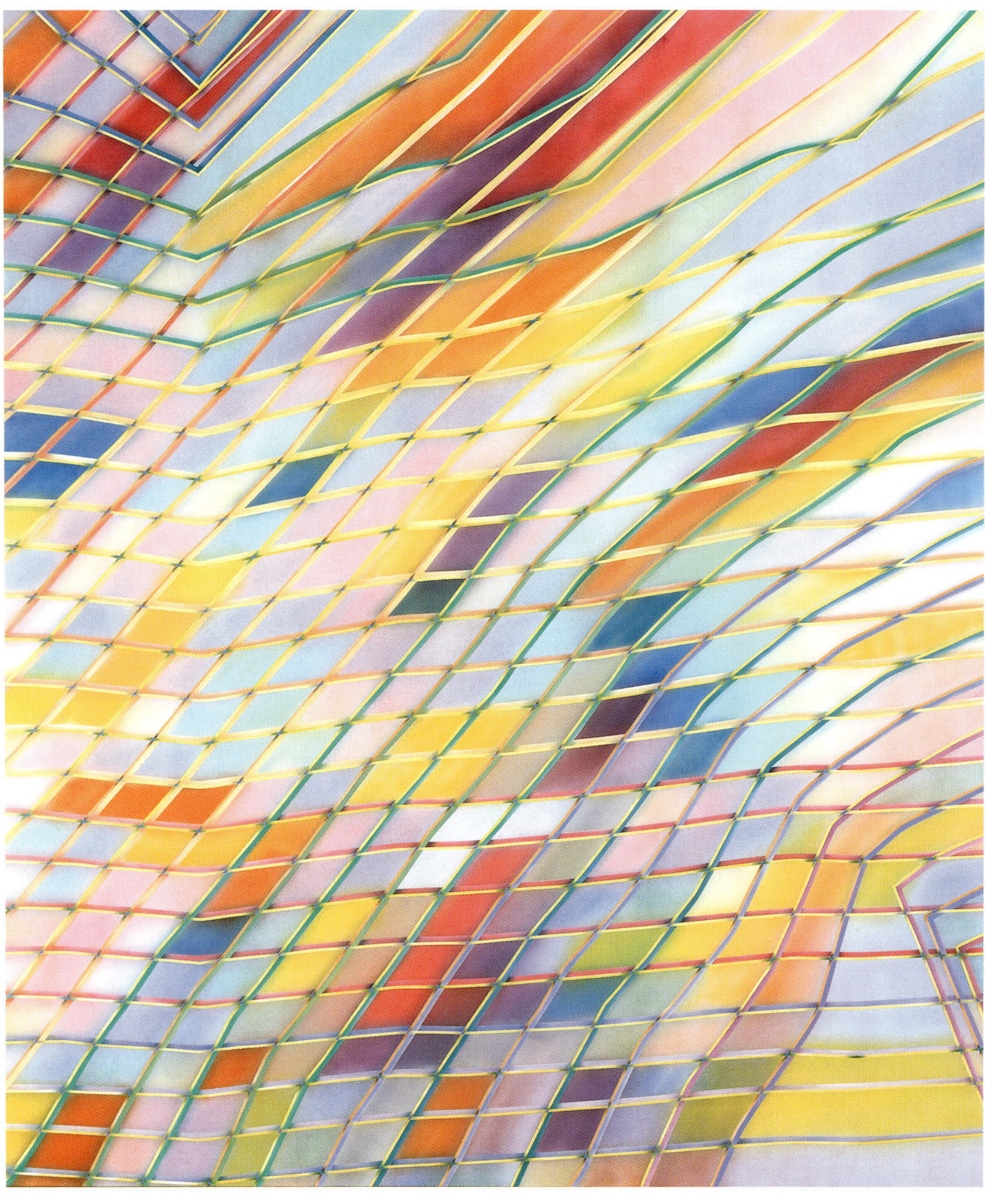

Figure 4. Kenneth Showell, *Besped*, 1967; sprayed acrylic on canvas, 108 × 90 in.; Gift of Mari and James A. Michener, G1968.118

Bellamy took in recommending such young artists, it's remarkable how historically significant many of the works are and how wise his choices have proven to be over time.

ALTERNATE WORLDS

When I visited the Michener Collection in May 2001, most of the paintings in the storage area were hung closely together on a series of rolling racks. When we pulled a rack all the way out, the paintings suddenly became visible in all their complexity, vulnerability, and strength. I was especially moved when a painting by Ken Showell, *Besped* (1967, figure 4), emerged in this way. The painting seemed so brave, so fresh, so youthful, so filled with "flower power" optimism and desire. I knew Ken slightly and, looking at the painting, remembered the last time I had seen him in Soho lugging heavy boxes of photographic equipment down the street, shoulders hunched. I could not reconcile the weightless, effervescent painting in front of me with the man I had seen. Ken's success as a painter came early and did not last, so, to make a living, he photographed other people's art and tended the bar at Fanelli's, a Soho hangout. I had seen other paintings by Ken but none like the one in the Blanton's collection. This painting seemed to transport me through a portal into a different, parallel future: into a new society that had achieved the goals of justice and equality that many of us believed in so strongly in the 1960s. This future was a vision from an ideal-filled time that now, because of Ken's painting, I remembered and longed to experience again.

EXPERIMENTAL ABSTRACT PAINTERS

Dissatisfied with the limitations of established painting discourses (Abstract Expressionism, geometric painting, and Clement Greenberg and the Color Field School), painters of both the 1930s and 1940s generations were trying to do something new. Given their understanding that art was under pressure from a number of historical shifts as well as changing social conditions, they wanted to find alternative possibilities within painting. Of course, in 1968 nobody could predict the power of the forces that would soon hit in the 1970s: the historical and aesthetic arguments declaring the end of painting, the anger and despair over the continuation of the war in Vietnam, the disillusionment of Watergate, and the strife and cultural differences that would divide the country. These paintings were made before all that happened, from a perspective of historical optimism and under the influence of strong and growing civil rights and feminist movements that made social change seem possible.

These are works by brash painters who had come to New York, the center of the art world, to make places for themselves. They thought that they could fit into a native tradition of painting, a tradition that included the masters of Abstract Expressionism and Minimalism, and that they could contribute their own innovations. They came from art schools around the country (several from the Kansas City Art Institute) with great hopes and ambitions. By the late 1960s some of them had achieved sudden art world fame: major galleries represented them, and major museums, both in New York and around the world, showed their work. But this fame lasted longer for some than for others. The works in the Michener Collection that I am discussing are, therefore, a kind of snapshot of the time—an archive, a historical record that can be deciphered and added to. One can see from the vantage point of time that these paintings display a consistency and share overlapping concerns to a degree that is unusual even for artists working during the same period.

All twenty-three paintings (except the Richard Tuttle) that Michener purchased under the advice of Bellamy assume the large size of Abstract Expressionist canvases. Their size is an indicator of the optimistic energy of the time. And because they establish a direct, visceral relationship to the viewer's body, one is made aware of one's smaller size and physical form while standing in front of them. Moreover, the paintings show an understanding of Minimalist installation, which was designed to intensify viewers' physical awareness as they moved around the artwork: these paintings extend and connect to the space in which they are installed and create new kinds of interactions with viewers.

The paintings are all structured in simple, direct, and blunt ways, yet they also incorporate sophisticated vocabularies derived from the innovations of the Abstract Expressionists and the Minimalists, especially Jackson Pollock and Barnett Newman. For example, each painting is "non-compositional," a phrase from the time used to describe a new way of structuring a painting, in which the parts have no hierarchy and relate primarily to the whole, thus focusing attention on the work in its entirety. "Allover" is another contemporaneous phrase that describes this approach to painting. The pictorial problem for these artists was how to work in adherence with this structure, while at the same time creating variety within the painting.

To my surprise, I noticed that many of the paintings have a square format (the Dan Christensens, Mary Corse, David Diao, Jane Logemann, and William Pettet; the John Torreano is circular but has a grid of squares within it). The Ralph Humphrey and Martin Canin are double squares. The frequent use of the square and the grid in these paintings relates to their "allover," "non-compositional" structure.

In addition to their structural or compositional approach, these twenty-three paintings share a type of surface indebted to Pollock and Newman. In an essay on Robert Mangold, art historian and critic Richard Shiff defined such surfaces as "declarative," with "paint applied 'very matter-of-factly.'" He stated, "Declarative painting is antithetical not only to the gestural drama of pictorial expressiveness, but also to the 'topical' and the 'beautiful.'"[4] The surface is not expressionistic because the paint handling does not aim to convey direct gesture or emotion; but neither is it as cool and subtly refined as in geometric painting. Rather, the surfaces in these paintings are workmanlike—as accomplished and skillful as a carefully painted wall. These artists (Canin, Christensen, Diao, Torreano, Steve Conley, Alan Cote, Neil Williams) often used tape to make edges in the manner of house painters and experimented with industrial tools to apply paint, such as squeegees and spatulas (Conley, Diao, Lipsky, Marden) and spray guns (Conley, Corse, Humphrey, Showell, Lawrence Stafford). The emphasis on a "declarative surface" also reveals the process of making the painting. The surface is a record of the making—to be deciphered and reconstructed by the viewer, thus uncovering the hidden performance of the painter. This is painting on a stage—self-conscious and active.

Stafford's *Untitled* from 1968 (figure 5) is an especially clear example of an artist's engagement with "declarative surface." Its surface is built up of many layers of sprayed acrylic paint, which was applied methodically with an airbrush as the artist walked back and forth in front of the canvas. In other paintings of this period, Stafford mechanized the painting process. He rolled the canvas around a large motorized horizontal cylinder that revolved at a constant rate. While this drum turned, he directed a spray of paint from an industrial spray gun at one spot along the turning drum, creating a blurry but straight line on the canvas. Next, the artist resumed spraying an inch or so to the side of the original location, which formed a second blurry but straight line, parallel to the first. He repeated this process across the length of the canvas. When Stafford removed the canvas from the drum and stretched it, he turned it so the lines became horizontal. The artist

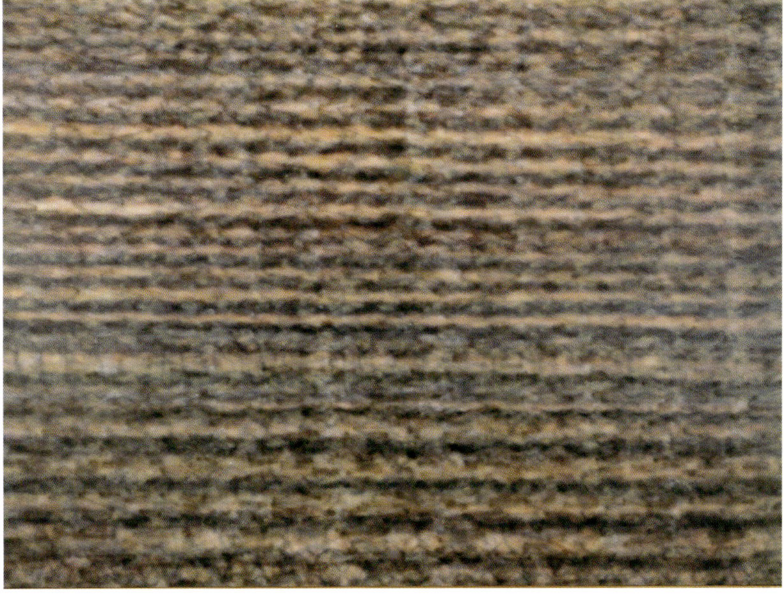

Figure 5. Lawrence Stafford, *Untitled*, 1968; sprayed acrylic on canvas, 72 × 96 in.; Gift of Mari and James A. Michener, G1968.121

then glazed transparent color over the surface with a brush or smaller spray gun, contrasting this final, more handmade finish with the mechanical look beneath.

COLOR: UNDERSHOOTING AND OVERSHOOTING

Color was an essential issue for all twenty-two painters recommended by Bellamy. They each avoided the three most familiar color strategies of their time: Constructivist color, which used systematic gradations of hue or value and often the three primary hues; classic Pop color (like Roy Lichtenstein's) with primary or easily identifiable hues used with graphic clarity; and Color Field painting, with its lush hues and limited range of values. The artists in the Michener Collection developed two basic alternative strategies. Some undershot color and devalued decoration by employing very light or very dark unnamable colors or strange metallic or industrial colors; others overshot the color—making it garish and kitsch—thus overstepping the "good taste" of decoration. In the latter case, hue becomes overly dominant and value is not controlled. Overshot colors often refer to those found in popular culture (interior decoration, clothes, cars, and toys) as well as other media (film, television, and posters), colors that are all around us and are made with artificial dyes.

Brice Marden's *Fave* (1968–1969, plate 111) is a classic example of the under-shooting strategy. Exactly what color is it? Green? Brown? Yellow? All these colors can be seen in the work in different lights and from different angles. Made by layering semitransparent paint mixed with a wax medium, the surface's color is very evocative because it is impossible to identify or remember. David Diao, in *Untitled* (1968, figure 6), used a different technique to reach a similar effect: he applied multiple glazes of transparent acrylic over a metallic underlayer. Dan Christensen's two untitled paintings from 1966 (figure 7) change color in an even more exaggerated way when seen from the side because of his use of interference (the tiny reflecting glass microspheres commonly found on highway signs) and pearlescent pigments. From the front, the vertical dash forms are lighter in value than the background, but from the side, they are darker. Sometimes, when this shift in value takes place, it activates the whole surface, creating a wavelike motion. Jane Logemann's *Untitled* from 1969 also uses a dark color that is hard to identify specifically. Is the painting black or a very dark hue? Trying to resolve this ambiguity keeps the viewer focused on the work.

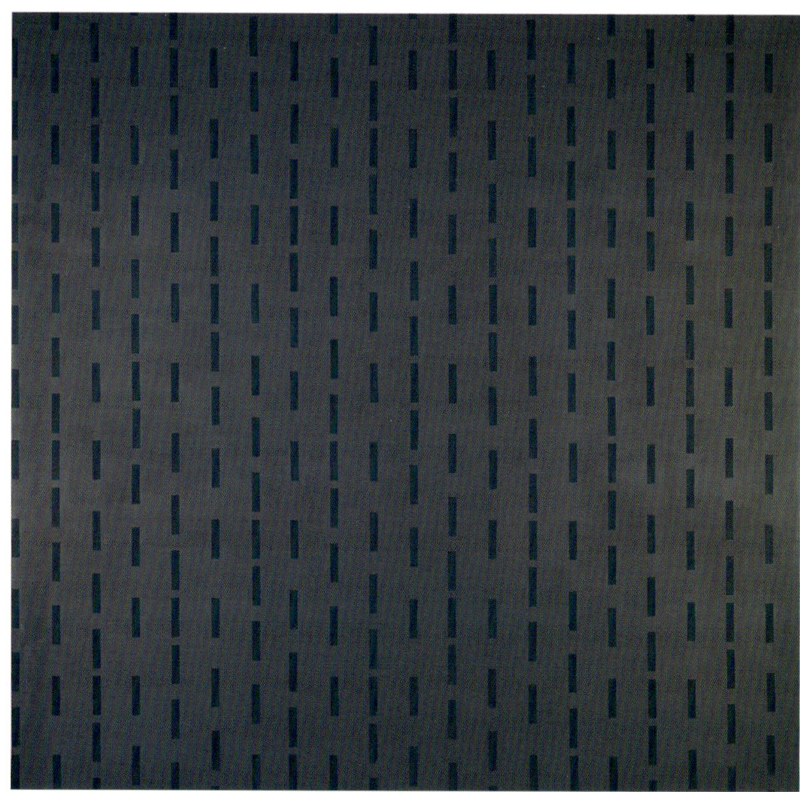

Figure 7. Dan Christensen, Untitled, September 1966; sprayed acrylic on canvas, 100 × 100 in.; Gift of Mari and James A. Michener, G1972.10.1

Figure 6. David Diao, *Untitled*, 1968; acrylic on canvas, 87⅜ × 87⅜ in.; Gift of Mari and James A. Michener, G1968.43

Other paintings rely on colors that are extremely light in value. Mary Corse is from Los Angeles but was working in New York in the late 1960s. She made her untitled painting from 1969 (plate 29) using white interference and pearlescent paint that changes in an astounding way into different rainbow hues when the work is viewed from the side. William Pettet also came to New York from California. His untitled painting from 1967 (not illustrated) looks just white at first but is in fact composed of layers of subtly varying grey over pink. In Richard Tuttle's *Light Pink Octagon* (1967, figure 8), a strange pale pink is soaked into unstretched canvas. The cloth is crumpled and the small folds create shadows, giving the color a permutable, grayed look.

To create *Untitled*, Stafford sprayed fuzzy black lines on a white ground and then glazed layers of magenta, blue, and yellow over them. This triad of colors relates to photographic print technology in ways that now seem prescient given the subsequent and continuing engagement of many painters with the interface between photography and painting.

The paintings by Peter Young and Ken Showell, with their wonderful sense of Pop psychedelic color, are examples of the overshooting strategy. Young's *Capitalist Masterpiece #26* (1968, plate 200) has an overabundance of hue possibilities in the diverse multicolored dots that lend optical dazzle to the painting. Even the slight figurative reference seems to support this overabundance. Both John Torreano's *I* (1968, figure 9) and Neil Williams's *Ship's Complement* (1964, not illustrated) refer to Constructivist color only to break the rules of good taste. The Torreano has too many colors, some even pearlescent, and we all know it is "wrong" to take a grid to such extremes of pattern and variation. The sources of the impure and exaggerated colors of this painting, which would include stylish clothing and desirable decorative objects, are even clearer in Torreano's later jewel paintings. Williams used transparency and colors referring to interior decoration to complicate seemingly Constructivist relations between colors. In her work *Clear Music* (1969, not illustrated), Pat Lipsky stained the canvas like Greenberg's Color Field painters, but unlike them she created hues. She used the techniques of staining but created hues that are too strong, too insistent—especially the yellow—to work together as they conventionally should. The colors have an independence from each other that gives the painting vitality. In *H.C.E.* (1967, not illustrated) by Philip Wofford (an artist born in 1935, between the two generations), there is a kind of painterly organic form unusual among Bellamy's choices, but the strange pinks and greens are not the kinds of earth colors usually employed with such forms. *Imperio II* (1966, not illustrated) by Steve Conley is perhaps the painting that hits the nadir with respect to taste. The sprayed pinks and mauves seem calculated to put one's teeth on edge, and the silver paint overlying thick textures is especially grotesque. These paintings try to push color into new territory by finding possibilities of structure and expression rarely explored in painting.

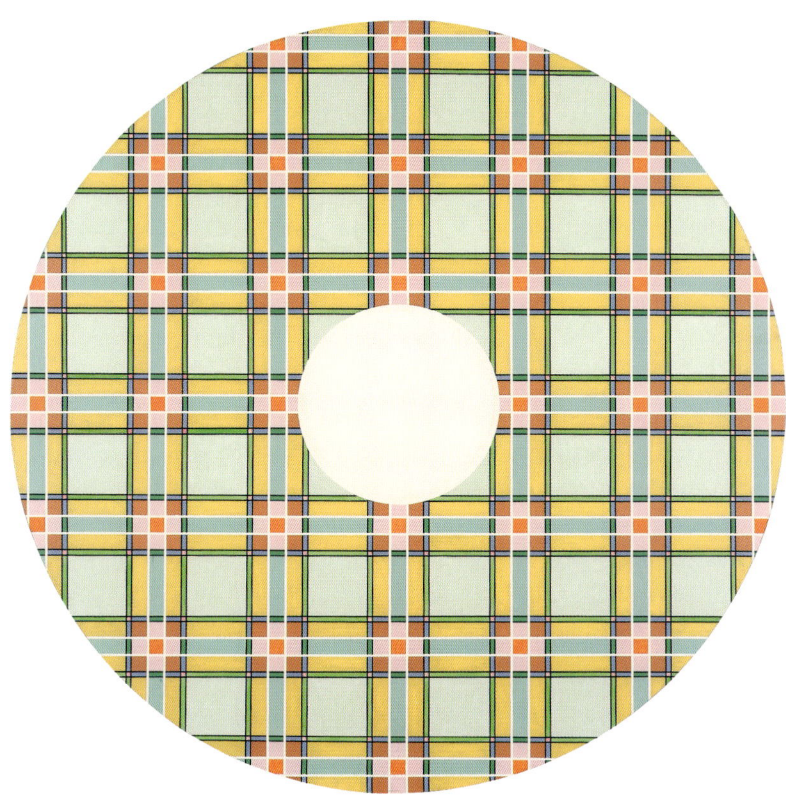

Figure 9. John Torreano, *I*, 1968; acrylic on canvas, 78 in. diameter; Gift of Mari and James A. Michener, 1979.31

Figure 8. Richard Tuttle, *Light Pink Octagon*, 1967; canvas dyed with Tintex, 56¾ × 53¹⁄₁₆ in.; Gift of Mari and James A. Michener, 1991.335

POST-MINIMAL PAINTING

Besides the shared subjects of structure and color, these paintings have other experiential issues in common. These are not paintings that can be seen quickly. To be appreciated, they need to be seen from various distances and angles over time. Many of the paintings feature fine detail as well as large areas of color. After moving in close and seeing the drips and underlayers on the bottom edge of Marden's *Fave*, for example, one can return to the monochromatic area above with an understanding of the tension between the thinness of the paint and the space implied by the color. And when one becomes aware of the variously layered undercolors in Pettet's painting, which at first glance seems to be a monochromatic white, the work springs to life. The triangles in Diao's *Untitled* tilt and move in a newly apparent shallow space once the viewer notices the reflective lines between them. The dots of paint in Young's *Capitalist Masterpiece #26* have a three-dimensional quality and reflect light off their shiny surfaces in a way that makes them seem to move as one walks by. All of these paintings engage the viewer by virtue of a tension between their simple, allover structure and the complex perceptual experiences that accumulate during the extended period spent in the act of viewing them. This sense of duration changes how the paintings can be understood.

There is often a separation, rather than an integration, of elements in these paintings. For example, one sees the form first and then the color, or the value first and then the hue, or vice versa in each case. This separation of elements makes viewing the paintings a puzzle that one wants to solve in a step-by-step manner, but often there is no clear solution. Vision cannot be taken for granted. Is the diagonal in Lee Lozano's *Ream* a perspectival recession or the edge of a positive form? It could be either or both. *Untitled* (1968, not illustrated) by Elliot Lloyd is a shaped canvas but a very unusual one: the format seems controlled by the marks inside it, a reverse of Frank Stella's method, in which the interior forms replicate the shape of the stretcher. How could a painting be made in this way—the shaped canvas following the painted form? The movements of the thin rectangular forms in *Tocqueville* (1969, plate 30) by Alan Cote seem to ignore the diagonal edges of the canvas. How are these forms ordered in relation to the shape of the canvas? Why do they seem to extend past its edges?

It almost seems that these paintings are uncomfortable being paintings. The squares and the grids form an underlying structure, but that structure is thrown out of balance, made to move or shift. What at first seems to be a rational structure instead is twisted into something antirational, distorted. The honeycomb grid of Showell's *Besped* is a good example of this. Trying to figure out how this strange structure varies from a regular grid keeps the viewer engaged in the act of viewing, while the physical quality of the structure itself creates a sense of movement and lift. The grid in *Besped* is not used for clarity but rather to show how quickly vision, when questioned, can become unstable and irrational.

A part of the self-consciousness of these paintings is that their physicality is both accepted and denied. *Light Pink Octagon* by Tuttle is radically materialistic, just a piece of cloth fixed to the wall. But its physical nature also generates an ephemeral quality that is accentuated by the shadows from the crumpled cloth. In Untitled Corse creates a kind of perceptual cloud that hovers in front of the actual work. Is Stafford's *Untitled* a photograph or a painting? Is Humphrey's *Untitled* paint or light? These paintings simultaneously assert and deny their own presence as paintings.

Because they were approaching painting from a perspective of inquiry rather than orthodoxy, these artists used forms that often changed in sudden and unexpected ways from painting to painting. There is none of the slow, steady development dictated by the reductive paradigm of modernism. Young could make paintings with separate vocabularies of dots and lines in the same year. Christensen could move quickly from thin rectangular forms to sprayed lines, then to large blocky rectangles, and then to thick, overall painterly surfaces. Humphrey could alternate from vertical elements to swirls of intertwining linear patterns in the same year. Diao changed from geometric paintings like the one in the Blanton's collection to very painterly, process-oriented works and then back to more geometric shapes. The variety of forms found in these artists' paintings stems from an additive approach, and the problems raised by adding elements are very different from the classic issues of reduction. How to go in the other direction? How to add? This is a complete break from the way art evolved in modernism.

To make the Blanton's collection even more unique and reflective of these radical approaches, it would be wonderful if additional representative works by these same artists could be acquired: a three-dimensional Humphrey; a wraparound Baer; a thickly painted David Budd; a linear painting by Young, or one of his paintings stretched over branches; a romantic gestural painting by Pettet; a Showell sprayed crumple painting; a Diao process painting; and a later, more painterly Cote.

It is satisfying to report that recent acquisitions made by the museum have already deepened the holdings by several of the artists I have discussed: a small but excellent "jewel" painting by Torreano (*Universe Painting*, 1975, plate 179); a later work by Williams (*Untitled*, n.d., not illustrated); an extraordinary and major late pierced painting, *Stroke* (1967–1970, plate 103), by Lozano; and a spray painting by Christensen (*LS*, November 1967, not illustrated) on long-term loan from Dick Bellamy's son, Miles Bellamy. There also have been recent gifts of works by artists whose efforts were related to the directions discussed above: a vibrant shaped painting by Edwin Ruda from 1966 (figure 9, page 384); a spare abstraction by Harriet Korman from 1972 (not illustrated); a lyrical white painting from 1967–1968 by Eleanore Mikus (plate 124); and two extremely beautiful optical paintings by Roy Colmer from the early 1970s (figure 10), which were made before he began to concentrate on photography and experimental film. I would love to see this extraordinary part of the Michener Collection further developed until it includes at least fifty works. Then it would be an indispensable, comprehensive, revelatory archive of this period of experimental abstraction—a time warp ready to be entered.

ILLUSION AND ILLUSIONISM

The differences between these painters and the preceding modernists, Abstract Expressionists, and Color Field painters were not adequately defined or appreciated at the time. Looking back now, after more than thirty years, I can see there was an astounding lack of insightful writing by contemporary critics and art writers, which only further confused and compromised the reception of the work.[5]

Some of the neglect experienced by these painters can be attributed to the fact that when their work was first shown and discussed, contemporary critics still equated steady and consistent development with authenticity and seriousness. Thus, writers were often extremely critical of what were, in fact, these paintings' most innovative attributes. The radical jumps and changes these artists made as they matured were timely and should have been understood and praised as a new way to open up possibilities for painting. Unfortunately, because the influence of Modernism was still too strong on those who were most influential in the public reception of new painting, this different and more challenging approach was neither appreciated nor acknowledged.

More specifically, Greenberg's "high Modernist" theories about painting were still very dominant at the time, and a number of the younger writers followed his thinking and misapplied his principles to these paintings. This lack of insight was decisive because, unlike Greenbergian Modernists, the painters discussed here did not want to separate painting from the influences of other forms of art and popular culture but rather embraced these influences as a way to find

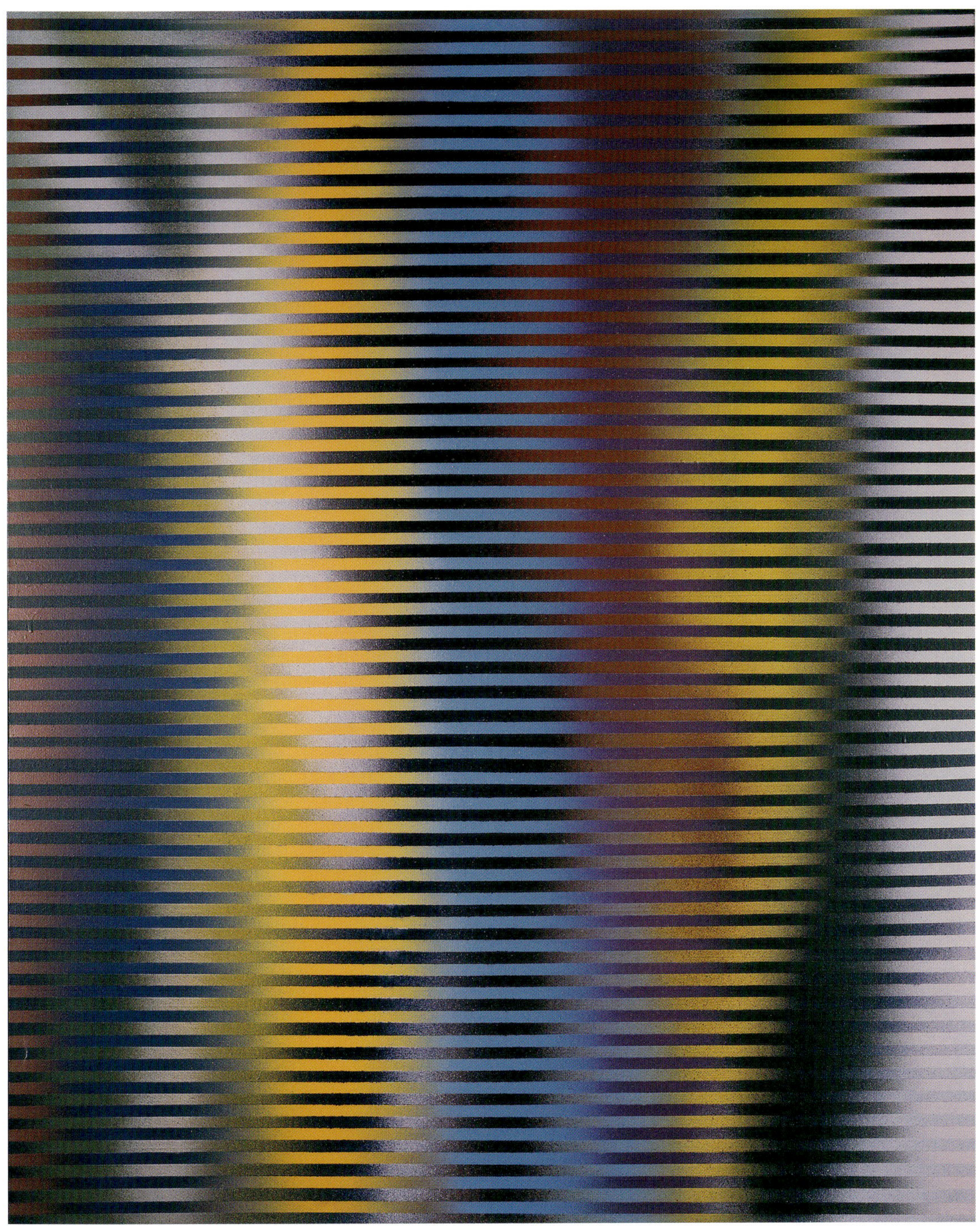

Figure 10. Roy Colmer, #56, 1974; acrylic on cotton duck, $75^{11}/_{16} \times 59^{3}/_{16}$ in.; Gift of Claudia Colmer, 2002.2838

new avenues for abstraction. In defiance of the imperatives for flatness and other formal properties that Greenberg thought unique and essential to painting, these artists sought painting's future outside the discipline. They made paintings to be experienced not at once but over time, and not in isolation but in relation to the world.

In addition to the unrelenting domination of Greenbergian orthodoxy, there was also a great deal of anti-painting rhetoric at the time that supported other forms of art and accused painting of being reactionary because it was inherently illusionistic. In a recent essay on Donald Judd, Richard Shiff, following a distinction made by the artist, clarified the difference between "illusion" and "illusionism": "illusion is a natural condition of vision, a physiological fact: illusionism is a constructed effect for the pictorially indoctrinated." Shiff continued:

> *Indeed, Judd did take pains, going so far as to point out that, among all the subjective psychological experiences people have, optical illusions (such as chromatic afterimages) are 'absolutely objective.' Everyone sees optical illusions in the same places, at the same times. Such illusions are not only objective but real—real illusions. They have little to do with illusionism. . . . Illusion is the way things are. Illusionism is the way things aren't.*[6]

In retrospect, we can now differentiate between "illusion" and "illusionism" in painting, whereas, at the time, "illusion" and "illusionism" were both attacked as if they were the same. Painting as a medium doesn't necessarily involve illusionism, as its critics insisted. Instead, painters can strategically employ illusion as part of the structures they invent. The painters that Bellamy recommended for the Michener Collection used illusion in their works, but not illusionism. The time-based, self-conscious structures of their paintings demonstrate their questioning of the possibilities of painting. They used separation and ambiguity to create illusions of form or color, but these illusions are not part of a system of illusionism, an acceptance of the conventions of painting. On the contrary, to understand these paintings, a viewer must question the illusions and discover them to have a physical and perceptual basis.

The only writing from the time, that I can find, in which a critic made a distinction between "illusion" and "illusionism" is an essay by Lucy Lippard titled "Perverse Perspectives." Published in *Art International* in 1967, this essay analyzed different kinds of illusionism and illusion in geometric painting and argued for what Lippard called the "new illusionism." (Following Shiff, it would be called "illusion.") Lippard wrote:

> *Within the last year or so, a new incongruous illusionism has appeared, incorporating the statement of the flat surface of a painting and the counterstatement of an inverse perspective that juts out into the spectator's space. Such "perverse perspectives" are founded on disunity, on a complex, tightly structured denial of pictorial logic that has its cake and eats it too, in the sense that it never wholly abandons the assertion of the picture plane arrived at by modernist or rejective painting, but distorts and reconstructs that plane outside of the conventions of depth simulation.*[7]

In the essay she advanced an opinion very similar to Shiff's:

> Trompe l'oeil *in the traditional sense merely presents the illusion as reality and depends upon the interest aroused by deception alone. The new perverse styles are both more direct and more devious. They make no claim to simulation of reality—concrete or figurative. The trickery is left unconsummated and exposed, but continuous. No actual three-dimensional substance is ever described, and illusion is established only to be discarded in favor of the painting as painting.*[8]

Just months after Lippard attempted to foster an appreciation for recent abstract painting with her explanation of "new illusionism," Baer defiantly and passionately defended it in a letter to the editor in the September 1967 issue of *Artforum*. Baer argued that, contrary to the allegations of Robert Morris and Judd, a painting is not necessarily inherently illusionistic, spacial, allusive, or generative of figure/ground contrast: painting does not equal "pictures in the . . . everyday sense of the word."[9] She contended that in their arguments against painting Morris and Judd were confusing illusion and allusion. She argued for a more complex reconsideration of the terms used to evaluate painting. After a point-by-point refutation of their positions, Baer ended by turning their language against them: "An 'inescapable' delusion moves the above critics. It is objectionable."[10]

Lippard's essay and Baer's letter represent the beginning of an argument that seeks to define new criteria for looking at paintings. But despite their efforts, critics rarely applied the distinctions that they insisted were necessary, and the dialogue never got underway. No debate about what kind of illusion was possible in painting was forthcoming. Instead, experimental painting was caught in the middle—condemned as outdated by unsympathetic critics and misunderstood by supporters, who, though well-meaning, used outmoded definitions of the medium and old-fashioned, no longer relevant for their judgements.

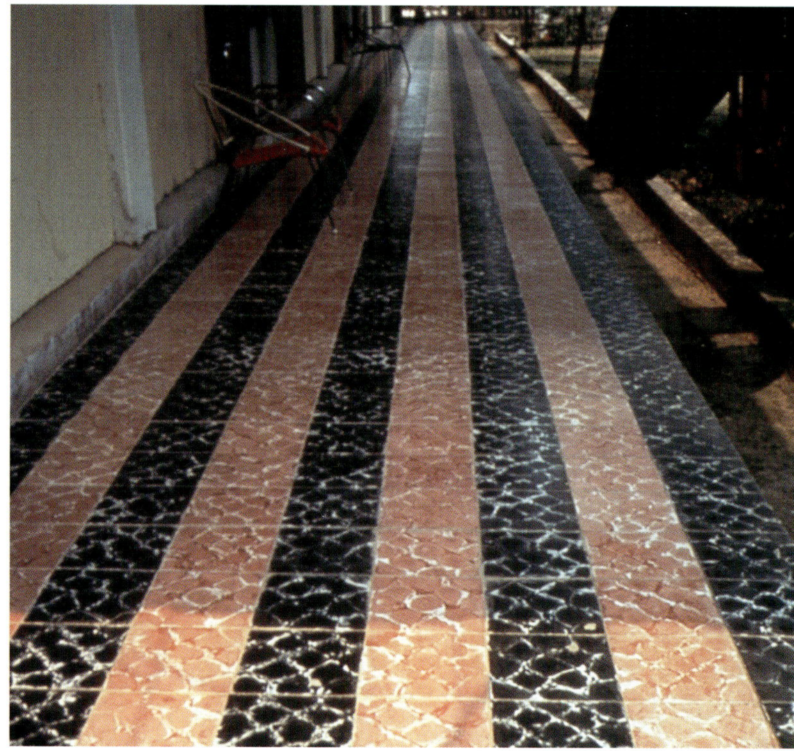

Figure 11. Robert Smithson, *Hotel Palenque* [detail], 1969; thirty-one chromogenic-developed slides and audio CD, dimensions variable; Solomon R. Guggenheim Museum, New York; Purchased with funds contributed by the International Director's Council and Executive Committee Members, 1999; Art © Estate of Robert Smithson/Licensed by VAGA, New York, NY

PORTALS AND DOORWAYS

While for a moment in the late 1960s it seemed that new possibilities were opening up in both art and society, this hopeful time soon ended. By the early 1970s most of the successes I cited had disappeared for these artists. From the older generation: Williams died young; Lozano dropped out of the art scene; Baer left for Amsterdam; and Humphrey did not achieve the recognition many expected. Of the younger artists, only Marden had a significant career. Tuttle was viciously attacked after his Whitney retrospective in 1975, but he continued to have a career because of support in Europe. Young, Stafford, Cote, and Wofford left New York. Others stayed but just held on, living in a distressed, divided, and decaying city.

Born in 1946, I am from a slightly younger generation. When I returned to New York in 1971, these were the artists just ahead of me. I saw their shows, discussed their work with my friends, and watched them carefully. I took their misfortunes as a warning. Looking back, I can certainly see how they were hurt by a lack of support, which had the effect of limiting their opportunities for exhibiting and for engaging in professional, intellectual dialogue. Often their greatest advocates were in Europe, but when support at home ended, they could no longer travel or maintain the credibility to sustain a career that only existed abroad.

And there is another factor that I have become aware of during this research. I have emphasized the year 1968 in the title because it seems to me that it sits at the tipping point of a drastic shift of mood in relation to art. By 1969, after assassinations and race riots and the escalation of the Vietnam War, youthful exuberance no longer seemed appropriate to these artists. Lozano's work accommodates this shift. The darkening and now somber light in Christensen's and Humphrey's work also acknowledges this change—but other artists seemed unable to alter their work to fit this adjustment of mood.

ROBERT SMITHSON'S QUESTION

In 1972 Robert Smithson spoke at the University of Utah and gave what might be the greatest artist's talk of all time, "Hotel Palenque." To the surprise and bewilderment of his audience, he didn't show slides of and talk about the Mayan ruins in Palenque, Mexico, as one might have expected from the title of his talk. Instead, he described in detail the architecture of the tourist hotel, itself in ruins, where he stayed. In this indirect and humorous way, he conveyed his innovative ideas about art.

Toward the beginning of the talk, one of Smithson's slides showed the floor of a partially enclosed walkway, a kind of veranda around a courtyard, which was articulated with receding bands of black and red tiles (figure 11). In an offhand manner, he said, "Actually I feel that these tiles are much more interesting than most of the paintings being done in New York City right now, showing far more imagination."[11] This comment is typical of much of the anti-painting rhetoric in the late 1960s and 1970s, and is characteristic of Smithson's attitudes as well. But why did this particular view of the hotel make Smithson think of New York painting? And why did he feel compelled to be so critical of that painting when looking at this slide? The receding bands of tiles, the grid of lines between them, and the diagonal repetition of organic rock shapes inside them echo then-current New York painting by providing an illusion without illusionism.

Just before his swipe at painting, Smithson said that he liked to think of the tile floor "as a black and white perspective" that seems to "lead towards something," but there is no point in figuring out where.[12] This issue of decentering, of throwing a grid off balance and making it move, is exactly the issue that was then most important to New York painting. How could a grid be made uneasy and troubled? Smithson experienced how the grid and the space around him changed as he walked down this veranda in the hotel. This is what the painters who Bellamy recommended also wanted a viewer to experience. They made paintings that could not be seen in a glance, that needed to be experienced over time, like Smithson's walk. This slide reminded Smithson that painting could have goals in common with his own. In a territorial maneuver, he attacked the competing influence of painting.

The image on the very last slide of Smithson's talk is of a door. Smithson observed, in his matter of fact way, "This is sort of the door . . . I mean it's just a green door."[13] It is a strange statement. What does he mean? He means that Palenque's forest, outdoors, is green. One can see light coming in from under the door. He is reminding us that the door can open. It leads outdoors. To me, this implies that the door is like a painting—it can lead to other spaces. Smithson concluded his talk with a brief, very poetic summary. He said: "The door probably opens to nowhere and closes on nowhere."[14] Sounds like a painting to me.

NOTES

1. There are several artists whose work Michener bought on Bellamy's advice that I have not written about in this essay because their work is figurative or because they were born earlier than the generations on which I have chosen to focus. They are Milet Andrejevic, Robert Beauchamp, Leon Berkowitz, Norman Carton, Miles Forst, Jules Olitski, John Martin Tweddle, John Wesley, and Tom Wesselmann.
2. Rolf Ricke, conversation with the author, Cologne, Germany.
3. See Reed's interviews in the Blanton Museum of Art Archives, The University of Texas at Austin. He spoke with Dan Christensen, David Diao, Pat Lipsky, Lawrence Stafford, John Torreano, and Peter Young (not recorded).
4. Richard Shiff, "Autonomy, Actuality, Mangold," in *Robert Mangold* (London: Phaidon, 2000), 21.
5. There are a few essays that are helpful. Carter Ratcliff wrote about new attitudes toward light in "New Informalists: Young New York Painters," *Artnews* 68 (February 1970): 47. Bill Wilson wrote on Humphrey's work: see his "Ralph Humphrey: An Apology for Painting," *Artforum* 16 (November 1977): 54–59, and "Ralph Humphrey," *Arts Magazine* 50 (February 1976): 5. And E. Johnson wrote a good essay on Peter Young: "Peter Young: A Chronology of the Work," *Artforum* 9 (April 1971): 58–63.
6. Richard Shiff, *Donald Judd: Late Work* (New York: PaceWildenstein, 2000), 9.
7. Lucy Lippard, "Perverse Perspectives," *Art International* 11 (March 1967), reprinted in Lucy R. Lippard, *Changing: Essays on Art* (New York: E.P. Dutton, 1971), 168–69.
8. Lippard, *Changing: Essays on Art*, 171.
9. Jo Baer, "Letter to the Editor," *Artforum* 6 (September 1967): 6.
10. Baer, 6.
11. Robert Smithson, "Insert Robert Smithson: Hotel Palenque, 1969–72," *Parkett* no. 43 (1995): 121.
12. Smithson, 121.
13. Smithson, 132.
14. Smithson, 132.

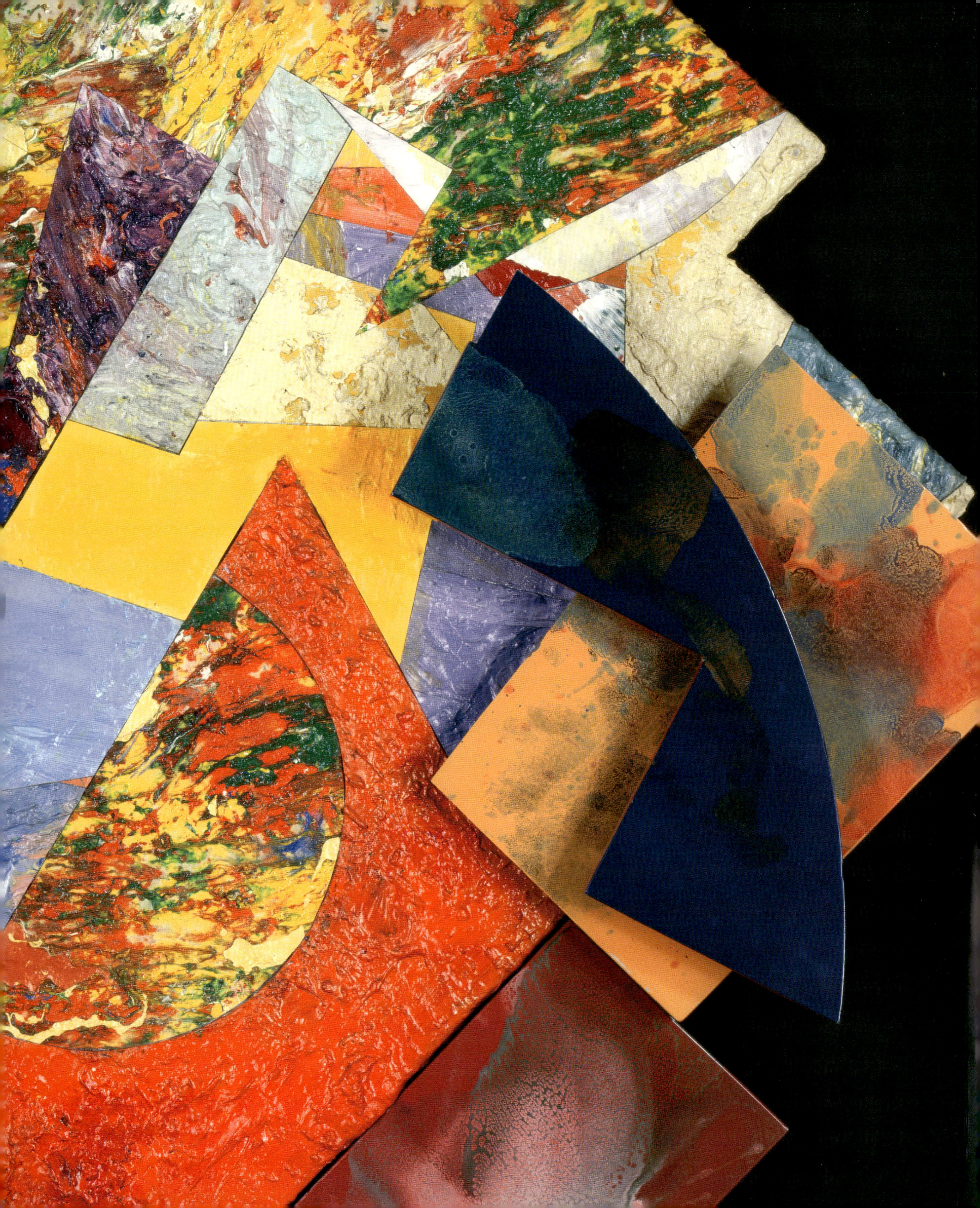

THE LOGICS OF COLOR
NOTES ON RICHARD ANUSZKIEWICZ AND SAM GILLIAM

Ann Eden Gibson

The image of my work has always been determined by what I wanted the color to do. Color function becomes my subject matter and its performance is my painting.

Richard Anuszkiewicz[1]

I think the most important thing that happened in the formation of my ideas about painting [was] . . . the acceptance of color as the major and the most dominant ingredient.

Sam Gilliam[2]

It is unlikely that a painting by Richard Anuszkiewicz ever would be mistaken for a Sam Gilliam, or vice versa. Although each artist paints abstractly and uses intense colors, in most respects their work is quite different. Yet color is crucial to both artists. They came to public attention in the United States in the 1960s, a decade in which color—in Color Field, Modernist, and Minimalist paintings—was a major consideration, as it was still in the work of most of their immediate predecessors, the Abstract Expressionists. But despite what seems as if it should have been a favorable entry, neither Anuszkiewicz nor Gilliam found quick acceptance and have always operated at a certain distance from the mainstream. Could their attitudes toward and approaches to color have had something to do with that? The following essay will compare their histories and then discuss in depth the role that color has played in the creation and reception of both Anuszkiewicz's and Gilliam's work.

Charles Harrison suggested that starting with Baudelaire, "to ask how colors mean," is close to asking "how color may be modern." To ask now, in the early twentieth century, "how colors mean"—which is really what I still want to know—is to be gloriously and hopelessly mired in time and place. Harrison most economically put into words an understanding of color that is crucial, but that has not been given the attention it is due: that *color cannot be separated from the particular instance in which it appears.*[3] In 1990 John Gage wrote that historians have been trying to address this problem for over a century, and that the best work on color has followed a German blend of aesthetic formalism and philosophical phenomenology (in general, the idea that one's subjective perception of the world is the only thing one can be said to really know). He proposed that the most promising approach at this point is likely to be broadly anthropological, perhaps impinging on the social history of art.[4] These are the directions I will follow in my investigation.

But what does it mean to say that for two distinctly different artists color counts more than any other tool at their disposal? What does it mean to say that of any artist's work? This is not easy to answer. Is this because it is neither easy, nor perhaps even possible, to predict color's psychological and emotional effects—or even to describe them effectively? As Jacqueline Lichtenstein noted in her study of color and rhetoric in seventeenth-century French painting, "like passion, the pleasure of *coloris* slips away from linguistic

Sam Gilliam, *Pantheon II*, 1983 (detail, figure 2)

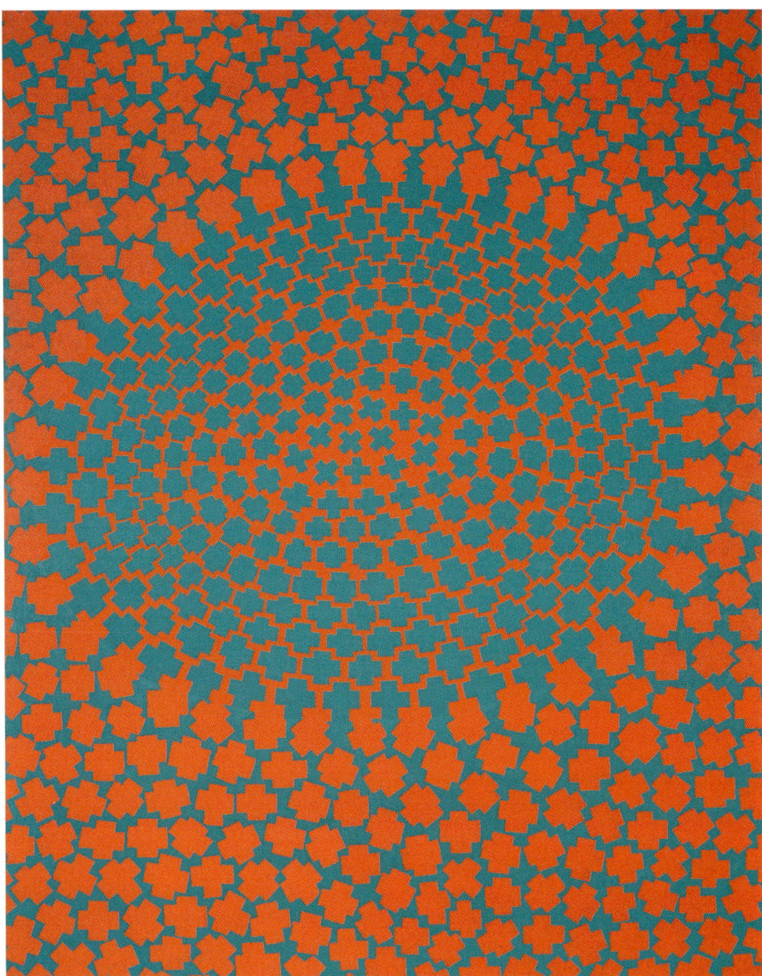

Figure 1. Richard Anuszkiewicz, *Plus Reversed*, 1960; oil on canvas, 75 × 58 in.; Gift of Mari and James A. Michener, 1991.177

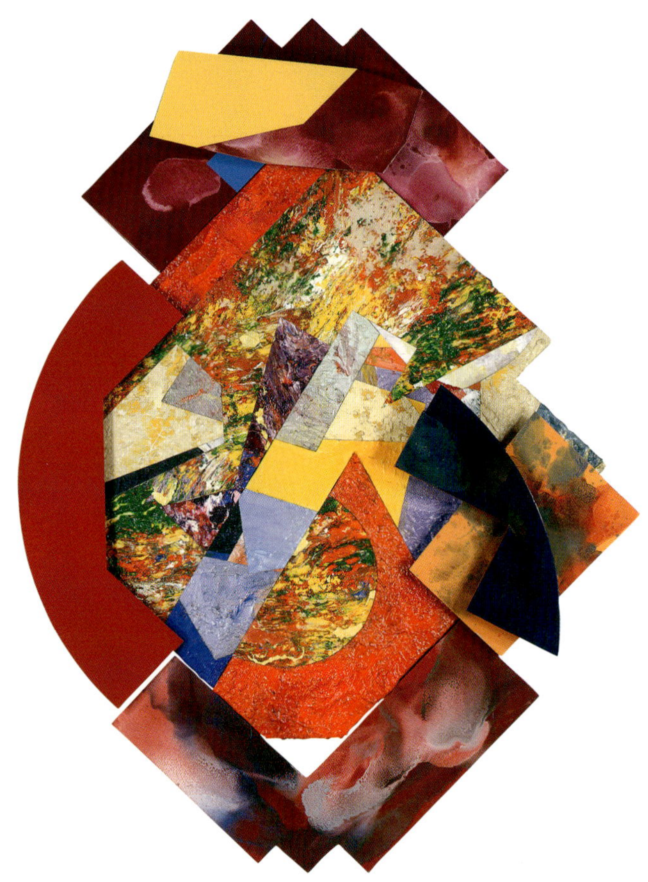

Figure 2. Sam Gilliam, *Pantheon II*, 1983; acrylic on canvas and polyurethane enamel on aluminum, 77 × 44 × 6 in.; Purchased through the Archer M. Huntington Museum Fund, 1985.35

determination."[5] In Western painting, color is dependent on its context. The scholar Norman Bryson wrote that the artist's emphasis on certain hues can establish "a unity which is there not from the moment of origin (or this is how the effect asks to be interpreted), but for the viewing subject, for the moment of reception."[6] I want to explore the ways that color's intransigence (its refusal to settle down and mean one thing in every instance)—recorded in its historical uses, in ideas about the psychophysiology of its reception, and in the varied cultural meanings that resulted—has been used by Anuszkiewicz, Gilliam, and their audiences to construct meanings for their work.

THE BACKSTORY: "HOW COLOR MAY BE MODERN" AFTER MID-CENTURY

Although Anuszkiewicz's *Plus Reversed* (1960, figure 1) was painted over twenty years before Gilliam's *Pantheon II* (1983, figure 2), the artists are near contemporaries: Anuszkiewicz was born in 1930, Gilliam in 1933. Neither was raised in a prominent art center and both received professional training in art schools on undergraduate and graduate levels before moving to the urban centers (New York and Washington, D.C., respectively) where their careers took hold. Anuszkiewicz's early work was indebted to American precedents such as Edward Hopper and Charles Burchfield, whereas Gilliam's early exposure was to German Expressionists such as Emil Nolde and Bay Area figurative painters David Park and Nathan Oliviera. Moreover, both encountered as young professionals intensely pursued and well informed approaches to color: Anuszkiewicz to Josef Albers at Yale, and Gilliam to Hans Hofmann and to the Washington Color School in the person of Tom Downing.[7] Anuszkiewicz and Gilliam each absorbed certain aspects of the methods and attitudes to which they had gained access; these became important elements of their later individual directions.

Anuszkiewicz, for instance, amped up the subtle interactions in Albers's Homage to the Square series (figure 3) with high intensity colors whose intersections are often so hard to focus on that the surfaces of his paintings flicker where the shapes meet, causing "film color," those little flares that appear around the pluses in *Plus Reversed* when you look steadily at the painting for half a minute or so.[8] He would have been exposed to teaching about this effect from Albers, who codified his lessons in the influential *Interaction of Color*, a looseleaf book put together with his students, in his last year at Yale in 1963. A collection of silkscreen prints of the sort that he did with his students over the years, the book instructs readers to view the studies in certain lights, or for certain periods of time, or to juxtapose unbound pages or hinged flaps of color—some with die-cut holes in them—to pages beneath them. When you follow the instructions, new colors appear where there were none, light colors darken and vice versa, and colors that were the same become unlike. It is hard to accept that you cannot believe what your eyes have just told you. The same color, in the same light, can change its appearance simply because of what it touches on one side.

Albers taught students extensively about simultaneous contrast—the way one hue unfailingly affects the way we see its neighbor—and that is the principle for which his teachings are best remembered. But for Albers, color's instability was more than an illuminating understanding: it was the axle around which his own paintings, as well as the color course he taught, turned. It became the principle on which Anuszkiewicz would eventually base his mature paintings, although integrating Albers's ideas into his own working process took some time.[9]

When he arrived in Washington in 1962, Sam Gilliam met artists in the developing Washington Color School.[10] It did not take the young out-of-towner long to realize that he might be able to achieve his goals more effectively without the figure, which he had explored intently during his schooling, though, as Anuszkiewicz had also learned, "unteaching yourself something about painting . . . wasn't easy."[11] However, it was the example of Hofmann to whom Gilliam cedes the immediate and decisive inspiration to jettison the figure. Significantly, Hofmann, who shares with Albers the honor of establishing the color tradition of the second half of the twentieth century in the United States, was, as Gilliam would become, something of an omnivore of painting.[12]

Hofmann's impasto brushwork and high key color, often in full strength primaries set off by a diverse range of neutrals, evident in the Blanton's *Elysium* (1960, figure 4), are also found in *Pantheon II.*

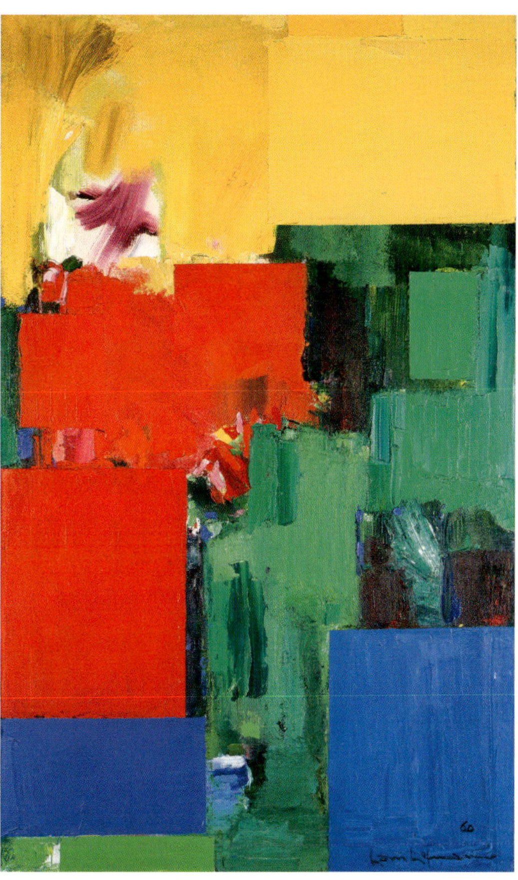

Figure 4. Hans Hofmann, *Elysium*, 1960; oil on canvas, 84 × 50 in.; Gift of Mari and James A. Michener, 1991.239; © 2005 Estate of Hans Hofmann/Artists Rights Society (ARS), New York

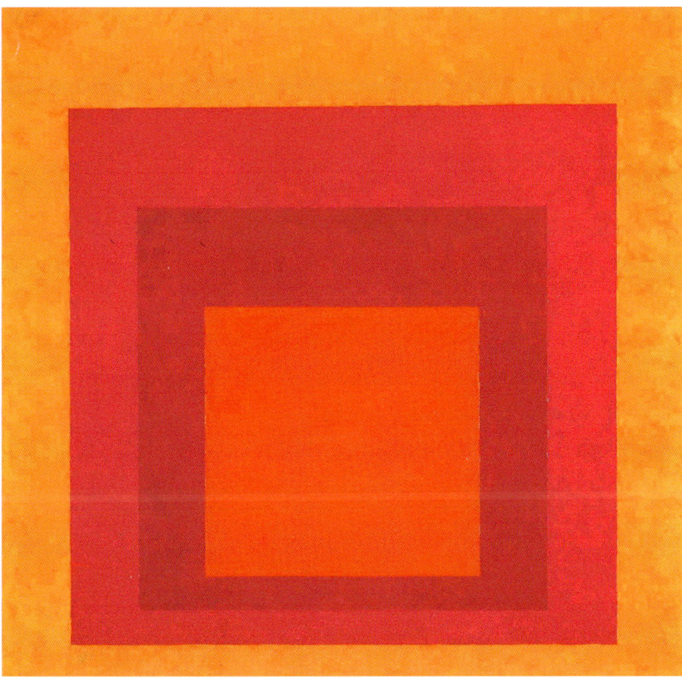

Figure 3. Josef Albers, *Homage to the Square (La Tehuana)*, 1951; oil on fiberboard, 30¾ × 30¾ in.; Collection of The Modern Art Museum of Fort Worth; Gift of Mrs. Anni Albers and The Josef Albers Foundation, Inc., 1980.3.G.P.; © 2005 The Josef and Anni Albers Foundation/Artists Rights Society (ARS), New York

Gilliam told critic Keith Morrison that he remembers the very moment that a rationale for Hofmann's abstract treatment of form clicked in: "It happened . . . when I was doing a figurative study; the construction of that composition paralleled a construction of an artist I was interested in—Hans Hofmann—so, immediately, instead of painting the figure I changed course and started to paint the structure."[13] Hofmann's slogan, "Push answers with Pull, and Pull with Push," has been often misunderstood to apply only to gesture. Gilliam seems to have understood the principle, as Hofmann meant it, as pertaining at least as much to the complementary forces of opposed colors or to dark and light as it did to gesture: to what the older artist called the differential "speeds" of vibrant and more neutral color areas—that is, their advancing and receding tendencies.[14] Before his plunge into the Washington Color School, Gilliam's aim "was to arrive at a format—a kind of a single format." His work grew at a crossing, he told another interviewer, "between the ideas of at least three artists: Hofmann, Rothko and Newman."[15]

If Albers and Hofmann supplied two of the pedagogical, theoretical, and art historical anchors of the available logics of color at the time that Anuszkiewicz and Gilliam began to make their way, Ludwig Wittgenstein's *Remarks on Color* (1977) and David Batchelor's *Chromophobia* (2000) provide useful frames through which other logics arise. Wittgenstein and Batchelor encapsulate with different emphases the various approaches that have occupied scholars as well as artists in the later twentieth century, ranging from physiological and psychological ones (Wittgenstein), to historical and social ones (Batchelor). Meditations on the psycho/physiological aspects of the perception of color and colored things occupied the last eighteen months of the life of philosopher Wittgenstein, known for his mapping of the dissolution of the ego and the social self. The characteristics of this dissolution—illogic, fragmentation, reduction, conceptualism, and a tendency to withdraw from what cannot be verbalized—have proven also to be characteristic of much modern art (and criticism).[16] In *Remarks on Color* these characteristics are illustrated in the development of Wittgenstein's idea that there might be a plurality of logics in the various ways of understanding how color means. But where and how to look for them? Twenty-three years later, artist and writer Batchelor's richly sociological discussion of color in an equally slim volume attempts to answer the question. While Wittgenstein analyzed the problems of rationalizing the disparity between sensation and intellectual apprehension that an experience of color reveals, Batchelor explores in social and emotional terms what these disparities have meant for various cultures.

The social meanings of color in Anuszkiewicz's and Gilliam's abstract forms have had a supplementary—repressed but integral—role in the construction of meaning not only in *their* paintings, but also in the paintings of those, such as Noland (figure 5), Frank Stella, and Jules Olitski, whose uses of color have been critically appraised as having different functions from theirs. Despite its resistance to being translated into words—in fact, partly as a result of this—color is a mighty purveyor of ideas and convictions, at the same time that the specific applications of that power are bound to time and place. That these circumstances coexist is because, although the representational mechanism that conveys color's affect may be metaphor (red is hot because many substances become red when they are heated), it can as well be metonym (the "red scare"), that avatar of conditionality. A familiar kind of metonymy is synecdoche, a figure in which the part may stand for the whole, but in a larger sense, metonymic relationships develop between objects and events (the USSR's predominantly red flag and the threat of communism) brought together arbitrarily (it could very well have been the "blue scare" if the flag had been blue). This is famously true of color. Metonymic figures take meaning from the pairing of two objects, regardless of their lack of necessary connection. Therefore, metonymic connections have been pejoratively categorized as weak or artificial, since their couplings seem so indiscriminate. (Metaphor, in contrast, was touted until the 1980s as a figure whose links are by definition composed of elements related by structural similarities rather than simply those of placement in space or time, as drawing was to color's arbitrary appearance.) Since color is an attribute of everything one sees, but whose meaning is determined by context, not definition, it shares qualities not only with shifters, such as pronouns, but with figures of relationality in general, like metaphor *and* metonymy.

Anuszkiewicz and Gilliam understood that color has many logics—the metaphoric, the metonymic, and the situational, the objective and the subjective, the physical and the emotional—and that they are often in play at the same time. That said, these artists subscribed to related but distinct schools of color: Anuszkiewicz to one particularly concerned with color's mechanics (Albers), and Gilliam to one more focused on its expression, that is, its emotional affect (Hofmann).[17] Despite their differences, however, both Hofmann and Albers taught with hands-on persuasion that the meaning of color for the viewer depends unfailingly on the specifics of its surroundings—and not only its surroundings within the work of art, but outside it as well. As Monet had so successfully demonstrated, and both Anuszkiewicz and Gilliam understood, in sunlight color changes continually as the earth's movement brings it closer or farther from the sun.[18] This is why Anuszkiewicz mixes his colors in a windowless room with the same incandescent lights under which they are most often viewed.[19] Add to this color's ability to affect us physically, whether we want it to or not, and you have a combination of instability and power that led generations of Western artists in the centuries since the Renaissance to distrust color as a carrier of meaning and to prefer line and the shadings of light and dark for the pursuit of "truth."

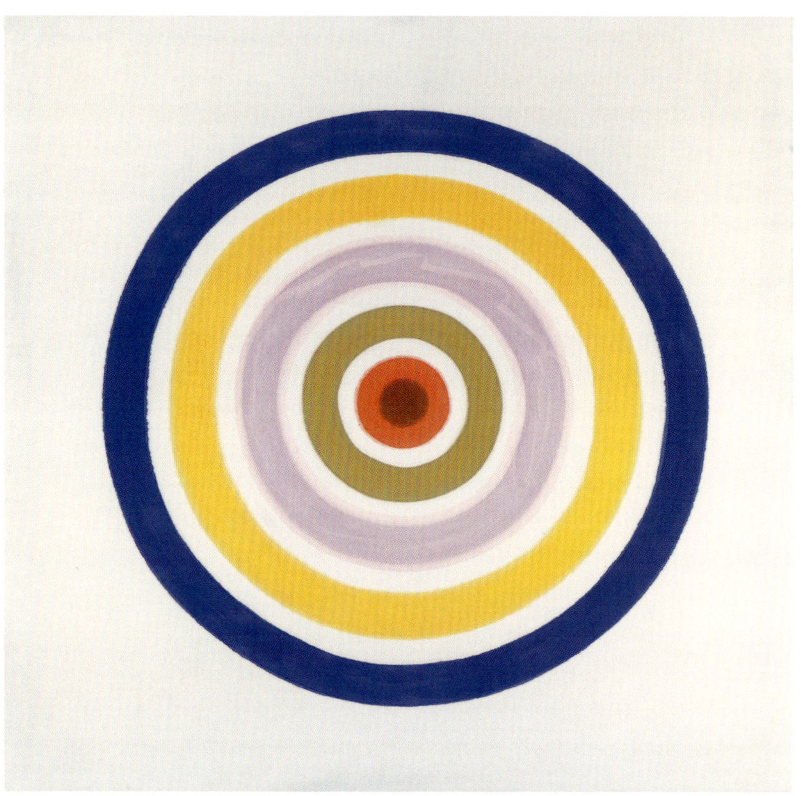

Figure 5. Kenneth Noland, *Split Spectrum*, 1961; acrylic on unsized canvas, 70 × 70 in.; Gift of Mari and James A. Michener, 1991.280

CRITICS RESPOND TO ANUSZKIEWICZ: TOO MUCH POWER OR TOO MUCH CONTROL?

As late as 1965 The Museum of Modern Art devoted an international exhibition entitled *The Responsive Eye* to an exploration of opticality broad enough to include Kenneth Noland, Bridget Riley, Frank Stella, Victor Vasarely, and Anuszkiewicz (figure 6). Curator William Seitz in an article in *Vogue* identified the apex of "Op art" with Anuszkiewicz.[20] Accordingly, Anuszkiewicz was acclaimed by *New York Times* critic Grace Glueck as an "Op Old Master." She called him "A virtuoso technician, whose sizzling colors, arranged in symmetrical bands, stripes

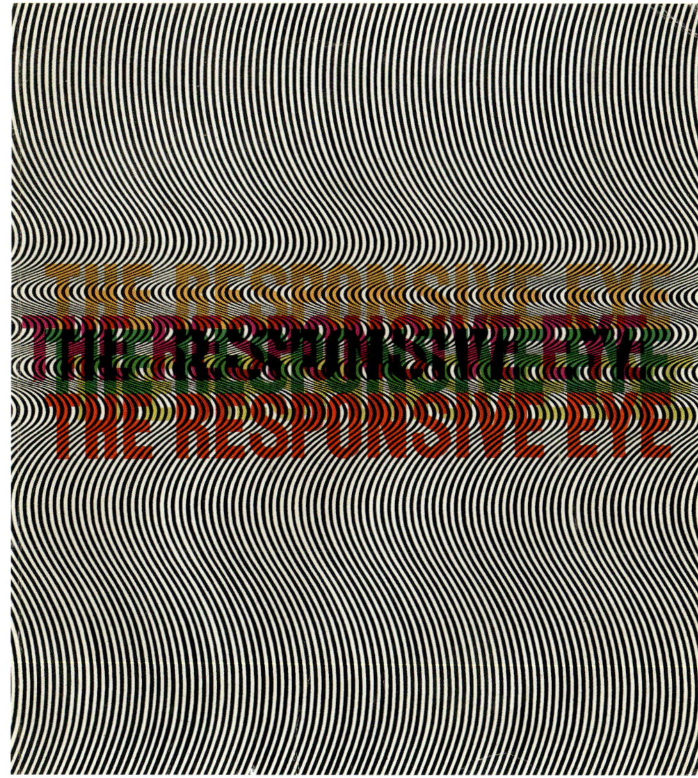

Figure 6. Cover of William Seitz's *The Responsive Eye,* The Museum of Modern Art, New York, 1965

and squares jump from the canvas to the eye," noting that he exhibited in New York "way back in 1960, long before the Op trend was up." "I really love color," he told her. "I try to manipulate it in schemes that give the viewer a particular feeling of excitement. If you want to call it emotion, that's fine," he said.[21] Although Anuszkiewicz pursued the dazzle labeled "Op," he claimed that optical flicker was not his primary goal. "It is important for me to have not just *a* color, but *the* color," he observed; critics followed suit, emphasizing that "pure color—not optical illusion—had always been his chief interest."[22]

But Anuszkiewicz's interactive pursuit of "not just *a* color, but *the* color" was not enough to attract lasting attention from significant critics. Despite the approbation of MoMA, his paintings, with their aggressive visual character, failed to find favor in scholarly and intellectual circles. The range of objections was broad, suggesting that Anuszkiewicz's painting assaulted the contemporary conventions accepted by a variety of critics. He flouted a Modernist tenet that had become especially strong in New York: the separation of fine art from the instruments of popular and mass culture. Unlike his predecessors in Abstract Expressionism, Anuszkiewicz enjoyed designing ashtrays, furs, nylon hose, floor coverings, sets of coasters—a pursuit for which he was not apologetic. Some critics were dismayed. Sniffed one, "few of his designs, which are fascinating superficially, are more than tasteful semi-commercial applications."[23] This did not make critics assume that his commercial efforts were "art," but that his art was debased. Another critic called his show of May 1973 at Sidney Janis Gallery "a good example of high-art *kitsch*."[24] Anuszkiewicz always had been a practical sort, and the Bauhaus attitudes that filtered through from Albers at Yale may have reinforced this. At any rate, he just could not see it as a problem: "I enjoyed doing those things," he said of his design of utilitarian objects, "and I got quite a bit of backfeed from them in the form of ideas for my other work."[25]

Anuszkiewicz's willingness to use the principles of interactive color as a basis for designing objects for everyday use in mass culture surely distanced his work from the reigning standards used by critics like Michael Fried to champion successful hard-edged paintings, like those of Noland and Stella. Critics who aligned themselves with Fried and Clement Greenberg saw these two artists, along with Jules Olitski, as the autonomous opposite of Pop art's renegotiation of the relation between high art and mass culture, while viewing Minimalist sculptors such as Donald Judd and Larry Bell as the theatrical antithesis of properly transcendent hard-edge abstraction. As a hard-edge abstractionist whose populist edge related him to Pop, Anuszkiewicz was in a double bind as far as these critics were concerned.

Nevertheless, supported by MoMA and Seitz, Anuszkiewicz's painting rose briefly to a prominence that peaked in the last half of the 1960s, spurred by publicity and events surrounding and extending from *The Responsive Eye* in 1965. This success, however, coincided with a flood of widely distributed and popular "psychedelic" painting and design with which it had some elements in common, further linking it to a socially radical popular art in the eyes of many critics as well as the public. Although the distinction between so-called high and low art recently had been rather successfully breached by Pop art, Pop was nevertheless considered unworthy of museum attention in some critical and museum circles in the 1960s and 1970s. Seitz well understood that damage control might be necessary, noting that only the best Op artists (of whom Anuszkiewicz would have been one of the first in line) managed to address the mind, the emotions, or even the aesthetic sense as opposed to settling for the direct and powerful stimulation of the anatomical reception centers of sight. Closer in the range of his appreciations to MoMA's Alfred Barr than to William Rubin, Seitz cited the proliferation of popular and commercial psychedelic art as an important part of the context in which Op art emerged.

Objections, then, ran from complaints about connections to popular culture and an appeal to the body or intellect rather than emotion to a naturalistic chauvinism, but a few were excited about Anuszkiewicz's project as the production of color *energy* at the place where colors with certain relationships meet. "Color energies are like word energies," wrote one enthusiastic promoter, Karl Lunde, suggesting that "Poets unlock the powers within words by rearranging them so that they transact and interact with one another in new ways." Lunde did not see the fluctuating ambiguity that makes it impossible to resolve the figure-ground relationship as a gimmick, but instead as a trigger, observing that it was "immensely stimulating to some observers, immensely disturbing to others."[26]

In the late 1960s, however—when Anuszkiewicz parsed the cool flatness of Modernist painting with colors calibrated to jolt viewers' spatial perception as well as their ability to tell what or where the "little flares" or "film colors" that this approach generated might actually be—some of the most powerful critics in the New York art world pronounced the phenomena he produced simply disturbing.[27] Instead

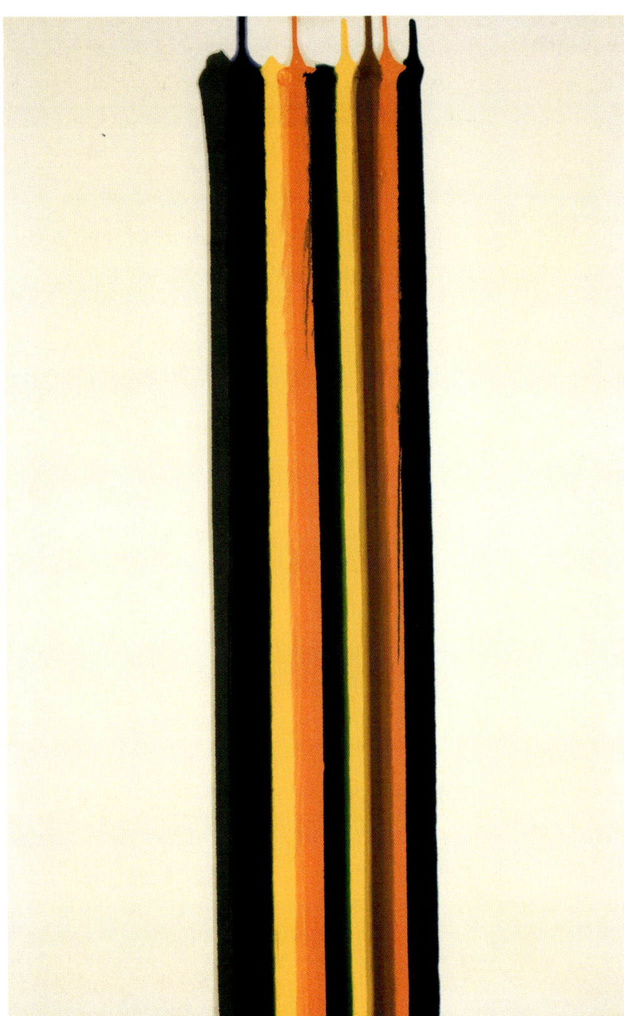

Figure 7. Morris Louis, *Water-Shot*, 1961; acrylic on unsized canvas, 84½ × 53¼ in.; Gift of Mari and James A. Michener, 1991.257

of what had been seen as the sublime breathability and openness of works by Barnett Newman, Helen Frankenthaler, and Morris Louis (figure 7)—from which one could step back and reassure oneself that if it could not be controlled, at least one could reflect on one's incapacity to do so—Anuszkiewicz's buzzing, throbbing colors produced effects that were at least equally unfathomable but that denied the viewer that step back. They were literally inescapable (as long as you were still looking, and if you looked back, they caught you again), suggesting the press of modern technologies—telephones, radios, televisions, cars—that unavoidably and increasingly shaped modern life.

Much more recently, Thomas Crow aptly suggested that Modernist critics' negative response to Bridget Riley's "neither trivial or transcendent" black and white Op paintings was due largely to the "temerity" Riley exercised in controlling to a noticeable degree the viewer's mental and physical state (figure 8).[28] Whereas the signature forms of Riley's dizzying play with viewers' perception began in black and white, Anuszkiewicz orchestrated in full color, using near-identical values and intensities. In *Plus Reversed* the opposites of red and green release a pale light that scintillates most strongly where each color turns from figure to ground for the other. Color explodes into light, obscuring Modernist painting's prime characteristic—flatness—in the process. An article on Op painting in *Life* magazine was entitled "Bringing Chaos out of Order."[29] Op technique might be precise, but its effect was unnerving. Responses to it make one think of the epithet for a group of early twentieth-century painters, the Fauves or "wild beasts," who declared their use of brilliant color a sign of their disdain for academic coloristic subtlety, but who ultimately meshed the simultaneous contrasts of Impressionistic color practice with the older French practice of Latinate *grande tradition*.[30] In their preference for innovation over tradition, they permitted color to devour their models, their studios, and the landscape itself. It could be said that Anuszkiewicz at first was considered "wild" by the intensity of his colors and their interactions, as well as by the relationship of his work to the willful evasion of psychic and social control associated with hallucinogenic drugs. His painting "jangles the nerves and assaults the eyeballs," as Barbara Rose observed.[31] Thomas Hess noted that the public was seen shaking their heads back and forth in front of Op art, "making little jumps like penguins at a mating dance."[32] But a decade later, Anuszkiewicz's work was acclaimed (or berated) less because of its violence and uncontrollability than for its deliberation and precision.[33] Critics found this disconcerting, too. Hayden Herrera concluded a thoughtful review in 1975 with praise for his control but with a caveat that she found his unsensual handling of disembodied color too slick—like commercial art—and therefore "disturbing."[34]

So impressions of the wildness of Op in general and of Anuszkiewicz's work as its quintessence were augmented by another alienated response. Despite his color's refusal to confine itself to a surface or an identifiable hue, Anuszkiewicz's alliance of elements of populism with

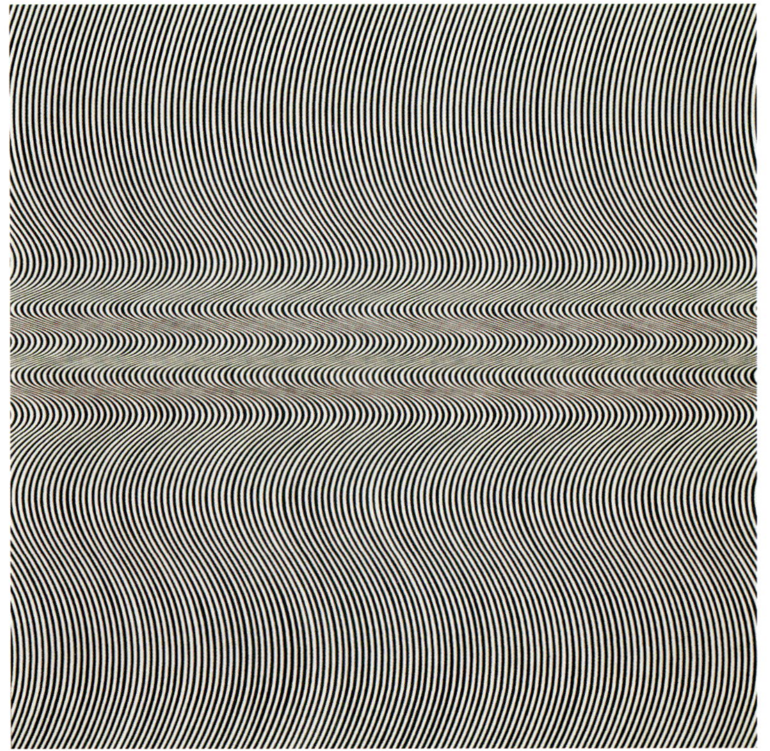

Figure 8. Bridget Riley, *Current*, 1964; synthetic polymer paint on composition board, 58⅜ × 58⅞ in.; Philip Johnson Fund, The Museum of Modern Art, New York, NY, U.S.A.; Digital Image © The Museum of Modern Art/Licensed by SCALA/Art Resource, NY; 2005 © Bridget Riley, all rights reserved.

"scientific" precision now caused concern among critics who found it too highly controlled to be sincere. They also relegated it to the category of the "other," not because of its wildness, but because it was in the domain of technology or popular culture, not "art." Too strong to be pleasantly decorative yet not redeemed by transcendence, its institutional reception was brief and fleeting.

CRITICS RESPOND TO GILLIAM: WHY CAN'T COLOR MOVE BEYOND RACE?

Critical perceptions of Sam Gilliam's painting followed a somewhat similar route, although the associations of its wildness, and then, as it became more familiar to viewers, of Gilliam's control of it, were those of "Black Power" versus integration, not commercial art and psychedelic culture versus scientific precision, as for Anuszkiewicz. Rather than linking his use of extravagant color with undisciplined and then controlling aspects of modern life, some of Gilliam's viewers in the 1960s and 1970s saw the revival of a "primitive" spirit and then its taming. And, as with Anuszkiewicz, some liked what they saw and others did not.

This might seem a strange claim, especially for resolutely nonfigurative art like Anuszkiewicz's and Gilliam's. So it is helpful to recall that for at least two centuries "wildness" was one of the supplementary loads carried by color, especially when multiple high-intensity colors were in close relationship. The influential view of color's negative social meanings (especially in regard to intense color), such as that published by Johann Wolfgang Goethe in 1810, is disturbingly contemporary, despite its quaint diction: "It is worthy of remark that savage nations, uneducated people, and children have a great predilection for vivid colors," wrote the philosopher; "Animals are excited to rage by certain colors; that people of refinement avoid vivid colors in their dress and the objects that are about them, and seem inclined to banish them altogether from their presence."[35] But the idea that one can "save" civilization if one can only destroy the wild ones did not end in the nineteenth century.

By the twentieth century, Freudian psychology and modern cultural anthropology had begun to convince the modern cultures of the West, as Hayden White pointed out, that wildness is in *us* as well as in *them*.[36] Modern French artists from Paul Gauguin through the Fauves, German Expressionists such as Ernst Kirchner, Wassily Kandinsky, and Franz Marc, and certain American Abstract Expressionists, Color Field painters, Pop artists, and Minimalists, all known for their taste for vivid color, had by the 1960s successively brought aspects of color's wildness home. To maintain its "wildness" in Modernism's increasingly institutional surroundings, modern taste for high intensity color was often fused with Western perceptions of African, Native American, or Asian cultures and their diasporic or emigrated survivors, bringing wildness home using that gesture called "primitivism," but denying it integral status.[37] In paintings by Gauguin, Henri Matisse, and Kirchner, signifiers of wildness, such as heightened color, projected desires for spontaneity, originality, sexual enjoyment, healthful physicality, and untrammeled nature.[38] While writers from W.E.B. DuBois through Alain Locke to Robert Farris Thompson and Keith Morrison have attempted to revise the Western understanding of African aesthetics as instinctive, spontaneous, unintellectual, and sensual, i.e., "wild," these connections have continued to inform the interpretation, but not necessarily the production, of work by artists of African heritage, as a brief look at some of the discussions around Sam Gilliam's *Pantheon II* and related works will demonstrate.[39]

Working in Washington for eight years without a teaching job, Gilliam exposed himself to the Washington Color School and the antifigurative drive of Greenberg's version of Modernist painting at the same time.[40] When he arrived in D.C. in 1962, his earlier aesthetic, based on German Expressionism and San Francisco Bay Area figurative painting, became intentionally *less* symbolic and referential.[41] By 1963, via the example of Hofmann, Gilliam had moved away from the figure.[42] In the years immediately following this move, he adapted his figurative expressionist style to the thinner and more abstract uses of color current in the Capitol, becoming known as a junior member of the Washington Color School. "My aspirations were very romantic, and they were very romantic at that time for a black person," Gilliam recalled in 1984, "for most of the environment I existed in, even the imagery I was pursuing, was considered white. . . . At that time I saw every show that Noland did . . . I knew where I had to go and what I wanted to accomplish."[43]

Gilliam's next move was shockingly literal. Some of its closest analogies were to be found not in Washington but in New York. According to the artist, by the end of 1968, "ideas of process through Robert Morris" were a part of the mix when he "started getting away, or flirting with how to get away [from strict color field painting], in doing the suspended paintings."[44] He first exhibited his suspended canvases in the late 1960s and early 1970s (figure 9) at a time when the better-known Morris was calling for art that demonstrated, in his words, "change . . . disorientation and shift . . . violent discontinuity and mutability . . . the willingness for confusion."[45] It is a description that also suits Gilliam's departure from flatness for sumptuous and unpredictable three-dimensionality, as Jane Addams Allen noted.[46] In retrospect, it is clear that Gilliam participated—with Morris and others such as Richard Tuttle (figure 10) and Joe Overstreet (figure 11)—in the formation of a wing of that extension of Abstract Expressionist procedures called Process art. It eventuated in the late 1960s, most publicly in 1969 at the *Anti-Illusion: Procedure/Materials* exhibition at the Whitney Museum. Process art rejected the precise calibrations of Minimalism, stressing the qualities and positions taken by materials whose forms are determined by their natural proclivities (i.e., the amorphous quality of loose dirt, the flexibility of fabric, and its tendency to wrinkle, fold, and absorb fluid). Gilliam cited Tuttle and Overstreet as significant innovators with fabric, a material that also particularly interested him: "Tuttle—using a thin cheesecloth—the idea of tacking fabric to a wall—it became so important. . . . Joe's work was very fresh—everyone else was thinking of painting or structure; Joe found a way to pick up, fabricate, and put painted forms into space. That was very important."[47] Each of these artists, like Gilliam, integrated a play of predetermined and sometimes geometric edges with more organic form.

But Gilliam did not use colors the same way Overstreet or Tuttle did. Tuttle often accepted the natural color of his unstretched canvas or dyed it a single color, like the pale pink of the Blanton's piece, which

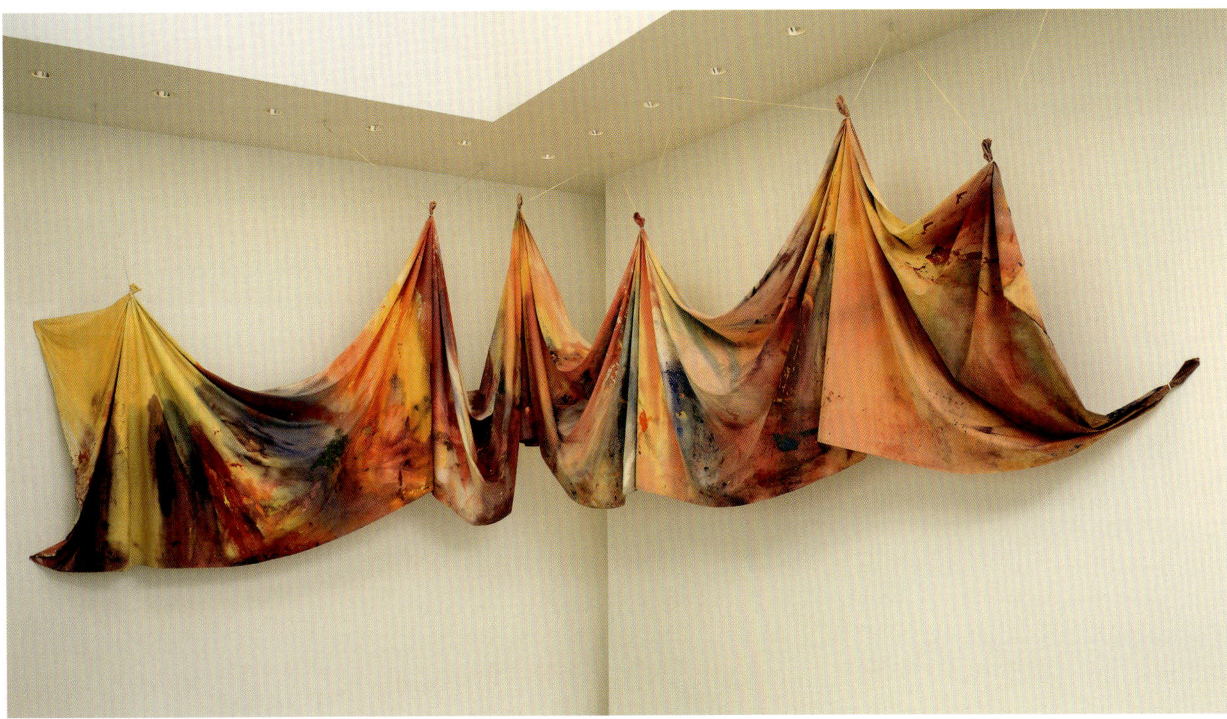

Figure 9. Sam Gilliam, *Carousel Merge*, 1971; acrylic on canvas, 120 × 900 in. (variable); Collection Walker Art Center, Minneapolis: Gift of Archie D. and Bertha H. Walker Foundation, 1971

Figure 10. Richard Tuttle, *Light Pink Octagon*, 1967; canvas dyed with Tintex, 56¾ × 53¹⁄₁₆ in.; Gift of Mari and James A. Michener, 1991.335

accentuates its tendency to buckle and wrinkle (and in doing so, recalls some of fabric's intimate associations with the human body as well). In his architectural scale and reference, as well as in his multicolored planes, Gilliam is closer to Overstreet.[48] Instead of coloring sculpture, Gilliam sculpted color. Or perhaps better yet, he sculpted painting. He continued to use the canvas, as seen in *Carousel Merge* (figure 9), as a support on which colors that already interacted in two dimensions were made to interact in three. Gilliam wanted his paintings, he recalled, "to get outside of the traditional framed space of paintings—like murals, in the Sistine, in the caves; to relate to sculpture and architecture like medieval painting did. *And* to catch up to the root of contemporary painting as it existed in Morris Louis and Tom Downing—they worked on the floor from around nineteen sixty three to sixty-six. Gene Davis, too."[49] At the same time, Gilliam emphatically encouraged viewers to experience the fluid three-dimensionality of the fabric itself, whose configurations changed at every installation.

If Anuszkiewicz floated and vibrated color free in a way that fascinated but discomfited viewers because it directly affected them physically, Gilliam's stained, painted, suspended, and collaged surfaces exponentially amplified the effect of his Hofmannian "push and pull" by expanding it into the literal space of three dimensions. And monumental size was a factor. Gilliam's *Autumn Surf East* (1972–1990) is 15 × 300 feet long.[50] The dominant critics of abstract art in the United States in the years that Gilliam made his decisive breakthroughs, from 1966 to 1969, had accepted one of two standards for abstract sculpture. The first (the Greenberg/Fried group) insisted that the internal relations of pure form were the basis on which abstract sculpture should be evaluated. The second (the group around Judd and Morris) evaluated abstract sculpture by how convincingly it appeared to be an *object* rather than a representation or a group of forms in relation to each other. For this group, the crucial issue was sculpture's relation to the viewer. The identity of *painting* for the first group was calculated in

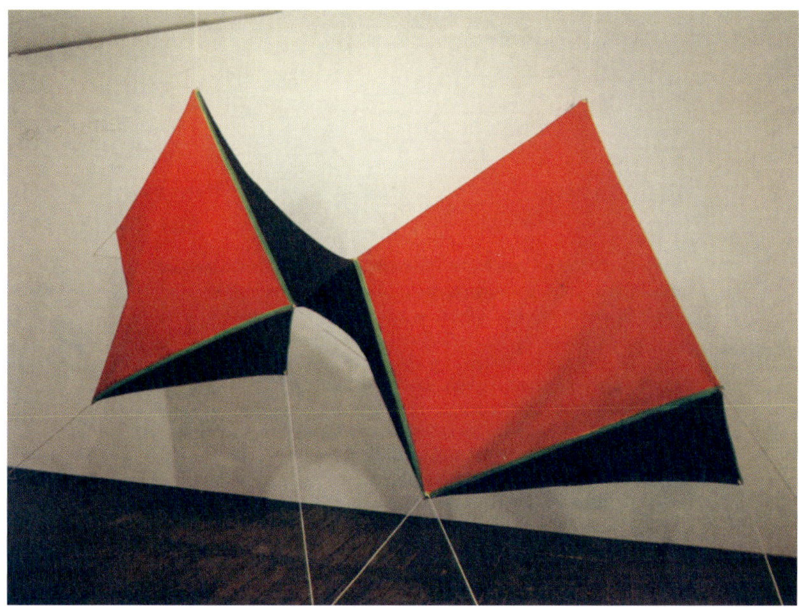

Figure 11. Joe Overstreet, *Power Flight*, 1971; acrylic on canvas with metal grommets and white rope, 8'2" × 13'8"; Brooklyn Museum; Gift of Mr. and Mrs. John de Meuil, 72.165

part by its distinction from sculpture and by the ingeniousness with which it analyzed the possibilities of its material distinction from not only sculpture but also from theater, literature, etc. However, the second seemed quite determined to negate that distinction in the service of moving beyond such formal concerns into a kind of theater in which the viewer was a participant. The "conflicting logics" of Gilliam's paint application—in which two-dimensional groups of forms on canvas were swept into three undulating dimensions from one suspension point to another in folds that repeatedly cut across the relations of one set of painted forms to another—shocked nearly everyone and pleased some critics. But few critics, even in Washington, attempted to analyze the development in detail and as it related to both sets of current values. Jonathan Binstock is perhaps the first scholar to pay prolonged attention to this development in Gilliam's career in the context of canonical criticism in New York. He has noted that not even now, in the new millennium, has the art world fully realized that what Gilliam did in Washington—with his Slice paintings and then even more noticeably in 1969 with the suspended ones—to upset Modernism, as it was understood in 1967, was as decisive for abstract painting as, and perhaps more so than, anything happening in New York.[51]

But another group of Washington, D.C.–based critics, following ideas advanced by Robert Farris Thompson and including Robert Douglas and Keith Morrison, took another track entirely. They argued that conflicting logics were the key to an Africanity that eyes and minds accustomed to European design in music and the visual arts could not recognize or appreciate. Nor were they the first to see in the use of color on three-dimensional form the possibility of affirming an identity connected to Africa. In 1935 the African American sculptor Sargent Johnson told an interviewer that he was interested in color on sculpture as were the Egyptians and the Greeks. "I am concerned with color, not solely as a technical problem," Johnson claimed, "but also as a means of heightening the racial character of my work."[52]

Thompson offered a related argument for the Africanity of certain design forms in music and visual production. In 1974 he claimed that "African music is distinguished from other world traditions by the superposition of several lines of meter. Broadly speaking, the difference between African and European rhythms is that whereas any piece of European music has at any one moment one rhythm in command, a piece of African music has always two or three."[53] Similarly, in the designs of African textiles like some of those from the Upper Volta, he observed, "what is 'on beat' at one level of the cloth is immediately 'off beat' in terms of another" so that "staggered motifs on certain chiefly cloths can be profitably compared to off-beat phrasing in music, dance, and decorative sculpture."[54] Citing, among others, these passages from Thompson, Douglas later argued that even in the case of Gilliam's "draped paintings," for which the artist himself made no claims of African influence or heritage as a source, the bright colors and the spontaneity of the hanging as well as the color design "may represent idiomatic elements more reminiscent of Africa than of Europe."[55]

Gilliam associated and showed principally with two sets of artists. One set included painter William T. Williams and sculptors Mel Edwards and Richard Hunt. These were African American artists who, like Gilliam, preferred that their work be judged on its aesthetic merits, although their forms and/or titles more than occasionally suggested African or African American references.[56] The other set was composed of the Washington Color painters and their antecedents.[57] Both groups stressed that the quality of the work was what counted, not the identity of its makers. Nevertheless, Gilliam's identity as an African-descended American *and* the way he handled pigments did associate him in the eyes of some with "black art."[58] At the same time, as Douglas observed, "It was once ardently debated by advocates of the Black Arts Movement that Gilliam's draped paintings were not representative of the black experience and difficult to identify as works by a black artist."[59]

So Gilliam's work was taken up in the debate about whether or not there was a "black aesthetic." An idea that found expression in the Black Power movement in the 1960s, it coalesced in the 1970s around an anthology edited by Addison Gayle, Jr. in 1971, *The Black Aesthetic*. In it Gayle argued that what mattered for black critics should not be how beautiful a melody, play, poem, or novel is, but how much more beautiful it had made the life of a single black man.[60] Some saw unacknowledged African references in the work of highly schooled artists such as Gilliam as learned or acculturated predilections. Douglas, on the other hand, felt that although "Afrocentrism" as an approach to culture was distinguished by a "particular world-view which artists of the African diaspora may use," it could only be employed properly to analyze the work of "artists of African descent who are unacculturated like the ghettoized masses or those who excavate their African roots."[61] In this, Douglas was closer to the latter group—one that proposed a black visual aesthetic—a group with whom Gilliam was allied in the eyes of some but not others, particularly not in the eyes of the members of the Washington-based AfriCobra group. The compositions of these artists featured brilliant and high-key color, freely geometric patterns, and often layered, "multi-dominant elements," whose purpose was to incorporate African aesthetics and African iconography with an "African Diasporan imagery in a positive response to contemporary political situations."[62] AfriCobra saw "transAfrican" references and tendencies as intrinsic components of their work as artists of African descent.[63] Although work by AfriCobra artists like Wadsworth Jarrell (figure 12) was often figurative, their use of a palette of multiple intense colors and the vitality of their allover compositions suggested to some that Gilliam might well have been a member of AfriCobra had he and the members of AfriCobra agreed on a common agenda.

AfriCobra artists, unlike those in either the Greenberg/Fried or Judd/Morris group, preferred compositions that could be described as "an orchestral quality of varying tones, shapes, harmonies, modulating off a blaze of poly-rhythms." These compositions featured high intensity colors that evoked "the deep, rich, brightness of African clothing, textiles, landscapes: strawberry, lime, orange, lemon yellow, green, violet, blue."[64] If for AfriCobrans such colors were charged with references explicitly African, Gilliam insisted that his use of color was multivalent. In an interview in 1977, he mentioned that color was "the major and most dominant ingredient," in his work. On the one hand, he used it as a material (paint, for instance, as a material that could be textured, which it certainly is in *Pantheon II*), exploiting its interactivity à la Albers to set up tension and the latitude of space in a work. At the same time, he was also conscious of its potential "in terms of an expressive way . . . color as a language."[65] Some critics recognized this complexity. Addams Allen remarked of Gilliam's uses of "flat color, atmospheric color, reflected color in incredible syncopations that amaze the eye and revive the senses."[66]

For Morrison in 1979, this use of color was what made Gilliam's work echo the "power of the cloth surface" and the color of garments worn by black people in Lagos, New York, and Kingston, and thus embody a visible part of the sensibilities of the Pan-African vernacular.[67] But the oscillating visual complexity of Gilliam's work around 1984 evoked effects that were also related to Anuszkiewicz's in the interactivity of some of their closest-valued colors—even if for Morrison and Douglas they were more like those of AfriCobra artists in their dizzying proliferation of rhythms and wide range of values and textures. The "conflicting logics" of the interactivity of their colors, their exuberant textures, and their three-dimensional play, as well as the additional color logic of the social meanings they evoked, made Gilliam's three-dimensional organizations of painted surfaces especially antithetical to the mainstream modernisms contemporary to them (just as had Anuszkiewicz's flat surfaces, whose apparently psychedelic colors would not allow them to stay put). This was so even though, on a purely formal level, the work of Minimalists such as Judd and Bell, like Gilliam's and Anuszkiewicz's, used color and form to incorporate viewers' perceptions as part of its subject matter. One might note that by the late 1970s other former Modernists were producing works that flaunted their "strawberry, lime, orange, lemon yellow, green, violet, blue" in "horror vacuii" or "jampack and jellytight" compositions (think of Stella's Indian Bird series, for instance, shown at Leo Castelli in 1979), as did those of a number of AfriCobrans.[68] Nevertheless, it was in Gilliam's work—not that of someone like Stella—that Morrison sought out, a year and a half later, in 1980, "the potential . . . irrationality" of sheer, bright color:

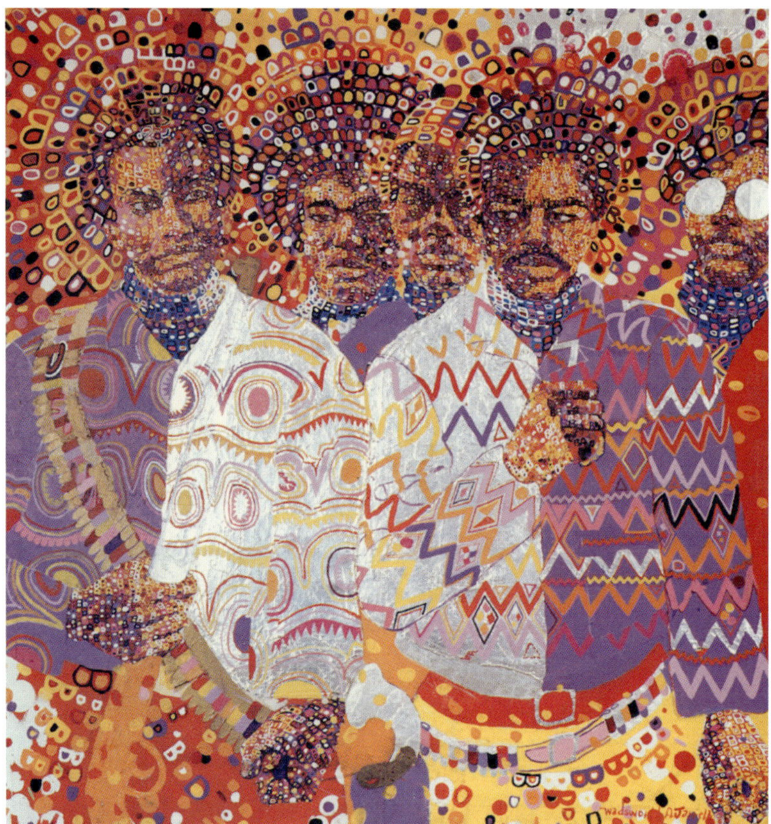

Figure 12. Wadsworth Jarrell, *Liberation Soldiers*, 1972; acrylic and foil on canvas, 50 × 48 in.; Collection of the Artist

> *Gilliam creates environments that undulate spectacularly through alternating shadows of folds and scintillating surfaces of color that often shimmer and actually move, especially when the work is placed out of doors. Gilliam's works have the quality of that which is tactile yet elusive to the actual touch, like the floating of some ethereal substance . . . creating a kind of environmental collage.*"[69]

This led the critic to observe that "color as an aspect of gaudy plumage, as expressive fantasy, a source of spiritual fervor goes back deep into the values of Black people as a group. Many people (I suspect mostly Black) have seen this value as a source of Gilliam's work."[70] Morrison had noted the year before that Gilliam himself did not subscribe to this idea. But "what the artist consciously means is not always the basis of art criticism," he reflected. Obviously basing his interpretation on audience reaction, not the artist's intention, Morrison nevertheless found Africanisms in Gilliam's work.[71]

As the comments of later critics of Gilliam demonstrate (as do some of Anuszkiewicz's earlier ones), the brilliant colors they used were associated in the United States with various degrees of willfulness and lack of decorum—with the kinds of refusal to conform to dominant standards that fit the definition of Hayden White's "wildness."[72] Like the critics of Anuszkiewicz who complained that his color controlled their vision, the language of Gilliam's critics also suggested an unease with its aggressive tenor: Vivien Raynor commented in the *New York Times* in 1978 that Gilliam's color, "always strong and threatening looking, has become fiercer."[73] Often critics would follow such comments with ameliorating qualifications, as did one, who, describing Gilliam's collaged acrylic paintings of the early 1990s, like *Crowned Upside Down* (1991), wrote, "The bright reds, oranges, and canary yellows, the greens and purples, shout a celebration of freedom and wildness." As if atoning for some rudeness, he added, "But this shout is answered elsewhere in the work with a quiet sense of order."[74] By the 1970s it seemed that Gilliam's color was linked by both black and white communities to what in the United States was seen as the blackness of his person. Some were determined to join them together, and some to sever them. Yet even arguments meant to accomplish the latter seemed, insidiously, to confirm the relationship, not to loosen it. Worrying about these associations has at times prevented viewers from being able to think about other aspects of Gilliam's achievements.

In the 1980s Gilliam's bas reliefs, such as *Wave Composition* (1981) and the Blanton's *Pantheon II* (figure 2), flooded viewers' perception with colors and shapes emanating a powerful sense of animation that depends on interactions among two-dimensional colors (as Op did, too); but some of Gilliam's works in that decade register their play of colors in the three-dimensional physicality of the bas-relief medium and its support.[75] Thus, his later relief treatments, like his earlier draped paintings, stepped outside the Modernist dictum that color in painting should be separated from the three-dimensionality of sculpture and the theatricality of installation. If we are accustomed to being able to parse a painting's meaning from its composition, as its color resonates with its flat surface within boundaries that are permanently set, and to measure the significance of a sculpture's articulation through its form and volumetric relations in terms of light and shadow, what are we to do with works like these, where one set of analytical tools regularly contradicts the other? *Pantheon II* displays real three-dimensional form not only in the distinctly different textures of the paint (figure 13) but also in the layers of aluminum held up by little rods at various elevations (figure 14). Moreover, the edges of these aluminum layers often are painted decisively eye-catching hues that contrast with the layer parallel to the wall, so that you are encouraged to walk around the piece, peering at it from different angles, as you might with a Gianlorenzo Bernini sculpture or a Victor Vasarely bas-relief.

Besides all this, Hofmann's "push and pull" is still operating on the color in *Pantheon II,* at both two- and three-dimensional levels, sometimes affirming and sometimes denying its actual three-dimensionality. A critic tellingly referred to Gilliam's painting as "guerilla warfare with color and form and space."[76] Seeing Gilliam as a "guerilla" painter suggests that he operates in independence from sanctioned authority, a reputation for intransigence much like that so often ascribed to color itself. Gilliam encourages this. Regarding his suspended paintings, he once said, "There are *no* associations in these paintings with human history—or rather, they are consistent with human history. The aesthetic experience is a part of human history." He added, "I don't *like* having them associated with the fact that I'm black."[77] Perhaps in response to such objections, most critics discussed Gilliam's work in apparently formal terms that struggled, nevertheless, with a quotient of "wildness" they felt it necessary to acknowledge and at the same time deny because of the racist associations that had accumulated around the term. They stressed the "non-violent" character of his regulation of an unruly cast of colors, textures, organic and geometric shapes, and two- and three-dimensional forms, referring to them as in constructions such as *Autumn Surf East* (1972) as "controlled chaos." The late Walter Hopps illustrates this vividly in a catalogue for the Speed Museum in 1976:

> *A sense of chaos, visual elements seemingly beyond conscious or rational control, is indeed present in Gilliam's work. However, a variety of structural means . . . are inevitably included to operate as controlling, posed visual forces. Indeed, in much of Gilliam's most powerful and beautiful work there exists a delicate balance between improvisation and structure, a sense of chaos controlled.*[78]

The use of phrases such as "nonviolent," reminiscent of the pacific aspirations of Martin Luther King's Civil Rights exhortations, continued to resonate in "multiculturalism" throughout the 1970s and 1980s. Gilliam did not always paint in bright colors. But when he did not, the fact was seen as an aberration. In 1973, remarking upon the painter's "remarkable gift for color," Washington critic and Gilliam supporter Paul Richard noted that of the thirteen paintings

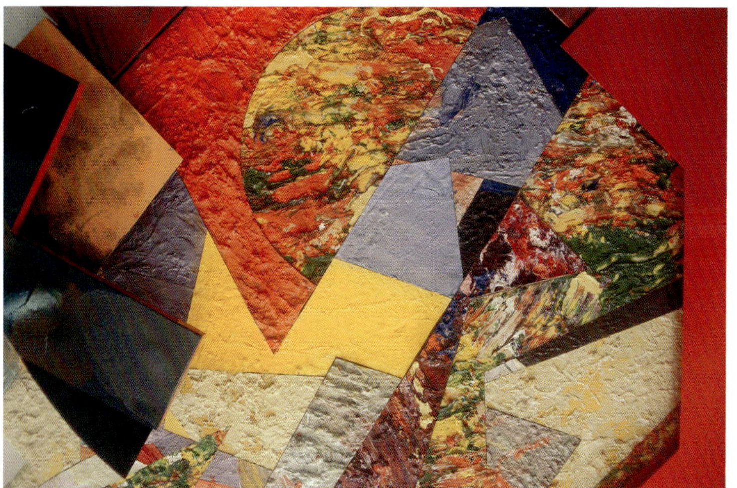

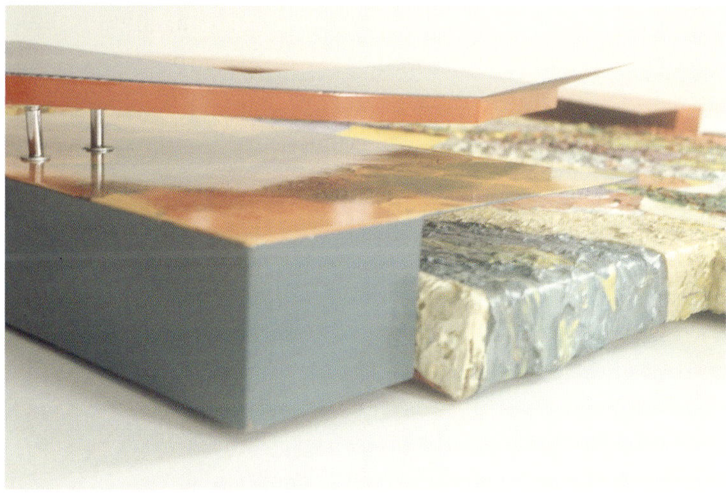

Figure 13. Sam Gilliam, *Pantheon II,* 1983 (detail)

Figure 14. Sam Gilliam, *Pantheon II,* 1983 (detail)

in the room (at the Jefferson Place gallery), "only one employs flashy, glaring colors."[79]

Critics regularly praised Gilliam for the "cultivation" or civility of his chaos—that is, for his "remarkable facility for coaxing potentially incompatible colors to cooperate and augment one another,"[80] as if it was necessary to convince readers that Gilliam could control the wildness he fostered. The fact that it was not the wildness that critics felt compelled to establish, but Gilliam's ability to harness it, speaks as eloquently about how critics wished their treatment of Gilliam to be perceived as a refusal to fall into racializing stereotypes as it does about the qualities they actually imputed to his use of color. A salvage paradigm was at work.[81] Reviewers' choice of language often belied what sounds now like their barely sublimated expectations of the "wildness" of color that, in tandem with Gilliam's ancestry, metonymically made his art "black." In the wake of the Black Power movement, it must have been difficult to read remarks about Gilliam's work like the following one as anything *but* a metaphor for race: "Color no longer steals the show but has been harnessed without loss of vibrancy to function within a tightly structured composition."[82]

By 1983 Gilliam's work—his "color" in both senses of the term—had come to represent pluralism in a way that becomes apparent in the criticism of Eleanor Green. On the occasion of the success of Gilliam's exhibition in Washington, D.C., Green remarked that

> *it seemed ungracious, however, for both the Corcoran catalogue and early reviews to dwell on the implications of Gilliam's black skin as if he were a Moby Dick of a different color. A picture of his Mount Pleasant Victorian house with its bric-a-brac and doodads bursting out in mauves and lavenders, yellows and reds like a massed spring bed of tulips and azaleas would have said more about Gilliam today.*[83]

The wildness of Gilliam's color was still an issue whose assumedly uncontrollable exuberance must be acknowledged even as it is defused. Not to comment on it would be (for whites) to implicitly accept effusive color as normal, which would remove one of the assumptions that has become accepted as a cultural distinction separating the tastes of blacks from whites. The fact that liking brilliant and even clashing colors and patterns was seen also as erasing the boundary between control and chaos indicates the fear that failing to distinguish between whiteness and blackness in the art world elicited. The barely submerged reference to blackness in the phrase a "Moby Dick of a different color," which is then linked to the physicalized vibrancy of "bursting out" in color in a domesticated setting of Floral Victoriana, also suggests that for some, it was in the perception of brilliant color (and perhaps in that most local of all settings, the home) that conflicts of race may be subsumed in desire.[84] Whether this is threatening or promising will depend on the values of the reader, in the case of the essay, and the viewer, in the case of the painting.

Gilliam continued to mix Hofmannesque formal procedures with forms, colors, and titles that meshed the aesthetics of a Western European avant-garde with African and African American aesthetic and cultural sources. Critics compared Gilliam's constructions to jazz and crazy quilts, associations the artist also encouraged—not only by titles such as *Memphis Jazz* and *Kansas City II* (figure 15), both 1984, and *Crazy Quilt*, but also by the irregularity of the cut-canvas shapes, the texture, and the seemingly random or "crazy" juxtapositions of patterned shapes with solid ones.[85] Gilliam insisted, however, that he used jazz titles, for instance, not because he is black, but because, like the rest of the Washington Color School, he enjoyed the music and discovered in it structural innovations like his own, as well as some he could use. Such references are buttressed by the inference of titles such as *Pantheon*. With it, Gilliam labels not only the Blanton painting, but the entire series to which it belongs, as places inhabited by Greek spirits. You can see that, indeed, *Pantheon II* exhibits what may be read as a profile facing right, as on ancient coins, and a head covering that might be thought of alternatively as a laurel wreath or an African headdress or hair arrangement. The artist presents the syncopated rhythms of African American music and visual forms ("crazy quilts" are the manifestations of a similar rhythm in African American visual folk tradition), as well as those of ethnic themes and traditions from

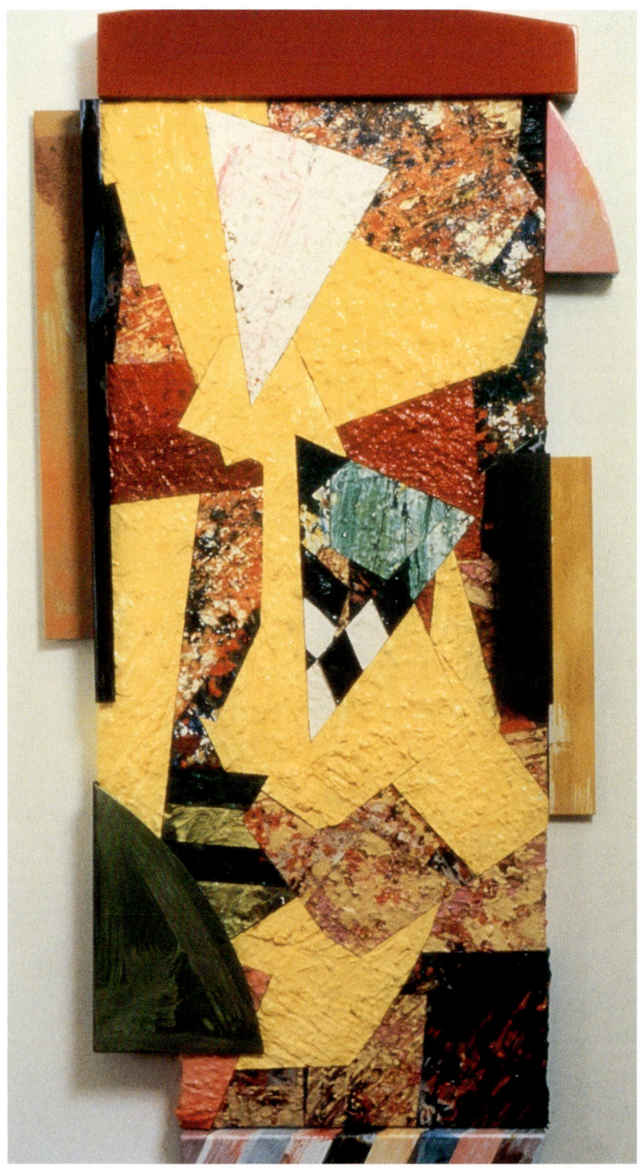

Figure 15. Sam Gilliam, *Kansas City II*, 1984; acrylic on aluminum, 67 × 32 × 3 in.; courtesy the Artist

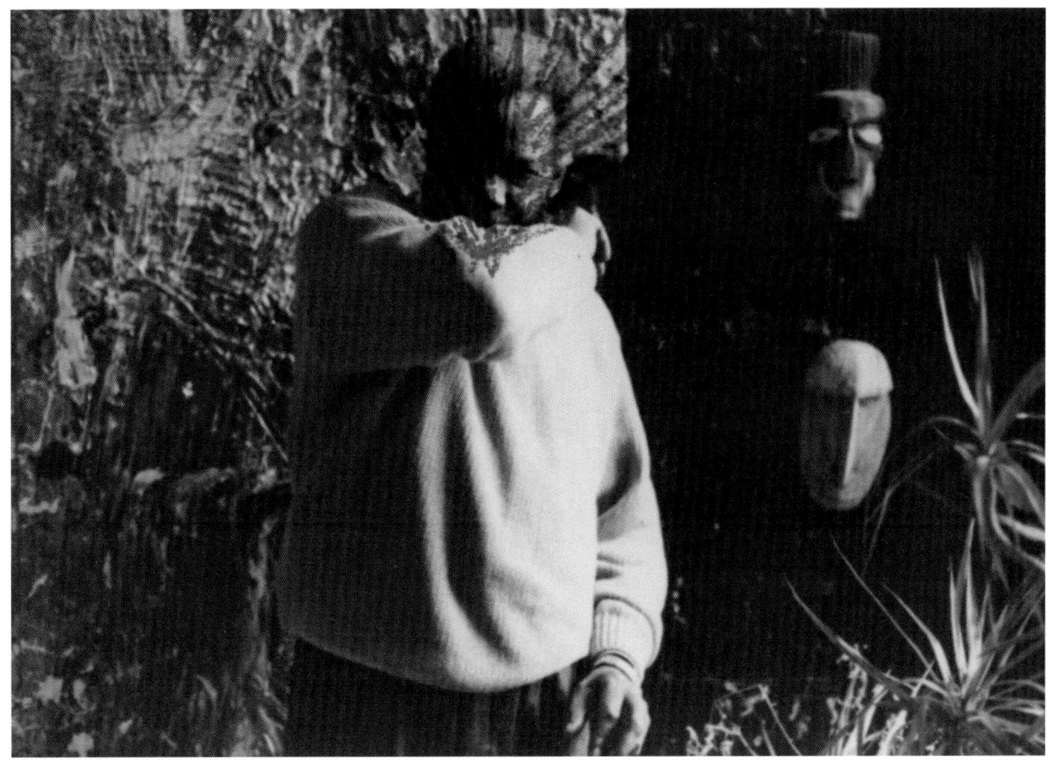

Figure 16. Adrian Piper and Sam Gilliam, *Green with Envy* [altered readymade of a photographic self-portrait by Sam Gilliam], in Adrian Piper's *Colored People*, Book Works, London, 1991

other cultures that have been opposed and united in various spheres over the centuries.[86] So it appears that Gilliam himself, and not only his critics, is controlling and interweaving various signs whose social implications involve them in a struggle in which African American interpreters have seldom had the upper hand.

Not surprisingly Gilliam, like Wittgenstein, is well aware of the differing registers of logic within which color may be played. And as he and most viewers are aware, "colored" is another word for the supposed difference of "race." The tension between these two logics of color is apparent in the contrast between the literal and metaphorical uses of "color"—the red, green, purple, etc., crayoned on photos of the "white" and "black" and now *literally* colored people (one of whom is Gilliam himself) (figure 16)—in Adrian Piper's book *Colored People.*[87] One might say that Piper puts us directly in the crucible of Wittgenstein's problems with color at a point of one of its cruelest and most ridiculous social "indeterminacies." In the 1930s and 1940s, in fact until the Civil Rights Era, African Americans called themselves "colored"—"'black' was not a word for polite company back then," Henry Louis Gates, Jr. recalls in the pages of his autobiography, *Colored People.*[88] In the United States, we are so well aware of the change of "colored" for "black" and then "African American" that one of the functions the word "colored" performs in Gates's book is to usher us believably back to the 1950s in Piedmont, West Virginia. But it also delivers us into a way of thinking about this aspect of color with which so-called "people of color" may be more experienced than whites:

> *I want to be black, to know black, to luxuriate in whatever I might be calling blackness at any particular time—but to do so in order to come out the other side, to experience a humanity that is neither colorless nor reducible to color. Bach* and *James Brown. Sushi* and *fried catfish.*[89]

CODA

Is it fair to inscribe a sociological interrogation into an analysis of color's phenomenological activity? (That is, does it invent, as well as find, meaning?) Wittgenstein, Gage, and Batchelor say no. Wittgenstein's insight that there are more color logics than one provides a working method to explore Harrison's remark that "to ask how colors mean" is close to asking "how color may be modern." The juxtaposition of such working methods, which I have attempted here, suggests that the relation between certain politics and color's empirical use in visual culture, both high and low, is indeed in desperate need of a more thoroughly anthropological context. Such a context might be profitably established by analyzing what Gilliam calls "technique"—how a painting is made and received—in its historical framework. What difference to interpretation should or must it make if Gilliam or Anuszkiewicz did or did not read Wittgenstein? If Anuszkiewicz was or was not interested in psychic or psychedelic effects? Are the reciprocal opinions of Gilliam and the AfriCobra artists about each others' work relevant? Anuszkiewicz is a "euroethnic," to use a term Adrian Piper has employed; his parents were born in Poland. Would the meanings of his paintings shift if they were explored in light of the arts of other Polish immigrants? Both men travel, but does where they have chosen to live matter? Probably. What might a formal, phenomenological, historical, and sociological analysis of the colors artists used at any point in their careers tell us if it were correlated with current events in the public sphere and in their personal lives? A lot? Different kinds of things than what we know now? Yes, perhaps. Whose history would that be? Maybe, partly, it would be theirs. But surely, it would be ours.

Notes

1. Richard Anuszkiewicz, quoted in United States Information Service, *Anuszkiewicz* (Washington, D.C.: United States Information Service, 1974), as quoted by Karl Lunde, *Anuszkiewicz* (New York: Harry N. Abrams, Inc., 1977), 9.
2. Sam Gilliam, interview with J. K. [Jay Kloner], 1977, p. 1 of ms., in "Biographical Material, writing on Gilliam," box 1, Sam Gilliam Papers, Archives of American Art, Smithsonian Institution, Washington, D.C. This archives is hereafter referred to as AAA/SI.
3. Charles Harrison, "On Color and Abstract Art, David Batchelor, Recent Work," *Art and Design* 12 (July/August 1997): 39.
4. John Gage, "Color in Western Art: An Issue," *Art Bulletin* 72 (December 1990): 518–19. One has only to read the remarks on twentieth-century art and artists by anthropologists Clifford Geertz, James Clifford, and Stanley Marcus to see how fruitfully anthropological frameworks illuminate cultural meaning in visual production.
5. Jacqueline Lichtenstein, *The Eloquence of Color, Rhetoric and Painting in the French Classical Age*, trans. E. McVarish (Berkeley, Calif.: University of California Press, 1993), 194. Such observations have become truisms in color study. Max Kozloff, for instance, wrote that criticism does not usually deal with color for two reasons: because it can be recalled with specificity only visually, not verbally, whereas criticism is made of words; and because color causes disturbances that run counter to art criticism's desire for uniform interpretation. See Max Kozloff, "Venetian Art and Florentine Criticism," *Artforum* 6 (December 1967): 42–45 and *Renderings* (New York: Simon & Schuster, 1968), 322–23. In 1978 John Gage quoted as still relevant S. Skard's observation in 1946 that the specificity of painters' hues "have little in common with the vague, suggestive, and elusive means of expression in language." See Gage, "Colour in History: Relative and Absolute," *Art History* 1 (March 1978): 104.
6. Norman Bryson, *Vision and Painting, The Logic of the Gaze* (New Haven, Conn.: Yale University Press, 1983), 119. Rosalind Krauss told readers that the "shifter," a term used by Roman Jacobson (in 1957) for words like "this," "I," and "you,"—"empty" words that waited each time they were used for their referent to be designated—was linked, in the case of "I," with children's self-identification and simultaneous alienation from the rest of the world, which occurs in what French psychologist and linguist Jacques Lacan names the "mirror stage." These observations occur in Krauss's "Notes on the Index, Part I," written in 1976, which stresses the indexicality of much art done in the 1970s. "Notes on the Index, Part II" (1977) begins with the note that, just as earlier in the century painters aspired in their work to the condition of music, so in the 1970s one might say that abstractionists aspired to the condition of photography—in its status as the indexical art *par excellence*. Like the shifter, the photograph was (in Roland Barthes's words, notes Krauss), a "message without a code." "Notes on the Index, Part I" and "Notes on the Index Part II" are reprinted in Krauss, *The Originality of the Avant-Garde and Other Modernist Myths* (Cambridge, Mass.: The MIT Press, 1985), 196–98, 210–11. In applying this argument to color, Bryson is also extending to color Derrida's "undecidability," discussed below.
7. Anuszkiewicz also mentioned his early interest in Andrew Wyeth (as well as Ivan Albright) to Paul Cummings in 1971, in an interview transcribed for the Archives of American Art. (Richard Anuszkiewicz Papers, AAA/SI, p. 9.) For his interest in Burchfield and Hopper, see Jay Jacobs, "Richard Anuszkiewicz," *The Art Gallery* 14 (March 1971): 27, 29. For Gilliam's early models, see Walter Hopps, " Introduction," in *Sam Gilliam, Painting and Works on Paper* (Louisville, Ky: The J. B. Speed Art Museum, 1976), n.p.; and especially Jonathan Binstock, "Sam Gilliam: The Making of a Career" (PhD diss., University of Michigan, 2000), 79, 81, 85–92.
8. Anuszkiewicz studied at Yale in the early 1950s, taking his MFA in 1955. Sasha M. Newman and Lesley K. Baier, eds., *Yale Collects Yale* (New Haven, Conn.: Yale University Press, 1993), 84.
9. Anuszkiewicz's painting did not immediately reflect Albers's teaching: the analytical approach was "too much" for him. "I just couldn't use it cold," he said. Anuszkiewicz continued painting figuratively while at Yale. It was not until the winter of 1957–1958, over two years after he graduated, that he began to explore what full complementary contrasts could do in his own work. The following spring he went to New York. Anuszkiewicz to Paul Cummings, December 28, 1971, Anuszkiewicz Papers, AAA/SI, 10.
10. Binstock (85–92) has argued compellingly for Downing's importance to Gilliam.
11. Quoted in Cornelia Noland, "Sam Gilliam, Jr.," in *Washington Forum Magazine* (September 1965). Clipping in "Scrapbook folder," box 1, Gilliam Papers, AAA/SI.
12. Hofmann, who came to the United States with a fully developed career in Europe, had studied in Germany and Paris, where he absorbed the lessons of Emile Nolde, Franz Marc, Wassily Kandinsky, Henri Matisse and Robert Delaunay. But while Gilliam's painting continued to suggest expressionist antecedents, the artist has acknowledged debts to Albers as well. Gilliam said to J. K., in fact, just after he said that color was the "dominant ingredient" in his work (in one of the epigrams for this essay), that (along with texture) color also set the spatial latitudes and established the tensions in his own paintings. Gilliam, interview with J. K., 1.
13. Sam Gilliam, "Interview with Sam Gilliam," by Keith Morrison, *New Art Examiner* 4 (June 1977): 4. Binstock (93–101) cites this realization, pointing out that Hofmann was one of a number of artists who would be important to Gilliam as he moved into abstraction. To Cornelia Noland, Gilliam mentioned Barnett Newman's *Onement I* as having a similar effect on him. Noland, "Sam Gilliam Jr."
14. Hans Hofmann in a 1951 typescript reproduced in Cynthia Goodman, *Hans Hofmann* (New York: Whitney Museum of American Art, 1990), 170–72. I have taken this useful gloss from Charles A. Riley II, *Color Codes, Modern Theories of Color in Philosophy, Painting and Architecture, Literature, Music, and Psychology* (Hanover and London: University Press of New England, 1995), 158.
15. Gilliam, interview with J. K., 29.
16. The similarities between Wittgenstein's *Tractatus* and modern art are striking, as Jorn K. Bramman demonstrates in *Wittgenstein's Tractatus and the Modern Arts* (Rochester, N.Y.: Adler Publishing Company, 1985). Bramman provided a summary of some of these similarities, which are taken up later in the book, 12–101.
17. For Eric Gibson, Albers and Hofmann were similar in that both artists were "so intellectually and morally involved with teaching that it constituted an ethic, a way of life." The difference, he said, is that one cannot say of Hofmann that without the teaching the artist would not have existed. "Josef Albers: In the Engine Room of Modern Art," *New Criterion* 4 (April 1986): 35.
18. "For me," Claude Monet commented of his Grainstacks in 1891, "a landscape does not exist in its own right, since its appearance changes at every moment, but the surrounding atmosphere brings it to life, the air and the light, which vary continually." Quoted in John House, "Monet, The Last Impressionist?" in Richard Tucker, ed., *Monet in the Twentieth Century* (London and Boston: Royal Academy of Arts and the Museum of Fine Arts, 1998), 8.
19. Richard Anuszkiewicz, interview with Paul E. C. Cummings, p. 20, Anuszkiewicz Papers, AAA/SI.
20. What has been called "Optical Art," he wrote, "is best exemplified, among the younger generation in colour, by the American, Richard Anuszkiewicz." William Seitz, "The New Perceptual Art," *Vogue* 145 (February 15, 1965): 80.
21. Grace Glueck, "Art Notes: Blues and Greens on Reds," *New York Times*, February 21, 1965: sec. 2, p. 19.
22. Hayden Herrera, "Richard Anuszkiewicz at Crispo," *Art in America* 65 (May 77): 118–19.
23. Anonymous review in the *Herald Tribune*, quoted by Jay Jacobs, "Richard Anuszkiewicz," *The Art Gallery* 14 (March 1971): 33.
24. Gerrit Henry, exhibition review, *Artnews* 72 (May 1973): 86.
25. Richard Anuszkiewicz, "Portrait of the Artist, Richard Anuszkiewicz," interview by Jay Jacobs, *The Art Gallery* 14 (March 1971): 33.
26. Karl Lunde, "Richard Anuszkiewicz," *Arts* 49 (March 1975): 56.
27. See Sandra Langer's summary of the reception of Anuszkiewicz's work, with a reevaluation of this response, in "Cosmic Genesis: A Critical Reappraisal of Richard Anuszkiewicz's Art," *Arts* 58 (April 1989): 118–20. For a discussion of the history of Optical painting and Anuszkiewicz, in particular, see Floyd Ratcliffe, "The Theory of Color and the Practice of Painting," especially 14–15; for "film color" in Anuszkiewicz and others, see Sanford Wurmfeld, "From Surface Color to Luminous Film Color in Abstract Painting," 16–21; both in *Color Function Painting: The Art of Josef Albers, Julian Stanczak and Richard Anuszkiewicz* (Winston-Salem, N.C.: Wake Forest University Fine Arts Gallery, 1996).
28. Thomas Crow, *The Rise of the Sixties* (New York: Prentice Hall and Harry N. Abrams, 1996), 113.
29. Warren Young, "Bringing Chaos Out of Order," *Life* (December 11, 1964): 38.
30. James Herbert, *Fauve Painting: The Making of Cultural Politics* (New Haven, Conn.: Yale University Press, 1992), 10.
31. Barbara Rose, "Beyond vertigo: Optical art at the Modern," *Artforum* 3 (April 1965): 30–31.
32. Thomas Hess, "You Can Hang It in the Hall," *Artnews* 63 (April 1965): 43.
33. See, for instance, Louis Chapin, "Gallery Andrew Crispo," *Artnews* 74 (May 1975): 98–99.
34. Hayden Herrera, "Richard Anuszkiewicz at Crispo," *Art in America* 65 (May 1977): 119.
35. David Batchelor, *Chromophobia* (London: Reaktion Books, 2000), 112, quoted from Johann Wolfgang von Goethe, *Theory of Colors*, trans. C. L. Eastlake (Cambridge, Mass. and London, 1970), 55.
36. Hayden White, *Tropics of Discourse* (Baltimore: Johns Hopkins University Press, 1978), 152, 154.
37. For more on the uses of Primitivism in modern art, see the remarks and bibliography in Mark Antliff and Patricia Leighton, "Primitive," in Robert S. Nelson and Richard Shiff, eds., *Critical Terms for Art History* (Chicago: University of Chicago Press, 1996), 170–84.
38. It is significant in this regard that Kirchner, (who, like Kandinsky, investigated available color theories with diligence), having studied Helmholtz, Rood, and perhaps Isaac Newton, returned to Goethe's *Theory of Colors*. Gage speculates that was because Goethe's discussion of after-images suggested that only strongly colored stimuli were necessary in a painting; their effects, the subjects of much nineteenth-century representation, would then be superfluous. John Gage, *Color and Culture: Practice and Meaning from Antiquity to Abstraction* (Boston: Little, Brown and Company, 1993), 207.
39. For summaries of some of this history, see Kariamu Welsh-Asante, "A Bibliographic Essay on African Aesthetics," 249–55, and Robert Douglas, "The Search for an Afrocentric Visual Aesthetic," 159–73, both in Kariamu Welsh-Asante, ed., *The African Aesthetic, Keeper of the Traditions* (Westport, Conn.: Praeger, 1993).
40. Despite his early involvement in Kentucky at the University of Louisville with NAACP programs, Gilliam stopped participating in activist politics about 1961. Of the relation between politics and art Gilliam observed in 1994, "I've always been too involved in art . . . to actually get involved in the other." Binstock, 80, 105.
41. Binstock, 79–91.
42. Binstock, 93–95, 99–100. In an interview, Gilliam noted that Washington Color painting originated in the 1950s, its ideas based on Frankenthaler and Pollock. "I was shocked," he recalled, "as a student coming in, to see Abstract Expressionism practiced so fluidly outside of New York." *Portraits in Black*, prod. Peter Jay Zabriskie, WETA, Washington, D.C., 1982, videocassette. Copy at AAA/SI.
43. Sam Gilliam, interview with Joseph Jacobs, in Joseph Jacobs, ed., *Since the Harlem Renaissance: 50 Years of African American Art* (Lewisburg, Penn.: Center Gallery of Bucknell University, 1985), 20.
44. Sam Gilliam, interview with Benjamin Forgey, November 4, 1989, Gilliam papers, AAA/SI, p. 5.
45. Robert Morris, "Notes on Sculpture 4: Beyond Objects," in Charles Harrison and Paul Wood, eds., *Art in Theory, 1900–2000: An Anthology of Changing Ideas*, new ed. (Malden, Mass.: Blackwell Publishers, 2003), 881.
46. Robert Morris, quoted in Jane Addams Allen, "Letting Go," *Art In America* 74 (January 1986): 99.
47. Gilliam, telephone interview with the author, September 25, 1995.

48. The history of painted and dyed fabric structures in the late 1960s has not been undertaken to my knowledge.
49. Gilliam, telephone interview with author.
50. John Beardsley, "Then and Now," in *Sam Gilliam, of Fireflies or Ferris Wheels* (Washington, D.C.: USIA, 1991), 18. Beardsley's essay charts the material and aesthetic development of Gilliam's suspended paintings.
51. Binstock, Chapter 3, "Maturation and Breakthrough, 1966–1968."
52. Sargent Claude Johnson in Evangeline J. Montgomery, *Sargent Johnson: Retrospective* (Oakland, Calif.: The Oakland Museum, 1971), 18.
53. Robert Farris Thompson, *African Art in Motion* (Los Angeles: University of California Press, 1974), 14.
54. Thompson, 11.
55. Douglas, "The Search for an Afrocentric Visual Aesthetic," 172.
56. Binstock, 175–80, 195–204.
57. Binstock, 205–18.
58. Keith Morrison did not think that all African American critics believed that African American artists produce work that has a "tangible or significant" relation to African American experience. For Morrison, for instance, Richard Hunt did not make "black art." Keith Morrison, "Black Art in America," *New Art Examiner* 7 (June 1980): 5.
59. Douglas, "The Search for an Afrocentric Visual Aesthetic," 172.
60. Addison Gayle, Jr., "Introduction," in *The Black Aesthetic* (Garden City, N.Y.: Doubleday, 1971), xxiii.
61. Douglas, "The Search for an Afrocentric Visual Aesthetic," 171–72.
62. Robert L. Douglas, "Formalizing an African-American Aesthetic," *New Art Examiner* 18 (June/summer 1991): 18–20; and Nubia Kai, "AfriCobra Universal Aesthetics," *AfriCobra, The First Twenty Years* (Atlanta Georgia: Nexus Contemporary Art Center, 1990). The quotation about the incorporation of African Diasporan imagery is from Jeff Donaldson in conversation with Michael Harris, quoted from his "From Double Consciousness to Double Vision, the Africentric Artist," *African Arts* 27 (April 1994): 45.
63. Donaldson, quoted in Kai, 6–7.
64. Kai, 7–8.
65. Gilliam, interview with J. K., 1.
66. Jane Addams Allen, "Jazz-Inspired Gilliam: Stretching the Rainbow," *Washington Times*, November 30, 1984: 2B.
67. Keith Morrison, "Art Criticism: A Pan-African Point of View," *New Art Examiner* 7 (February 1979): 6.
68. As Eleanor Heartney noted perceptively in 1985, "Stella and Gilliam have had to struggle with the content of abstraction as the pendulum swung away from the formalist tradition that was their first home." "Old Masters Meet the Eighties," *New Art Examiner* 12 (April 1985): 32–33. *Jam Packed and Jelly Tight* was the title of one of AfriCobra leader Jeff Donaldson's paintings of 1988; these were already terms Donaldson used to describe his own and other AfriCobrans' intricately detailed allover compositions.
69. Morrison, "Black Art in America," 4.
70. Morrison, "Black Art in America," 4.
71. Morrison, "Art Criticism," 7. Morrison must have had a sense that Gilliam, whom he clearly admired, might take issue with his view. Following the publication of this article, he sent Gilliam a copy of the page on which he discussed what he called his "Gothic Drapery" with a note that concluded, "Hope you approve of what I said of your work. If I am way off base, please forgive me." Keith Morrison to Sam Gilliam, March 5, 1979, "Clippings 1978–79," box 4, Gilliam Papers, SI/AAA.
72. See Chapter 7 ("The Forms of Wildness: Archaeology of an Idea") in White's *Tropics of Discourse*.
73. Vivien Raynor, "Art: Casting Space in a Different Light," *New York Times*, January 20, 1978: C18.
74. John Strand, "Flat Out," *Museum & Arts* (May/June 1991): 59.
75. Texture and bas-relief surfaces were seldom stressed by Op artists, nor were they particularly typical of the work of most AfriCobrans. The work of AfriCobra artists Akili Ron Anderson, Adger Cowans, Murry DePillars, Jeff Donaldson, Wadsworth Jarrell, James Phillips, Frank Smith, and Nelson Stevens, for instance, depended mostly on two-dimensional interchanges, whereas that of Michael Harris and Napoleon Jones-Henderson involved interactions between two- and three-dimensional forms.
76. Gerrit Henry, "A Metaphor for Human Being: New Paintings by Sam Gilliam," *Arts Magazine* 59 (February 1985): 78.
77. Sam Gilliam, telephone interview with the author.
78. Hopps, n.p.
79. Paul Richard, "Gilliam: Mellow and Calm," unidentified clipping, November 33, 1973, "Printed Material 1970–74," box 4, Gilliam Papers, AAA/SI.
80. Hugh M. Davies, "Sam Gilliam," *Arts Magazine* 53 (March 1979): 15.
81. See James Clifford, Virginia Dominguez, and Trinh T. Minh-Ha, "Of Other Peoples: Beyond the 'Salvage Paradigm,'" in Hal Foster, ed., *Discussions of Contemporary Culture* 1 (Seattle: Bay Press, 1987), 121–50.
82. Davies, 15.
83. Eleanor Green, "Modern Painters at the Corcoran: Sam Gilliam," *Washington Review* (June/July 1983): 23.
84. One could say that Greene describes Gilliam's home, to misquote Batchelor, as a place where "Whiteness is not woven into the fabric of Culture," and is therefore not idealized, not uncanny, and not Minimalist. See Batchelor's *Chromophobia*, Chapter 1, "Whitescapes," especially 18–19.
85. Henry, 79 and Addams Allen, "Letting Go," 146–47.
86. Addams Allen, "Letting Go," 147. References to crazy quilts and jazz abound in discussions of Gilliam's painting. Such remarks are typical: "When it comes to balancing solid colors and heavily impastoed mixtures with an eye to structure, Gilliam can hold his own with the most inspired of Afro-American quilters." Vivien Raynor, "Robert Beauchamp-Sam Gilliam," *New York Times*, February 22, 1985.
87. Adrian Piper, *Colored People* (London: Book Works, 1991). On the single page of text by Piper in this artist's book, she notes that the participants were self-selected from thirty-six original invitees, comprising an equal number of people of color and Euroethnics, each of whom was asked to submit eight photos of themselves, "each expressing facially the corresponding colloquial metaphor of color as mood." She notes that the project, which she had conceived as a "lighthearted conceptual gesture with serious implications," had serious potential in the professional arena for the participants, whose responses indicated not only their trust that Piper's project would be done in good faith, but also their sense of humor about themselves and their understanding of the serious social issues involved. I have chosen to reproduce here one of the photographs of Gilliam in the book, photographs whose inclusion in this project further demonstrates his understanding of the connections among the complex valences of color in the United States. Other art-worlders whose participation in this project is published in *Colored People*, and who can therefore be presumed also to understand the prevalence of associations between the phenomenological and social meanings of color and "race" in this country, are: Houston Conwill, Kinshasha Conwill, Jane Farver, David Frankel, Kellie Jones, Lucy Lippard, Rosemary Mayer, John Moore, John Marita, Clive Phillpot, Howardena Pindell, Lowery Stokes Sims, Kaylyn Sullivan, Judith Wilson, and Josephine Withers. In an essay from 1993, Piper locates Gilliam's use of color in the tradition of formalism, on the one hand, and politics, on the other. Piper also argued that, Greenberg's convictions to the contrary, the "role of *decisively* vanquishing the conceits of illusionistic pictorial space" should go not to the Color Field painters, but to Gilliam, "when he began to manipulate paint as itself a three-dimensional sculptural medium—a material that had its own formal properties, imposed its own formal demands, and required its own tools of formal manipulation." See Adrian Piper, Introductory essay, *New Observations 97: Color* (September/October 1993), 3.
88. Henry Louis Gates, Jr., *Colored People, A Memoir* (New York: Vintage Books, 1995), 7.
89. Gates, xv.

ABOUT THE CONTRIBUTORS

Ann Eden Gibson writes on contemporary art and theory and is a Professor in the Art History Department of the University of Delaware. She is the author of *Issues in Abstract Expressionism: The Artist-Run Periodicals* (University of Michigan Press, 1990); *Abstract Expressionism: Other Politics* (Yale University Press, 1997); and the forthcoming *Seeing Through Theory: Intention, Identity and Agency* (University of Chicago Press).

Linda Dalrymple Henderson is the David Bruton, Jr. Centennial Professor in Art History and Distinguished Teaching Professor at The University of Texas at Austin. In addition to numerous articles, she is the author of *The Fourth Dimension and Non-Euclidean Geometry in Modern Art* (Princeton University Press, 1983; new ed., MIT Press, 2006) and *Duchamp in Context: Science and Technology in the Large Glass and Related Works* (Princeton University Press, 1998).

Dave Hickey is an art critic who lives in Las Vegas, Nevada.

Robert Kushner was born and educated in California, but has considered himself a New Yorker for three decades. He lives, paints, and sometimes writes about art from his home and studio off Union Square. His art is represented by DC Moore Gallery, New York; Yoshiaki Inoue Gallery, Osaka; Bellas Artes Gallery, Santa Fe; and Gallery Camino Real, Boca Raton.

Karal Ann Marling is Professor of Art History and American Studies at the University of Minnesota and the author of more than twenty books on aspects of American art, social life, and popular culture. Her most recent titles are *Debutante! The Rites and Regalia of American Debdom* (University Press of Kansas, 2004) and *Norman Rockwell* (Taschen, 2005). She is currently completing a full-length study of Grandma Moses for Harvard University Press.

David Reed is an artist who lives and works in New York. He shows regularly with Max Protetch Gallery in New York, Galerie Xippas in Paris, Galerie Bob van Orsouw in Zürich, and Galerie Schmidt Maczollek (formerly Galerie Rolf Ricke) in Cologne. He is an advisor to "High Times, Hard Times: New York Painting 1967–75," an exhibition curated by Katy Siegel for Independent Curators International.

Raphael Rubinstein is a poet and critic whose books include *The Basement of the Cafe Rilke* (1997), *Postcards from Alphaville* (2000), and *Polychrome Profusion: Selected Art Criticism 1990–2002* (2004). He is a senior editor at *Art in America* and lives in New York.

Annette DiMeo Carlozzi is the curator of American and contemporary art for the Blanton Museum of Art at The University of Texas at Austin. Formerly a curator, director, and arts producer at a wide range of arts institutions across the United States, she is the author of numerous exhibition catalogues, essays, interviews, and reviews on contemporary art.

Kelly Baum is the assistant curator of American and contemporary art for the Blanton Museum of Art at The University of Texas at Austin. She received her PhD in Art History from the University of Delaware in 2005. She has written many essays on contemporary art for regional publications and arts organizations and has been working in the curatorial field for the last five years.

Erin Aldana is a PhD candidate in art history at The University of Texas at Austin

Ken Allan is a lecturer in the Department of Art History at the University of Southern California

Gwen Allen is visiting Assistant Professor of Art History at Maine College of Art

Charity Anderson has an MA in art history from Syracuse University

Claire Barliant is an associate editor at *Artforum*

Jennifer Barrett is a PhD candidate in art history at the University of Delaware

Regine Basha is an independent curator, consultant, and writer and is currently Adjunct Curator at Arthouse at the Jones Center, Austin

Alan C. Braddock is Assistant Professor of American Art History in the Department of Fine Arts at Syracuse University

Ann Clifton has an MA in art history from The University of Texas at Austin

Lea Cline is a PhD student in art history at The University of Texas at Austin

Rebecca S. Cohen is a freelance arts writer based in Austin

Feay Shellman Coleman is an independent scholar

Frances Colpitt is a critic and the Deedie Potter Rose Chair in Art History at Texas Christian University

Leo Costello is Assistant Professor of Art History at Rice University

Charlotte Cousins is a PhD candidate in art history at The University of Texas at Austin

Jennifer Davy is an independent critic and curator based in San Antonio

Nancy Deffebach is Assistant Professor of Art History at San Diego State University

John Devine is a freelance arts writer living in Houston

Amy Dove has an MA in art history from Columbia University and is currently an independent writer and art critic based in Los Angeles

Erina Duganne is Mellon Post-Doctoral Fellow in the History of Photography at Williams College

Alexander Dumbadze is Assistant Professor of Art History at George Washington University

Teresa Eckmann is a Center for Regional Studies Post-Doctoral Research Scholar at the Center for Southwest Research Special Collections at the University of New Mexico

Katie Robinson Edwards, a PhD candidate in art history at The University of Texas at Austin, is Visiting Assistant Professor at the Allbritton Art Institute at Baylor University

Rina Faletti is a PhD candidate in art history at The University of Texas at Austin

Jennifer Farrell is an art historian and critic based in New York

Mette Gieskes is a PhD candidate in art history at The University of Texas at Austin

Karen C. Gonzalez is a PhD student in art history at Duke University

Sue Graze is Executive Director of Arthouse at the Jones Center, Austin

Anjali Gupta is a freelance critic and video producer and the editor of *ARTL!ES* magazine

Stephanie Hanor is Curator at the Museum of Contemporary Art, San Diego

Valerie Hellstein is a PhD candidate at Stony Brook University

Sarah Holian is Assistant Curator of Collections and Exhibitions at the Grand Rapids Art Museum

James Housefield is Associate Professor of the History of Art at Texas State University and Adjunct Curator at the Austin Museum of Art

Madeline Irvine is an artist and writer living in Austin

Kathleen V. Jameson has a PhD in art history from the University of Delaware and is currently Assistant Director of Development at the Museum of Fine Arts, Houston

Jennifer Jankauskas is an independent curator and writer based in San Antonio

Lara Kuykendall is a PhD student in American art history at the University of Kansas

Rebecca E. Lawton is Curator of Paintings and Sculpture at the Amon Carter Museum, Fort Worth

Mary Leclère is Associate Director of the Core Residency Program at the Museum of Fine Arts, Houston and a PhD candidate in art history at the University of Virginia

Valerie Ann Leeds is Adjunct Curator of American Art at the Flint Institute of Arts, Michigan

Mariani Lefas-Tetenes is Lecturer in Art History in the Department of Art at Kingsborough Community College of the City University of New York (CUNY)

Ann Marie Leimer is Assistant Professor of Art History at the University of the Redlands

Laura A. Lindenberger has an MA in art history from The University of Texas at Austin

Heather E. Mathews has a PhD in art history from The University Texas at Austin

Dorothy Moss is a PhD candidate in art history at the University of Delaware and a Smithsonian Predoctoral Fellow

Sara-Jayne Parsons is Assistant to the Director at the University of North Texas Art Gallery and a PhD student in art history at The University of Texas at Austin

Lisa Pasquariello has a PhD in art history from Stanford University and is the managing editor of *October*

Justine Price is a PhD candidate in art history at The University of Texas at Austin

Karen M. Rapp is a PhD candidate in art history at Stanford University

Tiffany Rasco has an MA in Museum Education from The University of Texas at Austin

Katherine Roeder is a PhD candidate in American art history at the University of Delaware

R. Sarah Richardson has a PhD in art history from The Graduate Center of the City University of New York and currently works for Hollis Taggart Galleries in New York

Sue Scott is an independent curator and writer living in New York and a Consulting Curator for the Orlando Museum of Art

Cherise Smith is an Assistant Professor of Art History at The University of Texas at Austin

Patrick Tomlin is a PhD student in art history at Northwestern University

Melissa Warak is a PhD student in art history at The University of Texas at Austin

Kayaneh T. Wood is a master's degree candidate in Media Studies in the Department of Radio-Television-Film at The University of Texas at Austin

INDEX OF ARTISTS

Boldface page references indicate illustrations and color plates. Page references following artist's name indicate biography section.

PHOTO CREDITS

All photographs by Rick Hall and George Holmes, except the following:

Terry Adkins (plate 2): Ansen Seale, Courtesy Finesilver Gallery, San Antonio
Janine Antoni (plate 7): Larry Lamay, Courtesy Luhring Augustine Gallery, New York
Jeremy Blake (plate 22): Courtesy Feigen Contemporary, New York
Anne Chu (plate 28): Courtesy Victoria Miro Gallery, London
Sam Gilliam (page 413, figures 13 and 14): Ann Eden Gibson
Rachel Harrison (plate 58): Oren Slor, Courtesy Greene Naftali Gallery, New York
Joseph Havel (plate 60): David Wharton
Oliver Herring (plate 66): Chris Burke Studios, Courtesy Max Protetch Gallery, New York
Charles Hinman (plate 67): David Wharton
Emily Jacir (plate 73): Bill Haddad
Jesús Moroles (plate 127): the artist
Wangechi Mutu (plates 130 and 131): Gene Ogami, Courtesy Susanne Vielmetter Los Angeles Projects
Louise Nevelson (plate 133): Bill Jacobson, Courtesy PaceWildenstein Gallery, New York
Robyn O'Neil (plate 140): Courtesy Inman Gallery, Houston
John Pomara (plate 146): Harrison Evans
Dario Robleto (plate 152): Robert Wedemeyer Photography, Courtesy ACME Gallery, Los Angeles
Peter Rostovsky (plate 153): the artist
Shahzia Sikander (plate 163, video still): Bill Haddad
George Sugarman (plate 175): David Wharton